Seminars in Perinatal Psychiatry

College Seminars Series

For details of available and forthcoming books in the College Seminars Series please visit:
www.cambridge.org/series/college-seminars-series/

Seminars in Perinatal Psychiatry

Edited by
Liz McDonald
East London NHS Foundation Trust
Roch Cantwell
NHS Greater Glasgow and Clyde
Ian Jones
Cardiff University

CAMBRIDGE
UNIVERSITY PRESS

CAMBRIDGE
UNIVERSITY PRESS

Shaftesbury Road, Cambridge CB2 8EA, United Kingdom

One Liberty Plaza, 20th Floor, New York, NY 10006, USA

477 Williamstown Road, Port Melbourne, VIC 3207, Australia

314–321, 3rd Floor, Plot 3, Splendor Forum, Jasola District Centre, New Delhi – 110025, India

Cambridge University Press is part of Cambridge University Press & Assessment, a department of the University of Cambridge.

We share the University's mission to contribute to society through the pursuit of education, learning and research at the highest international levels of excellence.

www.cambridge.org
Information on this title: www.cambridge.org/9781911623502

DOI: 10.1017/9781911623496

When citing this work, please include a reference to the DOI 10.1017/9781911623496

First published 2026

Cover image: Cover image: chuvipro / DigitalVision Vectors / Getty Images.

A catalogue record for this publication is available from the British Library

A Cataloging-in-Publication data record for this book is available from the Library of Congress

ISBN 978-1-911-62350-2 Paperback

This book is dedicated to the memory of Dr Margaret Rose Oates (1934–2022), OBE FRCPsych FRCOG, whose achievements as an educator, service developer and, above all, clinician are legendary. Margaret's model of service delivery in Nottingham provided the template for perinatal mental health services as we know them today, and her work has improved the lives of countless women, infants and families.

Contents

List of Contributors x
Editor Biographies xiv
Foreword xv
Sally Wilson and Jamie Macdonald
Acknowledgements xvi
Gender-Sensitive Language xvii

Section 1 The Perinatal Context

1 **The Perinatal Frame of Mind** 1
Liz McDonald

2 **Experiencing Severe Perinatal Mental Illness: The Woman's Perspective** 23
Clare Dolman

3 **Physiological Changes in Pregnancy and Common Obstetric Medical Disorders** 39
Lin Foo and Shankari Arulkumaran

4 **Fetal Development and Routine Maternity Care** 56
Judith Meek, Adalina Sacco and Leigh Dyet

5 **Infant Development: Birth to 12 Months** 70
Angela Huertas-Ceballos, Emily Hills and Judith Meek

6 **Paternal Mental Health in the Perinatal Period: Impact on Family Relationships** 80
Jill Domoney, Jane Iles and Vaheshta Sethna

7 **The Perinatal Mental Health of Racial and Ethnic Minority Groups** 97
Raquel Catalao, Louisa Codjoe, Preety Das, Jacqui Dyer and Stephani L. Hatch

8 **Psychological Aspects of Infertility, Assisted Conception and Perinatal Loss** 113
Sarah Healy, Kyla Vaillancourt and Camilla Rosan

9 **The Evolving Leader in Perinatal Mental Health Services: Thinking, Practice and Relationships** 146
Michael Hobkirk and Graham Lee

Section 2 Maternal Mental Disorders

10 **Depression** 165
Lucy C. Barker, Cindy-Lee Dennis and Simone N. Vigod

11 **Anxiety Disorders** 186
Rose Meades, Heather O'Mahen, Antoinette Davey and Susan Ayers

12 **Postpartum Psychosis and Bipolar Disorder** 205
Ian Jones, Jess Heron and Arianna Di Florio

13 **Schizophrenia Spectrum Disorders** 221
Julia L. France, Lucy C. Barker and Simone N. Vigod

14 **Personality Disorder** 241
Gwen Adshead

15 **Complex Post-Traumatic Stress Disorder** 257
Alain Gregoire, Cerith Waters and Laura Richmond

16 **Eating Disorders** 281
Catia Acosta and Abigail Easter

17 **Medically Unexplained Symptoms** 306
Robby Steel

18 **Alcohol and Substance Use Disorders** 322
Claire Wilson and Emily Finch

19 **Intellectual Disability** 338
Sonya Rudra and Ken Courtenay

20 **Attention Deficit Hyperactivity Disorder** 355
Amanda Elkin and Sally Cubbin

21 **Autism** 376
Sam Porter

22 **Maternal Suicide, Deliberate Self-Harm and Other Mental Health Related Causes of Maternal Death** 393
Roch Cantwell

Section 3 Principles of Perinatal Assessment and Management

23 **Access, Assessment and Evaluation of Risk in Perinatal Mental Health Services** 407
Roch Cantwell, Liz McDonald and Lucinda Green

24 **Pre-pregnancy Advice and Planning** 423
Maddalena Miele and Shankari Arulkumaran

25 **Pre-birth Planning** 440
Lucinda Green

26 **Principles of Prescribing** 455
Liz McDonald

27 **The Reproductive Safety of Psychotropic Medication and Implications for Prescribing in the Perinatal Period** 468
Angelika Wieck

28 **Psychological Therapies for Parental Mental Health in the Perinatal Period: What Works?** 490
Heather O'Mahen, Rachel Mycroft and Camilla Rosan

29 **Effective Working across Health, Peer Support and Third-Sector Interfaces** 514
Judy Shakespeare, Jill Demilew and Jess Heron

30 **Perinatal Mental Health Service Development and Delivery** 536
Roch Cantwell and Giles Berrisford

31 **Perinatal Mental Health Services in Asia, Africa and Latin America** 546
Vandita Shanbhag, Bruma Palacios-Hernández, Tesera Bitew and Prabha Chandra

Section 4 Infant Mental Health in the Context of Maternal Mental Health

32 **Infant Mental Health: The Role of Perinatal Mental Health Services** 557
Anne McFadyen

33 **Maternal Mood and Stress during Pregnancy: Effects on the Fetus and the Child** 571
Vivette Glover

34 **Holding the Baby in Mind: How Does Infant Observation Contribute to Perinatal Practice?** 587
Biddy Youell

35 **Mother–Infant Focused Interventions: What Works to Improve the Mother–Infant Relationship?** 601
Jane Barlow

Section 5 Medico-Legal Issues in the Perinatal Period

36 **Child Safeguarding** 619
Lucinda Green

37 **Violence against Women** 638
Claire Wilson, Roxanne Keynejad, Siofra Peeren and Louise M. Howard

38 **When Mothers Kill Their Children** 648
Gwen Adshead

39 **Mental Health and Capacity Legislation in the Perinatal Period** 661
Livia Martucci, Alex Ruck Keene and Lucy Stephenson

40 **The Preparation of Psychiatric Reports for Court** 681
Gertrude Seneviratne and Susan Conroy

Index 699

Contributors

Catia Acosta, Consultant Psychiatrist in Liaison, Perinatal and Eating Disorders; previously at Vincent Square Eating Disorders Service and Perinatal Mental Health Services, Chelsea & Westminster Hospital, Central and Northwest London Mental Health Foundation Trust

Gwen Adshead, Consultant Forensic Psychiatrist and Psychotherapist, Broadmoor Hospital, West London Mental Health Trust

Shankari Arulkumaran, Consultant Obstetrician and Gynaecologist, St Mary's Hospital, Imperial College Healthcare NHS Trust

Susan Ayers, Professor of Maternal and Child Health, Centre for Maternal and Child Health Research, School of Health and Medical Sciences, City St George's, University of London

Lucy C. Barker, Psychiatrist and Scientist, Women's College Hospital, Toronto; Assistant Professor, Department of Psychiatry, Temerty Faculty of Medicine, University of Toronto

Jane Barlow, Professor of Evidence-Based Intervention and Policy Evaluation, Department of Social Policy and Intervention, University of Oxford

Giles Berrisford, National Specialty Advisor Perinatal Mental Health, NHS England; Consultant Perinatal Psychiatrist, Birmingham and Solihull Mental Health Trust and Maudsley Health – Abu Dhabi; Chair, Action on Postpartum Psychosis

Tesera Bitew, Associate Professor of Mental Health Epidemiology, Injibara University, Ethiopia

Raquel Catalao, Academic Clinical Fellow in Psychiatry, Section of Women's Mental Health, Institute of Psychiatry, Psychology & Neuroscience, King's College London and South London and Maudsley NHS Foundation Trust

Prabha S Chandra, Professor of Psychiatry and Dean, Behavioral Sciences Senior Professor of Psychiatry, National Institute of Mental Health and Neurosciences, Bangalore, India

Louisa Codjoe, Clinical Research Psychologist, Health Service and Population Research Department, Institute of Psychiatry, Psychology & Neuroscience, King's College London and South London and Maudsley NHS Foundation Trust

Susan Conroy, Researcher (retd.), Institute of Psychiatry, Psychology & Neuroscience, King's College London

Ken Courtenay, Consultant Psychiatrist in Intellectual Disability, North London NHS Foundation Trust

Sally Cubbin, Consultant Psychiatrist, Adult ADHD Clinic, Manor Hospital, Oxford

Preety Das, Academic Clinical Fellow in Psychiatry, Health Inequalities Research Group, Institute of Psychiatry, Psychology & Neuroscience, King's College London and South London and Maudsley NHS Foundation Trust

Antoinette Davey, Department of Psychology, Mood Disorders Centre, University of Exeter

Jill Demilew, Consultant Midwife (retd.), Kings College Hospital NHS Foundation Trust

Cindy-Lee Dennis, Professor in Nursing and Medicine, Department of Psychiatry, University of Toronto; Senior Scientist, Lunenfeld Tanenbaum Research Institute, Sinai Health; Heather Reisman Chair in Perinatal Nursing Research, Sinai Health; Fellow, Canadian Academy of Health Sciences

Arianna Di Florio, Professor of Psychiatry, Cardiff University

Clare Dolman, Co-chair, Bipolar Commission and Ambassador Bipolar UK; Trustee, Maternal Mental Health Alliance, the Global Alliance for Maternal Mental Health and Action on Postpartum Psychosis; Visiting Fellow, Edinburgh University

Jill Domoney, Research Clinical Psychologist, Section of Women's Mental Health, Health Service and Population Research Department, Institute of Psychiatry, Psychology & Neuroscience, King's College London

Jacqui Dyer, President of the Mental Health Foundation; Co-founder and Chair, Black Thrive Lambeth; Lambeth Cabinet member for Jobs, Skills and Community Safety; Chair, NHS England Advancing Mental Health Equalities Taskforce & Strategy; Chair, NHS England Patient & Carer Race Equality Framework Steering Group

Leigh Dyet, Consultant Neonatologist, University College London Hospitals; Honorary Associate Professor, University College London

Abigail Easter, Reader in Perinatal Mental Health, Department of Women and Children's Health, School of Life Course and Population Science, Faculty of Life Sciences and Medicine, King's College London

Amanda Elkin, Consultant Psychiatrist, Buckinghamshire Specialist Perinatal Mental Health Team, Oxford Health NHS Foundation Trust

Emily Finch, Consultant Psychiatrist and Clinical Director, Addictions Clinical Academic Group, South London and Maudsley NHS Foundation Trust

Lin Foo, Consultant in Obstetrics and Fetal Medicine, Royal Victoria Infirmary, Newcastle upon Tyne Hospitals NHS Foundation Trust

Julia L. France, Student, Women's College Hospital, Toronto

Vivette Glover, Visiting Professor of Perinatal Psychobiology, Imperial College London

Lucinda Green, Consultant Perinatal Psychiatrist, The Portland Hospital, London; Clinical Lead, Perinatal Masterclass Programme (Royal College of Psychiatrists)

Alain Gregoire, Perinatal Psychiatrist, Visiting Professor, Care Policy and Evaluation Centre, London School of Economics and Political Science; Honorary President, Maternal Mental Health Alliance UK; Chair, Global Alliance for Maternal Mental Health

Stephani L. Hatch, Professor of Sociology and Epidemiology, Institute of Psychiatry, Psychology & Neuroscience, King's College London

Sarah Healy, Clinical Director, The Perinatal Psychology Practice; Director, The Pearl Institute of Perinatal Psychology

Jess Heron, Chief Executive, Action on Postpartum Psychosis

Emily Hills, Neonatal Occupational Therapist, Royal Free London NHS Foundation Trust

Michael Hobkirk, Consultant Child Psychiatrist, Sussex Partnership NHS Foundation Trust and Associate Dean, NHS England in Kent, Surrey and Sussex

Louise M. Howard, Emeritus Professor, Section of Women's Mental Health, King's College London

Angela Huertas-Ceballos, Consultant Neonatologist (retd.), Neonatal Department, University College London Hospitals NHS Foundation Trust

Jane Iles, Associate Professor and Clinical Psychologist, Department of Psychology, University of Surrey, UK

Roxanne Keynejad, Clinical Senior Lecturer and Consultant Perinatal Psychiatrist, Section of Women's Mental Health, King's College London and South London and Maudsley NHS Foundation Trust

Graham Lee, Consultant Family and Systemic Psychotherapist, Associate Lecturer at the Universities of Surrey and Brighton, UK

Livia Martucci, Consultant Perinatal Psychiatrist, South London and Maudsley NHS Foundation Trust; Chair, Perinatal Faculty, Royal College of Psychiatrists

Anne McFadyen, Honorary Senior Lecturer in Child and Adolescent Psychiatry, Centre for Developmental Adversity and Resilience, School of Health and Wellbeing, University of Glasgow

Rose Meades, Senior Research Fellow, Centre for Maternal and Child Health Research, School of Health and Medical Sciences, City St George's, University of London

Judith Meek, Consultant Neonatologist and Honorary Associate Professor, University College London Hospitals NHS Foundation Trust

Maddalena Miele, Consultant in Perinatal Psychiatry and Honorary Senior Lecturer, St Mary's Hospital, Imperial College London and Central and North West London NHS Foundation Trust

Rachel Mycroft, Consultant Clinical Psychologist, South London and Maudsley NHS Foundation Trust

Heather O'Mahen, Professor of Perinatal and Clinical Psychology, Department of Psychology, Mood Disorders Centre, University of Exeter

Bruma Palacios-Hernández, Research Professor, Perinatal Mental Health Laboratory, Transdisciplinary Research Centre in Psychology, Autonomous University of the State of Morelos, Mexico

Siofra Peeren, Research Associate, Section of Women's Mental Health, King's College London

Sam Porter, Consultant Psychiatrist, Essex Partnership University NHS Foundation Trust; Honorary Lecturer, University College London

Laura Richmond, Honorary Research Fellow, Clinical, Educational and Health Psychology, University College London

Camilla Rosan, Consultant Perinatal Clinical Psychologist and Associate

Professor in Clinical Psychology, Anna Freud & UCL

Alex Ruck Keene, KC, Barrister; Professor of Practice at the Dickson Poon School of Law, King's College London; Visiting Professor, Geller Institute of Ageing and Memory, University of West London; Visiting Senior Lecturer, Institute of Psychiatry, Psychology & Neuroscience, King's College London; Research Affiliate, Essex Autonomy Project, University of Essex

Sonya Rudra, Doctoral Research Fellow, University College London; Honorary Consultant in Psychiatry of Intellectual Disabilities, Surrey and Borders Partnership NHS Trust

Adalina Sacco, Consultant in Obstetrics and Fetal Medicine, Birmingham Women's Hospital

Gertrude Seneviratne, Consultant Adult and Perinatal Psychiatrist, Channi Kumar Mother and Baby Unit, South London and Maudsley NHS Foundation Trust

Vaheshta Sethna, Senior Lecturer in Family Perinatal Mental Health Education, Social, Genetic & Developmental Psychiatry Centre, Institute of Psychiatry, Psychology & Neuroscience, King's College London

Judy Shakespeare, General Practitioner (retd.), Oxford

Vandita Shanbhag, Consultant Psychiatrist, Monash Health, Melbourne, VIC, Australia

Robby Steel, Consultant Liaison Psychiatrist, Royal Infirmary, Edinburgh; Honorary (Clinical) Senior Lecturer in Psychiatry, University of Edinburgh, Principal Medical Officer, Scottish Government

Lucy Stephenson, Consultant Psychiatrist, South London and Maudsley NHS Foundation Trust

Kyla Vaillancourt, Clinical Psychologist and Doctoral Research Fellow, Centre for Maternal and Child Health, City St George's, University of London

Simone N. Vigod, Professor, Department of Psychiatry, Temerty Faculty of Medicine, University of Toronto; Head, Department of Psychiatry, and Shirley A. Brown Memorial Chair in Women's Mental Health Research, Women's College Hospital, Toronto; Senior Adjunct Scientist, ICES (formerly the Institute for Clinical Evaluative Sciences), Toronto

Cerith Waters, Consultant Clinical Psychologist, Lead Psychologist for Perinatal Mental Health Services, Cardiff and Vale University Health Board and Cardiff University

Angelika Wieck, Honorary Consultant in General Adult and Perinatal Psychiatry, Greater Manchester Mental Health NHS Foundation Trust and University of Manchester

Claire Wilson, Advanced Fellow and Honorary Consultant Psychiatrist, Section of Women's Mental Health, King's College London and South London and Maudsley NHS Foundation Trust

Biddy Youell, Visiting Lecturer, Tavistock and Portman NHS Foundation Trust

Editor Biographies

Liz McDonald, MB BCh BAO MPhil FRCPsych DU
Liz is a consultant perinatal psychiatrist (retd.) who worked in developing and delivering services in east London, England. She was Chair of the Perinatal Faculty at the Royal College of Psychiatrists and the Pan-London Perinatal Mental Health Clinical Network and executive committee member of the Independent Advisory Group for MBRRACE-UK and the Association for Infant Mental Health (UK). Past roles also include Clinical Lead at the Royal College of Psychiatrists for developing the perinatal mental health workforce, Visiting Lecturer at the Tavistock and Portman NHS Trust and member of the Clinical Guideline Group for NICE Antenatal and Postnatal Mental Health Guidelines (2007, 2014).

Roch Cantwell, MB BCH BAO FRCPysch
Roch is a consultant perinatal psychiatrist (retd.) and professional advisor in perinatal mental health to the Scottish Government. He is a trustee of Aberlour Children's Charity. He was the founding lead clinician for Scotland's National Perinatal Managed Clinical Network and vice-chair of the Scottish Government's Perinatal and Infant Mental Health Programme Board, tasked with establishing specialist services across Scotland. Other past roles have included lead psychiatric assessor and chapter author for the Confidential Enquiries into Maternal Deaths from 2011 to 2021, chair of the College's UK and Scotland Perinatal Faculties, and of its Perinatal Quality Network Advisory Committee, and chair of the SIGN guideline development group on perinatal mood disorders. He led the development of Scotland's first Mother and Baby Unit and community perinatal mental health team.

Ian Jones, BSc MB BS MSc PhD FRCPsych
Ian is Professor Emeritus at the Division of Psychiatry and Clinical Neurosciences at Cardiff University. For over a decade he was Director of the National Centre for Mental Health and with colleagues leads the Bipolar Disorder Research Network. He was the clinical lead for the Cardiff University Psychiatry Service, and developed a clinical service offering pre-conception counselling to women with severe mental illness. He was Director of BEP-C, a group psychoeducation programme for bipolar disorder which received the British Medical Journal award for innovation in medicine. Ian is a trustee, past chair and scientific adviser to Action on Postpartum Psychosis, a trustee of the Maternal Mental Health Alliance and clinical advisor to Bipolar UK. He was Deputy Chair of the Perinatal Faculty, Royal College of Psychiatrists, President of the UK and Ireland Marcé Society and was a member of the Clinical Guideline Group for the NICE Antenatal and Postnatal Mental Health Guidelines. His research focuses on bipolar disorder and postpartum psychosis. He has authored or co-authored over 400 publications and book chapters. He has been awarded the Marcé Medal, the John Cox Medal and was named Academic Psychiatrist of the Year at the Royal College of Psychiatrists Awards.

Foreword

Sally Wilson, PhD, National Training Coordinator, Action on Postpartum Psychosis
Jamie Macdonald, PhD, Professor of Sport and Exercise Science, Institute for Applied Human Physiology, Bangor University

We sit together, laughing and combing the nits out of our daughters' hair, and remind ourselves how far we've come. The moments we now cherish – the seemingly 'normal', sometimes chaotic moments of parenthood – are ones we never imagined we would feel deeply grateful for back in 2015.

At that time, our world was completely upended. Just days after giving birth, Sally was diagnosed with postpartum psychosis, a diagnosis that led to her being separated from our newborn daughter and admitted to an acute adult psychiatric unit. The journey from there was nothing short of terrifying. We had no idea how – or if – Sally would recover. The experience was isolating, and we were overwhelmed by questions of whether life would ever feel 'normal' again.

Through this dark time, we encountered some incredible health professionals and individuals who helped us navigate a challenging and unfamiliar healthcare system. With the right treatment, including electroconvulsive therapy, Sally began her long and difficult road to recovery. The support we received from third-sector peer support organisations, in conjunction with clinical care, was invaluable and undoubtedly saved Sally's life.

We are reassured by how much the perinatal mental health landscape has evolved since we needed support but also recognise that there is still work to be done. Enhancing awareness and achieving equity of access to care remain key challenges, and we know that, unfortunately, some families still face tragic outcomes. We recognise that we were so fortunate – fortunate to have had access to the resources, care and support that made recovery possible for us. We are so excited that this textbook now exists. It brings together vital information in one place provided by a wealth of experts, offering essential information and support for professionals to help improve outcomes for families in their perinatal journey. We hope it provides you with what you need, and more.

We want to express our heartfelt gratitude to every healthcare professional, third-sector organisation, researcher and individual who supports women and their families during the perinatal period. Without your dedication and compassion, our family's story could have been very different. Today, we are fortunate to be able to do the things we love as a family, but also share simple moments with our daughter, like laughing together about nits. That is something we will never take for granted.

Thank you.

Acknowledgements

We are indebted to the women, their families and our colleagues, from whom we have learned so much throughout our clinical lives, the contributors to the book who have worked so hard to distil a vast amount of knowledge and experience, and our families, who have endured the book's long gestation with admirable forbearance.

Gender-Sensitive Language

The aim of this book is to improve healthcare for all people accessing perinatal mental healthcare, recognising that specialist perinatal mental health services may also be accessed by gender-divergent individuals and people whose gender identity does not align with the sex they were assigned at birth. In addition, we acknowledge that those working within perinatal mental health services – trainers, educators and learners – are also culturally and gender diverse.

In the perinatal context, language is especially important where it represents the individual's sense of identity, visibility and agency. Equality, diversity and inclusivity are constantly evolving aspects of society, and language changes in response. Inclusive language helps to break down barriers for people accessing services. While this textbook often uses the term *woman* to describe those who access our services, we recognise the importance of both preserving women-centred language and including language for those who do not identify as a woman or man.

Where the word *mother* is used, the context should also be seen as applying, where appropriate, to a trans man or non-binary person, or indeed to a gay man who is the primary carer of their infant. *Partner* refers to any significant other identified by the mother, who may also be a co-parent (including a father, co-mother or co-father). *Father* refers to the person identified as the father of the baby, regardless of biological connectedness or parental responsibility. Other *family members* denote anyone else in the family network who is significant to the mother. This could for example be the baby's grandparents, aunts, uncles and siblings. It can also include close friends.

The use of appropriate, respectful language is further addressed in Chapter 23, 'Access, Assessment and Evaluation of Risk in Perinatal Mental Health Services'.

Chapter 1

The Perinatal Frame of Mind

Liz McDonald

Introduction

The perinatal frame of mind is a concept that aims to capture the unique mental state, context and experiences of individuals planning a pregnancy and during the perinatal period, which spans from conception to one year postpartum. The term was coined by a group of clinicians tasked by Health Education England and The Tavistock and Portman NHS Trust in 2018 to develop a competency framework for professionals working with women who have perinatal mental health problems [1]. We hope that this chapter and textbook epitomise what they meant by the perinatal frame of mind: the concept that every aspect of the physical, social, psychological and psychiatric care of women in the perinatal period requires a deep understanding of them as individuals.

Such understanding needs to encompass many aspects of a woman's life, from childhood to her current context, including traumatic and positive experiences, cultural factors, both good and bad relationships, experiences of mental and physical illness and their risks and relevance to the perinatal context, her journey to becoming pregnant, and her personal strengths and challenges. The term asks that we think not only about the woman, her well-being and needs, but also those of the fetus or infant, the intimate partner and/or co-parent, and other family members. It means that we consider the relationships between the parents and the infant, as well as within the couple and among other family members. In essence, we don't just think about the individual woman, we hold in mind the community and cultural context surrounding them, which will include the partner, family, friends and, very often, and importantly, healthcare professionals, who can provide the right kind of support to help navigate any mental health challenges.

The focus of the perinatal frame of mind is on relating and relationships and how these affect and are affected by the woman's mental health condition and the perinatal context. Hence, working with the woman and her family means that we pay particular attention to who she is and where she has come from within her life. Vikram Patel has written about the universal right to mental health and how this must always be embedded in the right to be protected from known harms to mental health and the right to agency, freedom, inclusion, and dignity in mental health care [2]. His statement neatly pulls into our thinking the need to not only care for women with mental health problems but also to ensure that there is as little harm as possible to the woman and others, particularly the infant, caused by the disorders. It also implies that treatment should be provided with great care, respect and dignity within our services. The perinatal frame of mind, in addition, asks that we as clinicians develop the skills to reflect on and to be aware of our own emotional responses to the complex work of maternal mental health and perinatal psychiatry. We need to reflect on and understand our own attitudes, values and cultural influences in terms of how we view motherhood, and what our own expectations are of the families we meet. This will lead naturally to us thinking about our own experience of being parented and for many, being parents. Many clinicians training in perinatal psychiatry are at an age when they themselves are becoming, or considering becoming, parents with all that this entails for them. This may affect how they experience the clinical role and the often-unsettling themes and scenarios that they must deal with. Therefore, reflective practice, good and regular supervision and, when required, access to personal therapy, all play important roles in supporting the development of clinicians and ensuring best outcomes for services and the individuals and families they offer care to.

William Osler's (1849–1919) words, 'it is much more important to know what sort of a patient has a disease than what sort of a disease a patient has', serve as a reminder that there is an obligation to understand the individual woman, her relationships and her life experience so that we can best make sense of why she is presenting to clinical services now and what approaches can best help her at this critical time in both her and her family's lives. We want to know 'who is she?'.

The Experience of Pregnancy and New Motherhood

The term matrescence was coined by the anthropologist Dana Raphael as 'the process of becoming a mother – a developmental passage where a woman transitions, through preconception, pregnancy and birth, surrogacy, or adoption to the postnatal period and beyond' [3]. It alludes to the profound environmental, hormonal and neurobiological changes that mark the transition to motherhood as an extremely significant biopsychosocial life event and an important developmental stage in the lives of those who give birth. Orchards et al.'s paper [4] compared matrescence to adolescence where there are not only major hormonal and social changes but also morphological changes to the maternal brain occurring across pregnancy. The functional and structural neuroplasticity of matrescence primes the brain to prepare for developing and acquiring the skills and knowledge for parenthood.

Pregnancies may be planned or unplanned, wanted or unwanted, happen with ease or following years of lack of success, investigations and interventions, be a source of joy or fear and anxiety, be accompanied by optimism about the future or profound personal, political, economic and ecological pessimism. Each woman comes to her pregnancy with different circumstances and thinking, worries, preoccupations and hopes. The changes in her physical state and physiology may make her feel well and positive or may expose a vulnerability that makes her feel physically quite undone. Society, particularly through the media, often portrays an idealised picture of pregnancy and early motherhood. This may include unrealistic expectations of her appearance, her emotional state, the time needed for physical recovery and her ability to balance multiple aspects of her life. These ideas and images can be alienating and lead to feelings of inadequacy if the woman's experiences don't match these expectations.

Each woman will likely experience a profound shift in perspective accompanied by emotional, physical, social and intellectual upheaval during pregnancy. There will be much anticipation and preparation for the arrival of a new life, an increased focus on her health and well-being and that of the baby, heightened awareness of bodily changes, increased concern about potential risks, and a desire to create as safe and nurturing an environment for the child and family as possible. As new mothers they have additional responsibilities and increased cognitive demands, whilst attending to their own needs and existing responsibilities, and recovering physically and emotionally from childbirth. Her experience of childbirth is critical in how she adjusts to the early postpartum period. The birth is highly likely to be intense and transformative, often involving a mix of excitement, fear, joy, physical discomfort and pain. Traumatic births may lead to significant distress and morbidity (see Chapter 11, 'Anxiety Disorders') and may influence her adjustment and transition to parenthood. This transition often involves a significant shift in identity and role and with it the realisation that she now carries an immense responsibility for the new life of her infant, through their childhood and into early adulthood. She may begin to think about her own early relationships and how she will be as a parent, which can be particularly challenging for women who have experienced childhood adversity. There will be psychological and practical adjustments with changes in how she perceives herself, her relationships, daily routines, personal goals, values and priorities. As author Lucy Jones commented, 'the pregnant woman hovers between internal and external worlds, at a crossroads of past, present and future; self and other' and that motherhood took her 'to the edge of what it means to be human' [5].

There is likely to be a developing awareness by the mother of societal and cultural expectations of motherhood. This may come from social media, mainstream cultural influences, healthcare and other allied professionals, work colleagues, as well as from her partner, extended family and friends. Her perception of and response to these expectations may make her feel happy and accomplished or place her under strain, make her feel inadequate, frustrated, scrutinised and judged. Societal expectations of mothers vary by culture, and may shape the woman's experience in profound ways. Some cultures may place a high value on extended family support, while others expect mothers to be largely independent or return to work quickly after childbirth. Parenting practices vary considerably across cultures and within societies and include the role of the extended family, and approaches to feeding, sleeping and comforting the infant. These cultural expectations may complicate how an individual mother experiences the transition to parenthood with or without any mental health problems, as they may feel torn between their own needs, the style of caregiving they wish to deliver and the expectations placed on them by their families or communities. This can be additionally complex for intercultural couples if there are conflicting expectations from their different cultures.

In 1953, Donald Winnicott, a renowned British paediatrician and psychoanalyst, developed the concept of the 'good enough mother' as part of his work on early childhood development, psychoanalytic theory of attachment and the psychological formation of the child [6]. He introduced this idea to emphasise the importance of a mother's responsiveness to her child's needs, but also her ability to allow her child to experience some frustration and discomfort, which ultimately contributes to the child's emotional and psychological development. His idea of the 'good enough mother' challenged the idealised image of a mother who is attuned to her child's every need or want in a self-sacrificing way and suggested that it is more important for a mother to be 'good enough'. She must be sufficiently present and responsive in the early years but not perfect. He believed that the child develops resilience from not always having their needs met instantly. The 'good enough mother', while providing a secure environment for the infant to feel safe, loved and nurtured, would also allow the infant to experience the ordinary frustrations of life, enabling the child to gradually become more independent and develop a sense of self. Her imperfections – such as moments of frustration or fatigue – are seen as essential for the child's emotional growth because they help the child to understand that not all needs can be instantly fulfilled and that the world is not always perfectly responsive. By this, he attempted to reframe societal expectations of motherhood so that instead of striving for unattainable perfection, the more compassionate and realistic image of the 'good enough mother' allowed space for the child to grow, learn and adapt, whilst also enabling a secure and loving attachment to develop:

> A mother is neither good nor bad nor the product of illusion, but is a separate and independent entity: The good-enough mother . . . starts off with an almost complete adaptation to her infant's needs, and as time proceeds she adapts less and less completely, gradually, according to the infant's growing ability to deal with her failure. Her failure to adapt to every need of the child helps them adapt to external realities. [7]

Writers have tried to explore societal expectations and women's responses to them over many decades. Adrienne Rich, an American poet, essayist and feminist, wrote extensively about the complexities of motherhood, often exploring its psychological, political and social dimensions. One of her most significant works on the subject is her book *Of Woman Born: Motherhood as Experience and Institution*, written in 1976, where she delved into the duality of motherhood as both a deeply personal experience and an institution shaped by cultural expectations and power dynamics [8]. Her writings on motherhood presented a critical exploration of how motherhood is shaped by both personal feelings and societal structures, examining how motherhood is often idealised and romanticised in society as a pure, selfless role for women. She noted the way society has historically used motherhood to control and limit women's autonomy, contributing to women's oppression, and confining them to traditional roles that restrict their freedom and potential. She also, however, recognised that motherhood can be a profound, transformative experience and acknowledged the deep emotional connection that many mothers feel towards their children and the complexities and challenges of mother–child relationships, highlighting the tension between the personal experience of motherhood and the societal expectations that contain it. She said, 'but before we were mothers, we have been, first of all, women, with actual bodies and minds', highlighting the profound changes in self that motherhood can bring for many women.

Rachel Cusk, a British novelist and essayist, also addressed the complexities of motherhood in her memoir *A Life's Work: On Becoming a Mother*, with a frank perspective based on her own experience of becoming a mother [9]. She reflected on her struggle with the expectations placed on women, particularly in terms of how they are supposed to embody selflessness and nurturing qualities and grappled with the ambivalence and emotional difficulties that can accompany the transition into motherhood. She examined how culture can pressurise women to feel that they must be naturally fulfilled by motherhood or that they should feel entirely devoted to their children, without room for personal doubt or self-interest. She addressed her disorientation on becoming a mother and the way it affected her sense of identity, whilst noting the feelings of isolation, the overwhelming nature of caring for a child, and the way it reshaped both her inner life and her external relationships. She said: 'As it stands, motherhood is a sort of wilderness through which each woman hacks her way, part martyr, part pioneer; a turn of events from which some women derive feelings of heroism, while others experience a sense of exile from the world they knew.'

There can be an unspoken assumption that when a woman gives birth, she immediately experiences an instinctive, all-encompassing love for and connection with her baby. This of course does happen for many women, but it is not universal and often not immediate. The birth may leave the woman exhausted, frightened, traumatised and in pain so that she is unable to access a positive emotional response to the baby. Women can feel alienated, distressed, guilty and perplexed if they don't meet the expectation of an intense emotional connection to the infant. Following childbirth, the woman begins to adjust to her new role and the profound responsibilities of parenthood whilst recovering physically and emotionally. There is often a complex mix of joy, hope, love, anxiety, fear, profound fatigue and relief. Some women feel overwhelmed by their new responsibilities, the making of many small but important decisions and choices on an hour-by-hour basis, the worry about making mistakes and not being good enough, while coping with their physical recovery, the art of breastfeeding and sleep deprivation. The love that develops comes to be experienced as a new kind of love, not always joyful, as described here by Harold in *A Little Life* by Hanya Yangihara [10].

> I didn't feel that before Jacob, and I didn't feel that after. But it is a singular love, because it is a love whose foundation is not physical attraction, or pleasure, or intellect, but fear. You have never known fear until you have a child, and maybe that is what tricks us into thinking that it is more magnificent, because the fear itself is more magnificent. Every day, your first thought is not 'I love him' but 'How is he?' The world, overnight, rearranges itself into an obstacle course of terrors.

However, some women find that an intense, protective love for and attachment to their child does not present itself and they have a protracted ambivalence towards the infant. There may be a complex mix of conflicting emotions. It can be unsettling, frightening, shame- and guilt-inducing, and difficult for the woman to bear. The infant will not understand and may withdraw, making few demands or make increasingly desperate attempts to engage their mother. Ambivalence can develop from a variety of often overlapping factors including depression, anxiety, motherhood not meeting her expectations or conflicts with her own needs, frustration with the relentless tasks of caring for the infant, resentment if the birth was traumatic, unresolved issues with her partner, having poor emotional support, past trauma, and anger if the pregnancy was conceived through sexual violence.

The effects on the mother–infant relationship can vary and the ambivalence may resolve over time, as the mother adjusts to her new role and receives appropriate support for the underlying causative factors. It is therefore important to understand what the woman's expectations of early parenthood were and explore what factors are contributing to her difficulties.

And so, the discourse on how and what a mother is, or is expected to be, reveals a potential disconnect between the actual experience of the mother and what society at large expects from the role and relationship. What is clear is that there are a wide range of experiences, attitudes, pressures, challenges and opinions and that these change continually across generations, societies and cultures. As clinicians we must be aware of the societal and cultural narrative that a particular woman is operating within and how this affects her view of herself as a mother, whether she feels she fits in or is at odds with it, and how this affects her emotional well-being and mental health. Within perinatal mental health services and particularly within the Mother and Baby Unit context, mental health professionals need to be aware of how constant scrutiny and expectations that women will parent in a 'perfect way' may adversely affect her recovery and developing confidence as a mother. It is very important for perinatal mental health practitioners to understand that there is a range of parenting styles and cultural practices around child-rearing. As clinicians we need to be aware of the attitudes to and expectations of mothers we bring to our work and be able to reflect on whether these are helpful within the clinical context. We must strive to develop a compassionate, flexible and understanding approach that acknowledges the diverse experiences of mothers and to support them in confronting unrealistic ideals, of their own or society's making.

Individual Factors and Context for the Woman

There are many factors influencing the woman's experience of pregnancy and parenthood. Her life experience, coping strategies, resilience, expectations, social and emotional support, environmental factors, mental and physical health all play a part. Some of these will be explored below and many others are dealt with in detail in the relevant sections of this textbook.

Timing of Pregnancy

Teenage pregnancies occur for multifaceted reasons, have health and social consequences and are likely to be unplanned and unwanted. Young women are likely to be physiologically, psychologically and socially unprepared for what becomes an abrupt and often traumatic transition to adulthood and parenthood. Adolescence is a time during which major developments take place, at physiological and psychological levels, and in terms of the development of the personality. Early or teenage pregnancy is a worldwide phenomenon that occurs most frequently – but not only – in middle- and low-income countries. There are however some common risk factors and consequences particularly in terms of education and future life chances. Teenage pregnancy is often referred to as that which occurs within the first two years of gynaecological age (i.e. the time that has passed since menarche) and/or when the teenage girl is still dependent on her original family nucleus. The World Health Organization uses the expression 'early pregnancy' to refer to any pregnancy occurring before the age of 20 years and the United Nations defines teenage pregnancies as those in which the mothers are younger than 18 years. The young woman may be dependent on her family at this time in her life or she may become dependent on a third person because of pregnancy.

The body of the teenage girl or mother is not prepared for pregnancy and there is a major risk of dying from factors related to pregnancy, childbirth and post-childbirth, especially if the pregnancy occurs before the age of 15. It is estimated that complications arising from pregnancy and childbirth in girls between 15 and 19 years of age are the second most prevalent cause of death worldwide for this population group [11]. The numbers of teenage maternal psychiatric deaths in the UK and Ireland have increased in recent years (see Chapter 22, 'Maternal Suicide, Deliberate Self-Harm and Other Mental Health Related Causes of Maternal Death') and indicate that the mental health of pregnant teenagers has to be addressed rigorously. Furthermore, in addition to the physical consequences, there are psychosocial consequences that will impact the future lives of the mother and her offspring [12, 13, 14, 15] (see Box 1.1). However, the transition to the parenting role has more positive outcomes when there is strong family support.

Box 1.1 Factors Associated with Teenage Pregnancies

Factors associated with teenage pregnancies include:

- early and forced marriages
- low self-esteem
- history of child maltreatment and sexual abuse
- drug and alcohol misuse
- mental disorder in the individual and/or her family
- lack of sex education
- ignorance of, misinformation about and lack of access to contraception
- poor access to healthcare
- low educational level, interest and expectations
- poverty
- poor social support and absence of positive stereotypes

Consequences:

- complications with childbirth
- premature births
- underweight babies
- poor maternal weight gain
- higher maternal mortality
- higher infant morbidity and mortality
- higher rates of mental health problems
- economic and psychosocial consequences of single parenthood, lack of educational and occupational opportunities
- economic dependency increasing risk of future abusive relationships and sexual abuse
- children more likely to live in poverty and to have more accidents and behavioural problems

Lockwood Estrin's work in an inner-city environment found that young pregnant women under 25 had a very high prevalence of mental disorders, 67.2% versus 21.2% when compared with older women. They were also more likely to be Black and minority ethnic, single, to live in poverty, be homeless or in emergency accommodation, be unemployed or unable to work, and to have an unplanned pregnancy [16].

On the other hand, while older motherhood is not new, there is an increasing number of women becoming pregnant through technological means, often for the first time, at the end of their reproductive cycle [17]. Childbearing can be postponed for many reasons including higher educational attainment, focus on career, the ability to control fertility, waiting for a perfect partner or not finding a partner. However, there is a gendered anxiety associated with the often-painful reality of age-related fertility decline in women. Older mothers are more likely to be single, educated, use assisted reproductive technologies (ART), and have higher physical and psychiatric morbidity [18].

Pregnancy may also be delayed for reasons associated with the woman's mental health, including:

- effects of prescribed medication on ovulation, for example anti-psychotic drugs that raise prolactin levels
- fear of effects on the developing fetus of prescribed psychotropic medications
- medical advice to avoid pregnancy when taking specific medications, for example sodium valproate
- polycystic ovarian syndrome (PCOS) as a side effect of prescribed medication
- depression and anxiety affecting capacity to make decisions
- eating disorders with low BMI affecting fertility
- fearfulness of becoming a parent in the context of a personal history of child maltreatment, abuse and trauma
- tokophobia
- sexual trauma
- sexual dysfunction
- obsessional ideas or compulsions leading to avoidance of sex
- fear of relapse, for example for women who have severe mood disorders
- stigma including fear she will be regarded as a bad mother or that her infant will be removed

Women with some of the above dilemmas may present for pre-pregnancy advice (see Chapter 24, 'Pre-pregnancy Advice and Planning') and many of these conditions can be managed with appropriate interventions. It is also worth noting that many of these issues can be addressed through careful and sensitive exploration of the woman's sexual health and plans for parenthood as part of routine psychiatric care.

Trauma, Abuse, Neglect, Adversity

Niall Williams, in his novel *Time of the Child*, poignantly described a boy 'whose childhood tasted of tears' – a powerful image and one that resonates with our familiarity in clinical practice of women who have had jeopardised lives [19]. Childhood adversity is not uncommon, with 67% of the population having at least one adverse childhood event (ACE). However, when individuals have four or more ACEs there are clear effects on both physical and psychiatric morbidity with increased suicide attempts, depression, intravenous substance misuse, lung disease, liver disease and early sexual activity. Childhood adversity's profound effects on health are mediated through multiple hardships and cumulative stresses and are more common in deprived circumstances [20].

It stands to reason therefore that many of the women seen in perinatal mental health services have been exposed to adversity during their youth and that the effects of this will still be being felt when the woman is herself childbearing and parenting. There is evidence that the cumulative incidence of any postpartum psychiatric diagnosis is increased by the presence of different adversities experienced between age 0–15 years [21]. Early adversity may also make her more susceptible to abuse and trauma in adulthood. Additionally, parents with multiple ACEs may have post-traumatic stress disorder (PTSD) symptoms or complex PTSD (see Chapter 11, 'Anxiety Disorders' and Chapter 15, 'Complex Post-Traumatic Stress Disorder') and these are believed to be a key mediator of risk in the intergenerational transmission of ACEs. A history of trauma and abuse may haunt the woman and its viscerality be reawakened during pregnancy, childbirth and on becoming a parent, hence the importance of coming to know what might have happened to her. Work on preventing ACEs in children has begun to examine how children's risk for ACEs and potential for resilience may be linked to the early child-rearing experiences of their parents carried forward into parenting practices [22]. For clinicians this means that direct enquiry needs to be made to elicit the occurrence of ACEs during the mother's childhood with a view to prevention of breakdown, promptly and effectively treating underlying psychiatric problems and supporting her with parenting to reduce the risk of ACEs for her children, given the evidence that positive childhood experiences may be protective against intergenerational transmission.

Added to ACEs, many women face pregnancy and parenthood with a history of intimate partner abuse and violence [23, 24], sexual and non-sexual assault, loss which may be multiple and traumatic, displacement, exposure to war, civil conflict and natural disasters, as well as being victims of stigma and racism. These experiences also need sensitive enquiry though many women may not wish to explicitly recount them in detail. The principles of trauma-informed care (see Chapter 37, 'Violence against Women') need to be embedded in perinatal mental health services and practices as it is well established that high rates of trauma exist in women with mental disorders.

Relationships

Relationships are at the heart of the concept of the perinatal frame of mind and are central to all aspects of clinical work with women who have perinatal mental health problems and their families. It is essential to have a thorough understanding of a woman's experience of relationships with her parents and other key adult attachment figures during childhood as well as subsequent relationships with friends, family and intimate partners. Clinicians need to understand the nature of these relationships, how they may have affected the woman's mental health, and how any mental disorders have affected her relationships. Understanding what she experienced in her early relationships with parents and siblings and what that might mean for her current relationships with them is important, in order to gauge what support they may be able to provide, what caring responsibilities she has towards them, as well as being able to anticipate what unconscious repetition of early relating and behaviours may occur in her relationships with her family, infant and partner.

Some women may be isolated from family, friends and cultural groups during the perinatal period. There may be many reasons for this from personality-related factors which mean that she may have difficulty establishing or maintaining close relationships, to being a refugee following multiple losses. The lack of a close, confiding relationship is strongly associated with the development of depression [25]. Lack of practical support is hard for any new mother. Therefore, an exploration of the woman's relationships, her social network and the strengths and stresses associated with these, as well as the well-being of those close to her is vital to understanding her current situation and how to best support her and her family. Mothers and their infants are not alone and are part of families, be they nuclear, with a much wanted and treasured infant or a more complex family that may be extended, blended, broken or dispossessed with above-average stresses and strains.

The perinatal frame of mind includes exploration and consideration of the partner, father or non-birthing parent and the quality of the relationships between them and the mother. The physicality and uniqueness of childbearing and childbirth, and societal

Box 1.2 Questions to Address in Relation to the Partner

- How much does the partner know or understand about the mother's mental disorder?
- How do they respond to learning about the disorder and to experiencing their partner's symptoms? Do they feel able to cope, seek help appropriately, engage with healthcare professionals? Does the woman hide information or minimise her symptoms with them? Do they experience anger, blame, or feel abandoned and rejected and how do they cope with these feelings?
- What are their attitudes to mental illnesses and their treatments in general, and in the context of pregnancy and childbirth?
- What are the family, cultural or societal factors that affect the way they understand and deal with the illness in their partner?
- Does the partner have mental health problems too? If so, how does this interact with the woman's mental health problems? What support do they have with their mental health? And what does this mean for the infant if both parents are unwell at the same time?
- What is the history of the couple relationship? How have they reacted to the pregnancy, childbirth, early parenthood and associated changes to the emotional and physical relationship with the mother? Are there unresolved conflicts within the relationship? Is there intimate partner violence or abuse?
- What is their relationship with the infant like? How do they contribute to child-rearing tasks? Are there issues with their own parenting capacity?
- Is the current partner the parent of the unborn baby, or infant? If not how do they feel about the pregnancy?
- Do either the woman or partner have children from previous relationships and, if so, what is either or both of their relationships with their stepchildren like?

expectations around motherhood, may overshadow the roles and experience of fathers and non-birthing parents, contributing to them being overlooked and neglected (see Chapter 6, 'Paternal Mental Health in the Perinatal Period'). Asking sensitively but directly about the quality of the couple relationship is vital to determine how they support each other and to detect whether there is abuse within the relationship (see Chapter 37, 'Violence against Women') [23].

The questions that need addressing when thinking about the partner in the context of maternal mental disorder are set out in Box 1.2.

Physical Health

Some women come to pregnancy in optimal health, knowledgeable about diet and supplements and physically fit. Others bring with them physical vulnerabilities associated with their country of origin (infection, untreated congenital cardiac abnormalities, etc.), mental disorders, pre-existing physical conditions, environment, medication, family history, smoking and obesity. There are conditions that occur only in or are exacerbated by pregnancy (see Chapter 3, 'Physiological Changes in Pregnancy and Common Obstetric Medical Disorders'). More women are presenting to maternity services either overweight or obese and this poses a significant problem for both maternal and infant outcome. Both antipsychotic and antidepressant medication contribute to weight gain, which increases physical vulnerability in women taking these medications [26, 27].

Women with severe mental disorders are particularly vulnerable. Women with schizophrenia have worse physical health, are more likely to smoke and have higher rates of obesity than women in the general community. Symptoms of the disorder, poor diet, lifestyle factors, social isolation, poor self-care and hygiene as well as adverse treatment effects contribute to this. They have more autoimmune disorders, are more likely to die from cancer than men with schizophrenia, miss or are not offered opportunities for screening and routine care and reviews of their physical health, are subject to delays in diagnosis and receive suboptimal treatment. This means that women with schizophrenia are more likely to become pregnant in an unhealthy, malnourished state with consequences for both her and the infant's outcome (see Chapter 13 on schizophrenia). The combination of antipsychotic use and obesity causes a particular vulnerability in pregnancy. Studies in Canada and Denmark have shown that compared with women in the population who do not have a history of schizophrenia, women with schizophrenia tend to have higher risk outcomes including pre-eclampsia, venous thromboembolism, placental complications and haemorrhage, assisted deliveries such as caesarean sections, inductions of labour and maternal intensive care admissions, and more stillbirths and neonatal deaths [28]. There is also an increased risk of obstetric near misses during childbirth for women with severe mental illness even when age, ethnicity and socio-economic status are accounted for [29].

Women with bipolar affective disorder also have higher rates of physical comorbidities, obesity, smoking and obstetric complications (see Chapter 12, 'Postpartum Psychosis and Bipolar Disorder').

Therefore, the guidance offered within pre-pregnancy advice and planning (see Chapter 24, 'Pre-pregnancy Advice and Planning') needs to be considered for all women with severe mental disorders, even when they are not actively stating that they want to become pregnant. It affords the opportunity to address physical health problems, obesity and the effects of an unhealthy lifestyle, as it may be too late to address the risk issues once the woman is pregnant.

The woman may experience physical health complications due to new pregnancy and childbirth-related conditions, for example, pre-eclampsia, thrombosis, sepsis, liver disease (see Chapter 3, 'Physiological Changes in Pregnancy and Common Obstetric Medical Disorders') or fetal abnormalities may be detected during routine ultrasound scans (see Chapter 4, 'Fetal Development and Routine Maternity Care'), and require medical intervention, extended hospital stays for the woman or infant and cause considerable anxiety. Traumatic childbirth, previous pregnancy loss and years of infertility treatment (see Chapter 8, 'Psychological Aspects of Infertility, Assisted Conception and Perinatal Loss' and Chapter 11, 'Anxiety Disorders') can have both physical and psychological consequences for the woman and her partner.

Jardine's paper indicated that socio-economic and ethnic inequalities were responsible for a substantial proportion of stillbirths, preterm births and births with fetal growth retardation in England [30]. The largest inequalities were seen in Black and South Asian women in the most socio-economically deprived quintile and it was recommended that prevention should target the entire population as well as specific minority ethnic groups at high risk of adverse pregnancy outcomes, to address risk factors and wider determinants of health. The Mothers and Babies: Reducing Risk through Audits and Confidential Enquiries across the UK (MBBRACE) report finds that the risk of maternal death in 2020–22 was almost three times higher among women from Black ethnic minority backgrounds compared with white women, that women from Asian backgrounds also continued to be at higher risk than white women, and that women living in the 20% most deprived areas continue to have the highest maternal mortality rates, more than twice as high as the maternal mortality rate of women living in the 20% least deprived areas [31].

This means that the clinician needs to remain alert for the reality that there may be several cumulative risk factors that contribute to physical health problems for particular women in the perinatal period.

Mental Health

Perinatal psychiatry is not defined by a particular diagnosis. This textbook addresses individual disorders in terms of how the perinatal context affects their presentation, course, risks, treatment and care. It is essential however to have an up-to-date understanding of the entire range of psychiatric disorders that occur in adults and their recommended, effective and evidence-based interventions. This then allows for the perinatal psychiatrist/clinician to apply learning to the perinatal context and its effect on clinical practice. Clarification of the diagnosis and the exploration of comorbidities is an essential early task following referral (see Chapter 23 on perinatal assessment and evaluation of risk) and aids care-planning and risk assessment. Diagnoses can change over time and there are very high rates of both physical and psychiatric comorbidities in women with severe mental illness. Anxiety disorders are known to be both under- and mis-diagnosed and may be exacerbated by or arise de novo in the perinatal period.

Diagnosis is, however, just part of the clinician's task. Understanding what the diagnosis means for this individual woman during pregnancy, in labour and in early parenthood requires exploration of the history of the disorder. Areas that need clarification are set out in Box 1.3.

Residual symptoms and/or prior undertreatment of the disorder, need to be carefully considered by the clinical team, as these may impair maternal function and increase risk. Symptoms that may not have much influence on day-to-day functioning in the absence of parental responsibility may be highly problematic and potentially devastating in the context of child-rearing. Fatigue, low energy, poor drive, agitation, psychomotor retardation, social withdrawal, reduced facial expression and preoccupation will affect how the woman meets the physical and emotional needs of her infant. Comorbid substance misuse will also have potentially serious effects on parenting and attempts need to be made to address this (see Chapter 18, 'Alcohol and Substance Use Disorders'). Novel symptoms, that occur only within pregnancy (e.g. psychotic symptoms related to the fetus, denial of pregnancy, thoughts of feticide) or postpartum (e.g. estrangement from the infant, psychotic symptoms related to the infant, thoughts of infanticide or filicide), require careful exploration to both identify and assess the associated risks (see Chapter 36, 'Child Safeguarding' and Chapter 38, 'When Mothers Kill Their Children'). Suicide is a rare but devastating consequence of mental illness in the perinatal period, and this is discussed in Chapter 22, 'Maternal Suicide, Deliberate Self-Harm and Other Mental Health Related Causes of Maternal Death'.

What is unique about the perinatal period is of course the opportunity for early identification, assessment and, with it, prompt treatment and prevention in women who are either currently unwell or at risk of becoming unwell in pregnancy and postnatally

Box 1.3 Understanding the Woman's Diagnosis

- Is this a first episode or a recurrence of a long-standing mental disorder?
- Was there an acute or insidious onset?
- Is this an acute illness or is there a chronic condition with impairment of function?
- Have there been frequent relapses or has she remained well for many years?
- What do her most severe episodes look like?
- What treatments and interventions have been tried and what works?
- Does she achieve full remission or partial remission?
- What have been and what are the current risks to self and to others?
- Are there risks from others?
- What are the actual and potential effects of the disorder
  - on level of risk, when severely unwell, when relapsing, when stable
  - on self-care and daily functioning
  - on cognitive function
  - on pregnancy and childbirth
  - on parenting
  - on family, social network and health/social care relationships
- What may be the effects of pregnancy, childbirth and parenting on the disorder?

(see Chapter 23 on the perinatal assessment and evaluation of risk). National Institute for Health and Care Excellence Antenatal and Postnatal Mental Health guidance recommends that pregnant women are asked identification questions as part of a general discussion about their mental health and well-being at first contact with maternity services and primary care [32] (see Box 1.4). If women are identified as being unwell or at risk of relapse it is imperative that they are guided to the care pathway that meets their needs (see Chapter 29, 'Effective Working across Health, Peer Support and Third Sector Interfaces' and Chapter 30, 'Perinatal Mental Health Service Development and Delivery'), and that plans for monitoring and treatment are developed in partnership with and shared with the woman, her partner/family and teams and services working alongside her.

Once an assessment has taken place, working in partnership with the woman is essential. Psychoeducation about mental illness in the perinatal context is an important element of the woman's care. The development of a formulation and the sharing of and discussion with the woman of this can be helpful for her own understanding and self-compassion (see Chapter 23 on the perinatal assessment and evaluation of risk). The formulation and the woman's understanding of it may also be helpful in explaining to partners and family what is happening and can potentially change attitudes and reduce stigma.

The woman's previous experience of care needs to be explored, particularly if she has had unpleasant or traumatic experiences of general adult inpatient care. Women who are at high risk of breakdown in the perinatal period will benefit from discussions about what their treatment options might entail. A visit to their local Mother and Baby Unit may help to reduce any anticipatory anxiety they may have about a potential admission. Talking with the woman and her partner about setting out, in advance, plans to address particular issues that arise when she is most unwell may also be beneficial particularly when there are interventions she categorically does not want or if her symptoms

Box 1.4 Identifying Mental Health Problems in Pregnancy

At a woman's first contact with primary care or her booking visit, and during the early postnatal period, consider asking the following depression identification questions as part of a general discussion about a woman's mental health and well-being:

Depression and Anxiety Disorders

- During the past month, have you often been bothered by feeling down, depressed or hopeless?
- During the past month, have you often been bothered by having little interest or pleasure in doing things?

Also consider asking about anxiety using the two-item Generalized Anxiety Disorder scale (GAD-2):

- Over the last 2 weeks, how often have you been bothered by feeling nervous, anxious or on edge?
- Over the last 2 weeks, how often have you been bothered by not being able to stop or control worrying?

At all contacts after the first contact with primary care or the booking visit, the health visitor, and other healthcare professionals who have regular contact with a woman in pregnancy and the postnatal period (first year after birth), should consider:

- asking the two depression identification questions and the GAD-2 as part of a general discussion about her mental health and well-being and
- using the EPDS (Edinburgh Postnatal Depression Scale) or the PHQ-9 (Patient Health Questionnaire) as part of monitoring.

Severe Mental Illness

At a woman's first contact with services in pregnancy and the postnatal period, ask about:

- any past or present severe mental illness
- past or present treatment by a specialist mental health service, including inpatient care
- any severe perinatal mental illness in a first-degree relative (mother, sister or daughter)

negatively affect her relationships and she wishes to avoid the consequences of this (see Chapter 39, 'Mental Health and Capacity Legislation in the Perinatal Period').

The perinatal period is a time when women may be very afraid to admit to or to seek help for mental health problems because of fears that they will be judged negatively as a parent and/or that their children will be taken from them. Practitioners working with pregnant and postnatal women need to be aware that a reluctance to disclose and/or minimisation of symptoms might be present and needs careful elucidation. Women may also be reluctant to engage, or have difficulty in engaging, in treatment because of avoidance associated with their mental health problem or dependence on alcohol or drugs and clinicians need to be alert to this.

However, for the majority of women, pregnancy and early parenthood are times of great personal growth and development. The woman is likely to be highly motivated to remain well and to adjust lifestyle and relationship factors that contribute to her becoming unwell.

The perinatal frame of mind is not just for those working in perinatal mental health services. Clinicians working with women from menarche to menopause in child and adolescent and adult mental health services, that is, those women of childbearing potential, need to ensure that they optimise the treatment of psychiatric disorders from initial presentation and pre-conception so that women with the more severe disorders have the best chance of maintaining function to support their future parenting and caring roles. Clinicians in these services also need to regularly discuss and ask about the woman's sexual health, relationships and plans for pregnancy and parenthood, with this being embedded as part of routine care within secondary mental health services.

Culture, Ethnicity and Gender

The perinatal frame of mind involves understanding who this woman is and what are her relationships and influences. The contributions of the woman's culture, ethnicity and gender are of great importance in the perinatal period both on her physical and mental health. In Chapter 7, 'The Perinatal Mental Health of Racial and Ethnic Minority Groups', the authors address the striking inequities that persist in health outcomes for women of racial and ethnic minority groups beyond socio-economic and other demographic factors, and in particular what this means for women in the perinatal period.

Perinatal clinicians need to have a good understanding of the communities in which they practise. There is a need to know what, for example, are a particular religion's beliefs and attitudes to mental illness, mothers and mothers with mental illnesses. This needs to be accompanied by a knowledge of what behaviours may be exhibited towards the woman and her family, and what supports may be provided within her religious community for her as a mother and if she is unwell. In addition, it is important to understand the following within a particular culture:

- attitudes to mental health, including any issues to do with stigma, shame and honour
- beliefs and knowledge about mental illnesses and their treatment
- beliefs and practices regarding pregnancy, childbirth and parenting
- health-seeking behaviours
- beliefs and expression of these within the disorder
- language and words used for mental health symptoms and mental disorders

Watson found in her review of ethnic minority women's experiences of perinatal mental health conditions that there were problems in relation to healthcare professionals' attitudes, understanding and perceptions, that Black, Asian and minority ethnic women were less likely to be offered treatment when compared to white women and that there was limited availability of culturally appropriate services [33]. Language and interpreting services have a major role to play when working with women who have mental disorders. Ensuring that the options offered to women are of high quality and culturally appropriate is important. Women may lose their capacity to communicate clearly in their second language (English) when acutely unwell and it is better to err by providing an interpreter for these women rather that hoping that communication will be optimal [34].

Acculturation is an important factor for people within migrant groups. Having an understanding of women's identification within their own cultural group or within that of where they reside, helps us determine how this affects their mental health and how support for the woman can be developed within her community. People may acculturate in different ways, for example:

- integrated/bicultural: strong identification with host and cultural group
- separate: strong own group identification only
- assimilated: strong host identification
- marginalised: weak identification with host and cultural group

Marginalised women may find it very difficult to access perinatal mental health services, and those with a more separate identification may find it difficult to accept support from services. Women from diverse communities need to be stakeholders in the development of perinatal mental health (PMH) services to optimise access and engagement.

Within a culture there may be gender issues that affect the woman and her mental health in the perinatal period. For example, exploring the following may be critical to understanding her and how to support her:

- What is her role and status within the family?
- What autonomy does she have, for example access to money, her passport, travel locally, language classes and education, social pursuits, decision-making?
- What are the attitudes to fetal and infant loss?
- What are the attitudes towards the sex of the infant?
- Can she access healthcare (mental health, gynaecological, maternity) independently?
- What are attitudes to women seeing male healthcare professionals?
- Will male partners take advice from female healthcare professionals?
- Do families feel the need to consult either religious leaders, or traditional/faith-based healers before making decisions based on medical advice?

Relationship with the Infant and Safeguarding

The perinatal frame of mind includes holding in mind the infant and the parental relationships with the infant, alongside consideration of the mother (see Section 4, 'Infant Mental Health in the Context of Maternal Mental Health' and Chapter 36 'Child Safeguarding'). In addition, women worry about how their behaviours, relating and interpersonal difficulties associated with their perinatal mental illness, and their own childhood experiences, may affect the immediate and long-term development and outcome of their children. They may also have fears about the genetic transmission of their illness and the role that other factors associated with their illnesses (e.g. poor housing, poverty, unstable relationships, stigma) may have on their children's well-being. However, Stein's review purported that risks are not inevitable and in the absence of severe or chronic maternal disorder or other adversities, the effect sizes are generally small or moderate and that mechanisms underlying associations are complex and include a range of genetic, other biological, and environmental pathways [35]. Howard and Khalifeh noted that there is a limited understanding of protective factors that account for the large proportion of unaffected children, despite exposure to significant antenatal maternal illness, and that associations are attenuated or no longer evident after adjustment for confounders (e.g. young age, low educational level, interpersonal violence, poor social support, substance misuse) [36]. They also stated that the woman's own experience of being parented and early trauma, and the effects of these on her relating and attachment style (low maternal sensitivity and 'parental mentalisation') may be more significant influences on outcome for the exposed child. It is reiterated, therefore, that a careful developmental history needs to be undertaken within perinatal mental health services. Mental illness in both parents and inter-parental conflict are also clearly red flags for adverse child outcomes. Most importantly, the cumulative risk when parental mental illness is combined with other risk factors including domestic abuse and substance misuse may place the infant and other children at great risk of harm (see Chapter 36, 'Child Safeguarding'). However, positive parenting by a healthy co-parent (mother or father) can buffer children against the adverse effects of perinatal mental illness [37].

It is well established that stigma takes on an extra dimension in the perinatal period where women are afraid to seek help or admit that they have mental health problems as they fear they will be judged negatively as a parent and/or that their children will be taken from them. This contributes to women being fearful of services and can contribute to delays in accessing timely help. In women with the more severe mental disorders these ideas may become delusional and expose both the mother and infant to higher risk of harm. Clinicians need to be constantly aware that these fears may be present and concerning for the woman and seek to explore them in a sensitive and realistic manner.

However, when there are genuine concerns about risk to the infant (see Chapter 36, 'Child Safeguarding') difficult, often challenging and painful, conversations will need to take place between perinatal mental health practitioners and the woman and her family. Referral to children's social services can be alarming [38, 39] for the woman and her family, and the mother is particularly vulnerable to worsening of her mental state or the emergence of new risks when the infant is or might be removed from her care (see Chapter 2, 'Experiencing Severe Perinatal Mental Illness: The Woman's Perspective' and Chapter 22, 'Maternal Suicide, Deliberate Self-Harm and Other Mental Health Related Causes of Maternal Death'). Having the capacity to hold in mind that the mother, perinatal mental health services and other agencies all want the best outcome for the infant, that is, that they are safe and well cared for, is essential to ensuring that the mother remains supported at a very challenging time despite what might appear to be a perception of conflicting roles, interests and hopes.

What Does the Perinatal Frame of Mind Mean for Practitioners?

Perinatal psychiatrists need to develop their skills as clinicians, leaders (see Chapter 9, 'The Evolving Leader in Perinatal Mental Health Services') and as teachers. They also need to be mindful of the evidence base, and open to and able to critically appraise emerging research in the many disciplines which underpin perinatal psychiatry. These include but are not limited to, embryology, genetics, neuroscience, physiology, psychology, sociology, health services research, psychopharmacology, clinical trials and teratology. The clinical tasks are intellectually and emotionally demanding, as is leading a team and engaging with stakeholders to ensure that perinatal mental health services are developed, delivered and maintained. Teaching and training are key to not only the maintenance of optimal delivery of high-quality, effective and compassionate services within PMH teams [40] but also to ensure that primary care, general adult, liaison, home treatment and crisis team, as well as child and adolescent mental health services remain aware of the need to ensure that women of childbearing potential have their physical, sexual and mental health care needs addressed in a timely and holistic way. Health visitors, midwives, obstetricians, early years practitioners, workers in third-sector organisations as well as women and their partners and families, also need access to high-quality and regular perinatal mental health psychoeducation and training. It is vital that perinatal psychiatrists recognise and anticipate the need to deliver training in their local and regional areas to a wide breadth of professionals as well as ensuring high-quality training of medical students and trainee psychiatrists.

The perinatal frame of mind means that we have a number of people, not just the mother, and a range of relationships, to think about and hold in mind within our clinical practice, teams and when developing services. It also commits us to the vital task of working in partnership with women, their families, as well as the many professionals and services involved in a woman's care. These include maternity services, primary care professionals, universal services, general adult mental health teams, social care and third-sector services. Perinatal mental health clinicians need to work collaboratively, take responsibility and display trust, respect, compassion, transparency and resilience. NHS England's document *Involving and Supporting Partners and Other Family Members in Specialist Perinatal Mental Health Services: Good Practice Guide* (2021) sets out practical advice on how to work in partnership with women and their families [41]. The Royal College of Psychiatrists' (2021) *College Report CR232: Perinatal Mental Health Services: Recommendations for the Provision of Services for Childbearing Women* outlines how good perinatal mental health services should promote seamless, integrated, comprehensive care across the whole clinical pathway, with clear communication across organisational and professional boundaries [42].

Box 1.5 sets out who we need to consider and Box 1.6 what needs to be considered by the mother and by practitioners.

Women in the perinatal period, as with any other time, deserve to have safe, kind, compassionate, effective, continuous, personalised, co-produced and family-friendly services where they have access to specialist information and choice. Their practitioners need to uphold these values and be thoughtful, well-trained and competent, with access to training, supervision and mentoring. Box 1.7 sets out some of the skills, competencies and attributes the clinician must develop.

Box 1.5 Who Do We Consider in the Perinatal Period?

Who do we need to consider?

- the woman
- the infant
- the partner
- the family (older children, grandparents, extended family)
- other social relationships
- our own role
- the PMH team
- other mental health teams
- primary care
- health visiting
- children's social care
- other agencies
- voluntary and third-sector organisations

Box 1.6 What Do the Woman and Her Healthcare Practitioners Need to Consider in the Perinatal Period?

What does the woman think about in the perinatal period?

- not just one person
- conflicts between own needs and those of dependent others
- the fetus/infant and older children
- partner/co-parent
- wider family
- concerns about disclosure
- understanding of her disorder, insight
- how to remain well
- treatment/therapeutic issues and decisions to be made
- previous experience of care and treatment
- risk: what does it mean?
- influence of life experience, social and cultural issues
- what does it mean and feel like to be 'looked after'?
- fear, shame, stigma, grief, loss
- dealing with lots of professionals

What does the practitioner think about in the perinatal period?

- the perinatal frame of mind
- the concerns of the woman and her family
- illnesses may have a different course
- interventions may need to be adapted
- general principles and decision-making becomes more complex
- the unique opportunity for prevention
- risk assessment (always dynamic, e.g. stage of pregnancy, stage of illness) for both now and future, and for *at least two people*
- confidentiality – keeping and knowing when to share information
- communication
- the care to be delivered
- the woman's experience of care: autonomy, being listened to, heard, understood, coercion, helplessness

Box 1.7 Skills, Competencies and Attributes of the PMH Practitioner

- Knowledge of mental disorders, the perinatal context, culturally relevant issues
- discussing risk
- ability to hold difficult conversations
- information sharing/governance
- relationships and communication with team members and with other teams/agencies
- flexibility, compassion, curiosity, understanding
- awareness of own strengths and limitations
- ability to reflect on own experiences of being parented/parenting and how that affects relationships with patients
- knowing how and when to seek help, supervision and mentoring, recognising and managing stress and burnout

The team needs to be responsive, flexible, well-governanced, have clear aims, solid leadership, access to evidence-based interventions, with the skills and ethos of working with, communicating effectively with, working in partnership with, and managing conflict between the woman, partner, family, other teams, services and agencies. Perinatal mental health teams must face the challenges of not focusing exclusively on either the mother or the baby's well-being, of not excluding from services women with the 'wrong' diagnosis and of retaining the perinatal frame of mind, even when the workload is demanding or in the throes of clinical crises. Difficult decisions sometimes need to be made, as for example when a decision is reached that an infant be separated from their mother. Emotions may run high; opinions may become polarised and it may be hard to keep compassion alive. Supervision, mentoring, work-based discussion and striving to remain open and reflective will help at these times, as well as taking steps to avoid personal burnout and exhaustion.

Summary

This chapter shows how the perinatal frame of mind can help ensure that we are aware that women, their children, partners and families, and the relationships between them are of the utmost importance in our clinical work and that we work in partnership with the many professionals and services involved in the woman's care. Perinatal mental health is one of the most clinically complex areas within the practice of psychiatry. It can be challenging intellectually and emotionally for practitioners but also rewarding and a privilege to work with women and their families at one of the most important and motivated times of their lives. Our tasks are to instil hope, be effective, knowledgeable and compassionate clinicians, leaders and teachers and through this potentially make a huge difference to women and families, both in the perinatal period and the longer term.

References

1. Health Education England. The competency framework for professionals working with women who have mental health problems in the perinatal period. Health Education England; 2018. https://shorturl.at/Ts31h
2. V Patel. The right to mental health. *Lancet.* 2023;402(10411):1412–13.
3. D Raphael. *Being female: reproduction, power, and change.* Berlin; New York: De Gruyter Mouton; 1975. Chapter 12.
4. ER Orchard, HJV Rutherford, AJ Holmes, SD Jamadar. Matrescence: lifetime impact of motherhood on cognition and the brain. *Trends Cogn Sci.* 2023;27(3):302–16.
5. L Jones. *Matresence: on the metamorphosis of pregnancy, childbirth and motherhood.* London: Penguin; 2024. Chapter 2.
6. DW Winnicott. Transitional objects and transitional phenomena; a study of the first not-me possession. *Int J Psychoanal.* 1953;34(2):89–97.
7. DW Winnicott. *The child, the family, and the outside world.* London: Penguin; 1973.
8. A Rich. *Of woman born: motherhood as experience and institution.* New York: Norton; 1976.
9. R Cusk. *A life's work: on becoming a mother.* London: Faber & Faber; 2001.
10. H Yanagihara. *A little life.* London: Picador; 2015.
11. World Health Organization. *Global Accelerated Action for the Health of Adolescents (AA-HA!): guidance to*

support country implementation. 2nd edition. Geneva: WHO; 2023.

12. E Raya-Diez, C Serrano-Martínez, EDS Pedro, P Montañés-Muro. Risk factors and social consequences of early pregnancy: a systematic review. *Sage Open.* 2024;14(3):1–10.
13. MV Maheshwari, N Khalid, PD Patel, R Alghareeb, A Hussain. Maternal and neonatal outcomes of adolescent pregnancy: a narrative review. *Cureus.* 2022;14(6):e25921.
14. DG Reyna, MC Villarreal, AA Cruz, CCF Acosta, CR Colunga, JS López, et al. Sociodemographic and psychosocial factors associated with adolescent pregnancy. *J Pediatr Adolesc Gynecol.* 2023;37(2):297–8.
15. RS Siegel, AR Brandon. Adolescents, pregnancy, and mental health. *J Pediatr Adolesc Gynecol.* 2014;27(3):138–50.
16. G Lockwood Estrin, EG Ryan, K Trevillion, J Demilew, D Bick, A Pickles, LM Howard. Young pregnant women and risk for mental disorders: findings from an early pregnancy cohort. *BJPsych Open.* 2019;5(2):e21.
17. K Baldwin. The biomedicalisation of reproductive ageing: reproductive citizenship and the gendering of fertility risk. *Health, Risk & Society.* 2019;21(5–6):268–83.
18. ML Pettersson, E Nedstrand, M Bladh, AS Svanberg, C Lampic, G Sydsjö. Mothers who have given birth at an advanced age - health status before and after childbirth. *Sci Rep.* 2020:10(1):9739.
19. N Williams. *Time of the child.* New York: Bloomsbury Publishing; 2024.
20. Editorial. Childhood adversity: a profound determinant of health. *Lancet Public Health.* 2021;6(11):e755.
21. E Metzer-Brody, JT Larsen, L Petersen, J Guintivano, A Di Florio, WC Miller, et al. Adverse life events increase risk for postpartum psychiatric episodes. *J Clin Psychiatry.* 2017;78(1):e59–65.
22. AJ Narajan, AF Lieberman, AS Masten. Intergenerational transmission and prevention of adverse childhood experiences (ACEs). *Clin Psychol Rev.* 2021;85:101997.
23. P Greenfield, M Calcia, C McCree, M Sahota, H Thomas, K Kirkpatrick, et al. Identifying, assessing and responding to perpetration of domestic abuse: practice guide for mental health professionals. *BJPsych Adv.* 2025;31(1):8–19.
24. LM Howard, K Trevillion, R Agnew-Davies. Domestic violence and mental health. *Int Rev Psychiatry.* 2010;22(5):525–34.
25. SB Patten. Are the Brown and Harris "vulnerability factors" risk factors for depression? *J Psychiatry Neurosci.* 1991;16(5):267–71.
26. H Gill, B Gill, S El-Halabi, D Chen-Li, O Lipsitz, JD Rosenblat, et al. Antidepressant medications and weight change: a narrative review. *Obesity (Silver Spring).* 2020;28(11):2064–72.
27. M Dayabandara, R Hanwella, S Ratnatunga, S Seneviratne, C Suraweera, VA de Silva, et al. Antipsychotic-associated weight gain: management strategies and impact on treatment adherence. *Neuropsychiatr Dis Treat.* 2017;22;13:2231–41.
28. SN Vigod, PA Kurdyak, CL Dennis, A Gruneir, A Newman, MV Seeman, et al. Maternal and newborn outcomes among women with schizophrenia: a retrospective population-based cohort study. *BJOG.* 2014;121:566–74.
29. A Easter, J Sandall, LM Howard. Obstetric near misses among women with serious mental illness: data linkage cohort study. *Br J Psychiatry.* 2021;219(3):494–500.
30. J Jardine, K Walker, I Gurol-Urganci, K Webster, P Muller, J Hawdon, et al. Adverse pregnancy outcomes attributable to socioeconomic and ethnic inequalities in England: a national cohort study. *Lancet.* 2021;398:39–48.
31. M Knight, K Bunch, D Tuffnell, H Jayakody, J Shakespeare, R Kotnis, et al., editors. *Saving Lives, Improving Mothers'*

Care – Lessons learned to inform maternity care from the UK and Ireland Confidential Enquiries into Maternal Deaths and Morbidity 2020–22. Oxford: National Perinatal Epidemiology Unit, University of Oxford; 2023.

32. National Institute for Health and Care Excellence (NICE). Antenatal and postnatal mental health: clinical management and service guidance. Clinical Guideline (CG192). 2014. Updated 2020.
33. H Watson, D Harrop, E Walton, A Young, H Soltani. A systematic review of ethnic minority women's experiences of perinatal mental health conditions and services in Europe. *PLoS ONE*. 2019;14(1):e0210587.
34. R Tribe, P Lane. Working with interpreters across language and culture in mental health. *J Ment Health*. 2009;18(3):233–41.
35. A Stein, RM Pearson, SH Goodman, E Rapa, A Rahman, M McCallum, et al. Effects of perinatal mental disorders on the fetus and child. *Lancet*. 2014;384:1800–19.
36. LM Howard, H Khalifeh. Perinatal mental health: a review of progress and challenges. *World Psychiatry*. 2020;19(3):313–27.
37. B Barker, JE Iles, PG Ramchandani. Fathers, fathering and child psychopathology. *Curr Opin Psychol*. 2017;15:87–92.
38. R Smithson, M Gibson. Less than human: a qualitative study into the experience of parents involved in the child protection system. *Child Fam Soc Work*. 2017;22:565–74.
39. Royal College of Psychiatrists. Children's social services and safeguarding. www.rcpsych.ac.uk/members/your-faculties/perinatal-psychiatry/news-and-resources
40. Royal College of Psychiatrists. PQN community standards. www.rcpsych.ac.uk/docs/default-source/improving-care/ccqi/quality-networks/perinatal/pqn-standards/pqn-community-standards-6th-edition.pdf?sfvrsn=cf4efc12_4
41. NHS England. Involving and supporting partners and other family members in specialist perinatal mental health services: good practice guide. March 2021.
42. Royal College of Psychiatrists. Perinatal mental health services: recommendations for the provision of services for childbearing women (College Report CR232). 2021.

Chapter 2

Experiencing Severe Perinatal Mental Illness

The Woman's Perspective

Clare Dolman

Introduction

Fundamentally, a psychiatric patient's relationship with the health professionals treating her depends on developing trust and that trust relies on understanding on both sides: that is why it is so critical for a clinician to have as deep an understanding as possible of their patient's perspective. It's unusual for a patient with a physical ailment to feel a need to deliberately conceal things from her clinician but this is a common occurrence for women in a perinatal mental health setting. The main reason for this is fear: fear of having her children taken away, fear of being 'judged' for wanting to have a child while coping with a chronic mental illness. This chapter will provide an overview of the research I have conducted since 2010 to identify and record the experiences of women in receipt of perinatal services or, in some cases, of women not in receipt of the services they needed. As a researcher who is also a woman with a mental illness (bipolar disorder) and who has experienced an episode in the perinatal period (postpartum psychosis after the birth of my first child), I acknowledge that I inevitably bring that experience with its potential for bias to the undertaking but hopefully my professional training and supervision have mitigated against that. As with mental health provision generally, perinatal services have been lacking in the UK until very recent times. The work described here was undertaken from 2010 to 2019 and so, with the campaigning and extra services funded more recently, some of the challenges have decreased but many remain.

Pregnancy, childbirth and raising children present particular challenges to women with severe mental illness (SMI), often exacerbating existing symptoms or acting as a trigger for a severe episode, sometimes of psychosis. This does not, however, deter the majority from becoming mothers. Indeed, Howard and colleagues found that 63% of women with psychotic disorders were mothers [1]. There is also a subgroup of women with no history of mental illness who become psychotic in the postpartum, some of whom never have another episode. Most research in this area has focused on epidemiology and risk of recurrence, on the subjects' psychopathology and the potential harm to their children [2] or on service provision [3]. However, internationally there has been a growing awareness of the need to provide gender-sensitive mental health services, such as 'Mainstreaming Gender and Women's Mental Health' [4], and there is a developing literature on the experiences of mothers with severe mental illnesses including their experiences of health services. When I reviewed the qualitative literature on motherhood for women with severe mental illness in the study *Pre-conception to Parenting: Motherhood for Women with Severe Mental Illness, a Systematic Review and Meta-synthesis of the Qualitative Literature* [5] nine themes were identified: guilt; custody loss; concern over effect on the child; isolation; coping with dual identities; stigma; centrality of motherhood; problems with service provision; positive aspects of service provision. A second stage of synthesis was conducted which produced two overarching themes termed experiences of motherhood and experiences of services. Next I will give some examples of what women themselves said in relation to these themes, as recorded by the qualitative researchers who interviewed them.

Experiences of Motherhood

Guilt

Women referred to feelings of guilt in the majority of the papers examined, but this was for a number of different reasons. Some spoke of being deeply ashamed: '*my child deserves a lot better*' [6]. Many women, notably those who had postpartum psychosis (PP), felt they had failed their children by being separated from them for a time as infants: '*I still have pangs of guilt that she was in there [hospital] and cared for by members of staff and not me*' [7]. Many were ashamed that they '*couldn't cope as a mother*' [8] or that they hadn't lived up to the societal 'ideal of motherhood': '*I felt a failure, here we go again, I'm a failure as a mother*' [9].

Custody Loss

Fear of custody loss was related to severe chronic illnesses, with most studies reporting it as a concern. In Ackerson's study, for example, 11 of the 12 participants were worried about losing custody; this was not without reason as seven had lost custody of a child at some point [10]. Bassett said this fear 'permeated all they had to say' [11]. This fear of losing their child affected communication with care professionals, with some mothers saying they masked their symptoms because of it [12], while it made others reluctant to seek help [13]. In Sands' study [14] most interviewees struggled to maintain custody and were traumatised by separation, and she reported how traumatic most women found this: '*the greatest pain I've been through, drugs, prison, psychiatric clinics etc., was the loss of my children*'. For a number of the women with schizophrenia interviewed by Chernomas, the loss of a child was almost unbearable: '*you start to get feelings for them, and then they're gone, and you don't think you have a reason to live . . .*' [15].

Concern over the Impact on the Child

In a study on the perception of genetic risk among people with bipolar disorder, a large majority were concerned about their children's risk [16] and Meiser's interviews with the same diagnostic group found that half the women said it had affected their decision whether or not to have children [17]. My own study on the views of women with bipolar disorder confirmed that this was an issue, though some took the view that they were well-placed to help their child if they did inherit it: '*it wasn't enough to deter us from wanting to have a child but it was something that we . . . were concerned about*' [18].

Isolation

Women returned frequently to their feelings of isolation. Subthemes related to the damage done to social and family relationships by their illness and the difficulties of raising children alone. Because of their illness, they often had poor social networks and meagre financial resources, and many spoke of how much more difficult it was to parent alone, especially when they were ill. These studies generally involved women with the most severe enduring illness, including a high percentage of women with schizophrenia. This contrasted with the women who had PP who reported strong family support networks [19].

Coping with Dual Identities

Combining the persona of 'woman with mental illness' with that of 'mother' had both negative and positive effects on identity. Some studies reported the added pressure to be a 'perfect' mother: '*I had this vision of . . . how I would be as a mother and I didn't live up to that expectation, so it made me feel quite bad*' [8]. Others reported that motherhood '*motivated them to grow and develop*' [20]. Having interviewed and observed 10 chronically mentally ill mothers in a supported residential programme, Sands suggested that they 'saw childbearing and parenthood as ways to affirm their normalcy [as] parenthood is a pervasive human activity that connects one with the community' [14]. Although identity issues were referred to in the majority of papers, it was a particular problem for women whose first experience of severe mental illness came immediately after childbirth. Heron and colleagues described the shocking experience of suffering PP, especially with no history of mental illness, as 'an affront' to one's sense of personal and social identity [19]. Women who had suffered a PP described a theme of 'regaining self' as they gradually recovered [7].

Stigma

The corrosive effects of stigma were cited in over three-quarters of the studies, exacerbating women's problems by preventing them from discussing them openly [21], discouraging them from going out and making social contacts and making them more reluctant to seek help [10]. Some researchers found that the stigma associated with a psychiatric diagnosis was reinforced by also being a parent [22]. As Davies and Allen express it: 'Women who are mothers and also users of mental health services face particular challenges of identity management because of the inherent tension between the societal ideals around the "good mother" and social norms associated with mental illness' [9]. They feel stigmatised as women with SMI in their contact with professionals and society at large, and this contributed to many women feeling 'a pervasive sense of shame and guilt' [23]. Edwards and Timmons, who focused specifically on the effect of stigma in the postnatal period, found that all of the six women interviewed had experienced stigma from others, but that they also suffered from 'self-stigma' because they saw themselves as 'bad mothers'. The fact that these women felt unable 'to adhere to the "supermom" ideology depicted in the media further compounded their feelings of failure and the stigma they felt towards themselves' [8].

Centrality of Motherhood

Out of 23 studies, 18 highlighted the importance of being a mother to women with severe mental illness. This had negative implications when women were forced to relinquish their mothering role due to illness as it led to pervasive feelings of failure and lowered self-esteem [19]. This differed somewhat between women with a disabling chronic psychotic illness and women who experienced an episode of PP from which they had recovered. The former group often experienced a lifelong struggle to cope with parenting, often alone and impoverished [15]. In contrast, the PP group reported much better family and social support. Many in this group were upset that becoming a mother had not been the 'perfect' experience they had expected: *'My sisters had babies and nothing's gone wrong, it was just me . . .'* [7].

The vast majority of studies conveyed the positive effect of becoming a mother. The studies with the most severely ill samples contained particularly positive affirmations of the central role children played in these women's lives. Indeed, the latter study, which used a comparison group of well mothers attending a day-care centre, found that the women with SMI regarded being a mother as the most important thing in their lives: 'in contrast with . . . the day-care mothers [who] expressed more ambivalence about being a parent'. 'One way or another, all the mentally ill mothers said that being a mother was central to their existence, that it gave meaning and focus to their lives' [14].

Experiences of Services

Problems with Service Provision

Out of 23 studies, 22 reported problems with the provision of services, ranging from difficulties with interacting with medical staff [22] to feeling upset by the frequent changes in personnel [11]. This theme also included the different treatment needs of women with PP, who complained of treatment delay due to misdiagnosis [8] and not being able to have their baby with them in hospital [7]. Two studies cited drug side effects as impairments to parenting which were not fully recognised by professionals, [24, 25] and some reported the need for more practical help during a crisis, such as childcare provision [26].

A major subtheme in the negative experiences of service provision was the unmet need that many women identified for both information and peer support groups. Many researchers asked women what they felt would improve their lives in relation to becoming parents, and many suggested well-written information on discharge, especially on parenting issues [19]. The singular experience of women suffering from PP was evident in several themes. For women who had never experienced mental illness before and had anticipated a 'perfect' birth, the chasm between expectation and reality was hard to bear. Thus, comments on guilt, the centrality of motherhood and coping with dual identities were plentiful from this group of women, whereas they were far less likely to refer to suffering from isolation as they generally reported strong support from partners and family members [27]. This contrasted with the majority of studies where there was no mention of fathers or partners except in the context of their absence. In general mothers with SMI were enthusiastic about peer support. This would give them the opportunity to 'share their experiences and obtain guidance about coping with parenting' [21], and so could be viewed as an informal method of parenting education, which was also a popular request [28].

Positive Experiences of Services

Many studies gave examples of positive experiences with services but these were usually at the level of individual healthcare professionals rather than the healthcare system. An emergent subtheme was the desire to talk regularly to someone sympathetic; when this was available it was appreciated: *'To have someone you can talk to and trust like I can with my case manager ... that makes me stable'* [11]. Where specialist services were available, for example a Mother and Baby Unit, rehabilitation service or Women's Crisis House, women were appreciative [19].

Discussion

I found that, despite the heterogeneity of samples and methods in these studies, it was clear that the experience of motherhood evokes powerful emotions for women with SMI regardless of diagnosis or sociocultural context. Indeed, there is some evidence that women with SMI place a very high value on their role as mothers, perhaps because they have little else positive in their lives, or because the fear of having their children taken away makes them appreciate them all the more [14]. The vast majority of studies (19 of 23) emphasised the importance women attached to becoming mothers, both in terms of their own self-esteem and in the way that their children were central to their existence, conferring benefits such as 'love, purpose, identity and support' [15]. However, for many women, being a parent with a major mental illness is associated with stigma, guilt, isolation and concerns over the impact of illness on their children or the possibility of custody loss: a pervasive anxiety for many women in these studies. Consultations with health professionals for pre-conception advice, antenatal care or mental healthcare while parenting may therefore be influenced by these underlying concerns even if they are not disclosed during interviews.

Stigma was a particularly prominent theme which may impact on access to healthcare. Women described feeling stigmatised and felt that society's negative attitudes and assumptions impacted on professionals' views of their parenting abilities and the potential loss of custody of children. The stigma associated with mental illness was exacerbated by becoming a parent as women felt doubly stigmatised – by some health professionals as well as society generally – because their capacity to be 'a good mother' was automatically doubted [22]. This concurs with a quantitative survey which found that people with a mental illness rated 'being seen as a bad parent' as the second most important barrier to seeking psychiatric care [29]. This recurring theme overlapped with the consciousness of having 'dual identities' as a mentally ill woman who was socially stigmatised and in need of the State's help, while at the same time trying to fulfil the idealised role of extremely competent, nurturing and selfless mother.

Within the overarching theme of experiences of services, prominent subthemes were the lack of continuity of care and the need for childcare provision, especially in a crisis, confirming earlier findings from surveys. An unmet need for information was also evident as in other types of studies [3], and a need for peer support, which might prove particularly helpful to this population, isolated by both the stigma of mental illness and the need to care for an infant full-time. Unfortunately, there is a scarcity of good quality research on whether such support could improve social networks and childcare.

The singular experience of women suffering from PP was evident in several themes. For women who had never experienced mental illness before and had anticipated a 'perfect' birth, the chasm between expectation and reality was hard to bear. Thus, comments on guilt, the centrality of motherhood and coping with dual identities were plentiful from this group of women, whereas they were far less likely to refer to suffering from isolation as they generally reported strong support from partners and family members. This contrasted with the majority of studies where there was no mention of fathers or partners except in the context of their absence. This is similarly found in other studies, especially those looking at schizophrenia. In this review, excluding the PP subgroup, a large proportion of participants were single. The preponderance of single mothers also partly explains the prominence of concerns about custody loss and isolation; for example, Mowbray highlighted that single mothers 'felt they needed support from the children's fathers' and some mothers reported feeling deliberately isolated from their children by fathers [24].

Despite the heterogeneity of the studies included here, this review highlights the complexity of the challenges facing women with SMI when they have children and the ways in which issues such as stigma and fear of custody loss serve as barriers to the establishment of a positive therapeutic relationship with health professionals. Research into possible interventions such as pre-conception counselling, parenting programmes and peer support is needed. The results emphasise the central importance women with SMI assign to motherhood, a fact that should not be underestimated when caring for this population.

Focusing on the Experience of Women with Bipolar Disorder in Relation to Pregnancy

After conducting this review and qualitative meta-synthesis, I decided to gather the views of women with bipolar disorder about pregnancy and giving birth. I focused on this particular diagnostic group partly because there had been so little qualitative research on their views (only two studies involving a total of 14 women in the entire literature), but also because I had personal knowledge of some of the issues as I have bipolar disorder and suffered a PP with my first birth. Having run well-attended workshops with Professor Ian Jones for the charity Bipolar UK on Bipolar and Pregnancy, I was acutely aware of the dearth of information available to women with this condition thinking about having children. There were many tragic stories related by women attending the workshops of stopping medication abruptly and having to have an abortion followed by a lengthy stay in psychiatric hospital; of being told not to have children by clinicians – either directly or indirectly; and of leaving it too late because of lack of information and advice only to find they were too old to conceive. I found these stories distressing and was very keen to increase awareness of the situation and campaign to change it.

For this research project, *Women with Bipolar Disorder and Pregnancy: Factors Influencing Their Decision-Making*, I took evidence from 71 women with bipolar disorder about their experience of decision-making in the perinatal period [18]. Understanding how decisions are reached regarding pregnancy and identifying the barriers which prevent women from accessing the help with decision-making they need is critical for newly qualified perinatal specialists. Though my in-depth study focused on women with bipolar disorder, many of the lessons learned apply equally to women with other mental illnesses. Of the participants in this study, 50 contributed their views via the internet forum of the national charity Bipolar UK, while a further 21 were recruited for face-to-face interviews via a London mental health trust (76%) and Bipolar UK (24%) (see [18] for details of Methodology and Strengths and Limitations).

Not surprisingly, the themes that emerged were broadly similar to those described in the review and meta-synthesis but I am able to quote women themselves on the barriers to care they encountered and which factors most affected their decision-making. I have summarised them below:

Contextual Factors

- Cultural and religious
- Ticking biological clock
- Family history
- Local service provision
- Social support

Stigma

- Anticipated stigma
- Societal stigma
- Stigma around women who can't breastfeed
- Stigma from health professionals

Fear

- Of becoming ill
- Of being bad parents
- Of damaging her relationship
- Of passing on bipolar disorder
- Of harming the baby
- Of social services

In this section I give some examples of each of these themes.

Contextual Factors

Cultural and Religious Factors

These factors were important to some as attitudes to mental illness differ widely among different ethnic groups, and religious upbringing can influence attitudes to issues like abortion and optimal family size. One Asian woman said her family did not understand her illness because they 'didn't believe' in mental illness, while a woman of African descent described how her extended family were 'harassing' her to have a child as they thought it would benefit her mental health.

Physical and Psychological Readiness

Women highlighted the need to prepare physically as well as mentally for the pregnancy and the birth: *'I'm too fat at the moment to have a baby . . . I've got to lose 4 stone.'*

Time Pressure

Many women felt they needed to plan pregnancy well in advance because of the time involved in changing medications and preparing mentally and physically for motherhood. In addition, many had delayed having children due to their illness, or sometimes due to the associated instability in their lives, and were now very anxious that time was running out for them, as this woman on the e-forum expressed: *'Having bipolar has . . . greatly delayed the decision and now due to age . . . I have to make the choice.'*

Economic Factors

Women considering starting a family referred to delaying making a decision because of a desire to be financially secure enough to raise a child: *'[Because of] my illness, I haven't worked for years . . . I come from quite a secure background and . . . I wanted to re-create that . . . [but] due to my illness . . . I doubt . . . I could manage it.'*

Family History

For women who had had a parent with bipolar disorder, issues of whether they could do a better job of parenting were particularly important: *'We had a very . . . disrupted childhood and not a happy family life. My big fear is . . . I would end up reproducing that.'*

Social Support

For most married and cohabiting women in this study, their partner's involvement in the decision-making process was critical, with more than one woman saying she would not have considered having a baby without her partner's support: *'he is my rock in many, many ways'*. There was concern about how much support they would need during the pregnancy and after the birth, but also over the need to provide stability and continuity for the child growing up in case she suffered further episodes of illness. Not all partners were in favour of having a family (which was a big factor in some women deciding against it; two of the six women on the e-forum who had decided not to have children said it was because their partners were against it), and some had very different views about taking medications in pregnancy, as one said: *'I know he's dead against me taking any medication'* (e-forum). Most women – and not just the 48% of interviewees who were single mothers – said how important support from their family was, particularly if they were unwell postnatally.

Local Service Provision

Women's experiences of accessing local services varied. Some could readily access specialist perinatal service for pre-conception counselling, while others could not. The former reported a high level of satisfaction – describing it as 'absolutely invaluable' and 'vital'– while several women recounted how they had only finally got the information they needed when they had actively sought advice from such a specialist. On the whole, women felt that general psychiatrists – and general practitioners – lacked training and knowledge in this area, so those who were not referred to a specialist felt let down by the lack of information available. One woman, who had had two postpartum psychoses requiring admission to a Mother and Baby Unit, felt that if she had been properly advised it might have prevented the very damaging second episode: *'If I'd had a care plan I could have also been on medication . . . at the end of the pregnancy and just after birth . . . which might have meant this didn't happen at all.'*

Stigma

Women's consciousness of stigmatising attitudes towards them as people with a mental illness was evident and affected decisions they made about treatment choices such as their desire not to take medication postnatally because of the pressure to breastfeed and be a 'normal' mother. There are four subthemes in this category.

Anticipated Stigma

Participants worried that their friends might disapprove of them having children because of their mental health problems, or feared that people might consider them incapable of looking after their children: *'I worry whether some of my friends ... will say ... "Should you really be having children? ... You've got mental health problems! What happens if you, kind of, drown your baby?"'*

Experienced Stigma from Society

Rather than feeling supported, ignorance and stigma about bipolar alienated several women from friends and even family, and they described being treated in a discriminatory way. Some felt the stigma they experienced in society was partly driven by the 'very negative' media presentation of mental illness, especially sensationalist news stories focusing on the very rare instances of psychotic mothers harming their children: *'It's just the scare stories isn't it? It's the very occasional person with severe postnatal depression who harms her child that's in the media ... not the people who've managed ... it frustrates me the way that bipolar is depicted.'*

Stigma from Health Professionals

Some women also reported discriminating attitudes directly from health professionals. Frequently, women reported great difficulty in accessing information from health professionals about pregnancy, whom they looked to help them *'navigate the maze of medication and all the accompanying problems and mental fears and anxieties in order to have a child'*. Encountering a frustratingly negative attitude towards their desire for children was a common theme. One woman, who had asked her psychiatrist repeatedly for information and advice on pregnancy, was frustrated and angry when she wasn't given any. She said it *'was like bashing my head up against a brick wall'*. Some felt that the reluctance to give them information – or refer them to a specialist who could – was partly due to stigmatising attitudes towards them as potential mothers. For example, a woman for whom lithium had been the only successful treatment said that she had sought information on taking lithium during pregnancy from five different psychiatrists over a number of years but had been unsuccessful. She felt that they would not help her because they did not think she should have a child. Having sought out a specialist perinatal psychiatrist who gave her the information she needed, she commented: *'It would have been good ... to have some hard facts from them, rather than ... just sort of putting me off really.'* This participant went on to have a child without relapsing after receiving very supportive care from her perinatal team.

Some regarded the lack of information available in this area of healthcare as evidence in itself of discrimination against them for having a mental rather than physical illness: *'If you had a diagnosis of cancer, you'd get given every possible outcome of every medication – everything is given to you on a plate ... and with bipolar, it shouldn't be any different, really.'* This view was echoed on the e-forum with one woman posting that the doctor checking her baby after birth had said 'bipolar people shouldn't have kids'. Another reported feeling 'judged' by hospital staff: *'It's implicit that they view those of us that have got bipolar [as not having] adequate parenting skills.'* In light of the lack of advice available to them, a number of women thought it would be useful to have *'some kind of guide or booklet for women'*, which was *'not forbiddingly medical ... and "doomy and gloomy"'*. Since these interviews were done, there have been a number of booklets and websites providing high-quality information; please see Resources section at end of chapter.

Stigma against Women Unable to Breastfeed

Women described the stigma directed against them when they could not breastfeed because of the medication they needed to take to prevent relapse. Some felt they were 'judged' by maternity staff and other new mothers as inadequate, which upset them and added to their stress at a vulnerable time: *'it was always ... "Why don't you breastfeed?" ... it did really make me cry'*. This stigma also meant that some new mothers didn't receive the help they needed with bottle-feeding: *'... nobody showed us how to feed her [with a bottle] and we hadn't a clue'*. A systematic review of mothers' experiences of bottle-feeding (whether from choice or because of problems experienced) reported similar themes of shame, a sense of failure and worry [30]. Such stigma might be associated with a deterioration of a woman's mental state postnatally. Maternity services could mitigate the problems faced by women forced to bottle-feed their infants by adopting a more sensitive and non-judgemental approach to mothers in this situation. As suggested by nurse educator Professor John Mozingo: '[M]others should be reassured that bonding, attachment and infant health are not irreversibly damaged [by bottle-feeding] and the quality of their mothering should not be questioned because of the feeding method chosen.' They might also encourage mothers to use methods to enhance bonding such as 'skin-to-skin' contact and maintaining eye contact while bottle-feeding [31].

Fear

Because of the risk of having a serious episode, several women were very frightened at the prospect of being pregnant, especially at the thought that they would have to stop or change medication, and this had been a significant factor in delaying parenthood. Some reported searching on the internet and finding inaccurate accounts which had alarmed them and added to their anxiety.

Fear of Becoming Ill

Among those who had already had a child, fear of having another postnatal episode was a major reason why they had decided not to have any more; as one said: *'I couldn't face the prospect of getting ill again.'* Women who had suffered a PP were particularly scared of this happening again and so were more likely to state that they intended to have no further children as a result, both because of what they themselves would have to suffer and because they did not want their first child to suffer while they were in hospital. Some women were so frightened by the pregnancy and/or birth instigating an episode that they had considered adoption or surrogacy to try to avoid physically delivering the baby themselves. But those who had thought about this option said they had rejected it because – with their history of mental illness – they doubted they would be 'allowed' to adopt even if they had been well for some time.

Similarly, when planning for the birth, several said they had considered interventions such as induction and/or a caesarean section because they feared a long labour with no sleep would add to the risk of triggering an episode. Women who had already had a child were generally far more interested in the 'mechanics' of the birth and had firmer ideas on what treatments they wanted to receive; for example, one woman said she did not want to have another protracted labour which she felt had contributed to her becoming ill the first time: *'I want to make sure that I'm induced if it's dragging on.'*

Fear of Medication Causing Harm to the Baby

Many women in this study were also fearful that they might harm their baby by remaining on their medication. Some women who had been prescribed valproate and subsequently heard that it was teratogenic were very anxious to stop taking it or switch to an alternative. Weighing the chances of damaging their unborn child against the possibility of becoming ill when medication-free was described as extremely difficult and provoked much anxiety. Some women reported that their fear of getting ill when pregnant or postnatally was greatly exacerbated by being told their pregnancy was officially labelled 'high risk' – a common categorisation used by maternity services to flag up women who might need extra monitoring – though one said she regarded the label as 'a double-edged sword' as it made her feel anxious but also 'special'.

Fear of Social Services

A number of women were fearful that social services might be called in because of their mental health issues and were frightened that that could lead to their child being taken away from them, so much so that this fear had prevented them from asking for help when their condition was deteriorating. As one woman on the e-forum said: *'I am scared of getting pregnant again because I don't want my child to be taken away ... now that I have been diagnosed ... It scares me so much.'*

Fear of Passing on Bipolar Disorder

The 'genetic issue' was raised by several interviewees and was a particularly prominent concern among women posting on the e-forum, though some women who had become mothers expressed the view that at least they were well-placed to help if their child developed the condition.

Fear of Damage to Relationship

Women were also worried about the *'incredibly intense pressures on relationships that the illness brings'* and were anxious that if they felt they had made the wrong decision about treatment, or their partner had to look after a child while they were in hospital for several months, the strain might prove too much: *'I was scared that ... my marriage would really suffer.'*

When considering the factors influencing women with bipolar disorder (or other severe mental illnesses) in their decision-making around pregnancy and childbirth, it's also important to mention other matters which were raised such as concern over the weight gain associated with many medications, not only because of the detrimental effect that can have on a woman's self-esteem and vulnerability to depression, but also because obesity is known to increase the risk of birth complications [32]. Women were also concerned about the effects of a traumatic birth on their illness and coping with the sleep deprivation associated with caring for a young baby. A supportive partner and family were seen as important factors in mitigating these effects as well as access to some form of peer support.

This study was focused on the factors affecting decision-making around pregnancy but women also expressed views on their maternity and postnatal care and the seven main categories where they suggested improvements could be made are shown below:

- Information
- Continuity of care

- Training of health professionals
- To co-produce a detailed care plan
- Access to a Mother and Baby Unit
- Peer support
- More research on medications

The main points that emerged from both these papers and my doctoral research highlight the complexity of decision-making around pregnancy for women with SMI and the anxiety this causes them at a time when they need to be as stress-free as possible. Women described how much they wanted good advice to help them make difficult choices over medication, the conduct of labour and birth and treatment in the postpartum period, and how 'frustrated' and 'angry' they were that such information and support was often denied. More recently, the very welcome expansion of perinatal services and the growing interest in this area means that this is less often the case but gaps remain. For instance, though my work with Bipolar UK and the Bipolar/Pregnancy workshops, I've learned that many women who are not in regular touch with psychiatric services are unaware that they are entitled to pre-conception counselling when at the stage of thinking of having a child. The expression of fear about taking medication in pregnancy is in line with previous research indicating a high level of maternal anxiety over the teratogenicity of medications for depression in pregnancy [33].

Women suggested that information on the pros and cons of different treatments should be delivered in a comprehensible, jargon-free way, with a compassionate understanding of the potential it had for provoking greater anxiety in the recipients, who were understandably hoping that they would have a relatively 'normal' pregnancy and birth. Einarson and colleagues [33] demonstrated that a majority of women with depression resumed taking their medication while pregnant after receiving well-informed counselling on the subject; women in this study suggested that it is professionals as well as women who need to be informed of the up-to-date evidence base. Indeed, recent research found that perinatal suicides were associated with a lack of prescribing of medication [34].

Fear of social services removing the child is an issue that has been raised in many studies on perinatal mental disorders. Anxiety and stress caused by such fear could be detrimental for the baby in utero [35] as well as for the mother, and health professionals could potentially alleviate some of the distress by raising the subject themselves (as most women fear introducing it) and reassuring women about how rarely babies are removed or how, in some circumstances, social services can be a source of support. Peer support groups and parenting classes were suggested by participants as ways of improving their child-rearing abilities.

Along with the emotionally taxing dilemmas faced when contemplating pregnancy and the challenges of being a mother with mental illness, this study also attests to the enormous importance women with serious mental illness attach to having children. The testimony of these women demonstrates that it is not just psychiatrists who need to be better informed about the particular needs of women with mental illness in the perinatal period but general practitioners, social workers, psychiatric nurses and all maternity staff, and underlines the need to increase knowledge and reduce stigmatising attitudes.

Other Ways to Improve the Perinatal Care of Women with Serious Mental Illness

My doctorate was focused on decision-making in the perinatal period and when I asked women whether they thought a decision aid of some sort would be helpful the response was broadly positive (as it was from the psychiatrists interviewed too). To produce such a tool is challenging but if such a decision aid were developed and evaluated by means of a randomised controlled trial, I believe it has the potential to improve decision-making for this group. Meanwhile, an excellent internet platform has been developed by Tommy's with the help of Professor Louise Howard of King's College London, which women and their partners are reporting to be very useful (https://shorturl.at/oyfKt). A similar resource for health professionals advising women with SMI has also been launched through Public Health England on the same site (https://shorturl.at/RHChv).

Another resource with the potential to reduce anxiety in pregnancy for women with SMI and their families is an Advance Choice Document or ACD. This is not a legal document in England (though there are plans for it to become one in the near future) but a statement designed to provide key information to health professionals about contacts, treatment and other care issues, including relevant physical health issues (see www.advancechoice.org). Advance statements are already included in Scottish mental health legislation and plans are underway to produce digitalised ACDs which can be stored on a mobile phone. They are particularly valuable in psychiatric conditions with fluctuating capacity, such as bipolar disorder, schizoaffective disorder and schizophrenia. A pregnant woman with bipolar disorder 1 who has had a previous PP, for example, may be extremely anxious that she will be psychotic again after the birth and, when in this altered state, she might be both unable to make rational decisions or will deliberately make decisions which she would regret bitterly in retrospect (e.g. denying her husband access to the baby; insisting she won't take lithium). Both these examples have happened to women I know: if they are able to make an ACD detailing their true wishes and explaining that these should override their 'psychotic' self, it significantly reduces their anxiety levels. Such statements are also very useful for the medical team as they explain how the patient is likely to behave and how they want to be treated (e.g. my friend's statement meant that the team could give her lithium sooner and so accelerate her recovery) and it avoids the exclusion of the partner.

The development of perinatal ACDs illustrates the greater degree of collaboration and co-production between clinician and patient in today's health service. I believe that improving access to information on how mental illness and pregnancy interact, involving more people with lived experience in training programmes for all relevant health professionals and encouraging greater collaboration in decisions on treatment and the co-production of advance statements will all substantially improve perinatal care. Considered along with the country's great steps forward in provision of specialist care teams and universal access to Mother and Baby Units, such developments are to be greatly welcomed.

The greater involvement of people with lived experience in perinatal mental health research and clinical practice reflects the proliferation of personal accounts of having experienced everything from a traumatic birth to a PP. Such accounts have increasingly appeared in book or documentary form, press articles, blogs and on all forms of social media. This has definitely improved awareness of what were formerly even more stigmatised mental health conditions. Information from such sources will not always apply to every individual and need to be checked with trained medical professionals, but if it encourages people to speak up and ask for help it can only be viewed as a positive development.

Useful Resources

Maternal Mental Health Alliance: www.maternalmentalhealthalliance.org
Bipolar UK: www.bipolaruk.org
APP (Action on Postpartum Psychosis): www.app-network.org
Tommy's: www.tommys.org
Mind: www.mind.org.uk
Royal College of Psychiatrists' patient information leaflets on 'Before, during and after pregnancy': www.rcpsych.ac.uk/mental-health/mental-illnesses-and-mental-health-problems

References

1. LM Howard, R Kumar, G Thornicroft. Psychosocial characteristics and needs of mothers with psychotic disorders. *Br J Psychiatry.* 2001 May;178(5):427–32.
2. L Murray, P Cooper, A Hipwell. Mental health of parents caring for infants. *Arch Women's Ment Health.* 2003 Aug;6: s71–7.
3. LM Howard, K Hunt. The needs of mothers with severe mental illness: a comparison of assessments of needs by staff and patients. *Arch Women's Ment Health.* 2008 Jun;11:131–6.
4. Department of Health. Mainstreaming gender and women's mental health: implementation guidance. Department of Health; 2003.
5. C Dolman, I Jones, LM Howard. Pre-conception to parenting: a systematic review and meta-synthesis of the qualitative literature on motherhood for women with severe mental illness. *Arch Women's Ment Health.* 2013 Jun;16:173–96.
6. P Montgomery, S Mossey, P Bailey, C Forchuk. Mothers with serious mental illness: their experience of "hitting bottom". *ISRN Nurs.* 2011:708318.
7. E Robertson, A Lyons. Living with puerperal psychosis: a qualitative analysis. *Psychol Psychother.* 2003 Dec;76(4): 411–31.
8. E Edwards, S Timmons. A qualitative study of stigma among women suffering postnatal illness. *J Ment Health.* 2005 Jan 1;14(5):471–81.
9. B Davies, D Allen. Integrating 'mental illness' and 'motherhood': the positive use of surveillance by health professionals. A qualitative study. *Int J Nurs Stud.* 2007 Mar 1;44(3):365–76.
10. BJ Ackerson. Coping with the dual demands of severe mental illness and parenting: the parents' perspective. *Fam Soc.* 2003 Jan;84(1):109–18.
11. H Bassett, J Lampe, C Lloyd. Parenting: experiences and feelings of parents with a mental illness. *J Ment Health.* 1999 Jan 1;8(6):597–604.
12. P Montgomery, C Tompkins, C Forchuk, S French. Keeping close: mothering with serious mental illness. *J Adv Nurs.* 2006 Apr;54(1):20–8.
13. H Khalifeh, C Murgatroyd, M Freeman, S Johnson, H Killaspy. Home treatment as an alternative to hospital admission for mothers in a mental health crisis: a qualitative study. *Psychiatr Serv.* 2009 May;60(5):634–9.
14. RG Sands. The parenting experience of low-income single women with serious mental disorders. *Fam Soc.* 1995 Feb;76(2):86–96.
15. WM Chernomas, DE Clarke, FA Chisholm. Perspectives of women living

with schizophrenia. *Psychiatr Serv.* 2000 Dec;51(12):1517–21.

16. HL Peay, GW Hooker, L Kassem, BB Biesecker. Family risk and related education and counselling needs: perceptions of adults with bipolar disorder and siblings of adults with bipolar disorder. *Am J Med Genet A.* 2009 Mar;149(3):364–71.
17. B Meiser, PB Mitchell, H McGirr, M Van Herten, PR Schofield. Implications of genetic risk information in families with a high density of bipolar disorder: an exploratory study. *Soc Sci Med.* 2005 Jan 1;60(1):109–18.
18. C Dolman, IR Jones, LM Howard. Women with bipolar disorder and pregnancy: factors influencing their decision-making. *BJPsych Open.* 2016 Sep;2(5):294–300.
19. J Heron, N Gilbert, C Dolman, S Shah, I Beare, S Dearden, et al. Information and support needs during recovery from postpartum psychosis. *Arch Women's Ment Health.* 2012 Jun;15: 155–65.
20. CT Mowbray, D Bybee, L Hollingsworth, S Goodkind, D Oyserman. Living arrangements and social support: effects on the well-being of mothers with mental illness. *Social Work Research.* 2005 Mar 1;29(1):41–55.
21. A Diaz-Caneja, S Johnson. The views and experiences of severely mentally ill mothers: a qualitative study. *Soc Psychiatry Psychiatr Epidemiol.* 2004 Jun;39:472–82.
22. L Wilson, M Crowe. Parenting with a diagnosis bipolar disorder. *J Adv Nurs.* 2009 Apr;65(4):877–84.
23. I Engqvist, G Ferszt, A Åhlin, K Nilsson. Women's experience of postpartum psychotic episodes: analyses of narratives from the Internet. *Arch Psychiatr Nurs.* 2011 Oct 1;25(5):376–87.
24. CT Mowbray, D Oyserman, S Ross. Parenting and the significance of children for women with a serious mental illness. *J Ment Health Admin.* 1995 Mar;22:189–200.
25. I Savvidou, VP Bozikas, S Hatzigeleki, A Karavatos. Narratives about their children by mothers hospitalized on a psychiatric unit. *Fam Process.* 2003 Sep;42(3):391–402.
26. M Venkataraman, BJ Ackerson. Parenting among mothers with bipolar disorder: strengths, challenges, and service needs. *J Fam Soc Work.* 2008 Nov 24;11(4):389–408.
27. S Doucet, N Letourneau, ER Blackmore. Support needs of mothers who experience postpartum psychosis and their partners. *JOGNN.* 2012 Mar 1;41(2): 236–45.
28. R Ueno, K Kamibeppu. Narratives by Japanese mothers with chronic mental illness in the Tokyo metropolitan area: their feelings toward their children and perceptions of their children's feelings. *J Nerv Ment Dis.* 2008 Jul 1;196(7):522–30.
29. S Clement, E Brohan, D Jeffery, C Henderson, SL Hatch, G Thornicroft. Development and psychometric properties the Barriers to Access to Care Evaluation scale (BACE) related to people with mental ill health. *BMC Psychiatry.* 2012 Dec;12:36.
30. R Lakshman, D Ogilvie, KK Ong. Mothers' experiences of bottle-feeding: a systematic review of qualitative and quantitative studies. *Arch Dis Child.* 2009 Aug 1;94(8):596–601.
31. JN Mozingo, MW Davis, PG Droppleman, A Merideth. "It wasn't working": women's experiences with short-term breastfeeding. *MCN: Am J Matern Child Nurs.* 2000 May 1;25(3):120–6.
32. SD McDonald, Z Han, S Mulla, J Beyene. Overweight and obesity in mothers and risk of preterm birth and low birth weight infants: systematic review and meta-analyses. *BMJ.* 2010 Jul 20;341.
33. A Einarson, P Selby, G Koren. Abrupt discontinuation of psychotropic drugs during pregnancy: fear of teratogenic risk and impact of counselling. *J Psychiatry Neurosci.* 2001 Jan;26(1):44.

34. H Khalifeh, IM Hunt, L Appleby, LM Howard. Suicide in perinatal and non-perinatal women in contact with psychiatric services: 15 year findings from a UK national inquiry. *Lancet Psychiatry.* 2016 Mar 1;3(3):233–42.

35. H Beydoun, AF Saftlas. Physical and mental health outcomes of prenatal maternal stress in human and animal studies: a review of recent evidence. *Paediatr Perinat Epidemiol.* 2008 Sep;22(5):438–66.

Chapter 3

Physiological Changes in Pregnancy and Common Obstetric Medical Disorders

Lin Foo and Shankari Arulkumaran

Introduction

Pregnancy Adaptation

Pregnancy induces vast physiological shifts within several systems of the expectant mother's body, including haemodynamic, haematological, renal, endocrine and metabolic functions. These are necessary to adjust conditions for optimal growth and development of the fetus but are finely tuned to avoid subsequent compromise to maternal health; an imbalance of which may present with medical complications to both mother and baby.

It is essential to understand normal physiological changes in pregnancy in order to appreciate pathology, which may arise. This chapter aims to outline the main changes that occur, and further, to delineate a few common obstetric emergencies and complications that may develop during pregnancy.

Changes in Cardiovascular System: A 'Low Resistance, High Output' State

Normal pregnancy is associated with profound cardiovascular adaptation in order to optimise utero-placental perfusion without compromising the functioning of the maternal organs. These changes, as demonstrated in Figure 3.1, occur from very early pregnancy, and result in an overall 'hyperdynamic' circulation, in other words one of increased cardiac output, and low peripheral resistance. The resultant effects can commonly produce signs on examination of the cardiovascular system, which may be misinterpreted as pathological to those unfamiliar with pregnancy. Common signs may include a bounding or collapsing pulse and an ejection systolic murmur and/or peripheral oedema.

Blood Pressure

From as early as 6 weeks of amenorrhea in a conceptive cycle, the mean arterial pressure (MAP) is reduced by 3–5 mmHg, with an additional decline by only 1–2 mmHg in the remainder of the first trimester [2]. There is a general agreement that of the components of MAP, systolic blood pressure only undergoes minor changes, whilst the fall in diastolic component is slightly larger. This is most likely in conjunction with a higher arterial compliance. Diastolic blood pressure reaches a minimum level in mid-pregnancy and returns to non-pregnant levels nearer to term. After the first trimester, the MAP begins to increase again until 28 weeks, by approximately 2 mmHg. However, after the

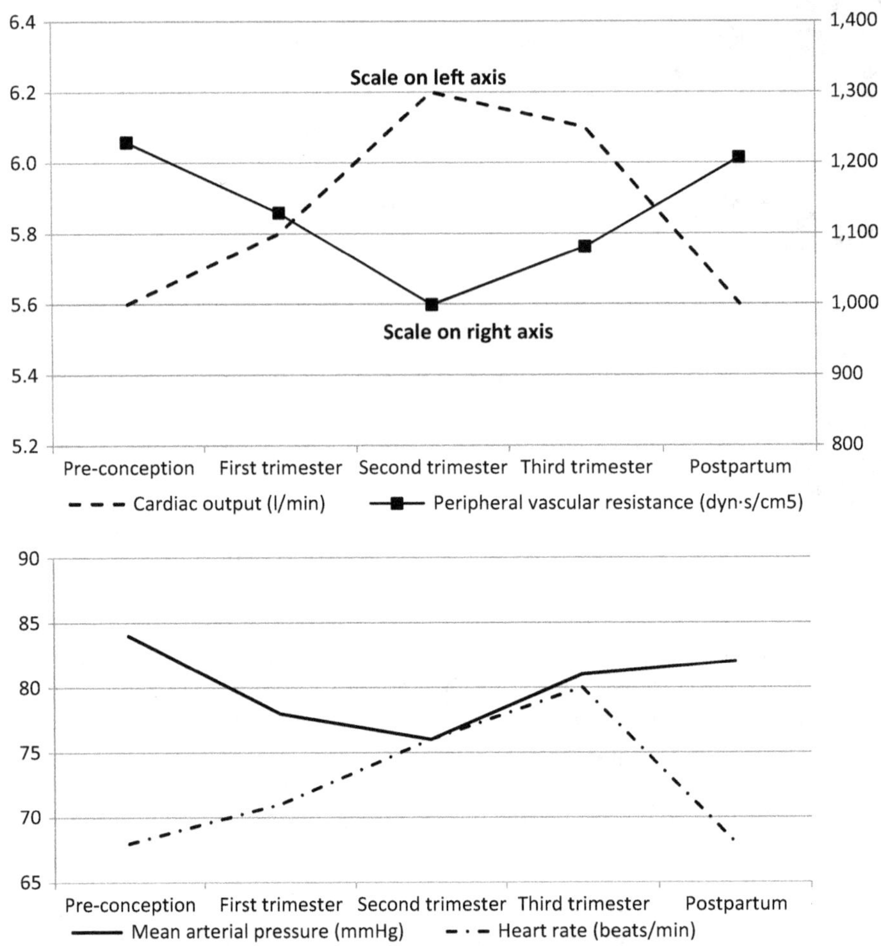

Figure 3.1 Cardiovascular changes from pre-conception to postpartum.
Graphical representation of changes in mean arterial pressure, heart rate, cardiac output and peripheral vascular resistance from pre-conception to postpartum. Data are from Mahendru et al. [1].

second trimester, the rise is about 6 mmHg to reach approximately non-pregnant levels nearer to term. Therefore, the blood pressure mainly drops in the first trimester, though low blood pressure is frequently misquoted as a dip 'mid-pregnancy' [2].

Cardiac Output, Stroke Volume and Heart Rate

A rise in cardiac output (CO) is detectable even in the first weeks of pregnancy. It has been reported that this is due to an initial rise in heart rate (HR), and then an increase in stroke volume (SV) during the subsequent weeks. Heart rate increase was observed by 5 weeks gestation and continued until 32 weeks [3]. Stroke volume increase occurs a little later at 8 weeks and reaches a maximum at approximately 20 weeks. The physiological importance or the drive that underlies this sequential rise in HR followed by SV is unclear. A plateau in CO is reached by the end of the second trimester, where it remains until term. Some studies report a further elevation of CO in the third trimester, thought to be driven by a combination of increased HR, volume-mediated pre-load augmentation and decreased after-load [4, 5, 6].

The magnitude of CO increment in pregnancy reported varies enormously within different studies, and is probably reflective of different measurement techniques, cohort design and reference points for pre-pregnancy data and pregnancy data. From longitudinal data, CO is observed to increase by approximately 45–50% above a non-pregnant level [3, 7].

During labour, there are further increases in cardiac output. Uterine contractions lead to approximately 300–500 ml of blood being pushed back into systemic circulation. The increase in CO is also driven by an adjunct sympathetic response to pain which further elevates the heart rate, and therefore output. Immediately following delivery, there is a profound increase in CO by a further 60–80% due to the elimination of vena-caval obstruction by the gravid uterus. Therefore, women with cardiovascular compromise are often most at risk of pulmonary oedema in the late stages of labour, delivery and the immediate postpartum period.

Structural Changes in the Heart

Left ventricular end-diastolic dimension, as measured by echocardiography, is reported to increase in the first trimester and remains elevated till full term. This is thought to be secondary with a rise in pre-load that occurs with pregnancy [8]. A consequence of these changes is an increase in left ventricular mass. Thereby pregnancy induces eccentric myocardial hypertrophy, resembling that observed in response to endurance sport [9, 10]. The increase in wall thickness is thought to minimise wall stress and maintain myocardial oxygenation in increased pre- and after-load.

Structural and positional changes in the heart can sometimes lead to ECG changes, which can be normal when observed in pregnancy. These include:

- Q wave (small) and inverted T wave in lead III
- ST-segment depression and T-wave inversion in the inferior and lateral leads
- left-axis shift of QRS

Furthermore, atrial and ventricular ectopics can also be relatively common in pregnancy and tend to resolve in the postpartum period.

Total Peripheral Resistance

One of the most prominent pregnancy-induced circulatory changes is that of a fall in systemic vascular tone. It is difficult to elucidate the mechanisms responsible for this effect, but it is thought to involve cell signalling molecules acting within immediate extracellular environments (paracrine) and the circulatory system (endocrine), as well as reflex loop systems.

Total peripheral resistance (TPR) has been observed to decrease significantly during the late luteal phase in women that subsequently are confirmed as pregnant. This suggests that a drop in TPR represents one of the earliest adjustments in physiological adaptation to pregnancy. The decrease in TPR continues till mid-pregnancy, followed by a slow rise till term. The magnitude of TPR reduction when comparing second trimester values to pre-pregnancy baseline has been reported to be as much as 35–40% [11].

Haematological and Coagulation Changes

A significant physiological change to circulation and blood viscosity is attributable to an increase in plasma volume, by approximately 50% by the third trimester. This increase is greater than that of red cell mass, resulting in a fall in haematocrit and red cell count but without changes in mean corpuscular volume or mean corpuscular haemoglobin concentration.

Iron requirements are greater in pregnancy than in the non-pregnant state. Although iron requirements are reduced in the first trimester because of the absence of menstruation, they rise steadily thereafter by approximately two- to three-fold. This is due to haemoglobin synthesis, fetal requirements and increased production of certain enzymes. Furthermore, there is a 10- to 20-fold increase in folate requirements. The World Health Organization recommends therefore a daily oral iron and folic acid supplementation with 30–60 mg of elemental iron and 400 μg (0.4 mg) of folic acid for pregnant women to prevent maternal anaemia, the need for blood transfusions, puerperal sepsis, low birth weight and pre-term birth. The equivalent of 60mg of iron is 300 mg ferrous sulphate, 180 mg of ferrous fumarate or 500 mg of ferrous gluconate. In the first and third trimesters, the threshold for diagnosis of anaemia is 110 g/L; in the second trimester, the threshold is 105 g/L.

There is a physiological decrease in platelet count during normal pregnancy due to haemodilution, increased consumption in peripheral tissue and increased aggregation (higher levels of thromboxane A2). The fall in platelet count usually remains within normal limits ($>100 \times 10^9$ cells/l) and has no adverse effects for the mother and fetus. From a practical standpoint, the consensus is that vaginal delivery is safe when platelet count is higher than 30×10^9 cells/l. For operative vaginal or caesarean deliveries, the safe platelet count should be at least 50×10^9 cells/l. Safe platelet counts for insertion of epidural anaesthesia are often considered around the region of $75–80 \times 10^9$ cells/l, with concerns related to the risk of epidural hematoma associated with lower platelet values.

Gestational thrombocytopenia is a benign condition with moderate thrombocytopenia (platelet count of $130–150 \times 10^9$ cells/l) in most cases. It is a diagnosis of exclusion, usually occurring in the second half of pregnancy, in the absence of a history of thrombocytopenia outside the pregnancy, and the platelet count is observed to return to normal levels within the first 2 months postpartum. It is not associated with maternal or fetal risks and does not require further investigation, except for periodical monitoring of the blood count, especially prior to delivery or interventions such as epidural anaesthesia.

Changes in the coagulation system during pregnancy produce a physiological hypercoagulable state (in preparation for haemostasis following delivery). Coagulation factor concentrations change dramatically throughout pregnancy, for instance fibrinogen levels rise significantly by up to 50% and fibrinolytic activity is decreased. Concentrations of endogenous anticoagulants such as antithrombin and protein S are also decreased, while clotting factors such as Factor VIII, IX and X are increased.

Therefore, overall, pregnancy predisposes the pregnant and postpartum woman to venous thrombosis. This increased risk is present from the first trimester and for at least 12 weeks following delivery. In vitro tests of coagulation (activated partial thromboplastin time (APTT), prothrombin time and thrombin time) remain normal in the absence of anticoagulants or a coagulopathy.

Finally, in view of liver function, pregnancy is associated with mild falls in alanine aminotransferase, aspartate aminotransferase, gamma-glutamyl transferase and bilirubin. Levels of alkaline phosphatase rise due to production of the placental iso enzyme. Serum amylase remains similar to non-pregnant cohorts. Total bile acid concentrations increase slightly from the first trimester to later pregnancy. However, markedly raised bile acid levels (19 micromol/L or more) in the presence of itching with no skin rash is usually indicative of intra-hepatic cholestasis.

Renal Changes

Pregnancy affects both the anatomy and physiology of the kidney. Overall kidney volume increases up to 30% in pregnancy due to increased kidney vasculature and interstitial volume. The kidney pelvis and calyceal systems tend to dilate in pregnancy under mechanical compressive force on the ureters, and possibly secondary to the effects of progesterone. Progesterone can reduce uretal tone, peristalsis and contraction pressure.

Hydronephrosis during pregnancy is reported quite commonly in pregnant women and is more prevalent in the third trimester. The dilated collecting system can hold 200–300 mL of urine, leading to urinary stasis, and therefore there is an increased risk of pyelonephritis in pregnant women with asymptomatic bacteriuria versus non-pregnant women. Of these cases, there is a right-sided preponderance. This is attributed to the right ureter crossing the iliac and ovarian vessels at an angle before entering the pelvis, whereas the left ureter travels at a less acute angle and in parallel with the ovarian vein.

There is an overall progressive increase in glomerular filtration rate (GFR) approximating 40–50% with peak increases sustained at term in uncomplicated pregnancies [12]. Increased filtration has been shown to continue at levels 20% above normal by the second postpartum week and resolve by the end of the first month.

Normal pregnancy is marked by an upregulation of the renin-angiotensin-aldosterone system (RAAS). Renin is released from extra-renal sources, specifically the ovaries and decidua. Activation of the RAAS system leads to increased plasma levels of aldosterone and subsequent salt and water retention in the distal tubule and collecting duct. The placenta also produces oestrogens that stimulate the synthesis of angiotensinogen by the liver, resulting in proportionally increased levels of aldosterone compared to renin. Plasma levels of aldosterone correlate well with those of oestrogens and rise progressively during pregnancy. The rise in GFR also increases distal sodium delivery, allowing excretion of excess sodium.

During pregnancy there are alterations in tubular handling of wastes and nutrients. Uric acid excretion increases due to the increases in GFR, decreases in proximal tubular reabsorption, or a combination of both. The increased clearance is thought to be necessary to handle the increased production from the fetus.

In normal pregnancy there is an increase in total urinary protein and albumin excretion, especially notable after 20 weeks. There is evidence that the amount of albuminuria increases in late pregnancy, albeit with levels that do not exceed the upper limit of normal. The rise in proteinuria during pregnancy is often attributed to the rise in GFR, although the timing does not fall within the peak increase in GFR.

Glucose is freely filtered at the glomerulus and almost completely reabsorbed in the proximal tubule, with a small amount reabsorbed in the collecting tubule. Glucosuria typically indicates that the filtered load of glucose has exceeded the maximal tubular reabsorptive capacity, for instance as seen in gestational diabetes.

Respiratory Changes

During a healthy pregnancy, pulmonary function, ventilatory pattern and gas exchange are affected through both biochemical and mechanical pathways. Breathlessness is commonly reported by healthy pregnant women during their daily living activities, starting from the very first trimester of gestation. Oxygen consumption and basal metabolic rate increase but to a lesser extent than ventilatory augmentation. Therefore, pregnancy-induced reduction in functional residual capacity combined with a rise in oxygen demand and consumption lowers the maternal oxygen reserve.

Progesterone increases the sensitivity of the neural respiratory centre to carbon dioxide and alters airway smooth muscle tone resulting in a bronchodilator effect. It also mediates hyperaemia and oedema of mucosal surfaces, causing nasal congestion. Concurrently, prostaglandins released during pregnancy stimulate uterine smooth muscle during labour and are present during all three trimesters of pregnancy. Prostaglandin $F_{2\alpha}$ increases airway resistance by bronchial smooth muscle constriction, whereas a bronchodilator effect can be a consequence of prostaglandins E_1 and E_2.

The progressive uterine distension associated with the growing pregnancy is a major cause of lung volume and chest wall changes, which comprise elevation of the diaphragm and altered thoracic configuration. The enlarging gravid uterus increases end-expiratory abdominal (gastric) pressure, thereby displacing the diaphragm upwards, with two consequences. Firstly, there is an increase in negative pleural pressure, leading to an earlier closure of the small airways with consequent reduction of functional residual capacity and expiratory reserve volume. Secondly, chest height becomes shorter, but the other thoracic dimensions increase in order to maintain constant total lung capacity.

Spirometry testing throughout pregnancy should, under normal circumstances, remain within normal limits, with no changes in forced vital capacity (FVC), forced expiratory volume in 1 second (FEV_1) and peak expiratory flow. Even with allowance for a moderate increase, the FEV_1/FVC index usually remains the same as pre-pregnancy values.

Conversely, lung volumes undergo major changes; the end residual volume gradually decreases during the second half of pregnancy, a reduction of 8–40% at term, because the residual volume reduces by 7–22% [13]. Functional residual capacity decreases by 9.5–25% while inspiratory capacity increases at the same rate in order to maintain stable total lung capacity.

Total pulmonary and airways resistances tend to decrease in late pregnancy as a consequence of hormonally induced relaxation of tracheobronchial tree smooth muscles. Minute ventilation (V'_E) starts to increase significantly during the first trimester of gestation, due to higher tidal volume (V_T) [14]. However, the respiratory rate remains unchanged. This ventilatory pattern is then maintained throughout the course of pregnancy.

With increasing gestation, the resting position of the diaphragm is splintered upwards by up to 5 cm. This allows the diaphragm to generate tension secondary to muscle fibre lengthening. The upward movement of the diaphragm contributes to the decrease in functional residual capacity.

Pregnancy-induced increased ventilation is a result of complex interactions between changes in chemo-reflex drives, acid–base balance, metabolic rate and cerebral blood flow. Increased ventilation and reduced levels of P_{CO2} increase arterial oxygen tension. Despite increased ventilation and respiratory alkalosis, blood pH remains almost constant at slightly alkalotic values (7.40–7.47), due to renal compensation by increasing the excretion of bicarbonate.

Obstetric Emergencies and Complications

There are a certain number of conditions that may occur uniquely to pregnancy and may arise in the antenatal, intra-partum or postpartum period. This section outlines a few: bleeding in early pregnancy, hyperemesis gravidarum, shoulder dystocia and maternal collapse. With regards to maternal collapse, potential causes include cardiac disease, hypertensive emergencies and venous thromboembolism. A brief summary of these conditions is also covered.

Early Pregnancy Bleeding

Pain and bleeding in pregnancy is relatively common and is in most cases harmless. However, in some cases, bleeding and/or pain could be a sign of an ectopic pregnancy or a miscarriage.

Ectopic pregnancies occur in approximately 11 out of 1,000 pregnancies. Miscarriages are fairly common, estimated to affect 1 in 3 to 5 pregnancies. Both conditions are associated with morbidity for the mother, and in some cases mortality, particularly in vulnerable populations who do not access medical help readily (recent migrants, asylum seekers or patients who have difficulty reading or speaking English).

Women with pain or bleeding should have an assessment with clinical history taking to include details of the last menstrual period and risk factors (e.g. previous miscarriage or ectopic, history of pelvic inflammatory disease). They should also have a physical examination including a vaginal examination, and a urine pregnancy test. Suspected cases should be referred for assessment in an early pregnancy unit where further investigations might include an ultrasound assessment and serial measurements of serum beta-HCG. However, if a patient is haemodynamically unstable, they should be referred directly from a primary care provider or inpatient mental health unit to A&E for assessment by the emergency gynaecology team, who will make a decision on whether to proceed straight to operative management.

Hyperemesis Gravidarum

Nausea and vomiting, known colloquially as 'morning sickness', can affect about 70% of pregnancies. A severe and intractable manifestation of this is hyperemesis gravidarum (HG), which is thought to affect up to 2% of pregnancies. Symptoms are usually confined to the first trimester, but some cases can persist till the late stages of pregnancy. Approximately 1.5% of cases require hospitalisation for complications such as severe dehydration, electrolyte imbalance, weight loss of >5% of body weight and muscle wasting from low dietary intake and malnutrition. Babies born of mothers with severe HG are more likely to be born prematurely and have a low birth weight. Aside from physical effects, HG carries a large psychological burden due to time lost from work and decreased quality of life. In a study of patients with HG, 82% were restricted in their everyday activities.

Treatment of HG revolves around dietary modifications, fluid replacement and anti-emetics. Having smaller amounts of food more often can help prevent mild cases from worsening. Protein-rich meals are thought to decrease symptoms. Thiamine supplementation (1.5 mg/day) should be prescribed, and if not tolerated orally, given as an IV replacement.

Fluid loss can be replaced with IV crystalloids, though one should be careful not to exacerbate electrolyte imbalances such as hyponatraemia.

Most anti-emetics are safe to use in pregnancy, and often combinations of different agents may be required. The Royal College of Obstetricians & Gynaecologists provides a guide for first-line (cyclizine, promethazine, prochlorperazine) to third-line agents (metoclopramide) that can be safely prescribed in all stages of pregnancy [15]. In severe cases of HG, steroids are prescribed, with maintenance doses ranging between 15 mg and 45 mg daily.

Shoulder Dystocia

Shoulder dystocia is defined as an 'arrest of spontaneous delivery due to impaction of anterior or posterior shoulder, or both on the symphysis pubis or sacral promontory' [16]. It occurs due to failure of the shoulders to rotate into the antero-posterior plane as the baby descends through the pelvis. Shoulder dystocia is a significant cause of fetal mortality at term. Following delivery of the head, the cord pH falls by 0.04 unit/min. As a result, delay in completing the delivery may result in asphyxia and neurological deficits.

Management of shoulder dystocia involves a sequence of manoeuvres which results in either an increase in the available pelvic diameter, a narrowing of the transverse diameter of the baby's shoulders or a movement of the shoulder axis into a more favourable angle relative to the antero-posterior pelvic diameter (often into the oblique plane).

Brachial plexus injuries are common with shoulder dystocia. Erb's palsy is the most common presentation (internal rotation and adduction of the shoulders, and extension and pronation of the elbow). A majority of cases occur without any risk factors, however there is a strong correlation between a higher fetal weight and shoulder dystocia. Therefore, in cases where macrosomic babies may be suspected, such as gestational diabetes, shoulder dystocia should be anticipated, and the couple counselled appropriately in the antenatal period as to mode of delivery choices.

Maternal Collapse

Cardiac arrest is a rare event in pregnancy, estimated to occur in 1 in 30,000 deliveries. This section will not cover resuscitation management, which to an extent follows the basic principles of adult life support. However, it is important to understand that certain physiological changes in pregnancy can affect resuscitation.

With a pregnancy beyond approximately 20 weeks gestation, the maternal vena cava is occluded by the gravid uterus when the women lies supine, thereby reducing venous return. Therefore, during a cardiac arrest, a left lateral tilt of greater than 15 degrees is recommended. Alternatively, manual displacement of the uterus to the left can be performed.

The Royal College of Obstetricians & Gynaecologists recommends a peri-mortem caesarean section with delivery within 5 minutes of a recognised arrest, again in order to improve venous return by removing the compression of the baby on the aorta and vena cava, to make ventilation easier and, thereby, improve maternal survival [17].

It is also difficult to provide effective ventilation breaths during CPR due to the increased weight of the abdominal contents and breasts. In addition, the oesophageal sphincter is more relaxed, therefore passive regurgitation of stomach contents is more likely. Therefore, it is recommended that adequate ventilation be achieved via an endotracheal tube if possible.

Common causes of maternal collapse include thromboembolism, hypovolaemia (e.g. haemorrhage following delivery or miscarriage, sepsis), hypoxia (e.g. fitting secondary to an eclamptic fit) and cardiac arrest. One of the most common causes of maternal collapse globally is secondary to pre-eclampsia, which is part of a spectrum of conditions known as hypertensive disorders in pregnancy.

Hypertensive Disorders in Pregnancy

Hypertensive disorders of pregnancy affect approximately 5–10% of all maternities and are major contributors of maternal and neonatal morbidity and mortality worldwide.

Over the last few decades, there has been a change in the demographics of motherhood with an increasing proportion of women entering first pregnancy at a later stage in life and with more chronic health conditions such as diabetes and obesity. The latter is particularly pertinent in women who are on psychotropic medications, with weight gain being a not uncommon side effect of a range of psychotropic drugs. Given these cumulative risk factors, it is expected the incidence of hypertensive disorders in pregnancy will continue to increase, and therefore increased awareness and action by both obstetric and mental health practitioners is important in providing adequate patient education and monitoring. It is good practice to screen for gestational diabetes in patients who are on anti-psychotic medication, due to the associations of these drugs with metabolic disease risk factors.

Hypertension can exist prior to (as chronic hypertension) or develop de novo in pregnancy within two well-defined disorders: pre-eclampsia and gestational hypertension (Figure 3.2). The latter group is thought to be part of the same continuum but with arbitrary division. Pre-eclampsia can often develop superimposed on established gestational or chronic hypertension. As pre-eclampsia carries the highest morbidity and mortality for mother and baby compared to gestational or chronic hypertension, it will be covered in more detail, with the understanding that the basic principles of blood pressure management is similar across all three disorders.

Defining Hypertension in Pregnancy

By convention, the threshold for diagnosis of hypertension in pregnancy is blood pressure levels of ≥140 mmHg systolic or ≥90 mmHg, confirmed by two readings at rest 4–6 hours apart. The National High Blood Pressure Education Program consensus report recommends that patients with blood pressure readings below the threshold for diagnosis but who have a 30 mmHg or 15mmHg rise in systolic and diastolic pressures, respectively, be streamlined as high-risk patients at risk of developing a hypertensive disorder in pregnancy [18]. The United Kingdom National Institute of Clinical Excellence further divides pregnancy-associated hypertension into risk tiers as below [19]:

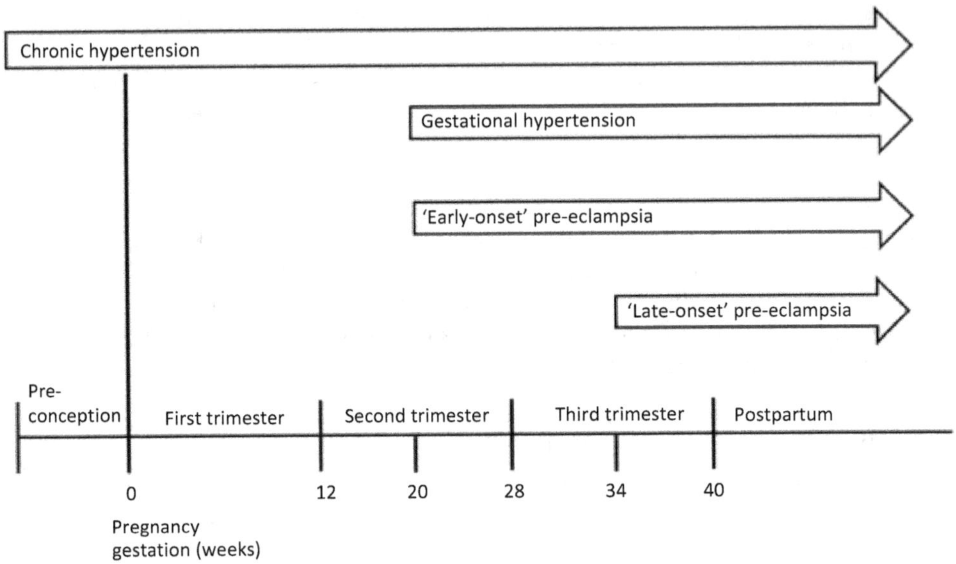

Figure 3.2 The clinical spectrum of hypertensive disorders in pregnancy.

- Mild: diastolic BP 90–99 mmHg, systolic BP 140–149 mmHg
- Moderate: diastolic BP 100–109 mmHg, systolic BP 150–159 mmHg
- Severe: diastolic BP 110 mmHg or greater, systolic BP 160 mmHg or greater

Readings in pregnancy are labile (especially in the context of pre-eclampsia which is often characterised by compartmental fluid shifts) and acutely sensitive to antihypertensive therapy. High blood pressure should therefore be reduced promptly but gradually with continuous monitoring of maternal and fetal parameters; overzealous reduction leads to a decrease in placental circulation and fetal distress. The recommendation is that diastolic blood pressure should not be reduced by more than 30 mmHg and that the mean arterial pressure be reduced by more than 25%.

Pre-eclampsia

Pre-eclampsia, pre-eclamptic toxaemia and proteinuric pregnancy-induced hypertension are roughly synonymous terms describing a syndrome characterised by new-onset hypertension with significant proteinuria (≥300 mg of protein in 24 h or two urine samples collected more than 4 h apart with ≥1+ proteinuria on stick test). This is diagnosed in the second half of pregnancy. The cause of pre-eclampsia is not known; however, it is observed to occur most commonly in nulliparous women usually after 20 weeks gestation and frequently late in the third trimester. There also appears to be a genetic pre-disposition: the risk of pre-eclampsia is increased threefold in women with an affected first-degree relative.

It is more widely accepted that there are two different phenotypes of pre-eclampsia: an early-onset phenotype, which is associated with poor placentation and fetal growth restriction, and a late-onset phenotype, which is not thought to be related to placental causes.

In general, early-onset pre-eclampsia (generally defined as <34 weeks gestation) is less common but is the more severe manifestation of pre-eclampsia. It is characterised by early sympathetic dominance in the cardiovascular system, elevated circulating markers of endothelial dysfunction, inadequate trophoblastic invasion of the uterine spiral arteries and early onset of fetal complications such as iatrogenic pre-term birth and low birth weights.

In contrast, late-onset pre-eclampsia is the most common, encompassing more than 80% of all cases, and is commonly observed on the background of pre-existing maternal morbidities such as chronic hypertension, renal disease and obesity.

Presentation of Pre-eclampsia

Women with pre-eclampsia are usually asymptomatic when the disease first manifests. Absence of the 'classic' signs of hypertension, proteinuria and oedema does not exclude diagnosis, and in practice, pre-eclampsia is diagnosed when there is a constellation of recognised features:

Symptoms

Headache
Nausea/vomiting
Peripheral oedema
Rapid weight gain
Visual disturbances
Right upper quadrant pain
Epigastric pain
Confusion
Convulsion (eclampsia)
Signs
Hypertension
Brisk reflexes
Clonus
Retinal oedema/haemorrhage
Pulmonary oedema
Oliguria
Jaundice
Fetal growth restriction
Placental abruption
Investigations
Proteinuria
Haematuria from acute tubular necrosis or HELLP syndrome
Thrombocytopenia
Disseminated intravascular coagulopathy

It is the association of hypertension with these features that allows distinction of pre-eclampsia from chronic and gestational hypertension.

Complications of Pre-eclampsia

A sudden increase in blood pressure above a critical threshold (commonly taken to be a mean arterial pressure >150 mmHg) can cause acute arterial damage, especially within the central nervous system, which is particularly sensitive to hypertensive pathology. The most common cause of death in pre-eclampsia is loss of cerebral auto-regulation leading to cerebral haemorrhage. A severe and uncommon complication of pre-eclampsia is eclampsia, a form of hypertensive encephalopathy which is defined as tonic-clonic (grand mal) seizures occurring in association with features of pre-eclampsia. Eclampsia may be associated with ischaemic or haemorrhagic stroke with cerebral vasospasm or oedema. Cortical blindness (usually reversible) is well described, although there is rare association with pre-eclampsia/eclampsia. Acute hypertension in pregnancy or after delivery can affect cerebral auto-regulation, which leaves permanent damage, and death can occur.

Other systemic complications include renal function impairment in the form of reduced uric acid clearance and glomerular hypofiltration. A rising plasma urate is an early sign of pre-eclampsia, but not always demonstrated, reflecting the heterogeneity of the disease. Hypo-albuminaemia causes a low colloid osmotic pressure which alters fluid transport across the capillaries, so that the vascular system in pre-eclampsia becomes 'leaky', with an abnormal distribution of fluid in the interstitial spaces from the vascular compartment, leading to intravascular depletion and possibly vasoconstriction. This extra-vascular fluid leads to uncommon complications such as ascites and pulmonary oedema. About 10–15% of pre-eclampsia cases can occur without oedema – 'dry pre-eclampsia' – which is recognised to be associated with higher perinatal mortality.

Liver dysfunction as a feature of pre-eclampsia may initially present with vomiting and epigastric pain and may progress to jaundice and hepatic failure. The clotting system which is normally activated in pregnancy (a 'hypercoagulable' state) is exaggerated in pre-eclampsia. There is an accentuation of the hypercoagulability of normal pregnancy which may in some cases decompensate into disseminated intravascular coagulation (DIC). This is particularly severe if there is concomitant hepatic involvement. If both are present with haemolysis, the acronym 'HELLP syndrome' has been used to identify the presence of haemolysis, elevated liver enzymes and low platelet count. HELLP syndrome is a dangerous complication, which is typified by epigastric pain and carries a maternal mortality rate of about 1%.

Management of Pre-eclampsia

A diagnosis of pre-eclampsia requires hospital admission, given the disorder's potential to worsen rapidly and the increased risk of placental abruption, especially when it develops superimposed on chronic hypertension. Delivery remains the only known 'cure'. At term, induction of labour or delivery is mandated. Attempts to prolong gestation to reduce the risk of neonatal morbidity by optimal blood pressure management should be undertaken if pregnancy is <34 weeks and there is good clinical response to therapy. Gestation is permitted to continue as long as blood pressure is sufficiently controlled, there are no signs of life-threatening maternal complications (such as DIC, HELLP, eclampsia) and fetal monitoring is reassuring.

Following diagnosis, women should receive regular blood pressure recording and monitoring of serum urea and creatinine, uric acid, haemoglobin, platelet count, liver function and coagulation screen if there is thrombocytopenia present.

Excessive fluid replacement should be avoided, as this may exacerbate interstitial oedema. Urine output as low as 10 ml/hr may be acceptable in the management of some cases of severe pre-eclampsia. Thromboprophylaxis with thromboembolic deterrent stockings and low molecular weight heparin should be administered.

There is no pharmacological cure for pre-eclampsia. Therapy is directed towards managing hypertension. Choices of pharmacological agents for treatment of pre-eclampsia and other hypertensive disorders in pregnancy are similar and in general are given if the blood pressure reaches 150/100 mmHg and are urgently required at 160/110 mmHg. Commonly used oral agents are labetalol, nifedipine and alpha-methyldopa.

In a hypertensive crisis, IV agents (labetalol or hydralazine) are used to achieve rapid blood pressure reduction, usually in concordance with IV magnesium sulphate to reduce the risk of eclampsia. Magnesium is not an anti-convulsant but is thought to work by increasing cerebral perfusion. Rapid reduction in blood pressure can reduce placental perfusion, and therefore it is important to monitor the fetus during therapy.

Cardiac Disease

In the UK, the overall maternal mortality rate from cardiac disease has risen from 7.3/million births in the 1982–4 triennium to 21/million births in the 2015–17 triennium. A major part of this increase is attributable to acquired heart disease. Since 2000, cardiac disease has been the overall leading cause of maternal death, and the leading case of indirect maternal death in the UK [20].

Patients with cardiac disease in pregnancy can be divided into two categories: congenital or acquired heart disease. One-third of deaths from cardiac disease in pregnancy are a result of myocardial infarction/ischaemic heart disease and a similar number of late deaths are associated with peripartum cardiomyopathy. Other significant contributors (5–10% each) are rheumatic heart disease, congenital heart disease and pulmonary hypertension.

Myocardial Infarction, Ischaemic Heart Disease and Aortic Dissection

Pregnancy raises the risk of acute myocardial infarction by three- to four-fold. This risk is 30 times higher for women aged >40 years compared with women aged <20 years. Traditional risk factors for cardiac disease such as hypertension, diabetes, obesity and hyperlipidaemia have been increasing over the last few decades, particularly in developed countries due to trends of mothers being older, having a higher body mass index and co-existing medical comorbidities. A majority of women who present with ischaemic heart disease in pregnancy were asymptomatic before pregnancy, with no history of heart disease, but possibly occult cardiovascular dysfunction in relation to their pre-existing risk factors. It is thought that the physiological strain of pregnancy on the cardiovascular system unmasks the predisposition to heart disease and decompensation.

It is therefore prudent to include myocardial infarction as a differential diagnosis in all pregnant woman who present with chest pain. Notably, acute myocardial infarction occurs most commonly in the latter half of pregnancy and can also present intra-partum and postpartum. Other causes of myocardial infarction aside from atherosclerosis include dissection of the coronary arteries, which is relatively more common in pregnancy than in the non-pregnant population. An electrocardiogram interpreted by someone who is trained at detecting signs of cardiac ischaemia and infarction should be performed. A serum troponin measurement can also be useful to further exclude or conclude the occurrence of myocardial infarction.

Management for acute ischaemia and infarction remains the same as it is for non-pregnant individuals, that is, heparin, nitrates and beta-blockers. Percutaneous transluminal angioplasty and stenting may be used if appropriate.

Peripartum Cardiomyopathy

Peripartum cardiomyopathy is a rare condition, but specific to pregnancy. It is the occurrence of heart failure without an identifiable cause, in pregnant women without a known history of cardiac disease. It usually presents in late pregnancy or early in the puerperium, but it can occur up to 6 months after delivery. Risk factors include multiple pregnancy, advanced maternal age and multiparity.

Symptoms are similar to that for congestive cardiac failure: dyspnoea, orthopnoea, paroxysmal nocturnal dyspnoea, reduced exercise tolerance, pulmonary and/or peripheral oedema and palpitations. As 25% of affected women will be hypertensive, it can be mistaken for pre-eclampsia. Investigations include an electrocardiogram, a chest X-ray and an echocardiogram. Diagnostic echocardiographic criteria include left ventricular ejection fraction <0.45 or M-mode fractional shortening $<30\%$ (or both) and end-diastolic dimension >2.7 cm/m^2.

Management usually involves elective delivery to offload the strain on the heart. Treatment for peripartum cardiomyopathy includes conventional pharmacologic heart-failure therapies – principally diuretics, angiotensin-converting enzyme inhibitors, vasodilators, digoxin, β-blockers, anticoagulants and peripartum cardiomyopathy-targeted therapies. Therapeutic decisions are influenced by drug-safety profiles during pregnancy and lactation. Mechanical support and transplantation might be necessary in severe cases.

Congenital Heart Disease

Although deaths from congenital heart disease are fortunately uncommon, the prevalence of this condition in pregnancy is about 0.8%. Congenital heart disease is one of the most common congenital abnormalities and, due to corrective surgery advances, the majority of those affected will survive to adulthood. Ideally, girls with congenital heart disease should be referred to a joint cardiology and obstetric clinic at a pre-conception stage for advice about contraception (and subsequently for pre-conception counselling) once they have reached puberty. Pre-conception counselling should also be offered to older women with a new diagnosis. At these clinics, women should be given an outline of the issues relating to pregnancy with congenital heart disease including the increased risk of mortality, congenital heart disease in the offspring (6% risk) and the need for increased medical surveillance during pregnancy.

All women with structural congenital heart disease should be offered a fetal echocardiogram during the second trimester. A further multidisciplinary meeting should take place early in the third trimester of gestation to establish a plan for delivery. Important details include deciding who should be involved in supervising the labour, whether a caesarean section is appropriate, whether pushing is advisable in the second stage and appropriate prophylaxis against postpartum haemorrhage. Routinely used uterotonics, which include prostaglandins, can have major cardiovascular adverse effects. A low-dose oxytocin infusion is probably the safest option, and at caesarean section prophylactic uterine compression methods such as uterine massage or sutures can be considered in place of uterotonics. The plan should also include postpartum management, including thromboprophylaxis, recovery within a high dependency unit and the timing of cardiac and obstetric review. The general principle of intrapartum management is to minimise cardiovascular stress. In most cases this will be achieved by the use of early slow incremental epidural anaesthesia and assisted vaginal delivery. Caesarean section is usually necessary only for obstetric indications.

Thromboembolism in Pregnancy

Pregnancy is a prothrombotic state; it epitomises all the components of Virchow's triad: venous stasis, endothelial damage and hypercoagulability. Therefore, pregnant women are more likely to experience thromboembolic events compared to non-pregnant women. For instance, the incidence of deep vein thrombosis (DVT) is five times higher in pregnancy compared to the non-pregnant population. The frequency of thrombosis is similar in all three trimesters, and also in the first 6 weeks postpartum. In addition to the acute complications of thromboembolic events, there is also an associated long-term morbidity of post-thrombotic syndrome.

Certain medical conditions increase the risk of pregnancy-related thrombosis such as inherited or acquired thrombophilias, a previous history of thrombosis, antiphospholipid syndrome, lupus, heart disease and sickle cell disease. Other risk factors include advanced maternal age, high body mass index, multiple pregnancy and immobility. In the puerperium, caesarean delivery increases the risk of thrombosis by two-fold and postpartum infection by four-fold.

Thromboprophylaxis in Pregnancy

Despite an increased risk for thrombosis during pregnancy, most women do not require anticoagulation. The risk of maternal haemorrhage with heparin and low molecular weight heparin (LMWH) is reportedly 2%. It is therefore imperative that formal risk assessments using a numerical score for pregnant and postpartum women is carried out and updated with developing clinical scenarios, for example, if mobility is impaired due to clinical complications.

Compared to unfractionated heparin, LMWH is the preferred agent for prophylaxis and treatment during pregnancy as it is just as effective and safer; the incidence of heparin-induced thrombocytopenia is much lower when compared to unfractionated heparin. However, a disadvantage of LMWH includes a longer half-life, which may be problematic at the time of delivery. Unfractionated heparin is preferable in patients with renal disease, as LMWH is primarily excreted by the kidneys. Warfarin crosses the placenta and is teratogenic. It is therefore used in pregnancy only if essential, but can safely be used in the puerperium, provided there are no haemorrhagic risks to the mother.

Where possible, anticoagulant therapy should be altered to avoid any unwanted anticoagulant effects during delivery. Women should be advised not to inject any further heparin once they go into labour. For elective delivery, LMWH should be stopped 24 hours before induction of labour or prior to a caesarean section. Subcutaneous unfractionated heparin should be discontinued 12 hours before and intravenous unfractionated heparin stopped 6 hours before an induction of labour or regional anaesthesia. Women who present in labour shortly after injecting LMWH can be reassured that bleeding complications are very uncommon with LMWH. If spontaneous labour occurs in women receiving therapeutic doses of subcutaneous unfractionated heparin, careful monitoring of the APTT is required. If it is markedly prolonged near delivery, protamine sulphate may be required to reduce the risk of bleeding. If unfractionated heparin is used after a caesarean section (or any other surgery), the platelet count should be monitored every 2–3 days for up to 2 weeks or until the heparin is stopped.

Diagnosis and Management of Thrombosis in Pregnancy

In any women with signs and symptoms of a DVT, objective testing should be expedited, and a treatment dose of anticoagulants given until a diagnosis is excluded. If a DVT remains untreated, 15–24% of these patients will go on to develop a pulmonary embolism (PE). In pregnancy, 15% of PE cases result in fatality. In a vast majority (66%), death occurs within 30 minutes of the embolic event [21].

Compression duplex ultrasound is the primary diagnostic test for DVT. Women presenting with signs and symptoms of an acute PE should have an electrocardiogram and a chest X-ray performed in the first instance. In women with suspected PE who also have symptoms and signs of DVT, compression duplex ultrasound should be performed. If compression ultrasonography confirms the presence of DVT, no further investigation is necessary and treatment for venous thromboembolism should continue. Despite a normal chest X-ray, if there is still a clinical suspicion of PE, a ventilation-perfusion (V/Q) scan should be organised as this carries a lower risk of breast cancer than a CT-pulmonary angiogram (CTPA). However, if the chest X-ray is abnormal, a CTPA is the preferred diagnostic tool. The D-dimer assay is positive in pregnancy, even in the absence of a thrombosis. This is due to increased thrombin activity and fibrinolysis in pregnancy. Therefore, this test is non-specific and not reliable in the diagnosis of thrombosis during pregnancy.

For treatment, LMWH should be given in doses titrated against the woman's booking or early pregnancy weight. Consideration should be given to the use of a temporary inferior vena cava filter in the peripartum period for patients with an iliac vein venous thromboembolism to reduce the risk of a PE or in patients with proven DVT and who have recurrent PE despite adequate anticoagulation. Treatment with therapeutic doses of subcutaneous LMWH should be employed during the remainder of the pregnancy and for at least 6 weeks postnatally or until at least 3 months of treatment has been given in total.

Conclusion

In conclusion, pregnancy involves vast physiological shifts that impact on several key systems within the mother, and such deviations carry implications for growth and development of her baby. Careful assessment of the pregnant patient with an understanding of what may be 'normal' for that stage of pregnancy is essential in diagnosis and management. Significantly, whilst it is important that women are reassured that fatality during or after pregnancy is rare in the UK and that many symptoms in pregnancy are unlikely to represent severe complications, raised awareness within both the clinical and patient community helps ensure that the small number of women who are seriously ill, are able to access care and are diagnosed early.

References

1. AA Mahendru, TR Everett, IB Wilkinson, CC Lees, CM McEniery. A longitudinal study of maternal cardiovascular function from preconception to the postpartum period. *J Hypertens.* 2014;32(4):849–56.
2. V Nama, TF Antonios, J Onwude, IT Manyonda. Mid-trimester blood pressure

drop in normal pregnancy: myth or reality? *J Hypertens.* 2011;29(4):763–8.

3. SC Robson, S Hunter, RJ Boys, W Dunlop. Serial study of factors influencing changes in cardiac output during human pregnancy. *Am J Physiol.* 1989;256(4 Pt 2):H1060–5.
4. MA Nickens, RC Long, SA Geraci. Cardiovascular disease in pregnancy: (women's health series). *South Med J.* 2013;106(11):624–30.
5. V Regitz-Zagrosek, C Blomstrom Lundqvist, C Borghi, R Cifkova, R Ferreira, JM Foidart, et al. ESC guidelines on the management of cardiovascular diseases during pregnancy: the Task Force on the Management of Cardiovascular Diseases during Pregnancy of the European Society of Cardiology (ESC). *Eur Heart J.* 2011;32(24):3147–97.
6. JM Sullivan, KB Ramanathan. Management of medical problems in pregnancy – severe cardiac disease. *N Engl J Med.* 1985;313(5):304–9.
7. EL Capeless, JF Clapp. Cardiovascular changes in early phase of pregnancy. *Am J Obstet Gynecol.* 1989;161(6 Pt 1):1449–53.
8. JJ Duvekot, EC Cheriex, WD Tan, GA Heidendal, LL Peeters. Volume-dependent echocardiographic parameters are not useful for estimating baseline blood volume but are useful for detecting acute changes in vascular filling state. *Basic Res Cardiol.* 1994;89(3):270–7.
9. E Chung, LA Leinwand. Pregnancy as a cardiac stress model. *Cardiovasc Res.* 2014;101(4):561–70.
10. K Melchiorre, R Sharma, B Thilaganathan. Cardiac structure and function in normal pregnancy. *Curr Opin Obstet Gynecol.* 2012;24(6):413–21.
11. AB Chapman, WT Abraham, S Zamudio, C Coffin, A Merouani, D Young, et al. Temporal relationships between hormonal and hemodynamic changes in early human pregnancy. *Kidney Int.* 1998;54(6):2056–63.
12. JM Davison, W Dunlop. Renal hemodynamics and tubular function normal human pregnancy. *Kidney Int.* 1980;18(2):152–61.
13. SE Weinberger, ST Weiss, WR Cohen, JW Weiss, TS Johnson. Pregnancy and the lung. *Am Rev Respir Dis.* 1980;121(3):559–81.
14. D Jensen, J Duffin, YM Lam, KA Webb, JA Simpson, GA Davies, et al. Physiological mechanisms of hyperventilation during human pregnancy. *Respir Physiol Neurobiol.* 2008;161(1):76–86.
15. Royal College of Obstetricians & Gynaecologists. The management of nausea and vomiting in pregnancy and hyperemesis gravidarum (Green-top Guideline No. 69). 2016.
16. Royal College of Obstetricians & Gynaecologists. Shoulder dystocia (Green-top Guideline No. 42). 2012.
17. Royal College of Obstetricians & Gynaecologists. Maternal collapse in pregnancy and the puerperium (Green-top Guideline No. 56). 2019.
18. Report of the National High Blood Pressure Education Program Working Group on High Blood Pressure in Pregnancy. *Am J Obstet Gynecol.* 2000;183(1):S1–22.
19. National Institute for Health and Care Excellence (NICE). Hypertension in pregnancy: diagnosis and management. NICE Guideline (NG133). 2019.
20. M Knight, K Bunch, D Tuffnell, J Shakespeare, R Kotnis, S Kenyon, JJ Kurinczuk, editors. *Saving Lives, Improving Mothers' Care – Lessons learned to inform maternity care from the UK and Ireland Confidential Enquiries into Maternal Deaths and Morbidity 2015–17.* Oxford: National Perinatal Epidemiology Unit, University of Oxford; 2019.
21. Royal College of Obstetricians & Gynaecologists. Thrombotic disease in pregnancy and the puerperium (Green-top Guideline No. 37b). 2015.

Chapter 4

Fetal Development and Routine Maternity Care

Judith Meek, Adalina Sacco and Leigh Dyet

This chapter contains an outline of fetal development, focusing on general organogenesis in the first trimester, and then brain development in the second and third trimesters. The effects of maternal well-being, therapeutic medication, tobacco and alcohol on the developing fetus are explored. Finally, the current format of antenatal care, screening and fetal medicine in the UK National Health Service (NHS) is described.

Fetal medicine is a rapidly evolving speciality, for example it has recently become possible to treat some babies with spina bifida with antenatal intrauterine surgery. However, the discovery of a problem during pregnancy clearly causes enormous distress with potential moral and ethical issues for both parents and their medical teams, especially when the fetus has a life-limiting diagnosis and the option of termination of pregnancy is considered and explained. Even when the fetus has an operable condition or a less serious diagnosis the emotional burden of the current and subsequent pregnancies is enormous. Therefore, the decisions that couples make have become extremely complex and there is a need for psychological support both during and after the pregnancy.

Although the chapter describes the effects of teratogens and poor maternal health on the developing fetus, it is important to emphasise that in most cases of fetal abnormality no obvious cause is found. Moreover, the majority of women who take prescribed or recreational drugs give birth to healthy full-term babies (see Chapter 25 on pre-birth planning).

Fetal Development

This section provides an outline of the embryological processes that are happening at each stage of gestation in the first trimester and highlights the time-dependent impact of abnormalities in development. The chapter then focuses on brain development over the second and third trimesters. The convention for timing for weeks of pregnancy is from the last menstrual period (LMP) rather than from fertilisation.

An understanding of basic embryology is extremely useful in providing insight into the effects of maternal illness and medication on the developing fetus. For a comprehensive review of this area see the relevant textbook [1]. Intrauterine development takes place with an orderly and time-sensitive course, and can be disrupted by genetic defects, teratogenic drugs, vascular accidents, placental insufficiency or maternal illness. In general, chromosome abnormalities, early infections and teratogens can also lead to miscarriage. The timing of an antenatal insult can often be inferred by the nature of a fetal abnormality. Severe neural, cardiac, palate, limb, eye and ear defects occur within the first 5 weeks of pregnancy often before a woman may be aware that she is pregnant.

However, most of these malformations are diagnosed in the early second trimester during the 19-week anomalies ultrasound scan.

Pre-conception

The main concern prior to conception is to ensure that there is sufficient folate available to ensure normal development of the neural tube. There is a well-established association between folate deficiency and neural tube defects such as spina bifida, and maternal pre-conception intake of folic acid at least 3 months before conception can reduce this risk [2]. It is therefore also important to consider stopping drugs that interfere with folate metabolism, such as sodium valproate, prior to pregnancy if possible. For valproate, it is important to adhere to Medicines & Healthcare products Regulatory Agency (MHRA) latest guidance on prescribing both during and outwith pregnancy.

The First Trimester

Following fertilisation, the zygote develops in the first few days into a morula (a single layer of cells) and then into a multidimensional blastocyst which implants into the uterine wall 6–10 days after ovulation. Gastrulation is the term for the process whereby the embryonic structures develop into the three germ layers: ectoderm, mesoderm and endoderm. These are the fundamental units of organogenesis and this is the most critical step and time of development. Gastrulation also provides axis formation (cranial/caudal, ventral/dorsal axes and left/right symmetry). Therefore, during this very critical period teratogens including alcohol, caffeine, tobacco, medication (including psychotropics, retinoic acid, etc.), radiation, viral infections and folic acid deficiency can cause abnormalities in cell signalling or proliferation that can be wide ranging and affect multiple developmental processes. Spontaneous abortion (miscarriage) usually occurs when one specific germ cell line is absent or when there is an abnormality in a major axis in the embryonic region.

During weeks 4–8 the gastrointestinal tract and portions of the lungs and glandular tissue arise from the inner ectoderm, and the musculoskeletal system, circulatory system, kidneys and internal sex organs arise from the mesoderm. The ectoderm is the outer layer of the embryo which gives rise to the external ectoderm (epidermis, hair and nails) and the neuroectoderm (neural crest and neural tube; brain/spinal cord) along with the lens of the eye and the inner ear.

The other major process that occurs at this time (weeks 4–8) is neurulation. This is the development of the brain, spinal cord and retina. A neural plate is formed which is broader cranially, to become the area that will form the brain. The plate develops a groove and then folds to form a tube. This tube then 'zips' closed, starting in the middle and ending at the cranial and caudal neuropores which remain open until days 38 and 40 respectively. The way this process occurs explains why neural tube defects tend to occur either towards the sacrum (spina bifida) or the head (anencephaly) as it is the closing of the neuropores that is the last part of the development to be completed. The most common caudal defects 'spina bifida' occur with an incidence of 0.06%. As this process occurs so early in pregnancy, often before a woman even knows she is pregnant, it is extremely important that folic acid supplementation is started pre-conception whenever possible to reduce the risk of neural tube defects. Continuing sodium valproate and carbamazepine during pregnancy is associated with a significant risk of neural tube defects, and concomitant use of folic acid does not appear to prevent these abnormalities [3].

During the 4–6 week period after the LMP the circulatory system also begins to develop. The heart starts as a simple tube which then undergoes a series of folds to change it into a shape that will become the four chambers. This occurs in weeks 5–7. The main abnormality that can occur at the earliest stage of cardiac development is dextrocardia, where the heart lies on the right with the apex of the left ventricle pointing to the right. This is often associated with situs-inversus where the organs of the abdomen are also positioned in a mirror image from their normal positions. This is most commonly an autosomal recessive inherited disorder.

The face develops between weeks 4 and 6. The surface of the external face is formed by fusion of facial swellings with mandibular and maxillary processes. The primary palate is formed in this period by fusion/merging of the medial nasal and maxillary processes. From week 6–12 the secondary palate is formed by fusion between palatal processes growing from the oral surfaces of the maxillary processes. Each merging and fusion site is also the site of a potential facial or palatal cleft.

Between weeks 5 and 10 (after the LMP) the body cavities form from a flat trilaminar disc of cells. Lateral plate mesoderm splits into splanchnic and somatic divisions and between these divisions, vacuoles form and merge creating a U-shaped cavity in the embryo. This is the intra-embryonic cavity, and it initially extends from the pelvis up into the thoracic region. The septum transversum then develops which eventually makes up part of the diaphragm. It divides the single cavity into a thoracic and peritoneal cavity. The separation of these cavities is not complete and there remain communications through the pericardioperitoneal canals. These communications are eventually closed off by pleuroperitoneal folds.

Failure of these processes results in the diaphragm not forming completely and the abdominal contents herniating into the thoracic cavity. This is a congenital diaphragmatic hernia. It occurs in 0.04% of births in the UK and results in poor lung development leading to pulmonary hypoplasia and hypertension. A left-sided diaphragmatic hernia is more common and its severity is dependent on whether the liver herniates into the thorax and how severely the lungs are affected. Most cases are surgically corrected postnatally with a mortality rate of 30%. Antenatal treatment which involves endoluminal tracheal occlusion is now available for some of the most severe cases. Congenital diaphragmatic hernia can be found as part of a syndrome or related to a genetic abnormality, but 80% have no known cause and there are no specific environmental factors that are known to cause it. The lung primordium is laid down as a diverticulum of the foregut and this phase lasts for about 7 weeks. From the 5th to the 17th week the lung resembles a tubule-acinar gland which sprouts epithelial tubes which then branch. This is termed the pseudoglandular phase. In the cannalicular phase (17th–26th week) the interface for gas exchange forms and the pneumocytes begin to make surfactant. This is important as the limit of viability for a premature baby's survival depends on having an adequate area for gas exchange using current ventilation techniques.

Herniation of the bowel can also occur, usually due to a defect in the anterior abdominal wall, and most often to the right of the umbilicus, and is called a gastroschisis. The viscera float in the amniotic fluid and are not covered in peritoneum or amnion. Herniation of the bowel requires surgical repair after birth, generally with good survival rates. Gastroschisis is more common in younger mothers in their late teens or early twenties. It occurs in about 0.03% of births in the UK and is associated with smoking and alcohol use and some studies have found associations with methamphetamine or other vasoactive recreational drugs, for example cocaine, amphetamine and ecstasy [4]. There have also been associations with maternal depression, antidepressant use and postnatal depression/psychosis following a previous pregnancy [5].

Brain Development

From 3 to 4 weeks as already described, primary neurulation occurs whereby the neural tube which is the precursor of the brain and spinal cord is shaped from the neural plate. Abnormalities at this stage are termed neural tube defects and are sometimes amenable to antenatal surgery which can lead to improved mobility and resolution or at least reduction of the associated hydrocephalus [6].

During the second and third month of pregnancy the neural tube grows, forms a rostral pouch and folds to form the primary brain which consists of the prosencepalon, mesencephalon and rhombencephalon. The prosencepahlon goes on to form the cerebral hemispheres, the lateral ventricles and the midline structures. The rhombencephalon forms the cerebellum, pons, medulla and fourth ventricle. The mesencephalon links the structures from the prosencephalon and rhombencephalon together. Any errors in these processes cause major structural abnormalities in the brain which lead to disability and epilepsy (e.g. holoprosencephaly). The corpus callosum, a large white matter tract connecting the left and right hemispheres, forms between 9 and 20 weeks. If is not seen on the antenatal scan, the prognosis depends on whether there are other abnormalities. An isolated absent corpus callosum is associated with a 75% chance of a normal outcome. Enlarged lateral ventricles can be related to a wide range of developmental or destructive causes and merit a fetal MRI scan for a more accurate diagnosis. Severe cases of fetal hydrocephalus may be cause by obstruction such as aqueduct stenosis.

During the third and fourth month there is a period of intense neural proliferation in the ventricular zone of the neural tube. Disorders of neuronal proliferation can cause microcephaly or macrocephaly. Microcephaly can have genetic causes, but can also result from viral infections such as cytomegalovirus (CMV), rubella or Zika, toxins such as alcohol, or be part of congenital syndromes. Macrocephaly can be associated with growth disturbance syndrome such as achondroplasia, Beckwith–Wiedemann syndrome, Fragile X and Sotos syndrome. It can also result from neurocutaneous syndromes.

From the third to the fifth months these neurones are destined to travel to their precisely predetermined final locations in layers in the cortex in a process called neuronal migration. During this phase the neurones develop an axon and dendrite which will form the basis of the white matter connections. Neuronal migration defects such as schizencephaly, lissencaphaly and polymicrogyria can result in developmental delay (which is often severe) and epilepsy.

The fifth month starts a protracted course of neuronal organisation where multiple synapses are made between neighbouring neurones, which will eventually be pruned into a network that results from the sensory experience of the fetus (or premature baby).

Disruption of brain formation at any of these early stages up to the fourth month results in gross anatomical abnormalities which are often visible on early ultrasound scans and would be sufficiently life-limiting to qualify for a termination of pregnancy even beyond 24 weeks (see the section on the pregnancy pathway). Any insult beyond this phase can result in developmental or behavioural problems, but may not be visible on antenatal ultrasound scans unless there is gross white matter damage from vascular accidents resulting from factors such as cocaine use. Most of the connections are not yet myelinated; this is a process that begins around birth and goes on for many years. It is the myelin which gives white matter its eponymous appearance.

Sensory Development

The fetus has a surprisingly rich sensory world, which feeds in to the individualised connectivity of the developing brain. Making parents aware of their unborn baby's abilities can aid bonding and attachment, and this is even more relevant for a baby who is born prematurely. The fetus is protected from intrusive noise and light and maintained at a comfortable temperature in utero. There is a continuous supply of nutrition and oxygen. The position is one of flexion, where flexor tone dominates over extensor tone, and movement results in sensations of touch and proprioception. Touch includes stretching the feet against the uterine wall, bringing the hands to the mouth, sucking the thumb and grasping the umbilical cord.

Fetal hearing begins at 24 weeks and auditory processing at 30 weeks; the sound is conducted by fluid rather than air. Newborns can therefore recognise their mother's voice and her first language, and respond to familiar music. The intrauterine environment is not completely dark, and this will depend on external light intensity, which varies with the time of day. In the third trimester a fetus in utero will track an external light stimulus [7].

Taste buds develop from 13 weeks onwards, transmitting signals to the brain from 20 weeks, and through swallowing amniotic fluid the fetus will experience a variety of flavours related to the mother's diet. Therefore fetal sensory input is dependent on the symbiotic relationship with the mother, and with her own environment, lifestyle and health.

Fetal Growth

Intrauterine growth restriction is an important cause of preterm delivery, postnatal hypoglycaemia and even stillbirth [8]. Up until the 19th week growth is usually predictably related to gestational age so that early scans can be reliably used for dating the pregnancy. If there is placental insufficiency the fetus will begin to display a fall-off in growth related to a poor intrauterine supply of nutrition and oxygen. High-risk mothers (women with hypertension, diabetes, lupus and other chronic illness) and twin pregnancies should be closely monitored (see the section on the pregnancy pathway). In some cases, poor growth may be a sign of a chromosome abnormality or an intrauterine infection.

In response to poor placental function the fetus will 'redistribute' the circulation to 'spare' vital organs such as the brain by increasing the resistance in all but the cerebral and adrenal vascular beds. Fat and muscle glycogen will be converted into glucose, giving the baby a 'wasted' appearance, with less resilience for enduring a normal labour and an increased risk of postnatal hypoglycaemia. Hypoxia may result in reactive polycythaemia. If the fetus is likely to die in utero early delivery is recommended.

In cases of poorly controlled diabetes, whereby the fetus is exposed to a high glucose load, this results in hyperinsulinaemia, and the fetus becoming macrosomic (greater than the 90th centile in birthweight). This causes excessive intrauterine growth with a typical distribution of visceral and central fat. The shoulders are wide relative to the head, leading to birth complications such as shoulder dystocia and maternal perineal lacerations. Continued production of insulin postpartum puts the baby at risk of hypoglycaemia. Maternal metabolic syndrome with diabetes, obesity and hypertension has adverse effects on fetal growth, with placental insufficiency or hyperinsulinaemia, and sometimes a combination of both. The timing and mode of delivery can be crucial for both mother and baby.

The Effect of Maternal Well-Being and Therapies on the Developing Fetus

The concept of maternal experience harming the unborn baby is ancient. The tragedy of Thalidomide in the 1950s brought the reality of teratogenic effects of drugs into public awareness, and this has resulted in an understandable reticence to take prescribed medication during pregnancy.

For women with psychiatric disease this issue has particular resonance, especially as the drugs themselves directly affect the action of neurotransmitters and therefore potentially the evolving brain. However, maternal distress, anxiety and use of tobacco and alcohol can also affect the fetus, particularly with respect to general growth and brain development.

The fetal brain is sensitive to chemical, hormonal and genetic influences, and also to vascular events and poor placental function. Factors such as maternal stress during pregnancy are known to be related to poor emotional and cognitive outcomes in children [9]. Therefore, the balance between the effects of treatment and the effects of mental illness needs to be established. There can be challenges in interpreting follow-up data and in how we advise and support women during their pregnancy on the basis of this information. Medication such as valproate [10] and addictive or recreational drugs such as alcohol, tobacco and cannabis can cause serious long-term cognitive and behavioural problems due to directly teratogenic effects on the developing brain (see chapters 18, 26 and 27).

For information about specific drugs or chemicals the UK Teratology Information Service is a useful resource [11].

Teratogenic Drugs

Alcohol

Alcohol is the most commonly ingested teratogen and the Royal College of Obstetricians & Gynaecologists recommends that women do not drink alcohol at any time during their pregnancy, advising that there is no safe lower limit [12]. Drinking during pregnancy is associated with placental insufficiency and poor growth, premature birth and stillbirth, but also has specific effects on brain development. Fetal alcohol spectrum disorder or fetal alcohol syndrome describe a specific syndrome of learning and behavioural difficulties, leading to lifelong emotional and psychiatric problems. Fetal alcohol spectrum disorder describes a range of disabilities, and fetal alcohol syndrome is at the most severe end of this spectrum. More details can be found on the NOFAS (National Organisation for Foetal Alcohol Syndrome-UK) website [13].

Tobacco

Exposure to tobacco either first- or second-hand can cause miscarriage, stillbirth, poor intrauterine growth, premature birth or placental abruption. Tobacco is teratogenic and is associated with developmental and behavioural problems, especially attention deficit hyperactivity disorder (ADHD) and poor school performance. Hackshaw et al. in a large review of 174,000 cases of birth defects concluded that for women who smoke while pregnant the risk was increased by around 30% for limb abnormalities, talipes, gastrointestinal defects, especially gastroschisis, craniofacial and occular abnormalities, and cleft lip/palate [14]. Children exposed to tobacco in utero have an increased incidence of respiratory diseases independent of their exposure to smoke, partly related to impaired lung development in utero and postpartum. For this reason, midwives are encouraged to test pregnant women for exhaled carbon monoxide and to offer support for smoking cessation.

Therapeutic Psychotropic Drugs

There is limited evidence that the majority of psychotropic drugs apart from valproate cause congenital malformation.

Valproate

The use of sodium valproate in pregnancy has been associated with a 40% risk of persistent neurodevelopmental disorders and a 10% risk of physical birth defects. There is a dose–response relationship. When taken in the first trimester it results in a 20-fold increase of congenital malformations including heart defects, neural tube defects, cleft lip and palate, craniosynostosis, hypospadias and polydactyly. Fetal valproate syndrome describes this wide range of physical, developmental and behavioural consequences, and the drug is now contraindicated as an anticonvulsant or psychotropic treatment in women who may become pregnant [3, 10, 11].

Further details on the prescribing of psychotropic medication and potential effects on the developing fetus can be found in Chapter 26, 'Principles of Prescribing', and Chapter 27, 'The Reproductive Safety of Psychotropic Medication and Implications for Prescribing in the Perinatal period'.

Maternal Well-Being

There is an increasing body of evidence that stress and depression during pregnancy are associated with an increased risk of developing depression, autism spectrum disorder (ASD), ADHD and cognitive and emotional problems [15]. The influence of maternal well-being on fetal brain development is borne out by animal models and is thought to be partially related to exposure of the fetus to stress hormones such as glucocorticoids and catecholamines, to an altered microbiome and to changes in cytokine levels. It is also increasingly recognised that conditions such as autism spectrum disorder (which is often diagnosed late or not at all in women) and ADHD have an inherited component, and are related to depressive illness.

The Pregnancy Pathway: Normal Screening and the Role of the Fetal Medicine Unit

Maternity care varies between countries and healthcare systems. In the UK, over 95% of women have their pregnancy care and birth within the NHS. Women get referred to an

NHS hospital by their general practitioner (GP) or can self-refer to most units in the UK. The NHS offers a series of antenatal appointments, ultrasound scans and blood tests to pregnant women which will be described further next.

Antenatal Appointments

Women in their first pregnancy will have approximately 10 appointments with a midwife, and women in their second and subsequent pregnancies will have approximately 7. This routine schedule of care is described on the NHS website [16]. Women may see midwives in a hospital, at a GP surgery or in the community. Routine appointments involve a discussion around the woman's health and well-being and their stage of pregnancy, measurement of blood pressure, testing of urine for protein and measurement of the symphysis-fundal height from 25 weeks' gestation. Women with additional risk factors, such as maternal physical or mental health problems or a complicated obstetric history, are identified at the first (also known as the booking) appointment and will also see an obstetrician or other specialty doctor (e.g. obstetric physician, anaesthetist, haematologist) as appropriate. Midwives are encouraged to ask about social factors specifically about domestic violence when the partner is not present. Women retain their pregnancy notes until the end of their pregnancy. There is a National Institute for Health and Care Excellence (NICE) guideline for antenatal care [17].

Ultrasound Scans

Two routine ultrasound scans are offered in all pregnancies by the NHS, one at 11–14 weeks of pregnancy (the 'dating' scan) and one at 18–21 weeks of pregnancy (the 'anomalies' scan). Details of the schedule and required standards for these scans are given in the Public Health England Fetal Anomaly Screening Programme guidance [18].

The purposes of the dating scan are to confirm the viability of the pregnancy, ascertain if it is a singleton or multiple pregnancy, estimate the gestational age and detect major structural anomalies that may be identified in early pregnancy, such as anencephaly. The scan also provides the first step of screening for common aneuploidies (trisomy 21, 18 and 13) if the woman opts for this. In the UK, first-line aneuploidy screening is performed by the combined screening test which uses maternal age, the nuchal translucency ultrasound measurement and two pregnancy hormones (human chorionic gonadotropin (hCG) and pregnancy-associated plasma protein-A (PAPP-A)) to produce a chance or risk estimation. If this is positive, non-invasive prenatal testing (NIPT, a blood test that detects fetal DNA fragments in the maternal circulation) is available in the NHS as a second-line screening test for women where screening tests have revealed a high risk of aneuploidy. It is also being used for fetal genotyping for rhesus negative women. Non-invasive prenatal testing is available in the private sector.

The purpose of the anomalies scan is to detect conditions that may benefit from treatment before or soon after birth. In addition, the scan is performed in order to detect conditions that mean the birth should be in an appropriate hospital and to optimise treatment after the baby is born. In some cases, the condition may mean that the baby might die shortly after birth in which case it is important to explore the parents' wishes and to plan a palliative care pathway that will minimise the baby's suffering, involving family and religious support as required. It is important to discuss these plans before the baby is born if possible.

A mid-gestation scan may also detect conditions which would lead to a substantial risk of physical or mental abnormalities and therefore allows patients in the UK the option to end the pregnancy legally under Section E of the Abortion Act 1967 (amended 1990). Identification of fetal sex and provision of photos are not national requirements for the anomalies scan, and are decided at a local level. As with all screening tests in pregnancy, women can choose not to have either or both of these scans if they do not wish. Some hospitals offer further routine ultrasound scans in pregnancy, for example a third trimester growth scan; this again is decided at a local level. There is now wide provision of Early Pregnancy Units (EPUs) across the UK, and women with problems such as pain or bleeding before the dating scan may have an early pregnancy scan in an EPU. If the baby is found to be in the breech position in the third trimester of pregnancy, then options can be discussed, such as external cephalic version, elective caesarean section and breech vaginal delivery.

The Fetal Medicine Unit

Fetal medicine is the branch of medicine that provides care for the fetus (or fetuses) and mother. In the UK, women are referred to be seen in a Fetal Medicine Unit (FMU) for a wide range of reasons, and they may be offered specialised imaging (ultrasound or MRI) and intrauterine interventions. The local unit may detect or suspect a fetal abnormality and refer for further diagnosis and management. The pregnancy may be complicated by a genetic abnormality (and sometimes this would be a suspected recurrence after an affected sibling). The pregnancy may be complicated by possible fetal infection, particularly CMV which may present as growth restriction or microcephaly. There may be severe fetal growth restriction or a twin pregnancy with complications such as twin to twin transfusion. Any triplet and higher order multiple pregnancy should be closely monitored in an FMU. Mothers with a previous history of isoimmunisation to red cells or platelets and those with rising rhesus antibody titres will need close follow-up and possibly intrauterine transfusions.

Patients at higher risk of preterm birth may also be referred to a fetal medicine unit if there is no preterm birth clinic available to them locally. Specialist fetal medicine centres provide ultrasound scanning and counselling, and link in with a number of other specialities and services such as medical genetics, palliative care, radiology, virology, neonatology, paediatric surgery, paediatric cardiology, paediatric nephrology/urology, paediatric neurology and facial cleft services. Specialist FMU centres are able to offer invasive testing (chorionic villus sampling or amniocentesis), feticide and in-utero treatment options such as in-utero blood transfusion in fetal anaemia or laser placental photocoagulation in complicated twin pregnancies.

In the eyes of the UK law only the mother has rights and the fetus is not yet an individual legal entity, but decisions are made by parents that may put the baby's well-being above that of the mother, for example opting for a caesarean section so that a baby with a lethal abnormality can be born alive. It is important for every family that the FMU team communicates the birth and care plans with the neonatal team.

Blood Tests

Women are offered the following blood and urine tests in the UK during pregnancy:

- a full blood count to screen for anaemia (offered at two points in pregnancy)
- a 'group and screen' to confirm maternal blood group and screen for red cell antibodies (offered at two points in pregnancy)
- haemoglobin electrophoresis to screen for thalassaemia and in some trusts sickle cell anaemia
- serology to screen for Hepatitis B, HIV and syphilis
- screening for common aneuploidies (trisomy 21, 18 and 13) if the woman opts for this
- screening for gestational diabetes with a urine glucose test, and further blood tests if the woman has a higher risk of this.

Summary

The NHS offers a series of antenatal appointments, ultrasound scans and blood tests to pregnant women as described above as a minimum. All screening tests are optional and women may decline any or all of those described. Many women will have additional appointments, ultrasound scans or tests depending on their individual conditions.

Chapter Summary

Pregnancy can be an exciting and happy experience, or one of mixed emotions, and for some families it is an anxious and stressful time when psychological support is needed. For some mothers there is a need to weigh up the benefits and risks of psychotropic medication, for others guilt around use of tobacco, alcohol or illegal drugs. Some women will face challenges linked to fetal abnormalities or other obstetric complications, where often a cause is unidentified. Often it is appropriate for several specialists and members of the family support network to be involved in helping to share information. Understanding the way that the fetus develops and having access to the most up-to-date information about potential insults to a pregnancy are essential if professionals are to collaborate well in supporting families during pregnancy in order to achieve the safest and healthiest outcome for mother and baby.

GLOSSARY: COMMON CONGENITAL MALFORMATIONS THAT CAN BE DETECTED ON ANTENATAL ULTRASOUND SCANS

Brain and Spinal Cord

Holoprosencephaly; failure of the prosencephalon to divide into the double lobes of the cerebral hemispheres. May be associated with severe skull and facial defects

Migration Disorders

- Absent/agenesis of corpus callosum; may be partially or completely absent. Prognosis will depend on associated abnormalities

- Lissencephaly; absence of the normal convolutions of the cerebral cortex with microcephaly
- Polymicrogyria; excess formation of gyral folds which are usually small
- Schizencephaly; formation of abnormal slits or clefts in the cerebrum

Neural Tube Defects

- Anencephaly; absence of a major portion of the brain, skull and scalp
- Encephalocele; sac-like protrusion of the brain and meninges through a defect in the skull
- Meningomyelocele (spina-bifida); sac-like protrusion of spinal cord nerves and meninges protruding through a defect in the lumbosacral spinal canal exposing and damaging nerves. Usually associated with hydrocephalus.

Neuromuscular disorders; congenital muscular dystrophy, spinal muscular atrophy. The fetus is hypotonic resulting in polyhydramnios due to failure to swallow amniotic fluid. The mother may notice a paucity of fetal movements.

Head and Neck

Cleft lip and palate; failure of fusion of frontonasal, maxillary or mandibular processes. Sometimes associated with micrognathia (Pierre Robin syndrome). May be difficult to intubate

Cystic hygroma; a lymphatic malformation causing multiple cysts in the neck and mediastinum. Masses obstructing upper airway and oesophagus will result in polyhydramnios

Heart

Aortic stenosis; narrowing of the aortic valve resulting in left ventricular hypertrophy

Atrioventricular septal defect (AVSD); often associated with Down's syndrome. A range of defects involving the AV valves

Coarctation of the aorta; narrowing of the aorta which may be critical, with a loss of systemic blood flow after closure of the patent ductus arteriosus

Double outlet right ventricle (DORV); the pulmonary artery and aorta are both connected to the right ventricle associated with a VSD

Heart block; atrioventricular heart block, associated with maternal anti-rho antibodies. Baby may need pacing

Hypoplastic left ventricle; the left side of the heart is critically underdeveloped. Staged surgery is offered but asymptomatic survival is unlikely

Pulmonary stenosis; narrowing of the pulmonary valve often occurring in conjunction with other congenital heart problems

Tetralogy of Fallot (TOF) (consider 22q deletion); VSD, pulmonary stenosis, overriding aorta and right ventricular hypertrophy

Transposition of the Great Arteries; a critical condition where the aorta and pulmonary veins are switched in relation to the ventricles. If there is an associated VSD there will be sufficient mixing of blood for short-term survival before surgery. Otherwise an urgent atrial septostomy may be performed

Truncus arteriosus; the pulmonary artery and aorta remain as a single vessel arising from both ventricles

Ventricular septal defect (VSD); (the most common abnormality in all babies)

Lungs

Congenital diaphragmatic hernia; a defect in the formation of the diaphragm allowing herniation of the abdominal organs into the thorax resulting in pulmonary hypoplasia

Congenital cystic adenomatous malformation; a benign lung lesion that may resolve during pregnancy. A cystic area of abnormal non-functional lung tissue

Pleural effusions and hydrops; multiple causes including chromosomal and syndromic. May need antenatal drainage

Abdomen

Duodenal atresia; obstruction of duodenum (double bubble on X ray)

Exomphalos/omphalocele; a rarer abdominal wall defect whereby the normal return of the intestine into the abdominal cavity via the umbilical ring at about 10 weeks does not occur. Intestine and sometimes liver are externalised within the umbilical cord. (consider Beckwith–Wiedemann syndrome, associated with neonatal hypoglycaemia)

Gastroschisis; abdominal wall defect lateral to the umbilicus whereby the intestines extend outside the abdomen

Imperforate anus; anomaly of anus; a surgical emergency. If there is only one opening for bladder, vagina and bowel this is termed a 'cloacal malformation'

Tracheo-oesophageal fistula; fistula between trachea and oesophagus. The most common type has a blind ending oesophageal pouch and a distal fistula

Renal

Horseshoe kidneys; the kidneys have fused into a U-shape; may cause urinary tract infection or renal stones

Hydronephrosis; a common finding on antenatal scans which may resolve. Sometimes due to obstruction at the ureteropelvic junction. Needs follow-up and prevention of urinary tract infection

Polycystic kidneys; an autosomal recessive condition with enlarged cystic kidneys. Poor renal function leading to anhydramnios causes pulmonary hypoplasia which may be incompatible with life

Posterior urethral valves (bilateral hydronephrosis in boys). A condition where there is a developmental obstructive membrane in the urethra causing obstruction to bladder emptying. This results in bladder wall hypertrophy and bilateral hydronephrosis.

Renal agenesis; associated with pulmonary hypoplasia and usually lethal

Musculoskeletal

Achondroplasia; a growth disorder formerly known as dwarfism caused by a mutation in the fibroblast growth receptor gene (FGFR3). Most are spontaneous mutations but some are inherited. Some forms are lethal if the chest wall is deformed and 'asphyxiating'

Arthrogryphosis; a wide range of conditions that result in multiple contractures

Limb defects

- Polydactyly where there are more than five digits (which is common and can be normal)
- Syndactyly where fingers are fused or webbed. There may be fusion of the underlying bones. Not usually associated with other malformations
- Interruption sequence of an upper or lower limb.

Talipes equinovarus; a foot deformity where the foot is rotated inward and downward. May be associated with chromosomal disorders, or may be an isolated finding.

Genetic disorders

Beckwith–Wiedemann syndrome (911p15 anomalies); macrosomia, asymmetry/hemihypertrophy, macroglossia, neonatal hypoglycaemia, umbilical hernia/exomphalos, renal or liver tumours in childhood

Noonan's syndrome; heart defects, typical facies, oedema and pleural effusions, short stature

Trisomy 13; Patau's syndrome associated with intra-uterine growth restriction, brain or spinal cord abnormalities, microphthalmia, cleft lip/palate, extra digits and low tone

Trisomy 18; Edward's syndrome associated with intra-uterine growth restriction, cleft palate, defects of heart, lungs, kidneys and intestines, hand and foot deformities

Trisomy 21; Down's syndrome associated with a wide spectrum of developmental delay, typical appearance, low tone, heart defects, hypothyroidism and myelodysplasia

Turner's syndrome; Single X chromosome, short stature, underdeveloped ovaries, lymphoedema, cardiac and renal abnormalities, webbed neck, cystic hygroma

22q11 deletion or DiGeorge syndrome; cleft palate, heart defects, absent thymus and immune deficiency, feeding difficulties, developmental delay, typical facies

Other syndromes

VACTERL syndrome; vertebral defects, anal atresia, cardiac defects, trachea-oesophageal fistula, renal anomalies and limb abnormalities

Twins

Monochorionic; sharing a placenta (identical)

Dichorionic; twins with separate placentas

Monoamniotic; sharing an amniotic sac (identical)

Diamniotic; separate amniotic sacs (if monochorionic the twins are identical)

Twin to twin transfusion syndrome; occurs in monochorionic twins when there are anastomoses of placental vessels resulting in imbalanced blood flow from the donor twin to the recipient twin. May be treated with laser coagulation of the anastomoses. A less severe version is called TAPS (twin anaemia polycythaemia sequence)

References

1. PP Pandya, R Wapner, D Oepkes, N Sebire. *Fetal medicine: basic science and clinical practice.* 3rd ed. Amsterdam: Elsevier; 2019.
2. MRC Vitamin Study Research Group. Prevention of neural tube defects: results of the Medical Research Council Vitamin Study. *Lancet.* 1991:338(8760): 131–7.

3. FJE Vajda, TJ O'Brien, JE Graham, AA Hitchcock, CM Lander, MJ Eadie. Valproate-associated foetal malformations: rates of occurrence, risk in attempted avoidance. *Acta Neurol Scand.* 2019;139(1):42–8.
4. L Elliott, D Loomis, L Lottritz. Case-control study of gastroschisis cluster in Nevada. *Arch Pediatr Adolesc Med.* 2009;163(11):1000–6.
5. JE Given, M Loane, E Garne, V Nelen, I Barisic, H Randrianaivo, et al. Gastroschisis in Europe: a case-malformed-control study of medication and maternal illness during pregnancy as risk factors. *Paediatr Perinatal Epidemiol.* 2017;31(6):549–59.
6. NS Adzick, EA Thom, CY Spong, JW Brock, PK Burrows, MP Johnson, et al. A randomized trial of prenatal versus postnatal repair of myelomeningocele. *N Engl J Med.* 2011;364(11):993–1004.
7. T Donovan, K Dunn, A Penman, R Young, V Reid. Fetal eye movements in response to a visual stimulus. *Brain Behav.* 2020;10(8):e01676.
8. ES Draper, JJ Kurinczuk, S Kenyon, editors. MBRRACE-UK Perinatal Confidential Enquiry: term, singleton, intrapartum stillbirth and intrapartum related neonatal death. MBRRACE-UK; November 2017.
9. D Kingston, SM McDonald, M-P Austin, S Tough. Association between prenatal and postnatal psychological distress and toddler cognitive development: a systematic review. *PLoS ONE.* 2015, May 21;10(5):e0126929.
10. GOV.UK. Valproate and risk of abnormal pregnancy outcomes: new communication materials. February 2016. https://shorturl.at/BNn8l
11. UK Teratology Information Service. www.uktis.org
12. Royal College of Obstetricians & Gynaecologists. Alcohol and pregnancy. May 2022. www.rcog.org.uk/en/patients/patient-leaflets/alcohol-and-pregnancy
13. National Organisation for Foetal Alcohol Syndrome-UK. www.nofas-uk.org
14. A Hackshaw, C Rodeck, S Boniface. Maternal smoking in pregnancy and birth defects: a systematic review based on 173 687 malformed cases and 11.7 million controls. *Hum Reprod Update.* Sep-Oct 2011;17(5):589–604.
15. E Fitzgerald, K Hor, AJ Drake. Maternal influences on fetal brain development: the role of nutrition, infection and stress, and the potential for intergenerational consequences. *Early Hum Dev.* 2020;150:1015190.
16. NHS website: antenatal appointments. www.nhs.uk/pregnancy/your-pregnancy-care/your-antenatal-appointments
17. National Institute for Health and Care Excellence (NICE). Antenatal care. NICE Guideline (NG201). 2021. www.nice.org.uk/guidance/ng201
18. NHS. NHS fetal anomaly screening programme handbook. 2024. www.gov.uk/government/publications/fetal-anomaly-screening-programme-handbook
19. NHS England. NHS standard contract for fetal medicine. www.england.nhs.uk/wp-content/uploads/2013/06/e12-fetal-medi.pdf

Chapter 5

Infant Development
Birth to 12 Months

Angela Huertas-Ceballos, Emily Hills and Judith Meek

Introduction

We are born with the promise of full potential in our lives. Our brain and body are designed according to an exact sequence of dots and chains, maps and pathways, sparks and lights, shapes, volumes and colours, all of which started at the moment of conception. This wonderful process of development is extraordinarily complex and, by approximately 280 days, when it is ready to be tested, we are born into a world with the expectation that it will give us the necessary stimuli to fulfil our potential.

Hence without doubt, the period of the first 1,001 days of our life, from conception to 2 years of age, is profoundly important [1]. During this time, the brain develops at such high speed that by the age of 2 years it has doubled in size. Synaptic connections are formed at a faster rate than in any other period and the organisation of its processes is directly affected by early life experiences [2].

It is therefore vitally important that healthcare professionals, early intervention providers and families understand early brain and infant development so that they can support individualised enriched environments that promote sensory, motor and social emotional well-being from the very first moment of life.

This chapter provides an insight into the process from birth to the first year of an infant's life. A framework of the core occupations of the infant and the sensory skills that underpin this development is used to illustrate a typical progression by age. The periods that will be reviewed are defined as from 0–3, 3–6 and 6–12 months, and there is a further section on social deprivation. As infant behavioural development would not be possible without parents' and carers' intervention, reference to their role will be highlighted throughout the chapter. Additional comments for healthcare professionals involved in early intervention are also included.

Core Occupations of the Infant

The main occupations of an infant in the first year of life are sleeping, playing and eating.

Sleeping

Sleep is essential for all humans, plays an important role in emotional regulation, attention and memory [3], and lack of good quality sleep may be associated with poor health indicators in children [4] and physical and mental health problems in adults [5].

The process of sleep develops rapidly in the first year of life, and a newborn that sleeps 16–20 hours a day may sleep for periods of up to 12–15 hours a day by 12 months of age [6].

Sleep in itself is complicated for both infant and parents as it may be disrupted for a number of reasons, including sensory, environmental, psychological and physiological factors. A predictable healthy sleep routine is essential for the infant's development and co-regulation. For this reason, it is vital for parents and healthcare providers to know the basics about infants' sleep to provide optimal sensory environments in which they can thrive.

Playing

Play is an activity that is 'intrinsically motivated, entails engagement and results in joyful discovery' [7].

Play is an essential childhood occupation, contributing to the cognitive, physical, social and emotional well-being of a child [8]. It is so important for optimal development that it has been recognised by the United Nations as a birth right of every child [9].

Play is mostly sensory based in the first year; as such, loving, appropriate and caring relationships by parents through play from day one, lead to well-defined developmental trajectories in infants [8]. To support infant development, healthcare professionals use model relationship-based care which supports sensory-enriched opportunities for reciprocal play.

Feeding

Breastfeeding is a total sensory experience. During breastfeeding, all the infant's awareness of inner body sensations or 'interoceptive' needs are met as a close loving relationship is formed. Touch, taste and smell are all experienced in a positive way through skin-to-skin contact. As the infant sucks, the benefit includes not only tailored nutrition but also stimulation of sense of balance or 'proprioception' which works as a regulatory activity. Vestibular and visual inputs are added to the olfactory and gustatory experience of the breast milk itself, as the infant turns to look at the mother's eyes and listens to the pleasant sound of her soft voice. Breastfeeding exclusively in the first 6 months of life is associated with optimal development of the infant into a child [10].

Eating during the first year is a 'dyadic' or parent–infant sensory experience, whether breastfeeding, bottle-feeding, infant-led or spoon-led feeding. It is through mealtimes that infants learn about communication, socialisation, families, celebration, growth and pleasure.

Feeding difficulties in infants are an important cause of emotional distress and anxiety for parents. Feeding problems, including food refusal, selective eating and poor weight gain may vary from 5% to 60% in the typical developing population and are much higher in the preterm population [11].

When supporting families, it is essential to understand feeding development, infants' behaviour and sensory environment. Feeding difficulties may initially occur due to physiological or respiratory difficulties, or as a result of sensory processing problems which then develop into a challenging behaviour [12]. Feeding difficulties should be addressed in the context of a whole family, and a play-based approach in a nurturing environment may be required.

The Sensory Systems

Sensation drives human development, and humans learn how to interact with the world through eight sensory systems or senses.

- *Tactile:* The tactile system is responsible for processing touch. Tactile receptors in the skin provide information about discrimination, temperature, pain, tickle, itch, vibrations and more.
- *Proprioception:* The proprioceptive system provides information about the body's position in space. Receptors for this system are found in muscle spindles and areas of interface between muscle and tendon (Golgi tendon organs) and provide information about position, location, orientation and movement of the body.
- *Vestibular:* The vestibular system located in the inner ear provides information about head position in relation to gravity.
- *Olfactory:* The olfactory system processes smell, via smell receptors located in the mucus membrane of the nasal cavity.
- *Gustatory:* The gustatory system processes taste, with receptors located in the cheeks, tongue and epiglottis and signals the five different types of taste, namely sweet, sour, bitter, salty and umami.
- *Auditory:* The auditory system processes auditory input, and the auditory receptors which are in the ear provide information on frequency, duration and pitch of sound.
- *Visual:* The visual system processes visual input; the visual receptors are in the retina of the eye and provide visual information including shape, orientation, colour and movement.
- *Interoception:* The interoceptive system processes information about internal body functions of digestion, bowel/bladder movement, feelings of hunger, thirst and the sleep/wake cycle.

Typical Development of Occupations and Sensory Systems by Age

0–3 Months

Occupations

Infants may sleep 16–20 hours a day. Infants' ability to sleep depend on their ability to habituate and block out unnecessary sensory input. Newborns will often prefer to sleep on their parents in skin-to-skin fashion. Although this is developmentally adequate for awake infants, safety issues have been raised regarding infants sleeping on their front. The Safe to Sleep international campaign recommends not to use this position for sleeping as it has been associated with an increased risk of sudden infant death syndrome [13].

Sensory and gastrointestinal systems before 3 months of age are designed to receive all the nutrients they require from breast- or bottle-feeding. During these first early months, they require regular and frequent feeds as their stomach is small and they may become easily tired. The World Health Organization recommends that breast milk is the infant's sole source of nutrition for the first 6 months of life [14].

From 0–3 months, play is a sensory experience that begins in a multi-modal fashion as the main source of learning. It starts as parents gradually recognise and respond to their infant's behavioural cues and progresses from there into a unique synchronised interaction that will continue a lifetime. Engaging in play by smiling, singing, reading, touching and smelling is recommended at this age [15].

Sensory Development

At this age, infants open their hands in respond to touch and grasp a toy for 3 seconds and begin to take their hand to their mouth. This activity is important for both regulation and visual development. By 3 months infants may smile and respond vocally at a pleasurable touch. Providing opportunities for hand-to-hand contact, foot-to-foot touch and for baby massage helps develop the infant's body patterns while also supporting sleep, digestion and social and emotional well-being.

Positioned on their back small infants may find difficult to turn to the side and, on their front, may not be able to raise their heads fully from the surface. In their carers' arms, infants are able to curl arms and legs towards midline and turn their face towards the breast. As differentiation of the nervous system evolves, infants begin to defy gravity: by 3 months they are able to support their head in the midline and lift it from the surface when on their front. Different positions for play, including tummy time, help develop head control, arm strength and body awareness.

The vestibular system at birth may be slightly immature and infants may experience frequent startles and tremors at their own movements or when their position is changed. By 3 months movements become complex, fluent and gentler in preparation for hand reaching. Providing gentle movement helps with the infant's ability to regulate and allows them to explore their body's position in relation to gravity.

The infant's primary caregiver, her clothes, hair, skin and breastmilk and any other environmental smells are readily identifiable by infants soon after birth, as pleasurable or not [16], information that may help carers in supporting infants with self-regulation.

Most infants at this age will continue to be breast- or bottle-fed. The taste of breastmilk depends on what the mother eats and infants like it because it's usually sweet. Infants may change their behaviour in response to flavours they dislike in breastmilk like medication, alcohol or other. Identifying infants' favourite/less favourite taste maybe very useful for supporting self-regulation and interoception.

Exposure and interaction with parents that read and sing to their infants from birth stimulates the auditory system and helps promote early language development and self-regulation. By 3 months infants are able to engage in 'conversation' with their carers. Encouraging this activity is not only very enjoyable but also really effective with self-regulation.

Infants have a natural sensitivity towards human eyes at birth. Just a few weeks after birth, infants spend a significant amount of awake time in mutual gaze with a parent [17]. They are able to track moving objects, with faces often being the most visually appealing, and they are also drawn towards bright, contrasting patterns. By 3 months they fix and focus their eyes on objects at a certain distance and smile in response to a smile. Contrast objects with black and white stripes or electronic screens tend to engage infants into 'staring' at them for long periods of time. Given the limited and not-real sensory experience, it is inadvisable for infants to use any screens before 3 years [18, 19, 20].

The interoceptive sensory system is continuously relaying information on the physiological maturation of bodily functions. As such, infants convey their message as to whether they are hungry, tired or sleepy by changing their state of alertness and behaviour. Activities such as skin to skin, baby wearing, breastfeeding, infant massage and sleep protection ensure that all the infant's interoceptive needs are met.

Most of what we know about infants' behaviour today is based on the work of Brazelton and colleagues and their observations of infants and their relationships with parents and carers. The Neonatal Behavioural Assessment Scale is described as the most comprehensive neuro-behavioural assessment available for newborns to 4 months. It gives an in-depth profile of an individual baby and is extremely informative for both parents and healthcare professionals providing early intervention to infants [21].

3–6 Months

Occupations

No two infants are alike, with some needing more sleep than others. At around 4 months of age, many infants experience a sleep regression. They often wake frequently during this period as a result of a change in their sleep cycle. They no longer fall straight into REM sleep but now move through four stages of sleep, which are similar to those found in adults. Due to this, multiple daytime naps are still very common.

At this stage, infants' primary form of nutrition continues to be breast or formula milk. Every baby though is different, and some may be still feeding regularly where others have fallen into a routine with longer periods of no milk. The infants' stomach is now larger than at the previous stage, and their gastrointestinal system is more mature, such that they are able to take larger quantities of milk at a time.

Play based on sensory experiences and purposeful movement is beginning to drive development and continues to help motor, sensory and cognitive development. Infants engage actively with their carers, by taking turns in conversation and laughing responsively. By 6 months, play is much more interactive. As the infant's motor system matures, they roll, pull to sit, sit independently, and individual play with both hands begins.

Sensory Development

Infants at this age learn about their world through touch. They begin exploring new objects, holding an object in one hand, transferring it to the other and successfully bringing it towards their mouth. Opportunities for different tactile sensations by caregivers will help support the infant's development.

Infants of 4–6 months make more sense of their bodies. They bring their hands to their knees and gradually towards their feet. Holding onto their feet helps them support their pelvis to lift it off the surface.

Lying on their front, infants are now able to prop themselves up onto their forearms, and when on their back they begin experimenting with different movement opportunities, such as rolling to their side and, soon after, to their front. To stimulate sitting, carers may place interesting toys in front of them to encourage leaning forward while supporting their body at the back. Learning to sit provides them with different vestibular sensations.

Smell continues to play a huge role in self-regulation. Most infants have a comfort toy that provides a reassuring scent, and some parents will place a cloth that smells of their parents in the baby's bed space. Most infants will continue to be breast- or bottle-fed at this stage and the taste of milk is sweet.

By 4 and moving into 5 and 6 months, infants focus on their carers mouth as they smile, laugh, speak or sing, and frequently mimic their gestures. They are able to follow the rhythms of their speech and the signs that may accompany these. Singing lullabies, nursery rhymes and other songs significantly helps with language development.

Interactive and visually stimulating objects capture the interest of infants after 5 months. They can see the colourful pictures in children's hard books and at the same time feel the different textures of soft textured books. By 6 months, they direct their attention to cause-and-effect toys. All of these visual experiences stimulate tactile, proprioceptive and vestibular development.

By 6 months, infants are equally likely to initiate an interaction by both staring at their parents as well as by responding. These early interactions require both mutual and interpersonal coordination of gaze [22].

The ability to communicate with intent begins when infants start referring to external objects. Parents transmit to infants the social and cultural use of objects, and infants progressively learn and master behaviours beyond their parents. The dyad infant–parent becomes a triad with the object, and the communication complexity increases with time. Infants begin to switch their gaze back and forth between the carer and the object. This type of communicative reference through infancy is central to early communication and essential for the development of behavioural cues [23].

Before 6 months, infants continue to rely on their parents for co-regulation. Baby massage, baby wearing in kangaroo fashion and good quality sleep continue to play an important role in development and maturation of internal body functions, behaviour and sleep/wake cycles.

6–12 Months

Occupations

At this stage infants often sleep for up to 15 hours a day and, by then, many families have established a routine that allows the baby to have long naps throughout the day.

Infants at 6 months have gastrointestinal, hormonal and renal systems mature enough to process foods different from milk, and baby foods are introduced at this stage in most cultures. Whether families adopt a baby-led or spoon-led approach to solids, new foods tend to be introduced depending on their sensory quality, grading from thinner to thicker consistency as they reach 12 months. As infants' hand skills develop, they are able to drink from a cup and also to finger feed and by their first birthday they are usually able to have their meals fit into their parents' routine. From 6 to 12 months feeding is a full sensory experience and parents and healthcare providers must be aware that difficulties may arise in any of the sensory domains.

After 6 months of age and as their hand skills develop, infants will explore different objects and mimic family members in household activities. Banging and shaking toys is seen at this age and this gives them information about cause and effect. Their progressively increased ability to move independently will continue to enhance their play and by 12 months of age pretend play will emerge. At around 6 months of age, babies have developed attachments to the people who care for them; when they are presented with unfamiliar carers they may become distressed, this is known as 'stranger anxiety' and may last in some children to 3 years of age.

Sensory Development

Infants will continue to develop their fine motor skills by using visual attention for grasping initially with the whole hand and progressively refining on to a neat pincer grip.

This hand exploration coordinated with their body movements allows them to become aware of the outside world.

By 12 months most infants are crawling, and many are standing and walking. During this process of weight bearing and balancing against gravity, their proprioception evolves, and they become aware of space, form and posture and learn to develop strategies that support their motor planning and problem solving.

From 6 to 12 months, as their vestibular system matures, most infants enjoy being carried, placed on rocking chairs and, as they grow older and stronger, taken to the swings at the park. Even after they've learnt how to walk, they might well continue to pivot on their tummies and roll as the movement sensations feel comforting to them.

Smell and taste continue to play an important role in regulation. Infants who throughout their first 6 months had a comfort toy, will continue seeking its reassuring scent. Some parents may place a cloth that smells of them in the infants' bed space for self-soothing.

Books are essential for optimal development at this stage. Most 6-month-old infants enjoy being read to and turn pages enthusiastically. Encouraging infants to turn the pages whilst listening promotes shared attention and turn taking.

At 6 months infants are often intrigued by mirrors and by reflections of themselves or others. Gradually, as they grow, they become interactive with their own reflection and, by one year, most understand the difference between the object and its reflection – they reach out and pat the mirror or smile and laugh. They look in the mirror at their mothers' reflection and then back to their mother. Play activities with mirrors helps develop social communication and cognition.

By 6 months infants may demonstrate social looking, social referencing and some humour perception [24]. By 10 months of age, they intentionally use conventional signals such as gaze and gestures as they start communicating. By 12 months children begin to attempt words to reference objects or acts. Research on different parenting styles has led to the theory of natural pedagogy that suggests that infants behave responsively following other's gaze because they refer to the framework of communication learnt much earlier on in life [25].

By 12 months babies still rely heavily on their parents for co-regulation and to meet their interoceptive needs. They continue to need a routine that supports good quality sleep, meals and play.

At this age, excessive media exposure carries developmental and behavioural health risks. Exposure to television and videos before 3 years of age is associated with later problems with language development, cognition, attention, executive functioning and school achievement. There is a replacement of enriching activities with caregivers, reduced language-based and play interactions with parents and less creative child's play when the TV is on [26].

Effects of Sensory Deprivation

There has been extensive research over the last century exploring sensory deprivation and its impact on development. In 'The Nature of Love', Harlow describes his experiment with two wire monkey mothers, one covered in cloth and the other with a bottle filled with milk. The paper reports on the behaviour of eight rhesus monkeys with access to both mothers. Not surprisingly, all monkeys fed from the wire monkey and then immediately moved to the cloth monkey where they hung on to the cloth mother for dear life. Harlow also noted that the monkeys, deprived of tactile input and early attachment experiences, developed abnormally, were socially isolated and were unable to parent their own young [27].

Spitz in 1945 demonstrated the importance of affection in infant development. He compared a group of infants raised in an orphanage with another group raised by imprisoned mothers who provided affection throughout the day. Outcomes at 1 year of age showed those raised in an orphanage had higher mortality rates and also had delays in motor and cognitive skills compared to the babies cared for by their mothers [28].

In Romania in 1989, psychologists explored the effects of human separation and sensory deprivation on 170,000 children living in orphanages. The Bucharest Early Intervention Project ran a randomised controlled trial of institutionalised versus foster family care for institutionalised children measuring outcomes over a 12-year period. The groups' cognitive function, physical growth, social skills and brain development were reviewed. Those children who remained institutionalised and were deprived of sensory input developed a variety of social and emotional disorders with significant brain changes compared to those in foster families [29].

Although much of the research has explored sensory deprivation, too much sensory input can also have an impact on brain development. Increased exposure to sensory stimuli in mice resulted in increased hyperactivity and impaired cognition, and in humans and can lead to attention problems later on in life [30].

In summary, in order to support infant development, it is essential that we understand that we humans live in a sensory world where our sensory systems drive our development and that our ability to process sensory input is unique to us. Severe and persistent under- or overstimulation can have a significantly detrimental effect on the child's development. To provide optimal infant development it is essential therefore that we understand what is too much or too little, in infant behaviour.

The Parent or Carer with Mental Health Issues

This chapter has described how infants need to be supported in their interactions with their environment in order to develop healthily and reach their full potential. Their environment is largely provided and moderated by the primary caregivers and risks being depleted if either parent is physically or psychologically unwell.

A core task of parents is the expectation that they provide a safe haven for their child. When a parent struggles to meet their own needs, formal safeguarding procedures may be warranted. Unique challenges arise, including medication effects leading to sedation, stigma impeding help-seeking, the disturbance of the nurturing and nutrition bond, and the potential inability to recognise and respond to the infant's emotions or needs.

When we look at the rich sensory and emotional interaction between an infant and their carer it seems obvious that any disruption of this complex process may have both long- and short-term effects [31].

Support needs to be both anticipatory and reactive. Mothers with current or pre-existing mental health problems should be offered interventions which enhance their ability to bond with their baby. Interventions should include fathers, as paternal postnatal depression is a well-recognised problem and is associated with emotional and behavioural problems, with an increased risk of conduct disorders in boys [32]. Every interaction with the family should be seen as an opportunity for assessment and support. Stein et al. summarise this by emphasizing the need to both treat the parent's disorder and help with associated caregiving difficulties [33]. Communication within the group of professionals caring for the family is essential. The challenge of balancing diagnosis, nurturing and safety needs skill and empathy, as well as teamwork with colleagues and the family. If this can be achieved the whole family will face a better future.

Conclusion

Without question parents are the single biggest influence on an infant's neurodevelopmental outcomes. The role of healthcare professionals is to support and model the behaviour, creating loving and nurturing relationships, while at the same time providing age-appropriate guidance on the next stage of development. Healthcare professionals concerned about an infant's development may wish to consider additional support from specialised early intervention providers.

References

1. A Leadsom. The best start for life: a vision for the 1,001 critical days. Review. 2021.
2. A Tierney, C Nelson. Brain development and the role of experiences in the early years. *Zero-Three.* 2009;30(2):9–13.
3. E Van der Helm, M Walker. Overnight therapy? The role of sleep in emotional brain processing. *Psychol Bull.* 2010;135(5):731–48.
4. JP Chaput, CE Gray, VJ Poitras, V Carson, R Gruber, T Olds, et al. Systematic review of the relationships between sleep duration and health indicators in school-aged children and youth. *Appl Physiol Nutr Metab.* 2016;41(6 suppl 3):S266–82.
5. JP Chaput. Is sleep deprivation a contributor to obesity in children? *Eat Weight Disord.* 2016;21(1):5–11.
6. E Tham, N Schneider, B Broekman. Infant sleep and its relation with cognition and growth: a narrative review. *Nat Sci Sleep.* 2017 May 15;9:135–49.
7. M Yogman, A Garner, J Hutchinson, K Hirsh-Pasek, R Golinkoff. The power of play: a pediatric role in enhancing development in young children. *Pediatrics.* 2018 Sep;142(3):e20182058.
8. K Ginsburg, American Academy of Pediatrics Committee on Communications, American Academy of Pediatrics Committee on Psychosocial Aspects of Child and Family Health. The importance of play in promoting healthy child development and maintaining strong parent-child bonds. *Pediatrics.* 2007 Jan;119(1):182–91.
9. United Nations, Convention on the rights of the child: Article 12, Committee on the rights of the child, Fifty-first session. 2009; CRC/C/GC/12 p. 2–136, Geneva.
10. M Kramer, F Aboud, E Mironova, I Vanilovich, RW Platt, L Matush, et al. Breastfeeding and child cognitive development. *Arch Gen Psychiatry.* 2008;65(5):578–84.
11. K Fleishcher Michaelsen, L Weaver, F Branca, A Robertson. Feeding and nutrition of infants and young children: guidelines for the WHO European Region, with emphasis on the former Soviet countries. World Health Organization. Regional Office for Europe; 2003. https://apps.who.int/iris/handle/10665/272658
12. M Hetherington, J Cecil, D Jackson, C Schwartz. Feeding infants and young children. From guidelines to practice. *Appetite.* 2011 Dec;57(3):791–5.
13. F Tratchenberg, E Haas, H Kinney, C Stanley, HF Krous. Risk factor changes for sudden infant death syndrome after initiation of back to sleep campaign. *Pediatrics.* 2012;129(4):630–8.

14. World Health Organization. Infant and young child feeding. 2021. www.who.int/news-room/fact-sheets/detail/infant-and-young-child-feeding
15. NHS. Baby and toddler play idea: ideas to help your child play and learn. 2018. www.nhs.uk/baby/babys-development/play-and-learning/baby-and-toddler-play-ideas/
16. S Lipchock, D Reed. The gustatory and olfactory systems during infancy: implications for development of feeding behaviors in the high-risk neonate. *Clin Perinatol.* 2011;38(4):627–41.
17. F Simion, E Di Giorgio. Face perception and processing in early infancy: inborn predispositions and developmental changes. *Front Psychol.* 2015 Jul 9;6:969.
18. Council on Communications and Media. Media and young minds. *Pediatrics.* 2016;138(5):e20162591.
19. Canadian Paediatric Society, Position Statement. Screen time and young children: promoting health and development in a digital world. *Paediatr Child Health.* 2017;22(8):461–8.
20. ACT Government Australia. Screen time and children. 2019. https://shorturl.at/cij01
21. K Nugent. Historical perspectives: Berry Brazelton: Le Magnifique. *NeoReviews.* 2019;20(11):e615–e621.
22. K Kaye, A Fogel. The temporal structure of face-to-face communication between mothers and infants. *Dev Psychol.* 1980;16(5):454–64.
23. N Dimitrova. The role of common ground on object use in shaping the function of infants' social gaze. *Front Psychol.* 2020;11(619):1–7.
24. G Mireault, SC Crockenberg, JE Sparrow, CA Pettinato, KC Woodard, K Malzac. Social looking, social referencing and humor perception in 6 and 12 month infants. *Infant Behav Dev.* 2014;37(4): 536–45.
25. G Csibra, G Gergely. Natural pedagogy. *Trends Cogn Sci.* 2009;13(4):148–53.
26. JS Radesky, M Silverstein, B Zucherman, D Christakis. Infant self-regulation and early childhood media exposure. *Pediatrics.* 2014;133:e1172–e1178.
27. H Harlow. The nature of love. *Am Psychol.* 1958;13:573–685.
28. R Spitz. Hospitalism: an inquiry into the genesis of psychiatric conditions in early childhood. *Psychoanal Study Child.* 1945;1(1):53–74.
29. NA Fox, CA Nelson, CH Zeanah. The effects of psychological deprivation on attachment: lessons from the Bucharest Early Intervention Project. *Psychodyn Psychiatry.* 2017;45(4):441–50.
30. DA Christakis, J Benedikt Ramirez, SM Fergusson, S Ravinder, JM Ramirez. How early media exposure may affect cognitive function: a review of results from observations in humans and experiments in mice. *PNAS.* 2018;115(40):9851–8.
31. D Kingston, SM McDonald, M-P Austin, S Tough. Association between prenatal and postnatal psychological distress and toddler cognitive development: a systematic review. *PLoS ONE.* 2015 May 21;10(5):e0126929.
32. P Ramchandani, A Stein, J Evans, TG O'Connor, ALSPAC study team. Paternal depression in the postnatal period and child development: a prospective population study. *Lancet.* 2005;365(9478):2201–5.
33. A Stein, RM Pearson, SH Goodman, E Rapa, A Rahman, M McCallum, et al. Effects of perinatal mental disorders on the fetus and child. *Lancet.* 2014;384(9956):1800–19.

Chapter 6

Paternal Mental Health in the Perinatal Period

Impact on Family Relationships

Jill Domoney, Jane Iles and Vaheshta Sethna

Introduction

Maternal mental health disorders in the perinatal period are inextricably linked with relationships and family. While the relationship with the baby is well established as a core feature of many perinatal mental health disorders (see Section 4 of this book), the quality of women's relationships with other family members, in particular with her partner, are also understood to be important factors in the course of mental health disorders and recovery. Poor quality relationships can trigger, exacerbate and perpetuate poor mental health, while strong supportive relationships can aid recovery and improve outcomes for all family members. Partners may be the first to notice a deterioration in maternal mental health, the best placed to pick up early signs of relapse, the main source of support following discharge from services, and the main caregiver for the infant and older children. Therefore, health professionals working with families in the perinatal period need to understand the factors that impact on the quality of these relationships and how they can support the whole family to manage the transition to parenthood.

The mental health of the partner is of particular significance. Similarly to women, poor paternal mental health is associated with impairments in the quality of the couple relationship, the co-parenting relationship and the father's relationship with his baby. Yet, while less is known about the impacts of poor mental health for lesbian, gay, bisexual, transgender and queer (LGBTQ+) parents, similar challenges with familial relationships are likely to occur. There may be potential additional stressors due to stigma and heteronormative health services, with often little support available to women's partners, and multiple barriers to help-seeking, which means that mental health disorders often go unidentified and untreated. Nevertheless, changes in policy and practice over recent years are creating new opportunities for supporting partners and taking a whole-family approach to perinatal mental health.

This chapter provides an overview of the evidence related to fathers and partners in the perinatal period. This chapter focuses on factors related to fathers' mental health, the couple relationship and the father–infant relationship. However, further work is necessary to understand and support the needs of co-mothers, and all partners who do not identify as a 'father'. Arguably, even more will need to be done to support equity of access for these families. Issues around engagement and inclusion of partners in perinatal services are briefly explored and practice implications are highlighted.

Background

Over the past 50 years, the role of fathers in Western cultures has changed substantially. Family structures and gender relationships have evolved, with women working as the norm, and men increasingly being involved in childcare, including as primary caregivers. For example, 40 years ago, men were not permitted to attend births in hospitals; now over 90% of fathers attend a birth in the UK [1, 2]. Alongside this, there has been an increasing understanding that fathers have significant, complex and multidimensional functions in their children's development [3, 4]. Father involvement has been linked with a range of positive child outcomes, and this has begun to be reflected in policy with the introduction of shared parental leave in the UK in 2015.

Nevertheless, the transition to parenthood can be extremely stressful for both parents; increased responsibility, changes in relationships, financial strain, lack of sleep and worry about the health of the baby can all contribute to feelings of being overwhelmed. For men, distress and confusion may be compounded by the need to construct their identity as a father amidst a rapidly changing social reality and unhelpful stereotypes of fathers as irresponsible or feckless [5].

Where women have mental health disorders, this can put significant strain on partners. As well as caring for the mother and dealing with worries and uncertainty about her well-being, they may also need to take on additional childcare and household duties alongside maintaining work commitments. Recognition of these challenges for the wider family has led to the development of specific guidance for perinatal mental health professionals around ways to involve and support partners and other family members where women are accessing specialist services [6]. This guidance includes consideration of the needs of a range of family members, including older children and grandparents who are also affected by maternal mental health disorders.

Fathers and partners may also be dealing with their own mental health difficulties. Fathers' mental health has increasingly been a focus of interest as studies have demonstrated the high prevalence of mental health disorders amongst fathers and the impact that these disorders can have on family well-being [7, 8]. Around 10–12% of fathers are thought have to symptoms of depression and anxiety, and research indicates that these disorders are linked with worse mental health in women, as well as increases in couple conflict. Indeed, the prevalence of paternal mental health disorders when their partner has a mental health disorder is thought to be between 25% and 50% [8, 9].

Maternal mental health disorders are not only associated with increased paternal depression and anxiety but also higher levels of paternal parenting stress [10]. Furthermore, mental health difficulties experienced by fathers can influence the father–infant relationship [11]. For instance, paternal depression is associated with a less-optimal father–infant relationship and less involvement with the child. These non-optimal patterns of parenting and poor-quality father–infant interactions are associated with behaviour problems, lower academic achievement and poorer mental health across childhood and adolescence [12, 13, 14]. Thus, aspects of parenting and the father–child relationship may mediate the familial transmission of risk [15].

In England, recognition of the concordance of maternal and paternal mental health and an understanding of the detrimental effects this can have on child development, led to the proposed introduction of mental health assessment for partners in cases where the mother is receiving support from specialist perinatal mental health services [16]. This would provide an opportunity to identify and support fathers who have mental health needs and to improve outcomes for the whole family.

And what of other partners and family members? There is little evidence on the experiences of LGBTQ+ people in relation to mental health in the transition to parenthood. Data is often not collected on the gender or sexual orientation of people who are pregnant or their partners, and so the number of LGBTQ people having babies is unknown. There are some existing studies on trans men's experiences of pregnancy [17] and on gay men's experiences of parenting through surrogacy [18], and there is a growing body of evidence around lesbian women's experiences of maternity care [e.g. 19]. However, there is much less known about mental health in these populations. Therefore, while mental health assessment of the partners of women who are accessing specialist perinatal mental health services may include LGBTQ people, little is known about whether existing support services are accessible or acceptable for those who may face particular structural and psychological barriers to receiving help, including stigma, lack of legal recognition as parents and heteronormative health services [20]. This is an important area of future research.

Fathers' Mental Health

To date, the focus of interest on paternal mental health has predominantly been on depression, with research indicating that around 10% of fathers are affected by perinatal depression [8, 21]. This is significantly higher than that reported in men in studies of the general population (approximately 4%, [22]), suggesting that fatherhood may be a time of increased vulnerability. Furthermore, these findings indicated that rates do not vary across the prenatal and postpartum time periods, although relatively higher rates of depression were reported between 3 and 6 months postnatally (13%, range 7.2–22.3%).

However, there may be challenges in the identification and measurement of perinatal depression in fathers. Studies have tended to conceptualise depression comparably to the experience of depression within mothers, yet men and women may experience depression differently. Studies of men's mental health suggest that men may be more likely to express distress through symptoms such as hostility, conflict and anger rather than sadness or apathy, and by disengaging through the use of substances or escape activities such as sports or overwork [23, 24]. Identification may therefore need to take these findings into account.

Paternal perinatal anxiety disorders have received comparably less attention. Nevertheless, a systematic review found that perinatal anxiety was common in fathers, occurring between 4.1–16.0% during the prenatal period and 2.4–18.0% during the postnatal period [7]. Anxiety disorders can take a number of different forms, ranging from generalised anxiety, specific phobias, panic disorder and obsessive-compulsive disorder [25]. A degree of increased anxiety may be seen as 'normal', or even protective, during the perinatal period. However, anxiety disorders can be incredibly debilitating, often leading to the development of a range of behaviours and coping strategies aimed at alleviating symptoms, which inadvertently prolong difficulties or have other detrimental outcomes on day-to-day functioning. This is particularly important when thinking about the well-being of fathers and the wider family during the perinatal period. Avoidance can be a common coping strategy; if a father is avoiding aspects of life which are key to psychosocial functioning and daily activities, for example, avoiding important others (including the mother or infant, or support networks), healthcare appointments or employment, this may impact on all of the family. Anxiety has also been found to be associated with poorer sleep, increased alcohol consumption, suicide attempts, poorer physical health and higher levels of depression [26, 27].

There is less available evidence for trauma symptoms in fathers. Nevertheless, it is increasingly recognised that partners may find elements of labour and childbirth incredibly distressing, fearing for the life of the mother or infant. For some, this distress continues into the postpartum and can result in the experience of posttraumatic stress disorder (PTSD) [28]. This can have a significant detrimental impact on functioning and relationships [29].

Risk Factors for Poor Paternal Mental Health

There are a range of risk factors for paternal mental health disorders, including psychological and social factors, and factors related specifically to pregnancy and the postpartum.

A key risk factor for poor postnatal mental health includes having a history of depression or anxiety prior to or during the partner's pregnancy [30]. In some cases this is because the transition to fatherhood acts as a stressor or trigger for men with an existing vulnerability to poor mental health, but there can also be a strong continuity of depression and anxiety from the prenatal period on through the postnatal period [30].

Previous experiences can create significant vulnerabilities. Adverse childhood experiences, such as parental mental health disorders, domestic violence, parental substance use, separation and divorce, are risk factors for mental health difficulties in adulthood [31]. The transition to parenthood can be a trigger for poor mental health in those with such early experiences. In pregnancy, memories of poor or traumatic early experiences can be triggered in expectant fathers, leading to worry and stress [32] and, postnatally, men may experience anxiety about the impact of their early experiences on their own parenting [33].

Qualitative studies highlight that worries about the relationship with the baby can increase stress, both during pregnancy and in the postnatal period. Men may struggle to bond with the unborn baby, not knowing what to expect of their role and feeling unprepared [34]. Unplanned pregnancy or history of pregnancy loss are also associated with paternal mental health disorders [35]. These experiences can increase worries about the viability of the current pregnancy, as well as triggering symptoms of grief. Postnatally, men frequently report feeling excluded from the relationship with the baby and may struggle to find a role [36]. These feelings of uncertainty, fear and exclusion can be compounded by experiences with perinatal health services. Studies have found that fathers often feel ignored and sidelined by healthcare professionals within maternity services [37], and describe their role as 'bystanders' or 'invisible parents' [38, 39]. Having to return to work soon after the birth can increase this sense of exclusion and lead to frustration [40].

In the men's mental health literature, adherence to masculine norms is associated with a higher likelihood of psychopathology [41]. In the perinatal period, typical masculine traits such as independence, self-reliance and an expectation to provide for the family can lead to lack of help-seeking, ignoring negative emotions and pressure to manage the increased responsibility of having a baby without support. Men report trying to meet expectations of being both a father and a man, juggling both personal and work-related contexts, and having to deal with economic pressures as well as the emotional needs of the family [36, 42]. In the context of internalised masculine stereotypes and associated gender role stress, this can lead to self-stigma and shame, which exacerbate stress and vulnerability to poor mental health [43].

Being unemployed, low job quality and financial hardship are associated with worse postnatal paternal mental health [44, 45]. In particular, jobs which have poor working hours, low job security and poor access to paid family-friendly leave lead to greater odds of psychological distress. These factors can lead to worries about financial stability and the ability to provide for the family, and may threaten fathers' sense of role competence [42, 46].

Lack of social support is a commonly cited risk factor for perinatal mental health disorders for both men and women [35, 47]. A report by Movember suggested that men may not recognise the importance of close relationships for their well-being and may lose friendships when they enter fatherhood, increasing their risk for poor mental health [48]. They may typically rely on their spouses for support, which becomes problematic when mothers are taking care of newborns and not able to offer the same levels of support as usual [49]. The impact of the couple relationship on paternal mental health is explored in more detail next.

Impact of Paternal Mental Health Disorders: A Family Affair

Fathers' mental health can cascade through the family, affecting not only the father himself, but also his partner and children. Consequently, the impact of paternal mental health is truly a family affair [50].

The Couple Relationship and Mental Health

There are significant stressors in the perinatal period which put strain on relationships as couples shift their time and energy away from a focus on their romantic relationship to parenting and child-rearing. They may experience uncertainty and worry about their new roles and responsibilities, must cope with a lack of sleep leading to fatigue, and have a substantial increase in household labour. This can lead to changes in expectations of partner support, whilst at the same time having less time to spend on each other.

Relationship quality is known to decline across the transition to parenthood, with longitudinal studies showing up to 70% of couples reporting increases in conflict and decreases in relationship satisfaction following birth [51, 52]. This decline has been demonstrated across a range of ethnic backgrounds and in same-sex couples, and research suggests it is rather persistent across the years following birth [53, 54].

A meta-synthesis of qualitative studies on men's mental health during the transition to parenthood identified that deterioration in the couple relationship was a common experience following the birth, including increased arguments, lack of support and reduced sexual contact [34]. Men report that the stress of having a baby means that the relationship becomes strained, there are more misunderstandings, problems remain unresolved and communication is poor [55]. Similarly, for women, qualitative literature indicates that partners may be perceived as not offering sufficient support in terms of validating feelings, taking the initiative and being more involved in infant care [56].

Women note there is less time to maintain their relationship and they may also begin to feel irritation and disappointment at a perceived lack of support and involvement by the father [57]. These experiences can increase vulnerability to poor perinatal mental health for both men and women.

Conversely, partner support and relationship satisfaction are strong protective factors against perinatal anxiety and depression [44, 49]. Supportive relationships facilitate an individual's capacity to adjust to significant life events by buffering against stress [58]. Therefore, improving the couple relationship and enhancing partner support are important targets for the prevention of perinatal mental health disorders.

For some couples, the transition to parenthood may be experienced in the context of intimate partner violence. In high-income settings the prevalence of domestic violence and abuse (DVA) in pregnancy ranges between 4 and 8% [59], while in low- and middle-income countries it is estimated to be as high as 49% [60]. While there is mixed evidence as to whether rates of DVA increase in the perinatal period, it is clear that pregnancy does not prevent the occurrence of violence and many women report being victims for the first time during pregnancy [61]. For women, there are strong associations between being a victim of domestic abuse and experiencing perinatal mental health disorders, including depression, anxiety and PTSD [62]. For this reason, National Institute for Health and Care Excellence (NICE) guidance recommends that assessment of women in perinatal mental health services should include asking about experiences of DVA, and it is important that practitioners know how to enquire and respond to disclosures [63] (see Chapter 37, 'Violence against Women').

Not all couples experience these difficulties in their relationship during the transition to parenthood. Factors such as functioning in the family of origin, unplanned pregnancy, relationship duration, income and pre-birth relationship quality are associated with the extent of decline [51, 53, 64]. However, given the associations between couple-related factors and both maternal and paternal mental health in the perinatal period, the relationship is an important target for preventive interventions [65].

Supporting the Couple Relationship

In qualitative studies of parents' needs in relation to their new role, women report finding it helpful if their partner has an attitude of respect and appreciation of the mother role, and a shift in the partner's priorities to include the whole family. This includes showing willingness to help, being reliable and offering praise [66]. Men report wanting to be included more by health professionals, acknowledged as equal partners and given more information both about infant development and about changes in the relationship with their partner [34].

Globally, there are a number of universal programmes which have been developed to enhance couple functioning across the perinatal period in order to prevent a decline in relationship quality (e.g. the Mindful Transition to Parenthood [67] and Bringing Baby Home [68]) or improve the co-parenting relationship (e.g. Family Foundations [69]). These vary in intensity and time commitment, including 'add-ons' to existing antenatal classes which focus specifically on the partner relationship, as well as couple programmes covering several sessions across the perinatal period. Many of these programmes have a secondary focus on preventing mental health disorders.

Where there are identified perinatal mental health disorders, there is less available evidence on the effectiveness of couple and family interventions. However, within specialist perinatal mental health services in England, some teams offer couple therapy or family interventions as part of the package of care, in recognition of the impact that relationship quality has on mental health outcomes. There is therefore an opportunity to build an evidence base for these interventions in the context of parental mental health disorders.

Paternal Involvement and Relationship with the Baby

Specific to the family system, paternal perinatal mental health difficulties are associated with less optimal parenting and reduced paternal involvement in childcare activities [11, 70]. Various features of the father–infant relationship are linked with paternal perinatal psychopathology, including low levels of sensitivity, withdrawal and disengagement in both verbal and behavioural features assessed. For instance, in observational studies, depressed and anxious fathers tend to be less responsive to their infants' signals, and display less warmth in their early interactions, than fathers without depression or anxiety [10, 71, 72]. They are also more likely to demonstrate negative affect [73]. Similarly, alcoholic fathers display lower warmth and higher negative affect when interacting with their infants [74]. These alterations may make the early socio-emotional environment suboptimal for the formation of a secure attachment bond, as well as for infants' emotional development.

However, effect sizes for the link between paternal perinatal psychopathology and father–infant relationship domains are small in magnitude [11] (but comparable to mothers for negative parenting behaviours [75]). Since current studies generally define paternal psychopathology as postnatal depression (assessed by self-reports of current depression symptoms in community samples) [70], it is possible that the strength of the relationship is underestimated. Moreover, it is likely that chronicity and severity of depression, as well as different types of paternal psychopathology and/or adversity, may give rise to different father–infant interactional patterns. Additionally, consideration of a broader range of environmental mechanisms, as well as gene–environment interactions that might account for the familial transmission of risk, is crucial, given the small effect sizes.

Nevertheless, in response to disruptions to paternal interactive behaviours, infants may also alter their interactive behaviours with increased negative affect and avoidance, such as gaze aversion [71, 73, 74]. Are fathers passing on negative interaction patterns portraying affective psychopathology during early interactions? While this might be the case, it is also possible that infant behaviours influence paternal mental health and parenting quality. Temperamentally "easy" children are more likely to be involved in more positive interactions with their fathers [76]. Conversely, Frodi et al. [77] report increased paternal involvement with difficult sons (but not with difficult daughters), also recently endorsed by Cabrera and colleagues [78].

Notably, not all studies report difficulties in the father–infant relationship in the context of paternal psychopathology in the perinatal period [70]. These studies, while emphasising that adverse outcomes are not inevitable, also give rise to important methodological considerations in research involving fathers – for instance, the use of standardised coding schemes with identified psychometric properties, universally established interaction features, tasks/techniques and coding tools for assessing the father–offspring relationship at various developmental stages.

The Couple Relationship and Child Outcomes

Does the father's relationship with his infant and/or mental health difficulties moderate the effects of maternal perinatal psychopathology on child outcomes? While less well studied, paternal depression does exacerbate the negative effects of maternal depression on internalising behaviours only when fathers are highly involved with their infant [79]. Similarly, partners of depressed mothers are less sensitive than partners of non-depressed mothers and, thus, children of depressed mothers are often raised in environments marked by a double risk [80], thus highlighting the necessity to involve fathers in intervention efforts in cases of maternal depression.

The quality of the couple relationship is also associated with child outcomes. Aspects of the couple relationship such as lack of mutual support and negative communication are associated with poor parenting practices such as insensitivity, harsh discipline and low expression of affection [81]. These practices are, in turn, associated with risk of adverse outcomes for the child including mental health disorders, poor social competence and effects on cognitive development [82, 83].

Furthermore, couple relationship satisfaction partly predicts the quality of co-parenting [84]. Co-parenting refers to the way that couples coordinate and support each other in their parental roles [85] and it may be more strongly related to parenting and child outcomes than the quality of the couple relationship itself [86]. Therefore, the co-parenting relationship represents an important causal mechanism on the pathway to child developmental outcomes. Infants require consistent, predictable responses from caregivers to help regulate emotions and behaviour, and so disparate or contradictory child-rearing practices may impact on the development of self-regulation [87].

Witnessing or being a victim of family violence has multiple negative consequences for children across the lifetime. Domestic violence and abuse in pregnancy increases the risk of poor obstetric outcomes such as low birth weight, preterm birth and miscarriage [88], and is associated with later child behavioural problems [89], while exposure during childhood is linked with both behavioural and emotional problems [90] (see Chapter 36, 'Child Safeguarding'). Adverse childhood experiences such as having a parent with a mental health disorder and living in a home with DVA have consistently been linked with poor mental and physical health in adulthood, and a higher likelihood of victimisation and perpetration of interpersonal abuse [31].

Paternal Engagement and Inclusion

Given the prevalence and impacts of paternal mental health disorders, there is a need to identify those with difficulties and to provide accessible, father-focused interventions, which can reduce the impact on fathers and improve outcomes for the whole family. However, despite robust evidence of the adverse impact of paternal mental health disorders, fathers are seldom engaged in perinatal mental health services or treatments and are less likely to seek support than women. There may be a number of reasons for this.

First, a key factor identified in the literature is an apparent reluctance of healthcare and mental health providers to adapt practices to encourage the inclusion of fathers [91, 92]. An evidence synthesis on the assessment of mental health of fathers, other co-parents and partners in the perinatal period [93] identified a number of service- and practitioner-level factors which impact on the acceptability of assessment and, therefore, identification, across community and clinical settings. These included, for example, the remit and culture of the service being geared towards women; the need for training and supervision; workload and time pressures; and knowledge, skills and confidence of staff. There may also be unhelpful attitudes about men as peripheral figures in the perinatal period or even as dangerous figures [92], which can serve to further marginalise fathers and perpetuate problems.

Second, fathers are less likely to attribute distress to mental health, as well as potentially feeling they are not legitimate users of services at this time [94]. Indeed, a survey of fathers' mental health help-seeking identified that only 3.2% of fathers sought counselling, and fathers reporting higher levels of distress were less likely to see help [95]. Barriers may include masculine stereotypes which lead to self-stigma and shame; expectations that fathers have to provide for their partners which leads to minimisation of their own needs; and the female partner's response to paternal depressive symptoms, for example, whether the partner's response tends to confirm or challenge stigma [43]. More practical barriers, such as treatment taking up too much time and being inconvenient, as well as being unsure where to go for help, have also been reported [96].

Third, men may struggle to express their needs in words [97] or express them in different ways. For example, men are typically more willing to acknowledge fatigue, irritability, anhedonia and sleep disturbances rather than reporting sadness, worthlessness or guilt [98]. They may also be more likely to withdraw socially or abuse substances, rather than talk about how they feel or cry [99]. This can lead to a lack of recognition of mental health needs by fathers themselves and by professionals that encounter fathers. Understanding these varying expressions of mental health is an important skill for those working with families.

Despite these challenges, some authors have noted that the transition to parenthood may be a 'teachable' moment for fathers, when they are potentially open to learning and receptive to information and support [100, 101]. Perceived negative impacts of their mental health on their baby and on their partner may be motivations for seeking help and for making changes in their health, relationships and work-life balance [32, 96]. There may also be opportunities for challenging rigid adherence to masculine norms, deepening the partner relationship and shaping the infant's experiences, which can empower men to embrace this new phase of life [102]. Therefore, the introduction in England of mental health assessment for partners provides an opportunity not only to identify mental health needs but also to harness fathers' motivation for change, to signpost to appropriate support and to improve outcomes for the whole family.

Practice Implications

As highlighted throughout this chapter, paternal mental health has multiple impacts on the wider family system. It is useful for practitioners to understand the associations between poor paternal mental health, the couple relationship and the relationship with the infant. This allows for a richer formulation of maternal mental health difficulties which can consider the multiple factors which may be maintaining and exacerbating problems and take steps to address these. This includes considering the need for interventions which target relationships, such as couple or family therapy, or parent–infant interventions; enquiring about DVA and responding appropriately to disclosures; and assessing and supporting partners' mental health.

There are a number of implications related to identifying and supporting partners' mental health. Perhaps the most notable clinical implication is evidence that screening programmes run the risk of not providing any benefit or worsening experiences in the absence of any suitable interventions [103, 104]. Therefore, there is a pressing need to develop and evaluate accessible interventions for partners alongside the introduction of mental health assessment. Indeed, many perinatal mental health services are beginning to offer couple therapy and family therapy, and researchers are exploring ways of adapting existing mental health interventions to meet the needs of new and expectant fathers [105] (see Chapter 28 on psychological therapies). Additionally, practitioners need to be aware of local services and resources which are available for fathers and other family members and signpost to these when needed.

A further consideration is awareness of the multiple barriers that exist for fathers in relation to help-seeking and receiving support. Stigma and shame around mental health, alongside a desire to focus on the needs of their partner and baby, can lead to minimising difficulties and reluctance to admit levels of distress. Even where support is wanted, time pressures, social norms and structures (e.g. having to return to work soon after the birth) can serve to exclude and marginalise partners, providing limited opportunities to take up offers of support.

Framing the content of intervention efforts around fatherhood (as opposed to mental health symptoms) and clarifying the benefits of engagement to maternal and infant well-being may be useful ways to reduce stigma and support engagement [106]. Practitioners need to be aware of existing stereotypes around being male, as well as the pressures on men to behave in certain ways and the negative impact of this. Evidence suggests that masculine socialisation contributes to and exacerbates mental health problems in men [107, 108], and practitioners' own gender biases may impact on interactions with male partners without appropriate training and supervision. Therefore, it is useful for practitioners to be aware of the different ways that men may express distress, to ensure gender competence in their practice and to build confidence in having conversations with fathers about how they can access support. Finding flexible ways to engage wider family members, for example, evening appointments or remote appointments (using online software) are also helpful ways to reduce barriers to engagement.

A related consideration highlighted in this chapter is the need for primary prevention of poor paternal mental health through active inclusion of fathers throughout the perinatal period and the provision of clear information about their role, including in the context of maternal mental health difficulties. This can mitigate against the experiences of uncertainty, exclusion and marginalisation which are risk factors for mental health disorders in partners.

Finally, as noted earlier in this chapter, there is a lack of evidence about the mental health needs of LGBTQ people in the transition to parenthood. Given that over half of LGBTQ people report having experienced depression [109], further evidence is urgently needed to ensure that the needs of these families can be adequately met within perinatal mental health services. One study found that the introduction of brief gender and sexuality awareness training for perinatal healthcare providers improved knowledge, attitudes and intended behaviour towards those identifying as LGBTQ [110]. Increased understanding and more inclusive practices within services may serve to reduce stress and exclusion, supporting family well-being across all family formations.

Conclusions

The transition to parenthood brings challenges and strains to all families. Where there are maternal mental health disorders, this is an additional challenge which impacts on the wider family system. Partners and other family members may have to take on additional responsibilities, manage worries about the mother's mental health and potentially deal with their own mental health difficulties. Recent guidance on how to involve and support partners of women who are accessing perinatal mental health services is a welcome step towards whole-family approaches.

The partner's mental health is an important aspect of family functioning that can impact on the whole family. There are multiple risk factors for poor paternal mental health across the perinatal period, and prevalence rates for depression and anxiety are high. These disorders affect the quality of the couple relationship, the co-parenting relationship and the relationship with the baby. The proposed introduction in England of mental health assessment for partners provides an opportunity to identify and support fathers who have mental health needs, and to improve outcomes for the whole family. This relies on practitioners supporting prevention efforts and working to reduce barriers to help-seeking and uptake of support where needed. These practices not only serve to improve the well-being of fathers and partners; well-supported family members who feel included and have their own mental health needs met will also have a significant positive impact on maternal recovery and well-being.

References

1. J Draper. Men's passage to fatherhood: an analysis of the contemporary relevance of transition theory. *Nurs Inq.* 2003;10(1):66–78.
2. A Burgess, R Goldman. *Who's the bloke in the room? Fathers during pregnancy and at the birth in the UK.* London: Fatherhood Institute; 2018.
3. A Sarkadi, R Kristiansson, F Oberklaid, S Bremberg. Fathers' involvement and children's developmental outcomes: a systematic review of longitudinal studies. *Acta Paediatr.* 2008;97(2):153–8.
4. V Sethna, E Perry, J Domoney, J Iles, L Psychogiou, NE Rowbotham, et al. Father–child interactions at 3 months and 24 months: contributions to children's cognitive development at 24 months. *Infant Ment Health J.* 2017;38(3): 378–90.
5. A Gregory, S Milner. What is "new" about fatherhood? The social construction of fatherhood in France and the UK. *Men Masculinities.* 2011;14(5): 588–606.
6. Z Darwin, J Domoney, J Iles, F Bristow, V Sethna. *Involving and supporting partners and other family members in specialist perinatal mental health services: good practice guide.* London: NHS England; 2021.
7. LS Leach, C Poyser, AR Cooklin, R Giallo. Prevalence and course of anxiety disorders (and symptom levels) in men across the perinatal period: a systematic review. *J Affect Disord.* 2016;190:675–86.
8. JF Paulson, SD Bazemore. Prenatal and postpartum depression in fathers and its association with maternal depression: a meta-analysis. *JAMA.* 2010;303(19): 1961–9.
9. JH Goodman. Paternal postpartum depression, its relationship to maternal postpartum depression, and implications for family health. *J Adv Nurs.* 2004;45(1): 26–35.
10. JH Goodman. Influences of maternal postpartum depression on fathers and on father-infant interaction. *Infant Ment Health J.* 2008;29(6):624–43.

11. S Wilson, CE Durbin. Effects of paternal depression on fathers' parenting behaviors: a meta-analytic review. *Clin Psychol Rev.* 2010;30(2):167–80.
12. PG Ramchandani, L Psychogiou, H Vlachos, J Iles, V Sethna, E Netsi, et al. Paternal depression: an examination of its links with father, child and family functioning in the postnatal period. *Depress Anxiety.* 2011;28(6):471–7.
13. PG Ramchandani, A Stein, J Evans, TG O'Connor. Paternal depression in the postnatal period and child development: a prospective population study. *Lancet.* 2005;365(9478):2201–5.
14. V Sethna, L Murray, E Netsi, L Psychogiou, PG Ramchandani. Paternal depression in the postnatal period and early father–infant interactions. *Parenting.* 2015;15(1):1–8.
15. A Stein, RM Pearson, SH Goodman, E Rapa, A Rahman, M McCallum, et al. Effects of perinatal mental disorders on the fetus and child. *Lancet.* 2014;384(9956):1800–19.
16. NHS England. The NHS long term plan. 2019.
17. R Charter, JM Ussher, J Perz, K Robinson. The transgender parent: experiences and constructions of pregnancy and parenthood for transgender men in Australia. *Int J Transgender.* 2018;19(1):64–77.
18. S Golombok, L Blake, J Slutsky, E Raffanello, GD Roman, A Ehrhardt. Parenting and the adjustment of children born to gay fathers through surrogacy. *Child Dev.* 2018;89(4):1223–33.
19. B Dahl, K Malterud. Neither father nor biological mother: a qualitative study about lesbian co-mothers' maternity care experiences. *Sex Reprod Healthc.* 2015;6(3):169–73.
20. SM Alang, M Fomotar. Postpartum depression in an online community of lesbian mothers: implications for clinical practice. *J Gay Lesbian Ment Health.* 2015;19(1):21–39.
21. EE Cameron, ID Sedov, LM Tomfohr-Madsen. Prevalence of paternal depression in pregnancy and the postpartum: an updated meta-analysis. *J Affect Disord.* 2016;206:189–203.
22. R Kessler, P Berglund, O Demler. The epidemiology of major depressive disorder: results from the National Comorbidity Survey Replication (NCS-R) *JAMA.* 2003;18(289):3095–3105.
23. SJB McCoy. Postpartum depression in men. In: MG Rojas Castillo, editor. *Perinatal depression.* New York: InTech; 2012. p. 163–76.
24. SV Cochran, FE Rabinowitz. Gender-sensitive recommendations for assessment and treatment of depression in men. *Prof Psychol Res Pract.* 2003;34(2):132–40.
25. American Psychiatric Association. *Diagnostic and statistical manual of mental disorders.* 5th ed. Washington, DC: American Psychiatric Association; 2013.
26. H Haller, H Cramer, R Lauche, F Gass, GJ Dobos. The prevalence and burden of subthreshold generalized anxiety disorder: a systematic review. *BMC Psychiatry.* 2014;14:128.
27. HU Wittchen. Generalized anxiety disorder: prevalence, burden, and cost to society. *Depress Anxiety.* 2002;16(4):162–71.
28. E Olde, O van der Hart, R Kleber, M van Son. Posttraumatic stress following childbirth: a review. *Clin Psychol Rev.* 2006;26(1):1–16.
29. E Daniels, E Arden-Close, A Mayers. Be quiet and man up: a qualitative questionnaire study into fathers who witnessed their partner's birth trauma. *BMC Pregnancy Childbirth.* 2020; 20:1–12.
30. JF Paulson, SD Bazemore, JH Goodman, JA Leiferman. The course and interrelationship of maternal and paternal perinatal depression. *Arch Womens Ment Health.* 2016;19(4):655–63.
31. K Hughes, MA Bellis, KA Hardcastle, D Sethi, A Butchart, C Mikton, et al. The effect of multiple adverse childhood experiences on health: a systematic review

and meta-analysis. *Lancet Public Health.* 2017;2(8):e356–66.

32. RM Tolman, TB Walsh. Ghosts in the ultrasound: expectant fathers' experience of trauma. In: HE Fitzgerald, K von Klitzing, NJ Cabrera, J Scarano de Mendonça, T Skjøthaug, editors. *Handbook of fathers and child development.* Cham: Springer; 2020. p. 195–208.
33. J Domoney, K Trevillion. Breaking the cycle of intergenerational abuse: a qualitative interview study of men participating in a perinatal program to reduce violence. *Infant Ment Health J.* 2021 Mar;42(2):206–21.
34. S Baldwin, M Malone, J Sandall, D Bick. Mental health and wellbeing during the transition to fatherhood: a systematic review of first time fathers' experiences. *JBI Database System Rev Implement Rep.* 2018;16(11):2118–91.
35. P Boyce, J Condon, J Barton, C Corkindale. First-time fathers' study: psychological distress in expectant fathers during pregnancy. *Aust N Z J Psychiatry.* 2007;41(9):718–25.
36. S Baldwin, M Malone, J Sandall, D Bick. A qualitative exploratory study of UK first-time fathers' experiences, mental health and wellbeing needs during their transition to fatherhood. *BMJ Open.* 2019;9(9):e030792.
37. C Gervais, F de Montigny, C Lacharité, K St-Arneault. Where fathers fit in Quebec's perinatal health care services system and what they need. *Psychol Men Masculinity.* 2016;17(2):126.
38. O Kowlessar, JR Fox, A Wittkowski. The pregnant male: a metasynthesis of first-time fathers' experiences of pregnancy. *J Reprod Infant Psychol.* 2015;33(2):106–27.
39. M Steen, S Downe, N Bamford, L Edozien. Not-patient and not-visitor: a metasynthesis fathers' encounters with pregnancy, birth and maternity care. *Midwifery.* 2012;28(4):422–31.
40. R Dallos, L Nokes. Distress, loss, and adjustment following the birth of a baby: a qualitative exploration of one new father's experiences. *J Construct Psychol.* 2011;24(2):144–67.
41. JL Oliffe, MJ Phillips. Men, depression and masculinities: a review and recommendations. *J Mens Health.* 2008;5(3):194–202.
42. JY Lee. The challenges and joys across the transition to fatherhood: a qualitative study on low-income fathers' perinatal experiences. *Soc Social Work Res.* 2019.
43. AR Dye. "It's a real thing": fathers' experiences with perinatal depression. 2020. California State University.
44. R Giallo, F D'Esposito, A Cooklin, F Mensah, N Lucas, C Wade, et al. Psychosocial risk factors associated with fathers' mental health in the postnatal period: results from a population-based study. *Soc Psychiatry Psychiatr Epidemiol.* 2013;48(4):563–73.
45. A Bruno, L Celebre, C Mento, A Rizzo, MC Silvestri, R De Stefano, et al. When fathers begin to falter: a comprehensive review on paternal perinatal depression. *Int J Environ Res Public Health.* 2020;17(4):1139.
46. Y Koh, C Chui, C Tang, A Lee. The prevalence and risk factors of paternal depression from the antenatal to the postpartum period and the relationships between antenatal and postpartum depression among fathers in Hong Kong. *Depress Res Treat.* 2014;2014:127632.
47. LM Howard, E Molyneaux, C-L Dennis, T Rochat, A Stein, J Milgrom. Non-psychotic mental disorders in the perinatal period. *Lancet.* 2014;384(9956):1775–88.
48. Movember. Fatherhood and social connections. 2019 June 7. https://shorturl.at/sA2nf
49. PD Pilkington, LC Milne, KE Cairns, J Lewis, TA Whelan. Modifiable partner factors associated with perinatal depression and anxiety: a systematic review and meta-analysis. *J Affect Disord.* 2015;178:165–80.
50. NL Letourneau, CL Dennis, K Benzies, L Duffett-Leger, M Stewart, PD

Tryphonopoulos, et al. Postpartum depression is a family affair: addressing the impact on mothers, fathers, and children. *Issues Ment Health Nurs.* 2012;33(7):445–57.

51. CP Cowan, PA Cowan. *When partners become parents: the big life change for couples.* Mahwah, NJ: Lawrence Erlbaum Associates; 2000.
52. E Lawrence, AD Rothman, RJ Cobb, MT Rothman, TN Bradbury. Marital satisfaction across the transition to parenthood. *J Fam Psychol.* 2008; 22(1):41.
53. BD Doss, GK Rhoades, SM Stanley, HJ Markman. The effect of the transition to parenthood on relationship quality: an 8-year prospective study. *J Pers Soc Psychol.* 2009;96(3):601–19.
54. AE Goldberg, A Sayer. Lesbian couples' relationship quality across the transition to parenthood. *J Marriage Fam Pract.* 2006;68(1):87–100.
55. M Edhborg, M Carlberg, F Simon, L Lindberg. "Waiting for better times": experiences in the first postpartum year by Swedish fathers with depressive symptoms. *Am J Mens Health.* 2016;10(5):428–39.
56. SM Haga, A Lynne, K Slinning, P Kraft. A qualitative study of depressive symptoms and well-being among first-time mothers. *Scand J Caring Sci.* 2012;26(3):458–66.
57. M Edhborg, M Friberg, W Lundh, A-M Widström. "Struggling with life": narratives from women with signs of postpartum depression. *Scand J Pub Health.* 2005;33(4):261–7.
58. B Figueiredo, T Field, M Diego, M Hernandez-Reif, O Deeds, A Ascencio. Partner relationships during the transition to parenthood. *J Reprod Infant Psychol.* 2008;26(2):99–107.
59. KM Devries, S Kishor, H Johnson, H Stöckl, LJ Bacchus, C Garcia-Moreno, et al. Intimate partner violence during pregnancy: analysis of prevalence data from 19 countries. *Reprod Health Matters.* 2010;18(36):158–70.
60. S Shamu, N Abrahams, M Temmerman, A Musekiwa, C Zarowsky. A systematic review of African studies on intimate partner violence against pregnant women: prevalence and risk factors. *PLoS ONE.* 2011;6(3):e17591.
61. C García-Moreno, H Jansen, M Ellsberg, L Heise, C Watts. *WHO multi-country study on women's health and domestic violence against women.* Geneva: World Health Organization; 2005;204:1–18.
62. LM Howard, S Oram, H Galley, K Trevillion, G Feder. Domestic violence and perinatal mental disorders: a systematic review and meta-analysis. *PLoS Medicine.* 2013;10(5):e1001452.
63. National Institute for Health and Care Excellence (NICE). Antenatal and postnatal mental health: clinical management and service guidance. Clinical Guideline (CG192). 2014.
64. ES Kluwer, M Johnson. Conflict frequency and relationship quality across the transition to parenthood. *J Marriage Fam.* 2007;69(5):1089–106.
65. PD Pilkington, L Milne, K Cairns, T Whelan. Enhancing reciprocal partner support to prevent perinatal depression and anxiety: a Delphi consensus study. *BMC Psychiatry.* 2016;16(1):23.
66. K Kirova, T Snell. Women's experiences of positive postnatal partner support. *J Reprod Infant Psychol.* 2019;37(2):206–18.
67. LE Gambrel, FP Piercy. Mindfulness-based relationship education for couples expecting their first child—Part 1: a randomized mixed-methods program evaluation. *J Marital Fam Ther.* 2015;41(1):5–24.
68. AF Shapiro, EY Nahm, JM Gottman, K Content. Bringing baby home together: examining the impact of a couple-focused intervention on the dynamics within family play. *Am J Orthopsychiatry.* 2011;81(3):337–50.
69. ME Feinberg, DE Jones, ML Hostetler, ME Roettger, IM Paul, DB Ehrenthal. Couple-focused prevention at the transition to parenthood, a randomized

trial: effects on coparenting, parenting, family violence, and parent and child adjustment. *Prev Sci.* 2016;17(6):751–64.

70. J Siew, J Iles, J Domoney, F Bristow, ZJ Darwin, V Sethna. The applicability and performance of tools used to assess the father-offspring relationship in relation to parental psychopathology and offspring outcomes. *Front Psychiatry.* 2021 Jan 5:11:596857. doi: 10.3389/fpsyt.2020.596857. eCollection 2020.
71. Y Parfitt, A Pike, S Ayers. The impact of parents' mental health on parent–baby interaction: a prospective study. *Infant Behav Dev.* 2013;36(4):599–608.
72. RD Eiden, C Colder, EP Edwards, KE Leonard. A longitudinal study of social competence among children of alcoholic and nonalcoholic parents: role of parental psychopathology, parental warmth, and self-regulation. *Psychol Addict Behav.* 2009;23(1):36–46.
73. S Koch, L De Pascalis, F Vivian, A Meurer Renner, L Murray, A Arteche. Effects of male postpartum depression on father-infant interaction: the mediating role of face processing. *Infant Ment Health J.* 2019;40(2):263–76.
74. RD Eiden, F Chavez, KE Leonard. Parent-infant interactions among families with alcoholic fathers. *Dev Psychopathol.* 1999;11(4):745–62.
75. MC Lovejoy, PA Graczyk, E O'Hare, G Neuman. Maternal depression and parenting behavior: a meta-analytic review. *Clin Psychol Rev.* 2000;20(5):561–92.
76. KG Mehall, TL Spinrad, N Eisenberg, BM Gaertner. Examining the relations of infant temperament and couples' marital satisfaction to mother and father involvement: a longitudinal study. *Fathering.* 2009;7(1):23–48.
77. AM Frodi, ME Lamb, M Frodi, CP Hwang, B Forsström, T Corry. Stability and change in parental attitudes following an infant's birth into traditional and nontraditional Swedish families. *Scand J Psychol.* 1982;23(1):53–62.
78. NJ Cabrera, J Fagan, V Wight, C Schadler. Influence of mother, father, and child risk on parenting and children's cognitive and social behaviors. *Child Dev.* 2011;82(6):1985–2005.
79. AH Mezulis, JS Hyde, R Clark. Father involvement moderates the effect of maternal depression during a child's infancy on child behavior problems in kindergarten. *J Fam Psychol.* 2004;18(4):575–88.
80. SH Goodman, MH Rouse, AM Connell, MR Broth, CM Hall, D Heyward. Maternal depression and child psychopathology: a meta-analytic review. *Clin Child Fam Psychol Rev.* 2011;14(1):1–27.
81. J Petch, WK Halford. Psycho-education to enhance couples' transition to parenthood. *Clin Psychol Rev.* 2008;28(7):1125–37.
82. L Murray, P Fearon, P Cooper. Postnatal depression, mother-infant interactions, and child development. In: J Milgrom, AW Gemmill, editors. *Identifying perinatal depression and anxiety: evidence-based practice in screening, psychosocial assessment, and management.* Chichester, UK: John Wiley & Sons; 2015. p. 139–64.
83. V Sethna, L Murray, O Edmondson, J Iles, PG Ramchandani. Depression and playfulness in fathers and young infants: a matched design comparison study. *J Affect Disord.* 2018;229:364–70.
84. I Gordon, R Feldman. Synchrony in the triad: a microlevel process model of coparenting and parent-child interactions. *Family Process.* 2008;47(4):465–79.
85. McHale JP. Coparenting in diverse family systems. In: JP McHale, KM Lindahl, editors. *Coparenting: a conceptual and clinical examination of family systems.* Washington, DC: American Psychological Association; 2011. p. 15–37.
86. G Margolin, EB Gordis, RS John. Coparenting: a link between marital conflict and parenting in two-parent families. *J Fam Psychol.* 2001;15(1):3–21.
87. JP McHale, L Negrini, Y Sirotkin. Coparenting. In: BH Fiese, M Celano,

K Deater-Deckard, EN Jouriles, MA Whisman, editors. *APA handbook of contemporary family psychology*. Washington, DC: American Psychological Association; 2019. p. 483–502.

88. G Feder, J Ramsay, D Dunne, M Rose, C Arsene, R Norman, et al. How far does screening women for domestic (partner) violence in different health-care settings meet criteria for a screening programme? Systematic reviews of nine UK National Screening Committee criteria. *Health Technol Assess*. 2009;13(16):iii–iv, xi–xiii, 1–113, 137–347.
89. C Flach, M Leese, J Heron, J Evans, G Feder, D Sharp, et al. Antenatal domestic violence, maternal mental health and subsequent child behaviour: a cohort study. *BJOG*. 2011;118(11):1383–91.
90. SE Evans, C Davies, D DiLillo. Exposure to domestic violence: a meta-analysis of child and adolescent outcomes. *Aggress Violent Behav*. 2008;13(2):131–40.
91. C Panter-Brick, A Burgess, M Eggerman, F McAllister, K Pruett, JF Leckman. Practitioner review: engaging fathers – recommendations for a game change in parenting interventions based on a systematic review of the global evidence. *J Child Psychol Psychiatry*. 2014;55(11):1187–212.
92. A Whitelock. Why do health visitors screen mothers and not fathers for depression in the postnatal period? *J Health Visit*. 2016;4(6):312–21.
93. Z Darwin, J Domoney, J Iles, F Bristow, J Siew, V Sethna. Assessing the mental health of fathers, other co-parents, and partners in the perinatal period: mixed methods evidence synthesis. *Front Psychiatry*. 2020;11.
94. Z Darwin, P Galdas, S Hinchliff, E Littlewood, D McMillan, L McGowan, et al. Fathers' views and experiences of their own mental health during pregnancy and the first postnatal year: a qualitative interview study of men participating in the UK Born and Bred in Yorkshire (BaBY) cohort. *BMC Pregnancy Childbirth*. 2017;17(1):45.
95. A Isacco, R Hofscher, S Molloy. An examination of fathers' mental health help seeking: a brief report. *Am J Mens Health*. 2016;10(6):NP33–8.
96. J Pirmohamed. Mental health care for common perinatal mental disorders: what do fathers need? 2020. University of Toronto.
97. S Doucet, N Letourneau, ER Blackmore. Support needs of mothers who experience postpartum psychosis and their partners. *J Obstet Gynecol Neonatal Nurs*. 2012;41(2):236–45.
98. CF Garfield, G Duncan, J Rutsohn, TW McDade, EK Adam, RL Coley, et al. A longitudinal study of paternal mental health during transition to fatherhood as young adults. *Pediatrics*. 2014;133(5):836–43.
99. KA Wilhelm. Men and depression. *Aust Fam Physic*. 2009;38(3):102–5.
100. D Da Costa, P Zelkowitz, N Letourneau, A Howlett, C-L Dennis, B Russell, et al. HealthyDads.ca: what do men want in a website designed to promote emotional wellness and healthy behaviors during the transition to parenthood? *J Med Internet Res*. 2017;19(10):e325.
101. A Venning, M Herd, D Smith, SJ Lawn, L Mohammadi, F Glover. Teachable moments: how can the community capitalise on existing and future support services to improve the mental health and wellbeing of 'new' fathers? Report No. 1920966579. 2018. Flinders University.
102. R Fletcher, T Knight, JA Macdonald, J StGeorge. Process evaluation of text-based support for fathers during the transition to fatherhood (SMS4dads): mechanisms of impact. *BMC Psychol*. 2019;7(1):63.
103. C Feltner, I Wallace, N Berkman, CE Kistler, JC Middleton, C Barclay, et al. Screening for intimate partner violence, elder abuse, and abuse of vulnerable adults: evidence report and systematic review for the US Preventive Services Task Force. *JAMA*. 2018;320(16):1688–701.

104. UK National Screening Committee. Criteria for appraising the viability, effectiveness and appropriateness of a screening programme. 2003.

105. J Domoney, K Trevillion, FL Challacombe. Developing an intervention for paternal perinatal depression: an international Delphi study. *J Affect Disord Reports.* 2020;2:100033.

106. H Rominov, R Giallo, PD Pilkington, TA Whelan. "Getting help for yourself is a way of helping your baby": fathers' experiences of support for mental health and parenting in the perinatal period. *Psychol Men Masculinity.* 2018; 19(3):457.

107. DS Berke, D Reidy, A Zeichner. Masculinity, emotion regulation, and psychopathology: a critical review and integrated model. *Clin Psychol Rev.* 2018;66:106–16.

108. JR Mahalik, GE Good, D Tager, RF Levant, C Mackowiak. Developing a taxonomy of helpful and harmful practices for clinical work with boys and men. *J Couns Psychol.* 2012;59(4):591–603.

109. C Bachmann, B Gooch. LGBT in Britain: Health Report. 2018. www.stonewall.org .uk/system/files/lgbt_in_britain_health .pdf

110. RB Singer, B Crane, EP Lemay Jr, S Omary. Improving the knowledge, attitudes, and behavioral intentions of perinatal care providers toward childbearing individuals identifying as LGBTQ: a quasi-experimental study. *J Contin Educ Nurs.* 2019;50(7):303–12.

Chapter 7

The Perinatal Mental Health of Racial and Ethnic Minority Groups

Raquel Catalao, Louisa Codjoe, Preety Das, Jacqui Dyer and Stephani L. Hatch

Despite increasing ethnic diversity [1] and a rising proportion of births to migrant women [2], inequalities in health and care experiences for racial and ethnic minority groups have been a persistent challenge in the UK [3], with perinatal mental health being no exception. Whilst it is important to acknowledge that inequities in maternal health are a global phenomenon, there is a clear and alarming pattern of people from racialised groups (i.e. those who, based on their skin colour, are disadvantaged due to normalisation of an array of dynamics that favour white people) experience worse maternal outcomes in many high-income countries [4]. Which specific groups experience worse outcomes is dependent on the sociocultural context rather than biological determinism. Childbirth has both a biological and a cultural definition. It is also a political and social phenomenon shaped by the society we live in [5]. Humans' actions such as the cultural creation of traditions, customs and rules affect childbirth practices directly. These actions take place through social interactions, communication and exchanges inside social institutions and can often be dismissed in the current culture of medicalisation of birth [5].

Racial and ethnic minority groups are not a homogenous entity and vary greatly in terms of migration history, culture, language and religion as well as health needs. Focusing merely on the ethnicity is likely to obscure differences on how distinct groups of women experience inequity and on the role of context. Women who belong to the same ethnic group may access and experience care differently depending on their migration status, language proficiency, marital status and recourse to public funds among many other factors. An intersectional approach, where the different components leading to women's experience of care are disaggregated and considered together, is often missing in mental health literature. Nevertheless, there is unequivocal evidence that race and ethnicity matter remarkably in access to treatment, experiences of care and outcomes.

A fundamental limitation in our ability to study and address these differences has to do with how these characteristics are coded in national databases. It is well recognised that ethnicity is poorly and inconsistently completed in health records and surveys [6]. In the last Census conducted in England in Wales in 2021, 81.7% of the population identified as White British, a figure that has been decreasing in recent years. People from Asian ethnic groups made up the second largest percentage of the population (9.3%), followed by Black (4.0%), mixed (2.9%) and other (2.1%) ethnic groups [7]. Although categorising people in groups is necessary to study their diverse health needs, these classifications represent an oversimplification of the cultural diversity in the UK and are likely to obscure within as well as between group disparities. Furthermore, these ethnic groups do not represent how all people identify.

Bearing these limitations in mind, evidence suggests that different ethnic minority groups are more likely to experience particular mental health disorders compared to the majority white population in the UK [8]. The risk of psychosis in Black men is considerably higher than in white men [9]. Black and Black British women experience common mental disorders (CMDs), for example depression and anxiety, at a higher rate than other ethnicities [10]. Non-European immigrant women including young South Asian women are a high-risk group for suicide attempts [11].

Crucially, despite the higher prevalence of certain conditions, ethnic minority groups face several barriers to accessing treatment particularly in the primary care setting [3, 12]. People in all ethnic minority groups, but most notably Black Caribbean, Black African and Black British people, are more likely to come into contact with mental health services via adversarial routes such as those involving the police and by compulsory admission to hospital [12, 13, 14, 15]. The reasons behind these disparities are complex and not fully elucidated [16]. Whereas poverty and social factors are likely to play a role, as are cultural beliefs regarding health and illness, the role of structural and systemic racism and xenophobia not only in health services but in the wider community is often overlooked [3].

Epidemiology of Perinatal Mental Illness in Minority Groups

A rapidly increasing proportion of UK births are to migrant women. Over a quarter (30.3%) of live births in England and Wales in 2021 were to women born outside the UK, the highest level on record [17]. Striking inequalities persist in outcomes and women of ethnic minorities are at higher risk of dying in pregnancy and in the postpartum. Data from the confidential reports into maternal mortality in the UK from 2020 to 2022 showed that Black women were over three times more likely to die than white women during the perinatal period and Asian women were twice more likely [18, 19]. Whereas mortality rates have been generally decreasing for babies in the UK, they remain high for Black, Black British, Asian and Asian British babies [20]. The COVID-19 pandemic accentuated these differences further and pregnant women of Black and other ethnic minority backgrounds were at higher risk of complications by the virus. Asian women were four times and Black women were eight times more likely to be admitted to hospital during pregnancy with COVID-19 than white women [21].

Despite recent reports highlighting how common perinatal mental disorders are [22] and their wide-ranging impacts for the mother, child, family and society [23], there has been limited research on the burden of these disorders in ethnic minorities in the UK [24]. The available literature suggests that migrant women and women from minority groups, particularly those from South Asian origin, have higher rates of distress and CMDs in the perinatal period [25, 26, 27, 28]. Importantly, whereas scales have been validated in specific ethnic minority groups (notably the Edinburgh Postnatal Depression Scale (EPDS) in South Asian women), and there are positive results for translated tools [29], challenges persist in the use of Western developed scales in women from different cultures [30]. This may partly explain the finding that Black women exposed to higher levels of risk factors were less likely to score above the EPDS threshold during pregnancy [31]. The use of EPDS also failed to identify depression in Japanese women who had given birth in England [32]. A study by the Postpartum Depression: Action Towards Causes and Treatment Consortium aggregated anonymous information on over 18,000 women from 19 institutions in 7 countries in Europe and North America. They reported that education but not ethnicity influenced the reporting of postpartum depression using the EPDS. There were however marked differences across continents [33]. This study concluded that postpartum women with lower levels of education may not disclose symptoms that usually trigger medical attention, such as crying and thoughts of self-harm. In these women, clinicians should focus on the presence of anhedonia and sensitively investigate other symptoms that may be present, but not disclosed, because they may be perceived as highly stigmatising [33].

Most available literature on perinatal mental health disorders focuses on depression and there is a paucity of studies on other mental health disorders such as anxiety disorders [29]. However, a study from an inner-city London maternity unit showed that Black women were at a particularly high risk of birth-related post-traumatic stress symptoms independently of level of deprivation or past mental health history [34]. Importantly, Black women report some of the worst experiences of maternity services, and qualitative evidence highlighted how systemic racism within maternity care – from individual interactions and workforce culture through to curricula and policies – can have a deep and devastating impact on basic rights in childbirth [35].

Whereas a population-based study from Sweden has reported that being an immigrant from a low-income country is associated with risk of dying from suicide in perinatal period [36], data from the UK did not see an increased risk of suicide for migrant or women of ethnic minority in the perinatal period compared to other periods [37].

Current National Institute for Health and Care Excellence (NICE) guidance recommends that women should be asked the two Whooley questions ('During the past month have you often been bothered by feeling down, depressed, or hopeless?'; 'During the past month have you often been bothered by having little interest or pleasure in doing things?') at first contact in primary care when pregnant, at the booking visit and during the early postnatal period [38]. This recommendation has been supported by a study in an ethnically diverse area of inner-city London which demonstrated that the Whooley questions have similar accuracy to the EPDS in identifying mental disorders in the antenatal period. Additionally, no differences in accuracy were seen between different ethnic groups [39].

Beyond concerns regarding the validity of screening tools, a more significant barrier to care is that women from ethnic minority groups, those living in more deprived areas and those who received less education, are less likely to be asked about their mental health in the perinatal period [40, 41]. Discriminatory practices, including opportunities for detection and early treatment, may contribute to the paradoxical finding that women from ethnic minority groups are less likely to be diagnosed with CMDs in primary care and nevertheless have a higher prevalence of severe mental illness [42]. It also brings to question what we currently know about the prevalence of CMDs in different ethnic groups.

A meta-analysis of studies from the UK showed consistently raised rates of psychosis in people of Black Caribbean and African origin controlling for effects of socio-economic deprivation [43]. However, not all migrant groups in England or elsewhere exhibit the same risk profile and there is considerable variation by ethnicity, gender and other socio-environmental factors. A global systematic review found five studies reporting the incidence of postpartum psychosis ranging from 0.89 to 2.6 in 1,000 women [44] and one study from the US reporting a prevalence of psychosis in the perinatal period of 5.0 in 1,000 [45]. Studies from Sweden [46] and the US [45] included in this review found that women from minority groups had higher rates of severe mental disorders in the perinatal period compared to women from the majority ethnic group. Furthermore, a study using data from UK General Practice reported that the prevalence of treated maternal non-affective psychosis was two times higher in Black and Asian children than white children [42].

In addition, data from a large South London electronic mental health case register showed that women of non-white ethnicities with affective or non-affective psychotic disorders are more likely to have a severe relapse in the perinatal period [47] and Black African mothers with psychotic disorders are more likely to have a history of a looked-after child by social services [48]. Importantly, studies looking at women discharged from mother and baby units reported that ethnicity is not associated with social service supervision but lone parenthood is and there is a higher proportion of lone parents in Black Caribbean families than other ethnic groups [49].

Risk Factors

The transition to motherhood is a unique point in women's lives, and its outcome is profoundly shaped by social determinants and health inequity. If we take forward the saying 'it takes a village to raise a child', this process will be more hazardous if the social context, 'the village', sees the mother as an 'other'. Several of the risk factors for the development of perinatal mental health disorders are not specific to this period or to specific disorders and include social risk factors whose prevalence is over-represented in minority groups, including low socio-economic status, migration, domestic violence, trauma, negative life events and low social support [50]. This greater exposure to unfavourable social, economic and environmental circumstances, in association with gender, only partly explains the increased rate of mental disorders in women from ethnic minority groups.

Socio-economic inequalities persist in the UK, and people from Asian and Black racial and ethnic groups are more likely to be in long-term unemployment than the general population [51]. People from Black ethnic groups are less likely to be in higher managerial and professional occupations than any other ethnicity. Furthermore, a higher percentage of men than women are in higher managerial and professional occupations and a higher percentage of women than men are classed as never worked or on long-term unemployment across all ethnicities.

Perceived lack of social support is a known risk factor for depression in the perinatal period and a qualitative study of minority ethnic women's experiences of accessing perinatal mental health care highlighted a lack of understanding from family and community members around their struggles. This could discourage disclosure and exacerbate women's mental distress [52].

Domestic abuse often starts during pregnancy and existing abuse may get worse during pregnancy and in the postpartum. Women from mixed ethnic groups, particularly those of mixed white and Black Caribbean background, are more likely to experience and report partner abuse whereas Asian/Asian British women are the least likely to report domestic abuse, according to the latest Crime Survey in England and Wales [53]. However, data also shows that Black women are 14% less likely to be referred to domestic abuse charities for support by police than white survivors of domestic abuse [54].

Beyond social risk factors women from ethnic minorities suffer an increased burden of pregnancy complications and perinatal loss. Black women are 43% more likely to have a miscarriage than white women [55], and over seven times more likely to experience a stillbirth [56]. Asian women are also over five times more likely to experience a stillbirth compared to White British women [56]. Data from the National Maternity and Perinatal Audit has shown socio-economic and ethnic inequalities are responsible for a substantial proportion of stillbirths, preterm births and births with fetal growth restriction (FGR) in England. The largest inequalities are seen in Black and South Asian women in the most socio-economically deprived quintile. It is estimated that 53.5% of stillbirths in South Asian women and 63.7% in Black women, and 71.7% of FGR in South Asian women and 55% in Black women, would not have occurred if women had the same risk as white women in the least deprived quintiles.

Ethnic disparities in outcomes exist despite socio-economic and demographic factors. Reasons behind these inequalities are complex and are likely to be in part explained by the racial bias of health systems and communities. While research studies have identified stigma as a barrier to accessing mental health services and/or supports, there is a paucity of research on how mental health stigma, when complicated by the experience of racism, sexism and ageism, affects access to services among women of ethnic minorities [57].

Racism can occur at both interpersonal and structural levels. Interpersonal racism might include prejudicial statements that are hurtful or attacking; as well as aggression, violence, bullying or harassment [58]. These adverse experiences might operate on the basis of casual slights, so-called micro-aggressions, that consist of chronic daily hassles, avoidance of people, places and contexts and thwarted aspirations. Indeed, they need not be directly experienced to have pernicious effects on the individual [59]. These subtle influences can result in pessimism, and difficulties adjusting to and recovering from trauma, and there is a growing and convincing body of evidence that psychosis and depression, substance misuse and anger are more likely in those exposed to racism [60, 61]. Alongside interpersonal racism, one set of explanations is based on the notions of structural racism and institutional racism. This means the way that institutions, such as health agencies, organise practices, policies and priorities, and reflect and replicate power dynamics in broader society [62]. This can happen knowingly or unknowingly but becomes established as ordinary behaviours, attitudes and practices within the institution. Institutional racism in organisations, such as mental health services, refers to not just unequal treatment of different ethnic groups but unfair outcomes [58].

Systemic Barriers to Care

The lack of recognition and awareness of the role of racism in mental health care, and its role in generating and perpetuating ethnic inequalities, has many consequences [58]. For those who require treatment, the ability to access appropriate therapy at a time they need it is potentially limited if services are seen as unwelcoming or negative, and are stigmatising. The experience of not being heard, or being mistrusted, or being treated with hostility, are commonly expressed by services users, and reveal implicit power dynamics that act as a context for inequalities [58]. Intersectionality is an important framework for the examination of experiences of mental health concerns among women of different ethnic minorities and the influences of the associated stigma on their help-seeking behaviour [57, 63, 64]. For example, Black Caribbean women, and particularly young Black Caribbean women, may not only experience exclusion from appropriate healthcare research but also may be hesitant to accept or seek help for mental health problems for fear of being further stigmatised. It has also been asserted that when young Black women do seek healthcare services for their health and mental health, they are often not taken seriously or their complaints are ignored [65]. The legacy of slavery, historical psychiatrisation of Black people, ignoring of the role of cumulative trauma, prevalence of the diagnosis of psychosis, and access to treatment via police or criminal justice system, engenders in many mistrust and fear of Western-based models of care [66, 67, 68].

A national review of provision of perinatal mental health services for Black and ethnic minority (BME) women in 2011 found that more than half of the respondents did not provide specific resources for minority women [24] and when they did the focus was on providing interpreting and translation services. Beyond efforts to improve communication, there was little acknowledgement on how cultural differences may impact patient care. Importantly, there was confusion on the definition and understanding of the construct 'BME' with a proportion unable to define the acronym or estimate what size of their patient group belonged to this group [24]. Qualitative work with health professionals has shown that they lack confidence and training to identify the specific needs of ethnic minority women and to manage perinatal mental health problems more generally, particularly in women with mild to moderate or 'subthreshold' depression [69].

Discrimination impacts on equitable access to healthcare services across the UK, and this is corroborated by the accounts of women and by analysis of routinely collected data [70]. Notably, women from all ethnic minority groups are consistently less likely to be diagnosed or offered treatment for perinatal mental health disorders, pharmacological or non-pharmacological, in primary care compared to white women [25, 26, 41]. There is also evidence that Black Caribbean women are more likely to be referred to secondary mental health services postnatally, as opposed to being treated in primary care [71]. A recent population-based study in England showed that Black African, Asian and White Other women have lower access rates to community mental health services and a higher proportion of involuntary admissions in the perinatal period. Importantly, women from these three groups had a higher number of attended community contacts and fewer non-attendances/cancellations of appointments than White British women, indicating that access rather than engagement appears to be a problem [72]. The White Other group was the largest ethnic minority group in this study and included 1 in 10 (10.4%) births in England [72]. The needs of this group require further study particularly bearing in mind the possible impact of political and societal changes, for example Brexit, on experiences of discrimination and access to care.

Focus groups with Black Caribbean women in community settings in the Northwest of England revealed they experience insensitive and uncompassionate encounters with health professionals regarding their physical health which drives them not to seek care for psychological problems for fear of similar experiences [73]. Importantly, experiences of racial and ethnic discrimination and its anticipation are related to increased psychological distress, including depressive and anxiety symptoms [74, 75]. In addition, the women reported that many of their consultations in the perinatal period felt formulaic and protocol driven with focus on the health of the infant at their expense. South Asian women often reported services to be culturally and religiously insensitive and that they felt uncomfortable to have to deal with male providers especially if their husbands were not present [76]. Lack of cultural awareness of staff as well as shortage of health professionals from minority ethnic backgrounds aggravates the lack of culturally appropriate services [16, 77]. British Pakistani mothers reported reluctance in taking antidepressant medication due to side effects and a perception medication 'numbs pain' but does not address the real issues. They were also less likely to be offered psychological therapy and if offered often discontinued due to lack of a culturally sensitive therapist [78].

Experiences of poor care do not seem to be limited to primary care but appear to be prevalent across different health settings. In the national maternity surveys, mothers from racial and ethnic minority groups were less likely to feel they were treated respectfully or always involved in decisions; their first antenatal contact and booking were later, they were less likely to be aware of all the possible options for place of birth, and less likely to say they were given enough information about the choices for maternity care. Results were similar if the women from minority groups were born in the UK or other countries [40]. Women from migrant groups can face additional barriers in accessing services including limited English proficiency, lack of awareness of services, presence of female genital mutilation and no entitlement to free healthcare [79].

Further obstacles to seeking treatment for poor mental health in the perinatal period resonate for all women independent of their ethnicity and include the intense fear of being considered to be an unsuitable parent due to their mental health problems and that this may result in their child being removed from their care [77, 80]. However, the threat or actual loss of identity for women from some minority ethnic groups extends further into other aspects of their identity, for example, where they are expected to continue the expression of matriarchal strength or uphold conflicting religious beliefs [77]. Further, women from minority ethnic groups are often not aware of the availability of services and may not conceptualise mental health symptoms as an illness, favouring explanations related to practical problems, financial or marital difficulties, physical and hormonal changes related to the perinatal period or the emotional burden of isolation [77].

Future Directions

Recognition of the need for action to address these inequalities is highlighted by the commitments stipulated in the Five Year Forward View for Mental Health [81] and the National Health Service (NHS) England's Long Term Plan [82]. The Five Year Forward View for Mental Health set the ambition that women in all areas of England should be able to access evidence-based specialist support, in the community or through inpatient mother and baby services, closer to their home, when they need it. Similar commitments have been made in the other devolved UK nations.

Whilst huge positive moves for perinatal health generally, the issue of how the NHS can practically target improving racial inequalities has presented long-standing challenges. The Black Lives Matter movement has propelled racial inequalities, historical injustice and the need for immediate action into everyone's mind. Within the recent NHS Advancing Mental Health Equalities Strategy [83], there is an explicit acknowledgement of the need for the NHS to do better as a sector and become a leading example of the fight against racialised healthcare inequalities. They suggest that to do this, it requires every component of the systems we operate within to acknowledge the stark reality of inequality. We will only tackle inequalities by understanding people's experience of them and acting to change [84]. The recently created NHS Race and Health Observatory has also identified maternal health as a key area for implementing change [85]. In 2018, the Patient and Carer Race Equality Framework (PCREF), first proposed in the review of acute adult inpatient psychiatric care [86], was introduced as a key recommendation from the national Mental Health Act Review as a practical approach to reducing inequality in access, experience and mental health outcomes that are seen in different ethnic groups [87]. The framework involves an organisation providing spaces to listen to its communities racialised lived experiences, especially where mental ill health is concerned, and developing competencies (the skills, knowledge and attributes required to complete a task well), that will enable it to better understand and meet the needs of the local population it serves [83, 88].

The ethos of PCREF (Figure 7.1) is underpinned by several national competencies a service should have in order to provide culturally responsive services. These include a commitment to co-production and co-learning at every level; partnership working with racialised communities, service users, carers and families; cultural awareness; a pledge to meet all needs; digital inclusion and use of data and intelligence to improve outcomes; staff knowledge and awareness; a whole system approach and accountability and transparency of the service provider who should be able to demonstrate their current gaps in equitable service provision and actions to reduce further inequity.

Good Practice Examples

A) Learning from the implementation of PCREF across the four London boroughs covered by South London and Maudsley NHS Foundation Trust can be used to provide an example of how PCREF could be utilised to address perinatal healthcare inequalities.

1. Co-production at all levels. A priority is to deliver a much wider reach into local racialised communities than achieved thus far. PCREF is a framework rooted in co-production to ensure it has integrity and co-ownership across staff, service users, carers and communities. A key aspect of this work is around developing or strengthening existing work with local communities to build trust and confidence. For example, the South London and Maudsley Trust (SLaM) has an established Partnership working model with Independent Advisory Groups consisting of community members working directly with service leads to co-create service improvements.
2. A whole system approach. The PCREF approach encourages mental health trusts to utilise and work with all available services, providers and institutions to improve experience and outcomes across a range of domains. SLaM is developing PCREF collaboratively with the Institute of Psychiatry, Psychology and Neurosciences and using research findings, data and expertise to better understand the local population and deliver more accessible and acceptable services.
3. Local, strategic needs assessment. As previously highlighted, a significant issue exists around data and how large organisations such as the NHS can collect and analyse data to identify inequalities. In 2019, monitoring against the national access ambition moved to the Mental Health Services Data Set, which has enabled us to better understand trends in access to perinatal mental healthcare.

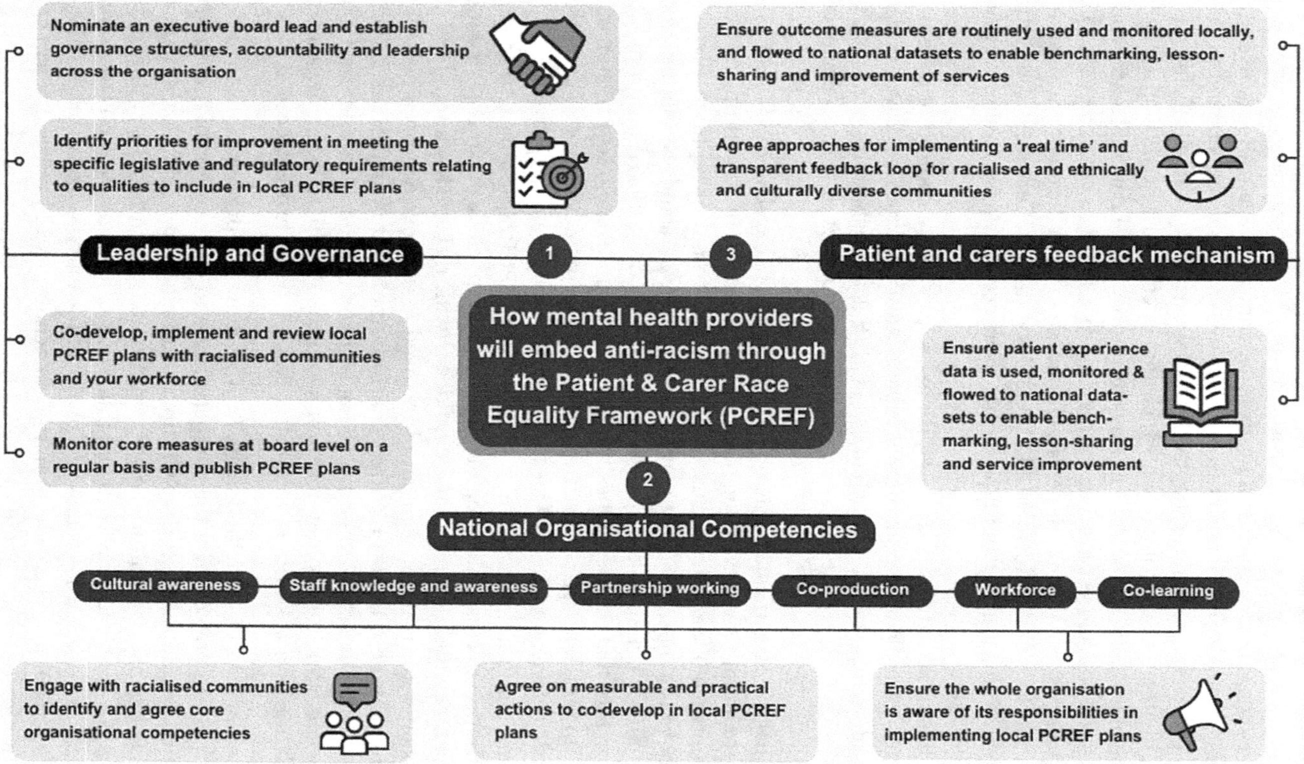

Figure 7.1 Patient and Carer Race Equality Framework components. www.england.nhs.uk/mental-health/advancing-mental-health-equalities/pcref/ Open government licence.

The perinatal mental healthcare dashboard enables viewing of access by age, ethnicity and deprivation at national, regional, Sustainability and Transformation Partnership, Clinical Commissioning Groups and provider level. However, to understand whether there are inequalities in access, there are some important considerations for mental health trusts to consider as they review how they collect and use data. For example, data needs to be compared against local, regional and national demographic data so the organisation can better understand population levels, prevalence and accurately assess racial variation. Ethnicity fields are typically often poorly completed, which makes comparisons difficult. It is vital that mental health trusts identify ways to improve local data collection and understand and address barriers to this. Improved data can then be used to better understand where inequalities exist within, the journey through perinatal mental health services, and to identify additional local data that are needed to better understand this journey and how service users access and experience services and their outcomes.

4. Engagement activity with staff, service users, carers and communities to develop activities to implement the national organisational competencies and to develop the local organisational competencies. PCREF is a collaborative approach that works with staff, service users, carers and communities to harness perspectives around the key priorities to be addressed.
5. Gap analysis. A gap analysis may then be conducted against the PCREF competencies to identify change ideas and service improvement projects which are co-owned by staff, service users, carers and community representatives. Using the above example, the Trust may further analyse data and see that treatment is being offered but not taken up by service users from specific ethnic groups. It may be from this, that the mental health trust seeks to understand why treatment is not taken up and develops a project to explore this. Findings from this can then lead to further developments and ideas for service change and improvement.
6. Accountability and transparency. In order for the PCREF approach to support the organisation to create meaningful change, it is imperative that there is a culture of transparency. Building trust and confidence with racialised communities necessitates an acknowledgement of the need to improve and open identification of where this need is most required. It is important that mental health services can demonstrate the actions they are taking to reduce inequalities and can be held accountable for this. Communication about the PCREF with the diverse populations being served is an integral part of the inclusive process.

B) Rather than being a rigid methodology, PCREF allows for organisations to be creative in the way they strive to meet the competencies and expectations of the framework. The Maudsley Cultural Psychiatry Group, an organisation within SLaM that aims to highlight issues on race, culture and intersectionality within staff training and education, is a good example. Using methods of staff engagement and co-production, they aim to: 1) provide an independent platform for staff discussion of these issues, 2) integrate material into the wider training curriculum and 3) bridge the gap between their institution and local communities.

C) Another helpful illustration of attending to the needs of a diverse population by applying PCREF national organisational competencies into practice is the

Birmingham and Solihull Mental Health Foundation Trust's new perinatal peer support model. Analysis of local data on access to mental health services identified that women of ethnic minorities were significantly less likely to access mental health services than white British women. In response to emerging data, the Birmingham specialist perinatal mental health community team have commissioned an innovative peer support model to ensure that peer workers are considered representative of their local population. Three peer workers with lived experience of perinatal mental illness are employed by third-sector organisations (Acacia Family Support, Approachable Parenting and Action on Postpartum Psychosis) and provided with honorary contracts to the trust as well as a supervision structure. This model demonstrates the importance of partnership working, use of data and intelligence, and co-production with lived experience representatives of local populations who were previously underserved. The aspirations of this peer support model are to help to raise awareness of existing community services and reduce stigma and fears of services within the local community, in order to improve access to perinatal services from the local ethnic minority communities [89].

Conclusion

Perinatal mental health teams are therefore uniquely placed to be at the forefront of changing outcomes for women of ethnic minority groups, by reaching out to the communities they serve and actively seeking feedback, critically assessing access to care interventions by ethnicity, educating all staff on diversity and inclusivity and co-developing interventions that serve the needs of the community. Importantly, the focus should be on providing person-centred care by showing openness and curiosity about the cultural beliefs women hold, their sociocultural context and how they make meaning of their distress in order to promote an inclusive supportive model for healing.

References

1. Office of National Statistics. Population of England and Wales – GOV.UK. Ethnicity facts and figures [cited 2020 Aug 20]. https://shorturl.at/7Xu5I
2. Office of National Statistics. Births by parents' country of birth, England and Wales. 2022.
3. K Bhui, K Halvorsrud, J Nazroo. Making a difference: ethnic inequality and severe mental illness. *Br J Psychiatry.* 2018 Oct 1;213(4):574–8.
4. R Catalao, L Zephyrin, L Richardson, Y Coghill, J Smylie, SL Hatch. Tackling racism in maternal health. *BMJ.* 2023;383: e076092.
5. R Behruzi, M Hatem, L Goulet, W Fraser, C Misago. Understanding childbirth practices as an organizational cultural phenomenon: A conceptual framework. *BMC Pregnancy Childbirth.* 2013 Nov 11:13:205.
6. RA Powell, C Njoku, R Elangovan, G Sathyamoorthy, J Ocloo, S Thayil, et al. Tackling racism in UK health research. *BMJ.* 2022 Jan 18;376.
7. UK Government. Population of England and Wales. 2022. https://shorturl.at/gOaGW
8. Mental Health Foundation. BAME and mental health. 2020. www.mentalhealth .org.uk/a-to-z/b/black-asian-and-minority-ethnic-bame-communities
9. NHS Digital. Adult Psychiatric Morbidity Survey: survey of mental health and wellbeing, England. 2014. https://shorturl .at/dzrOf
10. Office of National Statistics. Common mental disorders – GOV.UK. Ethnicity

facts and figures. 2020. https://shorturl.at/Sn0dk

11. A Forte, F Trobia, F Gualtieri, DA Lamis, G Cardamone, V Giallonardo, et al. Suicide risk among immigrants and ethnic minorities: a literature overview. *Int J Environ Res Public Health.* 2018 Jul 8;15(7):1438.
12. K Halvorsrud, J Nazroo, M Otis, E Brown Hajdukova, K Bhui. Ethnic inequalities and pathways to care in psychosis in England: a systematic review and meta-analysis. *BMC Med*; 2018 Dec 12;16(1):223.
13. SP Singh, N Greenwood, S White, R Churchill. Ethnicity and the Mental Health Act 1983: systematic review. *Br J Psychiatry.* 2007 Aug;191:99–105.
14. C Morgan, R Mallett, G Hutchinson, J Leff. Negative pathways to psychiatric care and ethnicity: the bridge between social science and psychiatry. *Soc Sci Med.* 2004;58(4):739–52.
15. Z Chui, B Gazard, S MacCrimmon, H Harwood, J Downs, I Bakolis, et al. Inequalities in referral pathways for young people accessing secondary mental health services in south east London. *Eur Child Adolesc Psychiatry.* 2020;30(7):1113–28.
16. Independent Review of the Mental Health Act 1983: supporting documents. 2019.
17. Office for National Statistics. Population and household estimates, England and Wales: Census 2021. 2021.
18. M Knight, K Bunch, D Tuffnell, H Jayakody, J Shakespeare, R Kotnis, et al. Saving Lives, Improving Mothers' Care – Maternal, Newborn and Infant Clinical Outcome Review Programme. 2018.
19. MBRRACE-UK. Maternal mortality 2020–2022. 2024. www.npeu.ox.ac.uk/mbrrace-uk/data-brief/maternal-mortality-2020-2022
20. ES Draper, ID Gallimore, JJ Kurinczuk, PW Smith, T Boby, LK Smith, et al. Maternal, Newborn and Infant Clinical Outcome Review Programme. MBRRACE-UK Perinatal Mortality Surveillance Report Summary Report. 2021.
21. M Knight, K Bunch, A Cairns, R Cantwell, P Cox, S Kenyon, et al. Saving Lives, Improving Mothers' Care Rapid report: learning from SARS-CoV-2-related and associated maternal deaths in the UK. Maternal, Newborn and Infant Clinical Outcome Review Programme. 2021.
22. LM Howard, P Piot, A Stein. No health without perinatal mental health. *Lancet.* 2014 Nov 15;384(9956):1723–4.
23. Centre for Mental Health, London School of Economics. The costs of perinatal mental health problems: report summary. 2014.
24. National Perinatal Mental Health Project Report. Perinatal mental health of Black and minority ethnic women: a review of current provision in England, Scotland and Wales. 2011.
25. L Moore, H Jayaweera, M Redshaw, M Quigley. Migration, ethnicity and mental health: evidence from mothers participating in the Millennium Cohort Study. *Public Health.* 2019 Jun 1;171:66–75.
26. SL Prady, KE Pickett, S Gilbody, ES Petherick, D Mason, TA Sheldon, et al. Variation and ethnic inequalities in treatment of common mental disorders before, during and after pregnancy: combined analysis of routine and research data in the Born in Bradford cohort. *BMC Psychiatry.* 2016 Apr 12;16(1):1–13.
27. FM Anderson, SL Hatch, C Comacchio, LM Howard. Prevalence and risk of mental disorders in the perinatal period among migrant women: a systematic review and meta-analysis. *Arch Womens Ment Health.* 2017;20(3):449–62.
28. K Onozawa, RC Kumar, D Adams, C Doré, V Glover. High EPDS scores in women from ethnic minorities living in London. *Arch Womens Ment Health.* 2003;6:S51–5.
29. RLR Playfair, B Salami, K Hegadoren. Detecting antepartum and postpartum depression and anxiety symptoms and

disorders in immigrant women: a scoping review of the literature. *Int J Ment Health Nurs.* 2017 Aug 1;26(4):314–25.

30. L Templeton, R Velleman, A Persaud, P Milner. The experiences of postnatal depression in women from Black and minority ethnic communities in Wiltshire, UK. *Ethn Health.* 2003 Aug;8(3):207–21.
31. D Edge, D Baker, A Rogers. Perinatal depression among black Caribbean women. *Health Soc Care Community.* 2004 Sep 1;12(5):430–8.
32. K Yoshida, MN Marks, N Kibe, R Kumar, H Nakano, N Tashiro. Postnatal depression in Japanese women who have given birth in England. *J Affect Disord.* 1997 Mar 1;43(1):69–77.
33. A Di Florio, K Putnam, M Altemus, G Apter, V Bergink, J Bilszta, et al. The impact of education, country, race and ethnicity on the self-report of postpartum depression using the Edinburgh Postnatal Depression Scale HHS Public Access. *Psychol Med.* 2017;47(5):787–99.
34. M Furuta, J Sandall, D Cooper, D Bick. Predictors of birth-related post-traumatic stress symptoms: secondary analysis of a cohort study. *Arch Womens Ment Health.* 2016 Dec 1;19(6):987–99.
35. Birthrights. Systemic racism, not broken bodies: an inquiry into racial injustice and human rights in UK maternity care. 2022.
36. A Esscher, B Essén, E Innala, FC Papadopoulos, A Skalkidou, I Sundström-Poromaa, et al. Suicides during pregnancy and 1 year postpartum in Sweden, 1980–2007. *Br J Psychiatry.* 2016 May 1;208(5):462–9.
37. H Khalifeh, IM Hunt, L Appleby, LM Howard. Suicide in perinatal and non-perinatal women in contact with psychiatric services: 15 year findings from a UK national inquiry. *Lancet Psychiatry.* 2016 Mar 1;3(3):233–42.
38. National Collaborating Centre for Mental Health. Antenatal and postnatal mental health: the NICE guideline on clinical management and service guidance (updated edition). The British Psychological Society and the Royal College of Psychiatrists; 2014.
39. LM Howard, EG Ryan, K Trevillion, F Anderson, D Bick, A Bye, et al. Accuracy of the Whooley questions and the Edinburgh Postnatal Depression Scale in identifying depression and other mental disorders in early pregnancy. *Br J Psychiatry.* 2018 Jan 1;212(1): 50–6.
40. M Redshaw, K Heikkila. Delivered with care: a national survey of women's experience of maternity care. Technical report. National Perinatal Epidemiology Unit, University of Oxford; 2010.
41. SL Prady, KE Pickett, ES Petherick, S Gilbody, T Croudace, D Mason, et al. Evaluation of ethnic disparities in detection of depression and anxiety in primary care during the maternal period: combined analysis of routine and cohort data. *Br J Psychiatry.* 2016 May 1;208(5):453–61.
42. KM Abel, H Hope, E Swift, R Parisi, DM Ashcroft, K Kosidou, et al. Prevalence of maternal mental illness among children and adolescents in the UK between 2005 and 2017: a national retrospective cohort analysis. *Lancet Public Health.* 2019 Jun 1;4(6):e291–300.
43. JB Kirkbride, A Errazuriz, TJ Croudace, C Morgan, D Jackson, J Boydell, et al. Incidence of schizophrenia and other psychoses in England, 1950–2009: a systematic review and meta-analyses. *PLoS ONE.* 2012 Mar 22;7(3): e31660.
44. R VanderKruik, M Barreix, D Chou, T Allen, L Say, LS Cohen, et al. The global prevalence of postpartum psychosis: a systematic review. *BMC Psychiatry.* 2017 Jul 28;17(1):272.
45. O Vesga-López, C Blanco, K Keyes, M Olfson, BF Grant, DS Hasin. Psychiatric disorders in pregnant and postpartum women in the United States. *Arch Gen Psychiatry.* 2008 Jul;65(7):805–15.
46. U Valdimarsdóttir, CM Hultman, B Harlow, S Cnattingius, P Sparén.

Psychotic illness in first-time mothers with no previous psychiatric hospitalizations: a population-based study. *PLoS Med.* 2009 Feb 10;6(2): e1000013.

47. CL Taylor, M Broadbent, M Khondoker, RJ Stewart, LM Howard. Predictors of severe relapse in pregnant women with psychotic or bipolar disorders. *J Psychiatr Res.* 2018 Sep 1;104:100–7.
48. LM Howard, R Kumar, G Thornicroft. Psychosocial characteristics and needs of mothers with psychotic disorders. *Br J Psychiatry.* 2001 May:178: 427–32.
49. L Howard, N Shah, M Salmon, L Appleby. Predictors of social services supervision of babies of mothers with mental illness after admission to a psychiatric mother and baby unit. *Soc Psychiatry Psychiatr Epidemiol.* 2003 Aug 1;38(8):450–5.
50. LM Howard, E Molyneaux, CL Dennis, T Rochat, A Stein, J Milgrom. Non-psychotic mental disorders in the perinatal period. *Lancet.* 2014 Nov 15;384(9956):1775–88.
51. Office of National Statistics. Socioeconomic status – GOV.UK. Ethnicity facts and figures. 2025 Jun 13. https://shorturl.at/i4DAm
52. S Pilav, K De Backer, A Easter, SA Silverio, S Sundaresh, S Roberts, et al. A qualitative study of minority ethnic women's experiences of access to and engagement with perinatal mental health care. *BMC Pregnancy Childbirth.* 2022;22(1) https://doi.org/10.1186/s12884-022-04698-9.
53. Office for National Statistics. Women most at risk of experiencing partner abuse in England and Wales. 2018 May 13. https://shorturl.at/kBqFw
54. Refuge. Ahead of Black History Month, Refuge calls for better protection for Black women experiencing domestic abuse. 2021 Sep 30. https://shorturl.at/rumqH
55. S Quenby, ID Gallos, RK Dhillon-Smith, M Podesek, MD Stephenson, J Fisher, et al. Miscarriage matters: the epidemiological, physical, psychological, and economic costs of early pregnancy loss. *Lancet.* 2021;397.
56. RJ Matthews, ES Draper, BN Manktelow, JJ Kurinczuk, AC Fenton, J Dunkley-Bent, et al. Understanding ethnic inequalities in stillbirth rates: a UK population-based cohort study. *BMJ Open.* 2022;12(2).
57. D Taylor, D Richards. Triple jeopardy: complexities of racism, sexism, and ageism on the experiences of mental health stigma among young Canadian Black women of Caribbean descent. *Front Sociol.* 2019 May 15;4:43.
58. The Synergi Collaborative Centre. The impact of racism on mental health. 2018.
59. PH Collins, P Essed. *Understanding everyday racism: an interdisciplinary theory.* Newbury Park, CA: Sage Publications, Inc.; 1992.
60. Y Paradies, J Ben, N Denson, A Elias, N Priest, A Pieterse, et al. Racism as a determinant of health: a systematic review and meta-analysis. *PLoS ONE.* 2015 Sep 23;10(9):e0138511.
61. AL Pieterse, NR Todd, HA Neville, RT Carter. Perceived racism and mental health among Black American adults: a meta-analytic review. *J Couns Psychol.* 2012 Jan;59(1):1–9.
62. K McKenzie, K Bhui. Institutional racism in mental health care. *BMJ.* 2007 Mar 31;334(7595):649–50.
63. PH Collins. Intersectionality's definitional dilemmas. *Annu Rev Sociol.* 2015 Aug 14;41(1):1–20.
64. SA Shields. Gender: an intersectionality perspective. *Sex Roles.* 2008;59: 301–11.
65. Women's Health in Women's Hands. Annual report 2006–2007. 2006.
66. T Beauboeuf-Lafontant. "You have to show strength": an exploration of gender, race, and depression. *Gend Soc.* 2007;21(1):28–51.
67. D Edge, SC MacKian. Ethnicity and mental health encounters in primary care: help-seeking and help-giving for perinatal

depression among Black Caribbean women in the UK. *Ethn Health.* 2010;15(1):93–111.

68. SC Faber, A Khanna Roy, TI Michaels, MT Williams. The weaponization of medicine: early psychosis in the Black community and the need for racially informed mental healthcare. *Front Psychiatry.* 2023;14.
69. D Edge. Falling through the net – Black and minority ethnic women and perinatal mental healthcare: health professionals' views. *Gen Hosp Psychiatry.* 2010 Jan;32(1):17–25.
70. H Watson, H Soltani. Perinatal mental ill health: the experiences of women from ethnic minority groups. *Br J Midwifery.* 2019 Oct 2;27(10):642–8.
71. D Edge, D Baker, A Rogers. Perinatal depression among black Caribbean women. *Health Soc Care Community.* 2004 Sep;12(5):430–8.
72. J Jankovic, J Parsons, N Jovanović, G Berrisford, A Copello, Q Fazil, et al. Differences in access and utilisation of mental health services in the perinatal period for women from ethnic minorities – a population-based study. *BMC Med.* 2020 Sep 11; 18(1):245.
73. D Edge. "It's leaflet, leaflet, leaflet then, 'see you later'": Black Caribbean women's perceptions of perinatal mental health care. *Br J Gen Pract.* 2011 Apr;61(585):256–62.
74. DM Quinn, G Camacho, B Pan-Weisz, MK Williams. Visible and concealable stigmatized identities and mental health: experiences of racial discrimination and anticipated stigma. *Stigma Health.* 2020;5(4):488–91.
75. MT Schmitt, T Postmes, NR Branscombe, A Garcia. The consequences of perceived discrimination for psychological well-being: a meta-analytic review. *Psychol Bull.* 2014;140(4):921–48.
76. A Wittkowski, A Zumla, S Glendenning, JRE Fox. The experience of postnatal depression in South Asian mothers living in Great Britain: a qualitative study. *J Reprod Infant Psychol.* 2011 Nov;29(5):480–92.
77. H Watson, D Harrop, E Walton, A Young, H Soltani. A systematic review of ethnic minority women's experiences of perinatal mental health conditions and services in Europe. *PLoS ONE.* 2019 Jan 1;14(1).
78. S Khan, K Lovell, F Lunat, Y Masood, S Shah, B Tomenson, et al. Culturally-adapted cognitive behavioural therapy based intervention for maternal depression: a mixed-methods feasibility study. *BMC Womens Health.* 2019 Jan 28;19(1):1–11.
79. GM Higginbottom, C Evans, M Morgan, KK Bharj, J Eldridge, B Hussain, et al. Access to and interventions to improve maternity care services for immigrant women: a narrative synthesis systematic review. *NIHR Journals Library*; 2020 Mar.
80. O Megnin-Viggars, I Symington, LM Howard, S Pilling. Experience of care for mental health problems in the antenatal or postnatal period for women in the UK: a systematic review and meta-synthesis of qualitative research. *Arch Womens Ment Health.* 2015;18:745–59.
81. NHS. NHS Five year forward view. 2014.
82. NHS. Fit for the future: 10 year health plan for England. 2025 Jul 3. www.longtermplan.nhs.uk
83. NHS. Advancing mental health equalities strategy. 2020.
84. National Collaborating Centre for Mental Health. Advancing mental health equality. 2019.
85. NHS Race & Health Observatory. Mapping existing policy interventions to tackle ethnic health inequalities in maternal and neonatal health in England: a systematic scoping review with stakeholder engagement. 2022. https://shorturl.at/pFZOG
86. N Crisp, G Smith, K Nicholson, editors. Old problems, new solutions: improving acute psychiatric care for adults in England. The Commission to review the

provision of acute inpatient psychiatric care for adults; 2022.

87. UK Government. Modernising the Mental Health Act: increasing choice, reducing compulsion. 2018.

88. J Dyer. How can we have the same outcomes when we're not having the same experiences? NHS England. 2019 Jul 12. https://shorturl.at/0kKCv

89. NHS. NHS long term plan. 2019.

Chapter 8

Psychological Aspects of Infertility, Assisted Conception and Perinatal Loss

Sarah Healy, Kyla Vaillancourt and Camilla Rosan

Introduction

For many people the journey to becoming a parent is not a straightforward one. The following chapter examines how experiences with infertility, assisted conception and perinatal loss can impact on an individual's mental health, relationships with others and future children. The chapter is divided into two sections: the first examining infertility and assisted conception and the second focusing on perinatal loss. Each section will briefly define key concepts, definitions and prevalence before describing the psychosocial impact of these difficulties and treatment options.

Although this chapter is divided into two sections, it should be noted that women who experience infertility and utilise artificial reproductive techniques are also highly likely to have experienced some form of perinatal loss. The experience of infertility alone is its own form of loss, and individuals who experience it may have a grief response and share similar psychological difficulties to those who experience pregnancy loss or baby loss. The aim of this chapter is to increase awareness around the often complex and lengthy journey to parenthood, and to support clinicians in understanding the experiences of those they come across at various stages of this journey and how they can best support them.

Infertility: Definitions and Prevalence

Infertility (sometimes referred to as subfertility) is defined as not being able to achieve a clinical pregnancy after 12 months or more of regular (every 2–3 days) unprotected sexual intercourse, or 12 cycles of artificial insemination (for those using a sperm donor). Primary infertility is when a pregnancy has never been achieved by a person, and secondary infertility is an inability to conceive or carry a pregnancy to term after having given birth before [1].

The World Health Organization recognises infertility as a global public health issue. Worldwide, an estimated 48.5 million couples are infertile, of which 19.2 million couples have primary infertility and 29.3 million couples have secondary infertility [2]. It is estimated that one in seven UK couples has difficulty conceiving, equating to around three million people across the country. It is likely that this is in part a hidden problem and that the prevalence of fertility problems has been seemingly increasing as a greater proportion of people come forward to seek help for such difficulties [3].

The authors would like to thank Dr Lucinda Green and Dr Fiona Seth-Smith for their review and contribution to the chapter. Our thanks also to Sharim Ponticelli and Anna Gine for the initial stages of the literature review.

The reasons behind infertility are varied and there may be more than one factor leading to difficulties in either the male or female partner. In the UK the main reasons for infertility are ovulatory disorders, tubal damage, low sperm count, poor sperm morphology or low motility, ejaculation issues, gamete or embryo defects; and uterine, endometrial or peritoneal disorders. Many medications such as some neuroleptics, chemotherapy, non-steroidal anti-inflammatory drugs and spironolactone can also adversely impact fertility. In general, approximately 30% of fertility problems are due to difficulties in the female partner, 30% due to the male partner and 30–40% to both or unknown causes [3].

Risk factors for infertility include smoking, obesity, occupational risks, excessive alcohol consumption and drug use. Female fertility declines with age; the effect of age on male fertility is less clear [3]. There is a known association between eating disorders and infertility, with anorexia and bulimia nervosa accounting for up to 60% of cases of anovulatory infertility [4].

Fertility treatment funded by the National Health Service (NHS) varies across the UK and often requires a longer period of attempted conception prior to accessing treatment. Waiting lists for treatment can be very long in some areas of the country. In most countries, the availability and quality of interventions to address infertility remain a challenge. Diagnosis and treatment of infertility is often not prioritised, and reproductive health strategies are rarely covered through public health financing. Additionally, a lack of trained personnel and the necessary equipment and infrastructure, and the currently high costs of medication, are major barriers even for countries that are actively addressing the needs of people with infertility [1].

When fertility problems are identified there are three main types of treatment:

- medical treatment to restore fertility (e.g. the use of drugs for ovulation induction)
- surgical treatment to restore fertility (e.g. laparoscopy for ablation of endometriosis)
- assisted reproduction techniques – any treatment that deals with means of conception other than vaginal intercourse; it frequently involves the handling of gametes or embryos [3]

Assisted Reproductive Techniques: Definitions and Prevalence

Assisted reproductive techniques (ART) comprise a range of interventions that involve the in vitro handling of human oocytes, spermatozoa and embryos for the purpose of reproduction. Among those interventions are in vitro fertilisation (IVF), embryo transfer, intracytoplasmic sperm injection (ICSI), embryo biopsy, pre-implantation genetic testing, assisted hatching and cryopreservation of either gametes or embryos. The request for ART treatments is on the rise all around the world. Fertility treatments provide many more families with the opportunity to become parents at older ages and offer a new avenue to parenthood for same-sex couples and those with no partner. Although treatment with a male partner still dominates in IVF treatment (94% in 2019 in the UK), there are an increasing number of cycles involving patients in female same-sex relationships or with no partner [5]. The Human Fertilisation & Embryology Authority which publishes the UK data on ART treatments does not include information on male same-sex couples, for whom surrogacy is the main treatment for those who want to have a genetic connection to their child.

In fertility treatments where a parent's egg or sperm are not able to be used to conceive or to support same-sex couples or solo parents in conception, donor eggs or sperm may be used. In some instances, both donor egg and sperm are used. Thus, the child and one or both of their parents will not share a genetic connection. The number of

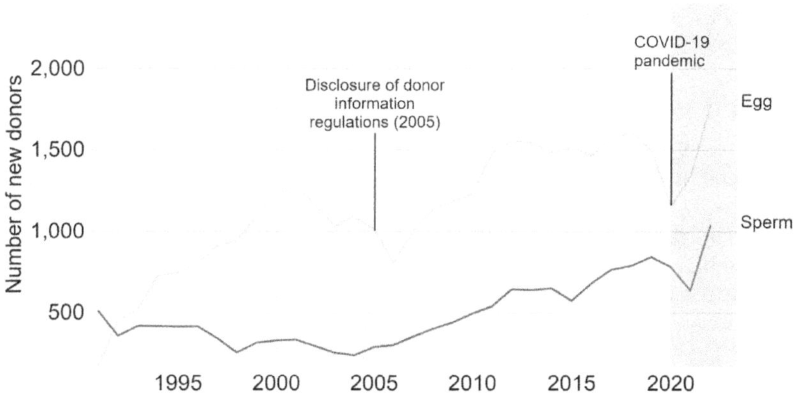

Figure 8.1 Number of new egg and sperm donors, 1991–2022 (preliminary 2020–2 data).
Fertility treatment 2022: preliminary trends and figure. Human Fertilisation and Embryology Authority (HFEA), July 2024.
Reproduced with permission from HFEA.

children born using donor conception increases yearly; see Figure 8.1 for a depiction of the number of IVF cycles using donor egg and/or sperm. In the US, there were over 10,000 live births from donor egg cycles in 2018 [6]; and in the UK over 1,200 babies were born following donor egg cycles and over 2,000 following donor sperm cycles in the same time period [5] (note donor sperm records are not maintained in the US).

In 2019, almost 53,000 patients had around 69,000 IVF cycles and around 5,700 donor insemination cycles at licensed fertility clinics in the UK. After years of rapid growth, there has recently been a levelling off in the number of IVF cycles, which are similar to 2017 levels [5].

Birth rates from IVF have steadily increased over time with the average birth rate per embryo transferred in the UK standing at 24% in 2018, compared with just 7% in 1991, with success rates decreasing with maternal age. As only about one in four patients get pregnant per attempted IVF cycle, a typical IVF programme can involve multiple cycles to achieve pregnancy. Fertility treatment is of course not guaranteed to be successful, and around 30% of patients do not achieve parenthood or end up having fewer children than they would like to [7, 8].

However, ART is not universally available within the NHS to all couples, and certain eligibility criteria have to be met. Although the National Institute for Health and Care Excellence (NICE) fertility guidelines make recommendations about who should be eligible for ART, access to treatment, as well as the type and length of treatment, is defined by each individual Clinical Commissioning Group/Integrated Care Systems (see Box 8.1 for NICE recommendations). Each local area will have their own exclusion criteria, such as women over 40, women with high BMIs, women who are smokers, women with secondary infertility and/or women who have already received a cycle of IVF.

Psychological Consequences of Fertility Difficulties and ART

The Mental Health of Women and Their Partners Experiencing Infertility

For many, fertility treatment opens up new possibilities for building a family, yet the diagnosis and treatment of infertility can also pose a significant psychological burden [9].

Box 8.1 NICE 2017 recommendations regarding fertility treatments [3]

Women under 40

Should be offered three cycles of IVF treatment on the NHS if:

- they've been trying to get pregnant through regular unprotected sex for 2 years
- they've not been able to get pregnant after 12 cycles of artificial insemination, with at least 6 of the cycles using a method called intrauterine insemination (IUI)

If you turn 40 during treatment, the current cycle will be completed, but further cycles shouldn't be offered.

If tests show IVF is the only treatment likely to help you get pregnant, you should be referred straight away.

Women aged 40–42

Should be offered one cycle of IVF on the NHS if all of the following criteria are met:

- they've been trying to get pregnant through regular unprotected sex for 2 years. Or they haven't been able to get pregnant after 12 cycles of artificial insemination, with at least 6 of the cycles using IUI
- they've never had IVF treatment before
- they show no evidence of low ovarian reserve (where eggs in your ovaries are low in number or quality)
- they've been informed of the additional implications of IVF and pregnancy at this age Again, if tests show IVF is the only treatment likely to help you get pregnant, you should be referred straight away.

Those with fertility issues can undergo an intense decision-making process throughout their fertility treatment, and for those seeking private treatment there can be considerable financial implications. Additionally, where egg or sperm donation has been part of the treatment, the transition to parenthood can involve an emotional loss related to missing the genetic connection and fears in relation to what this might mean for their relationship with their child [10].

There is limited research on the impact of assisted conception and infertility on mental health, with many studies having limitations in how generalisable their findings are given factors such as small sample sizes, use of self-report measures, lack of control groups and self-selecting participants. The vast majority of studies on fertility and ART focus on pregnancy outcomes or other physical symptoms, with limited research on the psychological impact [11]. This section aims to summarise the literature that is available currently, with an emphasis on meta-analyses and systematic reviews, where available.

The first reaction to the diagnosis of infertility is usually one of disbelief or even denial. Common reactions to a diagnosis of infertility include fear, sorrow, distrust and hostility [12], and for many these infertility difficulties will endure for several years adding to further psychosocial consequences. An American study surveying 200 heterosexual couples undergoing fertility treatment noted that half of the women and 15% of the men reported that infertility was the most upsetting experience of their lives [13]. Psychological distress has also been found to be the primary reason underlying the discontinuation of fertility treatment [14].

Mental Health during ART Treatment

Before starting IVF treatment, men and women score similar to normative samples in anxiety, self-esteem, mood and general psychological well-being, and life satisfaction [15]. Similarly, patients starting IVF treatments do not have worse marital or sexual relationships than the general population [15, 16, 17, 18]. However, undergoing treatment itself can adversely impact psychological well-being, including increases in anxiety, depression, feelings of loneliness, guilt and low self-esteem, as well as relationship issues and higher protective behaviours towards the infant, with emotional reactions found to be similar among men and women [12]. Even though the experience of IVF/ICSI cycles is highly stressful for both partners [19], the women trying to conceive appear to be affected to a greater extent by these treatments, as they show higher levels of anxious and depressive symptoms compared to their partners [20, 21, 22].

Several observational studies have investigated the prevalence rates for psychiatric disorders in women undergoing fertility treatments, with depression, anxiety disorders and adjustment disorders the most common diagnoses [22]. A Swedish study of over 500 heterosexual couples found a prevalence of mood disorders in around 30% of women and 10% of men, highlighting that major depression was the most common diagnosis. When compared to the general population, rates of depressive disorders were more common, while rates of anxiety disorders were similar [23]. In contrast with these findings in relation to depression, Salih Joelsson and colleagues compared depressive symptoms in pregnant women who received ART and those that did not and found no differences, suggesting a lack of negative effect of fertility treatments on psychopathological symptoms [24].

Mood changes are also associated with fertility medications. Commonly used medications in fertility treatment target hormones in the hypothalamic pituitary ovarian axis and alter levels of thyroid hormone, prolactin, oestradiol, progestogens, GnRH and gonadotrophins [11, 25]. Depression and anxiety are the most common, but some medications, for example clomifene, are associated with psychotic symptoms [26].

Fertility treatment can also impact other aspects of day to day life. During each IVF or ICSI cycle, 6 in 10 patients report treatment-related absences from work and, on average, miss 23 hours of work per cycle [27]. For those undergoing multiple treatment cycles, the impact on work and other domains of their life may also impact on their well-being. For example, it can be hard to plan holidays or think about changing jobs if there are ongoing fertility treatments that bring with them a level of uncertainty and unpredictability. Research has found that one of the most stressful components of IVF/ICSI is the 2-week waiting period related to hearing the results of a successful or unsuccessful embryo transfer, where anxiety and depressive symptoms are markedly increased [28, 29].

For those who are unsuccessful in their fertility treatments and are not able to have a biological child, a period of intense and prolonged grief can follow [30]. Multiple failures in conceiving a child are related to an increased level of anxiety and depression symptomatology [19, 22]. Cohort studies in Australia and Denmark suggest unsuccessful fertility treatment increases the risk of hospitalisation due to psychiatric disorders and increased suicide risk when compared to those who have successful treatments [31, 32, 33].

Positive adjustment has been suggested to be associated with a progressive acceptance of the loss, making meaning of past efforts to conceive and pursuing new life goals or activities. Social support was found to be a protective factor and the sociocultural context played a large role in shaping the experience of infertility and childlessness [34]. Factors associated with maladjustment include lack of partner and social support or a persistent and unresolved desire for children [28].

Historically, the psychological impact of infertility has been studied more intensely in women, yet there is a growing body of literature addressing the impact on men. A recent review noted that while the links between infertility and an increase in stress have been demonstrated, there is no clear evidence that indicates that emotional distress caused by fertility problems, or other life events co-occurring with treatment, decreases the chance of becoming pregnant [35]. However, there is some emerging evidence that post-traumatic stress disorder (PTSD) symptoms and childhood neglect may negatively impact on fertility. Further research is needed to explore this relationship as PTSD symptoms may have an impact on fertility via a range of factors including pelvic injury, vaginismus, neuroendocrine dysregulation and co-occurring mental health difficulties that may interfere with fertility such as eating disorders and alcohol and substance use [36, 37]. Additional research is required to further examine these findings, which rely on self-report measures, to further our knowledge of how trauma and trauma-related difficulties impact on fertility.

Mental Health Following Successful ART Treatment

Following successful ART treatment, pregnancies have been found to be perceived as more rewarding and satisfactory compared to women who conceived naturally. Women who have undergone ART have been found to have significantly higher levels of maternal-fetal attachment in pregnancy than women who conceived naturally [38].

A recent meta-analysis examining the association between infertility treatment and the risk of developing later perinatal depressive symptoms showed that women who receive infertility treatment do not appear to be at increased risk of significant perinatal depressive symptoms compared with those after spontaneous conception [39]. Similarly, a systematic review found that women who had undergone successful ART reported either the same or lower levels of depressive symptomatology than that of comparison groups or population norms [38]. A review of routine collected medical records of over 200,000 live births over a 10-year period in the UK found that women with a history of subfertility, or ART treatment, were not at increased risk of postpartum depression and/or anxiety compared to those with no fertility problems [40]. Mothers in the ART group were found to have a decreased likelihood of postnatal depression or anxiety, even when adjusting for socio-economic indicators, lifestyle and pregnancy-related factors. The authors acknowledge that further research would be needed to understand the mechanisms behind this further.

Findings in relation to antenatal anxiety following successful ART are also mixed [38]. A number of recent studies have shown increased antenatal anxiety in women following ART when compared to controls [22, 41, 42, 43]. However, other studies have found no significant difference in anxiety levels in ART groups compared to controls [44, 45, 46]. There does seem to be more consistency when research focuses on pregnancy-specific anxiety, which is found to be at higher levels (particularly worrying about perinatal loss) in women who have experienced ART when compared to control groups [38].

In relation to psychosis, a large Danish population-based study involving over 20,000 women conceiving with IVF treatments, found the risks of postpartum psychiatric episodes to be similar to those of the general population [47], which has also been found with a large Swedish sample [48].

Postnatally, evidence suggests that attachment to the baby and the parent–infant relationship quality among families who undergo ART is similar to comparison groups [12, 45, 49, 50, 51, 52]. Parental stress among IVF parents has been found to be lower when compared to controls, perhaps indicating an increased likelihood of being highly motivated parents. Those parents who had gone to the greatest lengths to achieve parenthood were the least likely to report distress resulting from the responsibilities of parenthood and the burdens associated with caring for a child [53]. Parents with children conceived through ART are more likely to show increased protectiveness towards their children than parents of children spontaneously conceived [22, 54].

In terms of the impact of unsuccessful treatment(s), even when pregnancy is achieved, there is some evidence to suggest that multiple failed treatments increase the likelihood of anxiety, depression and difficulties adjusting postnatally [19]. However, in looking at the longer-term impact, findings indicate that psychiatric disorders 5 years after ART are less common than at the time of ART treatment, and not more common than in the general population [23].

Studies have begun to examine the psychological impact where conception involves using donor egg or donor sperm. Findings suggest that mothers and non-gestational partners in both donor insemination and egg donation families were found to be psychologically well-adjusted. For the vast majority, parents' levels of depression, anxiety and parenting stress were found to be in line with comparison groups of non-donor fertility ART groups and pregnancies following natural conception [10, 55, 56]. Families created using donor conception have generally been found to be functioning well, with a high quality of parenting found across studies and few differences in child psychological adjustment, parent–child relationship quality or parental psychological well-being when compared to families formed using other types of assisted reproduction or unassisted conception [56, 57].

Impact on the Couple Relationship

Couples can be adversely affected by the stressful experiences related with fertility difficulties influencing the quality of the relationship. There has been some evidence to suggest that infertile couples have less stable marital relationships compared to fertile couples, impacted by a range of factors including differences in communication styles, the importance of biological parenthood, the meaning of infertility, mental health difficulties in one or both members of a couple and the emergence of psychosexual difficulties [58]. Findings in this area should be interpreted with caution as the research body is small, heavily reliant on small samples and descriptive in nature.

Qualitative research has found differences between couple members in the meaning and identity they attribute to what it is to experience infertility as well as the importance of biological parenthood, which can both feed into disagreements and couple relationship difficulties. Differences in communication style (in its amount, nature and purpose) have been suggested to play an important yet complex role in the experience of couple relationship problems [58].

Mental health problems have also been found to be associated with couple relationship distress. In fact, each partner's depressive symptoms have been found to be independently predicted by their partner's infertility-specific distress, so it is a complex interrelated relationship [59].

Additionally, for heterosexual couples, overcoming infertility is often predicated on sexual intercourse resulting in pregnancy. Therefore, research indicates that as couples focus on the technical timing and frequency of sexual intercourse, this can adversely impact on emotional closeness, pleasure, spontaneity and desire [60]. This secondary sexual dysfunction can have the opposite effect and actually lead to reduced frequency of intercourse, which can then serve to further exacerbate the fertility problems [3].

Vulnerability Factors for Mental Health Problems in Relation to Infertility and ART

The relationship between ART and mental distress is complex and requires a careful examination of the direction of effects between both variables. However, some women are more at risk of developing mental health problems when they are undergoing ART, with one of the major predictors being a history of mental health difficulties. Limited research has been done in this area, with the evidence that does exist suggesting that a history of mental health disorders is associated with an increased likelihood of depression, anxiety and/or psychiatric morbidity during treatment [61]. A past history of major depressive disorder (MDD) has been found to predict MDD during infertility treatment among both men and women, even after controlling for other well-established risk factors (i.e. baseline levels of depression, anxiety and partner support) [62].

As well as a history of mental health difficulties, another major risk factor for developing mental health problems is having an unsuccessful outcome of the ART intervention, with research showing those who do not manage to conceive with fertility treatment experience worse mental health and well-being than those who conceive [34]. Other risk factors include: using passive or avoidant coping strategies; having a lower educational level; being childless; having treatment-related physical or emotional complaints; experiencing high helplessness regarding infertility and its treatment; having undergone multiple ART cycles; and having a multiple pregnancy [19, 24].

Psychosocial Treatments, Infertility and ART

Psychologically Informed Care

According to the NICE guidance for fertility problems, women who experience difficulties in conceiving should be seen with their partner (when they are in a couple) because both partners can be affected by decisions surrounding investigation and treatment [3]. Women and couples value contact with sensitive and empathic staff members who provide support for their individual needs and pay attention to the emotional impact of infertility [63]. Examples of this include staff introducing themselves, their role and what will happen; offering the women and/or couple a chaperone if they would like one, ensuring the chaperone also introduces themselves and their role and what they will be doing through the procedure; asking permission for anyone else to be present in the room; acknowledging with the women and/or partner that they may be feeling worried or upset, which is common for fertility investigations, and inviting them to ask any questions.

Trauma-informed care should underpin the care that women receive from healthcare professionals throughout their journey. It is important for all staff to: understand what the impact of trauma could be for the individual, whether they disclose a trauma history or not; ensure they deliver trauma-informed care that is respectful and responds to care decisions; and consider how care interaction can affect an individual's future engagement with the healthcare system [64]. Principles of trauma-informed care include attention to: 1) safety; 2) trustworthiness and transparency; 3) peer support and mutual self-help; 4) empowerment, voice and choice; 5) collaboration and mutuality and 6) attention to cultural, historical and gender issues [64]. This should also be considered in relation to care following perinatal loss as discussed later in the chapter.

Mental Health Screening

As described, emotional distress is common and understandable during fertility difficulties and treatment. It is crucial for fertility specialists to be able to differentiate between more normative distress and clinical levels of mental health difficulties that may require treatment. Therefore, using validated screening measures for anxiety, trauma and depressive symptoms is crucial (such as the GAD-7, PHQ-9 and PCL-5) as women and men with higher levels may need a referral to specialised psychosocial care [23, 65, 66].

Different assessment measures have been developed specifically for the fertility context: SCREENIVF and FertiQoL. SCREENIVF can be used by fertility professionals to identify those people at risk of developing emotional or relational maladjustment at the beginning, during or after treatment, though has low predictive validity. The Fertility Quality of Life Tool (FertiQoL) also assesses the impact on fertility problems and treatment on personal, social and relational life domains [67]. It has been validated in various countries and has good overall psychometric characteristics [68]. The advantage of using the SCREENIVF or FertiQoL, with respect to other non-specific mental health instruments like PHQ-9, GAD-7 and PCL-5, is that they cover cognitions, emotions and support, using items worded in a way that will resonate with the lived experience of people undergoing this specific treatment [69, 70].

Psychological Therapy

Fertility clinics in the UK are licenced by the Human Fertilisation and Embryology Authority, who include in their guidance a requirement that women and couples be offered counselling when undergoing IVF, using donor gametes or embryos and for a range of other treatments [71]. Those at risk of experiencing clinically significant psychosocial or mental health problems should be referred to a specialist practitioner [63].

There are a range of psychological practitioners who may be involved in these different types of intervention, based on the needs of the women and her partner and the training of the practitioner. These include:

- *An infertility counsellor*: These practitioners will have a core training in counselling accredited by the British Association in Counselling and Psychotherapy. Most infertility counsellors go on to complete a further post-qualification foundation course in infertility counselling accredited by the British Infertility Counselling Association. The purpose of counselling for infertility and assisted conception is to: enable people to reflect upon and understand the implications of a proposed course of action for that person, their family, children born as a result and anyone else affected by the treatment or by donation of gametes and embryos; provide emotional support before, during and after treatment or donation of gametes and embryos (including legal considerations), particularly if the person is experiencing stress, ambivalence or distress; assist people in developing successful coping strategies for dealing with both the short- and longer-term consequences of infertility and treatment; and/or to help people to try to adjust and to accommodate to their particular situation [72].

- *A genetics counsellor*: Genetic counsellors are medical professionals trained in both genetic medicine and counselling and are accredited by the Genetic Counsellor Registration Board. They help people understand and adapt to the medical, psychological and family implications of genetic conditions.
- *A counselling/clinical psychologist*: These practitioners will have a doctorate-level training in a range of evidence-based psychological therapies such as cognitive behavioural therapy (CBT) and systemic couples therapy. Counselling and clinical psychologists are specifically trained in screening for, assessing and treating people with mental health problems.

Although a 2016 Cochrane Review was conducted into the effectiveness of psychological and educational interventions on the mental health of women and their partners experiencing infertility, they were not able to make any overall conclusions due to the very low quality of the evidence [73]. Thus, the summary below is brief in relation to what may be helpful to consider when delivering psychological interventions to those experiencing psychological distress in relation to fertility and/or fertility treatments. Further research in this area is needed to make more tailored recommendations.

Group interventions which emphasised education and skills training (e.g. relaxation training) appeared more effective in producing positive change across a range of outcomes than counselling interventions which emphasised emotional expression and support and/or discussion about thoughts and feelings related to infertility. Men and women appear to benefit equally from psychosocial interventions. The quality of the current evidence base does not allow for the comparison of effectiveness between different treatment modalities (e.g. CBT vs counselling) [32, 74]. A systematic review and meta-analysis published in 2023 [75] examining the effectiveness of group psychological interventions for women with infertility participating in fertility treatment found group support reduced depression, anxiety, fertility stress and marital dissatisfaction. Mindfulness-based interventions and CBT-based programmes were more widely researched and found to be more effective overall. The review also indicated that group programmes longer than 9 hours in duration that were also facilitated for more than six weekly sessions demonstrated larger effect sizes.

When mental health problems occur at any stage of fertility treatment or in relation to infertility, evidence-based treatments (that have been found to be effective in populations outside of an infertility context) should be offered where available (e.g. CBT for depression and anxiety, trauma-focused CBT or eye movement desensitisation and reprocessing (EMDR) for PTSD) [76, 77, 78]. There is some limited evidence that suggests that CBT could be efficacious in reducing symptoms of anxiety and depression (but not stress) in women experiencing fertility difficulties and/or going through ART [79, 80, 81]. Some support also exists for mind-body interventions (including mindfulness-based interventions and yoga) in reducing symptoms of anxiety and depression [82]. A systematic review and meta-analysis of 10 randomised controlled trials evaluating the effectiveness of mindfulness-based intervention programs in reducing mental and physical health in women with infertility found a significant reduction in depression and anxiety symptoms [83].

It is recommended that women who meet the criteria for perinatal mental health services (e.g. who have current or previous severe mental health problems) are referred for preconception advice when undergoing fertility treatment or in early pregnancy in line with NICE guidance [3, 78]. Their assessment, care planning and treatment should take their infertility and fertility treatment history and experience into account. Discussions about the use of psychiatric medication for women having fertility treatment should follow the same principles as for weighing up the risks and benefits of using medications in pregnancy [78, 84]. Women having fertility treatment may have concerns about the impact of psychiatric medications, including questions about the potential impact on the outcome on the fertility treatment itself. The evidence base for this is more limited than for the use of these medications during pregnancy. The current evidence suggests that selective serotonin reuptake inhibitor antidepressants are unlikely to reduce fertility or affect the outcome of infertility treatment, although they do have an adverse effect on semen parameters [85]. There is more limited evidence in relation to the use of other psychotropic medication [25] (see Chapter 28 on psychological therapies, Chapter 26 on prescribing and Chapter 25 on pre-birth planning.

As infertility can impact on the quality of the couple relationship, a couples approach can be helpful in working with relationship problems, particularly those involving communication, sexual difficulties, financial strain, decision-making and conflict resolution. A systematic review of couple therapy and infertility found couple therapy of six or more sessions to be effective in reducing depression, anxiety, stress and relational complaints in couples who present with a lengthier infertility history. Superior results were found with emotionally focused couple therapy, cognitive behavioural couple therapy and behavioural couples therapy [86].

Infertility and ART Summary

The literature, while limited in quality and quantity, highlights the possible impact of infertility and undergoing ART on mental health. As such, the experience a client may have had in their journey to becoming pregnant should be considered to build a comprehensive assessment and treatment plan when mental health issues arise, or for those women who may be at risk of mental health difficulties in the perinatal period.

Perinatal Loss

In the following section, we refer to perinatal loss as the loss of a pregnancy or death of an infant any time from conception until the end of the first postnatal year. A substantial proportion of women and couples will experience perinatal loss over the course of their childbearing years, and for some it may have a significant impact on their mental health, functioning and relationships. Parents can experience feelings of extreme grief within a society and culture that may mistakenly believe such a loss to be less traumatic or impactful than other kinds of death. Furthermore, there remains stigma and taboo associated with baby loss, all of which can exacerbate the devastation and isolation of the loss experience.

The research summarised in this section varies in quality, with some studies being limited by methods used to assess mental health (e.g. self-report vs diagnostic interviews), study designs (e.g. prospective or retrospective, nature of the comparison group), sample size or analytic quality (e.g. controlling for other key factors) and some areas lacking in research altogether. The section aims to describe the literature that is currently available, with an emphasis on studies which are of higher quality and conclusions drawn from meta-analyses, where possible.

Perinatal Loss: Definitions and Prevalence

Perinatal loss refers to different forms of pregnancy loss or the death of a baby during the perinatal period. This may include miscarriage, termination of pregnancy (including termination due to detection of fetal anomaly), ectopic pregnancy, molar pregnancy, stillbirth, neonatal death and sudden unexpected death in infancy (SUDI).

Box 8.2 provides an overview of common forms of perinatal loss with a brief description of the medical treatment and care, and processes that are involved for women and families who experience them. Although information included in this table pertains to England and the UK, there will be similarities across other developed nations. It should be noted that the gestation periods that define different forms of loss are done so for medical and legal reasons; but the subjective experience for women and couples will not necessarily match these delineations (e.g. the difference between a late miscarriage and a stillbirth is 1 day). As clinicians working with women in the perinatal period, it is helpful to understand the physical nature of pregnancy loss, stillbirth and neonatal death and to understand the processes (e.g. medical or coroner investigations, burials, etc.) that women and families will be navigating alongside their emotional response and grief. The nature of each kind of loss and the circumstances surrounding it will impact on a woman's experience. For example, the way in which women become aware of their loss, how this is communicated or shared, how physical and emotional pain are responded to by professionals, and other individual factors (e.g. prior trauma and mental health history) will influence a woman's experience. Some parents may also have encountered settings like a Neonatal Intensive Care Unit if a baby is born very sick. This environment can be frightening or overwhelming for parents, while they are also facing a poor or uncertain prognosis for their baby. Although there will be commonalities in the experience of perinatal loss, each person's particular circumstances and emotional response will be individual.

Approximately one in four pregnancies end in loss. Table 8.1 contains the estimated prevalence for different forms of loss. The experience of perinatal loss disproportionately affects women in terms of age, ethnicity and socio-economic deprivation. The incidence of stillbirth and neonatal death are significantly higher for women living in the most deprived areas of the UK, and for babies of Black, Black British, Asian and Asian British ethnicities [90]. Women over 35 years have increased risk of still birth, and higher neonatal mortality rates are found for women younger than 25 years and women over 35 years [90]. Women of Black ethnicity are also at increased risk of miscarriage [97]. Infant mortality rates are significantly higher in the most deprived areas of England [98]. The reasons for these inequalities are believed to be multifaceted, with social, biological and genetic factors likely contributing [97, 98]. Research is urgently needed to identify inequalities in care that may contribute to differences in perinatal and infant outcomes [99]. Efforts are underway including the use of personalised risk assessments in early pregnancy to proactively screen for placental dysfunction with encouraging results [100]. There is also evidence that women with severe mental illness are at increased risk of experiencing stillbirth and neonatal death,

Box 8.2 Overview of Different Kinds of Perinatal Loss [78, 87, 88, 89, 90, 91, 92, 93, 94]

Miscarriage

Definition: The spontaneous loss of a fetus or embryo during the first 24 weeks of a pregnancy. Symptoms include pain (cramping) and bleeding. Most occur within the first trimester, but risks of later miscarriage increase with maternal age. Recurrent miscarriage is defined as the loss of three or more consecutive pregnancies before 24 weeks. Note other relevant terms: A 'missed' miscarriage is when the fetus has stopped developing and there are no symptoms (e.g. pain or bleeding) and is detected during a routine pregnancy scan. A 'chemical' pregnancy refers to the loss of a pregnancy before or around 5 weeks, where a pregnancy was confirmed by pregnancy test only.

Medical treatment/care: Where miscarriage is suspected or confirmed, women will be advised to wait for the tissues to pass naturally ('expectant management'), be offered medical management (e.g. pessaries) or surgical management (i.e. removing remaining tissue in the womb surgically with local or general anaesthetic). The physical experience of miscarriage and treatment varies for each individual but for some will be associated with ongoing bleeding and discomfort after the procedure. Where women miscarry outside of hospital, they will manage heavy bleeding and may pass pregnancy tissue whilst at home or in another environment (e.g. public setting). There is no legal requirement to have a burial or cremation for losses before 24 weeks' gestation. Some hospitals and clinics will offer options for the sensitive disposal of the pregnancy remains (cremation or burial) but there is wide variability in practice with some hospitals treating pregnancy remains as clinical waste.

The UK recommends that women with recurrent miscarriage are referred to a specialist clinic for investigation. Treatment will depend upon the suspected cause but may include treatment for blood disorders, genetic counselling or surgery for anatomical problems. The UK guideline for recurrent miscarriage is currently under review to allow women to access investigations earlier.

Termination of Pregnancy (TOP) and Termination of Pregnancy for Fetal Anomaly (TOPFA)

Definition: A termination of pregnancy is the intentional end of a pregnancy with medical intervention. Access to TOP varies across the UK. It is legal in England, Scotland and Wales, for a termination of pregnancy for non-medical reasons to be conducted between conception and 24 weeks. In Northern Ireland there are more restrictions. Under conditions of fetal anomaly, a termination can be performed at any gestation. If a TOPFA takes place after 24 weeks, it may also be registered as a stillbirth.

Medical treatment/care:

- Termination of pregnancy for non-medical reasons: Options for a termination of pregnancy include medication or surgical intervention to remove the pregnancy depending on the gestation of pregnancy. This may be conducted in an NHS clinic or with an independent (non-NHS) provider. Women who chose medical intervention before 10 weeks have the option of taking medication and for the process to complete at home. The physical experience of TOP varies by individual in terms of the amount of pain, bleeding and discomfort someone may experience in response to the procedure.
- Termination of pregnancy for fetal anomaly: Where tests identify that the baby has a serious genetic anomaly, couples will be provided with information about the condition and likely impact on baby's life. Couples who decide to terminate the pregnancy will be offered the option of medical or surgical termination. Where the pregnancy is later in gestation, there may be interventions to end the life of the baby before a medical induction and birthing their baby. Families should be provided with

Box 8.2 *(cont.)*

the option to see or hold their baby or have a cremation or burial. In the UK post-mortem examinations of the fetus may be conducted to better understand the nature of the anomaly and any implications for future pregnancies.

Ectopic Pregnancy

Definition: When the fetus develops outside of the uterus, most often in the fallopian tube, it could also be in the ovary, abdomen or cervix. Pregnancies which are ectopic are not viable. Symptoms include vaginal bleeding, pain in lower abdomen or tip of shoulder, diarrhoea or pain when using the toilet, severe abdominal pain or collapse.

Medical treatment/care: Most ectopic pregnancies are detected between 6 and 10 weeks of pregnancy. Ectopic pregnancies vary in severity from mild to severe. In severe cases, it is considered a medical emergency due to risk of physical complications or maternal mortality if not promptly treated. Treatment will depend on the severity and when the ectopic pregnancy was detected, with options including expectant management, medical treatment or surgery. In severe cases, it may involve the removal of the affected fallopian tube. Where surgical intervention has been required, follow up with an obstetrician or consultant midwife may be offered.

Women may be asked their preferences and wishes in relation to the pregnancy remains, but like miscarriage, practice around the sensitive disposal of pregnancy remains varies widely hospital to hospital.

Molar Pregnancy and Gestational Trophoblastic Neoplasia (GTN)

Definition: Molar pregnancies are when chromosomes from the sperm and egg do not combine in the usual way, meaning that the fetus cannot develop. Molar pregnancies are a form of gestational trophoblastic disease. Molar pregnancies are usually identified before 12 weeks' gestation with severe hyperemesis gravidarum.

Medical treatment/care: Treatment involves surgery to remove the pregnancy tissue and specialist follow-up after surgery. There is a small chance that a molar pregnancy can progress to GTN, a rare form of cancer. Women will have follow-up to monitor the development of any disease before it is recommended that she conceive again.

As described above with other early pregnancy losses, women may be asked about their preferences and wishes for the pregnancy remains.

Loss in the Context of Twin (or Multiple) Pregnancies

Definition: Multiple pregnancies are associated with greater complications, including increased risk of loss compared to single pregnancies. Twin pregnancies which have separate placentae and separate amniotic sacs have the lowest complication rate.

Medical treatment/care: The treatment and care offered will depend on the gestation and health circumstances of the mother and baby. Forms of loss that may affect a twin pregnancy include a miscarriage or intrauterine death of one or both babies, or selective fetal reduction in cases where a fetal anomaly is detected in one twin or to increase the viability of the pregnancy. Twin pregnancies are also at greater risk of premature labour and delivery which may result in complications leading to babies being born sick and not surviving long after birth. A substantial proportion of twin births will have at least one baby that will spend some time in a Neonatal Intensive Care Unit (NICU).

Stillbirth

Definition: When a baby dies during pregnancy after 24 weeks' gestation (an intrauterine death) or during birth (an intrapartum stillbirth). Causes of stillbirth can include problems

Box 8.2 *(cont.)*

with the placenta (e.g. placental abruption, premature rupture of membranes), congenital abnormality, infection, problem with the umbilical cord, maternal health (e.g. high blood pressure). In the UK, over a third of stillbirths remain of unknown cause following investigation.

Medical treatment/care: For women who experience an intrauterine death, they will have to consider options for how to deliver their baby. Following birth, NICE guidance recommends that women and couples are given the opportunity to hold and see their baby if they wish and be offered opportunities for memory making. Memory making may include taking photographs, making handprints or footprints or spending time washing or dressing the baby. Post-mortem examinations and/or a coroner's inquest will be undertaken. All stillbirths are legally required to be buried or cremated and to be registered as a death. Women and families may wish to arrange a funeral or ceremony for their baby. Women may have ongoing physical symptoms which will require support (e.g. bleeding, pain and lactation).

For cases of stillbirth and neonatal death, hospitals will undertake an investigation and use the Perinatal Mortality Review Tool [95] as a framework to lead a hospital's review into a baby's death.

Neonatal Death

Definition: This is when a baby dies within the first 28 days after birth. The most common reasons for neonatal death are conditions related to prematurity, congenital anomalies and antepartum infection.

Medical treatment/care: Most babies who die within the first month of life will do so while being cared for in hospital or in a NICU. Parents may need to make difficult decisions to either not initiate or to withdraw intensive care from a baby. NICUs may provide support to families to prepare for death where this can be anticipated and coping with other challenges and tasks of this time (e.g. managing lactation). Where a baby dies in hospital parents should be offered the opportunity to hold, see and make memories with their baby.

Post-mortem examinations and/or a coroner's inquest are undertaken when there is a neonatal death. Neonatal deaths are legally required to be buried or cremated and to be registered as a death. Women and families may wish to arrange a funeral or ceremony for their baby and will be supported to do so.

For cases of stillbirth and neonatal death, hospitals will undertake an investigation and use the Perinatal Mortality Review Tool as a framework to lead a hospital's review into a baby's death.

Sudden Unexpected Death in Infancy (SUDI)

Definition: Sudden unexpected death in infancy is a term to describe the death of an infant which could not have been reasonably expected to occur 24 hours previously and in whom no pre-existing medical cause of death is apparent. It will include those deaths for which a cause is ultimately found following coroner investigation ('explained SUDI') and those that remain unexplained following investigation.

Sudden infant death syndrome (SIDS) describes the sudden and unexplained death of an infant during sleep and is a term that will be used when following investigation the coroner is satisfied that there is enough evidence to describe the death as a SIDS death.

Medical treatment/care: Most families who experience SUDI will no longer be in contact with maternity services. Hospital doctors and police provide the initial response with

Box 8.2 *(cont.)*

families. In all cases of SUDI, coroner and police investigations will be conducted to determine the cause of death. The coronial process can take 6 months or longer but parents can conduct a funeral once an initial post-mortem examination is complete and an interim certificate of the cause of death has been provided. In the UK, all child deaths are reviewed by a Child Death Overview Panel. Parents can input into this process if they wish. There are Multi-Agency Guidelines for Care and Investigation for Sudden Infant Death in Infancy and Childhood [96] and these guidelines describe how agencies can work together to share information and keep families included at every stage.

Table 8.1 Prevalence of perinatal loss in England and the UK [88, 93, 102, 103]

Type of loss	Prevalence
Miscarriage	Early (first trimester) miscarriage: 1 in 5 (20%), increases to 50% for those 40 years+ Late miscarriage (between 12–24 weeks): 1–2/100 (1–2%) Recurrent miscarriage: 1 in 100 (1% of couples). More than 6 in 10 of women who have a recurrent miscarriage go on to have a successful pregnancy
Ectopic or molar pregnancies	Ectopic: 1 in 90 (just over 1%) Molar: 1 in 714 (rare, less than 1%)
Stillbirth	1 in 250 births
Termination*	17.4/1000 pregnancies, 1.5% of all terminations in UK were due to detection of fetal anomaly in 2020 (3,083 in total)
Neonatal death	2.7/1000
SIDS	0.16 deaths per 1,000 live births (approximately 200/year)
Overall	1 in 4 pregnancies end in loss

although it is suspected that this is due to associated socio-economic and lifestyle factors rather than the psychiatric disorder itself [101].

Psychological Consequences of Perinatal Loss

Perinatal loss has differences to other forms of bereavement which can influence grief and psychological adjustment. The death of a baby means that individuals and couples face death where there was an expectation of new life, contrary to the 'natural order of things'. In contrast to other forms of bereavement, the loss is related to an emotional bond that may not have been witnessed by others and will be related to the hoped-for identity and future for themselves and their baby. Perinatal loss can be sudden and unexpected, often with no clear cause. It is commonly associated with physical changes (e.g. bleeding, lactation), distressing medical procedures, and ethical and moral dilemmas which can compound the trauma associated with perinatal loss. There is a lack of acknowledgement in society and an absence of bereavement rituals in relation to perinatal loss which can leave parents feeling isolated and that their grief is less legitimate to other forms of loss (known as 'disenfranchised grief') [104]. Perinatal loss has also been referred to as an 'ambiguous' loss because of the lack of (or brief) physical presence of the fetus or infant which can complicate the grieving process [104]. It is not uncommon for perinatal loss to be associated with self-blame due to a perception of personal failure or responsibility on the part of the woman or her body. It is common for women to report feeling isolated and disconnected from others following perinatal loss due to a lack of sensitivity and understanding in society around perinatal grief.

The loss of a pregnancy or death of a baby will be experienced as a stressful life event for nearly all people who are affected. Grief is common following the loss of a baby, with the most acute and pervasive symptoms occurring for most people within the first 6–24 months of the loss [105]. Common grief reactions following the loss of a baby include emotional numbness, shock, disbelief, denial, yearning, preoccupation, intrusive images, crying, anger, despair, insomnia, lack of appetite, withdrawal from social activities, fatigue and guilt.

The course of grief will vary for each individual and will be influenced by cultural, societal and personal factors. Modern theories of grief highlight the non-linear nature of grief to reflect how the intensity of grief will change and fluctuate over time [106]. Most people will experience a gradual reduction in psychological distress with time, whilst experiencing moments of intense grief at specific points indefinitely. In the context of perinatal loss, grief intensity may increase around meaningful dates or as the families of those around them expand. There is a proportion who following perinatal loss will go on to experience 'prolonged grief' (previously known as 'complicated' grief) reactions, adjustment difficulties, the new onset of mental health problems or the re-emergence of prior mental health problems. Persistent feelings of guilt and self-blame in response to perinatal loss have been found to be associated with the onset or recurrence of mental health problems and may interfere with the natural course of grieving [107, 108].

Incidence and Course of Grief and Mental Health Problems

The incidence of anxiety, depression and PTSD are significantly increased following the loss of a baby. In a sample of mothers who had experienced stillbirth, neonatal death or SIDS, approximately 18% of women experienced clinically significant symptoms of anxiety and 9% of women experience clinically significant symptoms of depression at 8 months following the loss [105]. In a meta-analysis of studies which looked at the prevalence of self-reported anxiety and depression in samples of women with a wide range of perinatal loss experiences, it concluded that perinatal loss is associated with elevated rates of anxiety and depression in comparison to non-bereaved women [109]. Women have also been found to be at increased risk for PTSD following all forms of perinatal loss. It is estimated that at 3–12 months following the loss of a pregnancy or loss of a baby, between 7% and 28% of women will meet diagnostic criteria for PTSD [110]. For those who have had an infant hospitalised in a NICU prior to their infant's death, the risk of mental health problems may be even greater [111]. For women who experience the onset of a mental health disorder or high levels of psychological distress following loss, these difficulties have been found to persist over time [105, 112, 113, 114, 115].

Research that has examined recurrence of illness in samples of women with bipolar disorder suggests that the risk of relapse following termination of pregnancy or miscarriage is greater than in pregnancy, but less than that of a live birth [116, 117]. It suggests that for those with a pre-existing bipolar illness, all pregnancy outcomes should be considered as a potential vulnerability for relapse and not solely focus on birth of a live baby [116]. To our knowledge, there are no studies which have examined risk of relapse in those with bipolar disorder following stillbirth or neonatal death. In the study by Di Florio and colleagues, outcomes following stillbirth were excluded from the analysis due to the rare occurrence of this outcome and small sample size.

Research suggests that women are also at increased risk for experiencing anxiety, depression and PTSD in subsequent pregnancies following a loss. A new pregnancy can serve as a physical and emotional reminder of the previous loss and is characterised by a period of heightened fear and uncertainty regarding the outcome [118, 119]. Women may also struggle with how to form a relationship with a new baby while maintaining a bond with the baby who has died [120, 121]. It is estimated that 13–20% of women will meet criteria for a clinical diagnosis of PTSD in a subsequent pregnancy following loss [110]. A meta-analysis of studies has found that the incidence of anxiety disorders, and to a lesser extent depressive disorders, are elevated in women who are pregnant following loss when compared to non-bereaved pregnant women [122]. In one large longitudinal study the number of previous perinatal losses significantly predicted symptoms of depression and anxiety in a subsequent pregnancy, and this remained relatively stable following the birth of a healthy child [115]. It is not uncommon for women in subsequent pregnancies to engage in self-protective strategies due to fear of further perinatal loss, including suppressing positive emotions related to the pregnancy, not thinking about the future and avoidance [123]. In some cases, these ways of coping may result in reduced feelings of bonding with the fetus which may or may not persist postnatally.

Where grief symptoms do not reduce in intensity or pervasiveness, and continue to cause significant impairment, a diagnosis of prolonged grief may be considered. Both the DSM-V and International Classification of Diseases (ICD-11) include a classification of prolonged grief disorder (PGD), when grief continues beyond 12 months (DSM-V) [124] or beyond 6 months after a death (ICD-10) [117]. Bereavement is no longer an exclusion for major depressive disorder in the DSM-V, with recognition that grief can precipitate an episode of depression in individuals who are vulnerable (e.g. history of depression). Prolonged grief differs from typical continuing grief in its chronicity, intensity and the degree of functional impairment, and that it exceeds social, cultural or religious norms (124]. A major feature of prolonged or persistent grief is unabated yearning and/or preoccupation with the deceased or the circumstances around the death. It is considered clinically distinct from PTSD and major depression, and thus it is important to effectively differentiate between diagnoses to guide the most effective treatment [125]. The prevalence of a clinical diagnosis of PGD has not been explored in perinatal samples. However, studies that have assessed complicated grief related to perinatal loss using self-report instruments have described varying prevalence of clinically significant symptoms, ranging from 12% to 50% of women being affected [107, 126, 127].

Fetal or infant death may be a risk factor for suicidality. A history of miscarriage has been associated with suicide attempts in subsequent pregnancies in a large sample of women who had been hospitalised in Mother and Baby Units in France [128]. In a US sample, fetal death or the death of an infant in the first year after delivery was associated with hospitalisation for a suicide attempt in a case-control study [129]. An association between attempted and completed suicide and perinatal loss (miscarriage, stillbirth, termination of pregnancy) has also been observed in Taiwan [130]. In the UK, the Confidential Enquiries into Maternal Deaths have highlighted the need for monitoring and support of the mental health of women who lose a baby, due to findings that women who have experienced pregnancy loss (including miscarriage, stillbirth or neonatal death, or when separated from a child in the context of safeguarding concerns) make up a significant proportion of those who died by suicide in pregnancy or the first postnatal year [131].

Impact on the Couple Relationship and Wider Family

Overall, research that has examined the impact of perinatal loss on partners suggests that they are less affected than women [132, 133]. However, it may also be that men cope with loss differently [134] and experience even further disenfranchisement of grief than women [135], an experience that has also been described for same-sex female partners [136]. The psychological needs of the woman and her partner may also have varying courses, with each partner having different needs at different times [137]. Couples may experience difficulties with communication, sex and intimacy, discordant coping and incongruent grieving following perinatal loss [138]. These factors may help to explain the finding that couple relationships have a greater risk of dissolving after miscarriage or stillbirth, when compared to couples who have had a live birth [139].

There is little research in relation to perinatal loss and the quality of the mother–infant relationship with subsequent children following loss. Two studies have examined the mother–infant attachment relationship in mothers with a history of perinatal loss. In a longitudinal study of mothers who previously had lost a baby after 18 weeks' gestation, a greater proportion of the next-born infants were classified as disorganised in their attachment relationship with their mother compared to a non-bereaved control group [140]. In this study, the relationship between perinatal loss and disorganised mother–infant attachment was accounted for by the mother's unresolved state of mind with respect to loss or trauma and not by PTSD status [140, 141]. However, follow-up assessments when the children were 6–8 years old found that infant disorganisation was not associated with later child vulnerability, and only modest differences were observed between index and control children [142]. Another study examined the impact of perinatal loss on maternal sensitivity and mother–infant attachment within a larger longitudinal study where mothers were recruited in pregnancy and followed up postnatally. In this community sample, 28% of the sample (N=58) experienced at least one experience of perinatal loss [143]. There was some evidence that a greater number of perinatal losses and later gestational age of the loss was associated with less optimal parent–infant attachment but this could not be explained by lower maternal sensitivity. Further research is needed with larger sample sizes.

There is some evidence that mothers report greater concern about children's physical well-being and have concerns about separation in next-born children following loss [144]. However, other studies which have examined mother's self-reported perceived bonding or maternal attitudes towards their subsequent child have found no or minimal differences between mothers who have or have not experienced perinatal loss [123, 145, 146]. It thus remains inconclusive about whether a history of perinatal loss poses any unique risk for difficulties in the relationship with a subsequent child. However, given that there is an increased risk of mental health problems in subsequent pregnancies amongst women who have a history of perinatal loss, and the known impact of maternal mental health for the fetus and infant [147], the treatment of mental health problems in women who have experienced loss should be seen as a priority for improving the long-term outcomes for future children.

Vulnerability Factors for Complicated Grief and Mental Health Problems Following Perinatal Loss

A history of mental health problems or psychiatric disorders is one of the most consistent predictors of mental health problems following perinatal loss [110, 148] and has been associated with prolonged or complicated grief [149] and with greater self-stigma following stillbirth [150]. Higher levels of subjectively perceived emotional support from friends and family have been found to be negatively correlated with grief intensity [151, 152] and with a reduced risk of mental health problems following loss [153]. There is also evidence that women's self-reported satisfaction with care from hospital staff and other support organisations is associated with reduced symptoms of depression and grief [154].

The research related to circumstances around perinatal loss and how this may contribute to the development of mental health problems is mixed. There is inconclusive evidence regarding gestational age and how this may impact women's psychological adjustment following loss. In the context of PTSD, neither type of loss nor gestational age appears to exert a significant effect [110]. In the case of grief intensity or symptoms of depression and anxiety, there is some evidence that the loss of a baby at an earlier gestational age may be associated with less psychological distress [151, 155]. However, this is not consistent with other findings that have shown significant mental health symptoms in samples of women who have had early pregnancy losses [112]. It is most likely that the impact of a loss on a woman's mental health will be dependent upon multiple factors, and individualised assessments should determine clinical need. Thus, it is recommended that all women who experience perinatal loss, no matter the gestational age, are seen as at an increased risk for experiencing a mental health problem and support and monitoring be provided.

There is mixed evidence as to the benefit of women seeing and holding their baby after death in cases of stillbirth or neonatal loss. Most women and couples describe finding this process helpful in legitimising their loss, but it may also increase risk of PTSD in some circumstances [110]. There is some evidence that professional support in preparing parents for seeing their baby and sharing memories of their baby with others may help to reduce risk of PTSD [156, 157].

Psychosocial Treatments and Perinatal Loss

In contrast to recommendations for antenatal and postnatal contacts with women to include screening for depression and anxiety, there is no targeted screening recommended for women following perinatal loss. However, NICE recommends that all women who experience stillbirth, neonatal death or miscarriage are given the opportunity to talk about their experience with a health professional and are offered an evidence-based psychological intervention (CBT or EMDR if PTSD is identified) [77]. NICE recommends that information about counselling and support services are provided to women following ectopic pregnancy and miscarriage [94]. Many people will find the support from charity organisations helpful, particularly for peer support and to meet others who can understand the experience of perinatal loss and the unique nature of this kind of grief.

The value of high-quality bereavement care in maternity should not be underestimated. The delivery of compassionate and sensitive care in maternity has been identified as essential by women who experience perinatal loss and is considered best practice by maternity professionals [158]. Maternity professionals can provide emotional support, physical health monitoring and guidance around investigations and options for making funeral and burial arrangements. The benefit of high-quality maternity care with continuity of carer has also been identified as beneficial for those pregnant following perinatal loss [122]. In the UK, National Bereavement Care Pathways (NBCP) have been established to guide healthcare organisations and professionals in providing parent-led and psychologically informed care for parents who experience perinatal loss [91, 159]. The NBCP place an emphasis on professionals' use of language and sensitive communication, continuity of care, involving parents in decisions relating to the care of themselves and their babies, offering opportunities for parents to make memories following the death of their baby, and ensuring professionals are aware of previous losses in subsequent pregnancies. It recommends that all bereaved parents are provided with information about how to access emotional support following loss and that professionals make referrals for mental health support when this is requested. The NBCP also promote training of healthcare staff in the delivery of high-quality bereavement care. Many hospital trusts across England have signed up to the NBCP standards and it is hoped that eventually NBCP will be adopted by all trusts. An initial evaluation of the NBCP standards has been favourable but does not include an evaluation of women's experience of accessing psychological support following perinatal loss [91].

Recent investment in Perinatal Mental Health Services in England and Scotland has resulted in the development of new psychological therapies services working closely with maternity units, called Maternal Mental Health Services in England [160] and Maternity and Neonatal Psychological Interventions (MNPI) services in Scotland [161]. In England, these services are designed to improve psychologically informed care in maternity and increase access to specialist psychological therapy for women who experience mental health problems following perinatal loss when this is needed. In Scotland, services have been established in larger delivery units in the first instance. The MNPI services have a similar remit to services in England, to support parents who have significant adverse mental health consequences following perinatal loss, as part of a wider bereavement pathway.

There have been limited randomised controlled trials (RCTs) evaluating the effectiveness of specific psychological interventions in the context of perinatal loss. Where there have been studies, CBT and interpersonal therapy (IPT) have been applied in the context of complicated grief and depression respectively [162, 163, 164, 165]. Kersting and colleagues delivered an online guided self-help CBT intervention to a community sample of help-seeking women. Results from the RCT showed a reduction in prolonged grief, depression, anxiety and post-traumatic stress for those in the treatment group [163]. In the study that applied IPT, it focused on those with a clinical diagnosis of major depression following loss and found group IPT to be superior to a group CBT intervention for depression on almost all measured outcomes [162].

There is one RCT that has been conducted with couples with the aim of preventing poor mental health adjustment following termination for fetal anomaly, randomising women to counselling support versus treatment as usual but found no difference between groups in terms of depression, anxiety or grief [166]. Another RCT compared different forms of support for couples who experienced miscarriage, including access to three sessions of nurse counselling, self-help or a combination of both and found the greatest benefit from the nurse counselling in reducing grief and depression [167]. A meta-analysis which evaluated a wide range of psychosocial interventions (e.g. counselling, psychoeducation, psychological interventions) following perinatal loss concluded that overall psychosocial interventions are effective in reducing symptoms of depression, anxiety and grief [168]. However, the majority of studies included in this review were of poor quality and few have specifically targeted those who develop a mental health problem. Given the paucity of high-quality research related to the application of psychological interventions in the context of perinatal loss, it is advised that women are referred for evidence-based psychological therapies in line with the presenting problem as would be the case for women who have a live baby in the perinatal period (see Chapter 28 on psychological therapies).

There is an urgent need for more research examining the efficacy of psychological therapy for different kinds of mental health problems following perinatal loss. Future studies need to include appropriate comparison groups and follow-up, where mental health and the quality of mother–infant relationship in future pregnancies can be assessed. Additional research regarding the acceptability of screening for mental health problems following perinatal loss and the impact of psychologically informed maternity care in reducing mental health problems following perinatal loss is also needed.

Perinatal Loss Summary

Women who experience perinatal loss are at increased risk of developing a mental health problem in the period following the loss event and in subsequent pregnancies. A woman's obstetric history and the impact of any perinatal loss should be considered in women's mental health assessment, formulation and treatment.

Chapter Summary and Key Clinical Implications

The journey to parenthood can be a complicated one for many, and where difficulties with conception or pregnancy occur, it can have a significant impact on mental health. It is estimated that one in seven couples in the UK will experience difficulties with conception, with ART treatments on the rise globally. When conception is achieved, approximately one in four pregnancies end in loss. While recognising the limitations in the quantity and quality of research in this area, current research suggests the following:

Infertility and ART

- Undergoing fertility treatments can adversely affect psychological well-being and impact on the couple relationship
- Women trying to conceive seem to be affected to a greater extent than men
- Those with a history of mental health difficulties appear more at risk of psychological difficulties
- Unsuccessful ART treatments increase the likelihood of mental health difficulties
- Pregnancies following ART are perceived as more rewarding and satisfying, though there is also an increased risk of pregnancy-specific anxiety

- Postnatal adjustment is similar to comparison groups, with the exception of an increased likelihood of protectiveness towards children
- Sensitive and empathic care from professionals is needed to attend to the emotional needs of those experiencing infertility or undergoing ART

Perinatal Loss

- Perinatal loss is common, with one in four pregnancies ending in loss
- Women are at increased risk for experiencing mental health problems following perinatal loss and in subsequent pregnancies, when compared with non-bereaved women and mothers
- Perinatal loss can have an impact on fathers and partners, and the quality of the couple relationship
- Research is inconclusive about the impact of perinatal loss on women's relationship with future children. However, the increased incidence of mental health problems in this group may convey risk to future children
- Women with a history of mental health problems are especially vulnerable to experiencing mental health difficulties following loss
- Satisfaction with support from friends and family and professionals may reduce the risk of mental health problems in parents following perinatal loss
- There is a need for more research to evaluate the effectiveness of psychological interventions in those who have pre-existing mental health problems or develop a mental health problems following perinatal loss

Based on these findings, it is recommended that:

- For all women, clinicians enquire about any fertility treatments, the number of previous pregnancies and her obstetric history to allow for discussion about infertility, any experiences of pregnancy or baby loss and the possible impact on her mental health
- Clinicians acknowledge any challenges to attaining pregnancy and the significance of loss for women and couples. Consider sensitivity in the language used when talking about fertility and loss with women and their families. Be led by the person and what language they prefer to use and feel comfortable with (e.g. baby, fetus, name of baby)
- Clinicians inquire about the presence of mental health problems, including any post-traumatic stress symptoms following ART and perinatal loss to inform appropriate onward referrals for psychological therapy
- Clinicians offer evidence-based psychological therapies when there is an identifiable mental health problem, with couples therapy being offered where appropriate
- Clinicians recognise the emotional impact of infertility, ART and perinatal loss in the absence of an identifiable mental health problem. If the woman believes that she would benefit from professional emotional support, ensure that she and her family are aware of what support is available locally (e.g. counselling and/or support from relevant charity organisations). It is also recommended that women are provided with information about how they can access support for their mental health in the future, should their needs change, or they become pregnant
- Clinicians include partners and families in mental health assessments. Partners or family members may need signposting to access their own psychological support

References

1. F Zegers-Hochschild, GD Adamson, J de Mouzon, O Ishihara, R Mansour, K Nygren, et al. International Committee for Monitoring Assisted Reproductive Technology (ICMART) and the World Health Organization (WHO) revised glossary of ART terminology, 2009. *Fertil Steril.* 2009 Nov; 92(5):1520–4.
2. MN Mascarenhas, SR Flaxman, T Boerma, S Vanderpoel, GA Stevens. National, regional, and global trends in infertility prevalence since 1990: a systematic analysis of 277 health surveys. *PLoS Med.* 2012 Dec 18;9(12).
3. National Institute for Health and Care Excellence (NICE). Fertility problems: assessment and treatment. Clinical Guideline (CG156). 2013. Updated 2017. www.nice.org.uk/guidance/cg156
4. The ESHRE Capri Workshop Group. Nutrition and reproduction in women. *Hum Reprod Update.* 2006 Jun 1;12(3):193–207.
5. Human Fertilisation and Embryology Authority. Fertility treatment 2019: trends and figures. 2021.
6. Centre for Disease Control and Prevention. 2019 assisted reproductive technology: fertility clinic and national summary report. 2021.
7. A Pinborg, CO Hougaard, A Nyboe Andersen, D Molbo, L Schmidt. Prospective longitudinal cohort study on cumulative 5-year delivery and adoption rates among 1338 couples initiating infertility treatment. *Hum Reprod.* 2008 Dec 26;24(4):991–9.
8. P Troude, G Santin, J Guibert, J Bouyer, E de La Rochebrochard. Seven out of 10 couples treated by IVF achieve parenthood following either treatment, natural conception or adoption. *Reprod Biomed Online.* 2016 Nov;33(5): 560–7.
9. J Stanhiser, AZ Steiner. Psychosocial aspects of fertility and assisted reproductive technology. *Obstet Gynecol Clin North Am.* 2018 Sep;45(3):563–74.
10. M Sälevaara, R-L Punamäki, L Unkila-Kallio, M Vänskä, M Tulppala, A Tiitinen. The mental health of mothers and fathers during pregnancy and early parenthood after successful oocyte donation treatment: a nested case-control study. *Acta Obstet Gynecol Scand.* 2018 Dec;97(12):1478–85.
11. A González-Rodríguez, J Cobo, V Soria, J Usall, C Garcia-Rizo, M Bioque, et al. Women undergoing hormonal treatments for infertility: a systematic review on psychopathology and newly diagnosed mood and psychotic disorders. *Front Psychiatry.* 2020;11:479.
12. A Malina, JA Pooley. Psychological consequences of IVF fertilization: review of research. *Ann Agric Environ Med.* 2017;24(4):554–8.
13. EW Freeman, AS Boxer, K Rickels, R Tureck, L Mastroianni. Psychological evaluation and support in a program of in vitro fertilization and embryo transfer. *Fertil Steril.* 1985 Jan 1;43(1):48–53.
14. RJ Edelmann, KJ Connolly. Gender differences in response to infertility and infertility investigations: real or illusory. *Br J Health Psychol.* 2000 Nov;5(4):365–75.
15. AD Domar, K Rooney, MR Hacker, D Sakkas, LE Dodge. Burden of care is the primary reason why insured women terminate in vitro fertilization treatment. *Fertil Steril.* 2018 Jun;109(6):1121–26.
16. P Slade, J Emery, BA Lieberman. A prospective, longitudinal study of emotions and relationships in in-vitro fertilization treatment. *Hum Reprod.* 1997 Jan 1;12(1):183–90.
17. CM Verhaak, JMJ Smeenk, MJ Nahuis, JAM Kremer, DDM Braat. Long-term psychological adjustment to IVF/ICSI treatment in women. *Hum Reprod.* 2007 Jan;22(1):305–8.
18. CM Verhaak, AME Lintsen, AWM Evers, DDM Braat. Who is at risk of emotional problems and how do you know? Screening of women going for IVF treatment. *Hum Reprod.* 2010 May 1;25(5):1234–40.

19. F Agostini, F Monti, M Paterlini, F Andrei, S Palomba, GB La Sala. Effect of the previous reproductive outcomes in subfertile women after in vitro fertilization (IVF) and/or intracytoplasmic sperm injection (ICSI) treatments on perinatal anxious and depressive symptomatology. *J Psychosom Obstet Gynecol.* 2018 Jan 2;39(1): 29–37.

20. Y El Kissi, AB Romdhane, S Hidar, S Bannour, K Ayoubi Idrissi, H Khairi, et al. General psychopathology, anxiety, depression and self-esteem in couples undergoing infertility treatment: a comparative study between men and women. *Eur J Obstet Gynecol Reprod Biol.* 2013 Apr;167(2):185–9.

21. B Kumbak, IE Atak, R Attar, G Yildirim, N Yesildaglar, C Ficicioglu. Psychological status of husbands and wives during the treatment in couples undergoing assisted reproductive treatment in Turkey. *Fertil Steril.* 2009 Sep 1;92(3):S256.

22. F Monti, F Agostini, P Fagandini, M Paterlini, GB La Sala, I Blickstein. Anxiety symptoms during late pregnancy and early parenthood following assisted reproductive technology. *J Perinat Med.* 2008 Jan 1;36(5).

23. H Volgsten, A Skoog Svanberg, L Ekselius, O Lundkvist, I SundstromPoromaa. Prevalence of psychiatric disorders in infertile women and men undergoing in vitro fertilization treatment. *Hum Reprod.* 2008 Jun 20;23(9):2056–63.

24. L Salih Joelsson, T Tydén, K Wanggren, MK Georgakis, J Stern, A Berglund, et al. Anxiety and depression symptoms among sub-fertile women, women pregnant after infertility treatment, and naturally pregnant women. *Eur Psychiatry.* 2017 Sep;45:212–19.

25. MA Becker, A Chandy, JLW Mayer, J Sachdeva, ES Albertini, C Sham, et al. Psychiatric aspects of infertility. *Am J Psychiatry.* 2019 Sep;176(9):765–6.

26. MV Seeman. Transient psychosis in women on clomiphene, bromocriptine, domperidone and related endocrine drugs. *Gynecol Endocrinol.* 2015 Oct 3;31(10):751–4.

27. CAM Bouwmans, BAME Lintsen, M Al, CM Verhaak, RJC Eijkemans, JDF Habbema, et al. Absence from work and emotional stress in women undergoing IVF or ICSI: an analysis of IVF-related absence from work in women and the contribution of general and emotional factors. *Acta Obstet Gynecol Scand.* 2008;87(11):1169–75.

28. S Gameiro, AW van den Belt-Dusebout, JMJ Smeenk, DDM Braat, FE van Leeuwen, CM Verhaak. Women's adjustment trajectories during IVF and impact on mental health 11–17 years later. *Hum Reprod.* 2016 Aug 1;31(8):1788–98.

29. F Gressier, A Letranchant, O Cazas, AL Sutter-Dallay, B Falissard, P Hardy. Post-partum depressive symptoms and medically assisted conception: a systematic review and meta-analysis. *Hum Reprod.* 2015 Nov;30(11):2575–86.

30. H Volgsten, AS Svanberg, P Olsson. Unresolved grief in women and men in Sweden three years after undergoing unsuccessful in vitro fertilization treatment. *Acta Obstet Gynecol Scand.* 2010;89(10):1290–7.

31. LM Stewart, CDJ Holman, JB Semmens, D Preen, Q Mai, R Hart. Hospital mental health admissions in women after unsuccessful infertility treatment and in vitro fertilization: an Australian population-based cohort study. *PLoS ONE.* 2015 Mar 25;10(3):e0120076.

32. B Baldur-Felskov, SK Kjaer, V Albieri, M Steding-Jessen, T Kjaer, C Johansen, et al. Psychiatric disorders in women with fertility problems: results from a large Danish register-based cohort study. *Hum Reprod.* 2013 Mar;28(3):683–90.

33. TK Kjaer, A Jensen, SO Dalton, C Johansen, S Schmiedel, SK Kjaer. Suicide in Danish women evaluated for fertility problems. *Hum Reprod.* 2011 Sep;26(9):2401–7.

34. S Gameiro, A Finnigan. Long-term adjustment to unmet parenthood goals

following ART: a systematic review and meta-analysis. *Hum Reprod Update.* 2017 May 1;23(3):322–37.

35. J Boivin, E Griffiths, CA Venetis. Emotional distress in infertile women and failure of assisted reproductive technologies: meta-analysis of prospective psychosocial studies. *BMJ.* 2011 Feb 23;342:d223.

36. R Wamser-Nanney. Trauma exposure, PTSD and indices of fertility. *J Psychosom Obstet Gynecol.* 2020 Apr 2;41(2):116–21.

37. R Wamser-Nanney. Types of childhood maltreatment, posttraumatic stress symptoms, and indices of fertility. *Psychol Trauma.* 2022 Nov;14(8):1263–71.

38. K Gourounti. Psychological stress and adjustment in pregnancy following assisted reproductive technology and spontaneous conception: a systematic review. *Women Health.* 2016 Jan 2;56(1):98–118.

39. S Chen, T Wang, S Zhang, L Zhao, L Chen. Association between infertility treatment and perinatal depressive symptoms: a meta-analysis of observational studies. *J Psychosom Res.* 2019 May;120:110–17.

40. FL Tianyi, Y Li, F Alderdice, MA Quigley, JJ Kurinczuk, C Bankhead, C Carson. The association between conception history and subsequent postpartum depression and/or anxiety: evidence from the Clinical Practice Research Datalink 1991–2013. *J Affect Disord.* 2022 Aug 1;310:266–73.

41. J Darwiche, C Lawrence, Y Vial, D Wunder, F Stiefel, M Germond, et al. Anxiety and psychological stress before prenatal screening in first-time mothers who conceived through IVF/ICSI or spontaneously. *Women Health.* 2014 Jul 4;54(5):474–85.

42. K Gourounti, F Anagnostopoulos, K Lykeridou. Coping strategies as psychological risk factor for antenatal anxiety, worries, and depression among Greek women. *Arch Womens Ment Health.* 2013 Oct;16(5):353–61.

43. C Hashemieh, L Neisani, H Taghinejad. Assessment of anxiety in pregnancy following assisted reproductive technology (ART) and associated infertility factors in women commencing treatment. *Iran Red Crescent Med J.* 2013 Dec 5;15(12).

44. E Harf-Kashdaei, M Kaitz. Antenatal moods regarding self, baby, and spouse among women who conceived by in vitro fertilization. *Fertil Steril.* 2007 Jun;87(6):1306–13.

45. A Hjelmstedt, A-M Widström, A Collins. Psychological correlates of prenatal attachment in women who conceived after in vitro fertilization and women who conceived naturally. *Birth.* 2006 Dec;33(4):303–10.

46. SC Klock, DA Greenfeld. Psychological status of in vitro fertilization patients during pregnancy: a longitudinal study. *Fertil Steril.* 2000 Jun 1;73(6):1159–64.

47. T Munk-Olsen, E Agerbo. Does childbirth cause psychiatric disorders? A population-based study paralleling a natural experiment. *Epidemiology.* 2015 Jan;26(1):79–84.

48. J Vikstrom, A Josefsson, M Hammar, M Bladh, G Sydsjo. Risk of postpartum psychosis after IVF treatment: a nationwide case-control study. *Hum Reprod.* 2017 Jan;32(1):139–46.

49. FL Gibson, JA Ungerer, CA McMahon, GI Leslie, DM Saunders. The mother-child relationship following in vitro fertilisation (IVF): infant attachment, responsivity, and maternal sensitivity. *J Child Psychol Psychiatry.* 2000 Nov;41(8):1015–23.

50. K Hammarberg, JRW Fisher, KH Wynter. Psychological and social aspects of pregnancy, childbirth and early parenting after assisted conception: a systematic review. *Hum Reprod Update.* 2008 May 22;14(5):395–414.

51. A Hjelmstedt, A Collins. Psychological functioning and predictors of father–infant relationship in IVF fathers and controls. *Scand J Caring Sci.* 2008 Mar;22(1):72–8.

52. JC Karatas, K Barlow-Stewart, B Meiser, C McMahon, KA Strong, W Hill, et al.

A prospective study assessing anxiety, depression and maternal-fetal attachment in women using PGD. *Hum Reprod.* 2011 Jan 1;26(1):148–56.

53. CA McMahon, F Gibson, G Leslie, J Cohen, C Tennant. Parents of 5-year-old in vitro fertilization children: psychological adjustment, parenting stress and the influence of subsequent in vitro fertilization treatment. *J Fam Psychol.* 2003;17(3):361–9.

54. CA McMahon, J Boivin, FL Gibson, K Hammarberg, K Wynter, D Saunders, et al. Age at first birth, mode of conception and psychological wellbeing in pregnancy: findings from the parental age and transition to parenthood Australia (PATPA) study. *Hum Reprod.* 2011 Jun 1;26(6):1389–98.

55. L Blake, V Jadva, S Golombok. Parent psychological adjustment, donor conception and disclosure: a follow-up over 10 years. *Hum Reprod Oxf Engl.* 2014 Nov;29(11):2487–96.

56. S Imrie, S Golombok. Impact of new family forms on parenting and child development. *Annu Rev Dev Psychol.* 2020 Dec 15;2(1):295–316.

57. S Imrie, S Golombok. Long-term outcomes of children conceived through egg donation and their parents: a review of the literature. *Fertil Steril.* 2018 Dec;110(7):1187–93.

58. P Tao, R Coates, B Maycock. Investigating marital relationship in infertility: a systematic review of quantitative studies. *J Reprod Infertil.* 2012;13(2):71–80.

59. BD Peterson, CS Sejbaek, M Pirritano, L Schmidt. Are severe depressive symptoms associated with infertility-related distress in individuals and their partners? *Hum Reprod.* 2014 Jan 1;29(1):76–82.

60. K Kainz. The role of the psychologist in the evaluation and treatment of infertility. *Womens Health Issues.* 2001 Nov;11(6):481–5.

61. I Zaig, F Azem, S Schreiber, A Amit, YG Litvin, M Bloch. Psychological response and cortisol reactivity to in vitro fertilization treatment in women with a lifetime anxiety or unipolar mood disorder diagnosis. *J Clin Psychiatry.* 2013 Apr 15;74(4):386–92.

62. SR Holley, LA Pasch, ME Bleil, S Gregorich, PK Katz, NE Adler. Prevalence and predictors of major depressive disorder for fertility treatment patients and their partners. *Fertil Steril.* 2015 May;103(5):1332–9.

63. S Gameiro, J Boivin, E Dancet, C de Klerk, M Emery, C Lewis-Jones, et al. ESHRE guideline: routine psychosocial care in infertility and medically assisted reproduction – a guide for fertility staff. *Hum Reprod Oxf Engl.* 2015 Nov;30(11):2476–85.

64. C Law, L Wolfenden, M Sperlich, J Taylor. NHS England: a good practice guide to support implementation of trauma-informed care in the perinatal period. NHS England and NHS Improvement; 2021 Feb.

65. CA Blevins, FW Weathers, MT Davis, TK Witte, JL Domino. The posttraumatic stress disorder checklist for DSM-5 (PCL-5): development and initial psychometric evaluation. *J Trauma Stress.* 2015;28(6):489–98.

66. RL Spitzer, K Kroenke, JBW Williams, B Löwe. A brief measure for assessing generalized anxiety disorder: the GAD-7. *Arch Intern Med.* 2006 May 22;166(10):1092–7.

67. K Kroenke, RL Spitzer, JBW Williams. The PHQ-9. *J Gen Intern Med.* 2001 Sep;16(9):606–13.

68. J Boivin, J Takefman, A Braverman. The fertility quality of life (FertiQoL) tool: development and general psychometric properties. *Hum Reprod Oxf Engl.* 2011 Aug;26(8):2084–91.

69. JWM Aarts, IWH van Empel, J Boivin, WL Nelen, JAM Kremer, CM Verhaak. Relationship between quality of life and distress in infertility: a validation study of the Dutch FertiQoL. *Hum Reprod.* 2011 May 1;26(5):1112–18.

70. HDL Ockhuijsen, M van Smeden, A van den Hoogen, J Boivin. Validation study of

the SCREENIVF: an instrument to screen women or men on risk for emotional maladjustment before the start of a fertility treatment. *Fertil Steril.* 2017 Jun;107(6):1370–9.e5.

71. Human Fertilisation & Embryology Authority. Code of practice. Ninth ed. 2021.

72. M Crawshaw, J Hunt, J Monach, S Pike. British Infertility Counselling Association: guidelines for good practice in infertility counselling. Third edition 2012. *Hum Fertil.* 2013 Mar 1;16(1):73–88.

73. J Verkuijlen, C Verhaak, WL Nelen, J Wilkinson, C Farquhar. Psychological and educational interventions for subfertile men and women. *Cochrane Database Syst Rev.* 2016;(3). Art. No.: CD011034. DOI: 10.1002/14651858.CD011034.pub2.

74. L Ying, LH Wu, AY Loke. The effects of psychosocial interventions on the mental health, pregnancy rates, and marital function of infertile couples undergoing in vitro fertilization: a systematic review. *J Assist Reprod Genet.* 2016;33(6):689–701.

75. E Warne, M Oxlad, T Best. Evaluating group psychological interventions for mental health in women with infertility undertaking fertility treatment: a systematic review and meta-analysis. *Health Psychology Review.* 2023 Jul 3;17(3):377–401.

76. National Institute for Health and Care Excellence (NICE). Obsessive-compulsive disorder and body dysmorphic disorder: treatment. Clinical Guideline (CG31). 2005 Nov 29. www.nice.org.uk/guidance/cg31

77. National Institute for Health and Clinical Excellence (NICE). Post-traumatic stress disorder. NICE Guidance (NG 116). December 2015. www.nice.org.uk/guidance/ng116

78. National Institute for Health and Clinical Excellence (NICE). Antenatal and postnatal mental health: clinical management and service guidance. Clinical Guideline (CG192). 2018. www.nice.org.uk/guidance/cg192

79. Y Frederiksen, I Farver-Vestergaard, NG Skovgard, HJ Ingerslev, R Zachariae. Efficacy of psychosocial interventions for psychological and pregnancy outcomes in infertile women and men: a systematic review and meta-analysis. *BMJ Open.* 2015 Jan 28;5(1):e006592.

80. N Katyal, CM Poulsen, UB Knudsen, Y Frederiksen. The association between psychosocial interventions and fertility treatment outcome: a systematic review and meta-analysis. *Eur J Obstet Gynecol Reprod Biol.* 2021 Apr;259:125–32.

81. S Abdollahpour, A Taghipour, SH Mousavi Vahed, R Latifnejad Roudsari. The efficacy of cognitive behavioural therapy on stress, anxiety and depression of infertile couples: a systematic review and meta-analysis. *J Obstet Gynaecol.* 2022 Feb;42(2):188–97.

82. H Gaitzsch, J Benard, J Hugon-Rodin, L Benzakour, I Streuli. The effect of mind-body interventions on psychological and pregnancy outcomes in infertile women: a systematic review. *Arch Womens Ment Health.* 2020;23(4):479–91.

83. G Wang, X Liu, J Lei. Effects of mindfulness-based intervention for women with infertility: a systematic review and meta-analysis. *Arch Womens Ment Health.* 2023 Apr;26(2):245–58. Erratum in: *Arch Womens Ment Health.* 2023 Dec;26(6):869.

84. RH McAllister-Williams, DS Baldwin, R Cantwell, A Easter, E Gilvarry, V Glover, et al. British Association for Psychopharmacology consensus guidance on the use of psychotropic medication preconception, in pregnancy and postpartum 2017. *J Psychopharm.* 2017 May;31(5):519–52.

85. C Sylvester, M Menke, P Gopalan. Selective serotonin reuptake inhibitors and fertility: considerations for couples trying to conceive. *Harv Rev Psychiatry.* 2019;27(2):108–18.

86. J Thompson. The effectiveness of couple therapy on psychological and relational variables and pregnancy rates in couples with infertility: a systematic review. *Aus N Z J Fam Ther.* 2021 Jun;42(2):120–44.

87. SCR Broderick. *Perinatal loss: a handbook for working with women and their families.* London: CRC Print; 2012.

88. Royal College of Obstetricians & Gynaecologists. Recurrent miscarriage, investigation and treatment of couples (Green-top Guideline No. 17). 2011 Apr. www.rcog.org.uk/en/guidelines-research-services/guidelines/gtg17

89. Royal College of Obstetricians & Gynaecologists. Gestational trophoblastic disease (Green-top Guideline No. 38). 2020 Jun. www.rcog.org.uk/en/guidelines-research-services/guidelines/gtg38

90. ES Draper, ID Gallimore, LK Smith, AC Fenton, JJ Kurinczuk, PW Smith, T Boby, BN Manktelow. MBRRACE-UK Perinatal Mortality Surveillance Report UK Perinatal Deaths for Births from January to December 2019. Department of Health Sciences, University of Leicester; 2021.

91. NBCP England. 2020 impact report: National Bereavement Care Pathway (NBCP). 2020. https://nbcpathway.org.uk/professionals/nbcp-england-2020-impact-report

92. Office for National Statistics. Child and infant mortality in England and Wales. 2021 Feb. https://shorturl.at/RhK4V

93. Office for National Statistics. Unexplained deaths in infancy, England and Wales. 2021 Feb. https://shorturl.at/JjKCg

94. National Institute for Health and Clinical Excellence (NICE). Ectopic pregnancy and miscarriage: diagnosis and initial management. NICE Guidance (NG 126). Updated Nov 2021. www.nice.org.uk/guidance/ng126

95. National Perinatal Mortality Tool. 2023. www.npeu.ox.ac.uk/pmrt (accessed 15 May 24).

96. The Royal College of Pathologists. Sudden unexpected death in infancy and childhood. Multi-agency guidelines for care and investigation. The report of a working group convened by The Royal College of Pathologists and endorsed by The Royal College of Paediatrics and Child Health. 2nd edition. London: The Royal College of Pathologists; 2016.

97. S Mukherjee, DR Velez Edwards, DD Baird, DA Savitz, KE Hartmann. Risk of miscarriage among Black women and white women in a US prospective cohort study. *Am J Epidemiol.* 2013 Jun 1;177(11):1271–8.

98. J Jardine, K Walker, I Gurol-Urganci, K Webster, P Muller, J Hawdon, et al. Adverse pregnancy outcomes attributable to socioeconomic and ethnic inequalities in England: a national cohort study. *Lancet.* 2021 Nov 20;398(10314):1905–12.

99. D Kapadia, J Zhang, S Salway, J Nazroo, A Booth. Ethnic inequalities in healthcare: a rapid evidence review. University of Sheffield. 2022 Feb;166.

100. B Liu, U Nadeem, A Frick, M Alakaloko, A Bhide, B Thilaganathan. Reducing health inequality in Black, Asian and other minority ethnic pregnant women: impact of first trimester combined screening for placental dysfunction on perinatal mortality. *BJOG.* 2022 Sep;129(10):1750–6.

101. King-Hele S, Webb RT, Mortensen PB, Appleby L, Pickles A, Abel KM. Risk of stillbirth and neonatal death linked with maternal mental illness: a national cohort study. *Arch Dis Child – Fetal Neonatal Ed.* 2009 Mar 1;94(2):F105–10.

102. Office of National Statistics (ONS). Births in England and Wales: 2020. 2021 Oct. https://shorturl.at/QrRwc

103. C Everett. Incidence and outcome of bleeding before the 20th week of pregnancy: prospective study from general practice. *BMJ.* 1997 Jul 5;315(7099):32–4.

104. A Lang, AR Fleiszer, F Duhamel, W Sword, KR Gilbert, S Corsini-Munt. Perinatal loss and parental grief: the challenge of ambiguity and disenfranchised grief. *OMEGA – J Death Dying.* 2011 Oct 1;63(2):183–96.

105. FM Boyle, JC Vance, JM Najman, MJ Thearle. The mental health impact of stillbirth, neonatal death or SIDS: prevalence and patterns of distress among

mothers. *Soc Sci Med.* 1996 Oct 1;43(8):1273–82.

106. M Stroebe, H Schut. The dual process model of coping with bereavement: a decade on. *OMEGA – J Death Dying.* 2010 Dec 1;61(4):273–89.

107. RD Goldstein, RI Lederman, WG Lichtenthal, SE Morris, M Human, AJ Elliott, et al. The grief of mothers after the sudden unexpected death of their infants. *Pediatrics.* 2018 May 1;141(5):e20173651.

108. M Frost, JT Condon. The psychological sequelae of miscarriage: a critical review of the literature. *Aust N Z J Psychiatry.* 1996 Jan 1;30(1):54–62.

109. D Herbert, K Young, M Pietrusińska, A MacBeth. The mental health impact of perinatal loss: a systematic review and meta-analysis. *J Affect Disord.* 2022 Jan 15;297:118–29.

110. DM Christiansen. Posttraumatic stress disorder in parents following infant death: a systematic review. *Clin Psychol Rev.* 2017 Feb 1;51:60–74.

111. R Malouf, S Harrison, HA Burton, C Gale, A Stein, LS Franck, F Alderdice. Prevalence of anxiety and post-traumatic stress (PTS) among the parents of babies admitted to neonatal units: a systematic review and meta-analysis. *EClinicalMedicine.* 2022 Jan 1;43: 101233.

112. J Farren, M Jalmbrant, L Ameye, K Joash, N Mitchell-Jones, S Tapp, et al. Post-traumatic stress, anxiety and depression following miscarriage or ectopic pregnancy: a prospective cohort study. *BMJ Open.* 2016;6(11):e011864.

113. KJ Gold, ME Boggs, M Muzik, A Sen. Anxiety disorders and obsessive compulsive disorder 9 months after perinatal loss. *Gen Hosp Psychiatry.* 2014 Nov 1;36(6):650–4.

114. KJ Gold, I Leon, ME Boggs, A Sen. Depression and posttraumatic stress symptoms after perinatal loss in a population-based sample. *J Womens Health.* 2016 Mar;25(3):263–9.

115. ER Blackmore, D Côté-Arsenault, W Tang, V Glover, J Evans, J Golding, TG O'Connor. Previous prenatal loss as a predictor of perinatal depression and anxiety. *Br J Psychiatry.* 2011 May;198(5): 373–8.

116. J Gilden, EMP Poels, S Lambrichts, A Vreeker, MPM Boks, RA Ophoff, et al. Bipolar episodes after reproductive events in women with bipolar I disorder: a study of 919 pregnancies. *J Affect Disord.* 2021 Dec 1;295:72–9.

117. A Di Florio, L Jones, L Forty, K Gordon-Smith, N Craddock, I Jones. Bipolar disorder, miscarriage, and termination. *Bipolar Disord.* 2015;17(1):102–5.

118. D Côte-Arsenault, N Mahlangu. Impact of perinatal loss on the subsequent pregnancy and self: women's experiences. *J Obstet Gynecol Neonatal Nurs.* 1999 Jun;28(3):274–82.

119. D Armstrong, M Hutti. Pregnancy after perinatal loss: the relationship between anxiety and prenatal attachment. *J Obstet Gynecol Neonatal Nurs.* 1998 Mar;27(2):183–9.

120. L Campbell-Jackson, J Bezance, A Horsch. 'A renewed sense of purpose': mothers' and fathers' experience of having a child following a recent stillbirth. *BMC Pregnancy Childbirth.* 2014 Dec 19;14(1):423.

121. J O'Leary. Grief and its impact on prenatal attachment in the subsequent pregnancy. *Arch Women's Ment Health.* 2004 Feb 1;7(1):7–18.

122. A Hunter, L Tussis, A MacBeth. The presence of anxiety, depression and stress in women and their partners during pregnancies following perinatal loss: a meta-analysis. *J Affect Disord.* 2017 Dec;223:153–64.

123. L Lee, K McKenzie-McHarg, A Horsch. The impact of miscarriage and stillbirth on maternal-fetal relationships: an integrative review. *J Reprod Infant Psychol.* 2017 Feb 1;35(1):32–52.

124. American Psychiatric Association. *Diagnostic and statistical manual of mental disorders (DSM-5).* Washington, DC: American Psychiatric Association; 2013.

125. KL Szuhany, M Malgaroli, CD Miron, NM Simon. Prolonged grief disorder: course, diagnosis, assessment, and treatment. *Focus.* 2021 Jun;19(2): 161–72.

126. A Kersting, M Dorsch, C Kreulich, M Reutemann, P Ohrmann, E Baez, et al. Trauma and grief 2–7 years after termination of pregnancy because of fetal anomalies – a pilot study. *J Psychosom Obstet Gynecol.* 2005 Mar;26(1):9–14.

127. M McSpedden, B Mullen, L Sharpe, LJ Breen, EA Lobb. The presence and predictors of complicated grief symptoms in perinatally bereaved mothers from a bereavement support organization. *Death Studies.* 2017;41(2).

128. F Gressier, V Guillard, O Cazas, B Falissard, NMC Glangeaud-Freudenthal, AL Sutter-Dallay. Risk factors for suicide attempt in pregnancy and the post-partum period in women with serious mental illnesses. *J Psychiatr Res.* 2017;84:284–91.

129. MA Schiff, DC Grossman. Adverse perinatal outcomes and risk for postpartum suicide attempt in Washington State, 1987–2001. *Pediatrics.* 2006 Sep 1;118(3):e669–75.

130. S-C Weng, J-C Chang, M-K Yeh, S-M Wang, C-S Lee, Y-H Chen. Do stillbirth, miscarriage, and termination of pregnancy increase risks of attempted and completed suicide within a year? A population-based nested case-control study. *BJOG Int J Obstet Gynaecol.* 2018;125(8):983–90.

131. R Cantwell, A Cairns, K Bunch et al. on behalf of the MBRRACE-UK mental health chapter-writing group. Improving mental health care and care for women with multiple adversity. In M Knight, K Bunch, D Tuffnell, R Patel, J Shakespeare, R Kotnis, et al. editors, on behalf of MBRRACE-UK. *Saving Lives, Improving Mothers' Care – Lessons learned to inform maternity care from the UK and Ireland Confidential Enquiries into Maternal Deaths and Morbidity 2017–19.* Oxford: National Perinatal Epidemiology Unit, University of Oxford; 2021. p. 34–51.

132. P Turton, W Badenhorst, P Hughes, J Ward, S Riches, S White. Psychological impact of stillbirth on fathers in the subsequent pregnancy and puerperium. *Br J Psychiatry.* 2006 Feb;188(2):165–72.

133. JC Vance, JM Najman, MJ Thearle, G Embelton, WJ Foster, FM Boyle. Psychological changes in parents eight months after the loss of an infant from stillbirth, neonatal death, or sudden infant death syndrome – a longitudinal study. *Pediatrics.* 1995 Nov;96(5 Pt 1):933–8.

134. HM Williams, A Topping, A Coomarasamy, LL Jones. Men and miscarriage: a systematic review and thematic synthesis. *Qual Health Res.* 2020 Jan 1;30(1):133–45.

135. KL Obst, C Due, M Oxlad, P Middleton. Men's grief following pregnancy loss and neonatal loss: a systematic review and emerging theoretical model. *BMC Pregnancy Childbirth.* 2020 Jan 10;20(1):11.

136. J Cacciatore, Z Raffo. An exploration of lesbian maternal bereavement. *Soc Work.* 2011 Apr 1;56(2):169–77.

137. J Vance, F Boyle, J Najman, M Thearle. Couple distress after sudden infant or perinatal death: a 30-month follow up. *J Paediatr Child Health.* 2002;38(4):368–72.

138. DG Wing, K Burge-Callaway, P Rose Clance, L Armistead. Understanding gender differences in bereavement following the death of an infant: implications of or treatment. *Psychother Theory Res Pract Train.* 2001;38(1):60–73.

139. KJ Gold, A Sen, RA Hayward. Marriage and cohabitation outcomes after pregnancy loss. *Pediatrics.* 2010 May 1;125(5):e1202–7.

140. P Hughes, P Turton, E Hopper, GA McGauley, P Fonagy. Disorganised attachment behaviour among infants born subsequent to stillbirth. *J Child Psychol Psychiatry.* 2001;42(6):791–801.

141. P Turton, P Hughes, P Fonagy, D Fainman. An investigation into the possible overlap between PTSD and

unresolved responses following stillbirth: an absence of linkage with only unresolved status predicting infant disorganization. *Attach Hum Dev.* 2004 Sep 1;6(3):241–53.

142. P Turton, W Badenhorst, S Pawlby, S White, P Hughes. Psychological vulnerability in children next-born after stillbirth: a case–control follow-up study. *J Child Psychol Psychiatry.* 2009;50(12):1451–8.

143. D Côté-Arsenault, EM Leerkes, N Zhou. Individual differences in maternal, marital, parenting and child outcomes following perinatal loss: a longitudinal study. *J Reprod Infant Psychol.* 2020 Jan 1;38(1):3–15.

144. SK Theut, HA Moss, MJ Zaslow, BA Rabinovich, L Levin, JJ Bartko. Perinatal loss and maternal attitudes toward the subsequent child. *Infant Ment Health J.* 1992 Sep;13(2):157–66.

145. C Bicking Kinsey, K Baptiste-Roberts, J Zhu, KH Kjerulff. Effect of miscarriage history on maternal-infant bonding during the first year postpartum in the First Baby Study: a longitudinal cohort study. *BMC Womens Health.* 2014 Jul 15;14(1):83.

146. SK Theut, HA Moss, MJ Zaslow, BA Rabinovich, L Levin, JJ Bartko. Perinatal loss and maternal attitudes toward the subsequent child. *Infant Ment Health J.* 1992;13(2):157–66.

147. A Stein, RM Pearson, SH Goodman, E Rapa, A Rahman, M McCallum, et al. Effects of perinatal mental disorders on the fetus and child. *Lancet.* 2014 Nov 15;384(9956):1800–19.

148. V Daugirdaitė, O van den Akker, S Purewal. Posttraumatic stress and posttraumatic stress disorder after termination of pregnancy and reproductive loss: a systematic review. *J Pregnancy.* 2015 Feb 5;2015.

149. R Neugebauer, J Kline, P Shrout, A Skodol, P O'Connor, PA Geller, et al. Major depressive disorder in the 6 months after miscarriage. *JAMA.* 1997 Feb 5;277(5):383–8.

150. D Pollock, E Pearson, M Cooper, T Ziaian, C Foord, J Warland. Breaking the silence: determining prevalence and understanding stillbirth stigma. *Midwifery.* 2021 Feb 1;93:102884.

151. HJEM Janssen, MCJ Cuisinier, KPHM de Graauw, KAL Hoogduin. A prospective study of risk factors predicting grief intensity following pregnancy loss. *Arch Gen Psychiatry.* 1997 Jan 1;54(1): 56–61.

152. LJ Toedter, JN Lasker, HJ Janssen. International comparison of studies using the perinatal grief scale: a decade of research on pregnancy loss. *Death Stud.* 2001 May;25(3):205–28.

153. MH Hutti, DS Armstrong, JA Myers, LA Hall. Grief intensity, psychological well-being, and the intimate partner relationship in the subsequent pregnancy after a perinatal loss. *J Obstet Gynecol Neonatal Nurs.* 2015 Jan;44(1):42–50.

154. F Demontigny, C Verdon, S Meunier, D Dubeau. Women's persistent depressive and perinatal grief symptoms following a miscarriage: the role of childlessness and satisfaction with healthcare services. *Arch Womens Ment Health.* 2017 Oct;20:655–62.

155. SM Bennett, BT Litz, S Maguen, JT Ehrenreich. An exploratory study of the psychological impact and clinical care of perinatal loss. *J Loss Trauma.* 2008 Nov 6;13(6):485–510.

156. K Ryninks, C Roberts-Collins, K McKenzie-McHarg, A Horsch. Mothers' experience of their contact with their stillborn infant: an interpretative phenomenological analysis. *BMC Pregnancy Childbirth.* 2014 Jun 13;14(1):203.

157. R Crawley, S Lomax, S Ayers. Recovering from stillbirth: the effects of making and sharing memories on maternal mental health. *J Reprod Infant Psychol.* 2013 Apr 1;31(2):195–207.

158. D Bakhbakhi, C Burden, C Storey, D Siassakos. Care following stillbirth in high-resource settings: latest evidence, guidelines, and best practice points.

Semin Fetal Neonatal Med. 2017 Jun 1;22(3):161–6.

159. The National Bereavement Care Pathway Project. The National Bereavement Care Pathway. 2024. www.nbcpscotland.org.uk (accessed 15 May 2024).

160. National Health Service. The NHS Long Term Plan. 2019 Jan. www.longtermplan.nhs.uk/publication/nhs-long-term-plan

161. NHS Scotland. Delivering effective services: needs assessment and service recommendations for specialist and universal perinatal mental health services. Perinatal Mental Health Network Scotland. 2019. www.pmhn.scot.nhs.uk/wp-content/uploads/2019/03/PMHN-Needs-Assessment-Report.pdf

162. JE Johnson, AB Price, JC Kao, K Fernandes, R Stout, RL Gobin, et al. Interpersonal psychotherapy (IPT) for major depression following perinatal loss: a pilot randomized controlled trial. *Arch Womens Ment Health.* 2016 Oct 1;19(5):845–59.

163. A Kersting, R Dölemeyer, J Steinig, F Walter, K Kroker, K Baust, et al. Brief internet-based intervention reduces posttraumatic stress and prolonged grief in parents after the loss of a child during pregnancy: a randomized controlled trial. *Psychother Psychosom.* 2013;82(6):372–81.

164. A Kersting, K Kroker, S Schlicht, K Baust, B Wagner. Efficacy of cognitive behavioral internet-based therapy in parents after the loss of a child during pregnancy: pilot data from a randomized controlled trial. *Arch Womens Ment Health.* 2011;14:465–77.

165. R Neugebauer, J Kline, J Markowitz, K Bleiberg, L Baxi, M Rosing, et al. Pilot randomized controlled trial of interpersonal counseling for subsyndromal depression following miscarriage. *J Clin Psychiatry.* 2006; 67(8):14541.

166. RJ Lilford, P Stratton, S Godsil, A Prasad. A randomised trial of routine versus selective counselling in perinatal bereavement from congenital disease. *BJOG Int J Obstet Gynaecol.* 1994;101(4):291–6.

167. KM Swanson, H-T Chen, JC Graham, DM Wojnar, A Petras. Resolution of depression and grief during the first year after miscarriage: a randomized controlled clinical trial of couples-focused interventions. *J Womens Health.* 2009 Aug 1;18(8):1245–57.

168. L Shaohua, S Shorey. Psychosocial interventions on psychological outcomes of parents with perinatal loss: a systematic review and meta-analysis. *Int J Nurs Stud.* 2021 May 1;117:103871.

Chapter 9

The Evolving Leader in Perinatal Mental Health Services

Thinking, Practice and Relationships

Michael Hobkirk and Graham Lee

Introduction

Perinatal mental health problems worsen outcomes for mothers, babies, families and society as a whole. About 20% of women experience mental health challenges in the first year after childbirth, with mental health causes contributing to 23% of maternal deaths [1]. In the UK, perinatal depression, anxiety and psychosis cost society approximately £8.1 billion in the long term, equating to roughly £10,000 for each birth. Surprisingly, improving recognition and treatment of these conditions would cost only about £400 per birth on average [2].

Despite these clear challenges, various barriers hinder access to perinatal mental health services at different levels [3]. One major obstacle is the lack of knowledge about perinatal mental health among healthcare providers, women and their families. This leads to difficulties in recognising symptoms, referral delays and uncertainty about the role of health visitors. Negative attitudes towards diagnosing and treating perinatal mental illness further discourage women from seeking help, adding to feelings of stigma and guilt. Organisational issues such as limited resources, fragmented services and poor communication between healthcare disciplines exacerbate these individual-level challenges. Operational issues like ineffective policy implementation and sociocultural factors such as tensions between different professional groups and language barriers also hinder access to services for this demographic.

An independent investigation into serious shortcomings in maternity services at Morecambe Bay NHS Trust underscored the importance of a professional culture prioritising high-quality care [4]. This culture, fostered by leadership and commitment from individual healthcare professionals, teams and senior management, emphasises collaboration across different professional disciplines. Partnering with mental health charities can strengthen women's resilience and improve mental health outcomes while integrating health and social care services benefits organisations, service users and caregivers alike [5, 6].

'Leadership' is a very fashionable term and firmly established in the lexicon of managers in both the private and public sectors and within domestic and international politics. As a concept, it is complex, multifaceted, dynamic and invariably influenced by the context and organisational culture in which it occurs.

The chapter begins with an overview of different ideas about leadership, examining 'wicked' and 'tame' problems, the distinction between leadership and management, psychiatrists as leaders and different leadership styles. We then discuss the recently emerging field of systemic leadership. We explore the role of contention, developing collaborative relationships, the centrality of developing relational trust, working with diversity and the ubiquitous influence of conflict in organisations. The chapter concludes with a discussion focused on service development, compassionate leadership and patient empowerment. Throughout, we will explore leadership through multiple lenses to unlock new possibilities for practice.

What Is Leadership?

There is little consensus on the basic meaning of leadership, how we should teach leadership or whether its effects can be measured and predicted [7]. Indeed, the concepts of leadership and management overlap [8]. However, the following four-fold typology encompasses a significant proportion of leadership definitions [7]:

1. **Leadership as person** – *who* leaders are; their personality traits, skills and standards of personal effectiveness
2. **Leadership as process** – *how* leaders get things done; social interactions, attempts at influence, communication, empathy, empowerment and coaching
3. **Leadership as position** – *where* leaders operate; as defined by organisational leadership roles, position, authority and professional status
4. **Leadership as results** – *what* leaders achieve

The above classification is practical and non-hierarchical, and real-world examples of leadership are likely to embody all four elements.

Wicked and Tame Problems

Leaders in complex systems tend to face what Rittel and Webber term 'wicked problems' [9].

Wicked Problems

Wicked problems are complex rather than just complicated (i.e. they are highly relational and cannot be removed from their environment, solved and returned without affecting the environment) [7]. There are no apparent answers; typically, applying several solutions to resolve the problem does not achieve sustained success. Wicked problems are common and tend to be sociopolitical, chronic and 'messy'. There is a high degree of uncertainty and no clear relationship between cause and effect, for example crime or poverty.

Examples of wicked problems in psychiatry include:

- the prevalence of perinatal mental illness in the community
- the contestable nature of professional knowledge; alternative views can be found (even in the same team) on the interventions which practitioners might use
- limited understanding of disease
- lack of suitable or available treatments
- a scarcity of appropriate teams and facilities
- maximising the quality of care while minimising the cost of care
- addressing central concerns (government, trust boards) as well as local needs.

Tame Problems

Applying logic and clear pathways or protocols solves tame problems even if they are complicated. They are likely to have occurred before and engender a limited degree of uncertainty. We primarily teach students and trainees to solve tame clinical problems. Examples of tame problems in psychiatry include:

- diagnosing perinatal mental health problems
- Mental Health Act assessments
- responding to complaints
- supporting an underperforming colleague
- workforce planning.

Modern Definitions of Leadership and Management

Grint suggests that leadership is 'the art of engaging a group or community into facing its wicked problems' [7]. In contrast, management provides an appropriate process to solve a 'tame problem'.

The Role of the Leader

Every psychiatrist will recognise the description of wicked problems; we face them daily. Wicked problems do not need leaders with the correct answers but leaders able to ask the right questions. By definition, wicked problems are not amenable to obvious solutions; finding solutions should lie with the practitioners facing the issue on the frontline. The role of the leader is to enable others to create their solutions to wicked problems. Successful leaders are leaders of teams and do not automatically assume the role of 'expert'; they acknowledge the strengths and expertise of all, activate the group's collective intelligence and reject the myth of the hero leader. Leading teams requires the leader to be less decisive and more reflective.

Unfortunately, in mental healthcare, the assumption often prevails that a logical and straightforward solution exists for most problems; for example, identify best practice examples, find the suitable management model, apply the lessons and fix the system. By behaving as if a wicked problem is a tame problem (through performance and change management, staff forums and conferences with expert panels), the wicked problem will, in time, surface with changed constraints, volatile requirements or resistance from colleagues and service users. This pretence is a recipe for disaster. One can also justify a lack of intervention by falsely labelling a tame problem as wicked.

The third type of problem is the 'crisis', such as a medical emergency or loss of critical funding. Crises require the leader to assume command, take decisive action (although it is also possible to be decisively wrong!) and answer the problem. These behaviours contrast with engaging standard techniques (management) or asking questions (leadership). When faced with a problem in the workplace, ask yourself – is this wicked, tame or a crisis (Figure 9.1)?

As psychiatrists, we might do well to adopt a healthy cynicism about most leadership theories. Many are ill-defined, poorly differentiated and lack empirical testing or predictive value. Few studies attempt to compare theories, and there is a reliance on common sense and intuition, for example, 'a good leader is a good listener'. Newly produced leadership texts and policies build on many existing discourses creating a mosaic of leadership themes through a stochastic process.

What Is Management?

Management is defined and described by the Royal College of Psychiatrists as 'getting things done well through and with people, creating an environment in which people can

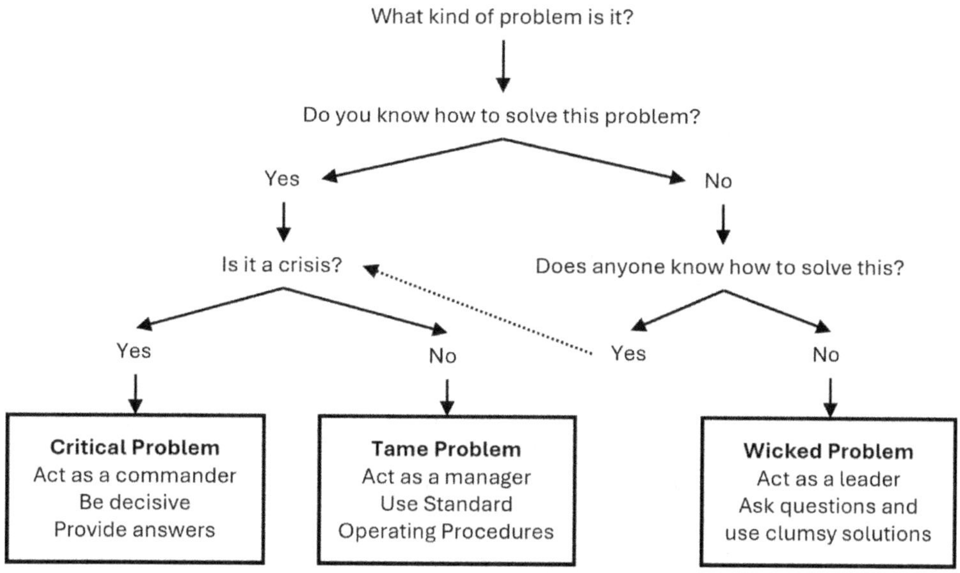

Figure 9.1 Wicked, tame and crisis problems.

perform as individuals and yet collaborate towards achieving group goals and removing obstacles to such performance' [10].

In essence, management directs flows of resources to achieve defined objectives and requires readiness and the ability to complete tasks [11]. Kotter distinguishes leadership from management as follows (Table 9.1) [12]:

Managers are central to maintaining performance in healthcare organisations and, like doctors, employ practical skills to improve patient care [13]. In addition to general administrative skills, managers often gain specialist expertise in disciplines beyond a doctor's practice, including human resources, procurement, IT and estates management. Managers face unique and significant challenges:

- They work in systems with intrinsic tensions where short-term political imperatives clash with long-term practical strategic management.
- Repeated reorganisations call for them to adjust their focus accordingly.
- Non-clinical managers change posts more frequently than medical leaders, and relationships must be re-established.
- Managers respond to public scrutiny.

Nearly all psychiatrists work alongside managers, but many psychiatrists fail to comprehend what managers do or recognise them as partners in enhancing patient care. This lack of awareness can create a harmful doctor-managerial divide despite most psychiatrists acting as managers in some capacity.

As psychiatrists, are we responsible for developing our relationships with managers? Should this relationship-building be a formal requirement? How can managers support this? The dynamic nature of doctor–manager relationships necessitates regular dialogue between both parties. In a successful partnership, the work of the doctor and manager is mutually enhanced, and there is agreement about optimal short- and long-term goals.

Table 9.1 Differences between leadership and management

	Leadership	Management
Focus	Establishing direction with vision and strategy	Planning and budgeting with actions and timetables
Colleagues	Aligning with vision through collaboration and influence	Organising through structure and allocation
Acts	Motivating, inspiring, engaging and energising	Controlling, monitoring and problem-solving
Results	Positive and potentially dramatic	Order, consistency and predictability

By developing a greater understanding of the function and purpose of managerial tasks, psychiatrists can contribute significantly to their impact.

A leader's key objective might be to foster and maintain complementarity between leadership and management.

What Is Medical Leadership?

In its broadest sense, the term 'medical leadership' encapsulates the concept of doctors undertaking leadership roles. The term 'clinical leadership' (leadership delivered by a spectrum of clinical professionals) is often used by commentators when the precise meaning is 'medical leadership' (leadership that doctors offer) [14]. This misuse is evident throughout the leadership development literature. This conflation is potentially problematic given that leadership provided by doctors is informed by a unique combination of professional values, practices and training.

Psychiatrists as Leaders

We deliver modern psychiatry through teamwork, and doctors thus require at least a fundamental leadership, management and relational skills competency. New psychiatrists report that they have not acquired leadership and management competency during their training, which focuses on producing competent clinicians [13]. Those aiming for senior management roles (clinical director or medical director) and managerial roles in medical education and academia will require higher competency levels. Historically, the National Health Service (NHS) prioritised investment in training individual technical skills rather than developing adaptive skills, such as teamwork and leadership.

Psychiatrists can provide leadership through enhancement of the skills required to be a good psychiatrist, including:

- an understanding of severe disturbance, interpersonal dynamics and pathological and healthy processes, particularly projection, splitting and mourning
- the ability to think in systems and groups
- expertise in managing boundaries, overcoming barriers and motivating and supporting others
- assimilating diverse and conflicting evidence.

Leadership and Excellence in Mental Health Services

The Royal College of Psychiatrists' occasional paper 'Role of the Consultant Psychiatrist: Leadership and Excellence in Mental Health Services' suggested the imperatives of leadership [15]. The authors state:

> A consultant doctor cannot usually see every patient (the money and the time are simply not there) or be personally responsible for every patient seen by a member of the team that they lead. However, a doctor can and indeed is uniquely positioned to lead a team in such a way that practice and outcomes for patients are good and are continuously improving. A doctor can be accountable for this leadership role.

An additional competency for the psychiatric leader is the ability to lead in the context of impoverished resources, low staff morale, rapid change and the threat of privatisation without compromising one's values. The idea of being 'uniquely positioned' is, of course, contestable in today's multidisciplinary thinking; other disciplines are just as well-positioned to lead a team.

Acts of Leadership

If we think of a respected and inspirational leader/manager with whom we have worked, we can consider what behaviours, skills and qualities we admire in this person. Influential acts of leadership suggested by consultant perinatal psychiatrists in 2018, and 2019 Royal College of Psychiatry Building Capacity in Perinatal Psychiatry programmes include:

Visibility: Being seen around the organisation; going to lunch/coffee with colleagues; attending ward rounds; actively teaching and attending educational meetings. Visibility allows leaders to demonstrate their passion and positivity and engage with others.

Awareness: Understanding organisation structures and power lines ('internal politics'); knowing the financial systems and funding streams; participating in social networks and being aware of critical 'hidden' roles (such as medical director, clinical director, educational supervisor) and committees (such as the ethics committee). Influential leaders keep in touch with what is going on, ask lots of questions, 'scan the environment' and keep their ears to the ground.

Integrity: Being open and upfront about one's vision, values, expectations (of others) and leadership approach. Teams value knowing their tasks and the strategic direction.

Role-modelling: Having a role model and being a role model for others increases confidence and competence.

Getting things done: Being task-orientated; awareness of how structures and systems help achieve goals. Healthcare systems are constantly evolving, and doctors must manage this change and maintain staff motivation and involvement; communication is vital and #saying what is happening as it happens'.

Adaptability: Asking, 'what does this situation need from me?'. Reflecting on colleagues and choosing the leadership style that best fits one's goals and circumstances.

Leadership Styles

Typically, the most influential leaders adapt to one or more of six distinct approaches to leadership and skilfully switch between the various styles in response to the situation

[16]. Four of these styles – visionary, coaching, affiliative and democratic – create a climate that boosts performance and builds motivation. Although useful in particular situations, two others – pace-setting and commanding – should be applied with caution. These six styles are the 'Repertoire of Leadership' (Table 9.2).

Reflective Opportunity

Which leadership style do you prefer, which are you wary of and which type would you like to demonstrate more? What would this look like if you were broadening your repertoire?

To illustrate switching between leadership styles, imagine a pregnant woman in the third trimester is admitted to the emergency department experiencing anxiety and panic attacks.

Commanding: The leader, a senior midwife, quickly assesses the situation and instructs the team to create a calm and private environment for the woman (directive approach due to the urgent need to reduce anxiety).

Pace-setting: The midwife demonstrates relaxation techniques such as deep breathing and guided imagery, encouraging the woman to participate (setting the pace for managing the anxiety).

Democratic: Once the woman is calmer, the midwife facilitates a discussion with her about her concerns and preferences for treatment, involving other healthcare professionals if needed (democratic approach to involve the woman in decision-making).

Affiliative: The midwife acknowledges the woman's distress and validates her feelings, providing emotional support and a sense of security (building trust and rapport).

Coaching: The midwife explores coping mechanisms the woman has used in the past and helps her identify strategies for managing future anxiety episodes (supporting the woman's self-management skills).

Visionary: Following the incident, the midwife leads a team meeting to discuss protocols for identifying and managing perinatal anxiety in the emergency department, aiming to improve the overall service for future patients (setting a clear vision for improved care).

This example showcases how a leader in perinatal mental health can adapt their style based on the evolving needs of the situation, from taking charge in an emergency to empowering the patient and fostering a collaborative team environment.

In daily practice, consider which style is most effective in each leadership scenario while mindful of its potential disadvantages. The positive impact of visionary leadership breaks down when middle managers misalign with senior management's strategic vision and causing change efforts to slow down or even fail. Coaching is seen as time-consuming and relies on skill, and affiliative may be unclear and unfocused. A democratic style may delay decision-making and dissipate a sense of direction, whilst pace-setting can impair communication, morale, flexibility and responsibility. Commanding may disempower and reduce job satisfaction, while authoritative may appear pompous or overbearing.

Groupthink and Confirmation Bias

We need to be alert to the dangers of groupthink and confirmation bias by using and encouraging a diversity of leadership styles and constructive criticism [17, 18].

Table 9.2 Leadership styles

Leadership Style	Description	Perinatal Mental Health Example
Democratic	Values team input and fosters buy-in for decisions.	A leader facilitates a meeting with staff from various departments (doctors, nurses, social workers, health visitors) to discuss implementing a new programme for perinatal anxiety screening. They encourage everyone to share their perspectives and collaborate on the program's design ('what do you think?').
Visionary	Motivates and inspires the team towards a shared goal.	A leader of a perinatal mental health service envisions a future where all new mothers receive postpartum depression screenings. They develop a strategic plan and inspire their team to work towards this goal, highlighting the positive impact on maternal well-being ('come with me').
Coaching	Develops staff by helping them connect their work with organisational goals.	A leader meets with a programme manager for a perinatal mental health support group. The leader helps the manager identify ways to improve group engagement and retention, aligning with the organisation's mission of providing long-term mental health support ('try this').
Affiliative	Builds trust and fosters collaboration within the team.	A leader organises a team-building activity for staff working in a perinatal mental health clinic. This activity fosters a sense of connection and strengthens communication within the team ('people come first').
Pace-setting (use with caution)	Sets a high bar for performance and motivates a skilled team.	A leader known for their expertise in perinatal mental health policy presents at a national conference, setting a high standard for advocacy and inspiring others to work towards improving access to mental health services for pregnant and postpartum women ('do as I do now').
Commanding (use with caution)	Provides clear direction and decisive action in a crisis situation.	A leader is notified of a staffing shortage in the perinatal mental health crisis team. They take decisive action to ensure continued service coverage, potentially including reassigning staff or securing temporary resources ('do what I tell you now'). It's crucial to follow up with clear communication and support for the team after the crisis.

In groupthink, we are influenced by the opinions and actions of others because we are wary of challenging others' views or creating conflict. Group members can be more concerned with reaching a consensus than discovering the best solution. Because of the lack of questioning, groupthink can also lead to overconfidence in decision-making. Confirmation bias is our tendency to seek for, interpret, prefer and recall information in a way that confirms or supports our prior beliefs or values [19]. People display this bias when choosing the data supporting their views, *ignoring* contrary data, or interpreting ambiguous evidence to support their existing attitudes. The effect is most potent for desired outcomes, emotionally charged issues and deeply entrenched beliefs. An example is online echo chambers, where people only encounter information or opinions that reflect and reinforce their own.

Compassionate Leadership

The King's Fund, a leading health think tank, asserts that 'compassionate leadership involves a focus on relationships through careful listening to, understanding, empathising with and supporting other people, enabling those we lead to feel valued, respected and cared for, so they can reach their potential and do their best work' [20]. These relational skills are further detailed by West and Eckert [21], who describe four components of compassionate leadership – attending, understanding, emphasising and helping – which are integral to patient care, staff engagement and the ability to change and innovate:

- *Attending:* Paying attention to accounts of challenges and problems experienced by colleagues. Active listening 'establishes the caring and compassionate connection necessary for strong and lasting bonds among leaders and employees'.
- *Understanding:* Empowering staff to make sense of the challenges they face. This sense-making emerges from a collaborative (non-hierarchical) approach that values individual perspectives and suspends judgement. In a diverse workforce, this is particularly important, enhancing self-efficacy and self-worth in teams. Equally, staff experiencing disempowerment or discrimination often describe an environment where they are *not* understood or valued.
- *Empathising:* Allowing oneself to experience your team members' frustrations. While this can feel exposing and uncomfortable, the proper acknowledgement of pain increases the likelihood of addressing it.
- *Helping:* Helping is the active component of compassionate leadership. Listening, understanding and empathy have less impact if the leader does not take 'thoughtful and intelligent action to help'.

Leaders can establish opportunities and processes where it is the norm for team members to behave compassionately. These include:

- structuring team meetings to include time for people to hear from and support each other
- creating time for team members to relate to each other as people with lives beyond work
- ensuring there are buddying arrangements in place to support people in situations such as joining the team, checking in on sick or self-isolating people

- holding listening events with teams, individuals and specific groups, for example ethnic minority colleagues, to accurately understand what people's experiences are and how we can lead them well

A Systemic Approach to Leadership

Leadership is an inherently relational phenomenon rather than a technical how-to-do-it issue. One cannot function as a leader without followers. The type and style of the relationship between leader and followers can significantly influence the identity and performance of the leader and, conversely, the followers. We often think of leadership as possessing specific traits and behaviours in individuals who occupy professional roles invested with authority within an organisation. While particular characteristics and behaviours are desirable in people occupying leadership positions within organisations, these characteristics or qualities are rarely sufficient in and of themselves.

In relational terms, the space between leader and followers is 'intersubjective', where the leader's subjectivity (personal feelings, preferences and opinions) meets the followers' subjectivities. Why is this important? Well, we are all familiar with those moments in life when we encounter people who draw out the best in us and those who manage to draw out the worst in us. Similarly, we can meet people inspired and motivated by us and people who claim to experience us as obstructive or unmotivating. The point here is that our best and worst qualities can be drawn out of us by others and vice versa. The leader/follower relationship is not immune from these processes. While working within one multidisciplinary team, we recall a new manager joining us. There was much anxious discussion about what they would be like and whether they would have certain qualities and characteristics. A reflective practice group comprising most of the team focused on these questions, and the facilitator asked, 'what can each of you do to ensure we bring out the best of the new manager?'. It surprised some team members that they could have a proactive role in influencing what sort of manager they wanted and needed to reach optimal performance and draw out the new manager's best qualities and characteristics. In patterns of relationships, both individual and group identities are mutually co-constructed by the parties involved over time, each subtly (and sometimes not so subtly) influencing the emergent leader and follower identities and imbuing them with ontological coherence.

A Few Thoughts about Systems

To better understand the idea of a systemic approach to leadership, it is essential to have some ideas about what we mean by 'systems'. Systems is a complex subject with substantial literature attached. However, we need only to touch upon a few salient ideas about organisations for our purposes.

At its most straightforward, a 'system' can be defined as two or more elements in a relationship with each other. We see that large organisations like the NHS or Social Care are indeed very complex systems. An important feature about organisations as systems is that a change in one part of a system can have a rippling impact on the whole system, and change in an entire system has a similar rippling effect on the components of the system. Within a system, we understand that everything is connected; no element remains isolated from other elements. The other vitally important aspect of systemic thinking is to embrace the idea that all systems are in a state of flux and change all of the time. The fast pace of modern life means that radical change is the most pervasive feature of organisational life. Complex organisations function in a social, cultural and political context that is in constant flux. To remain relevant and sensitive to this accelerating evolutionary process, individuals in leadership positions need to embrace the idea that disruption is the new normal. One of the main drivers of increasing complexity and accelerating change is the digital revolution in communication. Smartphones and other devices give virtually instant access to the world's knowledge, information and communication channels. This access means that post-industrial organisations now need to be understood as 'open systems' [22] and can thus be redescribed as 'complex adaptive systems'. They are 'complex' because they are the result of multiple interconnecting relationships. The way they respond to their environment creates new connections and, therefore, increases their complexity. They are 'adaptive' in the sense that they develop fit to the forces of change in their environment and developing technologies while working to retain an apparent coherence of their purpose. They are 'systemic' in that they survive by exchanging energy, information and materials with the broader community ecologies.

The follower is teacher to the leader.
– *Gerard Manley Hopkins* [23]

So what are the implications for leadership when thinking systemically about complex organisations? According to Amazon, there are over 60,000 books focused on leadership – having not read them all, we would guess that there will be at least one (and probably more) definition of leadership in each of them. No real shortage then! Here we will be selecting only a couple of definitions that fit a systemic approach to leadership. The simplest definition of leadership is someone who has followers and is therefore relational. However, the most critical aspect of followership is that it needs to be *active* and *engaged* to develop an authentic sense of a truly shared responsibility for the continuing success and productivity of the team/organisation. Creating dynamic, engaged followership needs to be understood in the context of complex organisations with hierarchical structures. Hierarchies tend to be organised vertically (although there are models of horizontal hierarchies [24]), with those with the highest levels of power, authority and status towards the top and those with less power, status and authority lower down. Inevitably this creates a power imbalance between leaders and followers, a relational context that often remains implicit and unspoken. People's relationships with authority and power vary and have very different dynamics. The implicit dynamics regarding power imbalances in the leader/follower relationship can and often lead to difficulties, problems and challenges in successfully leading a group through sustained and significant changes. No matter what the aspiration or strategy of the organisation is, it is the followers who make or break an organisation's strategies or aspirations. So, a vital aspect of leadership, according to Kouze, is developing 'the art of mobilising others to want to struggle for shared aspirations' [25].

Goodwin suggests that: 'Leadership is a dynamic process of pursuing a vision for change in which the leader is supported by two groups: followers within the leader's own organisation, and influential players and other organisations in the leader's wider external environment' [26]. The extent to which followers want to struggle for the shared aspirations of their organisation is largely dependent on the beliefs they have about themselves in the role they are in and the beliefs they have about the *value of their contribution* to the success of the organisation. Leaders are in a position to significantly influence such belief systems through the art of *framing* and *reframing*. Snow and Benford suggest that framing is 'the process by which leaders construct, articulate and put across their message in a powerful and compelling way in order to win people to their cause and call them to action' [27]. However, vital though the process of framing is, it is unlikely to be sufficient for people feeling undervalued or not valued in their role or believing they are not making a meaningful difference to the lives of others. In such instances, the gentle art of reframing is valuable.

A few years ago, in the NHS Trust where we worked, a very senior executive planned a formal visit to a child and adolescent psychiatric hospital. The staff were busy preparing for the visit. The day arrived, and the senior executive swept into the facility with a small entourage, walked straight past the reception and into the hospital. The same executive and staff finished their visit and swept back out a few hours later, passing reception without acknowledgement. This story was recounted to one of the authors (Graham) by the admin team some days later when he arrived to see a patient – the admin team was upset by this lack of an encounter. One of the admin team commented, 'well, we're the lowest of the low; we're just secretaries and receptionists', and other admin team members murmured their approval. Disconcerted, Graham openly disagreed with this comment. While expressing sadness and concern that they felt this way, he reframed their belief about their roles by saying that from his perspective, they played a vital role in enabling children and young people to recover from severe mental health difficulties. They are an essential part of an overall mental health project which is always a team effort, including every member and not just clinicians or senior executives. They can be very proud of the vital contribution and difference they make every day to the lives of young people and their families.

We subsequently emailed the senior executive with an account of this. To their credit, they made time to revisit the facility and reiterate and underline the reframe directly to the admin team. As later reported, the morale in the admin team significantly improved, and they expressed pride in their role of enabling the recovery of the patients in their hospital via their admin skills. While the big picture is vital in any complex adaptive organisation, the small reframes such as above are equally important because an organisation's direction of travel is influenced by all who participate in it. Leadership is a creative and collective process in this frame, distributed among diverse individuals collectively responsible for creating the organisation's future [28]. This way of understanding leadership enables us to distinguish between leadership roles, that is, a job that has leadership within its job description, and 'acts of leadership', which can be authored by anyone in the organisation. Complex adaptive organisations tend to be structured hierarchically, and the freedom to act increases the higher up the hierarchy one is positioned. Nevertheless, it is crucial to be mindful that intelligence and creativity exist at all hierarchy levels – not just at senior levels. Staff with leadership roles release this potential by promoting and supporting 'acts of leadership' from followers within the full range of hierarchical band levels within the parameters of their position.

The above anecdote is an example of *systemic blindness* in so far as within our organisations, we tend to see ourselves primarily in autonomous roles which we are required to discharge rather than in a relationship with one another. It simply did not occur to the senior executive above that ignoring the admin team while visiting the hospital might shape (or, more likely, misshape) the relationship between the admin team and senior executive staff, leading to the drearily familiar *us and them* scenario.

In any complex adaptive system, there are often powerful forces, dynamics and events at play all of the time. Again, leaders can often be blind to how they might characterise their relationship with these forces and dynamics. As a leader, it is helpful to ask, 'how do I find myself relating to these forces, dynamics, or events?' and 'how would I characterise these relationships?'. 'Is the way I relate to these issues productive or counterproductive?' and 'what modelling effect does my relationship with these issues have on my followers?' Working within complex adaptive systems, most of us are vulnerable to *unconsciously* falling into behaviour patterns towards both the forces and dynamics within an organisation and towards our peers and followers. We stress the word unconsciously because although these behaviours may be outside our awareness, they are not outside other colleagues' attention, particularly our followers. The only way to become aware of these behaviours is by creating a relational context with your followers in which it is safe for them to point them out. Such behaviours can include: being overly demanding of perfection in your followers; demanding a level of productivity that is unrealistic; showing little or no interest in the subjective experiences of your followers in the roles they have; being seduced by groupthink; behaviours that have a silencing effect on your followers; and passive rather than active listening to your followers. This list is not exhaustive, and it is worth asking oneself the question, 'what do I notice about the impact of my behaviours on my followers – what might this be telling me about my behaviours in relation to them?'.

Humans are narrative-generating beings – we create stories about ourselves, stories about others and stories about situations as a way of making sense of things. Unfortunately, we can become attached or very attached to specific accounts and imbue these stories often with unwarranted veracity. We have a preferred version, or story, about ourselves. If someone challenges this version of ourselves via negative feedback, we may find this difficult to bear, and we work hard to restore our preferred version of ourselves. Another consequence of systemic blindness is this process of generating narratives about situations, such as creating myths about the motives of others or myths about the competencies of others. When followers give negative feedback, we can react to it by taking it personally, as if they design feedback to hurt us deliberately. When this happens, we can get angry, seek to get even or withdraw from the encounter – the outcome being predictably unproductive.

Eliciting and Appreciating Contention

We have invited delegates to participate in a 'value clarification exercise' during many years of running training events. This exercise is lively, so we usually choose the graveyard slot, that is, the afternoon session, immediately after lunch. We place four pieces of flipchart paper (referred to as islands) at each corner of the room. On each is written either *AGREE, DISAGREE, AGREE with reservations* or *DISAGREE with reservations.* Everyone stands in a large circle, and we read out many contentious or morally ambiguous statements about aspects of mental health practice or services. We tell the delegates that when we read the first statement, they must not think about it – the idea is to react to it and go to the island that fits closest to their values. Once they have done this, the delegates find someone from a different island, and for one minute, explain to the other why they went to their island of choice. This exercise then repeats usually with four or five more statements. In every training event, each statement always splits the group.

This exercise demonstrates that whilst we may think or believe our colleagues share the same values as ourselves, the underlying reality is somewhat different. Large complex organisations have a set of values and beliefs that guide their clinical, managerial and administration practices. Quite reasonably, we expect staff to align themselves with these values. Staff in leadership positions then reasonably expect people to collaborate to realise their shared aspirations; however, since values, beliefs and ideals will always differ, reciprocal interaction will always involve constructive conflict. In addition, these differences in values, beliefs and standards also means that the idea of *consensus* is often a fantasy and needs to be replaced with the more realistic concept of *convergence*.

Each of us will have a different relationship with the idea and the reality of contention and conflict. It is worth pausing to ask yourself what your relationship is with disagreement and conflict. If you could video yourself when encountering a contentious or conflictual situation at work, what would you notice about yourself, what would you be doing and what would this tell you about yourself?

From a position of leadership, contention needs to be embraced and, more importantly, actively harvested. Silencing or ignoring contention means that potentially practical, creative and innovative ideas from the brightest and the best across hierarchical levels have no platform and therefore go underground or are lost to the organisation. However, actively harvesting contention requires the development of genuinely collaborative relationships between leaders and followers despite the power imbalance between them.

Fostering Collaborative Relationships

Achieving well-functioning sustained collaborative relationships is an essential prerequisite of optimal patient care and ensuring an optimal patient experience. From a leadership perspective there are two primary areas of focus in developing and maintaining collaborative relationships: collaborative relationships with followers and collaborative relationships with outside stakeholder agencies. Whilst the processes involved in developing collaborative relationships overlap within the two areas of focus there are also some significant differences. Firstly, for leaders within an organisation, collaborative relationships with peers and followers result from mutually influencing processes in which attention is paid to several key factors. First, language is constitutive of social realities; we create and live our social realities in and through language. Language practices in the workplace are critical in building the lived realities that people experience in their work. How we speak with one another, how leaders speak with their followers, their peers and the colleagues who lead them is vitally important – words have the capacity to both wound and inspire. Second, it is essential to understand respect as a relational activity. Pause for a moment and ask yourself, how do I actively show respect to my colleagues and followers – actively showing respect is also a modelling behaviour for others. Third, being genuinely curious and maintaining curiosity. It is all too easy to become enamoured with one's reactions and responses which sometimes need to be bracketed out in order to maintain a good enough level of curiosity. Fourth, try to be prepared not to understand too quickly. Again, feeling that you know or immediately understand what the other is saying is a seductive process. Give yourself time to understand, ask for further clarification, or hear more of what the other is saying to enable the other to feel they are genuinely being listened to. Finally, try to understand the importance of pauses in the other's speech – it is tempting not to let people finish if they need to pause to gather and formulate their thoughts and pitch in with your responses.

With regard to developing and maintaining optimal interagency collaborative relationships there are a number of processes that require persistent and constant attention. The thorny question of dedicated funding to support joint planning between agencies is an essential prerequisite. Unless this is in place leaders in their agencies often (quite rightly) claim they simply do not have the time to dedicate to joint planning. Lack of funding for this process can so easily act as a saboteur to effective interagency planning. Clear and effective communication is necessary to developing a mutual understanding of the aims and vision of each agency accompanied by dedicated work to establish the level of convergence of these visions and the barriers in place that may constrain an effective convergence of vision. Clear and effective communication is essential to this process – George Bernard Shaw commented that the problem with communication is the illusion it has been accomplished – the importance of verifying the understanding of the other cannot be overstated. Different agencies have different language practices and different vocabularies to describe their functions and the focus of their work. Take time to understand these practices and vocabularies and consider the question 'how do we co-construct a bridge across these differences?'. And lastly, ensure you have a focus on relationship-building – being exclusively task-centred at the expense of relationship-building can function as a constraint on both processes.

Building Trusting Leader/Follower Relationships

Trust in relationships is an essential prerequisite for an optimally functioning relationship. Whilst the idea of trust in working relationships tends to be an implicit phenomenon, it is worth thinking about what this involves. So, what is trust?

Anderson stated that it is '[t]he mutual confidence that no party to a relationship will exploit the vulnerability of the other' [29]. This straightforward definition demonstrates that issues around trust arise when one party to a relationship feels a sense of vulnerability – that there is a real possibility the other party will ride roughshod over this vulnerability. Trust is both relational and reflexive – as well as trusting the other, you have to trust yourself that you are acting with consistency, a sense of loyalty, openness and integrity. In addition to the moral values above, a sense of humility is a requirement for developing and maintaining trusting relationships. To quote Phil Carroll, CEO of Shell Oil: 'You need a healthy dose of humility . . . the truth is everyone can see your flaws . . . if you try to hide them, they wonder what else you are hiding' [28].

Celebrating Diversity: Drawing Out the Best in People

One cannot overstate the importance of developing awareness, sensitivity and competence in engaging and working with social differences. These are essential skills for all workers; however, they become crucial for effectively leading a socially and culturally diverse workforce. Alison Roper-Hall and John Burnham developed the mnemonic the 'Social GGRRAAACCEEESSS' to describe different aspects of people's identities [30, 31, 32]. The mnemonic stands for Gender, Geography, Race, Religion, Age, Ability, Appearance, Class, Culture, Ethnicity, Education, Employment, Sexuality, Sexual orientation, Spirituality. It is worth pausing to reflect on which aspects of the mnemonic or social graces you find yourself most readily drawn to and which you find yourself least attracted to, avoidant of or seek to actively hide from. What does this mean to you, and how may these aspects impact your relationship with your followers?

Conversely, which parts of the social graces in your followers do you find it easiest to engage with, which aspects do you find most challenging and which aspects do you avoid and thus remain unspoken? This mnemonic can be handy when we experience conversations as jarring or complex, and it offers a framework for thinking about what we stumble over. What might not be being said or acknowledged either by oneself or the other? How might one seek to create a relational context to give a safe voice to the not-yet-said?

The other issue to consider in terms of drawing the best out of people is personality. It is worth bearing in mind that we all have blind spots about our character and its impact on others. Trying to understand these blind spots in their entirety by yourself is rather like trying to see the back of your head without the aid of a mirror. The only way you can discover these aspects of your personality you are blind to is in the context of a trusting, collaborative relationship in which it is safe for the other to comment on this. Mason and Sawyer comment: 'If we can take the risk of learning to challenge cross culturally from respectful positions, rather than just play safe, we are more likely to develop collaborative, trusting relationships' [33].

Conflict

As alluded to earlier, conflict in the workplace due to differences in values, beliefs and ideals is inevitable. However, for many people, the idea of conflict fills them with dread, and they will take active steps to avoid it. Why do we avoid conflict? Some of the reasons for avoiding conflict can be:

- why should I talk with him?
- she'll bite my head off
- he won't listen anyway
- perhaps it will just go away
- let sleeping dogs lie
- if I talk to him, I'm making myself vulnerable – he should come to me
- if I bring it up, it will only make things worse.

There are numerous definitions of conflict; there are two definitions that are useful for our purposes: 'Conflicts are communicative interactions among people who are interdependent and who perceive that their interests are incompatible, inconsistent, or in tension' [34] and '[c]onflict is a disagreement through which the parties involved perceive a threat to their needs, interests and concerns' [35].

There are several essential points about a conflict that is worth trying to understand. Firstly, conflict usually develops when people *perceive a threat* to their well-being. This perception of a threat can be a threat to their physical integrity, emotional state or power or status, for example. When people perceive such a threat, they often respond based on their perceptions rather than an objective view of events. They filter the perception of a threat and their reactions through their values, beliefs, culture, experience, gender and some of the other social graces we have touched on. Whilst conflicts in the workplace are routine, predictable and should be expected, resolving them requires substantive procedural and psychological dimensions to be negotiated and creative problem-solving strategies.

Our society tends to reward alternative responses to conflict rather than through negotiation. Negotiation demands profound courage and determination. It takes courage to articulate your needs honestly and clearly and to sit down and listen with genuine curiosity to your adversaries. It takes courage and determination to look at your role in the dispute and to approach others with a sense of empathy, compassion, openness and respect for their perspective.

Concluding Thoughts

At its worst poor leadership in healthcare costs lives [18, 36]. In addition, the negative impact of poor leadership on the delivery of quality healthcare doesn't just impact the individual patient. It has a significant and ongoing ripple effect on the lives of those close to the patient who is on the receiving end of poor-quality care – whole families and close social networks are all negatively impacted by such leadership failures. As well as the personal costs for patients and their families and loved ones the costs to the taxpayer of poor leadership in healthcare are enormous – poor leadership is indeed costly. In this chapter, we have emphasised the importance of understanding oneself as a leader in relation to the role and to one's followers, to get the best out of people consistently. Leadership is a highly complex task that comes with great responsibility and accountability.

Nonetheless, leaders are human like everyone else, and they have egos, fears, anxieties, prejudices, aspects of themselves (and others) they would prefer to avoid rather than engage with. Successful leaders do not sit all day in their plush ivory tower office – they regularly reach out to their followers and engage; they don't conduct turf wars to wrestle power and build a power base; they understand that an organisation is hard-wired for conflict and therefore they have learnt to listen, exercise curiosity and engage; they don't surround themselves with sycophants who only tell them what they want to hear; and they don't believe, even when very highly qualified, that they know it all but rather have a good understanding of what they don't know. They understand the crucial influence their followers play in co-constructing their leadership identity. But, perhaps, most notably, together with the above, their clarity of vision regarding the organisation's direction successfully inspires their followers to want to follow and struggle to achieve the continuing success of their organisation.

References

1. NHS England. *Better births: improving outcomes of maternity services in England – a five year forward view for maternity care.* London: NHS England; 2016.

2. A Bauer, M Parsonage, M Knapp, V Lemmi, B Adelaja, S Hogg. *The costs of perinatal mental health problems.* London: Centre for Mental Health and London School of Economics; 2014 Oct 20.

3. MS Smith, V Lawrence, E Sadler, A Easter. Barriers to accessing mental health services for women with perinatal mental illness: systematic review and meta-synthesis of qualitative studies in the UK. *BMJ Open.* 2019 Jan 1;9(1):e024803.

4. B Kirkup. The report of the Morecambe Bay investigation. 2015 Mar.

5. M Steen, B Green. Mental health during pregnancy and early parenthood. In: M Steen, M Thomas, editors. *Mental health*

across the lifespan: a handbook. London: Routledge; 2015. p. 60–88.

6. A Cameron, R Lart, L Bostock, C Coomber. Factors that promote and hinder joint and integrated working between health and social care services: a review of research literature. *Health Soc Care Comm*. 2014 May;22(3): 225–33.
7. K Grint. A history of leadership. In: A Bryman, D Collinson, K Grint, B Jackson, M Uhl-Bien, editors. *The SAGE handbook of leadership*. London: SAGE; 2011. p. 3–14.
8. J Storey, editor. *Leadership in organisations: current issues and key trends*. London: Routledge; 2004.
9. HW Rittel, MM Webber. Dilemmas in a general theory of planning. *Policy Sci*. 1973 Jun;4(2):155–69.
10. Royal College of Psychiatrists. Leadership and management in psychiatry. A position statement. 2012.
11. C Pollitt. Justification by works or by faith? Evaluating the new public management. *Evaluation*. 1995 Jul;1(2):133–54.
12. JP Kotter. *Force for change: how leadership differs from management*. New York: Simon & Schuster; 2008.
13. PM Ginter, WJ Duncan, LE Swayne. *The strategic management of health care organisations*. Hoboken, NJ: John Wiley & Sons; 2018.
14. P Spurgeon, J Clark, C Ham, B Keogh. *Medical leadership: from the dark side to centre stage*. Boca Raton, FL: CRC Press; 2017.
15. Royal College of Psychiatrists. Role of the consultant psychiatrist. Leadership and Excellence in Mental Health Services (OP74). 2010.
16. D Goleman. *Leadership that gets results (Harvard business review classics)*. Boston, MA: Harvard Business Press; 2017.
17. R Francis. Report of the Mid Staffordshire NHS Foundation Trust public inquiry: executive summary. London: The Stationery Office; 2013 Feb 6.
18. M Flynn. Winterbourne View Hospital: a serious case review. Gloucestershire, UK: South Gloucestershire Council; 2012.
19. RS Nickerson. Confirmation bias: a ubiquitous phenomenon in many guises. *Rev Gen Psychol*. 1998 Jun;2(2):175–220.
20. The King's Fund. What is compassionate leadership? 2022. www.kingsfund.org.uk/insight-and-analysis/long-reads/what-is-compassionate-leadership
21. M West, R Eckert, B Collins, R Chowla. *Caring to change: how compassionate leadership can stimulate innovation in health care*. London: The King's Fund. 2017 May.
22. WR Scott. Organizations: natural, rational and open. *Can J Sociol*. 1988;29(1). 10.2307/2393090.
23. GM Hopkins. *The collected works of Gerard Manley Hopkins: Oxford essays and notes*. Oxford: Oxford University Press; 2006.
24. H Leblebici, DA Whetten. The concept of horizontal hierarchy and the organisation of interorganizational networks: a comparative analysis. *Soc Netw*. 1984 Mar 1;6(1):31–58.
25. JM Kouzes, BZ Posner. *The leadership challenge*. Hoboken, NJ: John Wiley & Sons; 2006.
26. N Goodwin. *Leadership in health care: a European perspective*. London: Routledge; 2013.
27. DA Snow, RD Benford. Master frames and cycles of protest. In: AD Morris, CM Mueller, editors. *Frontiers in social movement theory*. New Haven, CT: Yale University Press; 1992. p. 133–55.
28. P Senge, K Käufer. Communities of leaders or no leadership at all. In: B Kellerman, LR Matusak, editors. *Cutting edge leadership 2000*. College Park, MD: Center for the Advanced Study of Leadership, James MacGregor Burns Academy of Leadership. 2000.
29. JA Andersen. Trust in managers: a study of why Swedish subordinates trust their managers. *Bus Ethics: Eur Rev*. 2005 Oct;14(4):392–404.

30. J Burnham. Approach-method-technique: making distinctions and creating connections. *Human Systems.* 1992;3(1):3–26.

31. J Burnham. Systemic supervision: the evolution of reflexivity in the context of the supervisory relationship. *Human Systems.* 1993;4(19):349–81.

32. A Roper-Hall. Working systemically with older people and their families who have 'come to grief'. In: P Sutcliffe, G Tufnell, U Cornish, editors. *Working with the dying and bereaved: systemic approaches to therapeutic work.* London: Palgrave; 1998. p. 177–206.

33. B Mason, A Sawyer, editors. *Exploring the unsaid: creativity, risks and dilemmas in working cross-culturally.* Boca Raton, FL: Routledge; 2018.

34. C Conrad. Communication in conflict: style-strategy relationships. *Commun Monogr.* 1991 Jun 1;58(2):135–55.

35. University of Wisconsin-Madison. About conflict. n.d. https://tinyurl.com/mr2ducsp

36. NHS England. Stage 2 independent investigation into Southern Health NHS Foundation Trust. 2021 Sep. www.england.nhs.uk/south-east/publications/ind-invest-reports/southern-health

Chapter 10

Depression

Lucy C. Barker, Cindy-Lee Dennis and Simone N. Vigod

Introduction

Depression is common in pregnancy and postpartum and is linked to negative consequences for the affected person, and their family, including long-term adverse outcomes for the child. In the management of depression in pregnancy and postpartum, specific considerations include the role of reproductive hormones in the aetiology of the disorder, unique psychosocial stressors that may precipitate or perpetuate symptoms, and the safety of psychotropic medication in pregnancy and breastfeeding. This chapter is an overview of depression in pregnancy and the first year postpartum, including epidemiology, theories about aetiology, presentation, course, outcomes and an approach to management.

Epidemiology

Prevalence estimates for depression in pregnancy and postpartum range from 11.9% to 26.3% [1, 2]. Depression does not appear to be more common in pregnancy than in the non-pregnant state, but the risk may be elevated in the postpartum period [3, 4]. In low- and middle-income countries, perinatal depression appears to be more common than in high-income countries (odds ratio (OR) 1.8, 95% confidence interval (CI) 1.4–2.2) [1]. Over one-quarter of the time (~26.5%), people with postpartum depression report the onset of the depressive episode before pregnancy, highlighting that optimal management of depressive disorders before conception is likely to be an important target for consideration in the prevention of negative impacts of perinatal depression [5]. While depression is also common in partners, including fathers where the prevalence rate is estimated at ~8% [6], the focus of this chapter is on those who are pregnant or who recently delivered an infant (see Chapter 6 on paternal mental health).

Aetiology/Risk Factors

The etiology of perinatal depression is thought to be multifactorial, with biological, psychological and social factors often contributing to its development. Some, but not all, of these factors are similar to risk factors for depression occurring outside the perinatal period.

Psychiatric History

The strongest risk factor for depression in pregnancy is a personal history of depression [7]. In those with a history of severe depressive illness (i.e. multiple episodes, prior hospitalisations), antidepressant medication discontinuation is a strong risk factor for relapse in pregnancy (hazard ratio 5.0, 95% CI 2.8–9.1 for continuers vs. discontinuers in one classic study) [8]. With milder illness, antidepressant medication discontinuation may not play as much of a role [9]. The strongest risk factor for depression in the postpartum period is untreated depression in pregnancy (Cohen's effect size = 0.75), followed by untreated anxiety in pregnancy (Cohen's effect size = 0.68) [10]. Panic disorder, social phobia and post-traumatic stress disorder in pregnancy are specifically associated with an increased likelihood of postpartum depression [11]. There may be a reproductive subgroup who are susceptible to depression premenstrually, in the immediate postpartum and perimenopausally [12]. Those with prior depressive episodes in the first 4 weeks postpartum are at elevated risk of a repeat episode of postpartum depression after a subsequent pregnancy [12].

Neuroendocrine Factors

Given the substantive changes in sex hormones that occur during the perinatal period, there has been a focus on how these might relate to depression onset. Research suggests that perinatal depression is not the result of abnormal hormone levels but rather that some individuals are particularly vulnerable to mood changes in response to the normal physiologic changes of the perinatal period [13]. An experimental study aimed to mimic hormonal changes in pregnancy and postpartum in a sample with a history of postpartum depression. In this study, the add-back of estradiol and progesterone after induced hypogonadism (mimicking pregnancy) led to an increase in depressive symptoms, and these symptoms peaked during the rapid withdrawal of these hormones (mimicking childbirth) [14]. Also, oestrogen has been shown to effectively treat postpartum depression in some small studies, although it is not routinely used for this purpose due to the limited evidence and the potential risks of oestrogen treatment [15, 16]. While oestrogen and progesterone may impact mood directly, there is some evidence their effect occurs via important modulatory effects on glutamate, gamma-aminobutyric acid (GABA), serotonin and dopamine [17] and other systems that can influence mood [13]. For example, the GABAergic system has been studied for a role in both perinatal and non-perinatal depression – GABA, the primary inhibitory neurotransmitter, tends to be inversely correlated with depressive symptoms, although the specific role of GABA in perinatal depression has yet to be elucidated [18]. Allopregnanolone, a metabolite of progesterone and a potent allosteric modulator of the GABA type A receptor, has been hypothesised to play a role in postpartum depression. Allopregnanolone levels are low in postpartum depression, and exogenous allopregnanolone analogues have been newly approved as a postpartum treatment [19]. As another example, there is some evidence that monoamine oxidase A (MAO-A), a neurotransmitter responsible for the metabolism of serotonin, dopamine and noradrenaline whose level rises in the first week postpartum, may explain the onset of postpartum depressive symptoms in some cases [17].

Other pregnancy-related biological factors may increase the risk for perinatal depression. Oxytocin, a hormone important for social connection and emotion regulation that plays a significant role in childbirth, lactation and bonding, may also have a role in the etiology of depression, with low levels associated with increased risk for postpartum depression [20]. The hypothalamic-pituitary-adrenal (HPA) axis has been implicated in postpartum depression [18], and low morning cortisol is associated with depression in pregnancy and postpartum [21]. Since adversity, stress and trauma can reprogramme the HPA axis [18], this may represent a physiologic mechanism by which life events shape the risk for perinatal depression [15]. The link between elevated inflammatory markers and depression has been of great interest outside of the perinatal period [22]. Inflammatory markers change with normal pregnancy and are linked to many pregnancy complications such as pre-eclampsia, fetal growth restriction and fetal demise [23]. Pro-inflammatory cytokines are often elevated in depression in pregnancy and shifts in helper T cells may be related to the depression through complex interactions [18, 22, 24]. There is also emerging evidence for a bidirectional link between depression and alterations in the gut microbiome, and since the perinatal period is associated with changes in the gut microbiome, this has been identified as an area for further exploration [25, 26].

Heritability and Genetics

A family history of depression increases the risk for postpartum depression [27]. A perinatal-specific family history of depression explains ~14% of the risk for perinatal depression [27]. Where there is a family history of depression that starts in the first 4 weeks postpartum, there appears to be a specifically increased risk of developing depression in the first month postpartum (sibling concordance tetrachoric correlation coefficient for sibling concordance = 0.55, 95% CI 0.11–0.83) [12, 28]. These heritability studies have led to the investigation of genetic and epigenetic factors, mostly focused on the postpartum period, where the complex interplay of stress, sleep and hormonal changes are thought to interact with genetic factors to affect the likelihood of developing depression [29]. Most research in the area focuses on polymorphisms in genes that regulate neurotransmitters related to depression (e.g. monoamines, brain-derived neuropathic factor, the HPA axis) or reproductive hormones (e.g. oestrogen receptors, oxytocin) [29]. The most widely studied candidate gene is the serotonin transporter gene (5-HTT), with multiple studies demonstrating that being a carrier for the short allele of the 5-HTTLPR polymorphism is associated with depression risk with onset in the first 8 weeks postpartum [30]. A recent meta-analysis of genome-wide association studies found that no single-nucleotide polymorphisms reached genome-level significance; however, samples are smaller than for other mental health conditions, and larger samples are needed [31]. Epigenetic effects may also play a significant role, as interactions with environmental factors have been identified for many candidate genes including the oxytocin receptor, 5-HTT, MAO-A, tryptophan hydroxylase 2 [18]. At present, there are no genetic biomarkers ready for clinical use.

Social Risk Factors

Lack of social support, and specifically an unsupportive partner relationship, is a strong risk factor [7, 32]. Negative life events such as divorce and death in the family, as well as daily stressors such as time pressures, are also linked to perinatal depression risk [7, 33]. A history of adverse childhood trauma, particularly maltreatment starting in early childhood, increases the risk of depression in pregnancy [34] and the postpartum period [35]. Intimate partner violence has repeatedly been shown to increase the risk of perinatal depression [36]. Immigrants to a new country are at high risk of postpartum depression, with depression rates of 24–42% [37]. Migrants, particularly refugees, may have a history of trauma, a lack of social agency in their new country and a lack of support – all of which can precipitate and perpetuate depression [37]. Although research on perinatal depression in lesbian and bisexual women is limited, existing data suggest that rates of depression are at least as high and may be higher than for heterosexual women [38]. There is a lack of research on perinatal depression in transgender, non-binary and gender-diverse populations; given the much higher rates of depression in transgender populations generally, complex relationships to pregnancy for transgender men, non-binary and gender-diverse individuals, and disaffirming experiences in pregnancy care experienced by transgender men and non-binary individuals, this is likely to be a high-risk group [39, 40].

Social risk factors are generally consistent between high and low/middle-income countries (LMIC) [32]. In LMIC, specific important protective factors appear to include being of the ethnic majority, having an education and permanent employment [32]. Giving birth to a girl may increase the risk for postpartum depression, and when women move into the in-laws' residence following marriage, conflict with in-laws may put them at a higher risk of depression [32].

Concurrent Medical Conditions and Obstetrical Factors

Traditionally, the presence of a concurrent medical condition has been considered mostly in the context of a factor on the differential diagnosis for perinatal depression. Emerging evidence suggests, however, that concurrent medical conditions may also increase the risk for perinatal depression. For example, a systematic review found that a chronic medical condition increases the odds of peripartum depression (adjusted pooled OR 1.45, 95% CI 1.25–1.67) [41], as do physical, sensory and intellectual disabilities [42]. The nature of these associations is likely multifactorial; psychosocial factors including low-income status (possibly a shared risk factor, or low income due to an inability to work as a result of the medical illness), the effects of pain and sleeplessness, the stress of parenting in the context of a medical illness, as well as biological factors including shared genetics, proinflammatory cytokines, vascular pathology or HPA axis dysfunction [41]. Obstetrical factors such as perinatal pain may increase the risk for postpartum depression, although generally they are thought to have a relatively small contribution compared to other major risk factors such as psychiatric history [10, 43, 44].

Presentation, Course and Outcome

Presentation

Depression can present at any point in pregnancy or the postpartum period. Depression symptoms can include low mood, anhedonia, insomnia or hypersomnia, guilty thoughts, low self-worth, hopelessness, low or elevated appetite, poor motivation, low energy, poor concentration and suicidal thoughts [45]. In pregnancy, however, symptoms of increased appetite, oversleeping and agitation may be less helpful in identifying depression as they overlap with pregnancy symptoms [46]. In the postpartum, when waking up is often necessary multiple times through the night to care for infants, sleep disturbance and low energy may not represent depression – asking about the ability to sleep when the infant is sleeping may reveal more clinically useful information. Anxiety is a common feature of perinatal depression, with comorbid anxiety symptoms reported one-third to one-half of the time [47, 48]. Comorbid anxiety can lead to more severe symptomatology, greater treatment resistance and a higher risk for adverse maternal treatment outcomes [48].

Course

The course of depression in pregnancy and postpartum is variable and depends on a multitude of factors including a prior depressive history, the persistence versus resolution of stressors contributing to the depressive episode, the severity of symptoms and whether there has been appropriate treatment. While some depressive episodes will resolve spontaneously within a few weeks, approximately 20% of postpartum depressive episodes persist beyond the first year, and up to 40% will experience a relapse of their depression thereafter [49]; a similar relapse risk to that of non-perinatal episodes of depression [50].

Potential Consequences

Consequences of perinatal depression can include impaired quality of life and difficulty fulfilling roles at work and home. As with depression across the lifespan, perinatal depression carries a risk for suicide. Suicidal ideation is present in up to 21% of cases of perinatal depression [51]. While completed suicide is rare, it is a leading cause of maternal death in high-income countries where the maternal death rate for most other causes has reduced over time [52, 53]. In the UK, 29 of 229 maternal deaths in pregnancy and the first 6 weeks postpartum between 2018 and 2020 were due to suicide, and suicide was the leading cause of maternal death between 6 weeks and 1 year postpartum [54]. Those who die by suicide perinatally are more likely to have a diagnosis of depression compared to those who die by suicide outside of the perinatal period [55]. Infanticide is also a rare, but possible devastating consequence (see Chapter 22, 'Maternal Suicide, Deliberate Self-Harm and Other Mental Health Related Causes of Maternal Death' and Chapter 38, 'When Mothers Kill Their Children') [56].

Other specific consequences of perinatal depression are important to consider. Depression in pregnancy is associated with pregnancy complications such as gestational diabetes and pre-eclampsia [57, 58]. It is associated with adverse fetal and birth outcomes including an increased risk of preterm birth, intrauterine growth restriction and low birth weight. There is a particularly strong association between depression and low birth weight in lower-income countries [59]. Untreated depression during pregnancy can lead to hyperactivity and heart rate irregularities in the fetus, and altered EEG patterns, stress responses, along with altered cortisol, norepinephrine and dopamine levels in infants, which may contribute to the negative outcomes of premature death and neonatal intensive care unit admissions [60]. Postpartum depression is associated with a greater likelihood of breastfeeding challenges and discontinuation of breastfeeding [61]. There is also some evidence of an association with lower rates of infant well-baby visits, complete immunisation schedules, use of home safety devices and following of recommendations about sleep safety [62].

Effects of maternal depression can persist into childhood, but harm is not inevitable, and where there are risks to children, the effect sizes are generally small to moderate in the absence of severe or persistent maternal illness [63]. Depression in pregnancy may be associated with exposed children having higher cortisol levels and increased central adiposity, and a higher likelihood of internalising and externalising behaviours in childhood, and adolescent depression [60, 64]. Postpartum depression is associated with a higher incidence of gastrointestinal and lower respiratory infections [65] and higher overall adiposity in children [64]. It is also linked to problems with attachment and child bonding; depression may reduce attunement to children's cues, with parenting behaviours that can lead to child developmental and socioemotional problems [66]. These may include internalising and externalising behaviours, psychopathology, negative affect and depression [67, 68] as well as impaired cognition (with a particularly strong effect among boys) [69].

Perinatal depression also impacts the larger family unit including the partner and older children. One-quarter to one-half of men whose partners are depressed experience depression themselves, with rates much higher than among men without depressed partners [70]. This effect is thought to be related to factors such as shared external stressors and bidirectional impacts of depression on the other member of the relationship. Having two parents with depression leads to a higher risk of adverse outcomes in children, compared to when only one parent experiences depression [71].

Assessment

Case Identification

Pregnant and postpartum women and other childbearing individuals with possible depression may present to their primary care provider, maternity professional, health visitor/public health nurse or even an emergency department. They may have first contact with third-sector providers/community organisations or already be in contact with other mental health professionals. For many reasons, including shame, stigma and fear of having their child taken away, some may not present to their health professional with a subjective complaint of depression, and depression may not become apparent unless it is asked about specifically. Routine screening for perinatal depression is still being debated in the literature [72], although some evidence suggests that screening when combined with a treatment pathway may lead to improvements in depressive symptoms [73]. The Edinburgh Postnatal Depression Scale (EPDS) is the most widely used tool to identify perinatal depression [74, 75, 76]. It is a 10-question self-report questionnaire that asks a series of depressive and anxious symptoms rated on a scale of 0 to 3 (higher is more severe) based on the previous 7 days. Using a cut-off of 13 or greater, the English-language EPDS has a moderate to high sensitivity (0.67, 95% CI 0.18–0.96 to 1.00, 95% CI 0.67–1.00 across studies) and high specificity (0.87 or higher) for postpartum depression. It is also validated for depression in pregnancy. Different scores are recommended for other languages/cultural groups – for example, a cut-off of 9 or 10 is recommended when using the Chinese EPDS [77]. The final question asks about self-harm, and any positive response should prompt a thorough safety assessment. Two-question tools such as the Whooley and the Patient Health Questionnaire-2 (PHQ-2) may also be useful in busy clinics when it is less practical to use the EPDS [78, 79]. When potential cases are identified, it is important to follow up with a clinical assessment for diagnosis, risk management and treatment. Symptom scale results do not replace clinical assessment – of those who screen positive on the EPDS, over one-quarter have other disorders including bipolar, anxiety and substance use disorders [5].

Finally, regardless of the score on a screening tool, if a need for support is expressed, follow-up should be offered.

Diagnosis

In the *American Psychiatric Association's Diagnostic and Statistical Manual*, Fifth Edition, Text Revision (DSM-5-TR), a major depressive episode is defined as 2 weeks with at least five symptoms, of which at least one is depressed mood or anhedonia, as well as clinically significant distress or functional impairment (Box 10.1) [80]. Additional depressive symptoms include appetite/weight changes, insomnia or hypersomnia, psychomotor agitation or retardation, fatigue, worthlessness and/or guilt, poor concentration or indecisiveness, or thoughts of death or suicide. A specifier of 'with peripartum onset' can be applied if the depressive episode begins during pregnancy or the first 4 weeks postpartum, although many clinicians and researchers consider depression within the first year after delivery to be postpartum depression [81]. To count towards a diagnosis of a major depressive episode, symptoms must not be attributable to a medical condition, substance or psychotic disorder. Diagnosis using the International Classification of Diseases, 11th Revision (ICD-11) is similar, with a depressive episode being defined as 'a period of almost daily depressed mood or diminished interest in activities lasting at least two weeks accompanied by other symptoms such as difficulty concentrating, feelings of worthlessness or excessive or inappropriate guilt, hopelessness, recurrent thoughts of death or suicide, changes in appetite or sleep, psychomotor agitation or retardation, and reduced energy or fatigue' (Box 10.1) [82]. In ICD-11, depressive disorders are defined as single-episode depressive disorder or recurrent-episode depressive disorder, exclusionary criteria are bipolar disorder and adjustment disorders, and specifiers include severity and presence of psychotic symptoms. Collateral information should be obtained from sources close to the affected person whenever possible to assist with diagnosis.

Differential Diagnosis

The presence of depressive symptoms does not necessarily indicate the presence of a major depressive disorder, and a detailed assessment is required when a screening tool such as the EPDS is used to aid detection. The differential diagnosis for depression is generally similar perinatally to the differential diagnosis outside the perinatal period, but specific pregnancy- and postpartum-related conditions warrant consideration. Depression should be differentiated from normal feelings of sadness and grief in the face of a major loss, such as miscarriage, stillbirth or infant death. Careful clinical assessment and a longitudinal approach may be necessary to distinguish *bereavement* from depression. Pregnancy and the postpartum period are also times of major life change, and other major stressors (e.g. in relationships, financial stress) may produce symptoms that are similar to depression – when significant symptoms are present but do not meet full criteria for a major depressive episode, then a diagnosis of an *adjustment disorder* should be considered. Transient mood disturbances can occur early in the postpartum period, referred to as *postpartum blues* or *baby blues*. Estimates of prevalence vary between 26% and 84%, depending on the definition used [83, 84]. These mood disturbances, thought to be hormonally mediated [83], typically start shortly after delivery, tend to peak at 3–5 days postpartum, and resolve quickly, most often by 10–12 days

Box 10.1 Diagnosis of a Major Depressive Episode Using DSM-5-TR Criteria (Adapted from the DSM 5-TR [80])

Five or more of the following symptoms have been present nearly every day during a 2-week period and represent a change from baseline; at least one of the symptoms is (1) depressed mood or (2) anhedonia.

1. Depressed mood.
2. Anhedonia.
3. Weight loss or gain, or decrease or increase in appetite.*
4. Insomnia or hypersomnia.
5. Psychomotor agitation or retardation.
6. Fatigue or energy loss.
7. Feelings of worthlessness or excessive or inappropriate guilt.
8. Diminished ability to think or concentrate, or indecisiveness.
9. Recurrent thoughts of death, recurrent suicidal ideation or a suicide plan/attempt.

The symptoms cause clinically significant distress or impair functioning, are not attributable to the physiological effects of a substance or medical condition, are not better explained by a schizophrenia spectrum or other psychotic disorder, and there has never been a manic episode or a hypomanic episode.

Specify

- With anxious distress
- With mixed features
- With melancholic features
- With atypical features
- With mood-congruent psychotic features
- With mood-incongruent psychotic features
- With catatonia
- With peripartum onset
- With seasonal pattern

*Note that in pregnancy and postpartum, this should be measured in relation to the weight gain/loss expected with that perinatal stage

Diagnosis of a Depressive Episode Using ICD-11 Criteria (from ICD-11 [82])

A depressive episode is characterised by a period of almost daily depressed mood or diminished interest in activities lasting at least 2 weeks accompanied by other symptoms such as difficulty concentrating, feelings of worthlessness or excessive or inappropriate guilt, hopelessness, recurrent thoughts of death or suicide, changes in appetite or sleep, psychomotor agitation or retardation, and reduced energy or fatigue. There have never been any prior manic, hypomanic, or mixed episodes, which would indicate the presence of a bipolar disorder.

Exclusions: Bipolar or related disorders, adjustment disorder.

postpartum [85]. Depression can be differentiated from the blues by its greater severity and longer duration of symptoms.

Any psychiatric condition can present perinatally, so all may be considered on the differential diagnosis. Anxiety and related disorders such as *obsessive compulsive disorder* are common perinatally [7], and should be considered as alternate or comorbid diagnoses [86]. Obsessive compulsive disorder in particular may lead to high EPDS scores [11], highlighting the importance of not relying solely on the EPDS for diagnostic purposes. Trauma- and stressor-related disorders including *post-traumatic stress disorder* should also be considered, related either to trauma occurring prior to the pregnancy but also to trauma occurring perinatally, including around the time of delivery. Post-traumatic stress disorder can be differentiated from depression by asking about symptoms specific to the trauma, for example, nightmares, flashbacks, avoidance and hypervigilance. *Substance use disorders* can present with depressive symptoms, as the direct physiologic effects of intoxication and/or withdrawal and the impact of substance use disorders on individuals' lives can mimic depression. Many people reduce or abstain from substances during pregnancy, but not all will be abstinent (especially in the absence of treatment), and there is a risk for relapse in the postpartum period [87]. Hesitancy to disclose substance use in the perinatal period can be due to stigma or fears about child apprehension, so a non-judgmental, supportive and therapeutic environment should be established to help identify substance use.

Whether inside or outside the perinatal period, bipolar disorder should be considered as a possible diagnosis in anyone presenting with a major depressive episode. In a large American pregnancy and postpartum cohort study (n = 1396) 22.6% of those who screened positive (10 or higher) on the EPDS had bipolar disorders [5]. The index of suspicion for bipolar disorder should be especially high in those with symptom onset in the first 2 weeks postpartum [88]. Screening should include questions about any prior history of manic or hypomanic symptoms. The treatment and prognosis of bipolar disorders I and II differs significantly from that of unipolar depression and has specific implications for the perinatal period. Postpartum psychosis is a serious condition which can present initially with depressed mood. Careful screening for psychosis is important in all perinatal individuals presenting with depression due to the urgent need for diagnosis and treatment (see Chapter 12, 'Postpartum Psychosis and Bipolar Disorder') [89].

Physical health conditions should be on the differential diagnosis. Thyroid dysfunction, which is more common in pregnancy and the postpartum period due to the impact of chorionic gonadotropin on the thyroid gland, can be associated with depressive symptoms [90, 91]. Anaemia, which is linked to depression [92], is also more prevalent in pregnancy and postpartum. A thorough medical work-up should therefore be conducted including screening for anaemia and thyroid dysfunction.

Comorbidities

Comorbid anxiety and related disorders, including generalised anxiety disorder and obsessive-compulsive disorder, are common, and present in up to two-thirds of perinatal depression cases [5]. Sometimes, anxiety predates depression, and sometimes depression predates anxiety [93]. Depression can be also accompanied by comorbid substance use disorders, especially in the postpartum period. Between one-fifth and one-half of those with an active or recent substance use disorder will have depressive symptoms in the perinatal period [94]. Depression is also associated with a risk for self-medication with alcohol and drugs. While personality disorders continue across the perinatal period, relatively little research has evaluated the comorbidity between depression and personality disorders in the perinatal period. One cohort study found that of 42 women with personality disorders, approximately 20% developed depression in pregnancy [95].

Risk Assessment

Given the risk of suicide and self-harm in individuals with depression [96], health professionals should assess suicide risk at each clinical encounter [97]. The EPDS has a question on self-harm and, therefore, unlike shorter screens such as the Whooley or PHQ-2, can be part of ongoing self-harm/suicide risk assessment. If the EPDS is used, clinicians must always enquire further about any positive response to the question on self-harm. A diagnosis of depression is a major risk factor for suicide death in the perinatal period [55]. Other risk factors for suicidality in the perinatal period may include factors that can make the transition more difficult or lead to isolation, such as young age, single-parenthood, unintended pregnancy, lack of support or a partner who rejects paternity, nulliparity, being part of a minority, inadequate housing, rural residence, experiences of trauma such as family conflict/violence, gender and racial discrimination, and exposure to conflict or disaster [98]. Suicidality risk is higher for those with a personal and/or family history of suicide (completed suicide and suicidal ideation) and psychiatric disorders and for those with clinical factors such as psychiatric comorbidity, shorter illness duration and psychological symptoms such as negative attitudes towards pregnancy [98]. Ongoing assessment for psychotic symptoms is important, especially in the setting of severe depression (see Chapter 12 on postpartum psychosis). Violent thoughts towards others, including toward the infant(s) and other children, should be assessed, and any positive screen warrants careful clinical attention. In those with such severe depression who lack the motivation or capacity to care for their children, appropriate support will need to be put in place. Intimate partner violence is associated with an increased risk for depression [99], so should be considered as part of any risk assessment of perinatal depression. Jurisdictions vary regarding reporting obligations and management recommendations when safety concerns arise, and practitioners should be familiar with their local laws, guidelines and crisis resources.

Management

The approach to management described below is based on major English-language guidelines published by the American Psychiatric Association (APA, United States), the National Institute for Health and Care Excellence (NICE, England and Wales), Scottish Intercollegiate Guidelines Network (SIGN), the Canadian Network for Mood and Anxiety Treatments (CANMAT, Canada) and Beyond Blue (Australia) [100, 101, 102, 103]. For specifics about considerations around psychological and pharmacological treatments in the perinatal period, please see Chapter 26, 'Principles of Prescribing', Chapter 27, 'The Reproductive Safety of Psychotropic Medication and Implications for Prescribing in the Perinatal Period' and Chapter 28, 'Psychological Therapies for Parental Mental Health in the Perinatal Period'. Recommended treatments will depend on factors related to the specific presentation, including severity of the current depressive episode, what has been efficacious in the past, risk assessment, comorbidities, psychiatric history (e.g. severity of prior depressive episodes), social stressors, social supports and, for in the postpartum, breastfeeding status and patient preference. Stepped care approaches, in which treatment options escalate in intensity based on symptom severity and patient response, can be implemented (Box 10.2) [104]. However, this needs to be tempered by an awareness that severe illness can develop rapidly in the perinatal period and pathways

Box 10.2 Example of Stepped Care Approach [104] to Perinatal Depression Based on Guidelines [100, 101, 102, 103]

Note that in the context of severe symptoms, rapid escalation of Treatment Steps may be needed. Be aware that perinatal depression can progress rapidly. At any step, if symptoms are worsening quickly, consider going directly to a higher level of care.

Step 1: All, regardless of symptom severity, and may be adequate for mild symptoms alone

- Establish a therapeutic plan
- Self-management strategies (e.g. sleep protection, exercise where no contraindications)
- Psychosocial treatments (e.g. peer support, enabling access to housing, income, etc. where needed)
- Provider types: involve primary care provider, peer support worker, public health nurse and other community providers
- Setting: community, phone or online

Step 2: Moderate symptoms or inadequate improvement with Step 1 alone

- Add psychological treatment (e.g. cognitive behaviour therapy, interpersonal therapy)
- Provider types: involve a trained therapist (e.g. social worker, psychologist), primary care provider with psychotherapy training, psychiatrist
- Setting: community or outpatient clinic

Step 3: Severe symptoms or inadequate improvement with Step 2

- Add first-line SSRI
- If inadequate response, consider (a) a trial of another antidepressant, (b) augmentation with another agent or non-invasive neurostimulation (e.g. rTMS)
- Provider types: involve obstetrical or primary care provider with mental health expertise, and/or psychiatrist, perinatal psychiatrist with inadequate response to first-line SSRI
- Setting: outpatient clinic

Step 4: Very severe symptoms such as active suicidal ideation and plan or psychosis or very severe symptoms with inadequate response to Step 3

- Requires emergency risk assessment, with attention to the risk of harming self or others
- Until risk assessment is complete, should not have affected person alone or alone with the infant
- May require antipsychotic medication and/or ECT, usually in an inpatient setting
- Provider types: psychiatrist (perinatal psychiatrist, if available)
- Setting: initially inpatient hospital setting

need to be in place to allow direct access to specialist assessment and intervention where indicated by symptom pattern or mental health history.

Prevention

Since a pre-existing experience or diagnosis of depression is the strongest risk factor for perinatal relapse, and depression often begins before pregnancy, recommendations are increasingly focused on prevention. If identification and treatment of depression are part of preconception care, the management of this often chronic condition can be optimised before pregnancy, and perinatal depression and its consequences can be reduced or avoided [105]. Some psychosocial and self-management strategies may prevent depression in those with sub-syndromal symptoms and those with risk factors for depression, with evidence for peer-based telephone support, and interpersonal psychotherapy [106, 107]. Starting antidepressant medication to prevent perinatal depression if a person is asymptomatic is not routinely recommended [108].

Treatment Setting and Provider

Most perinatal depression is managed in primary care. There must be clear and explicit pathways of referral for individuals to access enhanced and specialist services, such as perinatal mental health midwifery, maternity psychological therapies services, perinatal mental health community care, outpatient perinatal psychiatric care and Mother and Baby Unit inpatient treatment (see Chapter 29, 'Effective Working across Health, Peer Support and the Third Sector' and Chapter 30, 'Perinatal Mental Health Service Development and Delivery').

Psychosocial Treatments and Self-Management Strategies

Most guidelines recommend guided self-management for mild depression [101]. Interventions such as telephone-based peer support have evidence for the prevention of postpartum depression and can be considered on their own for mild depressive symptoms [106]. Exercise is efficacious for the treatment of perinatal depression, at a dose of a minimum of 150 minutes of moderate exercise weekly [109]; an individualised approach should be considered in conjunction with the obstetrical care provider, to ensure that there are no contraindications to an exercise program. Sleep protection is important; in the postpartum period, when maternal sleep is heavily influenced by infant sleep patterns, interventions to improve infant sleep may improve maternal mood, although further research is needed to confirm this [110]. Mindfulness-based interventions and yoga have both been investigated in perinatal depression, with positive results [111, 112].

Psychological Treatments

Most guidelines recommend psychological treatments as a first-line treatment for mild to moderate depression in pregnancy and lactation [102, 103]. The largest bodies of evidence for the psychological treatment of perinatal depression are for cognitive behaviour therapy and interpersonal therapy, with fewer studies, and therefore less evidence, for psychodynamic psychotherapies [103, 113, 114]. Cognitive behaviour therapies target distorted thoughts (e.g. polarised thinking about being a terrible mother) and maladaptive behaviours (e.g. avoidance behaviours) to reduce depressive feelings, while interpersonal therapy focuses on improving interpersonal functioning related to relationships (e.g. improving relationship with one's partner in the context of parenting), and role transitions (e.g. transition to motherhood). In the postpartum, there is some evidence for the efficacy of mother–infant dyadic therapies, so these can be considered for those who do not improve with first-line treatments or where there are risk factors for impaired maternal–infant bonding [103]. There is increasing evidence that psychotherapy can be effectively delivered virtually [115]. For specifics around psychological therapy in the perinatal period, please see Chapter 28, 'Psychological Therapies for Parental Mental Health in the Perinatal Period'.

Pharmacotherapy

Pharmacotherapy should be considered when psychological treatment alone does not induce remission (or does not do so rapidly enough), for severe depression unlikely to respond to psychological treatment alone, or for mild-to-moderate symptoms when there is a history of severe depression (e.g. those who have relapsed with discontinuation of antidepressant medication) [101]. Other factors to consider in medication decisions include patient preference and prior response to treatment [7]. Antidepressants can be considered alone, or in combination with psychotherapy. In pregnancy and lactation, the potential benefits of pharmacotherapeutic treatment must be weighed against the potential risks of medication exposure to the fetus and/or infant.

The choice of pharmacological agent should be guided by the clinical presentation including symptoms, comorbidities and prior response to antidepressant medication. In pregnancy, for non-psychotic depression, the selective serotonin reuptake inhibitors (SSRIs) citalopram, escitalopram and sertraline may be considered first due to their favourable efficacy and safety profiles in pregnancy and lactation [102] (see Chapter 27, 'The Reproductive Safety of Psychotropic Medication and Implications for Prescribing in the Perinatal Period'). When these agents are ineffective or not tolerated, other first-line agents such as SSRIs, serotonin-norepinephrine reuptake inhibitors (SNRIs) and mirtazapine may be considered as there is some fairly reassuring information available regarding their safety in pregnancy [102]. For those taking antidepressant drugs before pregnancy in whom the decision to continue pharmacotherapy is thought to outweigh the potential risks of fetal exposure, switching to another medication is not generally recommended, as the risk profile across all of the above-mentioned medications is quite similar. In the postpartum period, as SSRIs, SNRIs and mirtazapine are all considered compatible with breastfeeding, for those already taking an antidepressant, switching to another medication is not generally recommended, although individualised discussions are always recommended [116]. For those newly starting medication, sertraline is generally recommended as a first-line agent due to its minimal passage into breastmilk [81]. Other first-line agents would also be a reasonable first choice, apart from fluoxetine, which, although still considered compatible with lactation, would not be a first choice of SSRI in someone newly starting a medication due to its long half-life (while not a focus of this chapter, there have been case reports of seizures in infants exposed through breastmilk to bupropion, also suggesting that this would not be a first choice of agent to start) (see Chapter 26, 'Principles of Prescribing').

For depression with psychotic features, antipsychotics should be part of first-line treatment, and specialist advice should be sought urgently. Specialist advice should also be sought when moving beyond first-line agents into augmentation strategies (e.g. with antipsychotics, lithium, etc.), switching to second- and third-line treatments (e.g. tricyclic antidepressants, monoamine oxidase inhibitors) or when somatic treatments such as electroconvulsive therapy (ECT) or non-invasive brain stimulation treatments are to be considered. Electroconvulsive therapy can be considered in pregnancy and postpartum for severe depression including those with mixed states, catatonia or psychosis, or with imminent risk to the affected person or fetus/infant (e.g. harm to self or others) [101, 102, 117, 118].

Emerging Therapeutics

Non-invasive localised brain stimulation therapies for depression that pose no theoretical risk to a developing fetus are being investigated for use in pregnant populations. These include repetitive transcranial magnetic stimulation (rTMS), which uses magnetic coils (typically targeted at the dorsolateral prefrontal cortex) to modulate activity [119, 120, 121, 122], and transcranial direct current stimulation (tDCS), which uses low-intensity direct current via electrodes placed to modulate regional brain activity in the prefrontal cortex [123]. New pharmacologic options are emerging for postpartum depression. Brexanolone, an allopregnanolone analogue that is infused over 60 hours, was the first pharmacologic treatment specifically for postpartum depression and was approved by the Food and Drug Administration in the United States in 2019 [19]. This was followed by zuranalone, an oral allopregnanolone analogue, which was approved in 2023 [124].

Ongoing Management

A plan should be developed to monitor progress, with frequency of follow-up determined based on the individual clinical scenario, with very close follow-up in the setting of any high-risk features (e.g. psychotic symptoms, suicidality, estrangement from infant, violent thought content). Health professionals should be aware of the possibility of rapid and distinctive patterns of change in presentation in the perinatal period (e.g., acute worsening postpartum), and therefore more frequent follow-up may be needed compared to other populations. At each appointment, the management plan should be revisited. Standardised measures (both clinician- and patient-rated) may be used to complement clinical evaluation and their use can improve care outcomes and future service provision [97, 125]. For effective measurement-based care, validated outcome scales should be used at regular intervals, and reviewed collaboratively by the patient and practitioner. Most research on measurement-based care comes from non-perinatal research, and further research is needed to identify the best outcome scales for use in perinatal populations. As individuals progress out of the perinatal period, there may also be transitions in care from specialised services to non-perinatal services; caution must be applied to ensure that these do not result in disruption of treatment. Since perinatal depression increases the risk of future depression, discussions should be started early to mitigate relapse risk going forward including specific discussion of risk in relation to future pregnancies and postpartum periods.

Summary

Pregnancy, childbirth and the postpartum period have unique biological and psychosocial characteristics that can affect the development, expression and course of depression. Special consideration needs to be given to many aspects of depression-related care and treatment in the perinatal period, such as using screening tools that are sensitive to mood changes perinatally, attending to co-morbidities and having an expanded differential diagnosis. Complexities in management include modifications of depression treatment to attend to specific social (e.g. childcare), psychotherapeutic (e.g. role transition) and biological (e.g. potential for fetal/infant medication exposure) factors.

References

1. CA Woody, AJ Ferrari, DJ Siskind, HA Whiteford, MG Harris. A systematic review and meta-regression of the prevalence and incidence of perinatal depression. *J Affect Disord.* 2017;219:86–92.
2. K Al-abri, D Edge, CJ Armitage. Prevalence and correlates of perinatal depression. *Soc Psychiatry Psychiatr Epidemiol.* 2023;58(11):1581–90.
3. NI Gavin, BN Gaynes, KN Lohr, S Meltzer-Brody, G Gartlehner, T Swinson. Perinatal depression: a systematic review of prevalence and incidence. *Obstet Gynecol.* 2005;106(5 Pt 1):1071–83.
4. O Vesga-López, C Blanco, K Keyes, M Olfson, BF Grant, DS Hasin. Psychiatric disorders in pregnant and postpartum women in the United States. *Arch Gen Psychiatry.* 2008;65(7):805–15.
5. KL Wisner, DKY Sit, MC McShea, DM Rizzo, RA Zoretich, CL Hughes, et al. Onset timing, thoughts of self-harm, and diagnoses in postpartum women with screen-positive depression findings. *JAMA Psychiatry.* 2013;70(5):490–8.
6. EE Cameron, ID Sedov, LM Tomfohr-Madsen. Prevalence of paternal depression in pregnancy and the postpartum: an updated meta-analysis. *J Affect Disord.* 2016;206:189–203.
7. LM Howard, E Molyneaux, CL Dennis, T Rochat, A Stein, J Milgrom. Non-psychotic mental disorders in the perinatal period. *Lancet.* 2014;384(9956):1775–88.
8. LS Cohen, LL Altshuler, BL Harlow, R Nonacs, DJ Newport, AC Viguera, et al. Relapse of major depression during pregnancy in women who maintain or discontinue antidepressant treatment. *JAMA.* 2006;295(5):499–507.
9. KA Yonkers, N Gotman, MV Smith, A Forray, K Belanger, WL Brunetto, et al. Does antidepressant use attenuate the risk of a major depressive episode in pregnancy? *Epidemiology.* 2011;22(6):848–54.
10. E Robertson, S Grace, T Wallington, DE Stewart. Antenatal risk factors for postpartum depression: a synthesis of recent literature. *Gen Hosp Psychiatry.* 2004;26(4):289–95.
11. M Mauri, A Oppo, MS Montagnani, C Borri, S Banti, V Camilleri, et al. Beyond "postpartum depressions": specific anxiety diagnoses during pregnancy predict different outcomes. *J Affect Disord.* 2010;127(1–3):177–84.
12. JL Payne, JT Palmer, H Joffe. A reproductive subtype of depression: conceptualizing models and moving toward etiology. *Harv Rev Psychiatry.* 2009;17(2):72–86.
13. CE Schiller, S Meltzer-Brody, DR Rubinow. The role of reproductive hormones in postpartum depression. *CNS Spectr.* 2015;20(1):48–59.
14. M Bloch. Effects of gonadal steroids in women with a history of postpartum depression. *Am J Psychiatry.* 2000;157(6):924–30.
15. AJ Gregoire, R Kumar, B Everitt, AF Henderson, JW Studd. Transdermal oestrogen for treatment of severe postnatal depression. *Lancet.* 1996;347(9006):930–3.
16. EL Moses-Kolko, SL Berga, B Kalro, DKY Sit, KL Wisner. Transdermal estradiol for postpartum depression: a promising treatment option. *Clin Obstet Gynecol.* 2009;52(3):516–29.
17. C Barth, A Villringer, J Sacher. Sex hormones affect neurotransmitters and shape the adult female brain during hormonal transition periods. *Front Neurosci.* 2015;9:37.
18. JL Payne, J Maguire. Pathophysiological mechanisms implicated in postpartum depression. *Front Neuroendocrinol.* 2019;52:165–80.

19. S Meltzer-Brody, H Colquhoun, R Riesenberg, CN Epperson, KM Deligiannidis, DR Rubinow, et al. Brexanolone injection in post-partum depression: two multicentre, double-blind, randomised, placebo-controlled, phase 3 trials. *Lancet.* 2018;392(10152):1058–70.
20. D Moura, MC Canavarro, M Figueiredo-Braga. Oxytocin and depression in the perinatal period: a systematic review. *Arch Womens Ment Health.* 2016;19(4):561–70.
21. MJ Szpunar, BL Parry. A systematic review of cortisol, thyroid-stimulating hormone, and prolactin in peripartum women with major depression. *Arch Womens Ment Health.* 2018;21(2):149–61.
22. LM Osborne, C Monk. Perinatal depression – the fourth inflammatory morbidity of pregnancy?: theory and literature review. *Psychoneuroendocrinology.* 2013;38(10):1929–52.
23. T Cotechini, CH Graham. Aberrant maternal inflammation as a cause of pregnancy complications: a potential therapeutic target? *Placenta.* 2015;36(8):960–6.
24. P Leff-Gelman, I Mancilla-Herrera, M Flores-Ramos, C Cruz-Fuentes, JP Reyes-Grajeda, M Del Pilar García-Cuétara, et al. The immune system and the role of inflammation in perinatal depression. *Neurosci Bull.* 2016;32(4):398–420.
25. G Winter, RA Hart, RPG Charlesworth, CF Sharpley. Gut microbiome and depression: what we know and what we need to know. *Rev Neurosci.* 2018;29(6):629–43.
26. SM Edwards, SA Cunningham, AL Dunlop, EJ Corwin. The maternal gut microbiome during pregnancy. *MCN Am J Matern Child Nurs.* 2017;42(6):310–17.
27. A Viktorin, S Meltzer-Brody, R Kuja-Halkola, PF Sullivan, M Landén, P Lichtenstein, PKE Magnusson. Heritability of perinatal depression and genetic overlap with nonperinatal depression. *Am J Psychiatry.* 2016;173(2):158–65.
28. L Forty, L Jones, S Macgregor, S Caesar, C Cooper, A Hough, et al. Familiality of postpartum depression in unipolar disorder: results of a family study. *Am J Psychiatry.* 2006;163(9):1549–53.
29. J Elwood, E Murray, A Bell, M Sinclair, WG Kernohan, J Stockdale. A systematic review investigating if genetic or epigenetic markers are associated with postnatal depression. *J Affect Disord.* 2019;253:51–62.
30. K McEvoy, LM Osborne, J Nanavati, JL Payne. Reproductive affective disorders: a review of the genetic evidence for premenstrual dysphoric disorder and postpartum depression. *Curr Psychiatry Rep.* 2017;19(12):94.
31. J Guintivano, EM Byrne, J Kiewa, S Yao, AE Bauer, KA Aberg, et al. Meta-analyses of genome-wide association studies for postpartum depression. *Am J Psychiatry.* 2023;180(12):884–95.
32. J Fisher, M Cabral de Mello, V Patel, A Rahman, T Tran, S Holton, W Holmes. Prevalence and determinants of common perinatal mental disorders in women in low- and lower-middle-income countries: a systematic review. *Bull World Health Organ.* 2012;90(2):139G–149G.
33. CA Lancaster, KJ Gold, HA Flynn, H Yoo, SM Marcus, MM Davis. Risk factors for depressive symptoms during pregnancy: a systematic review. *Am J Obstet Gynecol.* 2010;202(1):5–14.
34. VM Atzl, AJ Narayan, LM Rivera, AF Lieberman. Adverse childhood experiences and prenatal mental health: type of ACEs and age of maltreatment onset. *J Fam Psychol.* 2019;33(3):304–14.
35. KW Choi, KJ Sikkema, B Vythilingum, L Geerts, SC Faure, MH Watt, et al. Maternal childhood trauma, postpartum depression, and infant outcomes: avoidant affective processing as a potential mechanism. *J Affect Disord.* 2017;211:107–15.
36. LE Ross, CL Dennis. The prevalence of postpartum depression among women

with substance use, an abuse history, or chronic illness: a systematic review. *J Womens Health.* 2009;18(4):475–86.

37. CH Collins, C Zimmerman, LM Howard. Refugee, asylum seeker, immigrant women and postnatal depression: rates and risk factors. *Arch Womens Ment Health.* 2011;14(1):3–11.
38. LE Ross, L Steele, C Goldfinger, C Strike. Perinatal depressive symptomatology among lesbian and bisexual women. *Arch Womens Ment Health.* 2007;10(2):53–9.
39. AD Light, J Obedin-Maliver, JM Sevelius, JL Kerns. Transgender men who experienced pregnancy after female-to-male gender transitioning. *Obstet Gynecol.* 2014;124(6):1120–7.
40. OJ Fischer. Non-binary reproduction: stories of conception, pregnancy, and birth. *Int J Transgend Health.* 2021;22(1–2):77–88.
41. HK Brown, A Qazilbash, N Rahim, CL Dennis, SN Vigod. Chronic medical conditions and peripartum mental illness: a systematic review and meta-analysis. *Am J Epidemiol.* 2018;187(9):2060–8.
42. M Mitra, LI Iezzoni, J Zhang, LM Long-Bellil, SC Smeltzer, BA Barton. Prevalence and risk factors for postpartum depression symptoms among women with disabilities. *Matern Child Health J.* 2015;19(2):362–72.
43. HC Youn, S Lee, SW Han, LY Kim, T-S Lee, M-J Oh, et al. Obstetric risk factors for depression during the postpartum period in South Korea: a nationwide study. *J Psychosom Res.* 2017;102:15–20.
44. J Mo, Z Ning, X Wang, F Lv, J Feng, L Pan. Association between perinatal pain and postpartum depression: a systematic review and meta-analysis. *J Affect Disord.* 2022;312:92–9.
45. American Psyciatric Association. *Diagnostic and statistical manual of mental disorders, 5th edition (DSM-5).* Washington, DC: American Psychiatric Association; 2013.
46. KA Yonkers, MV Smith, H Lin, HB Howell, L Shao, RA Rosenheck. Depression screening of perinatal women: an evaluation of the healthy start depression initiative. *Psychiatric Serv.* 2009;60(3):322–8.
47. K Falah-Hassani, R Shiri, S Vigod, CL Dennis. Prevalence of postpartum depression among immigrant women: a systematic review and meta-analysis. *J Psychiatr Res.* 2015;70:67–82.
48. CL Dennis, K Falah-Hassani, R Shiri. Prevalence of antenatal and postnatal anxiety: systematic review and meta-analysis. *Br J Psychiatry.* 2017;210(5):315–23.
49. JH Goodman. Postpartum depression beyond the early postpartum period. *J Obstet Gynecol Neonat Nurs.* 2004;33(4):410–20.
50. W Coryell. The time course of nonchronic major depressive disorder. *Arch Gen Psychiatry.* 1994;51(5):405–10.
51. D Sit, J Luther, D Buysse, MH Nauta, SO de Vries, BWJH Penninx, et al. Suicidal ideation in depressed postpartum women: associations with childhood trauma, sleep disturbance and anxiety. *J Psychiatr Res.* 2015;66–67:95–104.
52. Australian Institute of Health and Welfare. Maternal deaths in Australia 2012–2014. 2017. www.aihw.gov.au
53. M Knight, M Nair, D Tuffnell, J Shakespeare, S Kenyon, JJ Kurinczuk, editors. *Saving Lives, Improving Mothers' Care – Lessons learned to inform maternity care from the UK and Ireland Confidential Enquiries into Maternal Deaths and Morbidity 2013–15.* Oxford: National Perinatal Epidemiology Unit, University of Oxford; 2017.
54. M Knight, K Bunch, R Patel, J Shakespeare, R Kotnis, S Kenyon, JJ Kurinczuk, editors. *Saving Lives, Improving Mothers' Care – Lessons learned to inform maternity care from the UK and Ireland Confidential Enquiries into Maternal Deaths and Morbidity 2018–2020.* Oxford: National Perinatal Epidemiology Unit, University of Oxford; 2022.
55. H Khalifeh, IM Hunt, L Appleby, LM Howard. Suicide in perinatal and non-

perinatal women in contact with psychiatric services: 15 year findings from a UK national inquiry. *Lancet Psychiatry.* 2016;3(3):233–42.

56. MG Spinelli. Maternal infanticide associated with mental illness: prevention and the promise of saved lives. *Am J Psychiatry.* 2004;161(9):1548–57.
57. SN Hinkle, GM Buck Louis, S Rawal, Y Zhu, PS Albert, C Zhang. A longitudinal study of depression and gestational diabetes in pregnancy and the postpartum period. *Diabetologia.* 2016;59(12):2594–602.
58. MK Thombre, NM Talge, C Holzman. Association between pre-pregnancy depression/anxiety symptoms and hypertensive disorders of pregnancy. *J Womens Health.* 2015;24(3): 228–36.
59. NK Grote, WJ Katon, MJ Lohr, K Carson, M Curran, E Galvin, et al. Culturally relevant treatment services for perinatal depression in socio-economically disadvantaged women: the design of the MOMCare study. *Contemp Clin Trials.* 2014;39(1):34–49.
60. S Gentile. Untreated depression during pregnancy: Short- and long-term effects in offspring. A systematic review. *Neuroscience.* 2017;342:154–66.
61. CL Dennis, K McQueen. Does maternal postpartum depressive symptomatology influence infant feeding outcomes? *Acta Paediatr.* 2007;96(4):590–4.
62. ML Zajicek-Farber. Postnatal depression and infant health practices among high-risk women. *J Child Fam Stud.* 2009;18(2):236–45.
63. A Stein, RM Pearson, SH Goodman, E Rapa, A Rahman, M McCallum, et al. Effects of perinatal mental disorders on the fetus and child. *Lancet.* 2014;384(9956):1800–19.
64. KA Ertel, KC Koenen, JW Rich-Edwards, MW Gillman. Antenatal and postpartum depressive symptoms are differentially associated with early childhood weight and adiposity. *Paediatr Perinat Epidemiol.* 2010;24(2):179–89.
65. L Ban, JE Gibson, J West, LJ Tata. Association between perinatal depression in mothers and the risk of childhood infections in offspring: a population-based cohort study. *BMC Public Health.* 2010;10(1):799.
66. E Lefkovics, I Baji, J Rigó. Impact of maternal depression on pregnancies and on early attachment. *Infant Ment Health J.* 2014;35(4):354–65.
67. SH Goodman, MH Rouse, AM Connell, MR Broth, CM Hall, D Heyward. Maternal depression and child psychopathology: a meta-analytic review. *Clin Child Fam Psychol Rev.* 2011;14(1):1–27.
68. L Murray, A Arteche, P Fearon, S Halligan, I Goodyer, P Cooper. Maternal postnatal depression and the development of depression in offspring up to 16 years of age. *J Am Acad Child Adolesc Psychiatry.* 2011;50(5):460–70.
69. SL Grace, A Evindar, DE Stewart. The effect of postpartum depression on child cognitive development and behavior: a review and critical analysis of the literature. *Arch Womens Ment Health.* 2003;6(4):263–74.
70. JH Goodman. Paternal postpartum depression, its relationship to maternal postpartum depression, and implications for family health. *J Adv Nurs.* 2004;45(1):26–35.
71. PJ Havinga, L Boschloo, AJP Bloemen, MH Nauta, SO de Vries, BWJH Penninx, et al. Doomed for disorder? High incidence of mood and anxiety disorders in offspring of depressed and anxious patients. *J Clin Psychiatry.* 2017;78(1):e8–e17.
72. The Lancet. Screening for perinatal depression: a missed opportunity (Editorial). *Lancet.* 2016;387(10018):505.
73. E O'Connor, RC Rossom, M Henninger, HC Groom, BU Burda. Primary care screening for and treatment of depression in pregnant and postpartum women. *JAMA.* 2016;315(4):388–406.
74. American College of Obstetrics and Gynecology. ACOG Committee Opinion

No. 757 Screening for Perinatal Depression. *Obstet Gynecol.* 2018;132(5): e208–e212.

75. MF Earls, MW Yogman, G Mattson, J Rafferty, Committee on Psychosocial Aspects of Child and Family Health. Incorporating recognition and management of perinatal depression into pediatric practice. *Pediatrics.* 2019;143(1): e20183259.

76. JL Cox, JM Holden, R Sagovsky. Detection of postnatal depression: development of the 10-item Edinburgh Postnatal Depression Scale. *Brit J Psychiatry.* 1987;150:782–6.

77. DT Lee, SK Yip, HF Chiu, TY Leung, KP Chan, IO Chau, et al. Detecting postnatal depression in Chinese women: validation of the Chinese version of the Edinburgh Postnatal Depression Scale. *Br J Psychiatry.* 1998;172:433–7.

78. K Bosanquet, D Bailey, S Gilbody, M Harden, L Manea, S Nutbrown, D McMillan. Diagnostic accuracy of the Whooley questions for the identification of depression: a diagnostic meta-analysis. *BMJ Open.* 2015;5(12):e008913.

79. D Gjerdingen, S Crow, P McGovern, M Miner, B Center. Postpartum depression screening at well-child visits: validity of a 2-question screen and the PHQ-9. *The Annals of Family Medicine.* 2009;7(1):63–70.

80. American Psychiatric Association. *Diagnostic and statistical manual of mental disorders, fifth edition, text revision (DSM-5-TR).* Washington, DC: American Psychiatric Association; 2022.

81. DE Stewart, S Vigod. Postpartum depression. *New Engl J Med.* 2016;375(22):2177–86.

82. World Health Organization. International classification of diseases for mortality and morbidity statistics (11th revision). 2018. https://icd.who.int/browse11/l-m/en

83. MW O'Hara, EM Zekoski, LH Philipps, EJ Wright. Controlled prospective study of postpartum mood disorders: comparison of childbearing and nonchildbearing women. *J Abnorm Psychol.* 1990;99(1):3–15.

84. A Oakley, G Chamberlain. Medical and social factors in postpartum depression. *J Obstet Gynaecol.* 1981;1(3):182–7.

85. MW O'Hara, KL Wisner. Perinatal mental illness: definition, description and aetiology. *Best Pract Res Clin Obstet Gynaecol.* 2014;28(1):3–12.

86. EJ Russell, JM Fawcett, D Mazmanian. Risk of obsessive-compulsive disorder in pregnant and postpartum women. *J Clin Psychiatry.* 2013;74(4):377–85.

87. A Forray, B Merry, H Lin, JP Ruger, KA Yonkers. Perinatal substance use: a prospective evaluation of abstinence and relapse. *Drug Alcohol Depend.* 2015;150:147–55.

88. T Munk-Olsen, TM Laursen, S Meltzer-Brody, PB Mortensen, I Jones. Psychiatric disorders with postpartum onset: possible early manifestations of bipolar affective disorders. *Arch Gen Psychiatry.* 2012;69(4):428–34.

89. V Bergink, N Rasgon, KL Wisner. Postpartum psychosis: madness, mania, and melancholia in motherhood. *Am J Psychiatry.* 2016;173(12):1179–88.

90. SJB McCoy, JM Beal, ME Payton, AL Stewart, AM DeMers, GH Watson. Postpartum thyroid measures and depressive symptomology: a pilot study. *J Am Osteopath Assoc.* 2008;108(9):503–7.

91. R Bunevicius, L Kusminskas, N Mickuviene, A Bunevicius, CA Pedersen, VJM Pop. Depressive disorder and thyroid axis functioning during pregnancy. *World J Biol Psychiatry.* 2009;10(4):324–9.

92. H Vulser, E Wiernik, N Hoertel, F Thomas, B Pannier, S Czernichow, et al. Association between depression and anemia in otherwise healthy adults. *Acta Psychiatr Scand.* 2016;134(2):150–60.

93. H Skouteris, EH Wertheim, S Rallis, J Milgrom, SJ Paxton. Depression and anxiety through pregnancy and the early postpartum: an examination of prospective relationships. *J Affect Disord.* 2009;113(3):303–8.

94. SLC Chapman, LT Wu. Postpartum substance use and depressive symptoms: a review. *Women Health.* 2013;53(5):479–503.

95. C Hudson, E Spry, R Borschmann, D Becker, P Moran, C Olsson, et al. Preconception personality disorder and antenatal maternal mental health: a population-based cohort study. *J Affect Disord.* 2017;209:169–76.

96. V Lindahl, JL Pearson, L Colpe. Prevalence of suicidality during pregnancy and the postpartum. *Arch Womens Ment Health.* 2005;8(2):77–87.

97. RW Lam, D McIntosh, J Wang, MW Enns, T Kolivakis, EE Michalak, et al. Canadian Network for Mood and Anxiety Treatments (CANMAT) 2016 clinical guidelines for the management of adults with major depressive disorder: Section 1. Disease burden and principles of care. *Can J Psychiatry.* 2016;61(9):510–23.

98. L Orsolini, A Valchera, R Vecchiotti, C Tomasetti, F Iasevoli, M Fornaro, et al. Suicide during perinatal period: epidemiology, risk factors, and clinical correlates. *Front Psychiatry.* 2016;7:138.

99. KM Devries, JY Mak, LJ Bacchus, JC Child, G Falder, M Petzold, et al. Intimate partner violence and incident depressive symptoms and suicide attempts: a systematic review of longitudinal studies. *PLoS Med.* 2013;10(5):e1001439.

100. AJ Gelenberg, MP Freeman, JC Markowitz, JF Rosenbaum, ME Thase, MH Trivedi, RS Van Rhoads. Practice guideline for the treatment of patients with major depressive disorder. Third ed. 2010. www.psychiatryonline.com/pracGuide/pracGuideTopic_7.aspx

101. National Institute for Health and Care Excellence (NICE). Antenatal and postnatal mental health: clinical management and service guidance. Clinical Guideline (CG192). 2014. https://shorturl.at/gZN3f

102. GM MacQueen, BN Frey, Z Ismail, N Jaworska, M Steiner, RJ Van Lieshout, et al. Canadian Network for Mood and Anxiety Treatments (CANMAT) 2016 clinical guidelines for the management of adults with major depressive disorder: Section 6. Special populations: youth, women, and the elderly. *Can J Psychiatry.* 2016;61(9):588–603.

103. MP Austin, N Highet, Guidelines Expert Advisory Committee. Clinical practice guidelines: depression and related disorders – anxiety, bipolar disorder and puerperal psychosis – in the perinatal period. 2011. https://shorturl.at/V8ckV

104. D Gjerdingen, W Katon, DE Rich. Stepped care treatment of postpartum depression. *Womens Health Issues.* 2008;18(1):44–52.

105. S Meltzer-Brody, I Jones. Optimizing the treatment of mood disorders in the perinatal period. *Dialogues Clin Neurosci.* 2015;17(2):207–18.

106. CL Dennis, T Dowswell. Psychosocial and psychological interventions for preventing postpartum depression. *Cochrane Database Syst Rev.* 2021;(11). Art. No.: CD001134. DOI: 10.1002/14651858.CD001134.pub3.

107. E Werner, M Miller, LM Osborne, S Kuzava, C Monk. Preventing postpartum depression: review and recommendations. *Arch Womens Ment Health.* 2015;18(1):41–60.

108. E Molyneaux, LA Telesia, C Henshaw, E Boath, E Bradley, LM Howard. Antidepressants for preventing postnatal depression. *Cochrane Database Syst Rev.* 2018;(4). Art. No.: CD004363. DOI: 10.1002/14651858.CD004363.pub3.

109. ID Morres, NA Tzouma, A Hatzigeorgiadis, C Krommidas, KV Kotronis, K Dafopoulos, et al. Exercise for perinatal depressive symptoms: a systematic review and meta-analysis of randomized controlled trials in perinatal health services. *J Affect Disord.* 2022;298(Pt A):26–42.

110. L Kempler, L Sharpe, CB Miller, DJ Bartlett. Do psychosocial sleep interventions improve infant sleep or maternal mood in the postnatal period? A systematic review and meta-analysis of randomised controlled trials. *Sleep Med Rev.* 2016;29:15–22.

111. KM Sheffield, CL Woods-Giscombé. Efficacy, feasibility, and acceptability of perinatal yoga on women's mental health and well-being: a systematic literature review. *J Holist Nurs.* 2016;34(1):64–79.

112. B Lever Taylor, K Cavanagh, C Strauss. The effectiveness of mindfulness-based interventions in the perinatal period: a systematic review and meta-analysis. *PLoS ONE.* 2016;11(5):e0155720.

113. CL Dennis, ED Hodnett. Psychosocial and psychological interventions for treating postpartum depression. *Cochrane Database Syst Rev.* 2007;(4). Art. No.: CD006116. DOI: 10.1002/14651858.CD006116.pub2.

114. S Stuart, H Koleva. Psychological treatments for perinatal depression. *Best Pract Res Clin Obstet Gynaecol.* 2014;28(1):61–70.

115. SN Vigod, CL Dennis. Advances in virtual care for perinatal mental disorders. *World Psychiatry.* 2020;19(3):328.

116. DE Stewart, SN Vigod. Postpartum depression: pathophysiology, treatment, and emerging therapeutics. *Annu Rev Med.* 2019;70:183–96.

117. HB Ward, JA Fromson, JJ Cooper, G De Oliveira, M Almeida. Recommendations for the use of ECT in pregnancy: literature review and proposed clinical protocol. *Arch Womens Ment Health.* 2018;21(6):715–22.

118. F Gressier, S Rotenberg, O Cazas, P Hardy. Postpartum electroconvulsive therapy: a systematic review and case report. *Gen Hosp Psychiatry.* 2015;37(4):310–14.

119. J Downar, ZJ Daskalakis. New targets for rTMS in depression: a review of convergent evidence. *Brain Stimul.* 2013;6(3):231–40.

120. G Hızlı Sayar, E Ozten, E Tufan, C Cerit, G Kağan, N Dilbaz, N Tarhan. Transcranial magnetic stimulation during pregnancy. *Arch Womens Ment Health.* 2014;17(4):311–15.

121. G Eryılmaz, G Hızlı Sayar, E Özten, I Göğcegöz Gül, Ö Yorbik, N Işiten, E Bağcı. Follow-up study of children whose mothers were treated with transcranial magnetic stimulation during pregnancy: preliminary results. *Neuromodulation.* 2015;18(4):255–60.

122. R de M Felipe, YA Ferrão. Transcranial magnetic stimulation for treatment of major depression during pregnancy: a review. *Trends Psychiatry Psychother.* 2016;38(4):190–7.

123. SN Vigod, KE Murphy, CL Dennis, TF Oberlander, JG Ray, ZJ Daskalakis, DM Blumberger. Transcranial direct current stimulation (tDCS) for depression in pregnancy: a pilot randomized controlled trial. *Brain Stimul.* 2019;12(6):1475–83.

124. KM Deligiannidis, S Meltzer-Brody, B Maximos, EQ Peeper, M Freeman, R Lasser, et al. Zuranolone for the treatment of postpartum depression. *Am J Psychiatry.* 2023;180(9):668–75.

125. CC Lewis, M Boyd, A Puspitasari, E Navarro, J Howard, H Kassab, et al. Implementing measurement-based care in behavioral health. *JAMA Psychiatry.* 2018;76(3):324–35.

Chapter 11

Anxiety Disorders

Rose Meades, Heather O'Mahen, Antoinette Davey and Susan Ayers

Introduction

Perinatal anxiety is characterised by intense symptoms of anxiety and fear and includes affective, cognitive and behavioural components. Anxiety disorders include generalised anxiety disorder (GAD), panic disorder, specific phobias, and social anxiety disorder. Obsessive compulsive disorder (OCD) and post-traumatic stress disorder (PTSD) were reclassified into their own sections in the fifth edition of the *Diagnostic and Statistical Manual of Mental Disorders* (DSM-5) but are included here to remain in line with the majority of published evidence, and because of agreement that anxiety is a central characteristic of these disorders [1, 2]. Some level of antenatal anxiety is common, but when it becomes extreme or persistent it can be associated with maternal, fetal and infant morbidity including poor fetal development, preterm birth and low birthweight [3], lower rates of breastfeeding and higher rates of postpartum depression [4], difficulties interacting with infants [5], attention, conduct, emotional and cognitive problems in children and teenagers and risk of the child developing an anxiety disorder [6]. In the UK, perinatal anxiety is estimated to cost £34,840 (in 2016) for each woman's lifetime. Together with perinatal depression, the total cost is £6.6 billion, 75% of which is attributed to impact on the child [7].

In this chapter we will first provide an overview of the different anxiety and associated disorders. Then, we focus on issues to consider in perinatal anxiety, namely the consideration of symptoms versus disorders, normal versus pathological anxiety and pregnancy-specific versus general anxiety. The subsequent sections of the chapter focus on each of the anxiety and associated disorders in turn: their epidemiology, aetiology, presentation, course and outcomes including for the infant and family; and, finally, their management.

Prevalence of Anxiety Disorders and Comorbidity

Anxiety disorders are among the most prevalent mental health disorders, are three times more prevalent in mothers than fathers, often have their first onset during the child-bearing years and are more prevalent in pregnancy than depression [2, 8, 9].

Meta-analytic evidence that included only studies using diagnostic interviews suggests 20.7% of women have at least one anxiety disorder during pregnancy or postpartum, and 5.5% of women have more than one anxiety disorder [2]. By trimester, across countries and settings, prevalence rates for any anxiety disorder were 18% in the first trimester, 15% in the second and third trimesters of pregnancy, and 9.3–9.9% in the first year after birth [9]. Prevalence and incidence differ between the disorders and more is known about anxiety disorders in pregnancy than postpartum. By disorder, estimates of prevalence are: GAD 1.3–3.8%; social phobia 1.6–3.5%; panic disorder 1.9%; agoraphobia 1.0–4.0%; specific phobia 2.4–7.7% (needle phobia being the most common subtype); OCD 1.2–3.6%; PTSD 0.5–2.0% [2]; and tokophobia (0.03%) [2, 10]. Although most anxiety disorders in the perinatal period have a similar prevalence as outside the perinatal period [2], there is evidence that OCD is more prevalent postnatally than at other times in life [11], and up to 50% of women retrospectively report their first onset of OCD in the postnatal period. Women who have pre-existing OCD are more likely to experience a worsening of symptoms in the perinatal period [11].

A notable proportion of women (0.8–4.5%) are diagnosed with anxiety disorder not otherwise specified, indicating their symptoms may not be captured by the other anxiety disorders [12]. For example, women suffering with pregnancy-specific anxiety may have high levels of worry that are disabling, but they do not meet criteria for GAD because their worries are focused on the pregnancy, their own health and/or childbirth, rather than on diffuse areas of worries as is typically characterised in GAD [12, 13].

Levels of self-reported symptoms of anxiety have a different pattern than disorders and are more prevalent in the second and third trimesters than at other points in the perinatal period. Evidence from cross-sectional or cohort studies (i.e. not self-selected or high-risk women) suggests that symptoms increase during pregnancy, with a prevalence of 18.2% in the first trimester of pregnancy, 19.1% in the second trimester, 24.6% in the third trimester, 17.8% in the first 4 weeks after birth and 15.0% after the first 24 weeks postpartum [9].

Perinatal anxiety may co-exist with other mental health problems and may be the presenting symptom for depressive and substance use disorders, autism spectrum disorder or attention deficit hyperactivity disorder. Severe anxiety may be the initial prodromal feature of an evolving psychotic illness. Commonly, perinatal anxiety is highly comorbid with depression. Women with comorbid anxiety and depression can also experience higher levels of anxiety symptoms, anger and daily hassles than those with anxiety or depression alone [9].

Course and Associated Outcomes

Although non-clinical levels of perinatal anxiety may resolve within 6 months of birth [8], without treatment, anxiety disorders, PTSD and OCD have chronic courses, with low rates of spontaneous remission, especially in women with histories of mental health problems before pregnancy [14]. Increased anxiety during pregnancy is also a strong risk factor for depression, both during pregnancy and postpartum [15]. Individuals with comorbid anxiety and depression are especially likely to experience a chronic course if their symptoms remain untreated [16].

Perinatal anxiety extends beyond the mother and is associated with problems in the intimate partner relationship [17], small for gestational age infants [18], increased infant cortisol levels in the first 15 months of life [19], lower rates of breastfeeding and longitudinally with increased social and behavioural problems in the infant [6]. Comorbid depressive and anxiety disorders are associated with higher levels of preterm birth and low birthweight [12], and women with anxiety and depression living in areas of neighbourhood deprivation are at higher risk of preterm birth than those who are not [14]. These problems may be mediated, in part, by the parent's preoccupation with their worries and fears, and inability to attend sensitively to the child [20] and by child temperament. Infant behavioural inhibition has been strongly linked to later risk for anxiety disorders [21, 22], though the epigenetic role of parental cortisol levels in pregnancy and parenting postnatally on the expression of temperament is not clear.

Aetiology

As a whole, anxiety disorders are characterised by excessive fear, distress and avoidant behaviours in response to perceived environmental or internal threats [1, 2]. Although associative learning processes are thought to be a core underlying learning process, variations in the age of onset across disorders, higher prevalence of anxiety in women and the fact that many individuals will encounter fearful learning contexts but not develop an anxiety disorder point to the importance of additional risk factors in the onset of anxiety disorders, including genetic and hormonal factors [22].

Associative learning processes include classical conditioning, where pairing a neutral stimulus (e.g. visit to midwifery clinic) with a negative stimulus (e.g. physically uncomfortable examination accompanied with perceived 'coldness' by midwife) results in fears of the previously neutral stimulus. Further recognised factors in associative learning include individual differences in sensitivities to acquiring fear and lack of previous experiences with stimuli in neutral contexts because of restricted environmental contact (e.g. through controlling parenting) – resulting in poor inhibition of associative fear learning. For example, a woman who has attended health checks and hospital clinics several times before she experiences the painful and emotionally uncomfortable visit is less likely to view these types of medical encounters as negative and fearful. Additionally, fear generalisation from one stimulus to another and poor fear extinction may be linked to repetitive processes such as worry and rumination, and behavioural avoidance of feared stimuli. Some of these processes are thought to be associated with women's increased risk of developing an anxiety disorder, including evidence that women are more likely to ruminate and worry, and that girls are more likely to experience restrictive and intrusive parenting [23]. Perinatally, new experiences, increased perceived levels of responsibility for the baby, new environments and having to encounter situations that may previously have been feared but avoided (e.g. blood/injection phobia) may prompt the onset of a new anxiety disorder, or the worsening or recurrence of an existing anxiety disorder. Research with a large population of perinatal women provided evidence of risk factors for anxiety across the perinatal period. These included higher educational level, history of depression, preterm birth, negative experience of birth and the first week postpartum, excessive infant crying, low maternity self-efficacy, low partner support and poor current maternal health [24].

Some of these factors may also be linked to individual differences. There is evidence from twin studies that the acquisition of fear is 35–40% heritable [25]. The serotonin transporter gene 5-HTTLPR, which is associated with amygdala reactivity, may underlie fear acquisition, whilst brain-derived neurotropic factor is critical for neural plasticity in the hippocampus and may be linked with fear generalisability. Critically, these may be moderated by epigenetic processes [25]. Further, although evidence on the role of hormones in associative learning is scarce, emerging evidence has shown that ovariectomised rats or those that were receiving estradiol showed greater fear generalisation [26], whereas higher levels of estradiol in humans were associated with better fear extinction.

During the perinatal period, these findings imply that, although parents may be more prone to developing over-general fears if exposed to traumatic or fearful stimuli, they may also be especially likely to respond well to exposure-based treatments that build on extinction learning. In contrast, rapidly dropping estradiol levels in the immediate postpartum period may equate to lowered sensitivity in women to exposure-based treatments.

Assessment

Normal versus Pathological Anxiety

Understanding whether anxiety is normal or pathological may be difficult for women as some worries and anxiety about the developing baby, birth and being a parent are a universal normal response to a life-changing event. However, understanding the severity, chronicity and perceived emotional and functional impact of anxiety symptoms can help to distinguish between normal and pathological anxiety. A further issue in characterising anxiety in the perinatal period includes understanding the extent to which somatic criteria are due to physical or psychological causes (e.g. being more fatigued than normal, difficulty sleeping, avoiding social situations because of pregnancy/postpartum health constraints or because of anxiety) [27]. Without consideration of the physical impact of pregnancy and the postpartum period on these somatic problems, perinatal anxiety levels may be inflated. Assessment should therefore query whether parents believe difficulties in these domains are due to pregnancy/postpartum or to their mood.

Assessment Measures

Clinical guidelines recommend assessment for anxiety should start with the GAD-2 (the first two items of the GAD-7), although criticisms of this measure include its specificity to GAD only, and that it has not been widely validated with perinatal women [28]. The GAD-2 has shown poor predictive validity, with low areas under the curve [29]. The Depression, Anxiety, and Stress Scales are validated for use in the perinatal period and detect a wider range of anxiety disorders [30]. The CORE-10 and Stirling Antenatal Anxiety Scale [31] have been validated against the Mini-Neuropsychiatric Interview in pregnant and postnatal women in the UK and both showed better diagnostic accuracy than the GAD-2 and GAD-7 at identifying anxiety disorders [32]. The Perinatal Anxiety Screening Scale (PASS) [33] includes a social anxiety subscale and the total score identified 68% of women with a diagnosed anxiety disorder but prevalence in the samples was low. A study of the PASS with an Italian sample of 298 perinatal women compared it to the Hamilton Anxiety rating scales and found that with a cut-off of 6 the area under the curve = 0.80, providing good support for its use as a screening scale [34]. There is some evidence that early pregnancy is the optimal time to screen for anxiety in order to pick up women who have or develop anxiety disorders [35].

Risk

Assessment during the perinatal period should always include assessment of risk to mother and to the infant. Intrusive thoughts about perinatal-related concerns are common in anxiety and depressive disorders, and should be carefully compared to more rare psychotic thoughts (see [36, 37] for helpful clinical guides). Domestic violence increases in the perinatal period and should be carefully assessed relative to parents' fears and anxieties. Although anxious parents are more likely to report worries about bonding, these do not accurately predict the quality of the parent–infant interaction [10], thus observational assessments are needed to determine risk and whether direct work with the parent–infant relationship is required.

Monitoring Anxiety and Distress in Response to Treatment

The CORE-10 is widely used in clinical practice to monitor progress and outcomes during therapy. The CORE-10 captures a wide range of emotional difficulties and includes two items measuring anxiety. In pregnancy and the early postpartum the CORE-10 has been validated against the Mini-International Neuropsychiatric Interview and Whooley Questions [38]. It may therefore be appropriate to use the CORE-10 as an outcome measure in perinatal treatment.

Because of the links between pregnancy-specific anxiety and infant birth outcomes [4, 5] and because pregnancy-specific anxiety content may not be detected on existing generic measures of anxiety, a pregnancy-specific measure or interview should be employed to augment other validated assessment. A number of measures of pregnancy-specific anxiety have been developed and validated including the Cambridge Worry Scale, the Wijma-Delivery Experience Questionnaire, the Stirling Antenatal Anxiety Scale and the Pregnancy-Related Anxiety Questionnaire (see [28] for review).

Interview-Based Measures

Interviews for diagnosing anxiety disorders in perinatal research include the Mini-International Neuropsychiatric Interview (MINI) [39], the Composite International Diagnostic Interview for Women (CIDI-V) [40], the Structured Clinical Interview (SCID) for DSM-IV (SCID-IV) [41] and the Psychiatric Diagnostic Screening Questionnaire (PDSQ) [42]. The CIDI-V is a women-specific platform embedded in the highly structured World Health Organization-Composite International Diagnostic Interview (WHO-CIDI), based on DSM-IV. It includes complete menstrual, perinatal and pregnancy history, providing clinically relevant information about women's mental health not included in other diagnostic interviews. In a large study of perinatal women, the PDSQ showed low agreement with another measure of anxiety (SCL-90), which has led some researchers to consider that the PDSQ is not suitable for perinatal populations [42].

Treatment of Perinatal Anxiety and Relation Disorders

Given the chronicity of untreated or partially treated perinatal anxiety and the potential for adverse impact on childbirth and infant outcomes, it is critical to provide timely access to evidence-based interventions for parents suffering from anxiety disorders during the perinatal period (see Chapter 28, 'Psychological Therapies for Parental Mental Health in the Perinatal Period: What Works?'). However, many women will not seek help, and when they do, anxiety disorders are especially unlikely to be diagnosed during the perinatal period (e.g. of those with GAD 1.5–62.2%; OCD 3–30.2%) and even fewer will be treated to remission [43], placing them and their infants at increased risk for ongoing problems. Perinatal women describe a number of barriers to care, including:

a) a preference to receive care embedded in antenatal care pathways; b) to be actively supported in accessing care; c) lack of knowledge about mental health problems and their treatment, especially anxiety disorders and non-depressive disorders; d) stigma about mental health treatment; and e) lack of time and/or childcare [44]. Addressing these barriers are essential to increasing access.

A number of strategies can increase perinatal women's engagement with treatment. Rapid referral to evidence-based and acceptable treatment, active outreach by practitioners to ensure initial engagement and continuing treatment adherence (e.g. repeated phone and text invitations), flexibility in treatment scheduling, blending in-person with remote treatment provision, expanding the offer of psychological interventions with other clinical and health providers, connecting women to peer supporters who may help to allay fears and normalise the treatment process, and allowing the infant to be present during treatment or providing childcare may facilitate sustained engagement.

Where there are comorbidities between anxiety disorders, or between anxiety disorders and other mental health disorders such as depression, the problem the individual considers to be the primary and most disabling problem should typically be treated first, as targeting this problem often results in amelioration of other comorbid problems. This is also supported by the fact that the interventions with the greatest support for each of the anxiety disorders use exposure-based techniques, and exposure for one disorder may have transtherapeutic effects across comorbid anxiety disorders. Exposure-based techniques involve the individual fully and repeatedly approaching feared stimuli, with the aim to *temporarily* increase emotional arousal until habituation is achieved. Many approaches incorporate emotion processing (e.g. eye movement desensitisation and reprocessing (EMDR) [45] and reappraisal of negative thoughts (trauma-focused cognitive behaviour therapy [46]) into exposure, and these strategies can be particularly helpful in creating strong logic for undertaking exposure-based work and addressing accompanying emotions of guilt and shame.

During pregnancy clinicians should weigh up the pros and cons of using exposure-based techniques with their clients. Evidence now suggests that exposure techniques are likely safe [47], with randomised controlled trials of EMDR and pre-post intervention using trauma-focused treatments demonstrating no evidence of negative outcomes for the infant [48, 49]. Key considerations for the clinician and patient in undertaking exposure during pregnancy may include: a) the risk that a pregnant woman with an anxiety disorder will already have chronically elevated levels of cortisol that will persist without appropriate treatment; b) the risk:benefit ratio of treating with antidepressants and their acceptability to the woman; c) evidence that non-pregnant individuals undergoing exposure demonstrate moderate, rather than high levels of self-reported and physiological arousal; and d) in PTSD treatment, thought to involve the most 'intensive' exposure, there may be a transient worsening of symptoms [47]. Other considerations by trimester include personalised decision-making in the first trimester about the strength of the individual's fears about associations between miscarriage and exposure, even though there is no association in the literature, and in the last trimester about potential time to childbirth. Practitioners should ensure during the third trimester that each session would be okay to be the last prior to childbirth. If exposure-based treatments are undertaken, they should be administered by a skilled practitioner with high-quality supervision to ensure the treatment is undertaken in a competent fashion, as research has demonstrated that non-exposure-based treatments for anxiety can fail to produce positive clinical outcomes, or where exposure is not competently undertaken, can cause harm by sensitising the individual to the feared stimulus [50]. Treatment should be reviewed regularly to ensure women are receiving optimal treatment.

Anxiety and Related Disorders

PTSD and Birth Trauma

Post-traumatic stress disorder was outlined by the *Diagnostic Statistical Manual 5th Revision* (DSM-5) of the American Psychiatric Association as occurring after an event in which: a) there is actual or threatened death; b) actual or threatened serious injury; or c) actual or threatened sexual violence [1]. It is possible for birth to fulfil these criteria if a woman thinks she or her baby will die or be severely injured. Birth may also involve actual or threatened violence. In law the term 'obstetric violence' has been defined as 'the appropriation of a woman's body and reproductive processes by health personnel, in the form of dehumanising treatment, abusive medicalisation and pathologisation of natural processes, involving a woman's loss of autonomy and of the capacity to freely make her own decisions about her body and her sexuality, which has negative consequences for a woman's quality of life' [51]. The World Health Organization has subsequently called for the prevention and elimination of disrespect and abuse in childbirth [52].

An example of a traumatic birth which involves both physical injury and disrespect was reported in a case study [53] of a woman who had an emergency caesarean section without effective anaesthesia in which 'she experienced excruciating pain during an operation which took 10 minutes. She was screaming, shouting, and struggling to get off the operating table during the procedure, and was held down by attendants while the anaesthetist attempted to supplement the epidural' (p. 526). The evidence supports the importance of the way women are treated and supported during birth. For example, Harris and Ayers [54] surveyed 675 women who had traumatic births and asked women to write about their worst moment during birth, or trauma 'hotspot'. This study found that the worst hotspots were due to obstetric complications and pain (36%), complications or separation from the baby (27%) but also interpersonal difficulties such as feeling abandoned, ignored or not supported (37%).

Symptoms of PTSD fall into four clusters: a) re-experiencing; b) avoidance; c) hyperarousal; and d) negative cognitions and mood. For a diagnosis, symptoms need to be evident for at least 1 month and cause significant disability and impairment to a person's life. It should be noted that PTSD is also highly comorbid with depression, with up to 72% of women reporting both PTSD and depression [53].

Reviews suggest that although between 3 and 5% of women develop PTSD after birth [55], there is increased prevalence (15–18%) in high-risk groups such as parents who have severe complications or a preterm or stillborn baby. Women may also have symptoms that do not meet criteria for a diagnosis of PTSD but still cause significant distress and disability. Perinatal parents may also have PTSD due to other traumatic events. A UK survey of 4,509 women found 9.3% had significant PTSD symptoms, 6.8% of which were due to non-childbirth-related traumatic events [56].

Symptoms of PTSD may have unique consequences when birth is the triggering trauma because of the involvement of the baby. If parents associate the baby with the trauma, some may avoid contact with the baby to reduce reminders about the event [57]. Quantitative research suggests that general PTSD symptoms (i.e. hyperarousal, negative cognitions and mood) may impact more negatively on the mother–infant relationship than birth-related PTSD symptoms (i.e. re-experiencing, avoidance) [58].

Another unique aspect is that, unlike other traumatic events, giving birth and having a baby is viewed positively in most societies. This means there can be a lack of acknowledgement by society and friends and family that birth can be traumatic. Parents may feel isolated and not able to talk about birth trauma. There may also be pressure for parents to have another baby and therefore revisit the trauma. However, this is speculative at this stage because there is little empirical evidence examining these factors.

Treatment for PTSD may involve trauma-focused cognitive behaviour therapy (CBT) or EMDR, though content may require adapting to manage feared trauma situations (i.e. childbirth) that in pregnant parents will inevitably happen. Strategies such as using imagery ('flashforward') may help parents to confront both their past traumatic events and future feared events and to 'rescript' these events to include successful coping. Reviews of current adapted treatments have highlighted the use of communication strategies to build interpersonal coping, particularly in managing interactions with obstetric/maternity health staff. A growing body of research suggests PTSD interventions during pregnancy and postnatally are effective and safe for mother and baby. A review contacted the authors of six small studies and none of them reported adverse parental events ranging from suicidal ideation to injurious behaviours or crisis contacts, suggesting that clinicians' fears of parents 'destabilising' in the course of treatment may be rare. Treatment regarding partners' PTSD and longitudinal research examining whether treatment of perinatal PTSD reduces risk of symptoms in subsequent pregnancies is also needed.

Tokophobia

Although fear of childbirth is common, clinical levels of extreme fears of childbirth, known as tokophobia, are relatively rare [59, 60]. Tokophobia can be primary, in women who have not given birth, or secondary in women who experienced a traumatic birth. Tokophobia is associated with a range of obstetric, psychological and socio-demographic factors [59] and can impact on women's birth choices and outcomes. For example, women with tokophobia are more likely to opt for an elective caesarean section (CS), choose an epidural, have longer labours or have an emergency CS [61].

Tokophobia is associated with poor psychological adjustment during pregnancy and after birth, such as antenatal depression and anxiety [62] and postpartum PTSD, depression and anxiety [63]. The long-term impact of tokophobia on mother–infant outcomes has yet to be investigated. However, research on antenatal anxiety suggests anxiety is associated with altered patterns of fetal behaviour and heart rate responses [64], more fearful or anxious behaviour in the infant and increased risk of poor development and adverse child outcomes [65]. Furthermore, antenatal depressive symptoms have been linked to poorer maternal responsiveness 12 months postnatally [20]. This research suggests tokophobia and comorbid affective disorders may have a negative impact on women and their infants.

A range of interventions for the prevention or treatment of tokophobia have been evaluated with women with moderate to severe fear of childbirth. Interventions include tailored antenatal education, enhanced midwifery care, CBT, alternative therapies and other talking therapies. Reviews and meta-analyses suggest most interventions lead to a reduction in symptoms of fear of childbirth, regardless of the approach [44] and that interventions with an educational component are particularly promising [66], although this may be because educational interventions have been more commonly evaluated. However, these reviews also highlighted the poor methodological quality of intervention studies which limits conclusions [44]. An expert consensus paper concluded that in order to improve our understanding, prevention and treatment of tokophobia, we need a better understanding of its aetiology and development[67]. This can then be used to underpin effective and evidence-based interventions.

Generalised Anxiety Disorder

Excessive, uncontrollable worry is the core symptom of GAD. Current research has demonstrated that individuals with GAD tend to experience negative emotion more easily, quickly and intensely than those who do not have GAD. Faced with these strong emotions, particularly in uncertain circumstances, individuals with GAD develop feelings of vulnerability to negative possible events. Fearful of possible bad outcomes, they adopt beliefs that worry will help them prepare or ward off the worst and protect them from 'let-down' if outcomes are poor [22].

Psychological strategies to manage these patterns of fear and worry in GAD include psychoeducation about anxiety and worry, addressing positive beliefs about the functions of worry, learning to tolerate uncertainty, and exposure to feared negative outcomes [68]. Evidence has shown that the efficacy of this latter approach may be enhanced if it follows a period of sustained relaxation. This may support individuals to learn to tolerate their fears about feeling emotionally 'let-down' when they transition from a pleasant mood state to a negative state [22].

The perinatal period presents a number of specific worries that inform treatment of GAD during this period. These worries centre around themes of fears of fetal well-being, maternal illness, parental ability, illness in the partner, negative effects on infant, and parental mortality [69]. Pregnancy-specific worries are of particular concern, as they are related to negative childbirth and neonatal outcomes in comparison to general, non-pregnancy-related worries [70]. Further, individuals who have low tolerance of uncertainty are especially likely to experience increases in worry and anxiety across the transition to parenthood [71]. In the perinatal period, GAD also has negative effects on interpersonal relationships during a period of enhanced need for support; midwives and obstetricians report excessive reassurance-seeking in women suffering from GAD [72], and GAD is associated with declines in relationship satisfaction [73]. Interventions should therefore take the impact of these factors into account in treatment.

Initial studies for psychological treatments adapted for GAD in the perinatal period have shown that group CBT is promising in randomised controlled trials [74, 75] and quasi-experimental designs [76]. There is also early evidence that mindfulness-based cognitive therapy helps reduce anxiety and worry [77].

Perinatal adaptations to these interventions include psychoeducation about anxiety during the perinatal period, tolerating pregnancy-related uncertainty, communication skills and mindfulness with baby exercises. Delivery modifications include delivery by midwives, either with or without a mental health practitioner co-facilitator, inclusion of partners and, postnatally, inclusion of babies. Intervention length typically ranges from three to eight sessions, indicating brief treatments can be effective. However, further sessions may be required in individuals with more severe functional impairment.

Psychological treatment should be a first-line treatment for pregnant women suffering from GAD when functional impairment is mild. When functional impairment is moderate to severe, or the individual has not responded to a brief psychological intervention, either psychological treatment or medication (but not benzodiazepines) may be considered, as there is no evidence of superiority of one form of treatment over the other.

Obsessive Compulsive Disorder

Intrusive thoughts and compulsions are common in parents during the perinatal period (up to 50%), although they are disabling in parents who develop OCD [37]. Parents with OCD are more likely than those in the perinatal period to have intrusive thoughts about fearing the baby will be contaminated, intentionally harming the baby, or that bad things will happen to the baby, and intrusive sexual thoughts about the baby. Parents with OCD report that they find these thoughts highly distressing, 'repugnant' (ego-dystonic) and shameful, and feel that they are personally responsible for causing or avoiding the feared outcome. They therefore spend significant periods of time compulsively attempting to neutralise the thoughts with reassurance, avoidance (of baby), behavioural and cognitive distraction, and performing ritualised behaviours. It is critical that healthcare providers are well-informed about the prevalence of intrusive thoughts and can distinguish between these types of thoughts and both depressive thoughts and psychotic delusions. Parents with OCD are clear that they do not *want* the feared outcomes to happen, and referrals to social services on these thoughts alone should not be made. Parents with psychosis express ego-syntonic thoughts, which makes it more likely they will want to act on the thought. Those with comorbid depression may feel that their children are better off without them; these two latter types of thoughts should be rapidly assessed further.

Individuals with OCD should be offered CBT for OCD. This typically consists of exposure and response prevention and cognitive restructuring. Trained OCD providers who offer CBT for OCD should receive ongoing supervision. Evidence from case studies [78] and a pilot randomised controlled trial [79] suggest that intensive CBT treatment (e.g., four to six 2–3 hour sessions delivered within 2 weeks) is as acceptable and effective in rapidly reducing OCD symptoms as weekly treatment [80]. Furthermore, improvement in intensive treatment lasts 3–6 months post-treatment [79].

Parents with mild to moderate/severe OCD can be treated in primary care mental health services, but those with severe impairment or complexity should be treated within perinatal mental health teams or collaboratively with specialist OCD services in secondary mental healthcare teams. These parents may also be offered medication, typically selective serotonin reuptake inhibitors (SSRI). Where the woman has especially severe OCD or is living in unstable conditions that are a barrier to treatment, admission to a Mother and Baby Unit may be considered. Parents who have other anxiety disorders or depression that persist beyond OCD treatment and OCD symptom remission should receive treatment for these disorders as well.

Parents with OCD may have difficulties with the parent–infant relationship, although many will not. Any suspected problems should be carefully assessed using well-validated observational assessments. Sometimes parents may avoid doing specific activities with the infant (e.g. washing them) or they may avoid the infant more generally because of specific OCD-related fears. In these cases, the OCD treatment should target these fears directly as they may be part of the OCD. There is a lack of data on whether OCD treatment alone helps when there are parent–infant relationship problems [81]. Therefore, persistent parent–infant problems, or problems in the relationship that are not explained by the OCD, should receive interventions that directly target the parent–infant relationship.

Specific Phobias

There is little research on treatment for specific phobias during the perinatal period. Effective psychological treatment approaches typically involve using exposure and habituation to extinguish learned responses to feared stimuli [82]. One quasi-experimental study found a two-session group (or individual) CBT treatment that involved graded exposure with applied tension (tensing muscles to temporarily increase blood pressure and reduce probability of fainting) to injections was acceptable to women and reduced their fears of injection and symptoms of anxiety and depression [83]. Individuals with specific phobias may also be treated with medications, typically SSRIs, but these are less often recommended because psychological treatments are very effective and have fewer side effects than medications, and there are as yet no controlled studies of SSRIs for specific phobias.

Social Anxiety Disorder

Studies assessing social anxiety disorder (SAD) in pregnancy and the postpartum are very limited despite it being one of the most prevalent common mental health disorders in the general population [84]. We therefore draw on a combination of evidence from the general population and the extant perinatal literature.

In common with other anxiety disorders, sub-threshold symptoms, as well as a diagnosed disorder, are associated with significant impairments in work, social and educational domains [83]. Because SAD usually precedes most comorbid conditions and it is highly comorbid with other disorders and anxiety disorders in particular, it is also an important focus for prevention [83]. Younger maternal age, lower socio-economic status and not breastfeeding are significant predictors of increased symptoms of social anxiety, but family and personal psychiatric history are not [85]. Not breastfeeding may be associated with concerns about public exposure, lack of self-confidence or lack of energy, or it could be due to the more dramatic drop in hormone levels experienced by women who do not breastfeed, triggering postpartum social anxiety [86]. Hormones implicated in the development of social anxiety include corticotropin-releasing hormone which is elevated in pregnancy and which is associated with a behaviourally inhibited temperament; serotonergic dysfunction possibly initiated by strong fluctuations in oestrogen; and oxytocin which is associated with fear during social functioning in those with insecure attachments or pre-existing social vulnerabilities [86].

Individuals with SAD have a marked and persistent fear of social interactions and/or performance situations, and fear judgement or acting in a humiliating or embarrassing way; social situations are endured with intense distress or avoided. Impairments in social life and close relationships are common, and work and managing the household can be impaired [84, 86]. Pregnancy and the postpartum period are times of increased social attention which could make this a particularly difficult time for women with SAD, for instance being the centre of attention at social gatherings, struggling with integrating at antenatal or parent–infant groups, or on re-entry to the workplace [87]. Postpartum women with SAD have reported difficulties in initiating and participating in meaningful conversations, inability to find common ground with others who do not have children, and beliefs that they could not talk about anything other than child-rearing, that led to further avoidance of social situations [86]. Further, socially anxious women report that their partners are less caring than women without symptoms, which may be associated with the reported negative impact of social anxiety symptoms on relationship stress [86]. Social anxiety symptoms in pregnancy are predictive of negative maternal reports of child behaviour, and less warmth towards children [88, 89].

Systematic reviews of treatment of perinatal anxiety disorders have found no studies to include on the treatment of SAD [2], and only one to treat multiple anxiety disorders in pregnancy (as opposed to 28 trials for depression) [2]. In the general population individual CBT is considered the best intervention for the initial treatment of SAD as it has lower risks of side effects and larger effect sizes [90].

Panic Disorder

Risk factors for perinatal panic disorder (PD) include a history of psychiatric illness, depression or any anxiety disorder, and lack of family support [91, 92]. There is some evidence that women experiencing life stress and women with lower socio-economic status are more likely to develop PD or panic symptoms in pregnancy [91, 92]. However, research on most predictors is inconclusive [91].

Postpartum women report the most common symptoms of a panic attack as heart palpitations, sweating, trembling and parasthesia [93]. In pregnancy, women report panic because of fear of pregnancy complications and when talking about feelings related to the pregnancy [93]. Whilst some of these symptoms may be physiological aspects of pregnancy and the postpartum period, panic disorder involves unexpected and sudden panic attacks that last for 10–15 minutes and which are accompanied by a fear of dying or of being mentally unstable. Agoraphobia may be diagnosed with PD if women are avoiding situations in which panic attacks are feared (e.g. being in a crowd or at home alone). Qualitative research suggests that postpartum women worry that their panic will have a negative impact on their child because they may have been so consumed with preventing panic they inadvertently neglected aspects of parenting [94]. Overwhelming exhaustion from trying to hide their panic from others, and a fear of leaving the house to take children to groups or activities can result in further concern about the impact on their children [92, 95].

Systematic reviews of treatments for antenatal and postpartum PD [2] have found very few studies to include. There is a strong evidence-base for CBT outside the perinatal period, and it is likewise suggested as a first-line treatment during pregnancy and postpartum [93, 96]. Tricyclic antidepressants and SSRIs have resulted in significant PD improvement and with no reported effects on babies in some studies [93]. However, the evidence base is small. One study found that pregnant women with untreated PD had significantly lower birth weight and gestational age at birth than both women treated with antidepressants for PD and a control group who had similar outcomes, suggesting that pharmacotherapy with SSRIs may have a beneficial impact on birth outcomes for women with PD [97]. Risks and benefits of SSRI treatment in pregnancy are discussed in detail in Chapter 27 ('The Reproductive Safety of Psychotropic Medication and Implications for Prescribing in the Perinatal Period') but any drug treatment should be used only after careful consideration of the benefits and costs for the individual woman. Benzodiazepine treatment is contraindicated for treatment for PD outside the perinatal period, and PD treatment with benzodiazepines during pregnancy was associated with more caesarean births, low birthweight and use of ventilatory support for neonates [98]. With this in mind, CBT may be offered as a first-line treatment, and medication treatment with SSRI undertaken if the individual would not like to undertake CBT or has not responded to CBT. However, the complexity of factors including severity of PD, impact on daily functioning, previous treatment responses and potential impact of medication treatment suggest that combined therapy may be appropriate for some women.

Summary and Conclusion

Anxiety disorders are highly prevalent during the perinatal period, but they are relatively unrecognised and may be misdiagnosed as depression or, in the case of intrusive thoughts, as postpartum psychosis. As anxiety disorders are frequently comorbid with other anxiety disorders and depression, tend to have an unremitting course if untreated and are associated with considerable distress and impairment in functioning, it is critical to accurately assess and promptly treat them. In most cases, psychological interventions such as CBT (and EMDR in the case of PTSD and tokophobia) should be the first-line treatment, though SSRIs may also be prescribed in conjunction with psychological treatment or if the parent prefers medication treatment. Evidence-based CBT and EMDR should be carried out by practitioners who are trained to competence in these treatments and who are supervised by specialists in these interventions. Treatment for anxiety during pregnancy and the postpartum period should be perinatally adapted, taking into account the stage of pregnancy, or infant-related content, and impact of the anxiety disorder on the infant. In particular, clinicians should be competent in assessing for and addressing pregnancy-related anxiety, childbirth and loss related fears, and intrusive thoughts about the infant. Where possible, problems in the parent–infant relationship should also be targeted in treatment. Delivery modifications are frequently needed in the perinatal period and may include having the infant present during treatment, and conducting treatment in health settings and/or including healthcare providers in supporting the delivery of the treatment. With appropriate, competent care there is a strong probability of recovery from perinatal anxiety disorders.

References

1. American Psychiatric Association. Highlights of changes from DSM-IV to DSM-5. *Diagnostic and statistical manual of mental disorders*. https://tinyurl.com/2539b4nk

2. EJ Fawcett, N Fairbrother, ML Cox, IR White, JM Fawcett. The prevalence of anxiety disorders during pregnancy and the postpartum period: a multivariate Bayesian meta-analysis. *J Clin Psychiatry*. 2019;80(4):18r12527.

3. XX Ding, YL Wu, SJ Xu, RP Zhu, XM Jia, SF Zhang, et al. Maternal anxiety during pregnancy and adverse birth outcomes: a systematic review and meta-analysis of

prospective cohort studies. *J Affect Disord.* 2014 Apr;159:103–10.

4. S Grigoriadis, L Graves, M Peer, L Mamisashvili, G Tomlinson, SN Vigod, et al. A systematic review and meta-analysis of the effects of antenatal anxiety on postpartum outcomes. *Arch Womens Ment Health.* 2019;22(5):543–56.
5. A Granat, R Gadassi, E Gilboa-Schechtman, R Feldman. Maternal depression and anxiety, social synchrony, and infant regulation of negative and positive emotions. *Emotion.* 2017;17(1):11–27.
6. V Glover. *Maternal stress during pregnancy and infant and child outcome.* Oxford: Oxford University Press; 2016.
7. A Bauer, M Knapp, M Parsonage. Lifetime costs of perinatal anxiety and depression. *J Affect Disord.* 2016 Mar 1;192:83–90.
8. L Vismara, L Rollè, F Agostini, C Sechi, V Fenaroli, S Molgora, et al. Perinatal parenting stress, anxiety, and depression outcomes in first-time mothers and fathers: a 3-to 6-months postpartum follow-up study. *Front Psychol.* 2016 Jun 24;7:938.
9. CL Dennis, K Falah-Hassani, R Shiri. Prevalence of antenatal and postnatal anxiety: systematic review and meta-analysis. *Br J Psychiatry.* 2017;210(5):315–23.
10. S Nath, P Busuulwa, EG Ryan, FL Challacombe, LM Howard. The characteristics and prevalence of phobias in pregnancy. *Midwifery.* 2020 Mar 1;82:102590.
11. EJ Russell, JM Fawcett, D Mazmanian. Risk of obsessive-compulsive disorder in pregnant and postpartum women: a meta-analysis. *J Clin Psychiatry.* 2013 Apr 15;74(4):18438.
12. ER Blackmore, H Gustafsson, M Gilchrist, C Wyman, TG O'Connor. Pregnancy-related anxiety: evidence of distinct clinical significance from a prospective longitudinal study. *J Affect Disord.* 2016 Jun;197:251–8.
13. S Matthey, C Ross-Hamid. The validity of DSM symptoms for depression and anxiety disorders during pregnancy. *J Affect Disord.* 2011 Oct;133(3): 546–52.
14. E Asselmann, SL Kunas, HU Wittchen, J Martini. Maternal personality, social support, and changes in depressive, anxiety, and stress symptoms during pregnancy and after delivery: a prospective-longitudinal study. *PLoS ONE.* 2020 Aug 24;15(8):e0237609.
15. A Biaggi, S Conroy, S Pawlby, CM Pariante. Identifying the women at risk of antenatal anxiety and depression: a systematic review. *J Affect Disord.* 2016 Feb 1;191:62–77.
16. MA Whisman, J Davila, SH Goodman. Relationship adjustment, depression, and anxiety during pregnancy and the postpartum period. *J Fam Psychol.* 2011 Jun;25(3):375–83.
17 P Hasanjanzadeh, M Faramarzi. Relationship between maternal general and specific-pregnancy stress, anxiety, and depression symptoms and pregnancy outcome. *J Clin Diagn Res.* 2017 Apr;11(4):VC04.
18. SL Warren, Gunnar, J Kagan, TF Anders, SJ Simmens, M Rones, et al. Maternal panic disorder: infant temperament, neurophysiology, and parenting behaviors. *J Am Acad Child Adolesc Psychiatry.* 2003;42(7):814–25.
19. A Stein, RM Pearson, SH Goodman, E Rapa, A Rahman, M McCallum, et al. Effects of perinatal mental disorders on the fetus and child. *Lancet.* 2014;384(9956):1800–19.
20. A Tang, H Crawford, S Morales, KA Degnan, DS Pine, NA Fox. Infant behavioral inhibition predicts personality and social outcomes three decades later. *Proc Natl Acad Sci.* 2020 May 5;117(18):9800–7.
21. A Sandstrom, R Uher, B Pavlova. Prospective association between childhood behavioral inhibition and anxiety: a meta-analysis. *J Abnorm Child Psychol.* 2020 Jan;48(1):57–66.

22. MG Newman, SJ Llera. A novel theory of experiential avoidance in generalized anxiety disorder: a review and synthesis of research supporting a contrast avoidance model of worry. *Clin Psychol Rev.* 2011 Apr 1;31(3):371–82.

23. S Nolen-Hoeksema, A Aldao. Gender and age differences in emotion regulation strategies and their relationship to depressive symptoms. *Pers Indiv Differ.* 2011 Oct 1;51(6):704–8.

24. AI van der Zee-van, MM Boere-Boonekamp, CG Groothuis-Oudshoorn, SA Reijneveld. Postpartum depression and anxiety: a community-based study on risk factors before, during and after pregnancy. *J Affect Disord.* 2021 May 1;286:158–65.

25. JM Hettema. What is the genetic relationship between anxiety and depression? *Am J Med Genet C Semin Med Genet.* 2008 May 15;148C(2): 140–6.

26. J Lynch, PK Cullen, AM Jasnow, DC Riccio. Sex differences in the generalization of fear as a function of retention intervals. *Learn Mem.* 2013 Nov 1;20(11):628–32.

27. S Matthey. *Anxiety and stress during pregnancy and the postpartum period.* Oxford: Oxford University Press; 2016.

28. A Sinesi, M Maxwell, R O'Carroll, H Cheyne. Anxiety scales used in pregnancy: systematic review. *BJPsych Open.* 2019;5(1):e5.

29. N Fairbrother, B Corbyn, DS Thordarson, A Ma, D Surm. Screening for perinatal anxiety disorders: room to grow. *J Affect Disord.* 2019 May 1;250:363–70.

30. A Osman, JL Wong, CL Bagge, S Freedenthal, PM Gutierrez, G Lozano. The Depression Anxiety Stress Scales–21 (DASS-21): further examination of dimensions, scale reliability, and correlates. *J Clin Psychol.* 2012 Dec;68(12):1322–38.

31. A Sinesi, H Cheyne, M Maxwell, R O'Carroll. The Stirling Antenatal Anxiety Scale (SAAS): development and initial psychometric validation. *J Affect Disord Rep.* 2022 Apr 1;8:100333.

32. S Ayers, R Coates, A Sinesi, H Cheyne, M Maxwell, C Best, et al. Assessment of perinatal anxiety: diagnostic accuracy of five measures. *Br J Psychiatry.* 2024 Apr;224(4):132–8.

33. S Somerville, SL Byrne, K Dedman, R Hagan, S Coo, E Oxnam, et al. Detecting the severity of perinatal anxiety with the Perinatal Anxiety Screening Scale (PASS). *J Affect Disord.* 2015 Nov 1;186:18–25.

34. A Koukopoulos, C Mazza, L De Chiara, G Sani, A Simonetti, GD Kotzalidis, et al. Psychometric properties of the perinatal anxiety screening scale administered to Italian women in the perinatal period. *Front Psychiatry.* 2021 Jun 22;12: 684579.

35. S Ayers, A Sinesi, R Coates, H Cheyne, M Maxwell, C Best, et al. When is the best time to screen for perinatal anxiety? A longitudinal cohort study. *J Anxiety Disord.* 2024 Feb 6;103:102841.

36. PJ Lawrence, MG Craske, C Kempton, A Stewart, A Stein. Intrusive thoughts and images of intentional harm to infants in the context of maternal postnatal depression, anxiety, and OCD. *Br J Gen Pract.* 2017 Aug 1;67(661):376–7.

37. FL Challacombe, M Bavetta, S DeGiorgio. Intrusive thoughts in perinatal obsessive-compulsive disorder. *BMJ.* 2019 Dec 5;367.

38. R Coates, S Ayers, R de Visser, A Thornton. Evaluation of the CORE-10 to assess psychological distress in pregnancy. *J Reprod Infant Psychol.* 2020 May 26;38(3):311–23.

39. DV Sheehan, Y Lecrubier, KH Sheehan, P Amorim, J Janavs, E Weiller, et al. The Mini-International Neuropsychiatric Interview (M.I.N.I.): the development and validation of a structured diagnostic psychiatric interview for DSM-IV and ICD-10. *J Clin Psychiatry.* 1998;59:22–3.

40. J Martini, H-U Wittchen, CN Soares, A Rieder, M Steiner. New women-specific diagnostic modules: the Composite International Diagnostic Interview for

Women (CIDI-VENUS). *Arch Womens Ment Health.* 2009;12(5):281–9.

41. MB First. Structured clinical interview for DSM-IV axis I disorders (SCID-I), clinician version (administration booklet). American Psychiatric Publishing, Inc.; 1997.
42. B Leung, N Letourneau, K Bright, GF Giesbrecht, H Ntanda, L Gagnon, et al. Appraisal of the Psychiatric Diagnostic Screening Questionnaire in a perinatal cohort: the APrON study. *Scand J Pub Health.* 2017;45(6):658–65.
43. CA Schofield, CL Battle, M Howard, S Ortiz-Hernandez. Symptoms of the anxiety disorders in a perinatal psychiatric sample: a chart review. *J Nerv Ment Dis.* 2014 Feb 1;202(2):154–60.
44. R Webb, N Uddin, E Ford, A Easter, J Shakespeare, N Roberts, et al. Barriers and facilitators to implementing perinatal mental health care in health and social care settings: a systematic review. *Lancet Psychiatry.* 2021 Jun 1;8(6):521–34.
45. F Shapiro. *Eye movement desensitization and reprocessing (EMDR) therapy: basic principles, protocols, and procedures.* New York: The Guilford Press; 2017.
46. A Ehlers, DM Clark. Post-traumatic stress disorder: the development of effective psychological treatments. *Nord J Psychiatry.* 2008 Jan 1;62(sup47):11–18.
47. JJ Arch, S Dimidjian, C Chessick. Are exposure-based cognitive behavioral therapies safe during pregnancy? *Arch Womens Ment Health.* 2012 Dec;15(6):445–57.
48. MA Baas, MG van Pampus, CA Stramrood, JW Vanhommerig. Treatment of pregnant women with fear of childbirth using EMDR therapy: results of a multi-center randomized controlled trial. *Front Psychiatry.* 2022 Feb 10;12:798249.
49. FL Challacombe, R Tinch-Taylor, K Sabin, L Potts, V Lawrence, L Howard, B Carter. Exposure-based cognitive-behaviour therapy for anxiety-related disorders in pregnancy (ADEPT): results of a feasibility randomised controlled trial of time-intensive versus weekly CBT. *J Affect Disord.* 2024 Jan 1;344:414–22.
50. A Ehlers, J Bisson, DM Clark, M Creamer, S Pilling, D Richards, et al. Do all psychological treatments really work the same in posttraumatic stress disorder? *Clin Psychol Rev.* 2010 Mar 1;30(2):269–76.
51. Belém do Pará Convention. *Second hemispheric report on the implementation of the Belém do Pará Convention.* Washington, USA; 2012. www.oas.org/en/mesecvi/docs/MESECVI-SegundoInformeHemisferico-EN.pdf
52. World Health Organization. *The prevention and elimination of disrespect and abuse during facility-based childbirth.* World Health Organization Statement; 2015. https://shorturl.at/qxzV3
53. CG Ballard, AK Stanley, IF Brockington. Post-traumatic stress disorder (PTSD) after childbirth. *Br J Psychiatry.* 1995 Apr;166(4):525–8.
54. R Harris, S Ayers. What makes labour and birth traumatic? A survey of intrapartum 'hotspots'. *Psychol Health.* 2012;27(10):1166–77.
55. PD Yildiz, S Ayers, L Phillips. The prevalence of posttraumatic stress disorder in pregnancy and after birth: a systematic review and meta-analysis. *J Affect Disord.* 2017 Jan 15;208:634–45.
56. SE Harrison, S Ayers, MA Quigley, A Stein, FJ Alderdice. Prevalence and factors associated with postpartum posttraumatic stress in a population-based maternity survey in England. *J Affect Disord.* 2021 Jan 15;279: 749–56.
57. S Ayers, A Eagle, H Waring. The effects of childbirth-related post-traumatic stress disorder on women and their relationships: a qualitative study. *Psychol Health Med.* 2006 Nov 1;11(4):389–98.
58. JE Handelzalts, IS Hairston, M Muzik, A Matatyahu Tahar, S Levy. A paradoxical role of childbirth-related posttraumatic stress disorder (PTSD) symptoms in the association between personality factors

and mother–infant bonding: a cross-sectional study. *Psychol Trauma.* 2022 Sep;14(6):1066–72.

59. C Nilsson, E Hessman, H Sjöblom, A Dencker, E Jangsten, M Mollberg, et al. Definitions, measurements and prevalence of fear of childbirth: a systematic review. *BMC Pregnancy Childbirth.* 2018 Jan 12;18(1):28.

60. MA O'Connell, P Leahy-Warren, LC Kenny, SM O'Neill, AS Khashan. The prevalence and risk factors of fear of childbirth among pregnant women: a cross-sectional study in Ireland. *Acta Obstet Gynecol Scand.* 2019 Aug;98(8):1014–23.

61. G Sydsjo, M Bladh, C Lilliecreutz, AM Persson, H Vyoni, A Josefsson. Obstetric outcomes for nulliparous women who received routine individualized treatment for severe fear of childbirth – a retrospective case control study. *BMC Pregnancy Childbirth.* 2014;14:126.

62. L Andersson, I Sundström-Poromaa, M Wulff, M Åström, M Bixo. Implications of antenatal depression and anxiety for obstetric outcome. *Obstet Gynecol.* 2004 Sep;104(3):467–76.

63. A Capik, H Durmaz. Fear of childbirth, postpartum depression, and birth-related variables as predictors of posttraumatic stress disorder after childbirth. *Worldviews Evidence-Based Nurs.* 2018;15(6):455–63.

64. MT Kinsella, C Monk. Impact of maternal stress, depression and anxiety on fetal neurobehavioral development. *Clin Obstet Gynecol.* 2009 Sep;52(3):425–40.

65. NM Talge, C Neal, V Glover. Antenatal maternal stress and long-term effects on child neurodevelopment: how and why? *J Child Psychol Psychiatry.* 2007 Mar–Apr; 48(3–4):245–61.

66. S Striebich, E Mattern, GM Ayerle. Support for pregnant women identified with fear of childbirth (FOC)/tokophobia: a systematic review of approaches and interventions. *Midwifery.* 2018 Jun;61:97–115.

67. J Jomeen, CR Martin, C Jones, C Marshall, S Ayers, K Burt, et al. Tokophobia and fear of birth: a workshop consensus statement on current issues and recommendations for future research. *J Reprod Infant Psychol.* 2021 Jan 1;39(1):2–15.

68. YI Nillni, A Mehralizade, L Mayer, S Milanovic. Treatment of depression, anxiety, and trauma-related disorders during the perinatal period: a systematic review. *Clin Psychol Rev.* 2018 Dec 1;66:136–48.

69. C Goldfinger, SM Green, M Furtado, RE McCabe. Characterizing the nature of worry in a sample of perinatal women with generalized anxiety disorder. *Clin Psychol Psychotherapy.* 2020 Mar;27(2):136–45.

70. M Kaitz, D Mankuta, AM Rokem, SV Faraone. Relation between maternal antenatal anxiety and infants' weight depends on infants' sex: a longitudinal study from late gestation to 1-month post birth. *J Psychosom Res.* 2015 Dec 1;79(6):620–7.

71. M Furtado, CH Chow, S Owais, BN Frey, RJ Van Lieshout. Risk factors of new onset anxiety and anxiety exacerbation in the perinatal period: a systematic review and meta-analysis. *J Affect Disord.* 2018 Oct 1;238:626–35.

72. SM Green, E Donegan, RE McCabe, DL Streiner, M Furtado, L Noble, et al. Cognitive behavior therapy for women with generalized anxiety disorder in the perinatal period: impact on problematic behaviors. *Behav Ther.* 2021 Jul 1;52(4):907–16.

73. B Figueiredo, C Canário, I Tendais, TM Pinto, DA Kenny, T Field. Couples' relationship affects mothers' and fathers' anxiety and depression trajectories over the transition to parenthood. *J Affect Disord.* 2018 Oct 1;238:204–12.

74. SM Green, E Donegan, RE McCabe, DL Streiner, A Agako, BN Frey. Cognitive behavioral therapy for perinatal anxiety: a randomized controlled trial. *Aust N Z J Psychiatry.* 2020 Apr;54(4): 423–32.

75. HA O'Mahen, PG Ramchandani, DX King, L Lee-Carbon, EL Wilkinson, C Thompson-Booth, et al. Adapting and testing a brief intervention to reduce maternal anxiety during pregnancy (ACORN): report of a feasibility randomized controlled trial. *BMC Psychiatry.* 2022 Dec;22(1):1–2.

76. F Salehi, M Pourasghar, A Khalilian, Z Shahhosseini. Comparison of group cognitive behavioral therapy and interactive lectures in reducing anxiety during pregnancy: a quasi experimental trial. *Medicine.* 2016 Oct;95(43).

77. JH Goodman, A Guarino, K Chenausky, L Klein, J Prager, R Petersen, et al. CALM Pregnancy: results of a pilot study of mindfulness-based cognitive therapy for perinatal anxiety. *Arch Womens Ment Health.* 2014 Oct;17(5):373–87.

78. FL Challacombe, PM Salkovskis. Intensive cognitive-behavioural treatment for women with postnatal obsessive-compulsive disorder: a consecutive case series. *Behav Res Ther.* 2011 Jun 1;49(6–7):422–6.

79. FL Challacombe, PM Salkovskis, M Woolgar, EL Wilkinson, J Read, R Acheson. A pilot randomized controlled trial of time-intensive cognitive–behaviour therapy for postpartum obsessive–compulsive disorder: effects on maternal symptoms, mother–infant interactions and attachment. *Psycholog Med.* 2017 Jun;47(8):1478–88.

80. VB Oldfield, PM Salkovskis, T Taylor. Time-intensive cognitive behaviour therapy for obsessive-compulsive disorder: a case series and matched comparison group. *Br J Clin Psychol.* 2011 Mar;50(1):7–18.

81. FL Challacombe, PM Salkovskis, M Woolgar, EL Wilkinson, J Read, R Acheson. Parenting and mother-infant interactions in the context of maternal postpartum obsessive-compulsive disorder: effects of obsessional symptoms and mood. *Infant Behav Dev.* 2016 Aug 1;44:11–20.

82. KB Wolitzky-Taylor, JD Horowitz, MB Powers, MJ Telch. Psychological approaches in the treatment of specific phobias: a meta-analysis. *Clin Psychol Rev.* 2008 Jul 1;28(6):1021–37.

83. L Fehm, K Beesdo, F Jacobi, A Fiedler. Social anxiety disorder above and below the diagnostic threshold: prevalence, comorbidity and impairment in the general population. *Soc Psychiatry Psychiatr Epidemiol.* 2008;43(4): 257–65.

84. AM Ruscio, TA Brown, WT Chiu, J Sareen, MB Stein, RC Kessler. Social fears and social phobia in the USA: results from the National Comorbidity Survey Replication. *Psychol Med.* 2007;38(1):15–28.

85. RP Mattick, JC Clarke. Development and validation of measures of social phobia scrutiny fear and social interaction anxiety. *Behav Res Ther.* 1998;36(4):455–70.

86. A Wenzel, EN Haugen, LC Jackson, JR Brendle. Anxiety symptoms and disorders at eight weeks postpartum. *J Anxiety Disord.* 2005;19(3): 295–311.

87. J Martini, J Petzoldt, F Einsle, K Beesdo-Baum, M Höfler, H-U Wittchen. Risk factors and course patterns of anxiety and depressive disorders during pregnancy and after delivery: a prospective-longitudinal study. *J Affect Disord.* 2015;175:385–95.

88. M Crosby Budinger, TK Drazdowski, GS Ginsburg. Anxiety-promoting parenting behaviors: a comparison of anxious parents with and without social anxiety disorder. *Child Psychiatry Hum Dev.* 2013;44(3):412–18.

89. ML Miller, BM Williams, JE McCabe, JA Williamson, S King, DP Laplante, et al. Perinatal anxiety and depressive symptoms and perception of child behavior and temperament in early motherhood. *J Dev Orig Health Dis.* 2020:1–10.

90. E Mayo-Wilson, S Dias, I Mavranezouli, K Kew, DM Clark, AE Ades, et al. Psychological and pharmacological interventions for social anxiety disorder

in adults: a systematic review and network meta-analysis. *Lancet Psychiatry.* 2014;1(5):368–76.

91. O Guler, V Kaya, K Gezginc, F Kayhan, E Cicek, O Sonmez, et al. Pregnancy-onset panic disorder: incidence, comorbidity and associated factors. *Noro Psikiyatr Ars.* 2015;52(3):216–20.

92. C Marchesi, P Ampollini, C Paraggio, G Giaracuni, P Ossola, C De Panfilis, et al. Risk factors for panic disorder in pregnancy: a cohort study. *J Affect Disord.* 2014 Mar;156:134–8.

93. C Marchesi, P Ossola, A Amerio, BD Daniel, M Tonna, C De Panfilis. Clinical management of perinatal anxiety disorders: a systematic review. *J Affect Disord.* 2016 Jan 15;190:543–50.

94. CT Beck. Postpartum onset of panic disorder. *Image J Nurs Sch.* 1998;30(2):131–5.

95. A Wenzel, LL Gorman, MW O'Hara, S Stuart. The occurrence of panic and obsessive compulsive symptoms in women with postpartum dysphoria: a prospective study. *Arch Womens Ment Health.* 2001;4(1):5–12.

96. PP Roy-Byrne, MG Craske, MB Stein. Panic disorder. *Lancet.* 2006 Sep 16;368(9540):1023–32.

97. F Uguz, G Yuksel, OS Onur, C Karsidag, K Gezginc, N Arpaci. Neonatal outcomes in pregnant women with untreated and treated panic disorder. *Compr Psychiatry.* 2018;87:107–11.

98. KA Yonkers, K Gilstad-Hayden, A Forray, HS Lipkind. Association of panic disorder, generalized anxiety disorder, and benzodiazepine treatment during pregnancy with risk of adverse birth outcomes. *JAMA Psychiatry.* 2017;74(11):1145–52.

Chapter 12

Postpartum Psychosis and Bipolar Disorder

Ian Jones, Jess Heron and Arianna Di Florio

Introduction

A young woman in childbed not well purged after birth and delivery, fell into a great delirium suddenly without any disease afore going. She was angry most with her best friends, husband and mother, but she spoke many things religiously . . .
– *Felix Plater, 1602*

The beautiful wife of Carcinator, who always enjoyed the best of health, was many times attacked by melancholia after childbirth and remained insane for a month, but recovered with treatment.
– *Jao Rodrigues de Castelo Branco, 1551*

Postpartum (puerperal or postnatal) psychosis is a condition with a long history. For as long as people have written about childbirth there have been accounts of severe mood or psychotic episodes occurring in the perinatal period. Certainly, by the time medical textbooks began to be written in Europe over 400 years ago there are accounts, as illustrated in the above quotes, of women with recurrent severe mood and psychotic episodes following childbirth [1]. The obstetrician F. B. Osiander, more famous for inventing the uterine traction forceps, was the first to clearly describe puerperal mania in 1797, and in 1858 Louis Victor Marcé published his famous treatise on the psychoses of pregnant women and newly delivered and nursing mothers [2, 3]. Postpartum psychosis, therefore, is clearly not a recent invention.

Postpartum psychosis also continues to be of great clinical and public health importance. Severe episodes of mental illness in the perinatal period can result in significant distress, may disrupt the developing relationship between mother and child, and have long-term implications for the well-being of the woman, her baby, family and wider society. In rare but tragic cases, the illness can lead to suicide, a leading cause of maternal death (see Chapter 22, 'Maternal Suicide, Deliberate Self-Harm and Other Mental Health Related Causes of Maternal Death') and even more rarely infanticide (see Chapter 38, 'When Mothers Kill Their Children').

Despite its long history and ongoing contemporary importance, the concept of postpartum psychosis is not without its problems, perhaps best illustrated by it not being adequately dealt with either by the International Classification of Disease (ICD) [4] or the *Diagnostic and Statistical Manual of Mental Disorders* (DSM) [5] (discussed below). There are certainly important questions and uncertainties, particularly around the boundaries of the concept.

Should we limit the label to those with an onset in the immediate perinatal period or include onsets many weeks or months following childbirth? Do we consider birth as the only trigger, or include other triggers in the perinatal period, such as the return of menstruation? Is postpartum psychosis a disorder in its own right, or should it be considered the perinatal expression of another condition such as bipolar disorder? Should we only include psychotic episodes in its definition, as its name would suggest, or should we also include severe episodes of mania with no psychotic symptoms? What about severe and psychotic postpartum depression and exacerbations of non-affective psychosis in the perinatal period? These are certainly difficult questions and highlight the lack of clarity around the boundaries of the condition. This situation, however, is no different from many mental and physical health conditions. Indeed, when it comes to the core concept of postpartum psychosis, we 'know it when we see it', and the term is still usefully employed – by both clinicians and, perhaps even more importantly, those with lived experience and their partners [6]. In this chapter we will discuss what we know about this condition, how it might best be defined, what we still need to find out, and consider how it should be managed.

What Do We Mean by Postpartum Psychosis and What Are Its Clinical Features?

The term postpartum psychosis is normally reserved to describe an episode of severe mental illness, with dramatic onset shortly after childbirth. Symptoms may occur as a recurrence of an existing relapsing and remitting condition, or as a new episode in those who have not previously experienced mental ill health. It normally does not include severe mental illness in the postpartum period that occurs as a continuation of a chronic psychotic condition that began in, or prior to, pregnancy [7, 8, 9, 10].

In the past (and perhaps still today in low- and middle-income contexts) other systemic conditions such as eclampsia, delirium, thyroid disorders or infection were important causes of psychosis occurring in relation to childbirth. It is important that physical conditions are excluded as their misattribution to psychiatric disorder has led to deaths in new mothers (see Chapter 22, 'Maternal Suicide, Deliberate Self-Harm and Other Mental Health Related Causes of Maternal Death').

Postpartum psychosis usually presents as a severe mood episode – mania, severe psychotic depression or, perhaps more commonly than at other times, a mixed affective state [11]. As the name suggests, psychotic symptoms such as delusions and hallucinations are common and women with postpartum psychosis may also demonstrate a marked confusion or perplexity [11, 12]. Sudden onset and rapid deterioration are typical and the clinical picture often changes rapidly, with wide fluctuations in the intensity of symptoms and severe swings of mood – which has been described as a kaleidoscopic presentation [1, 7, 9]. Compared to first onset bipolar disorder outside the perinatal period, episodes of postpartum psychosis show more irritability [11], anxiety and depressive symptoms [12]. Features of catatonia are also more commonly seen, with one case note review of 200 postpartum psychosis admissions to a Mother and Baby Unit finding catatonic signs in 20% of women [13].

It is a matter of debate as to whether women not experiencing psychotic symptoms should be labelled as postpartum psychosis. The name does suggest that psychotic symptoms are present and certainly this would not be a term appropriate for the much more common episodes of non-psychotic major depression. However, a small proportion of women experience manic or mixed episodes with early postpartum onset with no psychotic symptoms. These are often diagnosed as postpartum psychosis, which, given the similar prognosis of these episodes to postpartum mania with psychosis, may be appropriate. The majority of postpartum full manic episodes do manifest psychotic symptoms however, although it remains unknown if the rates of psychosis are higher than in severe non-postpartum bipolar I disorder where there is a lifetime prevalence of psychosis of over 70% [14].

How Is Postpartum Psychosis Dealt with in Classification Systems?

As discussed above, while the core of the concept of postpartum psychosis may be clear, there are issues around its boundaries and clarity is not helped by the way the condition is dealt with by the ICD [4] and DSM [5] classification systems. Neither system has a distinct, separate diagnosis specifically labelled 'postpartum psychosis', but episodes that would traditionally be labelled as postpartum psychosis are dealt with differently in the two systems.

DSM-5

For episodes meeting the criteria of a mood disorder the most recent fifth edition of the DSM allows for a peripartum onset specifier that indicates the episode had its onset in pregnancy or within the first 4 weeks following childbirth [5]. The onset specifier can therefore be given to women with both unipolar and bipolar mood disorders depending on the nature of the postpartum episode. Examples of DSM-5 diagnoses of postpartum psychosis episodes could therefore be: 'major depressive disorder with psychotic features, with peripartum onset' or 'bipolar I disorder, most recent episode manic, with psychotic features, with peripartum onset'.

The peripartum onset specifier is not directly applicable to primary psychotic disorders (like schizophrenia or schizoaffective disorder) in DSM-5. It is possible, however, that there are psychotic episodes that fit the postpartum psychosis concept but which are not diagnosed as a DSM-5 mood disorder, those receiving the label of a brief psychotic disorder, for example. For these episodes there is provision to record a 'with postpartum onset' specifier if within 4 weeks of delivery.

Other issues with the peripartum onset specifier approach include not distinguishing between episodes with onset in pregnancy from those, as in the case of postpartum psychosis, which have their onset following childbirth. In addition, there is an issue of the 4-week limit to onsets following delivery. While, as discussed below, most women with postpartum psychosis have their onset within this time frame, there are some women who become unwell later, or who have a more gradual onset that escalates in severity, for whom a label of postpartum psychosis may be appropriate. Finally, the lack of a postpartum psychosis diagnostic label and the ability to attach the peripartum onset specifier to both unipolar and bipolar disorder may underplay the specific relationship of postpartum psychosis to bipolar disorder, particularly concerning the increased risk of future bipolar episodes as discussed below.

ICD-11

In contrast to DSM-5, ICD-11 does not provide a perinatal onset specifier for mood disorder episodes or indeed for any conditions [4]. Instead, it has a separate section for mental and behavioural disorders associated with pregnancy, childbirth or the puerperium that have their onsets within 6 weeks of delivery. These include the category *mental and behavioural disorders associated with pregnancy, childbirth or the puerperium, with psychotic symptoms (6E21).* However, there is additional guidance that if the symptoms meet the diagnostic requirements for another mental disorder, the other diagnosis should *also* be assigned. While this approach may be an improvement on ICD-10, which permitted the classification of mental and behavioural disorders associated with the puerperium (F53) only if they could not be classified elsewhere, it remains likely that the perinatal labels will often not be used and will result in an underestimate of the true prevalence of postpartum psychosis.

In summary, both DSM and ICD, even in their most recent versions, do not deal helpfully with postpartum psychosis. We will return later to a discussion of why this is important.

How Common Is Postpartum Psychosis and When Does It Have Its Onset?

As discussed, there are issues around the definition, classification and boundaries of postpartum psychosis. These clearly impact on what we know about the epidemiology of the condition. Depending on the exact definition used, episodes of postpartum psychosis occur following approximately 1–2 in 1,000 deliveries (0.1–0.2%), and this is a dramatic increase in the incidence of mania and psychotic episodes [15, 16, 17]. Unlike other mood episodes in the perinatal period where onsets are spread throughout pregnancy and the postpartum, the majority of episodes of postpartum psychosis have their onset within 2 weeks of delivery [16], with over 50% of first symptoms occurring on days 1–3 in one retrospective study [18, 19].

What Is the Prognosis for Episodes of Postpartum Psychosis?

Women with postpartum psychosis can become unwell very quickly and experience very severe episodes of illness. Despite this, the prognosis for recovery from the initial episode is usually excellent, with a good recovery in weeks to months. A study of 78 women with postpartum psychosis, for example, found that by 9 months 74% reported good functioning on the domains of work, interpersonal relations, recreation and global satisfaction, and 88% had resumed their premorbid employment and household responsibilities [20]. Women who have experienced an episode of postpartum psychosis, however, remain at high risk of a recurrence of a mood disorder (specifically bipolar disorder) both following subsequent deliveries and at times unrelated to childbirth.

A meta-analysis has attempted to quantify that increased risk following an index episode of postpartum psychosis [21]. It included 6 studies of 645 patients with follow-up periods ranging from 11 to 26 years. Experiencing a recurrence was common, occurring in 64% of women, which meant 36% had no recurrence during follow-up. The study found 43.5% of women had 'isolated postpartum psychosis', experiencing no further episodes (36.1%) or only further postpartum episodes (7.1%). In contrast, over half of women (56.7%) experienced further episodes also occurring outside of the perinatal period. It is important to note that these results are from naturalistic, observational studies and can tell us little about the impact, for example, of prophylactic medication. It is also important to bear in mind that the period of observation in these studies may not include menopause – a known period of increased risk of mood episodes [22]. The risk of recurrence at menopause is an area of growing interest and an issue of undoubted importance to women. It has received limited direct research, however, with much of the work at the level of case series which have suggested that women who have experienced postpartum psychosis, even if well for many years, may be at risk of a severe recurrence in the perimenopause [23].

What Is the Relationship of Postpartum Psychosis to Bipolar Disorder?

Despite no major difference in incidence and prevalence there are important sex differences in bipolar disorder [24]. Women with bipolar have a later illness onset, experience more rapid cycling, more bipolar II, show a more seasonal pattern, are more impacted by depression, and experience more mixed and dysphoric manic episodes. Perhaps the biggest sex difference, however, is the impact in women of periods of hormonal change including puberty, menstruation, menopause and, in particular, childbirth [25, 26]. As will have become apparent, there is a strong relationship between bipolar disorder and postpartum psychosis. The symptom profile of postpartum psychosis shows considerable overlap with bipolar disorder [11, 12] and women with previous bipolar episodes are at a much higher risk of developing postpartum psychosis than either the general population or indeed those with any other mental health condition [25, 26]. The close link of postpartum psychosis to bipolar disorder is also underlined, as discussed above, by the high risk of subsequent episodes of bipolar disorder not related to childbirth in those women who have experienced postpartum psychosis [27].

There have been a number of systematic reviews and meta-analyses of the available literature which have examined the risk of perinatal recurrence in women with bipolar disorder. Combining this data is difficult due to considerable heterogeneity in the original studies, particularly regarding diagnosis of bipolar disorder and the nature of the perinatal recurrence. Overall postpartum recurrence rates for bipolar women have been reported at similar levels in systematic reviews of overlapping data sets which report a recurrence risk of 37% [28] and 36.7% [29], although another review did find a higher risk at 54.9% [30]. These recurrence figures, however, include episodes of depression in addition to postpartum psychosis and may also include women from across the bipolar spectrum. An important finding to emerge from the literature is a higher risk of postpartum psychosis in women with bipolar I disorder compared to bipolar II [25]. Although the risk of postpartum psychosis is lower for women with bipolar II, there is still a high risk (around 40%) of a mood episode, mostly depression, in the perinatal period [25]. There is less data on risk in the perinatal period for women with schizoaffective disorder. Although clearly on the mood psychosis spectrum, the evidence of treatment response, prognosis and from genetic studies [31] supports considering the bipolar subtype as if it were bipolar and the depressive subtype as schizophrenia. Therefore, to summarise the literature, given the caveats discussed, women with bipolar I disorder (and schizoaffective disorder bipolar type) are at the highest risk of postpartum psychosis which occur following around 200 in 1,000 deliveries (20%) – an approximate 200-fold increased risk compared to the general population.

For bipolar women there does seem to be a specific and strong childbirth-related trigger with a clustering of episode onsets in the immediate postpartum. This contrasts with episodes of major depression where perinatal onsets are spread out more evenly in pregnancy and the postnatal months (see Chapter 10, 'Depression'). The evidence suggests that the risk of bipolar episodes is lower in pregnancy with registry studies in Denmark finding low rates of both new onset [17] and recurrence during pregnancy [26]. In addition, a clinical study of 980 women with bipolar I disorder found only 8% of perinatal episodes had an onset in pregnancy [25]. Another study found conflicting results with a high rate of recurrence in pregnancy (85.5%) in a study of 62 bipolar women who discontinued prophylactic medication [32]. A study from the same group in an expanded sample of women with bipolar disorder (283 with BP I and 338 with BP II) did, however, find considerably higher rates of episodes in the postpartum (52%) compared to pregnancy (23%) [33].

What Are the Known Risk Factors for Postpartum Psychosis and What Do They Tell Us about Aetiology?

Although there is a strong case for postpartum psychosis being under-researched, due perhaps to the ongoing confusion around classification already discussed, the evidence points to a range of factors that affect risk. These are not just of potential clinical importance but also may provide clues to the aetiology of this condition.

Social and Psychological Factors

For psychiatric disorders in general, and for postpartum depression in particular there is strong and consistent evidence for psychosocial factors playing a major role (see Chapter 10, 'Depression'). These factors include, but are not limited to, lack of social support, relationship problems, socio-economic status, stigma and adverse childhood experiences. In contrast, the more limited evidence suggests that childbirth is not acting as a general, non-specific psychosocial stressor in the triggering of postpartum psychosis. Studies of high-risk women find no association between stressful life events and the occurrence of a postpartum psychotic episode [34, 35, 36] but have suggested that the presence of a supportive partner is associated with reduced risk [37].

Mental Health History

The strongest risk factor, and the one undoubtably of greatest clinical importance, is a woman's own mental health history. As we have discussed, a history of bipolar disorder, specifically bipolar I disorder (and schizoaffective disorder bipolar type), is a marker of high risk (around 20% of deliveries) [28]. Around half of women who develop postpartum psychosis have no previous mental health history, but the aetiology of postpartum psychosis is clearly interwoven with that of bipolar disorder.

An even higher risk (around 40% of deliveries) is seen in women with a previous episode of postpartum psychosis [38]. The impact of other clinical features is less studied and probably less dramatic, but age of onset, number of episodes, severity of episodes and recency of episodes may all play a role and need further study.

Family History and Genetic Factors

Although there are no twin or adoption studies of postpartum psychosis the evidence for genetic involvement in mood and psychotic disorders more generally is overwhelming.

The evidence from family studies does suggest, however, that a specific susceptibility to the puerperal triggering of bipolar disorder is familial [39, 40] and, moreover, that episodes of postpartum psychosis are a marker for a more familial subtype of bipolar disorder [41]. In women with a personal history of bipolar disorder a family history of postpartum psychosis is important to establish, as it doubles the risk of postpartum psychosis. For women without a personal history of mental illness the evidence is that a family history of both postpartum psychosis and bipolar disorder do increase risk, but due to the low rates of postpartum psychosis in the general population the risk is still low and it is not clear that screening women in the general population for their family history of these conditions is clinically indicated.

Finding the genetic factors that influence risk of postpartum psychosis is an important goal of current research. A number of genetic studies have been conducted including linkage [42] and candidate gene association studies [43, 44, 45] but no specific genetic variants have been replicated to date. A more promising approach has been an application of the genome-wide association study (GWAS) approach to perinatal disorders, both for postnatal depression [46] and a study of postpartum psychosis that involved the analysis of polygenic risk scores for schizophrenia [47]. This study, although small by GWAS standards – involving 1,428 women with bipolar disorder or postpartum psychosis – found differences in the polygenic risk score profiles for women with first onset postpartum psychosis compared to those experiencing their perinatal episode in the context of a bipolar disorder history. This supports the recognition of first onset as a separate nosological entity adding to the already complex issue of classification discussed above. Further GWAS studies and other approaches such as whole genome sequencing undoubtably have promise to bring further insights on the aetiology, though it is clear that much larger cohorts of women with postpartum psychosis will be needed to make progress.

Obstetric Risk Factors: Primiparity

There is a long list of obstetric factors that have been studied [48] including the sex of the baby, pregnancy complications, caesarean section and gestational length, but the only consistent finding is that first-time mothers have a higher risk of postpartum psychosis compared to those who have had more than one child [15, 16, 17, 25]. There are many possible explanations for this primiparity finding, including greater psychological stress in first pregnancies, although biological differences to subsequent pregnancies also need to be considered. One intriguing possibility is of shared aetiological factors with other disorders, such as pre-eclampsia, that show a similar increased risk in first pregnancies. Pregnancy and childbirth are associated with great immunological challenge, and therefore dysregulation of immune system function is a candidate for involvement in the aetiology of postpartum psychosis [49]. While more work is needed, there are reports of women with postpartum psychosis showing anti-NMDA receptor autoantibodies [49], autoimmune thyroid dysfunction [50] and of dysregulation of the immunoneuroendo crine set point in postpartum psychosis, with overactivation of the monocyte and macrophage arm of the immune system [49, 51].

Sleep Disturbance

There is a considerable body of work demonstrating how circadian rhythm disruption, such as sleep loss, plays a role in bipolar disorder, triggering the onset of mania in susceptible individuals, particularly in women [52, 53]. Given that some disruption of sleep is an almost universal consequence of having a baby it is an excellent hypothesis to explore and the limited work linking sleep loss and postpartum psychosis is promising [54, 55]. For example, in one study women with bipolar disorder who describe sleep loss as a trigger for manic episodes were twice as likely to experience postpartum psychosis than those whose episodes were not triggered by sleep loss [56]. Further, if indirect, evidence for the importance of sleep comes from the observation that interventions targeting sleep can lead to remission in about 6% of cases of postpartum psychosis [57].

Hormonal

Given the huge changes that occur in reproductive hormones through pregnancy and the postpartum period, hormonal factors would seem obvious candidates for involvement in the aetiology of postpartum psychosis. A number of hormonal systems have been suggested to play a role in postpartum mood disorders including gonadal steroid pathways [58], hypothalamic-pituitary-adrenal axis dysregulation [59] and thyroid hormone dysfunction [50]. Despite the interest, the evidence implicating hormones in postpartum psychosis remains mostly circumstantial resting on the typical onset in the immediate postpartum at a time of great hormonal flux. The intriguing possibility is that postpartum mood episodes do not represent gross abnormalities in endocrine physiology but rather represent an abnormal response to the normal hormonal fluctuations in the perinatal period [60], determined perhaps by genetic factors described above.

Management

We will first consider managing women at high risk before moving on to consider the care of women experiencing an episode of postpartum psychosis.

Care of Women at High Risk

While many risk factors have been explored, it is a personal history of bipolar disorder, particularly bipolar I (and schizoaffective disorder bipolar type), or a history of a previous postpartum psychosis that are the most important clinical markers of high risk. Women with bipolar II, while not at the same very high risk of postpartum psychosis, are also at high risk of a mood episode, mostly depression, in the perinatal period. For this reason, national guidelines on perinatal mental health, such as NICE [61] and SIGN [62], suggest referring a woman to secondary mental health services (preferably specialist perinatal mental health services) for preconception counselling if she has a current or past severe mental health problem and is planning a pregnancy (see Chapter 24, 'Pre-pregnancy Advice and Planning'). A history of bipolar disorder, of any form, would justify such a referral for further assessment.

It can be argued, however, that this is too late and that education of bipolar women about pregnancy and discussion of contraception should begin, ideally, at first diagnosis. The symptoms of bipolar disorder make this even more important, particularly as hypersexuality has been highlighted as an overlooked symptom that has a huge impact on women (88% experiencing hypersexuality when high, 54% finding themselves in potentially dangerous situations, 42% reporting being sexually assaulted, and 22% raped) [63].

Structured education about bipolar disorder (psychoeducation) has a substantial evidence base that demonstrates improved outcomes [64] and discussion of pregnancy and childbirth is important to be included in these programmes. Women may need information very quickly, and therefore easily accessible and relevant online information and support are needed, best delivered perhaps by third-sector organisations such as Bipolar UK (www.bipolaruk.org) and Action on Postpartum Psychosis (www.app-network.org).

Women with a history of bipolar disorder or postpartum psychosis may be currently well and not in contact with mental health services so it is important that their mental health history is explored at first contact in pregnancy. Perinatal mental health guidelines suggest asking women about any past or present severe mental illness, previous or current treatment, and any severe postpartum mental illness in a first degree relative [61, 62] (see Chapter 1, 'The Perinatal Frame of Mind'). Ideally, women at high risk will be referred preconception but if this risk is not identified until the women is pregnant then referral should be made to secondary mental healthcare, preferably a specialist perinatal mental health team. Once identified as in the high-risk group, monitoring through pregnancy and postpartum is essential (see Chapter 23, 'Access, Assessment and Evaluation of Risk in Perinatal Mental Health Services') accompanied by pre-birth planning at 32 weeks' gestation (see Chapter 25, 'Pre-birth Planning').

The preconception assessment (see Chapter 24, 'Pre-pregnancy Advice and Planning') for women at high risk is likely to include a review of diagnoses, establishing co-morbidities, exploring the expression of and risks associated with the illness, medication history, the woman's understanding of her illness and discussion of interventions to reduce risk of recurrence in the perinatal period. It will cover medication options in pregnancy, intra-partum and postpartum and strategies to optimise physical and mental health. For women with bipolar disorder the issue of medication in pregnancy is likely to be prominent, but other risk factors for adverse fetal outcomes, such as smoking, nutritional deficiencies and obesity should also be addressed [65, 66]. Some women and their partners may have concerns about passing on a susceptibility to severe mental illness to their children and discussions need to address this or in some circumstances may prompt referral for further genetic counselling.

With regard to medication, the potential risks and benefits of all options need to be discussed, including continuing the current regimen, discontinuing some or all medication and switching to drugs with greater evidence of safety in pregnancy (see Chapter 26, 'Principles of Prescribing'). The high risk of recurrence in the perinatal period for women with a history of bipolar disorder or previous postpartum psychosis should weigh heavily in the risk benefit analysis. Consideration must also be given to a woman's individual history of treatment response and to what has happened when medication stopped previously. As discussed in Chapter 27, there are issues with the reproductive safety of some medications used in women with bipolar disorder, with sodium valproate having the greatest reproductive safety concerns.

An important question for many women is whether prophylaxis can be started after delivery or whether it also needs to be taken during pregnancy. A study from the Netherlands suggests the answer may depend on whether episodes have previously occurred outside of the perinatal period [67]. Women with a history of postpartum psychosis alone were at high risk of recurrence following childbirth but not in pregnancy. However, for women who also had a history of bipolar episodes not related to childbirth, episodes were observed in pregnancy making it also a period of high risk. There is less data to guide how long prophylactic medication should be continued following delivery but at least 6 months to ensure it covers the period of high risk would be sensible.

There is limited data on the effectiveness of prophylactic medication in the immediate postpartum for women at high risk. Interpretation is further complicated by the observational nature of the data with no randomised controlled trials as these would be difficult practically and indeed ethically. Although some studies have failed to demonstrate a prophylactic benefit of medication [68], systematic reviews of the available data provide reassurance that medication reduces risk. One review reports a recurrence risk of 66% in those women who were medication free compared to 23% in women who continued prophylactic medication [28]. Another review of overlapping data found a risk of 58.1% with no medication use compared to 25.9% for those on medication [69]. Older studies support the use of lithium prophylaxis [70, 71], but there are issues relating to reaching therapeutic levels quickly for women starting medication in the postpartum and significant concerns around breastfeeding (see Chapter 27, 'The Reproductive Safety of Psychotropic Medication and Implications for Prescribing in the Perinatal Period'). Antipsychotics, typical or atypical, are therefore often used [72]. With regard to choice of prophylaxis, considering medication the woman has responded to previously should weigh heavily in the decision.

Care of Women with Postpartum Psychosis

Episodes of postpartum psychosis often have a sudden onset, become severe quickly and the symptoms can vary substantially from hour to hour. In around 50% of women it may be the first episode of severe mental illness with no indication that a woman was at high risk. For these reasons it is important for all healthcare professionals who come into contact with women in the postpartum to be aware of the presenting symptoms and to ensure it is identified quickly. Episodes of postpartum psychosis are a psychiatric emergency due to rapid onset, severity of symptoms and the perinatal context. Psychosis at other times can have a long prodromal phase and mental health services accustomed to such insidious onsets may not be aware of the urgency for intervention needed with postpartum psychosis.

Due to the severity of the illness, symptoms of psychosis and the presence of the baby, many, if not all, women with postpartum psychosis will require admission to hospital, preferably to a Mother and Baby Unit if available. Decisions about the need for admission will depend on several considerations but the following factors should lower the threshold for admission: severe symptoms, rapid deterioration with significant impairment; psychotic symptoms, particularly command hallucinations, passivity phenomena or delusions involving the baby; suicidal ideation or significant aggression to others; poor social support; lack of insight; poor nutrition and hydration; and risk of harm to infant including poor infant care and lack of bonding. It should be emphasised when discussing risk to the baby that infanticide is a very rare event in postpartum psychosis and linked more with other psychopathology (see Chapter 38, 'When Mothers Kill Their Children'). Infanticidal thoughts, however, are not uncommon, found in 8% of women with postpartum psychosis in one study [11]. Likewise, while suicide is a rare event, suicidal ideation is more commonly experienced in these episodes [73].

In addition to admission, medication is also a key component of treatment of the acute phase. There is an even sparser evidence base for the pharmacological treatment of postpartum psychosis than for its prophylaxis, so choice of medication is based on extrapolation from studies outside the perinatal period. Just as for prophylactic agents, a woman's previous response to medication should influence the specific drug chosen. Safety of medication in breastfeeding must also be considered (see Chapters 26 and 27) as should maternal side effects because excessive sedation, for example, could affect a mother's ability to care for the child, particularly at night.

A four-stage treatment algorithm for postpartum psychosis has been published based on the approach developed at the Erasmus Medical Centre in the Netherlands [57]. The four stages involve benzodiazepines, antipsychotics, mood stabilisers and finally electroconvulsive therapy (ECT). Results were reported for the treatment of 64 women with postpartum psychosis, and all women achieved remission with the first three stages, none needing ECT. Moreover, sustained remission was observed in 80% or women at 9 months, and women treated with lithium had a significantly lower rate of relapse compared with those treated with antipsychotic monotherapy. Although ECT was not needed in this study, and despite limited data on its use in the perinatal period, it is a potentially effective treatment in severe episodes, particularly in the presence of high suicidal risk [74].

As for prophylaxis, there is little data to guide how long medication should be continued following postpartum psychosis, but the decision should be individualised based on clinical factors such as symptom severity and the previous history, particularly of bipolar episodes. Continuing antipsychotic treatment for 6 months to a year after the acute symptoms of postpartum psychosis have resolved is often recommended, however, as the risk of relapse is high within the first postpartum year.

After the acute phase, women need to be counselled about the risk they have of further puerperal and non-puerperal episodes to ensure that they do not believe that avoiding further pregnancies is a way of guaranteeing no further episodes of illness.

Although postpartum psychosis responds well to medical treatment in the acute phase, women often need psychological treatment and support in the longer term to come to terms with their experience and regain their confidence. Some women have a longer course of illness with recovery taking many months or even years. The long-term emotional impact of postpartum psychosis for women and families has been explored in several studies, as well as their information and support needs during recovery [75]. As women recover sufficiently, input from psychology services may also be required. Peer support from women with lived experience of the condition plays an important role in this recovery and is available in the UK through Action on Postpartum Psychosis (www.app-network.org). This organisation is also an important source of support for the partner and wider family, the needs of whom are often neglected.

Summary and Conclusions

Postpartum psychosis has a long history, but there are still major gaps in our understanding of this condition. There is much work to do but also considerable excitement at the prospect of major advances in our knowledge of its aetiology and in the development of new and better treatments. Although it may have been under-researched to date, the link between childbirth and the triggering of severe mood episodes is one of the strongest and most robust findings in the mental health literature. It remains a fantastic clue to the aetiology of mood and psychotic disorders, for perinatal episodes certainly but also, it could be argued, for episodes not related to childbirth. The application of neuroscience, genetics and neuroimaging holds great promise, but important insights will also arise from epidemiology and clinical studies.

It is clear, however, that to make the progress women and their families need will require major international efforts, much larger cohorts and a willingness to share data. Encouragingly, we can already see the beginning of such collaborations.

We will also need better recognition of postpartum psychosis in classification systems and, again, important work is being done to this end. While a better understanding of aetiology will hopefully lead to new and better treatments, it is not the only goal of research. We need to gain a deeper understanding of how to assess a woman's individual risk and how to manage it effectively to achieve the best possible outcomes. We must improve our treatment of acute episodes of postpartum psychosis and understand better how to predict and reduce the risk of recurrence.

Underpinning all this work, however, must be a consideration of the perspective of women who experience these episodes [76] (see Chapter 2). Qualitative studies have clearly shown that women at high risk can struggle to get the information they need in order that they can make the difficult decisions they face when considering starting or extending their families [6, 77, 78]. We need to work in partnership with women and their partners, not only to improve the care and treatment of individual women, but to guide service design, development and evaluation, and contribute to the teaching and training needs of professionals working with women in the perinatal period. As clinicians, researchers and, most importantly, women and their families, we can, by working together, make a positive difference for those whose lives are touched by postpartum psychosis.

References

1. I Brockington. Puerperal psychosis. In: *Motherhood and maternal mental health.* Oxford: Oxford University Press; 1996. Chapter 4.
2. LV Marcé. *Traité de la folie des femmes enceintes, des nouvelles accouchées et des nourrices (Treatise on the madness of pregnant women, new mothers, and wet nurses).* Paris: J.-B. Baillière; 1858.
3. FB Osiander. *Entwurf einer Theorie der Entbindungskunst (Draft of a theory of obstetrics).* Göttingen: Vandenhoeck & Ruprecht; 1797.
4. World Health Organization. International classification of diseases for mortality and morbidity statistics (11th revision). Geneva: World Health Organization; 2019. https://icd.who.int
5. American Psychiatric Association. *Diagnostic and statistical manual of mental disorders.* 5th ed. Arlington, VA: American Psychiatric Publishing; 2013.
6. C Dolman, I Jones, LM Howard. A systematic review and meta-synthesis of the experience of motherhood in women with severe mental illness. *Arch Women Ment Health.* 2013;16:173–96.
7. I Jones, PS Chandra, P Dazzan, LM Howard. Bipolar disorder, affective psychosis, and schizophrenia in pregnancy and the post-partum period. *Lancet.* 2014;384(9956):1789–99.
8. A Di Florio, T Munk-Olsen, V Bergink. The birth of a psychiatric orphan disorder: postpartum psychosis. *Lancet Psychiatry.* 2016;3(6):502.
9. V Bergink, N Rasgon, KL Wisner. Postpartum psychosis: madness, mania,

and melancholia in motherhood. *Am J Psychiatry*. 2016;173(12):1179–88.

10. V Bergink, P Boyce, T Munk-Olsen. Postpartum psychosis: a valuable misnomer. *Aust N Z J Psychiatry*. 2015;49(2):102–3.
11. AM Kamperman, MJ Veldman-Hoek, R Wesseloo, E Robertson Blackmore, V Bergink. Phenotypical characteristics of postpartum psychosis: a clinical cohort study. *Bipolar Disord*. 2017;19(6):450–7.
12. S Ganjekar, G Desai, PS Chandra. A comparative study of psychopathology, symptom severity, and short-term outcome of postpartum and nonpostpartum mania. *Bipolar Disord*. 2013;15(6):713–18.
13. A Nahar, N Kondapuram, G Desai, PS Chandra. Catatonia among women with postpartum psychosis in a mother-baby inpatient psychiatry unit. *Gen Hosp Psychiatry*. 2017;45:40–3.
14. SR Aminoff, IN Onyeka, M Ødegaard, C Simonsen, TV Lagerberg, OA Andreassen, et al. Lifetime and point prevalence of psychotic symptoms in adults with bipolar disorders: a systematic review and meta-analysis. *Psychol Med*. 2022;52(13):2413–25.
15. IM Terp, PB Mortensen. Post-partum psychoses: clinical diagnoses and relative risk of admission after parturition. *Br J Psychiatry*. 1998;172:521–6.
16. RE Kendell, JC Chalmers, C Platz. Epidemiology of puerperal psychoses. *Br J Psychiatry*. 1987;150:662–73.
17. T Munk-Olsen, TM Laursen, CB Pedersen, O Mors, PB Mortensen. New parents and mental disorders: a population-based register study. *JAMA*. 2006;296:2582–9.
18. J Heron, E Robertson Blackmore, M McGuinness, N Craddock, I Jones. No 'latent period' in the onset of bipolar affective puerperal psychosis. *Arch Womens Ment Health*. 2007;10(2):79–81.
19. J Heron, M McGuinness, E Robertson Blackmore, N Craddock, I Jones. Early postpartum symptoms in puerperal psychosis. *BJOG*. 2008;115(3):348–53.
20. KM Burgerhout, AM Kamperman, SJ Roza, MP Lambregtse-van den Berg, KM Koorengevel, WJG Hoogendijk, et al. Functional recovery after postpartum psychosis: a prospective longitudinal study. *J Clin Psychiatry*. 2017;78(1):122–8.
21. J Gilden, AM Kamperman, T Munk-Olsen, WJG Hoogendijk, SA Kushner, V Bergink. Long-term outcomes of postpartum psychosis: a systematic review and meta-analysis. *J Clin Psychiatry*. 2020;81(2):19r12906.
22. LM Shitomi-Jones, C Dolman, I Jones, G Kirov, V Escott-Price, SE Legge, et al. Exploration of first onsets of mania, schizophrenia spectrum disorders and major depressive disorder in perimenopause. *Nat Ment Health*. 2024;2(10):1161–8.
23. E Robertson Blackmore, N Craddock, J Walters, I Jones. Is the perimenopause a time of increased risk of recurrence in women with a history of bipolar affective postpartum psychosis? A case series. *Arch Womens Ment Health*. 2008;11:75–8.
24. A Di Florio, I Jones. Is sex important? Gender differences in bipolar disorder. *Int Rev Psychiatry*. 2010;22(5):437–52.
25. A Di Florio, L Forty, K Gordon-Smith, J Heron, L Jones, N Craddock, et al. Perinatal episodes across the mood disorder spectrum. *JAMA Psychiatry*. 2013;70(2):168–75.
26. T Munk-Olsen, TM Laursen, T Mendelson, CB Pedersen, O Mors, PB Mortensen. Risks and predictors of readmission for a mental disorder during the postpartum period. *Arch Gen Psychiatry*. 2009;66(2):189–95.
27. E Robertson, I Jones, S Haque, R Holder, N Craddock. Risk of puerperal and non-puerperal recurrence of illness following bipolar affective puerperal (post-partum) psychosis. *Br J Psychiatry*. 2005;186(3):258–9.
28. R Wesseloo, AM Kamperman, T Munk-Olsen, VJ Pop, SA Kushner, V Bergink. Risk of postpartum relapse in bipolar disorder and postpartum psychosis: a systematic review and meta-analysis. *Am J Psychiatry*. 2016;173(2):117–27.

29. L Conejo-Galindo, ÁM Ortega-Galán, R Rodríguez-Blanque, C López-Díaz, MP García-Caro. Bipolar disorder and postpartum psychosis: a systematic review of risk factors and preventive strategies. *J Affect Disord.* 2022;297: 645–55.

30. GA Masters, J Hugunin, L Xu, CM Ulbricht, TA Moore Simas, JY Ko, N Byatt. Prevalence of bipolar disorder in perinatal women: a systematic review and meta-analysis. *J Clin Psychiatry.* 2022;83(5):21r14045.

31. N Craddock, MJ Owen. The Kraepelinian dichotomy – going, going... but still not gone. *Br J Psychiatry.* 2010;196(2):92–5.

32. AC Viguera, T Whitfield, RJ Baldessarini, DJ Newport, Z Stowe, A Reminick, et al. Risk of recurrence in women with bipolar disorder during pregnancy: prospective study of mood stabilizer discontinuation. *Am J Psychiatry.* 2007;164(12):1817–24.

33. AC Viguera, L Tondo, AE Koukopoulos, D Reginaldi, B Lepri, RJ Baldessarini. Episodes of mood disorders in 2252 pregnancies and postpartum periods. *Am J Psychiatry.* 2011;168(11):1179–85.

34. TF McNeil. A prospective study of postpartum psychoses in a high-risk group. 4. Relationship to life situation and experience of pregnancy. *Acta Psychiatr Scand.* 1988;77(6):645–53.

35. MN Marks, A Wieck, SA Checkley, R Kumar. Contribution of psychological and social factors to psychotic and non-psychotic relapse after childbirth in women with previous histories of affective disorder. *J Affect Disord.* 1992;24(4):253–63.

36. IF Brockington, C Martin, GW Brown, D Goldberg. Stress and puerperal psychosis. *Br J Psychiatry.* 1990;157(3):331–4.

37. D Dowlatshahi, ES Paykel. Life events and social stress in puerperal psychoses: absence of effect. *Psychol Med.* 1990;20(3):655–62.

38. A Di Florio, K Gordon-Smith, L Forty, MR Kosorok, C Fraser, A Perry, et al. Stratification of the risk of bipolar disorder recurrences in pregnancy and postpartum. *Br J Psychiatry.* 2018;213(3):542–7.

39. I Jones, N Craddock. Familiality of the puerperal trigger in bipolar disorder: results of a family study. *Am J Psychiatry.* 2001;158(6):913–17.

40. T Munk-Olsen, TM Laursen, CB Pedersen, O Mors, PB Mortensen. Family and partner psychopathology and the risk of postpartum mental disorders. *J Clin Psychiatry.* 2007;68(12):1947–53.

41. I Jones, N Craddock. Do puerperal psychotic episodes identify a more familial subtype of bipolar disorder? Results of a family history study. *Psychiatr Genet.* 2002;12(3):177–80.

42. I Jones, M Hamshere, JM Nangle, P Bennett, E Green, J Heron, et al. Bipolar affective puerperal psychosis: genome-wide significant evidence for linkage to chromosome 16. *Am J Psychiatry.* 2007;164(7):1099–104.

43. N Coyle, I Jones, E Robertson, C Lendon, N Craddock. Variation at the serotonin transporter gene influences susceptibility to bipolar affective puerperal psychosis. *Lancet.* 2000;356(9232):1490–1.

44. E Robertson, I Jones, F Middle, J Morey, N Craddock. No association between two polymorphisms at the 5HT2A gene and bipolar affective puerperal psychosis. *Acta Psychiatr Scand.* 2003;108(5):387–91.

45. F Middle, I Jones, E Robertson, J Morey, C Lendon, N Craddock. Variation in the coding sequence and flanking splice junctions of the estrogen receptor alpha (ERα) gene does not play an important role in genetic susceptibility to bipolar disorder or bipolar affective puerperal psychosis. *Am J Med Genet B Neuropsychiatr Genet.* 2003;118B(1):72–5.

46. J Guintivano, EM Byrne, J Kiewa, S Yao, AE Bauer, KA Aberg, et al. Meta-analyses of genome-wide association studies for postpartum depression. *Am J Psychiatry.* 2023;180(12):884–95.

47. A Di Florio, JMK Yang, K Crawford, V Bergink, G Leonenko, AF Pardiñas, et al.

Post-partum psychosis and its association with bipolar disorder in the UK: a case-control study using polygenic risk scores. *Lancet Psychiatry.* 2021;8(12):1045–52.

48. ER Blackmore, I Jones, M Doshi, S Haque, R Holder, I Brockington, N Craddock. Obstetric variables associated with bipolar affective puerperal psychosis. *Br J Psychiatry.* 2006;188(1):32–6.

49. V Bergink, KM Burgerhout, K Weigelt, V Pop, MP Lambregtse-van den Berg, HA Drexhage. Immune system dysregulation in first-onset postpartum psychosis. *Biol Psychiatry.* 2015;78(9):768–76.

50. V Bergink, SA Kushner, V Pop, H Kuijpens, MP Lambregtse-van den Berg, HA Drexhage, et al. Prevalence of autoimmune thyroid dysfunction in postpartum psychosis. *Br J Psychiatry.* 2013;202(5):264–8.

51. K Weigelt, V Bergink, KM Burgerhout, M Pescatori, A Wijkhuijs, HA Drexhage. Down-regulation of inflammation-protective microRNAs 146a and 212 in monocytes of patients with postpartum psychosis. *Brain Behav Immun.* 2013;29:147–55.

52. KS Lewis, K Gordon-Smith, L Forty, A Di Florio, N Craddock, L Jones, et al. Sleep loss as a trigger of mood episodes in bipolar disorder: individual differences based on diagnostic subtype and gender. *Br J Psychiatry.* 2017;211(3):169–74.

53. KJS Lewis, K Tilling, K Gordon-Smith, KEA Saunders, A Di Florio, L Jones, et al. The dynamic interplay between sleep and mood: an intensive longitudinal study of individuals with bipolar disorder. *Psychol Med.* 2023;53(8):3345–54.

54. A Perry, K Gordon-Smith, KJS Lewis, A Di Florio, N Craddock, L Jones, et al. Perinatal sleep disruption and postpartum psychosis in bipolar disorder: findings from the UK BDRN Pregnancy Study. *J Affect Disord.* 2024;346:21–7.

55. C Carr, D Borges, K Lewis, J Heron, S Wilson, MR Broome, et al. Sleep and postpartum psychosis: a narrative review of the existing literature. *J Clin Med.* 2023;12(24):7550.

56. KJ Lewis, A Di Florio, L Forty, K Gordon-Smith, A Perry, N Craddock, et al. Mania triggered by sleep loss and risk of postpartum psychosis in women with bipolar disorder. *J Affect Disord.* 2018;225:624–9.

57. V Bergink, KM Burgerhout, KM Koorengevel, AM Kamperman, WJ Hoogendijk, MP Lambregtse-van den Berg, et al. Treatment of psychosis and mania in the postpartum period. *Am J Psychiatry.* 2015;172(2):115–23.

58. I Kirpinar, I Coskun, A Caykoylu. Progesterone and estradiol levels in postpartum women with and without psychosis. *J Psychiatry Neurosci.* 2010;35(3):166–72.

59. SJ McCoy, JM Beal, GH Watson, ES Paykel. Stressor and HPA axis responses in women with psychotic postpartum depression. *Arch Womens Ment Health.* 2003;6(3):177–84.

60. M Bloch, PJ Schmidt, M Danaceau, J Murphy, L Nieman, DR Rubinow. Effects of gonadal steroids in women with a history of postpartum depression. *Am J Psychiatry.* 2000;157:924–30.

61. National Institute for Health and Care Excellence (NICE). Antenatal and postnatal mental health: clinical management and service guidance. Clinical Guideline (CG192). 2014. Updated 2020.

62. Scottish Intercollegiate Guidelines Network (SIGN). SIGN 169: perinatal mental health conditions: a national clinical guideline. Edinburgh: SIGN; 2023.

63. C Dolman, L Howard, GM Goodwin, A Young, IR Jones, V Bergink, et al. Hypersexuality in bipolar disorder: an overlooked symptom. *Lancet.* 2024;11:405–6.

64. F Colom, E Vieta. *Psychoeducation manual for bipolar disorder.* Cambridge: Cambridge University Press; 2006.

65. LM Howard, D Bekele, M Rowe, J Demilew, S Bewley, TM Marteau. Smoking cessation in pregnant women with mental disorders: a cohort and

nested qualitative study. *BJOG.* 2013;120:362–70.

66. H McColl, M Dhillon, LM Howard. A systematic review of the nutritional status of women of a childbearing age with severe mental illness. *Arch Womens Ment Health.* 2013;16:39–46.
67. V Bergink, PF Bouvy, JS Vervoort, KM Koorengevel, EAP Steegers, SA Kushner. Prevention of postpartum psychosis and mania in women at high risk. *Am J Psychiatry.* 2012;169:609–15.
68. CL Taylor, RJ Stewart, LM Howard. Relapse in the first three months postpartum in women with history of serious mental illness. *Schizophr Res.* 2019;204:46–54.
69. V Sharma, KN Wood, B Weaver, D Mazmanian, M Thomson. Occurrence of postpartum manic or mixed episodes in women with bipolar I disorder: a systematic review and meta-analysis. *Bipolar Disord.* 2024;26:240–8.
70. DE Stewart, JL Klompenhouwer, RE Kendell, AM van Hulst. Prophylactic lithium in puerperal psychosis: The experience of three centres. *Br J Psychiatry.* 1991;158:393–7.
71. MP Austin. Puerperal affective psychosis: is there a case for lithium prophylaxis? *Br J Psychiatry.* 1992;161:692–4.
72. V Sharma, A Smith, D Mazmanian. Olanzapine in the prevention of postpartum psychosis and mood episodes in bipolar disorder. *Bipolar Disord.* 2006;8:400–4.
73. V Bergink, N Rasgon, KL Wisner. Postpartum psychosis: madness, mania, and melancholy in motherhood. *Am J Psychiatry.* 2016;173(12): 1179–88.
74. GN Babu, H Thippeswamy, PS Chandra. Use of electroconvulsive therapy (ECT) in postpartum psychosis – a naturalistic prospective study. *Arch Womens Ment Health.* 2013;16:247–51.
75. J Heron, N Gilbert, C Dolman, S Shah, I Beare, S Dearden, et al. Information and support needs during recovery from postpartum psychosis. *Arch Womens Ment Health.* 2012;15(3):155–65.
76. JMK Yang, K Vaiphei, M Siliya, T Mkandawire, C Dolman, J Heron, et al. Postpartum psychosis: a public involvement perspective across three continents. *Arch Womens Ment Health.* 2023;26(6):831–7.
77. E Roxburgh, N Morant, C Dolman, S Johnson, BL Taylor. Experiences of mental health care among women treated for postpartum psychosis in England: a qualitative study. *Community Ment Health J.* 2023;59(2):243–52.
78. C Dolman, IR Jones, LM Howard. Women with bipolar disorder and pregnancy: factors influencing their decision-making. *BJPsych Open.* 2016;2(5):294–300.

Chapter 13

Schizophrenia Spectrum Disorders

Julia L. France, Lucy C. Barker and Simone N. Vigod

Introduction

Schizophrenia spectrum disorders, including schizophrenia and schizoaffective disorder, affect 0.3–0.7% of the population [1, 2, 3, 4]. The onset of schizophrenia spectrum disorders typically occurs in late adolescence or early adulthood [1], with a slightly later age of onset for women compared to men. This means that onset often occurs before and during reproductive and child-bearing periods [1]. About 30% of patients admitted with a first-episode psychosis are already parents [5], meaning that they became parents before the onset of their psychotic illness – others will become parents during the course of their illness. Psychotic symptoms present in a broad array of different conditions, including mood disorders (e.g. bipolar or major depressive disorder with psychotic features), personality disorders, medical conditions, and substance use (e.g. acute intoxication, substance-induced psychotic disorders) and can be transient (e.g. brief psychotic disorder). However, the nature of schizophrenia spectrum disorders with the resultant impact on daily function and quality of life, portend unique considerations in the perinatal period. This chapter focuses on the clinical presentation and course of schizophrenia spectrum disorders perinatally, and it addresses issues in management for this population from preconception to the postpartum period.

Epidemiology

Several studies dating back decades found that those with schizophrenia were less likely to bear children, and to have fewer children than individuals without schizophrenia [6, 7, 8, 9, 10, 11]. With the transition of individuals with schizophrenia spectrum disorders from institutional to community care programmes in the 1980s, and the introduction of fertility-sparing second-generation antipsychotic medications in the mid-1990s, birth rates have risen in this population [5, 6, 12]. While still having a lower fertility rate overall compared to those without schizophrenia, in one Canadian population-based study, the general fertility rate (the number of live births per 1,000 eligible women aged 15–49) in women with schizophrenia was 16% higher in 2007–9 than in 1996–8 (95% confidence interval (CI) 1.04–1.31) [6]. Among adolescents, those with major mental illnesses including schizophrenia and bipolar disorder have birth rates close to three times higher than those unaffected [13].

From an epidemiological perspective, those with schizophrenia spectrum disorders appear to become pregnant at a younger age than those without schizophrenia spectrum disorders, and are more likely to be single parents [1, 6, 14, 15]. They more frequently experience poverty, lack of employment and have fewer social and emotional supports than unaffected individuals; they also experience higher rates of childhood trauma and other adverse childhood experiences [14, 16, 17, 18, 19].

There is a higher risk of unplanned pregnancy among those with schizophrenia, including adolescents; contributing factors appear to be disproportionately higher rates of sexual assault and lower rates of contraception prescription [14, 20, 21]. Individuals with schizophrenia have higher therapeutic abortion rates and higher rates of rapid repeat pregnancies, when a second pregnancy occurs within 1 year from a prior delivery, a usually undesirable outcome due to the associated maternal and child morbidity that can result [21, 22, 23, 24].

Clinical Presentation

Symptomatology

Schizophrenia spectrum disorders are marked by the chronic presence of key symptoms including delusions (i.e. fixed, false beliefs that are in contradiction to reality and outside societal norms), hallucinations (i.e. perceptual experiences of any of the senses (visual, auditory, olfactory, gustatory or tactile) in the absence of external stimulus), disorganized thinking and behaviour (i.e. incoherence, 'word salad', tangentiality or derailment of speech in conversations, catatonic behaviour), negative symptoms (i.e. flattened affect, avolition, anhedonia, asociality) and cognitive symptoms (e.g. executive dysfunction, slowed processing speed and working memory deficits) [25, 26]. Perinatal individuals with psychotic disorders can experience all of the symptoms associated with psychotic disorders in non-perinatal populations (see Box 13.1 for DSM-5 and ICD-11 criteria and symptomology for common psychotic disorders).

Positive psychotic symptoms may include paranoid delusions, hallucinations or disorganised thinking that leads to isolation from family, friends or healthcare providers, and/or puts child or maternal health at risk. For instance, paranoid delusions might lead to the misinterpretation of external information, intent of individuals in the support system, or actions or cues from the child [28]. One study reported on semi-structured interviews conducted with 15 parents with psychosis who described the biggest struggles of managing psychosis as a parent were dealing with depression, fatigue and difficulty focusing as a result of hearing voices [29]. Parents indicated that these symptoms all impacted their ability to provide protection, reciprocity, control and maintain consistent routines for their child [29]. In rare but severe cases, postpartum psychotic illness has been linked to infanticide (i.e. the killing of a baby in the first year of life) [1, 21, 30]. In addition, some individuals experience 'denial of pregnancy', a fixed false belief characterised by denial or rejection of the fact that one is pregnant, despite physiological proof. The symptoms of pregnancy may be attributed to other phenomena [31]. For example, in a case study from the United States, a patient described 'her enlarged abdomen as a paranormal phenomenon that had been projected onto her and as a prolonged reaction to eating granola the month before' [30]. While its prevalence is unknown, denial of pregnancy increases risk for poor outcomes for both mother and child, including neonaticide (i.e. the killing of a baby in the first day of life) [32].

When assessing someone who reports pregnancy or presents with pregnancy features who does not have a positive pregnancy test, delusional pregnancy and pseudocyesis can be considered. Albeit rare, with estimates of 1–6 per 22,000 births in higher-income

Box 13.1 Schizophrenia Spectrum Disorders: Comparison of DSM and ICD Criteria

Adapted from the DSM-5 Criteria [25]

Schizophrenia. Two or more of delusions, hallucinations, disorganised speech, grossly disorganised or catatonic behaviour or negative symptoms have been present nearly every day during a 1-month period, with a period of at least 6 months of symptoms. At least one symptom must be a delusion, hallucination or disorganized speech. The symptoms must cause significant distress or impair function, and not be attributable to the physiological effects of a substance or medical condition or another mental disorder. *Schizophreniform disorder will be diagnosed if the symptoms last between 1 and 6 months.*

Schizoaffective Disorder. A diagnosis of schizoaffective disorder can be made if one meets the main criteria of symptoms for schizophrenia during a major depressive or manic episode, but the delusions or hallucinations persist for at least 2 weeks in the absence of a mood episode.

Delusional Disorder. A diagnosis of delusional disorder can be made if one has *never* met the main criteria for schizophrenia but has experienced the presence of one or more delusions for a 1-month period or longer, and functioning is not impaired outside of the context of the specific delusion. The symptoms must not be better explained by another medical, substance or psychiatric disorder.

Adapted from the ICD-11 Criteria [27]

Schizophrenia. Schizophrenia is characterised by a period of at least 1 month with persistent disturbances across multiple domains including thinking (e.g. delusions, disorganised thinking), perception (e.g. hallucinations), self-experience (e.g. delusions of being controlled), cognition (e.g. impaired social cognition), volition, affect (e.g. flattened affect) and behaviour (e.g. bizarre behaviour). Symptoms are not attributable to a medical condition, substance or medication.

Schizoaffective Disorder. Schizoaffective disorder is characterised by a period of at least 1 month with the presence of the diagnostic symptoms of schizophrenia with the addition of a simultaneous manic, mixed or depressive episode not attributable to a medical condition, substance or medication.

Delusional Disorder. Delusional disorder is characterised by a period of at least 3 months with a persistent delusion or set of delusions which otherwise lacks the other symptoms of schizophrenia and leaves other aspects of speech, thought, affect and behaviour unaffected while not being attributable to a medical condition, mood disorder, substance or medication.

countries, *delusional pregnancy and pseudocyesis* appear to be more common in cultures and families where there are strong pressures towards and values placed on a woman's reproductive capacity and fertility [27]. Delusional pregnancy presents as one believing they are pregnant with the absence of or presence of minimal physical pregnancy symptoms [27]. Pseudocyesis (i.e. false pregnancy) presents as physiological symptoms of pregnancy such as abdominal swelling, menstrual disturbance, breast tenderness in the absence of actually being pregnant [27]. Delusional pregnancy is closely related to psychosis whereas pseudocyesis is often considered a somatoform disorder [27]. That being said, it can be difficult to distinguish between these two disorders [27]. Importantly, this delusion does not occur in the perinatal period because the individual is not actually pregnant, however in the context of perinatal psychiatry it is important to note its similarity and overlap with individuals presenting across the perinatal period, particularly those with psychotic disorders.

Negative symptoms such as anhedonia, asociality, alogia, avolition, fatigue and blunted affect may also have unique impacts perinatally. For example, these symptoms can impact a parent's ability to model and teach effective social and emotional reactions, interactions and roles, solve conflict and emotional problems and be able to execute important aspects of responsivity such as higher levels of praise, warmth, consistency, reasonable limit setting, time spent engaged in activity with the child and lower levels of criticism [5, 33]. Lack of insight into the presence or severity of symptoms can impact the ability to effectively manage their symptoms and the impacts of their symptoms on parenting responsibilities [5]. Less research has been conducted on the impact of cognitive symptoms in the perinatal period, and research in this area is needed to understand how these could impact parenting (e.g. if executive dysfunction could make it challenging to manage the many organisational tasks of parenting).

Course of Illness

There is no evidence that the course of psychotic illness specifically worsens during pregnancy. In one population-based study of 1,433 people with schizophrenia who had given birth, risk of emergency department visits and psychiatric hospitalisation was lower in pregnancy than in the year before conception [34]. There has been a suggestion that high oestrogen levels during pregnancy may act as a protective factor against psychiatric symptoms [35, 36, 37]. In several qualitative studies, individuals with psychotic disorders have described increased motivation and pride as well as more closeness and connection with family members in pregnancy, which may protect against relapse [5, 37].

There does appear to be an increased risk of relapse in the early postpartum period [1, 34, 35, 38]. In one large population-based study, the incidence rate ratio of psychiatric hospitalisations was found to be higher in the first 9 days postpartum (3.59; 95% CI, 2.74–4.69) and decrease by 10–29 days postpartum (0.87; 95% CI, 0.56–1.24), and to be generally lower over the first year postpartum compared to the year before conception (0.66; 95% CI, 0.57–0.76) [34]. In a study of 452 full-term pregnancies, 28.3% were associated with relapse within 3 months postpartum [39], and medication was not found to have a prophylactic effect (crude odds ratio (OR) = 0.65; 0.34–1.25) (adjusted OR = 0.99; 0.54–1.83). Risk for relapse of psychotic symptoms may be at least partly related to the rapid oestrogen withdrawal that occurs immediately postpartum [21, 34, 35]. Factors such as sleep deprivation and the profound psychosocial adjustment of caring for a newborn combined with fluctuating levels of oestrogen may also increase risk of psychotic relapse in new mothers with schizophrenia spectrum disorders [21, 34]. A study exploring risk factors for postpartum relapse found that higher maternal age, lower income, antepartum psychiatric admissions and lack of consistent mental healthcare provider were all associated with a higher risk of psychiatric admission in the postpartum period [40].

Associated Conditions

Higher rates of sexually transmitted infections [14, 41], and diabetes [12], are among associated medical factors that can impact individuals with psychosis in the perinatal period. Perinatal individuals with schizophrenia are also at a higher risk of co-occurring mental disorders [34]. In a sample of 1,433 individuals with schizophrenia who gave birth in Ontario, Canada, 43.5% were also identified as having a co-occurring mood disorder and 14.4% were identified as having a co-occurring personality disorder [34]. Substance use rates are also higher – one study found that 51% of pregnant people with schizophrenia smoked during pregnancy compared to 24% of those without schizophrenia [42]. Rates of other substance use among people with schizophrenia such as cannabis, alcohol and cocaine can be as high as three times that of the general population [43, 44, 45, 46].

Pregnancy, Neonatal and Child Outcomes

Developmental origins influence most, if not all, chronic diseases, including cardiac, metabolic, lung and kidney diseases, mental illness and even some cancers [47, 48, 49]. Increased sensitivity in early life development is related to extensive plasticity during that time, where a wide variety of stressors (e.g. psychosocial, infectious, nutritional, chemical) can alter developmental trajectories [50]. Children born to people with schizophrenia may be at risk for a variety of such adverse early developmental exposures. *Prenatal* exposures might be social (such as those related to poverty, poor housing and unemployment) [51], behavioural (e.g. sub-optimal eating, smoking or substance use) [52] and/or medical (e.g. diabetes, hypertension in pregnancy, exposure to psychotropic medications) [53, 54, 55]. A child exposed to poorly controlled diabetes, in utero, may be at higher risk for multiple medical problems, including malformations and later metabolic disease [56, 57, 58]. In utero exposure to psychotropic drugs used to treat maternal schizophrenia (e.g. antipsychotics, anti-epileptics) may also impact the health of that child [59]. *Postnatal* factors, such as compromised parenting capacity (e.g. due to schizophrenia-related cognitive dysfunction), maternal separation, poverty, second-hand smoke and poor diet, could further increase a child's vulnerability to various chronic diseases [60].

Pregnancy and Neonatal Outcomes

Schizophrenia spectrum disorders appear to be linked to a higher risk of various obstetric complications [42, 61, 62, 63, 64, 65, 66]. Population-level studies have shown that pregnant individuals with schizophrenia experience a 1.5 to 2-fold higher risk of gestational hypertension and pre-eclampsia, venous thromboembolism, placental complications, postpartum haemorrhage, assisted deliveries such as caesarean sections, inductions of labour and maternal intensive care unit admissions/hospitalisations [1, 61, 63, 64]. Neonatally, maternal schizophrenia spectrum disorders are associated with 1.5 to 2-fold higher risks of preterm birth, small for gestational age, large for gestational age, low birth weight, seizures, sepsis, neonatal abstinence syndrome, lower Apgar scores, and miscarriage and possibly stillbirth and infant death [34, 61, 62, 64, 65]. While the mechanism for the increased risk for pregnancy and neonatal complications is not entirely clear, high rates of cigarette smoking in this population may be a large contributor, as well as substance use and various reproductive history variables [62]. In one study, smoking explained the greatest proportion of elevated adjusted relative risk (aRR) for prematurity (9.9%), small for gestational age (28.7%) and Apgar score <8 at 1 and 5 minutes (9.8%, 5.6%) [62], suggesting that behavioural interventions, such as in the area of smoking cessation, could help to improve outcomes. Having schizophrenia is associated with a lower likelihood of skin-to-skin contact (65.2% vs 78.1%; aRR 0.88, 95% CI: 0.82–0.94) and breastfeeding initiation post-delivery (38.9% vs 52.6% aRR 0.80, CI:

0.71–0.90) compared to those without schizophrenia [67], suggesting that further supports are needed around the time of delivery.

Longer-Term Child Outcomes

Large epidemiological studies have mostly evaluated the risk for schizophrenia in adult children of one or both parents with schizophrenia, and showed that the risk is elevated, due to the strong heritability of the disorders [68, 69, 70]. With respect to other outcomes, small clinical studies have focused on child neurodevelopment up to age 4 years; these studies observed delays in motor, language and cognitive development in children born to individuals with schizophrenia [68]. Whether related to developmental factors or to postnatal environmental factors, there is also evidence of slightly increased risks for child accidental injury, as well as injury due to assault in the child's early years and self-injury when approaching adolescence [71, 72]. This evidence comes from population-based data, and we do not know to what extent assault is from the parent (s) with schizophrenia or assault from other individuals (e.g. other parents or caregivers). Recent research has also found that risk of childhood chronic conditions are higher among children of mothers with schizophrenia [73, 74].

Financial disadvantage as well as judgement from others and life disruptions caused by increases in psychotic symptoms are all described as contributing to various long-term psycho-social impacts of paternal mental illness on children, including increased difficulty socialising and building relationships with peers, with paternal mental illness reported to undermine or prevent one's participation in social and recreation activities [75, 76]. Children have reported experiencing increased anxiety and depression as a result of being acutely aware of their parent's illness and fluctuating symptoms, in combination with feeling an obligation to alleviate, resolve or tend to their parent's illness [75, 76]. However, parental mental illness can also increase resiliency among children, resulting in longer-term resilience to mental illness and higher levels of positive traits such as adaptability and self-efficacy into adulthood [75].

Parenting and Child Custody Loss

Overall, parental competency is multi-faceted. While aspects such as abuse can be easier to assess, other aspects of parental competency can be more difficult to assess as many methods of assessing competency can be subjective and culturally biased. For example, spending time engaged in play with a child or providing toys are not parental responsibilities that are universal across all cultures and traditions [5]. However, environments where parents and their children experience higher levels of support and lower levels of isolation and negative judgments, bolster opportunities for better outcomes for both parent and child [75]. There is evidence that with comprehensive support and management, there are examples of positive parenting interactions between parents with serious mental illness and their children. For example, a study examining the outcomes of a 10-week Mental Health Positive Parenting programme for parents with serious mental illness based on Triple P programming, found decreases in laxness, over-reactivity, verbosity and the perception of child behaviour as problematic [77]. In a study comparing parenting among mothers with and without schizophrenia, there were no significant difference in over-reactivity and hostility scores between groups. This suggests that the sometimes cited perception of mothers with schizophrenia as being hostile or aggressive towards their children may not be based on evidence [33].

Given the nature of both the positive and negative symptoms of schizophrenia spectrum disorders, however, some parents with schizophrenia spectrum disorders may be unable to safely meet the needs of their infant or child, either periodically or over the longer term. As such, this maternal–child dyad population is at a high risk of child apprehension and custody loss [1, 5, 36, 75]. It is reported that custody loss among parents with a serious mental illness diagnosis is around 60% [5, 75] and in a sample of 5,000 Medicaid-eligible women, mothers with schizophrenia were three times as likely to be involved in the child welfare system or have experienced custody loss and child apprehension [5, 78]. This means that children are at higher risk of experiencing inconsistent or intermittent care by various different and revolving family members [5, 79]. Many parents with serious mental illness also experience familial disputes over parenting capacity and arrangements [80, 81, 82]. Further, loss of child custody is a difficult tragedy for parents to navigate and can highlight the tensions between maternal identity and one's management of their mental illness [80, 83]. In many cases, child removal can exacerbate maternal mental health difficulties and have devastating effects on children [84, 85, 86, 87].

It has also been suggested that individuals with schizophrenia spectrum disorders may face negative societal perceptions of their ability to effectively and adequately parent that are not necessarily backed by objective evidence of their parenting ability [5]. In the perinatal period, this may increase isolation and act as a barrier to prenatal and postnatal care, to engaging appropriate support systems such as family, friends or professionals or pursuing education surrounding pregnancy and parenting due to worry of judgement from others and fear of child removal [5, 82, 84, 88]. Comprehensive efforts at managing maternal mental illness and addressing custody loss risk factors should be considered [80, 89]. Ensuring an objective, fair and non-judgemental assessment of parenting capacity, including a person's support systems, is essential prior to making recommendations of maternal–child separation. When separation is needed, kinship placements are often preferred [80, 90] and seem to reduce some of the negative impacts of child removal on both mother and child [90, 91] (see Chapter 36, 'Child Safeguarding').

Management

Preconception Health

Women with serious mental illnesses such as schizophrenia have dealt with a difficult past when it comes to reproductive rights and freedoms. Women with schizophrenia have historically been separated from society and institutionalised, where they have had little option or ability for family planning or the expression of their reproductive desires [6, 23, 72, 92]. Additionally, women with schizophrenia have also been forcibly sterilised or sterilised without their knowledge and informed consent [24, 92]. To this end, preconception and perinatal care for women, transgender and non-binary individuals with psychotic disorders needs to be informed by the historical (and, in some cases, ongoing) wrongdoings and treatment of individuals with these disorders and address rights to reproductive and sexual knowledge, health, and choice, despite the presence of mental illness [22]. Both positive and negative symptoms of psychotic disorders, as well as associated social factors (e.g. financial difficulties), stigma and inadequately equipped services can create barriers to sexual and reproductive healthcare for those with psychosis; particular consideration needs to be paid to the unique circumstances that individuals with schizophrenia face when it comes to contraception and family planning [14, 93]. For example, symptoms such as disorganisation, avolition, fatigue and the management of distracting symptoms such as hallucinations or delusions might make it difficult to remember birth control, to use birth control on a reliable schedule, or to access a reliable supply of many birth control methods [14, 92]. Informing individuals who have the ability to become pregnant about emergency contraceptive options such as the morning-after pill, or long-acting reversible contraception methods such as intrauterine devices are examples of ways to address these individuals' unique experiences as they relate to sexual health. Pregnant individuals who are unsure about whether to proceed with the pregnancy should be provided with education about the continuation or termination of pregnancy, and providers should ensure that the patient has control over their reproductive options. For those whose schizophrenia spectrum disorders or comorbid conditions make communication about reproductive health more challenging, strategies such as demonstration (e.g. condom demonstration) and checking comprehension can be used where appropriate [94], although providers should not assume communication difficulties based on a diagnosis of schizophrenia.

For those planning a pregnancy, attention to optimising risk factors preconception is essential. For example, smoking has a significantly higher prevalence among individuals with schizophrenia than the general population and has been tied to a number of negative health outcomes in the perinatal period such as low birth weight [14, 64]. Pharmacological approaches to aid with smoking cessation have been tested among samples of people with schizophrenia and it has been found that certain medications such as bupropion have better smoking abstinence results without adverse effects on psychiatric symptoms unlike other pharmacological approaches such as varenicline [95, 96]. Furthermore, pharmacotherapy seems to be more important for achieving smoking abstinence among people with schizophrenia compared to the general population [95, 96]. A double-blind placebo-controlled trial of bupropion combined with cognitive behavioural therapy was found to result in sustained smoking cessation 2 years post trial [97]. Evidence suggests that attempts to manage smoking cessation need to be informed by the unique intersecting attributes of one's psychiatric illness, rather than the provision of uniform approaches to smoking cessation. As well, if pregnancy is imminent, then non-pharmacologic approaches to smoking cessation should be considered aligned with pregnancy-specific recommendations [98]. Treating concurrent substance use and serious mental illness such as schizophrenia requires consideration towards an integrated approach to care. Often, patients access different services to treat either the substance use disorder or the mental illness, separately [99]. However, attention should be paid to how aspects of both disorders intersect to create unique barriers to treatment accessibility and outcomes [99]. As such, treatment approaches integrating multiple interventions have the most success in managing these disorders [100]. Research continues on exploring best practices for treating concurrent disorders such as schizophrenia and substance use disorders. Additionally, unique approaches to weight management for people with schizophrenia have been explored, given the additional risk of weight gain due to antipsychotic medication [100]. A systematic review of weight management interventions found that behavioural modification programmes including dietary and exercise counselling were the most effective in managing weight, especially compared to the use of pharmacological interventions [100]. Finally, key members of the prospective mother/parent's psychosocial support network should be identified and solidified, and close connections to obstetric support are vital to support optimal health in the perinatal period (see Chapter 24, 'Pre-pregnancy Advice and Planning' and Box 13.2).

In the preconception period, the effects of antipsychotic medication deserve consideration. With respect to fertility, most first-generation and some second-generation antipsychotic medications (e.g. risperidone at higher dosages) can cause sustained hyperprolactinemia which will result in suppression of ovulation, and thus reduce fertility. Antipsychotic agents also increase risk for metabolic syndrome, which can leave individuals at risk for health problems in pregnancy and in delivery, so preconception optimisation is ideal when possible. Further, it is ideal for discussions about the risks and benefits of psychotropic medication use in pregnancy to be started early (i.e. when the medications are started) and revisited frequently to ensure that individuals have adequate information to make informed decisions related to their reproductive planning.

Box 13.2 Preconception Checklist (Can Be Implemented by Multidisciplinary Care Providers)

- Provide education to patient (and partner/family, when desired), on issues including presentation, course of illness, absolute risk increases for adverse pregnancy, neonatal and child outcomes, and offer information related to heritability of psychiatric illness
- Assess, optimise and educate around medical, sexual and reproductive health: sexual health check-up including testing for and education surrounding sexually transmitted infections, contraception and reproductive options, and management of medical comorbidities
- Assess and optimise psychosocial support network (e.g. partner, family, friends, support groups, social worker, occupational therapy, etc.) and economic resources, with connection to economic supports (e.g. government benefits, other financial support for new parents)
- Assess behavioural and metabolic risk factors, including smoking, substance use and weight and, if relevant:
    - Discuss risks of smoking, substance use, body mass index
    - Engage relevant treatment and support options
- Discuss and assist patient in making an informed decision about the benefits and risks of medication use in pregnancy, whilst breastfeeding and in the postpartum period
- Discuss who will provide mental health and obstetrical care during the perinatal period
    - Obstetrical care providers (e.g. obstetrician, general practitioner/family physician, midwife)
    - Psychiatric care provider (e.g. current psychiatrist, perinatal psychiatrist)
    - Other care providers as needed (e.g. psychologist, psychotherapist, health visitor, social worker)
- Consider resources that may be beneficial during and after pregnancy:
    - Prenatal education
    - Parenting education and support groups and resources

Always ensure patient is aware of how to access 24/7 crisis support resources

Reproductive plans can be considered when selecting a choice of agent for an individual who plans to become pregnant, and reproductive considerations should be part of ongoing follow-up care, including and especially when planning of pregnancy is imminent. While efficacy is paramount, considerations in choosing an agent in all reproductive-aged individuals with the ability to become pregnant may include its impact on fertility, its safety profile, including related to fetal and infant exposure in-utero and in lactation.

Pregnancy Care

In pregnancy, ongoing care should be taken to optimise health, with special attention to risk factors for negative outcomes as described above. Strategies for management of risk factors may differ compared to those for non-pregnant individuals. For example, behavioural strategies are used first-line for smoking cessation [98], and nutritional and exercise recommendations need to be adapted for pregnancy. Multidisciplinary care during pregnancy is recommended, including collaboration between the psychiatrist and obstetrician-gynaecologist or maternal/fetal medicine specialist [101]. Risk for intimate partner violence should be assessed in pregnancy [101]. During this time, a plan for postpartum management can be formulated, again with collaboration across disciplines including pediatrics [101] (see Chapter 25, 'Pre-birth Planning'). It is important to bolster economic and social support during this time [80].

Antipsychotic Medication Use in Pregnancy and Postpartum

Antipsychotic medications are the mainstay of treatment for individuals with schizophrenia spectrum disorders [102]. Psychosocial and psychotherapeutic treatments also have a place in the management of all mental illnesses, and individuals with schizophrenia spectrum disorders may be prescribed a number of other types of medications, including antidepressants, mood stabilisers, benzodiazepines or hypnotics, or may benefit from somatic therapies such as electroconvulsive therapy that come along with their own benefits and risks [102, 103, 104, 105]. Decisions about medication use during pregnancy involve weighing the potential benefits of medication use on maternal mental health against the potential risks of medication use to the mother/parent and the developing fetus. Discussion of risks and benefits with the individual is paramount for informed decision-making.

Risks associated with untreated psychotic illness (or relapse due to discontinuation of medication) in the perinatal period to pregnant/postpartum individuals, fetuses and children can be substantial [21, 106]. So, in most cases, stopping or changing medications is not recommended. That being said, there is evidence that as many as 62% of pregnant individuals on atypical antipsychotics and 81% of those on typical antipsychotics discontinue their antipsychotic medication during pregnancy, which may be at least partially due to their concerns about risk to the fetus [107]. Discontinuation often continues into the postpartum period, where the sedation caused by antipsychotic medications can be a concern for many parents who worry about staying vigilant or attentive to their newborns [5]. Some individuals worry that by taking medication they will be perceived as ill and thus unable to care for a child, and that showing that one is not taking medication would be perceived as positive [5]. In the postpartum period some mothers/parents with psychotic disorders may also worry about how not taking their medication could be perceived by others as being non-compliant and increase risk of interference or investigation into their fitness to parent [5].

The research on the safety of antipsychotics in pregnancy is limited to observational studies, which can be prone to confounding by indication and other factors (see Chapter 25). Medications under study have included first-generation antipsychotics, several second-generation antipsychotics (mainly olanzapine, quetiapine, risperidone and to some extent aripiprazole), including in long-acting injectable antipsychotic form (LAI-APs) and clozapine, although the size of studies varies by agent [59, 106, 108]. While a full review of the safety of each medication is outside the scope of this chapter, most large studies have not found a convincing link between the use of most antipsychotics in pregnancy and congenital malformations [109, 110, 111]. Some, but not all, studies have found an increased risk for metabolic complications of pregnancy (e.g. gestational diabetes) with second-generation antipsychotics [110, 111, 112]. Of note, recent research suggests that the risk for gestational diabetes is higher among those who take antipsychotics prior to pregnancy compared to those who do not, and the risk may not be reduced by discontinuing the antipsychotic [113, 114]. Studies have found at least some level of increased risk of adverse perinatal outcomes such as preterm labour, caesarean section births, small and large for gestation age infants, miscarriage loss, still birth, with some differences in findings across agents and across studies [109, 110]. However, once again, it is possible that these observational studies do not fully account for other factors that might increase the risk for adverse outcomes independent of medication exposure. There has been less data on developmental/long-term outcomes after exposure to antipsychotic medication in utero [106, 110, 115, 116, 117, 118], although recent research suggests that antipsychotic agents do not increase risk for attention deficit hyperactive disorder or autism spectrum disorder [119, 120]. Clozapine exposure specifically has been associated with increased rates of floppy infant syndrome at delivery, characterised by reduced muscle tone and associated with motor developmental delays, hyper-extensibility of joints, abnormal postures, decreased fetal heart rate variability, and seizures in infancy, although most studies in this area are case studies [117]. Outside the scope of this chapter, mood stabilisers may be prescribed for some schizophrenia spectrum disorders (e.g. schizoaffective disorder), and prescribers should be aware of the specific risks associated with these (e.g. the use of valproate is not recommended in those with pregnancy potential due to the risk of malformations including neural tube defects) [101, 121]. In general, across all agents, the lowest effective doses of medications should be used and polypharmacy should be avoided where possible [101]. Most guidelines suggest not initiating LAIs in pregnancy [101]. Further research is needed on the comparative safety of individual agents, LAIs and the concomitant use of antipsychotic agents with other psychotropics [122, 123]. It is important that prescribers keep up to date with research and evidence-based guidance on medication use in pregnancy and breastfeeding.

In the postpartum period, the risk of discontinuing antipsychotic medication is likely to be substantial given that this is the highest risk time for relapse [1, 34, 35]. Thus, the benefits of antipsychotic medication must be weighed against the potential risks for medication exposure through lactation for those choosing to breastfeed. While antipsychotic medications pass into breastmilk and have been detected in the plasma of infants, most have generally not been consistently associated with any adverse infant effects [124, 125]. Due to immature hepatic and renal systems, preterm infants are at risk for elevated plasma medication concentrations, which should be considered when deciding to use antipsychotics while breastfeeding for preterm infants [124, 125]. For example, the US Food and Drug Adminstration suggests not to breastfeed/chestfeed when taking olanzapine and warns about the development of extra-pyramidal symptoms among newborns who are exposed to olanzapine during the third trimester of pregnancy [126]. Clozapine could lead to agranulocytosis as it accumulates in breast milk and is able to cross the placenta, therefore testing is required and attention needs to be paid to the specific risks and benefits for each patient [117]. Additional considerations such as the risk of sleep deprivation from around-the-clock feeding and difficulty feeding the infant overnight due to sedation also play into decisions related to feeding method and should be part of medication planning discussions. If a new parent is taking a sedating medication, then ensuring that there is adequate overnight support for infant feeding and care is crucial, as is counselling on the risks of co-sleeping for all parents.

Parenting Interventions

Like all people who become parents, there are both new joys and new burdens experienced [5]. New mothers/parents with psychotic disorders experience all of the same difficulties associated with new motherhood/parenthood that mothers/parents without psychotic disorders experience, such as new schedules, routines and tasks, child behavioural challenges, difficulty with a child's eating or sleeping routines, or child illness or sickness. However, those with psychotic disorders experience the additional burden of managing their own illness symptoms and subsequent self-care needs, and parenting duties can be especially challenged by some of the key symptoms of psychotic disorders including anhedonia, avolition and cognitive symptoms such as disorganization, poor verbal memory, attention deficits and executive functioning [5]. These symptoms combined with additional symptoms such as flattened affect, alogia and asociality can also have an impact on the interactions between mother and child and on the mother–child bond [127]. In a study of mothers in the first 4 months of the postpartum period, interactions between mothers with schizophrenia and their newborns were observed as containing more negative interactions such as being remote, insensitive or intrusive. At 4 months, infants of mothers with schizophrenia were more avoidant [67, 127].

On top of factors surrounding illness symptoms and being a new parent, those with schizophrenia face additional difficulties because of their risk of poverty, lack of safe housing, domestic violence, substance abuse, social isolation, poor nutrition and other physical health challenges, and lack of a support network [5]. Therefore, appropriate and comprehensive care and support mitigate the risks associated with pregnancy and caring for an infant. There is increasing evidence supporting the efficacy of wrap-around, cross-agency approaches to care that are informed by a family-centred and strengths-based approach and utilise a network of organisations and relationships to provide the mother and child with a comprehensive system of care to reduce the risks associated with pregnancy and parenthood for people with psychotic disorders [5, 80]. These networks are able to support the needs and well-being of the mother/parent and child across a range of different domains and levels of acuity, including services that provide 24/7 support, substance abuse services, liaison with the legal and education system, financial and transportation aid, vocational support, trauma and abuse counselling, spiritual and cultural guidance, advocacy, respite services and family case management [5, 80, 128].

Respite services are one intervention specifically intended to aid parents in relieving stress, improving sleep and managing their illness [128, 129, 130]. Psychoeducation, didactic parenting classes, parenting coaching, parent support/mutual aid groups and co-parenting support are all programmes aimed at improving parenting skills that can be offered in different settings such as residential settings, community-based programmes or in-home [5, 80, 128]. During episodes of acute symptom exacerbation, Mother and Baby Inpatient Units have been used – primarily in the United Kingdom and Australia – to provide a space where mother–child contact can be maintained and more intensive support can be provided to the mother, including symptom management and assistance with parenting skills [5].

Schizophrenia spectrum disorders are chronic in nature, and therefore ongoing parenting support beyond the immediate postpartum period is important. Further research is needed on parenting interventions for this population to optimise long-term outcomes for mothers/parents and their children [131].

Conclusion

Women with schizophrenia spectrum disorders are increasingly becoming parents and are faced with managing the varying symptoms of psychotic disorders in addition to the unique effects of psychotic symptomology on pregnancy and parenting. Evidence suggests that the course of psychotic illness can be affected perinatally, including a high risk for relapse in the early post-partum period. Psychotic disorders are linked to a range of problems with pregnancy, neonatal and long-term child outcomes. Among the largest barriers for women with psychotic disorders around the perinatal period may be discrimination for their illness, and a lack of social and economic resources. Yet, with effective and comprehensive care and management around the perinatal period, outcomes for people with psychotic disorders and their children can be optimised. Attention to preconception health, the effects of antipsychotic medication and both prenatal and parenting education and support highlight key pillars of supporting perinatal individuals with schizophrenia spectrum disorders in the perinatal period. Research and practice in the area of perinatal psychotic disorders should further explore how to better address and reduce the structural vulnerabilities faced by those with psychotic disorders while supporting the pursuit of optimal health in the preconception, pregnancy and postpartum period.

References

1. CL Taylor, T Munk-Olsen, LM Howard, SN Vigod. Schizophrenia around the time of pregnancy: leveraging population-based health data and electronic health record data to fill knowledge gaps. *BJPsych Open*. 2020;6(5).
2. LC Barker, SN Vigod. Sexual health of women with schizophrenia: a review. *Front Neuroendocrinol.* 2020;57:100840.
3. B Moreno-Küstner, C Martín, L Pastor. Prevalence of psychotic disorders and its association with methodological issues: a systematic review and meta-analyses. *PLoS ONE*. 2018;13(4).
4. FJ Charlson, AJ Ferrari, DF Santomauro, S Diminic, E Stockings, JG Scott, et al. Global epidemiology and burden of schizophrenia: findings from the Global Burden of Disease Study 2016. *Schizophr Bull.* 2018;44(6):1195–203.
5. MV Seeman. Parenting issues in mothers with schizophrenia. *Curr Womens Health Rev.* 2010;6(1):51–7.

6. SN Vigod, MV Seeman, JG Ray, GM Anderson, CL Dennis, S Grigoriadis, et al. Temporal trends in general and age-specific fertility rates among women with schizophrenia (1996–2009): a population-based study in Ontario, Canada. *Schizophr Res.* 2012;139(1–3):169–75.

7. TM Laursen, T Munk-Olsen. Reproductive patterns in psychotic patients. *Schizophr Res.* 2010;121(1):234–40.

8. LM Howard, C Kumar, M Leese, G Thornicroft. The general fertility rate in women with psychotic disorders. *Am J Psychiatry.* 2002;159(6):991–7.

9. H Hope, R Parisi, DM Ashcroft, R Williams, S Coton, K Kosidou, et al. Fertility trends of women with serious mental illness in the United Kingdom 1992–2017: a primary care cohort study using the clinical practice research datalink. *J Affect Disord.* 2020;269:141–7.

10. RA Power, S Kyaga, R Uher, JH MacCabe, N Långström, M Landen, et al. Fecundity of patients with schizophrenia, autism, bipolar disorder, depression, anorexia nervosa, or substance abuse vs their unaffected siblings. *JAMA Psychiatry.* 2013;70(1):22–30.

11. H Bundy, D Stahl, JH MacCabe. A systematic review and meta-analysis of the fertility of patients with schizophrenia and their unaffected relatives. *Acta Psychiatr Scand.* 2011;123(2):98–106.

12. P Dazzan. Schizophrenia during pregnancy. *Curr Opin Psychiatry.* 2021;34(3):238–44.

13. SN Vigod, CL Dennis, PA Kurdyak, J Cairney, A Guttmann, VH Taylor. Fertility rate trends among adolescent girls with major mental illness: a population-based study. *Pediatrics.* 2014;133(3):e585–91.

14. A González-Rodríguez, A Guàrdia, A Álvarez Pedrero, M Betriu, J Cobo, S Acebillo, et al. Women with schizophrenia over the life span: health promotion, treatment and outcomes. *Int J Environ Res Public Health.* 2020;17(15):5594.

15. A Ranning, T Munk Laursen, A Thorup, C Hjorthøj, M Nordentoft. Children of parents with serious mental illness: with whom do they grow up? A prospective, population-based study. *J Am Acad Child Adolesc Psychiatry.* 2016;55(11):953–61.

16. A Topor, CG Stefansson, A Denhov, P Bülow, G Andersson. Recovery and economy; salary and allowances: a 10-year follow-up of income for persons diagnosed with first-time psychosis. *Soc Psychiatry Psychiatr Epidemiol.* 2019;54(8):919–26.

17. MV Seeman. Schizophrenia mortality: barriers to progress. *Psychiatric Q.* 2019;90(3):553–63.

18. J Read, J Van Os, AP Morrison, CA Ross. Childhood trauma, psychosis and schizophrenia: a literature review with theoretical and clinical implications. *Acta Psychiatr Scand.* 2005;112(5):330–50.

19. KL McCabe, EA Maloney, HJ Stain, CM Loughland, VJ Carr. Relationship between childhood adversity and clinical and cognitive features in schizophrenia. *J Psychiatr Res.* 2012;46(5):600–7.

20. LD de Mooij, M Kikkert, NM Lommerse, J Peen, SC Meijwaard, J Theunissen, et al. Victimisation in adults with severe mental illness: prevalence and risk factors. *Br J Psychiatry.* 2015;207(6):515–22.

21. NA Brzezinski-Sinai, A Brzezinski. Schizophrenia and sex hormones: what is the link? *Front Psychiatry.* 2020;11:537154.

22. R Gupta, HK Brown, LC Barker, CL Dennis, SN Vigod. Rapid repeat pregnancy in women with schizophrenia. *Schizophr Res.* 2019;212:86–91.

23. HK Brown, CL Dennis, P Kurdyak, SN Vigod. A population-based study of the frequency and predictors of induced abortion among women with schizophrenia. *Br J Psychiatry.* 2019;215(6):736–43.

24. L Simoila. Reproductive health among Finnish women with schizophrenia or schizoaffective disorder. Doctoral thesis. University of Helsinki; 2019. https://shorturl.at/mphkA

25. American Psychiatric Association. Schizophrenia spectrum and other psychotic disorders. In: *Diagnostic and statistical manual of mental disorders*. 5th ed. Washington, DC: American Psychiatric Association; 2013. p. 87–122.
26. RA McCutcheon, T Reis Marques, OD Howes. Schizophrenia: an overview. *JAMA Psychiatry.* 2020;77(2):201–10.
27. World Health Organization. International classification of diseases for mortality and morbidity statistics (11th revision). 2018. https://shorturl.at/XTnyZ
28. H Solari, KE Dickson, L Miller. Understanding and treating women with schizophrenia during pregnancy and postpartum. *J Popul Ther Clin Pharmacol.* 2009;16(1):23–32.
29. J Strand, P Boström, K Grip. Parents' descriptions of how their psychosis affects parenting. *J Child Fam Stud.* 2020;29(3):620–31.
30. T Ostler, S Kopels. Schizophrenia and filicide. *Curr Womens Health Rev.* 2010;6(1):58–62.
31. M Nau, HE Bender, J Street. Psychotic denial of pregnancy: legal and treatment considerations for clinicians. *J Am Acad Psychiatry Law.* 2011;39(1):31–9.
32. SH Friedman, A Heneghan, M Rosenthal. Characteristics of women who do not seek prenatal care and implications for prevention. *J Obstet Gynecol Neonatal Nurs.* 2009;38(2):174–81.
33. S Shenoy, G Desai, G Venkatasubramanian, PS Chandra. Parenting in mothers with schizophrenia and its relation to facial emotion recognition deficits: a case control study. *Asian J Psychiatr.* 2019;40:55–9.
34. G Rochon-Terry, A Gruneir, MV Seeman, JG Ray, P Rochon, CL Dennis, et al. Hospitalizations and emergency department visits for psychiatric illness during and after pregnancy among women with schizophrenia. *J Clin Psychiatry.* 2016;77(4):541–7.
35. JA Markham. Sex steroids and schizophrenia. *Rev Endocr Metab Disord.* 2011;13(3):187–207.
36. CL Taylor, M Broadbent, M Khondoker, RJ Stewart, LM Howard. Predictors of severe relapse in pregnant women with psychotic or bipolar disorders. *J Psychiatr Res.* 2018;104:100–7.
37. B Davies, D Allen. Integrating "mental illness" and "motherhood": the positive use of surveillance by health professionals. A qualitative study. *Int J Nurs Stud.* 2007;44(3):365–76.
38. NR Matevosyan. Pregnancy and postpartum specifics in women with schizophrenia: a meta-study. *Arch Gynecol Obstet.* 2011;283(2):141–7.
39. CL Taylor, RJ Stewart, LM Howard. Relapse in the first three months postpartum in women with history of serious mental illness. *Schizophr Res.* 2019;204:46–54.
40. SN Vigod, G Rochon-Terry, K Fung, A Gruneir, CL Dennis, S Grigoriadis, et al. Factors associated with postpartum psychiatric admission in a population-based cohort of women with schizophrenia. *Acta Psychiatr Scand.* 2016;134(4):305–13.
41. SF Chen, JH Chiang, CY Hsu, YC Shen. Schizophrenia is associated with an increased risk of sexually transmitted infections: a nationwide population-based cohort study in Taiwan. *Schizophr Res.* 2018;202:316–21.
42. E Nilsson, P Lichtenstein, S Cnattingius, RM Murray, CM Hultman. Women with schizophrenia: pregnancy outcome and infant death among their offspring. *Schizophr Res.* 2002;58(2):221–9.
43. DA Regier, ME Farmer, DS Rae, BZ Locke, SJ Keith, LL Judd, et al. Comorbidity of mental disorders with alcohol and other drug abuse: results from the Epidemiologic Catchment Area (ECA) study. *JAMA.* 1990;264(19):2511–18.
44. RA Chambers, JH Krystal, DW Self. A neurobiological basis for substance abuse comorbidity in schizophrenia. *Biol Psychiatry.* 2001;50(2):71–83.
45. ND Volkow. Substance use disorders in schizophrenia: clinical implications of

comorbidity. *Schizophr Bull.* 2009;35(3): 469–72.

46. JY Khokhar, LL Dwiel, AM Henricks, WT Doucette, AI Green. The link between schizophrenia and substance use disorder: a unifying hypothesis. *Schizophr Res.* 2018;194:78–85.

47. PD Wadhwa, C Buss, S Entringer, JM Swanson. Developmental origins of health and disease: brief history of the approach and current focus on epigenetic mechanisms. *Semin Reprod Med.* 2009;27(5):358–68.

48. B Medsker, E Forno, H Simhan, JC Celedón. Prenatal stress, prematurity, and asthma. *Obstet Gynecol Surv.* 2015;70(12):773–9.

49. CJ Smith, KK Ryckman. Epigenetic and developmental influences on the risk of obesity, diabetes, and metabolic syndrome. *Diabetes Metab Syndr Obes.* 2015;8:295–302.

50. JJ Heindel, LN Vandenberg. Developmental origins of health and disease: a paradigm for understanding disease cause and prevention. *Curr Opin Pediatr.* 2015;27(2):248–53.

51. Canadian Psychiatric Association. Clinical practice guidelines. Treatment of schizophrenia. *Can J Psychiatry.* 2005;50(13 Suppl 1):7S–57S.

52. MV Seeman. Clinical interventions for women with schizophrenia: pregnancy. *Acta Psychiatr Scand.* 2013;127(1):12–22.

53. JW Newcomer. Metabolic syndrome and mental illness. *Am J Manag Care.* 2007;13(7 Suppl):S170–7.

54. A Czeizel, I Dudás, A Vereczkey, F Bánhidy. Folate deficiency and folic acid supplementation: the prevention of neural-tube defects and congenital heart defects. *Nutrients.* 2013;5(11).

55. K Blighe, BL Chawes, RS Kelly, H Mirzakhani, M McGeachie, AA Litonjua, et al. Vitamin D prenatal programming of childhood metabolomics profiles at age 3 y. *Am J Clin Nutr.* 2017;106(4):1092–9.

56. M Balsells, A García-Patterson, I Gich, R Corcoy. Major congenital malformations in women with gestational diabetes mellitus: a systematic review and meta-analysis. *Diabetes Metab Res Rev.* 2012;28(3):252–7.

57. JS Sheffield, EL Butler-Koster, BM Casey, DD McIntire, KJ Leveno. Maternal diabetes mellitus and infant malformations. *Obstet Gynecol.* 2002;100(5 Pt 1):925–30.

58. CM Boney, A Verma, R Tucker, BR Vohr. Metabolic syndrome in childhood: association with birth weight, maternal obesity, and gestational diabetes mellitus. *Pediatrics.* 2005;115(3):e290–6.

59. M Galbally, M Snellen, J Power. Antipsychotic drugs in pregnancy: a review of their maternal and fetal effects. *Ther Adv Drug Saf.* 2014;5(2):100–9.

60. A Ranning, TM Laursen, A Thorup, C Hjorthøj, M Nordentoft. Serious mental illness and disrupted caregiving for children: a nationwide, register-based cohort study. *J Clin Psychiatry.* 2015;76(8):19263.

61. SN Vigod, PA Kurdyak, CL Dennis, A Gruneir, A Newman, MV Seeman, et al. Maternal and newborn outcomes among women with schizophrenia: a retrospective population-based cohort study. *BJOG.* 2014;121(5):566–74.

62. SN Vigod, K Fung, A Amartey, E Bartsch, R Felemban, N Saunders, et al. Maternal schizophrenia and adverse birth outcomes: what mediates the risk? *Soc Psychiatry Psychiatr Epidemiol.* 2020;55(5):561–70.

63. BE Bennedsen, PB Mortensen, AV Olesen, TB Henriksen, M Frydenberg. Obstetric complications in women with schizophrenia. *Schizophr Res.* 2001;47(2–3):167–75.

64. LM Ellman, M Huttunen, J Lönnqvist, TD Cannon. The effects of genetic liability for schizophrenia and maternal smoking during pregnancy on obstetric complications. *Schizophr Res.* 2007;93(1):229–36.

65. MC Magnus, A Havdahl, NH Morken, KA Wensaas, AJ Wilcox, SE Håberg. Risk of miscarriage in women with psychiatric

disorders. *Br J Psychiatry.* 2021;219(3): 501–6.

66. F Judd, A Komiti, P Sheehan, L Newman, D Castle, I Everall. Adverse obstetric and neonatal outcomes in women with severe mental illness: to what extent can they be prevented? *Schizophr Res.* 2014;157(1–3):305–9.

67. CL Taylor, HK Brown, NR Saunders, LC Barker, S Chen, E Cohen, et al. Maternal schizophrenia, skin-to-skin contact, and infant feeding initiation. *Schizophr Bull.* 2022;48:145–53.

68. KM Henriksson, TF McNeil. Health and development in the first 4 years of life in offspring of women with schizophrenia and affective psychoses: Well-Baby Clinic information. *Schizophr Res.* 2004;70(1):39–48.

69. EW Schubert, TF McNeil. Prospective study of adult mental disturbance in offspring of women with psychosis. *Arch Gen Psychiatry.* 2003;60(5):473–80.

70. LT Niemi, JM Suvisaari, JK Haukka, G Wrede, JK Lönnqvist. Cumulative incidence of mental disorders among offspring of mothers with psychotic disorder: results from the Helsinki High-Risk Study. *Br J Psychiatry.* 2004;185:11–17.

71. CL Taylor, HK Brown, NR Saunders, LC Barker, S Chen, E Cohen, et al. Accidental injury, self-injury, and assault among children of women with schizophrenia: a population-based cohort study. *Acta Psychiatr Scand.* 2021;143(5):406–17.

72. SW Yang, MA Kernic, BA Mueller, GE Simon, KCG Chan, A Vander Stoep. Association of parental mental illness with child injury occurrence, hospitalization, and death during early childhood. *JAMA Pediatr.* 2020;174(8): e201749.

73. SN Vigod, JG Ray, E Cohen, AS Wilton, NR Saunders, LC Barker, et al. Maternal schizophrenia and the risk of a childhood chronic condition. *Schizophr Bull.* 2022;48(6):1252–62.

74. A Toufeili, E Cohen, JG Ray, AS Wilton, HK Brown, NR Saunders, et al. Complex chronic conditions among children born to women with schizophrenia. *Schizophr Res.* 2022;241:24–35.

75. MV Seeman. Schizophrenia and motherhood. In: A Reupert, D Maybery, J Nicholson, M Göpfert, MV Seeman, editors. *Parental psychiatric disorder: distressed parents and their families.* 3rd ed. Cambridge: Cambridge University Press; 2015. p. 107–16.

76. P Bee, K Berzins, R Calam, S Pryjmachuk, KM Abel. Defining quality of life in the children of parents with severe mental illness: a preliminary stakeholder-led model. *PLoS ONE.* 2013;8(9):e73739.

77. RF Phelan, DJ Howe, EL Cashman, SH Batchelor. Enhancing parenting skills for parents with mental illness: the Mental Health Positive Parenting Program. *Med J Aust.* 2013;199(3):S30–3.

78. JM Park, P Solomon, DS Mandell. Involvement in the child welfare system among mothers with serious mental illness. *Psychiatr Serv.* 2006;57(4):493–7.

79. MV Seeman. The changing role of mother of the mentally ill: from schizophrenogenic mother to multigenerational caregiver. *Psychiatry.* 2009;72(3):284–94.

80. MV Seeman. Grappling with issues of motherhood for women with schizophrenia. *Healthcare.* 2023;11(21): 2882.

81. MS Salzer, KL Berg, K Kaplan, E Brusilovskiy. Custody challenges experienced by parents with serious mental illnesses outside of child protective services proceedings. *Psychiatr Rehabil J.* 2021;44(2):197–200.

82. KS Kenny, C Barrington, SL Green. "I felt for a long time like everything beautiful in me had been taken out": women's suffering, remembering, and survival following the loss of child custody. *Int J Drug Pol.* 2015;26(11):1158–66.

83. R Shor, M Moreh-Kremer. Identity development of mothers with mental illness: contribution and challenge of motherhood. *Soc Work Ment Health.* 2016;14(3):215–26.

84. P Weller. Mothers and mental illness: breaking the silence about child loss. *Int J Law Psychiatry.* 2019;67:101500.

85. E Wall-Wieler, LL Roos, J Bolton, M Brownell, N Nickel, D Chateau. Maternal mental health after custody loss and death of a child: a retrospective cohort study using linkable administrative data. *Can J Psychiatry.* 2018;63(5):322–8.

86. A Bilson, KEC Martin. Referrals and child protection in England: one in five children referred to children's services and one in nineteen investigated before the age of five. *Br J Soc Work.* 2017;47(3):793–811.

87. C Grant, J Radley, G Philip, R Lacey, R Blackburn, C Powell, et al. Parental health in the context of public family care proceedings: a scoping review of evidence and interventions. *Child Abuse Negl.* 2023;140:106160.

88. A Halsa. Trapped between madness and motherhood: mothering alone. *Soc Work Ment Health.* 2018;16(1):46–61.

89. L Ostrow, K Kaplan, Y Zisman-Ilani, E Brusilovskiy, C Smith, MS Salzer. Risk factors associated with child protective services involvement among parents with a serious mental illness. *Psychiatric Serv.* 2021;72(4):370–7.

90. M Cooley, J Krysik. Foster caregiving and child outcomes in relative and non-relative foster families. *Child Adoles Soc Work J.* 2022;39(5):539–44.

91. R Ueno, K Kamibeppu. Narratives by Japanese mothers with chronic mental illness in the Tokyo metropolitan area: their feelings toward their children and perceptions of their children's feelings. *J Nerv Ment Dis.* 2008;196(7): 522–30.

92. LJ Miller. Sexuality, reproduction, and family planning in women with schizophrenia. *Schizophr Bull.* 1997;23(4):623–35.

93. LC Barker, J Zaheer, Z Hussain, J France, A Rodriguez, S Lubotzky-Gete, et al. Experiences of sexual and reproductive health care access for women and nonbinary people with early psychosis: towards an integrated perspective of service users and clinicians. *Can J Psychiatry.* 2024;69(1):33–42.

94. World Health Organization. Promoting sexual and reproductive health for persons with disabilities: WHO/UNFPA guidance note. 2009. www.unfpa.org/sites/default/files/pub-pdf/srh_for_disabilities.pdf

95. C Cather, GN Pachas, KM Cieslak, AE Evins. Achieving smoking cessation in individuals with schizophrenia: special considerations. *CNS Drugs.* 2017;31(6):471–81.

96. DT Tsoi, M Porwal, AC Webster. Interventions for smoking cessation and reduction in individuals with schizophrenia. *Cochrane Database Syst Rev.* 2008;(3). Art. No.: CD007253. DOI: 10.1002/14651858.CD007253.

97. AE Evins, C Cather, NA Rigotti, O Freudenreich, DC Henderson, CM Olm-Shipman, et al. Two-year follow-up of a smoking cessation trial in patients with schizophrenia: increased rates of smoking cessation and reduction. *J Clin Psychiatry.* 2004;65(3):307–11.

98. LWS Leung, GA Davies. Smoking cessation strategies in pregnancy. *J Obstet Gynaecol Can.* 2015;37(9):791–7.

99. KT Mueser, AS Bellack, JJ Blanchard. Comorbidity of schizophrenia and substance abuse: implications for treatment. *J Consult Clin Psychol.* 1992;60(6):845–56.

100. G Faulkner, AA Soundy, K Lloyd. Schizophrenia and weight management: a systematic review of interventions to control weight. *Acta Psychiatr Scand.* 2003;108(5):324–32.

101. A Lefebvre, A Pouchon, S Bioulac, J Mallet, M Polosan, C Dondé. Management of schizophrenia in women during the perinatal period: a synthesis of international recommendations. *Expert Opin Pharmacother.* 2022;23(11):1337–50.

102. KR Patel, J Cherian, K Gohil, D Atkinson. Schizophrenia: overview and treatment options. *Pharm Therapeut.* 2014;39(9):638–45.

103. P Chue, JK Lalonde. Addressing the unmet needs of patients with persistent negative symptoms of schizophrenia: emerging pharmacological treatment options. *Neuropsychiatr Dis Treat.* 2014;10:777–89.

104. J Labad, I Montalvo, A González-Rodríguez, C García-Rizo, B Crespo-Facorro, JA Monreal, et al. Pharmacological treatment strategies for lowering prolactin in people with a psychotic disorder and hyperprolactinaemia: a systematic review and meta-analysis. *Schizophr Res.* 2020;222:88–96.

105. IM Zervas, C Theleritis, CR Soldatos. Using ECT in schizophrenia: a review from a clinical perspective. *World J Biol Psychiatry.* 2012;13(2):96–105.

106. GE Robinson. Treatment of schizophrenia in pregnancy and postpartum. *J Popul Ther Clin Pharmacol.* 2012;19(3):e380–6.

107. I Petersen, RL McCrea, DJP Osborn, S Evans, V Pinfold, PJ Cowen, et al. Discontinuation of antipsychotic medication in pregnancy: a cohort study. *Schizophr Res.* 2014;159(1):218–25.

108. M Ellfolk, MK Leinonen, M Gissler, AM Lahesmaa-Korpinen, L Saastamoinen, ML Nurminen, et al. Second-generation antipsychotics and pregnancy complications. *Eur J Clin Pharmacol.* 2020;76(1):107–15.

109. CG Coughlin, KA Blackwell, C Bartley, M Hay, KA Yonkers, MH Bloch. Obstetric and neonatal outcomes after antipsychotic medication exposure in pregnancy. *Obstet Gynecol.* 2015;125(5):1224–35.

110. P Damkier, P Videbech. The safety of second-generation antipsychotics during pregnancy: a clinically focused review. *CNS Drugs.* 2018;32(4):351–66.

111. SN Vigod, T Gomes, AS Wilton, VH Taylor, JG Ray. Antipsychotic drug use in pregnancy: high dimensional, propensity matched, population based cohort study. *BMJ.* 2015;350:h2298.

112. Y Park, S Hernandez-Diaz, BT Bateman, JM Cohen, RJ Desai, E Patorno, et al. Continuation of atypical antipsychotic medication during early pregnancy and the risk of gestational diabetes. *Am J Psychiatry.* 2018;175(6):564–74.

113. Z Wang, KKC Man, T Ma, LM Howard, L Wei, ICK Wong, et al. Association between antipsychotic use in pregnancy and the risk of gestational diabetes: population-based cohort studies from the United Kingdom and Hong Kong and an updated meta-analysis. *Schizophr Res.* 2021;229:55–62.

114. S Kucukgoncu, S Guloksuz, K Celik, MO Bahtiyar, JJ Luykx, BPF Rutten, et al. Antipsychotic exposure in pregnancy and the risk of gestational diabetes: a systematic review and meta-analysis. *Schizophr Bull.* 2020;46(2):311–18.

115. A Einarson, R Boskovic. Use and safety of antipsychotic drugs during pregnancy. *J Psychiatr Pract.* 2009;15(3):183–92.

116. M Trixler, A Gáti, S Fekete, T Tényi. Use of antipsychotics in the management of schizophrenia during pregnancy. *Drugs.* 2005;65(9):1193–206.

117. TM Mehta, RJ Van Lieshout. A review of the safety of clozapine during pregnancy and lactation. *Arch Womens Ment Health.* 2017;20(1):1–9.

118. Z Wang, R Brauer, KKC Man, B Alfageh, P Mongkhon, ICK Wong. Prenatal exposure to antipsychotic agents and the risk of congenital malformations in children: a systematic review and meta-analysis. *Br J Clin Pharmacol.* 2021;87(11):4101–23.

119. Z Wang, AYL Chan, D Coghill, P Ip, WCY Lau, E Simonoff, et al. Association between prenatal exposure to antipsychotics and attention-deficit/hyperactivity disorder, autism spectrum disorder, preterm birth, and small for gestational age. *JAMA Intern Med.* 2021;181(10):1332–40.

120. Ó Hálfdánarson, JM Cohen, Ø Karlstad, CE Cesta, MH Bjørk, SE Håberg, et al. Antipsychotic use in pregnancy and risk of attention/deficit-hyperactivity disorder and autism spectrum disorder: a Nordic cohort study. *BMJ Ment Health.* 2022;25(2):54–62.

121. J Jentink, MA Loane, H Dolk, I Barisic, E Garne, JK Morris, et al. Valproic acid monotherapy in pregnancy and major congenital malformations. *New Engl J Med.* 2010;362(23): 2185–93.

122. DL O'Sullivan, N Byatt, EC Dossett. Long-acting injectable antipsychotic medications in pregnancy: a review. *J Acad Consult Liaison Psychiatry.* 2022;63(1):53–60.

123. LC Barker, SN Vigod. Reproductive health among those with schizophrenia spectrum disorders: an overview of considerations related to the premenopausal period, pregnancy and postpartum, and the menopausal transition, with a focus on recent findings. *Curr Psychiatry Rep.* 2023;25(12):793–802.

124. SA Reinstein, J Cosgrove, T Malekshahi, KM Deligiannidis. Long acting injectable antipsychotics use during pregnancy: a brief review and concise guide for clinicians. *J Clin Psychiatry.* 2020;81(6):20ac13597.

125. N Kronenfeld, M Berlin, D Shaniv, M Berkovitch. Use of psychotropic medications in breastfeeding women. *Birth Defects Res.* 2017;109(12):957–97.

126. Food and Drug Administration. Zyprexa (Olanzapine) label. 2009. https://shorturl .at/iblu8

127. D Riordan, L Appleby, B Faragher. Mother-infant interaction in post-partum women with schizophrenia and affective disorders. *Psychol Med.* 1999;29(4):991–5.

128. MV Seeman. Intervention to prevent child custody loss in mothers with schizophrenia. *Schizophr Res Treatment.* 2011;2012:e796763.

129. EA Craig. Parenting programs for women with mental illness who have young children: a review. *Aust N Z J Psychiatry.* 2004;38(11–12):923–8.

130. T Jacobsen, LJ Miller, KP Kirkwood. Assessing parenting competency in individuals with severe mental illness: a comprehensive service. *J Ment Health Adm.* 1997;24(2):189–99.

131. J Radley, C Grant, J Barlow, L Johns. Parenting interventions for people with schizophrenia or related serious mental illness. *Cochrane Database Syst Rev.* 2021;(10).

132. MV Seeman. Pseudocyesis, delusional pregnancy, and psychosis: the birth of a delusion. *World J Clin Cases.* 2014;2(8):338–44.

Chapter 14

Personality Disorder

Gwen Adshead

Introduction

Perinatal services can expect to be asked to assess, treat and support mothers with personality disorder (PD). Yet we know that some services and clinicians feel anxiety about working with mothers with PD, perhaps because they feel less confident about how to make therapeutic relationships with people who often struggle to engage in treatment [1].

In this chapter I will discuss why PD is a complex concept and how it is still developing as a field of study. I will set out a model of understanding personality development from an evolutionary perspective of humans as group animals as a mental capacity that helps us understand other people's minds (mentalising [2, 3]). Disorders of personality function impair mentalising and thereby have a negative impact on social relationships of all kinds, but especially those that involve asking for care when vulnerable or providing care when vulnerable [4]. This problem inevitably affects relationships with mental healthcare professionals and may explain why people with PD have been so unpopular with professionals, and attract professional stigma, which leads to them being rejected from services [1, 5].

In the context of this textbook, personality disorders are especially problematic for women who become mothers; first because they may find the transition to motherhood especially painful and difficult and, second, because their personality dysfunction can have a negative impact on how they bond to their babies, relate to them and provide care for them. Although not all mothers with PD pose a risk to their children (especially if they get help and support), in a minority of cases maternal PD may be a risk factor for child maltreatment, especially if the woman in question has other mental health problems (including substance misuse) and is a victim of domestic violence [6].

Personality as a Function of the Social Mind and Brain

The human personality has evolved as a function of our enhanced neocortical volume, which is related to our identity as primates who live in groups [7]. Our personalities allow us to be recognised by other group members over time as both unique individuals and also as members of our identified social group. Successful membership of primate groups requires the capacity to make and maintain social relationships over time; especially relationships that involve seeking help when distressed, and cooperation when vulnerable. The human personality has therefore evolved to have an interpersonal and relational function; which is facilitated by the capacity to think about other people's minds as well as our own. This reflective capacity (or 'mentalising function') is crucial to maintaining relationships that endure over time, and thereby promote safety, welfare and social success with peers.

The human personality has therefore evolved to have an affect regulation function as part of its social function; and it also acts as an organising principle for those traits, dispositions and values that make up an individual sense of self. In this sense, a person's personality is best understood as an organic relational system which allows them to make successful relationships with others. Rather than a categorical 'box' in which people stick lifelong, the human personality is a dynamic dimensional system which ecologically has a genetic level, a cognitive belief level, a cultural level and a narrative level [8].

Diagnosis and Epidemiology

Space does not permit a full discussion of the diagnosis of PD. For many years, it was assumed that PD was not a disorder like schizophrenia or bipolar disorder because clinicians did not always 'see' the psychological problems faced by people with PD, and tended to focus on external behaviours that were self-destructive or antisocial. Increased study of post-traumatic stress disorder (PTSD) in the 1980s, and similar study of the long-term effects of childhood trauma in the 1990s, have helped clinicians to understand that the symptoms and signs of PD in adulthood may reflect what happens to children's minds and brains when exposed to different kinds of childhood adversity. Attachment theory as a paradigm for understanding the development of children's brains and minds has also proved a useful paradigm, and I discuss this in more detail below.

Box 14.1 sets out the International Classification of Diseases, 11th Revision (ICD-11) diagnostic criteria for PD [9]. Both the ICD-11 and the *Diagnostic and Statistical Manual of Mental Illnesses*, fifth edition (DSM-5) encourage clinicians to think of PD in terms of a spectrum of personality *dysfunction*, which is mild, moderate or severe. The dysfunction primarily involves (a) self-experience and (b) affect and arousal regulation which in turn lead to (c) interpersonal dysfunction, especially in relationships that involve caregiving or vulnerability.

Clinicians are therefore invited to rate a person's condition of PD in terms of (a) its impact on self-experience and social dysfunction and (b) the severity of this impact, in terms of social engagement and harm to self or others. Only emotionally unstable (or borderline) personality disorder remains as a discrete category, because research in the field indicated that most categories were too non-specific to be useful. Specific attention is paid to a person's self-experience, affect dysregulation and interpersonal problems together with the presence of maladaptive personality traits (psychoticism, antagonism, neuroticism, disinhibition and avoidance/detachment). It is important to note that acts of self-harm or destructiveness *on their own* are not evidence of PD; and this is especially true for women who only self-harm or have suicidal ideation for the first time in pregnancy.

The ICD-11 invites clinicians to rate a person's problems as mild, moderate or severe. The severe group are a minority in ordinary mental health services and tend to be found only in forensic populations [10]. The implication of a dimensional model is that it may be possible to help a person whose condition is moderate become mild, and a mild condition become non-clinical. The DSM-5 developed an alternative model for PD, which also emphasises the dimensional as opposed to categorical nature of PD [11].

The research underlying this focus on 'severity' and dysfunction is based on epidemiological studies of dysfunctional personality traits in the community. A study by Yang

Box 14.1 ICD-11 Personality Disorder Diagnostic Criteria

The central manifestations of personality disorder are impairments in functioning of aspects of the self (e.g. identity, self-worth, capacity for self-direction) and/or problems in interpersonal functioning (e.g. developing and maintaining close and mutually satisfying relationships, understanding others' perspectives, managing conflict in relationships).

Impairments in self-functioning and/or interpersonal functioning are manifested in maladaptive (e.g. inflexible or poorly regulated) patterns of cognition, emotional experience, emotional expression, and behaviour.

The following diagnostic requirements for personality disorder present a set of essential features, all of which must be present to diagnose a personality disorder. Once the diagnosis of a personality disorder has been established, it should be described in terms of its level of severity:

- 6D10.0 mild personality disorder
- 6D10.1 moderate personality disorder
- 6D10.2 severe personality disorder

A category relevant to this grouping is:

- QE50.7 personality difficulty

Personality difficulty is not classified as a mental disorder, but rather is listed in the grouping of Problems Associated with Interpersonal Interactions in the chapter on Factors Influencing Health Status or Contact with Health Services. Personality difficulty refers to pronounced personality characteristics that may affect treatment or health services but do not rise to the level of severity to merit a diagnosis of personality disorder.

Personality disorder and personality difficulty can be further described using five trait domain specifiers. These trait domains describe the characteristics of the individual's personality that are most prominent and that contribute to personality disturbance. As many as necessary to describe personality functioning should be applied.

Trait domain specifiers that may be recorded include the following:

- 6D11.0 negative affectivity
- 6D11.1 detachment
- 6D11.2 dissociality
- 6D11.3 disinhibition
- 6D11.4 anankastia

More detailed guidance about the personality characteristics reflected in the trait domain specifiers is provided in the respective sections.

Clinicians may also wish to add an additional specifier for 'borderline pattern':

- 6D11.5 borderline pattern

The borderline pattern specifier has been included to enhance the clinical utility of the classification of personality disorder. Specifically, use of this specifier may facilitate the identification of individuals who may respond to certain psychotherapeutic treatments.

A complete description of a particular case of personality disorder includes the rating of the severity level and the assignment of the applicable trait domain specifiers (e.g. mild personality disorder with negative affectivity and anankastia; severe personality disorder with dissociality and disinhibition).

The borderline pattern specifier is considered optional but, if used, should ideally be used in combination with the trait domain specifiers (e.g. moderate personality disorder with negative affectivity, dissociality, and disinhibition, borderline pattern).

Table 14.1 The *Diagnosis and Statistical Manual of Mental Disorders*, fourth edition, Text Revision (DSM-IV-TR) clusters PDs into three groups

Cluster	Types of PD
Cluster A	Includes paranoid, schizoid and schizotypal PDs, often characterised as odd or eccentric
Cluster B	Includes antisocial, borderline, histrionic and narcissistic PDs or the dramatic, emotional or erratic PDs
Cluster C	Includes avoidant, dependent and obsessive-compulsive PDs, and individuals with these disorders are often characterised as fearful or anxious

et al. [12] of PD traits in a large community sample found that only 23% of the population have *no* dysfunctional traits, but only 1% have *severe* personality dysfunction. The same study used a measure of PD which divides people into three clusters ([13]; see Table 14.1) and reported on the different clusters in women of childbearing age. They found high levels of both simple (mild) and complex (moderate) PD in all three clusters in women aged 15–44 (p. 195). These data would suggest that many women of childbearing age who present to perinatal services will have personality pathology which may complicate their experience of pregnancy. Similar studies in the USA [14] found that these clusters are not discrete and overlap with each other; and that there is a strong association with other mental disorders, such as depression. All PDs were associated with significant interpersonal dysfunction, even those with dysfunction in one area such as obsessive-compulsive PD [15].

These studies imply that it makes more sense to think of people with PDs as people with 'relational' disorders; who struggle dynamically with making and maintaining relationships; chiefly because they struggle with regulating affect and arousal when trying to understand other people's minds. Although much research on maternal PD has focused on women with cluster B forms of PD (presumably because this form can be associated with high levels of self-harm and suicidal ideation), women in the other clusters also struggle with relationships with others [16], and these struggles may be exacerbated after the birth of a baby.

Some service users and professionals do not like the term 'personality disorder', seeing it as a stigmatising label, rather than an actual diagnostic entity. They prefer to see the problems defined in the ICD-11 and DSM-5 as a form of 'complex PTSD, (see Chapter 15, 'Complex Post-Traumatic Stress Disorder'). However, there is good quality evidence that emotionally unstable personality disorder (EUPD) and complex PTSD are distinct disorders but which have some symptoms patterns in common [17, 18]. There is also good quality evidence that exposure to chronic childhood trauma increases the risk of *all* psychiatric disorders and is not specific to PD [19]. If there is stigma attached to the diagnosis, this is largely driven by professional anxiety and resistance, and needs to be addressed by better training and support for mental health professionals who work with people with PD.

Epidemiology in the Context of Maternity Services and Perinatal Mental Health

There have been several studies that have looked at the impact of maternal PD on maternal mental health, both antenatally and postnatally [20, 21, 22]. A study by

Crowley [23] found that 16.2% of women at an antenatal booking clinic had raised levels of dysfunctional personality traits (a higher prevalence than the general population prevalence estimates of PD). Those with raised dysfunctional traits were also likely to experience increased risk of anxiety, depression and other axis I disorders. Another study of mothers with newborn babies found high levels of all three clusters. especially in cluster C [16]. The commonest PDs diagnosed were obsessive-compulsive PD (19%) and borderline PD (BPD) (17%).

Younger women with dysfunctional PD traits may experience a range of problems associated with pregnancy, especially those with borderline traits. Yang's study ([12, p. 195]) reports a higher prevalence of PD in *all* clusters in young women aged 16–24 compared to older women. This is likely to be because personality dysfunction tends to first emerge in adolescence at a time of identity formation, and first experiments in interpersonal function outside the family. Teenagers with high levels of borderline traits are at increased risk of unplanned pregnancy [24], which may exacerbate their symptoms [25]. A mediating factor for risk is increased exposure to adverse childhood experiences in women (ACEs), which are associated with sexual risk behaviours leading to unplanned and unwanted pregnancies, and ambivalence about the pregnancy [26, 27]. A recent population-based study in Canada suggests that *all* teenage pregnancies are associated with increased mortality rate from a range of causes, including unnatural deaths, such as suicide [28]; in which dysfunctional personality traits may be a mediating factor.

Personality disorder symptoms can become exacerbated in pregnancy (just like other mental disorders) in response to several factors. First, the pregnant brain is one which is highly neuroplastic in response to hormonal changes, resulting in changes in grey matter volume and cognitive function similar to adolescence [29, 30, 31]. Hormone-related changes in the pregnant brain may affect serotonergic metabolism [32] which may contribute to the risk of disorders of affect regulation, including anxiety, depression and BPD. The exacerbation of PD symptoms may explain why so many studies have found that maternal PD is associated with less positive birth outcomes [33, 34].

Presentation

Women with personality dysfunction are more likely to experience the pregnancy as stressful and may experience suicidal thoughts and increased anxiety about the pregnancy [35]. In some cases, maternal anxiety in women with PD may manifest itself as unusual healthcare-seeking behaviour antenatally, including obstetric factitious disorders, including demands for opiates and early delivery by caesarean section [36]. After delivery, all kinds of maternal PD is associated with increased levels of postnatal anxiety and depression [16]. Mothers with cluster C PDs may experience increased obsessional thoughts about the baby and anxieties about being unable to provide 'perfect' care [37].

Perinatal psychiatrists can expect to see a prevalence of PD of at least 6% in an ordinary antenatal service (which is the community norm), but it could be double this figure. Maternal PD can be an issue for both primiparous women and for women who already have children. It is unlikely that all these women will need a formal psychological intervention, but they may benefit from education and advice about their feelings, and enhanced support during pregnancy and the first 6 months postnatally. Sadly adult mental health services rarely offer interventions for PD (seeing them as specialist interventions) and the model of care in specialist PD services excludes women who are pregnant or have small children.

Postnatally, the picture may be similar; mothers with PD have increased levels of personality dysfunction in the postnatal period, as mothers adjust to oscillating levels of mood-regulating hormones and the demands of motherhood, including lack of sleep and the need to prioritise the baby's needs above her own. But it is this emotional demand with which a mother with PD will struggle. Mothers with PD who cannot regulate their own distress and anxiety may resort postnatally to a range of externalising solutions such as obsessional rituals, eating disorders, substance misuse, health anxiety and self-harming behaviours; none of which may have been present *before* the pregnancy.

For those women who have used dysfunctional solutions to distress before pregnancy, these behaviours are likely to get worse. Intriguingly post-natal psychosis does not seem to be more prevalent in this group, despite the fact that affect dysregulation and brief periods of psychosis are recognised EUPD symptoms. A recent study suggested that bipolar women with BPD traits are more likely to develop depression postnatally [38].

Aetiology

There are many theories of personality development and function (see [39]) which cannot be reviewed in a short chapter. However, attachment theory, based on the work of Bowlby and Ainsworth, is especially useful in the context of this chapter. In the late 1950s and early 1960s, psychological therapists like Bowlby argued that babies instinctively form attachments to their caregivers based on how the caregiver responds to their emotional needs. Attachment theory draws on animal studies of how 'attachments' between a baby and their caregiver become the basis for a biobehavioural system that helps to regulate stress in situations of vulnerability and need.

The attachment system has both a physiological and a psychological form. Physiologically, a 'secure' attachment system influences both epigenetic mechanisms and development of parasympathetic and vagal nerve distribution affecting unconscious stress and distress responses [40, 41]. Psychologically, a 'secure' baby develops a internal working model of relationships where it is okay to be upset, it is safe to approach people when needy and they can trust that others will help when one is vulnerable [42]. With age and speech, this model becomes linguistically articulated into a narrative of attachment, and 'secure' attachment narratives typically read as fresh and coherent accounts of the experience of relationships of need and dependence [43].

By contrast, insecure attachment in children is associated with avoidance of care or disorganised responses to feeling vulnerable or afraid. Insecure children tend to grow up to be insecure adults [44] who are at increased risk of developing clinical psychiatric disorders [45]. Linguistically, insecure attachment narratives are often hard to understand: they may be lengthy rambling narratives, preoccupied with pain, fear and anger; or brief terse accounts that dismiss neediness and vulnerability and emphasise strength and normality.

Attachment insecurity is likely to occur in response to exposure to childhood adversity, especially childhood maltreatment. Thus attachment insecurity and PD diagnoses share an association with exposure to ACEs and childhood maltreatment. Several studies that have demonstrated a close relationship between insecure attachment, ACEs (including child maltreatment) and adult personality dysfunction [46, 47, 48, 49]. The mediating factors between childhood adversity, insecure attachment and personality dysfunction are likely to be unresolved traumatic distress and poor mentalising skills [50]. In general, studies of maternal attachment insecurity of mind find a strong relationship with infant insecurity; such that maternal insecurity of mind predicts infant insecurity [51].

Personality function is also influenced by genetic variations, whose expression is influenced by epigenetic environmental factors. For example, some variants of genes for proteins affecting serotonin transport and metabolism may be expressed differently under different conditions, such as maternal or offspring stress. Although theoretically some kinds of epigenetic interaction may render individuals more resilient, they are unlikely to present in clinical populations. Clinicians instead are likely to see people in whom genetic vulnerabilities have interacted with environmental stressors to render them even more vulnerable. Current thinking about personality dysfunction suggests that there may be a general 'p' factor for personality pathology that increases the risk of developing personality dysfunction under environmental stress [52].

Course and Outcomes

Personality disorder is generally understood to be a relapsing and remitting condition, which generally improves over time; although the interpersonal dysfunction aspect has less good a prognosis [53, 54]. In the context of maternal PD, the main clinical concern is that women with mild/moderate PD may find the process of becoming a mother (i.e. conception, pregnancy, labour and postnatal identity shift) so stressful that their personality dysfunction becomes worse, resulting in worsening subjective distress, acting out and impairment of parental function (see Box 14.2).

Not all mothers with PD will struggle to care for their babies. Much depends on how severe the dysfunction is, what external support is available and what other stressors they

Box 14.2 Case Example: Amelia

Amelia is a 24-year-old woman with mild EUPD. She has sometimes struggled with mood swings and comorbid anxiety disorder, which results in minor substance misuse (alcohol and cannabis). But she sees her general practitioner (GP) to get antidepressants when she needs to; and she is able to hold down a job and has never self-harmed.

Amelia becomes pregnant unexpectedly, and she is ambivalent about both the pregnancy and her relationship with Gary, the baby's father. Her personality function deteriorates; resulting in high levels of antenatal anxiety and somatisation, in increased alcohol abuse or drug-seeking behaviour and highly stressful rows with Gary, whom she accuses of being *'controlling'*.

Amelia comes up to A&E once or twice in the last trimester complaining of abdominal pain and demanding to have a C section *'because my body can't cope with this'*. She experiences her (normal) labour as highly stressful and calls it *'traumatic'*; she is tearful because she finds bonding with her newborn baby girl difficult.

Her antenatal anxieties persist into the postnatal period; and both the community midwife and the health visitor are concerned that she may be developing postnatal depression, as she describes occasional thoughts of self-harm and suicidal ideation. Her relationship with Gary ends amid accusations of domestic violence. Her somatic anxieties about the pregnancy now seem to transfer to anxieties about the baby's health, leading to frequent visits to the GP and A&E; where Amelia says tearfully that she thinks there is *'something wrong'* with the baby.

have to face, such as family stress and intimate partner violence. Midwives, health visitors and community support services have traditionally had an important role in supporting mothers with mild degrees of personality dysfunction.

Mothers with more severe dysfunction may develop more dysfunctional ways of coping in the postnatal period; including obsessive compulsive disorders, eating disorders and suicidal behaviours. The outcome for these disorders clearly depends on what treatment is provided; like any other people with a health condition, mothers with personality dysfunction do better if they get appropriate treatment, and do worse if no treatment is provided.

Implications for Infants, Children and Adolescents

As discussed above, pregnancy and motherhood are *relational* experiences, which can be impacted badly by poor maternal mental health. Any maternal mental health problem (including maternal PD) is a form of adverse childhood experience, and the greater the degree of maternal psychiatric morbidity, the greater the risk of the offspring developing psychopathology [55, 56].

The mediating factors that link maternal PD and offspring psychopathology have been shown to be mothers' reduced attunement to their babies' emotional cues and greater avoidance of their emotional cues. This effect is identifiable as early as 6 weeks postnatally [57]. The negative effect of maternal attachment insecurity on mothers' responses to babies' emotional cues can be identified using functional MRI scanning [58].

The most concerning implication for children and toddlers is that if their mother has PD, she may not be able to regulate a child's ordinary affects of anger, rage, boredom and fear. Poor mentalising skills means that mothers with PD may struggle to 'see' or 'read' her child's emotional experience and not confuse it with her own; and they may also struggle to 'see' themselves in adult and parental roles. Because of their mentalising problems, many mothers with PD may struggle to understand that their baby is a small person who has emotions that need containing; and they may find it hard to enjoy being with their baby, instead seeing them as challenging, difficult or 'naughty' which further increases their sense of stress.

The birth of a child may activate traumatic memories for a mother of her own experiences as a small child, and early relationships with parents. For a mother with PD, who has been exposed to ACEs, becoming a mother may activate memories of her own attachment to her mother, in a way which is disturbing [59]. Such a mother may be able to provide good enough *physical* care for her baby, but struggle to provide the psychological attunement that is needed, leading to a risk of transgenerational failure of attachment in her baby.

Maternal PD can increase the risk of child maltreatment, including filicide (see Chapter 36, 'Child Safeguarding' and Chapter 38, 'When Mothers Kill Their Children'). Studies of filicide repeatedly find that maternal PD is the commonest diagnosis in women who kill their children [60]. A subgroup of mothers with PDs may be at increased risk of an unusual form of child maltreatment, in which they give false or exaggerated accounts of their children's illnesses, and sometime fabricate or even induce illness in their child (the paediatric diagnosis of factitious and induced illness, or FII). Mothers who cause FII in their children are often diagnosed with EUPD [61], but may also be diagnosed with somatic symptom disorder which is a diagnosis which may be comorbid with PD diagnoses [62]. Maternal eating disorders are also conditions that are commonly comorbid with EUPD [63], and exacerbation of maternal eating disorder after pregnancy can also extend to child nourishment and potential harm (see Chapter 16, 'Eating Disorders' and Chapter 36, 'Child Safeguarding').

Mothers with PD may struggle with caregiving in indirectly harmful ways to children. Some mothers with PD may struggle to manage high levels of anxiety by developing a narrative in which not they but the children have the 'problem'; for example, they come to believe that the baby is 'difficult' or the toddler is naughty; or that the child has a food intolerance of a neurodevelopmental disorder. For these mothers with PD, these kinds of child-illness narratives reduce shame and fear and place the responsibility for making the child 'better' onto healthcare professionals. Mild variations of this dynamic are common in primary care and child and adolescent mental health services; more severe versions can acquire a malignant form in which a child's ordinary physical and psychological needs are medicalised into pathological belief systems resulting in harmful iatrogenic behaviour towards the child.

The Biopsychosocial Treatment of Personality Dysfunction

It used to be said that personality was fixed from birth and that disorders of personality were therefore 'untreatable'. However, research over the last 25 years has proved this statement comprehensively untrue. There are now national guidelines for the treatment of PD [64, 65], and although most research has focused on EUPD, the general principles are likely to apply for cluster A and cluster C.

The best evidence to date suggests the following:

1. there are a range of psychological interventions for PD that are effective in achieving remission amounting to recovery in some cases
2. these recovery gains can be maintained over time
3. these interventions are cost-effective in terms of prevention of later morbidity and mortality

The interventions that are most usually offered to women with PD are listed in Table 14.2. Only mentalisation-based therapies (MBT) have been adapted for use with maternal PD in the context of mother–child relationships, and evaluation is ongoing. Many perinatal services may offer parent–infant psychotherapy [66]; but some specialist services offer groups for mothers with PD that focus on improving maternal mentalisation skills [67, 68]. Such interventions may help mothers with PD 'see' their children's needs and their own needs with more compassion and less anxiety.

Before treatment can start, the following should take place. First, no treatment can be sensibly offered without a full *assessment* including an in-depth history (ideally going back three generations). The next step is a *formulation* of how the history and patient's experience provide a functional understanding of what the patient is struggling with. Second, there must be an assessment of *severity*: this is a condition of the diagnosis for ICD-11. It is clinically obvious that more severe conditions with multiple comorbid problems may be much harder to treat than milder more discrete conditions.

Third, there must be an assessment of the possible *risk* to self and family members, in this case children; treatment may not be possible in the short term if the risk is too great (see Chapter 36, 'Child Safeguarding'). Finally, the treatment must be available to be delivered by *trained professionals*; any disorder is 'untreatable' if there are no trained

Table 14.2 Assessment and interventions for maternal PD

Name of therapy	Group or individual	Focus	Comment
Dialectical behaviour therapy	Both	Emotional regulation and reduced impulsivity 12–18 month programme	Highly effective Requires trained therapists and supervisors Not relationally based
Mentalisation-based therapies	Both	Improved emotional regulation and empathic perspective taking 12–18 month programme	Highly effective. Requires trained therapists and supervisors Relationally based and has parental versions (see below)
Schema-focused therapy	Both	Improved understanding of self states 12–18 months	Effective in PD but not tested in maternal PD as yet
Transference-focused therapy	Individual	12–18 months	Improves mentalising but not tested in maternal group
Therapies for PTSD: including cognitive behavioural therapy (CBT), eye movement desensitisation and reprocessing (EMDR), narrative approaches and behaviour therapy	Individual work is more common	Improved affect regulation in response to intrusive memories; importance of self-compassion	May be indicated if trauma symptoms are complicating picture. No evidence about specific role in maternal function
Individual mother–infant therapy	Dyadic plus individual sessions for mothers	Length of treatment depends on local services: usually 12 months	Case reports positive and good service user feedback
Parental mentalising interventions	Usually group based	12–18 months	Include parental MBT; Lighthouse model; minding the baby
Parental mindfulness practises	Individually taught	Work in progress	May be useful as introduction to affect regulation and grounding techniques

professionals available to carry out the specific intervention. There is no prima facie reason why every member of a perinatal team could not be trained to deliver a relevant evidence-based intervention within a service.

Most mothers with PD will probably not need inpatient care (and evidence from other sources suggests it may make them worse). However, they may benefit from a short stay in a Mother and Baby Unit to complete assessment, especially of risk or to treat comorbid mental disorders such as depression. As outpatients, mothers with PD could benefit from the recommended evidence-based treatments; most take 12–18 months to complete. The advantage of this approach is that it allows for monitoring of mental states and also gentle inquiry into how this mother may be coping, not only with this child, but other young children in her care. It may be helpful to make links with other services that focus on infant care or third-sector services that support new mothers or mothers with multiple children. Some services have initiated parental mental health services which offer care up to school age.

In the past, perinatal mental health services have sometimes resisted offering treatment to mothers with PD, arguing that their problems are '*not related to the perinatal context*'. However, the evidence base in favour of treatment (and the dangers of not treating) is such that failure to treat cannot be ethically justified. However, staff may feel a lack of confidence in managing this group of mothers, and specialist training from people with this expertise can be helpful (e.g. the Anna Freud Centre in London).

For mild to moderate PD, a quite brief intervention may make a big difference, especially in terms of mother–child relationships. A mother with mild PD whose main problem is anxiety or obsessive-compulsive disorder or eating disorder symptoms may benefit from psycho-education and modified CBT for her anxiety, that is, modified to take account of her identity as a mother and her relationship with her baby and others. For women with PD who have PTSD-like symptoms that resemble PTSD, then EMDR can be offered; for those who have obvious affect dysregulation, there is evidence for the effectiveness of dialectical behaviour therapy, MBT, schema-focused therapy and structured clinical management. Even if it is not possible to offer the full programmes, the psycho-educational aspects can still be useful and patients say they find them of interest.

Experts by experience (ex-service users) are also known to play an extremely important role in services for the treatment of personality dysfunction; especially in helping people recover and develop a sense of autonomy. Some of the earliest evidence about the effectiveness of treatment for PD comes from studies of the effectiveness of therapeutic communities like the Cassell Hospital, where relationships with peers are crucial. Such 'experts by experience' can help develop trust and engagement, and they model the mentalising stance of being comfortable with uncertainty and not knowing. In the treatment of PD, they can also be extremely helpful in discussing their experiences of the more challenging experiences that mothers with PD face; such as the involvement of social services and potential for legal action.

Ideally all maternal mental health services would offer:

1. an "understanding personality and attachment" group
2. an "emotional regulation" group (based on the dialectical behaviour therapy intervention programme)
3. an "introduction to a mentalising" group (based on the MBT treatment manual)

These psycho-educational interventions alone may provide women with PD some understanding of why they struggle; and help them feel more empowered to ask for help, engage in any more formal intervention offered and self-soothe. These interventions should be integrated with any parent–infant psychotherapy service that is available; again, ideally each mother might get 4–6 sessions of such therapy just as an introduction.

There is still considerable professional debate about the role of medication in the treatment of PD. The National Institute for Health and Care Excellence guidelines do not recommend the use of antidepressants or antipsychotic medications; but there are both empirical studies and multiple case reports of the beneficial effects of these medications. There is a subgroup of people whose symptoms are well controlled with antidepressants combined with antipsychotic medication such as quetiapine. There are also extensive reports of the effectiveness of low-dose clozapine. It is also essential to consider the use of appropriate medications for comorbid conditions.

All medications are problematic in terms of harmful side effects (especially sedation) which must be weighed up with the patient against the benefits; especially in the context of child care and protection. Just as in other psychiatric disorders, there are a population of people who do not respond at all to any medications. In this group fiddling with dosages and types makes little difference and the focus should be on psychosocial treatments.

Long-term, PD is a relapsing and remitting condition; but the general trend is towards recovery, especially for milder conditions. There are few outcome or efficacy studies for the treatment of maternal PD because of the limited provision of services to date. However, there is no prima facie reason why the evidence from general psychotherapy research should not apply. It is well established that successful treatment outcomes in any therapy are more likely when there is (a) good engagement; (b) a therapeutic alliance between patients and therapists; and (c) when there is good communication between all professionals involved in a woman's care.

Conclusion

There is an irony that a great deal of attention is paid to identifying *physically* high-risk pregnancies antenatally but much less to identifying *psychologically* high-risk pregnancies. This may be because professionals assume that there are no interventions to offer or that it is not the role of a perinatal service to offer them. I hope this chapter has shown that this is not the case.

I hope I have also shown that professional stigma and rejection of women with PD is unkind and unjust, and may be based on ignorance and anxiety. An example from history makes the point. In medieval times, lepers were a group of people who were feared and excluded; and the word 'leper' itself was a stigmatising term (and is still a synonym for people we don't like). But when we understood what caused leprosy, and its frightening signs and symptoms, we developed treatments and our attitudes towards sufferers changed. It should be so for maternal PD.

References

1. D Chartonas, M Kyratsous, S Dracass, T Lee, K Bhui. Personality disorder: still the patients psychiatrists dislike? *BJPsych Bull.* 2017 Feb;41(1):12–17.
2. CD Frith. The social brain? *Philos Trans R Soc B: Biol Sci.* 2007 Apr 29;362(1480): 671–8.
3. CD Frith, U Frith. Mapping mentalising in the brain. In: M Gilead, KN Ochsner, editors. *The neural basis of mentalizing.* Cham: Springer International Publishing; 2021. p. 17–45.
4. K Norton, RD Hinshelwood. Severe personality disorder: treatment issues and selection for in-patient psychotherapy. *Br J Psychiatry.* 1996 Jun;168(6):723–31.
5. P Snowden, E Kane. Personality disorder: no longer a diagnosis of exclusion. *Psychiatr Bull.* 2003 Nov;27(11):401–3.
6. M Brandon. Child fatality or serious injury through maltreatment: making

sense of outcomes. *Child Youth Serv Rev.* 2009 Oct 1;31(10):1107–12.

7. RI Dunbar. Coevolution of neocortical size, group size and language in humans. *Behav Brain Sci.* 1993 Dec;16(4): 681–94.
8. DP McAdams. *The art and science of personality development*. New York: Guilford Publications; 2015.
9. World Health Organization. International Classification of Disease version 11. 2019. www.idc11.org
10. J Volkert, TC Gablonski, S Rabung. Prevalence of personality disorders in the general adult population in Western countries: systematic review and meta-analysis. *Br J Psychiatry.* 2018 Dec;213(6):709–15.
11. J Zimmermann, A Kerber, K Rek, CJ Hopwood, RF Krueger. A brief but comprehensive review of research on the alternative DSM-5 model for personality disorders. *Curr Psychiatry Rep.* 2019 Aug;21(9):92.
12. M Yang, J Coid, P Tyrer. Personality pathology recorded by severity: national survey. *Br J Psychiatry.* 2010 Sep;197(3):193–9.
13. American Psychiatric Association. *Diagnostic and statistical manual*; fourth-TR edition. Washington, DC: American Psychiatric Publishing; 2000.
14. BF Grant, FS Stinson, DA Dawson, SP Chou, WJ Ruan. Co-occurrence of DSM-IV personality disorders in the United States: results from the National Epidemiologic Survey on Alcohol and Related Conditions. *Compr Psychiatry.* 2005 Jan 1;46(1):1–5.
15. AE Skodol. Personality disorders: a burden in the community, neglected in the clinic? *J Clin Psychiatry.* 2015 Nov 25;76(11):14168.
16. S Conroy, CM Pariante, MN Marks, HA Davies, S Farrelly, R Schacht, P Moran. Maternal psychopathology and infant development at 18 months: the impact of maternal personality disorder and depression. *J Am Acad Child Adolesc Psychiatry.* 2012 Jan 1;51(1):51–61.
17. M Cloitre, DW Garvert, B Weiss, EB Carlson, RA Bryant. Distinguishing PTSD, complex PTSD, and borderline personality disorder: a latent class analysis. *Eur J Psychotraumatol.* 2014 Dec 1;5(1):25097.
18. JD Ford, CA Courtois. Complex PTSD and borderline personality disorder. *Borderline Personal Disord Emot Dysregul.* 2021 May 6;8(1):16.
19. BW Sahle, NJ Reavley, W Li, AJ Morgan, MB Yap, A Reupert, AF Jorm. The association between adverse childhood experiences and common mental disorders and suicidality: an umbrella review of systematic reviews and meta-analyses. *Eur Child Adolesc Psychiatry.* 2022 Oct;31(10):1489–99.
20. K Börjesson, S Ruppert, M Bågedahl-Strindlund. A longitudinal study of psychiatric symptoms in primiparous women: relation to personality disorders and sociodemographic factors. *Arch Womens Ment Health.* 2005 Nov 1;8(4):232–42.
21. G Blankley, M Galbally, M Snellen, J Power, AJ Lewis. Borderline personality disorder in the perinatal period: early infant and maternal outcomes. *Australas Psychiatry.* 2015 Dec;23(6):688–92.
22. C Hudson, E Spry, R Borschmann, D Becker, P Moran, C Olsson, et al. Preconception personality disorder and antenatal maternal mental health: a population-based cohort study. *J Affect Disord.* 2017 Feb 1;209:169–76.
23. G Crowley, E Molyneaux, S Nath, K Trevillion, P Moran, LM Howard. Disordered personality traits and psychiatric morbidity in pregnancy: a population-based study. *Arch Womens Ment Health.* 2020 Feb;23(1):43–52.
24. NM De Genna, U Feske, C Larkby, T Angiolieri, MA Gold. Pregnancies, abortions, and births among women with and without borderline personality disorder. *Womens Health Issues.* 2012 Jul 1;22(4):e371–7.
25. S Nannini, I Tung, JB Northrup, SD Stepp, K Keenan, AE Hipwell. Changes in

severity of depression and borderline personality disorder symptoms from pregnancy to three years postpartum in adolescent mothers. *J Affect Disord.* 2021 Nov 1;294:459–63.

26. SD Hillis, RF Anda, SR Dube, VJ Felitti, PA Marchbanks, JS Marks. The association between adverse childhood experiences and adolescent pregnancy, long-term psychosocial consequences, and fetal death. *Pediatrics.* 2004 Feb 1;113(2):320–7.

27. KC Young-Wolff, J Wei, N Varnado, N Rios, M Staunton, C Watson. Adverse childhood experiences and pregnancy intentions among pregnant women seeking prenatal care. *Womens Health Issues.* 2021 Mar 1;31(2):100–6.

28. JG Ray, L Fu, PC Austin, AL Park, HK Brown, SM Grandi, et al. Teen pregnancy and risk of premature mortality. *JAMA Netw Open.* 2024 Mar 4;7(3):e241833.

29. S Carmona, M Martínez-García, M Paternina-Die, E Barba-Müller, LM Wierenga, Y Alemán-Gómez, et al. Pregnancy and adolescence entail similar neuroanatomical adaptations: a comparative analysis of cerebral morphometric changes. *Hum Brain Mapp.* 2019 May;40(7):2143–52.

30. ER Orchard, HJ Rutherford, AJ Holmes, SD Jamadar. Matrescence: lifetime impact of motherhood on cognition and the brain. *Trends Cogn Sci.* 2023 Mar 1;27(3):302–16.

31. F Gholampour, MM Riem, MI van den Heuvel. Maternal brain in the process of maternal-infant bonding: review of the literature. *Soc Neurosci.* 2020 Jul 3;15(4):380–4.

32. JS Lonstein. The dynamic serotonin system of the maternal brain. *Arch Womens Ment Health.* 2019 Apr 8;22:237–43.

33. J Eyden, C Winsper, D Wolke, MR Broome, F MacCallum. A systematic review of the parenting and outcomes experienced by offspring of mothers with borderline personality pathology: potential mechanisms and clinical implications. *Clin Psychol Rev.* 2016 Jul 1;47:85–105.

34. CA Marshall, J Jomeen, C Huang, CR Martin. The relationship between maternal personality disorder and early birth outcomes: a systematic review and meta-analysis. *Int J Environ Res Public Health.* 2020 Aug;17(16):5778.

35. LM Howard, E Molyneaux, CL Dennis, T Rochat, A Stein, J Milgrom. Non-psychotic mental disorders in the perinatal period. *Lancet.* 2014 Nov 15;384(9956):1775–88.

36. J Jureidini. Obstetric factitious disorder and Munchausen syndrome by proxy. *J Nerv Ment Dis.* 1993 Feb;181(2):135–7.

37. S Oddo-Sommerfeld, S Hain, F Louwen, K Schermelleh-Engel. Longitudinal effects of dysfunctional perfectionism and avoidant personality style on postpartum mental disorders: pathways through antepartum depression and anxiety. *J Affect Disord.* 2016 Feb 1;191:280–8.

38. MC Dias, M Kelson, K Gordon-Smith, A Perry, N Craddock, L Jones, et al. Borderline personality traits are differently associated with postpartum psychosis and postpartum depression episodes in women with bipolar disorder. *J Affect Disord.* 2023 May 1;328:81–6.

39. WJ Livesley, R Larstone, editors. *Handbook of personality disorders: theory, research, and treatment.* New York: Guilford Publications; 2018.

40. AN Schore. Effects of a secure attachment relationship on right brain development, affect regulation, and infant mental health. *Infant Ment Health J.* 2001 Jan;22(1–2):7–66.

41. CE Izard, SW Porges, RF Simons, OM Haynes, C Hyde, M Parisi, B Cohen. Infant cardiac activity: developmental changes and relations with attachment. *Dev Psychol.* 1991 May;27(3):432–9.

42. I Bretherton. The origins of attachment theory: John Bowlby and Mary Ainsworth. *Dev Psychol.* 1992 Sep;28(5):759–75.

43. D Benoit. Infant-parent attachment: definition, types, antecedents,

measurement and outcome. *Paediatr Child Health.* 2004;9(8):541–5.

44. LA Sroufe. Attachment and development: a prospective, longitudinal study from birth to adulthood. *Attach Hum Dev.* 2005 Dec 1;7(4):349–67.

45. MJ Bakermans-Kranenburg, MH van IJzendoorn. The first 10,000 Adult Attachment Interviews: distributions of adult attachment representations in clinical and non-clinical groups. *Attach Hum Dev.* 2009 May 1;11(3): 223–63.

46. JG Johnson, P Cohen, J Brown, EM Smailes, DP Bernstein. Childhood maltreatment increases risk for personality disorders during early adulthood. *Arch Gen Psychiatry.* 1999 Jul 1;56(7):600–6.

47. CL Battle, MT Shea, DM Johnson, S Yen, C Zlotnick, MC Zanarini, et al. Childhood maltreatment associated with adult personality disorders: findings from the Collaborative Longitudinal Personality Disorders Study. *J Pers Disord.* 2004 Apr 1;18(2):193–211.

48. N Lorenzini, P Fonagy. Attachment and personality disorders: a short review. *Focus.* 2013 Apr;11(2):155–66.

49. TO Afifi, A Mather, J Boman, W Fleisher, MW Enns, H MacMillan, J Sareen. Childhood adversity and personality disorders: results from a nationally representative population-based study. *J Psychiatr Res.* 2011 Jun 1;45(6):814–22.

50. U Iyengar, S Kim, S Martinez, P Fonagy, L Strathearn. Unresolved trauma in mothers: intergenerational effects and the role of reorganization. *Front Psychol.* 2014 Sep 1;5:966.

51. MH Van IJzendoorn. Adult attachment representations, parental responsiveness, and infant attachment: a meta-analysis on the predictive validity of the Adult Attachment Interview. *Psychol Bull.* 1995 May;117(3):387–403.

52. S Selzam, JR Coleman, A Caspi, TE Moffitt, R Plomin. A polygenic p factor for major psychiatric disorders. *Transl Psychiatry.* 2018 Oct 2;8(1):205.

53. JG Gunderson, RL Stout, TH McGlashan, MT Shea, LC Morey, CM Grilo, et al. Ten-year course of borderline personality disorder: psychopathology and function from the collaborative Longitudinal Personality Disorders Study. *Arch Gen Psychiatry.* 2011;68(8):827–37.

54. AE Skodol. Impact of personality pathology on psychosocial functioning. *Curr Opin Psychol.* 2018 Jun 1;21:33–8.

55. JG Johnson, P Cohen, S Kasen, JS Brook. Maternal psychiatric disorders, parenting, and maternal behavior in the home during the child rearing years. *J Child Fam Studies.* 2006 Feb;15:96–113.

56. KR Steele, ML Townsend, BF Grenyer. Parenting and personality disorder: an overview and meta-synthesis of systematic reviews. *PLoS ONE.* 2019 Oct 1;14(10):e0223038.

57. LE Crandell, MP Patrick, RP Hobson. 'Still-face' interactions between mothers with borderline personality disorder and their 2-month-old infants. *Br J Psychiatry.* 2003 Sep;183(3):239–47.

58. L Strathearn, P Fonagy, J Amico, PR Montague. Adult attachment predicts maternal brain and oxytocin response to infant cues. *Neuropsychopharmacology.* 2009 Dec;34(13):2655–66.

59. A Murphy, M Steele, SR Dube, J Bate, K Bonuck, P Meissner, et al. Adverse Childhood Experiences (ACEs) questionnaire and Adult Attachment Interview (AAI): implications for parent child relationships. *Child Abuse Negl.* 2014 Feb 1;38(2):224–33.

60. GM Lattanzi, L Provini, R Williams, F Aceti, N Giacchetti. Personality structure and attachment models of women who kill their children: a systematic review on maternal filicide. *Child Abuse Negl.* 2020 Aug 1;1 (106):104532.

61. G Yates, C Bass. The perpetrators of medical child abuse (Munchausen syndrome by proxy): a systematic review of 796 cases. *Child Abuse Negl.* 2017 Oct 1;72:45–53.

62. C Macina, R Bendel, M Walter, JS Wrege. Somatization and somatic symptom

disorder and its overlap with dimensionally measured personality pathology: a systematic review. *J Psychosom Res.* 2021 Dec 1;151:110646.

63. M Martinussen, O Friborg, P Schmierer, S Kaiser, KT Øvergård, AL Neunhoeffer, et al. The comorbidity of personality disorders in eating disorders: a meta-analysis. *Eat Weight Disord.* 2017 Jun;22:201–9.

64. Simonsen S, Bateman A, Bohus M, Dalewijk HJ, Doering S, Kaera A, et al. European guidelines for personality disorders: past, present and future. *Borderline Person Disord Emot Dysreg.* 2019 May 21;6:9.

65. F Leichsenring, N Heim, F Leweke, C Spitzer, C Steinert, OF Kernberg. Borderline personality disorder: a review. *JAMA.* 2023 Feb 28;329(8):670–9.

66. SD Stepp, DJ Whalen, PA Pilkonis, AE Hipwell, MD Levine. Children of mothers with borderline personality disorder: identifying parenting behaviors as potential targets for intervention. *Personal Disord.* 2012 Jan;3(1): 76–91.

67. L Nijssens, P Luyten, DL Bales. Mentalization-based treatment for parents (MBT-P) with borderline personality disorder and their infants. In: N Midgley, I Vrouva, editors. *Minding the child: mentalization-based interventions with children, young people and their families.* London: Routledge; 2013. p. 93–111.

68. G Byrne, M Sleed, N Midgley, P Fearon, C Mein, A Bateman, P Fonagy. Lighthouse Parenting Programme: description and pilot evaluation of mentalization-based treatment to address child maltreatment. *Clin Child Psychol Psychiatry.* 2019 Oct;24(4):680–93.

Chapter 15

Complex Post-Traumatic Stress Disorder

Alain Gregoire, Cerith Waters and Laura Richmond

Introduction

Most psychiatric diagnoses are essentially syndromes, based on clusters of symptoms that tend to co-occur and sometimes predict, more or less usefully, risk factors, course or responses to treatments. Post-traumatic stress disorder (PTSD) and complex post-traumatic stress disorder (CPTSD) are rare examples of diagnoses based on aetiology. Complex post-traumatic stress disorder describes the mind's response to severe and sustained environmental adversity, particularly in the early years of life when we are learning about, and developing adaptive responses to, our environment. In our very earliest years, it is the human environment provided by our primary caregivers, and in pregnancy specifically our mother, that nurtures and sustains us. We now know that this nurturing care, or the absence of it, shapes the developing brain and our short- and long-term interactions with our physical, emotional and social environments. This affects multiple areas of our functioning including mental [1], brain molecular [2], autonomic [3], endocrine [4], immune [5] and gut–brain axis [6, 7] and powerfully predicts physical, mental and social outcomes for us and for those close to us. In particular, there is now consistent evidence that our own early experiences predict outcomes in our children [8, 9], and probably also our children's children [10, 11, 12, 13], and that part of this transmission is mediated by our mental well-being as parents during the perinatal period [14]. These phenomena are often referred to as the developmental origins, or intergenerational transmission, of health and disease. In most of the published literature in this field, and in the perinatal mental health literature, the mental health problems studied across the generations have not included CPTSD or the symptom profiles associated with the diagnosis. This is mainly because even recently published studies were designed before the inclusion of CPTSD in the World Health Organization's International Classification of Diseases (ICD-11) [15] or are using the USA's *Diagnostic and Statistical Manual* (DSM-5) [16], and/or simply because the researchers involved were not aware of the profound significance of CPTSD to intergenerational and perinatal mental health. We will briefly review what makes CPTSD so important, particularly in the perinatal period, for women and their families, for clinicians and researchers, and indeed for decision makers across society.

What Is CPTSD?

According to the ICD-11, CPTSD is a condition that can arise from prolonged exposure to traumatic events, and is typically characterised by symptoms such as hyperarousal, avoidance, intrusive thoughts, experiences or emotions, emotional dysregulation, negative self-concept, self-harming behaviours and difficulties in interpersonal relationships. This closely matches earlier descriptions of the condition, such as by Herman in 1992 [17]. For the purpose of clearer understanding, it is worth unpicking the term CPTSD word by word.

Although 'complex' generally refers to the features of the 'stress disorder' rather than the 'trauma', in some ways it applies to both. However, an understanding of current perinatal and intergenerational knowledge of these issues provides enough understanding of both the 'trauma' and the 'stress disorder' to lift this veil of apparent complexity. As the research specific to CPTSD is limited, we must sometimes draw on the wider literature relating to both childhood 'trauma' and the mental health effects associated with it.

In a memoir of her personal experience of CPTSD, Laura Richmond provides an important complementary perspective to objective descriptions:

> *I had come to view myself as they viewed me, as a complex case, but really, it was overwhelmingly simple. Not the symptoms – those were ever-shifting, overlapping, indistinct, because they were simply the manifestations of pain, or my responses to it. They were never the point. Eradicating them was never the point, not really. The symptoms – the behaviours, if you like – they were what happened when suffering exceeded my capacity to withstand it. Yet I did withstand it, by any means necessary. As I was shunted around, referred from this doctor to that, from this service to that, I was running in circles, holding up my pain to anyone who would listen, telling them, 'It hurts. Please believe me. It hurts too much, and I can't bear it.'* [18]

The Concept of 'Trauma' in Relation to CPTSD

The concept of 'trauma' in CPTSD refers to environmental factors or experiences, particularly in early life, that are associated with severe, long-term adverse effects on mental health and functioning. Cloitre et al. (2013) found that chronic trauma was more predictive of CPTSD than PTSD and that CPTSD resulted in significantly greater functional impairment than PTSD [19]. Herman's (1992) original description of CPTSD proposed that the aetiology was exposure to prolonged or repetitive traumatic events from which escape is difficult or impossible [17].

In the perinatal context the inadequacy of the word trauma to describe these adverse factors and experiences becomes particularly evident. For fetuses, the most consistently documented psychological factor with long-term developmental effects (i.e. 'trauma') is exposure to maternal anxiety [20]. For babies, who are dependent for their survival on nurturing care that responds to their cues and meets their needs, the blank face and unresponsive behaviour of a depressed mother could represent a potential risk to the baby's well-being. In adults with PTSD and CPTSD, a systematic review found the most common timing of traumatic experiences is childhood rather than adulthood and the most common source of trauma was interpersonal [21].

It has long been known that childhood adverse experiences predict not just the risk, but the severity, course and outcomes of mental health problems such as depression (e.g. [22]). The rapidly expanding literature on adverse childhood experiences (ACEs) has demonstrated that childhood adversity, including exposure to parental mental health problems, may be associated with a broad range of poor physical health, mental health and social outcomes (see Chapter 32, 'Infant Mental Health: The Role of Perinatal

Mental Health Services'). In particular, exposure to multiple ACEs greatly increases the risk of all forms of self-harming and high-risk behaviours, including drug and alcohol misuse, smoking, eating disorders, self-mutilation and suicide, as well as attachment and relationship problems [23, 24]. A recent systematic review has demonstrated consistent associations between exposure to ACEs and suboptimal maternal and infant outcomes during the perinatal period, especially in the context of emotional and sexual abuse during childhood and adolescence [25]. Studies of childhood exposure to significant ACEs (such as emotional or physical abuse or neglect, or sexual abuse) have found an increased risk of the full range of mental health problems/conditions even when accounting for familial confounders [26].

Furthermore, cumulative childhood maltreatment shows a dose–response relationship to symptom severity and complexity [27]. We can see how the intergenerational story emerges, as all of these ACEs may be associated not only with parental mental health problems, but also with parents' own exposure to the very same list of ACEs [28]. For example, maternal childhood maltreatment has been shown to be the most powerful predictor of depression in pregnancy and postnatally [29] and maternal antenatal depression in turn is associated with an increased risk of offspring experiencing future maltreatment (defined as harsh parental discipline, physical or sexual abuse) [30], though there was no evidence that mothers themselves were the source of the maltreatment. A dose–response relationship is emerging between the severity of maltreatment experienced by mothers in their own childhood and severity of emotional and behavioural problems in their children [31]. Possible mediating processes for this transmission have been explored. A systematic review by Vaillancourt and colleagues found a consistent relationship between maternal childhood abuse and dysfunctional mother–infant interactions [24]. Maternal perinatal mental health and infant maltreatment appear to mediate the effects of maternal childhood maltreatment on poor infant emotional and behavioural outcomes [32, 33]. Maternal childhood maltreatment also impacts biological markers, for example with maternal cortisol levels and hypothalamic-pituitary-adrenal effects in the offspring, further modulated by maternal depression [34].

It is not clear from the current literature exactly how these factors interact in their intergenerational transmission. However, evidence is beginning to emerge that poor maternal mental health may also be a mediator for the effects of wider environmental disadvantages (e.g. poverty) on children [35], and remain a predictor of later mental health even when potential genetic mediators of both ACEs and mental problems are taken into account [36].

The Features of the 'Stress Disorder' in CPTSD

The findings we have described suggest a particular range of mental health difficulties associated with exposure to adversity in the early years, and these are reflected in the ICD-11 descriptions of the defining features of CPTSD (listed below in italics), to which we have added comments in relation to presentation in the perinatal context.

The ICD-11 describes three core symptoms in common with PTSD:

- *Intrusions or re-experiencing of the event such as intrusive memories, nightmares, flashbacks and strong or overwhelming emotions and physical sensations triggered by reminders.* (In the perinatal context it is relevant to note that re-experiencing is not reliant on verbal or visual memories of traumatic events or environments. The ICD-11 states: 'Re-experiencing in the present can also involve feelings of being overwhelmed or immersed in the same intense emotions that were experienced during the traumatic event, without a prominent cognitive aspect, and may occur in response to reminders of the event.')

> *Once again, my body became a siren. I would act as if trivial things were emergencies because it made sense, then, that my muscles were tense, and my mouth was parched, and I could hear my heart banging away. Missed a bus? Emergency! Lost a sock? Emergency! I was ridiculous, and I knew it.* [18]

In the perinatal period women face multiple additional or new potential triggers, with changes in family relationships, body shape, and procedures such as intimate physical examinations, that can produce re-experiencing of trauma [37, 38, 39].

> *Every moment was a roll of the dice. It might be lights on and nobody home. It might be flashbacks and intrusive thoughts firing all over the place. I might be coldly suicidal. I might even be fine. Sometimes I seemed to exist in multiple states at once, as if I were two or three people jostling for space in this one battered body.* [18]

- *Avoidance of internal or external reminders, such as thoughts or memories, or people, places, conversations or situations.* (When related to very early interpersonal traumatic experiences such as neglect, abuse or exposure to domestic violence, the reminders that are avoided may include situations of separation or abandonment, conflict and interactions with others who hold greater power or control. During the perinatal period this may lead to avoidance of relationships that could offer sources of support. Indeed, women with CPTSD have been shown to have uniquely low levels of perceived social support [40]. This may also result in avoidance of much needed health and social care services.)
- *Persistent perceptions of heightened current threat, with hypervigilance, and enhanced startle response, either in specific situations or more generally.* (In women during the perinatal period this often shows as extreme anxiety in response to perceived immediate threat to herself or the fetus/baby. Wariness of others, particularly professionals with perceived potential power to do harm is common, especially amongst those with repeated contacts with health or social care systems. This may present as hypervigilance and repeated or intrusive worries and fears about the fetus/baby's health, for example checking and re-checking milk formulas and hygiene, waking frequently during the night to check the baby is alive, coupled with reluctance to ask for help for fear of being judged as incapable/not good enough. Fear that they will be judged incapable of looking after their baby is extremely common amongst women with mental health problems generally – 46% of women with mental health problems described this in a survey by the National Childbirth Trust [41] – and may be even more common in this group.)

And three additional groups of symptoms in CPTSD:

- *Severe problems in mood regulation including heightened emotional reactivity to minor stressors, violent outbursts, reckless or self-destructive behaviour, dissociative symptoms when under stress, emotional numbing, and inability to experience pleasure or positive emotions.* (This cluster of symptoms is often significantly intensified during the perinatal period, as women face the frequent additional triggers and perceived threats described above, coupled with the continuous additional pressures and responsibilities, the sleep deprivation, the physical changes and the interpersonal changes – including the increased risk of domestic violence – that occur at this time. In addition, women's ability and opportunities to engage in activities that might help are considerably reduced.)

- *Beliefs about oneself as diminished, defeated or worthless, accompanied by feelings of shame, guilt or failure related to the traumatic event.* (If the 'trauma' relates to the woman's own experiences of neglectful or otherwise abusive care in early childhood, her negative beliefs about herself in general and in particular about her functioning as a mother may be profound, and she may be unable to appreciate her strengths and successes, making video-interactive therapy approaches particularly useful in this group. See below and Chapter 35, 'Mother–Infant Focused Interventions: What Works to Improve the Mother–Infant Relationship?')
- *Difficulties in sustaining relationships and in feeling close to others.* (This is commonly expressed as lack of trust in others. In the perinatal context this is likely to include lack of trust in professionals, poor relationships with partners, weak social and family support networks, and difficulties in forming secure attachments with the baby. Complex PTSD increases vulnerability to intimate partner violence [42] adding to the cycle of trauma and poor mental health for the woman and her offspring.)

The most common 'additional clinical features' mentioned by the ICD-11 seen in perinatal practice include: self-harm in a variety of forms, including substance misuse [43]; 'unexplained' somatic symptoms, which are sometimes a very prominent and chronic feature (e.g. during the pregnancy, repeated presentations with 'unexplained' abdominal or pelvic pain); pseudo-psychotic experiences (e.g. vivid 'voices' or visions 'in my head' as opposed to externally experienced through a sensory organ); and dissociation or detachment in particularly challenging or stressful circumstances or interactions. The latter can in itself worsen difficulties and circumstances, as women will disengage from conversations and other attempts to explore, understand and help them. This may further lead to a judgemental negative reaction from professionals.

In perinatal clinical practice these features are often easy to identify (see below), but as with all health conditions, there is some individual variability in how, or how intensely each feature is experienced or expressed. This individual variability may be best understood with the concept of a spectrum of presentations [44], as is being increasingly recognised and applied across diagnostic groups in mental and physical health. This is particularly relevant when considering aetiologically defined conditions rather than syndromes, as the former are the developmental result of varying journeys from a common origin, whereas the latter are constructed on the basis of their symptoms patterns.

Development of CPTSD

Numerous bio-psycho-social mediating as well as modulating factors for the relationship between childhood adversity and subsequent CPTSD or poor mental health have been examined. As previously mentioned, the literature remains limited for links to subsequent CPTSD, but later poor mental health following childhood adversity has been associated with the interpersonal nature of the adverse experience [45] and poor parental mental health [46]. Other potentially adverse outcomes linked to early adversity include epigenetic [47, 48], endocrine [49] and inflammatory [50] changes.

An interesting emerging literature exists on benevolent childhood experiences (BCEs) [51], which can produce resilience [52]. The importance of considering a developmental pathway to CPTSD is reinforced by the finding that BCEs have a significant modulating influence in CPTSD that was not found in PTSD [53]. Furthermore, there is some evidence that future positive relationships can diminish the adverse effects of childhood maltreatment [54]. A review of this literature is beyond the scope of this chapter, but it is worth noting the multiple, interacting factors at play, which confirm that the links between traumatic childhood experiences and subsequent CPTSD or poor mental health are not inevitable and are potentially modifiable.

Prevalence

The prevalence of CPTSD from studies in a UK population exposed to at least one traumatic life event is around 13% (compared to PTSD just over 5%) and, in samples of trauma-exposed patients referred to mental health services, is over 40% [55, 56]. The first prevalence study in a population of mothers of older children (in Taiwan) found similar figures of 12.1% for CPTSD and 4.4% for PTSD [45]. Symptoms can re-emerge or intensify as a result of the context or experiences related to pregnancy, childbirth or the postpartum period [57].

> *I think most people would have found my birth experience traumatic, to some degree, but it was compounded by everything that had gone before. Traumatic events aren't isolated; they happen in the context of a whole life narrative.* [18]

No studies have yet been published of CPTSD prevalence amongst patients in perinatal mental health services. The ongoing Maternal Wellbeing, Mental Health and Life Experiences study based in the National Centre for Mental Health at Cardiff University is currently recruiting a sample of perinatal women and screening for PTSD and CPTSD. Among women under the care of community mental health services in this study, 4.2% met criteria for PTSD and 15% for CPTSD on the International Trauma Questionnaire (ITQ) [58]. Of the women meeting criteria for CPTSD on the ITQ in this study, only 3% had received a CPTSD diagnosis from a mental health professional. Alternate diagnoses given by mental health professionals for women meeting criteria for CPTSD in this sample included depressive, anxiety, psychotic and personality disorders [58]. No data are currently available on recognition of CPTSD in clinical practice across perinatal mental health services generally in the UK or elsewhere, but anecdotal evidence indicates that recognition levels are very low and, in some services, use or indeed awareness of the diagnosis is absent.

Diagnosis and Differential Diagnosis

Given that the diagnostic category has only recently been applied in UK health services, we must ask ourselves where women with CPTSD are in clinical and other samples or populations? The inevitable answer is that there are large numbers with either unidentified CPTSD comorbidity or misdiagnoses with depression, anxiety disorders, as well as ADHD, substance misuse, somatisation disorder, eating disorder, medically unexplained symptoms and, given the near identical features, borderline (emotionally unstable) personality disorder (BPD). In perinatal mental health practice, we should always be wary of adopting pre-existing diagnoses from adult or child mental health services without careful re-evaluation, and this is particularly relevant amongst women presenting with this CPTSD pattern of symptoms. The ICD-11 warns us that:

> Children and adolescents with Complex Post-Traumatic Stress Disorder often report symptoms consistent with Depressive Disorders, Eating and Feeding Disorders, Sleep-Wake Disorders, Attention Deficit Hyperactivity Disorder, Oppositional Defiant Disorder, Conduct-Dissocial Disorder, and Separation Anxiety Disorder. Additional co-occurring diagnoses should only be made if the symptoms are not fully accounted for by Complex Post-Traumatic Stress Disorder and all diagnostic requirements for each disorder are met.

> *It all began with the discovery of my self-harm. That moment in the locker room when time stopped and shuddered, like a film paused on an old television set, and the eyes of twenty girls were on me. My secret, exposed for all to see. Everyone was shocked. My parents were distraught. The doctor was concerned. The headmistress was disgusted. I was deeply ashamed. And yet I couldn't stop hurting myself. Since then, I had swallowed every tablet, listened to every theory, tried every self-help technique, and I still couldn't stop because I needed it to cope with being me. Once I was an adult, self-harm was easier to hide, and easier to ignore. I was allowed to get on with it, which was what part of me had wanted all along. Yet another part of me clearly did not want that because here I was, taking buses to the city centre of my own free will to tell mental health nurses about it. Somewhere, my thirteen-year-old self was scoffing at this.* [18]

The distinction with BPD deserves particular consideration, as the ICD-11 also warns us that individuals with CPTSD 'may also meet the diagnostic requirements for Personality Disorder. Generally, individuals with such disorders should not be given an additional diagnosis of Personality Disorder unless additional personality features are present that contribute to significant problems in functioning of aspects of the self or interpersonal functioning.'

Patients who have PTSD are reported to have BPD comorbidity ranging from 37% to 68% [59, 60] and, conversely, among BPD patients 58% are diagnosed with comorbid PTSD [61, 62, 63].

A key factor that is said to distinguish CPTSD from BPD, including in the ICD-11, is the association with childhood traumatic experiences. Yet studies have found a similar level of association between childhood traumas and BPD (e.g. 83%) [64] as found with CPTSD (93%) [65], despite those studies measuring an incomplete range of the known forms of childhood adversity. This is a significant omission, as one study has specifically examined the relationship between gestational stress and offspring risk of personality disorder, finding a threefold increase in risk of a personality disorder diagnosis associated with self-reported levels of prenatal stress [66]. Studies that have examined severity and type of childhood trauma have found more severe trauma to be associated with BPD compared to other conditions, as well as reported emotional abuse and neglect (e.g. [67]).

The descriptions in the ICD-11 of CPTSD and BPD (the 'borderline pattern' specifier relies on the DSM criteria for BPD) differ more in semantics than phenomenology. According to diagnostic criteria, both share the features in Table 15.1.

Cloitre et al. (2014) carried out an analysis of symptom profiles among 310 women with histories of childhood abuse [68]. The symptoms they included represented the diagnostic criteria for PTSD, CPTSD and BPD described above. In addition to a low-symptom group, this revealed three distinct patterns or classes of symptoms: all three groups had similar levels of the core PTSD diagnostic symptoms. The second group had,

Table 15.1 Shared features of ICD-11 CPTSD and BPD

ICD-11 CPTSD	ICD-11 BPD (specific borderline features from DSM-5)
Significant impairment in personal, family, social, educational, occupational or other important areas of functioning.	Substantial distress or significant impairment in personal, family, social, educational, occupational or other important areas of functioning.
Persistent difficulties in sustaining relationships and in feeling close to others. The person may consistently avoid, deride or have little interest in relationships and social engagement more generally. Alternatively, there may be occasional intense relationships, but the person has difficulty sustaining them.	Interpersonal dysfunction (e.g. ability to develop and maintain close and mutually satisfying relationships, ability to understand others' perspectives and to manage conflict in relationships). A pattern of unstable and intense interpersonal relationships characterised by alternating between extremes of idealisation and devaluation.
Severe and pervasive problems in affect regulation. Examples include heightened emotional reactivity to minor stressors, violent outbursts. Re-experiencing in the present ... can also include feelings of being overwhelmed or immersed in the same intense emotions that were experienced during the traumatic event, without a prominent cognitive aspect, and may occur in response to reminders of the event(s).	Maladaptive patterns of cognition, emotional experience, emotional expression and behaviour. Affective instability due to a marked reactivity of mood, for example, intense episodic dysphoria, anxiety or irritability, usually lasting a few hours and rarely more than a few days. Inappropriate, intense anger or difficulty controlling anger, for example, frequent displays of temper, constant anger or recurrent physical fights
Persistent perceptions of heightened current threat. Feel themselves or others close to them to be under immediate threat either in specific situations or more generally. Psychotic symptoms.	Transient, stress-related paranoid ideation.
Active internal avoidance of thoughts and memories related to the event(s), or external avoidance of people, conversations, activities or situations reminiscent of the event(s).	Frantic efforts to avoid real or imagined abandonment.
Dissociative symptoms when under stress and emotional numbing.	Severe dissociative symptoms.
Persistent beliefs about oneself as diminished, defeated or worthless, accompanied by deep and pervasive feelings of shame, guilt or failure.	Identity disturbance: markedly and persistently unstable self-image or sense of self.
Inability to experience pleasure or positive emotions.	Chronic feelings of emptiness.

Table 15.1 *(cont.)*

ICD-11 CPTSD	ICD-11 BPD (specific borderline features from DSM-5)
Suicidal ideation and behaviour, substance abuse. In adolescence, substance use, risk-taking behaviours (e.g. unsafe sex, unsafe driving, non-suicidal self-harm).	Recurrent suicidal behaviour, gestures or threats, or self-mutilating behaviour.
Reckless, self-destructive behaviours.	Impulsivity in at least two areas that are potentially self-damaging, for example, spending, substance abuse, reckless driving, sex, or binge eating.

in addition to the PTSD symptoms, high levels of the additional diagnostic CPTSD symptoms, plus feeling 'empty'. The third group showed high levels of the PTSD symptoms as well as CPTSD and BPD symptoms. The groups did not differ in the type or timing of abuse apart from sexual abuse being more common in the CPTSD group. The authors conclude that this demonstrates three distinguishable syndromes in populations with histories of abuse, but do not question the traditional labelling of two of these groups as post-traumatic stress disorders and one as a disorder of personality. The authors justify the continued usefulness of the construct of BPD as a separate clinical entity as it does not require the presence of historical trauma. However, as we have seen, rates of historical trauma are in fact the same in CPTSD and BPD, and studies are now beginning to disentangle the types of traumas that are more likely to lead to BPD or CPTSD presentations. For example, Yuan et al. [69], studying the impact of various forms of childhood abuse, found a most consistent association between emotional abuse and BPD, indicating its unique role in understanding the development of BPD symptoms. Schalinski et al. found a specific relationship between dissociation (a 'BPD symptom') and earlier childhood maltreatment [70], and Jowett found that dissociation mediates the relationship between reported childhood trauma exposure and the presence of CPTSD [71].

Studies have also found that dissociation acts as a mediating factor in the relationship between childhood trauma and later self-harm [72, 73]. More severe childhood adversity, which is more common in women than men [74], is more associated with CPTSD/BPD comorbidity [75]. These findings demonstrate a common trauma aetiology for all three symptom clusters, with different timings, types and severity of adversity leading to different recognisable patterns of symptoms. These distinctions appear clinically relevant and may eventually lead to the development of individually tailored treatment approaches. Conversely, mislabelling of people who have CPTSD may result in inappropriate or even harmful treatment approaches that fail to address the underlying trauma.

> *Trauma shouldn't be defined by the event. It should be defined by the effect that it has. PTSD and complex PTSD aren't mental illnesses: they're mental injuries. If you get a physical trauma, say something whacks you over the head and you turn up at A & E, they aren't going to assess that injury according to whether it was a brick or a spade that hit you. They're more likely to look at how much your head is bleeding.*

> *Most of us experience potentially traumatic events over the course of our lives: bereavement, assault, bullying, divorce . . . Shit happens, and none of us are exempt. Whether or not we're traumatised depends on a complicated range of factors: our genetics, our age at the time, and how we're supported or, indeed, not supported, to name only a few. Two people can have an identical experience and one will walk away relatively psychologically intact while the other is left in pieces. Many people with PTSD and complex PTSD, even those who have lived through the most shocking atrocities, will tell you that someone else has had it worse. It's the shame talking. It's saying, 'I don't matter.' What doesn't matter is whether what's happened to you is better or worse than what's happened to someone else. It's not a competition, certainly not a competition you'd want to win.* [18]

Indeed, if one considers the prevalence of CPTSD in populations of people with mental health problems, this may be one reason why response to evidence-based treatments is poor in so many, in both treatment trials and in clinical practice, as suggested by the range of evidence that childhood maltreatment adversely affects the course and response to treatment of mental disorders.

> *I wanted to believe I was worth helping even if I wasn't in mortal peril. I wanted to believe that my experience of being alive was something that mattered. That everyone's experience of being alive is something that matters. It was never about the self-harm, not to me. It was about why I needed to self-harm in the first place. It was about the suffering that, after all these years and all these diagnoses, I still didn't have a name for or a means to communicate.* [18]

In assessing and making a diagnosis, it is essential for professionals to adopt a trauma-informed lens that recognises the impact of past trauma on current functioning, thereby fostering a more compassionate, accurate and non-stigmatising understanding of their clients' experiences and enabling more effective intervention.

> *Much of my trauma was inflicted by the very people who were supposed to be helping.* [18]

Individuals with perinatal CPTSD risk the diagnosis being missed or being misdiagnosed with personality disorder or other disorders. The label of personality disorder is particularly highly stigmatised because it carries with it a range of assumptions of the mental health problems being inherent in the person and therefore subject to individual choice and untreatable, which are clearly false [76]. Institutional maltreatment can manifest in the form of inadequate support systems, lack of access to mental health resources, and a healthcare environment that may inadvertently perpetuate trauma [77, 78].

Impact on Mother–Baby Relationships and Child Development

Due to the lack of research relating to the impact of maternal CPTSD on the mother–baby relationship, we must draw on the limited literature relating to those with a history of exposure to childhood trauma and the significantly overlapping conditions of BPD and PTSD (see Chapter 11, 'Anxiety Disorders' and Chapter 14, 'Personality Disorder'). A recent systematic review has shown that women exposed to maltreatment in their own childhood are more likely to display disturbances in the mother–baby relationship and their infants are more likely to show poorer emotion regulation [25]. Similarly, studies of mothers who experience persistent problems in managing their emotions and interpersonal relationships, consistent with the label 'personality disorder', have also been shown to display greater problems in the mother–baby relationship [79]. Women diagnosed with a personality disorder (especially BPD) have been found to display reduced sensitivity, increased intrusiveness and decreased responsiveness during interactions with their baby [80, 81, 82]. The comorbidity of a personality disorder with depression, as well the combined impact of both conditions on the mother–baby relationship is highlighted in these studies [83, 84]. An association between a maternal BPD diagnosis and poorer child outcomes as well as the intergenerational transmission of 'maladaptive parenting' have long been documented [85].

A systematic review of the perinatal PTSD literature by Cook and colleagues (2018) concluded that there are contradictory findings regarding the impact of PTSD on the mother–baby relationship and child development [86]. The authors propose that the mixed findings likely reflect measurement inconsistencies and methodological weaknesses across the included studies. Where significant associations have been reported, elevated postnatal PTSD symptoms predict increased parenting stress and dysfunctional mother–baby interactions [87, 88]; increased bonding difficulties [89, 90, 91]; and lower breastfeeding rates [91, 92]. It is important to highlight that PTSD and depression are highly comorbid during the perinatal period [83, 90]. When measured within the same sample, both direct and indirect effects of PTSD and depression on the parent–baby relationship have been reported [84, 93, 94, 95]. The avoidance symptom cluster of PTSD, reduced maternal sensitivity and decreased responsiveness to babies' communication cues have been highlighted as potential mechanisms of effect in studies that have measured concurrent depressive and PTSD symptoms [83, 86].

Care and Treatment

Enquiry, Attitudes, Behaviour and Information

Given that enquiry levels about childhood trauma exposure are very poor amongst mental health professionals generally [96], it is likely, though undocumented, that this applies in perinatal mental health services. Once exposure to childhood trauma is identified, any consequences for the patient's mental health can be explored. Enquiry into the details of childhood trauma exposure needs to be handled sensitively and in the context of a trusted relationship. Crucially, it is not necessary for the purposes of a therapeutic conversation to enquire about the specific details of the trauma exposure; knowing that something has happened is usually enough to engage in the far more important process of exploring a plausible explanation of how this led to the current difficulties.

> *There's an unpleasantly voyeuristic, peanut-crunching feel to it, this relentless focus on what happened to you. I wonder when we will stop demanding that people hold up their worst memories and ask, 'Does this count?'* [18]

The developmental and intergenerational perspective that defines the field of perinatal mental health allows us to provide plausible explanations for the seemingly complex, and challenging patterns of features that emerge in CPTSD and the individual variations seen in clinical practice. Such a model is helpful to individual clinicians and teams, and can provide a therapeutic understanding for those affected, who frequently describe never experiencing recognition or plausible explanation for their mental health problems. It is therefore worth considering in more detail how to explain to patients the ways in which these features might emerge, at least in perinatal populations. Next is an example of patient information written for women with CPTSD in a specialist community and inpatient service, providing an explanation of the development of some of the most common difficulties they describe:

- If other people do bad things to you as a child, even when you are a baby, you may learn that you cannot be in control of what happened to you and you stop planning ahead, making decisions for yourself and you do not learn to solve problems you face in life. This makes life very difficult and makes more bad things happen. It can also mean it is hard to focus on and achieve long-term goals.
- If bad things happen whatever you do, you may develop the assumption that it is something about you, and have a negative or insecure view of yourself, easily blaming yourself if things go wrong.
- When children are trapped in stressful or traumatic situations and cannot get away from them, their brain learns to escape mentally by switching off or 'dissociating'. Another way of mentally escaping is to go into a fantasy world in various ways, making up a different reality or imagining things that only you can see or hear.
- If you have had bad experiences or been badly treated as a child, you may learn not to trust other people. You may build up barriers around yourself and not let people get too close. This makes it difficult to have good relationships. Often, the only people who break through your barriers are controlling or abusive.
- If you learnt as a child that bad things can suddenly happen to you, it teaches you to be on the lookout for danger, always on edge or anxious and jumpy.
- This can make you react strongly to everyday situations, events or problems. Normal life is full of these, so these strong reactions can make your emotions, your thinking and what you do appear very changeable and extreme. It is like having a very thin emotional skin.
- Because this extreme distress is very painful it can lead people to look for anything that will make the feelings go away, for example taking drugs, drinking alcohol, causing physical pain to drown the mental pain (sometimes by cutting), or by just shutting off mentally.

Psychological, Psychosocial and Pharmacological Treatments

The impact of childhood adversity on mental healthcare and treatment outcomes is striking. These include earlier first admissions, with greater severity (more symptoms), higher frequency of admissions, longer length of admissions, increased likelihood of seclusion, higher doses of medication, poorer response to treatment, elevated rates of relapse, higher suicide risk and increased rates of self-harm [97]. This is highly suggestive that the approaches taken by individuals and services are not well suited to this large subgroup of mental health patients, and that trauma-informed services are required throughout mental, and indeed general healthcare.

Reviews of interventions for parents in the perinatal period experiencing symptoms of CPTSD and/or with a history of childhood maltreatment concluded that there is currently a lack of high-quality evidence regarding the effectiveness of interventions to improve parenting capacity or parental psychological well-being [98, 99]. These authors pointed to the need for more high-quality research, whilst adding that even small benefits should not be dismissed. Similarly, De Jongh concluded that the paucity of research into the efficacy of treatments for CPTSD does not justify delaying or denying access to interventions [100]. As this is especially true among perinatal populations, we will refer to the most relevant evidence and treatment guidance for PTSD and BPD, given that these populations and conditions substantially overlap.

In the perinatal period, there are three areas of psychological and psychosocial intervention that broadly map onto the different symptom clusters of CPTSD. Namely: 1) trauma-focused psychological interventions that target the re-experiencing, avoidance and hypervigilance symptom clusters; 2) psychological and psychosocial interventions that target difficulties in emotion regulation and negative self-concept; and 3) relationally focused interventions that target difficulties in the mother–infant relationship, adjustment to the maternal role, problems in the couple relationship, and interventions that support the individual's wider social relationships.

Intervention plans for women in the perinatal period need to follow a comprehensive psychological assessment, and formulation of the presenting problems should be co-produced in terms of decisions around what interventions are prioritised and when, and should follow a discussion of the potential risks and benefits of a given intervention at a given time. For example, the possibility that treatments focused on trauma processing could result in an initial worsening of hyperarousal and reliving symptoms balanced with the current stage of pregnancy/postpartum and the woman's capacity to engage in treatment. Decisions regarding *which* interventions are to be prioritised and in *what order*, will be influenced by when in the perinatal period the interventions are being considered, the nature and severity of the presenting problems, the women's preferences and her readiness. Problems in the parent–infant relationship are often prioritised but are *not* inevitable for all women with CPTSD. It is important to recognise that intervention plans for women during the perinatal period are generated with the psychological needs of both the mother and the infant in mind, as well as the wider family context. See Chapter 28, 'Psychological Therapies for Parental Mental Health in the Perinatal Period: What Works?' and Chapter 35, 'Mother–Infant Focused Interventions: What Works to Improve The Mother–Infant Relationship?' for further discussion on evidence-based psychological treatment strategies in the perinatal period.

Trauma-Focused Interventions That Target the Re-experiencing, Avoidance and Hypervigilance Symptom Clusters

There is no specific treatment guidance for trauma-focused treatments for CPTSD (or PTSD) during the perinatal period. Drawing on the wider general-adult PTSD literature, there is consensus across guidance documents and systematic reviews of randomised controlled trials that eye movement desensitization and reprocessing psychotherapy (EMDR), trauma-focused cognitive behavioural therapy (TF-CBT), cognitive reprocessing therapy and prolonged exposure (PE) are the most effective individualised treatments for moderate-to-severe PTSD. Narrative exposure therapy, person-centred therapy and group-delivered TF-CBT are also indicated as effective treatments for PTSD [101, 102, 103, 104]. Karatzias and colleagues [105] conducted a systematic review and meta-analysis of treatment trials for complex PTSD symptoms that included clinically significant baseline measures of one or more disturbance of self-organisation (DSO) symptom clusters (e.g. affect dysregulation, self-concept and/or disturbed relationships). Across 51 studies, TF-CBT, EMDR and PE were superior to usual care for the treatment of PTSD symptoms. Regarding the additional DSO symptoms clusters, TF-CBT and PE each had moderate-to-large effects on measures of negative self-concept, whereas TF-CBT, PE and EMDR had moderate-to-large effects on measures of disturbances in relationships. Moderator analyses showed that exposure to childhood trauma was associated with poorer treatment outcomes.

Whilst in their infancy, treatment trials of trauma-focused treatments for perinatal women are emerging. Zolghadr and colleagues [106] conducted a small scale randomised controlled trial (RCT) comparing a brief EMDR intervention against usual care for pregnant women with a history of prior stillbirth. At post-treatment, women who had received EMDR reported a statistically significant reduction in childbirth-related anxiety compared to controls.

Emotion Regulation, Negative Self-Concept and Interpersonal Functioning Interventions

There is ongoing debate within the wider CPTSD literature regarding the need for psychological interventions for CPTSD to begin with an initial 'stabilisation phase' before commencing the trauma-focused element of the treatment [100]. The International Society of Traumatic Stress Studies treatment guidance for adults with CPTSD recommends a person-centred, phased-based approach – where the sequencing of interventions is tailored to the patient's dominant problems [107, 108]. Phase one typically begins with interventions that aim to improve the individual's safety and readiness for psychotherapy by teaching emotion and interpersonal regulation skills [109, 107, 100]. Phase two focuses on the processing of traumatic memories, and phase three the consolidation and generalisation of treatment gains in daily life. In line with these recommendations, Cloitre and colleagues [110, 111] have developed the Skills Training in Affect and Interpersonal Regulation (STAIR) intervention, which adopts this phased-based approach for adults with CPTSD. A number of studies have found the STAIR intervention to be effective in reducing PTSD and depression and increasing emotion regulation and social functioning for individuals with PTSD and complex trauma histories [112, 113]. Further, a recent systematic review has concluded that multicomponent interventions (including phase-based and modular approaches) are the most effective treatments for individuals with PTSD and complex trauma histories [114]. For further discussion of the rationale and evidence for modular and phased-based approaches for CPTSD see Karatzias and Cloitre [115].

Dialectical behavioural therapy (DBT) aims to treat emotion and interpersonal dysregulation and is a recommended treatment for BPD in non-perinatal populations [116, 117, 118]. A recent scoping review has identified DBT as a promising approach for the treatment of emotion regulation and interpersonal difficulties in perinatal samples [119], including samples of women with CPTSD [120]. None of the seven studies included in the review used an RCT design or included all of the four traditional DBT treatment components. Nevertheless, DBT-informed interventions appear to improve emotion regulation, interpersonal functioning, parenting outcomes and symptoms of PTSD in samples of perinatal women [120].

Mother–Infant and Couple Relationship Interventions

There is no specific treatment guidance for psychological and/or psychosocial interventions that address difficulties in the mother–infant or the couple relationship for perinatal women with CPTSD or PTSD. Psychological interventions for difficulties in the mother–infant relationship have grown out of the developmental psychology literature that has documented the qualities of the optimal early caregiving environment, as well as the adverse impact of postnatal depression on mother–infant interactions [121]. These interventions are underpinned by a strong empirical evidence base and detailed theories of change. The overarching aims of these interventions include increasing attuned, responsive and sensitive caregiving, improving mothers' reflective functioning, and augmenting infant attachment security.

Video feedback interventions, most notably video interaction guidance (VIG), and video feedback intervention to promote positive parenting (VIPP), have both been highlighted in systematic reviews and guidance documents as effective parent-infant interventions [122, 123]. Of relevance to the perinatal context, studies using an RCT design have found that VIG improves mother–infant bonding and attachment security following childbirth-related traumatic events [124], whereas VIPP has been shown to increase maternal sensitivity and decrease parenting stress for mothers with complex trauma histories and 'personality disorder' diagnoses [125].

Attachment and bio-behavioural catch-up (ABC) [126] has been identified as one of the most well-evidenced interventions for infants exposed to early adversity [123, 127]. It is a trauma-informed intervention that aims to address parents' trauma histories and improve infant attachment security and healthy biological regulation [128]. Numerous RCTs of the ABC intervention with children involved in child protection services (e.g. foster care, adoption, edge of care) have demonstrated the effectiveness of ABC in improving the quality of the parent–child relationship, attachment security and child behavioural and emotional outcomes [129, 130, 131]. Parent–infant psychotherapy is another intervention with a growing evidence base for mothers with a history of trauma exposure, with a recent systematic review concluding that findings are mixed, and more research is needed [132]. Finally, group programmes such as Circles of Security show promise, although large-scale RCTs in perinatal populations are required [133].

There is a dearth of research into the efficacy of interventions for difficulties in the couple relationship in the context of CPTSD or indeed PTSD. To our knowledge, treatment guidance for this domain of functioning is non-existent, despite paternal (as well as maternal) mental health problems and parental relationship difficulties having long been associated with adverse child developmental outcomes [134, 135]. In clinical practice, behavioural couples therapy and interpersonal psychotherapy have been indicated as effective treatments for parental depression and relationship difficulties during the perinatal period [136]. However, efficacy trials of interventions that address interpersonal difficulties in the parental relationship for CPTSD are lacking.

Psychotropic Medications

In specialist perinatal services at least, women with CPTSD commonly describe a long history of multiple previous and sometimes current unhelpful medications, and an understandable loss of faith in prescribed medications and the professionals prescribing them. Although there is some evidence that some antidepressants may reduce symptoms of PTSD, there is no published evidence to suggest that antidepressants are effective for CPTSD. They may help with comorbid moderate-severe depression, despite the reduced effectiveness of antidepressants in the presence of childhood trauma [137]. Patients with CPTSD commonly present with long histories of trying multiple antidepressants without benefit.

Although there is similarly no published evidence for its effectiveness, self-guided use of low-dose antipsychotics (e.g. quetiapine 50 mg) can be helpful for intense mood swings and facilitate more effective use of psychological techniques. Clinical experience suggests that if low doses don't work, higher doses are unlikely to.

Another common clinical observation, but without any RCT evidence [138], is that self-guided use of low-dose trazodone (50–100 mg) can be helpful for improving sleep and relief of nightmares. Again, it seems from clinical experience, that if a dose of 100 mg is unhelpful, higher doses are unlikely to be.

A range of promising innovative approaches are also starting to emerge from the burgeoning research into mediators of intergenerational trauma and poor mental health, and we can expect from this a further enriching of clinical practice in perinatal mental health. These include potential microbiome, immune system and neuroendocrine interventions [139, 140].

Conclusions

The relatively new diagnostic category of CPTSD offers researchers and clinicians an opportunity to use a term that reflects the origins, nature and symptom profile of an extremely common condition. The responsibility lies with us to ensure that those affected by perinatal CPTSD receive the recognition, support and care they need. Given that the source of their difficulties arises in so many cases from society's failure to genuinely support our population in the earliest stages of life this is surely a moral obligation. Given the huge impact on future health and functioning in this generation and the next and the inevitable economic implications, this is surely also an economic imperative.

A developmental, intergenerational approach to mental health and ill-health is fundamental to perinatal mental healthcare and provides us with an opportunity to recognise the life experiences of patients. Complex PTSD provides a positive, non-judgemental, evidence-based and effective therapeutic construct for those experiencing the effects of early life or intergenerational trauma. This can enhance the ethos and morale of the teams we work in, and the many other services and systems we work closely with.

References

1. E Crouch, E Radcliff, M Strompolis, A Srivastav. Safe, stable, and nurtured: protective factors against poor physical and mental health outcomes following exposure to adverse childhood experiences (ACEs). *J Child Adolesc Trauma.* 2019;12:165–73.
2. P Ibrahim, D Almeida, C Nagy, G Turecki. Molecular impacts of childhood abuse on the human brain. *Neurobiol Stress.* 2021;15: 100343.
3. RA Bates, L Militello, E Barker, HG Villasanti, K Schmeer. Early childhood stress responses to psychosocial stressors:

the state of the science. *Dev Psychobiol.* 2022;64(7):e22320.

4. NC Nicolaides, C Kanaka-Gantenbein, P Pervanidou. Developmental neuroendocrinology of early-life stress: impact on child development and behavior. *Curr Neuropharmacol.* 2024;22(3):461–74.
5. SH Shin, YK Kim. Early life stress, neuroinflammation, and psychiatric illness of adulthood. *Adv Exp Med Biol.* 2023;1411:105–34.
6. E Beurel, CB Nemeroff. Early life adversity, microbiome, and inflammatory responses. *Biomolecules.* 2024;14(7):802.
7. A Tremblay, L Lingrand, M Maillard, B Feuz, TA Tompkins. The effects of psychobiotics on the microbiota-gut-brain axis in early-life stress and neuropsychiatric disorders. *Prog Neuropsychopharmacol Biol Psychiatry.* 2021;105:110142.
8. S Pawlby, DF Hay, D Sharpe, CS Waters, CM Pariante. Antenatal depression and offspring psychopathology: the influence of childhood maltreatment. *Br J Psychiatry.* 2011;199(2):106–12.
9. DT Plant, S Pawlby, CM Pariante, FW Jones. When one childhood meets another – maternal childhood trauma and offspring child psychopathology: a systematic review. *Clin Child Psychol Psychiatry.* 2018;23:483–500.
10. Y Xerxa, MHJ Hillegers, E Mesman, H Tiemeier, PW Jansen. Intergenerational transmission of psychopathology across three generations: the role of social support. *Eur Child Adolesc Psychiatry.* 2025;34(4):1329–40.
11. T DeAngelis. The legacy of trauma: an emerging line of research is exploring how historical and cultural traumas affect survivors' children for generations to come. *Am Psychol Assoc.* 2019;50(2).
12. A Jawaid, M Roszkowski, I Mansuy. Transgenerational epigenetics of traumatic stress. *Prog Mol Biol Transl Sci.* 2018;158:273–98.
13. LL Braga, MF Mello, JP Fiks. Transgenerational transmission of trauma and resilience: a qualitative study with Brazilian offspring of Holocaust survivors. *BMC Psychiatry.* 2012;12:134.
14. DT Plant, FW Jones, CM Pariante, S Pawlby. Association between maternal childhood trauma and offspring childhood psychopathology: mediation analysis from the ALSPAC cohort. *Br J Psychiatry.* 2017;211(3):144–50.
15. World Health Organization. *International statistical classification of diseases and related health problems* (11th edition). 2019.
16. American Psychiatric Association. *Diagnostic and statistical manual of mental disorders* (5th edition). Washington, DC: American Psychiatric Association; 2013.
17. JL Herman. Complex PTSD: a syndrome in survivors of prolonged and repeated trauma. *J Traum Stress.* 1992;5(3):377–91.
18. L Richmond. *All my worldly joy: a memoir of motherhood and mental health.* Wilton Square, in press.
19. M Cloitre, DW Garvert, CR Brewin, RA Bryant, A Maercker. Evidence for proposed ICD-11 PTSD and complex PTSD: a latent profile analysis. *Eur J Psychotraumatol.* 2013;15:4.
20. S Rees, S Channon, CS Waters. The impact of maternal prenatal and postnatal anxiety on children's emotional problems: a systematic review. *Eur Child Adolesc Psychiatry.* 2019;28(2):257–80.
21. S Jowett, T Karatzias, I Albert. Multiple and interpersonal trauma are risk factors for both post-traumatic stress disorder and borderline personality disorder: a systematic review on the traumatic backgrounds and clinical characteristics of comorbid post-traumatic stress disorder/borderline personality disorder groups versus single-disorder groups. *Psychol Psychother.* 2020;93(3): 621–38.
22. V Nanni, R Uher, A Danese. Childhood maltreatment predicts unfavorable course of illness and treatment outcome in depression: a meta-analysis. *Am J Psychiatry.* 2012;169(2):141–51.

23. RF Anda, VJ Felitti, JD Bremner, JD Walker, C Whitfield, BD Perry, et al. The enduring effects of abuse and related adverse experiences in childhood: a convergence of evidence from neurobiology and epidemiology. *Eur Arch Psychiatry Clin Neurosci.* 2006;256(3):174–86.

24. K Vaillancourt, S Pawlby, RM Fearon. History of childhood abuse and mother-infant interaction: a systematic review of observational studies. *Infant Ment Health J.* 2017;38(2):226–48.

25. AJ Souch, IR Jones, KHM Shelton, CS Waters. Maternal childhood maltreatment and perinatal outcomes: a systematic review. *J Affect Disord.* 2022;302:139–59.

26. HB Daníelsdóttir, T Aspelund, Q Shen, T Halldorsdottir, J Jakobsdóttir, H Song, et al. Adverse childhood experiences and adult mental health outcomes. *JAMA Psychiatry.* 2024;81(6):586–94.

27. IM Steine, D Winje, JH Krystal, B Bjorvatn, AM Milde, J Grønli, et al. Cumulative childhood maltreatment and its dose-response relation with adult symptomatology: findings in a sample of adult survivors of sexual abuse. *Child Abuse Negl.* 2017;65:99–111.

28. AJ Narayan, AF Lieberman, AS Masten. Intergenerational transmission and prevention of adverse childhood experiences (ACEs). *Clin Psychol Rev.* 2021;85:101997.

29. DT Plant, ED Barker, CS Waters, S Pawlby, CM Pariante. Intergenerational transmission of maltreatment and psychopathology: the role of antenatal depression. *Psychol Med.* 2013;43(3):519–28.

30. S Pawlby, D Hay, D Sharp, CS Waters, CM Pariante. Antenatal depression and offspring psychopathology: the influence of childhood maltreatment. *Br J Psychiatry.* 2011;199(2):106–12.

31. V Clemens, D Wernecke, JM Fegert, J Genuneit, D Rothenbacher, S Braig. Maternal child maltreatment and trajectories of offspring behavioural and emotional difficulties from age 4 to 7 years: results from a prospective birth cohort study. *Eur Child Adolesc Psychiatry.* 2025;34(3):1039–50.

32. EM Bosquet, MM Englund, B Egeland. Maternal childhood maltreatment history and child mental health: mechanisms in intergenerational effects. *J Clin Child Adolesc Psychol.* 2018;47(suppl. 1): S47–S62.

33. M Harris, H MacMillan, J Mepham, D Joshi, C Wekerle, L Atkinson, et al. Maternal childhood maltreatment history and child behavior problems: developmental patterns and mediation via maternal depressive symptoms and parenting behavior. *Child Maltreat.* 2023;28(2):254–64.

34. N San Martín-González, J Moya-Higueras, E Eixarch, Á Castro-Quintas, L Marques-Feixa, F Crispi, et al. Intergenerational effects of maternal childhood maltreatment on newborns' stress regulation: the role of maternal depressive symptoms. *Child Abuse Negl.* 2024;155:106968.

35. C Rutherford, H Sharp, J Hill, A Pickles, D Taylor-Robinson. How does perinatal maternal mental health explain early social inequalities in child behavioural and emotional problems? Findings from the Wirral Child Health and Development Study. *PLoS ONE.* 2019;14(5):e0217342.

36. JR Baldwin, HM Sallis, T Schoeler, MJ Taylor, ASF Kwong, JJ Tielbeek, et al. A genetically informed Registered Report on adverse childhood experiences and mental health. *Nat Hum Behav.* 2023;7(2):269–90.

37. SS Adams, M Eberhard-Gran, A Eskild. Fear of childbirth and duration of labour: a study of 2206 women with intended vaginal delivery. *BJOG.* 2012;119(10):1238–46.

38. T Frazier, CJ Hogue, KM Yount. The development of the healthy pregnancy stress scale, and validation in a sample of low-income African American women. *Matern Child Health J.* 2018;22(2): 247–54.

39. NR Stevens, V Tirone, TA Lillis, L Holmgreen, A Chen-McCracken, SE Hobfoll. Posttraumatic stress and depression may undermine abuse survivors' self-efficacy in the obstetric care setting. *Psychosom Obstetr Gynecol.* 2017;38(2):103–10.

40. N Simon, NP Roberts, CE Lewis, MJ van Gelderen, JI Bisson. Associations between perceived social support, posttraumatic stress disorder (PTSD) and complex PTSD (CPTSD): implications for treatment. *Eur J Psychotraumatol.* 2019;10(1):1573129.

41. National Childbirth Trust. The hidden half report. 2017. www.nct.org.uk/sites/default/files/2019-04/NCT%20The%20Hidden%20Half_0.pdf

42. AM Speranza, B Farina, C Bossa, A Fortunato, C Maggiora Vergano, L Palmiero, et al. The role of complex trauma and attachment patterns in intimate partner violence. *Front Psychol.* 2022;12:769584.

43. R Rossi, F Reda, I Federico, TB Jannini, V Socci, G D'Aurizio, et al. The association between traumatic experiences and substance and behavioral addictions in late adolescence: a role for PTSD and cPTSD as potential mediators. *J Psychiatr Res.* 2023;168:82–90.

44. C Moreau, S Zisook. Rationale for a posttraumatic stress spectrum disorder. *Psychiatr Clin North Am.* 2002;25(4):775–90.

45. HW Fung, K Lee, EKS Wang, JY Wong. Trauma-related mental health problems among mothers in Taiwan and their relationship with children's emotional and behavioral problems. *Eur J Psychotraumatol.* 2024;15(1):2382554.

46. JG Green, KA McLaughlin, PA Berglund, MJ Gruber, NA Sampson, AM Zaslavsky, et al. Childhood adversities and adult psychiatric disorders in the national comorbidity survey replication I: associations with first onset of DSM-IV disorders. *Arch Gen Psychiatry.* 2010;67(2):113–23.

47. BJ Krause, R Artigas, AF Sciolla, J Hamilton. Epigenetic mechanisms activated by childhood adversity. *Epigenomics.* 2020;12(14):1239–55.

48. P Collender, AK Bozack, S Veazie, JC Nwanaji-Enwerem, L Van Der Laan, K Kogut, et al. Maternal adverse childhood experiences (ACEs) and DNA methylation of newborns in cord blood. *Clin Epigenetics.* 2023;15(1):162.

49. N Cattane, R Rossi, M Lanfredi, A Cattaneo. Borderline personality disorder and childhood trauma: exploring the affected biological systems and mechanisms. *BMC Psychiatry.* 2017;17(1):221.

50. TG O'Connor, MT Willoughby, JA Moynihan, S Messing, A Vallejo Sefair, J Carnahan, et al. Early childhood risk exposures and inflammation in early adolescence. *Brain Behav Immun.* 2020;86:22–9.

51. L Tadjine, L Swords. "I just wouldn't like him to go through what I went through as a kid": a qualitative study on the mitigating effects of positive childhood experiences in mothers with a history of adverse childhood experiences in an Irish population. *Community Ment Health J.* 2025;61(3):492–501.

52. L Bornscheuer, K Gauffin, YB Almquist. Mapping resilience: a scoping review on mediators and moderators of childhood adversity with a focus on gender patterns. *BMJ Open.* 2024;14(9):e080259.

53. T Karatzias, M Shevlin, C Fyvie, G Grandison, M Garozi, E Latham, et al. Adverse and benevolent childhood experiences in posttraumatic stress disorder (PTSD) and complex PTSD (CPTSD): implications for trauma-focused therapies. *Eur J Psychotraumatol.* 2020;11(1):1793599.

54. SR Jaffee, R Takizawa, L Arseneault. Buffering effects of safe, supportive, and nurturing relationships among women with childhood histories of maltreatment. *Psychol Med.* 2017;47(15):2628–39.

55. T Karatzias, M Cloitre, A Maercker, E Kazlauskas, M Shevlin, P Hyland, et al. PTSD and Complex PTSD: ICD-11

updates on concept and measurement in the UK, USA, Germany and Lithuania. *Eur J Psychotraumatol.* 2018;8(suppl 7):1418103.

56. M Knefel, B Lueger-Schuster, J Bisson, T Karatzias, E Kazlauskas, NP Roberts. A cross-cultural comparison of ICD-11 complex posttraumatic stress disorder symptom networks in Austria, the United Kingdom, and Lithuania. *J Trauma Stress.* 2020;33(1):41–51.

57. B Leeners, W Rath, E Block, G Görres, S Tschudin. Risk factors for unfavorable pregnancy outcome in women with adverse childhood experiences. *J Perinat Med.* 2014;42(2):171–8.

58. A Souch. Mothers' exposure to early life adversity and mental health and childbirth related outcomes. Unpublished PhD thesis, Cardiff University; 2023.

59. K Heffernan, M Cloitre. A comparison of posttraumatic stress disorder with and without borderline personality disorder among women with a history of childhood sexual abuse: etiological and clinical characteristics. *J Nerv Ment Dis.* 2000;188(9):589–95.

60. C Zlotnick, CL Franklin, M Zimmerman. Is comorbidity of posttraumatic stress disorder and borderline personality disorder related to greater pathology and impairment? *Am J Psychiatry.* 2002;159(11):1940–3.

61. JA Golier, R Yehuda, LM Bierer, V Mitropoulou, AS New, J Schmeidler, et al. The relationship of borderline personality disorder to posttraumatic stress disorder and traumatic events. *Am J Psychiatry.* 2003;160(11):2018–24.

62. MS Harned, SL Rizvi, MM Linehan. Impact of co-occurring posttraumatic stress disorder on suicidal women with borderline personality disorder. *Am J Psychiatry.* 2010;167(10):1210–17.

63. MC Zanarini, FR Frankenburg, ED Dubo, AE Sickel, A Trikha, A Levin, et al. Axis II comorbidity of borderline personality disorder. *Compr Psychiatry.* 1998;39(5):296–302.

64. M Westphal, M Olfson, M Bravova, MJ Gameroff, R Gross, P Wickramaratne, et al. Borderline personality disorder, exposure to interpersonal trauma, and psychiatric comorbidity in urban primary care patients. *Psychiatry.* 2013;76(4):365–80.

65. T Karatzias, M Shevlin, C Fyvie, P Hyland, E Efthymiadou, D Wilson, et al. An initial psychometric assessment of an ICD-11 based measure of PTSD and complex PTSD (ICD-TQ): evidence of construct validity. *J Anxiety Disord.* 2016;44:73–9.

66. R Brannigan, A Tanskanen, MO Huttunen, M Cannon, FP Leacy, MC Clarke. The role of prenatal stress as a pathway to personality disorder: longitudinal birth cohort study. *Br J Psychiatry.* 2020;216(2):85–9.

67. S Machizawa-Summers. Childhood trauma and parental bonding among Japanese female patients with borderline personality disorder. *Int J Psychol.* 2007;42:265–73.

68. M Cloitre, DW Garvert, B Weiss, EB Carlson, RA Bryant. Distinguishing PTSD, complex PTSD, and borderline personality disorder: a latent class analysis. *Eur J Psychotraumatol.* 2014;15:5.

69. Y Yuan, H Lee, CE Newhill, SM Eack, R Fusco, LN Scott. Differential associations between childhood maltreatment types and borderline personality disorder from the perspective of emotion dysregulation. *Borderline Personal Disord Emot Dysregul.* 2023;10(1):4.

70. I Schalinski, MH Teicher, D Nischk, E Hinderer, O Müller, B Rockstroh. Type and timing of adverse childhood experiences differentially affect severity of PTSD, dissociative and depressive symptoms in adult inpatients. *BMC Psychiatry.* 2016;16:295.

71. S Jowett, T Karatzias, M Shevlin, P Hyland. Psychological trauma at different developmental stages and ICD-11 CPTSD: the role of dissociation. *J Trauma Dissociation.* 2022;23(1):52–67.

72. A Vatanparast, S Shakiba, F Momeni, A Kamrani. The relationship between childhood maltreatment and self-harm: the mediating roles of alexithymia, dissociation, internalizing and posttraumatic symptoms. *Eur J Psychotraumatol.* 2024;15(1):2378642.

73. I Franzke, P Wabnitz, C Catani. Dissociation as a mediator of the relationship between childhood trauma and nonsuicidal self-injury in females: a path analytic approach. *J Trauma Dissociation.* 2015;16(3):286–302.

74. I Haahr-Pedersen, C Perera, P Hyland, F Vallières, D Murphy, M Hansen, et al. Females have more complex patterns of childhood adversity: implications for mental, social, and emotional outcomes in adulthood. *Eur J Psychotraumatol.* 2020;11(1):1708618.

75. S Jowett, T Karatzias, I Albert. Multiple and interpersonal trauma are risk factors for both post-traumatic stress disorder and borderline personality disorder: a systematic review on the traumatic backgrounds and clinical characteristics of comorbid post-traumatic stress disorder/borderline personality disorder groups versus single-disorder groups. *Psychol Psychother.* 2020;93(3):621–38.

76. JG Gunderson, RL Stout, TH McGlashan, MT Shea, LC Morey, CM Grilo, et al. Ten-year course of borderline personality disorder: psychopathology and function from the Collaborative Longitudinal Personality Disorders study. *Arch Gen Psychiatry.* 2011;68(8):827–37.

77. G Lewis, L Appleby. Personality disorder: the patients psychiatrists dislike. *Br J Psychiatry.* 1988;153:44–9.

78. S Flynn, J Raphael, J Graney, T Nyathi, A Williams, N Kapur, et al. The personality disorder patient pathway: service user and clinical perspectives. *Personal Ment Health.* 2019;13(3):134–43.

79. A May, R Balzan, AS Williams, TD Wade, SM Paranjothy. Interventions for perinatal borderline personality disorder and complex trauma: a systematic review. *Arch Womens Ment Health.* 2023;26:295–309.

80. S Conroy, CM Pariante, MN Marks, HA Davies, S Farrelly, R Schacht, P Moran. Maternal psychopathology and infant development at 18 months: the impact of maternal personality disorder and depression. *J Am Acad Child Adolesc Psychiatry.* 2012;51(1):51–61.

81. LE Crandell, MP Patrick, RP Hobson. 'Still-face' interactions between mothers with borderline personality disorder and their 2-month-old infants. *Br J Psychiatry.* 2003;183:239–47.

82. H White, TJ Flanagan, A Martin, D Silvermann. Mother–infant interactions in women with borderline personality disorder, major depressive disorder, their co-occurrence, and healthy controls. *J Reprod Infant Psychol.* 2011;29(3): 223–35.

83. S Garthus-Niegel, A Horsch, S Ayers, J Junge-Hoffmeister, K Weidner, M Eberhard-Gran. The influence of postpartum PTSD on breastfeeding: a longitudinal population-based study. *Birth.* 2018;45(2):193–201.

84. Y Parfitt, A Pike, S Ayers. Infant developmental outcomes: a family systems perspective. *Infant Child Dev.* 2014;23(4):353–73.

85. KR Steele, ML Townsend, BFS Grenyer. Parenting and personality disorder: an overview and meta-synthesis of systematic reviews. *PLoS ONE.* 2019;14(10):e0223038.

86. N Cook, S Ayers, A Horsch. Maternal posttraumatic stress disorder during the perinatal period and child outcomes: a systematic review. *J Affect Disord.* 2018;225:18–31.

87. N Feeley, P Zelkowitz, C Cormier, L Charbonneau, A Lacroix, A Papageorgiou. Posttraumatic stress among mothers of very low birthweight infants at 6 months after discharge from the neonatal intensive care unit. *Appl Nurs Res.* 2011;24(2):114–17.

88. S McDonald, P Slade, H Spiby, J Iles. Post-traumatic stress symptoms, parenting stress and mother-child relationships following childbirth and at

2 years postpartum. *J Psychosom Obstet Gynaecol.* 2011;32(3):141–6.

89. LJ Frankham, EB Thorsteinsson, W Bartik. Birth related PTSD and its association with the mother-infant relationship: a meta-analysis. *Sex Reprod Healthc.* 2023;38:100920.

90. YM Parfitt, S Ayers. The effect of post-natal symptoms of post-traumatic stress and depression on the couple's relationship and parent–baby bond. *J Reprod Infant Psychol.* 2009;27(2):127–42.

91. S Ayers, DB Wright, N Wells. Symptoms of post traumatic stress disorder in couples after birth: association with the couple's relationship and parent–baby bond. *J Reprod Infant Psychol.* 2007;25(1):40–50.

92. I Hairston, JE Handelzalts, C Assis, M Kovo. Postpartum bonding difficulties and adult attachment styles: the mediating role of postpartum depression and childbirth related PTSD. *Infant Ment Health J.* 2018;39(2):198–208.

93. N Erickson, M Julian, M Muzik. Perinatal depression, PTSD, and trauma: impact on mother–infant attachment and interventions to mitigate the transmission of risk. *Int Rev Psychiatry.* 2019;31(3):245–63.

94. SN Radoš, M Matijaš, M Anđelinović, A Čartolovni, S Ayers. The role of posttraumatic stress and depression symptoms in mother-infant bonding. *J Affect Disord.* 2020;268:134–40.

95. JS Seng, M Sperlich, LK Low, DL Ronis, M Muzik, I Liberzon. Childhood abuse history, posttraumatic stress disorder, postpartum mental health, and bonding: a prospective cohort study. *J Midwifery Womens Health.* 2013;58(1):57–68.

96. C Neill, J Read. Adequacy of inquiry about, documentation of, and treatment of trauma and adversities: a study of mental health professionals in England. *Community Ment Health J.* 2022;58(6):1076–87.

97. J Read, RP Bentall. Negative childhood experiences and mental health: theoretical, clinical and primary prevention implications. *Br J Psychiatry.* 2012;200(2):89–91.

98. C Chamberlain, G Gee, S Harfield, S Campbell, S Brennan, Y Clark, et al. Parenting after a history of childhood maltreatment: a scoping review and map of evidence in the perinatal period. *PLoS ONE.* 2019;14(3):e0213460.

99. KA Jones, I Freijah, SE Brennan, JE McKenzie, TM Bright, R Fiolet, et al. Interventions from pregnancy to two years after birth for parents experiencing complex post-traumatic stress disorder and/or with childhood experience of maltreatment. *Cochrane Database Syst Rev.* 2023;5(5):CD014874.

100. A De Jongh, PA Resick, LA Zoellner, A van Minnen, CW Lee, CM Monson, et al. A critical analysis of the current treatment guidelines for complex PTSD in adults. *Depress Anxiety.* 2016;33(5):359–69.

101. C Lewis, NP Roberts, M Andrew, E Starling, JI Bisson. Psychological therapies for post-traumatic stress disorder in adults: systematic review and meta-analysis. *Eur J Psychotraumatol.* 2020;11(1):1729633.

102. Matrics Cymru. Post-traumatic stress disorder. 2023. https://shorturl.at/4PEZN

103. Matrix Scotland. Post-traumatic stress disorder. 2023. https://shorturl.at/zcFsx

104. National Institute for Health and Care Excellence. Post-traumatic stress disorder. NICE Guideline (NG116). 2018. www.nice.org.uk/guidance/ng116

105. T Karatzias, P Murphy, M Cloitre, J Bisson, M Shevlin, P Hyland, et al. Psychological interventions for ICD-11 complex PTSD symptoms: systematic review and meta-analysis. *Psychol Med.* 2019;49(11):1761–75.

106. N Zolghadr, A Khoshnazar, M Moradibaglooei, Z Alimorad. The effect of EMDR on childbirth anxiety of women with previous stillbirth. *J EMDR Pract Res.* 2019;13(1):10–19.

107. M Cloitre, CA Courtois, A Charuvastra, R Carapezza, BC Stolbach, BL Green.

Treatment of complex PTSD: results of the ISTSS expert clinician survey on best practices. *J Trauma Stress.* 2011;24(6): 615–27.

108. International Society for Traumatic Stress Studies. Position paper on complex PTSD in adults. 2018. https://shorturl.at/TBslF

109. M Cloitre, CA Courtois, JD Ford, BL Green, P Alexander, J Briere, et al. The ISTSS expert consensus treatment guidelines for complex PTSD in adults. 2012. www.istss.org

110. M Cloitre, K Koenen, L Cohen, H Han. Skills training in affective and interpersonal regulation followed by exposure: a phase-based treatment for PTSD related to childhood abuse. *J Consult Clin Psychol.* 2002;70(5):1067–74.

111. M Cloitre, KC Stovall-McClough, K Nooner, P Zorbas, S Cherry, CL Jackson, et al. Treatment for PTSD related to childhood abuse: a randomized controlled trial. *Am J Psychiatry.* 2010;167(8):915–24.

112. S Jain, K Ortigo, J Gimeno, DA Baldor, BJ Weiss, M Cloitre. A randomized controlled trial of brief skills training in affective and interpersonal regulation (STAIR) for veterans in primary care. *J Trauma Stress.* 2020;33(4):401–19.

113. HB MacIntosh, M Cloitre, K Kortis, A Peck, BJ Weiss. Implementation and evaluation of the skills training in affective and interpersonal regulation (STAIR) in a community setting in the context of childhood sexual abuse. *Res Soc Work Pract.* 2018;28(5):595–602.

114. PA Coventry, N Meader, H Melton, M Temple, H Dale, K Wright, et al. Psychological and pharmacological interventions for posttraumatic stress disorder and comorbid mental health problems following complex traumatic events: systematic review and component network meta-analysis. *PLoS Med.* 2020;17(8).

115. T Karatzias, M Cloitre. Treating adults with complex post-traumatic stress disorder using a modular approach to treatment: rationale, evidence, and directions for future research. *J Trauma Stress.* 2019;32(6):870–6.

116. National Institute for Health and Clinical Excellence. Treatment and management of borderline personality disorder. Clinical Guideline (CG78). 2009.

117. Matrics Cymru. Borderline personality disorder. 2023. https://shorturl.at/AAjQ2

118. Matrix Scotland. Borderline personality disorder. 2023. www.nes.scot.nhs.uk/media/2ocnzsta/matrix_-_adultmentalhealthtables.pdf

119. SN Hellberg, AB Bruening, KA Thompson, TA Hopkins. Applications of dialectical behavioural therapy in the perinatal period: a scoping review. *Clin Psychol Psychother.* 2024;31(1).

120. H Wilson, AL Donachie. Evaluating the effectiveness of a dialectical behaviour therapy (DBT) informed programme in a community perinatal team. *Behav Cogn Psychother.* 2018;46(5):541–53.

121. L Murray. *The psychology of babies: how relationships support the development from birth to two.* London: Robinson; 2014.

122. L O'Hara, ER Smith, J Barlow, N Livingstone, NINS Herath, Y Wei, et al. Video feedback for parental sensitivity and attachment security in children under five years. *Cochrane Database Syst Rev.* 2019;11(11):CD012348.

123. MM Hare, TD Landis, ML Hernandez, PA Graziano. A systematic review of infant mental health prevention and treatment programs. *Infant Ment Health J.* 2023;44(4):499–522.

124. HN Hoffenkamp, A Tooten, RA Hall, J Braeken, MP Eliëns, AJ Vingerhoets, HJ van Bakel. Effectiveness of hospital-based video interaction guidance on parental interactive behavior, bonding, and stress after preterm birth: a randomized controlled trial. *J Consult Clin Psychol.* 2015;83(2):416–29.

125. K Barnicot, M Welsh, S Kalwarowsky, E Stevens, J Iles, J Parker, et al. Video feedback parent-infant intervention for mothers experiencing enduring

difficulties in managing emotions and relationships: a randomised controlled feasibility trial. *Br J Clin Psychol.* 2022;61(4):1188–210.

126. WA Grube, KW Liming. Attachment and biobehavioral catch-up: a systematic review. *Infant Ment Health J.* 2018;39(6):656–73.

127. B Wright, P Fearon, M Garside, E Tsappis, E Amoah, D Glaser, et al. Routinely used interventions to improve attachment in infants and young children: a national survey and two systematic reviews. *Health Technol Assess.* 2023;27(2):1–226.

128. M Dozier, K Bernard, CKP Roben. Attachment and biobehavioral catch-up. In: H Steele, M Steele, editors. *Handbook of attachment-based interventions.* New York: The Guilford Press; 2018. p. 27–49.

129. K Bernard, M Dozier, J Bick, E Lewis-Morrarty, O Lindhiem, E Carlson. Enhancing attachment organization among maltreated children: results of a randomized clinical trial. *Child Dev.* 2012;83(2):623–36.

130. T Lind, K Lee Raby, EB Caron, CK Roben, M Dozier. Enhancing executive functioning among toddlers in foster care with an attachment-based intervention. *Dev Psychopathol.* 2017;29(2):575–86.

131. AR Tabachnick, RD Eiden, MH Labella, M Dozier. Effects of an attachment-based intervention on autonomic regulation among opioid-exposed infants. *Dev Psychobiol.* 2022;64(6):e22286.

132. C Cucciniello, Y Melia. Effectiveness of parent–infant psychotherapy for infant development, parenting, parental mental health, and the attachment relationship: a review of the literature. *J Public Child Welfare.* 2024;1–35.

133. C Rosan, KA Dijk, Z Darwin, D Babalis, V Cornelius, R Phillips, et al. The COSI trial: a study protocol for a multi-centre, randomised controlled trial to explore the clinical and cost-effectiveness of the Circle of Security-Parenting Intervention in community perinatal mental health services in England. *Trials.* 2023; 24(1):188.

134. H Scarlett, S Moirangthem, J van der Waerden. The impact of paternal mental illness on child development: an umbrella review of systematic reviews and meta-analyses. *Eur Child Adolesc Psychiatry.* 2024;33(11):3693–706.

135. WM van Eldik, AD de Haan, LQ Parry, PT Davies, MPCM Luijk, LR Arends, P Prinzie. The interparental relationship: meta-analytic associations with children's maladjustment and responses to interparental conflict. *Psychol Bull.* 2020;146(7):553–94.

136. M Rathgeber, PC Bürkner, EM Schiller, H Holling. The efficacy of emotionally focused couples therapy and behavioral couples therapy: a meta-analysis. *J Marital Fam Ther.* 2019;45(3): 447–63.

137. N Nikkheslat, AP McLaughlin, C Hastings, Z Zajkowska, MA Nettis, N Mariani, et al. Childhood trauma, HPA axis activity and antidepressant response in patients with depression. *Brain Behav Immun* 2020;87:229–37.

138. C Geldenhuys, LL van den Heuvel, P Steyn, S Seedat. Pharmacological management of nightmares associated with posttraumatic stress disorder. *CNS Drugs.* 2022;36(7):721–37.

139. RR Dietert, JM Dietert. Using microbiome-based approaches to deprogram chronic disorders and extend the healthspan following adverse childhood experiences. *Microorganisms.* 2022;10(2):229.

140. V Mondelli, AC Vernon. From early adversities to immune activation in psychiatric disorders: the role of the sympathetic nervous system. *Clin Exp Immunol.* 2019;197(3):319–28.

Section 2 **Maternal Mental Disorders**

Chapter 16

Eating Disorders

Catia Acosta and Abigail Easter

Introduction

Eating disorders can have a profound impact on women during the pre-conception, antenatal and postnatal periods, and this has implications for their care and treatment. This chapter describes the rate, course and risk factors for eating disorders within the context of the perinatal period. It covers what is known from current research and clinical evidence about the effect of the most common eating disorders on pre-conception health, pregnancy and birth outcomes. Drawing on existing clinical guidance and research evidence, it provides an overview of the guidance and recommendations for the assessment, management and treatment of eating disorders from pre-conception through to the postnatal period.

Epidemiology and Aetiology

Diagnostic Classifications

Eating disorders are mental illnesses, which are characterised by disturbances of eating behaviours, and thoughts and beliefs about food, weight and body shape. Those with eating disorders can experience a variety of symptoms, categorised in the *Diagnostic and Statistical Manual of Mental Disorders* (DSM-5) and International Classification of Diseases (ICD-11) into four main types: anorexia nervosa, bulimia nervosa, binge eating disorder and other specified feeding or eating disorders [1>, 2]:

- Anorexia nervosa (AN) is defined as a persistent restriction of energy intake leading to significantly low body weight, accompanied by an intense fear or dread of gaining weight.
- Bulimia nervosa (BN) involves recurrent episodes of binge eating (eating an unusually large amount of food in a defined period) with a loss of control, that is followed by compensatory behaviours to prevent weight gain (e.g. self-induced vomiting (SIV), abuse of laxatives or other tablets, or excessive exercise).
- Binge eating disorder (BED) involves recurrent episodes of binge eating with a loss of control, accompanied by severe distress about binge eating but, unlike BN, it is not followed by any compensatory behaviours.
- Other specified feeding or eating disorders (OSFED), previously known as eating disorders not otherwise specified (EDNOS), refers to a group of eating disorders that cause significant distress or impairment but do not meet the full criteria for one of the eating disorders defined above.

Both AN and BN have purging and non-purging subtypes. There are often high rates of diagnostic crossover among eating disorder categories, where individuals may experience different eating disorders or subtypes across their lifespan. This section does not provide a full list of diagnostic criteria for each of the eating disorders, which is out of scope of this chapter.

Prevalence, Incidence, Risk and Comorbidity

Studies of the rate of eating disorders in community-based samples across Europe suggests that among females, AN is reported in between <1% and 4%, BN <1% and 2% and BED <1% and 4%. Sub-threshold eating disorders and OSFED are less frequently reported but the prevalence is thought to be approximately 2–3% of women in Europe. Eating disorders disproportionately affect females, and the male to female ratio is between 1:2 and 1:16 across the eating disorder spectrum, with European studies suggesting that between 0.3% and 0.7% of males meet diagnostic criteria for an eating disorder [3].

Global statistics are less frequently available, and epidemiological studies in non-Western countries are often conducted with high-risk female samples. A recent systematic review of worldwide trends in eating disorders suggests a point prevalence of AN 0–1%, BN 0.9–3% and BED 1.9–4.5% in studies from China, Japan, Africa, Latin America and Hispanic or Latinas samples in the USA [4]. This review reported substantially lower prevalence of AN in Africa and Latin America compared to Western countries, which is thought to be driven by sociocultural differences in attitudes to body image. Nevertheless, international evidence indicates that females during adolescence and early adulthood are at the highest risk of developing an eating disorder, highlighting the importance of considering their impact and manifestation during pregnancy and motherhood.

The aetiology of eating disorders is multifactorial, and as with many psychiatric disorders there is evidence of gene and environment interactions. Eating disorders aggregate in families, and AN, BN and BED are heritable disorders. Findings from large twin studies indicate heritability estimates for AN range between 0.48 and 0.74; for BN, between 0.55 and 0.62, and for BED, between 0.39 and 0.45 [5]. In addition, a wide range of risk factors have been reported, including social factors (e.g. gender, race and ethnicity), familial (e.g. parental obesity, parental psychopathology and family interaction and communication style), psychological (e.g. low self-esteem, perfectionism and dieting), developmental (e.g. adolescent age, childhood eating and feeding problems, early pubertal maturation) and biological factors (e.g. genetic factors, neuroendocrine and metabolic disturbances) [6]. However, there are few longitudinal studies, and it is difficult to differentiate risk factors between eating disorder types and untangle which risk factors precede the development of an eating disorder.

Morbidity and Mortality

Eating disorders are also highly comorbid with other mental illnesses and approximately 70% of individuals in a large Swedish clinical data registry study were found to experience psychiatric comorbidity [7]. Over 50% reported anxiety disorders and more than 40% mood disorders; self-harm (>20%) and substance use (>10%) were also found to be common [4]. Neurodevelopmental disorders are also recognised as comorbidities with eating disorders [8, 9, 10]; these include autism spectrum disorders (ASD) and attention deficit hyperactivity disorder (ADHD).

Nazar et al. [10] suggested that adult women with ADHD are at higher risk of developing an eating disorder, in particular BN, and less so for AN. Rates of BN found in ADHD groups ranged from 1% to 12%, versus 0% to 2% in control groups. Chapter 27 was strongly and significantly associated with lifetime BN, BED but not with AN or subthreshold BED, and that even after adjusting for demographic variables and psychiatric comorbidities, all associations of lifetime ADHD with eating disorders were substantially attenuated. Only the association of ADHD with BN remained statistically significant [11]. A systematic review highlighted significantly raised prevalence rates of ASD in eating disorder populations, especially AN with typical autistic eating behaviours like selective eating, compared with those in healthy control participants [12]. Moreover, these diagnoses can make treatments challenging, and adjustments to treatments should be made to suit the particular characteristics of these patients [13]. This requires taking into account that the ASD patient may require adjustments to how a treatment is delivered and how it may affect the expression of their eating disorder. In ADHD pharmacological treatments can have a major impact on appetite and eating which is also important to keep in mind. Moreover, these medications, when taken in the first trimester, may increase the risks for fetal cardiac malformations and therefore may be contraindicated. A careful risk-benefit analysis needs to be undertaken (see Chapter 26, 'Principles of Prescribing' and Chapter 27, 'The Reproductive Safety of Psychotropic Medication and Implications for Prescribing in the Perinatal Period').

Physical health problems also frequently co-occur and can be life-threatening, and in general the risks of morbidity and mortality are similar in the perinatal period to outside of the perinatal period [14]. Medical complications among individuals with AN and BN typically arise as an effect of starvation and purging, respectively, and conversely, metabolic syndrome is associated with BED, secondary to a raised BMI and obesity as in the general population. Numerous studies indicate that AN and BN can both have an adverse impact on skin, hair, teeth and bone health, as well as contribute to bone marrow, hepatic, cardiac, renal, reproductive system and endocrine disturbances [15]. During pregnancy the risk of gestational diabetes is also elevated, which increases the risk of maternal and perinatal mortality [16].

Although many of the physical complications seen among individuals with eating disorders can be effectively treated with improvements in nutrition, weight normalisation and ceasing of purging behaviours, they can in some instances be fatal if they are achieved too fast. The most critical impact on physical health is severe electrolyte disturbances including hyponatremia and hypokalaemia, often caused by excessive purging, which can result in life-threatening complications including seizures and cardiac arrhythmias [15].

Among all psychiatric disorders AN has the highest mortality rate, and although approximately half of all deaths are attributable to physical health complications, the risk of suicide is also elevated – approximately 50% of all deaths among individuals with AN are attributable to suicide [17, 18]. Suicide attempts in this group are also more likely to involve more violent methods, for example hanging or jumping, similar to those who die from suicide during the perinatal period [19, 20]. In BN, the risk of mortality from suicide is similar to the general population, but the rate of non-fatal suicide attempts is increased [21, 22]. Purging eating disorder subtypes have higher mortality risk when there is a history of child abuse, post-traumatic stress disorder, substance misuse, lower BMI, psychiatric comorbidities as well as a history of non-suicidal deliberate self-harm behaviours [23, 24].

Presentation, Course and Outcome during the Perinatal Period

The presentation of eating disorders during the perinatal period is comparable to other times. However, pregnancy is a unique opportunity for diagnosis and treatment of eating disorders, and there are specific implications and consequences in the perinatal period that should guide management and treatment during this time.

Pre-conception

Eating disorders can cause disruptions to a woman's menstrual cycle, ovulation and fertility, such as increasing the chance of amenorrhea or oligomenorrhea, reduction in uterine and ovarian size as well as in the endometrium lining [24, 25, 26]. Substantial weight loss is associated with reduced levels of luteinising hormone and follicle-stimulating hormone, and hormonal changes and irregular menstrual cycles have been observed across the spectrum of eating disorders.

Despite this, several studies have indicated no differences in the rate of pregnancy, fertility and infertility among women with eating disorders compared to the general population [24]. However, conflicting findings exist and some studies have found eating disorders to be common in women seeking fertility treatment, with reports of 16.7% and 20.7% of women attending fertility clinics meeting criteria for an eating disorder, and 58% among women who were diagnosed with amenorrhea or oligomenorrhea [27, 28]. Furthermore, polycystic ovarian syndrome (PCOS) is a common cause of fertility problems. Up to 75% of women with BN have been found to have polycystic ovaries, and PCOS is also associated with BED [29, 30].

A large prospective birth cohort in the UK found that women with a history of AN and BN were more likely to seek help for a fertility-related problem and took longer to conceive compared to the general population; nevertheless the majority of women with eating disorders in this study conceived within 1 year [25].

Conversely, several large studies have demonstrated a high rate of unplanned pregnancies, among both women with AN and BN, potentially due to misconceptions about their fertility [25, 31, 32]. Unplanned pregnancies may lead to poorer pre-conception and early antenatal health and behaviours, as well as delayed antenatal care, increasing the risk of adverse pregnancy and birth outcomes for mother and child. These findings highlight the importance of discussions about contraceptive methods, family planning and pre-conception health, particularly for women who are experiencing menstrual disturbances [24].

The Antenatal Period

Although few studies have investigated the prevalence of eating disorders during pregnancy, a recent systematic review estimated the prevalence of all eating disorder classifications to be around 5% and up to 7.5% [33, 34]. However, there is a notable scarcity of research in pregnant populations from non-Western, and low- and middle-income countries. A large study of 77,267 women from the Norwegian Mother and Child Cohort (MoBa) found 4.8% of women had an eating disorder in early pregnancy, the majority of whom met criteria for BED [35]. A UK study of women attending their first antenatal appointment indicated that 7.5% of women met diagnostic criteria for an eating disorder when self-reported [33]. Similarly, most women in this study reported EDNOS (5%) or BED (1.8%), and AN and BN were found to occur less frequently during pregnancy (0.5% and 0.1%, respectively). More recently, findings from a study in South-East London reported rates of active eating disorders in early pregnancy to be much lower when using a clinical diagnostic interview (1.5%). However, approximately 15% of the women in this sample had experienced an eating disorder at some point in their lifetime [36]. These findings emphasise that although active eating disorder symptoms during pregnancy are relatively uncommon, a significant proportion of women will have a history of an eating disorder, which may also have several implications for maternal and infant health [33, 36].

During pregnancy, many women report an improvement in eating disorder–related symptoms and behaviours. The MoBa study found remission rates in pregnancy of between 29% and 78% across the eating disorder categories. Notably, continuation rates of BED were considerably higher, with 61% of women continuing to experience BED during their pregnancy [4, 35]. Despite the general reduction in eating disorder symptoms during pregnancy, they typically remain higher than healthy control groups, and women who have previously recovered from an eating disorder may have an increased risk of relapse during pregnancy [37, 38]. Depression and anxiety are frequent comorbidities for women with eating disorders, which tend to remain elevated throughout the perinatal period [38, 39].

Remission rates during pregnancy are thought to be driven by three potential mechanisms: psychological, which includes maternal responsibility for recovery, changes in perception of body image during pregnancy, and a separation of pregnancy from their eating disorder; social, including greater social support from family and friends; and biological, for example via neuroendocrine changes such as increased levels of dehydroe piandrosterone [24]. Greater understanding of these factors can help inform the perinatal needs of women with eating disorders and emphasises the importance of a multidisciplinary approach that does not solely focus on a women's weight or eating behaviours.

Pregnancy and Birth Outcomes

Eating disorders during pregnancy have been associated with several adverse birth outcomes [40, 41]. However, the risk of different complications of pregnancy can vary considerably across the eating disorder spectrum and according to the duration and severity of symptoms during pregnancy. A recent systematic review found that eating disorders were associated with preterm birth in 36% of the studies identified and small for gestational age in 63% of studies. In particular, AN is associated with an increased risk of a low birthweight baby, particularly when a woman has low BMI and poor gestational weight gain during pregnancy. These findings may be further moderated by increased rates of smoking during pregnancy among women with eating disorders. Conversely, BED is more likely to be associated with large-for-gestational-age babies [40]. There is some evidence to suggest that BN may increase the risk of miscarriage among women who are symptomatic during pregnancy [40].

Evidence is lacking to determine whether these relationships are causal, although birth outcomes do appear to be more adversely affected among women with more severe symptoms and those for whom the eating disorder remains active during pregnancy. Furthermore, 36–39% of women with AN and around 59% of women with BN have an increased risk of antenatal depression [32, 39, 42, 43]. Given the high proportion of women who will experience comorbid depression or anxiety during their pregnancy, the role of antenatal stress is likely to play an important role [38].

Studies have shown greater and faster gestational weight gain among women with eating disorders. This also varies by eating disorder type and women with BN and BED have been observed to gain more weight during pregnancy compared to women without eating disorders. Although gestational weight gain may be protective against adverse obstetric outcomes for women with AN, those with BN and BED may be at risk of excessive gestational weight gain or gestational diabetes [35].

The Postnatal Period

The postnatal period is often considered a vulnerable time for mothers with eating disorders, and resurgence of eating disorder–related symptoms and behaviours is not uncommon [38, 40]. Women with AN in particular describe the loss of their pregnancy identity and postnatal weight retention as triggering a relapse of symptoms following birth [44]. However, some studies have indicated that remission rates observed during pregnancy can persist into the postpartum period. The Norwegian MoBa study found that remission rates in women diagnosed with an eating disorder in early pregnancy at 18 months were 50% for AN, 39% for BN, 46% for EDNOS (purging disorders) and 45% for BED [35]. Continuation or relapse of symptoms appears to be more common in clinical samples compared to general population samples, suggesting that women with more severe symptoms may be more likely to experience postpartum illness. In addition, women with eating disorders have heightened risk of postnatal depression and anxiety, compared to women without eating disorders. There is a risk of postnatal depression (PND) and anxiety of 40–46% and a third of women with BN have been found to develop PND, a risk similar to women with major depressive disorder without an eating disorder [32, 42, 43].

Maternal eating disorders have been found to impact on maternal–infant attachment, infant feeding, mealtime interactions and infant growth trajectories [45, 46]. Mealtimes may be a difficult time for mothers with eating disorders, with higher levels of mealtime conflicts and control over their child's food intake reported. Maternal eating disorders may increase the infant's exposure to critical attitudes towards weight and shape, food intake and eating patterns, and increase the risk of early childhood eating problems and disordered eating and body image in later childhood and adolescence.

These findings highlight the changes in eating disorder presentations many women experience during pregnancy. This is commonly echoed by the descriptions that women use to describe their transition to motherhood, and it's important to be aware and recognise the qualitative experiences of women during the perinatal period [44].

- During the first trimester, women often make statements such as 'I feel too sick to eat', 'I feel too fat', 'I can't look at myself', 'I feel huge and nothing fits me anymore', 'I cannot stop vomiting and medication just doesn't work', 'I cannot look at myself or touch my body, even in the shower', 'I can't stand my husband touching the bump or me!', 'I feel out of control of my eating and emotions', 'I don't feel connected with my baby.'

- In the second and third trimesters, some women adapt to their feelings and weight gain but continue to express negative feelings about their weight or pregnancy body image: 'people keep commenting on my big baby which makes me feel like a whale', 'the baby is a good reason for my weight and my shape', 'I can cope with that [weight] as I am pregnant', 'I need this baby out as I cannot cope any more with the way I look or how people keep wanting to touch my bump.'

In the postnatal period, especially in the early weeks, it is frequent to hear: 'I look awful', 'I look disgustingly fat', 'I still look like I'm pregnant', 'the only thing I think about is my weight and my body being deformed', 'my mind keeps telling me to restrict food' or 'to get rid of the food after I eat', 'I worry about my body weight and eating never getting into control.' During pregnancy, some women express concerns that 'they are afraid they will go back to their previous eating disorder behaviours and concerns', in particular in the postnatal period when 'the baby is safe outside' and they feel they 'can't cope with how they look and feel any longer'.

Assessment in the Perinatal Period

One of the challenges in the assessment of eating disorders in the perinatal period is identifying women at risk and women who are already unwell but not under the care of mental health services. Healthcare professionals often assume that women with eating disorders do not get pregnant and have little training or knowledge about eating disorders and their consequences [47, 48]. Women with eating disorders frequently do not disclose their mental illness diagnosis or symptoms during antenatal maternity assessments. Therefore, the illness might go unnoticed until the presentation becomes obvious or there are concerns about fetal growth and development. There are occasions where the eating disorder concerns are only raised in crisis situations, that is, women presenting with fainting, arrhythmias, chest pain or shortness of breath, after physical causes were excluded.

Identification of Eating Disorders

Assessment for the presence of an eating disorder is essential and should be part of the mandatory training for maternity staff. It is important to screen for hyperemesis gravidarum and for eating disorders and to recognise that symptoms of one may be misattributed to the other.

The first sign that a woman is suffering from an eating disorder can be severe hyperemesis, which does not respond to usual treatment. This can be a hyperemesis gravidarum or part of an eating disorder, purging subtype or a mixture of both. In eating disorder patients, the hyperemesis seems frequently more severe and persistent. Severe hyperemesis gravidarum can lead to low mood, exhaustion and even to women considering or terminating a pregnancy, so it is very important to assess if present, its likely cause and severity, and to treat appropriately and aggressively, by general practitioners (GPs) and/or obstetricians. This can help exclude vomiting as a symptom of an eating disorder plus reduce frequency of vomiting if part of hyperemesis gravidarum.

There are different ways of screening for the presence of an eating disorder. The SCOFF questionnaire is easy and quick to use in clinical practice, consisting of five questions with yes or no answers [49]:

- Do you make yourself **S**ick because you feel uncomfortably full?
- Do you worry you have lost **C**ontrol over how much you eat?
- Have you recently lost more than **O**ne stone (6 kg) in 3 months (or less)? (Holding in consideration that there is a fetus and associated expected weight gain per trimester, and pre-pregnancy weight. See below)
- Do you believe yourself to be **F**at when others say you are too thin?
- Would you say that **F**ood dominates your life?

One point is assigned for every 'yes' response, and a score of two or more indicates a likely case of AN or BN and it can also be an indication of a BED.

The Eating Disorder Examination Questionnaire is a well- established self-report questionnaire widely used which is easy to administer and can identify people with an eating disorder [50]. It can also be used for monitoring and outcome purposes. In case of a positive screening this can be administered to confirm.

In cases where initial assessment is indicative of an eating disorder, a referral to the local eating disorder service for further assessment and treatment should be completed as soon as possible in the perinatal period.

The care should then be shared between the eating disorders, perinatal and maternity service antenatally, and with GP/health visiting services postnatally. In cases where the patient declines initial referral to the specialist service, maternity, GP and health visiting services should liaise with the local eating disorder and/or perinatal mental health services for advice and recommendations and continue to offer referral to the specialist service(s). Who will lead the care should be decided on a case-by-case basis, depending on the multiple diagnoses if they exist, and their severity and impact on health and functioning. A multidisciplinary approach is usually the most appropriate. A referral to a dietician, preferably a specialist in eating disorders, may be helpful in some cases. It is also recommended that a named obstetrician and a caseload midwife, as well an enhanced health visitor, are nominated for women with perinatal eating disorders [51, 52]. Given the high risk of antenatal and postnatal depression and anxiety, women with eating disorders should be assessed by the perinatal mental health service for these risks, monitored if high risk and treated as required as per usual care.

Assessment

The assessment of eating disorders in the perinatal period contains the elements that would exist for the non-pregnant/breastfeeding woman. However, there is the need to also bear in mind the welfare of the fetus/infant and the maternal–fetal/infant relationship. The assessment will consist of history taking, physical examination and investigations and all results together inform the assessment of severity, risk and the care plan (see below). Maternity services need to complete a thorough assessment regarding the pregnancy as per usual care, with extra monitoring as addressed below. It is also essential, for joint eating disorders and perinatal care, having the fetus/infant in mind and understanding the implications of the eating disorder as well as any other comorbidity, for their biopsychosocial development, particularly around feeding, eating habits and behaviours.

The history should include questions about:

- Current symptoms: weight variation and how quickly they occurred, eating habits, for example rules for eating, typical daily food and fluid intake and self-perception of body and checking behaviour, for example ideal weight, avoiding mirrors, checking for fat, etc.
- Compensatory behaviours: including purging, SIV, abuse of tablets like laxatives or diuretics, and exercise regimen.
- Comorbidities and specialist assessment/treatment if required. However, note that screening for ASD or ADHD should take place once the treatment of the ED or other illnesses (e.g. depression) have been successful, as pharmacological treatment for ADHD can lead to deterioration of other untreated or unstable mental illnesses.
- Feeding and bonding with the unborn/newborn, expectations of pregnancy and motherhood, and wider support available for mother and infant. Insight into the possible impact any illness and comorbidities may have during gestation, and both short- and long-term outcomes for the offspring, including around nutrition of the child (e.g. breastfeeding and later socialisation around food).
- Physical examination: current height, weight and BMI and past highest and lowest weight as well as pre-pregnancy weight.

For women with mild symptoms or women refusing referral to the eating disorder service, follow-up questions in each review to monitor severity of the eating disorder should include:

- What is your current eating pattern and has it changed from previously?
- Are you restricting your dietary intake?
- Do you binge? (Eating an excessive number of calories in a short period of time, e.g. 1–2 hours)?
- Do you induce vomiting/vomit or take laxatives after eating?
- Do you feel exceedingly concerned about your shape or weight?
- What is your weight? Are you gaining weight appropriately? Are you losing more than 1 kg/week?
- What exercises are you doing? For how long? How often?
- What is your mood like? Do you feel anxious about food or feel that eating dominates your life?

Physical examination and investigations are essential to pick up signs of a more severe eating disorder or raise concerns of one when denied. Some of the signs include alopecia or thin hair, lanugo hair, ankle swelling, high sensitivity to cold even in pregnancy, jaundice, dental erosion and parotid hypertrophy. Blood pressure (BP), pulse, temperature and respiratory rate along with weight and BMI calculation should be conducted weekly in moderate/severe cases. Please see Table 16.1 for an interpretation of results relating to risk severity.

The danger signs of high risk of death in eating disorders are [53]:

- Rapid weight loss (>1 kg/week) and BMI <13 or food refusal or intake <400 Kcal/day (adjusting for pregnancy, especially after the first trimester, even if with hyperemesis gravidarum, weight reduction of more than 1–2% for normal weight women or BMI reduction by 0.2–0.5 points for women who started underweight pre-pregnancy requires addressing assertively).

Table 16.1 Assessing medical risks in eating disorders, including during pregnancy

	Investigation	Moderate risk	High risk	Physiological changes in pregnancy
Nutrition	BMI	**<14 kg/m^2**	**<12 kg/m^2**	(Refer to Table 16.2)
	Weight loss/week	**>0.5 kg**	**>1.0 kg**	-
	Skin breakdown	**<0.1 cm**	**>0.2 cm**	-
	Purpuric rash		*	-
Circulation	Systolic BP	**<90**	**<80**	**↓ in 1st/2nd T but Normal in 3rd T**
	Diastolic BP	**<70**	**<60**	**↓ in 1st/2nd T but Normal in 3rd T**
	Postural drop (sit – stand) mmHg	**>10**	**>20**	**<5–10 Sys and > up to 15 DYAS from mid 2nd T and normalises end of pregnancy**
	Pulse Rate/min	**<50**	**<40**	**↑ until 28/40**
Musculo-skeletal (Squat Test and Sit up test)	Difficulty to get up without using arms for balance or as leverage	*		**Possible from mid 2nd/3rd T**
	Unable to get up without using arms for balance or as leverage		*	**Possible from 3rd T**
Temperature		**<35 °C**	**<34.5 °C**	**↑↑**
Bone Marrow	WCC	**<4.0**	**<2.0**	**↑ 15–18x10^3/l**
	Neutrophil count	**<1.5**	**<1.0**	**↑**
	Hb	**<11**	**<9.0**	**↓Hb to 100–115, Htc, RCC**
	Acute Hb drop (↑MCV & MCH no acute risk)		*	**Progressive drop Hb, N MCV & MCHC**
	Platelets	**<130**	**<110**	**↓ but within normal values**
Salt /water balance	K+	**<3.5**	**<3.0**	**↓ until 3rd T ↓↓ if hyperemesis ↑↑ in 3rd T**
	Na+	**<135**	**<130**	**↓ from 10–28/40 ↑ from 28–37/40**
	Mg++	**0.5–0.7**	**<0.5**	**↓ 3rd T, raise labour**
	Phosphate	**0.5–0.8**	**<0.5**	**↓ 3rd T, raise labour**
	Urea	**>7**	**>10**	**< value 3.2 (also creatinine value to 44)**
Liver	Bilirubin	**>20**	**>40**	**↓ all T**
	Alkpase	**>110**	**>200**	**↑ from 2nd T**
	AsT	**>40**	**>80**	**N**
	ALT	**>45**	**>90**	**N**
	GGT	**>45**	**>90**	**↓ from 2nd T**

Table 16.1 *(cont.)*

	Investigation	Moderate risk	High risk	Physiological changes in pregnancy
Nutrition	Albumin Creatinine Kinase Glucose	**<35** **>170** **<3.5**	**<32** **>250** **<2.5**	**↓ (progressive to 3T)** **↑** **↑ if GDM (from 28/40) or N** **↓ HbA1c in 2nd & ↑ 3rd T**
ECG (if BMI<15, low K+, drugs prolonging QTC prescribed)	Pulse rate Corrected QT interval (QTC) arrhythmias	**<50**	**<40** **>450 msec** *	↑ left-axis shift of QRS **Due to changes of position of heart, it's possible to have:** • atrial and ventricular ectopics • Q wave (small) and inverted T wave in lead III • ST-segment depression and T-wave inversion in the inferior and lateral leads
Thyroid	TSH/T3/T4			**↓ 1st T/↓/↓ (up to 20%)**
Cholesterol	Total	↑↑	↑↑↑	**↑ up to 40%**
Vitamin D	Check if on supplements	↓	↓↓	↓

Source: Table adapted and modified by Dr Acosta, from Treasure, J. (2009) *A guide to the medical risk assessment for eating disorders.* Accessed via https://shorturl.at/Gq7Hr
Notes:

- *Any abnormal result is an indication for concern, monitoring and consultation/referral to specialist eating disorders service.
- Obtaining measurements pre-pregnancy or as early as possible in pregnancy is essential to be able to accurately assess risk.
- Baseline values for these tests may vary between labs.
- A tachycardia in the presence of signs and investigations of severe risk may be an indication of imminent cardiovascular collapse.

- Blood investigation abnormalities: low potassium, sodium, phosphate and glucose; low Hb (haemoglobin), WCC (white cell count) and platelets; significantly raised LFTs (liver function tests).
- Difficulty arising from squat, without using arms as levers (adjusting for the fact that in mid to late pregnancy this might not be possible for most women).
- Hypothermia, bradycardia, low blood pressure, dizziness, fainting, arrhythmias.
- Petechial rash, ulcers, cramps, seizures, tetany, coma.

It is important to understand what the woman's baseline measurements in relation to the above are pre-pregnancy. For example, when a woman with an eating disorder is chronically hypotensive when non-pregnant the finding of 'normal' blood pressure in pregnancy may indicate that her blood pressure is in fact raised and she should therefore be monitored for pre-eclampsia. Similarly, when someone has chronic low WCC and neutrophils, in pregnancy she may only reach a normal range WCC and neutrophils and not have these indices raised as would be expected in pregnancy (see Chapter 3, 'Physiological Changes in Pregnancy and Common Obstetric Medical Disorders').

Investigations

- At assessment, primary care or maternity services or psychiatric services if already involved, should request a set of investigations, as below. This will speed up the process of full assessment including physical risk when seen by the specialist services.
  - ✓ Bone Marrow: Full Blood Count
  - ✓ Salt and water balance: U&E, Magnesium and Phosphate
  - ✓ Liver: LFT, Bilirubin, GGT, Alkaline phosphate
  - ✓ Nutrition: albumin, CK, Glucose, HbA1C
  - ✓ Others: Lipid and bone profiles, amylase, TFT, ESR, CRP, vitamin B12 and folate
  - ✓ Iron
  - ✓ Coeliac disease screen if not previously done
  - ✓ 12 lead ECG when BMI is <16 or regular and moderate to severe purging

It is helpful to request investigations when the woman screens positive for an eating disorder or at referral, so the eating disorder service can review results and provide a full treatment plan on assessment, in order to save valuable time. It is important to bear in mind, and liaise with the obstetrician when required, that biochemistry and normal reference values change throughout pregnancy (see Table 16.1), whilst also remembering that obstetricians may not be familiar with changes that occur in an eating disorder patient. Liaison between services is essential.

The same can be said for BMI/weight, so it is important to have a pre-pregnancy weight or early pregnancy weight, to compare it to subsequent weight measurements during pregnancy. During a normal pregnancy, a 9–12 kg weight increase is to be expected, and for women with a weight below normal (i.e. below 18.5 kg) to have an increase between 12 and 15 kg (see Table 16.2). One can use BMI as a reference for monitoring, comparing it to pre-pregnancy BMI although one cannot rely on its values of normalcy during pregnancy as the fetus and all maternal physiological changes need to be taken in consideration as well. Psychiatrists need to be guided by and regularly liaise with maternity services and vice versa, including for obstetric ultrasound scans to monitor fetal growth. If there is normal fetal growth, but no maternal weight increase, one must assume that the mother is losing weight.

Several studies [54, 55, 56, 57, 58] have recommendations for ideal weight gain in pregnancy – see Table 16.2 for a consensus based on the different studies and practical experience. It is important to remember that insufficient weight gain as well as excess weight gain can have implications for pregnancy outcomes, delivery and fetal and infant growth and well-being; for example, too little weight gain can increase the risk of premature delivery and small babies that may require special care/NICU, and too much weight gain in pregnancy can come with complications including birth trauma, sometimes with fetal injury, or gestational diabetes, which increases the risk of stillbirth, for example.

Table 16.2 Recommendations for total and rate of weight gain during pregnancy, by pre-pregnancy BMI. Adapted from recommendation of several studies [55, 56, 57, 58]

Pre-pregnancy BMI (weight (kg)^2/height (cm))	Total weight gain		Rate of weight gain in 1st trimester		Rates of weight gain in 2nd and 3rd trimester	
	Range in kg	Range in lbs	Range in kg	Range in lbs	Range in kg	Range in lbs
Underweight (<18.5 kg/m^2)	12.5–18	28–40	0.5–2 kg (1.1–4.4 lbs) (if this is less or more, the weight gain in 2nd and 3rd trimesters will need to be adjusted accordingly)		0.51 (0.44–0.58)	1 (1–1.3)
Normal weight (18.5–24.9 kg/m^2)	11.5–16	25–35			0.42 (0.35–0.50)	1 (0.8–1)
Overweight (25.0–29.9 kg/m^2)	7–11.5	15–25			0.28 (0.23–0.33)	0.6 (0.5–0.7)
Obese (≥30.0 kg/m^2)	5–9	11–20			0.22 (0.17–0.27)	0.5 (0.4–0.6)

The frequency of investigations depends on the initial severity and ongoing deterioration or improvement of symptoms and weight; for example, weekly in severe cases to monthly in milder cases, and daily in very severe cases (e.g. inpatients in a specialist eating disorder unit or maternity setting with eating disorder service input ideally).

In BED and if there is an associated diabetes mellitus type 2, closer monitoring of blood sugars is essential. If there are no comorbidities, monitoring should be regular and screening for gestational diabetes mellitus should be completed before the usual 28 weeks' gestation.

Guidance for Eating Disorder Services

It is recommended that eating disorder services should prioritise women during the perinatal period for assessment and treatment as much as possible, given the impact on fetal growth and development which may be significantly impacted by delays in interventions. If an eating disorder service is not involved, it is important to make sure there is a designated service, usually the GP, that will routinely check blood results and address abnormalities. In our view, perinatal women with eating disorders should be considered and treated as a priority by all services involved, given the risks to both mother and fetus/infant, the time constraints associated with pregnancy and infant development and to maximise the opportunity to reduce, if not stop, the intergenerational transmission of illness. Joint working and early intervention are often dependent on local service arrangements, but in our clinical experience a good conversation between eating disorder services, perinatal and maternity, with GP and health visiting involvement locally, can be helpful in setting local guidance for joint care, until national guidance can be developed.

Additional recommendations for universal services in monitoring the fetus/infant/child include:

- Maternity – regular growth ultrasound scans of fetus
- Health visitor/GP – regularly monitor growth of the baby/child, with close monitoring of quantity and quality of food intake

- For all, monitoring of eating disorders requires regular weight and BMI measurement, physical examination and blood investigations as outlined above

The severity of eating disorders is based on several criteria, including symptoms, physical examination and investigation results, including obstetric scans if no other causes for abnormalities are found by maternity, which in our experience are frequently forgotten. Treatment and monitoring frequency are based on severity. The reference values below apply to pregnancy, although for AN they are not pregnancy specific. A BMI of greater than 17–18 is required for fetal growth. Those with BMI below 15 are unlikely to conceive.

It is important to keep in mind that it can take at least 6 months post-delivery for the woman's weight and shape to return to pre-pregnancy levels, although in AN and BN weight loss can happen more quickly, that is, within a few weeks if women are relapsing or worsening postnatally. Weight gain in binge eating can also be quicker during the postnatal period. Nevertheless, BMI is a good guide for the severity of the eating disorder in the perinatal period. By comparing values in the same patient across time, it informs future risks and guides follow-up and monitoring. Pre-pregnancy or early pregnancy weight should be used as a reference to guide assessment and monitoring, and recording weight at the end of and post-delivery is essential for comparison purposes in the postnatal period. Guidance is summarised in Box 16.1, including for the other types of eating disorders.

Risks and Risk Assessment

A frequent risk for women with eating disorders in the perinatal period is that of deterioration or relapse. This risk is higher in the postnatal period, as during pregnancy the woman may feel protective towards her baby and in general be more motivated to maintain healthy behaviours. Other risks include antenatal and postnatal depression,

Box 16.1 Indicators of Disorder Severity

AN and monitoring of BMI (pre-pregnancy):

- *Mild:* BMI > 17
- *Moderate:* BMI 15.6–16.9
- *Severe:* BMI 13.6–15.5
- *Very severe:* BMI < 13.5

BN and monitoring of the number of episodes of inappropriate compensatory behaviours, for example SIV or abuse of tablets:

- *Mild:* average of 1–3 episodes per week
- *Moderate:* An average of 4–7 episodes per week
- *Severe:* An average of 8–13 episodes per week
- *Very severe:* An average of 14 or more episodes per week

BED and monitoring of number of binge-eating episodes:

- *Mild:* 1–3 episodes per week
- *Moderate:* 4–7 episodes per week
- *Severe:* 8–13 episodes per week
- *Very severe:* 14 or more episodes per week

Box 16.2 Physical Risks of Eating Disorders

- Compromised immune system with increased risk of infections in patients with low weight or BMI
- Electrolyte imbalances that can lead to cerebral oedema or cardiac arrhythmias
- Refeeding syndrome in patients with very little or no food intake (over 10 days) before restarting eating
- Metabolic syndrome in BED and some BN patients (with long-term physical comorbidities such as diabetes mellitus or hyperlipidaemias)

anxiety, and death by suicide and alcohol-related illnesses, which are more common in AN and BN respectively [39].

Box 16.2 summarises the physical risks including the risk of death.

Therefore, the risk assessment needs to include not only assessment of the mental health risks to self (i.e. deliberate self-harm or suicide), but also an assessment of neglect of nutrition or abuse of substances, for example:

- assess the rapidity of the onset of illness and weight loss
- the duration of the eating disorder
- food consumed in the last 2 weeks to assess the risk of refeeding syndrome
- frequency of purging behaviours and any associated complications like haematemesis, erosions in mouth, frequency of diarrhoea and possible dehydration

Routine regular blood investigations are important and need to be repeated along with an ECG if there are any sudden changes in presentation, for example:

- onset of chest pains or shortness of breath
- increase/cessation in SIV
- onset of severe diarrhoea (abuse of laxatives, that can lead to water and electrolyte imbalance)

In such circumstances it is frequently recommended that the patient is sent to A&E, medical or maternity assessment units, for assessment and treatment as required. The referral needs to contain the important information about the case as above and clearly stated concerns in case of poor awareness by A&E staff of eating disorders and their complications.

Refeeding Syndrome Risk

Refeeding syndrome can be very serious and is more frequent in women with very low weight, when starting to eat again. There is a high risk of rapid deterioration of the physical health that can ultimately lead to death. It is therefore essential to regularly monitor electrolytes namely phosphate, magnesium and potassium for early detection and correction of abnormalities. Refeeding syndrome can start within 4 days and up to 2 weeks after the patient starts refeeding. The alert symptoms include:

- muscle weakness
- low blood pressure
- increased heart rate
- shortness of breath
- palpitations

Box 16.3 Risk Factors for Refeeding Syndrome

- BMI below 16, or 3 BMI points lower than previously in pregnancy
- very low food intake in the previous 10 days
- weight loss of more than 15% of total body weight in the past 3–6 months, 2 months if pregnant
- low WCC, which in pregnancy can be normal/lower side of normal WCC
- low potassium, phosphate and magnesium

- swelling
- abdominal pain
- neurological symptoms like confusion or seizures

The risk factors for refeeding syndrome are show in Box 16.3.

More severe cases, or acute deteriorations, should be monitored and treated by specialist services (medical and eating disorders), but it is important to recognise the following important clinical signs and how to manage abnormalities [54]:

- *Potassium* is often chronically low in purging patients, with no immediate consequence. However, acute changes in purging behaviour can lead to rapid changes in potassium levels. Regular feeding, with control of purging, is usually enough to correct this. If replacement is required it is best given as an oral rehydration solution. Regular monitoring of fluid and water status should include lying and standing blood pressure measurement. Refractory hypokalaemia can occur due to concurrent low magnesium or calcium, and this should be rectified. If vomiting persists, potassium can remain low, and a proton pump inhibitor may reduce metabolic alkalosis and help to conserve potassium.
- Rebound *hypophosphatemia* can occur in the initial refeeding because of the sequestrated carbohydrate metabolism, and can be fatal. Therefore, in initial refeeding it is important to include foods with high phosphate content, for example milk-based products, >2 pints a day. If necessary oral phosphate supplements can be prescribed for about 4 days alongside 10 days of thiamine.
- *Multivitamin and mineral deficiencies are frequent in restrictive illnesses*, so it is recommended to prescribe a multivitamin and mineral tablet during the whole pregnancy and breastfeeding period, and possibly even longer. In certain cases, it is also worth increasing it to two a day for a period if the restriction is severe or the variety of foods consumed is poor.
- *Refeeding oedema* is common and can be harmless, resolving spontaneously in a few weeks, but should be assessed to differentiate from oedema secondary to heart failure.

Care and Treatment during the Perinatal Period

Treatment for eating disorders is most effective when received early and should ideally be provided prior to pregnancy. Women with active eating disorders wishing to conceive should be advised to postpone pregnancy until they have received specialist treatment for their disorder and are largely recovered. Screening and treatment for abuse of laxatives, appetite suppressants, diuretics or any other tablets which may be harmful in pregnancy, should always be considered.

Women with eating disorders planning to conceive should be offered the opportunity within pre-conception services to receive advice and education about body changes, cravings, the possibility of hyperemesis gravidarum, expected weight gain in pregnancy and nutritional requirements during pregnancy. During pregnancy and postnatally, women with a past history of eating disorders should also be informed of their nutritional needs, risk factors and be monitored for signs of relapse and any comorbidities by maternity, primary care and perinatal mental health services.

During pregnancy and postnatally, eating disorder treatment depends on the specific diagnosis and the associated risks that the eating disorder poses to the patient and fetus/infant. The overall management is based on the patient's BMI, current presentation and investigation results, comorbidities (physical and mental) and past risks. More perinatal-specific recommendations are outlined below.

The gold standard treatments for eating disorders are: [51]

- psychological interventions (see below)
- occupational therapy
- specialist dietician input
- family therapy when indicated

Treatment should be delivered by specialist eating disorder service/specialists, as soon as possible after diagnosis, and preferably within the first 3 years after onset for better prognosis. The recent First Episode Rapid Early Intervention for Eating Disorders intervention is recommended for patients within 3 years of onset of illness, in a similar way to the early intervention services for psychosis. It consists of quick and easy-to-access multidisciplinary intervention, and it has been rolled out in multiple eating disorder services throughout the UK [59].

The treatment for eating disorders can be delivered, again depending on risks, in:

- medical or specialist eating disorder inpatient units (for high-risk patients)
- day-care specialist eating disorder units (for moderate risk and acute on chronic patients)
- outpatient specialist eating disorder services (for low-risk and well-engaged patients)

Evidence-based psychological interventions include: [51, 60, 61, 62]

- ➢ CBT-ED (cognitive behaviour therapy for eating disorders)
- ➢ MANTRA (Maudsley Model of Anorexia Nervosa Treatment for Adults)
- ➢ CAT (cognitive analytical therapy)
- ➢ psychodynamic psychotherapy
- ➢ family therapy when indicated

For more severe and treatment refractory cases, trials with rTMS (repetitive transcranial magnetic stimulation) show promise [63, 64], among others.

During the perinatal period, eating disorder services should prioritise women's treatment, using as per usual interventions, given the effects the disorder can have on the mother's health and fetal and infant development, offering assessment within 2 weeks and treatment within 4 weeks of referral. Ideally, women with active eating disorders should have joint care between maternity, eating disorders and perinatal mental health services and the GP/health visiting/paediatric services when required. Joint working protocols and guidance are required. Involving the husband or partner as much as possible in the care and treatment will also improve outcomes of eating disorders treatments and, postnatally, being able to see women with their infant if childcare is an issue should be facilitated.

Antenatal in Mental Health Settings

In inpatient psychiatric units, whether specialist eating disorder unit or a Mother and Baby Unit (MBU), good practice should be for services to support each other, for example women in an MBU having meals plans and catering from the eating disorder unit or mothers in the eating disorder unit having access to facilities from the MBU specifically designed for mother–baby interaction and feeding, and attending the different group and activities on each ward as appropriate. This is easier if both units are on the same hospital site, if there is cooperation between both units and joint protocols which can be tailored to individual cases. Services on different sites should be able to provide video links and guide each other's interventions and treatments remotely.

Antenatal in General Hospital Settings

Inpatient units in medical hospitals should be supported by both local community perinatal and eating disorder services. If there is a severe eating disorder with risks of refeeding syndrome antenatally, the ideal would be the antenatal maternity ward, where the mother's physical and mental health, and that of the pregnancy and fetus can be monitored. In addition, a registered medical nurse may need to be present and the Mental Health Act utilised if required. Input from the eating disorder service would address meal plans and monitoring and, with the perinatal mental health service, advise on medication if required, and on the fetal–maternal relationship.

Postnatally

If the above occurs postnatally, then it would be best for a short stay in an eating disorder inpatient unit or general hospital until there is a reduction in physical risk with subsequent transfer to an MBU with close support and intervention from the eating disorder unit as above.

If within 12 months postpartum and the eating disorder is mild to moderate, and there are other associated risks or an adjustment disorder to motherhood that would require admission, admit to an MBU; continuing engagement with the local eating disorder service for treatment of the eating disorder is recommended as is ensuring continuity of care post-discharge.

Recommendations about Weight and Nutrition in the Perinatal Period

In pregnant women with an active eating disorder, care should include recommendations for [37, 65, 66, 67, 68]:

- Desired weight gain during first, second and third trimesters as per BMI pre-pregnancy (or earliest one in pregnancy) – see Table 16.1 for details. Be aware the GP might have previous weight records as well as any previous eating disorder services/interventions the women may have been offered or engaged with.
- Close monitoring and assertive treatment of nausea and vomiting.

- Monitoring of macronutrient intake – e.g. usually less protein and fat intake in AN, which can negatively impact the neurological development of the fetus – possible dietician referral.
- Monitoring for micronutrient intake – advise the use of one multivitamin and mineral supplement tablet a day, plus extra folic acid, especially if taking other pharmacotherapy.
- Micronutrients – in severe cases it is recommended, according to presentation and investigation results to prescribe: thiamine 100 mg once a day, vitamin B compound strong one tablet three times a day, Calcichew D3 forte twice a day, and Dioralyte PRN after purging to replace potassium or use oral tablet replacement as recommended above if severe deficiency.

In breastfeeding women, it is important to [37, 65, 66, 67, 68]:

- Monitor if breastfeeding is being used to lose weight or if women are too preoccupied to breastfeed (the latter is frequently due to the severe body weight and shape concerns).
- Advise that to sustain breastfeeding an extra 500–600 kcal a day intake is required.
- Advise that restrictive food intake can affect milk quality, including volume and fat content, which may affect child outcomes, including neurological and cognitive development.
- Monitor macro and micronutrients intake and recommend continuing multivitamins and mineral supplements as during pregnancy.
- Recommend mixed feeding for women with AN, some women with BN and low BMI, instead of exclusively breastfeeding. This ensures that infant nutrition is adequate and includes all micro and macronutrients required for growth and development, independent of the mother's eating content and frequency, and moreover that the mother's own health and nutrition are not compromised by exclusively breastfeeding, particularly if she cannot increase nutrition intake during this period or until treatment is effective.
- Inform the health visitor and GP of the risks for the infant's development and recommend close monitoring of the child's growth and development. It is well known that, for example, good neurological development is dependent on fat in the diet, which is not infrequently restricted by women with eating disorders.

Psychotropic Medication

The use of psychotropic medication in the treatment of eating disorders is almost exclusively to manage comorbidities. These should be managed by the eating disorder service providing treatment, with perinatal mental health services advising on the risks and benefits in the perinatal period. Women with low BMI, particularly if below 16 kg/m^2 (higher in pregnancy), will respond poorly to low doses of medications. It is recommended that psychotropic medications doses are quickly titrated to their maximum therapeutic dose, if they are used. However, it is also important to recall that certain medications, such as paracetamol or antibiotics, may require paediatric doses according to liver function.

The recommendations for psychotropic treatment for depression, anxiety or obsessive-compulsive disorder (common comorbidities in eating disorders), are the same as those for women without eating disorders, but with higher doses as per above [69, 70].

In some cases, medication may be used to facilitate psychological treatment and feeding. Specific recommendations include [71, 72, 73]:

- In AN, olanzapine may be helpful to improve weight gain and treatment adherence, as well as to reduce psychological symptoms such as agitation, pre-meal anxiety or obsessional and abnormal beliefs. We recommend 2.5 mg at night and occasionally will titrate to 5 mg if only partial benefit at lower dose. These should be guided by the eating disorder specialist who has experience in using olanzapine for this purpose. Doses above 5 mg are not recommended.
- In BN, it is usual to prescribe the maximum doses of selective serotonin reuptake inhibitors, such as sertraline or fluoxetine, to reduce the frequency of bingeing and purging, although evidence is slim for this.
- In BEDs in the perinatal period, topiramate was previously used to help reduce binges and improve weight loss when combined with psychological treatments. However, recent Medicines and Healthcare products Regulatory Agency guidance is that this is no longer recommended [74]. There are other potential pharmacological treatments, not expanded on here as they are generally not recommended during the perinatal period and are only to be prescribed by specialist services.

For the most common physical symptoms:

- For abdominal cramps, which are common in eating disorder women, the recommendation in the perinatal period is metoclopramide rather than mebeverine, taken before meals, as it has a better safety profile in pregnancy.
- For constipation, Fybogel is first-line medication or lactulose as second line, being mindful of balancing need against possible risks for abuse.

It is also recommended that women with eating disorders should be provided with support in breastfeeding and feeding their other children, by the health visitor and GP, or even paediatrician in more severe cases, to ensure adequate nutrition.

The Role of the Perinatal Mental Health Services in Managing Eating Disorder Patients as We See It

Box 16.4 summarises the primary tasks for mental and physical health professionals and teams in assessing and managing eating disorders in the perinatal period.

Conclusion

After reading this chapter, and despite how complex and challenging eating disorders are for patients and clinicians, we hope that you:

- feel more aware and at ease to suspect, screen, discuss risks, monitor and refer on women with eating disorders that require specialist care, at any particular point in the perinatal period
- know and understand that early diagnosis and specialist treatment are crucial for better outcomes in all cases

Box 16.4 Primary Tasks for Perinatal Mental Professionals and Teams, Looking after Women with Eating Disorders during the Perinatal Period as well as Other Health Professionals

For patients with an active eating disorder who accept referral to the eating disorder service, the perinatal mental health service role is to:

- discuss antenatal and postnatal risks of relapse, diagnosis and treat any comorbidities
- recommend psychopharmacological treatment if indicated
- monitor postnatally for relapse and parent–infant difficulties and treat as required
- inform the GP and health visitor of risks to infant development
- provide maternity liaison as required

For patients with an active eating disorder who decline eating disorder referral, the perinatal mental health service role is to:

- get specialist advice from the local eating disorder service
- monitor mental state and risks and discuss perinatal risks including risks of the untreated eating disorder
- consider mental capacity and mental health act assessment if high risk
- inform the health visitor of risks to infant development and liaise with GP

For patients who decline both perinatal and eating disorder referrals and have an active eating disorder, maternity and GP role is to:

- liaise with the local perinatal and eating disorder services for advice on monitoring and management
- monitor mental state and risks throughout the perinatal period
- continue to offer referral to both services throughout pregnancy
- inform the health visitor of risks to infant development and GP to monitor

For patients who have a past eating disorder but are in remission, the perinatal mental health services should (GP or maternity should inform the perinatal service, or eating disorder service if know previous patient is now pregnant, as per yellow recommendation by MBBRACE):

- inform of perinatal risks and monitor for relapse
- monitor weight gain and fetal development (maternity to do this)
- refer to eating disorder service if signs of relapse for early intervention
- inform the health visitor/GP of potential risks to infant development

For patients who need admission to an inpatient unit, the choice of unit should depend on:

- the severity of the eating disorder, where in the perinatal journey they are and risks to mother and fetus/infant (as above)

- feel you can make recommendations for monitoring and jointly manage the pharmacological treatment of these patients with maternity, GP/health visiting and eating disorder services
- remember the importance of monitoring and treating any comorbidities even if there is an eating disorder present
- refer to safeguarding as required given that malnutrition/neglect of nutrition is a risk, and always inform GP and health visiting services of this risk for the mother as well as the infant/child/adolescent

References

1. American Psychiatric Association. *Diagnostic and statistical manual of mental disorders* (5th ed., text revision). Washington, DC: American Psychiatric Association; 2013.
2. World Health Organization. International classification of diseases for mortality and morbidity statistics (11th revision). 2018.
3. A Keski-Rahkonen, L Mustelin. Epidemiology of eating disorders in Europe: prevalence, incidence, comorbidity, course, consequences, and risk factors. *Curr Opin Psychiatry.* 2016;29(6):340–5.
4. HW Hoek. Review of the worldwide epidemiology of eating disorders. *Curr Opin Psychiatry.* 2016;29(6):336–9.
5. CM Bulik, SC Kleiman, Z Yilmaz. Genetic epidemiology of eating disorders. *Curr Opin Psychiatry.* 2016;29(6):383–8.
6. C Jacobi. Psychosocial risk factors for eating disorders. *Eat Disord Rev.* 2005; 1:59–84.
7. S Ulfvebrand, A Birgegård, C Norring, L Högdahl, Y von Hausswolff-Juhlin. Psychiatric comorbidity in women and men with eating disorders results from a large clinical database. *Psychiatry Res.* 2015;230(2):294–9.
8. A Hambleton, G Pepin, A Le, D Maloney, National Eating Disorder Research Consortium, S Touyz, S Maguire. Psychiatric and medical comorbidities of eating disorders: findings from a rapid review of the literature. *J Eat Disord.* 2022;10(1):132.
9. V Huke, J Turk, S Saeidi, A Kent, JF Morgan. Autism spectrum disorders in eating disorder populations: a systematic review. *Eur Eat Disord Rev.* 2013;21(5):345–51.
10. BP Nazar, CM Pinna, G Coutinho, D Segenreich, M Duchesne, JC Appolinario, P Mattos. Review of literature of attention-deficit/hyperactivity disorder with comorbid eating disorders. *J Braz Psychiatry.* 2008;30(4):384–9.
11. H Ziobrowski, TD Brewerton, AE Duncan. Associations between ADHD and eating disorders in relation to comorbid psychiatric disorders in a nationally representative sample. *Psychiatry Res.* 2018;260:53–9.
12. L Karjalainen, M Råstam, G Paulson-Karlsson, E Wentz. Do autism spectrum disorder and anorexia nervosa have some eating disturbances in common? *Eur Child Adolesc Psychiatry.* 2019;28(1):69–78.
13. CS Stewart, FS McEwen, A Konstantellou, I Eisler, M Simic. Impact of ASD traits on treatment outcomes of eating disorders in girls. *Eur Eat Disord Rev.* 2017;25:123–8.
14. PS Mehler, DV Blalock, K Walden, S Kaur, J McBride, K Walsh, et al. Medical findings in 1,026 consecutive adult inpatient–residential eating disordered patients. *Int J Eat Disord.* 2018;51(4):305–13.
15. U Voderholzer, V Haas, CU Correll, T Körner. Medical management of eating disorders: an update. *Curr Opin Psychiatry.* 2020;33(6):542–53.
16. MS Linna, A Raevuori, J Haukka, JM Suvisaari, JT Suokas, M Gissler. Pregnancy, obstetric, and perinatal health outcomes in eating disorders. *Am J Obstet Gynecol.* 2014;211(4):392.e1–e8.
17. PF Sullivan. Mortality in anorexia nervosa. *Am J Psychiatry.* 1995;152(7):1073–4.
18. M Pompili, I Mancinelli, P Girardi, A Ruberto, R Tatarelli. Suicide in anorexia nervosa: a meta-analysis. *Int J Eat Disord.* 2004;36(1):99–103.
19. M Knight, K Bunch, D Tuffnell, H Jayakody, J Shakespeare, R Kotnis, et al., editors. *Saving Lives, Improving Mothers' Care – Lessons learned to inform maternity care from the UK and Ireland Confidential Enquiries into Maternal Deaths and Morbidity 2014–16.* Oxford: National Perinatal Epidemiology Unit, University of Oxford; 2018.
20. M Knight, K Bunch, D Tuffnell, J Shakespeare, R Kotnis, S Kenyon, JJ

Kurinczuk, et al., editors. *Saving Lives, Improving Mothers' Care – Lessons learned to inform maternity care from the UK and Ireland Confidential Enquiries into Maternal Deaths and Morbidity 2015–17*. Oxford: National Perinatal Epidemiology Unit, University of Oxford; 2019.

21. S Guillaume, I Jaussent, E Olie, C Genty, J Bringer, P Courtet, et al. Characteristics of suicide attempts in anorexia and bulimia nervosa: a case–control study. *PLoS ONE*. 2011;6(8):e23578.

22. DL Franko, PK Keel. Suicidality in eating disorders: occurrence, correlates, and clinical implications. *Clin Psychol Rev*. 2006;26(6):769–82.

23. K Kostro, JB Lerman, E Attia. The current status of suicide and self-injury in eating disorders: a narrative review. *J Eat Disord*. 2014;2(1):19.

24. M Kimmel, E Ferguson, S Zerwas, C Bulik, S Meltzer-Brody. Obstetric and gynecologic problems associated with eating disorders. *Int J Eat Disord*. 2016;49(3):260–75.

25. A Easter, J Treasure, N Micali. Fertility and prenatal attitudes towards pregnancy in women with eating disorders: results from the Avon Longitudinal Study of Parents and Children. *BJOG*. 2011;118(12):1491–8.

26. K Lai, R De Bruyn, B Lask, R Bryant-Waugh, M Hankins. Use of pelvic ultrasound to monitor ovarian and uterine maturity in childhood onset anorexia nervosa. *Arch Dis Child*. 1994;71(3):228–31.

27. DE Stewart. Reproductive functions in eating disorders. *Ann Med*. 1992;24(4):287–91.

28. M Freizinger, DL Franko, M Dacey, B Okun, AD Domar. The prevalence of eating disorders in infertile women. *Fertil Steril*. 2010;93(1):72–8.

29. SE McCluskey, JH Lacey, J Pearce. Binge-eating and polycystic ovaries. *Lancet*. 1992;340(8821).

30. M Ålgars, L Huang, AF Von Holle, CM Peat, LM Thornton, P Lichtenstein, et al. Binge eating and menstrual dysfunction. *J Psychosom Res*. 2014;76(1):19–22.

31. CM Bulik, ER Hoffman, A Von Holle, L Torgersen, C Stoltenberg, T Reichborn-Kjennerud. Unplanned pregnancy in anorexia nervosa. *Obstet Gynecology*. 2010;116(5):1136.

32. JF Morgan, JH Lacey, E Chung. Risk of postnatal depression, miscarriage, and preterm birth in bulimia nervosa: retrospective controlled study. *Psychosom Med*. 2006;68(3):487–92.

33. A Easter, A Bye, E Taborelli, F Corfield, U Schmidt, J Treasure, et al. Recognising the symptoms: how common are eating disorders in pregnancy? *Eur Eat Disord Rev*. 2013;21(4):340–4.

34. R Baskin, R Galligan. Disordered eating and the perinatal period: a systematic review and best evidence synthesis of mental health and psychosocial correlates. *Eur Eat Disord Rev*. 2019;27(5):462–80.

35. HJ Watson, L Torgersen, S Zerwas, T Reichborn-Kjennerud, C Knoph, C Stoltenberg, et al. Eating disorders, pregnancy, and the postpartum period: findings from the Norwegian Mother and Child Cohort Study (MoBa). *Norsk Epidemiologi*. 2014;24(1–2):51–61.

36. A Bye, S Nath, EG Ryan, D Bick, A Easter, LM Howard, et al. Prevalence and clinical characterisation of pregnant women with eating disorders. *Eur Eat Disord Rev*. 2020;28(2):141–55.

37. N Micali, J Treasure, E Simonoff. Eating disorders symptoms in pregnancy: a longitudinal study of women with recent and past eating disorders and obesity. *J Psychosom Res*. 2007;63(3):297–303.

38. A Easter, F Solmi, A Bye, E Taborelli, F Corfield, U Schmidt, et al. Antenatal and postnatal psychopathology among women with current and past eating disorders: longitudinal patterns. *Eur Eat Disord Rev*. 2015;23(1):19–27.

39. M Martinez-Olcina, J Rubio-Arias, C Reche-García, B Leyva-Vela, M Hernández-García, JJ Hernández-Morante, A Martínez-Rodríguez. Eating

disorders in pregnant and breastfeeding women: a systematic review. *Medicina (Kaunas)*. 2020;56(7):352.

40. KD Charbonneau, JA Seabrook. Adverse birth outcomes associated with types of eating disorders: a review. *Can J Diet Pract Res*. 2019;80(3):131–6.
41. HJ Watson, S Zerwas, L Torgersen, K Gustavson, EW Diemer, GP Knudsen, et al. Maternal eating disorders and perinatal outcomes: a three-generation study in the Norwegian mother and child cohort study. *J Abnorm Psychol*. 2017;126(5):552–64.
42. SE Mazzeo, MC Slof-Op't Landt, I Jones, K Mitchell, KS Kendler, MC Neale, et al. Associations among postpartum depression, eating disorders, and perfectionism in a population-based sample of adult women. *Int J Eat Disord*. 2006;39(3):202–11.
43. N Micali, E Simonoff, J Treasure. Pregnancy and post-partum depression and anxiety in a longitudinal general population cohort: the effect of eating disorders and past depression. *J Affect Disord*. 2011;131(1–3):150–7.
44. E Taborelli, A Easter, R Keefe, U Schmidt, J Treasure, N Micali. Transition to motherhood in women with eating disorders: a qualitative study. *Psychol Psychother*. 2016;89(3):308–23.
45. HJ Watson, A O'Brien, S Sadeh-Sharvit. Children of parents with eating disorders. *Curr Psychiatry Rep*. 2018;20(11):101.
46. E Astrachan-Fletcher, C Veldhuis, N Lively, C Fowler, B Marcks. The reciprocal effects of eating disorders and the postpartum period: a review of the literature and recommendations for clinical care. *J Womens Health*. 2008;17(2):227–39.
47. MA Leddy, C Jones, MA Morgan, J Schulkin. Eating disorders and obstetric-gynecologic care. *J Womens Health*. 2009;18(9):1395–401.
48. A Bye, J Shawe, D Bick, A Easter, M Kash-Macdonald, N Micali. Barriers to identifying eating disorders in pregnancy and in the postnatal period: a qualitative approach. *BMC Pregnancy Childbirth*. 2018;18(1):114.
49. JF Morgan, F Reid, JH Lacey. The SCOFF questionnaire: assessment of a new screening tool for eating disorders. *BMJ*. 1999;319(7223):1467–8.
50. CG Fairburn, SJ Beglin. Eating disorder examination questionnaire. *Cogn Behav Ther Eat Disord*. 2008:309–13.
51. National Institute for Health and Care Excellence. Eating disorders: recognition and treatment. NICE Guideline (NG69). 2017.
52. National Institute for Health and Care Excellence. Antenatal and postnatal mental health: clinical management and service guidance. Clinical Guideline (CG192). 2014.
53. P Robinson, WR Jones. MARSIPAN: management of really sick patients with anorexia nervosa. *BJPsych Adv*. 2018;24(1):20–32.
54. J Treasure. A guide to the medical risk assessment for eating disorders. King's College London, Section of Eating Disorders, Institute of Psychiatry. 2004. www.iop kcl ac uk/sites/edu
55. KM Rasmussen, AL Yaktine. Weight management before, during and after pregnancy. Public Health Guideline (PH27). National Institute for Health and Care Excellence; 2010.
56. AM Siega-Riz, LS Adair, CJ Hobel. Institute of Medicine maternal weight gain recommendations and pregnancy outcome in a predominantly Hispanic population. *Obstet Gynecol*. 1994;84(4):565–73.
57. B Abrams, SL Altman, KE Pickett. Pregnancy weight gain: still controversial. *Am J Clin Nutr*. 2000;71(5 Suppl):1233S–1241S72.
58. KM Rasmussen, AL Yaktine, editors. *Weight gain during pregnancy: reexamining the guidelines*. Institute of Medicine and National Research Council Committee to Reexamine IOM Pregnancy Weight Guidelines. Washington, DC: National Academies Press; 2009.

59. KL Allen, V Mountford, A Brown, K Richards, N Grant, A Austin, et al. First episode rapid early intervention for eating disorders (FREED): from research to routine clinical practice. *Early Interv Psychiatry.* 2020;14(5):625–30.

60. U Schmidt, N Magill, B Renwick, A Keyes, M Kenyon, H Dejong, et al. The Maudsley Outpatient Study of Treatments for Anorexia Nervosa and Related Conditions (MOSAIC): comparison of the Maudsley Model of Anorexia Nervosa Treatment for Adults (MANTRA) with specialist supportive clinical management (SSCM) in outpatients with broadly defined anorexia nervosa: a randomized controlled trial. *J Consult Clin Psychol.* 2015;83(4):796–807.

61. CG Fairburn, S Bailey-Straebler, S Basden, HA Doll, R Jones, R Murphy, et al. A transdiagnostic comparison of enhanced cognitive behaviour therapy (CBT-E) and interpersonal psychotherapy in the treatment of eating disorders. *Behav Res Ther.* 2015;70:64–71.

62. P Hay. A systematic review of evidence for psychological treatments in eating disorders: 2005–2012. *Int J Eat Disord.* 2013;46(5):462–9.

63. J McClelland, M Kekic, N Bozhilova, S Nestler, T Dew, F Van den Eynde, et al. A randomised controlled trial of neuronavigated repetitive transcranial magnetic stimulation (rTMS) in anorexia nervosa. *PLoS ONE.* 2016;11(3):e0148606.

64. J McClelland, M Kekic, IC Campbell, U Schmidt. Repetitive transcranial magnetic stimulation (rTMS) treatment in enduring anorexia nervosa: a case series. *Eur Eat Disord Rev.* 2016;24(2):157–63.

65. C Acosta, J Treasure. Eating disorders. In: J Studd, editor. *Current progress in obstetrics & gynecology*, Vol. 2. Kothari Medical Subscription Services Pvt Limited; 2014.

66. CM Bulik, A Von Holle, AM Siega-Riz, L Torgersen, KK Lie, RM Hamer, et al. Birth outcomes in women with eating disorders in the Norwegian Mother and Child cohort study (MoBa). *Int J Eat Disord.* 2009;42(1):9–18.

67. N Micali. Management of eating disorders during pregnancy. *Prog Neurol Psychiatry.* 2010;14(2):24–6.

68. S Kouba, T Hällström, C Lindholm, AL Hirschberg. Pregnancy and neonatal outcomes in women with eating disorders. *Obstet Gynecol.* 2005;105(2):255–60.

69. W Milano, A Capasso. Psychopharmacological options in the multidisciplinary and multidimensional treatment of eating disorders. *Open Neurol J.* 2019;13(1).

70. MH Bloch, J McGuire, A Landeros-Weisenberger, JF Leckman, C Pittenger. Meta-analysis of the dose-response relationship of SSRI in obsessive-compulsive disorder. *Mol Psychiatry.* 2010;15(8):850–5.

71. KC Dunican, D DelDotto. The role of olanzapine in the treatment of anorexia nervosa. *Ann Pharmacother.* 2007;41(1):111–15.

72. A Capasso, C Petrella, W Milano. Pharmacological profile of SSRIs and SNRIs in the treatment of eating disorders. *Curr Clin Pharmacol.* 2009;4(1):78–83.

73. DL Reas, CM Grilo. Review and meta-analysis of pharmacotherapy for binge-eating disorder. *Obesity.* 2008;16(9):2024–38.

74. Medicines and Healthcare products Regulatory Agency. Topiramate (Topamax): introduction of new safety measures, including a pregnancy prevention programme. Drug Safety Update. 2024. https://tinyurl.com/mr3p7zwp

Chapter 17

Medically Unexplained Symptoms

Robby Steel

Introduction

Published studies examining medically unexplained symptoms (MUS) in perinatal women are thin on the ground. Keyword searches of research databases bring up titles such as 'Psychosomatic Obstetrics and Gynaecology – A Neglected Field?' [1]. However, whilst there is little research on this narrow topic, there is an extensive literature on MUS in other populations. This chapter draws mainly upon that literature and attempts to apply it to pregnancy and the puerperium in a way that will, it is hoped, prove clinically useful.

What Are Medically Unexplained Symptoms?

The term MUS is generally used to refer to physical symptoms that do not appear to be caused by a recognised physical disease. As a clinician, it is important to remember that a symptom feels the same to the patient whether it invites a clear medical explanation or none. The terminology in this area reflects the variety of competing explanatory models and is therefore unavoidably messy: 'functional' implies that, whilst the sufferer's body appears to be structurally intact, it is not working ('functioning') as it ordinarily would; 'somatoform' (literally translated as 'body like') captures the fact that the patients' presentations resemble those of patients presenting with organic pathology; 'psychogenic' ('arising from the mind') implies that psychological factors are key to the aetiology; 'conversion' stems from the Freudian concept of inner conflict being 'converted' into a symbolically representative physical symptom; 'hysteria' attributes symptoms to a 'wandering uterus'! For the purposes of this chapter the author has accepted the widely used phrase medically unexplained symptoms (MUS) as a catch-all for these types of presentations but there are a number of problems with this term. First, it perpetuates the idea that somatoform syndromes such as irritable bowel syndrome (IBS) or fibromyalgia cannot be diagnosed through the conventional diagnostic process of identifying positive features and excluding differentials (in day-to-day clinical practice, *they can*). Second, it confuses the message we give to patients – we are giving them a positive diagnosis (e.g. of IBS), whilst in the same sentence telling them their symptoms are 'unexplained'. Finally, the term implies a false dichotomy between 'medically unexplained' conditions and other conditions that are, by implication, 'explained' – does medical science really have a complete understanding of inflammatory bowel disease or rheumatoid arthritis (or, for that matter, psychiatric disorders such as depression and schizophrenia)?

Sadly, the diagnostic manuals offer little clarity – the limitations of both the International Classification of Diseases, 10th revision (ICD-10) and *Diagnostic and*

Statistical Manual of Mental Disorders, fifth edition (DSM-5) in this area are widely acknowledged. In recent years potentially less problematic alternatives such as 'functional somatic disorders' have been proposed [2]. The recently released ICD-11 brings some order to the previous nosological chaos with a new overarching category of 'bodily distress disorder', divided into the usual ICD subcategories: 'mild', 'moderate', 'severe', 'unspecified' and 'other'. The ICD-11 views 'factitious disorders' and 'malingering' as distinct entities and categorises 'hypochondriasis' as an 'obsessive compulsive disorder' (rather than a 'bodily distress disorder').

Figure 17.1 presents a pragmatic clinicians' guide to diagnosis that is intended to provide a useful framework for thinking about these presentations. Of course, as with any area of medicine, patients do not always fit neatly into predetermined categories – many patients display features from more than one. Most psychiatrists are familiar with the archetypes of specific personality disorders listed in the ICD and DSM and recognise that, in clinical practice, they rarely present in their pure form – it is probably best to think of the archetypes presented in Figure 17.1 (and described below) in a similar way.

Whilst the definition and classification of MUS remain essentially contested, the assertion that MUS are extremely common is incontrovertible. In a seminal study published in 1989, Kroenke and Mangelsdorff followed a cohort of 1,000 consecutive patients presenting to an internal medicine clinic in Canada (roughly equivalent to a general practitioner (GP) surgery in the UK) for 3 years after their initial presentation with a physical symptom [3]. They found that a clear physical cause for the presenting complaint was identified in only 16% of patients. Even when the presenting complaint was an objective clinical sign such as oedema, in two-thirds of patients the presentation remained medically unexplained 3 years later. Comparable studies in secondary care outpatient settings report rates of MUS of 25–50% [4, 5]. Perhaps the most methodologically robust study, examining almost 4,000 new patient assessments at neurology

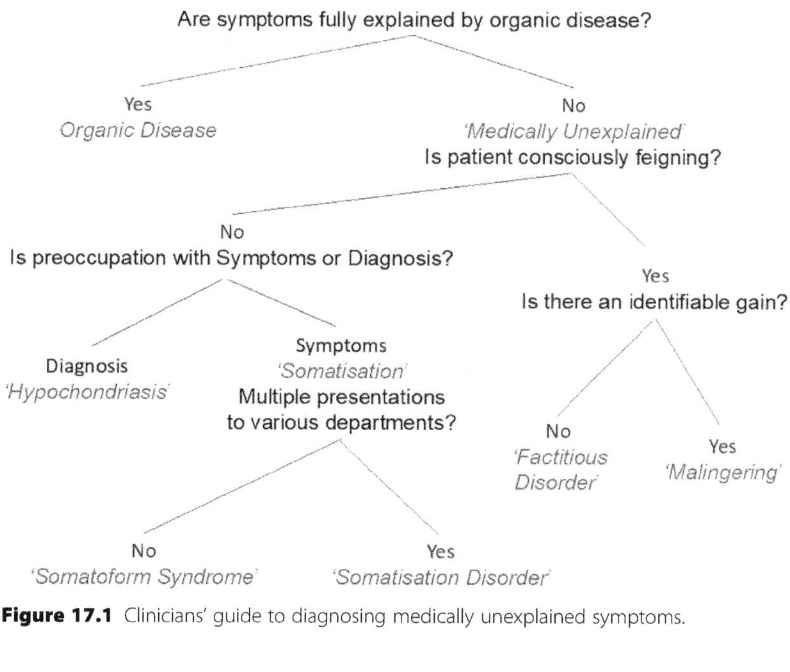

Figure 17.1 Clinicians' guide to diagnosing medically unexplained symptoms.

clinics across Scotland, found that 30% of patients had symptoms that were 'not at all' or only 'somewhat' explained by organic disease [6]. Interestingly, the study found that the initial clinical impression of a neurologist in relation to MUS is remarkably reliable – only 2–3% of the MUS cohort went on to develop organic disease. The authors' adoption of the category 'only somewhat explained by organic disease' acknowledges the limitations of a dichotomous model of physical symptoms as either entirely 'organic' or entirely 'medically unexplained'. The experiencing, and indeed reporting, of symptoms is driven by a multitude of factors: some physical, some psychological and some cultural.

In clinical practice, most clinicians and most patients are familiar with the idea that the disease model rarely provides a complete explanation for the patient's presentation. Most of the time both parties are able to tolerate the uncertainty. Only a tiny proportion of patients presenting with MUS are referred on to mental health services. Hence a mental health professional in receipt of such a referral should always ask the question, 'what was it about this particular case that prompted the referral to psychiatry?' As a general rule, referral to psychiatry is a marker of something unusual in the presentation: the patient may be unusually anxious, unusually distressed, unusually disabled, expressing unusual ideas or exhibiting unusual behaviours. Sometimes the referral to psychiatry reflects tension in the doctor–patient relationship.

Symptoms that do not appear to be caused by physical disease present a challenge to both patient and doctor – the patient can feel frustrated by 'not having an answer' or feeling they have 'not been listened to', meanwhile the doctor can feel frustrated that all their years of training and an extensive compendium of high-tech tests have failed them. It is not uncommon for such tension to manifest as an accusation (overt or implied) that the patient is 'faking it' or 'lying'. Whilst there are undoubtedly situations where patients seek to knowingly deceive clinicians (see the sections on malingering and factitious disorders below), in the absence of clear evidence of deception, it is safest to proceed on the assumption that the patient is presenting a sincere account of their subjective experience. Recent functional brain imaging studies identifying neural correlates of MUS provide powerful evidence that patients with MUS are not 'putting on' their symptoms [7].

As explained in the introduction, there are very few published studies to guide us as to how the general principles outlined above manifest specifically in the perinatal population. One study from the team led by eminent liaison psychiatrist, Wayne Katon [8], found somatic symptoms to be very common during pregnancy and, as in non-pregnant populations, somatic symptoms were found to be more common among those patients with comorbid depression/anxiety than in those without. These findings align with clinical experience – anybody with experience of pregnancy will be aware that it is associated with a wide array of physical symptoms from nausea and vomiting to fatigue, insomnia, dyspepsia, abdominal discomfort, lower back pain, frequency of micturition, disturbed bowel function, leg swelling, etc. Whilst there are no studies to support or refute the proposition, it would be understandable if, in the context of very high levels of somatic symptomatology, both patients and clinicians should tend to attribute to pregnancy symptoms that under other circumstances might attract the label of MUS (or even a somatoform diagnosis such as cyclical vomiting syndrome, functional back pain, fibromyalgia, CFS/ME, IBS or angioedema). For the practising psychiatrist, the upshot is that the threshold for referral of patients with MUS is probably raised during pregnancy. Hence in the perinatal population, it is more especially important to ask the question, 'what was it about this particular case that prompted the referral to psychiatry?'

Diagnosing Medically Unexplained Symptoms

This section takes the reader through the decision tree shown in Figure 17.1.

The first question, 'are the symptoms fully explained by organic disease?', is primarily for the referrer. In perinatal psychiatry this will often be the patient's obstetrician or midwife. As the psychiatrist, it is judicious to resist the temptation to play amateur obstetrician and instead defer to the referrer's professional judgement that there is something about the patient's presentation that is not readily or fully explained by their current pregnancy and/or medical condition. It is usually worth speaking with the referrer to clarify relevant medical/obstetric details and to ascertain exactly what the referrer feels is unusual about the presentation. Many patients are understandably sceptical about being sent to see a psychiatrist when they present with physical symptoms, hence being able to demonstrate that you have a good handle on the medical/obstetric issues can make it easier for the patient to trust you.

The second question, 'is the patient consciously feigning?', will be addressed in more detail below (under Malingering and Factitious Disorders). Whilst the decision tree presents this as a dichotomous choice, as clinicians, we recognise that it is often not as simple as that – patients frequently exaggerate or underplay elements of their history for a variety of reasons. The diagnostic concepts of hypochondriasis and somatisation are broad enough to accommodate boundary cases, it is therefore best to reserve malingering and factitious disorders for cases where there is unambiguous evidence of a deliberate attempt to deceive.

The third question can be expanded to: 'Is the patient's primary preoccupation with their symptoms or with a particular condition/diagnosis?' Again, in clinical practice this dichotomous distinction can sometimes feel artificial as many patients will express concern about both. However, the distinction remains useful because, even in patients with an element of both, separating out fears of a particular condition from concerns about symptoms helps when it comes to the practical task of producing a formulation and management plan.

Hypochondriasis

The ICD-11 describes hypochondriasis as follows:

> The persistent preoccupation or fear about the possibility of having one or more serious, progressive or life-threatening illnesses. The preoccupation is accompanied by either: 1) repetitive and excessive health-related behaviours, such as repeatedly checking the body for evidence of illness, spending inordinate amounts of time searching for information about the feared illness, repeatedly seeking reassurance (e.g. arranging multiple medical consultations); or 2) maladaptive avoidance behaviour related to health (e.g. avoids medical appointments). [9]

In clinical practice, pure hypochondriasis is rare (even in liaison psychiatry), whereas hypochondriacal cognitions are relatively common in depression and anxiety disorders and can arise in obsessive-compulsive disorder and even schizophrenia.

In the general population hypochondriacal thoughts are most commonly centred around conditions that engender fear or stigma – the archetype being cancer.

Hypochondriasis can arise at any time in a person's life but is often precipitated by an experience of physical illness (either first-hand or in a loved one). Pregnancy and childbirth introduce various changes in bodily appearance and function that can trigger hypochondriacal cognitions and a plethora of potential diagnoses that can become the focus: miscarriage/premature labour; gestational diabetes; pre-eclampsia; and, of course, hypochondriacal concerns about the unborn child or infant – 'I fear there is something wrong with my baby.'

Somatisation

Under the decision tree, the patient who is focused more upon their symptoms than on a particular diagnosis falls into the broad category of somatisation. There is no universally accepted definition of the term but it refers to the physical (or bodily) expression of stress and emotions. Somatisation is normal; most of us are familiar with common physical manifestations of psychological stress: headaches, fatigue, insomnia, gastrointestinal upset, etc. As explained above, the vast majority of patients with somatisation are not referred to psychiatry and the threshold is probably even higher in pregnancy. Hence if a patient is referred to perinatal psychiatry on account of somatisation, it is likely that it is giving rise to significant problems.

Somatoform Syndromes

Each specialty within medicine has its own diagnosis (or diagnoses) for patients presenting with persistent and disabling somatic symptoms: cardiology has atypical chest pain; rheumatology has fibromyalgia; gastroenterology has IBS; neurology has non-epileptic seizures, functional gait disorders, etc. Collectively, these are referred to as the somatoform syndromes. The term functional disorder is often used where the predominant feature is a loss of function, such as a loss of normal speech (functional aphonia) or loss of normal gait (functional gait disorder). There is substantial overlap between the various somatoform syndromes; indeed some authors argue that they ought to be considered a single entity – the differences between syndromes reflecting the perspectives of different specialists more than differences in patient symptoms [10]. The fact that the predisposing factors for the various syndromes are shared (and are the same as those for depression, which also displays substantial symptom overlap with somatoform disorders) lends weight to this argument; however, the symptom overlap is far from absolute and the precipitating factors, or triggering risk markers, appear to be unique for each condition [11].

Somatoform syndromes are common in the general population and the prevalence is higher in women than in men [12]. These syndromes are therefore common in the perinatal population. There is no published research on the impact of pregnancy on the course and severity of somatoform disorders, but clinical experience suggests that those syndromes characterised by general malaise, pain and fatigue (fibromyalgia, CFS/ME, persistent somatoform pain disorder, etc.) tend to worsen, whereas those characterised by specific functional symptoms or impairments tend to improve. The most plausible explanation is that generalised symptoms such as fatigue are exacerbated by the physical challenges of pregnancy; meanwhile, many patients with functional disorders have symptoms perpetuated by abnormally focused attention from which pregnancy offers relief by providing opportunities for a shift of focus. New somatoform syndromes can emerge during pregnancy as physical symptoms associated with pregnancy become more severe and more disabling than expected. Referrals for suspected non-cardiac chest pain are fairly common in later pregnancy although the underlying diagnosis is often panic disorder. Childbirth can precipitate somatoform symptoms such as acute functional weakness of the lower limbs (typically following spinal or epidural anaesthesia) and somatoform pain disorder, particularly if the delivery is traumatic and/or frightening.

There is no somatoform syndrome specific to pregnancy and the puerperium, although an argument could be made for classifying pseudocyesis and even Couvade syndrome as somatic syndromes.

Hyperemesis gravidarum (HG) has historically been viewed by some clinicians as a somatoform syndrome – 'psychogenic vomiting'. However, whilst there is some evidence that a past history of depression conveys an increased risk of HG [13], the effect size is small and the evidence for an 'organic' cause is far stronger. In recent years the enormous range of severity, (from mild nausea to intractable vomiting), that was previously interpreted by some as evidence of a solely psychological aetiology, has now been associated with genetic variations in a gene (GDF15) that encodes for a receptor expressed in areas of the brain associated with appetite loss, taste aversion, nausea and vomiting [14]. Women suffering from HG may be referred to mental health services for a number of reasons. First, the experience of unremitting nausea and vomiting can be so distressing as to give rise to a request for termination of pregnancy or even suicidal thoughts. Second, when HG symptoms persist beyond the usual resolution phase (early second trimester), the maternity team may seek a psychological explanation for the unusual clinical course. By taking a detailed clinical history it is sometimes possible to identify a conditioned vomiting response (triggered either by a range of smells and foodstuffs or by physiological symptoms such as hunger), and/or psychological perpetuating factors such as hypervigilance, catastrophisation and avoidance behaviours.

Somatisation Disorder

Whilst somatisation (the experiencing of physical symptoms as a consequence of stress or emotions) is ubiquitous and somatoform syndromes common, the term somatisation disorder is reserved for rare and severe cases where recurrent somatoform presentations become a life-long pattern of behaviour. Under ICD-11, patients with somatisation disorder fall within the category 'bodily distress disorder: severe' but the term remains clinically useful. The description in the ICD-10 neatly captures the presentation:

> The main features are multiple, recurrent and frequently changing physical symptoms of at least two years duration. Most patients have a long and complicated history of contact with both primary and specialist medical care services, during which many negative investigations or fruitless exploratory operations may have been carried out. Symptoms may be referred to any part or system of the body. The course of the disorder is chronic and fluctuating, and is often associated with disruption of social, interpersonal, and family behaviour. [9]

No psychiatrist reading that description will be surprised to learn that somatisation disorder is often associated with, or best understood as, personality disorder. The key to confirming a diagnosis of somatisation disorder lies in reviewing the hospital case notes and speaking with the patient's GP. In the UK, the majority of patients with somatisation disorder are managed extremely effectively by their GP, sometimes with support from

Liaison Psychiatry. However, hospital specialists such as obstetricians can get drawn into an unproductive and potentially dangerous cycle of over-investigation and unnecessary physical treatment. The role of the psychiatrist is to support the obstetrician in protecting the patient from iatrogenic harm, whilst at the same time remaining vigilant for 'red flag' symptoms (i.e. new onset physical symptoms recognised to be indicative of underlying pathology).

Conscious Feigning of Symptoms

We will now return to the second question in the decision tree: 'Is the patient consciously feigning?' The phenomenon of patients purposefully simulating signs and symptoms of disease is probably as old as medicine itself. It was first documented by nineteenth-century Edinburgh physician Hector Gavin in a paper describing behaviours observed in soldiers and seamen [15]. Gavin coined the term factitious disease from the Latin *facer*, 'to make', and drew a distinction between those who engaged in these behaviours for obvious material gain – what we now call malingering – and those for whom no objective external benefit could be identified – factitious disorder. The deception inherent to these presentations renders them inaccessible to conventional scientific study. We don't know how common they are nor what the demographic distribution looks like, for the simple reason that we do not see the lies that we believe! Furthermore, as doctors we are used to working within a framework of mutual trust and are therefore not primed to identify deception. What doctors *are* good at is identifying inconsistencies: histories that change, are internally inconsistent or contradicted by objective clinical findings or corroborative accounts. When we see such inconsistencies we should seek an explanation.

By far the commonest clinical inconsistency is a discrepancy between the reported severity of symptoms and observed level of disability, for example, 'my back pain is so bad I can't get out of bed', yet the patient has just walked into the clinic room. This is rarely evidence of a deliberate attempt at deception (if it is, it is not a particularly sophisticated one), rather it is a sincere attempt to communicate distress, to be heard. Inconsistencies more indicative of conscious deception include demonstrable falsifying (underplaying or gross exaggeration) of the medical history, barriers to obtaining corroborative accounts (not registered with a GP, next of kin uncontactable, no visitors, etc.), symptoms arising only when the patient is not observed, symptoms escalating following negative test results, unusual response to treatment such as a wound failing to heal. In medical and surgical specialties patients will sometimes go to extraordinary lengths to deceive doctors, particularly if their aim is to secure hospital admission: dripping blood into samples, injecting themselves with insulin, etc. However, such extreme presentations are vanishingly rare in obstetrics, not least because the threshold for hospital admission is low – a report of per vaginal bleeding, abdominal cramping or reduced fetal movements will usually suffice.

Malingering

The ICD-11 states:

> Malingering is the feigning, intentional production or significant exaggeration of physical or psychological symptoms, or intentional misattribution of genuine symptoms to an unrelated event or series of events when this is specifically motivated by external incentives

> or rewards such as escaping duty or work; mitigating punishment; obtaining medications or drugs; or receiving unmerited recompense such as disability compensation or personal injury damages award. [9]

This is not listed under 'Mental, behavioural or neurodevelopmental disorders' but under 'Factors influencing health status or contact with health services' (it attracts a 'Q' code).

There are a host of reasons why someone might feign or fabricate illness. In the perinatal population there are three specific scenarios that one should bear in mind. The first is the woman attempting to secure a termination of pregnancy, particularly in the face of religious or other sociocultural barriers. The second is the woman seeking to affect the mode or date of delivery (usually driven by anxiety). Finally, it is always important to be vigilant for the woman escaping domestic violence or abuse.

Anxiety and depression can be mistaken for malingering as a patient exaggerates or fabricates symptoms in order to secure the reassurance and support that hospital admission brings. This is relatively common in obstetrics both antenatally, when a woman is anxious that she may lose her baby and feels safer in hospital, and postnatally when a mother is either anxious about the baby's health or feels she is struggling to cope (perhaps due to postnatal depression).

Factitious Disorders

The ICD-11 states:

> Factitious disorders are characterised by intentionally feigning, falsifying, inducing, or aggravating medical, psychological, or behavioural signs and symptoms or injury in oneself or in another person, most commonly a child dependent, associated with identified deception. A pre-existing disorder or disease may be present, but the individual intentionally aggravates existing symptoms or falsifies or induces additional symptoms. Individuals with a factitious disorder seek treatment or otherwise present themselves or another person as ill, injured, or impaired based on the feigned, falsified, or self-induced signs, symptoms, or injuries. The deceptive behaviour is not solely motivated by obvious external rewards or incentives (e.g., obtaining disability payments or evading criminal prosecution). This is in contrast to Malingering, in which obvious external rewards or incentives motivate the behaviour. [9]

Factitious disorders are rare but in the obstetric context they carry potentially serious implications, particularly for any children in the woman's care. This is a challenging topic to study and the literature is sparse; however, in a case series of 28 women facing prosecution for fabricating or inducing illness in a child, Bass and Jones found that 64% had a history of factitious disorder [16]. Although 'factitious disorder imposed on another' (previously called 'fabricated or induced illness' or Munchausen's syndrome by proxy) is not limited to the neonatal period, the opportunity to identify it early may be. The perinatal psychiatrist is well placed to identify mothers displaying abnormal illness behaviours that appear to be factitious. Where a factitious disorder is suspected or identified, the author would advise involving a liaison psychiatrist. The message for child protection agencies is that factitious disorder in a mother ('imposed on the self') is only one step away from factitious disorder imposed on the child.

It is important to note that a factitious act is not pathognomonic of a factitious disorder. It is not uncommon for patients who are anxious about their health, and feel that their concerns have not been heard, to 'up the ante' in an act of desperation. This may lead to them overstating their symptoms or even presenting false accounts or interfering with tests. For this reason, even where unambiguous evidence of deception is found, the patient should be offered an opportunity to come clean: 'We appreciate that sometimes when people are under stress they behave in a way that they would not normally behave, do you think that might have happened here?' [17].

Clinical Assessment

An unflattering caricature of the General Adult Psychiatry response to a MUS referral might be: 'No major mental disorder. Discharge to GP.' As a perinatal psychiatrist accepting referrals from obstetricians, it is important to appreciate the referrer's expectations. Diagnosing or excluding major mental disorder is the bare minimum – but still important, as is psychiatric risk assessment. In addition to these core psychiatric tasks, you will probably be expected to help the patient (and obstetrician) navigate the hinterland between the psychological and the physical – to provide insights into the role that psychological factors may be playing, ultimately using your medical, psychiatric and psychological understanding to provide a coherent explanation as to why this patient is presenting with these symptoms at this time (and why they are affecting her in the way that they are). The obstetrician may also hope that you can help to alleviate the woman's distress, repair a fractured patient/service relationship, and generally ensure that the woman's obstetric care runs as smoothly as possible! This is a big ask but it is surprising how much impact a thorough and empathic bio-psycho-social assessment can make. Table 17.1 shows the types of aetiological factors to consider, presented in the hopefully familiar format of bio-psycho-social predisposing, precipitating and perpetuating factors.

History

Chapter 23 ('Access, Assessment and Evaluation of Risk in Perinatal Mental Health Services') addresses the art of history taking in Perinatal Psychiatry, the essential message

Table 17.1 Aetiology of MUS in pregnancy/puerperium

	Biological	*Psychological*	*Social*
Predisposing	Genetic History of physical illness	Depression/anxiety Personality traits (anxious, dependent, perfectionistic, etc.)	Adverse childhood events Modelling of illness behaviours
Precipitating	Physical illness/injury or physiological change (such as pregnancy)	Worry about physical symptoms or change	Life events
Perpetuating	Physical deconditioning Neuroendocrine changes (e.g. up-regulation of HPA axis)	Illness beliefs Hypervigilance/attentional bias Avoidance behaviours Secondary depression	Not being believed Stigma of MUS Secondary gain: 'Reward' from family, healthcare system, etc.

being: 'take a conventional psychiatric history and add in perinatal elements' – psychiatric history and family history of puerperal mental disorder being particularly important. When assessing a perinatal woman referred with MUS, the task is to take a conventional perinatal psychiatric history and add in MUS elements – medical history and family history of physical illness being the obvious focal points. It is always best to review the patient's medical records before the appointment and, as with any clinical assessment, a corroborative account can add valuable information. As well as adding specific elements to the history, a referral for MUS can add a new dimension to the task of establishing a therapeutic rapport: 'Why am I seeing a mind doctor when my symptoms are physical?' In a large majority of cases, by agreeing to see a psychiatrist, the woman is demonstrating a degree of openness to the idea that psychological factors may have a role to play and a rapport is easily established. Sometimes referral to psychiatry prompts reflection and research, the woman arriving at the appointment with her own comprehensive and accurate bio-psycho-social formulation and management plan – she has done your job for both of you! Where the patient remains sceptical it can be helpful to start the consultation by reading the referral letter and then exploring obstetric issues – this is safe ground for someone who is wary of psychiatry and also helps to establish that, as a psychiatrist, you are medically qualified and closely aligned to the obstetric team.

There is no right or wrong way to take a psychiatric history but many psychiatrists adopt a narrative approach, following the patient's biographical timeline. This is particularly helpful in perinatal psychiatry where the biographical timeline lends itself to exploration of the trajectory of the woman's maternal identity: What was her own experience of being parented? As a young child, did she see herself becoming a mother one day? When did she start trying for children? How did she feel when she saw the positive pregnancy test? What course has each of her pregnancies and deliveries followed? Etc. As mentioned above, when assessing any patient experiencing MUS, it is important to explore, in detail, the medical history and the medical history of family and close friends. In the perinatal context particular attention should be given to any pregnancy-related experiences or fears the woman may have: 'Many families have stories about pregnancy and childbirth – stories like, "such-and-such was born with the cord around their neck" – are there any stories like that in your family?' 'Have any of the women in your family experienced health issues in pregnancy?' 'What about among your friends, or just stories you have heard?'

The psychiatrist exploring a patient's (medically unexplained) physical symptoms is faced with two tasks. First, to be a doctor taking a detailed history of the symptoms; second, to be a psychiatrist exploring the patient's beliefs about their symptoms and emotions associated with them. It is not uncommon for patients presenting with MUS to have multiple somatic symptoms [12]; the first task involves eliciting all of them ('draining the symptoms dry'), and documenting them in the form of a list constructed in collaboration with the patient, ordered from what they regard as the most troublesome/serious to the least troublesome. It is often helpful to focus in detail upon the onset of symptoms as this can provide useful insights into the patient's beliefs about causality. Sometimes patients with MUS feel that doctors have not listened to them (and they are often right); the act of working with the patient to co-construct their symptom list is a robust demonstration that this doctor *is* listening to them. Once the symptom list has been agreed, a natural way to progress to the second task is to ask the patient what other doctors have said and/or how other doctors have made them feel. This can be quite illuminating. It can also be valuable to ask whether the patient has obtained advice or opinions from anywhere else: family, friends, the internet, etc. Sometimes such sources can plant or reinforce unhelpful misconceptions. Then ask the patient what their best-guess explanation for their symptoms would be. Finally explore how the symptoms make them feel and if there is anything specific they are worried about.

Examination including Mental State Examination

The history-taking tasks described above can be time-consuming but it is important not to neglect the mental state examination (MSE): keep an eye out for features suggestive of depression, anxiety and other major mental disorders. With respect to MUS, it is important to remain vigilant for inconsistencies and to explore whether the patient's primary concern is with symptoms or with a particular diagnosis. Historically emphasis has been placed upon '*la belle indifférence*': an apparent lack of concern about potentially serious physical symptoms said to be suggestive of conversion disorder (or 'hysteria'), but in clinical practice most patients are extremely anxious about and distressed by their symptoms, whilst others put on a brave face. Recent studies suggest *la belle indifférence* probably has no diagnostic value [18].

Physical examination can sometimes be a useful adjunct to the history and MSE, particularly as an extension of 'active listening' – 'could you possibly show me the rash', 'let me take a look at the swelling', etc. – but as a psychiatrist it is always important to remain within the boundaries of your clinical competence. Where a more detailed physical examination is indicated it can be helpful to conduct a joint assessment with a clinician from the relevant specialty. There are some specialist physical examinations particular to the field of MUS; for example, eliciting Hoover's sign in the patient with functional weakness [19] but these are beyond the scope of this chapter.

Investigations

The most important investigations in any patient presenting with MUS are a review of the medical notes and a discussion with the GP. Most patients with MUS will have been thoroughly investigated by the referring hospital specialist before being referred to psychiatry. It is important that the psychiatrist has reviewed the results and has a good understanding of what they mean (if in doubt, ask the referrer). A proper explanation of negative investigation results can help challenge misguided beliefs and concerns about physical causality/risk, thereby helping shift the patient's understanding of their symptoms from the physical towards the psychological. Conversely, where the patient is not reassured, or only briefly reassured, by negative results, this is an indicator of poor prognosis.

One of the challenges in the perinatal population is that certain investigations, that would under other circumstances help reassure the patient, may be contraindicated – X-ray, CT, diagnostic laparoscopy, etc. – and this can contribute to the perpetuation of distressing and disabling clinical uncertainty. If your assessment is that a negative test result could have a significant clinical impact, it may be worth exploring safe alternatives (such as MRI) with the referrer.

Management

As in any area of psychiatric practice, assessment is an important first step in management. For many patients with MUS, the perception that they have not been heard or believed by doctors serves to perpetuate their difficulties. There is an adage in Liaison Psychiatry of 'if you have to prove you are ill, you can't get well' [20]. The assessment described above includes the detailed and comprehensive elucidation of all physical symptoms and collaborative production of a personalised symptom list. If done well, this can be a powerful exercise in validation, which allows the patient to move on. This validating effect of the assessment interview can be further reinforced by copying the clinical letter to the patient.

Doctors referring patients to psychiatry for assessment and management of MUS often report that they have 'reassured' the patient. However, all too often they are describing 'negative reassurance' – offering the patient a list of serious conditions that they don't have – rather than 'positive reassurance' – reaching a shared plausible and acceptable explanation for the patient's symptoms. The aim of the psychiatric assessment is to achieve such a shared explanation: a coherent formulation linking the physical and psychological, which can form the basis of a rational management plan. Diagnosis (particularly the positive diagnosis of a somatoform syndrome) may be an important component of formulation but it is not a substitute, particularly in the area of MUS where the diagnostic nomenclature is imperfect. Often the best explanation incorporates both physical and psychological elements; for example, unusually strong Braxton-Hicks contractions and a disproportionate fear of premature labour, driven by a belief that 'women in our family have their babies early'. It is important to present both physical and psychological components in a positive, confident manner whilst acknowledging that there are some things that medical science does not yet fully understand. A good formulation will be simple enough for the patient to understand and remember and will lead naturally to therapeutic interventions. Given the importance of validation in allowing the patient to move on, it is important that the formulation does not attribute blame.

Psychological Management

Psychological management of MUS builds upon the formulation. At the time of writing, in most parts of the UK the limited access to dedicated National Health Service psychological therapy services is not compatible with obstetric timescales and, even if it were, few psychological therapists have expertise in the management of MUS. It therefore falls to the assessing psychiatrist to adopt a pragmatic, psychologically informed approach to treatment. Certain cognitive and attentional biases have been described in patients with MUS: restrictive or oversimplistic assumptions about health and bodily functions; a tendency to overinterpret physical sensations as evidence of organic disease; hypervigilance for bodily change; an amplifying perceptual style; and a recall bias for illness-related memories. Perhaps unsurprisingly, a range of abnormal or dysfunctional illness behaviours have also been described, including: excessive checking; a tendency to catastrophisation; extreme conscientiousness; and a tendency to boom-and-bust activity. All of these are potentially amenable to cognitive behavioural therapy–informed intervention.

Once the patient's symptoms have been validated and a plausible explanatory model has been agreed, the next stage is to explore possible aggravating/perpetuating and relieving factors. This discussion will often generate simple problem-solving strategies that involve tackling perpetuating factors and maximising the patient's current positive coping strategies. Where unhelpful cognitions are a barrier to progress these should be identified and subjected to challenge. In some cases, the obstetrician or other specialist can be a powerful ally in challenging such cognitions (e.g. 'pain is evidence that something is seriously wrong. I must not do anything that might trigger pain'). In other cases, a behavioural experiment can be a powerful intervention (e.g. bed rest vs a short walk as approaches to fatigue). Where anxiety is giving rise to counter-productive safety behaviours or avoidance these should be tackled in a graded way. It can be useful to involve partners or other family members as it is not uncommon to find that they are inadvertently reinforcing such behaviours. Where fear of premature labour or intrauterine death is prominent, the most pragmatic approach may be to work with safety behaviours (such as frequent midwife review, or weekly growth scans), even accepting a degree of escalation confident in the knowledge that they will not be needed after delivery.

Pharmacological Management

The principles of psychotropic prescribing in the perinatal population are outlined in Chapter 26. Suffice to say, the threshold for prescribing is higher in pregnancy and breastfeeding than at other times and the palette of available drugs is restricted. Furthermore, there is research evidence to suggest that the preference for psychological therapy over pharmacotherapy is more marked during pregnancy [21], which may have an impact upon patient engagement and ultimately treatment efficacy. Hence, within perinatal psychiatry, there is a strong argument for pursuing psychological treatment options as first line and reserving medication for the most severe or intractable presentations, at least when treating non-psychotic disorders. The presence of MUS strengthens this argument further: patients with MUS are unusually prone to medication side effects and to the nocebo effect (a reverse placebo effect – the chance of a drug proving ineffective or harmful is largely driven by expectation) [22]. Furthermore, the idea of prescribing a psychotropic drug for physical symptoms is often met with (understandable) resistance. Having said that, medication does have a role to play in the management of MUS and there is a robust evidence base to support its efficacy.

Clearly if the assessment for MUS reveals comorbid mental disorder (anxiety, depression, etc.) then this should be treated appropriately. However, there is good evidence to support the use of antidepressants in certain types of MUS even in the absence of mental disorder. Chronic pain syndromes, chronic fatigue, fibromyalgia and IBS have all been shown to respond to antidepressants, typically with a number needed to treat (NNT) of around 4 (which is comparable to the NNT for antidepressants in depression) [23]. There may also be a role for antidepressants in functional neurological disorders although the evidence base is less strong. Studies suggest that, where pain is a prominent feature, agents with combined serotonergic and noradrenergic activity are more effective than selective serotonin reuptake inhibitors (SSRIs). Interestingly tricyclic antidepressants (TCAs) have been found to be effective in pain at doses that would be regarded as subtherapeutic in depression (typically 50–100 mg daily of Amitriptyline). Gabapetinoids are often prescribed in primary pain disorders but their efficacy is unclear and the fact that they are contraindicated in pregnancy renders them unsuitable for use in the perinatal context.

Functional imaging studies support the hypothesis that the effects of combined seotonergic/noradrenergic antidepressants are due to the normalising of descending antinociceptive systems that are defective in patients with functional pain. Antidepressant drugs may also help to normalise attentional bias for noxious stimuli.

Most clinicians prescribing an antidepressant for MUS would choose a TCA or serotonin-norepinephrine reuptake inhibitor (SNRI) where pain is prominent, a TCA where sedation is desirable and an SSRI where pain is not prominent and sedation is undesirable. In the perinatal population the restricted palette of drugs renders this choice relatively straightforward: Amitriptyline is the TCA of choice during pregnancy, Nortriptyline during breastfeeding [24] (SNRIs are relatively contraindicated), meanwhile Sertraline is currently the preferred SSRI. Whilst choosing a drug may be relatively easy, care needs to be taken over how the drug is prescribed. As mentioned, many patients are understandably sceptical about the idea of taking an antidepressant when they do not feel depressed. It is important to explain that drugs can have more than one mode of action – a useful example is aspirin, which most patients recognise can be taken for a headache or to thin the blood. Furthermore, patients with MUS are prone to side effects so it is prudent to start with very low doses and build up gradually at a rate determined by the patient. It is also important to manage the patient's expectations of side effects but a balance needs to be struck between warning them about common side effects and feeding the nocebo effect by raising their expectations of side effects.

Managing the Healthcare System

Most clinicians are motivated by a desire to help – to use their expertise and the tools at their disposal to alleviate their patients' distress. The patient whose symptoms appear to defy medical explanation challenges the clinician's sense of agency. This can be profoundly egodystonic for the clinician. Whilst most clinicians tolerate this discomfort most of the time, it can give rise to feelings and behaviours that are unhelpful. One common response to this sense of clinical impotence is to double-down – to look ever harder for a medical explanation by doing more tests, trying speculative treatments, etc. This places patients with MUS at very high risk of iatrogenic harm, often in the form of unnecessary and ineffective prescribing, for example, cardioprotective drugs prescribed to a patient with non-cardiac chest pain. Perhaps the most frequently encountered overprescribing issue is the patient with medically unexplained pain being prescribed long-term opiates. Whilst primary responsibility for reducing and discontinuing unnecessary prescriptions lies with the prescriber, the psychiatrist can be a useful ally. Another common response to the uncomfortable sense of professional impotence is to become angry with the patient, who is then at risk of malignant alienation with consequent under-investigation and undertreatment. Again, the psychiatrist has an important role in helping their colleagues to recognise and understand this and in protecting the patient from any potential harm. New symptoms, particularly new 'red flag' symptoms, reported by a patient with MUS should be examined and (ideally non-invasively) investigated as they would be in any other patient.

Conclusions

Medically unexplained symptoms are extremely common but only a tiny minority of patients are referred to psychiatry, and it is likely that the threshold for referral is raised in the perinatal population. When in receipt of a referral for MUS the psychiatrist should always ask, 'what was it about this particular case that prompted the referral to psychiatry?' Whilst there are situations where a patient consciously attempts to deceive their doctor (malingering and factitious disorders), the vast majority of patients with MUS are presenting a sincere account of their subjective experience. A distinction can be drawn between preoccupation with a particular diagnosis (hypochondriasis) and with physical symptoms (somatisation). Comorbid mental disorders are common, particularly depression and anxiety, which are approximately twice as common in patients with MUS as in patients with equivalent physical disability from organic disease. Clinical assessment comprises a conventional perinatal psychiatry assessment with additional focus upon medical history and physical illness affecting family and friends. It is always wise to review the patient's medical notes and ideally to speak with their GP. Within the assessment it is important to validate the patient's symptoms; this can be done by documenting them in a comprehensive list that is shared with the patient. The aim of assessment is to produce a plausible and acceptable formulation linking the physical and psychological, which can form the basis of a rational management plan. Management is largely pragmatic but informed by the principles of psychological therapy. Antidepressant medication is an evidence-based treatment for MUS but the threshold for prescribing in the perinatal population is high. Patients with MUS are at increased risk of iatrogenic harm. The psychiatrist has a role in protecting them from this.

Further Reading

1. C Burton, editor. *ABC of medically unexplained symptoms*. BMJ Books; 2013.
2. www.neurosymptoms.org
3. E Guthrie, A Nayak. Medically unexplained symptoms. In: E Guthrie, S Rao, M Temple, editors. *Seminars in liaison psychiatry*. London: Royal College of Psychiatrists; 2012. p. 66–85.
4. R Mayou, A Farmer. Functional somatic symptoms and syndromes. In: C Burton, editor. *ABC of psychological medicine*. London: BMJ Books; 2002. p. 265–8.

References

1. PS Chandran, S Ranjan. Psychosomatic obstetrics and gynaecology – a neglected field? *Curr Opin Psychiatry*. 2007;20(2):168–73.
2. C Burton, P Fink, P Henningsen, B Löwe, W Rief. Functional somatic disorders: discussion paper for a new common classification for research and clinical use. *BMC Med*. 2020;18(1):34.
3. K Kroenke, AD Mangelsdorff. Common symptoms in ambulatory care: incidence, evaluation, therapy, and outcome. *Am J Med*. 1989;86(3):262–6.
4. U Baitha, KS Deb, P Ranjan, A Mukherjee, NK Bauddh, GS Kaloiya, et al. Estimated prevalence of medically unexplained physical symptoms in the medicine outpatient department of a tertiary care hospital in India. *Gen Hosp Psychiatry*. 2019;61:47–52.
5. S Mangawa, S Burlinson, F Creed. Medically unexplained symptoms presenting at secondary care – a comparison of white Europeans and people of South Asian ethnicity. *Int J Psychiatry Med*. 2009;39(1): 33–44.
6. J Stone, A Carson, R Duncan, R Coleman, R Roberts, C Warlow, et al. Symptoms 'unexplained by organic disease' in 1144 new neurology out-patients: how often does the diagnosis change at follow-up? *Brain*. 2009;132(10):2878–88.
7. SM Kim, JS Hong, KJ Min, DH Han. Brain functional connectivity in patients

with somatic symptom disorder. *Psychosom Med.* 2019;81(3):313–18.

8. RH Kelly, J Russo, W Katon. Somatic complaints among pregnant women cared for in obstetrics: normal pregnancy or depressive and anxiety symptom amplification revisited? *Gen Hosp Psychiatry.* 2001;23(3):107–13.
9. World Health Organization. *The ICD-10 classification of mental and behavioural disorders.* Geneva: World Health Organization; 1993.
10. S Wessely, C Nimnuan, M Sharpe. Functional somatic syndromes: one or many? *Lancet.* 1999;354(9182):936–9.
11. WT Hamilton, AM Gallagher, JM Thomas, PD White. Risk markers for both chronic fatigue and irritable bowel syndromes: a prospective case-control study in primary care. *Psychol Med.* 2009;39:1913–21.
12. K Kroenke, RL Spitzer. Gender differences in the reporting of physical and somatoform symptoms. *Psychosom Med.* 1998;60(2):150–5.
13. HK Kjeldgaard, M Eberhard-Gran, JS Benth, H Nordeng, ÅV Vikanes. History of depression and risk of hyperemesis gravidarum: a population-based cohort study. *Arch Womens Ment Health.* 2017;20(3):397–404.
14. M Fejzo, N Rocha, I Cimino, SM Lockhart, CJ Petry, RG Kay, et al. GDF15 linked to maternal risk of nausea and vomiting during pregnancy. *Nature.* 2024;625:760–7.
15. H Gavin. *On feigned and factitious disease, chiefly of soldiers and seamen; on the means used to simulate or produce them and on the best modes of discovering impostors.* London: Churchill; 1843.
16. C Bass, D Jones. Psychopathology of perpetrators of fabricated or induced illness in children: case series. *Br J Psychiatry.* 2011;199(2):113–18.
17. RM Steel. Factitious disorder (Munchausen's syndrome). *J Roy Coll Phys Edin.* 2009;39:343–7.
18. J Stone, R Smyth, A Carson, C Warlow, M Sharpe. La belle indifférence in conversion symptoms and hysteria: a systematic review. *Br J Psychiatry.* 2006;188:204–9.
19. MM Mehndiratta, M Kumar, R Nayak, H Garg, S Pandey. Hoover's sign: clinical relevance in neurology. *J Postgrad Med.* 2014;60(3):297–9.
20. N Hadler. If you have to prove you are ill, you can't get well. *Spine.* 1996;21(20):2397–400.
21. JJ Arch. Cognitive behavioural therapy and pharmacotherapy for anxiety: treatment preferences and credibility among pregnant and non-pregnant women. *Behav Res Ther.* 2014;52: 53–60.
22. L Colloca, AJ Barksy. Placebo and nocebo effects. *New Engl J Med.* 2020;382(6):554–61.
23. BA Fallon. Pharmacotherapy of somatoform disorders. *J Psychosom Res.* 2004;56:455–60.
24. Scottish Intercollegiate Guidelines Network. Management of perinatal mood disorders (SIGN Guideline 127). 2012.

Chapter 18

Alcohol and Substance Use Disorders

Claire Wilson and Emily Finch

Introduction

Substance misuse is defined as the harmful or hazardous use of psychoactive substances, including alcohol and nicotine. Psychoactive substances are defined by the World Health Organization (WHO) as those affecting mental processes, including cognition and affect [1]. Psychoactive substance misuse is associated with adverse physical, psychological and social outcomes. Repeated use of such substances can sometimes lead to dependence syndrome, although the term 'psychoactive' does not imply that the drug will produce dependence. Similarly, the term 'substance misuse' does not always imply dependence. The International Classification of Diseases, 11th edition (ICD-11) criteria for dependence state that for any substance, three or more of the following should have been present together at some time during the previous year [2]:

- strong desire or compulsion to take the substance
- difficulty in controlling substance-taking behaviour, for example onset, termination or levels of use
- physiological withdrawal state when substance use is stopped or reduced (symptoms vary depending on the substance); may also be associated with use of the substance (or a closely related one) to relieve or avoid the withdrawal symptoms
- tolerance, whereby increased doses of the substance are required to achieve effects originally produced by lower doses
- neglect of alternative pleasures or interests other than the substance
- persistence of substance use despite knowledge of its potential harms

An overview of substances misused, effects of intoxication and effects of withdrawal are provided in Table 18.1.

Substance misuse may be comorbid with mental disorder and physical ill health. It may also increase the risk of exposure to violence, abuse and exploitation; substance misuse in either partner within a relationship is a well-established risk factor for domestic violence [3]. It may result in decline in functioning, loss of employment and family breakdown.

Substance misuse in the perinatal period may also increase the risk of adverse maternal and child sequelae. These include reduced engagement with antenatal care [4] and obstetric and neonatal complications such as low birth weight and prematurity [5, 6]. Substance misuse has also been implicated in maternal deaths in the UK; 23% of those who died between 2019 and 2021 were smokers and 14% were using other substances [7]. Clearly, studying longer-term outcomes in offspring is challenging, with small sample sizes and unmeasured confounding factors characteristic of many of the

Table 18.1 Summary of common substances of misuse

Substance	Effect of intoxication	Effect of withdrawal
Alcohol	Confusion, nausea and vomiting, disinhibition, ataxia, drowsiness or coma	Tremor, anxiety, sweating, palpitations, nausea and vomiting, seizures (life threatening)
Benzodiazepines	Slurred speech, unsteadiness, impaired judgement, attention and memory, nystagmus, drowsiness or coma	Tremor, anxiety, nausea and vomiting, insomnia, psychomotor agitation, seizures (life threatening)
Cannabis and synthetic cannabinoid receptor agonists	Conjunctival injection, hyperphagia, euphoria, dry mouth, heightened perceptual sensitivity, depersonalisation, derealisation, paranoid ideas	Irritability, insomnia, anorexia (but physical withdrawal symptoms are uncommon)
Opioids, e.g. heroin	Pupillary constriction, psychomotor agitation or retardation, slurred speech, drowsiness or coma	Pupillary dilatation, nausea and vomiting, myalgia, lacrimation, rhinorrhoea, piloerection, sweating, diarrhoea, insomnia
Stimulants, e.g. cocaine, methamphetamine	Pupillary dilatation, euphoria, sweating, nausea and vomiting, increased sociability, psychomotor retardation or agitation	Hypersomnia, fatigue, anhedonia, depression, anxiety

studies in this area. Despite this there is some evidence from prospective, longitudinal birth cohorts that maternal substance misuse is associated with a range of emotional and behavioural difficulties in exposed children [6] and even in a recent US cohort with future substance misuse at age 30 [8].

In this chapter we discuss how psychiatrists and other healthcare professionals can support families affected by substance misuse, from the preconception period, through pregnancy and in the postpartum.

Epidemiology

Globally, harmful use of alcohol results in 3.3 million deaths annually and at least 35 million people have drug use disorders [1]. Estimating the prevalence of substance misuse during pregnancy is often difficult, perhaps due to reluctance by health professionals to enquire about it or women to disclose it. However, 20% of people starting treatment for substance misuse in England between 2017 and 2018 reported living with a child under the age of 18 [9]. Data from the Health Survey for England and General Household Survey from 2004 found that 30% of children in the UK under the age of 16 were living with at least one binge-drinking parent [10]. In an analysis of maternal deaths in the UK between 2009 and 2013, substance misuse was one of the leading factors associated with increased odds of maternal death (adjusted odds ratio of 12) [11]. Among those who misuse substances, poly-drug use is common. There is also likely to be an increased risk of comorbid mental disorder, for example a systematic review of prevalence for postpartum depression in a population of women misusing substances suggests a higher prevalence than in the general pregnant population [12]. However, pregnancy may be a motivator for some women to reduce or stop substance misuse [13].

Alcohol

Global prevalence of alcohol use during pregnancy is 9.8% [14]. There is no known safe alcohol consumption level in pregnancy. Heavy drinking (greater than 70 grams per week) and binge drinking (four or more drinks or greater than 50 grams on one occasion) in pregnancy may be associated with an increased risk of prematurity and low birth weight [15, 16] and a range of physical, behavioural and learning problems, collectively known as fetal alcohol spectrum disorders. The association between lower levels of consumption (less than four units per week) and adverse outcomes is less clear [17]. Current advice from UK and Australian Departments of Health and US Centres for Disease Control and Prevention (CDC) is to abstain completely from alcohol in pregnancy or when trying to conceive [18, 19, 20]. Men are also advised not to drink alcohol excessively to improve fertility [21]. As such, National Institute for Health and Care Excellence (NICE) and UK Department of Health guidelines advise that pregnant women using alcohol be provided with brief, or if necessary more extended, interventions to stop or at least reduce their alcohol consumption, even if they decline assisted alcohol withdrawal [22, 23].

Tobacco

In England, 10.4% of pregnant women were known to be smoking tobacco at the time of delivery [24]. Smoking during pregnancy is often comorbid with mental disorder and other substance misuse and is associated with a range of adverse offspring outcomes, including reduced fetal growth [25]. It is also associated with an increased risk of miscarriage, prematurity, placental abruption and still birth [25].

Opioids

Use of opioids may include misuse of and/or dependence on both illicit opioids and opioids prescribed by a medical practitioner. While there is a lack of evidence to support a direct association between fetal teratogenicity and opioid exposure, fluctuating levels in the maternal blood may lead to withdrawal in the fetus and/or overdose in the mother [26]. Other possible risks include the effects of comorbid substance misuse, the risks of injecting (such as infected injection sites and blood-borne viruses), poor diet and malnutrition, neglect of personal care, domestic violence and poor engagement with obstetric services.

Neonatal abstinence syndrome (NAS) occurs in between 70 and 95% of the neonates of mothers who have misused opioids during pregnancy [26]. Signs include a high-pitched cry, rapid breathing, ineffective sucking and excessive wakefulness [27] and onset is between 24 and 48 hours following delivery, although can occur up to 10 days postpartum, particularly if the woman is taking methadone in conjunction with benzodiazepines [26]. As with all substances used in pregnancy, psychiatrists should be aware of the importance of neonatal monitoring for withdrawal and liaise with obstetric and neonatal services to ensure that they are aware of the infant's exposure.

Benzodiazepines

Benzodiazepines are often used by those misusing other substances [28]. This is important when one considers that comorbid benzodiazepine misuse may exacerbate the NAS associated with opioid misuse during pregnancy. Psychiatrists should consider and enquire about benzodiazepine use (including prescribed benzodiazepines) in all women who are pregnant or planning pregnancy.

The teratogenicity of benzodiazepines during pregnancy is unclear and evidence is conflicting regarding longer-term impacts on the developing infant [29, 30, 31, 32]. Risks must be weighed against the benefits of their short-term use in alcohol detoxification during pregnancy. 'Floppy baby syndrome' has been reported in neonates exposed to benzodiazepines in utero. Symptoms include poor muscle tone, hypothermia, lethargy and breathing and feeding difficulties; management is supportive.

Cannabis and Synthetic Cannabinoid Receptor Agonists

Cannabis is one of the most commonly used substances during pregnancy, with some women believing it to be safe during pregnancy [33]. A recent review identified one potential reason for this perceived absence of risk was a lack of communication by healthcare professionals about the potential adverse outcomes of cannabis use in the perinatal period [33]. However, tetrahydrocannabinol: the major psychoactive component of cannabis, readily crosses the placental barrier [34]. Synthetic cannabinoid receptor agonists (SCRAs), for example, 'Spice', are also potent stimulators of the endocannabinoid system and their safety during pregnancy is unknown. There is some evidence associating cannabis with a range of adverse obstetric and neonatal outcomes such as low birth weight and preterm birth and with adverse neurobehavioral outcomes, although data are inconclusive [35, 36, 37]. As such, British Association for Psychopharmacology (BAP) guidelines advise complete abstinence from cannabis during pregnancy [21, 38]. Likewise for SCRAs, while there are now UK management guidelines for the non-pregnant population [39], there is little guidance for women during pregnancy.

It is important for healthcare professionals working with women who are pregnant or planning pregnancy to enquire about cannabis use, quantify how much cannabis is being used, counsel women on the potential risks and consider offering referral to specialist drug and alcohol services for heavy users. It is also important to be aware of the potential for cannabis, when smoked with tobacco, to potentiate adverse effects of both substances.

Stimulants (Including Cocaine, Amphetamines and Mephedrone)

Stimulants such as cocaine, mephedrone and amphetamines are all potent vasoconstrictors so can affect the fetus at any stage of gestation [40, 41]. Women using non-prescribed stimulants in pregnancy should be encouraged to stop completely [21, 22].

A neonatal withdrawal syndrome has been reported in some cases of infants exposed to stimulants in utero; it involves withdrawal symptoms such as vomiting and restlessness, although stimulant withdrawal in infants is not as well defined a syndrome as the

NAS associated with opioid exposure, and withdrawal symptoms are thought to be less severe [42]. Studies report between 4% and 6% of those infants exposed to stimulants experiencing withdrawal; this increases when there is concomitant use of opioids but also appears to decline when evaluators are blinded to whether or not the infant has been exposed to stimulants [42]. Given these potential risks, close monitoring of the pregnancy and infant, particularly fetal growth, is required in women who have used stimulants in pregnancy.

Assessment

For many women and their partners who misuse substances, pregnancy may be the first time that they have engaged with health services. As such, it provides an opportunity for health services to support women, their partners and their wider social networks with their substance misuse. Psychiatrists should routinely and sensitively enquire about substance use, including alcohol and tobacco, in all women who are pregnant or planning pregnancy. Dependence on prescribed medication such as opioids and benzodiazepines should also be considered.

Regarding specific assessment tools, many have been used in the non-pregnant population but few have been validated for use in the perinatal period. NICE suggests using the AUDIT questionnaire for alcohol use as per NICE guidelines for the non-pregnant population [23]. There is a briefer three-question version of this: the AUDIT-C [43], although there is limited evidence for its validity during pregnancy [44, 45, 46]. There has been even less validation in the perinatal period of tools for other substances, with performance varying greatly between different populations [47, 48].

Those with children or who are expecting a baby may worry that their parenting ability will be questioned if they disclose substance use [49]. The most effective way to create an environment conducive to disclosure is a collaborative, individualised discussion considering the broader stressors, not the substance use alone. This is best done by a trusted professional who has established a rapport. Clearly such discussions are even more effective if conducted in the preconception period [50].

Questions to Consider Asking about Substance Use during Pregnancy or in Women Planning a Pregnancy

- What types and amounts of substances is she using? What is the method and frequency of use?
- Is her partner or anybody else in the family also using substances?
- What is her understanding of the impact of the substance use on her pregnancy and unborn infant?
- Are there other physical and mental health conditions or needs, and social vulnerabilities?
- Is she engaged with maternity services and receiving antenatal care?
- Is she known to any other services such as a specialist addictions service? What are those services currently providing?
- Who is supporting her during pregnancy and in the postpartum?
- Would she like to breastfeed?
- Does she have any other children?

Safeguarding

Variation in type and quantity of substances used is important to consider when evaluating risk. Some histories may raise safeguarding concerns for the mother, her unborn infant, other children and/or wider family. Such risks should always be considered and conditions under which confidentiality may be breached should be clearly communicated. Potential safeguarding referrals should always be discussed with the woman prior to making them, unless there are overwhelming risk issues. More discussion on safeguarding issues can be found in Chapter 36.

Management

The optimal approach to managing substance misuse when identified within a family is likely to be a multidisciplinary and multi-agency one. Information may need to be shared (within the confines of data protection regulations) between agencies to ensure a coordinated approach to care and to deliver a care plan which considers needs, risks, goals and wider social networks. Where available, disciplines that may be involved in care include social work, primary care, maternity and addiction services as there will often be multiple physical and mental health needs and social stressors. A number of integrated programmes have been developed to bring together the many professionals supporting parents who use substances. A meta-analysis of these interventions indicate a medium effect size in reducing maternal substance use but more randomised trials are required [51].

Brief Interventions

For those wishing to reduce or stop their substance use, brief interventions can be offered by a range of healthcare professionals working in the mental health team. These are currently recommended by the UK Department of Health in its clinical guidelines on drug misuse and dependence [22] and by NICE in its clinical guidelines on antenatal and postnatal mental health [23]. Brief interventions are short structured therapies, usually a maximum of 30 minutes in duration designed to be delivered by non-specialists, to explore ambivalence and encourage behaviour change in those who have had little previous support with their substance use. Motivational interviewing using the FRAMES model may form part of a brief intervention [52].

The FRAMES Model [52]

- Feedback: information about the risks of the substance on the pregnancy and developing infant
- Responsibility: emphasise responsibility of the individual to make decision regarding her substance use
- Advice: information about how to reduce or stop substance use
- Menu of options: offer different options to facilitate shared decision-making
- Empathy: be empathic and non-judgmental at all times
- Self-efficacy: instil hope that she is capable of change

However, many will require additional support. Both NICE and the UK Department of Health recommend that pregnant women seeking to engage in treatment of their substance misuse be fast-tracked in to a treatment programme as early in pregnancy as possible [22, 23].

Those who may particularly benefit from referral to drug and alcohol services are those dependent on substances such as alcohol and opioids, who require substitute prescribing or have complex comorbidities. Here they will receive individualised support from a drug and alcohol keyworker, including developing a treatment and recovery plan and monitoring its progress, support with social needs and delivery of psychosocial interventions. Other services that may be offered include smoking cessation, training on the use of naloxone to those using opioids, needle exchange facilities and blood-borne virus testing for those using drugs intravenously and sexual health services. Some midwifery teams also have a specialist midwife for substance misuse. There is evidence that engagement in a drug treatment programme during pregnancy results in improvements in antenatal care and general health of both mother and baby, regardless of whether or not abstinence is achieved [5].

Smoking Cessation

NICE guidelines advise that all pregnant women who are currently smoking or who have stopped in the last 2 weeks be referred to smoking cessation services [49]. Such advice could also be usefully employed in the preconception period in those planning pregnancies. There is strong systematic review evidence that smoking cessation programmes improve rates of smoking cessation during pregnancy and in turn reduce rates of prematurity and low birth weight [53]. However, it is also important to note that certain groups may find it more difficult to stop smoking; for example there is evidence that women with mental disorders may find it more difficult, even if they are referred to smoking cessation services [54].

Carbon monoxide testing is now being offered routinely within maternity services at antenatal booking and as required throughout pregnancy to identify women exposed to tobacco [55]. This may be conducted within a 'very brief advice' framework of 'Ask' (about smoking status), 'Advise' (on the results of carbon monoxide screening) and 'Act' (refer to smoking cessation services) [55]. While psychiatrists are unlikely to be able to offer carbon monoxide screening they can liaise with maternity services providing this and adapt their care to deliver similarly brief interventions to women and their partners who are smoking, as discussed above.

Psychosocial Interventions

UK Department of Health guidelines recommend a number of different psychosocial interventions for drug misuse and dependence [22]. For many substances such as cannabis, stimulants such as cocaine, and many of the newer psychoactive substances, they are the mainstay of treatment. These guidelines outline interventions that can support individuals at different stages from assessment and engagement, through to behaviour change and into early recovery [22]; many of them can be offered by non-specialists. However, evaluation of psychosocial interventions in the perinatal period to date has been limited. Moreover, there is increasing awareness of the importance of optimising health of potential parents in the preconception period [50], with some preconception interventions recently trialled in the US resulting in reduced tobacco and alcohol exposure during pregnancy [56].

Engagement strategies may involve offering support to address social issues or incentivising attendance [22]. One form of incentivising is through contingency management. Contingency management uses positive reinforcement techniques to support and reward positive behaviour, for example use of vouchers as a reward for regular attendance. A systematic review of psychosocial interventions for pregnant women in outpatient drug treatment programmes compared to other interventions yielded 14 studies, most of which involved women misusing opioids or cocaine [57]. Studies looked at motivational interviewing and contingency-based management strategies. Compared to treatment as usual, which was often specialist substance misuse services, neither was able to demonstrate superiority in terms of significant improvements in maternal outcomes (retention in treatment or abstinence) or neonatal outcomes (prematurity and low birth weight), although contingency management did result in neonates remaining in hospital for fewer days after delivery [57]. Moreover, a systematic review of randomised controlled trials (RCTs) of psychoeducational interventions to reduce alcohol consumption in women during pregnancy or who are planning a pregnancy yielded four studies. While some studies demonstrated improved rates of abstinence, results were inconsistent, with little evidence to support the use of one specific type of intervention [58].

There are a number of ways in which behaviour change can be supported. These include setting SMART goals (specific, measurable, agreed-upon, realistic, time-limited) [22] and rewarding their achievement. The use of more intensive psychosocial interventions for behaviour change such as cognitive behavioural therapy (CBT) based approaches has not been widely evaluated in the perinatal period, although there is some limited evidence to support the use of CBT in the management of opioid dependence during pregnancy. In a study of pregnant women on methadone treatment, CBT significantly reduced risky injecting behaviours but there was no change in sexual risk behaviours, drug use or injection frequency [59]. Building self-efficacy and coping skills is a central component of the management plan employed by many keyworkers within drug and alcohol services. Other resources to support abstinence include 12 Step programmes such as Alcoholics Anonymous, which are also recommended in the Department of Health guidelines [22]. Relapse prevention work is also done by keyworkers.

Women and their families will likely require ongoing support in the postpartum, including management of comorbid mental disorders and social support, particularly around parenting. Risks to young children living in homes with those who misuse substances include those from substitute medications such as methadone. Lessons emerging from case reviews conducted by the agency Adfam highlight the importance of healthcare professionals being able to educate parents who misuse substances on the importance of safely storing drugs out of reach of children [60]. This may include the provision of safe storage boxes.

Prescribing

Management of substance use in both specialist and non-specialist settings involves a range of approaches, both pharmacological and psychosocial, as discussed above. The aim of medication use is to achieve stability; as with all prescribing in pregnancy, a balance must be struck between minimising exposure of the fetus to prescribed medication or illicit drugs versus a potential increase in relapse risk if prescribed substitutes are withdrawn [22]. Currently UK Department of Health guidelines recommend that breastfeeding be encouraged unless the risks clearly outweigh the benefits, even in women who continue to misuse substances, except in those using cocaine or crack cocaine or high doses of benzodiazepines [22]. It may even reduce the intensity and length of neonatal abstinence syndrome [5].

Alcohol Detoxification

The WHO recommend that, if necessary, pregnant women dependent on alcohol be referred to a service that can support detoxification at the earliest opportunity [61]. Women should be advised against stopping drinking suddenly due to the life-threatening complications of alcohol withdrawal, such as seizures and delirium tremens. They should also be offered thiamine and vitamin B as per the usual protocol. BAP addictions and perinatal guidelines advise that long-acting benzodiazepines such as chlordiazepoxide or diazepam should be used to prevent these complications of alcohol withdrawal (see section on benzodiazepines) [21, 38]. Detoxification should ideally be in the inpatient setting to facilitate close monitoring and liaison between obstetric and addictions teams [21, 38].

There are insufficient data on safety to support the use of relapse prevention medications such as acamprosate, disulfiram and naltrexone [21, 22, 38]. However, clearly the risks of relapse to alcohol use versus maintaining abstinence with the help of a relapse prevention medication need to be weighed for each individual.

Neonates exposed to alcohol in pregnancy may experience a withdrawal syndrome. If psychiatrists are aware that an unborn infant may have been exposed to alcohol, this is another reason to inform maternity care providers of the woman's alcohol use.

Nicotine Replacement Therapy

A number of guidelines recommend that nicotine replacement therapy (NRT) only be considered if smoking cessation interventions without NRT have failed and there is complete smoking cessation [21, 38, 49]. However, a systematic review of RCTs of NRT in pregnancy found insufficient evidence that it improved rates of smoking cessation or reduced risks of miscarriage, stillbirth, prematurity, low birthweight, admission to neonatal intensive care or neonatal death compared to control groups [62]. Nonetheless, alternatives such as NRT are likely to be safer than cigarettes so should be considered within the context of an informed discussion with the woman.

At the time of writing, the use of electronic cigarettes remains controversial [63, 64], with the CDC advising against their use in pregnancy due to their unknown safety profile [65] but NHS England advising that they are safer than smoking tobacco in their guidelines on smoking in pregnancy [66]. Bupropion and varenicline should not be prescribed to pregnant or breastfeeding women [21, 38].

Opioid Substitution Therapy

Methadone and buprenorphine are recommended in the non-pregnant population for the management of opioid dependence [67]. Department of Health and BAP guidelines also recommend their use in the pregnant population at a dose that stops or minimises illicit opioid use, with a focus on maintaining stability [21, 22, 38]. Methadone maintenance treatment compared to heroin misuse is associated with a number of improved outcomes for mother and baby, including earlier antenatal care, reduced risk of prematurity [68] and reduced risk of low birth weight [69].

Methadone metabolism is increased in the third trimester of pregnancy and it may be necessary to increase the dose or split it, from once-daily to twice-daily consumption, or both [22]. Split dosing may minimise fetal intoxication or withdrawal [70]. The obstetric team should be made aware that a woman is dependent on opioids. Management of pain in labour and method of delivery should be discussed in advance with the woman and obstetric team [38].

The choice of buprenorphine or methadone should be individualised to the patient, and switching during pregnancy, particularly if well maintained, is discouraged [38]. There have been a number of trials comparing methadone and buprenorphine in pregnancy and both appear to be associated with NAS, although an international RCT comparing the two suggests that NAS may be less severe with buprenorphine [28]. However, a subsequent systematic review which also included this study suggested that methadone may be associated with better retention in treatment [71]. There is inconsistent evidence that dose of methadone is associated with severity of NAS [72, 73, 74]. Thus it is important that neonates exposed to opioid substitutes such as methadone and buprenorphine are also monitored for signs of withdrawal [61].

Opioid Detoxification

BAP guidelines are clear that opioid detoxification should generally be avoided while pregnant, as relapse rates are high and risks are greater from failed detoxification and relapse to illicit drug use than from opioid maintenance treatment [21, 38]. Low rates of detoxification completion and high rates of relapse were also found in a recent systematic review [75]. However, if women are particularly stable and keen to pursue detoxification, it should be done in the second trimester due to an increased risk of spontaneous abortion with detoxification in the first trimester. Detoxification in the second trimester may be undertaken in small reductions of, for example, 2–3 mg methadone every 3–5 days. If there is any ongoing illicit use, there should be a focus on re-stabilisation on an opioid substitute. Detoxification in the third trimester is also not advised as maternal withdrawal has been associated with fetal distress, preterm delivery and stillbirth [21].

There may be an increased risk of relapse in the postpartum; women should also be warned that they may have lost their tolerance and could overdose unexpectedly [23]. Another risk in cases where the child has been removed from the mother is an increased risk of suicide in the mother [11].

Benzodiazepine Detoxification

UK Department of Health guidelines strongly recommend that pregnant women undergo a gradual dose reduction using long-acting benzodiazepines such as diazepam at the lowest effective dose, but only for as long as is required to manage the symptoms of withdrawal [22]. A gradual taper will reduce the symptoms of withdrawal and reduce the risk of exacerbation of symptoms in those being prescribed benzodiazepines as part of the treatment of a mental disorder. WHO and BAP guidelines also suggest that inpatient admission be considered during this time given the serious risks of benzodiazepine withdrawal, which include seizures [38, 61]. They also recommend that psychosocial interventions be provided during the period of benzodiazepine withdrawal [38, 61].

Breastfeeding

Alcohol

While alcohol use is not a complete contraindication to breastfeeding, WHO guidelines recommend a careful consideration of risks and benefits and advise that in cases of heavy alcohol consumption, for example in alcohol dependence, breastfeeding exposes the infant to high risks which could be avoided if safe breast milk alternatives are available. They also suggest that it is possible to reduce exposure in women using alcohol intermittently by avoiding breastfeeding 2 hours after consuming one standard drink or 4–8 hours after consuming more than one drink in a single occasion [61]. Caregivers should also be made aware of the potential impact of alcohol intoxication on their ability to care for the child.

Tobacco

There is little nicotine transferred to breast milk and the benefits of breastfeeding likely outweigh the risks in mothers who smoke. Nonetheless, 50% of smokers report that smoking affected their breastfeeding decisions and 10% reported smoking being the reason for stopping breastfeeding [25].

Opioids

Women who are stable on opioid maintenance treatment with methadone or buprenorphine should be encouraged to breastfeed, unless the risks outweigh the benefits [22]. Children should be weaned off breast milk gradually to reduce the risk of withdrawal [61]. However, a number of challenges to breastfeeding by women on methadone maintenance therapy have been identified, many of them relating to prolonged hospital stays by neonates in the postpartum, sometimes in the intensive care setting [76].

Benzodiazepines

There is transfer of benzodiazepines into breast milk; while there is less concern about breastfeeding when benzodiazepines are taken at normal prescribed doses, higher doses may lead to infant sedation, irritability and withdrawal symptoms. Thus the WHO cautions against breastfeeding when benzodiazepines are being used at high doses [61]. Clearly, 'normal prescribed doses' may vary internationally and with guidelines not providing an indication of this and the limited evidence, this advice should be applied with caution.

Other Substances

As with many other substances used during pregnancy, the decision as to whether or not to breastfeed should be on an individual, case by case basis, in discussion with the mother; there is some evidence of transfer of cannabis into breastmilk [77] and guidelines are conflicting as to whether or not breastfeeding should be undertaken in women who continue to misuse cannabis [34]. However, guidelines are clear that women using stimulants should not breastfeed [61].

Conclusion

Many women and their partners use substances; during pregnancy this may be associated with adverse obstetric and child outcomes, although clearly this differs depending on the type and level of use. Healthcare providers, including psychiatrists, should routinely enquire about substance use, including alcohol and tobacco, in all women who are pregnant or planning pregnancy. Pregnant women misusing substances and their partners should be fast-tracked into treatment and psychosocial interventions considered. Psychiatrists working with families affected by substance misuse may need to liaise with other agencies, including social work, primary care, maternity and addiction services, where available. A risk-benefit discussion, informed by the latest evidence, ensures a collaborative management plan, ultimately helping to improve outcomes for all those affected.

References

1. WHO. Management of substance abuse: facts and figures. n.d. www.who.int/substance_abuse/facts/en
2. WHO. The ICD-11 classification of mental and behavioural disorders: clinical descriptions and diagnostic guidelines. Geneva: World Health Organization; 2024.
3. G Gilchrist, K Hegarty. Tailored integrated interventions for intimate partner violence and substance use are urgently needed. *Drug Alcohol Rev.* 2017;36(1):3–6.
4. H Klee. Drug-using parents: analysing the stereotypes. *Int J Drug Policy.* 1998;9(6):437–48.
5. S Mayet, T Groshkova, L Morgan, T MacCormack, J Strang. Drugs and pregnancy—outcomes of women engaged with a specialist perinatal outreach addictions service. *Drug Alcohol Rev.* 2008;27(5):497–503.
6. K Kaltenbach, L Finnegan. Children of maternal substance misusers. *Curr Opin Psychiatry.* 1997;10(3):220–4.
7. M Knight, K Bunch, A Felker, R Patel, R Kotnis, S Kenyon, et al., editors. *Saving Lives, Improving Mothers' Care – Lessons learned to inform maternity care from the UK and Ireland Confidential Enquiries into Maternal Deaths and Morbidity 2019–21.* Oxford: National Perinatal Epidemiology Unit, University of Oxford; 2023. www.npeu.ox.ac.uk/mbrrace-uk/reports
8. CA Essau, S Sasagawa, PM Lewinsohn, P Rohde. The impact of pre- and perinatal factors on psychopathology in adulthood. *J Affect Disord.* 2018;236:52–9.
9. Public Health England. *Adult substance misuse statistics from the National Drug Treatment Monitoring System (NDTMS): 1 April 2017 to 31 March 2018.* London: Public Health England; 2018. https://shorturl.at/HtkMU
10. V Manning, DW Best, N Faulkner, E Titherington. New estimates of the number of children living with substance misusing parents: results from UK national household surveys. *BMC Pub Health.* 2009;9:377.
11. M Nair, M Knight, JJ Kurinczuk. Risk factors and newborn outcomes associated with maternal deaths in the UK from 2009 to 2013: a national case–control study. *BJOG.* 2016;123(10):1654–62.
12. LE Ross, C-L Dennis. The prevalence of postpartum depression among women with substance use, an abuse history, or chronic illness: a systematic review. *J Womens Health.* 2009;18(4):475–86.
13. K Kendler, H Ohlsson, D Svikis, K Sundquist, J Sundquist. The protective effect of pregnancy on risk for drug abuse: a population, co-relative, co-spouse, and within-individual analysis. *Am J Psychiatry.* 2017;174(10):954–62.
14. S Popova, S Lange, C Probst, G Gmel, J Rehm. Estimation of national, regional, and global prevalence of alcohol use during pregnancy and fetal alcohol syndrome: a systematic review and meta-analysis. *Lancet Global Health.* 2017;5(3):e290–9.
15. AL Flak, S Su, J Bertrand, CH Denny, US Kesmodel, ME Cogswell. The association

of mild, moderate, and binge prenatal alcohol exposure and child neuropsychological outcomes: a meta-analysis. *Alcohol Clin Exp Res.* 2014;38(1):214–26.

16. C O'Leary, N Nassar, J Kurinczuk, C Bower. The effect of maternal alcohol consumption on fetal growth and preterm birth. *BJOG.* 2009;116(3):390–400.
17. L Mamluk, HB Edwards, J Savović, V Leach, T Jones, THM Moore, et al. Low alcohol consumption and pregnancy and childhood outcomes: time to change guidelines indicating apparently 'safe' levels of alcohol during pregnancy? A systematic review and meta-analyses. *BMJ Open.* 2017;7(7):e015410.
18. Australian Government Department of Health. National Health and Medical Research Council's Australian guidelines to reduce health risks from drinking alcohol. 2009. www.nhmrc.gov.au/health-topics/alcohol-guidelines
19. US Centers for Disease Control and Prevention. Alcohol and pregnancy. 2016. https://shorturl.at/254UG
20. Department of Health. *UK Chief Medical Officers' alcohol guidelines review: summary of the proposed new guidelines.* London: Department of Health; 2016. https://shorturl.at/4r9uj
21. AR Lingford-Hughes, S Welch, L Peters, D Nutt. BAP updated guidelines: evidence-based guidelines for the pharmacological management of substance abuse, harmful use, addiction and comorbidity: recommendations from BAP. *J Psychopharmacol.* 2012;26(7):899–952.
22. Department of Health and Social Care. *Drug misuse and dependence: UK guidelines on clinical management.* London: Department of Health; 2017. https://shorturl.at/FxsfX
23. NICE. Antenatal and postnatal mental health: clinical management and service guidance. Clinical Guideline (CG192). 2020. www.nice.org.uk/guidance/CG192
24. Public Health England. *Health matters: stopping smoking – what works?* London: Public Health England; 2018. https://shorturl.at/W0Xsl
25. A Cohen, R Osorio, LM Page. Substance misuse in pregnancy. *Obstet Gynaecol Reprod Med.* 2017;27(10):316–21.
26. B Winklbaur, N Kopf, N Ebner, E Jung, K Thau, G Fischer. Treating pregnant women dependent on opioids is not the same as treating pregnancy and opioid dependence: a knowledge synthesis for better treatment for women and neonates. *Addiction.* 2008;103(9):1429–40.
27. LM Jansson, M Velez. Neonatal abstinence syndrome. *Curr Opin Pediatrics.* 2012;24(2):252–8.
28. HE Jones, K Kaltenbach, SH Heil, SM Stine, MG Coyle, AM Arria, et al. Neonatal abstinence syndrome after methadone or buprenorphine exposure. *New Engl J Med.* 2010;363(24):2320–31.
29. L Ban, J West, JE Gibson, L Fiaschi, R Sokal, P Doyle, et al. First trimester exposure to anxiolytic and hypnotic drugs and the risks of major congenital anomalies: a United Kingdom population-based cohort study. *PloS ONE.* 2014;9(6):e100996.
30. LR Dolovich, A Addis, JMR Vaillancourt, JDB Power, G Koren, TR Einarson. Benzodiazepine use in pregnancy and major malformations or oral cleft: meta-analysis of cohort and case-control studies. *BMJ.* 1998;317(7162):839–43.
31. MM Iqbal, T Sobhan, T Ryals. Effects of commonly used benzodiazepines on the fetus, the neonate, and the nursing infant. *Psychiatr Serv.* 2002;53(1):39–49.
32. JT Mortensen, J Olsen, H Larsen, J Bendsen, C Obel, HT Sørensen. Psychomotor development in children exposed in utero to benzodiazepines, antidepressants, neuroleptics, and anti-epileptics. *Eur J Epidemiol.* 2003;18(8):769–71.
33. H Bayrampour, M Zahradnik, S Lisonkova, P Janssen. Women's perspectives about cannabis use during pregnancy and the postpartum period: an integrative review. *Prev Med.* 2019;119: 17–23.

34. LM Jansson, CJ Jordan, ML Velez. Perinatal marijuana use and the developing child. *JAMA.* 2018;320(6):545–6.

35. SN Conner, EB Carter, MG Tuuli, GA Macones, AG Cahill. Maternal marijuana use and neonatal morbidity. *Am J Obstet Gynecol.* 2015;213(3):422.e1–4.

36. MR Hayatbakhsh, VJ Flenady, KS Gibbons, AM Kingsbury, E Hurrion, AA Mamun, et al. Birth outcomes associated with cannabis use before and during pregnancy. *Pediatric Res.* 2011; 71:215.

37. TD Warner, D Roussos-Ross, M Behnke. It's not your mother's marijuana: effects on maternal-fetal health and the developing child. *Clin Perinatol.* 2014;41(4):877–94.

38. RH McAllister-Williams, DS Baldwin, R Cantwell, A Easter, E Gilvarry, V Glover, et al. British Association for Psychopharmacology consensus guidance on the use of psychotropic medication preconception, in pregnancy and postpartum 2017. *J Psychopharmacol.* 2017;31(5):519–52.

39. D Abdulrahim, O Bowden-Jones. *Harms of synthetic cannabinoid receptor agonists (SCRAs) and their management.* London: Novel Psychoactive Treatment UK Network (NEPTUNE); 2016.

40. A Forray, D Foster. Substance use in the perinatal period. *Curr Psychiatry Rep.* 2015;17(11):91.

41. LP McLafferty, M Becker, N Dresner, S Meltzer-Brody, P Gopalan, J Glance, et al. Guidelines for the management of pregnant women with substance use disorders. *Psychosomatics.* 2016;57(2):115–30.

42. American Academy of Pediatrics Committee on Drugs. Neonatal drug withdrawal. *Pediatrics.* 1998;101(6):1079–88.

43. JB Saunders, OG Aasland, TF Babor, JR De La Fuente, M Grant. Development of the Alcohol Use Disorders Identification Test (AUDIT): WHO Collaborative Project on Early Detection of Persons with Harmful Alcohol Consumption-II. *Addiction.* 1993;88(6):791–804.

44. E Burns, R Gray, LA Smith. Brief screening questionnaires to identify problem drinking during pregnancy: a systematic review. *Addiction.* 2010;105(4):601–14.

45. DA Dawson, BF Grant, FS Stinson, Y Zhou. Effectiveness of the Derived Alcohol Use Disorders Identification Test (AUDIT-C) in screening for alcohol use disorders and risk drinking in the US general population. *Alcohol Clin Exp Res.* 2005;29(5):844–54.

46. EA O'Connor, LA Perdue, CA Senger, M Rushkin, CD Patnode, SI Bean, et al. Screening and behavioral counseling interventions to reduce unhealthy alcohol use in adolescents and adults: updated evidence report and systematic review for the US Preventive Services Task Force. *JAMA.* 2018;320(18):1910–28.

47. G Chang, EJ Orav, JA Jones, T Buynitsky, S Gonzalez, L Wilkins-Haug. Self-reported alcohol and drug use in pregnant young women: a pilot study of associated factors and identification. *J Addict Med.* 2011;5(3):221–6.

48. SJ Ondersma, G Chang, T Blake-Lamb, K Gilstad-Hayden, J Orav, JR Beatty, et al. Accuracy of five self-report screening instruments for substance use in pregnancy. *Addiction.* 2019;114(9):1683–93.

49. NICE. Pregnancy and complex social factors: a model for service provision for pregnant women with complex social factors. Clinical guideline (CG110). 2010. www.nice.org.uk/guidance/cg110

50. Public Health England. *Making the case for preconception care: planning and preparation for pregnancy to improve maternal and child health outcomes.* London: Public Health England; 2018. https://shorturl.at/XGKp8

51. K Milligan, A Niccols, W Sword, L Thabane, J Henderson, A Smith, et al. Maternal substance use and integrated treatment programs for women with substance abuse issues and their children:

a meta-analysis. *Subst Abuse Treat Prev Policy*. 2010;5(1):21.

52. RK Hester, WR Miller. *Handbook of alcoholism treatment approaches*. 2nd ed. Boston, MA: Allyn & Bacon; 1995.
53. C Chamberlain, A O'Mara-Eves, J Porter, T Coleman, SM Perlen, J Thomas, et al. Psychosocial interventions for supporting women to stop smoking in pregnancy. *Cochrane Database Syst Rev*. 2017;(2).
54. LM Howard, D Bekele, M Rowe, J Demilew, S Bewley, TM Marteau. Smoking cessation in pregnant women with mental disorders: a cohort and nested qualitative study. *BJOG*. 2013;120(3):362–70.
55. NHS England. *Saving babies' lives version two: a care bundle for reducing perinatal mortality*. London: NHS England; 2019. https://shorturl.at/LrzSg
56. MM Velasquez, KL von Sternberg, RL Floyd, D Parrish, A Kowalchuk, NS Stephens, et al. Preventing alcohol and tobacco exposed pregnancies: CHOICES Plus in primary care. *Am J Prevent Med*. 2017;53(1):85–95.
57. M Terplan, S Ramanadhan, A Locke, N Longinaker, S Lui. Psychosocial interventions for pregnant women in outpatient illicit drug treatment programs compared to other interventions. *Cochrane Database Syst Rev*. 2015;(4).
58. BC Stade, C Bailey, D Dzendoletas, M Sgro, T Dowswell, D Bennett. Psychological and/or educational interventions for reducing alcohol consumption in pregnant women and women planning pregnancy. *Cochrane Database Syst Rev*. 2009;(2): CD004228-CD.
59. K O'Neill, A Baker, M Cooke. Evaluation of a cognitive-behavioural intervention for pregnant injecting drug users at risk of HIV infection. *Addiction*. 1996;91(8):1115–25.
60. Adfam. Medications in drug treatment: tackling the risks to children. 2014. https://adfam.org.uk/files/docs/adfam_ost_fullreport_web.pdf
61. WHO. *Guidelines for the identification and management of substance use and substance use disorders in pregnancy*. Geneva: World Health Organization; 2014. www.who.int/substance_abuse/publications/pregnancy_guidelines/en
62. T Coleman, C Chamberlain, MA Davey, SE Cooper, J Leonardi-Bee. Pharmacological interventions for promoting smoking cessation during pregnancy. *Cochrane Database Syst Rev*. 2015;(12).
63. A Bush, J Coutts, R Langley. Vaping in pregnancy: caution required! *Addiction*. 2024;119(8):1491–2.
64. F Pesola, KM Smith, A Phillips-Waller, D Przulj, C Griffiths, R Walton, et al. Safety of e-cigarettes and nicotine patches as stop-smoking aids in pregnancy: secondary analysis of the Pregnancy Trial of E-cigarettes and Patches (PREP) randomized controlled trial. *Addiction*. 2024;119(5):875–84.
65. US Centers for Disease Control and Prevention. *E-cigarettes and pregnancy*. Atlanta, GA: US Centers for Disease Control and Prevention; 2024. www.cdc.gov/maternal-infant-health/pregnancy-substance-abuse/e-cigarettes.html
66. NHS England. *Stop smoking in pregnancy*. London: NHS England; 2023. www.nhs.uk/pregnancy/keeping-well/stop-smoking
67. NICE. Methadone and buprenorphine for the management of opioid dependence. Technology Appraisal Guidance (TA114). 2007. www.nice.org.uk/guidance/TA114
68. L Burns, RP Mattick, K Lim, C Wallace. Methadone in pregnancy: treatment retention and neonatal outcomes. *Addiction*. 2007;102(2):264–70.
69. GK Hulse, E Milne, DR English, CDJ Holman. The relationship between maternal use of heroin and methadone and infant birth weight. *Addiction*. 1997;92(11):1571–9.
70. BK Wittmann, S Segal. A comparison of the effects of single- and split-dose methadone administration on the fetus: ultrasound evaluation. *Int J Addict*. 1991;26(2):213–18.

71. S Minozzi, L Amato, C Bellisario, M Ferri, M Davoli. Maintenance agonist treatments for opiate-dependent pregnant women. *Cochrane Database Syst Rev.* 2013;(12).

72. BJ Cleary, J Donnelly, J Strawbridge, PJ Gallagher, T Fahey, M Clarke, et al. Methadone dose and neonatal abstinence syndrome—systematic review and meta-analysis. *Addiction.* 2010;105(12):2071–84.

73. C Dryden, D Young, M Hepburn, H Mactier. Maternal methadone use in pregnancy: factors associated with the development of neonatal abstinence syndrome and implications for healthcare resources. *BJOG.* 2009;116(5):665–71.

74. CA Kuschel, L Austerberry, M Cornwell, R Couch, RSH Rowley. Can methadone concentrations predict the severity of withdrawal in infants at risk of neonatal abstinence syndrome? *Arch Dis Child Fetal Neonatal Ed.* 2004;89(5):F390–3.

75. M Terplan, HJ Laird, DJ Hand, TE Wright, A Premkumar, CE Martin, et al. Opioid detoxification during pregnancy: a systematic review. *Obstet Gynecol.* 2018;131(5):803–14.

76. J Hicks, E Morse, DK Wyant. Barriers and facilitators of breastfeeding reported by postpartum women in methadone maintenance therapy. *Breastfeed Med.* 2018;13(4):259–65.

77. T Baker, P Datta, K Rewers-Felkins, H Thompson, RR Kallem, TW Hale. Transfer of inhaled cannabis into human breast milk. *Obstet Gynecol.* 2018;131(5):783–8.

Chapter 19

Intellectual Disability

Sonya Rudra and Ken Courtenay

Introduction

This chapter focuses on women with intellectual disabilities (ID). It does not apply to other neurodevelopmental disorders such as autism and ADHD except in the context of dual diagnosis with ID.

Various terms have been used historically to refer to people with ID such as 'mental retardation', 'mental handicap' and 'learning disabilities'. In this chapter, the term 'intellectual disabilities' (ID) is used reflecting its use in internationally accepted classification systems [1].

The American Psychiatric Association's *Diagnostic and Statistical Manual of Mental Disorders*, 5th edition (DSM-5) defines an intellectual disability as a condition in which the below criteria are met:

1. Impairments in intellectual functions, such as reasoning, planning and problem solving, confirmed by both clinical assessment and intelligence testing.
2. Loss of adaptive functioning resulting in failing to meet developmental and societal standards for personal independence and social responsibility. Daily activities such as communicating, living independently, or working, require ongoing support.
3. Intellectual and adaptive deficits during the developmental period. [2]

The term 'intellectual developmental disorder' is placed in parentheses and listed after the DSM-5 diagnosis, to mirror the language used in recent revisions of the International Classification of Diseases [1].

The severity of an intellectual disability can be defined as mild, moderate, severe or profound based on adaptive functioning in the conceptual, social and practical domains [2]. There is a thus a great degree of heterogeneity in ID with considerable variation in underlying intellectual functioning and adaptive behaviour.

Prevalence rates of ID vary depending on the study design and the population studied, but is often cited close to 3% [3]. Individuals with mild ID represent the largest proportion, approximately 2.5%, with the other levels accounting for 0.5% of the population [3].

In order for a perinatal psychiatrist to deliver optimum care to women with ID, it is essential to have a broad understanding of the social, psychological and biological contexts of their presentations in order to deliver tailored, holistic and effective care. The existing literature in the field of perinatal psychiatry and ID compares women with ID with women without ID in the general population. This comparison may be less useful in perinatal mental health where women experiencing mental illness during the perinatal period are the focus and would be the ideal comparison group when attempting to understand the additional needs of mothers with ID. However, due to a sparsity of literature on perinatal mental health in women with ID, it is often necessary to draw conclusions from the evidence on women without ID in the general population.

In this chapter, maternal health, perinatal mental health, parenthood and pregnancy outcomes of women with ID are explored along with the support options available to clinicians supporting women with ID.

Background

Women with Intellectual Disability as Parents

Mothers with ID have faced a long struggle to prove their parental competence. Historically, childbearing among women with ID was uncommon because of sterilisation, institutionalisation and pressures not to parent [4]. De-institutionalisation and changing attitudes, coupled with policy and legislative changes recognising the rights of people with ID to parent [5] and to have a family life [6], have resulted in more people with ID becoming parents. With more community-based care, women with ID now have more opportunities to develop relationships and have children.

Unfortunately, many mothers with ID continue to experience negative attitudes from society, healthcare professionals, social services practitioners and their own families and close friends about their pregnancies [7, 8, 9, 10]. They are faced with discrimination, stigma and negative attitudes about their ability to be effective parents [11] and face a battle to prove to professionals and society that they are competent parents [12]. This is in spite of evidence indicating that there is no clear relationship between parental competency and intelligence for parents with mild ID [13, 14].

Although international data suggest that the number of parents with ID is increasing [15], the estimates of the number vary widely. Data in England indicate that 1 in 15 (7%) people with ID have children [16]. In Australia, it is estimated that up to 2% of families with a child under 18 years of age has at least one parent with ID [17]. Reasons for the lack of reliable data include fragmented services, poor record-keeping, lack of common definitions of ID over time, the variety of terms used to represent the same condition, the invisibility of many parents to official agencies, and that many cases are 'borderline' and therefore included in some datasets but not in others [18].

In general, mothers with ID have a mild form of ID. Parents with moderate and more severe forms of ID have a much lower prevalence of parenthood because they are more likely to lack the mental capacity to consent to sexual intercourse. Among such women, a pregnancy would raise concerns of abuse, sexual exploitation or rape [19].

Women with Intellectual Disabilities and Pregnancy Outcomes

Women with ID are at increased risk of adverse maternal and neonatal outcomes compared with those without ID [20]. Several studies show that pregnancies are more likely to be complicated by common pregnancy complications such as gestational hypertension and gestational diabetes, as well as rare but serious complications including pre-eclampsia, venous thromboembolism, placental abruption and antepartum haemorrhage [21, 22, 23, 24]. Delivery is more likely to result in caesarean section [22] and there is increased risk of stillbirth [20, 25, 26], perinatal death [25] or neonatal mortality [20, 27].

Among live births, infants are more likely to be of low birth weight [27, 28], small for gestational age [21, 29] and born preterm [27, 28, 29]. They experience more neonatal morbidities [27], increased rates of admissions to neonatal intensive care units [29] and longer stays in hospital [30]. Pregnancy outcomes are worse still for mothers with comorbid ID and mental illness [31].

Such disparities, both in maternal and neonatal outcomes, reflect cumulative social and economic disadvantages. Women with ID are a vulnerable population who experience poverty, violence or abuse, chronic medical disease and mental illness disproportionately, all of which are risk factors for poor reproductive outcomes. These indicators are discussed in more depth throughout this chapter.

Contextual Factors

The model proposed by Aunos and Feldman highlights the importance of understanding contextual factors in parents with ID [4]. These factors drive services, policy and cultural attitudes, which together produce specific outcomes.

Research has suggested that mothers with ID are more likely to be unemployed, struggle financially, have low educational attainment, reside in poor housing and in deprived neighbourhoods compared to mothers without ID [21, 32, 33]. Socio-economic factors are associated with mental illness in women whether with or without ID [34]. Therefore, for women with a dual diagnosis of ID and mental illness, their social circumstances can present significant challenges to them [31]. Furthermore, women with ID have been found to suffer from more trauma than women without disabilities, such as being victims of assault [32]. A systematic review has highlighted the link between the increased levels of interpersonal trauma in parents with ID and parental mental illness [35].

In terms of support, mothers with ID are less likely to be married or have a partner compared to mothers without ID [21, 36, 37, 38, 39]. They have smaller support networks, often relying on formal professional relationships [40] or close family for support [8, 41]. A perceived lack of a support network is associated with high levels of stress and poor mental health [42]. Pregnant women with ID may also avoid contact with individuals whom they perceive as prejudiced towards them [43], which can lead to their already small support networks becoming smaller and delay them seeking support from professionals.

Contextual factors play a big role in increasing the stress faced by mothers with ID to levels higher than those in the general adult population of women who have given birth [42]. Conceptualising stress as a form of overload on an individual's adaptive resources, women with ID face a double jeopardy due to their cognitive impairment and their role as parents [13]. Additionally, they are more likely to experience parenting under conditions of adversity, making them even more susceptible to stress. This is important as increased stress is linked to maternal mental health problems [44].

Maternal Mental Health in Women with Intellectual Disabilities

Women with ID compared with those without, are more likely to experience mental illness. Although accurate figures vary, Brown and colleagues found that women with ID were twice as likely to have mental health problems including psychotic disorders, mood and anxiety disorders and substance use disorders [45]. Rates are even higher for women with an existing dual diagnosis of ID and mental illness, compared with those with ID only [31].

Risk factors independently associated with the development of mental illness in this group of women have some similarities to that of the general population, such as experiencing a higher number of preceding life events, a higher number of general practitioner consultations, and being a smoker [46]. However, some differences have been suggested, such as no association between residing in more deprived areas, not having a daytime occupation, and marital status [46].

Mothers with ID are particularly more prone to mental illness during the perinatal period [37, 47]. A population-based study from Canada found that among women with no pre-pregnancy history of mental illness, those with ID had 1.38 times the risk of new-onset mental illness in the perinatal period compared to women without a disability. Among mothers with distal mental illness, women with ID had 1.24 times the risk of recurrent disorders in the perinatal period compared to those without a disability. Among women with a recent history of mental illness, those with intellectual disabilities had 1.31 times the risk of ongoing use of mental health services perinatally, compared to those without a disability [33].

These findings align with studies from Mitra and Brown that have shown that during pregnancy and after childbirth, women with ID have higher rates of visits to emergency departments for psychiatric reasons such as postpartum depression, anxiety disorder and other mood disorders [37, 47]. Following childbirth, women with ID have a ten-fold higher rate of hospital admission for psychiatric reasons where the most common reasons for hospital admissions after childbirth are schizophrenia/psychosis, postpartum depression and bipolar affective disorder [47].

Physical Health

Women with ID, compared with those without, have also been found to have higher rates of some physical health conditions such as diabetes mellitus, herpes or HIV, and epilepsy [48]. Furthermore, women with an existing dual diagnosis of ID and mental illness have higher rates of physical health conditions than women with ID only [31].

This puts women with ID presenting to perinatal services at greater risk of suffering from or developing new physical health problems during pregnancy. This risk is compounded by the finding that women with ID are more likely to receive inadequate prenatal care [49].

In the postpartum period, the greater need for physical healthcare continues. Women with ID have a two-fold higher rate of visits to emergency departments for medical reasons when compared with women without ID and have longer lengths of hospital stays [30]. Common reasons include puerperal infections, abdominal/pelvic pain and postpartum haemorrhage [47].

Sexual Health

There remain mixed attitudes towards sexuality, sterilisation, procreation and parenting by people with ID [4, 50], often with assumptions that they are not engaging in sexual intercourse. This may therefore be a topic of discussion that is neglected completely by clinicians, families and teachers. Thus, contact with perinatal services could be the first opportunity to open a discussion about sexual health and safe reproductive practices.

Exploring the views and practices regarding contraception in a woman with ID is important. A previous form of contraception may not have been successful or the woman does not feel ready for the demands of another pregnancy and may opt to start a form of contraceptive. Different methods of contraception have specific modes of administration, interactions with other drugs and side effects. Decisions about the contraceptive method need to be tailored to a woman's specific circumstances and preference. In women who lack mental capacity regarding contraception, such decisions should be made in her best interest.

Lifestyle Factors

Women with ID presenting to perinatal services have a range of lifestyle factors that may impact on their physical and mental health. Some lifestyle factors have been linked to increased risks of mental illness in the mother. Therefore, by addressing these factors we can support women and their children to remain healthy and reduce the risks of mental illness and relapse.

Mothers with ID are more likely to smoke during pregnancy [21, 38, 49, 51, 52] and obesity in pregnant women with ID is higher than in women without ID [51]. Weight gain could be explained by an increased appetite from medication, a lack of understanding about the importance of healthy weight, a lack of support to eat healthily or sedentary behaviours. Sedentary lifestyle behaviours may be related to the side effects of psychotropic medication, lack of knowledge about health, lack of support to access activities and limitations due to physical disabilities.

Support to access information on healthy lifestyle behaviours during and after pregnancy is integral to making informed decisions and lifestyle choices [53]. The provision of accessible information by trained professionals reduces the reliance on unreliable sources such as the internet. Information should be timely to support decision-making, optimise healthy pregnancies and early childhood development and well-being [54].

Child Outcomes

The findings on child developmental outcomes for children of parents with ID are inconclusive [55]. Many of the existing studies include small cohorts and are conducted on selected groups. There are a few larger studies, although the definitions of ID used in these studies is inconsistent. The contextual-interactional model of parenting in ID posits some intergenerational effects that are supported by research [56]; for example, the impact of parental childhood trauma on parenting, child and family outcomes [35]. Therefore, supporting mothers can help improve outcomes for their children.

One of the biggest concerns among mothers with ID is seeking support from professionals because of the risk of being judged incompetent and having their children removed from their care. Such concerns are not unfounded. Parents with ID are significantly over-represented in child protection proceedings, and their children are removed from their care significantly more often than their peers without ID [57, 58]. Data from Ontario, Canada indicate that up to 5.7% of newborn children of women with ID were discharged to child protection services immediately after birth compared to 0.2% of women without ID [58]. Qualitative data has highlighted the distressing impact of child removal processes. Women may suffer severe depression and anxiety which reoccurs even years after the pregnancy and increases risks of maternal suicide [59].

Assessment

Mental Health Assessment

Women with ID as parents may present late to mental health services. They may delay seeking help for a number of reasons that include the fear of being judged or having their children removed. By the time they present to mental health professionals, their symptoms may be more frequent and severe [60]. They may minimise symptoms and distress, in which case the psychiatrist needs to conduct a careful and thorough assessment of risk which may only be achieved after conducting a number of reviews, during which time trust has been built with the mother. Seeking information from an informant who knows the woman well can be useful in understanding how the current presentation differs from her usual level of functioning.

In general, it is useful to look for similar symptomatology that would indicate mental illness in the general population. This is best achieved using clinical interview and professional judgement. Most screening/diagnostic tools have not been validated in the ID population and therefore risk missing a diagnosis of mental illness [61]. If using standardised instruments, it is essential they are adapted to reflect the educational and comprehension levels of the woman with ID [62].

Before an assessment takes place, it is important to optimise communication with the mother. Communication can be difficult in mothers with ID for a number of reasons which include their cognitive impairment, associated speech problems, or autistic traits where she may have difficulty describing her symptoms. It can be helpful to utilise communication aids or to consult others who know the mother well [63]. This essential consideration could help earlier recognition of mental disorders in women with ID.

Mental Capacity Assessment

A person's ability to make decisions relies on their mental capacity to accept and understand information on the decision to be taken, to weigh up the information and to communicate their decision. All persons are assumed to have mental capacity unless it is proved otherwise. Some people with ID do not have the mental capacity to make some or all decisions for themselves. Regardless of this, women with ID should be involved in all the steps of the decision-making process on matters that affect their health and welfare.

Mental capacity should be assessed when making any decision and complex decisions may require a formal capacity assessment by an appropriate professional. In women with ID these decisions include capacity to consent to clinical interventions, to consent to arrangements with social care and to consent to sexual relations.

The Mental Capacity Act 2005 (England and Wales) sets out a two-stage test of capacity [64]. Specific steps should be taken to support people with ID to make decisions on matters that affect them. Examples of support include making 'reasonable adjustments' to enhance their mental capacity and to optimise their ability to communicate their decision effectively. This may require the involvement of other people such as family members, speech and language therapists or social workers. For other suggestions refer to the section on Reasonable Adjustments and Box 19.1.

For those who lack capacity, in England and Wales, the Mental Capacity Act 2005 provides that any act done, or decision made, on their behalf must be in their best

Box 19.1 Examples of reasonable adjustments/adaptations for working with people with ID

Prior to review

- Offering appointments at times/locations which are accessible to the person
- Sending easy-read appointment letters to professionals/carers supporting the individual as well as the individual themselves (with permission)
- Sending additional appointment reminders
- Developing visual aids of what occurs in the appointment

During review

- Starting appointments on time or ensuring there is a quiet/private area to wait
- Conducting reviews in a location appropriate for the person's sensory needs
- Allowing the duration of reviews to be flexible
- Allowing additional presence and support during reviews from family/carers
- Maintaining consistency in professional involvement

Ending review

- Providing information in easy-read and different formats after the review, e.g. written, visual and audio
- Providing additional appointments and long-term follow-up

interests. Best interest decisions must include consultation of family members and the decision-maker to consider previously expressed wishes and behaviour of the person.

Mental capacity legislation in other areas of the UK (Adults with Incapacity (Scotland) Act 2000; Mental Capacity (Northern Ireland) Act 2016) are founded on similar principles.

Therapeutic Approaches

Psychotropic Medication in Women with Intellectual Disabilities

A large proportion of people with ID are prescribed antipsychotic medication without a diagnosed psychotic illness [65]. Women with ID are likely to use psychotropic medication to treat mental disorders such as anxiety or depression or to help with behavioural challenges such as impulsivity or aggression. The rate of epilepsy among people with ID is high, and therefore women with ID are also more likely to use antiepileptic medication [45].

Women with ID, in common with other pregnant women, face a number of other difficult decisions involving medication. The decision to breastfeed can be a particularly important decision for any mother and may be associated with feelings of motherhood and empowerment. However, the decision to breastfeed will need to be balanced against the benefits from the medications they are using, and particular medications may need to be altered or discontinued in women who choose to breastfeed (see Chapter 26).

Women with ID who have epilepsy require careful monitoring of their response to anti-epileptic medication during pregnancy, when breastfeeding and in the puerperium because of changes in therapeutic blood levels. Women with ID using sodium valproate should be managed according to the accepted protocols for all women but extra care may be needed to support their decisions on using it [19, 66, 67]. Such complex decisions on using medication require detailed discussions that may need to be conducted over a number of consultations with the support of augmented communication and 'reasonable adjustments' to enhance the woman's understanding of information to reach an informed decision.

Psychological Therapies in Women with Intellectual Disabilities

In many instances it will be appropriate to offer psychological therapies to women with ID, although the woman should possess certain prerequisite skills to effectively engage with the therapy. There may be a need to adapt psychological therapies developed for the general population; however, there is a balance to be made as large adaptations can impact the evidence base for the intervention. The format of psychotherapy also varies depending on the individual. In people with milder levels of ID, guided self-help approaches based on cognitive behavioural therapy or psychoeducation have been found to be feasible [68]. A meta-analysis of psychological treatment for people with an ID [69] reported that group-based interventions had a moderate but smaller treatment effect than individual-based interventions. Professionals should also consider the usefulness of parental mentalising interventions given the heightened proclivity for pre-mentalising identified in some parents with ID [70]. Thus, input from a psychological therapist trained in working with people with ID is essential for developing an appropriate individualised psychological therapy plan.

Social Support

Social networks are key to providing emotional and practical support to mothers. They play a role in establishing and maintaining a woman's identity as a mother, an important part of becoming a parent [40, 71]. Strengthening social supports can help imbue resilience in mothers with ID which can promote mental health. This can be achieved using the following approaches:

1. *Enhancing existing social supports:* Existing social supports include support from fathers, family, friends and neighbours. These people can be encouraged to come together voluntarily and intentionally to help promote and progress the goals and interests of the person with ID in 'Circles of Support' [72]. For many parents with ID they may not have these close social relationships. Therefore, support may be necessary to develop strategies to identify, reconnect, and strengthen existing social relationships.
2. *Providing compensatory support to isolated and/or at-risk individuals and families:* Increased support and monitoring of women with ID during the perinatal period can enhance mental well-being. This may take the form of input from voluntary services such as local peer support groups [40] or professional input from a social worker, doula or independent advocate [73].
3. *Adult learning*: Adult learning allows one to develop the awareness, understanding and skills to strengthen social relationships. This can take a variety of forms from using written information to participating in parent training workshops. Parent training for parents with ID has been shown to increase childcare skills, home safety skills and reduce parent stress [18].

Overall, support should be competence-promoting, recognising and valuing the abilities of the person. This positive approach enhances feelings of self-confidence, promotes autonomy and fosters better engagement with services [41, 74].

Additional Considerations

Reasonable Adjustments

Reasonable adjustments ensure that a disabled person receives the same level of service as a non-disabled person, which is a statutory requirement under the Equality Act (2010) in the UK. 'Intellectual disability' masks a wide range of abilities and with every person it is essential to consider if all reasonable adjustments have been made by services to ensure equity of access to services. Reasonable adjustments can cover a broad range of adjustments made to accommodate the needs of a person with disabilities. Greater efforts by healthcare providers to enhance their practice through reasonable adjustments is essential if women with ID are to benefit from the care offered to them [75].

As an example, making small but significant adjustments in communicating information to support pregnant women with ID could deliver better outcomes in practice. Providing optimal perinatal informational support to women with ID is challenging because of their varying abilities in intellectual and adaptive functioning. *The key to such interventions is to make them specific and adapted to the person with ID.* Table 19.1 describes other examples of reasonable adjustments to consider incorporating into all appointments and interactions with women with ID.

Safeguarding

Safeguarding refers to the procedures and processes to protect adults and children who experience harm or are at risk of harm. This may differ between organisations and countries. In the UK, safeguarding adults is defined in the Care Act 2014 as 'protecting an adult's right to live in safety and free from abuse and neglect' [76].

Women with ID, as with all women, should be protected from all forms of abuse. Women with disabilities are particularly vulnerable to intimate partner violence, defined as physical, sexual or emotional abuse perpetrated by a spouse or current/former partner [77, 78]. In becoming a mother, women may face violent conceptions, they may be pregnant or mothering whilst living with domestic violence and exposed to a broad spectrum of abuse [79].

Women with ID are especially vulnerable to abuse because of their cognitive, adaptive and sometimes physical limitations [80]. They may depend more on others for their support needs and not understand that what they experience is abuse, particularly where abuse is part of a relationship which they value. Societal devaluation, the desire for social status and the need to have a partner have all been highlighted as factors that influence women's experiences to remain in violent relationships [81]. Additionally, fears of child removal may make parents with ID reluctant to confide in professionals. Therefore, professionals working with parents with ID need training and support to recognise and respond appropriately to signs of abuse. They should not conflate domestic violence with risks to child safety or overstate parenting risks that lead to the automatic removal of the child [82].

There will be times when children of parents with ID, as with other parents, need to be removed from the family home to ensure their health, safety and well-being are maintained. The United Nations Convention on the Rights of the Child (1990) and the laws of many countries around the world make it necessary to intervene when a child's welfare is at stake [83]. This is implemented through local pathways ensuring the mother is supported and kept informed throughout the process (see Chapter 36, 'Child Safeguarding').

Perinatal Services for Women with Intellectual Disabilities

Mothers with ID face considerable inconsistencies in the care and support they receive from healthcare services. A population-based study from Canada highlighted that this group were more likely to receive inadequate or no prenatal care – entering care later and with fewer than the recommended number of visits, compared to women without disabilities [84]. For those women with ID who do receive care, many report negative experiences related to barriers at the societal (e.g. cultural norms of motherhood), policy/institutional (e.g. child protection policies and practices), interpersonal (e.g. inadequate formal and informal support) and intrapersonal levels (e.g. internalised stigma) [85].

Currently, in the UK and other countries, services caring for mothers with ID vary from specialised teams to general services. This is partly due to different thresholds for severity of ID for accepting referrals into specialist teams. When mothers with ID are reviewed by mainstream services, advice can be sought from specialised ID teams. Conversely, specialist ID teams require clear pathways to refer their patients to perinatal services. The optimum scenario consists of joint working and collaboration between perinatal mental health services and ID services. For inpatients this would involve in-reach from specialist ID teams into inpatient Mother and Baby Units.

In general, 'good practice' requires a positive and proactive approach to identifying need; reasonable adjustments to communication and providing information; and professionals working together to support and enable parents [86]. Therapeutic approaches should be flexible and individualised and sensitive to individual context. A number of qualitative studies emphasise the need for family-based approaches [87, 88, 89]. The training and support of professionals is key for ensuring consistently high-quality care. Brown and Mitra's perinatal health framework for people with intellectual disability highlights the importance of interactions across policy, community, institutional, interpersonal and individual levels in producing perinatal outcomes and identifies areas of need when delivering care for people with ID [90]. Thus, care needs to be holistic, multidisciplinary and multi-agency, paired with policy efforts to address social determinants of health and trauma [90].

Training of Professionals

In their journey from pregnancy to motherhood, women with ID are likely to encounter many professionals offering advice and support. A benchmarking exercise for the Learning Disability Improvement Standards in the NHS in the UK found that a little over half of staff (53%) confirmed they had the necessary training to meet the requirements of the Learning Disability Standards in delivering care to people with ID, autism or both that took account of their rights and needs [91]. There are particularly large gaps in the training of professionals for working with women with ID during the perinatal period [92, 93].

The understanding and attitudes of professionals regarding ID are likely to have direct impacts on the quality of care they receive. Without training, medical staff can lack the knowledge to support mothers with ID effectively [94]. Even professional staff such as midwives who have contact with pregnant women with ID, do not always consider they have the skills to support women with ID [95, 96, 97]. Training and education on ID in general, and on pregnancy in women with ID specifically, can improve communication with them, and increase the confidence of healthcare providers to support this group of women [98]. This is particularly crucial as many parents with ID often consider professionals as part of their support network [40], therefore better relationships with professionals could impact on health-seeking behaviours leading to better health outcomes [8, 10].

The Core Capabilities Framework for Supporting People with a Learning Disability/ Autistic People in England sets out the core skills and knowledge that staff supporting people with ID and autistic people should have, depending on the nature and intensity of support and care that they give [99]. Providers of education in higher educational institutions and health services should ensure that specific training for professional staff is available on assessing and meeting the needs of parents with ID who have professional contact with them and their families. To ensure true service-user participation, training needs to be delivered in a co-produced way with parents with ID and their supporters.

Conclusion

Intellectual disability is a lifelong disorder that affects up to 3% of the population [3]. More women with ID are parents than previously because of changes in society and how they are perceived and treated. However, they experience higher rates of mental and physical health disorders than women in the general population including in the perinatal period. The maternal and neonatal health outcomes of women with ID are worse than women in the general population compounded by adverse socio-economic factors and fewer social supports.

Professionals delivering services to women with ID need to be aware of the issues affecting women with ID in order to deliver high-quality effective care to this vulnerable group who face many adversities in life, not least the assumptions made by society and professionals regarding their ability to parent their children. Gaining support from family members or carers is essential in helping to construct accurate professional opinions and treatment plans. On account of the higher rate of comorbid disorders affecting women with ID, prescribing practice needs to take account of drug interactions and side effects. Making adjustments to clinical practice can effectively enhance the care that women with ID receive, leading to better outcomes for mothers and their children.

Overall, knowledge of the perinatal mental health needs of women with ID is patchy with challenges in identifying mental disorders in mothers with ID. Standardised objective tools to assess mental health in women in general when evaluated in women with ID indicate that results are not valid in this group of women. Given the complexities and vulnerabilities of this highly heterogeneous group, more research is required into the perinatal mental health care of women with ID.

References

1. World Health Organization. *ICD-11 for mortality and morbidity statistics*. Geneva: WHO; 2018. https://icd.who.int/browse11/l-m/en
2. American Psychiatric Association. *Diagnostic and statistical manual of mental disorders (DSM-5®)*. Washington, DC: American Psychiatric Association; 2013.

3. PK Maulik, MN Mascarenhas, CD Mathers, T Dua, S Saxena. Prevalence of intellectual disability: a meta-analysis of population-based studies. *Res Dev Disabil.* 2011;32(2):419–36.
4. M Aunos, M Feldman. Attitudes towards sexuality, sterilization and parenting rights of persons with intellectual disabilities. *J Appl Res Intellect Disabil.* 2002;15(4):285–96.
5. Equality Act 2010. London: HMSO. www.legislation.gov.uk/ukpga/2010/15/contents
6. Human Rights Act 1998. London: HMSO; 2020. www.legislation.gov.uk/ukpga/1998/42
7. B Hoglund, M Larsson. Professional and social support enhances maternal well-being in women with intellectual disability: a Swedish interview study. *Midwifery.* 2014;30(11):1118–23.
8. S Wilson, K McKenzie, E Quayle, GC Murray. The postnatal support needs of mothers with an intellectual disability. *Midwifery.* 2013;29(6):592–8.
9. R Malouf, J McLeish, S Ryan, R Gray, M Redshaw. 'We both just wanted to be normal parents': a qualitative study of the experience of maternity care for women with learning disability. *BMJ Open.* 2017;7(3):e015526.
10. LA Potvin, BM Barnett, HK Brown, V Cobigo. "I didn't need people's negative thoughts": women with intellectual and developmental disabilities reporting attitudes toward their pregnancy. *Can J Nurs Res.* 2019;51(3):154–67.
11. B Höglund, M Larsson, P Lindgren. Pregnancy and birth among women with intellectual disability in Sweden: experiences and outcomes. *Acta Obstet Gynecol Scand.* 2012;91:90–1.
12. CN Shpigelman, M Bar. "I'm a good mother; I play with her; I love her": the motherhood experience of women with intellectual disabilities from empowering and intersectional approaches. *Disabil Health J.* 2023;16(4):101504.
13. T Booth, W Booth. Parenting with learning difficulties: lessons for practitioners. *Br J Social Work.* 1993;23(5):459–80.
14. L Dowdney, D Skuse. Parenting provided by adults with mental retardation. *J Child Psychol Psychiatry.* 1993;34(1):25–47.
15. U Pixa-Kettner. Parenting with intellectual disability in Germany: results of a new nationwide study. *J Appl Res Intellect Disabil.* 2008;21(4):315–19.
16. NHS Digital. *Adults with learning difficulties in England, 2003–2004.* England: NHS; 2005. https://shorturl.at/GzLI4
17. A Lamont, L Bromfield. *Parental intellectual disability and child protection: key issues.* Melbourne: Australian Institute of Family Studies; 2009.
18. E Coren, K Ramsbotham, M Gschwandtner. Parent training interventions for parents with intellectual disability. *Cochrane Database Syst Rev.* 2018;(7).
19. H Angus-Leppan, R Shankar, H Cock. Valproate, women, and exceptional circumstances. *BMJ.* 2018;362:k3625.
20. HK Brown, V Cobigo, Y Lunsky, SN Vigod. Maternal and offspring outcomes in women with intellectual and developmental disabilities: a population-based cohort study. *BJOG.* 2017;124(5):757–65.
21. J Fairthorne, J Bourke, M O'Donnell, K Wong, N de Klerk, G Llewellyn, et al. Pregnancy and birth outcomes of mothers with intellectual disability and their infants: advocacy needed to improve well-being. *Disabil Health J.* 2020;13(2):100871.
22. E Rubenstein, DB Ehrenthal, DC Mallinson, L Bishop, H-H Kuo, M Durkin. Pregnancy complications and maternal birth outcomes in women with intellectual and developmental disabilities in Wisconsin Medicaid. *PloS ONE.* 2020;15(10):e0241298.
23. W Horner-Johnson, B Garg, BG Darney, FM Biel, AB Caughey. Severe maternal morbidity and other perinatal complications among women with physical, sensory, or intellectual and

developmental disabilities. *Paediatr Perinat Epidemiol.* 2022;36(5):759–68.

24. JL Gleason, J Grewal, Z Chen, AN Cernich, KL Grantz. Risk of adverse maternal outcomes in pregnant women with disabilities. *JAMA Netw Open.* 2021;4(12):e2138414.

25. B Hoglund, P Lindgren, M Larsson. Newborns of mothers with intellectual disability have a higher risk of perinatal death and being small for gestational age. *Acta Obstet Gynecol Scand.* 2012;91(12):1409–14.

26. I Akobirshoev, SL Parish, M Mitra, E Rosenthal. Birth outcomes among US women with intellectual and developmental disabilities. *Disabil Health J.* 2017;10(3):406–12.

27. LA Tarasoff, F Murtaza, A Carty, D Salaeva, AD Hamilton, HK Brown. Health of newborns and infants born to women with disabilities: a meta-analysis. *Pediatrics.* 2020;146(6).

28. JE Shin, GJ Cho, S Bak, SE Won, SW Han, SB Lee, et al. Pregnancy and neonatal outcomes of women with disabilities: a nationwide population-based study in South Korea. *Sci Rep.* 2020;10(1):1–8.

29. HK Brown, S Chen, A Guttmann, SM Havercamp, SL Parish, JG Ray, et al. Neonatal outcomes of mothers with a disability. *Pediatrics.* 2022;150(3).

30. W Horner-Johnson, BG Darney, FM Biel, AB Caughey. Prolonged postpartum length of hospital stay among women with disabilities. *Disabil Health J.* 2020;13(4):100934.

31. HK Brown, V Cobigo, Y Lunsky, CL Dennis, S Vigod. Perinatal health of women with intellectual and developmental disabilities and comorbid mental illness. *Can J Psychiatry.* 2016;61(11):714–23.

32. LA Tarasoff, Y Lunsky, S Chen, A Guttmann, SM Havercamp, SL Parish, et al. Preconception health characteristics of women with disabilities in Ontario: a population-based, cross-sectional study. *J Womens Health.* 2020;29(12):1564–75.

33. HK Brown, SN Vigod, K Fung, S Chen, A Guttmann, SM Havercamp, et al. Perinatal mental illness among women with disabilities: a population-based cohort study. *Soc Psychiatry Psychiatr Epidemiol.* 2022;57(11):2217–28.

34. Commission on Social Determinants of Health. *Closing the gap in a generation: health equity through action on the social determinants of health.* Final Report of the Commission on Social Determinants of Health. Geneva: World Health Organization; 2008.

35. M Hammarlund, P Granqvist, T Forslund. Experiences of interpersonal trauma among parents with intellectual disabilities: a systematic review. *Trauma Violence Abuse.* 2023;24(4):2843–62.

36. M Redshaw, R Malouf, H Gao, R Gray. Women with disability: the experience of maternity care during pregnancy, labour and birth and the postnatal period. *BMC Pregnancy Childbirth.* 2013;13(1): 1–14.

37. M Mitra, SL Parish, KM Clements, J Zhang, TAM Simas. Antenatal hospitalization among US women with intellectual and developmental disabilities: a retrospective cohort study. *Am J Intellect Dev Disabil.* 2018;123(5):399–411.

38. AD Goldacre, R Gray, MJ Goldacre. Childbirth in women with intellectual disability: characteristics of their pregnancies and outcomes in an archived epidemiological dataset. *J Intellect Disabil Res.* 2015;59(7):653–63.

39. NW Man, C Wade, G Llewellyn. Prevalence of parents with intellectual disability in Australia. *J Intellect Dev Disabil.* 2016;42(2):173–9.

40. I Strnadová, J Bernoldová, Z Adamčíková. 'She will know that her mother's doing something for her': women with intellectual disabilities assuming the mother identity. *Disabil Soc.* 2018;34(1):68–94.

41. LA Potvin, HK Brown, V Cobigo. Social support received by women with intellectual and developmental disabilities

during pregnancy and childbirth: an exploratory qualitative study. *Midwifery.* 2016;37:57–64.

42. D McConnell, R Mayes, G Llewellyn. Prepartum distress in women with intellectual disabilities. *J Intellect Dev Disabil.* 2008;33(2):177–83.
43. R Mayes, G Llewellyn, D McConnell. Misconception: the experience of pregnancy for women with intellectual disabilities. *Scand J Disabil Res.* 2006;8(2–3):120–31.
44. LM Schwab-Reese, EJ Schafer, S Ashida. Associations of social support and stress with postpartum maternal mental health symptoms: main effects, moderation, and mediation. *Women Health.* 2017;57(6):723–40.
45. HK Brown, Y Lunsky, AS Wilton, V Cobigo, SN Vigod. Pregnancy in women with intellectual and developmental disabilities. *J Obstet Gynaecol Can.* 2016;38(1):9–16.
46. SA Cooper, E Smiley, J Morrison, A Williamson, L Allan. Mental ill-health in adults with intellectual disabilities: prevalence and associated factors. *Br J Psychiatry.* 2007;190:27–35.
47. HK Brown, V Cobigo, Y Lunsky, S Vigod. Postpartum acute care utilization among women with intellectual and developmental disabilities. *J Womens Health.* 2017;26(4):329–37.
48. HK Brown, YA Kirkham, V Cobigo, Y Lunsky, SN Vigod. Labour and delivery interventions in women with intellectual and developmental disabilities: a population-based cohort study. *J Epidemiol Community Health.* 2016;70(3):238–44.
49. BA Mueller, D Crane, DR Doody, SN Stuart, MA Schiff. Pregnancy course, infant outcomes, rehospitalization, and mortality among women with intellectual disability. *Disabil Health J.* 2019;12(3):452–9.
50. W de Wit, D Roeg, N Frielink, PJCM Embregts. Exploring sexual health in people with mild intellectual disabilities: a concept mapping study on the perspectives of relatives and support staff. *J Intellect Dev Disabil.* 2024:1–12.
51. B Hoglund, P Lindgren, M Larsson. Pregnancy and birth outcomes of women with intellectual disability in Sweden: a national register study. *Acta Obstet Gynecol Scand.* 2012;91(12):1381–7.
52. M Mitra, SL Parish, I Akobirshoev, E Rosenthal, TAM Simas. Postpartum hospital utilization among Massachusetts women with intellectual and developmental disabilities: a retrospective cohort study. *Matern Child Health J.* 2018;22(10):1492–501.
53. L Potvin, R Lindenbach, H Brown, V Cobigo. Preparing for motherhood: women with intellectual disabilities on informational support received during pregnancy and knowledge about childbearing. *J Dev Disabil.* 2020;25(1).
54. A Guay, M Aunos, D Collin-Vézina. Mothering with an intellectual disability: a phenomenological exploration of making infant-feeding decisions. *J Appl Res Intellect Disabil.* 2017;30(3): 511–20.
55. E Emerson, P Brigham. The developmental health of children of parents with intellectual disabilities: cross sectional study. *Res Dev Disabil.* 2014;35(4):917–21.
56. MA Feldman, M Aunos. Recent trends and future directions in research regarding parents with intellectual and developmental disabilities. *Curr Dev Disord Rep.* 2020;7(3):173–81.
57. F Lima, M O'Donnell, J Bourke, B Wolff, A Gibberd, G Llewellyn, et al. Child protection involvement of children of mothers with intellectual disability. *Child Abuse Negl.* 2022;126:105515.
58. HK Brown, LA Potvin, Y Lunsky, SN Vigod. Maternal intellectual or developmental disability and newborn discharge to protective services. *Pediatrics.* 2018;142(6).
59. E Wall-Wieler, LL Roos, NC Nickel, D Chateau, M Brownell. Mortality among mothers whose children were taken into care by child protection services: a

discordant sibling analysis. *Am J Epidemiol.* 2018;187(6):1182–8.

60. AJ Tymchuk. Depression symptomatology in mothers with mild intellectual disability: an exploratory study. *Aust N Z J Dev Disabil.* 1994;19(2):111–19.

61. K Gaskin, H James. Using the Edinburgh Postnatal Depression Scale with learning disabled mothers. *Community Pract.* 2006;79(12):392–6.

62. LV Darbyshire, BS Kroese. Psychological well-being and social support for parents with intellectual disabilities: risk factors and interventions. *J Pol Pract Intellect Disabil.* 2012;9(1):40–52.

63. J Rotheram. *Pregnancy and disability: RCN guidance for midwives and nurses.* London: Royal College of Nursing; 2007.

64. NHS England. Mental Capacity Act 2005. London: HMSO; 2020. www.legislation.gov.uk/ukpga/2005/9/pdfs/ukpga_20050009_en.pdf

65. R Sheehan, A Hassiotis, K Walters, D Osborn, A Strydom, L Horsfall. Mental illness, challenging behaviour, and psychotropic drug prescribing in people with intellectual disability: UK population based cohort study. *BMJ.* 2015;351:h4326.

66. I Sawhney, A Zia, D Adams, B Gates. Use of valproate: implications for women with intellectual disabilities and the wider interdisciplinary healthcare team. *Br J Learn Disabil.* 2019;47(3):195–200.

67. LV Watkins, HR Cock, H Angus-Leppan, R Shankar. Valproate and the Pregnancy Prevention Programme: exceptional circumstances. *Br J Gen Pract.* 2019;69(681):166–7.

68. E Chaplin, T Craig, J McCarthy, N Bouras. The SAINT: a guided self-help approach for people with intellectual disabilities. *J Ment Health Res Intellect Disabil.* 2017;10(3):237–52.

69. L Vereenooghe, PE Langdon. Psychological therapies for people with intellectual disabilities: a systematic review and meta-analysis. *Res Dev Disabil.* 2013;34(11):4085–102.

70. M Hammarlund, M Breitholtz, P Granqvist, T Forslund. Parental mentalising among mothers with intellectual disability or ADHD: links with experiences of abuse, neglect and psychosocial risk. *J Appl Res Intellect Disabil.* 2023;36(6):1206–17.

71. R Mayes, G Llewellyn, D McConnell. "That's who I choose to be": the mother identity for women with intellectual disabilities. *Womens Stud Int Forum.* 2011;34(2):112–20.

72. C Burke, K Ball. A guide to Circles of Support UK: foundation for people with learning disabilities. n.d. www.mentalhealth.org.uk/sites/default/files/a-guide-to-circles-of-support.pdf

73. A McGarry, B Stenfert Kroese, R Cox. How do women with an intellectual disability experience the support of a doula during their pregnancy, childbirth and after the birth of their child? *J Appl Res Intellect Disabil.* 2016;29(1):21–33.

74. M Tucker, O Johnson. Competence promoting vs. competence inhibiting social support for mentally retarded mothers. *Hum Organ.* 1989;48(2):95–107.

75. C Homeyard, E Montgomery, D Chinn, E Patelarou. Current evidence on antenatal care provision for women with intellectual disabilities: a systematic review. *Midwifery.* 2016;32:45–57.

76. Department of Health and Social Care. Care and support statutory guidance. 2020. https://shorturl.at/zZgEg

77. M Mitra, SL Parish, KM Clements, X Cui, H Diop. Pregnancy outcomes among women with intellectual and developmental disabilities. *Am J Prev Med.* 2015;48(3):300–8.

78. MM García-Cuéllar, G Pastor-Moreno, I Ruiz-Pérez, J Henares-Montiel. The prevalence of intimate partner violence against women with disabilities: a systematic review of the literature. *Disabil Rehabil.* 2023;45(1):1–8.

79. M McCarthy. 'All I wanted was a happy life': the struggles of women with learning

disabilities to raise their children while also experiencing domestic violence. *J Gend-Based Violence.* 2019;3(1): 101–18.

80. SB Plummer, PA Findley. Women with disabilities' experience with physical and sexual abuse: review of the literature and implications for the field. *Trauma Violence Abuse.* 2012;13(1):15–29.
81. K Pestka, S Wendt. Belonging: women living with intellectual disabilities and experiences of domestic violence. *Disabil Soc.* 2014;29(7):1031–45.
82. S Collings, I Strnadová, J Loblinzk, J Danker. Benefits and limits of peer support for mothers with intellectual disability affected by domestic violence and child protection. *Disabil Soc.* 2020;35(3):413–34.
83. United Nations. Convention on the Rights of the Child. New York: United Nations; 1989. www.ohchr.org/documents/professionalinterest/crc.pdf
84. F Nishat, Y Lunsky, LA Tarasoff, HK Brown. Prenatal care adequacy among women with disabilities: a population-based study. *Am J Prev Med.* 2022;62(1):39–49.
85. M Khan, HK Brown, Y Lunsky, K Welsh, SM Havercamp, L Proulx, et al. A socio-ecological approach to understanding the perinatal care experiences of people with intellectual and/or developmental disabilities in Ontario, Canada. *Womens Health Iss.* 2021;31(6):550–9.
86. A Cox, T Parsons, S Watkin, A Gallagher. Supporting the delivery of good maternity care for parents with learning disabilities. *Midwifery.* 2021;102:103073.
87. R Rinaldi, M Legierski, E Wauthia, E Mazza, E Batselé. Exploring professionals' practices and perspectives on supporting parents with intellectual disabilities: a qualitative study. *Front Rehabil Sci.* 2023;4:1153570.
88. K Wos, D Baczała. Parenting by mothers with intellectual disabilities in Poland: A photovoice study. *J Appl Res Intellect Disabil.* 2021;34(6):1452–62.
89. J Nicholson, S Mazel, K Faughnan, A Silverman. Mothers with intellectual/developmental disabilities and behavioral health conditions and community experts provide recommendations for treatment/services, systems, and research. *Internat J Environ Res Pub Health.* 2023;20(10):5876.
90. HK Brown, M Mitra. Perinatal health framework for people with intellectual disability. *Disabil Health J.* 2023:101576.
91. NHS England and NHS Improvement. *Performance against the learning disability improvement standards.* England: NHS; 2019. https://shorturl.at/kYhvL
92. N Amir, LD Smith, AM Valentine, M Mitra, SL Parish, TA Moore Simas. Clinician perspectives on the need for training on caring for pregnant women with intellectual and developmental disabilities. *Disabil Health J.* 2022;15(2):101262.
93. LD Smith, A Valentine, TA Moore Simas, SL Parish, A Levy, M Mitra. Clinician-reported barriers to providing perinatal care to women with intellectual and developmental disabilities. *J Intellect Dev Disabil.* 2023;48(1):12–22.
94. I Strnadová, J Bernoldová, Z Adamčíková, J Klusáček. Medical personnel's knowledge, attitudes, and experiences with regard to mothers with intellectual disability in the Czech Republic. *J Intellect Dev Disabil.* 2019;44(1):81–91.
95. B Höglund, P Lindgren, M Larsson. Midwives' knowledge of, attitudes towards and experiences of caring for women with intellectual disability during pregnancy and childbirth: a cross-sectional study in Sweden. *Midwifery.* 2013;29(8):950–5.
96. E Castell, BS Kroese. Midwives' experiences of caring for women with learning disabilities: a qualitative study. *Midwifery.* 2016;36:35–42.
97. S Beake, LL Clark, T Turner, D Bick. A mixed methods study to develop and pilot a competency assessment tool to

support midwifery care of women with intellectual disabilities. *Nurse Educ Today.* 2013;33(8):901–6.

98. I Strnadova, S Collings, J Loblinzk, J Danker. Parents with intellectual disabilities and their perspective of peer support: "It depends on how they give it". *J Appl Res Intellect Disabil.* 2019;32(4):879–89.

99. Department of Health and Social Care. *Core Capabilities Framework for Supporting Autistic People.* England: Health Education England; 2019. https://shorturl.at/SMn3Q

Chapter 20

Attention Deficit Hyperactivity Disorder

Amanda Elkin and Sally Cubbin

ADHD in Women in the Perinatal Period

In this chapter, we first consider issues relating to attention deficit hyperactivity disorder (ADHD) in general, focusing on the female population. We then address ADHD in the perinatal period, thinking about issues as they present during the pre-conceptual period, pregnancy and postnatally.

Adult ADHD is a common neurodevelopmental disorder present in up to 3.6% of adults, featuring symptoms of inattention, impulsivity and hyperactivity [1]. It is now recognised that it occurs across the lifespan, often presenting for the first time in adulthood. In addition, 80% of childhood cases are likely to persist into adulthood, frequently leading to significant disability [2]. It is a highly treatable condition with evidence-based guidelines yet is commonly confused with other mental health disorders.

Diagnosis may be made for the first time in adults, and as awareness of the condition improves, this is an increasingly common scenario. In adults, ADHD is associated with significant impairment, including lower levels of academic achievement and employment, frequent job changes, higher levels of divorce, a higher chance of being arrested as well as being less satisfied with family, social and professional lives [3]. It is associated with an increase in rates of serious road traffic accidents and of deliberate self-harm [4]. It is also associated with much psychiatric comorbidity, and in adults, often these are diagnosed first, and ADHD is identified later. Over 60% of those with adult ADHD present with one or more comorbid disorders [5] ranging from anxiety, mood disorders (including postnatal depression) and substance use [6] to other neurodevelopmental disorders, including autism [7]. Bipolar disorder, personality disorders, post-traumatic stress syndromes and other neurodevelopmental disorders such as Tourette's syndrome are also common. In fact, ADHD is 10 times more common in patients with three or more psychiatric diagnoses [8]. Physical health comorbidities, including asthma [9], obesity [10], sleep disorders [11], traumatic brain injury, joint hypermobility [12], chronic fatigue, migraine and fibromyalgia [13] as well as chronic pain, type 2 diabetes [14] and polycystic ovary syndrome also commonly occur and complicate the diagnostic picture.

Research has highlighted that few cases are treated for ADHD. Instead, treatment is often provided for other psychiatric disorders [15] with no thought given to the possibility that ADHD may also be present and may be the underlying (and treatable) perpetuating factor fuelling other comorbidities. Sometimes emotional instability, common in ADHD, may be misattributed to bipolar disorder, personality disorders, depressive disorders or 'cyclothymia'.

Features of ADHD

In adults, ADHD is often characterised by mental restlessness with patients describing ceaseless mental activity, overthinking and an inability to switch off. This commonly impairs sleep. Rather than more obvious physical hyperactivity, body-focused repetitive behaviours can be more subtle presentations of fidgeting, including nail biting, skin picking or chewing the inside of the mouth or inner lip. Fiddling with jewellery or a 'fidget toy' is also common. Mind wandering is often described as a significant factor contributing to distractibility and poor concentration, in addition to sensitivity to environmental distractions. Severe procrastination and disorganisation lead to a sense of overwhelm and underachievement. Adults commonly suffer with mood instability, often being very sensitive to criticism and rejection. Irritability, impatience and anger can damage relationships. Impulsivity, including impulsive spending and promiscuity, as well as saying things without thinking, are common and commonly damage relationships both at home and work. This combination of diverse yet impairing symptoms also makes it more challenging to maintain the consistency and patience required for good parenting.

Classification of Adult ADHD

The 18 core symptoms of ADHD are described in both the International Classification of Diseases, 11th revision (ICD-11) [16] and the *Diagnostic and Statistical Manual of Mental Disorders*, fifth edition (DSM-5) [17]. For an ICD-11 adult diagnosis to be made, the patient needs impairment from several symptoms of either inattention or hyperactivity/impulsivity (or both for combined type). Symptoms should be 'persistent, and sufficiently severe that they have a direct negative impact on academic, occupational, or social functioning', with evidence of symptoms prior to age 12 (but not necessarily impairment).

It is important to note that childhood impairment is not needed for an adult diagnosis. Commonly, the support structure of school and home life, and the less demanding life of childhood compared to adulthood, means that symptoms do not necessarily result in significant impairment for many. The ICD-11 states that 'some individuals may first come to clinical attention later in adolescence or as adults, often when demands exceed the individual's capacity to compensate for limitations'. We know that females are typically recognised later in adulthood. One precipitant resulting in the demands of life becoming greater than their ability to cope is often parenthood.

Inattentive symptoms are where the patient:

- often fails to give close attention to detail or makes careless mistakes (e.g. overlooks or misses details, work is inaccurate)
- often has difficulty sustaining attention (e.g. has difficulty remaining focused during lectures, conversations or reading)
- often does not seem to listen when spoken to directly (e.g. mind seems elsewhere, even in the absence of any obvious distraction)
- often does not follow through on instructions and fails to finish work (e.g. starts tasks but quickly loses focus, is easily side-tracked)
- often has difficulty organising tasks (e.g. messy, disorganised work; has poor time management; fails to meet deadlines)

- often avoids, dislikes or is reluctant to engage in tasks that require sustained mental effort (e.g. puts off preparing reports, has difficulty completing forms)
- often loses things necessary for tasks and activities (e.g. wallets, keys, paperwork, glasses, mobile telephones, tools)
- is often easily distracted by extraneous stimuli (or by unrelated thoughts and mind wandering)
- is often forgetful in daily activities (e.g. doing chores, running errands, returning calls, paying bills, keeping appointments)

Symptoms of hyperactivity-impulsivity are where the patient:

- often fidgets or taps with hands or feet, or squirms in seat
- often leaves seat in situations when remaining seated is expected
- often feels restless
- often is unable to engage in leisure activities quietly
- is often 'on the go' or acting 'as if driven by a motor' (e.g. is uncomfortable being still and finds sitting for long meals or meetings difficult)
- often talks excessively
- often blurts out an answer before a question has been completed
- often has difficulty waiting his or her turn in a queue
- often interrupts or intrudes on others (e.g. may take over what others are doing)

Identifying Females with ADHD

In childhood up to nine times as many boys are diagnosed than girls [18]. However, many studies have shown that the sex ratio in adult ADHD clinics is equal [19]. Females with ADHD experience later recognition and treatment. There are mixed research findings on subtypes of ADHD. The inattentive presentation is more common in women than men, but the most common type of ADHD overall in both genders is the combined type. Hyperactive-impulsive symptoms may be less obvious in females [20] and easily missed, including fiddling with hair and jewellery, skin picking, nail biting, cheek or lip chewing or being restless internally, 'on the go' and unable to relax. Talkativeness may be seen as a socially acceptable character trait. Ceaseless mental activity is often associated with sleep disturbance. The disorder causes a frequent sense of overwhelm and chronic stress and is highly comorbid and often manifests with symptoms of low self-esteem, anxiety, low mood and emotional dysregulation, which females are more likely to seek help for than males. Females with ADHD present with more 'internalising' (depression and anxiety) than the more obvious 'externalising' (disruptive and aggressive) symptoms. They are more likely to have been diagnosed with a mood disorder and are more likely to suffer problems with emotional dysregulation [21].

A lack of awareness among clinicians as to how ADHD may present, gender stereotypes of ADHD as a disruptive, male condition and the diagnostic overshadowing from other mental health conditions, including anxiety and depression, means that ADHD in women is commonly missed or misdiagnosed [22]. This is exacerbated by the misunderstanding that it must cause impairment in childhood. Compensatory behaviours in females that mask symptoms [23] may also contribute to a missed diagnosis of ADHD. Working hard, appearing to cope – usually under stress and at the last minute – can work against women with ADHD, and there is ultimately a significant detrimental cost to their mental or physical well-being. They are more likely to be 'people pleasers' closely attending to the needs of others, willing to work extra hours. Most women with ADHD lack self-confidence. They feel disorganised, regularly overwhelmed, 'hanging on by a thread' and have had background levels of stress and anxiety their entire lives, often worrying about the possibility of yet another unpredictable 'mess up'. It is unsurprising therefore that they may instead receive a diagnosis of low self-esteem and anxiety. It is not unusual for women to present after a promotion at work, or after the birth of a child when the challenges of work or parenting makes life even more demanding. It is crucial to appreciate that high intelligence, academic success or apparent high functioning does not exclude a diagnosis of ADHD. There may be a lifetime of underachievement relative to ability, and of significant detrimental personal cost associated with that achievement. Educational, occupational and financial difficulties are more common in individuals with ADHD.

Emotional dysregulation is recognised as an associated, but not diagnostic features of ADHD in the DSM-5 and ICD-11. There is evidence that these symptoms may also be responsive to ADHD medication [24]. Sadly, ADHD is highly treatable yet is commonly both a misdiagnosis and a missed diagnosis especially in women. This has detrimental implications for long-term social, educational and mental health outcomes [25].

Relationship difficulties are common in those with ADHD. Whilst some women may rush impulsively into new relationships, others lack the confidence to enter such relationships. The tendency to spend money impulsively can cause difficulties, and it is perhaps not surprising that those with ADHD have twice the risk of marital separation and divorce.

It is also important to appreciate the high comorbidity associated with ADHD. Clinicians should be alert to its presence as a treatable disorder that may fuel other mental health problems. Substance misuse is common, and many patients self-medicate with alcohol or cannabis because of the unpleasant absence of physical and mental calm, and to facilitate sleep. The binge eating disorders and bulimia nervosa are more common in patients with ADHD as is obesity – both conditions with an associated lack of impulse control (see Chapter 16 on eating disorders).

Diagnosing Adult ADHD

There are geographical variations in the quality of care offered to adults with ADHD, with only 27% of UK services providing the full range of services recommended by the National Institute for Health and Care Excellence (NICE) [26]. Transition from child to adult services is often poorly managed, and many adults with ADHD are not receiving adequate or appropriate care [27]. At the time of writing, NHS England had set up a Task Force to address these inequalities [28]. The Competency Based Curriculum for Specialist Training in Psychiatry produced by the Royal College of Psychiatrists in 2017 [29] does not require competence in adult neurodevelopmental disorders, including ADHD. Evaluation of neurodevelopmental disorders has recently been added as a core requirement (2022 curriculum), although specific points about ADHD assessment and medications are not included [30].

The UK Adult ADHD Network (UKAAN), a professional body providing support, education and training for mental health professionals working with adults with ADHD, have produced the Adult ADHD Assessment Quality Assurance Standard (AQAS) [31]

Box 20.1 Essential Components for Diagnostic Assessment

- presenting complaint(s)
- full psychiatric history
- neurodevelopmental evaluation
- past medical history for potential differentials and contraindications to treatment
- semi-structured ADHD interview with open questions and elaboration; not merely a checklist; not simply 'yes or no' questions; careful use of, not reliance on, questionnaires or rating scales – with adequate probing during the interview. All relevant areas of life (e.g. education, employment, leisure, relationships, daily task and health management) need to be reviewed in detail to establish the impact of symptoms and the degree of impairment
- explicit detailing of which DSM-5 symptoms of inattention, hyperactivity and impulsivity are present, pervasive and persistent; and how they cause at least moderate impairment in at least two domains, with detailed illustrative examples
- discussion of independent evidence (informant-based and other objective data such as school reports) used to support the diagnosis
- consideration of differential diagnoses and comorbidity (including physical health comorbidity)

in response to the lack of consistency observed in the quality and reliability of adult ADHD assessments.

Box 20.1 provides a summary from the AQAS of what a quality assessment should constitute:

Information on the assessment and treatment of women with ADHD is also found in two chapters of the 2021 publication *Understanding ADHD in Girls and Women* [32] but is beyond the scope of this chapter. For detailed training on how to diagnose adults with ADHD, and for more information on treatment approaches, UKAAN provide in-person and online workshops for healthcare professionals (see UKAAN Events at www.ukaan.org/ukaan_events.htm).

No screening tool is diagnostic but may be helpful to prompt the clinician to explore ADHD symptoms in more depth. A widely used screening tool is the World Health Organization Adult ADHD Self-Report Scale [33] which is free to download (ASRS v1.1: www.caddra.ca/wp-content/uploads/ASRS.pdf). An additional useful screening tool highlighting impairment rather than symptoms is the Weiss Functional Impairment Rating Scale (self-report) (WFIRS-S): www.caddra.ca/wp-content/uploads/WFIRS-S.pdf.

Guidelines on the Treatment of ADHD in Adults

There are several published international guidelines on the treatment of ADHD, including, in the UK, NICE [34] and the British Association of Psychopharmacology (BAP) [35]. Advice seen across guidelines is similar.

Pharmacological Treatments

Pharmacological treatment is the first-line treatment of choice in adults with either stimulants or non-stimulant drugs. We will refer to prescribing issues in the perinatal period below but will start with a general outline of current commonly used treatments for ADHD.

Now, NICE recommends use of a stimulant drug in the first instance, which can be either (any brand or formulation of) methylphenidate or the long-acting amphetamine drug lisdexamfetamine. The latest NICE guidance did not incorporate a 2018 systematic review and network meta-analysis which reviews both the efficacy and tolerability of ADHD treatments [36]. This suggested that stimulant drugs based on amphetamines may have some benefit over methylphenidate in adults with ADHD.

Following the initiation of ADHD treatment, wider benefits are often seen beyond the reduction of ADHD symptoms. ADHD medication has been shown to improve depression and reduce suicide as well as reduce rates of teenage pregnancy, sexually transmitted infections, traumatic brain injury, bone fractures and reduce accidental injuries [37], reduce road traffic accidents [38] and lead to a reduction in criminality of 32% for men and 41% for women [39]. It has also been shown to reduce the misuse of substances (illegal drugs) [40] as well as cigarette smoking, reduce hospital admissions [41] and lead to better educational outcomes [42]. There is even evidence suggesting that mortality rates for individuals with ADHD may decrease when taking ADHD medication [43, 44]. Medication has also been shown to improve self-report scores for daily functioning, general well-being and productivity [45].

Baseline Investigations Prior to Starting Medication and Ongoing Physical Health Monitoring

Initial physical investigations should include measurement of heart rate, blood pressure and weight. The main reason for the latter is to monitor for weight loss, and this is more complex in the perinatal period when significant weight changes are to be expected. NICE suggests 'an examination of the cardiovascular system'. A routine ECG or any routine blood tests are not needed. A medical, and particularly a cardiac history, including a family history of sudden unexpected death or cardiac disease, should be obtained. Consider an ECG if there is a past medical or family history of serious cardiac disease, a history of sudden death in family members, abnormal findings on cardiac examination or if other treatments might affect the QT interval (especially if using atomoxetine).

In terms of ongoing monitoring, NICE recommends that blood pressure and pulse are measured after each dose adjustment, and then six monthly, and weight six monthly.

Treatment Options

Stimulant Drugs -- The stimulant medications methylphenidate and lisdexamfetamine are both first-line treatments. The doses of each need to be titrated, with regular monitoring for effects and side effects in order to obtain the optimal dose. The dose should always be started low and increased gradually according to response as per British National Formulary (BNF). Medication should be reduced or stopped if unwanted side effects, which outweigh the benefits, occur. For a more detailed discussion of dosing regimes, especially above BNF dosing, we strongly recommend UKAAN training for clinicians (see www.ukaan.org).

Table 20.1 summarises the main characteristics of commonly used medications in the UK.

Practical Tips on the Use of Methylphenidate

Long-acting, extended-release formulations have a smoother profile of release and longer duration of action, usually lasting up to 10–12 hours. This is preferable in the

Table 20.1 Diagnostic assessment

STIMULANTS					
Amfetamine-based drugs					
Drug	**Brand name**	**Form**	**Dose range**	**Use**	**Lenth of action**
Lisdexamfetamine	Elvanse or Elvanse Adult	Capsules	20–70mg OD	OD	Up to 14 hrs
Dexamfetamine	Amfexa	Tablets	5–60mg TDD*	2–4 divided doses	Around 4 hrs
Methylphenidate-based drugs					
Long-acting drugs	Concerta XL	Tablets	18mg–108mg**	OD	Up to 12 hrs
	Xenidate XL	Tablets	18mg–108mg**	OD	Up to 12 hrs
	Xaggitin XL	Tablets	18mg–108mg**	OD	Up to 12 hrs
	Affenid XL	Tablets	18mg–108mg**	OD	Up to 12 hrs
	Matoride XL	Tablets	18mg–108mg**	OD	Up to 12 hrs
Medium-acting drugs	Equasym XL	Capsules	10–100mg	OD or 2 divided doses	Up to 8 hrs
	Medikinet XL	Capsules	10–100mg	OD or 2 divided doses	Up to 8 hrs
	Meflynate XL	Capsules	10–100mg**	OD or 2 divided doses	Up to 8 hrs
Short-acting drugs	Ritalin	Tablets	5–100mg TDD*	2-4 divided doses	Around 4 hours
	Medikinet	Tablets	5–100mg TDD*	2-4 divided doses	Around 4 hours
	Tranquilyn	Tablets	5–100mg TDD*	2-4 divided doses	Around 4 hours
NON-STIMULANT DRUGS					
Atomoxetine			80–120mg TDD*	OD or 2 divided doses	
Bupropion M/R	eg Zyban		150mg–450mg TDD*	Usually 2 divided doses	
Guanfacine M/R	eg Intuniv		1–7mg	OD	

* Total Daily Dose
** Licenses vary but dose reflects limits of common practice for methylphenidate formulations

perinatal population. In the antenatal period lower peak plasma levels confer less theoretical risk to the developing baby. In the postnatal period this is also true in a breastfeeding mother. Long-acting preparations include Concerta XL, Xenidate XL, Matoride XL, Xaggitin XL and Affinid XL. Start with a dose of 18 mg once daily in the morning and increase by 18 mg increments at weekly intervals according to response in order to find the minimum effective dose. Sometimes, the medication may be metabolised rapidly, so a twice-daily dosing regime can be helpful if the patient feels that the effects do not last as long as expected. An alternative when the drug wears off too soon is to follow with a 'top up' of an immediate release formulation to provide evening symptom cover, as long as this does not cause insomnia.

Medium-release formulations (e.g. Medikinet XL, Equasym XL, Meflynate XL and Metyrol XL) usually last around 6–8 hours. Prescribe 10 mg once a day, increasing in 10 mg increments with 5 mg increments possible for Medikinet XL usually to 60–80 mg total daily dose as per BNF. Immediate-release methylphenidate (e.g. Ritalin, Medikinet, Tranquilin or prescribed generically as methylphenidate) lasts 3–4 hours. Prescribe 5 mg orally initially twice a day after breakfast and lunch, and increase to 10 mg doses if tolerated and if needed up to three times a day, with further increases usually in 5 mg increments. Frequent small doses may be needed, for example every 3–4 hours.

For those who do not suffer from the side effect of insomnia, later doses may be helpful to prevent the return of evening symptoms, which, for those sensitive to this side effect and therefore unable to tolerate a later dose of stimulant, can be harder to control.

Long-acting and medium-acting formulations start to work and wear off more gradually, which may be advantageous compared to immediate-release formulations, which are often perceived as less smooth in effect. Some people find that they sleep better with some stimulant taken later in the day, and so insomnia is not a universal problem as for some, the drug can actually cause mental calm and enhance sleep. Many brands of stimulants are licensed for the treatment of ADHD in childhood only. Therefore, prescriptions of ADHD medication in adults are sometimes off-licence but are supported by NICE and BAP guidance.

Formulations and Modes of Action of Amphetamine-Based Drugs -- Formulations available in the UK include immediate-release (i.e. short-acting) dexamfetamine, sometimes branded Amfexa (not recommended for first-line use due to its immediate release nature and therefore greater risk of misuse) and long-acting lisdexamfetamine (branded Elvanse and Elvanse Adult in the UK).

Amphetamines stimulate the release of dopamine and noradrenaline into the synapse and also block their reuptake. Lisdexamfetamine is an extended-release pro-drug and is metabolised to become dexamfetamine. As this takes around an hour, patients often report that this smoother onset of action is preferable. This gradual effect probably prevents its use as a recreational drug. Formulations of amphetamines available outside Europe include formulations of mixed amphetamine salts branded Adderall in the USA.

Practical Tips on the Use of Amphetamine-Based Drugs -- *Lisdexamfetamine* dosing starts at 20 mg or 30 mg once in the morning for adults. The dose can be titrated in 10 mg increments to a maximum of 70 mg once each morning.

Dexamfetamine is a short-acting formulation and can be used as long as there are no concerns about the risk of diversion or misuse. Dosing starts at 5 mg twice to three times a day and increases in 5 mg increments. As it is a short-acting amphetamine it is not recommended as a first-line drug as it is the ADHD drug most vulnerable to misuse and diversion as a recreational drug.

Non-stimulant Drugs -- If stimulants have been unsuccessful or not well tolerated, NICE suggests that the non-stimulant drug atomoxetine is used for second-line management. Some patients find it useful as an adjunct in combination with stimulants. It is suggested by NICE that other medications (e.g. clonidine, bupropion, guanfacine) should only be used in adults by tertiary care specialists.

Monitoring -- Monitoring of dose titration is commonly completed by online video or telephone. Initially frequent, brief consultations every few weeks may be required. The aim is for symptom reduction and improved functioning. Stimulants reduce symptoms quickly (often less than an hour after taking a dose) but are not a cure and the effect lasts transiently with symptoms returning when the drug wears off. The goal is to minimise symptoms for as long as possible rather than symptom eradication.

Issues to explore at follow-up include:

- the dose, frequency and timing of medication use and response of the patient's key symptoms
- adverse effects such as appetite loss, insomnia, dry mouth, anxiety or cardiac symptoms and the effect of missed doses / periods of no treatment
- is there a need for premenstrual dose adjustments? Sometimes slightly higher doses are needed premenstrually. An increase in dose may help combat premenstrual worsening of cognitive and emotional symptoms [46]
- changes in existing psychiatric symptoms, for example mood or anxiety
- any concerns about misuse or diversion
- the opinions of carers / partners on treatment response
- the results of physical health monitoring, for example blood pressure, pulse and weight usually by home monitoring

Long-Term Use of Medication -- Following dose stabilisation, if the primary care physician is willing to take over the prescribing, this is usually with a local shared care agreement. As treatment should be reviewed at least annually, it is usual for a patient to remain under the care of a psychiatrist, so referral to a local adult ADHD service may be needed. We hope the outcome of the NHS Task Force will improve service provision in the UK as arranging ongoing specialist treatment to continue monitoring of ADHD medication after the perinatal period can be problematic.

Non-pharmacological Treatments

Psychotherapeutic Treatments

'Pills don't build skills', and therapy, coaching and mindfulness can also be very helpful. In fact, there is likely to be a greater effect from medication if also benefiting from other strategies to improve focus and memory [34].

In an ideal world, individuals with ADHD would be offered both psychotherapy and support as well as medication. NICE suggests that if, following medication, there is either residual impairment or no response, or if medication is not an option, or if the person chooses to avoid medication, then cognitive behavioural therapy (CBT) should be considered. It can be provided on an individual or group basis. It helps the patient to develop a more reflective and goal-oriented approach to everyday activities and helps with problem-solving. Regular sessions of CBT have been shown to reduce ADHD symptoms in children, adolescents and adults.

Other psychotherapeutic treatments are sometimes offered and can also be individual or group-based and could include skills training [47], mindfulness or dialectical behavioural therapy, especially for those suffering significant emotional dysregulation.

Psychoeducation

Psychoeducation provides more in-depth information about the disorder to individuals with ADHD, their families or people close to them. Giving the opportunity to learn more about pharmacological treatments is also important as are suggestions for lifestyle modification. This may help their ability to cope and function with ADHD. Information on ADHD and self-help materials can be given in the form of brochures, books, internet resources and educational videos/podcasts. Patients can be taught self-monitoring and self-management of their disorder. The importance of a balanced diet, good nutrition and regular exercise should also be highlighted.

Coaching and Other Group Therapies

Although an unregulated industry, there is anecdotal evidence that coaching can be helpful individually and as a group. A female-specific treatment group for women with ADHD and premenstrual worsening of their ADHD and mood symptoms has been found to be successful [46]. Other specialist types of therapy may sometimes be useful, for example, relationship/marital counselling, family therapy, vocational coaching and educational study skills support although further research is needed.

Self-Help Groups

Informal psychosocial support from local self-help groups is often highly valued.

ADHD in the Perinatal Period

As the number of people with an ADHD diagnosis, or waiting for an assessment, continues to dramatically rise, perinatal mental health services are similarly seeing more women with diagnosed or suspected ADHD. They may present at all stages of the perinatal journey – in the preconceptual clinic, during pregnancy or postnatally – and are seen in both community and in-patient services.

In the general population it is sadly known that the prevalence and incidence of intimate partner violence increases during pregnancy and the first 18 months after childbirth [48]. Females diagnosed with ADHD in childhood are at increased risk of intimate partner violence in young adult relationships (30.7% vs 6.3%) [49] and clinicians should be especially alert to this risk in mothers with ADHD.

Preconceptual Issues

Specialist community perinatal mental health teams in the UK offer pre-conception advice for women with a complex or severe mental health problem (current or past) who are planning a pregnancy [50]. Access to good quality advice, information and support helps women make informed decisions around the options to manage their mental health condition during the perinatal period. At the time of writing, anecdotal experience suggests that it is unusual for women with ADHD to be referred for pre-conception advice.

Clinicians in the pre-conceptual clinic should be alert to the fact that some women may suffer from undiagnosed or misdiagnosed ADHD. The disorder may be missed, particularly when the core symptoms are clouded by prominent mood instability. In our experience, symptoms can be instead attributed to bipolar affective disorder (mainly type II and rapid cycling subtypes), cyclothymia and emotionally unstable or borderline personality disorder. An accurate diagnostic reformulation may result in more appropriate medications being prescribed with better symptom control and functioning and other positive outcomes in the perinatal period. The risk profiles and general management plans for these disorders are quite different in the perinatal period, and diagnostic clarity from the outset is desirable.

Young women with ADHD are vulnerable; they tend to become sexually active earlier than their peers and have more sexual partners. Rates of sexually transmitted infections are raised four-fold and teenage unplanned pregnancies ten-fold [51]. Youths with ADHD are almost four times as likely to be victims of sexual violence [52]. Of teenage girls with ADHD, 15.2% become mothers, with 6.23 times higher odds compared to those without ADHD [53]. These facts highlight that prescribers who initiate ADHD medication should appreciate the possibility of a future pregnancy, including one which is unplanned with unintended exposure to stimulants in early pregnancy. Pre-emptive advice should be given at initiation. Girls and young women with ADHD should also be strongly encouraged to access contraceptive advice, and mental health services, including child and adolescent mental health services, have a role in highlighting this. Long-acting reversible contraceptives are a more effective alternative to a daily oral contraceptive for someone with difficulties with planning, organisation and memory. The required annual reviews are also an opportunity to remind and reinforce these messages.

There is a substantial familial risk for the development of ADHD. It is one of the most heritable conditions; twin and adoption studies have demonstrated an average heritability of 76%. Estimates vary, but it is thought that up to 40% of parents with ADHD will have children who develop ADHD [54].

Pregnancy

There is anecdotal evidence that impairment from some symptoms of ADHD spontaneously improve during pregnancy. This is hypothesised to be an oestrogen effect, also explaining reports of changes in symptom profile during the menstrual cycle, perimenopause and post-menopausal period.

Women with ADHD appear to be at slightly higher risk of adverse pregnancy outcomes regardless of current medication status [55]. The increased rates of risk factors for adverse pregnancy outcomes may explain this finding. Pregnant women with ADHD are more likely to smoke during the third trimester (odds ratio (OR), 6.88), have a body mass index of less than 18.50 (OR, 1.29) or more than 40.00 (OR, 2.01) or suffer from a comorbid alcohol and substance use disorder (OR, 20.25). Enhanced obstetric care in this group of women may, therefore, be considered.

ADHD Medication in Pregnancy

There are no specific guidelines regarding the pharmacological treatment of ADHD in pregnancy.

The use of any medication during this period should always be based on an individualised risk assessment, balancing the known and possible unknown risks of continuing medication against the advantages of continuing medication for both mother and baby. There may be significant risks associated with stopping ADHD medication, including poor planning and organisation resulting in, for example, suboptimal attendance for antenatal care; poor diet; increased chaotic, impulsive and risk-taking behaviours, including self-harm; higher rates of smoking, using recreational drugs and alcohol; and the emergence of, or worsening of, comorbid psychiatric disorders such as anxiety and depression. These issues may impact the assessment of a mother's capacity to parent the unborn child and any older children.

As recognition of female ADHD increases, more women of child-bearing age are using pharmacological treatment, the first-line treatment in adults. Indeed, a study looking at trends in the use of ADHD medication during pregnancy showed that between 2003 and 2010 use increased 100-fold from 5 to 533 per 100,000 person-years. This mirrored an increase in prescribing among women of childbearing age [56].

Two subsequent large population-based cohort studies described the trajectories of use in more detail [57, 58]. Both showed that the use of ADHD medication before, during and after pregnancy followed four distinct patterns: continuation, discontinuation, interruption and initiation.

'Discontinuers' (who were taking medication before pregnancy and stopped it when pregnant) formed the largest group in both studies, approaching 50%. In recent years, the proportion of 'continuers' has increased (2014–19) most recently accounting for 23.3%. This group differed in sociodemographic and clinical factors, which may reflect more severe ADHD. Approximately one-fifth of women were 'interrupters' (stopped medication during pregnancy, resumed postpartum). A similar proportion initiated treatment in the postnatal period. Compared to other groups, most of these mothers were diagnosed late, were more likely to be taking antidepressant treatment and were more likely to have had inpatient or outpatient hospital contacts for non-psychiatric disorders.

A relatively common scenario encountered in community perinatal mental health services concerns a woman who has unexpectedly conceived whilst taking stimulant medication for ADHD, the question being if it is 'safe' to continue to take it. Ideally, this will have already been addressed at initiation and/or annual reviews. There are a few management options.

Given the anecdotal evidence that symptoms may spontaneously improve, consideration may be given to a trial without medication, particularly in the first trimester when the baby's major organs are forming, and the theoretical risks are greatest. Compared to most other psychotropic medications, it is not necessary to wean off stimulant medications; their short half-life means that they can usually be stopped abruptly without a withdrawal reaction (although the absence of the drug may cause a return of ADHD symptoms). The short half-life also allows women to limit fetal exposure to stimulant medication by only taking it on days when ADHD symptoms need to be better controlled, such as at work. Medication may be omitted on other days when symptom control is less critical. This contrasts with advice for most other psychotropic medications.

Non-stimulant medication should be stopped gradually over a short period of a week or two. Therefore, they cannot be taken on an ad-hoc basis like the stimulants. An initial trial of medication at a lower dose may be worthwhile. The aim should always be to treat any condition with the minimum effective dose, especially in the perinatal period.

Non-pharmacological treatments are often more acceptable to women during pregnancy and include psychological, educational, behavioural, social and lifestyle interventions. It is unlikely that perinatal services would have the skill or resource to offer these, and collaboration with local ADHD services to develop local pathways is needed.

Restarting or continuing ADHD medications may be considered if the risks of stopping medication are significant. Those with mild to moderate symptoms are more likely to function relatively well without medication.

For pregnant women who restart or continue stimulant medication, consideration should first be given to switching from an immediate-release formulation to a modified-release one. Their lower peak plasma levels confer less theoretical risk to the developing baby.

Compared to the other main classes of psychotropic medication, the evidence base around the use of ADHD medications in pregnancy is relatively poor. It is more robust for stimulant as compared to non-stimulant treatments. In the United Kingdom, the latter are classified as Schedule B under the Misuse of Drugs Act (1971) [59].

When the evidence base is relatively poor, it can be helpful to go back to data from animal studies, and the literature around fetal exposure to common ADHD medications in animals is largely reassuring. Congenital malformations were only seen at well above the equivalent maximum recommended human dose (MRHD), and these associations seem to be dose-related. With methylphenidate, for an increased incidence of fetal spina bifida to be seen, pregnant rabbits needed to have been exposed to 40 times the MHRD [60]. For amphetamines, embryotoxic and teratogenic effects in mice were seen at 41 times the MHRD [61] but not at lower levels in rabbits and rats [62, 63].

In recent years, two systematic reviews have suggested that the risks in humans are lower than previously understood. These older views are perhaps influenced by the legacy of studies in the 1980s looking at mothers who took crack cocaine, an illegal stimulant medication, during pregnancy. These 'crack-babies' had poor birth outcomes, but the predicted poor long-term cognitive and physical effects have not been borne out by subsequent follow-up studies.

The first systematic review and meta-analysis, published in 2019 [64], reviewed eight large cohort studies (700 to 2 million offspring) and concluded that 'exposure to ADHD medication during pregnancy does not appear to be associated with serious adverse maternal or neonatal outcomes'.

A further high-quality systematic review in 2020 [55] assessed the same eight cohort studies. It concluded that 'the current evidence does not suggest that the use of ADHD medication during pregnancy results in significant adverse consequences for mother or offspring'. Twenty-four wide-ranging outcomes were considered during pregnancy, during labour and delivery, congenital malformations and perinatal morbidity. Both systematic reviews made conclusions about the class of ADHD medications as a whole. Currently, there is insufficient evidence to clearly differentiate between the individual medications in pregnancy although it seems that risks with methylphenidate may be very slightly more significant than for dexamphetamine when taken in the first trimester.

A 2018 study [65] compared over 4 million pregnancies, including almost 3,500 live births exposed to stimulants. Whilst there was no association observed for methylphenidate and 13 congenital malformations, overall, there was a small increase in cardiac malformations. The relative risk was 1.28 (95% confidence interval (CI) 1.00–1.64), an increase calculated to correspond to three additional infants born with congenital cardiac malformations for every 1,000 women who took methylphenidate in the first trimester. First-trimester dexamphetamine use was not associated with any congenital malformations, including cardiac ones.

This, and a further three studies, were included in a subsequent meta-analysis [66] examining the association between first-trimester exposure to methylphenidate and major congenital malformations. This showed an increased risk for major congenital malformations (OR 1.26; 95% CI 1.05–1.51) overall, the majority of this being accounted for by cardiac malformations (OR 1.59; 95% CI 1.02–2.49). The cardiac malformations were of varying clinical severity, and the clinical significance was estimated to be small, with the baseline risk for congenital malformations rising from 1.07% to 1.7%. This translates to a number needed to harm of 159. Fetal echocardiography in pregnant women using methylphenidate may therefore be considered.

The authors of both papers note that the data is too limited to make unequivocal recommendations and that further research is needed, particularly prospective studies that control for important confounders.

Data around the risk of a newborn suffering from withdrawal symptoms, if prescribed stimulants are taken close to labour, are lacking. Acknowledging this potential, local guidelines for Neonatal Abstinence Syndrome (NAS) should be referred to. Breastfeeding is also known to reduce the severity of NAS symptoms. As a class of drugs, ADHD treatments have not been associated with neonatal resuscitation, low Apgar scores, stillbirth/perinatal death or neonatal intensive care unit admission.

Of the eight cohort studies in the systematic reviews and meta-analysis, only half included atomoxetine. The data is too limited to make any definitive statements about its safety in pregnancy at the current time.

Concerns have been raised as to whether taking ADHD medication during pregnancy has long-term adverse effects on the offspring, particularly neurodevelopmental disorders and growth later in life. Two recent studies are largely reassuring.

A large Danish cohort study followed up those exposed to in-utero stimulants, atomoxetine and clonidine [67]. After adjusting for confounders, no increased risk of developmental disorders was found. Neurodevelopment and growth in offspring also did not differ based on antenatal exposure to ADHD medication.

A study from the United States studied outcomes for antenatal exposure to amphetamines and methylphenidate only [68]. After strict adjustment for confounders neither were associated with neurodevelopmental outcomes. These findings suggest that amphetamines and methylphenidate exposure in utero are not likely to meaningfully increase the risk of childhood neurodevelopmental disorders.

The Postnatal Period

Periods of transition often unmask previously unidentified ADHD. It goes without saying that becoming a parent is a massive transition requiring, among others, skills around attention, planning, organisation and multitasking. It is also invariably associated with a degree of sleep deprivation. It may therefore be that ADHD presents for the first time during the postnatal period, as a new mother struggles to meet these challenges and her pre-existing ADHD symptoms start to cause more impairment. These difficulties can also lead to symptoms of low mood and anxiety.

If a woman has stopped treatment for ADHD in the antenatal period, she will almost certainly benefit from restarting it early in the postnatal period. This should not be overlooked, and it is useful to have already planned for this during pre-conceptual counselling and/or pregnancy.

Furthermore, if a new mother with untreated ADHD presents with mild to moderate symptoms of anxiety and/or depression it is likely that, in the first instance, restarting ADHD medication will be more useful than prescribing a selective serotonin reuptake inhibitor or other pharmacological treatments for these disorders. Whilst separate treatment for a depressive illness may also be needed, particularly for a more severe presentation, it is important not to underestimate the benefits from restarting ADHD drugs. Evidence in the general population suggests that the occurrence of depression is 20% less common during periods of treatment with ADHD medication [69].

Emotional lability and dysregulation are common features in patients with ADHD. This can lead to increased levels of irritability and anger, a low frustration tolerance and emotional lability. A meta-analysis of 32 studies demonstrated that parental ADHD symptoms are significantly associated with elevated rates of harsh, lax or negative parenting styles. Furthermore, greater ADHD symptoms were more strongly associated with less positive and more harsh and lax parenting behaviours [70]. Although these effect sizes were small, they are comparable to the associations found between other parental psychopathologies and parenting. It has not yet been shown if treatment which reduces ADHD symptoms improves parenting style, but it can be hypothesised that it would.

A later study attempted to separate the impact of maternal ADHD symptoms and emotion dysregulation on parenting difficulties [71]. Maternal ADHD symptoms were associated with difficulties responding to children's negative emotions, whereas emotional dysregulation was associated with problems with discipline practices.

The transition in returning to work is often challenging for new mums; for those with ADHD, this may be particularly difficult.

Using ADHD Medications during Breastfeeding

Some relatively recent and influential guidance [21] suggests that it would be generally safer to advise the cessation of medications for ADHD during breastfeeding altogether, and where ADHD medication is necessary, then an alternative to breastfeeding is needed to minimise any risk to the baby.

We suggest that a more nuanced approach is taken to support women who wish to breastfeed.

As in pregnancy, consideration should first be given to switching an immediate-release formulation to a modified-release one.

For estimating the risk to the breastfed infant, one of the more popular methods is the relative infant dose (RID). This estimates how much of the 'maternal dose' an infant receives. Generally, a RID of <10% is considered safe, assuming that the baby is born at term and is otherwise fit and well.

The RID for methylphenidate is extremely low at 0.2–0.4% [72]. Even for a woman taking higher doses, levels are probably too low to be clinically relevant and data suggest that breastfeeding is probably compatible. No paediatric concerns have been reported from milk, but this does not exclude potential risk. Nonetheless, it is recommended that the infant be monitored for agitation, poor sleeping patterns, changes in feeding and poor weight gain. The RID for lisdexamfetamine is greater than for methylphenidate but still low at 1.8–6.2% [72]. Data suggests that at normal therapeutic doses, the dose of dexamfetamine in breastmilk is probably subclinical and breastfeeding is presumed compatible. There is, therefore, no reason to switch a breastfeeding mother, whose ADHD symptoms are well-controlled on a dexamfetamine preparation, to methylphenidate. Paediatric concerns include possible insomnia, irritability, anorexia, reduced weight gain or poor sleeping patterns in infants, but in limited studies, no infants were affected [72]. Suggested infant monitoring as is for methylphenidate.

Atomoxetine metabolism is highly variable and no data is available on the transfer of atomoxetine into human milk. Mothers should probably be cautioned about its use whilst breastfeeding until more data is available [72].

Clonidine may reduce prolactin secretion and could conceivably reduce milk production early postpartum. In small studies, excretion of human milk was minimal; the RID was 0.9–7.1%. Clinical symptoms of neonatal toxicity are unreported and unlikely in normal full-term infants. Although paediatric concerns have not been reported via milk, this does not exclude potential risk. Infant monitoring is recommended for drowsiness, lethargy, pallor, dry mouth, poor feeding, constipation and weight gain [72].

There are no current studies looking at the long-term consequences of a breastfed infant being exposed to ADHD medications.

Summary and Conclusions

Whilst there are still many barriers to the recognition of ADHD in females, in recent years there have been huge increases in those of reproductive age being recognised as having the condition and taking stimulant medication, the first-line treatment for adults. The proportion of women continuing medication throughout the perinatal period has also dramatically increased. Recent data suggests it will take the NHS over 8 years to clear its current waiting list for adult ADHD assessments if service provision does not change [73]. The impact of these issues and more are felt in all parts of the specialist perinatal pathway, resulting in a pressing need for perinatal clinicians to better understand and manage this condition.

Irrespective of medication use, women with ADHD are particularly vulnerable. In the pre-conceptual period, there are notable risks around sexual activity at a younger age, high rates of sexually transmitted infections and being victims of sexual violence. Adverse pregnancy outcomes are more likely regardless of medication status, and risks of intimate partner violence are especially high, the perinatal period being a time when the risk is already raised.

Anecdotal evidence suggests that some ADHD symptoms improve in pregnancy, perhaps mediated by oestrogen, and a better understanding of the changing symptom profile during the perinatal period would better inform management options.

In the postnatal period, clinicians should be mindful that unidentified ADHD may present for the first time, perhaps being confused for an affective disorder, anxiety or personality difficulties. Effective pharmacological treatment should be started, leading to improved outcomes for both mother and baby. Swift improvements in symptoms are expected, which can be very rewarding to see. The amount of stimulant medication transferred into breast milk is low, and breastfeeding is not contraindicated, providing the infant is born at term and otherwise fit and well.

Parental ADHD symptoms are significantly associated with negative parenting styles and there is scope to develop parenting interventions to support parents with the specific difficulties they have been shown to struggle with.

Gathered experience and the evidence base around using medications for ADHD in the perinatal period continue to evolve and is largely reassuring, including recent studies considering the risks of neurodevelopmental disorders after in-utero exposure. However, compared to other classes of psychotropic medications, the evidence base is poor, and a lack of specific clinical guidelines is concerning. This results in inconsistent treatment and guidance dependent on the level of knowledge of the treating clinician. Interfaces between specialist ADHD and specialist perinatal services also vary locally and impact the care received. Collaboration between these specialist services is strongly encouraged to improve outcomes for women, their babies and wider family.

References

1. J Fayyad, NA Sampson, I Hwang, T Adamowski, S Aguilar-Gaxiola, A Al-Hamzawi, et al. The descriptive epidemiology of DSM-IV adult ADHD in the World Health Organization World Mental Health Surveys. *Atten Defic Hyperact Disord.* 2017;9(1):47–65.
2. B Franke, G Michelini, P Asherson, T Banaschewski, A Bilbow, JK Buitelaar, et al. Live fast, die young? A review on the developmental trajectories of ADHD across the lifespan. *Eur Neuropsychopharmacol.* 2018;28(10):1059–88.
3. J Biederman, SV Faraone, TJ Spencer, E Mick, MC Monuteaux, M Aleardi. Functional impairments in adults with self-reports of diagnosed ADHD: a controlled study of 1001 adults in the community. *J Clin Psychiatry.* 2006;67(4):524–40.
4. S O'Grady, S Hinshaw. Long-term outcomes of females with attention-deficit hyperactivity disorder: increased risk for self-harm. *Br J Psychiatry.* 2021;218(1):4–6.
5. NN Rommelse, ME Altink, EA Fliers, NC Martin, CJ Buschgens, CA Hartman, et al. Comorbid problems in ADHD: degree of association, shared endophenotypes, and formation of distinct subtypes. Implications for a future DSM. *J Abnorm Child Psychol.* 2009;37(6):793–804.
6. CP Jacob, J Romanos, A Dempfle, M Heine, C Windemuth-Kieselbach, A Kruse, et al. Comorbidity of adult attention deficit/hyperactivity disorder with focus on personality traits and related disorders in a tertiary referral center. *Eur Arch Psychiatry Clin Neurosci.* 2007;257(6):309–17.
7. CM Jensen, H-C Steinhausen. Comorbid mental disorders in children and adolescents with attention-deficit/hyperactivity disorder in a large nationwide study. *Atten Def Hyperact Disord.* 2015;7(1):27–38.
8. JS Kooij, D Dijlenga, L Salerno, R Jaeschke, I Bitter, J Balazs, et al. Updated European Consensus Statement on diagnosis and treatment of adult ADHD. *European Psychiatry.* 2019;56: 14–34.
9. S Cortese, S Sun, J Zhang, E Sharma, Z Chang, R Kuja-Halkola, et al. Association between attention deficit hyperactivity disorder and asthma: a systematic review and meta-analysis and a Swedish population-based study. *Lancet Psychiatry.* 2018;5:717–26.

10. S Cortese, CR Moreira-Maia, D St Fleur, C Morcillo-Penalver, LA Rohde, SV Faraone. Association between ADHD and obesity: a systematic review and meta-analysis. *Am J Psychiatry.* 2016;173:34–43.

11. B Libutzki, B Neukirch, A Reif, CA Hartman. Somatic burden of attention-deficit/hyperactivity disorder across the lifecourse. *Acta Psychiatr Scand.* 2024;150(2):105–17.

12. JLL Csecs, V Iodice, CL Rae, A Brooke, R Simmons, L Quadt, et al. Joint hypermobility links neurodivergence to dysautonomia and pain. *Front Psychiatry.* 2021;12:786916.

13. R van Rensburg, HP Meyer, SA Hitchcock, CE Schuler. Screening for adult ADHD in patients with fibromyalgia syndrome. *Pain Med.* 2018;19:1825–31.

14. MH Chen, TL Pan, JW Hsu, KL Huang, TP Su, CT Li, et al. Risk of type 2 diabetes in adolescents and young adults with attention-deficit/hyperactivity disorder: a nationwide longitudinal study. *J Clin Psychiatry.* 2018;79(3):788–93.

15. J Fayyad, R De Graaf, R Kessler, J Alonso, M Angermeyer, K Demyttenaere, et al. Cross-national prevalence and correlates of adult attention-deficit hyperactivity disorder. *Br J Psychiatry.* 2007;190:402–9.

16. World Health Organization. ICD-11 international classification of diseases, 11th revision. Geneva: WHO; 2019. https://icd.who.int/en

17. American Psychiatric Association. *Diagnostic and statistical manual of mental disorders*, 5th edition. Washington, DC: American Psychiatric Association; 2013. p. 59–60.

18. J Waddell, MM McCarthy. Sexual differentiation of the brain and ADHD: what is a sex difference in prevalence telling us? *Curr Top Behav Neurosci.* 2012;9:341–60.

19. M Faheem, W Akram, H Akram, MA Khan, FA Siddiqui, I Majeed. Gender-based differences in prevalence and effects of ADHD in adults: a systematic review. *Asian J Psychiatr.* 2022;75.

20. M Gaub, CL Carlson. Gender differences in ADHD: a meta-analysis and critical review. *J Am Acad Child Adolesc Psychiatry.* 1997;36:1036–45.

21. S Young, N Adamo, BB Ásgeirsdóttir, P Branney, M Beckett, W Colley, et al. Females with ADHD: an expert consensus statement taking a lifespan approach providing guidance for the identification and treatment of attention-deficit/hyperactivity disorder in girls and women. *BMC Psychiatry.* 2020;20:404.

22. J Martin, K Langley, M Cooper, OY Rouquette, A John, K Sayal, et al. Sex differences in attention-deficit hyperactivity disorder diagnosis and clinical care: a national study of population healthcare records in Wales. *J Child Psychol Psychiatry.* 2024;65(12):1648–58.

23. PO Quinn, M Madhoo. A review of attention-deficit/hyperactivity disorder in women and girls: uncovering this hidden diagnosis. *Prim Care Companion CNS Disord.* 2014;16.

24. P Asherson. Clinical assessment and treatment of attention deficit hyperactivity disorder in adults. *Expert Rev Neurother.* 2005;5(4):525–39.

25. J Gershon. A meta-analytic review of gender differences in ADHD. *J Atten Disord.* 2002;5:143–54.

26. S Young, P Asherson, T Lloyd, M Absoud, M Arif, WA Colley, et al. Failure of healthcare provision for attention deficit/hyperactivity disorder in the United Kingdom: a consensus statement. *Front Psychiatry.* 2021;12:649399.

27. W Retz, P Retz-Junginger, J Thome, M Rosler. Pharmacological treatment of adult ADHD in Europe. *World J Biol Psychiatry.* 2011;12(Suppl 1):89–94.

28. NHS England News. NHS to launch cross-sector ADHD taskforce to boost care for patients in England. 2024 28 Mar. https://shorturl.at/KysOt

29. Royal College of Psychiatrists. *A competency based curriculum for specialist training in psychiatry.* London: Royal College of Psychiatrists; 2017.

30. Royal College of Psychiatrists. Curricula documents and resources. N.d. https://shorturl.at/3hmnd

31. M Adamou, M Arif, P Asherson, S Cubbin, L Leaver, J Sedgwick-Müller, et al. The adult ADHD assessment quality assurance standard. *Front Psychiatry.* 2024;15.

32. J Steer, editor. *Understanding ADHD in girls and women.* London: Jessica Kingsley; 2021. p. 211–314.

33. RC Kessler, L Adler, M Ames, O Demier, S Faraone, E Hiripi, et al. The World Health Organization Adult ADHD Self-Report Scale (ASRS): a short screening scale for use in the general population. *Psycholog Med.* 2005;35:245–56.

34. National Institute for Health and Care Excellence. Attention deficit hyperactivity disorder: diagnosis and management. NICE Guidance (NG87). 2018. www.nice.org.uk/guidance/ng87

35. B Bolea-Alamañac, DJ Nutt, M Adamou, P Asherson, S Bazire, D Coghill, et al. Evidence-based guidelines for the pharmacological management of attention deficit hyperactivity disorder: update on recommendations from the British Association for Psychopharmacology. *J Psychopharmacol.* 2014;28(3):179–203.

36. S Cortese, N Adamo, C Del Giovane, C Mohr-Jensen, AJ Hayes, S Carucci, et al. Comparative efficacy and tolerability of medications for attention-deficit hyperactivity disorder in children, adolescents, and adults: a systematic review and network meta-analysis. *Lancet Psychiatry.* 2018;5:727–38.

37. SV Faraone, T Banaschewski, D Coghill, Y Zheng, J Biederman, MA Bellgrove, et al. The World Federation of ADHD International Consensus Statement: 208 evidence-based conclusions about the disorder. *Neurosci Biobehav Rev.* 2021;128:789–818.

38. Z Chang, PD Quinn, K Hur, RD Gibbons, A Sjölander, H Larsson, et al. Association between medication use for attention-deficit/hyperactivity disorder and risk of motor vehicle crashes. *JAMA Psychiatry.* 2017;74(6):597–60.

39. P Lichtenstein, L Halldner, J Zetterqvist, A Sjölander, E Serlachius, S Fazel, et al. Medication for attention deficit-hyperactivity disorder and criminality. *New Engl J Med.* 2012;367(21):2006–14.

40. PD Quinn, Z Chang, K Hur, RD Gibbons, BB Lahey, ME Rickert, et al. ADHD medication and substance-related problems. *Am J Psychiatry.* 2017;174(9):877–85.

41. H Taipale, J Bergström, K Gèmes, A Tanskanen, L Ekselius, E Mittendorfer-Rutz, M Helgesson. Attention-deficit/hyperactivity disorder medications and work disability and mental health outcomes. *JAMA Netw Open.* 2024;7(3).

42. Y Lu, A Sjölander, M Cederlöf, BM D'Onofrio, C Almqvist, H Larsson, et al. Association between medication use and performance on higher education entrance tests in individuals with attention-deficit/hyperactivity disorder. *JAMA Psychiatry.* 2017;74(8):815–22.

43. L Li, N Zhu, L Zhang, R Kuja-Halkola, BM D'Onofrio, I Brikell, et al. ADHD pharmacotherapy and mortality in individuals with ADHD. *JAMA.* 2024;331(10):850–60.

44. VC Chen, HL Chan, SI Wu, ML Lu, ME Dewey, R Stewart, et al. Methylphenidate and mortality in children with attention-deficit hyperactivity disorder: population-based cohort study. *Br J Psychiatry.* 2020;14:1–9.

45. L Adler, B Dirks, P Deas, A Raychaudhuri, M Dauphin, K Saylor, et al. Self-reported quality of life in adults with attention-deficit/hyperactivity disorder and executive function impairment treated with lisdexamfetamine dimesylate: a randomized, double-blind, multicenter, placebo-controlled, parallel-group study. *BMC Psychiatry.* 2013;13:253.

46. M de Jong, DSMR Wynchank, E van Andel, ATF Beekman, JJS Kooij. Female-specific pharmacotherapy in ADHD: premenstrual adjustment of

psychostimulant dosage. *Front Psychiatry.* 2023;14:1306194.

47. V Nimmo-Smith, A Merwood, D Hank, J Brandling, R Greenwood, L Skinner, et al. Non pharmacological treatments for adult ADHD: a systematic review. *Psychol Med.* 2020;50:529–41.
48. H Finnbogadottir, AK Dykes. Increasing prevalence and incidence of domestic violence during pregnancy and one and half year postpartum, as well as risk factors: a longitudinal cohort study in Southern Sweden. *BMC Pregnancy Childbirth* 2016;16:327.
49. MD Guendelman, S Ahmad, JI Meza, EB Owens, SP Hinshaw. Childhood attention-deficit/hyperactivity disorder predicts intimate partner victimization in young women. *J Abnorm Child Psychol.* 2016;44(1):155–66.
50. National Collaborating Centre for Mental Health. The Perinatal Mental Health Care Pathways: full implementation guidance. 2018.
51. RA Barkley, M Fischer, L Smallish, K Fletcher. Young adult outcome of hyperactive children: adaptive functioning in major life activities. *J Am Acad Child Adolesc Psychiatry.* 2006;45(2):192–202.
52. MN Christoffersen. Sexual crime against schoolchildren with disabilities: a nationwide prospective birth cohort study. *J Interpers Violence.* 2022;37: 3–4.
53. C Skoglund, KH Kopp, A Skalkidou, AK Wikström, C Lundin, S Hesselman, et al. Association of attention-deficit/ hyperactivity disorder with teenage birth among women and girls in Sweden. *JAMA Netw Open.* 2019;2(10).
54. M Uchida, H Driscoll, M DiSalvo, A Rajalakshmim, M Maiello, V Spera, et al. Assessing the magnitude of risk for ADHD in offspring of parents with ADHD: a systematic literature review and meta-analysis. *J Atten Disord.* 2021;25(13):1943–8.
55. L Li, AC Sujan, A Butwicka, Z Chang, S Cortese, P Quinn, et al. Associations of prescribed ADHD medication in pregnancy with pregnancy-related and offspring outcome: a systematic review. *CNS Drugs.* 2020;34:731–47.
56. KB Haervig, LH Mortensen, AV Hansen, K Strandberg-Larsen. Use of ADHD medication during pregnancy from 1999 to 2010: a Danish register-based study. *Pharmacoepidemiol Drug Saf.* 2014;23(5):526–33.
57. C Srinivas, Ø Karlstad, H Stigum, K Furu, CE Cesta, J Reutfors, et al. Trajectories of ADHD medication use before, during, and after pregnancy: a population-based study from Norway and Sweden. *Pharmacoepidemiol Drug Saf.* 2023;32(10):1152–60.
58. K Bang Madsen, M Bliddal, CB Skoglund, H Larsson, T Munk-Olsen, MG Madsen, et al. Attention-deficit hyperactivity disorder (ADHD) medication use trajectories among women in the perinatal period. *CNS Drugs.* 2024;38(4):303–14.
59. Home Office.gov.uk. List of most commonly encountered drugs currently controlled under the misuse of drugs legislation. Updated 2022 8 Aug. https://shorturl.at/KUrOa
60. DA Beckman, M Schneider, M Youreneff, FL Tse. Developmental toxicity assessment of D,L-methylphenidate and D-methylphendiate in rats and rabbits. *Birth Defects Res B Dev Repro Toxicol.* 2008;83(5):489–501.
61. JJ Nora, DG Trasler, FC Fraser. Malformations in mice induced by dexamphetamine sulphate. *Lancet.* 1965;2(7420):1021–2.
62. G Kasirsky. Teratogenic effects of metamphetamine in mice and rabbits. *J Am Osteopath Assoc.* 1971;70(10):1119–20.
63. Y Yamamoto, K Yamamoto, T Hayase, Y Fukui, K Shiota. Effects of amphetamine on rat embryos developing in vitro. *Repro Toxiocol.* 1998;12(2):133–7.
64. HY Jiang, X Zhang, CM Jiang, HB Fu. Maternal and neonatal outcomes after exposure to ADHD medication during

pregnancy: a systematic review and meta-analysis. *Pharmacoepidemiol Drug Saf.* 2019;28(3):288–95.

65. KF Huybrechts, G Bröms, LB Christensen, K Einarsdóttir, A Engeland, K Furu, et al. Association between methylphenidate and amphetamine use in pregnancy and risk of congenital malformations: a cohort study from the international pregnancy safety study consortium. *JAMA Psychiatry.* 2018;75(2):167–75.

66. G Koren, Y Barer, A Ornoy. Fetal safety of methylphenidate-A scoping review and meta analysis. *Reprod Toxicol.* 2020;93:230–4.

67. K Bang Madsen, TK Robakis, X Liu, N Momen, H Larsson, JW Dreier, et al. In utero exposure to ADHD medication and long-term offspring outcomes. *Mol Psychiatry.* 2023;28(4):1739–46.

68. EA Suarez, BT Bateman, S Hernandez-Diaz, L Straub, CJ McDougle, KL Wisner, et al. Prescription stimulant use during pregnancy and risk of neurodevelopmental disorders in children. *JAMA Psychiatry.* 2024;81(5):477–88.

69. Z Chang, BM D'Onofrio, PD Quinn, P Lichtenstein, H Larsson. Medication for attention-deficit/hyperactivity disorder and risk for depression: a nationwide longitudinal cohort study. *Biol Psychiatry.* 2016;80(12):916–22.

70. JL Park, KL Hudec, C Johnston. Parental ADHD symptoms and parenting behaviors: a meta-analytic review. *Clin Psychol Rev.* 2017;56:25–39.

71. KE Woods, H Mazursky-Horowitz, SR Thomas, LR Dougherty, A Chronis-Tuscano. The unique effects of maternal ADHD symptoms and emotion dysregulation on parenting behavior. *J Atten Disord.* 2021;25(5):672–84.

72. Hale's Medications & Mothers' Milk. 2025. www.halesmeds.com

73. BBC News. Eight-year ADHD backlog at NHS clinics revealed. 2024 24 Jul. www.bbc.co.uk/news/articles/c720r1pxrx5o

Chapter 21

Autism

Sam Porter

What Is Autism?

The landscape of neurodevelopmental medicine is in a period of significant change, as our understanding of autism enters a new era. Diagnosis rates are climbing (UK diagnosis rates increased 787% between 1998 and 2018 [1]), as are prevalence rates (which increased from 0.05% in the 1960s [2] to 1% globally in 2022 [3] – higher in developed countries, with estimates as high as 2.6% in South Korea [4]). These changes are a reflection of not only increased awareness among practitioners and the public, but increasingly refined and inclusive diagnostic criteria. As diagnosis rates have increased, we have also observed a change in the demographics of the autistic population. The proportion of autistic people with an intellectual disability (ID) is currently estimated at 33% [3], down from 69% in the 1980s [5], with growing recognition that autistic people without an ID are able to mask or camouflage their traits and so go undiagnosed, as well as evidence that traditional intelligence tests can underestimate intelligence in autistics [6, 7]. Our estimation of the male to female ratio of autistic people has undergone a similar change over time – from 8:1 in 1995 to 3:1 in 2010 [8]. (NB, as well as focusing on autistic females, this chapter is primarily focused on autistic people without an ID. Whilst many aspects will be relevant to both populations, many autistic people with an ID will have additional needs related to their ID.)

These changes have occurred in part as a result of a richer dialogue, with increasing involvement of autistic individuals in clinical research – as researchers rather than subjects – and far stronger autistic-led advocacy organisations. Perhaps the most important change that increasing autistic involvement in the conversation about autism has led to is a change in how we conceptualise what autism actually is. The development of the neurodiversity paradigm and subsequent neurodiversity movement has stimulated a shift towards viewing autism as being part of the natural extraordinary diversity of human minds – with autism representing a phenotype of divergence that will inevitably occur in the presence of such diversity, rather than a pathology of normal developmental processes creating an impairment. The term 'disorder' is slowly falling out of fashion, and whilst the official name of 'autistic spectrum disorder' (ASD) remains in diagnostic manuals, NHS England recommends using 'autism' instead [9], with autistic people overwhelmingly preferring identity-first language (autistic people) to person-first language (people with autism) [10] – reflecting the view that autism is not a disorder or condition that somebody has, it is an indelible part of who they are. And whilst proponents of person-first language argue that it is destigmatising – allowing the person to not be defined by their diagnosis – a study of 225 autistic doctors found that those who preferred person-first language were more likely to consider autism a disorder rather than a difference and were more likely to have attempted suicide [11].

Proponents of person-first language are generally more likely to view autism itself as a disorder, and prefer the traditional ASD terminology. The proposition that autism is a disorder can largely be founded upon two arguments – that even with optimised environmental and social interventions and in the absence of diagnosable pathology autism can be disabling for some people just by its nature and the disproportionately high rates of psychiatric and medical illness seen in the autistic population. However, as perinatal psychiatrists we have to hand a useful analogy for a state of human existence that the same could broadly be said for – that of pregnancy.

Pregnancy is a normal and natural – though atypical – state of human existence. Each individual will have a different experience of being pregnant – in each there will be some ubiquitous features, and some unusual. Some aspects of a typical pregnancy experience will be unique to pregnancy, some that are universal human experiences but intensified in those that are pregnant (nausea, fatigue, nocturia). Some common aspects of a normal pregnancy experience will be unpleasant to many, even disabling to some, in a manner that is not ameliorable by social intervention nor attributable to separate pathology. But we would not think of pregnancy as a 'disorder' nonetheless. Nor do we talk about pregnancy with 'comorbid' deep vein thrombosis.

Why Is It a Perinatal Mental Health Issue?

Despite this shift of conceptualisation away from a disorder framework, another change in the conversation around autism is an increased recognition of the importance of a good understanding of autism for the general adult psychiatrist – with a drive to move diagnosis out of specialist services, and a recognition that many psychiatric conditions are more common in autistic patients and may require a different treatment approach. It is possible that autistic people make up about 20% of referrals to psychiatric outpatients [12], with autistic people having a significantly higher risk of a whole host of mental disorders than the general population [13], with such diverse conditions as obsessive-compulsive disorder, psychotic illnesses, mood disorders, post-traumatic stress disorder, alcohol misuse disorders and eating disorders. Perhaps the starkest argument for autism being a psychiatrist's business is the nine-fold increased incidence of suicide for autistic adults without an ID, suicide being the second biggest premature killer of autistic adults behind seizures [14]. Furthermore, with the exception of schizophreniform disorders, late diagnosis of autism is a risk factor for any mental disorder compared to people with childhood diagnoses [13, 15]. Contrary to perceptions that late diagnosis indicates a 'less severe' autistic presentation, it would seem that the process of navigating the world as an undiagnosed autistic has a significant toll on mental health.

Therefore, even if autism need not be conceptualised as a psychiatric diagnosis in itself, it is of vital importance that the general adult (or perinatal) psychiatrist can confidently recognise their autistic patient and allow this recognition to inform their assessment and management of her mental illness. Indeed, for perinatal psychiatrists, working exclusively with female patients, this becomes particularly pertinent, as female autistics are less likely to have been diagnosed and more likely to have received a previous misdiagnosis, with those that are diagnosed more likely to have been diagnosed later in life [16, 17]. This has predictable mental health consequences – autistic women are more likely than both neurotypical women and autistic men to have psychiatric diagnoses, have been admitted to a psychiatric hospital [18], to die during an inpatient stay and to complete suicide [14] – with autistic people being one of the few groups in which being female is a risk factor for completed suicide.

The relationship between autism and perinatal mental health specifically is an area of growing interest and research, but from the studies that we do have available it seems apparent that autism affects the entirety of the perinatal journey, with evidence of worse mental health during pregnancy [19] and higher rates of postnatal depression [20], as well as worse pregnancy outcomes, increased complications [21] and a lower sense of satisfaction with the care that they received ante and postnatally [20]. This is to be expected, however, as autistic people face a wide range of barriers when accessing healthcare. In one study autistic people reported lower quality of care than non-autistic adults across 50/51 dimensions, with non-autistic people being five times more likely to endorse statements like 'I usually understand what my healthcare professional means when they discuss my care', and 'I am provided with appropriate support after I receive a diagnosis of any kind'. Indeed, so consistent was the difference in the experiences of accessing healthcare that the tool used to assess healthcare inequality could predict autism with an accuracy of 73% and higher sensitivity than the standard screening tools [22].

It is inarguable, therefore, that autism is a primary part of the perinatal psychiatrist's business, and that it is vital that they are equipped to recognise which patients are autistic, and work to ensure that they can access healthcare appropriately, both psychiatric and obstetric.

What Does Autism Look Like?

The diagnostic criteria for autism have changed over time, and are likely to change again in future, if nothing else to change the language towards a less deficit-based approach. It is worth remembering that for adults without an ID, autistic to autistic communication is at least as efficient and effective as non-autistic to non-autistic, and that the problems with communication between autistic and non-autistic people are bidirectional [23]. A similar result would be seen with groups of people who speak different languages – and the communication difficulties would not be perceived as one of the languages being deficient.

Is it therefore necessary to consider autistic traits 'deficits', as is typically done? Doing so eventually leads us to needing to perceive every deviation from the norm as inferior to it – sometimes with perplexing outcomes. In a 2021 paper, one researcher, having determined that autistic people were 'much more likely to reject the opportunity to earn ill-gotten money by supporting a bad cause' determined that this was down to a 'core-deficit in theory of mind ability, which extends to perturbations in moral judgment and decision making', with autistic people showing 'undue concern about their ill-gotten gains and the moral cost' [24]. What led them to conceptualise moral consistency and integrity as the result of a deficiency? Who determines when concern about the moral cost of our activities tips into the realm of undue? How do deficiencies in theory of mind – the ability to appreciate the cognitive state of others – correlate with deprioritising personal financial gain in favour of justice?

Nonetheless, but with that caveat in mind, the *Diagnostic and Statistical Manual of Mental Disorders*, fifth edition (DSM-5) criteria as currently published can be summarised in Box 21.1:

Box 21.1 Summary of Autism DSM-5 Criteria

Persistent deficits in social communication and social interaction across multiple contexts, as manifested by significant problems with all of:

Social emotional reciprocity (the naturalness of back-and-forth conversation). This may present in many ways: a tendency towards overinclusivity when speaking, going on at length about things apparently oblivious that the other person is not interested, not asking many questions, difficulties with small talk and telephone conversation, a tendency to only volunteer information directly asked for, not picking up on social cues, etc. (the list is not exhaustive nor is anything on it ubiquitous).

Non-verbal communication. Many autistic people talk about often feeling 'misunderstood' or 'not heard'. As touched upon above, autistic to non-autistic information transfer is poor in both directions, and a large part of this is due to differences in naturalness of communicating non-verbally. Autistic people may take things very literally, misunderstanding turns of phrase or interpreting sarcasm or exaggeration as genuine. Many will have repeatedly been misunderstood because of their tones, gestures, expressions or demeanour not conveying to others what they intended it to, and many will misinterpret the same things in other people – either by ignoring them altogether or through over-interpreting and actively looking for subtext that isn't there, because they're so prone to missing it.

Developing and/or maintaining relationships. Whilst many autistic people are socially isolated, with a lifelong history of difficulty with (or lack of interest in) forming relationships, many other autistic people want to and can make and keep friends and romantic partners. Some of the following may be observed, however: a tendency towards a small number of close friends, a preference for friendships with people of the opposite sex, a tendency towards friendships with people older or younger rather than peers, a tendency to drift from friendship to friendship, friends being very situational – for example, work friends are not seen outside of work or kept in touch with when they leave that place of employment (but are very important during that period), a disproportionate amount of autistic friends, a history of bullying and exclusion, a repeated history of unequal friendships (where the autistic person takes a long while to realise the friendship is a lot more important to them than it is the other person) and a history of many friendships fizzling out due to a lack of energy to pursue them, and deprioritising socialisation over solo activities when fatigued.

AND

Restricted, repetitive patterns of behaviours, interests or activities as manifested by abnormalities in at least two of:

Stereotypies. Stereotyped or repetitive movements, use of objects or speech may not be immediately obvious in an adult without an ID – especially in a clinic setting, but can be uncovered on exploration. As well as the archetypal hand-flapping, rocking, neologisms and echolalia, stereotypies can involve repetitious manipulation of objects, skin-picking or hair-pulling, coughing, joint-cracking, licking or sucking objects and much more.

Routines and rituals. Whilst the stereotypical anankastic picture of autistic adults in much of the popular imagination – bookish and nerdy, highly organised, set in their ways, overly fastidious, myopic, anxious and totally unfashionable – presents one picture of this area of autism, many autistic people will appear the total opposite of this – chaotic and disorganised, with a sense of total loss of control over every part of their life. Her need for perfection, and an inability to move on from a task until it has been completed to her satisfaction – regardless of relative importance to other tasks, leaves her in a perpetual state of disarray. Her need for things to be just so and done in specific ways leaves her unable to tolerate her partner's way of doing things, leading her to take on a disproportionate share of the labour and burn out.

Box 21.1 *(cont.)*

Restricted and fixated interests. Whilst there are stereotypical activities – birdwatching, metal detecting, train-spotting, etc. – and intense fandoms – Dr Who, Star Wars, Harry Potter – special interests can be anything, and sometimes in women can be missed if they are stereotypically 'feminine' interests – shoes, celebrities, soap operas, etc. – or indeed reinforced and encouraged if they are seen as positive – reading, schoolwork, drawing. They can often focus on fact and statistic collection but this is not ubiquitous. There is a strong emotional and well-being connection to the special interest and they can have a huge role in breaking down barriers to social interaction. Autism can often become a special interest of autistic people, and pregnancy/motherhood commonly becomes a special interest of the pregnant autistic woman.

Sensory hypo/hypersensitivities. Sensory hypo/hypersensitivities can be present in any sense, and it is important to remember that there are more than five senses. Proprioceptive hyposensitivity – leading to clumsiness – is common. Interoceptive hypersensitivity can lead to significant distress in pregnancy as unfamiliar internal feelings become common. Autistic women often have profound sensitivity to female hormones, and premenstrual dysphoric disorder is common [25]. When prescribing to autistic people, remember that they can be hypo- or hypersensitive to medication, so start low and build the dose slowly, believing them about side effects even at very low doses, but be prepared to use very high doses if necessary.

These features have to have been present from early childhood, not better attributable to another known cause and be present in multiple contexts. It must be remembered that no autistic traits are unique to autistic people nor are any universal, but are simply traits that are more common in autistic people. Left-handedness could be considered an autistic trait, as research shows that autistic people are around three times more likely to be left-handed, and left-handed people around 2.5 times more likely to be autistic. Most autistic people are, however, right-handed, and most left-handed people are not autistic.

The final diagnostic criterion is that these traits should cause some level of impairment, but it is important to recognise that the individual's strengths, along with appropriate accommodation, support and scaffolding can significantly reduce the impairment, and can mask the diagnosis, with sometimes objective impairment only becoming apparent at moments of transition to increased levels of demand – secondary school, leaving home or indeed having a baby. This can present a picture of everything being fine until that point that can throw clinicians off the scent of the diagnosis. It is also worth remembering that autistic people, especially autistic women, can mask their autistic traits, making it less obvious in certain contexts, but with an unseen cost. Masking is profoundly exhausting, and many autistic people describe the effort of masking throughout the day leaving them able to do nothing else when they get home; housework piles up, any semblance of a social life goes out the window – life is spent at school/work or recovering from school/work.

Autistic children may face challenges in getting a diagnosis because school see no evidence of any problems, whilst the parents describe severe problems at home. The home becomes the focus, with no consideration given to an autism diagnosis – if the child were autistic the problems would be present at school. However, as time goes on, it becomes apparent that they had been putting so much effort into holding things together at school, that by the time they got home they were unable to regulate at all, leading to the two extremes. Similarly, an autistic woman may be able to manage working but really struggle to be productive at home. This isn't an issue when it is just herself to worry about, or when she has a partner to pick up the slack, but when a baby is added to the mix it becomes overwhelming. Masking is associated with poor outcomes for autistic people and is a risk factor for suicidal behaviours [26]. Remember therefore to proactively ask about these traits when considering if a patient is autistic, rather than judging it by your impression of their interpersonal style, or their superficial level of function (job, partner, etc.).

Qualitative research on the autistic perinatal experience is minimal but beginning to appear and gathering pace. Early themes from research are in keeping with existing anecdotal evidence, clinical experience and general axiom: that autistic women can face profound challenges on their perinatal journey – some of which could be ameliorated by appropriate accommodations by healthcare professionals. These challenges may not be common for neurotypical women and may be ignored or overlooked, and they can pervade the entire course of the perinatal journey. Going through different stages of the perinatal journey we can consider what these challenges might be. Whilst none of them is unique to or ubiquitous in autism, remember, many of your autistic patients will be undiagnosed, and observation of difficulties of similar natures should prompt the perinatal psychiatrist to consider autism and explore this with the patient. The examples of some of the potential difficulties used below are all from real-life autistic patients.

Autism and the Perinatal Period

Sex and Conception

The sexual health of disabled people has long been overlooked, but it is impossible to consider the perinatal journey without some consideration to sex. Autistic people can have very specific sexual health needs. A far higher proportion of autistic people are LGBT [27]. Autistic women also report dramatically higher rates of sexual violence [28]. Whilst most autistic people are sexually active, they are less likely to be sexually active than non-autistics, but have similar rates of sexually transmitted infections [27], which may suggest that they are more likely to engage in riskier sexual activity.

Planned conception may be more difficult – with autism being associated with endometriosis, polycystic ovaries and idiopathic menstrual irregularities [29] – but even an autistic woman without any fertility problems may find the process of planned pregnancy immensely difficult. Many will get drawn into carefully planning attempts at conception – measuring body temperature, tracking ovulation, etc. Patients who describe (or whose partners do) a highly regimented conception process, planned as if pregnancy was the goal of a military mission, are worth screening for autism. Perfectionist traits and a tendency towards intense introspection can make difficulties in conception particularly painful, as the inability to conceive becomes a personal failing. And for a cohort of people who, in general, prefer things to be carefully planned and timed, being at the mercy of nature can feel very disruptive, with the autistic tendency to monotropism leading to the rest of life being put on the shelf whilst pregnancy is pursued – which might not be a problem for a few weeks, but after several months of trying can lead to significant difficulties.

Antenatal

Advances in antenatal healthcare over the years have contributed to a significant improvement of maternal and infant outcomes, especially for women who have problems with their pregnancy, with the standard antenatal pathway having mutated significantly from the experiences of our grandparents. Multiple appointments in brightly lit clinics, a new midwife every time, extra scans because of anomalies that are 'probably nothing to worry about', decisions to make about birthing preferences, masses of (often contradictory) information being fired at you from all angles, a list of things to avoid, blood tests and blood pressure monitoring – the potential to overwhelm an autistic patient simply by using routine pathways is significant. Simple changes can be very powerful. Consistency of staff, consistency of location and minimising the number of trips back and forth by aligning scans with blood tests and perinatal appointments, etc. can all be hugely beneficial. Thinking about the environment in which the patient is seen is important too. An autistic person in a very bright room, overwhelmed by the light to the point that they are struggling to communicate, even think, may present as depressed. An intrusive, repetitive noise – a ticking clock or dripping tap – may constantly distract them and cause them to miss important pieces of information. Adopting an approach of taking a minute at the start of each appointment to check the patient's comfort with the sensory environment (and modifying it as needed) will not harm neurotypical patients but may profoundly improve an autistic patient's experience.

Whilst some autistic patients will be paragons of organisation, arriving 10 minutes early for every appointment, with all of the correct paperwork in a neatly arranged file, others may find it impossible to keep on top of the increase in organisational demand antenatally – especially if they are juggling work and/or older children. Many areas have automatic safeguarding referrals in place if women miss a certain number of antenatal appointments – and autistic women can often end up triggering these because they have been unable to manage one or multiple aspects of attending all their appointments – for example, difficulties with navigation or timekeeping, profound anxiety about meeting new people or because the appointments are distressing. Where autistic women are missing appointments, every effort should be made to find out why and see how they can be supported to attend them. It may also be necessary to recognise that her capacity to attend appointments may be limited, or that indeed they are harmful to her in some way – some autistic women may find themselves profoundly exhausted by their appointments, others may find that they trigger profound anxiety about the health of the pregnancy – occasionally to the point that they are considering a termination to end the misery of worrying about the unborn! In such cases it is worth taking a backwards step and reviewing the necessity of the various appointments and allowing her the freedom to capaciously decline some of them, especially those that will not change the immediate management plan and are primarily for monitoring. Allowing patients to opt out of some appointments may increase the total number that they attend.

Pregnancy can often become an area of special interest for the pregnant autistic, and whilst education and knowledge can be beneficial and empowering, there are multifaceted risks associated. A patient who is well read and tends towards bluntness in conversation can be perceived as intimidating by professionals, especially if there is an area of disagreement, and this can lead to a strained therapeutic relationship or, worse, make the professional (ironically) more rigid and monotropic in their approach to treating the patient. The research itself can also be incredibly anxiety provoking, as women read multiple (often contradictory) things about what to do or not do. Combining this with a tendency to think through every possible outcome of everything in order to avoid feeling unprepared can lead to anxiety which can be so extreme as to cause suicidal ideation; profound antenatal anxiety should always lead the perinatal psychiatrist to at least pause to consider if the patient might be autistic.

Consider further the potential problems that can arise when we tell somebody with a tendency towards anxiety, pattern recognition, hypersensitivity to change and hypersensitive interoception to monitor her baby's movements and seek help if there are any changes (any undiagnosed patients who repeatedly present with altered fetal movements with no concerns identified should be screened for autism). There is a fine line to walk between not wanting to feed her anxieties and not wanting to under-investigate a person who is at a baseline higher risk of adverse outcomes. Managing these and other health anxieties for autistic people can be a challenge. Some autistic people will be reassured about their worries by a trusted professional to a significant effect (in a way that somebody with a health anxiety disorder would not), generally when they feel that their concerns have been properly listened to and they have had the reasons that the professional is not as worried as they are explained clearly – but many will remain profoundly anxious throughout, and may require pharmacological or psychological interventions.

Pregnancy can also be a time of significant change in a woman's life. There may be a need to move to a bigger home, an unprecedented acceleration in a previously casual relationship with the father, a first foray into cohabitation, the trigger for abandonment by a partner or rejection by family, the precipitant for a partner to change and become abusive, significant changes in work role, effects on physical health and knock-on impact on other important activities or hobbies. Change can be very difficult for many autistics, and multiple significant changes together can be disabling. Explore the changes that are going on in your autistic patient's life, and be aware that those going through multiple changes may need heightened levels of support. Consider screening undiagnosed patients who begin to decompensate when going through periods of significant change.

Delivery

The lack of control a woman has over her own pregnancy can be incredibly distressing for an autistic woman and drive a need to control every aspect that she can, will often be observed, often followed by profound dysregulation if those things don't go to plan. This can be particularly problematic during the delivery process and can be a driver behind autistic women requesting elective caesarean sections, as the process feels brought under control – which feels preferable to worrying that everybody will think you are mad because you have had a meltdown because your partner packed the wrong slippers, or being on your own because your birthing partner couldn't get there. Autistic women who, having been given the information, are requesting an elective section, should be given one, and again, women without a diagnosis who are requesting one because of the sense of control should be thought about from a neurodevelopmental perspective.

For those that do opt for a vaginal delivery, birth planning is important. Autistic women can range from feeling so overwhelmed by the unpredictability of birth that she is unable to engage with birth planning or considers it pointless, to arriving to the meeting having drawn up a plan with military precision, with a lot of emotional investment in the birth proceeding as anticipated. When thinking about birth planning it's helpful to try and take a middle approach – acknowledging the inherent unpredictability of birth but identifying the predictable stressors. There is a growing recognition of the need to consider in advance what modifications might need to be made to the sensory environment.

All women should have pain management discussed but this requires greater attention for autistic women. It is well established that nociceptive hyper- and hyposensitivity are both autistic traits, which may mean that autistic women are far more debilitated by the pain of early labour than neurotypical women. Whilst some autistic patients are hyposensitive to pain and may consider labour little more than discomfort, this is still atypical for autistics, and practitioners should not rush to assume that a lack of apparent pain during labour is due to nociceptive hyposensitivity. Idiosyncrasies in their response to pain may lead them to shut down when in pain, rather than display the usual outward signs, and their verbal communication may be inhibited, so they may not be able to ask for help. Ask patients ahead of time how they respond to pain; think about how their pain might best be managed during labour ahead of time. If they are hypersensitive to pain, make a plan for them to be allowed to be admitted for analgesia at an earlier stage of labour than normal if necessary. Encourage labour ward staff to treat pain to the patient's experience rather than the stage of labour or regularity of contractions, and remember that these early interactions can, if they are negative, considerably damage the trust the patient has in their care. The phrase 'you need to wait for the real pain to begin before you get an epidural', said to a woman bent over and sobbing in agony immediately makes the patient feel uncared for, and reduces their likelihood of raising matters of concern in future – with potentially disastrous consequences.

Delivery can involve a lot of physical contact between healthcare providers and the patient – holding hands, rubs on shoulders, hands on backs may all be done as natural responses to the woman, and indeed be welcomed by many women, including many autistic women. Staff may also need to touch women for the purposes of examination or recording of observations. It is important that autistic patients are warned in advance of any physical contact that they are not initiating – small sentences like: 'Would it help to squeeze my hand?' or 'I just need to pop this SATS probe back on your finger' can make big differences.

Immediate Postnatal Period

Although change often represents a major challenge for autistic patients, the transition to motherhood is at least usually accompanied with months of notice, which is usually plenty of time for them to prepare themselves (mentally as well as practically) for the change, and many autistic women, especially those who have an uncomplicated delivery and are in an otherwise stable situation, will thrive during early motherhood. Prematurity or unexpected complications in the delivery process, however, can be particularly unsettling, and whilst a multiparous woman will have the advantage of early motherhood not being new to them, a baby with a significantly different temperament to previous ones can also lead to decompensation, as many autistic people also struggle when eventualities deviate from expectations significantly.

One change that is more difficult to prepare for, however, is the environmental change of the postnatal ward, and for many autistic women who have acute decompensations in their emotional regulation abilities postnatally this is the driving factor. Some autistic people are very uncomfortable sleeping outside of their own home at all – one patient's delivery was her second night spent outside of the home she grew up in (she went to university for a night and returned the next day; when she got married, her husband moved into her parents' home). Even those that are more tolerant of it will struggle immensely on a noisy ward, with staff coming in and out, surrounded by strangers and potentially in a very sensorily challenging environment. Single rooms should be offered where available so that the patient can have as much control as possible over her sensory environment, and discharge facilitated as quickly as possible if there are no medical concerns. Staffing should be kept as consistent as possible, and a balance may need to be struck at times between monitoring physical observations and allowing the patient to have space – some patients may prefer to sometimes have a competent partner or parent take their observations and advise staff of the results, or timings slightly changed so that they can be done by a familiar healthcare assistant rather than a stranger.

Staff interacting with the patients should also remember that in the immediate postpartum – exhausted, in pain, perhaps anaemic, and dealing with all the complex emotions common to having just delivered a newborn – many autistic women will have lost their capacity to mask. Certain autistic traits may become more pronounced – they may become more inflexible or monotropic, for instance – and there may be an increased discordance between the emotions they are feeling and the emotions that others consider them to be projecting. This may lead to miscommunications and misunderstandings (even with familiar staff who have only known the patient whilst she was masking) that the patient does not have the emotional capacity for – precipitating periods of acute dysregulation that lead to concerns about the mother's mental health – prompting assessments by more strangers, prolonging the admission and increasing the dysregulation. At this time more than ever it is vital to communicate clearly and directly – indeed given the likelihood that the patient will interpret things literally then communication should be literal. Similarly, without very good reason not to, take patients literally. If unsure as to whether or not something is meant literally, ask. Patients who have a monotropic focus on an issue and are not moving past it will not be aided by having their concerns ignored or being forced to move on to another matter, and even if conversation diverts to new topics their mind is unlikely to – asking patients what further information or reassurances that they might need to be able to move on to a new subject and then providing them has far more utility.

Patients should be encouraged ahead of delivery to think about the things that will help them to regulate whilst they are inpatients and be supported to access those and use them without judgement. These may be sensory items, stereotyped movements or other behaviours. For example, a patient may find using a dummy incredibly soothing when distressed, and will use them at home to regulate distress. Should she find herself on a maternity ward in a distressed state, she might choose not to use a dummy on the ward for fear of being perceived in a negative light. Her coping mechanism thus removed, she is more prone to acute emotional decompensation – any incidence of which may lead to staff developing negative perceptions of her and even questioning her parenting capacity. Having a side room, knowing staff have been made aware ahead of time and that it is not a concern for them will be of great help. It is even better if the woman can be reassured that staff will use the information to inform their communication style and awareness of the need to avoid sensory overstimulation.

Moving Forward

There are many challenges to raising a baby and the majority of the problems that autistic parents face are common to all parents. However, as noted previously, autistic women are more likely to develop postnatal depression than non-autistic women. The reasons for this are likely to be multifactorial, and it is important to adopt a holistic approach to moderating these risks – exploring the factors that are contributing to the presentation and considering whether she is depressed or burnt out by the change and increase in responsibilities, especially for primiparous women, as motherhood presents difficulties across the areas covered by the diagnostic criteria – especially social, sensory and routine.

The first few weeks are often overwhelming for the autistic woman as she deals with all the normal difficulties of having a baby, along with the increase in social contact as family and in-laws come to coo at the baby – on top of professional visits and appointments (the principles of minimising appointments, travel and staff involved are never more important). A social expectation (perceived or otherwise) to attend baby groups and exercise sessions can be disastrous for people who are highly driven to be (or to be seen to be) doing the 'right' thing and are depleted by social contact, and it is important that socialisation for its own sake is not promoted. Social activities attended out of a sense of duty but are not particularly rewarding – for example, a weaning group or a family visit to a noisy soft play – deplete her energy without rewards, leaving no energy for social interactions that she may enjoy. Each time an unrewarding social activity takes precedence over a rewarding one, social interaction is negatively reinforced. Encourage patients to engage in social activities that they wish to, but at a pace and regularity that suits them. Some will force themselves to attend groups that they hate because they have already paid for them. It is worth pointing out that attending the groups will not gain them the money back, and that attending groups that they don't enjoy or gain from just because they have paid for them is somewhat akin to eating something they're allergic to because they hadn't read the ingredients before purchasing it.

Humans are hardwired by millions of years' evolution to be driven to despair by the crying of a baby – particularly their own – and it is certainly not a uniquely autistic trait to experience auditory overwhelm in response to one. Indeed, it can be a useful comparator for people who do not have acoustic hypersensitivity to understand what it is like – imagine the impossibility to relax, talk, even think in the presence of a screaming baby, and suffering that whenever in the room with a running washing machine, or background chatter in a bar. However, whilst it is a normal human response to be overwhelmed by your baby's crying when you were already at the point of breakdown because the aforementioned washing machine has been running all day and the only escape has been to a noisy café with a friend, prolonged crying spells can potentially trigger significant acute decompensations presenting as shutdowns or meltdowns, and any history of the same should prompt further exploration. Breastfeeding presents a new sensory experience that some autistic women find deeply unpleasant (but endure because doing the 'right' thing is more important than being comfortable, or because the subjective sense of bond and connection with the baby whilst she is breastfeeding outweighs the unpleasant sensory experience). Many autistic women love to cuddle their babies, but some find themselves constantly feeling worn down from the amount of physical contact that their baby requires. Some autistic women find the smells associated with a new baby around toileting, etc. absolutely intolerable and spend their time between nappy changes dreading the next, whilst the author has observed many autistic women smelling their baby's head repeatedly when talking about difficult subjects, using it as a regulatory sensation. This new sensory world can have a potentially significant impact on mental health and well-being, and many undiagnosed women will either not make the connection or be embarrassed by it and not wish to share it.

Autistic women may find the unpredictability of a baby, especially a newborn, very difficult to manage, and may describe being unable to do anything whilst the baby naps because they don't know how long they will have and do not wish to start anything they will not have time to finish. Attending to a baby at the drop of a hat may mean that rituals as part of day-to-day life that they would normally complete suddenly become impossible – and people who have never lacked the time to count every tile on the wall behind the hob after turning it off may not realise how destabilising they find it if a crying infant prevents them. Some will feel intensely bound to do everything 'by the book' and have an enormous sense of pressure to make sure that everything is done absolutely 'correctly'; for example, times between feeds correct to the minute, and a great deal of distress if it is impossible to do so. Many autistic mothers will be profoundly anxious, and women who describe being unable to sleep whilst their baby does because they are listening for their breathing, or are constantly checking baby's temperature should be considered for screening.

It is, however, important to note that most autistic mothers take to motherhood well, and many flourish and enjoy it, and whilst the presence of any or many of the above may make parenting more difficult and challenging at times, with appropriate support and understanding there is no reason to believe that autistic women are any more or less likely to be good enough mothers than non-autistic women. However, stigma and outdated perceptions still persist, and the perinatal psychiatrist must be prepared at times to be a staunch advocate for autistic patients whose child(ren) are the subjects of social services plans. Sometimes concerns will arise that are entirely rooted in prejudice or stigma, and this must be challenged where it is seen. At other times concerns may arise that simple accommodation may have overcome (e.g. a referral made because of a number of missed appointments without accessibility difficulties being addressed), and it is better that such needs are identified and addressed before making safeguarding referrals that eventually prove a source of stress for the patient and a consumption of stretched social care resources.

There are, of course, situations where the concerns raised are serious and justified – indeed it may be the perinatal psychiatrist themselves who are raising the concerns – but the psychiatrist's role of advocate nonetheless continues. Whilst not all autistic women, for diverse reasons, are safe mothers, it is important that the assessment process is fair and enables those women who are able to be good parents to be able to demonstrate that. Therefore it is important that her perinatal psychiatrist advocates that the process be conducted and interpreted in an autism-aware manner.

Consider the expectations on the mother – a plan that places an expectation on a mother to attend multiple groups and appointments could have an overall detrimental effect as alluded to above, and it is important that such activities are restricted to what is objectively necessary, and focus on social activity that is rewarding and more likely to positively reinforce social contact. Where groups are considered essential, the mother's participation in the group must be assessed in the context of the amount of effort and energy she is expending just to sit in the room and tolerate being there.

Organising meetings in brightly lit rooms with multiple people, with a number of them previously unknown to the mother, is likely to leave her feeling overwhelmed, and increase the risk of bilateral miscommunications and misunderstandings. The perinatal psychiatrist should educate the wider network that making judgements about the mother's general mental stability based on a difficulty in regulating her emotions in such environments is inappropriate.

Whilst unannounced visits by social workers are an essential aspect of safeguarding at times, services should be encouraged that these should be completed by people well known to the mother, and that even as little as a minute or two's advanced notice by text could be enough to make a big difference to the mother's experience – as might allowing the mother to take 5 minutes in another room to compose herself after the social worker arrives. Whether these accommodations can be made or not, it is important that the social worker is supported to understand that autistic people will struggle with unannounced visitors – before we even consider the stakes of the visit – and to recognise that any anxiety or agitation they encounter is not necessarily reflective of their day-to-day state of being.

Where it is not considered safe for an assessment to be completed with baby and mother at home together, the suitability of the environment for the assessment should be considered. Being flung into any new environment is incredibly destabilising for most autistic people, but when that new environment is a mother and baby assessment unit, living communally with strangers, with enforced socialisation, regimented approaches that can be intolerant of idiosyncrasy, cameras in bedrooms and timers on visits to communal bathrooms that are not maintained to your particular standards of hygiene it is unremarkable that the author's experience is that such placements often break down within weeks for autistic women. Acutely aware of the need to be perceived as 'normal' they fatigue themselves through social contact, they distress themselves immeasurably by dispensing of all stereotypies and rituals that may be overt and lead them to be considered unusual (they are on camera all the time after all), and they are generally isolated from family, friends and special interests that may help to restore them. The author always advocates for such assessments to be carried out in mother and baby foster placements, ideally with an autistic foster care or a foster carer with training and/or experience in working with autistic people. If an autistic patient is in unit, it is helpful to meet with the management of the unit, the patient and the social worker to come up with a tailored plan that meets safeguarding requirements within an autistic friendly way.

What To Do if You Suspect a Patient Is Autistic

It can be difficult to broach the conversation with an undiagnosed patient who has not themselves brought it up as a possibility. There is a wide range of public understanding and views about autism, and patients can react in a variety of ways to the diagnosis being suggested. For this reason, if there are historical features or issues occurring that give you cause to suspect that the patient is autistic, it is worth asking them what they know about or understand about autism. Starting with something along the lines of:

> 'Studies have shown that up to a fifth of people referred to mental health services are autistic, but that many of them – especially women – will not have been diagnosed. For that reason, it is always worth considering – if only to rule it out – if patients referred to our service are autistic, especially those with a history of (relevant historical features), which are more common in the autistic population. What do you know about autism?' Further helpful questions might be: 'Is it something you have ever wondered about in relationship to yourself?' 'Has anybody ever suggested you might be autistic?'

Some patients may shut down the conversation then and there, and their wishes not to explore it should be respected, whilst others will at this point reveal that they were already fairly sure that they were autistic. Many patients, perhaps most, however, will be a little taken aback, but willing to explore if it is felt to be worth exploring. These patients should be given information about autism – particularly helpful is autobiographical lived experience testimony – and given time to go through this information and ask questions if they wish. You may wish to complete screening tools, of which the Autism Quotient 50 [30] and Ritvo Autism Asperger's Diagnostic Scale-Revised [31] are both validated, with the Camouflaging Autistic Traits Questionnaire [32] helpful for detecting masking, and are worth completing with the patient together, as the questions themselves can be used as prompts for further exploration in the history.

If you and the patient are both in agreement that autism seems a good fit, then the ideal scenario would be for the perinatal psychiatrist, having taken a thorough history from the patient and where possible a collateral and developmental history from a parent, to make a formal diagnosis, but, if this is not practicable or possible, then a referral for an assessment via the appropriate route should be made. In such instances, it is best practice to work with the patient as if they were autistic. One useful framework for guiding how to work with autistic patients is encapsulated by the mnemonic Autistic SPACE [33]. The paper itself provides further details, but can be summarised thus:

S - Sensory – think about the sensory environment you are seeing the patient in and modify it as far as possible to the patient's preferences.

P – Predictability – avoid last-minute changes, do the things that you are going to say that you are going to do, give advance warning of major changes.

A – Acceptance – accept the patients as they are, explicitly give them the freedom to choose to eschew eye contact, or to communicate in a blunt and direct way, or prefer a life of relative solitude and not to be judged for that.

C – Communication – remember to be clear about what you are saying, sharing information explicitly and specifically, bearing in mind that it may take some time to be processed. Ensure that you respond to your patient's words, rather than what you think they may have meant by them – clarify with the patient if you think there is some subtext and check that your inferences are correct.

E – Empathy – remember that autistic people do not typically lack empathy, but that autistic and non-autistic people struggle to interpret each other properly. Be aware of the bidirectionality of the potential empathy gap, and that interpreting autistic patients may be more difficult.

The acronym taken as a whole prompts us to remember that autistic people will need space to access healthcare effectively – physical space, processing space and emotional space.

Key Messages

1. No autistic traits are unique to autism nor ubiquitous among autistics. A propensity of traits across various diagnostic area is required for diagnosis. A trait is not pathological in an autistic person and non-pathological in a non-autistic person, and may require the same accommodations, regardless of diagnosis.
2. Remember that autistic people can conceal autistic traits, and so you must be proactive in considering whether patients are autistic if there are historical clues or autistic traits described or observed.
3. Many of your autistic patients will be undiagnosed, so considering the sensory and communication style preferences of all of your patients will ensure that all your autistic patients benefit whether diagnosed or not, with no detriment to your non-autistic patients.
4. Most autistic mothers thrive and do well, and flourishing in the role is not an exclusion criterion for the diagnosis.

References

1. G Russell, S Stapley, T Newlove-Delgado, A Salmon, R White, F Warren, et al. Time trends in autism diagnosis over 20 years: a UK population-based cohort study. *J Child Psychol Psychiatry.* 2022 Jun;63(6):674–82.
2. CJ Newschaffer, LA Croen, J Daniels, E Giarelli, JK Greher, SE Levy, et al. The epidemiology of autism spectrum disorders. *Annu Rev Public Health.* 2007;28:235–58.
3. J Zeidan, E Fombonne, J Scorah, A Ibrahim, MS Durkin, S Saxena, et al. Global prevalence of autism: a systematic review update. *Autism Res.* 2022 Mar;15(5):778–90.
4. YS Kim, BL Leventhal, YJ Koh, E Fombonne, E Laska, EC Lim, et al. Prevalence of autism spectrum disorders in a total population sample. *Am J Psychiatry.* 2011 Sep;168(9):904–12.
5. J Miller, D Bilder, M Farley, H Coon, J Pinborough-Zimmerman, W Jenson, et al. Autism spectrum disorder reclassified: a second look at the 1980s UTAH/UCLA autism epidemiologic study. *J Autism Dev Disord.* 2013 Jan; 43(1):200–10.
6. M Dawson, I Soulieres, MA Gernsbacher, L Motrron. The level and nature of autistic intelligence. *Psychol Sci.* 2007 Aug;18(8):657–62.
7. V Bal, T Katz, SL Bishop, K Krasileva. Understanding definitions of minimally verbal across instruments: evidence for subgroups within minimally verbal children and adolescents with autism spectrum disorder. *J Child Psychol Psychiatry.* 2016 Jul;57(12):1424–33.
8. CM Jensen, HC Steinhausen, MB Lauritsen. Time trends over 16 years in incidence – rates of autism spectrum disorders across the lifespan based on nationwide Danish register data. *J Autism Dev Disord.* 2014 Aug;44(8):1808–18.
9. NHS England. Making information and the words we use accessible. https://shorturl.at/0PiOp
10. A Taboas, K Doepke, C Zimmerman. Preferences for identity-first versus person-first language in a US sample of autism stakeholders. *Autism.* 2023 Feb;27(2):565–70.
11. SK Shaw, A Fossi, L Carravallah, K Rabenstein, M Doherty. The experiences of autistic doctors: a cross-sectional study. *Front Psychiatry.* 2023 Jul;14:1160994.
12. J Nyrenius, J Eberhard, M Ghaziuddin, C Gillberg, E Billstedt. Prevalence of autism spectrum disorders in adult outpatient

psychiatry. *J Autism Dev Disord.* 2022 Jan;52:3769–79.

13. SJ Rim, KJ Kwak, S Park. Risk of psychiatric comorbidity with autism spectrum disorder and its association with diagnosis timing using a nationally representative cohort. *Res Autism Spect Disord.* 2023;104:102–34.
14. T Hirvikoski, E Mittendorfer-Rutz, M Boman, H Larsson, P Lichtenstein, S Bölte. Premature mortality in autism spectrum disorder. *Br J Psychiatry.* 2016 Mar;208(3):232–8.
15. MC Lai, C Kassee, R Besney, S Bonato, L Hull, W Mandy, et al. Prevalence of co-occurring mental health diagnoses in the autism population: a systematic review and meta-analysis. *Lancet Psychiatry.* 2019 Oct;6(10):819–29.
16. L Fusar-Poli, N Brondino, P Politi, E Aguglia. Missed diagnoses and misdiagnoses of adults with autism spectrum disorder. *Eur Arch Psychiatry Clin Neurosci.* 2022 Mar;272(2): 187–98.
17. C Gesi, G Migliarese, S Torriero, M Capellazzi, AC Omboni, G Cerveri, et al Gender differences in misdiagnosis and delayed diagnosis among adults with autism spectrum disorder with no language or intellectual disability. *Brain Sci.* 2021 Jul 9;11(7):912.
18. MI Martini, R Kuja-Halkola, A Butwicka, E Du Rietz, BM D'Onofrio, F Happé, et al. Sex differences in mental health problems and psychiatric hospitalization in autistic young adults. *JAMA Psychiatry.* 2022 Dec 1;79(12):1188–98.
19. CA Lancaster, KJ Gold, HA Flynn, H Yoo, SM Marcus, MM Davis. Risk factors for depressive symptoms during pregnancy: a systematic review. *Am J Obstet Gynecol.* 2010 Jan;202(1):5–14.
20. S Hampton, C Allison, E Aydin, S Baron-Cohen, R Holt. Autistic mothers' perinatal well-being and parenting styles. *Autism.* 2022 Oct;26(7):1805–20.
21. CG McDonnell, EA DeLucia. Pregnancy and parenthood among autistic adults: implications for advancing maternal health and parental well-being. *Autism Adulthood.* 2021 Mar 1;3(1):100–15.
22. E Weir, C Allison, S Baron-Cohen. Autistic adults have poorer quality healthcare and worse health based on self-report data. *Mol Autism.* 2022 May 26;13(1):23.
23. CJ Crompton, D Ropar, CV Evans-Williams, EG Flynn, S Fletcher-Watson. Autistic peer-to-peer information transfer is highly effective. *Autism.* 2020 Oct;24(7):1704–12.
24. Y Hu, AM Pereira, X Gao, BM Campos, E Derrington, B Corgnet. Right temperoparietal junction underlies avoidance of moral transgression in autism spectrum disorder. *J Neurosci.* 2021 Feb;41(8):1699–715.
25. H Obaydi, BK Puri. Prevalence of premenstrual syndrome in autism: a prospective observer-rated study. *J Int Med Res.* 2008 Mar–Apr;36(2):268–72.
26. SA Cassidy, K Gould, E Townsend, M Pelton, AE Robertson, J Rodgers. Is camouflaging autistic traits associated with suicidal thoughts and behaviours? Expanding the interpersonal psychological theory of suicide in an undergraduate student sample. *J Autism Dev Disord.* 2020 Oct;50(10):3638–48.
27. E Weir, C Allison, S Baron-Cohen. The sexual health, orientation, and activity of autistic adolescents and adults. *Autism Res.* 2021 Nov;14(11):2342–54.
28. V Gibbs, J Hudson, E Pellicano. The extent and nature of autistic people's violence experiences during adulthood: a cross-sectional study of victimisation. *J Autism Dev Disord.* 2023 Sep;53(9):3509–24.
29. T Simantov, A Pohl, A Tsompanidis, E Weir, MV Lombardo, A Ruigrok, P Smith, et al. Medical symptoms and conditions in autistic women. *Autism.* 2022 Feb;26(2):373–88.
30. S Baron-Cohen, S Wheelwright, R Skinner, J Martin, E Clubley. The autism-spectrum quotient (AQ): evidence from Asperger syndrome/high-functioning

autism, males and females, scientists and mathematicians. *J Autism Dev Disord.* 2001 Feb;31(1):5–17.

31. RA Ritvo, ER Ritvo, D Guthrie, MJ Ritvo, DH Hufnagel, W McMahon, et al. The Ritvo Autism Asperger Diagnostic Scale-Revised (RAADS-R): a scale to assist the diagnosis of autism spectrum disorder in adults: an international validation study. *J Autism Dev Disord.* 2011 Aug;41(8):1076–89.
32. L Hull, W Mandy, MC Lai, S Baron-Cohen, C Allison, P Smith, KV Petrides. Development and validation of the Camouflaging Autistic Traits Questionnaire (CAT-Q). *J Autism Dev Disord.* 2019 Mar;49(3):819–33.
33. M Doherty, S McCowan, SC Shaw. Autistic SPACE: a novel framework for meeting the needs of autistic people in healthcare settings. *Br J Hosp Med (Lond).* 2023 Apr 2;84(4):1–9.

Chapter 22

Maternal Suicide, Deliberate Self-Harm and Other Mental Health Related Causes of Maternal Death

Roch Cantwell

Introduction

The shadow of maternal death has long been a presence in the care of women during pregnancy and the postnatal period. With the development of modern obstetric practice, rates of maternal death have plummeted in much of the Western world. In stark contrast, rates remain stubbornly high in low-income countries, with rates in 2020 in sub-Saharan Africa 136 times those of Australia and New Zealand, where the maternal mortality rate (MMR) is lowest [1]. However, in many high-income countries, relative to the absolute reduction, mortality associated with mental ill health has emerged as a leading cause of maternal death. Between 6 weeks and 1 year after delivery, mental illness is now the leading cause of maternal death in the UK and Ireland [2].

Given its rarity, much of the data on maternal suicide and other mental health related deaths are derived from nationally collected information which monitors the performance and safety of maternity care. The longest-running and most extensive dataset is provided through the UK and Ireland Confidential Enquiries into Maternal Deaths (referred to hereafter as 'the Enquiries'), covering over 30 years of information on psychiatric deaths.

The UK and Ireland Confidential Enquiries into Maternal Deaths

History of the Enquiries

First published in 1952, the Enquiries are the longest established in the world. Up to 2015, with some exceptions, they provided triennial reports. From 2015, reports have been published annually, but each still produces rolling triennial data, and specific themes, such as deaths due to psychiatric causes, are analysed in greater detail every 3 years.

Deaths related to psychiatric disorder were first identified for more detailed review in the report covering 1994–6 and then in each triennial report up to that of 2007–9. From that point, reports focusing on mental health related deaths include those published in 2015 (covering 2009–13), 2018 (2014–16), 2021 (2017–19) and 2022 (covering a detailed review of mental health related deaths in 2020, due to a significant rise in rates). In addition, in recent years the Enquiries have conducted yearly themed morbidity reviews. The 2017 report reviewed the care of a cohort of women who were at increased risk of early postpartum major mental illness to learn lessons from their subsequent management.

Since the early 1990s, the Enquiries have repeatedly reported on the twin themes of lessons learned to improve individual clinical care, and those which suggest improvements to the structure and function of services that address the mental health needs of women and their infants in the perinatal period.

Methodology

The Enquiries' philosophy is to go 'beyond counting numbers to listen and tell the stories of the women who died so as to learn lessons that may save the lives of other mothers and babies, as well as aiming to improve the standard of maternal health overall' [3]. In practice, this means a synthesis of data from multiple sources, both quantitative and qualitative, including national data reporting and case records from maternity, mental health and primary care, where available, along with other sources, to build up as complete a picture as possible of the woman's background and care. All deaths receive obstetric, midwifery, anaesthetic and pathology initial review, with deaths where there have been psychological factors or mental health diagnosis or care, being reviewed in addition by two psychiatrists.

Reports combine quantitative data on prevalence, demographics and treatment-related factors, alongside anonymised vignettes of women's health difficulties and care. Where patterns emerge, recommendations can be made for improving clinical care or service organisation. Given the nature of the Enquiries, all information is anonymised prior to review and, in generating recommendations, reviewers can set a threshold of 'gold standard' clinical care or service provision to ensure that all possible lessons can be learnt.

Other International Maternal Deaths Audits

The conducting of national or regional maternal deaths reviews has become more commonplace in the past several decades, but not all separate psychiatric deaths or continue their enquiries beyond the first 42 postnatal days. Other national reviews are also more limited in the completeness of data, often relying solely on reporting structures, without the benefit of national data linkage to ensure comprehensiveness. This is particularly important for capturing psychiatric deaths, which may occur in the late postpartum and are less likely to be reported through maternity services. As such, they are more limited as a means to understanding the causes of psychiatric death and the adequacy of care received. Furthermore, the majority of national maternal deaths reviews come from high-income countries and lessons learned may not be directly applicable to middle- and low-income settings. For example, differences in classification were noted in a comparison of national maternal deaths reviews in Suriname, Jamaica and the Netherlands [4].

Countries which have reviewed deaths by suicide up to the end of the first postnatal year include the Nordic countries [5], France [6], Switzerland [7] and Canada [8], alongside many, but not all, states in the USA [9]. However, even among European countries which only report on deaths up to 42 days postpartum, suicide is highlighted as a leading cause of maternal death [10]. A number of recent reports have commented on the rising numbers of women who die by suicide, though it is difficult to know whether any rise reflects improvements in case ascertainment rather than a true increase. Where reviews specifically report on lessons learned to inform future practice, these tend to mirror those of the UK and Ireland Enquiries, including the need to improve multidisciplinary collaboration between maternity and mental health professionals, better screening for current or previous mental health conditions at point of contact with maternity services, and the development of specific care pathways.

Maternal Suicide

Classification

The World Health Organization (WHO) defines maternal death as any death occurring during or within 42 days of the end of pregnancy, from any cause related to or aggravated by the pregnancy or its management, but not from accidental or incidental causes [11]. Maternal death is further classified as *direct* or *indirect*. *Direct deaths* are those arising from complications of pregnancy, labour or the puerperium, or from interventions, omissions and incorrect treatment. Examples include postpartum haemorrhage or eclampsia. *Indirect deaths* result from pre-existing disease or disease which developed or worsened during pregnancy or the puerperium, and which were not due to a direct obstetric cause but were aggravated by the effects of pregnancy. These would include deaths such as those arising from malignancy or pre-existing cardiac disease. In addition, *coincidental deaths* are those arising from unrelated causes (such as road traffic accidents or homicide) which happen to occur in pregnancy or the puerperium. In the production of maternal mortality rates (MMR) for international comparison, only direct and indirect deaths, occurring during or within 42 days of the end of pregnancy, are counted.

Direct and indirect deaths occurring between 43 and 365 days after the end of pregnancy are defined as *late deaths*. These are not included in WHO-derived MMR but comprise a significant proportion of all deaths, particularly from indirect causes.

Previously, all deaths related to psychiatric disorder were classified as indirect or coincidental. In 2012, the WHO reclassified maternal suicide as a *direct* cause of death, irrespective of the underlying psychiatric diagnosis. The reclassification has undoubtedly raised the awareness of the importance of addressing mental ill health in maternity care though it has been controversial and has led to a questioning of the usefulness of maintaining a distinction between direct and indirect causes of maternal death in general [12].

Epidemiology

Overall, rates of suicide are lower in pregnancy and the postnatal period, when compared with suicide in the general female population [13]. The reduction is greater in pregnancy, but the absolute difference in the postnatal period may be less marked than previously reported [14]. The 2021 UK and Ireland Confidential Enquiry (covering 2017–19) found a rate of 2.64 deaths by suicide per 100,000 maternities for deaths in pregnancy and up to the end of the first postnatal year [15]. There has been no consistent decline in the rate over the course of the Enquiries' reporting, despite a fall in other (direct) causes of maternal death. Psychiatric deaths were not due to be reviewed in detail again for a further 3 years, but a significant increase was noted in the following year's data (2020) and so reported in detail in the 2022 Enquiry. Psychiatric deaths by suicide in that year occurred at a rate of 3.84 per 100,000 maternities, representing a 45% increase over the 2017–19 period. When limited to pregnancy and the early postpartum period (up to 6 weeks), the increase was three-fold [16].

The presence of severe mental disorder after delivery and prior history of deliberate self-harm are strong predictors of completed suicide in the first postnatal year [14]. In an analysis of deaths reported to the Confidential Enquiries compared with female suicide at other times, women who died in the perinatal period were more likely to have a diagnosis of depressive disorder and less likely to be receiving active treatment [17]. Appleby found a 70-fold increase in suicide risk in the first postnatal year for women who had required postpartum psychiatric admission [18].

Studies focusing on major mental illness with onset in the 3 months following delivery demonstrated a risk of suicide which was significantly higher than in childbearing women who had mental illness onset outwith the early postpartum [19]. Even more notable was the elevated risk of progression to completed suicide following deliberate self-harm in women with early postpartum onset who have self-harmed (hazard ratio (HR) 8.7; 95% confidence interval (CI): 3.5–21.7, compared to women without a mental disorder), which was significantly greater that the risk for women with non-postpartum mental disorder (HR 2.7; 95% CI: 1.9–3.7) and for childless women with mental disorder (HR 2.8; 95% CI: 2.1–3.8) [20]. Together, these demonstrate the specific risk of suicide associated with severe perinatal mental disorder, particularly where there is additional self-harm, and there are clear parallels with the distinctive pattern of progression of mental illness symptoms and risk in the early postnatal period identified in repeated Enquiries.

Findings from the 2021 Enquiry showed that 60% of women who died by suicide were aged 30 or older, and the overwhelming majority had previous children. Nearly one in five had a history of domestic violence and over a third were known to social services. Almost half were from the two most deprived quintiles of areas of residence. Fewer than half received National Institute for Health and Care Excellence recommended levels of antenatal care.

Of particular concern in the 2021 report was the increased proportion of women who died by suicide who were teenagers – 11%, giving an MMR of 11 per 100,000 teenagers. Findings from the 2022 report suggest that this trend continues with a rate of 27 per 100,000.

Mirroring the findings of other research, the Enquiries show that suicide is less prevalent in pregnancy but is fairly evenly distributed throughout the first postnatal year (Figure 22.1). This does not follow the pattern of increased risk in the early postpartum for major mental disorder and suggests that risk is not solely associated with early onset severe disorder.

Psychiatric Diagnosis

A review of 15 years of the UK Enquiries data (1997–2012) found that women who died by suicide in the perinatal period were more likely to have had a diagnosis of depressive disorder and less likely to have associated substance misuse [17]. The Enquiries have persistently described depressive disorder, including recurrent depressive disorder, as the commonest diagnosis.

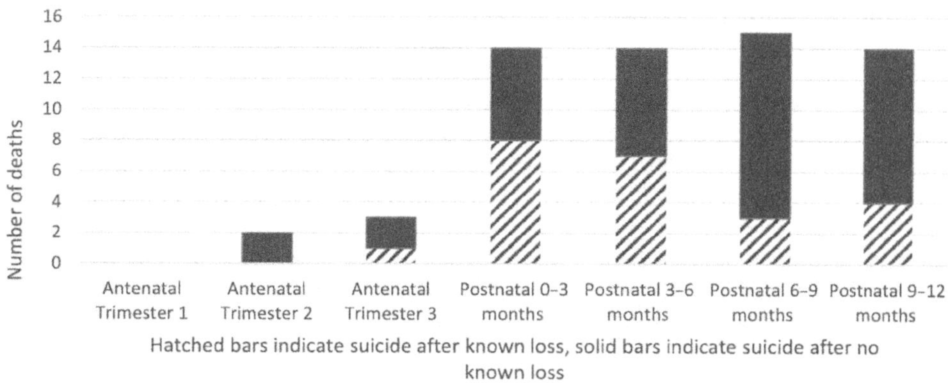

Figure 22.1 Timing of suicide in pregnancy and the first postnatal year (2017–19) [2].

Making a retrospective diagnosis for the women who died by suicide can be challenging, given the frequent lack of psychiatric records available to the Enquiries. Nevertheless, in the majority of cases there is enough information for assessors to reach confident conclusions. Throughout the history of the Enquiries the most common diagnosis has been depressive disorder, whether recurrent or newly arising in the perinatal period. Psychosis (most commonly depressive psychosis) has been diagnosed in 20–40% of women dying by suicide. A small but consistent proportion of women in this group have a primary diagnosis of substance misuse. Although particularly important in terms of prevention, the numbers of women with bipolar disorder or previous postpartum psychosis are low.

Mode of Suicide

A striking finding of the Enquiries is the use of violent (i.e. non-overdose) methods to complete suicide, consistently accounting for more than 80% of all deaths by suicide, with hanging being the most common modality. Office of National Statistics data from the UK indicate that the proportion of women in the general population who die by hanging (as opposed to other methods) has been increasing steadily over the past 20 years, and this trend is most marked in those of reproductive age [21]. However, it still appears that violent methods overall remain more common in the perinatal period [16]. This feature of maternal suicide accords with the specific nature of the symptomatology and pattern of progression in the perinatal period and speaks to a significant level of risk among women who are affected by major mental illness during this time.

Extended Suicide

Issues around infanticide are described in Chapter 38, 'When Mothers Kill Their Children' but very little is known of infanticide associated with completed suicide in the perinatal period. An early estimate from data in the Confidential Enquiries suggested a rate of 5% in maternal suicide [22] though the consequences of both reporting bias and underreporting of suicide in the earlier days of the Enquiries suggests that the true rate is almost certainly significantly lower.

Lessons for Clinical Practice

Prevention of Illness Occurrence or Re-occurrence

There is a unique opportunity for preventative interventions in perinatal mental health. Based on the first case descriptions, the Enquiries recommended that antenatal screening for history of mental disorder should be universal. This is now standard practice in maternity services, with screening questions for identification of significant past mental illness and for evidence of current depression and anxiety usually incorporated into booking documentation. A further recurrent theme is the importance of good communication between primary care, mental health and maternity services to ensure that all relevant mental health history is known to those involved in the woman's care.

Recognising the frequency with which opportunities to intervene were missed, a repeated message has been that women who have a history of significant mental disorder should have psychiatric assessment in pregnancy, they should be counselled about their risk of recurrence (in this and future perinatal periods) and about ways of mitigating that risk through preventative engagement with services. A management plan for their care should be shared with them and with all professionals involved in their care. The use of late pregnancy mental health management plans has now become universal in specialist perinatal mental health services. Women at specific risk of early postpartum mental disorder should receive preconception specialist advice which covers the same points.

Acute Risk Assessment and Management

Repeated messages in the Enquiries highlight the need to be aware of the distinctive patterns of illness progression in the perinatal period when conducting acute assessments or implementing risk management strategies. Multiple reports have identified failures in making comprehensive assessments, completing mental state evaluation, recognising escalating symptoms or acting on any suicide risk identified.

Patterns of symptoms presentation may include initial relatively non-specific changes in mental state which are nevertheless unusual for that woman. The pattern of rapid progression, often distinctive to perinatal mental illness, means that any emergent symptoms should be followed up over a short timescale – generally days rather than weeks – to ensure early detection of more significant illness and risk. Clinicians must take care that conclusions about risk flow from comprehensive history and mental state examination, paying particular attention to the presence of continuing disturbed, or rapidly deteriorating, mental state. Related lessons from the Enquiries include that clinicians should guard against the use of simplistic categorisations of risk as high or low, for example, by inappropriately using terms such as 'impulsive' or 'no planning' (in relation to self-harm) to suggest low risk of future suicide. Similarly, the presence of children was sometimes incorrectly seen as a protective factor, even in cases where the woman had already indicated risk by self-harming. There is also a danger of diagnostic overshadowing or 'stickiness' in clinical evaluation of risk, where a prior diagnosis (often of personality difficulties or substance use) is retained, even when all the evidence of clinical assessment points to newly emerging illness with associated increased risk.

In the 2015 report [23], a triad of 'red flags' highlighted certain (though not all) factors which could be linked to increased suicide risk (Box 22.1). The 2018 report broadened concern to include all acts of self-harm, suggesting that, as they are unusual in

Box 22.1 Red Flag Presentations Which Should Prompt Urgent Senior Psychiatric Assessment

- Recent significant change in mental state or emergence of new symptoms
- New thoughts or acts of violent self-harm (*broadened to all self-harm in the 2018 Enquiry*)
- New and persistent expressions of incompetency as a mother or estrangement from the infant

Source: M Knight, D Tuffnell, S Kenyon, J Shakespeare, R Gray, JJ Kyrinczuk, editors, on behalf of MBRRACE-UK. *Saving Lives, Improving Mothers' Care – Surveillance of maternal deaths in the UK 2011–13 and lessons learned to inform maternity care from the UK and Ireland Confidential Enquiries into Maternal Deaths and Morbidity 2009–13*. Oxford: National Perinatal Epidemiology Unit, University of Oxford; 2015.

pregnancy or the early postpartum, they should therefore prompt referral, ideally to a perinatal mental health service [24].

Reports repeatedly caution that women from marginalised communities or with multiple adversity can be particularly vulnerable, and disengagement from care or alterations in presentation may be indicators of worsening mental state. There is a particular need for women with substance misuse, or a history of complex trauma, to have careful risk evaluation.

Lastly, in making decisions on risk management, the option of inpatient care was often not reviewed. The 2015 Enquiry suggested that, in the presence of a red flag symptom, pervasive guilt or psychosis, there should be a clearly documented consideration of whether inpatient care would most appropriately address risk.

Partner and Family Involvement

Partner and family involvement for women with mental illness is recognised in several reports. Three broad messages have emerged: (i) the need to listen to relatives' concerns, remembering that they will know the woman better than any professional; (ii) the importance of educating relatives about the significance and serious nature of perinatal mental illness so they know when to be concerned; and (iii) a caution that relatives are not mental health professionals and should not be asked to manage risk at an inappropriate level. A particularly important message from the 2015 report emphasised that a clinician's duty of confidentiality does not prevent engagement with or listening to relatives' concerns.

Prescribing Issues

For women and their families, decisions to continue or stop prescribed medication in pregnancy or breastfeeding can be fraught with concern. The 2018 report cautioned against a tendency to prioritise potential risks over benefits resulting in a failure to give women a balanced account which enables them to make informed decisions about their care.

If women, alone or in discussion with their care provider, decide to discontinue medication on discovering a pregnancy, they may remain well in pregnancy. However, the postnatal period can be a time of greater risk. The 2021 Enquiry reported that women who had stopped medication during pregnancy were not re-evaluated postpartum to ascertain whether they should recommence previously effective medication. A new recommendation suggests that any women who had discontinued medication before or during pregnancy should be assessed early in the postpartum period regarding the need to restart. This should be included in the prebirth plan (see Chapter 25).

Loss or Threatened Loss

A significant proportion of deaths by suicide are associated with experiences of loss (see Figure 22.1). These include not only pregnancy or neonatal loss but also loss through removal of a child into care or threatened loss in the context of child safeguarding proceedings. There is a pattern of support falling away from the mother following child removal, at a time when she is likely to be most vulnerable. Although we cannot infer a causal link between loss and suicide, it is clear that there is a need for continuing support and risk assessment where loss or threatened loss has occurred.

Lessons for Service Organisation

Improvements to individual practice cannot make up for poorly designed systems surrounding the practitioner and their patient. The 1998 report recommended that a clinician should be identified in each area who would be responsible for providing a perinatal mental health service. In the mid 1990s, such services were present in only a handful of larger cities in England and barely at all in the other nations of the UK. In subsequent reports, there has been an evolving pattern of guidance for service development, beginning with recommendations that Mother and Baby Unit (MBU) and specialist community team provision should be available to every woman who required them. Later Enquiries expanded on this to require that there should be close integration between regional MBUs and local specialist perinatal mental health community teams, and that community teams are adequately resourced to provide senior clinical assessment and to case manage all women requiring secondary care.

The last piece of the service organisation jigsaw fell into place in the 2015 report which recommended the establishment of perinatal mental health regional networks to coordinate care provision.

As specialist services have expanded rapidly throughout the UK and Ireland over the past 5–10 years, new lessons on how community perinatal mental health teams and MBUs should function are emerging. The 2021 report highlighted four areas of concern including: (i) failure to refer to specialist services; (ii) restrictive referral criteria acting as a block to appropriate care; (iii) response times from services not taking into account the maternity context; and (iv) the increasingly complex landscape of specialist, enhanced and universal services surrounding the woman and her infant risking confusion in developing clear pathways into care. The report took the opportunity to reiterate the need for specialist services to have the capacity to assess and case manage any woman who would meet criteria for general adult mental health services and, in addition, to be able to adjust for the altered (usually lowered) thresholds for assessment in the perinatal period. This recognises the need for rapid intervention given the time constraints imposed by pregnancy, childbirth and the importance of the mother–infant relationship to early child development. Further discussion on service development and organisation can be found in Chapter 30.

With the increasing subspecialisation of adult mental health services, a particular message arose in the 2015 report around the requirement for liaison, crisis and home treatment teams to have specific training in the distinctive symptom profile, progression and risk management of perinatal mental illness. More concerns of a similar nature arose in the 2021 report.

Deliberate Self-Harm in Pregnancy and the Postnatal Period

Thoughts of self-harm are not uncommon in the perinatal period, particularly in those with mental disorder. A recent systematic review and meta-analysis found a pooled prevalence of suicidal ideation in pregnancy and the postpartum of 8% (10% in pregnancy, 7% postpartum) [25]. For a sample of women diagnosed with major depressive or bipolar II disorder, one report found that, in the first postnatal year, 16.97% of women reported thoughts of self-harm and 6.16% reported suicidal ideation [26].

In contrast, perinatal self-harm appears to be less common, with ranges of 0–2.39% in pregnancy and 0–2.41% in the postpartum period in a recent systematic review [27]. However, in those with a history of severe mental illness, prevalence ranges were significantly higher at up to 23.78% in pregnancy, and 21.9% in the postpartum year.

Two recent large cohort studies have provided additional understanding of rates and risk factors associated with perinatal self-harm. A Danish register-based cohort study found overall rates of deliberate self-harm (defined as self-harm leading to inpatient or outpatient contact) of 32.2 per 100,000 deliveries in pregnancy and 63.3 per 100,000 deliveries in the postnatal period [28]. Pregnancy-related self-harm was 4.3 times more prevalent, and postnatal-related self-harm 5 times more prevalent, in those with a psychiatric history when compared to those without. In terms of specific disorders, women with personality disorder had the highest risk of self-harm in pregnancy, while in the postnatal period those with psychotic disorders were most at risk. Other factors associated with increased risk of self-harm included younger age, non-Danish birth, preconception self-harm and parental psychiatric history. Multiparity and preterm birth were additional factors in the postnatal period. Johannsen et al. also found an increased risk of deliberate self-harm for women with a first presentation of mental disorder in the 90 days after delivery, compared with the general population, but also that the postpartum group who self-harmed were at significant risk of progression to completed suicide [20].

A UK primary care based large cohort study used a broader definition of self-harm to include any event recorded as such in primary care clinical notes. When compared to non-perinatal women, overall rates of self-harm halved in pregnancy, returning to non-perinatal rates between 0 and 6 months postnatal and to slightly higher than non-perinatal rates between 6 and 12 months postnatal [29]. Furthermore, women with mental illness had a larger relative decrease in both pregnancy and postpartum, even though they were more likely than non-ill women to self-harm.

Maternal Deaths Related to Substance Misuse

Women who are affected by substance misuse form a small but important subsection of those dying by suicide. However, a much larger number will die in relation to accidental overdose or to the effects of substance use on the aetiology, course or treatment of underlying physical ill health. Substance misuse is also a contributory factor in a number of deaths due to homicide. The proportion of women who die in relation to substance use has increased steadily throughout the Enquiries and, in the most recent three reports focusing on mental health related deaths (2018, 2021, 2022), now accounts for very nearly as many deaths as those by suicide. It is also likely that, in a number of the deaths categorised as accidental, there was suicidal intent. However, the Enquiries will only classify a death as suicide where there is unequivocal evidence to support that attribution.

In comparison to women dying by suicide, women who die in relation to substance use are more likely to be late bookers and less likely to receive minimum or recommended maternity care. More frequently, they come from socio-economically deprived backgrounds. They are much more likely to be known to social services and to have experienced child protection procedures or the removal of a child into care, though comprehensive data are less available in this regard than for the women dying by suicide.

Lessons learned to improve care have been consistent throughout those enquiries which have looked in detail at substance misuse related deaths. There are greater challenges to engagement and consequent great risk of discontinuities of care. Repeated recommendations have been made about the need to ensure good communication between agencies and effective co-ordination of care.

Mental Health in Relation to Other Causes of Maternal Death

Women with a history of mental ill health are over-represented among those who die by homicide. For women with underlying physical ill health, the presence of comorbid mental disorder may place them at increased risk of diagnostic overshadowing, where symptoms are misattributed to mental illness. The 2011 Report detailed a number of case histories of women who died from a wide range of illnesses, where correct diagnosis was delayed or not made, due to misattribution to mental disorder [30]. Examples included the misattribution of agitation to 'anxiety' when the underlying diagnosis was eclampsia, or weight loss seen as due to an eating disorder in a woman who had tuberculosis. A helpful guide to exercising caution around making a psychiatric diagnosis in the absence of positive indications was included with the Report (Box 22.2).

Near-Miss Audits of Perinatal Mental Healthcare

The 2016 report saw a new departure for the Enquiries. An audit on a specific maternal morbidity topic was included to widen the scope of lessons learned. In 2017, a mental health themed morbidity report examined the care received by a cohort of women who,

Box 22.2 Unexplained Physical Symptoms

Unexplained physical symptoms should not be attributed to psychiatric disorder:

- unless there is a clear pathway to symptom production
- unless there is a known previous psychiatric history
- when they represent a marked change from normal functioning
- when the only psychological symptoms are behavioural and non-specific for example, distress and agitation
- when the woman does not speak English or is from an ethnic minority group

Source: Centre for Maternal and Child Enquiries (CMACE). Saving Mothers' Lives: reviewing maternal deaths to make motherhood safer 2006-08: the Eight Report of the Confidential Enquiries into Maternal Deaths in the United Kingdom. *BJOG*. 2011;118(Suppl. 1):16–21.

by reason of previous bipolar disorder or postpartum psychosis, were at significant risk of recurrence of illness in the early postpartum [31]. A number of recommendations, described as 'amber flags', highlight factors to consider regarding the risk of recurrence of severe mental disorder (Box 22.3) for women who have experienced a postpartum psychosis in an earlier pregnancy or who have a pre-existing diagnosis of psychotic disorder. The concept of the preventative triad was introduced to describe appropriate actions to assist women and their families in minimising risk in future postnatal periods (Figure 22.2).

Box 22.3 Amber Flags Which Should Prompt Heightened Awareness of Change in Mental State [2]

- Women with any past history of psychotic disorder, even when not diagnosed as postpartum psychosis or bipolar disorder, should be regarded as at elevated risk in future postpartum periods and should be referred to mental health services in pregnancy to receive an individualised assessment of risk and development of a postpartum plan.
- Women with a family history of postpartum major mental illness should be closely monitored by maternity and primary care service in late pregnancy and the early postpartum period. Where they themselves are currently unwell in pregnancy or have had previous postpartum mood destabilisation, they should be referred to mental health services as soon as possible to receive an individualised assessment of risk and development of a management plan.
- The personal and familial pattern of occurrence and re-occurrence of postpartum mood disorder should inform risk minimisation strategies.

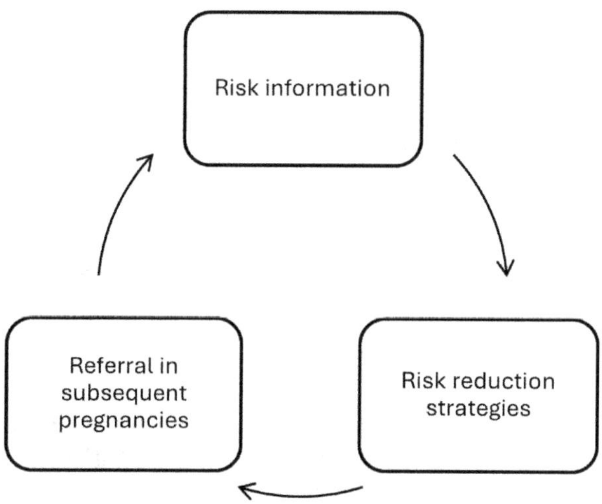

Figure 22.2 Preventative triad for the management of women at high risk of severe postpartum mental illness. Source: Adapted from M Knight, M Nair, D Tuffnell, J Shakespeare, S Kenyon, JJ Kurinczuk, editors, on behalf of MBRRACE-UK. *Saving Lives, Improving Mothers' Care – Lessons learned to inform maternity care from the UK and Ireland Confidential Enquiries into Maternal Deaths and Morbidity 2013–15.* Oxford: National Perinatal Epidemiology Unit, University of Oxford; 2017.

Conclusions

Suicide remains a leading cause of maternal death in the UK and in other high-income countries. While there are clear risks in severe mental disorder, those who die have experienced a range of mental illnesses and often come from more deprived communities. The Confidential Enquiries highlight the distinctive patterns of occurrence and progression in perinatal mental illness and the need for improvements in clinical evaluation of risk, effective risk management and the availability of high-quality perinatal mental healthcare as important factors in helping reduce progression to suicide.

References

1. World Health Organization. Trends in maternal mortality 2000–2020: estimates by WHO, UNICEF, UNFPA, World Bank Group and UNDESA/Population Division. Geneva: WHO; 2023.
2. M Knight, K Bunch, D Tuffnell, R Patel, J Shakespeare, R Kotnis, et al., editors, on behalf of MBRRACE-UK. *Saving Lives, Improving Mothers' Care – Lessons learned to inform maternity care from the UK and Ireland Confidential Enquiries into Maternal Deaths and Morbidity 2017-19.* Oxford: National Perinatal Epidemiology Unit, University of Oxford; 2021.
3. G Lewis. Introduction: aims, objectives and definitions used in this report. In Centre for Maternal and Child Enquiries (CMACE). Saving Mothers' Lives: reviewing maternal deaths to make motherhood safer: 2006–08. The Eighth Report on Confidential Enquiries into Maternal Deaths in the United Kingdom. *BJOG.* 2011;118(Suppl. 1):1–203.
4. LR Kodan, KJC Verscheuren, AM McCaw-Binns, RTK Fat, JL Browne, MJ Rijken, KWM Bloemenkamp. Classifying maternal deaths in Suriname using WHO ICD-MM: different interpretation by Physicians, National and International Maternal Death Review Committees. *Reprod Health.* 2021;18(1):46.
5. B Bodker, L Hvidman, T Weber, M Møller, JL Sørensen. An audit of 70 maternal deaths. *Dan Med J.* 2021;68(9):A02210144.
6. MN Vacheron, V Tessier, M Rossignol, C Deneux-Tharaux. Mortalité maternelle par suicide en France 2013–2015 [Maternal deaths due to suicide in France 2013–2015]. *Gynécol Obstét Fertil Sénol.* 2021;49(1):38–46.
7. L Perotto, R Zimmermann, KC Quack Lotscher. Maternal mortality in Switzerland 2005–2014. *Swiss Med Wkly.* 2020;150:w20345.
8. S Grigoriadis, AS Wilton, PA Kurdyak, AE Rhodes, EH VonderPorten, A Levitt, et al. Perinatal suicide in Ontario, Canada: a 15-year population-based study. *CMAJ.* 2017;189:E1085–92.
9. JT Howard, CS Sparks, AR Santos-Lozada, SA Olowolaju, JC Janak, KJ Howard. Trends in mortality among pregnant and recently pregnant women in the US, 2015–2019. *JAMA.* 2021;326(16): 1631–3.
10. C Diguisto, M Saucedo, A Kallianidis, K Bloemenkamp, B Bødker, M Buoncristiano, et al. Maternal mortality in eight European countries with enhanced surveillance systems: descriptive population based study. *BMJ.* 2022;379:e070621.
11. World Health Organization. The WHO application of ICD-10 to deaths during pregnancy, childbirth and the puerperium: ICD-MM. Geneva: WHO; 2012. https://apps.who.int/iris/handle/10665/70929
12. M van den Akker, M Nair, M Goedhart, J Schutte, T Schaap, M Knight, et al. Maternal mortality: direct or indirect has become irrelevant. *Lancet.* 2017;5; e1181–2.
13. L Appleby. Suicide during pregnancy and in the first postnatal year. *BMJ.* 1991;302:137–40.

14. H Lysell, M Dahlin, A Viktorin, E Ljungberg, BM D'Onofrio, P Dickman, B Runeson. Maternal suicide: register based study of all suicides occurring after delivery in Sweden 1974–2009. *PLoS ONE.* 2018;13(1):e0190133.

15. R Cantwell, A Cairns, K Bunch, M Knight, on behalf of the MBRRACE-UK mental health chapter-writing group. Improving mental health care and care for women with multiple adversity. In: M Knight, K Bunch, D Tuffnell, R Patel, J Shakespeare, R Kotnis, et al. editors, on behalf of MBRRACE-UK. *Saving Lives, Improving Mothers' Care – Lessons learned to inform maternity care from the UK and Ireland Confidential Enquiries into Maternal Deaths and Morbidity 2017–19.* Oxford: National Perinatal Epidemiology Unit, University of Oxford; 2021. p. 34–51.

16. A Cairns, S Kenyon, R Patel, K Bunch, M Knight on behalf of the MBRRACE-UK mental health chapter-writing group. Improving mental health care and care for women with multiple adversity. In: M Knight, K Bunch, R Patel, J Shakespeare, R Kotnis, S Kenyon, JJ Kurinczuk, editors, on behalf of MBRRACE-UK. *Saving Lives, Improving Mothers' Care: Core report – Lessons learned to inform maternity care from the UK and Ireland Confidential Enquiries into Maternal Deaths and Morbidity 2018–20.* Oxford: National Perinatal Epidemiology Unit, University of Oxford; 2022. p. 21–33.

17. H Khalifeh, IM Hunt, L Appleby, LM Howard. Suicide in perinatal and non-perinatal women in contact with psychiatric services: 15 year findings from a UK national inquiry. *Lancet Psychiatry.* 2016;3:233–42.

18. L Appleby, PB Mortensen, EB Faragher. Suicide and other causes of mortality after post-partum psychiatric admission. *Br J Psychiatry.* 1998;173:209–11.

19. BMW Johannsen, JT Larsen, TM Laursen, V Bergink, S Meltzer-Brody, T Munk-Olsen. All-cause mortality in women with severe postpartum psychiatric disorders. *Am J Psychiatry.* 2016;173:635–42.

20. BM Johannsen, JT Larsen, TM Laursen, K Ayre, LM Howard, S Meltzer-Brody, et al. Self-harm in women with postpartum mental disorders. *Psychol Med.* 2019;50:1563–9.

21. Office for National Statistics. Suicides in England and Wales: 2019 registrations. 2020. https://shorturl.at/DTz95

22. L Appleby. Suicidal behaviour in childbearing women. MD Thesis. University of Edinburgh; 1995.

23. R Cantwell, M Knight, M Oates, J Shakespeare on behalf of the MBRRACE-UK mental health chapter writing group. Lessons on maternal mental health. In: M Knight, D Tuffnell, S Kenyon, J Shakespeare, R Gray, JJ Kyrinczuk on behalf of MBRRACE-UK. *Saving Lives, Improving Mothers' Care – Surveillance of maternal deaths in the UK 2011–13 and lessons learned to inform maternity care from the UK and Ireland Confidential Enquiries into Maternal Deaths and Morbidity 2009–13.* Oxford: National Perinatal Epidemiology Unit, University of Oxford; 2015. p. 22–41.

24. R Cantwell, E Youd, M Knight on behalf of the MBRRACE-UK mental health chapter-writing group. Messages for mental health. In: M Knight, K Bunch, D Tuffnell, H Jayakody, J Shakespeare, R Kotnis, et al., editors, on behalf of MBRRACE-UK. *Saving Lives, Improving Mothers' Care – Lessons learned to inform maternity care from the UK and Ireland Confidential Enquiries into Maternal Deaths and Morbidity 2014–16.* Oxford: National Perinatal Epidemiology Unit, University of Oxford; 2018: p. 42–60.

25. M Xiao, Y Hu, S Huang, G Wang, J Zhao, J Lei. Prevalence of suicidal ideation in pregnancy and the postpartum: a systematic review and meta-analysis. *J Affect Disord.* 2022;296:322–36.

26. CJ Pope, B Xie, V Sharma, MK Campbell. A prospective study of thoughts of self-harm and suicidal ideation during the postpartum period in women with mood disorders. *Arch Womens Ment Health.* 2013;16(6):483–8.

27. K Ayre, HG Gordon, R Dutta, J Hodsall, LM Howard. The prevalence and correlates of self-harm in the perinatal period: a systematic review. *J Clin Psychiatry.* 2020;81(1):19r12773.

28. K Ayre, X Liu, L Howard, R Dutta, T Munk-Olsen. Self-harm in pregnancy and the postnatal year: prevalence and risk factors. *Psychol Med.* 2023;53(7):2895–903.

29. H Hope, M Pierce, CS Osam, C Morgan, A John, KM Abel. Self-harm risk in pregnancy: recurrent-event survival analysis using UK primary care data. *Br J Psychiatry.* 2022;221:621–7.

30. M Oates, A Harper, J Shakespeare, C Nelson-Piercy. Back to basics. In Centre for Maternal and Child Enquiries (CMACE). Saving Mothers' Lives: reviewing maternal deaths to make motherhood safer 2006-08: the Eight Report of the Confidential Enquiries into Maternal Deaths in the United Kingdom. *BJOG.* 2011;118(Suppl. 1):16–21.

31. R Cantwell, R Gray, M Knight on behalf of the MBRRACE-UK psychosis chapter-writing group. Caring for women with psychosis. In: M Knight, M Nair, D Tuffnell, J Shakespeare, S Kenyon, JJ Kurinczuk, editors, on behalf of MBRRACE-UK. *Saving Lives, Improving Mothers' Care – Lessons learned to inform maternity care from the UK and Ireland Confidential Enquiries into Maternal Deaths and Morbidity 2013–15.* Oxford: National Perinatal Epidemiology Unit, University of Oxford; 2017. p. 37–49.

Chapter 23

Access, Assessment and Evaluation of Risk in Perinatal Mental Health Services

Roch Cantwell, Liz McDonald and Lucinda Green

General Considerations

This chapter describes access, assessment, communication and risk management from a specialist perinatal mental health service perspective. It also addresses how the outcomes of a specialist assessment might be communicated to women, partners, families and professionals. However, many of the principles and areas of enquiry are relevant to assessments carried out in maternity, primary care and other clinical settings.

We know that there are many obstacles between a woman's, or her family's, recognition of her difficulties and her receiving an assessment by a specialist perinatal mental health service. In the broadest terms these include her, and her family's, understanding of mental ill health and her fear of stigmatisation (influenced in turn by societal and cultural views on mental illness and motherhood), her appreciation of her symptoms as warranting further support or investigation, the knowledge and attitudes of those from whom she seeks help, and the pathways into (and availability of) specialist provision [1]. Women from disadvantaged backgrounds or more excluded groups within society often face additional hurdles in accessing appropriate care [2].

Women's fear of being judged negatively as a parent, fear of losing custody of her child and feeling a sense of shame and stigma in relation to having a mental illness have repeatedly been identified as some of the most significant barriers to engagement [3, 4, 5, 6]. It is therefore important to address and challenge these beliefs and to help women in understanding that having care and support for their mental health is just as important as it is for physical well-being. Having an assessment will enable access to the most effective care and treatment which will be beneficial for the woman, her baby and their relationship. Addressing stigma at societal, service provision and individual levels is particularly important, and good guidance to minimise its effects now exists for perinatal mental health professionals and commissioners [7].

Perinatal mental health professionals have an important role in training for maternity staff and other referrers, to highlight the importance of how they discuss perinatal mental illness and perinatal mental health services with women, as their knowledge and attitudes can influence engagement [3, 4]. Professionals should encourage women to recognise the benefits of being under the care of the perinatal mental health team from the point of referral.

Access and Referral Management

The rapid expansion and complexity of perinatal mental health provision in recent years has had unintended consequences, including confused referral pathways leading to adverse outcomes [8]. As a first step, those providing specialist care have a duty to ensure clarity on referral criteria and pathways, and to work closely with others providing related services, such as maternity psychological therapies services (maternal mental health services in England; maternity and neonatal psychological interventions services in Scotland), specialist maternity and health visiting staff (perinatal mental health midwives, etc.) and primary care psychological services, so that there are systems in place for triage and redirection (both routine and urgent) where appropriate. National referral guidance exists in a number of the UK nations [9, 10, 11]. In some areas, access to mental health secondary care may be via a single point of referral or common triage system, and perinatal mental health professionals must ensure that those operating such systems (and those providing unscheduled care) have the appropriate understanding of perinatal mental illness and its attendant risks, so that there is no delay in the pathway to specialist care [12].

Clear local pathways and joint working protocols are also important. Women who have pre-existing severe and complex mental illness, whether currently well or unwell, and regardless of already being under the care of a general adult mental health service, should have the opportunity of an assessment by a perinatal mental health service. This is particularly important for women who have any current or previous psychotic illness. While this is well recognised for women who have a diagnosis of bipolar disorder, who need specialist advice about the risk of illness in pregnancy and the postnatal period, referrers may be less aware of the importance of referral of women with other psychotic disorder diagnoses. Child safeguarding needs careful consideration when a woman has chronic schizophrenia with significantly impaired functioning. It is also important to carefully review the course and presentations for women who have been given a diagnosis of acute and transient psychotic disorder or unspecified non-organic psychosis, or indeed of psychotic depression, to clarify whether a diagnosis of bipolar disorder, schizophrenia or schizoaffective disorder may be more appropriate given the significance of these diagnoses and associated risks in the perinatal period (see Chapter 12, 'Postpartum Psychosis and Bipolar Disorder', Chapter 13, 'Schizophrenia Spectrum Disorders' and Chapter 22, 'Maternal Suicide, Deliberate Self-Harm and Other Mental Health Related Causes of Maternal Death').

Given the nature of perinatal mental illness, triaging of referrals will usually take place at least daily and referrers will be encouraged to make telephone contact where there are more urgent concerns. Many community teams operate a duty or advice system during working hours to provide advice on referral appropriateness and urgency. Referral thresholds and response times must always take into account the particular modifying effects of pregnancy, childbirth and childcare on the course of mental illness, and the timescales of pregnancy and child development.

It is not uncommon for teams to assess a proportion of referrals as not being appropriate for the service. For the referrer and woman herself, it is most helpful that the team takes time to consider what alternative care might be more useful and for our language to move from *rejected* to *redirected* referrals. The best way to reduce the need for redirection is to support referrers' awareness of clear referral pathways and criteria, and to use each redirected referral as an opportunity to promote that awareness. Women and professionals should be informed of the referral decision. When a woman is considered not to need assessment by the perinatal mental health service, both she and the professionals involved in her care should be offered the option of re-referral at a later stage in the perinatal period should there be a significant deterioration in her mental health, or new risks identified.

The Pathway to Assessment

Information should be provided for women prior to the assessment explaining the assessment process, providing the name and role of the professional they will see, and information on who can accompany them to the assessment [13]. They should be informed that they are welcome (and indeed encouraged) to bring their infant to the appointment, and there is a responsibility on services to ensure that there are appropriate facilities to support the mother in caring for her baby, including baby feeding and changing facilities. It may be preferable for a woman not to bring older children to the assessment due to the nature of the information discussed.

Practical difficulties in terms of lack of childcare or the logistics or timing of contacts can prevent women attending appointments [3, 14]. Offering women some choice about the timing and location of appointments, holding clinics in child-friendly locations and having home visits can all be helpful [15]. Since the Covid-19 pandemic, it has become increasingly common to offer women the option of video or telephone consultation. There are important considerations when deciding whether it is more clinically appropriate to conduct a face-to-face assessment and what precautions particular to the perinatal context are relevant for virtual consultations, for instance clarifying whether somebody else is present or within earshot, not discouraging her from having the baby with her if she can manage, and having clear pathways to further assessment where required [16].

The attitudes of partners and families to mental ill health can act as a barrier or facilitator to engagement [3, 4, 12, 17]. Services should provide information for partners and families and offer women the option of involving their partner, or another person identified by the woman, in part or all of the assessment. However, it is also important to address individual women's concerns about involving partners and sharing information about her mental health prior to or during the initial assessment. It is good practice to allocate time in the initial appointment for the woman to be seen on her own and to explain that this is normal for mental health assessments. Some women may prefer to be seen alone for the first appointment. Partners can then be invited to a subsequent appointment and women can consider what they are, and are not, keen to share. It might be helpful to give the partner an explanation of the woman's diagnosis and the factors which have contributed to her illness, to discuss the fact that it is not her fault that she is ill and to outline the plan for her care.

Cultural and language barriers can also influence women's decision to attend appointments offered by perinatal mental health services [4]. Women should be asked about the need for an interpreter, and the specific language should be clarified. Family members should not be relied on for this purpose. Teams require access to effective interpretation services, which have awareness of the personal and cultural significance and sensitivity of the perinatal period and the challenges that women may face. Cultural differences between the patient and assessor may leave the woman feeling that the assessment has been formulaic and lacking in a true understanding of her needs (see Chapter 7, 'The Perinatal Mental Health of Racial and Ethnic Minority Groups').

Engagement and Rapport Building

The assessment of any pregnant or postnatal woman needs to be thorough, attuned and carried out with compassion, sensitivity and curiosity. The historical and current information gleaned alongside an understanding of the woman's personality, coping mechanisms, attitudes, hopes and ability to think about her present state and potential future illness will inform and enable the development of a rapport, care planning and treatment. It is the starting point for the practitioner and team to demonstrate their commitment and desire to working collaboratively and in a trustworthy manner, to offer choice and safety, and to engender empowerment for the individual who has come to them for help. The assessment provides women and partners with their first impression of the service. The importance of this experience and the relationship established with the assessing clinician cannot be overstated. There is good evidence that non-judgemental, compassionate care from staff who are sensitive and warm and who inspire confidence can foster hope and optimism in the therapeutic relationship [3, 5, 15].

Language is an all-important factor in the assessment process. Language evolves continually and there are theoretical, ideological and geographical influences that may at times be in conflict with each other. In the perinatal context, language is especially important where it represents the individual's sense of identity, visibility and power. One must take care to distinguish between the interrelated terms of gender, sex and gender-identity. Gender denotes a primarily sociocultural construct; sex denotes biological assignment; and gender identity primarily denotes a person's psychological sense of their gender. Ask the individual what language they use to describe themselves and how they are described by others, and use and record identified pronouns [18, 19]. Errors are human and it is important to acknowledge and apologise when one gets it wrong.

The physical environment can also help or hinder engagement. An explicitly baby- and family-friendly space helps women to feel at ease. Ways to avoid an overstimulating environment are discussed in more detail in Chapter 21, 'Autism', and can be just as relevant for those who are not neurodivergent.

It is helpful to consider the questions women may have when they attend the assessment as outlined in Box 23.1. These may include general questions about the experience of assessment and the likely attitude of professionals as well as more specific questions about their illness and its potential consequences.

Issues of confidentiality should be raised early in the consultation (and in material about the service sent prior to the appointment). Women have the right to expect that what they discuss remains confidential, but they also need to be aware of the limits of confidentiality, particularly in relation to child safeguarding. Appealing to a shared desire for the best outcomes for their infant can be a sensitive and acceptable way of introducing the discussion and helping to allay the often unspoken fear that they will be judged negatively as a parent.

Confidentiality must also be seen in the context of involvement of partners, fathers and other family members. There is a responsibility on services to support the developing relationship between the infant and other family members, particularly where they have parental rights, so long as that does not compromise the infant's safety or welfare. Equally, a misunderstanding of the obligations of confidentiality where clinicians refuse to listen to the concerns of those who may know the woman well, is not helpful to

Box 23.1 Questions Women May Have Prior to Assessment

General Questions

- Will I be listened to and understood?
- Does the clinician have the expertise to ensure I have the right care?
- Does the clinician have a genuine interest in my history and context including my previous experience, family and cultural context?
- Can I trust the professionals?
- Will I be judged negatively as a mum?

Questions about Illness and Its Consequences

- Why do I have mental health problems?
- Is it my fault?
- Is it because of hormones?
- What's my diagnosis?
- Is my previous diagnosis correct?
- Will I become unwell in pregnancy or after birth?
- How will I cope with sleep deprivation when this has previously meant that I have become unwell?
- Will I get better?
- Will my baby be taken away because I have (or have had) a mental health problem, or if I develop a perinatal mental illness?
- What if I don't love my baby because I'm so unwell?
- What will happen if I can't look after my baby because I am too unwell?

Questions about Care and Treatment

- What will help me stay well?
- What will help me get better if I become unwell?
- If I take medication in pregnancy, or when breastfeeding, will this harm my baby?
- Are you going to make me have treatment I don't want?
- What else will help? For example, talking therapies?
- What other treatment and support is available?
- What care and treatment can my partner access?
- Can you help me with problems which are causing stress and making pregnancy more difficult, for example housing, immigration issues, etc.?
- Can I have a caesarean section because I'm scared of vaginal birth?
- If I become unwell, will I have to go back to the ward I was on last time?
- If I become unwell who will look after my baby?
- Will you keep information confidential? Do you have to tell my partner, my family and the other professionals involved in my care?

thorough assessment, adequate risk management or to developing a relationship with and engaging partners, families and other carers [20, 21].

Content of the Assessment

Essential training for all those working in mental health services is the taking of an accurate, detailed and wide-ranging personal history and performing a comprehensive mental state examination. A review of previous mental health records is an integral part of a thorough assessment. Some women may have little memory of symptoms and behaviours during a psychotic episode of illness many years ago. Others may be reluctant to share information about risks to themselves or others associated with past episodes of illness, for example due to concerns about negative judgement in the perinatal context.

Whilst this chapter will not set out the basics of history taking it will guide the reader to consider what extra contextual information needs to be sought. History taking is the foundation of our practice and all new members to a perinatal team must be encouraged to develop their competencies (skills, knowledge and attitudes) in this area, through practice and supervision. Having in mind a set of general headings with associated probes to elicit detail is required to guide the interviewer. Interviewee factors will however have a dynamic effect on how the assessment proceeds with language, cultural factors, mental state, physical health, emotional state (fear, guilt, self-blame, anxiety, despair, etc.), the influence of stigma, the presence of others (baby, partner, other relatives, other professionals, trainees), whether they feel safe, and the establishment or not of a rapport affecting the individual's capacity or willingness to reveal very personal information. Interviewer factors may also affect the process including their professional and personal experience, competencies, fatigue, time pressure, curiosity and desire to understand the individual.

It is vital to keep in mind that the perinatal period is, by its very nature, a time of understandable anxiety and vigilance. The perinatal mental health clinician must be able to delineate this expected level of anxiety from thoughts or preoccupations which have become more overvalued, obsessional or even psychotic in nature, driven by an underlying mental illness. Careful history taking is at the core of this evaluation.

The contents of a perinatal mental health history and mental state examination are summarised in Box 23.2, with emphasis on factors that are more particular to the perinatal period. Note that assessments of capacity and vulnerability have a bearing not only on the woman herself but also on her ability to safeguard her infant.

As an aid to assessment, the use of assessment and outcome tools is increasingly encouraged. These help monitor and evaluate individual care, but can also be an essential component of service quality improvement. Generic measures, such as the CORE or HONOS, should be supplemented, in a perinatal mental health setting, by measures of the mother–infant relationship and of infant development. Scales may include clinician- and patient-rated outcome measures (CROMs, PROMs) and ratings of patient experience of care (PREMs). Suggested core and supplementary measures are provided in the Royal College of Psychiatrists College Report 216 [22] and their use in infant assessment is further discussed in Chapter 35, 'Mother–Infant Focused Interventions: What Works to Improve the Mother–Infant Relationship?'.

Formulating and Communicating Assessments

A high-quality, thorough and skilled assessment enables a relationship to be established with the woman, and sometimes also her partner, in which she can feel understood, her experience can be validated and she can start to benefit from compassionate and non-judgemental care. Having taken a thorough history, it is important to summarise the key points, incorporating information provided by her partner or other carer where appropriate, and relevant history from her previous mental health records. The diagnosis, or diagnoses, should be discussed and explained. Diagnosis has many functions [23].

Box 23.2 Contents of the Perinatal Mental Health History and Mental State Examination

- Reason for referral
- Pregnant/postnatal/planning pregnancy
- Expected date of delivery or date of birth (DOB) and name of infant/s
- Intended/current method of feeding
- DOBs, names and care arrangements for other children in family
- Involvement of other health, social care and third sector services and agencies (including names and contact details)
- Where is the infant currently (if not with mother)? Who has parental responsibility?
- Child safeguarding measures in place?

Current/Index Pregnancy

- Was the pregnancy planned/unplanned, wanted/unwanted; partner's attitude to the pregnancy and how conceived
- Psychological adjustment to pregnancy – reaction to pregnancy; reaction of others; consideration of not continuing the pregnancy; concealment of pregnancy; how did feelings about the pregnancy develop over time; concerns about changes in body shape and appearance; timing and course of any changes in mood, anxiety, irritability, self-harm in relation to pregnancy or delivery; what worries and concerns emerged/developed over the course of the pregnancy
- Physical adjustment to pregnancy: nausea and vomiting, weight gain, medical complications, fatigue, concerns about obstetric care, for example, physical examinations and procedures, delivery plans; obstetric complications and interventions
- Social adjustment to pregnancy: effects on lifestyle (stopping alcohol, changes to social life); anxiety about work, housing and finance; effects on relationship with partner, family, friends; planning for arrival of infant
- Beliefs and attitudes about pregnancy, delivery and postnatal care, and childcare (which may be influenced by religious, cultural and family practices)
- Labour, delivery and early postnatal experience
- Current supports – partner, family, friends, workplace, other teams and agencies
- Relationship with partner and/or father of infant

Relationship with Fetus/Infant

- Preparation for and adjustment to parenthood
- Perception of relationship with fetus/infant; sense of attachment/bonding and emotional care
- Physical care and feeding (or plans for feeding); general health and immunisations

Current Symptoms

- Detailed account directed by presenting problems and information from other sources paying particular attention to new or unusual symptoms for this woman
- Specific enquiry regarding thoughts of harm to self/pregnancy/baby/others; enquire if acts of self-harm have occurred (and not previously disclosed)

Psychiatric History

- Past diagnoses, treatments, hospital admissions, involuntary detention, self-harm, suicide attempts
- Any past perinatal mental ill health including diagnoses, interventions, admissions, involvement of social services/child protection

Box 23.2 *(cont.)*

- In absence of formal prior diagnosis, enquire about changes to mental well-being over the course of previous pregnancies and postnatal periods
- Exacerbations of mental health problems around menstruation
- Effects of sleep deprivation on mental health

Substance Use

- Cigarettes, alcohol, drugs, including modifications to use during/after current and previous pregnancies

Personal History

- Birth, early development, childhood trauma and abuse, education, sexual development, occupation, abuse and trauma in adulthood, relationship history, current stressors
- Social network and supports
- Specific enquiry about her own experiences of being parented
- Evidence of neurodivergence

Family History

- Parents – marital relationship, physical health, mental health and current relationship with parents
- Siblings – physical and mental health, relationships with siblings
- Family psychiatric history with particular focus on perinatal mental illness (including patterns of occurrence and recurrence), bipolar disorder, psychosis, mood disorders, suicide

Medical History

- Physical development, illnesses in childhood, current health including chronic illnesses, history of head injuries, operations/surgery
- Medication, allergies to medication, alerts re. medication including interactions, supplements

Obstetric History

- Contraception
- Previous pregnancies, obstetric complications, miscarriages, terminations of pregnancy, perinatal loss
- Infertility, infertility interventions

Personality

- Consider hobbies/interests/passions, managing conflict, coping with success, stress and failure, sociability, strengths, attitudes and belief systems, words to describe self

Forensic History

Mental State Examination

- In addition to a standard mental state examination, particular focus on evidence of (i) rapidly changing/deteriorating mental state or emergence of new symptoms; (ii) unusual thoughts regarding pregnancy/baby; (iii) feelings of incompetence with or estrangement from baby; (iv) new thoughts of self-harm or suicide
- Observation of mother–infant interaction where possible

Assessment of Capacity (in Relation to Self and Pregnancy/Infant)

- Ability to make informed decisions about care and treatment
- Ability to plan ahead and organise in relation to pregnancy health and childcare
- Ability to recognise and prioritise the infant's needs
- Ability to provide a safe, nurturing and stimulating environment for the infant

Assessment of vulnerability to abuse, neglect or exploitation

Having a diagnosis can help a woman make sense of her experience, recognise she is not alone in having this combination of difficulties, reduce shame and self-criticism, and provide reassurance that there is knowledge, understanding and evidence-based treatment which she can benefit from. In perinatal psychiatry it is particularly important to clarify the diagnosis because of the implications for the perinatal period, such as in the case of a woman with a diagnosis of bipolar disorder who is at high risk of postpartum psychosis [24]. The diagnosis should be discussed in the context of a formulation which can help the woman to understand the combination of factors that have contributed to her being unwell and demonstrate an understanding of her history, her experience and her family and cultural context.

Diagnosis and formulation provide a basis for discussing the woman's risk of becoming unwell in the perinatal period and options for care and treatment, taking into account her history, experience and preferences. The assessment should inspire a sense of trust that perinatal mental health professionals will work in partnership with the woman, her partner and family and the other involved professionals. It should also instil hope that the woman can be helped to stay well and that illness can be effectively treated, whilst supporting the mother–infant relationship and the family as a whole.

All of this needs to be communicated not only verbally at the assessment, but also in writing. Letters are important for conveying key information to referrers and other professionals about the woman's history, the diagnosis, risks, the information discussed with the woman and the plan for care and treatment. Letters can improve other professionals' understanding of the woman's history, the reasons for her illness, her insight and engagement and the role they can play in her care. Arguably letters are even more important as a written record for the woman of what has been discussed at the assessment. Research has identified that patients can find it hard to recall all the detail discussed at medical appointments for a variety of reasons [25, 26, 27]. This is particularly relevant for assessments in perinatal psychiatry where a huge amount of complex information may be discussed, and women's anxiety about being judged negatively in the context of pregnancy and parenting can affect her retention and recall.

Guidance from the Royal College of Psychiatrists (RCPsych) [28] and the General Medical Council [29] outlines key issues in communicating with referrers and patients and the important functions of clinical letters. RCPsych guidance states that letters can either be written directly to the patient and copied to the general practitioner (GP), or can be written to the GP with a copy sent to the patient. However, in 2018 the Academy of Medical Royal Colleges developed guidance on writing outpatient letters [30] which encourages doctors to write outpatient clinical letters directly to patients and to send a copy of the letter to the GP and other professionals. Whilst this may not be routinely applied in psychiatric practice it is encouraged [31] and recommended in National Institute for Health and Care Excellence guidance on shared decision-making [32]. Writing directly to women can be particularly useful in perinatal psychiatry where there is an emphasis on partnership and shared decision-making with women and families and on the woman being at the centre of her care. Skilled clinical letter writing involves documenting important information discussed at the assessment, whilst also conveying a compassionate, non-judgmental and non-blaming approach. For some women reading information about traumatic experiences discussed at their assessment can be distressing and it is important to agree with women how much detail will be documented and what will be shared with others, keeping in mind that it is normal practice in perinatal mental health for letters to be shared with key health professionals which include the GP, midwife, obstetrician and health visitor. When child safeguarding concerns are identified, relevant information must also be shared with children's social workers.

The summary and formulation needs to include relevant information about the woman's current pregnancy, her experience of the birth and her feelings about these as well as relevant obstetric history including fertility treatment, pregnancy loss and experiences of traumatic birth. It should also summarise her mental health history including the diagnosis, severity, associated risk and previous experience of and response to treatment. It should state whether she is currently unwell or not and summarise her current presentation. It should describe the factors which have contributed to her illness including predisposing, precipitating and maintaining factors, particularly highlighting those that relate to pregnancy and parenting. In addition to highlighting concerns, for example about a high risk of perinatal mental illness and the potential impact of this on her care of, and relationship with, her baby, the letter should also clearly identify her strengths. Information about diagnosis, perinatal mental illness and risk needs to be outlined. The letter should also document what has been discussed about care and treatment, including the risks and benefits of medication in pregnancy and breastfeeding, psychological therapies, lifestyle factors, other interventions and support. It is particularly important, for the woman and referrer, to have a clearly articulated plan of care which is well demarcated within the letter. All this information can give the woman a chance to reflect on complex information, consider treatment options and, if she chooses, to share and discuss this information with her partner or another carer.

The language and tone of letters is very important. Whether or not letters are written to the woman, or written to her GP and copied to her, medical jargon should be avoided and professionals should consider the messages they want to convey, using clear, concise and thoughtful language. This should include a non-judgemental, collaborative approach, with concerns being taken seriously and strengths being recognised. It should leave women with a sense that the assessment itself has been a helpful intervention, improving their understanding of their illness and the contributing factors and reducing shame and self-criticism. It should enable women to feel hopeful that specialist care can help them to be as well as possible, to develop their confidence as a mother and to enjoy family life.

Risk Assessment and Management

Risk assessment is integral to history taking and mental state examination, and usually enhanced by corroborative histories from people who know the woman well and a thorough review of her mental health records. In the perinatal period, risk needs to be assessed across a number of domains, keeping in mind at all times that risk must be considered not only in relation to the woman but also to the fetus/infant. It should always be informed by an understanding of the distinctive presentations and course of perinatal mental illness. The relevant domains of perinatal risk assessment are listed in Box 23.3.

Risk assessment must be effectively communicated, alongside a clear management plan, which addresses immediate, short-term and medium/longer-term plans. Immediate risk management should include consideration of inpatient care where appropriate, with thresholds for admission altered to account for the risk of rapid

Box 23.3 Domains of Risk Assessment and Management in the Perinatal Period

- Risk of occurrence or recurrence of illness
- Risks associated with treatment or no treatment
- Risks from misattribution of mental illness to adjustment to pregnancy or from misdiagnosis of an underlying physical illness as a mental disorder
- Risk of harm to the woman through self-neglect, self-harm or suicide
- Risk of harm to the pregnancy/infant (and older children) through neglect or intentional harm
- Risk to the evolving parent–infant relationship and to optimal infant development
- Risk of harm to others within or outwith the family
- Risk of harm from others including sexual, physical, emotional, financial or coercive harms

Risks may also be compounded by systemic disadvantages related to socio-economic status, race, culture, lifestyle and age, and by a lack of appropriate family, social and professional supports.

Box 23.4 Red Flag Signs in Risk Assessment

- Recent significant changes in mental state or emergence of new symptoms
- New thoughts or acts of violent self-harm (subsequently expanded to include any acts of self-harm in the perinatal period)
- New and persistent expressions of incompetency as a mother or estrangement from the infant

deterioration in certain conditions, and the importance of supporting the mother–infant relationship and infant development. The Confidential Enquiries into Maternal Deaths have highlighted certain warning signs which should alert the assessing clinician to circumstances of significant risk of self-harm or suicide. These are listed in Box 23.4. Where they exist (or other significant concerns are raised), and if inpatient care is not deemed the most appropriate response, any management plan should include how and when any early reassessment will be carried out. This must take into account the risk of rapid deterioration. Risk, and therefore risk management, is dynamic and, in the perinatal period, may alter significantly within short time periods. For that reason, *risk re-evaluation* should be a continuing process throughout contact with the service.

Risk management must include measures to safeguard both the mother and infant. In inpatient (Mother and Baby Unit (MBU)) settings organisational guidance on observation levels can be applied for the woman, but these are not easily translated to safeguarding for the infant. For infants, there is a need to address (i) direct risk of harm or neglect, and (ii) risk to the parent–infant relationship and (iii) infant development. A mother with psychotic beliefs driven by severe mental illness may pose a direct risk to her infant but, more commonly, she may fail to be able to provide safe, consistent care because of disorganisation, mood disturbance or treatment side effects. Any supervision of the infant needs to take all these factors into account and put in place measures to ensure that both safety and developmental needs are met. An example of such a system was developed by Scottish MBUs, and provides a five-point *Support and Supervision Scale* describing what (if any) risks are posed to the infant, what the mother capacity is to meet her infant's needs and the support that staff are required to provide to her and to her infant to ensure that all her infant's needs are met (see Box 23.5). This system recognises the central importance of supporting the mother–infant relationship while, at the same time, ensuring that all the infant's needs are met.

Box 23.5 **Framework for Support and Supervision to Ensure Infant Needs Are Met in an MBU Setting**

Adapted from NHS Greater Glasgow & Clyde West of Scotland Mother and Baby Unit Support and Supervision Form

Principles

- Mothers should be assessed jointly by a nursery nurse and a mental health nurse to determine mother's support and supervision needs in relation to provision of the child's care, and based on Getting it Right for Every Child principles.
- An overall required level 1–5 of support and supervision should be agreed.
- Levels should be reviewed at the start of every shift, and more frequently if required.
- Fathers should be involved and informed of the level of care required, wherever appropriate.
- Assessment and programme of intervention should be agreed by mental health nurse / nursery nurse / health visitor in collaboration with mother (and partner where appropriate).

Levels of Support and Supervision

Level 1 Can provide adequate and safe care to baby independently in and outside the unit. Responds to advice and support.

Level 2 Can provide **some** aspects of care to baby across **most** domains but requires support and supervision in some aspects of care.

May require support and supervision when out of the unit, although this can be reviewed by the multidisciplinary team.

Level 3 Can provide **limited** aspects of care to baby across **most** domains and may require an increased level of support and supervision.

Requires support and supervision when out of the unit, either by staff member or carer.

Level 4 Difficulty or inability to provide **most** aspects of safe care to baby without support and supervision. This may be due to unpredictability, inconsistency or incapacity.

Requires that baby must be within sight of designated member of staff at all times.

Level 5 Difficulty or inability to provide **most** aspects of safe care to baby without support and supervision. This may be due to unpredictability, inconsistency, incapacity or may have significant thoughts of harming baby where there are concerns she may act upon these thoughts, based on clinical risk assessment. Therefore, poses **significant** and **imminent** risk to baby.

A designated member of staff must provide all care of baby at all times.

(If level 5 is applied for a prolonged period, it is expected that the multidisciplinary team will promptly review if MBU admission for mother and baby remains appropriate.)

Box 23.5 *(cont.)*

Aspects of Care

1. **Providing a safe environment** e.g. takes safety precautions when using baby equipment such as pram, highchair; changes unsafe practice in response to advice; is self-reliant and has a routine for the infant
2. **Safe handling of child** e.g. holds the infant safely and gently; keeps infant within eye or hearing distance; attends to crying infant; is in attendance if infant is in an open cot, changing table or bed; does not place the infant near hot water
3. **Nutrition, feeding and hydration** e.g. feeds infant at appropriate times; prepares formula milk appropriately and at correct temperature
4. **Bathing and hygiene** e.g. changes infant's nappy when required; has safe bathing/changing routines
5. **Dressing and temperature control** e.g. dresses infant appropriately
6. **Play and exploration** e.g. smiles, talks and sings to the infant; engages in reciprocal interaction and play, taking cues from infant; attempts to stimulate the infant appropriately
7. **Promotion of child development** e.g. infant has a content disposition; is easily settled when distressed; enjoys being handled; snuggles in at feed times; responds to parent smiles; responds to stimuli; settles easily in different environments; sleeps well for developmental stage; reaches developmental milestones
8. **Mother–infant interaction and relationship** e.g. speaks to infant appropriately, not yelling or swearing; maintains good eye contact with the infant; holds infant close; addresses infant by name; looks to enjoy the infant

Summary

Difficult lessons from the Confidential Enquiries into Maternal Deaths remind us that thorough clinical assessment, detailed mental state examination and an appreciation of the dynamic nature of risk and its management are central to the effective treatment of women with perinatal mental illness. This is underpinned by the establishment of a trusting, respectful and honest relationship with the woman, which sees her as a partner in decision-making, and a detailed knowledge of the distinctive presentations and risks associated with illness in pregnancy and after childbirth, and its consequences for the woman and her infant. The first, and every subsequent encounter with the woman and her family are opportunities for therapeutic engagement and instillation of hope.

Services must have clear referral pathways and criteria, training for referrers, and an awareness of barriers to access and engagement which women may face. Clinicians need to develop skills in communicating assessment outcomes to referrers and to women in language which is compassionate, non-blaming and jargon free.

The assessment provides the foundation for the woman's relationship with the perinatal mental health service and for ensuring she has effective care and treatment. It should enable the woman, her partner and family and the professionals involved in her care to have a shared understanding of her illness, the contributing factors and the associated risks. It should leave the woman and her family feeling confident that she will have safe, effective, evidence-based care and treatment by professionals working in partnership who genuinely want to ensure the best possible outcomes for her and her family.

References

1. R Webb, E Ford, J Shakespeare, A Easter, F Alderdice, J Holly, et al. Conceptual framework on barriers and facilitators to implementing perinatal mental health care and treatment for women: the MATRIx evidence synthesis. *Health Social Care Deliv Res.* 2024;12(2).
2. N Jovanović, KC Packer, M Conneely, S Bicknell, A Copello, R McCabe, et al. Barriers to accessing perinatal mental health services and suggestions for improvement: qualitative study of women of Black and south Asian backgrounds. *BJPsych Bull.* 2024:1–8.
3. D Daehn, S Rudolf, S Pawils, B Renneberg. Perinatal mental health literacy: knowledge, attitudes, and help-seeking among perinatal women and the public – a systematic review. *BMC Pregnancy Childbirth.* 2022; 22(1):574.
4. M Sambrook Smith, V Lawrence, E Sadler, A Easter. Barriers to accessing mental health services for women with perinatal mental illness: systematic review and meta-synthesis of qualitative studies in the UK. *BMJ Open.* 2019;9(1): e024803.
5. O Megnin-Viggars, I Symington, LM Howard, S Pilling. Experience of care for mental health problems in the antenatal or postnatal period for women in the UK: a systematic review and meta-synthesis of qualitative research. *Arch Womens Ment Health.* 2015;18(6):745–59.
6. C Dolman, I Jones, LM Howard. Pre-conception to parenting: a systematic review and meta-synthesis of the qualitative literature on motherhood for women with severe mental illness. *Arch Womens Ment Health.* 2013;16(3): 173–96.
7. See Me. Perinatal and infant mental health stigma. 2022. https://shorturl.at/bP2gH
8. R Cantwell, A Cairns, K Bunch, M Knight on behalf of the MBRRACE-UK mental health chapter-writing group. Improving mental health care and care for women with multiple adversity. In: M Knight, K Bunch, D Tuffnell, R Patel, J Shakespeare, R Kotnis, S Kenyon, JJ Kurinczuk, editors, on behalf of MBRRACE-UK. *Saving Lives, Improving Mothers' Care – Lessons learned to inform maternity care from the UK and Ireland Confidential Enquiries into Maternal Deaths and Morbidity 2017–19.* Oxford: National Perinatal Epidemiology Unit, University of Oxford; 2021. p. 34–51.
9. NHS England and NHS Improvement. The perinatal mental health care pathways. 2018. https://shorturl.at/e8oXs
10. Perinatal Mental Health Network Scotland. The Scottish perinatal mental health care pathways. 2021. www.nn.nhs.scot/pmhn/professionals/delivering-effective-services
11. NHS Wales Executive. Perinatal mental health pathways. n.d. https://shorturl.at/ZsHst
12. R Cantwell, M Knight, M Oates, J Shakespeare on behalf of the MBRRACE-UK mental health chapter writing group. Lessons on maternal mental health. In: M Knight, D Tuffnell, S Kenyon,

J Shakespeare, R Gray, JJ Kurinczuk, editors, on behalf of MBRRACE-UK. *Saving Lives, Improving Mothers' Care – Surveillance of maternal deaths in the UK 2011–13 and lessons learned to inform maternity care from the UK and Ireland Confidential Enquiries into Maternal Deaths and Morbidity 2009–13.* Oxford: National Perinatal Epidemiology Unit, University of Oxford; 2015. p. 22–41.

13. Royal College of Psychiatrists College, Centre for Quality Improvement (CCQI). Perinatal Quality Network: standards for community perinatal mental health services. 6th ed. CCQI; 2023. https://shorturl.at/4MAV5
14. A Ayres, R Chen, T Mackle, E Ballard, S Patterson, G Bruxner, et al. Engagement with perinatal mental health services: a cross-sectional questionnaire survey. *BMC Pregnancy Childbirth.* 2019; 19(1):170.
15. E Moran, M Noonan, MM Mohamad, P O'Reilly. Women's experiences of specialist perinatal mental health services: a qualitative evidence synthesis. *Arch Womens Ment Health.* 2023;26(4): 453–71.
16. R Cantwell. Coronavirus resilience planning: telepsychiatry quick reference guide 4 – telepsychiatry in perinatal mental health settings. Digital Health & Care Scotland; 2020. https://shorturl.at/57Ayr
17. B Lever Taylor, J Billings, N Morant, D Bick, S Johnson. Experiences of how services supporting women with perinatal mental health difficulties work with their families: a qualitative study in England. *BMJ Open.* 2019;9(7):e030208.
18. American Psychological Association. APA style: gender. 2019. https://apastyle.apa.org/style-grammar-guidelines/bias-free-language/gender
19. Coalition for Diversity and Inclusion in Scholarly Communication. Gender, gender identity, and sexual orientation. 2022. https://c4disc.pubpub.org/pub/4hyglwhz/release/1?readingCollection=8dea2bef
20. General Medical Council. Confidentiality: good practice in handling patient information. 2017.
21. Mental Welfare Commission for Scotland. Carers, consent and confidentiality: how families can be involved in their relative's care and treatment. 2024.
22. Royal College of Psychiatrists. College report 216: framework for routine outcome measures in perinatal psychiatry. 2018. http://bit.ly/40Tp8hi
23. N Craddock, L Mynors-Wallis. Psychiatric diagnosis: impersonal, imperfect and important. *Br J Psychiatry.* 2014;204(2):93–5.
24. R Wesseloo, AM Kamperman, T Munk-Olsen, VJ Pop, SA Kushner, V Bergink. Risk of postpartum relapse in bipolar disorder and postpartum psychosis: a systematic review and meta-analysis. *Am J Psychiatry.* 2016;173(2):117–27.
25. MB Laws, Y Lee, T Taubin, WH Rogers, IB Wilson. Factors associated with patient recall of key information in ambulatory specialty care visits: results of an innovative methodology. *PLoS ONE.* 2018;13(2):e0191940.
26. C Richard, E Glaser, MT Lussier. Communication and patient participation influencing patient recall of treatment discussions. *Health Expect.* 2017;20(4):760–70.
27. RP Kessels. Patients' memory for medical information. *J R Soc Med.* 2003;96(5):219–22.
28. Royal College of Psychiatrists. Writing clinic letters: College guidance on improving engagement with patients. 2021. www.rcpsych.ac.uk/members/supporting-your-professional-development/writing-clinic-letters
29. General Medical Council. Good medical practice. 2024. www.gmc-uk.org/professional-standards/good-medical-practice-2024
30. Academy of Medical Royal Colleges. Please, write to me. Writing outpatient letters to patients: guidance. 2018. www.aomrc.org.uk/wp-content/uploads/2018/

09/Please_write_to_me_Guidance_010918.pdf

31. D Martin, K Weetman. Writing letters to patients attending psychiatry clinics. *BMJ*. 2023;383:2857.

32. National Institute for Health and Care Excellence. Shared decision making. Clinical Guideline (CG197). 2021. www.nice.org.uk/guidance/ng197

Chapter 24

Pre-pregnancy Advice and Planning

Maddalena Miele and Shankari Arulkumaran

Introduction

National guidelines recommend that all women of childbearing potential who have a new, existing or past mental health condition be offered advice on planning a pregnancy [1, 2]. The Royal College of Psychiatrists' Perinatal Quality Network recommends including pre-conception and contraception advice as part of the discharge planning process from both inpatient and community specialist services [3].

Over the past decades, advances in the research on pre-conception health and care in the general population have informed and shaped international and national guidelines [4, 5]. Although guidance about what pre-conception advice should be offered to women of childbearing age with a mental illness has been published, research on family planning and contraception use for those with perinatal mental health difficulties is sparse. The same applies with regard to the effectiveness of pre-conception advice on maternal mental health and pregnancy outcome.

In this chapter we will briefly review the current evidence for approaches to general pre-conception health and care and then provide an overview of pre-conception care for women with a mental illness. The last part of the chapter will focus on implementing pre-conception care in clinical mental health settings.

Approaches to Pre-conception Health and Care

Maternal health and care has attracted increasing attention as a means of improving pregnancy and birth outcomes [6]. Interventions to optimise maternal health have focused on the early gestational period. Smoking, alcohol consumption, substance misuse, obesity and maternal undernutrition have been repeatedly associated with pre-eclampsia, gestational diabetes, intrauterine growth retardation, low birth weight, preterm birth and still birth. There is public awareness that avoidance of smoking [7] and alcohol [8] in pregnancy is associated with improved pregnancy outcomes and reduced risk of fetal alcohol spectrum disorders.

In the early 1990s, the seminal epidemiological work of David Barker highlighted the relationship between the timing of exposure to environmental factors and critical stages of fetal development (fetal programming). The hypothesis of the developmental origin of health and disease (DOHaD) has shaped our understanding of illness aetiology and focused research on the relationship between the timing of exposure and critical stages of development.

Interventions delivered during pregnancy to redress diet, gestational weight gain and obesity [9, 10, 11] or antenatal supplementation of micronutrients [12] yielded minimal or no benefit on common adverse pregnancy outcomes. These results suggest that interventions such as the reversal of obesity and micronutrient supplementation have to be implemented before the endpoint of critical stage of fetal development in order to mitigate the risk of adverse pregnancy and birth outcomes.

Additional evidence indicates that reproductive health and care should extend beyond early gestation and focus on the pre-conception period. The timescale for folate supplementation to achieve adequate intracellular concentrations, thus reducing the risk of neural tube defects, is 4–6 weeks before conception [13]. Supplementation trials seem to confirm that interventions need to occur at least 3 months prior to conception in order to have an effect on birth weight [14]; maternal weight optimisation does not improve outcomes unless is achieved 2–3 years before conception [15]. Additional evidence suggests that interventions should target the adolescent period if pre-conception risks are to be mitigated [16].

To this end, Stephenson and co-workers have proposed a more radical approach for pre-conception care [17]. Drawing from the tenets of life-course epidemiology [18], they conceptualise pre-conception health and care within a life-course framework and identify three points of interventions: biological, individual and population level. The embryological stage (gamete maturation, fertilisation and embryo development) is the most sensitive to environmental factors, such as alcohol, teratogens, insufficient nutrients; from an individual perspective, pre-conception effectively coincides with the decision to have a baby; the evidence suggests however that some health behaviours need to change when women are not planning for a pregnancy; this requires a public health approach with long-term strategies at population level.

A detailed description of pre-conception health and care from a public health perspective is outside the scope of this chapter and pre-conception planning will be discussed primarily from an individual perspective.

Pre-conception Health and Care in Women with Mental Illness

Many women and couples affected by a mental illness often face the prospect of a pregnancy with profound apprehension. They are concerned about exposure to medication, the risk of a relapse precipitated by the physical adaptation to pregnancy and by parenthood, the impact of psychiatric symptoms on their ability to care for their baby, and the risk of losing child custody. All these aspects should be carefully discussed and incorporated in the pre-conception consultation.

Pre-conception Attitudes

A prospective study investigating the association of pre-conception adolescent and young adult mental health, substance use, and socio-economic characteristics with child outcomes, estimated that 18% of parents had a pre-conception common mental disorder [19].

Qualitative research on pre-conception attitudes in women attending antenatal clinics has identified three groups of women: women with high levels of pregnancy planning who take up interventions; women who plan but have poor awareness; and women for whom the pre-conception period has little meaning [20]. Pregnancy is categorised as intended, mistimed or unwanted; mistimed and unwanted pregnancies are considered together as unintended. The average time to conception for fertile couples is 3 months [21] and pregnancy planning is common; a study combining information from several surveys reported that 60% of pregnancies are intended; 38% of unintended pregnancies led to an unplanned birth [22].

Unintended pregnancies limit the scope of action for pre-conception health and care and many women access healthcare only when pregnant. The risk of an unintended pregnancy is increased in women with a mental illness [23]. Women with pre-existing mental illness often experience stigma from healthcare professionals regarding their desire for motherhood [24].

Risk of Relapse

Women with a pre-existing or a new onset mental illness in the perinatal period, like those with a pre-existing or new onset medical condition, are at increased risk of a recurrence or a relapse; 43% of women with a history of depression experience a relapse in pregnancy [25], increased rates of relapse in pregnancy in non-affective psychosis and in bipolar affective disorders have also been reported [26, 27]. Women with a family history of postpartum psychosis or a diagnosis of bipolar affective disorder type I or schizoaffective disorders are at increased risk of postpartum psychosis (see Chapter 11).

Parenting and Mental Illness

The risk of intergenerational transmission of dysfunctional parenting and of child psychopathology [28] is, with very good reason, an extremely sensitive and anxiety-provoking aspect of pre-conception management. However, it can no longer be ignored, and a tactful exploration of the parents' expectations and fantasies about the pregnancy and the baby should be an integral part of the consultation. The pre-conception consultation is an opportunity to look at reproductive choices in a holistic manner and should include a sensitive discussion of the importance of the quality of parenting and other factors mediating and moderating the risk of intergenerational transmission of psychological disturbance and psychopathology.

Physical Health Considerations

The chance of having a healthy, live birth may be impacted upon by a number of factors such as weight, diet, smoking, substance misuse, environmental pollutants, infections, medical conditions, medications and family medical history. Women with perinatal mental illness have a higher prevalence of well-established obstetric risk factors including proximal risk factors (such as obesity, gestational diabetes, hypertension and smoking) and distal risk factors (such as domestic violence and poor or delayed antenatal care). These risks are elevated regardless of pharmacotherapy during pregnancy.

The susceptibility to factors affecting fetal development varies throughout the different stages of pregnancy, depending on the timing of organ development. Teratogens are especially damaging in the first 12 weeks of gestation because it is a critical period in perinatal development. The timely recognition and management of obstetric complications, for example pre-eclampsia and pre-eclamptic toxaemia, can be instrumental in minimising the risk of adverse outcomes. The evidence suggests that untreated (or sub-optimally treated) maternal mental illness is associated with an increased risk of adverse obstetric outcomes [29] although it is unclear if this is secondary to health behaviour or is a direct effect of maternal mental illness.

A data linkage cohort study comparing a cohort of women with a live or still birth with or without a history of secondary mental healthcare before delivery showed that after adjusting for maternal socio-demographic characteristics, the overall risk of an obstetric near miss remained higher for women with a severe mental illness (adjusted odds ratio 1.6, 95% confidence interval 1.3–2.0, $P < 0.001$) [30] (Figure 24.1).

The woman's physical health may not be the primary focus from a specialist perinatal mental health perspective; however, the pre-conception consultation is an important opportunity for the woman/couple before conceiving to be informed about vitamin supplements (e.g. folic acid) and nutrition in pregnancy, to discuss smoking cessation, alcohol consumption, weight optimisation as well as considering screening tests (e.g. sickle cell).

Prescribing Strategies in Pregnancy

Prescribing in pregnancy is common; there is evidence that the mean number of medications taken in pregnancy has almost doubled over the past 5 years. The average pregnant patient in the US and Canada uses more than two drugs during the course of their pregnancy [31]; 95.8% of participants in a longitudinal study took prescription medications; excluding prenatal formulations and oral iron prescriptions, 59.7% of the patients used a prescription medication during their pregnancy, 92.6% self-medicated with over-the-counter medication (excluding vitamins and iron supplements) and 45.2% used herbal medications [32].

Physiological adaptation to pregnancy results in changes affecting the majority of organ systems often from the early stages of the pregnancy. These alterations influence drugs pharmacokinetics, that is, absorption, distribution, metabolism and elimination, and pharmacokinetics. For example, the increase in renal clearance (20–65%) doubles the clearance of lithium (which is not protein bound) during the third trimester of pregnancy compared with the non-pregnant state, leading to subtherapeutic drug concentrations. The increased insulin resistance may exacerbate the diabetogenic effect of antipsychotics such as olanzapine (Box 24.1).

Most treatments and dosing strategies are based on data from healthy male volunteers and non-pregnant women. Pregnant women are actively excluded from phase 3 clinical trials, which establish the safety and efficacy of a drug. The evidence from observational studies must be interpreted with caution also because of individual variability.

Therefore, there is very limited data to guide clinicians in dosing strategies in pregnancy, and clinicians must understand: a) what is already known about pharmacokinetics in pregnancy; b) the critical stages of fetal development; c) the rate of major birth defects in the general population is around 3% [33] and also use basic principles of prescribing, namely: use the lowest beneficial dose, monitor mental state and response to medication closely and adjust dosage accordingly in a timely fashion and avoid polypharmacy.

The discussion of the 'risks versus benefits' for specific classes of medication has to be based on relevant guidelines, for example those of the British Association of Psychopharmacology, National Institute for Health and Care Excellence and the recommendations of the UK Teratology Information Service, and when relevant should incorporate pharmaco-vigilance alerts (e.g. Pharmacovigilance Risk Assessment

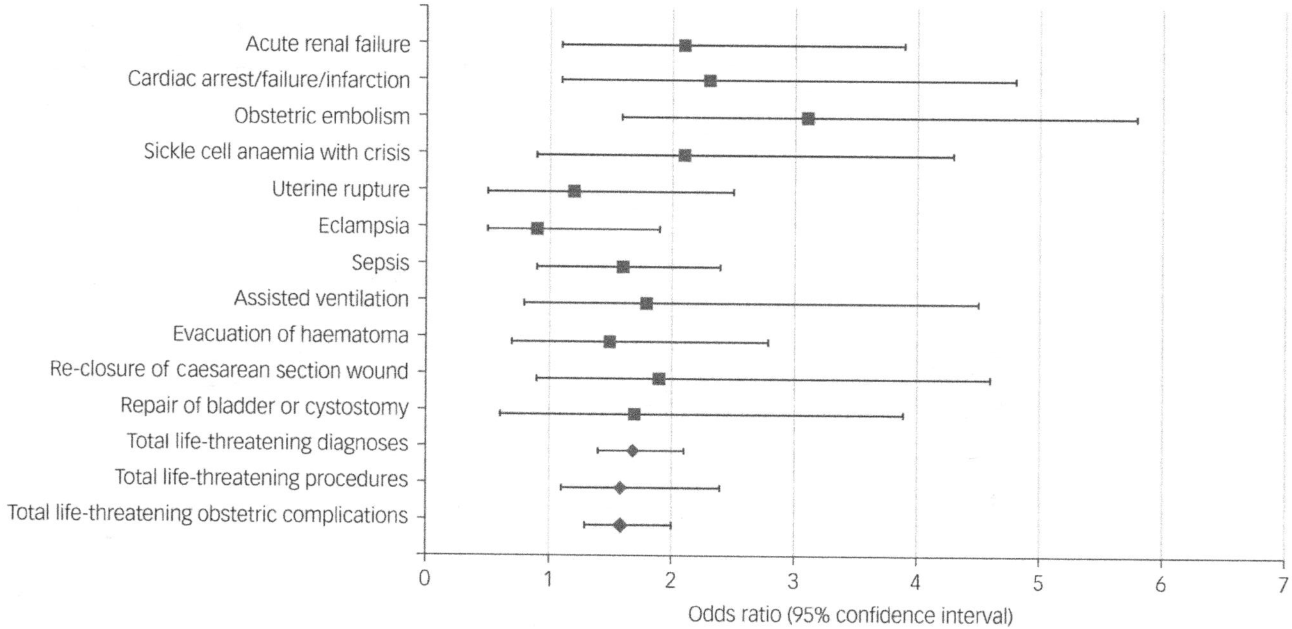

Figure 24.1 Comparison of obstetric near misses among women with and without serious mental illness [30].

Box 24.1 **Pharmacokinetic Changes Secondary to Physiological Adaptation To Pregnancy**

- Reduced gastric motility
- Increased gastric PH
- Reduced gastric secretion
- Reduced intestinal motility
- Increased cardiac output (30–50%)
- Increased maternal blood volume
- Increased blood flow to the kidneys and utero-placental unit
- Decreased blood pressure
- Increased tidal volume (30–50%)
- Increased body fat and total body water
- Decrease plasma protein binding, especially albumin
- Increased renal blood flow and glomerular filtration rate increase of 50%
- Increased activity of P450 CYP enzyme family
- The placental MAO and COMT can accelerate the metabolism of some drugs
- Increased insulin resistance

Committee of the European Medicine Agency recommendations on valproate use in pregnancy).

To date intrauterine exposure to psychotropic medication has been varyingly associated with an increased risk of teratogenesis, obstetric complications, neonatal withdrawal symptoms, neonatal persistent pulmonary hypertension, autism and other child psychopathology. Many of these associations have not been confirmed by larger studies and it is difficult to draw firm conclusions. Newborn babies exposed to psychotropic medication in utero should be monitored after delivery (see also Chapter 25).

Prescribing Strategies in Lactation

On average, nursing mothers produce 600–1,000 ml of milk daily [34].

All psychotropic medications are transferred in the breast milk by simple diffusion processes. Maternal drug concentration (controlled by maternal pharmacokinetics) and milk plasma ratio are major determinants of infant dose via breast milk [35].

Lipophilic compounds tend to have concentrations higher in the hind milk because of its high lipid content. Therefore, hind milk has a higher concentration of maternal (lipophilic) medication than fore milk [34].

The relative infant dose (RID), that is, the ratio between the infant dose/kg body weight (BW) and the maternal dose/kg BW is considered the best index of safety for medication in lactation. A RID <10% is regarded as relatively safe [36] and most psychotropic drugs have a RID <10%.

The World Health Organization recommends exclusively breastfeeding for at least 6 months and continuing breastfeeding for at least 2 years ('breast is best'). A large meta-analysis indicates protection against child infections and malocclusion, increase in intelligence and probable reductions in obesity and diabetes. For nursing women, breastfeeding gives protection against breast cancer and it improves birth spacing. It might also protect against ovarian cancer and type 2 diabetes [37]. Despite this evidence, the UK has one of the lowest rates of breastfeeding. Worldwide it is estimated that one-third of infants are exclusively breast fed to 6 months. In the UK, however, it has been reported that by 6 weeks just 21% of infants are exclusively breast fed, and by 6 months less than 1% of infants are exclusively breastfed [36].

The PROBIT study [38], a randomised controlled trial of an effective breastfeeding support intervention in 17,000 women in Belarus, followed the children to early adulthood; the clearest long-term effect was an increase in IQ in the breastfed group (mean 6 points increase at age 6.5 years).

Advice on breastfeeding to women with a mental illness should consider additional aspects not routinely incorporated in the discussion on breastfeeding choices. Lactation may be influenced by level of stress, maternal nutritional state, maternal medication and prematurity. Difficulties in establishing breastfeeding can lead to significant sleep deprivation, which is one of the identified risk factors for postnatal relapse. If the woman chooses to do so, breastfeeding should be encouraged. Mixed feeding, either with expressed milk or formula, should be suggested to help reduce sleep deprivation. Women should not be made to feel guilty if they wish to stop breastfeeding to prioritise their mental health.

Interface between Mental Illness and Parenting

A number of longitudinal studies indicate that children of parents suffering from a mental illness are at increased risk of developing psychological and psychiatric conditions later in life; however, it is not possible to infer a causal relationship. The mechanisms underlying the intergenerational transmission of mental disturbance are complex and include both genetic and environmental effects.

Fetal Programming

The maternal hypothalamic-pituitary-adrenal axis and the placenta, which produces corticotrophin-releasing hormone, are a source of programming information to adapt fetal development to survival in response to threats. Prenatal exposure to excessive levels of glucocorticoids may increase the risk of adverse neurodevelopmental outcomes. Persistent maternal stress is likely to increase the risk of pervasive programming consequences for both brain and behaviour by means of prenatal exposure to high cortisol [39, 40].

Parenting

Some of the identified mediating variables and moderators are potentially modifiable, for example social, emotional and material support, duration of the parental disorder and the quality of parenting [28].

There is ample evidence that the quality of the parenting – sensitive, unresponsive or controlling – shapes the organisational attachment patterns, and these in turn are predictive of future functioning. Sensitive parenting promotes the development of secure attachment, resilience and emotional well-being.

The research on parent sensitivity identified two main correlates of sensitive parenting:

- Attunement (or contingency, defined as the temporal relationship between two events that involve sequential coordination) between parent and infant [41]
- Mind-mindedness or reflective function. The parent's capacity to understand the infant behaviour in terms of internal feeling states [42, 43]

Risk factors for the intergenerational transmission of psychopathology are not routinely considered in mental health assessments, but this aspect can no longer be overlooked and should be an integral component not only of pre-conception advice but also of all generic mental health assessment of the childbearing (female and male) population. Exploring the interface between mental illness and parenting is extremely anxiety provoking for women or couples with lived experience. The ability to meet the baby's needs adequately can be affected by a number of factors; and so, identifying factors that women recognise as potentially impacting on their ability to meet infants' needs, and finding ways to mitigate them, is an integral part of empowering women and couples to plan for parenthood.

Having a mental illness does not equate to 'bad parenting'; many women and couples with lived experience are perfectly capable of caring for their children adequately and well. Women and couples should be reassured that if they experience difficulties in bonding and parenting, they would be able to be assessed and receive appropriate help. Interventions that enhance sensitivity, like those based on reflective video feedback (e.g. video interactive guidance and positive parenting [44]) have a positive impact on the developing child.

Many women and couples are deeply apprehensive at the prospect of being referred to social care on account of maternal mental illness. Often the fear that social services 'will take the baby away' discourages women from being open about their diagnosis and from seeking help. The consultation offers the opportunity to explain the referral criteria and remits of social care and clarify that their primary role is to support parenting and empower families.

Doctors should be mindful of the language used to explore sensitive areas during the consultation and formulate the relevant recommendations. Experts by lived experience feedback indicates that they feel overwhelmed by the notion that maternal mental illness is associated with an increased risk of adverse pregnancy outcomes and child psychopathology. A thoughtful and well-informed pre-conception consultation can empower women and their partners to make informed choices and plan for a pregnancy knowing that their mental health will receive the same consideration as their physical health and that they will be supported in their decisions, whatever these may be.

Pre-conception Consultation

Referral Pathways

Access to mental health pre-conception advice for women varies widely depending on commissioning arrangements, service provisions and level of clinical expertise within teams. Specialist perinatal mental health services are unlikely to have the capacity to offer pre-conception advice and planning to all women of childbearing age affected by a mental disorder. Women with a severe mental illness, even if they are in remission, are at high risk of relapse in the event of a pregnancy and should be referred for specialist pre-conception care either by primary (general practitioner) or secondary services. Women with mild to moderate mental illness may also benefit from pre-conception advice and planning; specialist services may not be able to provide this through direct care, but they still have a role in facilitating access to pre-conception care for these women by delivering supplemented care, that is, providing specialist training, advice and clinical supervision to primary and non-specialist secondary care and by liaising with the mental health pharmacists attached to other services. Pre-conception advice should be an integral part of discharge planning from specialist Mother and Baby units and acute mental health inpatient units.

Purpose of the Consultation

It is helpful to clarify that the scope of the consultation extends beyond the discussion on the risk of intrauterine (and through breastfeeding) exposure to medication. The overall aims should include the following: advice on optimising general and reproductive health; a sensitive discussion of the possible impact of the illness on the pregnancy and on the neonatal outcomes; how the transition to parenthood can be affected by mental illness but also impact on mental illness (e.g. sleep deprivation); an exploration of the adjunctive role of non-pharmacological interventions. The consultation should also cover access to specialist perinatal mental healthcare at pregnancy recognition and a detailed discussion of the package of care the woman is entitled to, clarifying that the multidisciplinary care can be extended to the infant and the partner if necessary. Women should be informed that specialist services work in partnership with other health professionals and agencies involved in their care, for example midwifery, health visiting; the consultation should offer the opportunity to clarify the role of children and family social care, with an emphasis on their supportive role, and explore fears and concerns women may have to this end.

The time to conceive can be stressful for couples and it may increase the woman's vulnerability to relapse, especially if medication is modified or discontinued. Therefore, an additional aim of the consultation is the development of a personalised relapse prevention plan with recommendation on the timing for suspending contraception which should be aligned with the titration/discontinuation medication regimen.

Perinatal mental health specialist services are not commissioned to provide ongoing care to couples who are trying to conceive. At the end of the consultation, it is important to clarify who will take responsibility for overseeing the care of the individual woman prior to conceiving, to ensure close monitoring of their mental health, management of the medication regimen and implementation of the relapse prevention plan. The aims of pre-pregnancy advice and planning discussed above are summarised in Box 24.2.

Box 24.2 Aims of Pre-pregnancy Advice and Planning

Pre-conception advice should extend beyond the remits of prescribing in pregnancy and lactation and it should include:

- Discussion of general and reproductive health
- Impact of maternal mental illness on the pregnancy and neonatal outcomes
- Effect of maternal mental illness on the transition to parenthood
- Risk-benefit analysis of prescribing psychotropic medication
- Role of adjunctive non-pharmacological interventions
- Access pathways to specialist perinatal mental health services at pregnancy recognition
- Explanation of the perinatal mental health package of care for women, infants and significant others
- Relapse prevention plan inclusive of signposting to emergency care

Structure of the Consultation

The initial appointment should last between 1 and 1.5 hours to gather a comprehensive history and to discuss formulation, risks, protective factors and well-being recommendations. Partners should be invited to attend with the woman's consent if this is her preference; however, healthcare professionals should be mindful of the risk of domestic abuse and reproductive coercion [45], ensuring that women can be seen on their own and with an independent interpreter when necessary. In-person appointments are preferable to remote consultations.

At times it may be prudent to arrange a dedicated follow-up appointment with partner/significant others to revisit the plan and provide psychoeducation.

The duration of the consultation should be sufficient to allow time to assess all aspects specific to pre-conception care in addition to the conventional headings of the initial personal history (Box 24.3).

Initial Assessment/Intake History

Taking a thorough mental and physical health history is the fundamental pre-requisite for formulating a tailored pre-conception plan and establishing the basis for a meaningful therapeutic relationship. Confirming or clarifying the psychiatric diagnosis in association with a detailed evaluation of previous pharmacological treatments can help in

Box 24.3 Pre-conception Care: Areas to Explore in the Initial Assessment

- Exploring fears, including fear of loss of child custody, expectations and empowering the woman or the couple to make an informed decision about pregnancy and parenthood
- Physical and mental health risks deriving from adaptation to pregnancy and parenthood
- Impact of physical and mental health risks on the unborn and the infant
- Risk of intergenerational transmission of psychopathology
- Risk of intergenerational transmission of dysfunctional parenting
- Pharmacological options

  a. Continue medication throughout conception, pregnancy and lactation
  b. Continue medication but switch to a different psychotropic medication with a better teratogenic profile; this however may well increase the risk of relapse and there is always the uncertainty related to the clinical response to medication
  c. Discontinue prior to conceiving, be mindful that the timescale for conceiving cannot be fully controlled and explore the timing (early warning signs or *relapse signature*) of resuming medication at pregnancy recognition
  d. Reinstate medication after 12 weeks of gestation even if there is no evidence of symptoms breakthrough
  e. Reinstate medication after delivery or at any stage of the pregnancy if there is evidence of a relapse/recurrence

- Woman's preferences and choices of maternity care and entitlement to perinatal mental healthcare provided locally
- Access to mental healthcare while trying to conceive

assessing the risk of relapse or recurrence. Increasing awareness of early warning signs and agreeing on what the *relapse signature* looks like helps to establish the points of intervention.

The psychiatric anamnesis in the context of pre-conception care should elicit biological, psychosocial, behavioural and cognitive factors likely to impact on adaptation to pregnancy and parenthood (Box 24.4).

Risk Benefit Analysis in the Outcome of the Consultation

As clinicians we need to support women to make informed choices, and we must present information in an unbiased way. The final decision of whether to prescribe or not relies upon the balance between risks versus benefits. Women should also be asked routinely about over-the-counter medication, and this information should be incorporated to guide the final choice.

The discussion on prescribing should be formulated not in the restrictive context of the teratogenic risk but in the wider context of the cost of untreated maternal mental illness. The choice of language and the general tone of the discussion are important to establish a non-judgemental environment allowing women or couples to make an informed choice. Words such as 'risk', 'teratogenic', 'psychopathology' and 'adverse outcomes' can be deeply anxiety provoking and therefore require further explanation and checking that they are understood by the woman. Psychiatric illnesses and the associated risks should not be downplayed, but a transparent risk benefit analysis balanced by the inclusion of protective factors as well as information on accessing specialist professional help is likely to empower women and couples to make the best choice.

Using words such as 'chance' or 'likelihood' rather than 'risk' may be less anxiety provoking; and a clear explanation of relative versus absolute risk can empower women and couples to make an informed decision. The risk benefit analysis should be based on the assumption that absolute certainty can never be achieved and that each decision will entail a margin of risk.

The outcome of the consultation should be summarised with a view to generating a formulation which will guide the management plan. It is helpful to highlight protective factors, such as no relevant medical or obstetric history, healthy lifestyle, adaptive coping strategies, uneventful childhood with positive experiences of being parented, and ability to take responsibility for health. It is prudent to inform women at particularly elevated risk that a low maintenance dose of medication may be preferable to the high dose of psychotropics and the poly-pharmacy necessary to manage an acute and severe recurrence or relapse.

Women should be offered access to non-pharmacological interventions. It is helpful to discuss the evidence for psychological interventions clarifying that at the early signs and symptoms of relapse they may need to be supplemented by pharmacological ones to manage risk effectively.

Non-pharmacological interventions are not a substitute for pharmacological treatment; psychological therapies also have potential adverse effects [47]. However, there is evidence supporting the effectiveness of modified psychological interventions in relapse prevention, such as cognitive behavioural therapy for the relapse prevention of bipolar affective disorder [48, 49].

Box 24.4 Intake History Outline

Past Psychiatric History. Focus: Prognostic Factors and Health Behaviour

- Age of onset, characteristics of episodes, frequency and duration of relapses, number and modalities of admissions to hospital, factors precipitating relapses (e.g. sleep deprivation), compliance with treatment, response to interventions (pharmacological and non), insight and ability to take responsibility for health
- Impact of the symptoms on level of functioning and cognitive processing
- Post-traumatic stress disorder secondary to previous traumatic birth
- *Does the current diagnosis need revisiting?*

Family and Personal History. Focus: Risk of Intergenerational Transmission of Parenting Style and Psychopathology

- Genetic predisposition
- Exposure to developmental stressors, experience of being parented ('I want to give my baby what I have never had'), refer to the neurobiological evidence for intergenerational transmission of parenting style. The Adverse Childhood Experience Questionnaire is a helpful tool to evaluate exposure to developmental stressors

Pre-morbid Personality. Focus: Coping Styles at Times of Stress

- Consider a screening tool for mild, moderate and severe personality disorders (Standardised Assessment of the Severity of Personality Disorders, SAS-PD [46]); the degree of severity of personality disorder influences adaptation to parenthood; for example, are the usual coping strategies, such as smoking, alcohol, substances use, over-reliance on fitness, comfort eating, etc. compatible with physical adaptation to pregnancy and motherhood? Is there a risk that the baby will be used to regulate negative emotions?

Relationships and Social Circumstances. Focus: Protective Factors

- Quality of the relationship with the father of the baby and the extended family (domestic violence, 'parents as partners', partner's understanding and acceptance of mental illness; family dynamics, e.g. intrusive, controlling parents-in-law, additional family obligations)
- Resources to outsource household management, childcare. Be specific about 'support', clarify that material and social support is not substitutive of interventions; one should be realistic about what statutory and non-statutory agencies can offer
- Entitlement to maternity pay. Harassment in the workplace

Reproductive History and Attitude towards Conception. Focus: Vulnerability and Ability to Prioritise the Baby's Need

- Termination of pregnancies, miscarriages, sexual health and behaviour – this is also helpful for assessing the risk of vulnerability
- Try to get a sense of the 'role of the baby', for example replacement baby; the desire to have a baby can be driven by unmet emotional needs or the wish to consolidate an unstable relationship

Medical and Obstetric History. Focus: Risk Factors for Pregnancy

- Pre-existing health condition
- High blood pressure (uncontrolled)
- Polycystic ovarian syndrome is associated with a reduction in fertility and an increased risk of obstetric complications

Box 24.4 *(cont.)*

- Diabetes
- Kidney disease
- Auto-immune diseases (e.g. lupus, multiple sclerosis)
- Thyroid disease
- Infertility (in 8–12% of couples) – fertility treatment is associated with increased risk of obstetric complications and multiple gestation
- Obesity (52% of UK female population is overweight)
- Age (early or advanced maternal age is associated with increased risk of adverse obstetric and neonatal outcomes)
- Previous pregnancies; history of traumatic birth

Lifestyle factors: alcohol, tobacco, recreational drugs, physical exercise

Medication: prescribed presently, in the past; over-the-counter medication

Irrespective of the decision made in regard of medication or the choice of psychological treatment, it is prudent to monitor the woman's mental state. The professionals responsible for the woman's mental healthcare (primary care physician or the adult community mental health service) should oversee this, and women should be reassured that the care they will receive will not be affected by their choices. Tracking changes indicative of relapse/recurrence/escalation of symptoms while trying to conceive, especially if the medication is changed or discontinued, can assist patients and clinicians to time interventions and monitor response to treatment. This can be achieved by disorder specific rating scales (e.g. PHQ, GAD) self-administered at regular intervals; and the use of mobile medical apps by clinicians and patients has grown considerably since the introduction of mobile phones [50]. The management plan should include information on access to mental health services with a recommendation to refer to specialist perinatal mental health services at pregnancy recognition (Box 24.5).

Conclusions

Optimising physical healthcare has attracted increasing attention as a means of improving pregnancy and birth outcomes. The hypothesis of DOHaD has shaped our understanding of illness etiology and focused research on the relationship between the timing of exposure and critical stages of development. Additional evidence indicates that reproductive health and care should extend beyond the early gestation and focus on the pre-conception period. Pre-conception health and care is increasingly conceptualised within a life-course framework with a view to identifying consequential points of interventions. The research on family planning and contraception use for those with perinatal mental health difficulties is sparse. The same applies for the effectiveness of pre-conception advice on maternal mental health and pregnancy outcome. Thus, there is no current evidence-based guideline about what pre-conception advice should be offered to women of childbearing age with a mental illness. However, there is consensus among professionals and national guidelines that for those women at significantly increased risk of relapse or recurrence in the perinatal period, pre-conception advice should be an integral part of routine care.

Box 24.5 Perinatal Mental Healthcare Package

Perinatal mental healthcare should be coordinated by a specialist team. Alternatively adult mental health services should take the lead in coordinating the care.

The essential remits of perinatal mental health management are:

- Monitoring the mental state for early signs and symptoms of relapse or recurrence (early warning signs or *relapse signature*)
- Monitoring the response to medication and adjusting the dosage accordingly
- Assessment of suitability and referral for psychological interventions
- Ensuring effective communication and sharing of information (e.g. the lead clinician takes responsibility for creating a distribution list of all the professionals and significant others involved in the care of the woman to share all the relevant care plans). This is extremely important when clinical and other relevant information is held on separate, not-interfaced database and therefore not universally accessible
- Working in partnership with the maternity services, ensuring that the woman receives enhanced obstetric care and additional obstetric monitoring where indicated and that her birth choice is carefully discussed
- Arranging a pre-birth multidisciplinary planning meeting at 32 weeks to ensure the woman and her family have the care and support they need during the remainder of the pregnancy, her maternity admission for the birth of her baby and for the early postnatal period (6–8 weeks). This can include discussions regarding the timing and mode of delivery, care during labour and post-delivery, as well as discharge planning, such as a prophylactic admission to a specialist Mother and Baby Unit where indicated or involvement with the local home treatment team
- When possible, arranging for the woman to visit the nearest Mother and Baby Unit. Meeting the team and visiting the premises can reduce anxiety and assist families to make an informed decision on in-patient treatment, should this be necessary at any point
- Working in partnership with health visiting services to deliver infant mental health psycho-education and implement screening of bonding and attachment difficulties

The clinical approach guiding pre-conception advice requires a shift towards a collaborative model of care, using a strengths-based formulation, inclusive of an integrated physical and mental health assessment combined with an appraisal of the future ability to meet the needs of the baby.

The final formulation should actively incorporate protective factors as well as triggers and maintaining factors in order to help parents to make changes to promote positive mental health, improve their reproductive choices and the chances of having a healthy pregnancy outcome.

Providing pre-conception advice, not only to mothers but also in the wider context to health professionals, is an integral part of perinatal mental healthcare and risk management.

This knowledge can promote an informed, shared decision-making process in relation to the timing of the pharmacological and non-pharmacological interventions and motivate women and couples to implement lifestyle changes in preparation for parenthood.

References

1. National Institute for Health and Care Excellence. Antenatal and postnatal mental health: clinical management and service guidance. Clinical Guideline (CG192). 2018.
2. Scottish Intercollegiate Guidelines Network. Perinatal mental health conditions. 2023.
3. Z Schneider. Standards for community mental health services In: *CCQI Quality Network for Perinatal Mental Health Services*. Royal College of Psychiatrists; 2017.
4. World Health Organization. Preconception care: maximising the gains for maternal and child health. Policy Brief 1–8. 2013.
5. SC Davies. Chief Medical Officer annual report 2014: women's health. Department of Health and Social Care; 2015.
6. National Institute for Health and Care Excellence. Antenatal care for uncomplicated pregnancies. Clinical Guideline (CG62). 2008.
7. JV Been, UB Nurmatov, B Cox, TS Nawrot, CP van Schayck, A Sheikh. Effect of smoke-free legislation on perinatal and child health: a systematic review and meta-analysis. *Lancet.* 2014;383(9928):1549–60.
8. British Medical Association. Alcohol and pregnancy: preventing and managing fetal alcohol spectrum disorders. 2007.
9. AC Flynn, PT Seed, N Patel, S Barr, R Bell, AL Briley, et al. Dietary patterns in obese pregnant women; influence of a behavioral intervention of diet and physical activity in the UPBEAT randomized controlled trial. *Int J Behav Nutr Phys Activ.* 2016;13(1):124.
10. JM Dodd, D Turnbull, AJ McPhee, AR Deussen, RM Grivell, LN Yelland, et al. Antenatal lifestyle advice for women who are overweight or obese: LIMIT randomised trial. *BMJ.* 2014;348:g1285.
11. B Muktabhant, TA Lawrie, P Lumbiganon, M Laopaiboon. Diet or exercise, or both, for preventing excessive weight gain in pregnancy. *Cochrane Database Syst Rev.* 2015;(6):Cd007145.
12. D Devakumar, CH Fall, HS Sachdev, BM Margetts, C Osmond, JC Wells, et al. Maternal antenatal multiple micronutrient supplementation for long-term health benefits in children: a systematic review and meta-analysis. *BMC Med.* 2016;14:90.
13. GJ Cuskelly, H McNulty, JM Scott. Effect of increasing dietary folate on red-cell folate: implications for prevention of neural tube defects. *Lancet.* 1996;347(9002):657–9.
14. RD Potdar, SA Sahariah, M Gandhi, SH Kehoe, N Brown, H Sane, et al. Improving women's diet quality preconceptionally and during gestation: effects on birth weight and prevalence of low birth weight: a randomized controlled efficacy trial in India (Mumbai Maternal Nutrition Project). *Am J Clin Nutr.* 2014;100(5):1257–68.
15. D Aune, OD Saugstad, T Henriksen, S Tonstad. Physical activity and the risk of preeclampsia: a systematic review and meta-analysis. *Epidemiol.* 2014;25(3):331–43.
16. USAID, Strengthening Partnerships, Results, and Innovations in Nutrition Globally (SPRING). Nutrition of adolescent girls and women of reproductive age in low- and middle-income countries: current context and scientific basis for moving forward. 2015.
17. J Stephenson, N Heslehurst, J Hall, DAJM Schoenaker, J Hutchinson, JE Cade, et al. Before the beginning: nutrition and lifestyle in the preconception period and its importance for future health. *Lancet.* 2018;391(10132):1830–41.
18. Y Ben-Shlomo, D Kuh. A life course approach to chronic disease epidemiology: conceptual models, empirical challenges and interdisciplinary perspectives. *Int J Epidemiol.* 2002;31(2):285–93.
19. E Spry, CA Olsson, SJC Hearps, S Aarsman, JB Carlin, LM Howard, et al.

The Victorian Intergenerational Health Cohort Study (VIHCS): study design of a preconception cohort from parent adolescence to offspring childhood. *Paediatr Perinat Epidemiol.* 2020;34(1):86–98.

20. G Barrett, J Shawe, B Howden, D Patel, O Ojukwu, P Pandya, et al. Why do women invest in pre-pregnancy health and care? A qualitative investigation with women attending maternity services. *BMC Pregnancy Childbirth.* 2015;15(1).

21. RG Potter, MP Parker. Predicting the time required to conceive. *Pop Stud.* 1964;18(1):99–116.

22. G Sedgh, S Singh, R Hussain. Intended and unintended pregnancies worldwide in 2012 and recent trends. *Stud Fam Plann.* 2014;45(3):301–14.

23. KS Hall, JR Steinberg, CA Cwiak, RH Allen, SM Marcus. Contraception and mental health: a commentary on the evidence and principles for practice. *Am J Obstet Gynecol.* 2015;212(6):740–6.

24. C Dolman, I Jones, LM Howard. Pre-conception to parenting: a systematic review and meta-synthesis of the qualitative literature on motherhood for women with severe mental illness. *Arch Women Ment Health.* 2013;16(3):173–96.

25. LS Cohen, LL Altshuler, BL Harlow, R Nonacs, DJ Newport, AC Viguera, et al. Relapse of major depression during pregnancy in women who maintain or discontinue antidepressant treatment. *JAMA.* 2006;295(5):499–507.

26. AC Viguera, L Tondo, AE Koukopoulos, D Reginaldi, B Lepri, RJ Baldessarini. Episodes of mood disorders in 2,252 pregnancies and postpartum periods. *Am J Psychiatry.* 2011;168(11):1179–85.

27. CL Taylor, LM van Ravesteyn, MP van denBerg, RJ Stewart, LM Howard. The prevalence and correlates of self-harm in pregnant women with psychotic disorder and bipolar disorder. *Arch Womens Ment Health.* 2016;19(5):909–15.

28. A Stein, RM Pearson, SH Goodman, E Rapa, A Rahman, M McCallum, et al. Effects of perinatal mental disorders on the fetus and child. *Lancet.* 2014;384(9956):1800–19.

29. AV Jablensky, V Morgan, SR Zubrick, C Bower, LA Yellachich. Pregnancy, delivery, and neonatal complications in a population cohort of women with schizophrenia and major affective disorders. *Am J Psychiatry.* 2005;162(1):79–91.

30. A Easter, J Sandall, LM Howard. Obstetric near misses among women with serious mental illness: data linkage cohort study. *Br J Psychiatry.* 2021:1–7.

31. AA Mitchell, SM Gilboa, MM Werler, KE Kelley, C Louik, S Hernández-Díaz. Medication use during pregnancy, with particular focus on prescription drugs: 1976–2008. *Am J Obstet Gynecol.* 2011;205(1):51.e1–8.

32. DD Glover, M Amonkar, BF Rybeck, TS Tracy. Prescription, over-the-counter, and herbal medicine use in a rural, obstetric population. *Am J Obstet Gynecol.* 2003;188(4):1039–45.

33. FG Cunningham, KJ Leveno, SL Bloom, JC Hauth, D Rouse, C Spong. *Williams obstetrics.* New York: McGraw-Hill; 2018.

34. VK Burt, R Suri, L Altshuler, Z Stowe, VC Hendrick, E Muntean. The use of psychotropic medications during breast-feeding. *Am J Psychiatry.* 2001;158(7):1001–9.

35. J Rampono, LP Hackett, JH Kristensen, R Kohan, M Page-Sharp, KF Ilett. Transfer of escitalopram and its metabolite demethylescitalopram into breastmilk. *Br J Clin Pharmacol.* 2006;62(3):316–22.

36. P Bennett, A Astrup-Jensen, CJ Bates, EJ Begg, S Edwards, C Lazarus, et al. *Drugs and human lactation.* Amsterdam: Elsevier; 1996.

37. CG Victora, R Bahl, AJ Barros, GV Franca, S Horton, J Krasevec, et al. Breastfeeding in the 21st century: epidemiology, mechanisms, and lifelong effect. *Lancet.* 2016;387(10017):475–90.

38. MS Kramer, B Chalmers, ED Hodnett, Z Sevkovskaya, I Dzikovich, S Shapiro, et al. Promotion of Breastfeeding Intervention Trial (PROBIT): a randomized trial in the

Republic of Belarus. *JAMA.* 2001;285(4):413–20.

39. V Glover, TG O'Connor, K O'Donnell. Prenatal stress and the programming of the HPA axis. *Neurosci Biobehav Rev.* 2010;35(1):17–22.
40. CA Sandman, EP Davis, C Buss, LM Glynn. Exposure to prenatal psychobiological stress exerts programming influences on the mother and her fetus. *Neuroendocrinol.* 2012;95(1):7–21.
41. B Beebe, J Jaffe, S Markese, K Buck, H Chen, P Cohen, et al. The origins of 12-month attachment: a microanalysis of 4-month mother-infant interaction. *Attach Hum Dev.* 2010;12(1–2):3–141.
42. E Meins, C Fernyhough, E Fradley, M Tuckey. Rethinking maternal sensitivity: mothers' comments on infants' mental processes predict security of attachment at 12 months. *J Child Psychol Psychiatry.* 2001;42(5):637–48.
43. A Slade, J Grienenberger, E Bernbach, D Levy, A Locker. Maternal reflective functioning, attachment, and the transmission gap: a preliminary study. *Attach Hum Dev.* 2005;7(3): 283–98.
44. K Barnicot, E Stevens, F Robinson, S Labovitch, R Ballman, M Miele, et al. Feasibility and acceptability of the video feedback intervention for positive parenting adapted for young babies of mothers experiencing perinatal mental health difficulties. *J Reprod Infant Psychol.* 2024;1–17.
45. S Rowlands, R Holdsworth, A Sowemimo. How to recognise and respond to reproductive coercion. *BMJ.* 2022;378:e069043.
46. K Olajide, J Munjiza, P Moran, L O'Connell, G Newton-Howes, P Bassett, et al. Development and psychometric properties of the Standardized Assessment of Severity of Personality Disorder (SASPD). *J Pers Disord.* 2018;32(1):44–56.
47. JR Vittengl, RB Jarrett, E Weitz, SD Hollon, J Twisk, I Cristea, et al. Divergent outcomes in cognitive-behavioral therapy and pharmacotherapy for adult depression. *Am J Psychiatry.* 2016;173(5):481–90.
48. JR Geddes, DJ Miklowitz. Treatment of bipolar disorder. *Lancet.* 2013;381(9878):1672–82.
49. W Mansell, S Tai, A Clark, S Akgonul, G Dunn, L Davies, et al. A novel cognitive behaviour therapy for bipolar disorders (Think Effectively About Mood Swings or TEAMS): study protocol for a randomized controlled trial. *Trials.* 2014;15(1):405.
50. TL Lewis, JC Wyatt. mHealth and mobile medical apps: a framework to assess risk and promote safer use. *J Med Internet Res.* 2014;16(9):e210.

Chapter 25

Pre-birth Planning

Lucinda Green

Introduction

Guidelines and enquiries [1, 2, 3, 4, 5, 6, 7, 8, 9] repeatedly highlight the potential risks for pregnant women who have a current or previous history of severe mental illness (see chapters 11, 21 and 33) and the importance of early identification, preventative care planning, multi-agency working and good communication to ensure these women and families have the best possible outcomes. The National Institute for Health and Care Excellence (NICE) guidelines for antenatal and postnatal mental health [1], Scottish Intercollegiate Guidelines Network (SIGN) perinatal mental health conditions guideline [2] and the Royal College of Psychiatrists' standards for community perinatal mental health services [3] specifically recommend that these women should have a written care plan covering pregnancy, birth and the postnatal period. This should be recorded in the woman's maternity, primary care and mental health records and a copy given to the woman and all involved professionals.

There are usually many different professionals involved in the care of pregnant women with a diagnosis of a severe mental illness. It is important that each woman can be confident that all these professionals have a shared understanding of her and her family, including the concerns, strengths and potential risks. It is essential that all the professionals work in partnership with the woman, her family and with each other so that there is an agreed plan for the woman's care and clarity about the roles of the professionals involved. Having a pre-birth planning meeting facilitates this information sharing and the collaborative development of an individualised plan covering all aspects of the woman's care throughout the perinatal period.

This chapter provides information about how to organise a pre-birth planning meeting and how to develop a perinatal mental healthcare plan.

What Is a Pre-birth Planning Meeting?

A pre-birth planning meeting is a multidisciplinary meeting which brings together a pregnant woman, her partner and/or other close relatives, and all the professionals involved in her care. The meeting is usually held between 30 and 32 weeks' gestation.

The meeting provides an opportunity to share information relevant to the individual woman's mental healthcare and treatment. This should include current and historical concerns and risks as well as information about the woman and family's strengths and

This chapter is based on the content of the Pan London Perinatal Mental Health Network Best Practice Toolkit for Pre-Birth Planning – with permission.

the available support. The information discussed is used to inform the perinatal mental healthcare plan, which is devised and agreed collaboratively by all those present at the pre-birth planning meeting.

The perinatal mental healthcare plan highlights the key concerns, risks and strengths and outlines the plan for the woman's care during the remainder of her pregnancy, her maternity admission for the birth of her baby and for the early postnatal period. It should include contact details for all the involved professionals and a crisis plan so that the woman and her family know how they can access urgent assessment should this be needed.

A document summarising the discussions held at the pre-birth planning meeting and the perinatal mental healthcare plan should be sent to the woman and all those invited to the meeting (including those who may have been unable to attend) and filed in her maternity, mental health and primary care medical records. An example template from the Pan London Perinatal Mental Health Network's perinatal mental health pre-birth planning toolkit [10] is shown in Figure 25.1.

Organising the Meeting

Pre-birth planning meetings should usually be organised and led by a clinician from the perinatal mental health service. For areas without a perinatal mental health service, the community mental health team or specialist mental health midwife may organise and lead the meeting.

A pre-birth planning meeting is essential when a woman has a current or previous serious mental illness including bipolar disorder, schizophrenia, schizoaffective disorder, any other psychotic illness and severe depression with a significant impact on the woman's daily functioning. It can also be useful for women with other diagnoses where there are also multiple risk factors or complexities involved such as substance misuse, child protection concerns, poor engagement with services, personality disorder, complex social difficulties, forensic history, physical health problems or obstetric complications.

The psychiatrist, or other professional, who is organising the pre-birth planning meeting should explain the purpose of the meeting to the pregnant woman and discuss how this can help to ensure she and her family have the care they need. She should also be given written information about pre-birth planning meetings. There should be a discussion with her about who needs to be invited to the meeting. It is important to invite the woman's partner or other relatives who will be supporting her after her baby is born. They need to understand the risk of postnatal mental illness and to know how to contact professionals if there are any concerns.

If a woman does not want to attend or declines to have a pre-birth planning meeting, the reasons for this should be explored with her. All attempts should be made to accommodate her concerns and enable her to attend. For example, if she finds large meetings difficult it may be agreed that fewer professionals will attend and information can be gathered from the others prior to the meeting. If the woman is concerned about distressing historical information being discussed she may prefer professionals to meet for a short time to share this information before she joins the meeting. Every effort should be made to involve the woman in decisions about her care, but it is still essential that a perinatal mental healthcare plan is agreed, even if the woman chooses not to be involved in devising this. In a small number of cases a professionals' meeting will be needed if a

Name:	DOB:	
Address:	Tel:	
NHS No:		
Date of meeting:		
Professionals involved:	**Contact details**	**Attended meeting? Yes/no**
Community midwife		
Consultant Obstetrician		
Specialist mental health midwife		
Health Visitor		
GP		
Consultant Perinatal Psychiatrist		
Perinatal Mental Health Nurse		
Community Mental Health Team – Consultant Psychiatrist		
Community Mental Health Team – care co-ordinator		
Social Worker		
Other		

Partner, family or friends who can be contacted		
Name	**Relationship**	**Contact number**
Details of anyone who should not be contacted		
Pregnancy		
Estimated Delivery Date: **Maternity Service:**		
Mental Health		
Diagnosis: **Mental Health History:**		

Figure 25.1 Template for recording the pre-birth planning meeting and perinatal mental healthcare plan [9].

Relapse Indicators
Risk of Postnatal Mental Illness
Risk
To self: **To others:** **From others:**
Current Psychiatric Medication
Current sources of stress
Other children
Number of children:
Support
Partner: **Family support:** **Other:**
Safeguarding concerns
Previous concerns: **Current concerns:** *State if there is a current Child in Need or Child Protection Plan and/or a separate Safeguarding Plan which professionals should refer to* **Plan:**
Contraception
Plans for contraception:
Other

Figure 25.1 (*cont.*)

PERINATAL MENTAL HEALTH CARE PLAN	
ANTENATAL	
MATERNITY ADMISSION FOR BIRTH	
POSTNATAL	
CRISIS PLAN What helps in a crisis? Let……….know how I'm feeling Contact: • Community mental health team – number – opening hours • Perinatal Mental Health Team – number – opening hours • 24 hour support line • Crisis team Attend A&E If admission is needed this should be to a psychiatric Mother & Baby Unit (*unless exclusion criteria apply).* The nearest MBU is….. contact details. If no MBU bed is available…..	
Minutes written by:	Date:
If you or any of the professionals involved in your care have any questions about this information or the plan please contact our team administrator on……	

Figure 25.1 (*cont.*)

Box 25.1 List of People to Be Invited to the Pre-birth Planning Meeting

- The pregnant woman
- Her partner or other family member or friend
- Community midwife
- Specialist mental health midwife
- Health visitor
- Obstetrician
- Primary care physician

The other professionals involved in the woman's care will vary but the following should be invited if involved:

- Consultant perinatal psychiatrist
- Specialist perinatal mental health nurse
- Other perinatal mental health professionals, such as psychologist, occupational therapist
- Care coordinator (community mental health team)
- Consultant psychiatrist (community mental health team)
- Psychologist/psychotherapist
- Maternity safeguarding lead
- Children and families' social worker
- Neonatologist
- Substance misuse service worker
- Specialist services such as eating disorders, learning disabilities, personality disorder service
- Other agencies such as domestic violence services, voluntary organisations
- Independent advocate
- Interpreter (sometimes the interpreter may be needed for a partner or carer rather than for the pregnant woman)

woman is not engaging with services. If it is not possible to have a meeting with the woman, or to bring the professionals together, then a plan should be written by one of the clinicians in the perinatal mental health team and shared with the woman (unless there are risks that mean this is not appropriate) and all the involved professionals.

It is important to ensure the meeting is held at an accessible location. The timing of the meeting should take into account the needs of the family. For example, if the woman has older children the meeting needs to be held within school hours. The venue should be child friendly for women who need to bring young children. It is important to consider the age of the children and whether it is appropriate for them to hear discussion about some potentially distressing issues.

Written invitations should be sent to everyone invited to the meeting. The list of people to be invited will vary according to the individual woman's needs. Box 25.1 provides a list of people who might be invited.

Information to Be Discussed, Shared and Clarified at the Pre-birth Planning Meeting

In order to decide what should be included in an individual woman's perinatal mental healthcare plan it is important to discuss relevant information about her mental health history, treatment and any risk concerns, her obstetric history and current pregnancy and other relevant information. This ensures that everyone involved has a shared understanding of the key concerns and risks as well as the woman and family's strengths. Usually, all the professionals will have seen the woman for an assessment, and in some cases for care and treatment, but they may hold different information. Some professionals, for example the health visitor, may be meeting the woman for the first time at the pre-birth planning meeting. If a woman has only recently moved to the area, if her mental health problems have developed during pregnancy or have not been identified as early as they could be, it may be that assessments have not been completed prior to the pre-birth planning meeting.

The following should be discussed at the meeting:

1. **Current pregnancy and obstetric history**

   It is important to identify any relevant previous obstetric history which may impact on the current pregnancy and any risk of obstetric complications. It is helpful to understand whether this was a planned or unplanned pregnancy and how the woman feels about her pregnancy and unborn baby. It is important to clarify where she plans to deliver. Every effort should be made to accommodate the woman's wishes. For example, if she wants a home birth or a delivery on a midwife-led birth unit her mental health history and treatment should not be a barrier to this unless there is a good reason why she needs to deliver in a hospital birth centre.

   It is important to clarify whether the woman has attended, or booked, antenatal classes. Some women may find attending an antenatal class with other women difficult and may need one-to-one antenatal education which a specialist mental health midwife may be able to offer. It is also essential to identify anything which may make labour particularly difficult. For example, for a woman who has a history of sexual abuse, vaginal examinations or birth may have the potential to trigger flashbacks. A woman with obsessive compulsive disorder who has obsessional thoughts about the risk of contamination may find hospital environments challenging. For these women there will need to be an individualised plan identifying what will help to make her feel safer during labour.

   The pre-birth planning meeting provides an opportunity to check whether the woman has started to think about the practical preparations for the birth of her baby and whether she will be able to obtain baby clothes and equipment that she will need. For some women with limited finances it may be that charitable funding is needed to enable to her purchase some of these items.

2. **Mental health history**

   In order that all the involved professionals understand the woman's mental health history and how she is affected during episodes of illness, a summary of her mental health history including her diagnosis, typical symptoms, the pattern of illness, any previous postnatal episodes and any previous need for hospital admission should be shared. It is important that there is an understanding of previous triggers for relapse, for example sleep deprivation or stressful life events. Her usual level of functioning when she is well and the impact of her illness on her daily functioning and self-care should be clarified. This may have implications for her ability to safely care for her baby if she becomes unwell. Other factors such as engagement with services, adherence to treatment and any drug or alcohol misuse are also essential to understand.

3. **Risk**
   Any risk history, however long ago the incidents occurred, should be discussed. For example, a woman who has been well for many years may have had a history of significant self-neglect and serious suicide attempts during previous episodes of illness. Her partner may not have known her when she was unwell and needs to know about these risks. Professionals visiting in the postnatal period also need to understand this history in order to ask about these issues and to take any depressive symptoms and suicidal thoughts seriously. Any risk of harm to others, particularly if there may be a risk to the unborn baby and/or other children needs to be highlighted (see below).

   It is essential to identify any risk from others. Domestic abuse is more common in pregnancy and in women with mental health problems [11].
4. **Relapse indicators**
   The woman, her partner and family and all the involved professionals need to be able to recognise early signs of relapse. Identifying relapse indicators will help to ensure that if the woman does become unwell this can be identified promptly so she can get the care and treatment she needs as early as possible.
5. **Current mental health**
   At the pre-birth planning meeting the woman's current symptoms and the impact these have on her functioning should be clarified. Any changes needed to her treatment should be discussed and implemented. For women who are psychiatric inpatients at the time of the pre-birth planning meeting, careful consideration should be given to the care the woman will need prior to the birth of her baby. Women who have a history of poor engagement with services and poor adherence to treatment should not be discharged too early without a clear plan to ensure there is no risk of a further deterioration in her mental health prior to the birth of her baby.
6. **Risk of postpartum relapse and plan to address this**
   It is essential that everyone at the pre-birth planning meeting understands the woman's risk of postpartum psychosis, postnatal depression or other postnatal mental illness. This may be the first time that professionals have had an opportunity to discuss this with the woman's partner or relatives. They may need to be given written information about the relevant disorders. In the case of postpartum psychosis they need to understand when the risk is highest, and that urgent psychiatric assessment is essential if the woman has any possible symptoms. Family members need to know how they can contact services if they have any concerns the woman is becoming unwell. If the woman lives alone, there needs to be a discussion about whether her partner, a family member or friend can stay with her in the early postnatal period, or whether she can stay with them so that any signs of relapse can be identified promptly. Other options, such as involving the home treatment team, can be considered. Family and professionals need to be informed about the care available if the woman does become unwell and how to access this, particularly if Mother and Baby Unit admission may be needed.
7. **Medication**
   The woman's current medication should be discussed and reviewed. Any plans to change or start medication during the remainder of her pregnancy or immediately after birth should be highlighted. The woman, her partner, relatives or the

professionals may have questions about the risks and benefits of using medication in pregnancy and breastfeeding which should be answered. There needs to be a clear plan to ensures doses can be changed if the woman's mental health deteriorates, or if medication levels (e.g. lithium) indicate dose changes are needed.

It is essential to clarify whether the woman needs to bring her own medication into hospital when she is admitted for the birth of her baby. There is also a need to be clear about who will write up the medication on the woman's drug chart and how medication will be administered on the maternity unit. It is good practice for women's medication to be prescribed rather than for women to self-medicate. Where there are concerns about adherence to medication there will need to be a plan to address this. Other issues that maternity staff need to know about include any investigations needed, for example blood tests for lithium levels, and routine investigations for women who are planning to start an antipsychotic on the postnatal ward to reduce the risk of postpartum psychosis.

Midwives and neonatologists need to be informed of any potential concerns for the baby, for example a risk of neonatal adaptation syndrome.

8. **Feeding**

   The woman should be asked about her preference for breast, bottle or mixed feeding. It is important that she, her partner and family understand how feeding methods may impact on her mental health. For example, when sleep deprivation may precipitate a relapse, staying awake to breastfeed during the night may increase the woman's risk of becoming unwell. For some women medication (e.g. lithium or clozapine) will mean that breastfeeding is not advised. It is important that professionals caring for the woman during her maternity admission and at home understand and respect the woman's decision about feeding. It is not helpful for a woman who has made a difficult but considered decision not to breastfeed to be told that breastfeeding is best for babies. It is equally unhelpful, if a woman has made a decision to breastfeed, or to mixed feed, having carefully weighed up the risks and benefits of taking medication, to be told that this medication is not safe in breastfeeding. This can sometimes happen when women are seen by junior obstetricians or neonatologists on the postnatal ward.

   It is helpful to have a discussion with women and families about breastfeeding. If a woman is keen to breastfeed it is helpful to acknowledge the benefits of breastfeeding for babies but also that for some women exclusively breastfeeding, or mixed feeding, can become a source of stress which can have an adverse impact on their mental health. Midwives and health visitors can tell women about the help and support that will be available to support breastfeeding if women find this difficult.

9. **Current sources of stress**

   For many women difficulties such as housing, finances and immigration issues can be a significant source of stress. Professionals should identify how they can support women and families to resolve any factors which may affect their mental health or ability to care for their baby as far as possible.

10. **Other children**

    The needs of other children in the family should be considered. It is important that the woman knows who can look after her other children while she is in hospital for the birth of her baby.

11. **Child safeguarding concerns**
    In the majority of cases where there are child safeguarding concerns these will have been identified prior to the pre-birth planning meeting and a social worker will have been allocated and invited to the meeting. Sometimes child safeguarding concerns may only be identified based on information discussed at the pre-birth planning meeting.

    Not all professionals have a good understanding of how mental illness can affect a woman's ability to care for her children. Assumptions should not be made based on a diagnosis. The discussion at the pre-birth planning meeting should help professionals to understand any concerns in this individual woman's case. If there are concerns it is important to clarify whether these are only relevant during episodes of illness, or whether there are also potential concerns about children's well-being even when the woman is at her best. Some women can still care for children well despite a high level of symptoms. For others there may be a risk of unintentional neglect or other harm during episodes of illness. In many cases family members may be available to support or take over the majority of care for children whilst a woman is very unwell. Many women and families are worried that their child or children will be removed from their care if they are unwell. It is important to acknowledge this fear and to reassure women and families where appropriate.

    When there are serious child safeguarding concerns the pre-birth planning meeting provides an opportunity to clarify current plans and progress. Cases may need to be escalated if there needs to be a child protection conference or legal planning meeting but no date has been set. In the relatively small number of cases where there is a potential for a formal parenting assessment to be needed, or for a baby to be removed from a woman's care at birth, the pre-birth plan needs to take account of the various possible outcomes.
12. **Adult safeguarding concerns**
    As with child safeguarding concerns any adult safeguarding concerns need to be identified and relevant referrals and plans made in relation to these.
13. **Family, culture and support**
    The pre-birth planning meeting provides an opportunity to clarify any relevant issues regarding the partner and family, whether these are positive factors about helpful and supportive relationships or concerns about difficult family dynamics, negative attitudes to mental health or other factors which increase concern or risk. It is also important to identify and clarify any culturally important factors relating to pregnancy, birth, parenting or mental illness. Professionals should not make any assumptions about the amount of practical support partners and family members can provide and this should be clarified at the meeting. A woman's partner or parents may have work commitments which limit what they can offer in terms of support with night feeds and care of the baby and children during the day. Elderly parents may have good intentions but can be limited by their own physical health problems. Starting to think about the help and support a woman needs at the pre-birth planning meeting allows families time to come up with solutions.

    The partner's needs should always be considered in terms of their role as carer, their own mental health needs and the transition to parenthood.

It is also a good time to discuss peer support from charities such as Action on Postpartum Psychosis or Maternal OCD, third-sector services such as HomeStart and Family Action, mother and baby groups in local children's centres and other local sources of support.

14. **Professionals and roles**
    The roles and responsibilities of all the involved professionals should be clarified. Joint working and coordination of appointments and visits should be agreed. For example, it is helpful if one professional can organise a rota for postnatal visits to ensure that visits are spread out across the week. It is important to consider the balance between having enough visits in the postnatal period to provide the woman with the advice and support she needs and to identify any signs of relapse promptly, and not overwhelming the family with too many professionals.

    Some women move to a different area in late pregnancy, or plan to stay with family for a few weeks or months in the postnatal period. In that case appropriate handover needs to be organised to local maternity, perinatal mental health and other services.
15. **Contraception**
    Rates of unplanned pregnancy are even higher for women with severe mental illness than for the general population [12]. It helps to discuss the woman's plans for contraception after birth at an early stage and to encourage her to seek information and advice if needed. Long-acting reversible contraception can sometimes be organised before discharge from the postnatal ward.

Perinatal Mental Healthcare Plan

The information from the discussion is used to inform the woman's perinatal mental healthcare plan which everyone at the pre-birth planning meeting can contribute to and devise collaboratively. The following sections outline what might be included in each section of the perinatal mental healthcare plan depending on the individual woman's needs.

Antenatal

Plan for the Remainder of the Pregnancy

1. **Antenatal care**
2. **Antenatal classes**
3. **Frequency of contact with professionals**
4. **Psychiatric medication**
5. **Psychological intervention**
6. **Information to be sent to the woman, her partner or family.** This may include information about perinatal mental health problems, treatments and sources of support.
7. **Referrals to other services.** Examples include eating disorder services or third-sector services. Referral to maternity, mental health and health visiting services in another area may be needed if the woman plans to stay with family, or to move, before or immediately after the birth.
8. **Information sharing.** If it is possible the woman may deliver at a unit other than where she is booked, the maternity service, liaison psychiatry or perinatal mental

health service in the relevant maternity unit should be informed about concerns, risks and the plan for her care.

9. **Additional information needed or aspects of the postnatal plan to be clarified.** It may not be possible to finalise all the details of the plan for the woman's care at the time of her pre-birth planning meeting. An example of information that may need to be clarified is the plan for the care of other children when the woman is admitted for the birth of her baby. The family may need more time to consider who can stay with the woman in the first few weeks after birth when she has a high risk of relapse. Children's social care may not have finalised plans for a parenting assessment.

Maternity Admission for the Birth

This part of the plan should cover the woman's care during maternity admission for delivery. A small number of women will plan a home birth and, in that case, a similar plan will be made for labour and the first 24 hours at home.

1. **How will the woman get to hospital when she is in labour?**
2. **Who will be looking after her other children during her maternity admission?**
3. **Which professionals should be informed that she has been admitted** in labour, or for a planned induction of labour or caesarean section? This might include the perinatal mental health team, specialist mental health midwife, safeguarding midwife, children's social worker and/or care coordinator.
4. **Any specific needs during labour.** It is important to clarify whether the woman hopes to deliver in a midwife-led unit or labour ward, but also to note that this may change depending on obstetric factors. Women with a history of sexual abuse may request female-only staff. Maternity staff may need to be informed about specific symptoms, such as flashbacks in post-traumatic stress disorder, or obsessional thoughts in obsessive-compulsive disorder and what triggers and helps these. There may be instructions in relation to medication, for example a plan to stop lithium at the onset of labour and to ensure good hydration. Medication may need to be prescribed in case of acute behavioural disturbance. The woman can still make a birth plan with her midwife with more detail about her plans for the birth including pain relief.
5. **Care and support on the postnatal ward immediately after birth.** Some women, for example those with a diagnosis of bipolar disorder, may have an increased risk of relapse if they are sleep deprived [13]. For these women having an individual room on the postnatal ward to provide a calm environment and allow her to have as much sleep and rest as possible can be helpful. The woman's partner, or a family member, may need to stay on the postnatal ward with her to support her in caring for her baby. For a small number of women one-to-one supervision may be needed due to concerns about the woman's current mental health (e.g. women who are psychiatric inpatients) or due to significant safeguarding concerns. The plan needs to state the member of staff who may be needed, for example a registered mental health nurse, maternity support worker or healthcare assistant. It is also important to clarify whether the maternity or mental staff will organise this.
6. **Psychiatric medication.** It helps maternity staff to know what medication the woman should take before, during and after labour. The dose may need to change or a new medication may be started. The woman should be advised whether she should bring her medication to hospital with her or whether this can be prescribed during her

admission. Potential additional medication that may be needed, such as lorazepam, should be included in the plan. Any investigations the woman might need, such as an ECG or blood tests if she is starting an antipsychotic postnatally, should be specified.

7. **Feeding.** The woman's preference for breast, bottle or mixed feeding should be stated in the plan. It should be clear what advice has been given regarding the safety of medication in breastfeeding. It is important that maternity staff know to support the woman to feed her baby in the way she has chosen.
8. **Neonatology review.** If a woman is prescribed psychiatric medication the neonatology team should be informed of this and her baby should be seen for a neonatal check within the first 24 hours after birth [14]. The woman should be given written information from the clinician completing the newborn examination informing her of symptoms to be aware of and how she can ensure her baby is reviewed if there are any concerns.
9. **Psychiatric review.** It is important to state in the perinatal mental healthcare plan whether or not the woman needs a review of her mental health before she is discharged from the maternity unit. If a psychiatric review is needed it should be clear who should see her during and outside normal working hours. This may be the perinatal mental health team, liaison psychiatry team or the care coordinator. It should be made clear whether review is essential or only needed if there are concerns about the woman's mental health at the time.
10. **Urgent concerns.** The plan needs to include details of who maternity staff can contact if there are urgent concerns about the woman's mental health during labour or the remainder of her maternity admission. This may be the perinatal mental health or liaison psychiatry team. Contact numbers should be included. Advice for maternity staff, for example to move the woman to an individual room with one-to-one care, or to give lorazepam or other medication, is also helpful.
11. **Informing professionals that the woman has given birth and when she will be discharged.** The plan should clearly state which professionals need to be informed that the woman is being discharged. This may include the health visitor, perinatal mental health professionals, care coordinator and social worker. If the woman is staying with relatives in a different area from where she lives, it is essential to ensure that professionals in that area are informed.
12. **Discharge planning.** It helps to state whether a discharge meeting is needed on the postnatal ward before the woman goes home with her baby. This should not usually be necessary if a pre-birth planning meeting has been held. However, if there are likely to be significant changes in her circumstances between the time of the pre-birth planning meeting and the birth, a discharge meeting may be needed. The social worker may request a discharge planning meeting if the baby is the subject of a child protection plan or if there are planned care proceedings. If it is likely the woman may need a psychiatric admission it should be clear what the plans are and whether this will be to a Mother and Baby Unit.

Postnatal Period

This is the plan for the first 6–8 weeks after birth.

1. **Professionals visits.** The professionals who will visit the woman at home after birth and the frequency of visits should be clear. These may include the midwives, health

visitor, perinatal mental health professionals, community mental health team care coordinator, children's social worker and home treatment team. It is helpful to identify a professional who can coordinate visits so these are spread throughout the week.

2. **Support from family.** Specific help and support can be included in the plan. The woman's partner or relatives may help with night feeds, cooking or taking older children to school. The woman may need support to develop confidence in caring for her baby.
3. **Medication.** The woman's medication, any dose changes and any monitoring should be clearly stated.
4. **Psychological interventions.** These may be ongoing or new interventions.
5. **Supporting the woman to care for her baby.** This can include support at home from relatives and local postnatal support in children's centres. Referrals to third-sector agencies may be helpful.
6. **Physical health.** The woman should be informed about how she can access physical healthcare, for example by seeing her primary care physician or attending maternity triage. She may have a planned health check, for example the standard 6-week postnatal check.
7. **Crisis plan: What to do if there are signs/symptoms of relapse.** The woman and her family should be advised to ask for help if there are any concerns. The plan should include contact numbers for crisis services. The crisis plan should include options for admission, for example to a Mother and Baby Unit and how this can be accessed.
8. **Contraception.** This is an essential part of the plan to reduce the chance of an unplanned pregnancy. It should be clear who the woman needs to see in order to organise contraception and to ensure this is arranged as soon as possible after the birth of her baby.
9. **Review care plan.** It is sometimes useful for the professionals to meet with the woman and her family to review the care plan at 6–8 weeks postnatal.

The discussion and plan should be documented. Copies should be sent to the woman and all those invited to the meeting (including professionals unable to attend). The plan should be recorded in all versions of the woman's notes including her maternity, mental health and primary care notes. A copy should be sent to the neonatologist when the woman has taken psychiatric medication during pregnancy. Some maternity services have systems, such as an alert on the electronic records, or a printed plan on coloured paper, to ensure that professionals are aware that there is a perinatal mental healthcare plan.

References

1. National Institute for Health and Care Excellence. Antenatal and postnatal mental health: clinical management and service guidance. Clinical Guideline (CG192). 2014. www.nice.org.uk/guidance/cg192
2. Scottish Intercollegiate Guidelines Network (SIGN). Perinatal mental health conditions. SIGN publication no. 169. 2023. www.sign.ac.uk
3. Royal College of Psychiatrists. Standards for community perinatal mental health services. 6th edition. 2023. https://tinyurl.com/4rdh3wam
4. Royal College of Obstetricians & Gynaecologists. Management of women with mental health issues during pregnancy and the postnatal period. Good

Practice No. 14. 2011. https://tinyurl.com/3zpu3zh8

5. G Lewis, editor. *Confidential Enquiries into Maternal and Child Health. Why Mothers Die. The Sixth Report of the United Kingdom Confidential Enquiries into Maternal Deaths in the United Kingdom.* London: RCOG Press; 2004. www.cemach.org.uk
6. MR Oates, R Cantwell. Deaths from psychiatric causes. In: G Lewis, editor. Saving Mothers' Lives: reviewing maternal deaths to make motherhood safer: 2006–08. The Eighth Report on Confidential Enquiries into Maternal Deaths in the United Kingdom. *BJOG.* 2011;118 Suppl 1:1–203.
7. M Knight, D Tuffnell, S Kenyon, J Shakespeare, R Gray, JJ Kurinczuk, editors. on behalf of MBRRACE-UK. *Saving Lives, Improving Mothers' Care – Surveillance of maternal deaths in the UK 2011–13 and lessons learned to inform maternity care from the UK and Ireland Confidential Enquiries into Maternal Deaths and Morbidity 2009–13.* Oxford: National Perinatal Epidemiology Unit, University of Oxford. 2015.
8. M Knight, K Bunch, D Tuffnell, H Jayakody, J Shakespeare, R Kotnis, et al., editors, on behalf of MBRRACE-UK. *Saving Lives, Improving Mothers' Care – Lessons learned to inform maternity care from the UK and Ireland Confidential Enquiries into Maternal Deaths and Morbidity 2014–16.* Oxford: National Perinatal Epidemiology Unit, University of Oxford; 2018.
9. A Cairns, S Kenyon, R Patel, K Bunch, M Knight on behalf of the MBRRACE-UK mental health chapter-writing group. Improving mental health care and care for women with multiple adversity. In: M Knight, K Bunch, R Patel, J Shakespeare, R Kotnis, S Kenyon, JJ Kurinczuk, editors. *Saving Lives, Improving Mothers' Care Core Report – Lessons learned to inform maternity care from the UK and Ireland Confidential Enquiries into Maternal Deaths and Morbidity 2018–20.* Oxford: National Perinatal Epidemiology Unit, University of Oxford; 2022. p. 10–16.
10. Pan-London Perinatal Mental Health Networks. Pre-birth planning: best practice toolkit for perinatal mental health services. 2019. https://tinyurl.com/4xkm8heu
11. LM Howard, S Oram, H Galley, K Trevillion, G Feder. Domestic violence and perinatal mental disorders: a systematic review and metaanalysis. *PLoS Med.* 2013;10(5):e1001452.
12. L Green, S Elliott, L Anwar, E Best, M Tero, A Sarkar, et al. An audit of pregnant women with severe mental illness referred during the first 2 years of a new perinatal mental health service. *Arch Womens Ment Health.* 2008;11(2):149–58.
13. KJS Lewis, A Di Florio, L Forty, K Gordon-Smith, A Perry, N Craddock, et al. Mania triggered by sleep loss and risk of postpartum psychosis in women with bipolar disorder. *J Affect Disord.* 2018;225:624–9.
14. Pan-London Perinatal Mental Health Network and the London Neonatal Operational Delivery Network. Perinatal mental health: guidance for newborn assessment. 2017. www.londonneonatalnetwork.org.uk/wp-content/uploads/2016/10/FinalNeodoc-v3.pdf

Chapter 26

Principles of Prescribing

Liz McDonald

Introduction

We know that pregnancy is not protective against occurrence or recurrence of mental illness, and it is well recognised that women experience high rates (10–20%) of mental disorder in the perinatal period [1]. Moreover, it is known that women have a higher prevalence of certain psychiatric illnesses, are the largest users of psychotropic drugs (particularly antidepressants), have differential treatment responses and course of illness compared to men, and seek help from healthcare services differently [2]. Ethical and other significant challenges in recruitment to clinical trials in the perinatal period exist despite approximately 13% of pregnant women taking psychotropic medication [3]. Women are not a homogenous group, and individual personal factors (physiological, social, emotional, cultural, ethnicity) need to be considered when thinking of why, when and how to prescribe psychotropic medication before and during the perinatal period. These factors also need to have a bearing on how we discuss risk with and communicate information about medication to women to ensure that there is an individualised and compassionate approach to what can be a challenging task.

Talking with women in the pre-conception or perinatal periods about psychotropic medication is an essential, sometimes difficult, part of the work of the perinatal psychiatrist (see Chapter 27, 'The Reproductive Safety of Psychotropic Medication and Implications for Prescribing in the Perinatal Period'). Offering the woman pre-pregnancy advice, an opportunity to plan what interventions may be required (see Chapter 24, 'Pre-pregnancy Advice and Planning'), and the opportunity to engage with advance planning before or during pregnancy (see Chapter 39, 'Mental Health and Capacity Legislation in the Perinatal Period') are seen as optimal particularly if she is at risk of a severe episode of illness. Once the woman is pregnant, pre-birth planning meetings at 32 weeks' gestation are imperative to ensure that the woman, her family and all involved agencies are fully aware of any prescribed psychotropic medication, including its indications, risks and benefits (see Chapter 25, 'Pre-birth Planning').

Other disciplines within the perinatal mental health team will also have to respond to questions about medication, as this is an issue that considerably preoccupies women, who will seek reassurance and opinions from those around them. It is important therefore that all clinicians have an up-to-date understanding of the effectiveness of medication side-effect profile and safety within pregnancy and breastfeeding. Team members also need to know when to seek further advice and to be able to comfortably acknowledge uncertainty in discussions with women and families. While knowledge of individual drugs is essential, there is also a need to have an overview of the general principles of prescribing and how to advise women. A central tenet is that it should not be assumed that it is always better to stop medication and that decisions on continuing, stopping or changing medication in pregnancy should be made only after careful review of the *benefits and risks* to both mother and infant of doing so [4].

Pharmacology

In Europe, Australia and the Americas 80% of pregnant women use at least one medication during pregnancy [5]. In 1977, the US Food and Drug Administration recommended that women of childbearing age should be excluded from phase 1 and early phase 2 clinical trials. This was because of potential risks to the developing fetus and greater hormonal variability during the menstrual cycle causing additional complexity to study design and analysis [6]. This recommendation has limited our knowledge of the influence of sex and hormones as biological variables in prescribing for women, and contributed to recommended treatments and dosing strategies being based largely on data from male volunteers. In 1993, the US National Institute of Health policy made the inclusion of women and minorities in trials mandatory, but drugs already registered at that time were never retested in large female study populations [7].

Significant sex differences have been clearly documented in blood, immune system, liver, kidneys, stomach, gut, heart and brain. Such differences can impact pharmacokinetic and pharmacodynamic mechanisms and predict sex-specific adverse drug reactions in women.

In comparison to men, women have a less acidic stomach, which increases the absorption of weak acids but decreases that of weak bases. They have slower gastric and colonic emptying increasing absorption time. Levels of protein-transporter p-glycoprotein are two-fold lower in women of childbearing age, increasing absorption in the body and the brain, while decreasing renal excretion. Blood volume and blood protein fraction are lower, decreasing dilution and binding capacity. Women have more fat tissue, which can lead to stacking of lipophilic drugs. In the gut and liver, many cytochrome P450 (CYP) enzymes are influenced by oestrogens, which can lead to higher (for CYP3A4, and to a lesser degree for CYP2D6) or lower (for CYP1A2 and CYP2C19) metabolic activity in women of reproductive age [8]. Renal blood flow, glomerular filtration, tubular secretion and resorption are all lower in women [9]. These sex differences are numerous and sizeable – a 10–50% sex difference per mechanism – and can significantly affect the efficacy and tolerability of pharmacotherapy if women are prescribed similar doses to men. Women generally have a lower body weight and organ size and a higher percentage of body fat, which affects the absorption and distribution of drugs. The larger the volume of distribution, the more likely the drug will be found in body tissues [9].

For psychotropic drugs, sex differences in pharmacodynamics further contribute to inequalities in efficacy and tolerability. Dopamine release regulation and synaptic elimination are influenced by sex hormones and differ significantly between men and women [10]. Although less well studied, such sex differences in neurotransmitter trafficking are also described in the serotonergic, GABAergic and glutamatergic circuitry [11].

Many of the above mechanisms – such as increased or reduced activity of CYP enzymes or p-glycoprotein, gastric acid production, gastric and colonic emptying, and dopaminergic and serotonergic trafficking – are oestrogen-dependent. This means that changes in pharmacokinetics and pharmacodynamics occur over the phases of the menstrual cycle, affecting the efficacy and tolerability of psychotropic drugs. Robust changes in efficacy and safety occur when hormonal changes are large, such as during pregnancy and menopause. With menopause, pharmacokinetic and pharmacodynamic mechanisms may both reduce the bioavailability of drugs, inducing a dramatic reduction in their efficacy [7]. Currently, few drugs have different dosing recommendations for women (zolpidem being a notable exception), while there are over 100 commonly prescribed drugs with unequal pharmacokinetics between men and women [7]. This suggests that women are at high risk for both over- and under-dosing of many drugs across medical specialties.

There are sex differences in every major part of the brain. Sex hormones affect the brains of men and women differentially and there may be differences in how biological mechanisms underlie male and female responses to stress [12]. There have been few studies that adequately evaluate sex differences in neuropsychopharmacological research, despite clear sex differences in the epidemiology, presentation and clinical course of many psychiatric disorders. A review of the literature demonstrated that of 251 neuropsychopharmacology studies that included both sexes and considered sex as a biological variable, in subsequent analyses, 80% used methodologies that eliminated the effect of sex (e.g. by including sex as a covariate to control for its effect). Only 20% of the studies adequately evaluated sex differences either by testing for an interaction involving sex or by stratifying analyses by sex. Of these, 72% found statistically significant sex differences in at least one outcome. The majority of studies conducted noted sex differences for antidepressants (13 out of 16), antipsychotics (10 out of 12), sedative-hypnotics (6 out of 10) and stimulants (6 out of 10). Only two studies of mood stabilisers evaluated sex as a biological variant, with one noting a sex difference [13].

Women are more likely to use polypharmacy. In addition, compared to men, women have an almost doubled risk of exhibiting adverse drug reactions (ADRs) across all drug classes, and are significantly more likely to be hospitalised as a consequence. This disparity is pervasive with one paper reporting that, among 668 drugs of the 20 most frequent treatment regimens in the USA, 307 (46%) describe significant sex differences in ADRs [14].

Changes in Pregnancy

Alterations in the woman's physiology in pregnancy facilitate the development and growth of the placenta and fetus, but also affect both the pharmacodynamics and the pharmacokinetics of psychotropic medication. An understanding of pregnancy physiology (see Chapter 3, 'Physiological Changes in Pregnancy and Common Obstetric Medical Disorders') and, from that, gestation-specific pharmacology of different drugs, is necessary to achieve effective treatment and to minimise risk (see Chapter 27, 'The Reproductive Safety of Psychotropic Medication and Implications for Prescribing in the Perinatal Period').

The effect of a drug on a person (pharmacodynamics) is determined by the drug's concentration and duration at its sites of action. As these sites are relatively inaccessible, plasma levels of the drug act as proxies [15]. Plasma levels are determined by pharmacokinetics (the effect of the body on the drug), which in turn are influenced by the dose, mode and timing of drug intake, the time course of drug absorption, the volume of distribution (Vd) in the body, the bioavailability after liver metabolism and protein binding, and the rate of excretion.

Distribution describes the reversible transfer of a drug between different locations following its entry into the systemic circulation. Drugs that predominantly remain within the vascular system will have a Vd estimate close to plasma volume, whereas drugs that are not bound to any proteins in the body will have a Vd estimate close to total body water. Drugs that are highly bound to tissues, with a small proportion remaining in the intravascular space, will have a very high Vd.

Drug metabolism involves chemical modification of a drug through specialised enzymatic systems. Oxidative reactions are predominantly carried out by the cytochrome P450 (CYP) family of enzymes that differ in their substrate specificity. The effects of pregnancy on enzyme activity can also vary with maternal genotype. Enzyme activity varies with ethnicity, gender, age and certain disease states that are unrelated to pregnancy.

Changes in drug metabolism can have implications for drug dosages in pregnancy. For drugs with a narrow therapeutic window, an increased clearance during pregnancy can lead to sub-therapeutic concentrations and worsening disease control. Conversely, to avoid increased toxicity, drug doses may need to be adjusted in the postpartum period, when pregnancy-related metabolic enzyme activity changes resolve. Renal drug excretion depends on glomerular filtration rate (GFR), tubular secretion, and reabsorption. Table 26.1 indicates some of the metabolic and physiological changes in pregnancy and potential effects on medication [16].

Concerns about fetal safety have historically limited prescribing during pregnancy and drug studies during pregnancy, despite pregnant women requiring medications for a range of disorders while pregnant. Much evidence on psychotropic medication in the perinatal period has been garnered from observational data which can be variable in quality. Failure to adequately adjust for confounders can lead to misleading associations between medication and adverse perinatal outcomes. For example, comorbid risk factors such as obesity and substance misuse have been implicated in the aetiology of pregnancy complications which had previously been ascribed to psychotropic medication. Observational studies often have not accounted for the severity and type of psychiatric illness, and few studies have compared women with untreated perinatal mental illness to women taking psychotropics [17]. However, in studies where confounders are better controlled for, apparent differences in outcome for infants exposed to psychotropic medication diminish.

Prescribing Psychotropic Drugs in Pregnancy

The weighing of risks and benefits of psychotropic medications in pregnancy and breastfeeding is one of the greatest challenges of working in perinatal psychiatry. The task clinicians face is to ensure that up-to-date knowledge and evidence is communicated and applied effectively and compassionately to the individual woman, and that this is done in in conjunction with the woman's own preferences and prior treatment experiences. The high prevalence of confounding factors in women with severe mental illness is a challenge for both the application of research data and the communication with the woman about potential risks and benefits.

Firstly, the clinician must establish the diagnosis, comorbidities and illness course; secondly, the indications must be clarified (e.g. maintenance, prophylaxis, acute treatment) and thirdly, the treatment options outlined alongside any associated risks. The

Table 26.1 Pharmacokinetic changes in pregnancy

Change in Pregnancy	Potential Consequence
Nausea and vomiting in the first trimester	Reduction in amount of drug available for absorption
Decrease in gastric acid production and increased mucus secretion, leading to an increase in gastric pH	Increase in ionisation and reduction in absorption of weak acids (e.g. aspirin) and weak bases (e.g. caffeine) will diffuse more readily since they will be primarily un-ionised
Slower intestinal motility and increased intestinal blood flow	Increase in drug absorption
Increased cardiac output, increased stroke volume, increased plasma volume, increased total body water and in all body fluid compartments	Increase in volume of distribution for hydrophilic drugs, leading to lower plasma concentrations
Increased maternal body fat	Increased volume of distribution for lipophilic drugs
Plasma protein binding of drugs decreases during pregnancy due to reduced concentrations of both albumin and alpha 1-acid glycoprotein Certain pathophysiologic conditions can lead to even lower albumin levels	Decrease in protein binding leads to higher concentrations of free drug (for drugs that have limited clearance) and favours more distribution to tissues. Drugs that are highly bound to plasma proteins and/or have a large molecular weight will tend to concentrate intravascularly and will have a small volume of distribution
Increase in uterine perfusion and the addition of the feto-placental compartment	Small-molecular-weight and lipophilic drugs readily cross the placenta
Fetus and the amniotic fluid act as additional compartments	Increase in drug accumulation and an apparent increase in volume of distribution of certain drugs
Increase in CYP3A4 (50–100%), CYP2A6 (54%), CYP2D6 (50%) and CYP2C9 (20%)	Changes in CYP3A4 activity lead to increased metabolism of some drugs
GFR is 50% higher by the first trimester and continues to increase until the last week of pregnancy	If a drug is solely excreted by glomerular filtration, its renal clearance is expected to parallel changes in GFR during pregnancy. Despite a uniform increase in GFR during pregnancy, differences in renal tubular transport (secretion or reabsorption) can result in differing effects on renally cleared drugs

thinking behind using a particular drug will also be affected by whether this is the first time psychotropic medication has been prescribed for the woman or whether she has a known medication history. The clinician is required to calculate risk profiles for two individuals involving multiple predictors and outcomes, taking into account the woman's subjective experience of how she views risk (e.g. risk of breakdown versus risk to the developing fetus). It is important to know who or what may be influencing the woman's decision-making outside of the mental health team and to understand what their opinions might be (e.g. maternity services, friends, family, religious leader). These are likely to be important factors influencing adherence (see Chapter 1, 'The Perinatal Frame of Mind').

Risks related to medication must be weighed against the risks of not treating and the benefits of treating. See Box 26.1.

The National Institute for Health and Care Excellence (NICE) antenatal and postnatal mental health: clinical management and service guidance [18] offers substantial guidance to the prescribing clinician on the issues to be considered in the perinatal period and how they may be addressed in consultation with the woman and her partner. If a woman declines pharmacological treatment, after discussion of the risks and benefits of both stopping and taking medication, it is important that she is offered support, monitoring, psychoeducation, psychological therapy if appropriate, and that a robust, well-communicated plan is in place should her condition deteriorate or relapse.

Detailed discussions, weighing up the risks and benefits of medication and the risks of non-treatment, need to take place with the woman. Box 26.2 sets out the areas to be covered. Depth of discussion will depend on the woman's current circumstances, including taking into consideration her current mental state. Optimally, discussions would take place with the woman at several points, such as pre-conception, at first consultation with

Box 26.1 Weighing risks and benefits of medication

Risks related to medication

- teratogenicity
- neonatal toxicity and withdrawal
- longer-term neurobehavioural/cognitive problems
- fetal growth
- incompatibility with breastfeeding
- physical risks to mother, gestational diabetes, obesity, etc.
- effects on parenting and social function (fatigue, drowsiness, general dulling, lack of emotional responsivity/availability)

Risks related to illness/non-treatment

- effects on birth weight and gestational age at delivery
- not accessing antenatal care, labour ward
- impairment of relationships with family, carers and professionals
- poor diet, smoking, alcohol, illicit drugs, risk-taking behaviours
- possible detrimental effect of the mental disorder in pregnancy on the fetus
- potential impact on mother–infant attachment and capacity to parent
- relapse, hospitalisation, worsening of prognosis, suicide

Benefits of treating

- woman remains well
- woman maintains relationships
- accesses maternity, mental healthcare
- optimises lifestyle and health
- avoids possible detrimental effect of the mental disorder in pregnancy on the fetus
- avoids potential impact on mother–infant attachment and capacity to parent
- avoids relapse, hospitalisation, worsening of prognosis, suicide

Box 26.2 Discussing Medication with Women [18]

Mental health professionals providing detailed advice about possible risks of mental health problems or the benefits and harms of treatment need to include discussion of the following, depending on individual circumstances:

- exploration of the individual woman's views, wishes, fears, priorities and preference
- risk of relapse/deterioration and ability to cope with this
- severity of previous episodes, previous response to treatment
- the likely benefits of each treatment, considering severity of the problem
- the risks or harms to the woman and the fetus or baby associated with treatment options
- the risk or harms to the woman and the fetus or baby associated with stopping or changing a treatment, that switching medication may not benefit and may increase risk
- the risks of sudden discontinuation, such as relapse and need to taper dose if discontinuing
- the uncertainty about the benefits, risks and harms of treatments to the individual woman
- the background risk of harm to the woman and the fetus or baby and that stopping drug with known teratogenicity may not remove risk of malformation
- the risk to mental health and parenting associated with no treatment
- the possibility of sudden onset of symptoms, particularly in the first few weeks after childbirth (e.g. in bipolar disorder)
- the need for prompt treatment
- breastfeeding

the perinatal mental health team and at the pre-birth planning meeting (when consideration will be given to medication in late pregnancy, intra-partum and following childbirth, including need for dose adjustments or medication reinstatement) or in the event of her becoming unwell in pregnancy or postpartum.

Once the prescriber has addressed individual factors for the woman (e.g. her views, fears, preferences) and general risk advice (e.g. of sudden discontinuation, background risk of fetal anomalies) (see Box 26.3), then the clinician's knowledge of individual drugs comes to the fore. For example, while in most instances stopping or switching medications would be approached with great caution, the woman who is taking sodium valproate would be most likely advised to discontinue the drug, supported by a care plan to address the effects on her health of doing so [19]. In general terms, the advice would be to use the least number of drugs at the lowest *effective* doses. The woman's previous response to treatment is one of the most important pieces of information the clinician relies on during the consultation. Women do not, in clinical experience, begin to respond to a medication that has *not* worked in the past (if prescribed at adequate dosage and duration). A thorough medication history is of vital importance, including prior patterns of response to treatment. Drug dosages may need to be adjusted in pregnancy and postnatally, which should be addressed in all treatment plans and discussions. If the woman has taken psychotropic medication with known teratogenic risk at any time in the first trimester, then the pregnancy needs to be confirmed as soon as possible along with screening for fetal abnormalities, and appropriate obstetric and fetal medicine consultation, in accordance with the woman's wishes.

Box 26.3 Explaining Risk [18]

When discussing likely benefits and risks of treatment with the woman and, if she agrees, her partner, family or carer:

- acknowledge the woman's central role in reaching a decision about her treatment and that the role of the professional is to inform that decision with balanced and up-to-date information and advice
- use absolute values based on a common denominator (that is, numbers out of 100 or 1,000)
- acknowledge and describe, if possible, the uncertainty around any estimate of risk, harm or benefit
- use high-quality decision aids in a variety of numerical and pictorial formats that focus on a personalised view of the risks and benefits (in line with the guidance on patient experience in adult National Health Service services, NICE guideline CG138)
- consider providing records of the consultation, in a variety of visual, verbal or audio formats

Rapid Tranquillisation

Rarely, a pregnant woman may display a level of acute disturbance that requires de-escalation, and failing that more active management to prevent risk of harm to herself or others. A pregnant woman requiring rapid tranquillisation should be treated according to the NICE guidelines on the short-term management of violence and aggression in mental health, health and community settings [20] with the following additional advice:

- she should *not be secluded* after rapid tranquillisation
- restraint procedures should be *adapted* to avoid possible harm to the fetus and woman
- when choosing an agent for rapid tranquillisation in a pregnant woman, an antipsychotic or a benzodiazepine with a short half-life should be considered; if an antipsychotic is used, it should be at the minimum effective dose because of neonatal extrapyramidal symptoms; if a benzodiazepine is used, the risks of floppy baby syndrome should be taken into account
- during the perinatal period, the woman's care should be managed in close collaboration with a paediatrician and an anaesthetist

Perinatal community, Mother and Baby Unit and acute ward mental health staff need to be aware of the adaptations to rapid tranquillisation that are required, and aids to support the pregnant woman (e.g. beanbags) need to be present in all areas where this situation may potentially present itself.

Assessment of the Neonate

If a woman has taken psychotropic medication during pregnancy, a full assessment and examination of the newborn for abnormalities and withdrawal or toxic effects due to exposure to medication needs to be carried out by an appropriate professional, bearing in mind:

- the variation in the onset of adverse effects of psychotropic medication and the need for continued monitoring

- the need to inform relevant healthcare professionals and the woman and her partner, family or carer of any further monitoring that may be required, particularly if the woman has been discharged early

The Pan-London Perinatal Mental Health Guidance for Newborn Assessment [21] offers general guidance and advice for the examination of the newborn who has been exposed to psychotropic medication in utero and Chapter 27, 'The Reproductive Safety of Psychotropic Medication and Implications for Prescribing in the Perinatal Period', highlights effects on the neonate due to specific drugs to be alert for.

Breastfeeding

Breastfeeding is advantageous for the mother's long-term health, improves birth spacing and contributes to a reduction in infections and an increase in intelligence in infants. It is recommended by The Royal College of Paediatrics (2021) that exclusive breastfeeding for healthy term infants takes place for up to 6 months followed by partial breastfeeding while weaning onto suitable solid foods [22].

Women with mental disorders who are taking psychotropic medication can almost always be encouraged to breastfeed, either solely or as part of a mixed breast/formula regime, and medication should very rarely be a reason not to breastfeed (breastfeeding is discussed in Chapter 24, 'Pre-pregnancy Advice and Planning' and Chapter 27, 'The Reproductive Safety of Psychotropic Medication and Implications for Prescribing in the Perinatal Period'). However, if the woman decides for various subjective reasons not to breastfeed then she should be supported with this choice.

The following need to be borne in mind when discussing breastfeeding with women:

- milk supply in the mother may be affected by maternal stress, nutrition and medication
- sleep deprivation induced by night feeds may be a risk factor for women with severe mood disorders relapsing (see Chapter 12, 'Postpartum Psychosis and Bipolar Disorder') and in this context shared feeding of the infant at night may be most appropriate
- preterm or unwell neonates may have underdeveloped processes for metabolising medication
- psychotropic medications are transferred to breast milk (BM) by simple diffusion, and levels of drug in BM are affected by the level of protein binding of drug in maternal plasma and by lipophilic drugs penetrating BM in higher concentrations and concentrating in hind milk
- the infant is exposed, in general, to lower amounts of the drug when breastfeeding compared to exposure in utero
- most psychotropic medication is compatible with breastfeeding. Contraindications to breastfeeding include taking carbamazepine, clozapine or lithium and sodium valproate (which is not recommended to treat mental disorders in women or girls of childbearing potential) [18]
- discarding BM or adjusting feeding times based on when the drug is taken is not supported by evidence. It is also potentially an anxiety-provoking and complex task for a woman dealing with an episode of mental illness
- women need to be supported in the choice of feeding method that best suits them and their families

- with all women who may need to take psychotropic medication in pregnancy or in the postnatal period, discussion needs to include the benefits of breastfeeding, the potential risks associated with taking psychotropic medication when breastfeeding and with stopping some medications to breastfeed, and treatment options that would enable her to breastfeed if she wishes [18]
- the need to monitor the breastfed baby for adverse effects of medication

A measure of exposure that is used in clinical practice based on milk concentrations is the relative infant dose (RID). This is defined as the daily amount of drug ingested by an infant, who is fully breastfed, per kg bodyweight divided by the maternal daily dose per kg body weight (see Chapter 27). The infant is assumed to ingest 150 ml breast milk per kg body weight daily. When the RID <10%, the drug is generally considered to pose a low risk to the breastfeeding infant; a RID of 10–25% means the drug needs to be used cautiously, with potential for monitoring or special considerations and a RID >25% indicates that the drug may pose a higher risk, and its use should be reconsidered, an alternative medication recommended or advice not to breastfeed given. Therefore, the RID helps determine whether the amount of the drug transferred via breast milk can potentially cause harm to the infant and is a factor influencing prescribing decisions.

Prescribing Off-Licence

No psychotropic medication is licensed for use in pregnancy or in breastfeeding mothers. The British National Formulary and product information advise at least caution in their prescription or, in many cases, contraindication. Drug trials exclude pregnant or breastfeeding women, and no randomised controlled trials of psychotropic medication have been conducted in pregnancy or in lactating women. There are implications from this for clinicians as the majority of the psychotropic drugs that are prescribed in perinatal mental health are off-licence. The Scottish Intercollegiate Guidelines Network guideline on *Off-licence Use of Medicines* [23] states: 'Generally, the unlicensed use of medicines becomes necessary if the clinical need cannot be met by licensed medicines; such use should be supported by appropriate evidence and experience.'

Prescribers must be satisfied that an alternative treatment would not meet the patient's specific needs before prescribing the unlicensed medicine and that there is sufficient evidence and/or experience of using the medicine to show its safety and efficacy following a risk benefit analysis. The prescriber needs to take responsibility for prescribing the medicine and for overseeing the patient's care, including monitoring and follow-up; record the medicine prescribed and the reasons for prescribing this medicine; record the discussion held with the patient; give the patient sufficient information about the proposed treatment, including known serious or common adverse reactions, to enable her to make an informed decision; and answer questions from patients (or 'carers') about medicines fully and honestly [24].

Communication

The wide range of issues involved in prescribing for women in the perinatal period that need to be part of the discussion between women, their partners/family and the prescribing clinician are set out above in Box 26.1. There are however additional principles that the clinician needs to be aware of in framing discussions about individual medications, set out in Box 26.2. It is important that the woman's central role in decision-making is acknowledged as is the role of the advising clinician who informs that decision with balanced and up-to-date information and advice. In optimal circumstances there is shared decision-making and responsibility is not placed solely on the woman.

The clinician needs to be attuned to women's feelings of anxiety or guilt about taking medication. Acknowledging that the clinician and parent/s have a shared desire to see best outcomes for fetus/pregnancy/infant and for the mother to remain well and, by extension, better able to meet baby's needs can help set the tone of the conversation. Information needs to be set out clearly in a manner that is understandable to the woman and should be supported by a written record of the discussion to enable her to review decisions made after the consultation (see Chapter 1, 'The Perinatal Frame of Mind' and Chapter 23, 'Access, Assessment and Evaluation of Risk in Perinatal Mental Health Services'). Other teams and services involved with the woman's care also need to be aware of discussions held and decisions made about medication. This will include primary care and maternity services, but may also include colleagues in anaesthetics, fetal medicine, neonatology and health visiting. It is important that a record is kept in the infant's records of medication prescribed when in utero or whilst being breastfed to inform any current or future monitoring. It must be recognised that there may be differences in clinical opinion about the advice to prescribe. These differences must be identified, acknowledged and resolved through multidisciplinary, collaborative working practices to ensure best outcome for the woman, her pregnancy, fetus and infant. It is also important to recognise that family members and friends may hold different opinions and to ensure that these are also addressed appropriately. Women often find it difficult to receive conflicting advice from other clinicians and from friends and family, and this may lead them to developing mistrust, anxiety and secretiveness. Occasionally, the woman and her partner/family may request a second opinion. This should be facilitated if possible and an opinion sought from either a perinatal pharmacist or specialist second opinion psychiatric service.

Summary

Prescribing psychotropic medication in the perinatal period can be challenging. Understanding the current evidence base; knowing how and when to acknowledge the uncertainty inherent in current knowledge and how that translates to the individual woman; balancing risks of medication with risks of not treating and benefits of treating; sharing decision-making while not putting all of the responsibility on the woman; communicating clearly and effectively with the woman, her partner, other professionals, services and agencies; and knowing when and how to seek further help or advice, are all essential components of good practice when prescribing in pregnancy and breastfeeding. It is also important to recognise that the information needs of each woman are highly individual and that the level of detail, as well as when and how the information is given, needs to be tailored to meet her needs. It addition, the prescriber also needs to have an awareness of their own attitudes towards risk and the cognitive biases that may affect their approach [25].

Ideally discussions with women about medication in pregnancy and postnatally should begin at first diagnosis within community mental health services and primary care services, as part of a wider discussion on pregnancy planning and contraception, once she is well enough to participate or failing that before conception when planning a pregnancy within specialist perinatal mental health services. Discussions need to be revisited throughout contact in the perinatal period.

Useful Resources

- UK Teratology Information Service (UKTIS). https://uktis.org
- Best Use of Medicines in Pregnancy (BUMPS). www.medicinesinpregnancy.org
- Drugs and Lactation Database (LactMed). www.ncbi.nlm.nih.gov/books/NBK501922
- Royal College of Psychiatrists. Patient information leaflets. www.rcpsych.ac.uk/members/your-faculties/perinatal-psychiatry/news-and-resources

References

1. LM Howard, H Khalifeh. Perinatal mental health: a review of progress and challenges. *World Psychiatry.* 2020;19(3):313–27.
2. M Mazza, D De Berardis, G Marano. Keep in mind sex differences when prescribing psychotropic drugs. *World J Psychiatry.* 2024;14(2): 194–8.
3. N Fabiano, S Wong, A Gupta, J Tran, M Bhambra, KK Min, et al. Safety of psychotropic medications in pregnancy: an umbrella review. *Mol Psychiatry.* 2025;30(2):327–35.
4. R Cantwell, E Youd, M Knight, on behalf of the MBRRACE-UK mental health chapter-writing group. Messages for mental health. In: M Knight, K Bunch, D Tuffnell, H Jayakody, J Shakespeare, R Kotnis, et al., editors. *Saving Lives, Improving Mothers' Care – Lessons learned to inform maternity care from the UK and Ireland Confidential Enquiries into Maternal Deaths and Morbidity 2014–16.* Oxford: National Perinatal Epidemiology Unit, University of Oxford; 2018. p. 42–60.
5. A Lupattelli, O Spigset, MJ Twigg, K Zagorodnikova, AC Mårdby, ME Moretti, et al. Medication use in pregnancy: a cross-sectional, multinational web-based study. *BMJ Open.* 2014;4:e004365.
6. M Romanescu, V Buda, A Lombrea, M Andor, I Ledeti, M Suciu, et al. Sex-related differences in pharmacological response to CNS drugs: a narrative review. *J Pers Med.* 2022;12(6):907.
7. IE Sommer, BA Brand, CCM Stuijt, D Touw. Sex differences need to be considered when treating women with psychotropic drugs. *World Psychiatry.* 2024;23:151–2.
8. M Oliva, M Muñoz-Aguirre, S Kim-Hellmuth, V Wucher, ADH Gewirtz, DJ Cotter, et al. The impact of sex on gene expression across human tissues. *Science.* 2020;369:eaba3066.
9. I Zucker, BJ Prendergast. Sex differences in pharmacokinetics predict adverse drug reactions in women. *Biol Sex Differ.* 2020;11(1):32.
10. JE Zachry, SO Nolan, LJ Brady, SJ Kelly, CA Siciliano, ES Calipari, et al. Sex differences in dopamine release regulation in the striatum. *Neuropsychopharmacol.* 2021;46(3):491–9.
11. KN Krolick, Q Zhu, H Shi. Effects of estrogens on central nervous system neurotransmission: implications for sex differences in mental disorders. *Prog Mol Biol Transl Sci.* 2018;160:105–71.
12. B Bolea-Alamanac, SJ Bailey, TA Lovick, D Scheele, R Valentino. Female psychopharmacology matters! Towards a sex-specific psychopharmacology. *J Psychopharmacol.* 2018;32(2):125–33.
13. KA Duffy, CN Epperson. Evaluating the evidence for sex differences: a scoping review of human neuroimaging in psychopharmacology research. *Neuropsychopharmacol.* 2022;47(3):430–43.

14. Y Yu, J Chen, D Li, L Wang, W Wang, H Liu. Systematic analysis of adverse event reports for sex differences in adverse drug events. *Sci Rep.* 2016;6:24955.

15. MV Seeman. Men and women respond differently to antipsychotic drugs. *Neuropharmacol.* 2020;163:107631.

16. M Feghali, R Venkataramanan, S Caritis. Pharmacokinetics of drugs in pregnancy. *Semin Perinatol.* 2015;39(7):512–19.

17. RH McAllister-Williams, DS Baldwin, R Cantwell, A Easter, E Gilvarry, V Glover, et al. British Association for Psychopharmacology consensus guidance on the use of psychotropic medication preconception, in pregnancy and postpartum. *J Psychopharmacol.* 2017;31(5):519–52.

18. National Institute for Health and Care Excellence. Antenatal and postnatal mental health: clinical management and service guidance. Clinical Guideline (CG192). 2014. Updated 2020.

19. Medicines and Healthcare Products Agency. Antiepileptic drugs in pregnancy: updated advice following comprehensive safety review. *Drug Safety Update.* 2021;14(6).

20. National Institute for Health and Care Excellence. Violence and aggression: short-term management in mental health, health and community settings. NICE Guideline (NG10). 2015. www.nice.org.uk/guidance/ng10

21. Healthy London Partnership. Pan-London Perinatal Mental Health: guidance for newborn assessment (v3). 2020. www.healthylondon.org/wp-content/uploads/2020/01/FinalNeodoc-v3.pdf

22. Royal College of Paediatrics. Breastfeeding in the UK – position statement. 2021. https://tinyurl.com/4jrevmvt

23. Scottish Intercollegiate Guidelines Network (SIGN). Off-licence use of medicines: a national clinical guideline (SIGN 145). 2015.

24. General Medical Council. Good practice in prescribing and managing medicines and devices. 2013.

25. CC Dobler, AS Morrow, CC Kamath. Clinicians' cognitive biases: a potential barrier to implementation of evidence-based clinical practice. *BMJ Evid Based Med.* 2018;23(3):85–7.

Chapter 27

The Reproductive Safety of Psychotropic Medication and Implications for Prescribing in the Perinatal Period

Angelika Wieck

Introduction

Treatment with psychotropic drugs in pregnancy and lactation is one of the most challenging tasks in clinical psychopharmacology. It is highly complex requiring to take into account the simultaneous drug exposure of a woman with an illness and her developing healthy child, a gamut of possibilities that may pose a risk to mother and child and constantly changes as pregnancy progresses, as well as the many pregnancy-induced pharmacokinetic and physiological changes, the various mechanisms involved with drug transfer from the mother through the placenta and breast milk to the infant and finally what this means for the health of the child.

The field of reproductive safety of psychotropics is developing fast and this chapter aims to give an overview of recent developments relevant to the clinical context. It will outline the principal ways in which psychotropic drugs could adversely affect embryonic and fetal development, pregnancy outcomes, neonatal health and long-term child development. It will discuss why it is often so difficult to interpret published papers in this area but also highlight recent progress in research methodology. A detailed analysis of the large evidence base for psychotropic drug classes and individual compounds is beyond the scope of the chapter. Rather, current evidence will be summarised whilst highlighting methodological strengths and limitations of influential and landmark studies. Implications for clinical practice and key principles of prescribing in pregnancy and lactation will be considered. Further guidance on the principles of prescribing in this period are outlined in Chapter 1, 'The Perinatal Frame of Mind'.

How Could a Psychotropic Drug Affect the Developing Fetus?

As small and lipophilic molecules, all psychotropic drugs can pass through the placenta and into breast milk. In the first 2 weeks after conception, maternal medication has an 'all or nothing' effect on the embryo; it can either kill it or have no effect at all. From week 3 until about week 16, an embryo is sensitive to gross structural defects although each organ system has its own specific sensitive window. For example, major heart defects, which are the most common major congenital anomalies, can result from drug exposure during fetal weeks 3–8, when many women are not yet aware of their pregnancy. In contrast, the central nervous system remains vulnerable to major congenital anomalies until about week 16.

Medication use in the second and third trimester may result in minor congenital anomalies, functional defects and abnormal organ or fetal growth. The outcomes that may result from drug exposure at this stage are wide ranging and include gestational diabetes in the woman, premature delivery, small and large size for gestational age, and neonatal toxicity or withdrawal symptoms. In the context of psychotropic drugs it is particularly important to highlight that a fetus is thought to be sensitive to neurodevelopmental disruptions by medications until birth.

What Are the Difficulties with Perinatal Safety Studies?

Because it is not possible on ethical grounds to use randomised controlled designs in perinatal safety studies, data in this area comes from case reports and observational studies, including pregnancy registries, cohort and pharmaco-epidemiological studies. The inherent risk of confounding in such data is particularly important for the childbearing situation. This is because a wide range of factors other than medication have been shown to affect pregnancy and child outcomes. An example of this is maternal BMI which is associated with an increase in major congenital malformations in a dose-dependent fashion, with significant results including anomalies of the heart and central nervous system that have also been associated with psychotropic drug exposure [1]. Similarly, nicotine use in pregnancy has been associated with congenital defects of the heart and other anomalies. Interestingly, the risks are of a similar magnitude to those that have been reported for some psychotropic drugs in the older literature.

Other important confounders include a family history of adverse pregnancy outcomes, substance misuse, concomitant medication, physical illnesses, poverty, social stress, environmental exposures and others. Almost all of these are more prevalent in women with mental illnesses, particularly if the illnesses are severe. Many studies investigating psychotropics – and this applies particularly to the older literature – have not, or only incompletely, been able to adjust for such confounders. An important reason is that obstetric and neonatal databases have often been set up for clinical and administrative rather than investigational purposes.

Observational studies are also prone to detection bias because pregnancies and newborn infants exposed to medication tend to be more closely scrutinised for adverse outcomes. Another fundamental problem that is difficult to tackle is the verification of actual drug exposure in pregnancy since it is not known whether drugs dispensed are actually taken, especially if exposure definitions rely on single prescriptions.

An oft-neglected issue in reproductive safety studies is that no corrections are made for the significance levels when numerous outcomes are being included; these sometimes number in the hundreds. Uncertainties about the clinical significance of some findings also make their interpretation difficult. An issue that is the most difficult and has hardly been addressed so far is the measurement of the mother's illness severity during pregnancy. This is particularly problematic when women who continue medication in pregnancy are compared with those who stopped it before conception. Ongoing treatment is likely to indicate persistent symptoms or a more severe form of illness and this can lead to overestimates of medication-induced adverse effects.

However, over recent years research methodology has made significant progress in overcoming some of the pitfalls, and this will be highlighted in the discussion of drug classes and individual compounds.

Setting Risks and Benefits into Context

When considering therapeutic options in pregnancy it is important to be aware of the size of the risk that can be attributed to medication exposure. It has been estimated that about 3% of babies in the general population are born with major congenital anomalies. Although the majority of women take prescribed or over-the-counter drugs at some time during pregnancy, it is thought that only a minority of all birth defects, about 2–3%, are caused by drugs used to treat an illness or a symptom.

In addition, when positive associations between psychotropic medication use in pregnancy and adverse obstetric or child outcomes are reported in studies, the relative risks (RR) or odds ratios (OR) tend to be small, typically two or less. The exception to this is the high figures that have been reported for valproate's harmful effects.

The risks of using medication in pregnancy must be weighed with the consequences of a mother having no treatment and deteriorating in her mental health and the risk that untreated mental illness presents to the unborn child. When a pregnant woman suffers poor mental health there is now evidence that this and associated lifestyle, physical health and psychosocial problems can contribute to impaired behavioural, emotional and cognitive development of her offspring. This has been shown for mood disorders [2] but has been largely unexplored for other conditions.

The benefits and risks of using or not using psychotropic medication during childbearing are highly dependent on the specific circumstances of each woman and her family, and overall conclusions will differ. It is clear, however, that if the mental illness is severe and the risk of recurrence is high, that the prescribing of effective medication will prevent significant harm to mother and baby in most cases. If a decision has been made to use medication, careful consideration also needs to be given to the choice of drug and incorporating medication plans into the overall antenatal and postnatal care plan.

Antidepressant Medication

Major Congenital Malformations

Selective Serotonin Reuptake Inhibitors

Selective serotonin reuptake inhibitors (SSRIs) antidepressants have been the most investigated psychotropic drug class in respect of their reproductive safety. Most studies have concerned the incidence of major congenital anomalies following first trimester exposure and the most commonly reported risk has been for cardiac malformations. These are also the most common congenital anomalies in the general population with a reported prevalence of usually less than 1%.

The meta-analysis by Gao et al. is the first to examine in detail the impact of confounding by indication on this association [3]. For the 29 included cohort studies with over 9 million births very small increases in the rate of all congenital malformations and all heart defects were reported (RR 1.11, 95% confidence interval (CI) 1.03–1.19 and RR 1.24, 95% CI 1.11–1.37) but the findings lost significance when women using SSRIs were compared with those with unmedicated psychiatric illness. Individual SSRIs were also not associated with overall heart defects when the analysis was restricted to women with a psychiatric illness.

In a population cohort study from five Nordic countries, Furu et al. showed that small increases in the rate of any type of malformation or cardiac anomalies, which had remained after adjustment for a number of confounders, resolved when children exposed to SSRIs or venlafaxine were compared with their unexposed siblings [4]. This suggests that it is important to control for familial factors in these studies.

Overall, these findings suggest that SSRIs are not major teratogens and that reported effects on the fetal development of the heart are likely to be due to maternal factors other than psychotropic medication.

Other Antidepressants

There is much less evidence on the teratogenic potential of other antidepressants since they are not first-line treatments in clinical practice.

Lassen et al. systematically reviewed studies examining the teratogenic potential of *venlafaxine* and did not find an association (RR 1.12; CI 0.92–1.35) [5]. Focusing on pregnancies ending in terminations, miscarriages, stillbirths, postnatal death or surgery, Kolding et al. found in their recent Danish population register study that first trimester use was associated with an increased risk of hypoplastic left heart syndrome (HLHS) (crude prevalence ratio 17.4; 95% CI 6.41–47.2) [6]. Among live births, there was neither an increase in serious or non-serious cardiac malformations. Confounding could only be partially taken into account. This is particularly important because venlafaxine tends to be prescribed to patients who are treatment resistant and are likely to have more confounding risk factors which are also more likely to be severe. Sample sizes in the exposure and the control group of former users were also small relative to the incidence of HLHS. Further investigation of this finding is needed before any conclusions can be drawn for clinical practice.

The evidence base for the reproductive safety of *duloxetine* has recently been markedly expanded by two large population-based cohort studies using propensity scoring and several sensitivity analyses [7, 8]. The compound did not appear to be a major teratogen, but in one study [7] there was a small almost significant effect on cardiovascular malformations (RR 1.29; CI 0.99–1.68). Total numbers of first trimester exposures are still small and further studies are needed.

There is as yet little data on the safety of *mirtazapine* in pregnancy, but no teratogenic signals were reported in a meta-analysis of studies with a total of 390 cases [9]. A nationwide study with a small (N=895) cohort of babies exposed to mirtazapine in the first trimester of pregnancy found no association with major congenital anomalies [10].

In a systematic review Hendrick et al. reported a link of *bupropion* use in the first trimester with a small elevation in the risk of cardiovascular defects in several studies [11]. Although the absolute risk was low, the specific heart defects concerned differed between studies and confounding by indication could not be excluded.

Early studies looking at the teratogenicity of *tricyclic antidepressants* are difficult to interpret because of numerous methodological problems. More recently, a population study with improved methodology included almost 6,000 children exposed to tricyclic antidepressants in the first trimester and did not find that they were more likely to be born with a defect, after adjustment for confounders [12].

Little is known about the safety of individual agents in this antidepressant class. A cohort study of early pregnancy exposures to tricyclic antidepressants, mostly represented by clomipramine, reported a two-fold increased risk of congenital cardiac defects [13]. However, the sample size was small and it could not be examined whether indication and several other confounders could explain the finding.

Preterm Delivery

Preterm birth is defined as occurring more than 21 days before the expected delivery date. It is an important pregnancy outcome because it can cause multiple health problems for the child, including neurological and long-term developmental disorders. Both depression and antidepressant medication have been associated with premature birth but causality has been difficult to disentangle.

Vlenterie et al. combined and analysed databases from 27 studies with individual patient data on depressive symptoms and diagnoses of depression in pregnancy [14]. Increased risks of preterm birth were observed for both women with a clinical diagnosis of depression during pregnancy irrespective of antidepressant use (OR 1.6; 95% CI 1.2–2.1) and women with depression who did not use antidepressants (OR 2.2; 95% CI 1.7–3.0). Use of SSRIs specifically was associated with preterm birth with or without restriction to women with depressive symptoms/depression in pregnancy (OR 1.6; 95% CI 1.0–2.5 and OR 1.9; 95% CI 1.2–2.8, respectively).

These findings suggest that depression or depressive symptoms and SSRI use during pregnancy are independently associated with small increases in the rate of preterm delivery.

Poor Neonatal Adaptation Syndrome

Late pregnancy use of antidepressant medications has consistently been linked with poor neonatal adaptation and increases its incidence three-fold [15] from a general population baseline of about 10%. The core features are respiratory distress and tremors but newborns may also have poor muscle tone, difficulties in temperature regulation and feeding, sleep disturbances and hypoglycaemia. The condition usually starts within 48 hours of birth, is usually mild and transient, and resolves within a few days. Usually, no major interventions are required although some babies require a longer stay in hospital for monitoring and treatment.

Persistent Pulmonary Hypertension of the Newborn

Persistent pulmonary hypertension of the newborn (PPHN) is a rare condition with an incidence of less than 6/1,000 births and multiple known causes. Symptoms range from mild respiratory problems to respiratory failure. It has repeatedly been shown that SSRIs increase the risks of PPHN with estimated odds ratios of 1.82 (CI 1.31–2.54) and 1.52 (1.04–2.00) in two meta-analyses [16, 17]. This seems to be linked with exposure in late pregnancy. The biological mechanism may be related to higher infant serotonin plasma levels causing constriction and smooth muscle proliferation in pulmonary vasculature. However, considering the low base rate the absolute risk is small.

Neurodevelopment

Initial research reporting increased risks for autism spectrum disorders (ASDs) and attention deficit hyperactivity disorder (ADHD) after pregnancy exposure to antidepressants led to intense debate in medical journals and fear among affected patients. More recent publications attributed the findings to previously unmeasured confounding. In the most extensive study to date, Suarez et al. used US healthcare and insurance data and the sample was large enough (145,702 antidepressant-exposed and 3,032,745 unexposed) to examine three drug classes (selective serotonin reuptake inhibitors (SSRIs), tricyclic antidepressants and serotonin and noradrenaline reuptake inhibitors) and five of the most commonly used drugs individually (sertraline, fluoxetine, bupropion, citalopram and escitalopram) [18]. Outcomes included diagnoses of seven different neurodevelopmental disorders (ASD, ADHD, specific learning disorders, developmental speech/language disorders, developmental coordination disorders, intellectual disabilities or behavioural disorders). A large range of confounders was measured. Approaches to confounding adjustment included propensity score fine stratification, comparisons with mothers discontinuing antidepressants before conception, and sibling analyses.

Although the risk of neurodevelopmental disorders was significantly increased following pregnancy exposure to any antidepressant versus no exposure and pre-conception discontinuation and, albeit to a lesser extent, adjusted analyses, no differences were found in sibling analyses. This suggests that the increase is due to genetic or shared environmental factors. Exposure in early and late pregnancy yielded similar results. This confirmed findings of other recent studies of ASD and ADHD.

In this study, analyses of drug classes and individual antidepressants did also not reveal any significant associations except for a small increase in the risk of coordination disorder in comparisons with non-exposure and pre-conception discontinuation. This could not be further tested in sibling analyses because samples did not have the required size, so that coordination disorder requires further attention.

One can conclude that there is now extensive evidence that antidepressant exposure in pregnancy does not pose significant neurodevelopmental risks.

Antipsychotics

Congenital Malformations

Previous studies examining the risk for congenital malformations after first trimester exposure to antipsychotic drugs usually reported up to two-fold increases of all congenital malformations taken together, and sometimes found a specific increase of cardiovascular malformations. This literature is difficult to interpret because of methodological limitations, mostly concerning small sample sizes and inadequate accounting for known or suspected confounders.

Significant progress was recently made by a landmark cohort study of women enrolled in the Medicaid programme in the United States by Huybrechts et al. [19]. It used propensity scoring to control for underlying psychiatric disorder and other potential confounders. The large sample included 9,258 women who had filled a prescription of a second-generation antipsychotic (SGA) (aripiprazole, olanzapine, quetiapine, risperidone, ziprasidone) in the first trimester and 733 women who had filled a prescription for a first-generation antipsychotic, and over 1.3 million controls. This sample size allowed, for the first time, to assess the safety of individual SGAs within one database. A small increase was seen of all congenital malformations and cardiac anomalies in particular when second-generation antipsychotics were considered together or individually. However, after a broad range of confounders were taken into account, the only finding that remained significant was a small increase of the general malformation rate in children exposed to risperidone (RR 1.26; 95% CI, 1.02–1.56). Interestingly, an update of this study with a larger sample from the same database confirmed these results except for the association with risperidone [20], suggesting that it had arisen by chance. Overall, these findings suggests that antipsychotic drugs are not major teratogens.

Gestational Diabetes

Since the endocrine and metabolic changes accompanying pregnancy enhance women's vulnerability to dysglycaemia, and some antipsychotic medications are well known to cause weight gain and diabetes, the question arises whether antipsychotic therapy also increases the risk of gestational diabetes. This is an important issue, since gestational diabetes places the infant at risk of poor outcomes, such as preterm birth, macrosomia and stillbirth.

Previous evidence was conflicting. A recent large US cohort study with improved methodology and a sample of almost 10,000 women prescribed SGAs was able to differentiate between agents (1,924 aripiprazole, 673 ziprasidone, 4,533 quetiapine, 1,824 risperidone and 1,425 olanzapine users) [21]. Women who discontinued SGAs before conception were compared with women who continued medication until week 20 of pregnancy or beyond. They found that quetiapine and olanzapine use was associated with a small increase in the incidence of gestational diabetes (adjusted RR 1.28; 95% CI, 1.01–1.62 and 1.61; 95% CI, 1.13–2.29) whereas other SGAs (aripiprazole, ziprasidone or risperidone) were not. A similar Swedish population register study with a smaller sample [22] found a relationship of comparable size with 'high risk' antipsychotics as a group (quetiapine, olanzapine, clozapine).

Current evidence suggests that caution is advised with the use of these drugs in pregnancy, especially if other predisposing factors for gestational diabetes are present. However, for a patient who has responded well to her medication, a switch to another agent may well carry greater risks. Maternity services in the UK routinely screen women taking antipsychotics across pregnancy to identify dysglycaemia early and mitigate its risks.

Poor Neonatal Adaptation Syndrome and Extrapyramidal Symptoms

Results of previous studies of neonatal health following intrauterine exposure to antipsychotic medication have been conflicting. In a population study with a large sample, Heinonen et al. were able to compare exposure in pregnancy (N=2,677) with exposure limited to only the pre-conception and postnatal period (N=34,492) thus accounting for indication [23]. After adjusting for maternal factors, including other prescribed neurotropic co-medications and smoking, exposure in pregnancy was associated with a higher rate of withdrawal symptoms, neurological symptoms and neonatal admissions, with adjusted relative risks ranging between 1.5 and 3.3. Risks were generally similar between first- and second-generation antipsychotics. This study also found for the first time a small increase in the risk of persistent pulmonary hypertension of the newborn (aRR 1.5; CI 1.0–2.2).

However, these findings may be subject to unmeasured confounding since neither misuse of illicit drugs or alcohol was considered nor the likelihood that women who continued medication in pregnancy had more severe illnesses and more severe comorbidities. In addition, the numbers of affected infants were low and the findings should not prevent antipsychotic treatment in pregnancy.

Neurodevelopmental Outcomes

In a recently published large population-based retrospective cohort study with up to 6 years of follow-up data, Wang et al. examined whether exposed children were more likely to develop ADHD or ASD [23]. Following propensity score weighting with potential confounders, including psychiatric illness, they found no effect. Sensitivity and sibling analyses supported this result. Interestingly, children born to mothers with psychiatric disorders who had never taken antipsychotic medication had an about two-fold increased risk compared to unexposed control children suggesting that genetic, social or environmental factors are important. Several other studies published since have supported these findings [24]. Similarly, academic performance in childhood does not seem to be compromised [25, 26]. Whether there are differences between individual antipsychotics is too early to say.

Newer Antipsychotics

No or very sparse reproductive safety data are as yet available for the newer compounds paliperidone, asenapine, lurasidone and cariprazine.

Prescribing Long-Acting Injectable Antipsychotic Drugs in Pregnancy

There are currently only case reports of long-acting injectable (LAI) antipsychotic use in pregnancy. Since LAI preparations are not more likely to cause serious side effects than oral medication [27], treatment should be continued in pregnancy if it is well established and effective for the patient.

Prescribers should be aware that aripiprazole can impair lactation in some women (see below). If an LAI preparation is used, its long half-life means that the effect may persist for several weeks into the postnatal period even if the medication is stopped or switched after childbirth.

Antipsychotic Plasma Levels in Pregnancy

In the first systematic study of plasma concentrations of three SGAs across the perinatal period, Westin et al. found progressive decreases for quetiapine and aripiprazole that reached –76% ($p<0.001$) and –52% ($p<0.001$) in the third trimester [28]. No significant changes were seen for olanzapine.

The findings are consistent with the known pregnancy-induced changes in activity of the hepatic cytochrome P450 enzymes involved with the breakdown of these three drugs [28]. Although the clinical consequences are as yet unknown, the findings suggest that women taking quetiapine or aripiprazole should be particularly closely monitored during pregnancy. If available, it is recommended to measure plasma levels in the perinatal period, preferably beginning before conception, and repeating in intervals until the first

2 weeks postpartum. Any changes in management need to consider alternative explanations for worsening mental states and all treatment options.

If the dose of aripiprazole needs to be increased in a woman receiving an LAI preparation oral medication should be added whilst maintaining the dose of the depot. This avoids overdosing in the early postnatal period since oral medication can be tapered more quickly.

Anti-epileptic Mood Stabilisers

Valproate

It is well established that valproate causes widespread harm to unborn children. About 11% of exposed children are born with congenital malformations [29], a roughly three times higher risk than in the general population. Anomalies can be severe and affect several organ systems. Compared with children of mothers without epilepsy or who have untreated epilepsy, exposed children have been reported to be intellectually less able [30], seven times more likely to have developmental delay [31] and three and five times more likely to have ASD or autism, respectively [32]. Taking into account other developmental problems, it has been estimated that 30–40% of exposed preschool children may be affected [33]. Although dose–response relationships have been described, there is no known safe dose in pregnancy and folic acid supplementation cannot prevent or only partially prevents harm.

Carbamazepine

Children exposed to carbamazepine in early pregnancy are up to twice more likely to be born with major congenital malformations than unexposed controls [34] whereas findings on neurodevelopmental outcomes have been variable [35].

Lamotrigine

There is extensive evidence that lamotrigine in monotherapy does not place the unborn child at an increased risk of major congenital malformations [34, 36]. Increasing data also suggest that this anti-epileptic does not cause neurodevelopmental disorders [35, 36].

Prescribing Anti-epileptic Drugs in Pregnancy

Because regulatory measures have only been partially successful, the European Commission passed a law in 2018 that restricts valproate prescriptions to pregnant women who suffer from a severe form of epilepsy and are at risk of uncontrollable life-threatening seizures during alternative treatments. In psychiatry, valproate should not be prescribed to pregnant women, and only to non-pregnant women with childbearing potential, if there are no alternative options and a pregnancy prevention programme is followed.

It has been widely recognised that the implementation of these restrictions raises difficult issues in clinical practice, and a series of tools have been published to address these. The Royal College of Psychiatrists and British Association of Psychopharmacology have published a position statement discussing the evidence for alternatives to valproate, and providing advice on valproate withdrawal in pregnancy [37]. A number of medical colleges and other professional and patient organisations jointly prepared guidance for difficult clinical circumstances, such as for example questions of oral contraception in girls and women with learning disability [38]. The Medicines and Health Care Products Regulatory Authority has also released a series of helpful tools for patients and healthcare professionals available on its website (www.gov.uk/guidance/valproate-use-by-women-and-girls#clinical-resources).

In recent years valproate prescriptions to women or girls who are pregnant or are of childbearing age have steadily declined in the UK [39]. Nevertheless, recent audits of clinical records from individual mental health trusts across the UK have shown that still too few prescribers inform women of the reproductive risks of valproate, discuss contraception or complete the necessary documentation (e.g. [40]). In addition, the implementation of the pregnancy prevention programme is currently still unsatisfactory [41].

The National Institute of Health and Care Excellence (NICE) in the UK recommends that carbamazepine should not be offered to women who are pregnant or are planning a pregnancy [42]. Given its uncertain efficacy in bipolar disorder, it is not commonly used in psychiatric practice. But if this drug is considered for a woman with bipolar disorder and childbearing potential, she should be informed about the teratogenic risk and offered reproductive counselling.

Plasma Levels of Lamotrigine in Pregnancy

When prescribing lamotrigine to women who are pregnant or planning a pregnancy, substantial pharmacokinetic changes need to be expected. After glucuronidation in the liver, lamotrigine is to 90% eliminated by the kidney. In pregnancy, rising oestradiol levels progressively enhance the activity of the responsible hepatic enzyme resulting in large drops of lamotrigine plasma levels. Substantial interindividual variability has been observed and Polepally et al. identified two subgroups of women, one with an only 20% increase in renal clearance (23% of women) and another with significantly larger changes (77% of women), with increases up to 220% being reported [43]. They hypothesised that this difference could be due to genetic polymorphisms of the responsible enzyme from the glucuronosyl-transferase family. Following the rapid decline of oestradiol synthesis after delivery, levels increase again within a few days and return to non-pregnant baselines within the first month postpartum.

The implications for clinical psychiatric practice are not clear. Prospective studies of mental state in pregnant women with bipolar disorder and its relationship to mental state do not exist. The only randomised controlled trial of therapeutic drug monitoring in pregnant women with epilepsy was regarded as inconclusive by the National Guideline Centre UK [44]. However, in the context of epilepsy, it supports the recommendations by the Medicines and Health Care Products Authority of the UK [45] that 'lamotrigine serum concentrations in the woman should be monitored before, during, and after pregnancy, including shortly after birth. If necessary, the dose should be adapted to maintain the lamotrigine serum concentration at the same level as before pregnancy or adapted according to clinical response. In addition, dose-related undesirable effects should be monitored after birth.'

Regarding bipolar disorder, it seems reasonable to assume that knowing the extent of plasma level drops can, in combination with considering any changes in the woman's psychosocial circumstances, help to identify the cause of any deterioration of mental state and therefore, choose appropriate interventions.

Lithium

In the UK, the use of lithium in pregnancy has been low and prescriptions are discontinued in two-thirds of women in early gestation, reflecting historical concerns about its reproductive safety. Currently only 1 in 10,000 pregnant women are prescribed lithium in the UK beyond the sixth week of pregnancy [46].

Reproductive Safety

In the late 1970s a study, that was subsequently criticised for its considerable methodological flaws, reported a large increase in the incidence of cardiovascular congenital anomalies, and in particular the severe and exceedingly rare Ebstein anomaly in children exposed to lithium in the first trimester of pregnancy. A review of later studies suggested that these observations were most likely a large overestimate [47]. Nevertheless, the original finding has influenced clinical practice until the present time.

Results from two recent studies that assessed the teratogenic risk with much larger samples and improved methodology should be highlighted. A European registry-based study covering 5.6 million deliveries found no cases of lithium exposure among 173 babies with otherwise unexplained Ebstein's [48]. A retrospective cohort study investigated cardiac malformations in 663 women treated with lithium in the first trimester [49]. After adjustment for several confounders, the rate of cardiac congenital anomalies was slightly increased with an odds ratio of 1.65 (CI 1.02–2.68). The effect was related to the daily dose and only significant when more than 900 mg were prescribed. At this level, the risk was increased three-fold. A similar result was found when first trimester exposures to lithium and lamotrigine were compared. Lithium plasma levels were not available.

These results should be interpreted with caution and regarded as preliminary for two reasons, firstly because of the small sample size and secondly because of the likelihood of unmeasured confounding. Women in the highest dose group had higher rates of bipolar disorder and were more likely to suffer from severe mania that is difficult to control, and associated with a greater severity of confounding risk factors for congenital heart defects. This includes obesity, nicotine use and misuse of other substances such as alcohol. These were either incompletely or not measured in the study.

There have been few studies of other pregnancy outcomes and no systematic studies of the physical health in newborns exposed to lithium in late pregnancy. At birth the child's lithium levels are similar to maternal values and a variety of symptoms, mostly consistent with impaired neonatal adaptation and side effects seen in adults, have been described in case reports [50]. No neonatal deaths have been reported. An increased rate of neonatal admissions has been found and it has been proposed that the neonate should be monitored for a few days on an appropriate inpatient unit [51].

There is one 5-year prospective study of 60 children that showed no excess of physical or mental anomalies compared to their unexposed siblings [52].

Lithium Use in Pregnancy

In view of this evidence and the recent recommendation to use lithium as first-line initial long-term therapy for the prevention of bipolar episodes [53] a switch of lithium to an antipsychotic in early pregnancy or when a woman is planning a pregnancy, is now less compelling. Lithium therapy could therefore be continued if it is clear that the patient requires maintenance treatment, there is evidence that she has responded to lithium and that the risk of relapse would be high if it was discontinued and replaced by an antipsychotic. If the woman requires a second drug for maintenance treatment in addition to an antipsychotic the choice should include lithium but not valproate or carbamazepine.

Lithium Dosing and Monitoring in the Perinatal Period

Since lithium readily equilibrates across the placenta, blood levels higher than necessary to maintain mood stability should be avoided. Because of the dynamic changes in renal function lithium plasma levels change as pregnancy progresses. Wesseloo et al. analysed 1,001 blood samples taken before, during and after pregnancy, and found that the plasma level to dose ratio significantly dropped in the first trimester, reached a nadir at week 17 of pregnancy and gradually returned towards pre-conception levels in the third trimester or shortly after birth [54]. The creatinine levels showed a similar longitudinal pattern. The proportion of sub-therapeutic lithium levels also mirrored this course and rose from a preconception baseline of 15% to 62% in the first and second trimester, dropped to 39% in the third trimester and fell below pre-conception levels after delivery.

The NICE antenatal and postnatal mental health clinical guideline recommended measuring plasma levels once a month until 4 weeks before the expected delivery date and then once weekly until delivery [42]. Because of the general risk of pre-eclampsia and other conditions with renal impairment, creatinine levels should always be included. In order to prevent toxic lithium levels, the antenatal care plan should include urgent action by psychiatric and maternity services in case of deteriorating renal function.

If possible, the dose of lithium should be kept at the lower range of the therapeutic window in pregnancy. It is also sometimes suggested to reduce the lithium some time before the expected delivery date in order to reduce neonatal symptoms. However, reports about the relationship between lithium levels in infants exposed before delivery and neonatal symptoms are conflicting [55, 56], and lowering the dosage or discontinuing lithium prior to delivery is not recommended [55]. This is particularly important in view of the very high risk of bipolar recurrence in the early postnatal period.

It is advisable to monitor lithium levels during labour and delivery by taking measurements 12 hours after a lithium dose, and to repeat this on the first postnatal day. If the result is not at the aimed target level dose adjustments should be continued at intervals until this is achieved.

Principles of Overall Management and Prescribing in Pregnancy and the Early Postnatal Period

In the childbearing context, psychiatric assessments should be akin to those in the forensic setting: a careful analysis of diagnosis and longitudinal course of the woman's illness; the risks and burden it represents to her, her developing child and others around her; the success of her previous treatments and the optimal mental state she could possibly achieve. This should precede any discussions with her and her partner about treatment plans for the ante- and postnatal period. When the woman's illness is severe and complex, this highly personalised approach is not only time-consuming but also requires a high degree of clinical skill and experience – and it is also essential for successful outcomes.

In order to maximise benefits for mother and child any effective non-pharmacological treatments should be exploited as appropriate, and this includes referral for dietary advice, weight management, smoking cessation and treatment of substance misuse. A well-coordinated team which includes all involved health and social care professionals, the patient and her partner is essential in the perinatal context. A single and comprehensive plan for the antenatal, delivery and postnatal periods should be ready by at least 32 weeks of pregnancy (see Chapter 25, 'Pre-birth Planning'). It should include clear instructions that the medication plan should not be altered without discussion with a senior medical member of the perinatal mental health team.

When selecting a drug for treatment in pregnancy, any agent with higher reproductive risks or little safety data should be avoided. Any drug discontinuation should be gradual to avoid precipitating recurrence of the illness. Once a decision has been made to initiate or continue a medication, it is important that the dose is not above but also not below the therapeutic range so that the patient receives the full treatment benefit and the child is not unnecessarily exposed to potential adverse effects.

Although few head-to-head comparisons have been made, we have seen from the available evidence that the differences in reproductive safety profiles of psychotropic drugs within one class appear small – the exception, of course, being the anti-epileptic drugs valproate and carbamazepine. Which agent within one psychotropic class is chosen for a perinatal patient should, in the majority of cases, be guided by her individual history, circumstances and preferences.

Neonatal withdrawal symptoms usually manifest themselves within 48–72 hours of birth. The maternity service should have a neonatal assessment and management programme in place for infants who have been exposed to psychotropic drugs before childbirth. In addition to opiates and benzodiazepines, this should also include antidepressants, antipsychotics, hypnotic benzodiazepine receptor agonists and polytherapy with several psychotropic drugs. The length of stay will depend on the level of risk and physical condition of the baby. On discharge the mother should receive written advice on observations of the baby and when and whom to ask for advice [57].

Breastfeeding

Current Breastfeeding Recommendations

Breastfeeding confers a number of physical, developmental and psychological benefits to mothers and their infant, some of them large, especially with exclusive breastfeeding. The Royal College of Paediatrics therefore strongly recommends exclusive breastfeeding for healthy term infants up to 6 months followed by partial breastfeeding while complementary foods are introduced [58].

Pharmacokinetics

Because drugs active in the central nervous system are lipophilic and tend to be small, they can be expected to penetrate milk in higher concentrations than other drugs. Important other factors that control the amounts entering breastmilk are the mother's individual metabolic capacity and the extent of protein binding in maternal plasma. Milk concentrations rise and fall depending on maternal levels, albeit with a delay.

Once the drug has been ingested by the breastfed infant, its fate depends on a number of processes which are as yet poorly understood. In the limited number of studies reporting measurements in infant plasma, levels have tended to be highly variable but generally low or below assay detection apart from lithium and lamotrigine. Likewise, studies of potential adverse medication effects in breastfed infants are limited and tend to consist of uncontrolled observations made on single cases or case series, usually without standardised assessments, and long-term effects remain largely unstudied.

Relative Infant Dose

Overall, infants are exposed to much smaller amounts during breastfeeding than in pregnancy, but there are exceptions. A measure of exposure that is based on milk concentrations and used in clinical practice is the relative infant dose (RID). This is defined as the daily amount of drug ingested by an infant, who is fully breastfed, per kg bodyweight divided by the maternal daily dose per kg body weight. The infant is assumed to ingest 150 ml milk per kg body weight daily. A RID of more than 10% is regarded as generally indicating a higher probability of side effects in the infant [59]. RID values have been published for most drugs, but are often only based on small case numbers.

Antidepressants

Most antidepressants are transferred in very low concentrations to breast milk whereas venlafaxine, fluoxetine and citalopram are reported to result occasionally in moderately high RIDs (less than 20%; [60]).

Breastfeeding and Antidepressant-Related Poor Neonatal Adaptation Syndrome

Kieviet et al. reported in a retrospective study of 247 neonates exposed to SSRIs, mirtazapine or venlafaxine that exclusive feeding with formula milk was associated with a markedly higher rate of poor neonatal adaptation than breastfeeding or mixed feeding (OR 3.16; 95% CI 1.40–7.13; p=0.003) [61]. Other potential risk factors for poor neonatal adaptation did not contribute significantly to the outcome. This suggests that the relatively low levels of these antidepressants the infant ingests during early breastfeeding may reduce antidepressant withdrawal symptoms or, alternatively, that at-risk neonates benefit from another mechanism associated with breastfeeding.

Antipsychotics

Small case numbers to date suggest low or very low transfer for the majority of antipsychotic drugs into breastmilk at therapeutic doses but higher RIDs have been found for sulpiride and amisulpride. For these agents the estimated values can exceed 10% [60, 62, 63]. Relatively few side effects have been reported although only limited clinical observations are available [64]. Some authors advise against clozapine therapy during breastfeeding because there is little clinical experience, and sedation and adverse haematological effects have been reported in the infants [60].

Lamotrigine

This drug is one of the best researched psychotropic agents in regard to lactational use and findings have been described comprehensively in the Drugs and Lactation Database [60]. The mean RID for lamotrigine has been estimated in case series as 7.6–9.2% albeit with wide confidence intervals. Reported plasma levels in breastfed infants vary widely and in one study about a fifth reached serum levels within the therapeutic range for epilepsy within the first 2 months postpartum [65].

There have been occasional reports of adverse effects, including withdrawal symptoms after abrupt weaning. One infant, who had a high plasma level in the context of a high maternal dose of lamotrigine (850 mg daily), was reported to have experienced a severe apnoeic episode. Recommendations for clinical practice [60] include that:

- breastfed infants should be carefully monitored for side effects such as respiratory problems, skin rash, drowsiness or poor sucking
- that infant serum levels should be measured if toxicity is suspected
- that monitoring of infant platelet count and liver function is advisable

However, the advice to measure infant serum concentrations before and after increases of maternal lamotrigine dosage will be difficult to implement in clinical practice.

Breastfeeding should not be abruptly discontinued to avoid the infant developing withdrawal symptoms. However, if the infant develops a skin rash, breastfeeding should be stopped until the cause has been established.

In the long term the mother's use of lamotrigine during breastfeeding does not seem to affect the child's development.

Lithium

Because lithium is not protein bound in maternal plasma, it easily enters breast milk and, in several case reports, breastfed infants had serum levels up to 50% of the maternal value [60]. Several cases of infant health problems have been described, including suspected lithium intoxication, abnormal thyroid function tests, slow weight gain and delay in motor development [60]. It has also been highlighted that numerous reports exist of infants without any signs of lithium toxicity or developmental problems and that maternal lithium therapy should not be an absolute contraindication to breastfeeding of full-term infants [60]. Great caution is advised when making decisions about breastfeeding during lithium therapy. It is sometimes recommended to monitor infant serum lithium, renal and thyroid function in intervals but these precautionary measures may not be possible in most countries. Breastfeeding should be discontinued immediately, and the infant evaluated if they appear restless or lethargic or have feeding problems. In the UK, clinicians generally advise against breastfeeding during lithium therapy.

In a recent study of 24 cases Imaz et al. measured lithium levels in the first 2 months postpartum in infants exposed to lithium in late pregnancy and found that they rapidly decreased when the mothers did not breastfeed [66]. They were below the detection limit in 80% of infants by the end of the first week. In fully breastfeeding infants this level was reached only at about 2 months. Interestingly, however, partial breastfeeding was similar to formula feeding so that this is an option available to mothers treated with lithium. These results are encouraging but require confirmation in other studies and an infant monitoring protocol that is feasible and locally agreed.

Principles of Prescribing during Breastfeeding

The relative infant dose is useful as a rough guide for the likelihood of side effects in the child and choice of drug. For example, if a breastfeeding woman requires an antidepressant or antipsychotic drug but has no past history of treatment for her illness, an agent with a low RID should be selected. If a woman with a psychiatric history has, however, responded to an antidepressant or antipsychotic medication with a moderately high RID, for example, then it is reasonable to continue this medication because otherwise the therapeutic effect might be lost for a relatively uncertain gain for her child. Drugs with very high RIDs need to be considered with caution.

It is sometimes suggested that mothers should 'pump and dump' breast milk after taking a medication dose. There are no or only limited data on time courses of milk concentrations for most psychotropic drugs and there is no clinical evidence to support this approach; in fact, it would probably mean adding to the mother's burden of mental illness.

Medication that causes recently delivered mothers significant sedation should be avoided if possible, since it can hinder nursing and baby care. If a mother feels sedated, she should be advised not to breastfeed unsupervised. If the sedative effect of a medication does not resolve, switching to a less sedative agent should be considered and support put in place regarding another adult being present to care for the infant.

During breastfeeding, mothers should be advised to monitor their baby for adverse effects such as excessive sedation and poor feeding and side effects seen in adults. If in doubt, mothers should seek advice from their health visitor or primary care physician.

Premature babies have little ability to metabolise psychotropic drugs and breastfeeding may lead to drug accumulation. Many maternity services in the UK offer donor milk in these circumstances.

Helpful Resources

There are multiple resources readily available on the internet to prescribers in mental health. The Royal College of Psychiatrists (www.rcpsych.ac.uk/mental-health/treatments-and-wellbeing) has published leaflets on perinatal mental illnesses and brief overviews of the reproductive safety of the main psychotropic classes. For rapid access to brief summaries and recommendations for busy mental health professionals the *Pocket Prescriber Psychiatry* (2024) includes a section on perinatal prescribing. Individual drug monographs of the UK Teratology Information Centre (https://uktis.org) are available for health professionals in general via institutional subscription. This service also provides patient information leaflets at no cost. In the US the Organization of Teratology Information Specialists (OTIS) publishes similar factsheets (https://mothertobaby.org/about-otis). An excellent resource specifically for breastfeeding issues is the Drugs and Lactation Database of the Toxicology Data Network in the US (https://toxnet.nlm.nih.gov/newtoxnet/lactmed.htm) which is free of charge. It provides regularly updated clinical summaries of current evidence related to medication and breastfeeding and a more detailed account of recent research studies.

For more in-depth study three helpful resources should be mentioned: the extensive analyses of the evidence and consensus guidelines by the British Association of Psychopharmacology [2], the Maudsley Prescribing Guidelines in Psychiatry [67] which include a chapter on pregnancy and lactation, and the guidance for multi-disciplinary assessment and management of neonates exposed to psychotropic medication before delivery [57].

Summary and Conclusions

This chapter aims to provide an overview of the current evidence base regarding the reproductive safety of the main psychotropic drug classes and implications for clinical practice. We have seen that in recent studies of antidepressant and antipsychotic drugs, lamotrigine and lithium, risks of major congenital malformations are much lower than previously reported or, more frequently, are completely accounted for by confounding factors. Improvements have also recently been made in investigations of other reproductive outcomes, especially the neurodevelopment of exposed children, and similar trends are being seen here. This is a welcome development for prescribers, but uncertainties remain about pregnancy outcomes and the health of neonates and infants exposed during breastfeeding where significantly more high-quality research is required.

Evidence that the use of valproate in pregnancy causes a large increase of major congenital malformations and major disruptions of children's neurodevelopment has gradually strengthened and has recently led to major restrictions of its use in psychiatric practice.

We have also in recent years gained more insights into those non-medication factors that cause adverse reproductive outcomes but were previously difficult to disentangle from drug effects. These 'confounders' include diabetes, obesity, smoking, substance misuse, maternal physical comorbidities, poverty, high levels of stress, suboptimal nutrition and environmental exposures. Most of these are significantly more prevalent in pregnant women with severe mental disorders and now require more attention in research and clinical practice. That such issues need to be tackled long before conception emphasises the importance of reproductive counselling for women with childbearing potential by general adult mental health teams. This is a neglected area at present. Once a woman is planning a pregnancy she can be referred to a specialist perinatal mental health team whose services are increasingly available in the UK (see Chapter 24, 'Pre-pregnancy Advice and Planning').

Because the rate of publications on the reproductive safety of psychotropic drugs has been increasing rapidly and research methodologies are steadily growing more complex, it has become very challenging for prescribers to remain up-to-date with and interpret recent findings. However, the latest research papers will rarely have immediate implications for clinical practice; these are rather based on accumulating evidence which undergoes a careful and ongoing evaluation of the balance of risks and benefits. There are several helpful resources available that provide summaries and interpretation for prescribers.

Further Reading

MZ Ankarfeldt, J Petersen, JT Andersen, H Li, SP Motsko, T Fast, et al. Exposure to duloxetine during pregnancy and risk of congenital malformations and stillbirth: a nationwide cohort study in Denmark and Sweden. *PLoS Med.* 2021;18(11):e1003851.

M Butler, TRJ Nicholson, JP Rogers, editors. *Pocket prescriber psychiatry.* Boca Raton, London, New York: CRC Press; 2024.

KM Deligiannidis, S Meltzer-Brody, H Gunduz-Bruce, J Doherty, J Jonas, S Li. Effect of zuranolone vs placebo in postpartum depression: a randomized clinical trial. *JAMA Psychiatry.* 2021;78(9): 951–9.

H Hummels, D Bertholee, D van der Meer, JP Smit, B Wilffert, P Ter Horst. The quality of lactation studies including antipsychotics. *Eur J Clin Pharmacol.* 2016;72(12): 1417–25.

GN Konstantinou, SN Vigod, S Mehta, ZJ Daskalakis, DM Blumberger. A systematic review of non-invasive neurostimulation for the treatment of depression during pregnancy. *J Affect Disord.* 2020;272:259–68.

DR Morales, J Slattery, S Evans, X Kurz. Antidepressant use during pregnancy and risk of autism spectrum disorder and attention deficit hyperactivity disorder: systematic review of observational studies and methodological considerations. *BMC Med.* 2018;16(1):6.

PB Pennell, L Peng, DJ Newport, JC Ritchie, A Koganti, DK Holley, et al. Lamotrigine in pregnancy: clearance, therapeutic drug monitoring, and seizure frequency. *Neurology.* 2008;70:2130–6.

E Poels, L Schrijver, AM Kamperman, MHJ Hillegers, WJG Hoogendijk, SA Kushner, SJ Roza. Long-term neurodevelopmental consequences of intrauterine exposure to lithium and antipsychotics: a systematic review and meta-analysis. *Eur Child Adolesc Psychiatry.* 2018;27(9):1209–30.

AC Sujan, AS Öberg, PD Quinn, BM D'Onofrio. Annual Research Review: maternal antidepressant use during pregnancy and offspring neurodevelopmental problems – a critical review and recommendations for future research. *J Child Psychol Psychiatry.* 2019;60(4):356–76.

SN Vigod, T Gomes, AS Wilton, VH Taylor, JG Ray. Antipsychotic drug use in pregnancy: high dimensional, propensity matched, population based cohort study. *BMJ.* 2015;350:h2298.

References

1. M Persson, S Cnattingius, E Villamor, J Söderling, B Pasternak, O Stephansson, M Neovius. Risk of major congenital malformations in relation to maternal overweight and obesity severity: cohort study of 1.2 million singletons. *BMJ.* 2017;357:j2563.
2. RH McAllister-Williams, DS Baldwin, R Cantwell, A Easter, E Gilvarry, V Glover, et al. British Association for Psychopharmacology consensus guidance on the use of psychotropic medication preconception, in pregnancy and postpartum 2017. *J Psychopharmacol.* 2017;31(5):519–52.
3. SY Gao, QJ Wu, C Sun, T Zhang, Z Shen, C Liu, et al. Selective serotonin reuptake inhibitor use during early pregnancy and congenital malformations: a systematic review and meta-analysis of cohort studies of more than 9 million births. *BMC Med.* 2018;16(1):205.
4. K Furu, H Kieler, B Haglund, A Engeland, R Selmer, O Stephansson, et al. Selective serotonin reuptake inhibitors and venlafaxine in early pregnancy and risk of birth defects: population based cohort study and sibling design [published correction appears in BMJ. 2015;350: h2235]. *BMJ.* 2015;350:h1798.
5. D Lassen, ZN Ennis, P Damkier. First-trimester pregnancy exposure to venlafaxine or duloxetine and risk of major congenital malformations: a systematic review. *Basic Clin Pharmacol Toxicol.* 2016;118(1):32–6.
6. L Kolding, V Ehrenstein, L Pedersen, P Sandager, OB Petersen, N Uldbjerg, LH Pedersen. Antidepressant use in pregnancy and severe cardiac malformations: Danish register-based study. *BJOG.* 2021;128(12):1949–57.
7. KF Huybrechts, BT Bateman, A Pawar, LG Bessette, H Mogun, R Levin, et al. Maternal and fetal outcomes following exposure to duloxetine in pregnancy: cohort study. *BMJ.* 2020;368:m237.
8. MZ Ankarfeldt, J Petersen, JT Andersen, H Li, SP Motsko, T Fas, et al. Exposure to duloxetine during pregnancy and risk of congenital malformations and stillbirth: a nationwide cohort study in Denmark and Sweden]. *PLoS Med.* 2021;18(11): e1003851.

9. M Smit, KM Dolman, A Honig. Mirtazapine in pregnancy and lactation: a systematic review. *Eur Neuropsychopharmacol.* 2016;26(1):126–35.

10. A Ostenfeld, TS Petersen, LH Pedersen, HB Westergaard, ECL Løkkegaard, JT Andersen. Mirtazapine exposure in pregnancy and fetal safety: a nationwide cohort study. *Acta Psychiatr Scand.* 2022;145(6):557–67.

11. V Hendrick, R Suri, MJ Gitlin, E Ortiz-Portillo. Bupropion use during pregnancy: a systematic review. *Prim Care Companion CNS Disord.* 2017;19(5):17r02160.

12. KF Huybrechts, K Palmsten, J Avorn, LS Cohen, LB Holmes, JM Franklin, et al. Antidepressant use in pregnancy and the risk of cardiac defects. *N Engl J Med.* 2014;370(25):2397–407.

13. BAJ Källén, PO Olausson. Maternal drug use in early pregnancy and infant cardiovascular defect. *Reprod Toxicol.* 2003;17(3):255–61.

14. R Vlenterie, MMHJ van Gelder, HR Anderson, L Andersson, BFP Broekman, G Dubnov-Raz, et al. Associations between maternal depression, antidepressant use during pregnancy, and adverse pregnancy outcomes: an individual participant data meta-analysis. *Obstet Gynecol.* 2021;138(4): 633–46.

15. EL Moses-Kolko, D Bogen, J Perel, A Bregar, K Uhl, B Levin, KL Wisner. Neonatal signs after late in utero exposure to serotonin reuptake inhibitors: literature review and implications for clinical applications. *JAMA.* 2005;293(19):2372–83.

16. R Masarwa, B Bar-Oz, E Gorelik, S Reif, A Perlman, I Matok. Prenatal exposure to selective serotonin reuptake inhibitors and serotonin norepinephrine reuptake inhibitors and risk for persistent pulmonary hypertension of the newborn: a systematic review, meta-analysis, and network meta-analysis. *Am J Obstet Gynecol.* 2019;220(1): 57.e1–57.e13.

17. QX Ng, N Venkatanarayanan, CYX Ho, WS Sim, DY Lim, W-S Yeo. Selective serotonin reuptake inhibitors and persistent pulmonary hypertension of the newborn: an update meta-analysis. *J Womens Health.* 2019;28(3):331–8.

18. EA Suarez, BT Bateman, S Hernández-Díaz, L Straub, KL Wisner, KJ Gray, et al. Association of antidepressant use during pregnancy with risk of neurodevelopmental disorders in children. *JAMA Intern Med.* 2022;182(11):1149–60.

19. KF Huybrechts, S Hernández-Díaz, E Patorno, RJ Desai, H Mogun, SZ Dejene, et al. Antipsychotic use in pregnancy and the risk for congenital malformations. *JAMA Psychiatry.* 2016;73(9):938–46.

20. KF Huybrechts, L Straub, P Karlsson, L Pazzagli, K Furu, M Gissler, et al. Association of in utero antipsychotic medication exposure with risk of congenital malformations in Nordic countries and the US. *JAMA Psychiatry.* 2023;80(2):156–66.

21. Y Park, S Hernandez-Diaz, BT Bateman, JM Cohen, RJ Desai, E Patorno, et al. Continuation of atypical antipsychotic medication during early pregnancy and the risk of gestational diabetes. *Am J Psychiatry.* 2018;175(6):564–74.

22. E Heinonen, L Forsberg, U Nörby, K Wide, K Källén. Antipsychotic use during pregnancy and risk for gestational diabetes: a national register-based cohort study in Sweden. *CNS Drugs.* 2022;36(5):529–39.

23. Z Wang, AYL Chan, D Coghill, P Ip, WCY Lau, E Simonoff, et al. Association between prenatal exposure to antipsychotics and attention-deficit/ hyperactivity disorder, autism spectrum disorder, preterm birth, and small for gestational age. *JAMA Intern Med.* 2021;181(10):1332–40.

24. Z Wang, AS Yuen, KH Wong, AY Chan, D Coghill, E Simonoff, et al. Association between prenatal antipsychotic exposure and the risk of attention-deficit/ hyperactivity disorder and autism spectrum disorder: a systematic review

and meta-analysis. *Neurosci Biobehav Rev.* 2024;160:105635.

25. X Liu, BB Trabjerg, T Munk-Olsen, J Christensen, JW Dreier. Association of maternal antipsychotic prescription during pregnancy with standardized test scores of schoolchildren in Denmark. *JAMA Intern Med.* 2022;182(10):1035–43.
26. C Bruno, CE Cesta, V Hjellvik, SP Ulrichsen, MH Bjørk, BÖ Esen, et al. Antipsychotic use during pregnancy and risk of specific neurodevelopmental disorders and learning difficulties in children: a multinational cohort study. *EClinicalMedicine.* 2024;70:102531.
27. F Misawa, T Kishimoto, K Hagi, JM Kane, CU Correll. Safety and tolerability of long-acting injectable versus oral antipsychotics: a meta-analysis of randomized controlled studies comparing the same antipsychotics. *Schizophr Res.* 2016;176(2–3):220–30.
28. AA Westin, M Brekke, E Molden, E Skogvoll, I Castberg, O Spigset. Treatment with antipsychotics in pregnancy: changes in drug disposition. *Clin Pharmacol Ther.* 2018;103(3):477–84.
29. K Meador, MW Reynolds, S Crean, K Fahrbach, C Probst. Pregnancy outcomes in women with epilepsy: a systematic review and meta-analysis of published pregnancy registries and cohorts. *Epilepsy Res.* 2008;81:1–13.
30. R Bromley, J Weston, N Adab, J Greenhalgh, A Sanniti, AJ McKay, et al. Treatment for epilepsy in pregnancy: neurodevelopmental outcomes in the child. *Cochrane Database Syst Rev.* 2014;(10):CD010236.
31. AA Veroniki, P Rios, E Cogo, SE Straus, Y Finkelstein, R Kealey, et al. Comparative safety of antiepileptic drugs for neurological development in children exposed during pregnancy and breast feeding: a systematic review and network meta-analysis. *BMJ Open.* 2017;7:e017248.
32. J Christensen, TK Grønborg, MJ Sørensen, D Schendel, ET Parner, LH Pedersen, M Vestergaard. Prenatal valproate exposure and risk of autism spectrum disorders and childhood autism. *JAMA.* 2013;309(16):1696–703.
33. European Medicines Agency. CMDh agrees to strengthen warnings on the use of valproate medicines in women and girls. Press release. 2014 21 Nov. https://tinyurl.com/jpzv6j43
34. R Bromley, N Adab, M Bluett-Duncan, J Clayton-Smith, J Christensen, K Edwards, et al. Monotherapy treatment of epilepsy in pregnancy: congenital malformation outcomes in the child. *Cochrane Database Syst Rev.* 2023;8(8):CD010224.
35. E Honybun, E Cockle, CB Malpas, TJ O'Brien, FJ Vajda, P Perucca, G Rayner. Neurodevelopmental and functional outcomes following in utero exposure to antiseizure medication: a systematic review. *Neurology.* 2024;102(8):e209175.
36. Medicines and Healthcare Products Regulatory Authority. Public Assessment Report of antiepileptic drugs: review of safety of use during pregnancy. https://tinyurl.com/375m2zh8
37. D Baldwin, A Wieck. Withdrawal of, and alternatives to, valproate-containing medicines in girls and women of childbearing potential who have a psychiatric illness. Royal College of Psychiatrists Position Statement (PS 04/18). 2018. www.bap.org.uk/pdfs/PS04-18-December2018.pdf
38. J Shakespeare, SM Sisodia. Guidance document on valproate use in women and girls of childbearing years. Royal College of General Practitioners and Association of British Neurologists and Royal College of Physicians, Version 2. 2021 23 Jan. https://tinyurl.com/4js25dk7f
39. Medicines and Healthcare Products Regulatory Authority. CPRD study monitoring the use of valproate in girls and women in the UK: January 2010 to December 2019. 2020. https://tinyurl.com/49rpsmx2
40. A Mohamed, AR Ramos, A Memon, A Crutchlow, A Marshall. Re-audit of sodium valproate: Risk minimization in

women of childbearing age. Abstract. Royal College of Psychiatrists, International Congress, 21–24 June. 2021.

41. MM Watila, A James, K Milne, G Mackay. Valproate pregnancy prevention scheme: What are the barriers to enrolling patients and how do we meet them? *BMJ Neurol Open*. 2023;5(2):e000433.

42. National Institute for Care and Health Excellence. Antenatal and postnatal mental health: clinical management and service guidance. Clinical Guideline (CG192). 2014.

43. AR Polepally, PB Pennell, RC Brundage, ZN Stowe, DJ Newport, AC Viguera, et al. Model-based lamotrigine clearance during pregnancy: clinical implication. *Ann Clin Trans Neurol*. 2014;1(2):99–106.

44. National Guideline Centre (UK). *Evidence review: Therapeutic drug monitoring in women and girls: Epilepsies in children, young people and adults: diagnosis and management: Evidence review 8*. London: National Institute for Health and Care Excellence; 2022.

45. Medicines and Health Care Products Agency. Antiepileptic drugs in pregnancy: updated advice following comprehensive safety review. *Drug Safety Update*. 2021;14(6).

46. RL McCrea, I Nazareth, SJ Evans, DPJ Osborn, V Pinfold, PJ Cowen, I Petersen. Lithium prescribing during pregnancy: a UK primary care database study. *PLoS ONE*. 2015;10(3):e0121024.

47. RF McKnight, M Adida, K Budge, S Stockton, GM Goodwin, JR Geddes. Lithium toxicity profile: a systematic review and meta-analysis. *Lancet*. 2012;379(9817):721–8.

48. B Boyle, E Garne, M Loane, M-C Addor, L Arriola, C Cavero-Carbonell, et al. The changing epidemiology of Ebstein's anomaly and its relationship with maternal mental health conditions: a European registry-based study. *Cardiol Young*. 2017;27(4):677–85.

49. E Patorno, KF Huybrechts, BT Bateman, JM Cohen, RJ Desai, H Mogun, et al. Lithium use in pregnancy and the risk of cardiac malformations. *N Engl J Med*. 2017;376(23):2245–54.

50. ACOG Committee on Practice Bulletins – Obstetrics. ACOG Practice Bulletin: Clinical management guidelines for obstetrician-gynecologists number 92, April 2008 (replaces practice bulletin number 87, November 2007). Use of psychiatric medications during pregnancy and lactation. *Obstet Gynecol*. 2008;111(4):1001–20.

51. M Torfs, T Hompes, M Ceulemans, K Van Calsteren, C Vanhole, A Smits. Early postnatal outcome and care after in utero exposure to lithium: a single center analysis of a Belgian tertiary university hospital. *Int J Environ Res Public Health*. 2022;19(16):10111.

52. M Schou. What happened later to the lithium babies? A follow-up study of children born without malformations. *Acta Psychiatr Scand*. 1976;54(3):193–7.

53. GM Goodwin, PM Haddad, IN Ferrier, JK Aronson, T Barnes, A Cipriani, et al. Evidence-based guidelines for treating bipolar disorder: revised third edition recommendations from the British Association for Psychopharmacology. *J Psychopharmacol*. 2016;30(6):495–553.

54. R Wesseloo, AI Wierdsma, IL van Kamp, T Munk-Olsen, WJG Hoogendijk, SA Kushner, V Bergink. Lithium dosing strategies during pregnancy and the postpartum period. *Br J Psychiatry*. 2017;211(1):31–6.

55. NM Molenaar, E Poels, T Robakis, R Wesseloo, V Bergink. Management of lithium dosing around delivery: an observational study. *Bipolar Disord*. 2021;23(1):49–54.

56. WE Heinonen, K Tötterman, K Bäck, I Sarman, L Forsberg, J Svedenkrans. High lithium concentration at delivery is a potential risk factor for adverse outcomes in breastfed infants: a retrospective cohort study. *Int J Bipolar Disord*. 2023;11(1):36.

57. The Pan-London Perinatal Mental Health Network and the London Neonatal Operational Delivery Network. Pan-London perinatal mental health: guidance

for newborn assessment. 2017. https://tinyurl.com/ymnajrm4

58. Royal College of Paediatrics. Breastfeeding in the UK – position statement. 2021. https://tinyurl.com/4jrevmvt
59. PN Bennett. Use of monographs in drugs. In: PN Bennett, editor. *Drugs and human lactation*. Amsterdam: Elsevier Science Publishers; 1996. p. 67–74.
60. Drugs and Lactation Database (LactMed). Bethesda, MD: National Library of Medicine; 2024. www.ncbi.nlm.nih.gov/books/NBK501922
61. N Kieviet, C Hoppenbrouwers, KM Dolman, J Berkhof, H Wennink, A Honig. Risk factors for poor neonatal adaptation after exposure to antidepressants in utero. *Acta Paediatr.* 2015;104(4):384–91.
62. F Uguz. A new safety scoring system for the use of psychotropic drugs during lactation. *Am J Ther.* 2021;28(1): e118–e126.
63. T Hale. *Medications and mother's milk.* Amarillo, TX: Hale Publishing; 2012.
64. F Uguz. Second-generation antipsychotics during the lactation period: a comparative systematic review on infant safety. *J Clin Psychopharmacol.* 2016;36(3):244–52.
65. I Alvarez, E Heinonen, J Svedenkrans. Lamotrigine exposure during lactation: concentrations and effects in the newborn. *Neurotoxicol Teratol.* 2023;98:2.
66. ML Imaz, K Langohr, M Torra, D Soy, L García-Esteve, R Martin-Santos. Neonatal feeding trajectories in mothers with bipolar disorder taking lithium: pharmacokinetic data. *Front Pharmacol.* 2021;22;12:752022.
67. DM Taylor, TRE Barnes, AH Young. *The Maudsley® prescribing guidelines in psychiatry*. 14th edition. Chichester, UK: John Wiley & Sons Ltd; 2021.

Chapter 28

Psychological Therapies for Parental Mental Health in the Perinatal Period

What Works?

Heather O'Mahen, Rachel Mycroft and Camilla Rosan

The perinatal period is a time of significant psychological change and adaptation (see Chapter 3, 'Physiological Changes in Pregnancy and Common Obstetric Medical Disorders' and Chapter 8, 'Psychological Aspects of Infertility, Assisted Conception and Pregnancy Loss'). This includes managing a strong sense of responsibility for the baby (or babies), high levels of uncertainty and potential associated worries for the baby and childbirth, changes in roles and identity (e.g. changes in paid work and parenting); rapidly learning new skills and adapting to significantly different routines; changes in relationships, particularly forming a new relationship with the baby (during pregnancy and after the baby is born); and adjustments in existing relationships, particularly the couple and family relationship and changes in body shape and body image. Together, these changes can present challenges that contribute to existing mental health problems, a relapse in previous problems or a new onset of problems. Emerging research is also demonstrating that hormonal changes in oestrogen and progesterone across pregnancy and the early postnatal period can have an impact on learning, such that fears may be more likely to be overgeneralised across contexts when there are higher levels of oestrogen and progesterone (as occurs in the later stages of pregnancy), and this may give rise to increased risk for clinical levels of anxiety [1]. At the same time, increases in oestrogen are related to improvements in extinction (weakening an association between a feared object or situation and a negative outcome), suggesting that exposure-based treatments may be especially effective during these periods [2]. These challenges occur against a backdrop of strong societal and cultural beliefs about parenthood which can shape individuals' reactions and evaluations of the impact of perinatal changes in their lives.

Together, these social and psychological factors point to the value of psychological interventions adapted to the perinatal period. There is a strong evidence base for psychological interventions for a range of mental health disorders, particularly in the anxiety disorders, post-traumatic stress disorder (PTSD), obsessive-compulsive disorder (OCD), depression and prolonged grief disorder. For example, given the strength of evidence for cognitive behavioural therapy (CBT) compared to both treatment-as-usual and medication, and its longer-lasting impact [3, 4, 5], they are recommended as first-line treatments for PTSD, OCD, panic and social anxiety disorders in international

The authors would like to thank Dr Hannah Wilson for their review and contribution to the chapter. Our thanks also go to Hannah Hopson and Dr Alex Tsefos for their support with the literature review and referencing.

clinical guidance [3, 6, 7]. For PTSD, medication is recommended as an option where the patient prefers it. For severe OCD, social anxiety or panic disorder, or those who have not responded to previous psychological treatment, a combination of psychological treatment with medication is recommended [8]. There is also evidence for the utility of psychological therapies for depression [9], eating disorders (particularly bulimia nervosa [10, 11, 12], borderline personality disorder [13] and for managing prevention/relapse prevention of psychosis/bipolar disorder [14] and depression (mindfulness-based cognitive therapy [6] and CBT [15]). For severe and/or treatment-resistant problems, a combination of psychological treatment and medication is recommended for these latter mental health disorders. The National Institute for Clinical Excellence (NICE) recommendation for depression is a combination of psychological therapies like CBT or interpersonal therapy, and antidepressant medications for moderate to severe depression while also promoting self-help strategies and lifestyle changes [6]. Regular monitoring and tailored approaches are essential, especially for individuals with specific needs or risks. Guidelines from NICE for bulimia nervosa suggest using CBT as the first-line treatment, along with nutritional counselling and medical monitoring [11]. For severe cases, combining CBT with medication and ensuring ongoing support and follow-up is crucial. For borderline personality disorder (BPD) NICE guidelines recommend dialectical behaviour therapy (DBT) as a primary treatment, with a focus on developing coping skills and emotional regulation [13]. For severe cases, combining DBT with medication and regular follow-up care is essential. Recommendations from NICE for managing psychosis/bipolar disorder include a combination of antipsychotic medication and psychotherapy, such as CBT [14]. For bipolar disorder, a combination of mood stabilisers, antipsychotic medication and psychological therapy is advised, with ongoing monitoring and support tailored to individual needs.

Although there are fewer trials of perinatally adapted interventions, particularly large, fully powered trials, the extant research base suggests that psychological interventions in the perinatal period are on par with similar interventions (e.g. interpersonal psychotherapy for depression) offered to non-perinatal populations [16, 17, 18]. For these reasons, 15 of 16 clinical guidelines that address the treatment of perinatal-specific depression (from 12 different countries) recommend psychological therapies [19]. This chapter focuses on psychological therapies which target parental mental health, commonly in the mother or birthing person. Therapies focused on the parent–infant relationship are reviewed in Chapter 35, 'Mother–Infant Focused Interventions: What Works to Improve the Mother–Infant Relationship' and interventions for partners and fathers in Chapter 6, 'Paternal Mental Health in the Perinatal Period: Impact on Family Relationships'.

Decision-Making about Use of Psychological Treatment in the Perinatal Period

At assessment, the patient should be informed about available evidence-based interventions. Decision-making about which treatments to use should also take into account the patient's preferences (e.g. for type of treatment, mode of delivery such as in-person or remote, and whether to have individual, couple or group treatment), history of treatment and readiness to undertake treatment (e.g. 'stage of change' [20]). A key issue of concern for women and birthing people is the potential risk of medication use during pregnancy and breastfeeding, with a number expressing a preference for psychological treatments over medication as a result [21]. A careful, individualised discussion about the cost-benefit ratio of medication can support women and birthing people in personalising their care (Chapter 26, 'Principles of Prescribing'). Psychological interventions may be important alternative or adjunctive treatments. Likewise, the patient's history with different psychological treatments should be considered, as this may influence decisions about what has worked and what they might prefer. It should be noted that lack of success with a given treatment modality should not necessarily rule that treatment out as the individual may not have been ready for the treatment at the time, or it may have been delivered in a less-adherent fashion. Careful consideration of these issues and the patient's current state of readiness to undertake specific interventions, including their stage of pregnancy (see Timing of Psychological Therapy section), can help to ensure appropriate treatment 'matching'.

General Principles for Psychological Therapy in the Perinatal Period

Psychological Assessment and Formulation

Parents in the perinatal period point to the importance of psychological therapy recognising and addressing pregnancy and having a newborn [22], and an unwillingness to engage with interventions that do not address these factors [23, 24]. Perinatally adapted psychological therapy differs from treatment outside this period in that it simultaneously holds in mind the needs of the parent, the infant, the relationship between them and other family members. This 'perinatal frame of mind' (see Chapter 1, 'The Perinatal Frame of Mind'), makes psychological therapies different to those which focus on one individual. As such, a psychological assessment will include a biopsychosocial assessment of the parent's mental health, an assessment of the relationship of the parent and infant, including the parent's perceived bond with the baby, meanings of this baby to the parent and, postnatally, interactions between the parent and infant, using observations of the mother or father with the baby wherever possible. Indications of support and conflict with close others and their impact on shared parenting and the parent's mood are also assessed. This information is then included in the formulation and, where appropriate, may also be a target for intervention.

In addition to an overlap with problems presenting at other points in the lifespan, it is also important to consider perinatal issues relating to pregnancy (e.g. fear of miscarriage, uncertainty about baby or mother's health), childbirth (e.g. fear of childbirth) and parenting (e.g. impact of challenges in feeding or with infant sleeping, lack of confidence in parenting) and to adapt interventions to suit the stage of the perinatal period. For example, different types of activities and exercise are suitable in early versus late pregnancy and in the postnatal period. Commonly the focus of a woman or birthing person's anxiety may shift from pregnancy and childbirth to parenting over time. It is important that therapists can follow a woman through her perinatal journey, for example, by providing postnatal follow-up. Having the same therapist and working on an integrated episode of psychological therapy across the perinatal period wherever possible can provide continuity, even though a variety of different service settings in maternity/obstetrics, primary care and other mental health services may also be involved.

Formulation and Treatment Planning

Information from the psychological assessment will be used to draw up a psychological formulation (an explanation of how the problems came about and what keeps them going). The formulation may include behaviours (e.g. avoidance, reassurance-seeking) or styles of thinking that maintain negative cycles in the here and now and may include important events and influences that have shaped the individual's beliefs and behaviours. It may focus on a particular presenting problem (e.g. OCD, PTSD) and/or be specific to a particular therapeutic orientation. Perinatal formulations will include the baby/unborn baby and the impact of relevant perinatal issues. The formulation will also consider risk to parent and baby, both direct risks (such as domestic violence, alcohol and substance use, self-harm and suicide, and safeguarding concerns) and indirect risks (such as the impact on the baby of maternal mental health problems in the short, medium and longer term) (see Chapter 23, 'Access, Assessment and Evaluation of Risk in Perinatal Mental Health Services').

Timing of Psychological Therapy

As in other areas of perinatal mental health treatment, it is important that parents can access psychological therapy in a timely way in the perinatal period because of the impact that parental mental health problems can have on the developing fetus and/or baby [25] and because, during pregnancy, it is crucial to address issues related to childbirth prior to delivery (see Chapter 33, 'Maternal Mood and Stress during Pregnancy: Effects on the Fetus and Child').

Psychological therapy typically involves consideration of difficult topics and problems, and these can be emotionally challenging for individuals undertaking treatment. Some individuals may not feel ready for this process, while others may wish to undertake these treatments in order to help them to achieve important changes in their life, relationships and mood. A careful individualised weighing up of the pros and cons of this process and expected benefits of undertaking an evidence-based intervention should be undertaken with each parent. Perinatal-specific considerations should be included; for example, parents may view treatment-related changes as giving them opportunities to be the parent they would like to be to their new baby. Others may perceive the disruptiveness of therapy as not appropriate during a busy, emotionally challenging, intensive period of life.

Of note, some treatments, such as CBT for anxiety and OCD and both eye movement desensitisation and reprocessing (EMDR) and CBT for PTSD, involve 'exposure' components that involve deliberately and repetitively approaching anxiety-producing stimuli (see Exposure-Based Approaches in CBT for Anxiety, OCD, PTSD and Eating Disorders section). There is evidence that exposure components are active mechanisms in these therapies [7, 26, 27, 28] which in several studies have enhanced outcomes. For example, where exposure was a component in treatment, effect sizes on perinatal anxiety were greater ($d = 1.33$ vs $d = 0.82$) [29]. However, it is important to note that exposure can be challenging to undertake and may result in temporary increases in distress during the most intensive parts of the treatment (typically between 3 and 5 weeks). Some therapists have expressed reluctance to conduct exposure-based procedures in pregnancy [30, 31], citing worries about the potential for negative effects on mother or infant because of possible temporary increases in cortisol in the pregnant mother or birthing person. However, research from trials using exposure during pregnancy has not reported any untoward effects on the unborn baby relative to those in the control condition or relative to population-level expected problems [31, 32, 33]. Other considerations include the timing of these procedures relative to childbirth. Research on hormones suggests that the later stages of pregnancy may be an especially effective time in which to undertake exposure-based treatment because extinction-based learning is stronger when oestrogen and progesterone levels are higher (though there are complex interactions with progesterone) [34]. For women close to their delivery date, guidance may include considering increasing the intensity of delivery (i.e. multiple times/week vs once/week) and joint decision-making about which content to undertake if, for example, this is the last session that can happen before delivery. A recent study of treatment for anxiety disorders during the perinatal period found that intensive delivery was perceived as highly acceptable and feasible to parents [32]. The weighing up of options for psychological intervention should be done by a psychological therapist with appropriate training who is practising under specialist perinatal supervision [35].

Delivery of Treatment

Psychological therapy may be accessed in a variety of settings or modalities and in accordance with stepped and collaborative care models, where available (i.e. [36, 37]). For example, individuals may first undertake guided self-help or group treatment but, if these do not result in improvements, may then engage in one-on-one psychological therapy. The existing evidence suggests that the effectiveness of treatment does not vary across mode of delivery (e.g. home, in-clinic, remote) [17]. Across the perinatal period, parents' circumstances may change their preferences for treatment delivery modality (e.g. medical complications, managing transport with a baby and other children, availability of support). Consideration may also include issues related to privacy/confidentiality and digital poverty.

Generic Therapeutic Factors in Psychosocial Treatments

All approaches to psychological therapy emphasise the importance of the therapeutic relationship as a key ingredient of change: it is seen as the foundation of therapeutic change – the 'necessary' component of treatment – from which emerge patient expectations for improvement and the ability to use specific therapeutic strategies to improve. In a review of specific common therapeutic factors associated with change, goal consensus, empathy, alliance between the therapist and patient, positive regard and therapist genuineness are key components and explain a significant proportion of patient improvement [38]. This evidence is important to consider in the perinatal period, a key life transition and point where the parent's identities, relationship with the co-parent and new relationship with the infant are tested. As such, people often reflect upon their own experiences of being parented and whether they would like to be the same or different. They may have increased contact with their own parents, or, where their parents are no longer present in their life due to bereavement or estrangement, they may notice their absence more. The importance of their attachment with their own parents and with their partner (where there is a partner) may be especially salient during this period, and this may be heightened as they seek to develop a new relationship with their infant(s) [39]. As such, therapists should remain alert to the importance of attachment styles during the perinatal period, and endeavour to provide a secure therapeutic relationship where the patient can feel safe to explore their attachment-related concerns [40].

Specific Therapeutic Factors in Psychological Treatments

With a strong therapeutic relationship in place, the evidence base supports the use of structured, personalised approaches focused on specific approaches to understanding and/or changing particular domains (interpersonal, behavioural, thoughts/learning, etc.). Critical to each of these approaches is the ability to administer the approach in a competent and adherent fashion, under appropriate perinatal specific supervision [41].

Types of Psychological Therapy

In the next sections, evidence-based therapeutic approaches that have been included in national guidance documents or, where there is not national guidance available for a particular mental health disorder, have guidance-level empirical support for them, are presented in turn, along with any specific perinatal considerations. Where perinatal-specific evidence is not available, it has been extrapolated from the general literature. Further work with perinatal populations is urgently needed, both to assess effectiveness of interventions with this population and also to examine what adaptations are appropriate and/or necessary to enable them to be applied effectively in the perinatal period. Table 28.1 provides an overview of psychological therapies for parental mental health problems in the perinatal period for which there is an established or emerging evidence base, with further details given in the text. Structured clinical management is not included in the scope of this chapter as it is a psychologically informed approach rather than a formal psychological therapy; however, it is noted that there is an evidence base for its effectiveness in emotionally unstable personality disorder (EUPD)/BPD.

Individual Therapies

Cognitive Behaviour Therapy

Cognitive behaviour therapy is a widely practised structured, present-oriented psychological therapy, associated with the greatest body of evidence across a wide range of presenting problems. The central tenet of CBT is that thoughts, behaviours and mood are interrelated [42]. It posits that problems with mood can be reduced through changing thoughts and associated behaviours. This is achieved through a set of procedures aimed at directly modifying unhelpful thinking patterns (cognitions and beliefs) and testing these modified beliefs with more effective behaviours (i.e. 'behavioural experiments') [43, 44].

The therapeutic 'stance' in CBT assumes that the therapist is a 'coach' rather than an expert, there to *collaboratively* support the patient to identify targets to work on, thoughts and beliefs to challenge, and behavioural domains in which to practise new thoughts. The principles and procedures of CBT are individualised to each patient's needs while sustaining a focus within treatment on changing thoughts and behaviours. To achieve this, the therapist takes a 'guided discovery' approach in which they try to gain an understanding of how the patient views their own situation and difficulties, help the patient to become aware of their underlying beliefs and assumptions, and work together to discover alternative perspectives and solutions. 'Socratic questioning' is a key strategy in CBT. It involves a shared dialogue of thought-provoking questions between the therapist and patient which is used to explore the patient's thoughts and behaviours and their relationship to their mood. Ultimately, the aim is to support the patient to become their own 'therapist'.

For depression, CBT typically starts with scheduling activities [45, 46]. This consists of identifying important behaviours such as self-care, diet, exercise or sleep that have

Table 28.1 Summary of which psychological therapies work for whom in the perinatal period

Psychological therapy	Perinatal mental health problem	Delivery modality
Individual therapies		
Cognitive behavioural therapy (CBT) including - Behavioural activation - Problem-solving treatment - Exposure-based interventions	• Depression • Anxiety disorders (social anxiety disorder, panic disorder, generalised anxiety disorder, health anxiety, obsessive compulsive disorder) • Bipolar disorder* • PTSD/complex PTSD (must be a trauma-focused treatment, i.e. trauma-focused cognitive therapy, cognitive processing therapy or prolonged exposure)* • Tokophobia (emerging evidence) • Bulimia nervosa and binge eating disorder* • Anorexia nervosa* • Psychosis* • Prolonged grief	• Individual • Group • In-person, clinic and home-based • Remote, guided self-help
Interpersonal psychotherapy (IPT)	Depression	• Individual • Group • In-person, clinic and home-based • Guided self-help
Eye movement desensitisation and reprocessing (EMDR)	• PTSD • Tokophobia (emerging evidence)	• Individual • In-person, clinic • Remote
Dialectical behaviour therapy (DBT)	• Complex needs associated with a diagnosis of EUPD/BPD*	• Individual + group • In-person, clinic • Remote
Prolonged grief disorder therapy (previously known as complicated grief therapy)	• Prolonged grief*	• Individual • In-person, clinic
Mentalisation-based treatment	• Complex needs associated with a diagnosis of EUPD/BPD*	• Individual, group • In-person, clinic
Short-term psychodynamic therapy	• Depression	• Individual • In-person, clinic
Couples therapies		
Behavioural couples therapy (BCT)	• Depression*	• Dyadic • In-person, clinic
Couples therapy for depression	• Depression*	• Dyadic • In-person, clinic

Table 28.1 *(cont.)*

Psychological therapy	Perinatal mental health problem	Delivery modality
Group treatment		
Mindfulness-based cognitive behavioural therapy	• Prevention of depression relapse in individuals with three or more previous episodes of depression	• Group

Note: * Evidence base for non-perinatal populations.

become imbalanced in the individual's life and setting up a schedule for achievable daily goals in these domains, which takes account of the context of pregnancy or caring for a baby (e.g. putting on music that baby and parent both enjoy, taking a short period of time to pause and message a friend or family member, agreeing and implementing a plan for eating a balanced meal each day, or drinking enough liquid, or a feasible calming bedtime routine for parent and baby and aiming for a regular bedtime). Scheduling behaviours is used throughout treatment, and as individuals build success in a particular domain they may choose to deepen their activity in that domain or to extend to other domains. Evidence has shown they are a key mechanism of mood improvement [47]. Where there are high standards, sometimes parents may be encouraged to do less of some behaviours (e.g. tidy and clean the home less frequently).

Restructuring cognitions is a key technique in CBT. The therapist and patient work together to identify negative or unhelpful thoughts, evaluate how reactions to these thoughts impact on behaviour and mood, identify alternative, more helpful thoughts, and then test these alternative thoughts in different behavioural contexts [45]. A variety of strategies and tools may be used to accomplish those aims, including keeping track of thoughts, moods and behaviours on a daily basis using thought records, identifying unhelpful patterns of thoughts, such as 'thinking biases', behavioural experiments to test beliefs and problem-solving to overcome challenges [48]. In the perinatal period, experiments commonly relate to the baby. For example, they may include challenging beliefs about needing to hide being a poor parent by being open about the struggles of parenting with other parents, rather than pretending that all is well; or letting someone else look after the baby for a short while where the parent is overinvolved and believes that bad things will befall their infant if they are not present. Lastly, CBT may also involve communication and relaxation skills.

Although CBT focuses on how current cognitions are impacting on behaviour and mood in the present, it acknowledges that early experiences can shape long-standing or 'core' beliefs. For example, a patient may see themself as worthless or a failure, and this can generalise to seeing themself as a bad parent. Another may see the world as an extremely dangerous place where bad things are very likely to happen: this might translate into hypervigilant and anxious parenting. Cognitive therapy works with the individual's unwritten rules for interacting with the world (i.e. 'conditional assumptions') that often present as 'if... then...' formats or as 'shoulds' or 'musts'. For example, 'if my baby struggles to feed, then I have failed as a mother' or 'I should always be able to soothe my baby quickly.' Reworking these rules can allow for greater flexibility in responding, such as 'there are lots of reasons why a baby might cry and it can be difficult to know why: I will try to systematically work my way through different solutions. Sometimes there is not an immediate solution to crying but it does pass: it does not reflect on my ability as a parent.'

Behavioural Activation

Another type of a CBT treatment that emphasises addressing the links between behaviour and mood without specifically addressing the *content* of negative thoughts is called behavioural activation (BA) [49]. It rests on the well-established observation that mood and behaviour are linked (e.g. [50]). Being able to engage in valued and/or pleasurable activities, and having a regular pattern of activities is associated with improved mood [51]. Ferster noted that when individuals encounter key blocks to valued or pleasurable activities (e.g. because of stressful events, transitions and/or environmental barriers) their response is often negative emotion, and a natural first reaction to negative emotion is to withdraw or avoid [52]. Although this is natural in most individuals and may in some circumstances be adaptive, it becomes problematic when the avoidance persists, reducing possibilities of overcoming barriers/problems and reducing the likelihood of experiencing positives associated with engaging in meaningful/rewarding behaviours. Depression can result when people become stuck in patterns of avoidance.

Behavioural activation aims to address these patterns of avoidance and to support individuals to re-engage with meaningful and rewarding/pleasurable behaviours. It acknowledges that to do this may, in the first steps, involve doing things that at first feel distressing and challenging, but in the longer term help to allow the person to live a more meaningful, engaged life. Like CBT, BA uses scheduling, but it also goes further to focus in-depth on working through patterns of avoidance in meaningful domains. It does not assume more activity per se is needed, but focuses on balance and self-care. This may be especially important to remember in the perinatal period, where parents may struggle with doing too much and may use activity in one domain to avoid activity in another. Because BA has a more specific focus on behaviours, it is perceived to be more straightforward to learn and carry out than CBT. In the perinatal period, where parents often have little time, may be significantly sleep deprived and have few opportunities for sustained attention focus, a straightforward approach such as BA may prove beneficial.

Exposure-Based Approaches in CBT for Anxiety, OCD, PTSD and Eating Disorders

A number of CBT treatments include exposure-based components in their interventions (EMDR and prolonged grief disorder therapy (PGDT) also use an exposure-based approach). Exposure involves purposively and repetitively confronting objects or situations that prompt distress and staying in those situations long enough for anxiety to decrease. There are two primary forms of exposure. *In vivo* exposure involves 'real life' confrontation of the feared object or situation. For example, a parent with OCD who fears that changing their infant's nappy in a public place will result in contamination, may purposefully undertake an exposure exercise where they go to a public toilet and change their baby's nappy there, staying in the situation long enough for their anxiety to decrease. Alternatively, a parent who has social anxiety and worries that other parents are judging their parenting skills may set up an exposure exercise where they ride a bus or go to a parenting group and stay in the situation until their anxiety decreases. The second form of exposure is called *imaginal exposure.* In imaginal exposure, the individual purposefully brings to mind a detailed and comprehensive 'here and now' image of the feared and/or traumatic situation. As part of the experience they may also imagine themselves successfully coping with the feared situation. A commonly used procedure in treatment for PTSD is to have the person call to mind the traumatic event(s) associated with their PTSD and to go through a detailed recollection of the event: this is known as 'reliving'. A parent who has experienced childbirth trauma, for example, may systematically and carefully go over a detailed recounting of the event with their therapist, who will attend to a number of features of the story, including 'hot spots' (highly emotional parts of the story) [53], gaps in the story and issues related to shame and guilt (e.g. 'I should have been more assertive about getting some support from the midwife, then things wouldn't have gone so wrong'). Extra attention is paid to retelling 'hot spots', reviewing contextual factors related to gaps in the story or finding other sources of information that might support filling in these gaps (e.g. a birth review with a midwife). Cognitive restructuring may also be a part of the process, whereby memories are updated with information that was not available at the time (e.g. 'at the time I thought I was going to die, however I now know that I didn't die and I am now safe and looking after my baby') and alternative compassionate interpretations may be used (e.g. 'I did my best to manage my labour and birth, and circumstances meant that in the end a caesarean section was the best thing for me and my baby').

Often, people are reluctant to engage in exposure because they believe that their anxiety will not decrease and will simply stay indefinitely and unbearably high. Not surprisingly, this leads people to want to avoid these situations, objects or memories, and if they encounter them, to escape them as quickly as possible. Together, these actions serve to confirm their negative beliefs. Some patients will point out that they have inadvertently encountered cues, objects or reminders associated with their distress or trauma previously and these have proven to be very upsetting events. The differences in exposure are that the encounter is not a surprise, it is purposefully approached, and that the person does not escape the situation or engage in other 'safety' behaviours or responses (e.g. compulsions). This is known as *response prevention.* Escape, safety and compulsive behaviours are associated with ongoing sensitisation to the object or event, but by preventing the response the individual is fully exposed to the anxiety. The individual then stays in the situation until anxiety decreases (anxiety cannot stay indefinitely high); and the individual repeats exposure exercises related to the feared/distressing stimulus until it results in less anxiety or distress even in the first moments of encounter, a process known as *habituation.* Thus, exposure gives the individual control over approaching feared stimuli and the opportunity to learn that their fears and anxieties can reduce and that they are not beholden to unexpected and often terrifying experiences.

Exposure-based approaches, although often very challenging to undertake, when followed through with can make a significant difference in patient's lives. 'I really hated that [exposure] with a fiery passion, but I did it and I think it was really useful…' (patient with PTSD). The therapist's competence and attitude in using exposure strategies can help provide the patient with the confidence to tolerate the temporary worsening of affect associated with exposure and see it through to its successful conclusion. To support the therapist, it is critical that they have skilled supervision in exposure. 'Being really clear on what the work involves and being really confident in how some of the work involves exposure and increasing anxiety and how that's safe, is really important in this population...' [54].

Some patients may experience inter-sessional distress and dysregulation during the acute initial phases of exposure. Those patients with social support and some life stability will likely find weathering these possible periods of dysregulation easier than those in more challenging circumstances or for those with other emotion dysregulation challenges. These latter factors should be considered when weighing up undertaking treatments with exposure-based components. Different approaches may be considered, including spending a preparatory period getting ready for the exposure components and managing dysregulation that might occur; starting with a less intensive approach to exposure initially to help the individual begin to manage the process first; or using newer approaches to exposure that do not require a graded, hierarchical approach to exposure, but instead require only that the individual engages in repetitive exposure. In PTSD treatment, the therapist and patient may begin with stabilisation and grounding techniques, particularly where there is a tendency to dissociation. They may also consider using narrative exposure or EMDR-based approaches, which some patients report they find gentler to undertake. Lastly, the patient may choose to delay an exposure approach to another time. In all instances, the patient should be clearly advised of the efficacy and pros and cons of each approach and have the option of full access to each approach (where they are available) so they are able to engage in fully informed decision-making.

Interpersonal Psychotherapy

Interpersonal therapy (IPT) is a time-limited, structured treatment for depression. It focuses on the connection between low mood and disturbing interpersonal life events, noting that depression often follows bereavements, life transitions or conflict with close others. Depression symptoms further complicate these situations, creating a difficult downward cycle. It may have particular relevance in the perinatal period, given the importance of relationships, support and conflict in managing the life transition of having a baby. It is also of relevance in cases of baby loss in the form of miscarriage, stillbirth or neonatal death [55]. Accordingly, there is a strong evidence base for IPT in perinatal depression [56, 57].

A key part of IPT is that it uses the medical model as a conceptual framework for patients' mood symptoms. It describes depression as a medical illness, and frames this as a way of understanding that depression is not the patient's fault but requires steps to help treat the depression. It focuses on providing patients with the support and skills to resolve the interpersonal components in their life situation. It is a pragmatic intervention. It recognises that there may be other factors that are impacting on the person and contributing to depression, but IPT also posits that to help treat depression it is important to make progress on at least one of the contributing factors, as often other factors will improve as a result. Thus, there is a strong premise around retaining focus throughout the treatment.

The therapy consists of typically around 12–16 weekly sessions. It consists of three phrases. In the first, the individual is assessed for depression and the interpersonal context is reviewed in depth. An interpersonal formulation is provided and the therapist and patient collaboratively determine one or two IPT areas to focus on in stage 2. The

IPT areas of focus are complicated bereavement, role dispute, role transition and interpersonal sensitivity. Role transition is particularly relevant to becoming a parent, where there are significant changes in role and identity. In stage 2, specific strategies are employed to support the patient to help resolve problems they are having. In contrast to some other empirically supported treatments, such as CBT, IPT focuses on affect. In complicated bereavement or role transitions, for example, this may be used in helping the patient to experience and mourn the loss of the baby or person who has passed or of the life domain that has been left behind (e.g. the professional career of someone who is now parenting full time). In role disputes and interpersonal sensitivity, feelings about the conflict or isolation are explored and skills to help the person approach and manage the dispute, such as communication analysis and role play, may be used. In the third phase, the therapist and patient prepare for the ending of treatment. Booster sessions may be scheduled in the upcoming year.

Although IPT is typically delivered in an individual one-on-one format, it has also been delivered in group and couples-based formats. Individual IPT can flexibly accommodate partners or other important supporters. It may therefore be particularly appropriate for individuals who have relationship conflict but where the partner is unwilling or unable to regularly attend conjoint treatment. It is also the only treatment recommended for depression that specifically addresses loss and grief, when that is the major cause of depression.

Eye Movement Desensitisation and Reprocessing

This is an integrative therapy with a significant experiential component that is guideline recommended for the treatment of PTSD. The EMDR method is time efficient, consisting of a structured treatment package that integrates techniques from cognitive behavioural, psychodynamic and body-oriented therapy. Adaptive information processing, which is the theory guiding EMDR, considers dysfunctional memories to be the source of psychopathology, as they interfere with current functioning. In EMDR therapy, the patient spends brief amounts of time attending to emotionally disturbing material associated with unprocessed traumatic experiences while also focusing on a bilateral stimulation, such as following a moving light from left to right (eye movement), alternate hand-tapping or having sounds presented to alternate ears. This is done sequentially during the treatment session and is hypothesised to facilitate accessing the traumatic memory network, thus enhancing information processing and developing new associations with more adaptive memories or information, cognitive insights and reducing emotional distress. In contrast to other treatments, EMDR does not focus on talking about traumatic experiences in a detailed fashion, rather the patient focuses on their experiences in terms of thoughts, emotions and physical sensations as they happen in the moment. It is effective in treating PTSD, and there is evidence that this includes PTSD after a traumatic experience of childbirth [58, 59]. It is also sometimes used to address fear of childbirth where there has been a previous traumatic birth (secondary tokophobia) [33, 60].

Treatment is weekly and typically completes in around 20 sessions or fewer. It is structured into eight phases which include: (1) *history taking* and treatment planning; (2) *preparation*, in which the therapist prepares the patient with skills to manage emotional disturbances that might arise during processing (e.g. grounding techniques, safe place imagery, relaxation); (3) *assessment*, during which the patient accesses each treatment target and undertakes processing; (4) *desensitisation*, when the patient focuses on the emotional and physical sensation responses they have to the target event, whilst engaging in a form of bilateral stimulation, giving them the opportunity to focus on aspects of the event that are as yet unprocessed; (5) *installation of positive cognition*, wherein the patient focuses on increasing positive beliefs; (6) *body scan*, in which the patient scans the body for residual tension, and then targets these domains for reprocessing; (7) *closure* includes preparation for ending treatment; (8) *re-evaluation* occurs throughout the treatment, ensuring the therapist and patient are in agreement about how treatment is progressing in relation to therapy goals.

Dialectical Behaviour Therapy

Emotional dysregulation refers to extreme and often unpredictable fluctuations in emotions that are experienced as difficult to manage. It can occur in the context of EUPD or BPD (see Chapter 14, 'Personality Disorder') or to a lesser non-clinical extent with or without comorbidities. Research suggests that emotional dysregulation and suicide are related [61, 62], and with the MBRRACE confidential enquiry into maternal deaths repeatedly finding suicide to be a leading cause of death following birth, emotion regulation provides a possible intervention target [63]. It also follows that if parents find it hard to regulate and soothe themselves, supporting an infant in distress might be even harder. An association between emotional dysregulation and the ability to hold a child's mental state and their needs in mind has been found [64]. A key task of parenting is to support children in learning to understand and regulate their own emotional states. If left untreated, parental emotional dysregulation may lead to a potential perpetuation of emotional vulnerability and invalidating environments for future generations [65]. Emerging research [66] reports that emotional dysregulation associated with BPD has more impact on child development than maternal depression and therefore the importance of providing timely treatment for both the benefit of the mother and child.

The perinatal period is full of important life changes and transitions [67] and even if effective strategies for coping and regulating emotions have been learnt before becoming a parent, the set of new challenges faced with parenting an infant mean it can be difficult to know how to apply and generalise these skills. Within the perinatal context, these skills can be tested especially as common emotional vulnerabilities can increase such as physical pain and lack of sleep [68, 69, 70, 71] in which emotion dysregulation can play a key role.

Dialectical behaviour therapy is an evidence-based treatment for BPD, which Linehan postulated is a disorder of emotion regulation showing itself as a pattern of instability in affect regulation, impulse control, interpersonal relationships and self-image [72]. It is a comprehensive programme of treatment. It is team based, and typically lasts for 12 months. It consists of four main components: weekly group skills training, which focuses on enhancing patient capabilities; individual psychotherapy, which seeks to personalise the application of skills learned in the group; in-between session telephone coaching that allows for in-the-moment use of skills; and a therapist consultation team that helps therapists stay motivated and competent in their work with BPD patients.

It is premised on realising a synthesis in the dialectic between acceptance and change, exploring the idea that opposite experiences can simultaneously be valid or important. The skills group, for example, balances the acceptance strategies of mindfulness and distress tolerance, against the change strategies of emotion regulation and interpersonal effectiveness. It can be validating to know, for example, that you simultaneously love your baby and yet also need some time apart from them. The therapy focuses on the following target outcomes: life-threatening behaviours, therapy-interfering behaviours (e.g. cancelling appointments, coming late to treatment, being non-collaborative), quality-of-life behaviours (relationship problems, occupational, housing, financial problems) and skills acquisition. It seeks to move the patient through three stages to help them achieve on each of these outcomes. In the first stage it helps the patient achieve behavioural control, in the second it helps them to safely experience emotion, and lastly, in stage 3, to learn to live and thrive, with opportunities for both normal happiness and regular sadness.

This therapy's compassionate stance towards problems may be especially important during the perinatal period, when parents struggle with heavy perceptions of judgement regarding their parenting behaviours and perceived failures. Parents with BPD may have both heightened emotional sensitivity and histories of invalidation which may make them more vulnerable to black and white thinking (e.g. 'I am completely useless as a parent'). Having a dialectical approach that works on finding what is effective rather than what is 'right' (e.g. 'this is challenging, I am doing my best right now and still have more to learn') can help navigate these extremes with more compassion and kindness whilst still being clear about what needs to be changed or improved. Skills can be adapted to the perinatal context, for example, a mindfulness exercise while holding the baby, or sharing soothing experiences in the five senses with the baby where appropriate (this might include watching bubbles, listening to music together, snuggling into a soft blanket).

Prolonged Grief Disorder Therapy

Loss related to death is a normal part of life, and grief responses are a natural reaction to these highly distressing events. Prolonged grief disorder differs from normal grief responses in that individuals continue to have significant ongoing challenges in adapting to the loss after a period of at least 12 months. They may struggle to accept the reality of the loss, avoid reminders of it, continue to experience intense, overwhelming and disruptive emotions and/or feel numb. They may feel isolated from others, fail to reintegrate back into day-to-day life and have strong ongoing feelings that life is meaningless. Prolonged grief disorder is more likely to occur in individuals who experience the sudden, unexpected loss of a loved one, particularly under traumatic circumstances [73]. Perinatal loss can take the form of miscarriage, stillbirth (usually defined as after 24 weeks of pregnancy) or neonatal death (within 28 days of birth) or the death of a baby during the first year of life. Inevitably, parents report they find these experiences traumatic, and this is often compounded by the intense sense of responsibility they feel for the health of their baby and the impact of the death on their identity as a parent [74, 75]. Further, parents often report the challenges they experience in trying to share their grief with others. This therapy may therefore be especially useful for parents who have experienced perinatal loss.

It is a structured, time-limited treatment, usually lasting around 12–16 sessions [76]; it has the largest evidence base for treatment for prolonged grief disorder. Although trials of PGDT have included perinatal parents and addressed perinatal loss, there is as yet no specific trial of PGDT in the perinatal period. It is based on both CBT and IPT approaches. It integrates reliving/exposure-based strategies from CBT for PTSD with restorative interpersonal strategies from IPT; the treatment was developed alongside leaders in both treatment approaches. The research on PGDT is particularly strong, in a randomised controlled trial it was twice (70%) as effective as IPT (31%) for prolonged grief [77]. Notably, although PGDT does well on its own, results are measurably improved when patients are also taking antidepressant medication [78].

The therapy is divided into three sections. In the first, the therapist provides psychoeducation, introduces the patient to the grief monitoring diary, discusses aspirational goals and works towards building support. A key aim of these sessions is to develop a strong and companionable alliance. The next part of treatment (sessions 4–9) focuses on revisiting the time of the death in an effort to reinvigorate a successful mourning process. These sessions include situational revisiting and memory work. The therapist guides the patient around working through grief derailers (e.g. seeing other babies or pregnant people) and coming to terms with the reality of the loss. During sessions, the therapist also guides the patient towards consideration of rewarding activities, aspirational goals and building support, to help retain a focus on not only processing the grief but also rebuilding a meaningful life. In the last component of treatment, from sessions 10–16, the focus is on completing and consolidating treatment gains and preparing for the ending of therapy. This includes supporting the patient to make peace with the loss while also recognising the permanence of grief. This includes, usually around session 11, an imaginal conversation with the deceased. The patient also focuses with the therapist on restoring a sense of possibility for a life with purpose and meaning, rebuilding and growing new relationships, and regaining a sense of competence in their role in the world. For perinatal parents, this may include rebalancing perspectives on grief over the loss of the baby whilst also approaching potential new pregnancies, and redirecting relationships with any existing children.

Mentalisation-Based Treatment

Mentalisation-based treatment (MBT) is a psychotherapy that focuses on teaching patients to mentalise. Mentalising is an individual's ability to attend to both their own mental states (thoughts, feelings, wishes and desires) and the mental states of others as they attempt to understand their own and other's actions. If someone is mentalising successfully, they are able to understand what is going on in their own mind and in the minds of other people, and realise how this is affecting the emotions, thoughts and actions of themselves and others. This treatment, which is grounded in attachment theory and integrates cognitive and relational therapy components, aims to support the individual to gain an understanding of their own perspectives as well as those of other people. It proposes this as the key mechanism of change which may result in improved social interactions and relationships and subsequently improved mood and well-being. In the perinatal period, MBT may support parents to gain an understanding of both their own and their baby's perspective.

The treatment is typically structured over 12–18 months and can be delivered in both individual and group formats. The group setting can help foster interpersonal awareness and emotional regulation, as participants learn from both their own experiences and the mental states of others. Key therapeutic components include fostering a secure attachment between the therapist and patients, stabilising emotional expression and encouraging reflective exploration of mental states. It takes a collaborative, non-knowing stance, where the therapist and patient work together to develop insight. Mental health professionals such as psychiatrists, psychologists, and nurses can be trained to deliver MBT with relatively modest additional training.

This treatment has garnered substantial evidence, particularly in relation to treating what is often referred to as borderline personality disorder. Studies have demonstrated its effectiveness in reducing core symptoms of BPD, such as emotional instability, impulsivity and interpersonal difficulties, and in decreasing self-harm, suicidal behaviour and the need for hospitalisation [79, 80]. In individuals with co-occurring BPD and antisocial personality disorder, MBT has been shown to mitigate adverse outcomes, including self-harm, suicide attempts, negative mood, overall psychiatric symptoms and social functioning challenges [81].

While MBT's evidence base is strongest for BPD, it has an emerging evidence base for eating disorders [82] and managing psychotic disorders [83]. Specifically within perinatal populations, MBT has been found to be effective in mothers with substance use disorders [84].

Short Term Psychodynamic Therapy

Brief psychodynamic psychotherapy is based on psychoanalytic theory. It focuses on the unconscious thoughts and feelings that are believed to cause unhealthy thinking and behaviour patterns. The main aim of this therapy is to help people become aware of hidden emotions like anger, shame or guilt, which they have pushed away because these feelings are too painful or cause anxiety. To achieve this, the therapist challenges the person's defences, such as self-blame or having an overly high opinion of oneself, which have kept these feelings hidden [85].

The therapy is called 'brief' because it aims to resolve emotional problems quickly by addressing these defences as soon as possible. It is considered 'dynamic' because it deals with unconscious feelings related to both past and present experiences. During sessions, the therapist often identifies a person's psychological defences by observing how they interact with the therapist. Though therapy can sometimes be upsetting as it brings up painful emotions that may have been avoided over time, the therapist's role is to provide a safe and supportive space where the person can face these emotions without fear. For example, a parent who is struggling to form a bond with their infant may be encouraged to consider internalised self-critical thoughts that they may have learned from early life experiences and then separate those thoughts and experience from their current interactions with their baby. The patient would then be encouraged to develop practical strategies to manage their critical thoughts and to engage in affirming behaviours that reinforce their view of themselves as a loving parent.

Brief psychodynamic therapy is recommended for the treatment of depression [86]. Typically, it involves 10–20 sessions, depending on the severity of a person's psychological issues and the strength of their defences.

Couples Therapies

The arrival of a baby is linked to far-reaching changes in the couple relationship with research indicating a decline in overall couple relationship satisfaction across the perinatal period [87], which is both a risk factor for new onset and/or recurrence of mental health problems and is more pronounced in women experiencing mental health difficulties [88] (see Chapter 6, 'Paternal Mental Health in the Perinatal Period: Impact on Family Relationships'). Meta-analytic and systematic reviews have consistently found robust associations between family functioning, conflict, gender role stress, lack of partner availability and low couple intimacy with perinatal mental health problems [89, 90]. There are also high rates of low-level inter-partner violence (defined as pushing, shoving, slapping) during the transition to parenthood [91], which has been found to be perpetrated at approximately equal prevalence by men and women and is also associated with parental mental health difficulties [92]. Further, relationship conflict has been shown to have a significant impact on parent–infant interaction and is associated with less sensitive parenting [93, 94]. A 2018 Early Intervention review by Harold et al. [95] found that the way couples communicate and engage with each other in managing relationship conflicts both affects their ability to engage in effective parenting practices and can influence children's mental health outcomes in infancy, childhood and adolescence, with extended impacts on academic/educational attainment, physical health and well-being, employability and future relationship stability in later life.

Unlike many other risk factors for perinatal mental illness, the couple relationship and family functioning are highly modifiable and respond to intervention. In a recent meta-analysis, communication, emotional and instrumental support, and conflict emerged as key, modifiable factors that could impact on depression [96].

There are a range of couple-focused interventions that have been developed to improve mental health symptoms. However, only two have an evidence base robust enough at the time of this writing to have been recommended in guidelines, that is behavioural couples therapy and couples therapy for depression. Each is described, in turn, next.

Behavioural Couples Therapy

Behavioural couples therapy (BCT) typically involves 16–20 sessions of treatment [97] for couples where there is both relationship distress and mental health difficulties, typically depression in one of the partners. The BCT model focuses on the relational aspects of depression and on factors that reduce stress and increase support within the couple. In the initial part of treatment, the therapist works with the couple to understand how relational patterns are reciprocally associated with mood. Depending on the couple's perspective on their patterns and depression, either a diagnosis may be used as a way to understand behaviours and thoughts that affect the relational pattern, or the patterns of behaviours and thoughts themselves may be described without the use of a diagnosis. The therapy often includes a focus on specific skills, such as teaching couples communication and problem-solving skills, and helps coach couples to set up positive behaviour exchanges. It may also use cognitive-restructuring exercises about the relationship as a way to interrupt partners' typical thoughts and create different experiences of their relationship. Together, these treatment activities aim to reset the negative trajectory of the couple's relationship and to alter meta-level cognitions about the relationship.

Couples Therapy for Depression

Couples therapy for depression builds on BCT approaches but includes aspects of emotion and acceptance drawn from DBT and then used in integrative behavioural couples therapy [98]. These additions include promoting empathy between the couple, helping them to build emotion regulation in relation to common conflict areas (e.g. sex, finance, parenting), and helping the couple to understand, accept and tolerate unresolvable differences that often lead to conflict.

Group Treatments

Mindfulness-Based Cognitive Therapy

Mindfulness-based cognitive therapy (MBCT) combines elements of CBT with mindfulness practices. It emphasises a recovery perspective that encourages the person to understand their individual risk factors for depression and allow them to non-judgementally experience negative (and positive) mood, whilst also giving them practices that allow them to live a meaningful life. It accomplishes this through mindfulness practices such as meditation, body scan and mindful breathing. Each of these practices helps the individual to pay attention to and remain anchored in present moments without judgement. These are combined with cognitive restructuring, behavioural activation and problem-solving techniques from CBT. It aims to break cycles of negative thinking and improve emotion regulation through the cultivation of this non-reactive awareness to thoughts and emotions. It also purports to reduce risk for relapse and enhance well-being by generating a more compassionate and accepting self-attitude. This can be particularly important in the context of the perinatal period, when life changes radically, and parents may feel out of their depth in learning how to care for a baby. Although there is nascent evidence supporting mindfulness in reducing symptoms of anxiety and depression in an at-risk population of pregnant women [99, 100], there is otherwise a lack of evidence for mindfulness approaches in the perinatal period [101, 102].

Typically, MBCT is delivered in a group format over 8 weeks, with each session lasting around 2 hours. Participants are guided through mindfulness practices and CBT exercises and are often given homework assignments to practise these techniques between sessions. Guidelines support the use of MBCT for reducing the risk of depression relapse, particularly in those who have had three or more previous episodes of depression. Although MBCT has been tested in other populations, the results are mixed to date. There is some evidence suggesting that MBCT may be as effective as continuation medication for individuals with multiple episodes of depression. As a time-limited, group-based, non-pharmaceutical treatment, it may therefore be especially helpful for pregnant women and may be a particularly promising option for pregnant women who want to stop taking medication and/or who are worried about their risk for depression relapse. Adaptations [103] of MBCT for parenting have also found positive effects on emotion regulation in the context of parenting, thus, there is the possibility that the treatment may have prophylactic effects on parenting.

Summary

Psychological therapies are of key importance in the perinatal period. There are significant psychological adjustments associated with the transition to parenthood, there are adjusted risks and benefits of prescribing at this time, parents state they prefer psychological approaches, and therapy may also be appropriate to address problems in the parent–infant relationship. It is important that psychological therapies are based on a perinatal frame of mind and can be accessed promptly when needed. Psychological therapy is most effective and accessible when it is adapted to take account of the perinatal context and issues related to pregnancy, childbirth or parenting. It is encouraging that therapies in the perinatal period are increasingly supported by a growing evidence base.

References

1. A Sartin-Tarm, MC Ross, AA Privatsky, JM Cisler. Estradiol modulates neural and behavioral arousal in women with posttraumatic stress disorder during a fear learning and extinction task. *Biol Psychiatry Cogn Neurosci Neuroimaging.* 2020 Dec 1;5(12):1114–22.
2. EM Glover, T Jovanovic, SD Norrholm. Estrogen and extinction of fear memories: implications for posttraumatic stress disorder treatment. *Biol Psychiatry.* 2015 Aug 1;78(3):178–85.
3. Department of Veterans Affairs and Department of Defense. VA/DOD clinical practice guideline for the management of posttraumatic stress disorder and acute stress disorder. 2023. www.healthquality.va.gov/guidelines/MH/ptsd
4. J Merz, G Schwarzer, H Gerger. Comparative efficacy and acceptability of pharmacological, psychotherapeutic, and combination treatments in adults with posttraumatic stress disorder. *JAMA Psychiatry.* 2019 Sep 1;76(9):904–13.
5. DJ Lee, CW Schnitzlein, JP Wolf, M Vythilingam, AM Rasmusson, CW Hoge. Psychotherapy versus pharmacotherapy for posttraumatic stress disorder: systemic review and meta-analyses to determine first-line treatments. *Depress Anxiety.* 2016 Apr 29;33(9):792–806.
6. National Institute for Health and Care Excellence. Depression in adults: treatment and management. NICE Guideline (NG222). 2022. www.nice.org.uk/guidance/ng222/chapter/recommendations
7. Veterans Affairs. Overview of psychotherapy for PSTD. n.d. https://tinyurl.com/58xv6557
8. P Skapinakis, DM Caldwell, W Hollingworth, P Bryden, NA Fineberg, P Salkovskis, et al. Pharmacological and psychotherapeutic interventions for management of obsessive-compulsive disorder in adults: a systematic review and network meta-analysis. *Lancet Psychiatry.* 2016 Aug 1;3(8):730–9.
9. P Cuijpers, G Andersson, T Donker, A Van Straten. Psychological treatment of depression: results of a series of meta-analyses. *Nord J Psychiatry.* 2011 Jul 20;65(6):354–64.
10. S Barakat, S Maguire. Accessibility of psychological treatments for bulimia nervosa: a review of efficacy and engagement in online self-help treatments. *Int J Environ Res Public Health.* 2022 Dec 22;20(1):119.
11. National Institute for Health and Care Excellence. Eating disorders: recognition and treatment. NICE Guideline (NG69). 2017. www.nice.org.uk/guidance/ng69/ifp/chapter/Bulimia-nervosa-treatment-for-adults
12. CE Loucas, CG Fairburn, C Whittington, ME Pennant, S Stockton, T Kendall. E-therapy in the treatment and prevention of eating disorders: a systematic review and meta-analysis. *Behav Res Ther.* 2014 Dec 1;63:122–31.
13. National Institute for Health and Care Excellence. Borderline personality disorder: recognition and management. Clinical Guideline (CG78). 2009. www.nice.org.uk/guidance/CG78
14. National Institute for Health and Care Excellence. Bipolar disorder: assessment and management. Clinical Guideline (CG185). 2014. www.nice.org.uk/guidance/cg185
15. RB Jarrett, JR Vittengl. The efficacy of cognitive behaviour therapy for depression. In: A Wells, P Fisher, editors. *Treating depression: MCT, CBT and third wave therapies.* Chichester, UK: Wiley Blackwell; 2016. p. 52–80.
16. P Cuijpers, AS Geraedts, P Van Oppen, G Andersson, JC Markowitz, A Van Straten.

Interpersonal psychotherapy for depression: a meta-analysis. *Am J Psychiatry*. 2011 Jun 1;168(6): 581–92.

17. D Pettman, H O'Mahen, O Blomberg, AS Svanberg, L Von Essen, J Woodford. Effectiveness of cognitive behavioural therapy-based interventions for maternal perinatal depression: a systematic review and meta-analysis. *BMC Psychiatry*. 2023 Mar 29;23(1):208.
18. CL Dennis. Psychosocial interventions for the treatment of perinatal depression. *Best Prac Res Clin Obstet Gynaecol*. 2014 Jan 1;28(1):97–111.
19. NM Molenaar, AM Kamperman, P Boyce, V Bergink. Guidelines on treatment of perinatal depression with antidepressants: an international review. *Aust N Z J Psychiatry*. 2018 Mar 5;52(4):320–7.
20. WR Miller, S Rollnick, et al. *Motivational interviewing*. New York: The Guilford Press; 2002.
21. J Milgrom, AW Gemmill, J Ericksen, G Burrows, A Buist, J Reece. Treatment of postnatal depression with cognitive behavioural therapy, sertraline and combination therapy: a randomised controlled trial. *Aust N Z J Psychiatry*. 2015 Jan 13;49(3):236–45.
22. L Fisher, A Davey, G Wong, S Morgan-Trimmer, LM Howard, H Sharp, et al. Women's engagement with community perinatal mental health services: a realist evaluation. *BMC Psychiatry*. 2024 Jul 8;24(1):492.
23. HA O'Mahen, DA Richards, J Woodford, E Wilkinson, J McGinley, RS Taylor, FC Warren. Netmums: a phase II randomized controlled trial of a guided internet behavioural activation treatment for postpartum depression. *Psychol Med*. 2014 Jun;44(8):1675–89.
24. R Webb, N Uddin, E Ford, A Easter, J Shakespeare, N Roberts, et al. Barriers and facilitators to implementing perinatal mental health care in health and social care settings: a systematic review. *Lancet Psychiatry*. 2021 Jun 1;8(6):521–34.
25. A Stein, RM Pearson, SH Goodman, E Rapa, A Rahman, M McCallum, et al. Effects of perinatal mental disorders on the fetus and child. *Lancet*. 2014 Nov 1;384(9956):1800–19.
26. BV Watts, PP Schnurr, L Mayo, Y Young-Xu, WB Weeks, MJ Friedman. Meta-analysis of the efficacy of treatments for posttraumatic stress disorder. *J Clin Psychiatry*. 2013 Jun 15;74(6):e541–50.
27. JM Lohr, SO Lilienfeld, GM Rosen. Anxiety and its treatment: promoting science-based practice. *J Anxiety Disord*. 2012 Oct 1;26(7):719–27.
28. ZJ Parker, G Waller, PGS Duhne, J Dawson. The role of exposure in treatment of anxiety disorders: a meta-analysis. University of Northampton's Research Explorer. 2018. https://tinyurl.com/347s9ccc
29. PN Maguire, GI Clark, BM Wootton. The efficacy of cognitive behavior therapy for the treatment of perinatal anxiety symptoms: a preliminary meta-analysis. *J Anxiety Disord*. 2018 Dec 1;60:26–34.
30. JM Meyer, NR Farrell, JJ Kemp, SM Blakey, BJ Deacon. Why do clinicians exclude anxious patients from exposure therapy? *Behav Res Ther*. 2014 Mar 1;54:49–53.
31. YMGA Hendrix, MAM Baas, JW Vanhommerig, A De Jongh, MG Van Pampus. Fear of childbirth in nulliparous women. *Front Psychol*. 2022 Jul 12;13:923819.
32. FL Challacombe, R Tinch-Taylor, K Sabin, L Potts, V Lawrence, L Howard, et al. Exposure-based cognitive-behaviour therapy for anxiety-related disorders in pregnancy (ADEPT): results of a feasibility randomised controlled trial of time-intensive versus weekly CBT. *J Affect Disord*. 2024 Jan 1;344:414–22.
33. MAM Baas, MG Van Pampus, CAI Stramrood, LM Dijksman, JW Vanhommerig, A De Jongh. Treatment of pregnant women with fear of childbirth using EMDR therapy: results of a multi-center randomized controlled trial. *Front Psychiatry*. 2022 Feb 10;12:798249.

34. J Lynch, PK Cullen, AM Jasnow, DC Riccio. Sex differences in the generalization of fear as a function of retention intervals. *Learn Mem.* 2013 Oct 16;20(11):628–32.

35. British Psychological Society Faculty of Perinatal Psychology. Perinatal service provision: The role of perinatal clinical psychology. Briefing Paper (No. 8). 2016.

36. National Institite of Health and Care Excellence. Anxiety disorders. Quality Standard (QS53). 2014. www.nice.org.uk/guidance/qs53

37. American Psychological Association. Professional practice guidelines for evidence-based psychological practice in health care. 2021. www.apa.org/about/policy/psychological-practice-health-care.pdf

38. BE Wampold. How important are the common factors in psychotherapy? An update. *World Psychiatry.* 2015 Sep 25;14(3):270–7.

39. M Flykt, K Kanninen, J Sinkkonen, R Punamäki. Maternal depression and dyadic interaction: the role of maternal attachment style. *Infant Child Dev.* 2010 Apr 12;19(5):530–50.

40. J Davila, KN Levy. Introduction to the special section on attachment theory and psychotherapy. *J Consult Clin Psychol.* 2006 Jan 1;74(6):989–93.

41. National Health Service. The competency framework for professionals working with women who have mental health problems in the perinatal period. 2018 Jul. https://tinyurl.com/2dk8ju2r

42. D Westbrook, H Kennerley, J Kirk. *An introduction to cognitive behaviour therapy: skills and applications.* London: Sage; 2011.

43. L Lorenzo-Luaces, RE German, RJ DeRubeis. It's complicated: the relation between cognitive change procedures, cognitive change, and symptom change in cognitive therapy for depression. *Clin Psychol Rev.* 2015 Nov 1;41:3–15.

44. J Bennett-Levy. *Oxford guide to behavioural experiments in cognitive therapy.* Oxford: Oxford University Press; 2004.

45. JS Beck. *Cognitive therapy: basics and beyond.* New York: The Guilford Press; 1995.

46. MW O'Hara, LP Rehm. Self-monitoring, activity levels, and mood in the development and maintenance of depression. *J Abnorm Psychol.* 1979;88(4):450–3.

47. F McManus, K Van Doorn, J Yiend. Examining the effects of thought records and behavioral experiments in instigating belief change. *J Behav Ther Experiment Psychiatry.* 2012 Mar 1;43(1):540–7.

48. K Rouf. *Oxford guide to behavioural experiments in cognitive therapy.* Oxford: Oxford University Press; 2004.

49. NS Jacobson, CR Martell, S Dimidjian. Behavioral activation treatment for depression: returning to contextual roots. *Clin Psychol Sci Pract.* 2001 Jan 1;8(3):255–70.

50. SJH Biddle. Emotion, mood and physical activity. In: R Kaney, editor. *Behavioural aspects of physical activity.* London: Routledge; 2003. p. 63–87.

51. KS Dobson, R Joffe. The role of activity level and cognition in depressed mood in a university sample. *J Clin Psychol.* 1986;42:264–71.

52. CB Ferster. Sustained behavior under delayed reinforcement. *J Experiment Psychol.* 1953 Jan 1;45(4):218–24.

53. N Grey, K Young, E Holmes. Cognitive restructuring within reliving: a treatment for peritraumatic emotional 'hotspots' in posttraumatic stress disorder. *Behav Cogn Psychother.* 2002 Jan 1;30(1):37–56.

54. FL Challacombe, K Sabin, S Jacobson, R Tinch-Taylor, L Potts, B Carter, et al. Patient and therapist experiences of exposure therapy for anxiety-related disorders in pregnancy: qualitative analysis of a feasibility trial of intensive versus weekly CBT. *BJPsych Open.* 2023 Oct 12;9(6):e189.

55. JE Johnson, AB Price, JC Kao, K Fernandes, R Stout, RL Gobin, et al.

Interpersonal psychotherapy (IPT) for major depression following perinatal loss: a pilot randomized controlled trial. *Arch Womens Ment Health.* 2016 Mar 22;19(5):845–59.

56. M Miniati, A Callari, S Calugi, P Rucci, M Savino, M Mauri, et al. Interpersonal psychotherapy for postpartum depression: a systematic review. *Arch Womens Ment Health.* 2014 Jun 24;17(4):257–68.
57. MW O'Hara, S Stuart, LL Gorman, A Wenzel. Efficacy of interpersonal psychotherapy for postpartum depression. *Arch Gen Psychiatry.* 2000 Nov 1;57(11):1039–45.
58. V Chiorino, MC Cattaneo, EA Macchi, R Salerno, S Roveraro, GG Bertolucci, et al. The EMDR Recent Birth Trauma Protocol: a pilot randomised clinical trial after traumatic childbirth. *Psychol Health.* 2019 Dec 5;35(7):795–810.
59. LW Kranenburg, HH Bijma, AJ Eggink, EM Knijff, MPLVD Berg. Implementing an eye movement and desensitization reprocessing treatment-program for women with posttraumatic stress disorder after childbirth. *Front Psychol.* 2022 Jan 21;12:797901.
60. N Zolghadr, A Khoshnazar, M MoradiBaglooei, Z Alimoradi. The effect of EMDR on childbirth anxiety of women with previous stillbirth. *J EMDR Pract Res.* 2019 Feb 1;13(1):10–19.
61. C Zlotnick, BA Wolfsdorf, B Johnson, A Spirito. Impaired self-regulation and suicidal behavior among adolescent and young adult psychiatric inpatients. *Arch Suicide Res.* 2003 Apr 1;7(2):149–57.
62. C Zlotnick, D Donaldson, A Spirito, T Pearlstein. Affect regulation and suicide attempts in adolescent inpatients. *J Am Acad Child Adolesc Psychiatry.* 1997 Jun 1;36(6):793–8.
63. A Felker, M Knight. MBRRACE-UK update: key messages from the UK and Ireland Confidential Enquiries into Maternal Death and Morbidity 2023. *Obstet Gynaecol.* 2023 Nov 28;26(1):27–31.
64. R Schacht, L Hammond, M Marks, B Wood, S Conroy. The relation between mind-mindedness in mothers with borderline personality disorder and mental state understanding in their children. *Infant Child Dev.* 2012 Jul 15;22(1):68–84.
65. SE Crowell, TP Beauchaine, MM Linehan. A biosocial developmental model of borderline personality: elaborating and extending Linehan's theory. *Psychol Bull.* 2009 Jan 1;135(3):495–510.
66. F Huntley, N Wright, A Pickles, H Sharp, J Hill. Maternal mental health and child problem behaviours: disentangling the role of depression and borderline personality dysfunction. *BJPsych Open.* 2017 Nov 1;3(6):300–5.
67. J Belsky, DL Vandell, M Burchinal, KA Clarke-Stewart, K McCartney, MT Owen. Are there long-term effects of early child care? *Child Dev.* 2007 Mar 1;78(2):681–701.
68. JL Cox, D Murray, G Chapman. A controlled study of the onset, duration and prevalence of postnatal depression. *Br J Psychiatry.* 1993 Jul 1;163(1):27–31.
69. A Davies, RJ McIvor, RC Kumar. Impact of childbirth on a series of schizophrenic mothers: a comment on the possible influence of oestrogen on schizophrenia. *Schizophr Res.* 1995 Jul 1;16(1):25–31.
70. MW O'Hara, AM Swain. Rates and risk of postpartum depression: a meta-analysis. *Int Rev Psychiatry.* 1996 Jan 1;8(1): 37–54.
71. I Jones, N Craddock. Bipolar disorder and childbirth: the importance of recognising risk. *Br J Psychiatry.* 2005 Jun 1;186(6):453–4.
72. MM Linehan. *DBT® skills training manual.* 2nd ed. New York: Guilford Press; 2015.
73. MK Shear, CG Bloom. Complicated grief treatment: an evidence-based approach to grief therapy. *J Ration-Emot Cogn-Behav Ther.* 2016 May 24;35(1):6–25.
74. A Kersting, B Wagner. Complicated grief after perinatal loss. *Dialogues Clin Neurosci.* 2012 Jun 30;14(2):187–94.

75. P Hughes, S Riches. Psychological aspects of perinatal loss. *Curr Opin Obstet Gynecol.* 2003 Apr 1;15(2):107–11.

76. MK Shear, N Skritskaya, C Bloom. Prolonged grief disorder therapy (PGDT). In: U Schnyder, M Cloitre, editors. *Evidence based treatments for trauma-related psychological disorders.* Cham: Springer; 2022. p. 329–44.

77. K Shear, E Frank, PR Houck, CF Reynolds. Treatment of complicated grief. *JAMA.* 2005 Jun 1;293(21):2601–8.

78. MK Shear, CF Reynolds, NM Simon, S Zisook, Y Wang, C Mauro, et al. Optimizing treatment of complicated grief. *JAMA Psychiatry.* 2016 Jul 1;73(7):685–94.

79. A Bateman, P Fonagy. Randomized controlled trial of outpatient mentalization-based treatment versus structured clinical management for borderline personality disorder. *Am J Psychiatry.* 2009 Dec;166(12):1355–64.

80. C Hajek Gross, SM Oehlke, K Prillinger, A Goreis, PL Plener, OD Kothgassner. Efficacy of mentalization-based therapy in treating self-harm: a systematic review and meta-analysis. *Suicide Life Threat Behav.* 2024 Apr;54(2):317–37.

81. A Bateman, J O'Connell, N Lorenzini, T Gardner, P Fonagy. A randomised controlled trial of mentalization-based treatment versus structured clinical management for patients with comorbid borderline personality disorder and antisocial personality disorder. *BMC Psychiatry.* 2016 Dec;16(1):304.

82. P Robinson, F Skårderud, B Sommerfeldt. *Mentalization-based treatments for eating disorders.* Cham: Springer; 2018.

83. J Weijers, C Ten Kate, W Viechtbauer, LJ Rampaart, EH Eurelings, JP Selten. Mentalization-based treatment for psychotic disorder: a rater-blinded, multi-center, randomized controlled trial. *Psychol Med.* 2021 Dec;51(16): 2846–55.

84. NE Suchman, JL Borelli, CL DeCoste. Can addiction counselors be trained to deliver Mothering from the Inside Out, a mentalization-based parenting therapy, with fidelity? Results from a community-based randomized efficacy trial. *Attach Hum Dev.* 2020 May 3;22(3):332–51.

85. D Malan, L Parker. *Individual psychotherapy and the science of psychodynamics.* Hoboken, NJ; CRC Press; 1995.

86. P Cuijpers, E Karyotaki, L de Wit, DD Ebert. The effects of fifteen evidence-supported therapies for adult depression: a meta-analytic review. *Psychother Res.* 2020 Apr 2;30(3):279–93.

87. MO Treter, GK Rhoades, SB Scott, HJ Markman, SM Stanley. Having a baby: impact on married and cohabiting parents' relationships. *Fam Process.* 2020 Jul 18;60(2):477–92.

88. Department for Work and Pensions. Department for Work and Pensions annual report and accounts 2014–15. 2015. https://tinyurl.com/fd57hftb

89. F Cluxton-Keller, ML Bruce. Clinical effectiveness of family therapeutic interventions in the prevention and treatment of perinatal depression: a systematic review and meta-analysis. *PLoS ONE.* 2018 Jun 14;13(6):e0198730.

90. MN Norhayati, NHN Hazlina, AR Asrenee, WMAW Emilin. Magnitude and risk factors for postpartum symptoms: a literature review. *J Affect Disord.* 2015 Apr 1;175:34–52.

91. K Halford, JF Petch, D Creedy. Promoting a positive transition to parenthood: a randomized clinical trial of couple relationship education. *Prev Sci.* 2009 Oct 15;11(1):89–100.

92. J Archer. Sex differences in aggression between heterosexual partners: a meta-analytic review. *Psycholog Bull.* 2000 Sep 1;126(5):651–80.

93. MT Owen, MJ Cox. Marital conflict and the development of infant–parent attachment relationships. *J Fam Psychol.* 1997 Jun 1;11(2):152–64.

94. A Pittig, I Heinig, S Goerigk, F Thiel, K Hummel, L Scholl, et al. Efficacy of temporally intensified exposure for anxiety disorders: a multicenter

randomized clinical trial. *Depress Anxiety.* 2021 Jul 22;38(11):1169–81.

95. Early Intervention Foundation. What works to enhance interparental relationships and improve outcomes for children? 2018. https://tinyurl.com/mpdbzkrj
96. PD Pilkington, LC Milne, KE Cairns, J Lewis, TA Whelan. Modifiable partner factors associated with perinatal depression and anxiety: a systematic review and meta-analysis. *J Affect Disord.* 2015 Jun 1;178:165–80.
97. DH Baucom, MS Fischer, S Corrie, M Worrell, SE Boeding. *Treating relationship distress and psychopathology in couples.* London: Routledge; 2019.
98. A Christensen, BD Doss. Integrative behavioral couple therapy. *Curr Opin Psychol.* 2017 Feb 1;13:111–14.
99. G Lönnberg, W Jonas, E Unternaehrer, R Bränström, E Nissen, M Niemi. Effects of a mindfulness based childbirth and parenting program on pregnant women's perceived stress and risk of perinatal depression: results from a randomized controlled trial. *J Affect Disord.* 2020 Feb 1;262:133–42.
100. LG Duncan, N Bardacke. Mindfulness-based childbirth and parenting education: promoting family mindfulness during the perinatal period. *J Child Fam Stud.* 2009 Oct 10;19(2):190–202.
101. Z Shi, A MacBeth. The effectiveness of mindfulness-based interventions on maternal perinatal mental health outcomes: a systematic review. *Mindfulness.* 2017 Jan 19;8(4):823–47.
102. BL Taylor, K Cavanagh, C Strauss. The effectiveness of mindfulness-based interventions in the perinatal period: a systematic review and meta-analysis. *PLoS ONE.* 2016 May 16;11(5):e0155720.
103. J Mann, W Kuyken, H O'Mahen, OC Ukoumunne, A Evans, T Ford. Manual development and pilot randomised controlled trial of mindfulness-based cognitive therapy versus usual care for parents with a history of depression. *Mindfulness.* 2016 May 25;7(5):1024–33.

Chapter 29

Effective Working across Health, Peer Support and Third-Sector Interfaces

Judy Shakespeare, Jill Demilew and Jess Heron

Introduction

The appropriate response from all healthcare professionals in contact with women and families in the perinatal period is key to them being able to access the right level of support from the right person at the right time. From a woman's viewpoint what matters are trusting relationships with professionals and timely, responsive access to treatment.

A small but significant proportion of women require referral to specialist mental health services in the perinatal period [1]. Women at risk of severe mental illness, or those developing severe illness, need to be carefully identified and receive timely and appropriate referral to specialist services. During their care by specialist services there needs to be joint working between specialist services and other agencies, including with general practitioners (GPs), midwives, health visitors (HVs) and appropriate third-sector organisations. Following discharge from specialist care, women with severe illness will be recovering and coming to terms with the impact of their illness long after specialist support has ended [2].

The vast majority of women who do not see specialist services in the perinatal period may have less severe symptoms, but they and their families may still experience significant distress. Some women do not seek help, but many reach out to friends, family, peer support organisations and healthcare professionals, including midwives, HVs, GPs, practice nurses and primary care psychological services, such as NHS Talking Therapies in England and equivalent services in other jurisdictions.

One of the biggest challenges for services is working together effectively. Specialist perinatal mental health services sit at the pinnacle of the pyramid of care for perinatal mental illness, but unless all parts of the pyramid work together, the pathway of care will not work for women.

Women with multiple deprivations are massively overrepresented in the postnatal illness population. The challenge is all the greater when we consider the impact of health and social inequalities on perinatal mental health [3].

In the UK, change has happened rapidly throughout all services. While specialist services have expanded, there have been workload and workforce issues within universal services. Now, GPs do not take any significant part in routine maternity care and may not meet a woman until after the birth of the baby. Many children's centres have closed or have changed their remit to offer services only to vulnerable families.

There is a strong evidence base for the management of perinatal mental illness and all healthcare professionals should be aware of that; women can be offered hope of recovery with treatment [4, 5].

NHS England and Scotland have published pathways of care for perinatal mental healthcare, but these do not deal with illness below the threshold of specialist care [6, 7]. Each area needs to develop effective local pathways of care that cover the full spectrum of disease and include all services.

The purpose of this chapter is to describe the building blocks that contribute to the rest of the pathway for women with perinatal mental illness. Although the chapter mainly covers the situation in England, it also gives information about the devolved nations, Scotland, Wales and Northern Ireland.

What follows covers principles of teamwork and stepped care.

What Does a Joined-Up Team Look Like?

Some Principles

- All members of the team are competent, keep themselves up to date with evidence-based practice, are compassionate, kind and curious.

This means they listen, understand and can develop therapeutic relationships with women.

- They put the woman and her family at the centre of their work, not the health and social care systems that may seem to block communication.

This means 'going the extra mile'. For example, if a woman with complex mental health moves house during or just after pregnancy (as so many do!), her midwife might speak to the new team, so the woman does not have to start again from square one.

Everyone should be flexible, prioritising time and resource for support in this area. Listening to women, advocating for them, giving the time when it is most needed could save time in the long run. Most healthcare professionals will also have more job satisfaction if they take this approach.

- The team should make efforts to get to know one another.

A consultant perinatal psychiatrist might go out to meet groups of GPs or invite them to visit a Mother and Baby Unit (MBU); they might speak to a GP if a referral is declined, so that learning can take place; they should be able to speak on the phone to a GP with concerns. Easy communication up and down the pathway of care educates and 'greases the wheels' for a future difficult time or conversation. Equally, good relationships with relevant peer support providers and community organisations can ease the transition to and from clinical services for women and families, decreasing barriers to care and improving support on recovery. Facilitating access to long-term support networks ultimately reduces the burden on clinical services.

- The team should be proactive not reactive.

This means they anticipate problems and set up early interventions, referrals and seek to support a woman to a position of strength and trust. If there isn't time at a first consultation, then promise to get back to the woman (and don't forget!). Otherwise, you will lose trust.

- Leaders and coordinators are both needed.

These are not necessarily the same person, but they could be. A consultant perinatal psychiatrist might develop a treatment plan with a woman, but the HV may have to implement and coordinate it. After discharge from an MBU the hospital team need to coordinate follow-up in the community. If it's complex, always use the telephone in preference to email, but email can help to set up a convenient time to call.

- Local knowledge.

Ensure you know about relevant local and national services. Signposting to third-sector organisations is a role for everyone, wherever they work in the pathway.

- Shared records.

If these have yet to be developed in your area of work, it needs to be a priority. Some places, such as London, already have this facility and it is a 'game changer'; everyone (including the woman) can be up to date, correct any errors in information and know names and contacts of other professionals.

- Things can go wrong, either for the woman or within the team. There should be a culture of learning and not of blame.

If a woman is getting worse and you don't think her risk is being taken seriously enough, escalate up the pyramid as far as you need to go, both in your own or another service provider, if necessary, above your line manager. If a woman requests a second opinion, to which she is entitled, help to facilitate the contact. Never denigrate another health professional to a patient or her family. If a referral is declined by specialist services, ask for an explanation and alternative approaches.

Afterwards look at any significant adverse incidents across the team and engage the family fully, fulfilling your professional duty of candour.

Stepped-Care Model for Perinatal Mental Illness

The model used for care in universal services is illustrated in Table 29.1.

In keeping with the model, women should be offered the lowest-intensity intervention appropriate to their needs in the first instance, with review and escalation to more intensive interventions if these are not suitable, acceptable or do not work [8]. As far as possible, women should be offered options and make their own treatment decisions. At a higher step the assumption should be that the options at a lower step are also available. Psychological therapies would normally be the first choice over medication.

Important exceptions to this are women who present with severe illness or suicidality. If postpartum psychosis is suspected, a woman should be seen within 4 hours [4]. All health professionals should be aware that postpartum psychosis can escalate rapidly. Women with postpartum psychosis are unlikely to be aware themselves that they are unwell and considerable ingenuity may be needed to ensure they are assessed within this timeframe. Same-day admission is likely to be required for the safety of mother and baby. Pregnant women, or women considering pregnancy, with a previous history of severe mental illness (bipolar disorder, schizophrenia, depression with psychosis) should be referred prior to conception or early in pregnancy to a specialist team, even if they are well at the time. Written management plans for the period of risk should be made with the woman and her family and shared with all agencies.

The following sections look at other services that a woman with perinatal mental health problems may encounter and discusses:

- what each service outside specialist services routinely offers

Table 29.1 Stepped care for perinatal mental health. The aim of the stepped-care model is to provide the most effective, yet least intensive treatment. It starts at step 1 (least intensive) and goes up to step 5 (most intensive)

Who is responsible for care?	What is the focus?	What do they do?
Step 1: GP, practice nurse, HV and midwife	Recognition	Assessment, social support
Step 2: Primary care team, HV, psychological well-being practitioner (low-intensity interventions)	Mild mental health problems	Watchful waiting, guided self-help, listening visits, computerised cognitive behavioural therapy, brief psychological intervention
Step 3: Primary care team, cognitive behavioural therapists and high-intensity therapists	Moderate or severe mental health problems	Medication, psychological interventions
Step 4: Perinatal mental health specialists, including crisis teams	Recurrent, atypical and those at significant risk	Medication, complex psychological interventions, combined treatments
Step 5: Inpatient care, crisis teams	Risk to life, severe self-neglect	Medication, combined treatments, electro-convulsive therapy

- what the recent policy changes are
- what the future challenges may be and
- what that means for consultant perinatal psychiatrists

Obstetrics and Midwifery Routine Care

Midwives

Every woman will have a 'named midwife' responsible for providing and coordinating her maternity care from antenatal booking through birth to postnatal care until discharge from maternity services to the GP and HV between Day 10 and 28 postnatal. If the woman is healthy her lead carers will be the midwife and her team. The named midwife works in a midwifery team, and a woman is provided with all contact details at her booking.

A key commitment in England is that all women have equitable access to specialist care in pregnancy, as specified in the National Institute for Health and Clinical Excellence (NICE) antenatal care guidelines [9], the Perinatal Mental Health Programme [10], the Maternity Transformation Programmes [11] and the National Health Service (NHS) Long-Term Plan [12]. In Scotland and Wales there are similar programmes [13, 14]. Women and families have said they wanted to have trusting relationships and continuity of carer from their maternity professionals. In addition, women and healthcare professionals all identified issues with variable mental health provision and expertise.

Some maternity services have a specialist mental health midwife in post [15]. This midwife will have expertise in perinatal mental health and act as local champion leading work in service development to ensure women with perinatal mental health problems receive specialist care and support. The role includes education and training, advising other maternity clinicians, quality improvement and helping women and other professionals navigate the system. Consultant midwives in some maternity services may run clinics for women with tokophobia (primary or secondary) or other complex situations for birth planning and parenting support in first postnatal month. Perinatal mental health midwives in some jurisdictions, such as Scotland and Ireland, may also have a role in delivering low-level psychological interventions.

Obstetrics

If a woman has any illnesses, previous pregnancy complications or relevant family history she will have a 'named obstetrician' who provides her obstetric care and plans care with all relevant healthcare professionals. Increasingly maternity services are appointing an obstetrician with a special interest in perinatal mental health, who can work with specialist perinatal mental health services.

Standard Maternity Care Schedule for Healthy Women (Women Have Midwife Care) [9]

10–12 weeks	Booking screening and history, initial maternity care plan completed including haemoglobinopathy screening
11–14 weeks	Nuchal scan
16–18 weeks	Midwife visit
20 weeks	Anomaly scan
25 weeks	Additional visit if first ongoing pregnancy
28 weeks	Midwife visit
31 weeks	Additional visit if first ongoing pregnancy
34 weeks	Midwife visit
36 weeks	Midwife visit for birth discussion
38 weeks	Midwife visit
40 weeks	Midwife visit
41 weeks	Midwife visit to discuss induction

(See Chapter 4, 'Fetal Development and Routine Maternity Care', for further information.)

For women with any physical, mental or social complexity, additional consultations are added. Women with social complexity may remain with the named midwife as lead for maternity care. Additional consultations in the schedule may be with a variety of professionals; for example, GP, psychological well-being practitioner, early intervention HV, perinatal psychiatrist, perinatal mental health team psychologist, psychotherapist; social worker (mother, unborn child, siblings); independent domestic violence advocate; sexual health service staff; addictions workers/hostel staff; outreach workers.

Maternity Transformation, Local Maternity Systems and Current Policy Changes

There are currently major issues with recruitment and retention of midwives [16] and this has led to a series of reports about the safety of maternity care in England [17].

In addition, there has been a recognition of the level and significance of birth trauma [18].

As a response, NHS England published a 3-year delivery plan for maternity and neonatal services in March 2023 [19]. The aim is to make care safer, more personalised and more equitable for women, babies and families. Integrated care boards (ICBs) commission most maternity services through their local maternity and neonatal system. The ICB commissions the local maternity and neonatal voice partnership that facilitates participation by women and families in local decision-making. The ICB is responsible for commissioning and implementing community perinatal mental health services including maternal mental health services (see below).

The core principles underpinning current priorities for system-wide change in England are:

- all pregnant women receive personalised care and support plan
- improve access to specialised perinatal mental healthcare, including new maternal mental health services in England
- integrated care systems to publish equity and equality plans to take action to reduce inequalities in experience and outcomes
- provide targeted and enhanced continuity of carer for Black, Asian and Minority Ethnic (BAME) women and women from deprived communities as soon as required midwifery staffing levels are met.

For psychiatrists and perinatal mental health teams, refocusing on maternity service transformation is an opportunity to develop practical steps to develop services that truly 'follow the woman' across organisational boundaries and administrative borders. The challenge locally is to ensure that women experiencing social exclusion or marginalisation are not left out.

When Babies Require Neonatal Care: Neonatal and Paediatric Services

Maternity and neonatal services are becoming more aligned in Scotland and England [13, 17]. For example, The Best Start document recommends:

> Maternity and neonatal care should be co-designed with women and families from the outset, with information and evidence provided to allow her to make informed decisions in partnership with her family, her midwife and the wider care team as required. [13]

Neonatologists and neonatal staff need to be involved with pre-birth perinatal mental health planning for women where babies may require care in the neonatal unit or in a transitional care cot. They need a copy of the pre-birth perinatal plan in the records.

The aim is that mother and baby are not separated, anxiety is reduced and a loving relationship is established. Neonatologists can provide advice on maternal medications that may affect a baby's transition to ex-utero life, especially in more complex and challenging treatment decisions. Neonatal staff may have limited ability to support women experiencing perinatal mental illness, who may need additional help to ameliorate any stress from having a baby in a neonatal unit. Perinatal services working with the neonatal team and family, providing education and information during the antenatal and postnatal periods, can help staff and families alike [20]. In Scotland, Maternity and Neonatal Psychological Interventions (MNPI) services also have a specific remit to support parents and infants where the infant is under the care of neonatal intensive or special care.

Maternity Psychological Services

In 2019, NHS England announced that new specialist Maternal Mental Health Services (MMHS) would be in place across England by 2024 for women experiencing moderate to severe or complex mental health difficulties arising from their maternity or perinatal or neonatal experience [12]. As well as moderate to severe mental illness, this may include birth trauma, perinatal loss (for any reason, including removal for safeguarding reasons), post-traumatic stress disorder or tokophobia (severe fear of childbirth). Forty MMHS are currently established across England with different combinations of staff, all including psychologists, and midwives, who are able to help with a range of issues. The MMHS and community PMH teams should work closely together to ensure women are directed to the appropriate service.

An evaluation of one pilot for services has shown a 'story of two halves': an unsustainable degree of pressure and stress experienced by staff who reported feeling insufficiently supported 'from above'; and life-saving, life-changing treatment experienced by women [21].

In Scotland, MNPI services provide a similar function. (See Chapter 30, 'Perinatal Mental Health Service Development and Delivery', for more discussion.)

What the Challenges May Be

These centre on establishing and maintaining relationships of trust with everyone providing care for a woman and her family. This may be particularly challenging where a woman is being moved to different locations for housing, physical or social service requirements. Women who have a long-standing chronic illness with little social support and periods of chaotic living are especially vulnerable. Careful, persistent and responsive working across the health, social and voluntary sectors can provide effective care in the perinatal period.

What That Means for Perinatal Mental Health Services

When assessing and planning care for a woman with an existing or developing mental illness, who is newly pregnant, it is important for clinicians to identify where she is booked for maternity care and the names and contacts of her named midwife and named obstetrician. The perinatal mental health team should have established contacts with local maternity services and know the specialist midwives, specialist midwifery teams and lead obstetrician for perinatal mental health. Where they do not, they should call local maternity service, asking for the midwifery manager on call, available 24/7. A woman will not routinely see her midwife from 16 weeks until either 25 weeks if first baby or 28 weeks if subsequent babies. Unless there is planned additional contact for monitoring a woman's mental health during this time, she may have no contact with a maternity professional for 2 or 3 months. Care plans should be shared with the patient (and birth partner as appropriate), GP, midwifery team, psychiatric team and other relevant professionals involved in the person's care. In cases where mental healthcare monitoring in the early postpartum days is essential (e.g. history of bipolar disorder, postpartum psychosis, other psychosis, suicidality or severe depression), the psychiatric team must be alerted to the delivery.

For women who are experiencing difficulties with housing, domestic abuse, working very closely with the named midwife and her team is integral to effective care planning during the perinatal period.

Primary Care Routine Care

In the UK, GPs hold the complete historic clinical record for individual patient NHS care. They have no criteria for whom they will and will not see. They do not have supervision of their clinical practice, but they have to undergo annual appraisal and 5-yearly revalidations on the basis of their appraisals. GP partners are effectively running the business of their practices; they are self-employed and contract with the NHS to care for patients.

Pregnant women no longer see a GP during their routine antenatal care. However, pregnant women and new mothers frequently consult GPs about themselves and their new infant. Some of these contacts are urgent, intercurrent problems. A routine maternal postnatal consultation has been included within the GP contract since April 2020 and this will generally take place at 6–8 weeks [22].

A GP consultation is usually scheduled to last 10 minutes. Surgeries are held in the morning from 8.30am until about 11am, but afternoon surgeries vary in time. It is difficult for GPs to be interrupted in their short consultation time, to speak to consultants. It is much more effective to leave a message and a mobile telephone number, so GPs can call back. Be aware that this may be at lunchtime or fairly late in the evening. Two-thirds of GPs technically work less than full-time, but most GPs work very long days, often about 12 hours.

Practice nurses are employed by GPs directly. Their training is managed by their employers. They may have more contact with pregnant women than GPs; they may take blood from pregnant women (as do many practice-employed phlebotomists), see women for contraceptive advice and immunise infants. More information is available in a paper about their role [23].

Practice receptionists control the availability of appointments for patients, although most GP systems also offer online bookings. In addition, they are likely to be the access point for external phone calls from specialists. They have no clinical knowledge, but often have local knowledge and intelligence that helps them in their work.

Current Policy Changes

General practice is under considerable pressure, faced with a recruitment and retention crisis. In January 2019 NHS England announced a deal offering £2.4 billion extra a year for general practice and 5,000 more GPs [24]. It also introduced the additional roles reimbursement scheme which has funded 20,000 more staff (pharmacists, physiotherapists, paramedics, physician associates and social prescribing link workers) to help GP practices work together [25]. This was intended to free up GPs' time, so they could spend more time with the patients who needed them most. In practice it has had the adverse consequence of suppressing GP recruitment and placing even more stress on GPs and has led to declining patient experience of GP practices since 2021 [26].

The Covid-19 epidemic has fundamentally changed the ways in which GPs work, so that there are more consultations than before, but less face-to-face contact and more telephone consultations, and less continuity of care [27].

Since 2022/3 each GP practice has employed a social prescribing link worker, meaning that patients can be referred to a range of local, non-clinical services [28]. There is a lot of positive experience about social prescribing, but the quality of evidence is still limited.

GPs are no longer responsible for 24-hour care of their patients. In reality there is more 'out of hours' time in a week than 'in hours'. Urgent treatment centres are accessible through 111 to provide urgent medical help for non-life-threatening emergencies [29].

What the Challenges May Be

GPs may not know their pregnant and postnatal women, especially during pregnancy. Women may not know their GP and poor access and lack of continuity of care may mean that they have not established trusting relationships. The nature of perinatal crises is that they are likely to happen out of hours when neither the usual GP nor the perinatal psychiatrist may be available.

What That Means for Perinatal Mental Health Services

It may seem difficult to have a telephone discussion with a GP. Book a call with receptionists in advance, unless it is an emergency that cannot wait until later in the day. The daytime pressure for GPs means that they are unlikely to attend care planning meetings, especially at short notice, but a conversation on the phone could always be arranged to share information.

GPs will be reliant on their local specialist perinatal mental health services for training and direction. They have a particular need for education and advice about medication in pregnancy and breastfeeding. Make efforts to get to know the GPs in your area: they are a fount of information about patients and their families, want to do their best for women with perinatal mental health and learn to improve their practice. They generally learn best from the cases that turn up in their everyday work.

Health Visitors Routine Care

Health visitors are public health nurses who work mainly with children and families from before birth to 5 years. They are responsible for women, infants and families after discharge by the midwife, usually at 10–14 days. They focus on supporting families and have a strong health promotion and prevention agenda to ensure every child has the best start in life and to reduce health inequalities. They are registered nurses/midwives who have an additional BSc or MSc in community public health nursing. Maternal, infant and family mental health are core components of health visiting provision and most HVs are trained to support women with mild to moderate mental health problems.

Across the four nations of the UK, there are also significant differences between the health visiting services offered – this is driven by different levels of prioritisation and investment by their respective governments. Health visitors work holistically making an assessment of all potential health issues (physical, mental and social) in the family that may impact the child. In addition to checking the baby the HV should also assess maternal sensitivity to her infant and, if present, paternal mental health. In England (where there are fewer contacts than in other parts of the UK) routine care includes contact at:

- antenatal check at 28 weeks of pregnancy
- new baby check
- at 6–8 weeks, specific perinatal mental health focus
- 1 year
- 2–2½ years

A targeted approach is used to improve outcomes and reduce inequalities using four tiers of care: *community*, *universal* (offered to all mothers), *targeted* (a more intense programme of interventions that are delivered by the HV team based on the needs of the individual, such as listening visits for perinatal mental health) and *specialist* (a more intense programme of interventions that are delivered by a multidisciplinary group of professionals or agencies based on the needs of the individual, usually including safeguarding) [30].

Specialist HVs in perinatal and infant mental health provide an expert resource, both through direct intervention with families needing specialist help and through training, offering consultation and specialist supervision to their colleagues. As well as the benefit to families, they also provide specialist expertise within the wider health system [31].

Current Policy Changes

Local authorities have been responsible for commissioning HVs in England since 2013. In England this has led to a 40% reduction in HV numbers, with staff under huge pressure and families dissatisfied with the service that they receive [32]. This is not the case in other parts of the UK.

What That Means for Perinatal Mental Health Services

The reduction in numbers of HVs in England will inevitably affect their current ability to support all women in the way that they would wish and to identify those mothers with perinatal mental health promptly. However, they provide a universal service and HVs should know women with identified perinatal mental health problems as well as their family context. Once identified, the mother becomes part of the HV's targeted caseload allowing her to follow her up with a package of support, including step 0–2 psychological support. Health visitors should also alert the mother's GP when working with a mother with mild to moderate perinatal mental health problems and will refer those with more serious illness to the GP, or in some areas directly to the perinatal mental health team or Mother and Baby Unit. Health visitors can be contacted by leaving a message on the local team answerphone or directly. Every mother should have a phone number for her HV in her child's parent held record.

Role of the Institute of Health Visiting

The Institute of Health Visiting (iHV) is a professional body and charity established in 2012 whose main focus is to strengthen health visiting services and reduce health inequalities. It has made perinatal mental health an organisational priority since foundation, due to its impact on the whole family, and especially the well-being of the child. It offers a range of training courses to the whole multi-professional team Perinatal and Infant Mental Health Champions programme. For more details see: https://ihv.org.uk/training-and-events/training-programme.

Talking Therapies in England and Equivalents in Other Devolved Nations

The NHS Talking Therapies for anxiety and depression programme (formerly known as Improving Access to Psychological Therapies) is part of primary care mental health services available in England. These services successfully treat many women experiencing depression and anxiety disorders (such as generalised anxiety, social anxiety, obsessive-compulsive disorder (OCD), post-traumatic stress disorders and comorbid illness) during the perinatal period. These women will be generally at Step 2–4 on the stepped-care pathway. Services can be accessed directly by patients or referrals can be made by others, such as healthcare professionals.

Talking therapy services generally do not accept women who are already receiving specialist psychiatric services, and mostly they do not have the facility to treat women with their babies. They work in targeted and structured ways to deliver treatments, but all services are locally focused and so they may offer slightly different options.

Talking therapy services prioritise perinatal women for treatment. NICE guidelines recommended rapid access to evidence-based psychological therapies for parents and infants during the perinatal period assessment within 2 weeks, and treatment started within 4 weeks [4]. There is an existing guide for talking therapy therapists [33].

One study about women's perinatal experiences of talking therapy reports overall positive experiences of receiving support from talking therapy for perinatal mental health difficulties. Nevertheless, issues were highlighted by women and therapists relating to barriers to access and a need to better tailor therapy to the perinatal context [34]. Therapists similarly expressed frustration that the constraints of talking therapy prevented them from adapting treatment sufficiently. Yet some also worried that deviating from protocols, or allowing babies in sessions, could reduce treatment efficacy or create other risks. Overall, therapists expressed anxiety working with perinatal mental health difficulties and wanted perinatal-specific training, supervision and resources. A more recent study shows that current services are broadly acceptable to women [35].

Current Policy Changes

Talking therapy services were expanded in the NHS Long-Term Plan and this has led to additional services for women with perinatal mental health problems [12]. They are also mentioned in the NHS perinatal mental healthcare pathways [6].

What the Challenges May Be

It may be a significant hurdle for a woman with perinatal mental health to make direct contact with her local service; she may need help and advocacy to help her pick up the phone or complete a form. In addition, if she is unable to take her baby there may be issues about childcare. Many women might feel going to a group that is not focused specifically on perinatal issues is not helpful.

What That Means for Perinatal Mental Health Services

It is worth getting to know your local talking therapy services and developing training or links with specific therapists with extended skills, especially within Step 3 services.

Devolved Nations

Throughout Scotland NHS provision of evidence-based interventions for mild to moderate mental distress and disorder at universal/primary care level is variable, but most areas offer an MNPI team [7].

In Wales primary care psychology services also exist [36].

Children's Centres

The Sure Start Children's Centre programme was introduced in England in 1998 and brought together services for young children and their families under one roof. Initially it was focused on the most disadvantaged areas in England, but the programme was later extended to all areas. In their short history, children's centres became a vital local resource for many families offering open access services such as 'Stay and Play' free of charge. By its peak in August 2009, there were 3,632 centres, with over half (54%) in the 30% most disadvantaged areas. However, in recent years, its status as a key national programme has diminished and severe local authority budget cuts have led to increasingly uneven local provision. An academic study from 2018 found that as many as 1,000 Sure Start centres across the country have closed since 2009 [37].

Andrea Leadsom was commissioned to lead a review of early years by the government and reported in 2021 [38]. After this the Conservative government announced 75 family hubs in England at a cost of £300 million and that it would implement Andrea Leadsom's Start for Life agenda [39].

Following the recent General Election in July 2024 Labour's plans are yet to become clear, but there was no specific mention of family hubs in Labour's Child Health Action Plan, which focused mainly on school-aged children [40].

What That Means for Perinatal Mental Health Services

The universal availability, accessibility and services from Children's Centres can no longer be relied upon in England. Practitioners need to be aware about what is available locally.

Social Care

Safeguarding women and children are discussed in Chapters 36 and 37. Most women's social issues in the community will be to do with employment, housing, benefits, childcare, marital breakdown and domestic abuse. Specialist services need to know how to signpost women to sources of practical help in these areas.

Peer Support for Perinatal Mental Health

Peer support has received strong backing at a national policy level, with recommendations that it is available in: MBUs; community perinatal mental health teams; and in the community, both for those recovering from severe perinatal mental health problems as well as those experiencing mild to moderate perinatal mental health, distress and adjustment disorders [12, 41, 42, 43].

Peer support has been reported to facilitate recovery in a wide range of mental illnesses, improving well-being, quality of life, decreasing social isolation, decreasing days in hospital, reducing readmission and reducing health service use [44, 45, 46, 47, 48, 49, 50].

Fewer studies have examined peer support in the perinatal context. It is theorised that peer support may be particularly valuable during recovery from perinatal mental illness, given the changes in identity that occur during the transition to motherhood, the value placed on managing the transition well, and the perceived negative impact of mental illness on this transition. Face-to-face and telephone peer support for postnatal depression and anxiety appear to aid recovery, reducing symptoms and improving access to social support [48, 51, 52, 53, 54, 55]. In a study of 10 voluntary sector organisations in England, McLeish and Redshaw report that peer support may reduce symptoms, by reducing isolation, disempowerment and stress, and increasing feelings of self-esteem, self-efficacy and parenting competence [56].

Peer support is also important for those recovering from severe forms of perinatal mental illness. Following postpartum psychosis (PP), women report a sense of shock, anger, shame and guilt about the experience. They question why this has happened to them, and mourn the loss of the motherhood they expected. Recovery involves building a new sense of self, and coming to terms with the impact of the illness on their relationships. Women face stigma, misunderstanding and poor knowledge about PP in families and the community. Most women who are affected will not meet another woman who has experienced it in their everyday lives [2, 57, 58]. Recovering women and their partners want access to reliable information and describe needing to talk to other women who have experienced the illness [2, 59, 60]. A service evaluation by Action on Postpartum Psychosis found that peer support for PP reduces isolation; increases feelings of support; increases hope for the future; decreases the impact of societal and family stigma; and is described by many as 'life-changing' and 'lifesaving'. It is not viewed by those who receive it as an alternative to medication or professional support but as an adjunct that supports a more holistic recovery [61].

Peer support has also been shown to have benefits for the peer supporters, enabling them to 'deepen' their recovery; bring about positive outcomes from difficult experiences; feel part of an active engaged peer community; and feel that they are 'giving back' and improving the future for other women and families [62, 63].

Key Ingredients of Effective Peer Support

Peer support happens naturally in our lives, in our friendship groups: we relate over shared experience as 'equals'. Its use in mental health settings can be seen as far back as the 1790s, in Bicetre Hospital, Paris, where former patients were recruited as staff. They found that staff with personal experience were 'gentle, humane, and disposed to kindnesses', and their presence improved outcomes and eliminated the cruelty that was commonplace in psychiatric treatment in France at that time.

Even the most formal peer support should be as free from power differentials as possible. Meeting and talking to others who have experienced and recovered from perinatal mental illness can normalise and destigmatise the experience; provide understanding; insight; hope for the future; friendship; empathy; and a role model for healthy recovery, growth and learning. Those who receive support report that there is a level of trust and credibility that comes from knowing that the person providing the support 'has been there' and provide real evidence that recovery is possible [2, 54].

Models of Peer Support

Peer support comes in many forms. It can be specific to certain illness (e.g. PP, depression and anxiety, maternal OCD) or more general (e.g. a group for women with any form of perinatal mental health problem). It can be provided 'in person', individually or in groups; during a practical activity (art and craft, pram pushing, learning parenting skills) or as an activity of itself (one-to-one conversation, social group). It can be conversational (e.g. tea and talk) or practical (e.g. support with household chores). It can also be provided effectively through online forums, email, messaging, telephone, video call and social media platforms. Services may vary in their formality: some peer support may be delivered as a course of evidence-based therapeutic groups, others may be social and informal. Peer support workers can be based within an NHS team, services can be commissioned by the NHS from third-sector peer support organisations, or referral arrangements can be more informal, using trained and supported volunteers, or third-sector agencies funded via charitable donations.

Assessing Quality of Peer Support in Perinatal Mental Health

Given this vast array of ways to deliver peer support, how do perinatal services determine which is best? There has not yet been enough research into the most effective or acceptable models of providing perinatal peer support, and therefore peer support can vary widely. The Maternal Mental Health Alliance commissioned a set of principles to outline the key ingredients of high-quality peer support. The principles outline what is meant by safe, nurturing, accessible, inclusive peer support. Peers should be meaningfully involved, and it should demonstrably benefit everyone, including the peers providing it [62]. A similar document exists in Scotland [63].

Things to Consider When Commissioning/Setting Up a Peer Support Service

Training

Training should cover the theory behind peer support and explain what peer support is and isn't. Peer supporters should have a role description [63]. They should understand their responsibilities and how far this responsibility extends. Providing sensitive, empathetic and nurturing support to others comes naturally for some people; for others training in peer support, listening and facilitation, can help to develop these skills. It is easy to fall into the role of offering advice and taking responsibility for a person's care. Training should include information relevant to their specific area of peer supporting, as well as information about other common perinatal problems (e.g. other diagnoses, infant feeding, birth trauma). Training should include an explanation of safeguarding concerns, and the processes they are required to follow – including modelling how these conversations can be best managed to minimise damage to the peer support relationship. Peers must also understand their responsibilities in terms of data protection, confidentiality and cyber security. Training should also increase the confidence of peers in managing some of the difficult situations that might arise while peer supporting, as relevant to their service (e.g. managing suicidality, psychosis, personal boundaries). Peers should know how to assess their own health and well-being to determine if they are in a good personal place to offer support to others. They should understand how they will be supported and managed as they support others, as well as the advice, supervision, debriefing time, ongoing support and training available to them.

Training about peer support for other staff in the team is essential. Peer support cannot work when line managers or other staff in the team do not understand the role of a peer supporter. An example guide for other professionals working with peer workers is available at www.app-network.org/get-help/peer-support-in-your-area

Recruitment

Having the experience of a specific illness does not necessarily make a person an effective peer supporter. Peer supporting requires a specific set of qualities and includes: empathy and understanding; ability to communicate warmth and friendliness with ease; being sensitive to other's feelings and needs; being a role model of good recovery and mental health management; having an awareness of one's own personal judgements; and being interested, enquiring, nurturing, reflective and resilient. Good training can help peers to develop an explicit awareness of how we demonstrate these skills in person or in writing, but good recruitment processes will help identify committed, passionate and resilient staff. Setting an adequate pay band for the personal and organisational skills required is essential. Media work demonstrating the work of the service or the value placed upon lived experience involvement, or offering local volunteer training in peer support can help increase the pool of people with lived experience and relevant skills from which to recruit from.

Developing a close relationship with the rest of the NHS team is essential for peer supporters to know who and how best to support, to share information as needed, and to influence thoughtful care practices in the entire NHS team. Clear and regular line management/supervision is necessary. Close contact with other peers and ongoing training alongside other peers is necessary to retain objectivity, adhering to different principles of operation from health professionals. Peer support should be built in at all levels – so peer support workers have a forum to provide support for each other.

Facilitation of Long-Term Support Post-Discharge

It is unlikely that one peer will be able to provide adequate peer support for all women, with all conditions. As an example, women with PP describe that peer support in an anxiety and depression support group can leave them feeling more isolated, self-conscious and not understood [2]. Discussions will be needed in the clinical team about who appropriate peers would be, and how many peers might be needed to cover the range of experience seen within the service – the different diagnoses, cultural backgrounds, the different family members who might also require support (partners, grandparents), bereaved families, LGBTQ+ families, etc.). Peers may be able to, with the right supporting networks, act as a gateway to meet other individuals, signpost to organisations in the community, or facilitate involvement with a third-sector peer support community that will enable families to meet others with a vast array of experiences.

Protocols That Adhere to Peer Support Principles

Consideration should be given to protocols: ensuring that peer support is as free from barriers or power differentials as possible. For example, sitting at a desk, taking notes, completing consent forms, laying ground rules, reading confidential and safeguarding statements, talking about people in team meetings, writing in patient notes, participating in routine documentation, reading files, writing treatment plans, may not be consistent with the peer role. Some of these, however, may be essential in delivering a safe, effective service that can follow patients through their recovery process and can be well evaluated.

Some note taking and record keeping is clearly needed: forgetting key facts impairs the formation of a relationship, but how will this be done without affecting the power dynamic? How will peers be transparent about confidentiality and limits of it, without impairing the developing peer relationship? How will peer support be delivered in your service? How can it be made as informal, friendly, stress reducing and pleasurable as possible?

Despite this, a peer support relationship is not a friendship. Safety procedures and methods of managing personal boundaries should be in place. Consideration needs to be paid to the level of risk appropriate for a peer supporter; should it be the same as for professional staff working within the NHS? Will walks and café trips be acceptable when a patient is well enough? Who will assess this? What about lone home visits in the community? Do peers have the required level of professional training to manage the risks they might be exposed to in lone working situations in people's homes?

NHS personal boundary policies might require that staff do not share details of their personal lives, but sharing selective and pertinent details of their personal life is essential for peers. Most NHS policies do not allow ongoing contact with patients once discharged. Peers should be advised how the service plans to manage this blurring of professional boundaries. Providing advice for peers about not sharing personal contact details, not connecting with patients they are supporting on social media, securing social media personal accounts, are common sense. However, because of the mutuality and shared experience, and because peers often support the post-discharge transition, some contacts may develop into friendships. This needs active consideration.

Line Management, Ongoing Training and Support

Peer supporters should not feel alone whilst supporting women. There should be internal methods of quality control, through access to advice and support, supervision, client feedback and discussions regarding ongoing training needs. Peers should have the opportunity to reflect on the support provided and share ideas or concerns about how they managed difficult issues. Where peer support services are commissioned from the third sector, peers will have an NHS team line manager and a line manager from the peer organisation, linking them to other peers and ongoing training. Generally, the NHS line manager will be the ward manager, occupational therapist or psychologist, and supervisions should happen monthly, or more as needed. Peer support must have benefits to those providing it, and should not overburden or cause undue stress. Peers should have access to others in similar roles. This is invaluable for learning and support, and for peers to feel part of a supportive like-minded community. Peers should also be included in any staff in-house multi-disciplinary team education and practice development activities [32].

Training and ongoing support will help to manage difficult issues like working with women with ongoing depression, suicidal thoughts, psychosis, high mood, personality disorders, fear of services, childhood trauma, difficulties forming a connection, boundary difficulties or talking to people with very different opinions to their own. For peers running face-to-face or online groups, strategies for managing difficult group dynamics, such as one person dominating the conversation, affecting group morale, or groups splitting off into cliques are useful.

Processes need to be put in place for self-care or support for the supporter *and* must be carefully considered, not patronising and patriarchal. These processes should recognise that while rewarding, peer support can be intense and worrisome, and that a peer supporter needs to be in the right place to support others. Peers should be included in designing self-care processes.

Managing Illness Cover and Succession Planning

Service flexibility needs consideration at an early stage of planning. Sometimes people need time away from supporting. In addition, whilst peer supporting may be a career calling for some, for others, who may be skilled and able peer supporters, this may be part of the process of recovery – giving back to the service that supported them, and bringing about positive change from a traumatic experience. Peer supporters will move on as their life moves on. The service will function best if it builds in succession planning processes, for example by training assistants, or volunteers to work alongside peer support staff, rather than accepting long delays while new staff are recruited and trained.

Commissioning Peer Support from Third-Sector Organisations

Working with third-sector organisations can have advantages and disadvantages. Peer support delivered in the third sector ensures patients are supported for much longer than the length of time a perinatal service can hold a patient, and may provide access to other relevant services that will improve social support and recovery outcomes.

Organisations specialising in peer support are set up with tested protocols, and have training, support and succession planning processes in place. Peer supporters working in this way are 'in' but not 'of' the system: making it easier to retain values that are true to the peer role and peers are able to access support from a large network of other peers.

However, greater efforts may be needed to embed third-sector employed peer workers in the NHS team. Agreements need to be in place for sharing data, communication and evaluation.

When working with smaller third-sector organisations or lived experience user groups, finance departments should be aware of good practice guidelines for contracting from the charitable sector, including the importance of making payments on time. NHS contract 'legalese' can be hard for small third-sector organisations and user-led groups to manage, meaning they have to buy in legal services to review contracts. When contracting directly with those with lived experience, processes for paying expenses should be straightforward, rapid and respectful.

Despite perinatal teams throughout the UK considering how to implement peer support in their region, little is known about the most effective models, or the situations where peer support has the most benefit. The Scottish Government report into perinatal mental health services outlines the urgent need for NHS boards and third-sector funders to review peer support models and develop an evidence and evaluation base [44].

Good Case Example

In Birmingham, three third-sector organisations have been contracted to cover the spectrum of experience. Action on Postpartum Psychosis employs a peer support facilitator to support families managing severe mental illness in pregnancy or the postpartum period (PP, bipolar disorder, schizophrenia); Acacia employs a peer support worker to work with women with anxiety and depression; and Approachable Parenting employs a worker to provide additional support to women from BAME backgrounds. The peer supporters work together and co-support as necessary. They are key members of the NHS team, as well as having access to the expertise, learning and peer community from their respective organisations. The NHS employs a region-wide lived experience involvement coordinator to connect peers throughout the region and ensure that their input is an integral part of service planning and delivery.

Working with Third-Sector Organisations and Community Groups

Third-sector providers in particular areas may also offer other specialist care services, for example counselling or formal psychological interventions. These not-for-profit services are worth understanding as they sometimes offer highly specialist and well-evaluated interventions, such as after baby loss, trauma or for postnatal depression and anxiety. NHS subcontracts or service-level agreements are needed to specify joint working, referral pathways and processes for data sharing.

Royal College of Psychiatrists guidelines outline that for every patient, the specialist team should provide information and encouragement to access local organisations for peer support and social engagement [42, 43]. This should be documented in the patient's care plan. This might include:

- activities that promote enjoyment and interaction with the baby and social engagement (such as swimming lessons, sensory activities, music groups)
- voluntary organisations
- community centres
- local religious/cultural groups
- peer support networks
- recovery colleges

The team should have a good knowledge about the range of local and national voluntary and community sector services available, and a member of staff should be responsible for keeping a database up to date, and sharing this knowledge with other staff.

Involving third-sector and community organisations in training days, perinatal networks and community events can encourage close links and ensure awareness of the support available and referral processes.

Lived Experience Co-production

National guidelines suggest that experts by experience should be involved in service planning and the delivery and development of staff training [28, 33, 34]. For effective co-production, lived experience representatives and third-sector organisations should be involved early in planning, and be present at the same meetings as commissioners and providers, rather than as a good practice after-thought. Lived experience speakers can be a powerful aid to help providers understand the needs of families. Innovative creative days can be used to gain broad lived experience input and understand the needs that are most important to users of the service. However, the support needs of those sharing their story and lived experience expertise should be a priority, with sufficient support time ahead of talks, training and debriefing time provided for lived experience speakers. Providers should recognise that giving lived experience talks can be emotionally draining, and bring up unexpected and difficult emotions, even for experienced speakers. Regular check-ins are also needed to ensure speakers are in a healthy place from which to be speaking. Expenses should be paid and remuneration appropriate to the expertise and time required. Various third-sector organisations (e.g. Action on Postpartum Psychosis, Maternal Mental Health Alliance) train and support lived experience speakers and can support co-production projects and ensure good support is in place.

Building Networks

The following links are a starting point for developing local and national directories that can be shared with parents. Networks should include perinatal mental health organisations, but may also include groups working with: diverse communities; bereaved parents; supporting relationships; parent–infant mental health; and those providing legal advice and finance support. Health professionals can connect with organisations on social media and in person, host events and help to build networks in the region.

- https://maternalmentalhealthalliance.org/resources/mums-and-families
- www.app-network.org/useful-links
- https://bump2babywellbeingguide.org
- www.bestbeginnings.org.uk/charities-uk-support
- www.sands.org.uk/professionals/projects-improve-bereavement-care/national-bereavement-care-pathway
- www.turn2us.org.uk/Your-Situation
- https://parentinfantfoundation.org.uk/useful-resources/information-for-parents

Summary

This chapter has tried to set out for specialist perinatal mental health services how community services work, their current challenges and changes. The last few years have been a time of massive change and we anticipate that these will continue, meaning that specialist perinatal mental health services need to keep up to date with changes and new developments in their local areas. The more closely specialist and community services can work together, the better the outcomes for women and their families in the shorter and longer terms.

References

1. Royal College of Psychiatrists. Perinatal mental health services: recommendations for the provision of services for childbearing women. 2021. https://tinyurl.com/ypnbrp35
2. J Heron, N Gilbert, C Dolman, S Shah, I Beare, S Dearden, et al. Information and support needs during recovery from postpartum psychosis. *Arch Women Ment Health*. 2012;15:155–65.
3. Public Health England. Place-based approaches for reducing health inequalities: main report. Guidelines to support local action on health inequalities. 2019. https://tinyurl.com/3tvay9t8
4. National Institute for Health and Clinical Excellence. Antenatal and postnatal mental health: clinical management and service guidance. Clinical Guideline (CG192). 2014. www.nice.org.uk/guidance/cg192
5. Healthcare Improvement Scotland. Perinatal mental health conditions (SIGN 169). 2023. www.sign.ac.uk/media/2172/sign-169-perinatal.pdf
6. National Collaborating Centre for Mental Health. *The perinatal mental health care pathways: full implementation guidance*. London: National Collaborating Centre for Mental Health; 2018. www.england.nhs.uk/publication/the-perinatal-mental-health-care-pathways

7. NHS Scotland Access to Specialist Care in Scotland. The Scottish perinatal mental health care pathway. 2024. www.pmhn.scot.nhs.uk/women-and-families-2/access-to-specialist-care-in-scotland
8. National Health Service. NHS talking therapies for anxiety and depression manual. 2024. https://tinyurl.com/2waucapk
9. National Institute for Health and Clinical Excellence. Antenatal care. NICE Guideline (NG201). 2021. www.nice.org.uk/guidance/ng201
10. NHS England. Perinatal mental health. n.d. https://tinyurl.com/37t278rb
11. NHS England. National Maternity Review. Better births: improving outcomes of maternity services in England – a five year forward view for maternity care. 2016. www.england.nhs.uk/wp-content/uploads/2016/02/national-maternity-review-report.pdf
12. NHS England. The NHS long-term plan. 2019. www.longtermplan.nhs.uk.
13. Scottish Government. The best start: a five year forward plan for maternity and neonatal care in Scotland. 2017. https://tinyurl.com/5n7u2w2w
14. Welsh Government. Maternity care in Wales: a five-year vision for the future (2019–2024). 2019. https://gov.wales/maternity-services-strategy-2019-2024
15. Maternal Mental Health Alliance. Specialist mental health midwives: what they do and why they matter. 2013. https://tinyurl.com/swvwk273
16. G Moncrieff, S Downe, M Maxwell, H Cheyne. Mapping factors that may influence attrition and retention of midwives: a scoping review protocol. *BMJ Open*. 2023;13:e076686.
17. J Shakespeare, E Duff, D Bick. How many more reviews are needed? Joined-up policy and investment in England's maternity units is needed now to improve postnatal and inter-pregnancy care. *Midwifery*. 2022 Oct;113:103469.
18. The All-Party Parliamentary Group on Birth Trauma. Listen to mums: ending the postcode lottery on perinatal care. 2024. https://tinyurl.com/mvpt6b45
19. NHS England. Three-year delivery plan for maternity and neonatal services. 2023. https://tinyurl.com/2t464usu
20. NHS England and NHS Improvement. Implementing the recommendations of the neonatal critical care transformation review. 2019. https://tinyurl.com/5h6a8kyv
21. National Health Service and McPin Foundation. Regional evaluation of the London pilot of maternal mental health services. 2023. https://tinyurl.com/2jnaf5nk
22. NHS England. GP six to eight week maternal postnatal consultation – what good looks like guidance. https://tinyurl.com/y6xsvc3s
23. C Bagness, J Shakespeare. Perinatal mental health and general practice nursing. *J Gen Pract Nurs*. 2016;2;56–60.
24. NHS England. Five-year deal to expand GP services and kick start NHS long-term plan implementation. 2019. https://tinyurl.com/yfb7bxer
25. NHS England. Additional roles reimbursement scheme. n.d. www.england.nhs.uk/gp/expanding-our-workforce
26. The Health Foundation. General practice data dashboard. 2024. www.health.org.uk/general-practice-data-dashboard
27. C Fraser, C Fisher. How has the COVID-19 pandemic impacted primary care? The Health Foundation; 2021. https://tinyurl.com/r5add69j
28. D Buck, L Ewbank. What is social prescribing? The King's Fund; 2020. https://tinyurl.com/33uata4k
29. NHS England. Urgent treatment centres. n.d. www.england.nhs.uk/urgent-emergency-care/urgent-treatment-centres
30. Public Health England. Health visiting and school nursing service delivery model. 2021. https://tinyurl.com/yeywvcxe
31. Health Education England. Specialist health visitors in perinatal & infant

mental health. https://tinyurl.com/ycykv2bw

32. Institute of Health Visiting. State of health visiting. UK survey report. 2023. https://tinyurl.com/3c7nb359
33. S O'Mahen, S Healy, N Haycock, S Igwe, R Chilvers, R Butterworth. NHS talking therapies for anxiety and depression: perinatal positive practice guide. University of Exeter; 2023. https://tinyurl.com/ymk2ca3m
34. L Millett, B Taylor, L Howard, D Bick, N Stanley, S Johnson. Experiences of improving access to psychological therapy services for perinatal mental health difficulties: a qualitative study of women's and therapists' views. *Behav Cogn Psychother.* 2018;4:421–36.
35. J Ingram, D Johnson, HA O'Mahen, R Law, I Culpin, D Kessler, et al. 'Asking for help': a qualitative interview study exploring the experiences of interpersonal counselling (IPC) compared to low-intensity cognitive behavioural therapy (CBT) for women with depression during pregnancy. *BMC Pregnancy Childbirth.* 2021;21:765.
36. NHS Wales. Perinatal mental health programme and pathways. n.d. https://tinyurl.com/bdhw633p
37. G Smith, K Sylva, T Smith, P Sammons, A Omonigho. Stop start: survival, decline or closure? Children's centres in England. Sutton Trust; 2018. www.suttontrust.com/wp-content/uploads/2018/04/StopStart-FINAL.pdf
38. A Leadsom. The best start for life: a vision for the 1,001 critical days. Gov.UK; 2021. https://tinyurl.com/5n92btbt
39. Gov.UK. Thousands of families to benefit from local support in rollout of family hubs. Press release. 2023. https://tinyurl.com/2wwupxmj
40. The Labour Party. Action plan will create the healthiest generation of children ever. 2024. https://tinyurl.com/yb657cah
41. Perinatal Quality Network for Perinatal Mental Health Services and Royal College of Psychiatrists. Standards for community perinatal mental health services. 4th edition. Z Schneider, editor. 2013. https://tinyurl.com/yzvxzmzc
42. Perinatal Quality Network for Perinatal Mental Health Services and Royal College of Psychiatrists. Standards for inpatient perinatal mental health services. 6th edition. 2018. https://tinyurl.com/ywyt2wsy
43. Scottish Government. Perinatal mental health services: needs assessment and recommendations. 2019. https://tinyurl.com/muk2rcur
44. S Lawton-Smith. Peer support in mental health: where are we today? *J Ment Health Train, Educ Pract.* 2013;8(3):152–8.
45. V Gidugu, ES Rogers, S Harrington, M Maru, G Johnson, J Cohee, J Hinkel. Individual peer support: a qualitative study of mechanisms of its effectiveness. *Community Ment Health J.* 2015;51(4):445–52.
46. G Nelson, J Ochocka, R Janzen, J Trainor. A longitudinal study of mental health consumer/survivor initiatives: Part 2 – a quantitative study of impacts of participation of new members. *J Community Psychol.* 2006;34(3):261–72.
47. N Pistrang. Mutual help groups for mental health problems: a review of effectiveness studies. *Am J Comm Psychol.* 2008;42:110–21.
48. C-L Dennis, E Hodnett, L Kenton, DE Stewart. Effect of peer support on prevention of postnatal depression among high-risk women: multisite randomised controlled trial. *BMJ.* 2009;338:a3064.
49. P Seebohm, S Chaudhary, M Boyce, R Elkan, M Avis, C Munn-Giddings. The contribution of self-help/mutual aid groups to mental well-being. *Health Soc Care Community.* 2013;21(4):391–40.
51. G Johnson, C Magee, M Maru, K Furlong-Norman, ES Rogers, K Thompson. Personal and societal benefits of providing peer support: a survey of peer support specialists. *Psychiatr Serv.* 2014;65(5):678–80.
52. C-L Dennis. The process of developing and implementing a telephone-based peer support program for postpartum

depression: evidence from two randomized controlled trials. *Trials.* 2014;15:131.

53. I Caramlau, J Barlow, S Sembi, K McKenzie-McHarg, C McCabe. Mums 4 Mums: structured telephone peer-support for women experiencing postnatal depression. Pilot and exploratory RCT of its clinical and cost effectiveness. *Trials.* 2011;12:88.
54. LJ Biggs, HL McLachlan, T Shafiei, R Small, DA Forster. Peer supporters' experiences on an Australian perinatal mental health helpline. *Health Promot Int.* 2018;34(3):479–89.
55. F Cust. Peer support for mothers with postnatal depression. *J New Writing Health Social Care.* 2016;2(2):21–31.
56. J McLeish, M Redshaw. Mothers' accounts of the impact on emotional wellbeing of organised peer support in pregnancy and early parenthood: a qualitative study. *BMC Pregnancy Childbirth.* 2017;17:28.
57. S Doucet, N Letourneau, ER Blackmore. Support needs of mothers who experience postpartum psychosis and their partners. *JOGN Nurs.* 2012;41:236–45.
58. E Robertson, A Lyons. Living with puerperal psychosis: a qualitative analysis. *Psychol Psychother.* 2003;76:411–31.
59. A Blackwell, J Heron, J Ives, et al. The experiences and support needs of men when their partners suffer postpartum psychosis. APP Report, email: info@app-network.org.
60. L McGrath, S Peters, A Wieck, A Wittkowski. The process of recovery in women who experienced psychosis following childbirth. *BMC Psychiatry.* 2013;13:341.
61. L Tait, J Heron, A Waters, et al. Evaluation of peer support for women affected by postpartum psychosis. APP Report, email: info@app-network.org.
62. MIND and McPin (commissioned by Maternal Mental Health Alliance). Peer support principles for maternal mental health. Project report. 2019. https://tinyurl.com/32jskvx7
63. Scottish Government, Evaluation Support Scotland and Inspiring Scotland. Peer support evaluation toolkit for perinatal and infant mental health services. 2020. https://tinyurl.com/56svf9z2

Chapter 30

Perinatal Mental Health Service Development and Delivery

Roch Cantwell and Giles Berrisford

Background

This chapter outlines the development of specialist perinatal mental healthcare in the UK and Ireland, and the importance of continuing quality improvement for services. International developments and challenges are addressed in Chapter 31, 'Perinatal Mental Health Services in Asia, Africa and South America'.

The development of specialist perinatal mental health services in the UK began with reports in the 1950s of joint admissions of mothers and babies for the treatment of maternal mental illness [1, 2]. The first ward dedicated to the care of mothers accompanied by their infants opened in 1959 [3]. In 1984, Margaret Oates established the first specialist community perinatal mental health team, in Nottingham [4], introducing the principle of comprehensive services across the inpatient and community spectrum. The diffusion of perinatal mental health services across the UK happened at a slow and steady pace over the subsequent two decades, usually led by local clinicians with a passionate desire to see improvements in the care of women with mental illness related to childbearing [5].

An increase in the pace of service development began in the new millennium, driven by findings from the Confidential Enquiries into Maternal Deaths (see Chapter 22, 'Maternal Suicide, Deliberate Self-Harm and Other Mental Health Related Causes of Maternal Death') which showed that mental illness is a major reason why women die in the postnatal period across the UK and Ireland, with prevalence data showing that morbidity from perinatal mental illness is the most common comorbidity of pregnancy. The enquiries highlighted the dangers of inadequate treatment and, over successive reports, made concrete recommendations to improve service delivery. Other important drivers included the actions of campaigning organisations such as the Maternal Mental Health Alliance, which highlighted inequities in the provision of care [6] and research demonstrating the economic costs of untreated maternal illness [7], and National Institute for Health and Care Excellence (NICE) and Scottish Intercollegiate Guidelines Network (SIGN) clinical guidelines showing a strong evidence base for treatment of perinatal mental health conditions. At a professional level, recognition by the Royal College of Psychiatrists (RCPsych) of perinatal psychiatry as a distinct speciality of mental healthcare, alongside the production of guidelines for service provision and the College's inauguration of an accreditation system for specialist services – the Perinatal Quality Network (PQN) – was complemented by the growing voice of women with lived experience demanding improvements in services. All these factors contributed to the political decision of governments to invest in perinatal mental health services across the UK.

There was a significant increase in Mother and Baby Unit (MBU) bed numbers in England, a new unit for Wales, and ongoing evaluations of the need for more bed provision in Scotland and inpatient beds for Northern Ireland. That has been accompanied by a dramatic expansion of specialist community teams in all parts of the UK. In 2014, eight teams were inaugural members of the RCPsych Community PQN. Seven years later, the number of members stood at 55.

An established model for inpatient and community perinatal mental health services is described in the RCPsych's report on the provision of services for childbearing women [8]. Many of its earlier recommendations evolved into the accreditation standards of the PQN, thus ensuring a high degree of consistency of service design, subsequently reflected in what was recommended in individual UK nations' documents guiding service development.

From the earliest stages, there has been a recognition of the twin roles of perinatal mental health services in (i) the assessment, prevention and management of maternal mental illness and (ii) the promotion of the parent–infant relationship and infant development. The case for *why* specialist services should be developed has been well-articulated, focusing on the importance of avoiding prolonged separation for mother and baby, the distinctiveness in presentation, risk and management of perinatal mental illness, the unique opportunities for prevention both of illness occurrence and recurrence, and of intergenerational harm, and the need for different service organisation, professional relationships and clinical expertise [9]. While these arguments are now widely accepted, the paucity of research evidence to demonstrate improvements in patient outcomes has only recently begun to be addressed [10, 11].

Evolution of Service Development in the Nations of the UK

England

Pioneering perinatal mental health services (usually centred on an MBU) were already in place by the 1980s in Birmingham, London, Manchester, Newcastle and Nottingham. A further long-established service, based in Stoke-on-Trent, provided specialist day-patient care. The subsequent decades saw the gradual establishment of more inpatient and community provision, but significant gaps remained in many regions.

In 2016 National Health Service (NHS) England announced a 5-year programme of investment in perinatal mental health specialist services to widen inpatient and community provision with the aim of treating an additional 30,000 women each year [12]. This investment resulted in a significant increase in bed numbers from 110 in 15 units to 164 beds in 20 units and in the number, size and complexity of perinatal mental health teams, ensuring that 100% of the country had access to specialist teams – increased from just 15% in 2014. In 2019 the NHS England Long-Term Plan made additional commitments in response to lessons from the original expansion to widen access to specialist services even further, offering care up to 24 months after delivery, expanding provision of psychological therapies, providing fathers/partners with assessment and signposting as required, and developing maternity outreach clinics (later renamed maternal mental health services) – services for women experiencing mental health difficulties directly arising from, or related to, the maternity experience [13]. The pivotal role of peer support workers, experts by experience and specialist pharmacy was recognised.

Other elements supporting the expansion of perinatal mental health provision included publication of the perinatal mental health care pathways [14] to reduce unwarranted variation in care, and the perinatal mental health competency framework [15], to provide a template for staff knowledge and skills acquisition, both in 2018. Health Education England also collaborated with RCPsych to produce a training programme for psychiatrists new to perinatal mental healthcare – the building capacity in perinatal mental health services project. This was echoed with similar collaborations between the Royal College of Occupational Therapists, the British Psychological Society and the Tavistock Clinic to develop perinatal mental health training resources for multidisciplinary teams.

This expansion contributed to the developing evidence base for perinatal mental health services. The National Institute for Health Research funded research specifically to evaluate the expansion, whilst routine collection of outcome measures was standardised and implemented, supported by the RCPsych evaluation and recommendations on use of outcome measures in perinatal psychiatry [16].

Scotland

By the mid 2010s Scotland already had two regional MBUs and some community provision in 4 of its 14 health board areas. In 2017, a national managed clinical network for perinatal mental health was established. Its first task was to produce recommendations on service development, published in the Delivering Effective Services report [17]. Recommendations were not restricted to specialist mental health provision, also encompassing universal services and the third sector, reflecting a desire to see greater integration of provision across all tiers of care. For specialist provision, a distinctive model of community provision reflected Scotland's different geography, particularly designed to meet the needs of smaller, more rural and island communities. Additional bed numbers were recommended and new services, entitled maternity and neonatal psychological interventions (MNPI) teams, were designed to deliver psychological therapies to parents (and their infants) experiencing mental health difficulties related to pregnancy or neonatal care.

All recommendations were accepted by the Scottish government which in 2019 committed funding to the expansion of perinatal and infant mental health services. A perinatal and infant mental health programme board was tasked with the delivery of this programme of investment over 4 years (2019–23), with an additional explicit remit also to develop infant mental health statutory services and enhance third-sector provision.

In addition, a perinatal mental health curricular framework set out learning objectives for both specialist and universal staff [18], alongside a suite of educational tools to equip new staff to deliver expert care [19]. Meanwhile, the perinatal mental health network published guidance on service development for community perinatal mental health teams, MNPI services and infant mental health services, five national perinatal and infant mental health care pathways, and a suite of professional role definitions for staff working within specialist services [20].

Wales

The Welsh government committed to enhancing community specialist perinatal mental health services and developing inpatient beds, establishing an MBU in 2021 [21] and commissioning additional beds in a new English MBU to ensure good access for patients from north Wales. More recently, Wales has established a perinatal mental health network which in turn has developed a perinatal and infant mental health curricular framework and training plan [22].

Northern Ireland

Following on recommendations for service provision [23], Northern Ireland has recently invested in a model of community provision specific to each health board and has plans for the establishment of an inpatient MBU. The challenges of developing specialist services in the Northern Ireland context are described by Mongan et al. [24].

Ireland

In 2017 Ireland launched a model of care for perinatal mental health services [25] which described a network of specialist multidisciplinary community hub teams, with spoke services led by perinatal mental health midwives, based on the network of maternity hospital care provision. There is a parallel development of education and training resources, an online app resource for perinatal mental health professionals and ongoing work to establish inpatient MBU provision [26].

Innovations in Service Design and Delivery

Peer Support Workers

Alongside the movement for true co-production between professionals and patients, there has been a steady expansion of peer support, provided by people with lived experience, within specialist inpatient and community settings. Peer support workers are recommended as core members of MBU and community teams in England and Scotland, and are now included in CCQI standards, with guidance provided about core roles and how to incorporate peer support workers into healthcare teams [27, 28, 29]. Challenges remain to ensure that peer workers have adequate support and supervision in a mental health setting. Different models have been used in different teams; varying from being directly employed by the service, to subcontracting to third-sector independent organisations which can provide supervision, training and support to maintain the peer aspect of the worker. Evaluations of effectiveness are beginning to become available [30] (see Chapter 29, 'Effective Working across Health, Peer Support and Third-Sector Interfaces').

Parent–Infant Therapists

While the importance of sustaining the mother–infant relationship and promoting infant development has long been recognised as a core function of perinatal mental health services, in practice, much of specialist team training and function has focused on the management of maternal mental disorder. The development of a small number of exemplar services, coupled with the wider recognition of the importance of the early years environment, led to a re-evaluation of the need for greater inclusion of parent–infant interventions in specialist services. Both England and Scotland now include parent–infant therapists as recommended core members of MBU and community teams (see Chapter 32, 'Infant Mental Health: The Role of Perinatal Mental Health Services').

Maternity Psychological Services

Providing liaison to maternity units has always been a core function of specialist services, but it has tended to focus on women with, or at risk of, the range of disorders typically presenting to secondary care mental health services. There has been a gap in provision for women experiencing more common mental health difficulties, generally amenable to psychological interventions, in a maternity setting. These would include those with birth trauma, pregnancy or neonatal loss and parents adjusting to significant obstetric or neonatal complications.

In response to this need, Scotland recommended the development of MNPI services, based in larger maternity units, staffed by psychologists and perinatal mental health midwives [17], A similar initiative in England, termed Maternal Mental Health Services, has been implemented as part of the Long-Term Plan for the NHS in England [13]. This has resulted in the implementation of a trauma-informed care approach across maternity services, with training often delivered by these teams for maternity staff. More is still needed to support those women who have their baby removed by social services as part of a child protection plan.

Continuity Up to 2 Years

NHS England's Long-Term Plan proposed that community perinatal mental health services should extend their remit to the end of the second postnatal year [13]. This was to overcome the cliff edge seen by many women and families due to the sharp cut-off of 12 months implemented by some of the new services. Extended engagement ensures that therapy and interventions can continue until completion rather than halted prematurely based on the age of the baby. It also means that those women who present later in the first postpartum year can still receive an assessment and appropriate intervention. There are a number of compelling arguments for continuing engagement beyond 1 year but there is a need for continuing evaluation to support the change. In Scotland, a different approach has been taken, which focuses more on improving integration of, and seamless transition between, perinatal, infant and child mental health provision, with 'soft' boundaries around transitions of care. This too requires further evaluation.

Challenges for Service Delivery

Ethnicity

It is important that the developing teams meet the needs of the entire population. By starting from such a low base of available services, it was inevitable that the first wave of expansion would enable access to those women actively seeking services. The future has to ensure that services are acceptable and accessible to all communities [31]. This means that developing services must be engaged with the local communities, overcoming stigma and barriers, co-producing services and developing the evidence base to ensure that interventions are appropriate across cultures and communities.

Remote and Rural Provision

There is a particular challenge for areas with low or very dispersed birth population numbers in ensuring they have access to specialist care. In dispersed populations, travelling time can be a significant barrier to face-to-face contact. The pandemic has provided an unexpected response in the rapid adoption of digital technologies. While useful, there can be problems in making thorough clinical assessments online, particularly in a perinatal setting. Guidance has been developed around these particular challenges [32].

For very low birth areas, suggested service models should include enhanced skills for mental health professionals in generic teams accompanied by regional links to specialist perinatal mental health teams who can provide additional supervision and support in clinical decision-making [8].

Widening Existing Access in Relation to Sex and Gender

Families may be constituted in many different ways. Services are increasingly likely to be challenged to provide a clinical response to parents and their infants who have not been included in mother and baby mental healthcare previously. These include not only fathers who are the sole primary carer of their infant or who are in same-sex relationships, and who develop significant mental illness, but also transsexual men who are pregnant or postnatal.

Widening access in this regard increases demand on services and, for MBUs in particular, challenges the traditional model of delivering care. It also requires reflection on our use of inclusive language to describe the services we provide.

Services for Substance Misuse

The needs of pregnant and postnatal women with substance misuse, and their infants, have often been overlooked in the development of perinatal mental health provision. Women with substance misuse are at greater risk of suicide and death by accidental overdose in the perinatal period, and vulnerability increases in the context of child protection proceedings [33]. Their infants are more likely to be removed into care and, for alcohol misuse in particular, to experience developmental difficulties. Yet there is no one accepted model of care to address need and limited models of preventative interventions. Models of specialist maternity provision have evolved but enhanced care tends to stop soon after delivery, which may be the time of greatest risk.

While traditional perinatal mental healthcare might not be adaptable to this group, we have a clear duty to assist in the development of suitable care. In Scotland, the managed clinical network for perinatal mental health published a review of existing care and recommendations for future delivery [34] and there is emerging guidance on how such care should be provided [35].

Neurodiversity

Identification and diagnosis of neurodevelopmental disorders is improving, specifically in women, as is our knowledge of the impact that this can have on adaptations to motherhood. A clear understanding of this needs further development to ensure that women with attention-deficit hyperkinetic disorders, autistic spectrum disorders and other neurodevelopmental conditions are not inadvertently discriminated against and can access the assessment, diagnosis and support required. For further discussion on the needs of this group, see Chapter 21, 'Autism'.

Young Mothers

Findings from the Confidential Enquiries into Maternal Deaths and research by Lockwood Estrin et al. [36] show that young mothers are at particular risk of having perinatal mental illnesses and also of dying. This challenges developing community perinatal teams to identify this risk and ensure services meet the needs of this small but risky population.

Maintaining Existing Access

With rapid expansion comes the risk that the core roles of perinatal mental health services are lost. In the face of increasing demand there may be a tendency to narrow the definition of perinatal mental illness to those conditions which show a clear association with pregnancy or the postnatal state (e.g. postpartum psychosis, newly arising depressive disorders). This fundamentally misunderstands the critical role of specialist services in assessment and treatment given the modifying effects of pregnancy and parenting on the course of pre-existing mental illness, the need for a distinctive response in terms of liaison with maternity, primary care and child welfare colleagues, pharmacological management in pregnancy and breastfeeding, and the need for interventions tailored at addressing the parent–infant relationship and infant development.

As the landscape of other services alters, there is also a need for closer liaison, not only between specialist perinatal, maternity psychological and infant mental health services, but also with teams who may have joint care of women and their infants at this time, such as early intervention in psychosis services, home treatment teams and mental health assessment centres. Perinatal mental health services need to make the case for continued involvement, in many circumstances as the lead care coordinating service.

Covid-19

The Covid-19 pandemic increased demand for mental healthcare and the perinatal period is a time of particular vulnerability [37]. Women were isolated from the family and social supports usually expected during pregnancy and early parenting. Infants had less opportunity to engage with extended family and peers. Maternity and mental healthcare was altered, with reduced face-to-face contact and almost complete cessation of group interventions.

Paradoxically, the increased use of telemedicine has increased access for some women and families but comes at a price of restricting ability to make comprehensive assessments of women at high risk or in vulnerable social circumstances. Guidance is available to help services recognise and overcome these limitations in clinical encounters [32]. As services have emerged from the pandemic, we need to hold on to the changes in ways of working which have benefited our patients, but also recognise that demand, and the pattern of that demand, may remain altered from what we had encountered before. As ever, services should be responsive to change, keeping in mind that it is our job to design services which meet our patients' needs rather than, from an often very vulnerable position, they are forced to adapt to our unchallenged models of care.

Quality Improvement in Perinatal Mental Health Provision

In 2008, Rothera and Oates qualitatively examined areas for improvement in perinatal mental healthcare, identifying need across five domains – knowledge and skills; access;

pathways and protocols; comprehensiveness and integration; and roles and responsibilities [38]. It is fair to say that the focus for quality improvement has not shifted significantly in the intervening years.

In the UK, drivers of quality improvement for perinatal mental health services have come from three broad sources: (i) the Confidential Enquiries into Maternal Deaths; (ii) the RCPsych; and (iii) evidence-based recommendations from NICE and SIGN.

The Confidential Enquiries have included recommendations on standards of service provision since the 1990s, providing more detailed advice with every new iteration. These have included recommendations on knowledge, skills and training, communication and record keeping, engagement with patients and families, therapeutic interventions and safe care. More discussion on Confidential Enquiry recommendations can be found in Chapter 22, 'Maternal Suicide, Deliberate Self-Harm and Other Mental Health Related Causes of Maternal Death'.

The RCPsych produced recommendations on service provision, including staffing, for MBUs and community teams in a seminal college report, subsequently updated in 2015 and again in 2021 [8]. A significant step forward occurred in 2009 with the establishment of the College's PQN, providing a suite of standards and an accreditation process for MBUs and, subsequently, community services. The PQN has an iterative process of reviewing standards every 2 years, driven by member clinicians and informed by the developing evidence base. All MBUs across the UK and the majority of community specialist teams are members of the PQN [39].

NICE has produced, and updated, evidence-based guidelines on perinatal mental health since 2007, the latest in 2020 [40]. SIGN published its first guideline in the area in 2002, updated in 2012, and again in 2023 [41].

This guidance is supplemented by clinical networks established in England, Scotland and Wales, postgraduate curricula with associated training provided by national NHS training organisations and a range of other materials produced by the independent sector and by government to support the development and improvement of perinatal mental health provision.

A fundamental principle of quality improvement has been the inclusion of voices of experience across all aspects of service development and delivery. This is reflected in the PQN standards [39] and co-production should be integral to service development, delivery and evaluation.

Good quality improvement is an iterative and responsive process and should be built into the day-to-day running of services. It should include regular evaluation to reduce known and emerging barriers to access to the highest quality perinatal mental healthcare for all [42, 43].

References

1. G Douglas. Psychotic mothers. *Lancet.* 1956;270:124–5.
2. TF Main. Mothers with children in a psychiatric hospital. *Lancet.* 1958;272:845–7.
3. AA Baker, M Morrison, JA Game, JG Thorpe. Admitting schizophrenic mothers with their babies. *Lancet.* 1961;278:237–9.
4. MR Oates. The development of an integrated community-orientated service for severe postnatal mental illness. In: R Kumar, IF Brockington, editors. *Motherhood and mental illness, vol. 2.* London: Wright; 1988. p. 133–58.

5. K Robertson. The diffusion of joint mother and baby psychiatric hospital admissions in the UK: an historical analysis. D Nursing doctoral thesis. School of Nursing, Midwifery and Health, University of Stirling, 2012.
6. Maternal Mental Health Alliance). The Everyone's Business campaign. n.d. https://maternalmentalhealthalliance.org/campaign
7. A Bauer, M Parsonage, K Knapp, V Iemmi, B Adelaja. The costs of perinatal mental health problems. LSE Research Online; 2014. http://eprints.lse.ac.uk/59885
8. Royal College of Psychiatrists. cr232: perinatal mental health services: recommendations for the provision of services for childbearing women. 2021.
9. Joint Commissioning Panel for Mental Health. Guidance for commissioners of perinatal mental health services. 2012.
10. LA Stephenson, AJD Madonald, G Seneviratne, F Waites, S Pawlby. Mother and baby units matter: improved outcomes for both. *BJPsych Open.* 2018;4:119–25.
11. LM Howard, K Tevillion, L Potts, M Heslin, A Picckles, S Byford, et al. Effectiveness and cost-effectiveness of psychiatric mother and baby units: quasi-experimental study. *Br J Psychiatry.* 2022;221:628–36.
12. National Health Service England. Implementing the five year forward view for mental health. 2016.
13. National Health Service England. The NHS long-term plan. 2019.
14. NHS England, NHS Improvement, National Collaborating Centre for Mental Health. The perinatal mental health care pathways. 2018.
15. E-Learning for Heath Care. The perinatal mental health competency framework. 2017. https://perinatalcompetency.e-lfh.org.uk
16. Royal College of Psychiatrists. Framework for routine outcome measures in perinatal psychiatry. 2018.
17. Perinatal Mental Health Network Scotland. Delivering effective services: needs assessment and service recommendations for specialist and universal perinatal mental health services. 2019.
18. NHS Education for Scotland. Perinatal mental health curricular framework: a framework for maternal and infant mental health. 2019.
19. NHS Education for Scotland. Perinatal mental health training plan. 2023. www.nes.scot.nhs.uk/our-work/perinatal-and-infant-mental-health
20. Perinatal Mental Health Network Scotland. Delivering effective services. n. d. www.nn.nhs.scot/pmhn/professionals/delivering-effective-services
21. National Assembly for Wales Children, Young People and Education Committee. Perinatal mental health in Wales. 2017.
22. Heath Education and Improvement Wales. Perinatal and infant mental health curricular framework. n.d. https://tinyurl.com/bdcptkfa
23. The Regulation and Quality Improvement Authority. Review of perinatal mental health services in Northern Ireland. 2017.
24. D Mongan, J Lynch, J Anderson, L Robinson, C Mulholland. Perinatal mental healthcare in Northern Ireland: challenges and opportunities. *Ir J Psychol Med.* 2023;40:601–6.
25. Health Services Executive. Specialist perinatal mental health services: model of care for Ireland. 2017.
26. M Wrigley, F O'Riordan. Developing specialist perinatal mental health services: the door of opportunity. *Ir J Psychol Med.* 40:577–83.
27. McPin Foundation. Peer support principles for maternal mental health: project report. 2019. https://tinyurl.com/5aa4khz7
28. Perinatal Mental Health Network Scotland. Specialist perinatal mental health professionals: role definitions and support structures: perinatal mental health peer support worker. 2021. https://tinyurl.com/4han2znn

29. Inspiring Scotland. Peer support evaluation toolkit for perinatal and infant mental health services. 2023. https://tinyurl.com/56svf9z2

30. J McLeish, S Ayres, C McCourt. Community-based perinatal mental health peer support: a realistic review. *BMC Pregnancy Childbirth.* 2023;23:570.

31. J Jankovic, J Parsons, N Jovanovic, G Berrisford, A Copello, Q Fazil, et al. Differences in access and utilisation of mental health services in the perinatal period for women from ethnic minorities: a population-based study. *BMC Med.* 2020;18(1):245. Published 2020 Sep 11. doi:10.1186/s12916-020-01711-w.

32. Digital Health and Care Scotland. Coronavirus resilience planning: telepsychiatry quick reference guide 4: telepsychiatry in perinatal mental health settings. 2020. https://tinyurl.com/3ez3zbsa

33. Centre for Maternal and Child Enquiries. Saving Mothers' Lives: reviewing maternal deaths to make motherhood safer: 2006–08. The Eighth Report on Confidential Enquiries into Maternal Deaths in the United Kingdom. *BJOG* 2011;118 (Suppl. 1):1–203.

34. Perinatal Mental Health Network Scotland. Supporting women, reducing harm: review of services for substance using women and their infants in pregnancy and the postnatal period. 2021. https://tinyurl.com/yszt2t8c

35. L Gilmore, L Honeybull, S Lewis, E Smith, H Cheyne, N Aladangady, et al. Scoping review: mapping clinical guidelines and policy documents that address the needs of women who are dependent on drugs during the perinatal period. National Institute for Health Research; 2024. www.stir.ac.uk/research/hub/publication/1990652

36. G Lockwood Estrin, EG Ryan, K Trevillion, J Demilew, D Bick, A Pickles, et al. Young pregnant women and risk for mental disorders: findings from an early pregnancy cohort. *BJPsych Open.* 2019;5(2):e21.

37. R Papworth, A Harris, G Durcan, J Wilton, C Sinclair. Maternal mental health during a pandemic: a rapid evidence review of Covid-19's impact. Centre for Mental Health; 2021. https://tinyurl.com/3yc85dv6

38. I Rothera, M Oates. Managing perinatal mental health disorders effectively: identifying the necessary components of service provision and delivery. *Psychiatr Bull.* 2008;32:131–3.

39. Royal College of Psychiatrists. Perinatal Quality Network (PQN). n.d. https://tinyurl.com/4ddcu4s6

40. National Institute for Health and Care Excellence. Antenatal and postnatal mental health: clinical management and service guidance. Clinical Guideline (CG192). 2024. www.nice.org.uk/guidance/cg192

41. Scottish Intercollegiate Guidelines Network. Perinatal mental health conditions. Clinical Guideline (SIGN 169). 2023.

42. M Sambrook Smith, V Lawrence, E Sadler, A Easter. Barriers to accessing mental health services for women with perinatal mental illness: systematic review and meta-synthesis of qualitative studies in the UK. *BMJ Open.* 2019;9:e024803.

43. R Webb, N Uddin, E Ford, A Easter, J Shakespeare, N Roberts, et al. MATRIx study team. Barriers and facilitators to implementing perinatal mental health care in health and social care settings: a systematic review. *Lancet Psychiatry.* 2021;8(6):521–34.

Chapter 31

Perinatal Mental Health Services in Asia, Africa and Latin America

Vandita Shanbhag, Bruma Palacios-Hernández, Tesera Bitew and Prabha Chandra

Introduction

Most health professionals consider perinatal mental health (PMH) services a priority; however, there exist many variations in the availability and quality of specialist services in various parts of the world. In low- and middle-income countries (LAMIC) where mental health systems are still not well developed and often concentrated in large psychiatric facilities or urban areas, PMH services are very few.

In this chapter, we have reviewed PMH services available in several countries of Asia, Africa and South America. These include community-based services, hospital-based facilities and the training and involvement of health workers and midwives. We have also attempted to highlight some specific successful initiatives in service development that can serve as a model in LAMIC and be a source of inspiration in developed countries.

South and South-East Asia

Published literature on PMH services in South and South-East Asia is sparse. In this section, we focus on PMH services in countries where some data is available, for example in South Asia (India, Pakistan and Sri Lanka) as well as South-East Asia (Thailand, Malaysia and Indonesia).

Inpatient Services

Low- and middle-income countries in Asia have high rates of postpartum psychiatric disorders with comorbid organic and medical conditions necessitating the need for specialised care and Mother and Baby Units (MBUs). The first MBU in Asia was established in 2004 in Colombo, Sri Lanka. In 2009, the National Institute of Mental Health and Neurosciences (NIMHANS), Bengaluru opened a five-bedded MBU which offers joint mother and infant care for all psychiatric disorders. A multidisciplinary team provides additional specific interventions for bonding disorders, breast feeding problems, developmental assessment and interventions for the infant, psychoeducation to family members and spousal support [1]. Keeping the cultural aspects in mind, the MBU allows a family caregiver to stay with the mother and baby throughout admission. This helps in handling challenges related to infant safety and feeding and provides additional support to the mother as she recovers.

In Sri Lanka, inpatient perinatal care is provided by a few MBUs established in urban areas in secondary and tertiary care hospitals [2]. The National Institute of Mental

Health located in Colombo has the largest MBU in the country with eight beds. Other smaller MBUs are located in North Colombo Teaching Hospital, Western Province (one bed), Northwestern province (two beds), the Sabaragamuwa province (two beds) and Central province (two beds). In most South Asian countries, due to lack of specialised MBUs, inpatient PMH care is offered through general hospital psychiatric units or adult psychiatry units which may sometimes find difficulty in admitting the baby along with the mother, leading to the baby being admitted under paediatric services or being cared for at home.

Outpatient Services

In India, the only specialist perinatal psychiatry clinic operates once a week and offers treatment for pregnant and postpartum women as well as preconception counselling for women with psychiatric illness planning for pregnancy. This service also runs a support group for families and developmental assessments for infants [1]. A multidisciplinary team of psychiatrists, psychologists, a developmental psychologist and psychiatric social workers organise the service. One unique aspect of the perinatal psychiatry outpatient service at NIMHANS is the collaborative model where obstetricians also offer their service at the same facility as the psychiatric clinic. This enables joint consultations and holistic care for pregnant and postpartum women and supports training of psychiatry residents. The perinatal outpatient service also offers partner support groups and family therapy.

A few other countries such as Hong Kong, Singapore, Malaysia and Taiwan have specialist outpatient perinatal psychiatry services integrated into different levels of public health systems [3]. In Indonesia and Malaysia, perinatal psychiatry care is offered through consultation liaison psychiatry by referrals from obstetricians to psychiatrists both in the public and private sector. In Kuala Lumpur, Malaysia, the women and children's hospital, Hospital Tunki Azizah, runs a combined PMH clinic with liaison between the obstetrics and psychiatry departments. In Doha, Qatar, Sidra Medical and Research Centre established the first and the only specialist perinatal psychiatric outpatient service, the Women's Wellbeing Clinic, in 2017. The clinic, co-located with obstetric outpatient services, offers evaluation and management for perinatal psychiatric illness. The Hamad Medical Corporation Mental Health Service, Primary Health Care Corporation and other private psychiatrists assess and refer women who need specialist perinatal psychiatric services to Sidra Centre [4].

Integration of Mental Health into Maternal Health Services

In resource-limited Asian countries, upskilling primary care workers and establishing access pathways has played a key role in providing perinatal psychiatry care [5]. In Sri Lanka, the medical officers in primary health care services running the maternal and child health programme screen for depression using the validated Sinhala translation of the Edinburgh Postnatal Depression Scale (EPDS). Women found to have perinatal psychiatric illnesses are referred by them to psychiatric services in the public or private sector [2]. Similarly, routine screening for perinatal mental illness is conducted in one secondary maternity hospital and one tertiary hospital in Shanghai, China. Women with higher scores on the Patient Health Questionnaire (PHQ-9) and/or General Anxiety

Disorder Scale (GAD-7) are referred to a team of psychiatrists, clinical psychologists, obstetricians and midwives [6].

Kerala state, India, has developed a state-wide maternal mental health screening programme – Amma Manasu (Mother's Mind). Under this programme, mothers are assessed for psychiatric illness during their antenatal and postnatal visits by trained nurses. Referral pathways to primary care doctors and a district mental health Programme are established [7]. Several states in India have now followed an integrative model and are in the process of systems strengthening, training and developing monitoring systems. This is indeed a great step towards creating a national policy on maternal mental health.

Pakistan has a well-established community health worker (CHW) programme called the Lady Health Workers programme. However, due to shortage of CHWs, many women do not receive the help they need. A randomised control trial of a peer-led version of the World Health Organization's (WHO) Thinking Healthy Programme (THP) was conducted in Pakistan and India for postpartum depression. The programme included elements such as empathetic relating, problem solving, facilitating family support and behavioural activation. The THP showed improvements in social, functional and clinical outcomes of postpartum women. It has been in operation for the past 5 years in Pakistan. Being peer delivered, the THP is acceptable, feasible, cost-effective and shows promise for long-term sustainability [8, 9].

Though no structured programmes or services are available in Afghanistan, psychological interventions based on the WHO's THP for women who screened positive using PHQ-9 showed improvement in 65% of women who attended the sessions. This emphasises the importance of manualised evidence-based psychological interventions which could be delivered by non-specialists in resource-scarce settings [10].

Singapore has a postnatal depression screening and intervention programme initiated in 2008, funded by the health ministry and developed within a public hospital, which handles around 12,000 deliveries every year. The programme is delivered by a multidisciplinary team and includes screening of postpartum women using the EPDS, and individualised clinical management for postpartum depression with supportive counselling, psychoeducation, spousal support and antidepressant recommendations for those with severe depression. A study examining the 4-year (2008–9) outcome of this programme reported that 1,369 women were screened with the EPDS of which 9% had depression. With early intervention, 74% of women with depression showed improvement in EPDS scores emphasising the importance of screening and early intervention [11].

In Japan, public health nurses perform home visits for all mother and babies within 4 months of delivery and screen women for depression using the EPDS along with a psychosocial risk assessment. Japan also has two national home visit programmes (the 'newborn home visit programme' and the 'Home Visit Project for All Infants') conducted by nurses and midwives for infants, which provides support and interventions to new mothers and families around care for infants.

Nepal has recently prioritised maternal mental health and uses the WHO model for training health professionals for integrating mental health into routine maternal and childcare.

It appears that most countries in South and South-East Asia are involved in some training in PMH and integrating it into routine care as well as establishing specialised services and stepped care.

Involvement of Midwives, Nurses, Community Health Workers and Training Initiatives

Despite the importance of PMH, there are few formal training programmes. The perinatal psychiatry service at NIMHANS in Bengaluru, India, offers a 1-year postdoctoral fellowship programme for psychiatrists in women's mental health, which includes perinatal psychiatry. The institution is also involved in training psychiatrists in the district mental health programme so that they can manage PMH disorders. This is done through distance education programmes and on-site training [12]. There is also a 3-month certificate course for health professionals in PMH. The Royal College of Obstetricians and Gynaecologists All India Coordination Committee South Zone has also been conducting online training of obstetricians in PMH in collaboration with the task force of PMH of the Indian Psychiatric Society.

In India, various CHWs such as auxiliary nurse midwives, Anganwadi workers and accredited social health activists play a role in enrolling pregnant women into antenatal services, encouraging regular antenatal check-ups, immunisation and supplements and promoting institutional delivery. Training of CHWs to identify perinatal psychiatric illness is undertaken in some centres. However, studies have shown that even after training knowledge of psychiatric illness is low [13, 14].

In Shanghai, China, women with postpartum depression receive online services which include online therapy, access to chat groups, videos and reading material on mental health, mother–infant bonding and breastfeeding. Women with severe mental illnesses are referred to the Shanghai Mental Health Centre or secondary psychiatric hospitals. Though similar services are available and the number of community health centres offering PMH services is gradually expanding in other provinces of China, access to qualified mental healthcare services is limited. Some possible reasons are limited resources, a dearth of trained professionals and social stigma [6].

In Japan, the Japan Association of Obstetricians and Gynecologists conducts regular workshops to train midwives and nurses in screening mothers for depression using the EPDS and offering support and referrals when high EPDS scores are recognised [15].

In Thailand, the surveillance and care system for depressive disorders programme supported by the Department of Mental Health and Department of Public Health carries out screening of all high-risk groups including women visiting antenatal clinics, using a screening tool developed in Thai dialects. Primary healthcare providers are trained to recognise, diagnose and treat major depressive disorders and to also make referrals when necessary [16].

In Indonesia, MotherHope Indonesia is a non-profit organisation that provides psychological support to mothers with psychiatric illness during pregnancy, childbirth, postpartum and breastfeeding. It collaborates with health professionals including experts in maternal mental health and aims to improve maternal mental health through support groups and providing access to education and information to families [17].

Africa

Hospital-Based Services and Other Maternal Mental Health Services

The delivery of mental health services in general and PMH services in particular is still underdeveloped in Africa. Hospital-based specialist PMH services are not found in most countries in Africa. Due to scarcity of resources, service development focuses on integrating PMH services within the existing health system rather than establishing a separate PMH service. Challenges in integrating PMH care in existing services include normalisation of perinatal mental disorders by stakeholders, already overburdened frontline workers, lack of training in evaluating and treating perinatal mental disorders, stigma, low levels of mental health literacy and poor political will, all of which are barriers to developing and maintaining PMH services [18].

Integration of Mental Health into Maternal Health Services

To enhance outreach and improve feasibility and sustainability of psychological interventions, healthcare models that involve assigning particular tasks to workers with less training or sharing tasks among a team of healthcare practitioners (task-sharing models) have been considered for delivering PMH services [19]. Some clinical trials have examined the feasibility and effectiveness of delivering psychological interventions in task-sharing models. For example, a group problem-solving therapy delivered by community grandmothers was efficacious for women with depressive symptoms in Zimbabwe [20]. A programme called Expanding Care for Perinatal Women with Depression in Nigeria trained community midwives to provide 'psychoeducation, problem solving treatment, and parenting skills' to women who had screened positive for postpartum depression [21]. The study evaluating this programme demonstrated the potential for midwives and CHWs to successfully deliver basic mental healthcare services to improve maternal and child health outcomes [21]. Other community-based PMH interventions that are in progress in the region include peer support in Rwanda, problem-solving therapy for women with antenatal depression and intimate partner violence in Ethiopia [22], group interpersonal therapy in Uganda and Partners in Health in Lesotho.

The development of the Practical Approach to Care Kit has been underway in Ethiopia since 2020 [21]. This programme aims to provide practical guidelines for the diagnosis and care of mental disorders in primary healthcare settings. However, lack of adequate training to promote healthcare workers' knowledge and skills may be obstacles for proper implementation. A study in Uganda reported significant gaps in knowledge about mental health problems as well as negative attitudes among mothers and healthcare providers towards sufferers. Poverty and inability to afford transport to services, poor partner support and stigma were thought to add to the difficulties of perinatal women accessing care [23].

Involvement of Midwives, Nurses, Community Health Workers and Training Initiatives

In South Africa, a district mental healthcare plan was developed to integrate mental health into existing chronic disease care [24]. The stepped care model in Cape Town provided integrated mental healthcare service in a maternity hospital. The model service provided screening and counselling to women attending antenatal care in an obstetric hospital which informed the need for development of services in similar primary health settings [25]. In a scoping review of the role of midwives with respect to the mental healthcare service, lack of access to training and education was a key barrier to the delivery of midwife-led mental healthcare. Heavy workload and organisational barriers were additional barriers to delivery of mental healthcare by the midwives [26]. Stigma is an issue related to accessing perinatal mental healthcare and therefore digital-based interventions have been suggested to make mental healthcare available and accessible for young mothers both in urban and rural Africa [27].

The Perinatal Mental Health Project is a non-profit independent initiative located within the Alan J Fisher Centre for Public Mental Health at the University of Cape Town, South Africa. It works in partnership with the Departments of Health and Social Development for providing PMH services. It also focuses on other challenging issues such as teenage pregnancy and gender-based violence through clinical engagement, training of staff, research projects and advocacy [28].

As a potential response to the challenges, the Alliance of African Maternal Mental Health (AAMMH), an alliance of organisations working together to improve the mental health of mothers in Africa, was launched in Malawi in 2018 [29]. The AAMMH aims to educate care providers and the wider community about recognition, prevention and treatment of maternal mental health problems; advocate for maternal mental health to be prioritised in the strategies, policies and budgets of governments and NGOs; and to act together to develop reproductive and child health services in which the mental health of the mother is centrally integrated.

Latin America

The Latin American and Caribbean region has adopted maternal and child health as a priority in national health plans [30]; however, the inclusion of PMH as part of the public health agenda has lagged. Latin America reports high levels of violence, especially intimate partner violence and child abuse, high rates of adolescent pregnancy, low exclusive breastfeeding rates during the first 6 months postpartum and frequent natural disasters, armed conflict and mass migration [31]. Perinatal mental health work has focused on these issues [32, 33].

Hospital-Based Services Including MBUs

Perinatal mental health services are mainly initiated and located in general and high-speciality hospitals. The first MBU in the region was established but later closed, in a national public hospital in Mexico in 2008 (the National Medical Center in Mexico City), with hospitalisation of mothers with postpartum depression and their babies [34].

Community-Based Services

The kangaroo model was designed in Colombia by medical doctors [35] for care of babies with high perinatal risks focused on maintaining skin-to-skin contact with the parent with positive impacts on breastfeeding [36], bonding and stress reduction in parents [37]. The WHO has supported its implementation in public hospitals.

In Mexico, PMH services are associated with research, screening and psychological intervention in women with high-risk pregnancies (e.g. National Institute of Perinatology) [38], or group psychoeducational interventions aimed at reducing perinatal depression with favourable effects on the mother–infant bonding (e.g. National Institute of Psychiatry) [39].

The Pan American Health Organization has recommended mental health support across the life cycle, and significant advances have been made in community mental health using this approach in Chile [40], Cuba [41] and Argentina [42].

Some hospitals have included community groups to focus their attention on the mother and baby, such as the WHO-UNICEF Baby-Friendly Hospital Initiative with strong implementation support in Latin America since 1991 [43]. Another example is the family-centred maternity model in Argentina with a psychosociocultural approach to the perinatal period focusing its attention on the whole family, with interventions to promote breastfeeding, support for adolescent parents, preterm births and prevention of family violence through counselling within voluntary and community groups [42].

Chile has developed several health protocols and clinical guides that prioritise the screening of psychosocial well-being of the mother from conception to postpartum [44, 45] detection and treatment of drug use in pregnancy and maternal depression [46]. Guidelines in Colombia help in the care of adolescent mothers with counselling, education for bonding with the baby, breastfeeding and prevention of child abuse [47]. Peru has guidance for screening for sexual violence and perinatal depression in women from the first prenatal check-up [48]. In Mexico, national health regulations promote screening, prevention, diagnosis and treatment of depression during pregnancy and postpartum and of intimate partner violence and sexual violence with an emphasis on pregnancy [49]. However, these guidelines have not been implemented at all levels of the public healthcare system in most of these countries.

Involvement of Midwives, Nurses, Community Health Workers and Training Initiatives

In most countries, nurses conduct home visits to women with problems accessing health services during pregnancy and in rural areas. In Chile (the Chile Crece Contigo programme) and Colombia, nurses visit mothers at home and support maternal mental health, parenting and attachment skills with babies [50, 51].

Midwives are key non-healthcare practitioners in the region, recognise the traditional medicine of indigenous peoples, and are supported by international agreements and agencies (e.g. the UN and United Nations Population Fund (UNFPA)). With the support of the UNFPA, midwifery has been promoted in countries such as Brazil, Uruguay, Argentina, Chile, Bolivia, Haiti, Ecuador, Paraguay, Barbados, Trinidad and Tobago, Guyana, Belize and Jamaica, with regional training initiatives in collaboration with universities, ministries of health and national partnership centres [52]. However, training in PMH is still inadequate. In Mexico, there are initiatives to train nurses and midwives and to conduct research on their role in promoting PMH [53] as well as in preventing obstetric violence [54]. Some countries such as Argentina and Colombia [55] have promoted the participation of doulas – women trained to provide psychological support for women especially during childbirth, in order to support the reduction of stress and unnecessary caesarean sections.

Bolivia, Honduras, Nicaragua and Peru have included community promoters of maternal and perinatal health with local health teams with support from universities and international agencies [56]. In Colombia, a primary care programme was developed with an emphasis on the training of volunteer women from the community in charge of visiting the homes of families for the promotion of family health, antenatal care, breastfeeding, with funding and participation from health authorities, communities and non-profit foundations [55].

Perinatal mental health training is still scarce in the region, but advances in the form of continuing professional development courses primarily aimed at mental health professionals and gynaecologists are being conducted in Argentina, Chile, Mexico and Colombia.

Conclusion

This chapter gives an overview of PMH services in Asia, Africa and South America. These are areas where service delivery, training and funding for PMH remain major challenges, whether in universal or specialist provision. Identified barriers to the delivery of care include limited resources (practitioners and finance), difficulties in the implementation of guidelines and training, and the heavy workload of overburdened frontline workers. Other challenges for women include stigma, normalisation of PMH problems, poor mental health literacy, poverty and poor partner support.

There are innovative developments in resource-scarce communities that include the training of CHWs, doulas, traditional midwives and even volunteers, to deliver care to women with mental health problems in the perinatal period. In some instances this can involve the delivery of manualised evidence-based psychological interventions by non-specialists.

In many areas there is no or limited MBU provision and little specialist perinatal outpatient care even within major urban areas. In response, attempts are often made to integrate perinatal mental healthcare into the existing healthcare system.

Investing in PMH services is vital for any country to ensure that the physical and mental well-being of mothers and their families is optimised. It is important to note that through baby steps each of these regions in the world are using innovative methods like alliances and networks to ensure that maternal mental health is not ignored.

References

1. PS Chandra, G Desai, D Reddy, H Thippeswamy, G Saraf. The establishment of a mother-baby inpatient psychiatry unit in India: adaptation of a Western model to meet local cultural and resource needs. *Indian J Psychiatry.* 2015;57:290–4.

2. A Hapangama, KALA Kuruppuarachchi. Maternal mental health services in Sri Lanka: challenges and solutions. *BJPsych Int.* 2021;18(4):100–2.

3. I Brockington, R Butterworth, N Glangeaud-Freudenthal. An international position paper on mother-infant (perinatal) mental health, with guidelines for clinical practice. *Arch Womens Ment Health.* 2017;20:113–20.

4. Your Mind Matters. Services in Qatar. n.d. https://tinyurl.com/23zpabm8

5. A Bagadia, PS Chandra. Starting the conversation: integrating mental health into maternal health care in India. *Indian J Med Res.* 2017;145:267–9.

6. SE Schwank, Q Zhou, Y He, G Acharya. Perinatal mental health around the world: priorities for research and service development in China. *BJPsych Int.* 2020;17(3):50–3.

7. S Ganjekar, AV Thekkethayyil, PS Chandra. Perinatal mental health around the world: priorities for research and service development in India. *BJPsych Int.* 2020;17(1):2–5.

8. S Siham, A Ikhlaq, A Najia, Z Ahmed, F Vanobberghen, HA Weiss, et al.

Delivering the Thinking Healthy Programme for perinatal depression through volunteer peers: a cluster randomised controlled trial in Pakistan. *Lancet Psychiatry.* 2019;6(2):128–39.

9. D Singla, A Lazarus, N Atif, S Sikander, U Bhatia, I Ahmad, et al. 'Someone like us': delivering maternal mental health through peers in two South Asian contexts. *J Affect Disord.* 2014;168:452–8.

10. M Tomlinson, D Chaudhery, H Ahmadzai, S Rodríguez Gómez, C Rodríguez Gómez, T van Heyningen, et al. Identifying and treating maternal mental health difficulties in Afghanistan: a feasibility study. *Int J Ment Health Syst.* 2020;14:1–8.

11. H Chen, J Wang, YC Ch'ng, R Mingoo, T Lee, J Ong. Identifying mothers with postpartum depression early: integrating perinatal mental health care into the obstetric setting. *ISRN Obstet Gynecol.* 2011:1–7.

12. National Institute of Mental Health & Neurosciences. District Mental Health Program – Uttarakhand. n.d. https://nimhans.co.in/district-mental-health-program-uttarakhand

13. A Mary Kapanee, K Meena, P Nattala, N Manjunatha, P Sudhir. Perceptions of accredited social health activists on depression: a qualitative study from Karnataka, India. *Indian J Psychol Med.* 2018;40:11–16.

14. QN Shah, PA Dave, DA Loh, RK Appasani, CL Katz. Knowledge of and attitudes towards mental illness among ASHA and Anganwadi workers in Vadodara District, Gujarat State. *India Psychiatr Q.* 2019;90:303–9.

15. S Suzuki, S Takeda, T Okano, K Kinoshita. Recent strategies in perinatal mental health care in Japan. *Hypertens Res Pregnancy.* 2018;6:11–14.

16. T Kongsuk, S Supanya, K Kenbubpha, S Phimtra, S Sukhawaha, J Leejongpermpoon. Services for depression and suicide in Thailand. *WHO South-East Asia J Public Health.* 2017;6(1):34–8.

17. Beranda – MotherHope Indonesia. www.mhinnovation.net/organisations/motherhope-indonesia-foundation

18. NDP Sarkar, F Baingana, B Criel. Integration of perinatal mental health care into district health services in Uganda: why is it not happening? The Four Domain Integrated Health (4DIH) explanatory framework. *Soc Sci Med.* 2020;296:113464.

19. M Ng'oma, T Bitew, M Kaiyo-Utete, C Hanlon, S Honikman, RC Stewart. Perinatal mental health around the world: priorities for research and service development in Africa. *BJPsych Int.* 2020;17:56–9.

20. D Chibanda, P Mesu, L Kajawu, F Cowan, R Araya, MA Abas. Problem-solving therapy for depression and common mental disorders in Zimbabwe: piloting a task-shifting primary mental health care intervention in a population with a high prevalence of people living with HIV. *BMC Public Health.* 2011;11.

21. O Gureje, BD Oladeji, R Araya, AA Montgomery, L Kola, L Kirmayer, et al. Expanding care for perinatal women with depression (EXPONATE): study protocol for a randomized controlled trial of an intervention package for perinatal depression in primary care. *BMC Psychiatry.* 2015;15:136.

22. T Bitew, R Keynejad, B Myers, S Honikman, G Medhin, F Girma, et al. Brief problem-solving therapy for antenatal depressive symptoms in primary care in rural Ethiopia: protocol for a randomised, controlled feasibility trial. *Pilot Feasibility Stud.* 2021: 7(1):35.

23. JEMM Nakku, ES Okello, D Kizza, S Honikman, J Ssebunnya, S Ndyanabangi, et al. Perinatal mental health care in a rural African district, Uganda: a qualitative study of barriers, facilitators and needs. *BMC Health Serv Res.* 2016;16:1–12.

24. I Petersen, L Fairall, A Bhana, T Kathree, O Selohilwe, C Brooke-Sumner, et al. Integrating mental health into chronic care in South Africa: the development of a

district mental healthcare plan. *Br J Psychiatry.* 2016;208:s29–39.

25. S Honikman, T van Heyningen, S Field, E Baron, M Tomlinson. Stepped care for maternal mental health: a case study of the perinatal mental health project in South Africa. *PLoS Med.* 2012;9: e1001222.
26. D Coates, M Foureur. The role and competence of midwives in supporting women with mental health concerns during the perinatal period: a scoping review. *Health Soc Care Community.* 2019;27(4):e389–e405.
27. L Kola. Making a case for use of digital interventions to manage adolescent perinatal depression in Nigeria. *Am J Biomed Sci Res.* 2019;6:327–8.
28. Perinatal Mental Health Project. About us. n.d. https://pmhp.za.org/about-us
29. African Alliance for Maternal Mental Health. https://aammh.org
30. UNICEF. Breastfeeding: a mother's gift, for every child. 2018. https://data.unicef.org/resources/breastfeeding-a-mothers-gift-for-every-child
31. Organización Panamericana de la Salud [Pan-American Health Organization]. Plan de acción de salud mental 2015–2020 [Mental health action plan 2015–2020]. 2014. www.paho.org/hq/dmdocuments/2015/plan-de-accion-SM-2014.pdf
32. MB Rondon. Perinatal mental health around the world: priorities for research and service development in South America. *BJPsych Int.* 2020;17:85–7.
33. ME Gomez. Avances en la investigación de la salud mental perinatal en Latinoamérica [Advances in perinatal mental health research in Latin America]. *Acta psiquiátrica y psicológica América Lat.* 2011;57:226–34.
34. LA Lara, JR Ornelas, WA Rivera, EC Bocanegra, GO Madrigal, M Camacho Díaz, et al. Modelo de intervención temprana en la depresión posparto en un hospital de tercer nivel [Model of early intervention in postpartum depression in a tertiary care hospital]. *Rev Espec Médico-Quirúrgicas.* 2012;17:100–8.
35. ES Rey, HG Martínez. Manejo racional del niño premature [Rational management of the premature child]. *Curso de Medicina Fetal Univ Nac.* 1983;137–51.
36. AG Mekonnen, SS Yehualashet, AD Bayleyegn. The effects of kangaroo mother care on the time to breastfeeding initiation among preterm and LBW infants: a meta-analysis of published studies. *Int Breastfeed J.* 2019;14:12.
37. Y Takubo, T Nemoto, Y Obata, Y Baba, T Yamaguchi, N Katagiri, et al. Effectiveness of kangaroo care for a patient with postpartum depression and comorbid mother-infant bonding disorder. *Case Rep Psychiatry.* 2019;9157214.
38. ME Gómez-López. Guía de intervención psicológica para pacientes con embarazo de alto riesgo [Guideline for psychological intervention for patients with high-risk pregnancy]. *Perinatol y Reprod Humana.* 2007;21:111–21.
39. MA Lara, C Navarro, L Navarrete. Outcome results of a psycho-educational intervention in pregnancy to prevent PPD: a randomized control trial. *J Affect Disord.* 2010;122:109–17.
40. Ministerio de Salud de Chile. Plan Nacional de Salud Mental 2017–2025 [Mental Health National Plan 2017–2025]. 2017.
41. D Liuba, P Galbán, DA Clavijo, L Alberto, B Mendoza, D Yohanys Fernández, et al. La psiquiatría comunitaria en Cuba [Community psychiatry in Cuba]. *Rev Cub Med Mil.* 2014;43(1): 91–104.
42. A Uranga, J Urman, C Lomuto, I Martínez, MJ Weisburd, O García, et al. Guía para la atención del parto normal en maternidades centradas en la familia [Guide for the care of normal childbirth in family-centered maternity hospitals]. Minsterio de Salud de la Nación; 2010.
43. Organización Panamericana de la Salud and Oficina Mundial de la Salud. Iniciativa Hospital Amigo del Niño, revisada, actualizada y ampliada para la

atención integral [Friend of the Child Hospital Initiative, revised, updated, and expanded for comprehensive care]. 2008.

44. Ministerio de Salud del Gobierno de Chile. Manual de atención personalizada en el proceso reproductivo [Manual of personalized care in the reproductive process]. 2008.

45. Ministerio de Salud del Gobierno de Chile. Guía perinatal [Perinatal guide]. 2015.

46. Ministerio de Salud del Gobierno de Chile. Protocolo de detección de la depresión durante el embarazo y posparto, y apoyo al tratamiento [Protocol for the detection of depression during pregnancy and postpartum, and support for treatment]. 2014.

47. Ministerio de Salud y Protección Social del Gobierno de Colombia and Fondo de Población de las Naciones Unidas. Protocolo de atención de la menor de 15 años embarazada [Protocol for the care of a 15-year-old pregnant girl]. 2014.

48. Ministerio de Salud del Perú. Guías nacionales de atención integral de la salud sexual y reproductiva [National guidelines for comprehensive sexual and reproductive health care]. 2004.

49. Consejo de Salubridad General. Guía de referencia rápida: detección y atención de la violencia de pareja y violencia sexual en el primer y segundo nivel de atención [Quick reference guide: detection and management of partner violence and sexual violence at the first and second levels of care]. https://tinyurl.com/t8mwwrb9

50. M Irarrázaval, F Prieto, J Armijo. Prevenção e intervenções precoces em saúde mental: uma perspectiva internacional [Prevention and early interventions in mental health: an international perspective]. *Acta Bioeth.* 2016;22:37–50.

51. DM Uribe Bustamante, M Viveros. Modelo de atención en salud 'doulas', para mejorar la calidad del cuidado perinatal en instituciones de primer nivel de atención en Bogotá [Model of care in health 'doulas', to improve the quality of perinatal care in first-level care institutions in Bogotá]. *Cuad Latinoam Adm.* 2009;5:95–119.

52. UNFPA. Parteras profesionales: clave para mejorar la salud materna y neonatal en la región [Professional midwives: key to improving maternal and neonatal health in the region]. 2017. https://tinyurl.com/ys4tby6e

53. Instituto Nacional de Salud Pública and Instituto Nacional de las Mujeres. El uso y rol de proveedores no-médicos para la atención prenatal y obstétrica en México: parteras profesionales técnicas y enfermeras obstetras. Evidencias y áreas de oportunidad [The use and role of non-medical providers for prenatal and obstetric care in Mexico: technical professional midwives and obstetric nurses. Evidence and areas of opportunity]. 2011.

54. JA González Almaguer, HJ García Ramírez, V Vargas Vite, LF Pimienta. Guía de implantación: modelo de atención a las mujeres durante el embarazo, parto y puerperio. Enfoque humanizado, intercultural y Seguro [Implementation guide: care model for women during pregnancy, childbirth, and postpartum. Humanized, intercultural, and safe approach]. 2018.

55. EU Compass Consortium. Good practices in mental health and well-being. 2017. https://tinyurl.com/2uwa892d

56. Centro Latinoamericano de Perinatología y Desarrollo Humano O and U de C. Manual de salud materno-perinatal para promotores comunitarios [Maternal-perinatal health manual for community promoters]. 1996.

Chapter 32

Infant Mental Health

The Role of Perinatal Mental Health Services

Anne McFadyen

Introduction

Those familiar with families that include babies and very young children have some understanding of how parenthood can be both exhilarating and exhausting. Working in perinatal mental health (PMH) services, whether in the National Health Service (NHS) or the third sector, affords a close-up view of the earliest relationship as it develops, first between fetus and pregnant woman, and then between new mother and infant. In this context, staff, volunteers, relatives and parents themselves have a responsibility to ensure that the infant's mental health is attended to. Perinatal mental health problems 'can have lasting effects on the emotional, behavioural, intellectual and social development of children exposed as foetuses or infants' [1]. Perinatal mental health clinicians and support workers have a particular role to play as their relationship with their patients or clients affords them opportunities to change things for the better for women, their infants and their developing relationships.

What Is Infant Mental Health?

Infant mental health (IMH) is the developing capacity of the child 'to experience, regulate and express emotions, form close and secure relationships, and explore the environment and learn' [2]. It concerns both 'being and becoming mentally healthy' [3].

Importantly, this development requires the baby to have a close, attuned relationship with a primary caregiver, most often their mother. When this is not present, babies' development is significantly affected, and they are more likely to experience mental distress and disorder and to have mental health difficulties later in life.

Like all child and adolescent mental health problems, infants' emotional difficulties 'can be understood only within the framework of many layered contexts, ranging from the molecular through to the societal' [4]. Both genetic and environmental factors are important with the latter including the in-utero environment and conditions surrounding their birth, parental mental health, the care they receive, their home environment and wider social and economic factors.

Following Felitti et al.'s description of the relationship between adverse childhood experiences (ACEs) and later morbidity and mortality [5], it has been shown that the risk of physical and mental health problems is influenced in a dose–response way [6]. The ACEs approach focuses on the characteristics of parents and carers, or the wider family environment, which impact on the child and are seen as risk factors for later poor health. These include maternal age, maternal mental health, domestic violence and parental substance use, all of which are also associated with developmental delay and disorder in young children. However, as Turner points out, 'these associations are at a population level' [7]. They are not deterministic and do not indicate that an individual child will have a poor outcome [8, 9]; for example, many younger mothers will have children who thrive.

Some babies' genetic vulnerabilities or physical status may make them more challenging to care for, and this may be even harder for mothers who are experiencing their own mental health difficulties.

The time from conception until the age of 2 years is the most important for ensuring that the baby's brain and mind develop optimally. During this period 'more than 1 million new neural connections form every second' [10]. In the UK, The First 1001 Days Movement has campaigned widely to educate the public about this and lobby for better early years services: 'Exposure to early adversity, particularly in the absence of nurturing relationships, can have long lasting effects on development. There is, therefore, a clear case for reducing adversity and supporting early caregiving in the earliest years of a child's life' [11]. Berens and Nelson (2019) [12] have summarised the many research studies which have contributed to our understanding of functional brain development. This happens sequentially from the brainstem regulatory systems essential for life, through to emotion and memory in the limbic system to the development of cortical functions such as empathy, decision-making, logic and reasoning. Early relationships affect brain circuitry as neuronal pathways are laid down in response to interactions with the world. Over time the neural pathways used most are made stronger and faster through myelination while others are pruned back as the brain responds and adapts to its environment [13].

Importantly, research supports the view that 'the infant comes into the world bringing formidable capabilities to establish human relatedness' with the ability to cue us into what they are thinking and feeling through their behaviour including their body movements, vocalisations and gaze [14]. Mothers have to tune into these communications in order to support their babies' cognitive and emotional development.

There are many ways of thinking about this attunement. Brazelton and Cramer described 'six characteristics of parent-infant interaction – synchrony, symmetry, contingency, entrainment, games (play) and autonomy' [15]. They conceptualised the dance between infant and adult and broke it down into component steps. By helping the infant to self-regulate, pay attention and prolong periods of attention, adults facilitate 'synchronous communication'. This is supported in a symmetric dialogue between parent and infant. Contingency is central to this communication, referring to babies' realisation that their actions have consequences. It 'requires availability on the mother's part' [15]. Agency is closely linked to contingency and refers to the infant's capacity to have an effect on other people or objects.

Reciprocity between infant and caregiver is essential for the development of communication, with the process by which meaningful interaction evolves relating to each one's interpretation and fit with their partner's actions. The rhythmicity of interaction seems to be as important, if not more important, in the development of the relationship than each participant's contribution [16].

The term 'perinatal mental illness' covers a range of presentations including florid psychosis, depressive illnesses, obsessive compulsive disorder, anxiety and eating disorders. Each woman's presentation and behaviour towards her baby will be unique and assessment should always include examination of the relationship between baby and mother. This will inform a treatment plan which may include specific therapeutic approaches to improve maternal sensitivity and attunement, and thus optimally support the baby's development.

Why Is Infant Mental Health Important?

The importance of the period from conception to the second birthday for subsequent mental and physical health has been highlighted in a number of reports, including from The First 1001 Days Movement [11], UNICEF [3], the Royal College of Psychiatrists [17] and the Academy of Medical Sciences [18].

It is not only important for babies *at the time*, but also for their later life. Infants experience upset and distress, but this is often short-lived. Emde and Sameroff use the term *perturbation* to describe this [19]. They refer to degrees of relationship problem as *perturbation*, *disturbance* and *disorder* and contrast these as follows:

> The concept of perturbation is implicit in development. Development advances through the meeting of challenges and the overcoming of problems ... For most children these perturbations are soon resolved as competence is reached in a new area. For others, however, a failure to attain a given developmental milestone becomes a disturbance if it interferes with other areas of adaptation and a disorder if it persists far beyond normative bounds. [19]

Relationships and development need to be evaluated hand in hand as they reflexively influence each other. The Royal College of Psychiatrists' Council Report 238, *Infant and Early Childhood Mental Health* [17], notes the paucity of prevalence studies of IMH disorder but does report that in England in 2017, 5.5% of 2- to 4-year-olds experienced a mental health condition [20].

Many babies will experience perturbation and disturbance during their development, and these include transient difficulties such as sleeping or eating problems, being fearful or anxious about specific things or more generally, being upset by separations and showing frustration through temper tantrums or refusal to cooperate with parental demands. For mothers struggling with their own mental health these 'ordinary' hiccoughs can be interpreted as persecutory. They may feel it is their failure to parent properly, and their inadequacy in understanding their child's needs. Here, members on the PMH team can offer support and reassurance but also have to be ready to arrange more focused specialist intervention for mother and infant if required.

Disorders arising in infancy include attachment disorders and neurodevelopmental disorders such as autism spectrum disorder, hyperactivity and fetal alcohol spectrum disorder, all of which require specialist assessment and management.

'Being mentally healthy in this life stage also enables children to develop the capacities to be mentally healthy throughout life' [3]. Good mental health in infancy underpins the development of empathy and self-regulation, the capacity to make and sustain relationships, achieve one's potential and have a sense of purpose and satisfaction. This aligns with the World Health Organization (WHO)'s definition of mental health as 'a state of mental well-being that enables people to cope with the stresses of life, realise their abilities, learn well and work well, and contribute to their community' [21]. It is not simply the absence of mental health conditions or psychiatric illness.

Further, the economic benefits for society in general of investing in the early years have been made by the WHO, United Nations Children's Fund and the World Bank

Group [22] who report that 'for every $1 spent on early childhood development interventions, the return on investment can be as high as $13'.

A Healthy and Safe Start

Galloway et al. describe the 'key ingredients' needed 'for babies to have a healthy and safe start in life' as a healthy pregnancy, healthy early relationships, effective care and support for caregivers, and a safe and stimulating environment [23].

A Healthy Pregnancy

Mothers' mental and physical health in pregnancy is crucially important for babies' later well-being and development. Adequate nutrition and the absence of toxins plays an important role in ensuring the healthy development of a fetus, as does the psychological well-being of the mother. Poor maternal health during pregnancy is associated with low birth weight and premature birth, postnatal depression, and longer-term cognitive and emotional difficulties for the child. In Chapter 33, Glover draws attention to the impact of stressors during pregnancy on the outcomes for the child. Alcohol use in pregnancy is associated with fetal alcohol spectrum disorder [24], a neurodevelopmental disorder, while substance use impacts on development in a number of ways [25], and in the case of opiates may lead to neonatal abstinence syndrome.

Healthy Early Relationships

Babies need caregivers to provide sensitive, attuned and consistent care. They thrive when their caregivers have healthy relationships with one another. An infant's brain develops through interaction with others, and is particularly influenced by their primary caregivers, who may not be able to develop secure relationships with their baby for many reasons. These include domestic abuse, poor mental health, their own history of poor attachment relationships or childhood abuse and neglect, and wider contextual issues such as poverty and insecure housing. The baby's own developmental difficulties, which may be related to prematurity, inherited illness, congenital abnormality or maternal alcohol or substance use in pregnancy, may also interfere with bonding.

The association between maternal mental health problems and infant development has been well made. Perinatal mental health problems can have lasting effects on the emotional, behavioural, intellectual and social development of children [1, 13]. Children of mothers with mental health issues are twice as likely to develop a psychiatric disorder, with poor maternal mental health/well-being at 9 months and 3 years strongly associated with challenging child behaviour at age 5. Postnatal depression and other mental illness have been linked to behavioural disturbance at home, less creative play and greater levels of disturbed or disruptive behaviour at primary school, poor peer relationships and a decrease in self-control with an increase in aggression [26].

Effective Care and Support for Caregivers

Parents and other primary caregivers need respectful care and support in addressing the problems they face, so that they have the emotional resources to care for their baby. This is especially the case for parents who have mental health or addiction problems, or past experiences of poor care themselves, and for those who are facing stressors such as poverty, housing insecurity and domestic abuse. They may find it harder to engage with services because of the demands of their life, or because they feel blamed and stigmatised [27]. According to Fonagy and Campbell, those labelled as 'hard to reach' may be 'simply showing an adaptation to a social environment where information from attachment figures was likely to be misleading' [28]. Introducing the concept of 'epistemic trust', that is, trust in the authenticity and personal relevance of interpersonally transmitted knowledge, they highlight its importance in the development of therapeutic relationships.

A Safe and Stimulating Environment

Good infant mental health is underpinned by adequate nutrition, protection from harm and positive, responsive caregiving [11]. Babies need a safe and stimulating environment providing appropriate sensory, social and emotional stimulation, with the space and encouragement to play, explore, learn and be creative.

Infants need attuned caregivers, who notice and respond to their baby's cues or miscues. This to-and-fro of interaction is known as 'serve and return' [29]. Sometimes the ball will be dropped and there will be an interruption or disconnection in this relational dance. It is impossible for caregivers to be attuned all the time. What matters is how this rupture is repaired and how the dyad gets back on track. 'Rupture and repair' is an important experience for infants and children and helps rather than impedes their development. In Winnicott's words: 'Human beings fail and fail; and in the course of ordinary care a mother is all the time mending her failures. These relative failures with immediate remedy undoubtedly add up eventually to a communication, so that the baby comes to know about success. Successful adaptation thus gives a sense of security, a feeling of being loved' [30]. Infants rely on parents and caregivers who can be with them through their range of feelings, showing that they've understood, and are not overwhelmed, and can help them cope. 'Maternal reverie', a concept described by Bion, refers to the mother's capacity to receive her baby's projections, and contain and modify them [31]. 'In other words, the mother takes in the infant's emotions, experiences them herself, helps to sort them out and give them meaning, and then, of course, lets the baby get on with having the experience' [32].

It is not hard to imagine that a mother lacking liveliness or preoccupied with her own thoughts or even delusions may find this task very difficult.

Addressing Systemic and Intergenerational Issues

NHS England's 'Good Practice Guide: Involving and Supporting Partners and Other Family Members in Specialist Perinatal Mental Health Services' [33] has three underpinning principles: 1) 'Think Family'; 2) 'The Perinatal Frame of Mind'; and 3) 'Stay Curious'. 'Mothers who are well supported by their family . . . are likely to recover more quickly and require less input from specialist services' [33]. Further, the baby's mental health and development may be afforded a degree of protection by their relationship with another primary caregiver. For women whose illness is severe enough to require admission to a Mother and Baby Unit, it will be important to consider how best to support other family relationships while also helping the mother to tune into her infant if she is well enough.

The life-stage model in Scotland's mental health and well-being strategy (see Figure 32.1) draws attention to the importance of intergenerational health and well-being

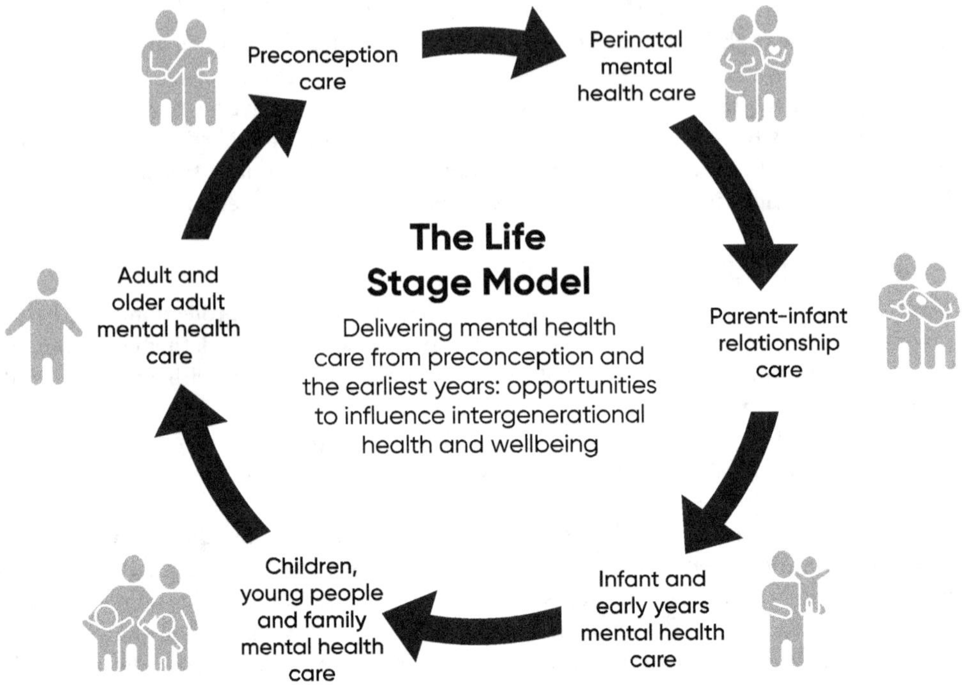

Figure 32.1 The Life Stage Model.

and emphasises the importance of the perinatal period: 'Establishing the conditions for good mental health is essential even before birth and throughout infancy, and we know that mental health within the perinatal period (before, during and after birth) has lifelong implications in relation to later mental and physical health' [34]. A systems approach to family well-being supports consideration of the importance of relationships not just between mothers and babies but also within the wider family, including partners and/or fathers, other children and grandparents.

The burgeoning of research into child development and early relationships necessitates the development of a model of understanding which embraces many different viewpoints. Like young children who are often at the centre of a complex system of relationships, especially if deemed to be vulnerable or at risk, so too must our understanding reflect a synthesis of the complex relationships between different theoretical models.

Much of the recent research in the field of IMH considers intergenerational factors. A key example is attachment research. Attachment theory was first described by Bowlby and provides one way of understanding the relationship between childhood experience and adult functioning, and also of integrating different theoretical models [35]. It was developed by Bowlby and other researchers to conceptualise in more detail the ways in which early experience and relationships link to later mental well-being and patterns of behaviour. He summarised this in a later paper, where he made links between the relationship and both the parent's and the infant's neurobiology:

1. Emotionally significant bonds between individuals have basic survival functions and therefore primary status.

2. They can be understood by postulating cybernetic systems situated within the central nervous system of each partner that have the effect of maintaining proximity or ready accessibility of each partner to the other.
3. In order for the systems to operate efficiently, each partner builds in their mind working models of self and of other and of the patterns of interaction that have developed between them.
4. Present knowledge requires that a theory of developmental pathways should replace theories that invoke specific phases of development in which it is postulated a person may become fixated and/or to which they may regress [36].

Sroufe described this as a reflexive process: 'Inner working models are constructed over time and are continually elaborated and, at times, fundamentally changed. At the same time, inner working models influence both the child's experience and how these experiences are processed' [37].

The impact of parental functioning on an infant's development is mediated through the quality of parent–infant interaction. A depressed mother may not tune into her baby's emotional state while someone experiencing acute psychosis may be incongruent in their responses. Traumatised parents may withdraw from their infants while anxious or obsessive parents can be over-organised and intrusive. Harm to the infant's mental health and personality development is not inevitable; however, the resilience of some babies in these situations is not yet fully understood.

The process by which the infant's development is influenced by the behaviours or attachment status of their mothers has been explored and it seems likely that there are several possible mechanisms. Murray et al. addressed the question of whether the quality of early communication might be a key mediator [38]. They suggested that the early use of infant-focused speech, or 'motherese', led to a better outcome for the infant at 9 months of age. In Chapter 35, Barlow explores more recent research on the impact of maternal reflective functioning, mind-mindedness and adult attachment status and describes the impact of dyadic interaction, such as being frightening or frightened, on the development of emotional regulation in the baby.

What happens between baby and mother can be supported and optimised by PMH clinicians and other specialists. It is important that timely referral is made if there are concerns about mother, infant or their interaction.

How Can Perinatal Mental Health Services Help?

All staff working in universal and specialist services for babies and their parents should know about perinatal and infant mental health, in particular the importance of the period from before conception to the end of the second year for both mother and baby.

The Perinatal Mental Health Network Scotland (PMHNS) and NHS Education Scotland have developed a curricular framework [39] with training organised around the levels of knowledge and competence required by professionals working in different settings (see Table 32.1). Similarly, the Association for Infant Mental Health (AiMH-UK)'s IMH competencies framework [40] details the skills required by specialists working with infants and their parents.

The roles and responsibilities of key personnel in maternity and PMH services are described by the Royal College of Psychiatrists in Council Report 232 and by PMHNS [41, 42]. All have an important role to play in ensuring that the baby is well cared for,

Table 32.1 Training levels as described in the perinatal mental health curricular framework

Level	For which professionals
Informed	Baseline knowledge and skills required by all staff working in health, social care and third sector settings. (All staff)
Skilled	Knowledge and skills required by staff who have direct contact and/or substantial contact with women during pregnancy and the postnatal period, their infants, partners and families. (All maternity, health visiting, primary care, children and families social work, relevant third sector)
Enhanced	Knowledge and skills required by staff who have more regular and intense contact with women who may be at risk of/affected by perinatal mental ill health, their infants, partners and families. (All mental health, including adult, child and adolescent mental health services, addictions, etc. as well as maternity, primary care, health visiting and third-sector staff who work in an enhanced role)
Specialist	Knowledge and skills required by staff who, by virtue of their role and practice setting, provide an expert specialist role in the assessment, care, treatment and support of women who may be at risk of/affected by perinatal mental ill health, their infants, partners and families. They will often have leadership roles in education, training and service coordination and development. (Staff working within specialist perinatal and infant mental health services)

Source: NHS Education for Scotland, 2019.

and that the early mother–infant relationship is supported. Clinicians should use every encounter as an opportunity to assess and to facilitate the mother–infant relationship. Noticing and talking to the baby and giving voice to their verbal and non-verbal communications can help the mother to appreciate her little one's agency and attachment. Commenting on interactions and especially actions or communications by the mother which elicit positive responses from the infant, and vice versa, can help reinforce the importance of these early exchanges. For this to happen, clinicians should always encourage the presence of the baby where possible in clinical encounters and ensure that the clinical environment is suitable for infants.

Midwives are usually the lead professional and first point of contact for women in pregnancy and the early postnatal period. All midwives should be at the 'Skilled' level in understanding PMH issues, promoting positive mental health, discussing mental health difficulties with women and helping women to access appropriate care and support when needed. They also require an understanding of their role in promoting and enhancing the developing mother–infant relationship and supporting other family members. Those working as members of more specialist mental health teams aligned to maternity service will have 'Enhanced' level skills.

Perinatal mental health nurses work in both inpatient and community settings. In addition to core nursing skills, they have a role in assessment and intervention, working as part of the PMH multidisciplinary team and alongside midwives, health visitors and other members of the primary care team. They have a key role in the promotion of IMH as they work with parents to support the developing parent–infant relationship and optimise infant development. All PMH nurses will have an 'Enhanced' or 'Specialist' level of knowledge and skills, depending on their seniority and training. Nurse consultants will have knowledge, skills and attitudes commensurate with the Specialist level of the curriculum.

Nursery nurses provide specialist infant care in inpatient and community settings. In addition to core skills, nursery nurses often support women as they adjust to pregnancy and begin to bond with their unborn child. Later they work alongside other key professionals providing advice on infant care, promoting and enhancing the developing parent–infant relationship and optimising infant development. In inpatient settings they may provide much of the direct care of the baby when the mother is unwell. Their sensitivity to the primary attachment relationship and the mother's capacity to tune into her baby requires 'Enhanced' or 'Specialist' training.

Peer support workers can now be found in third-sector and NHS PMH services. Their own lived experience gives them a unique perspective on the challenges faced by the patient and their baby. Their focus is mostly to support mothers, but the issues discussed will of course include feelings about their babies and how to do the best for them. Having experienced adversity themselves, they bring a unique set of skills and can offer support, hope and encouragement. The nature of their relationship will be slightly different to that of 'the clinicians', and support to them should include sufficient flexibility to maintain their own recovery and well-being. Training about perinatal and infant mental health should be at the 'Informed' or 'Skilled' levels.

Mental health occupational therapists (OTs) offer holistic assessment and treatment, incorporating the needs of the mother, infant and other family members. A collaborative approach focuses on the mother's goals and covers a range of interventions. This includes facilitating the mother–infant relationship and, if inpatients, thinking about and planning for discharge. Many OTs have specialist training in interventions to support the parent–infant relationship, working at an 'Enhanced' or 'Specialist' level.

Most *clinical psychologists* in PMH services will have been trained to 'Specialist' level. They have a leadership role in the development, supervision, delivery and evaluation of psychological informed interventions and evidence-based psychological therapies and are core to specialist PMH provision in inpatient, community, maternity and neonatal settings. They deliver direct services to patients and support other members of the team to do so. Many will have been trained in specialist interventions which support the developing mother–infant relationship, with some being employed in their service as a *parent-infant therapist*. Parent-infant therapists come from a range of professional backgrounds including psychology, psychiatry and child psychotherapy with some having an Allied Health Professionals or systemic therapy background. All should have had 'Specialist' training in line with those offered alongside the perinatal curricular framework or AiMH competencies. Their role will include conducting psychological assessments and developing a psychological formulation of the mother, her infant and the relationship between them, and delivering or supervising the delivery of effective, evidence-based interventions to address any bonding or attachment issues. Parent–infant therapists working within PMH teams act as an expert resource for other team members to supplement their own knowledge and training.

Perinatal psychiatrists have a leadership role in the assessment, diagnosis, care coordination and management of perinatal mental illness. Psychiatrists form the core of specialist mental health provision in inpatient and community settings and have a leadership role within the multidisciplinary team. In addition to core medical and psychiatric skills, perinatal psychiatrists will work in collaboration with women, their babies and other family members, coordinating and delivering complex biopsychosocial interventions. They have a key role in promoting and enhancing the developing parent–infant relationship and optimising infant development. Their knowledge and expertise reflect their 'Specialist' training.

Health visitors and *family nurses* have a central role in the lives of young children and their parents. Sometimes they will meet the family in late pregnancy but failing that their first meeting will be in the early days following the baby's birth. They are skilled members of the universal services workforce, with most having completed Solihull training in addition to their training as nurses and health visitors [43]. They are often the first to flag concerns about the developing relationship or the mother's mental health. It is important that their relationship with the family is supported to continue even if mother and baby have been admitted to hospital or are receiving intensive support in the community. Their role will continue long after any period of crisis, and ongoing communication with the PMH team should be seen as paramount.

Perinatal mental health services have evolved in different ways across the UK. In some areas, in the absence of an 'in-house' parent–infant therapist, the local parent–infant team or infant mental health team may be called upon to offer therapy to address and treat early relationship difficulties and promote sensitive and attuned parenting. Good links between perinatal and infant mental health services are essential, and ideally joint triage will be used in conjunction with clear care pathways between primary care and specialist services, and between specialist services.

The Journey

Women known to have a mental illness who are planning a pregnancy are encouraged to seek pre-conception advice. It is at this point that they may first be referred to the PMH team. In this context, the clinician's task is to consider how to optimise maternal and fetal well-being. As well as advising about the benefits and physical effects of prescribed and non-prescribed medication, and of alcohol and 'street' drugs, on both, they will seek to ensure that the mother maintains good mental health during pregnancy and postnatally. Thinking about the infant there may be questions about heritability as well as the impact of maternal mental illness.

Other women may become mentally unwell for the first time during pregnancy or in the postnatal period. Again, referral to the PMH team is indicated. They may already be known to addiction services, social work, early years services or third-sector agencies. Their first presentation may be in maternity or primary care. Therefore, it is important that those in the wider system around the pregnant woman and her unborn child, or mother and baby, are aware of the importance of the period from conception onwards for IMH. Timely referral is important for both the mother, whose presentation may change very quickly, and the baby, whose developmental trajectory may be knocked awry by the interruption to time-sensitive interactions which promote good mental health.

The wider system around the couple includes general practitioners, midwives, health visitors and family nurses, and may also include general psychiatrists and community psychiatric nurses, workers in addiction services and the third sector, and social workers.

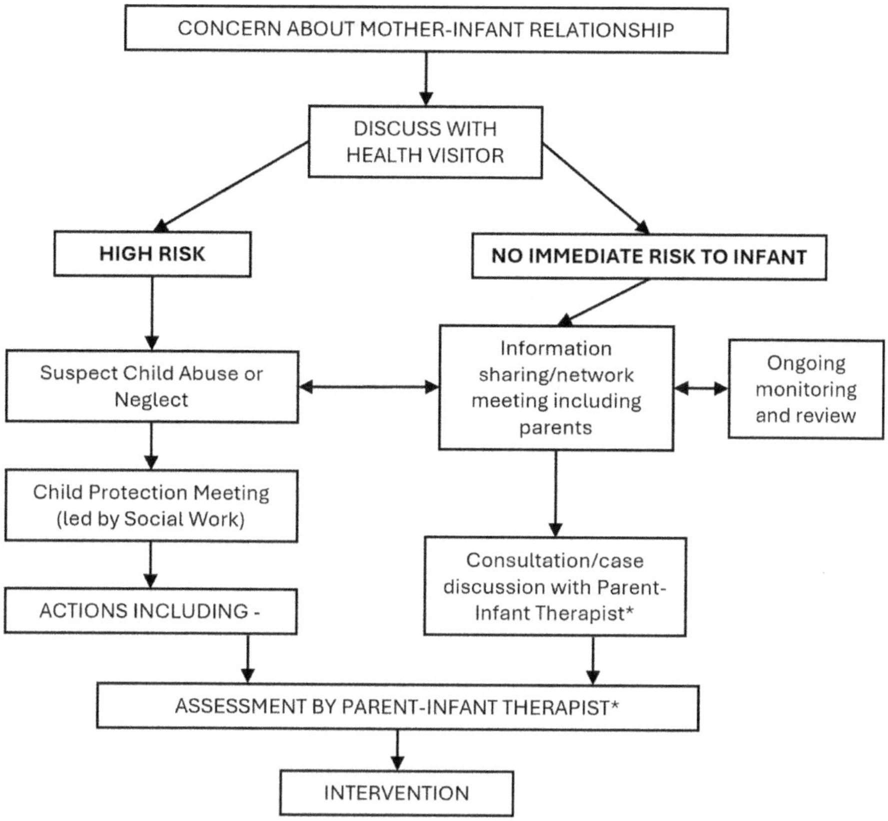

*The Parent-Infant Therapist may be a member of the perinatal mental health team or a parent-infant specialist service and may be from a range of progressions (e.g., psychiatrist, psychotherapist, psychologist, VIG practitioner).

Figure 32.2 Concern for mother–infant relationship pathway [44].

If concerns about the mother–infant relationship are encountered in any of these settings, specialist referral should be informed by the principles set out in Pathway 5 of the Scottish Mental Health Care Pathways [44] (Specialist assessment and intervention for mother–infant relationship difficulties), or equivalent in other jurisdictions (see Figure 32.2).

Concerns should be discussed with the baby's health visitor in the first instance. An immediate priority may be to think about the child's safety and any potential or actual child protection issues. Ideally, this initial exploration will include members of the family and support agencies already involved with the baby. As noted by Youell in Chapter 34, babies are often overlooked. They are present but not necessarily observed closely. Sharing what has been noticed about the mother, the baby and what transpires between them is crucial. If there is a risk to the child, then safeguarding/child protection protocols should be initiated. If it is deemed that the infant is not at immediate risk, the network discussion should ideally include a parent–infant therapist. This professional may be a part of the PMH team or of the local IMH team.

The relationship should continue to be monitored and, if deemed necessary, a specialist assessment should inform a therapeutic plan to address ongoing difficulties. In Chapter 35, Barlow has summarised the main interventions which can be offered to support the developing relationship, classifying them as follows:

1. psychotherapeutic interventions (e.g. parent–infant psychotherapy)
2. mentalisation-based treatments (e.g. Minding the Baby and the Mothers and Toddlers Programme)
3. sensitivity-based interventions, both individual (e.g. videotape feedback intervention to promote positive parenting and sensitive discipline; video interaction guidance) and group-based (e.g. infant massage and Circle of Security)
4. eclectic approaches underpinned by a range of theories, for example behavioural and attachment (e.g. Mellow Babies).

Treatment of the mother and the mother–infant relationships should always be accompanied by wider support to family members. This should include psychoeducation and may embrace family therapy approaches.

Conclusion

Perinatal mental illness impacts on mothers, their babies and the wider family. Concerns about the developing relationship between mother and infant may be the primary reason for referral to PMH services and, even if this is not the case, assessment of this relationship should be undertaken at the earliest opportunity.

The promotion of infant mental health and well-being, and prevention of disturbance and disorder in very young children and in later life, are key tasks of the PMH team. Timeliness is important for the woman, the baby and the relationship. There is now clear evidence of the efficacy of interventions which promote parent–infant attunement and support the development of good infant mental health and development more broadly.

References

1. A Gregoire. Antenatal and postnatal mental ill health. In: P Leach, editor. *Transforming infant wellbeing. research, policy and practice for the first 1001 critical days.* Abingdon: Routledge; 2018. p. 89–97.
2. Zero to Three. *Definition of infant mental health.* Washington, DC: Zero to Three Infant Mental Health Steering Committee; 2001.
3. S Hogg, J Moody. Understanding and supporting mental health in infancy and early childhood – a toolkit to support local action in the UK. 2023. UNICEF.
4. A McFadyen, J Roberts. Professionals must offer a multifaceted approach (letter). *BMJ.* 1997;315:312.
5. VJ Felitti, RF Anda, D Nordenberg, DF Williamson, AM Spitz, V Edwards, et al. Relationship of childhood abuse and household dysfunction to many of the leading causes of death in adults: the Adverse Childhood Experiences (ACE) Study. *Am J Prev Med.* 1998;14:245–58.
6. JR Baldwin, A Reuben, JB Newbury, A Danese. Agreement between prospective and retrospective measures of childhood maltreatment: a systematic review and meta-analysis. *JAMA Psychiatry.* 2019;76(6):584–93.
7. F Turner. Short term foster care in context: how do temporary child-carer relationships contribute to the development and recovery of maltreated young children? PhD thesis. 2022. University of Glasgow.

8. RE Lacey, H Minnis. Practitioner Review: Twenty years of research with adverse childhood experience scores – advantages, disadvantages and applications to practice. *J Child Psychol Psychiatry.* 2020;61:116–30.

9. RE Lacey, LD Howe, M Kelly-Irving, M Bartley, Y Kelly. The clustering of adverse childhood experiences in the Avon Longitudinal Study of Parents and Children: are gender and poverty important? *J Interpers Violence.* 2022;37(5–6):2218–411.

10. Centre on the Developing Child. Brain architecture. 2023. https://developingchild.harvard.edu/science/key-concepts/brain-architecture

11. Parent–Infant Foundation. The First 1001 Days Movement. 2024. https://parentinfantfoundation.org.uk/1001-days

12. AE Berens, CA Nelson. Neurobiology of fetal and infant development: implications for infant mental health. In: CH Zeanah, editor. *Handbook of infant mental health.* 4th ed. New York: The Guilford Press; 2019. p. 37–59.

13. R Balbernie. Circuits and circumstances: importance of earliest relationships and their context. In: P Leach, editor. *Transforming infant wellbeing: research, policy and practice for the first 1001 critical days.* Abingdon: Routledge; 2018. p. 19–27.

14. D Stern. *The first relationship: mother and infant.* Cambridge, MA: Harvard University Press; 1977.

15. TB Brazelton, BG Cramer. *The earliest relationship: parents, infants, and the drama of early attachment.* London: Karnac Books; 1990.

16. TB Brazelton, B Koswalski, M Main. The origins of reciprocity: the early mother-infant interaction. In: M Lewis, LA Rosenblum, editors. *The effect of the infant on its care-giver.* New York: John Wiley & Sons; 1974.

17. Royal College of Psychiatrists. Infant and early childhood mental health: the case for action (Council Report no. 238). 2023. https://tinyurl.com/3hyuka8h

18. Academy of Medical Sciences. Prioritising early childhood to promote the nation's health, wellbeing and prosperity. 2024. https://acmedsci.ac.uk/policy/policy-projects/child-health

19. RN Emde, AJ Sameroff. Understanding early relationship disturbances. In: AJ Sameroff, RN Emde, editors. *Relationship disturbances in early childhood.* New York: Basic Books; 1989.

20. NHS Digital. Mental health of children and young people in England, 2017. 2018. https://tinyurl.com/28wcvhen

21. World Health Organization. Mental health factsheet. 2023. www.who.int/news-room/fact-sheets/detail/mental-health-strengthening-our-response

22. World Health Organization, United Nations Children's Fund and World Bank Group. *Nurturing care for early childhood development: a framework for helping children survive and thrive to transform health and human potential.* Geneva: World Health Organization; 2023.

23. S Galloway, A Haynes, C Cuthbert. An unfair sentence: all babies count. 2014. NSPCC. https://tinyurl.com/25ba34ae

24. Scottish Intercollegiate Guidelines Network. Children and young people exposed prenatally to alcohol: a national clinical guideline (SIGN 156). 2019. www.sign.ac.uk

25. Perinatal Mental Health Network Scotland. Supporting women, reducing harm: review of services for substance-using women and their infants in pregnancy and the postnatal period. 2021. https://tinyurl.com/4e4knrmu

26. Wave Trust and Department of Education. Conception to age 2 – the age of opportunity. 2013. www.wavetrust.org/conception-to-age-2-the-age-of-opportunity

27. Mental Health Foundation. Stigma and discrimination. 2023. www.mentalhealth.org.uk/explore-mental-health/a-z-topics/stigma-and-discrimination

28. P Fonagy, C Campbell. Mentalizing, attachment and epistemic trust: how psychotherapy can promote resilience. *Psychiatr Hung.* 2017;32(3):283–7.

29. Centre on the Developing Child. Serve and return. 2024. https://tinyurl.com/ywn8b8p8
30. DW Winnicott. Communication between infant and mother, and mother and infant, compared and contrasted. In: WG Joffe, editor. *What is psychoanalysis?* London: Bailliere, Tindall & Cassell; 1968. p. 227–38.
31. WR Bion. *Second thoughts: selected papers in psychoanalysis*. New York: Aronson; 1967.
32. A McFadyen. *Special care babies and their developing relationships*. London and New York: Routledge; 1994.
33. NHS England. Good Practice Guide: Involving and supporting partners and other family members in specialist perinatal mental health services. 2021. www.england.nhs.uk/wp-content/uploads/2021/03/Good-practice-guide-March-2021.pdf
34. Scottish Government and COSLA. Scotland's mental health and wellbeing strategy. 2023. www.gov.scot/publications/mental-health-wellbeing-strategy
35. J Bowlby. *Attachment and loss, vol. 1: Attachment*. Harmondsworth: Penguin; 1969.
36. J Bowlby. Developmental psychiatry comes of age. *Am J Psychiatry*. 1988;145(1):1–10.
37. LA Sroufe. The role of infant-caregiver attachment in development. In: J Belsky, T Nezworski, editors. *Clinical implications of attachment*. Hove and London: Lawrence Erlbaum Associates; 1988. p. 18–38.
38. L Murray, C Kempton, M Woolgar, R Hooper. Depressed mothers' speech to their infants and its relation to infant gender and cognitive development. *J Child Psychol Psychiatry*. 1993;34(7):1083–1101.
39. NHS Education for Scotland. Perinatal mental health curricular framework: a framework for maternal and infant mental health. 2018. https://tinyurl.com/4wjn8m85
40. AiMH UK. Infant mental health competencies framework. 2022. https://aimh.uk/wp-content/uploads/2022/11/IMHCF-PDF-Download.pdf
41. Royal College of Psychiatrists. Perinatal mental health services: recommendations for the provision of services for childbearing women (Council Report no. 232). 2021. https://tinyurl.com/5n843crc
42. Perinatal Mental Health Network Scotland. Role definitions. 2021. www.nn.nhs.scot/pmhn/professionals/delivering-effective-services
43. Solihull. Solihull approach training for practitioners. 2024. https://solihullapproachparenting.com/solihull-approach-training-for-practitioners
44. Perinatal Mental Health Network Scotland. Care pathways. 2021. www.pmhn/scot.nhs.uk/care-pathways

Chapter 33

Maternal Mood and Stress during Pregnancy

Effects on the Fetus and the Child

Vivette Glover

Introduction

When caring for pregnant women it is important to consider not only the woman herself but her developing fetus and her future child. There is now considerable evidence that the emotional state of the woman during pregnancy may have a long-lasting effect on her developing baby. And it is not just a diagnosed mental illness, or extreme or toxic stress, that can have such effects. Many types of stress can affect a pregnant woman in a way that can alter the development of the baby in the womb. This is an aspect of fetal programming. Fetal programming occurs when the environment in the womb, during sensitive periods for specific outcomes, alters the development of the fetus, with a potentially long-lasting effect on the child and subsequent adult.

Stress is a complex umbrella term and has been used to describe both cause and effect. The World Health Organization (WHO) defines stress as a state of worry or mental tension caused by a difficult situation. It is a natural human response that prompts us to address challenges and threats. Stressors can be both physical, such as exercise, and psychological, such as fear. Stress can be acute or chronic. But there is no adequate definition or measure to differentiate mild or severe, or acute or chronic. It can be caused by external conditions such as natural disasters, or poverty, and can include feelings of anxiety or depression. The effects on the body of acute stress include the rapid release of adrenaline and noradrenaline, and the slower rise of cortisol. We all, including pregnant women, experience some stress as part of our daily lives but the way we respond to stress impacts on our overall well-being; when it becomes severe and long-lasting it can become damaging.

The concept of fetal programming has been advanced by the work of David Barker and his colleagues, who have shown that if a human infant is born small for gestational age, and grows less well before birth than expected, they are at increased risk of dying of cardiovascular disease several decades later. They are also at increased risk of developing metabolic syndrome, obesity, type 2 diabetes and hypertension [1]. These findings have been replicated in many studies around the world, and much work has been done on identifying the underlying mechanisms. These include the activation of the hypothalamic-pituitary-adrenal (HPA) axis, which releases cortisol, and the immune system [2].

Fetal programming does not imply that all the effects are irreversible; indeed there is much evidence that with some outcomes, although probably not all, it is possible to bring about change postnatally [3]. Many organs, including the brain, are very plastic, or susceptible to alteration by environmental stimuli, during the time in the womb. It is well known that certain drugs, such as thalidomide or alcohol, can alter fetal development. Alterations in the levels of some endogenous hormones, such as cortisol, can have major effects also [2].

Types of Antenatal Stress That Affect Fetal Development

Many studies from around the world have shown that a wide range of types of antenatal stress exposure can be associated with altered child development. Symptoms of anxiety and depression can alter the mother's chemistry in a way that alters the development of her fetus. But raised levels of daily hassles can have these effects too [4]. There have not been any studies so far, however, of the effects of psychosis or very severe mental illness.

Table 33.1 shows examples of the various types of antenatal stress that have been shown to be associated with increased risk of altered child outcomes. Many studies have found associations between symptoms of depression [5, 6, 7] and symptoms of anxiety [5, 8], and child development. Rather few have examined the effects of a diagnosed depressive or anxiety disorder. However, many have shown associations with other types of stress. Pregnancy-related anxiety, rather than general symptoms of anxiety, has been shown in several studies to be associated with increased risk of an altered outcome [4, 9]. Self-reported perceived stress, psychosocial stress and exposure to life events, especially a difficult relationship with the partner [10], have been measured in other research. Experience of natural disasters during pregnancy, such as an earthquake in China [11], an ice storm in Canada [12] or man-made disasters such as Chernobyl [13], have also been shown to increase the risk of changes in the child. Finally, a group of studies have found that maternal exposure to early trauma or abuse, with or without symptoms of anxiety or depression during pregnancy, can alter child development [14, 15]. Many of these studies, especially the large population studies, have included a wide range of

Table 33.1 Types of antenatal stress which have been shown to be associated with altered child outcome and development

Type of stress	Reference
Diagnosed depressive disorder	[91, 92, 93]
Symptoms of depression	[5, 6, 7, 22, 29, 31, 94, 95, 96]
Symptoms of anxiety	[5, 8, 22, 97, 98]
Pregnancy-related anxiety	[4, 9, 21, 34]
Daily hassles	[4]
Psychosocial stress	[99, 100]
Self-reported/perceived stress	[101, 102]
Life events	[10, 23, 103]
Relationship with partner	[10]
Natural disaster such as earthquake, ice storm, flood, hurricane	[11, 12, 24, 25, 28, 104]
Man-made disaster such as Chernobyl	[13]
Exposure to early childhood trauma	[14, 15]

confounders including obstetric risk, postnatal maternal mood, paternal pre- and postnatal mood, parenting and socio-economic status.

Effects on the Fetus and the Child

Maternal stress during pregnancy is associated with an increased risk of a wide variety of emotional, behavioural and cognitive problems in the child [16, 17] (Table 33.2). It has been questioned whether these associations are actually causal. Certainly, genetic vulnerabilities may play a role. If the mother is susceptible to depression she may pass on the relevant genes to her child. There is evidence of gene environment interactions for several of these outcomes, for example for memory and attention deficit hyperactivity disorder (ADHD) in O'Donnell et al. (2017) [18]. But there is also evidence for a causal role for prenatal stress independent of genetic vulnerabilities. Chen et al. (2024) have shown that maternal prenatal depression and anxiety and child polygenic risk scores for ADHD, schizophrenia or depression independently and additively predicted behavioural and emotional symptoms in the child until to at least mid-adolescence [19].

Many animal studies, which can control for the postnatal environment by cross-fostering to non-stressed mothers after birth, have shown that fetal programming by prenatal stress is biologically possible [20]. Many of the outcomes in such animal studies, such as increased symptoms of anxiety in the offspring, are analogous to those found in humans. Research on the effects of maternal antenatal exposure to disasters shows that effects can occur independently of the mother's original emotional state and are therefore unlikely to be due to genetic transmission [12]. Observations of the infant at birth show effects independently of postnatal care [21]; and several large-cohort studies have allowed for multiple confounders, including maternal postnatal mood, paternal mood, maternal smoking and alcohol consumption and maternal education and socio-economic status [22]. So, although genetics and quality of postnatal care certainly can

Table 33.2 Child outcomes associated with antenatal stress

Child outcome	Reference
Symptoms of depression	[5, 8]
Symptoms of anxiety	[5]
Symptoms of ADHD	[5]
Symptoms of conduct disorder	[5]
Behavioural regulation	[7]
Internalising problems	[102]
Criminality	[105]
Cognitive impairment/academic achievement	[27]
Schizophrenia	[11, 23]
Autism/autistic spectrum	[28, 106]
Infant temperament	[24]
Sleep problems in infants	[25]

affect child outcome, there is evidence that maternal stress during pregnancy can also play a causal role.

We do not know yet whether different types of stress have different effects on the fetus or fetal brain. So far there is little evidence for this. We do know that timing in pregnancy can make a difference. The risk of schizophrenia is increased, but only by exposure to very severe stress, such as the death of an older child, or exposure to a severe earthquake, in the first trimester [11, 23]. The increased risk for most of the other outcomes seems to be associated with stress throughout pregnancy (and often postnatally too). More research is needed to understand more about both timing and dose effects.

Table 33.2 shows examples of the wide range of neurodevelopmental and behavioural outcomes that can be associated with antenatal stress. Infants can have a more difficult temperament [24], be harder to soothe and sleep less well [25]. Children have been found to show more symptoms of ADHD, conduct disorder and anxiety and depression [5, 22, 26] as well as more cognitive problems, and do less well at school [27]. They can be more likely to be on the autistic spectrum [28], and adults are at increased risk of schizophrenia [11, 23].

Prospective, longitudinal analyses suggest these effects can persist through adolescence into early adulthood and are of a magnitude to be of clinical and public health relevance [22, 29, 30]. However, children are affected in different ways, and most are not affected at all [3, 17]. O'Donnell et al. (2014) have shown in the large UK community sample, ALSPAC, that if the mother was in the top 15% for symptoms of anxiety or depression while pregnant, her child at age 13 years had a 13% risk of a probable mental disorder, compared to a 7% risk for the children of the other 85% [22]. This was after allowing for a wide range of possible confounders. The effects of antenatal maternal mood were greater than those of paternal mood. Thus, in this O'Donnell et al. (2014) study, the risk from antenatal symptoms of anxiety or depression of a mental disorder in the child was approximately doubled, and clinically significant, although nearly 90% of the children were not affected [22]. The effects of antenatal and postnatal maternal symptoms on a later child mental disorder were similar and additive [22].

Many of these neurodevelopmental outcomes can be explained in evolutionary terms. In the animal kingdom, or for our ancestors, stress can be due to real external danger, as from a predator, for example. Increased anxiety and increased vigilance, and readily distracted attention, can help to detect external danger quickly, and so be protective.

The risk for many non-neurodevelopmental outcomes has been found to be increased by antenatal stress too. Examples of these are shown in Table 33.3 and include an increased risk of alterations to the immune system [31], asthma [32] and being mixed-handed [33]. Handedness is known to be formed in utero. Alterations in the pattern of the microbiome in the offspring have been described too [34]. This is increasingly recognised as having an influence on mental health [35].

Several of these altered outcomes are part of the life history. This is the pattern that describes the life cycle including the stage at which birth occurs, and ages of puberty, reproduction and death. The occurrence of these events can be affected by changes in the early environment and subject to evolutionary pressures. Antenatal stress has been found to increase the risk of early delivery [36], preterm birth [37], age of menarche [38] and telomere length [39] (which is associated with the duration of the lifespan). All this may also be explained in evolutionary terms. In situations of external danger, which makes

Table 33.3 Child physical health outcomes associated with antenatal stress

Child outcome	Reference
Reduced birthweight	[36, 92]
Reduced gestational age	[36]
Preterm delivery	[36, 37]
Earlier age of menarche	[38]
Decreased telomere length	[39]
Altered immune function	[31]
Asthma	[32]
Type 2 diabetes	[107]
Altered microbiome	[34]
Mixed handedness	[33, 108]
Sex ratio/more girls born	[109, 110]

the pregnant mother feel stressed, it may be of adaptive value to accelerate the life cycle of the offspring, to enable them to be born and reproduce early.

Many of the changes found in the child, associated with antenatal stress, are different in boys and girls. There is strong evidence, from many different laboratories, that prenatal stress in animal models has different effects in male and female offspring on brain structure, behaviour and stress responses [40, 41, 42, 43, 44]. Female offspring often show more anxiety and males more cognitive deficits and aggression. There have been fewer studies showing sex differences in the effects of prenatal stress in humans, but several are starting to be published, especially in infants [45, 46, 47]. Tibu et al. (2014) found that lower birth weight for gestational age predicted higher vagal reactivity only in girls, and prenatal maternal anxiety predicted lower vagal reactivity only in boys [48]. They conclude that their findings are consistent with sex differences in fetal programming with increased stress reactivity in females and decreased reactivity in males.

Underlying Biological Mechanisms

The Mother

While postnatal effects of the mother's mood on her young child are through psychological mechanisms, during pregnancy they are biological. Many different types of stress can have similar effects on the body, so it is not surprising that a wide range of types of stress exposure can alter fetal, and later child, development.

Based on work on animal models, many of the studies of underlying mechanisms in humans have focused on the HPA and the role of cortisol [49]. In rodent models, removing the adrenal gland or injecting corticosteroids in the pregnant dam can block or replicate some of the effects of prenatal stress on the offspring [50]. Several different types of study have shown that fetal brain development in humans can also be altered by increased exposure to cortisol or corticosteroids in utero, with later effects on the child.

Maternal exposure to synthetic glucocorticoids during pregnancy is associated with poorer mental health in childhood and adolescence [51]. Bergman et al. (2010) showed that altered cognitive function in infants was associated with higher levels of cortisol in the amniotic fluid [2]. The children of mothers who had consumed high levels of liquorice during pregnancy (which contains a natural inhibitor of 11-β-hydroxysteroid dehydrogenase type II (11β-HSD2), the enzyme which converts cortisol to its inactive form cortisone in the placenta), and were thus exposed to higher levels of cortisol in utero, were over three times more likely to show ADHD symptoms, as well as lower IQ scores and earlier puberty [52]. Davis et al. (2013) have shown that babies exposed to synthetic glucocorticoids in utero have altered brain structure, including a thinner cortex, as shown by MRI scans [53].

It is not likely that prenatal stress is altering fetal neurodevelopment primarily via raised maternal cortisol levels. The human maternal HPA axis functions differently in pregnancy than in most mammals, because of the placental production of corticotrophin-releasing hormone, which in turn causes an increase in maternal cortisol. The maternal HPA axis becomes gradually less responsive to external stressors as pregnancy progresses, and there is only a weak, if any, association between maternal mood and cortisol level, especially later in pregnancy. Bleker et al. (2017), for example, with a large cohort of pregnant Dutch women, have shown that none of the psychosocial stressors they examined was significantly associated with maternal serum cortisol levels [54].

However, the fetus is still likely to be exposed to more cortisol in response to maternal stress, even if the stress does not raise maternal levels, because of alterations in the function of the placenta [55]. The placenta filters what passes from the maternal blood to the fetal circulation, and the function of this filter can be altered by signals received from the mother. A study that measured levels of amniotic fluid cortisol and maternal blood cortisol at the same time showed that the correlation between these levels was dependent on the anxiety of the mother [56]. The greater the levels of symptoms of anxiety in the mother, the greater the correlation. This suggests that maternal anxiety can increase fetal exposure to cortisol even if her own cortisol levels are not increased by her own mood or stress.

The increased exposure of the fetus to cortisol with raised levels of maternal stress is probably due to a reduction of cortisol metabolism by the placenta, allowing more cortisol to pass through from mother to baby. There are high levels of the enzyme which breaks down cortisol to inactive cortisone, 11-β-hydroxysteroid dehydrogenase type II (11β-HSD2), lining the interface between the maternal and fetal blood streams. The expression of the placental messenger RNA which controls 11β-HSD2 activity has been shown to be downregulated in response to maternal antenatal anxiety, depression or stress [57, 58]. Other biological systems in the placenta are likely to be affected too, and also alter fetal exposures. For example, monoamine oxidase A, which metabolises the monoamines 5-HT, dopamine and noradrenaline to inactive forms, has been shown to be downregulated in association with symptoms of antenatal depression [59].

We still do not know what biological changes in the mother drive the alterations in the function of the placenta. There is currently much interest in the immune system and inflammation as a mediator of the effects of prenatal stress on offspring neuropsychiatric risk [60]. Maternal immune activation can occur in response to a number of triggers, such as infection and diet, as well as psychosocial stress. Animal models have shown that immune activation of the pregnant dam can lead to an increased risk for symptoms of anxiety and depression in the offspring [49]. There is increasing human evidence linking depression with altered functioning of the immune system including raised levels of pro-inflammatory cytokines [60]. Exposure to early-life stressful events can act through the modulation of inflammatory responses over the entire lifespan. A history of exposure to intimate partner violence, for example, has been associated with raised levels of the cytokine TNF-α during pregnancy [61]. However, we do not yet know how, if at all, this affects the functioning of the placenta or the development of the fetus.

The Child

The fetal period is critical for the development of the human brain, and the way it develops can be influenced by the environment. The developing brain contains billions of neurons, most of which are produced by mid-gestation. Neuronal migration peaks between gestational weeks 12 and 20 and is largely complete by weeks 26 to 29. During the later fetal period there is specialisation in the different brain regions, and connective pathways and synapses start to form. At week 34, approximately 40,000 new synapses are formed every second, a process that continues into early postnatal life [49]. Thus, the fetal brain is under construction, and how it is constructed can be affected by the biological signals it receives from the mother, including those caused by alterations in her own mood or stress.

Research is now starting to show associations between antenatal stress and alterations in the brain structure of the child. Table 33.4 shows studies which have shown an enlarged amygdala, which is generally associated with increased anxiety, alterations in the uncinate fasciculus (white matter associated with social behaviour), as well as a thinning of the cerebral cortex, which was associated with adolescent depressive symptoms. The biological signals from the mother which cause these alterations in fetal and child brain structures are not yet known, but cortisol is again one plausible mediator.

There has been much research on the associations between antenatal stress and the function of the HPA system in the child. In evolutionary terms it may be advantageous for a child born into a stressful environment to have a more reactive cortisol response. However, the findings are complex and may depend on the age when the child is tested, and the type of stress, among several other factors [62]. Mothers with antenatal depression have been shown to have infants with a greater cortisol response to immunisation at 1 year [63]. Nazzari et al. (2019) showed an association between maternal prenatal diurnal cortisol and the newborn's stress reactivity [64]. O'Connor et al. (2013) measured amniotic fluid cortisol levels and found that these predicted the infant cortisol response to a separation–reunion stress at 17 months [65]. However, others have failed to find an

Table 33.4 Examples of antenatal stress and altered brain development in the child

Brain change	Reference
Enlarged amygdala	[104]
Reduced cortical thickness	[47]
Altered uncinate fasciculus (white matter underlying child social behaviour)	[111]
Thinner superior frontal cortex and larger caudal middle frontal area in the left hemisphere	[112]

association between maternal antenatal depressive symptoms and the infant's cortisol response to inoculation at 2 months [66]. O'Donnell et al. (2013) found that symptoms of maternal antenatal anxiety or depression were associated with an alteration of diurnal cortisol in adolescent offspring, shown by a reduced cortisol awakening response and flatter diurnal slope, although the effects were small [67]. Most studies have found little association between the function of the child's HPA axis and altered phenotypes [62]. Although alterations in the HPA axis of the child may mediate some of the effects of antenatal stress on neurodevelopment and other outcomes, many different mechanisms are likely to be involved too.

Although there is a clinically significant increased risk from various forms of antenatal stress on later child psychopathology, most children are not affected – and those that are are affected in different ways. This is due, at least in part, to the genetic make-up of the child and gene–environments interactions. Qiu et al. (2017) have shown that both the effects of antenatal maternal depressive symptoms and the effect of socio-economic status on neonatal brain development are modulated by genetic risk [68]. Others have examined gene–environment interactions looking at specific genes. Chen et al. (2015) have shown that a genetic variant in *BDNF* affects the degree of association between maternal antenatal anxiety and neonatal DNA methylation, as well as neonatal brain structure [69]. O'Donnell et al. (2014), using the ALSPAC cohort, showed an interaction between prenatal anxiety and different genetic variants of *BDNF* and later child internalising symptoms from age 4 to 15 years [70]. O'Donnell et al. (2017) have also found a significant interaction between child *COMT* genotype and symptoms of both ADHD and working memory in the child [18]. There was no interaction between *BDNF* and working memory or ADHD, or between *COMT* and internalising symptoms. The interactions in both the O'Donnell studies only explained a small part of the variance, and there are probably very many genes involved in the predisposition to the many types of psychopathology outcomes affected by antenatal stress.

Epigenetics

There is much interest in the potential role of epigenetics in underlying the long-term effects of antenatal stress on the development of the fetus and the child [71, 72, 73, 74]. Epigenetic changes after prenatal stress have been found in animal models [75]. However, although epigenetics remains a promising mechanism for the mediation of antenatal stress on fetal development, evidence for its importance in humans is still quite limited.

Several studies have looked at alterations in the methylation of specific genes, and especially in the promoter region of the glucocorticoid receptor (*NR3C1*), the receptor for cortisol. Hompes et al. (2013) have shown epigenetic changes in this region using the cord blood from mothers who suffered from pregnancy-related anxiety [21]. Oberlander et al. (2008) have shown altered *NR3C1* promoter methylation in cord blood from neonates born to mothers with antenatal depression [76]. Mulligan et al. (2012) found methylation changes in this site in newborns of mothers exposed to prenatal stress in the Democratic Republic of Congo [77]. Epigenetic changes have also been found in older children whose mothers experienced stress during pregnancy. Maternal antenatal stress, caused by violence by the partner, has been shown to be associated with increased methylation of the *NR3C1* promoter in the blood of their adolescent children [78].

Epigenetic changes can last throughout the lifetime, although they can also be reversed. Some studies have found changes that last until the grandchild generation. Serpeloni et al. (2017) have shown that if a grandmother was exposed to the psychosocial stress of domestic abuse, her grandchildren had an altered genome-wide methylation pattern, an indication of an altered epigenetic profile [79].

Global Aspects

Most of the research on these topics has been in high-income countries, but the effects may be different and have an even greater impact in low- and middle-income countries. Levels of antenatal stress may be much higher due to wars, high levels of interpersonal violence [80], natural disasters and poverty. In a study in the Swat valley, Pakistan, an area affected by armed conflict, over a third of women showed significant psychological distress [81]. There may also be special reasons for raised levels of pregnancy-specific anxiety, with high rates of maternal and infant mortality. There are possible potential interactions with infections [82], food insufficiency, dietary deficiencies, crowded housing and extremes of temperature [83].

There may also be biological differences, including genetic, which alter the effects of antenatal stress on fetal and child development in different ethnic groups. Capron et al. (2017) found, in a small study, that the association between antenatal maternal stress and alterations in the expression of HPA-related genes in the placenta depended on the ethnicity of the mother [84]. While in Caucasians there was a clear downregulation of 11-βHSD2 expression and upregulation of the glucocorticoid receptor *NR3C1*, confirming previous studies, this was absent in the non-Caucasians, with a significant interaction with ethnicity. Genetic make-up can affect epigenetic changes too. Teh et al. (2014) have shown both that different ethnic groups in Singapore can be separated by their genetic profile, and that genotype influences epigenetic variation [85]. They further showed substantial interaction between genotype, different in utero environments, including maternal antenatal depression, and variably methylated regions.

This raises the interesting possibility that the effects of antenatal stress on later child psychopathology may be different in different ethnic groups, with some being more resilient and some more susceptible. This is a subject about which we know little and needs more research in the future.

Implications for Intervention

The evidence therefore suggests that stress in pregnancy can influence a range of negative outcomes in offspring. Further work is needed, however, to understand better the influence of the timing, nature and severity of stress on the magnitude of effect.

A pregnant women may be experiencing a wide variety of different types of stress, and it is likely that the earlier she can receive help, the less the risk to her child. She may be suffering from interpersonal violence, pregnancy-related anxiety or have suffered from childhood abuse or trauma. These may not be asked about by health professionals looking after women during pregnancy. Although universal, these problems can be especially common in some lower-income countries and may be present in recent immigrants to higher-income countries.

The risk for schizophrenia later in the child's life seems to be from very severe stress (as from the death of an older child) in the first trimester. With all the other outcomes the stress can have an effect all through pregnancy, so it is never too late to intervene. It is important to emphasise to women who may have heard about the effects of stress, that most children are not affected. We are only seeing an increase in risk. It is also important to emphasise that we all experience some stress, whether pregnant or not. And it is important not to induce more guilt in women. The aim of publicising these findings is to obtain more help and support. Further consideration of the impact on levels of guilt and how these issues should be discussed with women by clinicians is given in Chapter 1 ('The Perinatal Frame of Mind').

For women experiencing mental illness it is important they receive timely treatment with the usual pharmacological and psychological interventions. For other women experiencing stress there is some evidence for interventions that can help both antenatally for the woman and postnatally for the child. This is especially important in countries where there is little professional support. We must distinguish, however, between the evidence for the intervention reducing stress and evidence that this reduces adverse outcomes. The latter is more difficult to demonstrate and there is consequently a lower evidence base. For less severe stress, low mood and anxiety, directed or passive relaxation can be helpful for alleviating maternal symptoms [86]. There is considerable evidence that listening to suitable music can help the mother too [87], including in the antenatal period [88]. Postnatally it has been shown that the effects of antenatal anxiety on child behavioural problems is less in mothers who stroke their babies more [89]. Although still debated, there is some evidence that breastfeeding improves cognitive outcomes [90]. But the main implication of the research reviewed here is that clinicians, and all those caring for pregnant women, need to be aware that even if the woman is not suffering from a diagnosed mental illness, her emotional state may have consequences for both herself and her fetus.

References

1. DJ Barker. The developmental origins of adult disease. *Eur J Epidemiol.* 2003;18(8):733–6.
2. V Glover. Prenatal stress and its effects on the fetus and the child: possible underlying biological mechanisms. *Adv Neurobiol.* 2015;10:269–83.
3. K Bergman, P Sarkar, V Glover, TG O'Connor. Maternal prenatal cortisol and infant cognitive development: moderation by infant-mother attachment. *Biol Psychiatry.* 2010;67(11):1026–32.
4. AC Huizink, PG Robles de Medina, EJ Mulder, GH Visser, JK Buitelaar. Stress during pregnancy is associated with developmental outcome in infancy. *J Child Psychol Psychiatry.* 2003;44(6):810–18.
5. TG O'Connor, J Heron, J Golding, M Beveridge, V Glover. Maternal antenatal anxiety and children's behavioural/emotional problems at 4 years. Report from the Avon Longitudinal Study of Parents and Children. *Br J Psychiatry.* 2002;180:502–8.
6. CA Sandman, C Buss, K Head, EP Davis. Fetal exposure to maternal depressive symptoms is associated with cortical thickness in late childhood. *Biol Psychiatry.* 2014;77(4):324–34.
7. S Faleschini, SL Rifas-Shiman, H Tiemeier, E Oken, MF Hivert. Associations of prenatal and postnatal maternal depressive symptoms with offspring cognition and behavior in mid-childhood: a prospective cohort study. *Int J Env Res Public Health.* 2019;16(6):1007.
8. BR Van den Bergh, B Van Calster, T Smits, S Van Huffel, L Lagae. Antenatal maternal anxiety is related to HPA-axis dysregulation and self-reported depressive symptoms in adolescence: a prospective

study on the fetal origins of depressed mood. *Neuropsychopharmacology.* 2008;33:536–5.

9. C Buss, EP Davis, CJ Hobel, CA Sandman. Maternal pregnancy-specific anxiety is associated with child executive function at 6-9 years age. *Stress.* 2011;14(6):665–76.
10. K Bergman, P Sarkar, TG O'Connor, N Modi, V Glover. Maternal stress during pregnancy predicts cognitive ability and fearfulness in infancy. *J Am Acad Child Adolesc Psychiatry.* 2007;46(11): 1454–63.
11. C Guo, P He, X Song, X Zheng. Long-term effects of prenatal exposure to earthquake on adult schizophrenia. *Br J Psychiatry.* 2019:215(6):730–5.
12. DP Laplante, A Brunet, S King. The effects of maternal stress and illness during pregnancy on infant temperament: Project Ice Storm. *Pediatr Res.* 2016;79(1-1):107–13.
13. AC Huizink, DM Dick, E Sihvola, L Pulkkinen, RJ Rose, J Kaprio. Chernobyl exposure as stressor during pregnancy and behaviour in adolescent offspring. *Acta Psychiatr Scand.* 2007;116(6):438–46.
14. DT Plant, FW Jones, CM Pariante, S Pawlby. Association between maternal childhood trauma and offspring childhood psychopathology: mediation analysis from the ALSPAC cohort. *Br J Psychiatry.* 2017;211(3):144–50.
15. NK Moog, S Entringer, JM Rasmussen, M Styner, JH Gilmore, N Kathmann, et al. Intergenerational effect of maternal exposure to childhood maltreatment on newborn brain anatomy. *Biol Psychiatry.* 2018;83(2):120–7.
16. V Glover. Annual Research Review: prenatal stress and the origins of psychopathology: an evolutionary perspective. *J Child Psychol Psychiatry.* 2011;52(4):356–67.
17. BRH van den Bergh, MI van den Heuvel, M Lahti, M Braeken, SR de Rooij, S Entringer, et al. Prenatal developmental origins of behavior and mental health: the influence of maternal stress in pregnancy. *Neurosci Biobehav Rev.* 2020;117: 26–64.
18. KJ O'Donnell, V Glover, J Lahti, M Lahti, RD Edgar, K Raikkonen, et al. Maternal prenatal anxiety and child COMT genotype predict working memory and symptoms of ADHD. *PLoS ONE.* 2017;12(6):e0177506.
19. LM Chen, I Pokhvisneva, M Lahti-Pulkkinen, T Kvist, JR Baldwin, C Parent, et al. Independent prediction of child psychiatric symptoms by maternal mental health and child polygenic risk scores. *J Am Acad Child Adolesc Psychiatry.* 2024;63(6):640–51.
20. M Weinstock. The long-term behavioural consequences of prenatal stress. *Neurosci Biobehav Rev.* 2008;32(6):1073–86.
21. T Hompes, B Izzi, E Gellens, M Morreels, S Fieuws, A Pexsters, et al. Investigating the influence of maternal cortisol and emotional state during pregnancy on the DNA methylation status of the glucocorticoid receptor gene (NR3C1) promoter region in cord blood. *J Psychiatr Res.* 2013;47(7):880–91.
22. KJ O'Donnell, V Glover, ED Barker, TG O'Connor. The persisting effect of maternal mood in pregnancy on childhood psychopathology. *Dev Psychopathol.* 2014;26(2):393–403.
23. AS Khashan, KM Abel, R McNamee, MG Pedersen, RT Webb, PN Baker, et al. Higher risk of offspring schizophrenia following antenatal maternal exposure to severe adverse life events. *Arch Gen Psychiatry.* 2008;65(2):146–52.
24. Y Nomura, K Davey, PM Pehme, J Finik, V Glover, W Zhang, et al. Influence of in utero exposure to maternal depression and natural disaster-related stress on infant temperament at 6 months: the children of Superstorm Sandy. *Infant Ment Health J.* 2019;40(2):204–16.
25. G Simcock, VE Cobham, DP Laplante, G Elgbeili, R Gruber, S Kildea, et al. A cross-lagged panel analysis of children's sleep, attention, and mood in a prenatally stressed cohort: the QF2011 Queensland

flood study. *J Affect Disord.* 2019;255: 96–104.

26. S Pawlby, DF Hay, D Sharp, CS Waters, V O'Keane. Antenatal depression predicts depression in adolescent offspring: prospective longitudinal community-based study. *J Affect Disord.* 2009;113(3):236–43.
27. RM Pearson, MH Bornstein, M Cordero, G Scerif, L Mahedy, J Evans, et al. Maternal perinatal mental health and offspring academic achievement at age 16: the mediating role of childhood executive function. *J Child Psychol Psychiatry.* 2016;57(4):491–501.
28. DK Kinney, AM Miller, DJ Crowley, E Huang, E Gerber. Autism prevalence following prenatal exposure to hurricanes and tropical storms in Louisiana. *J Autism Dev Disord.* 2008;38(3):481–8.
29. RM Pearson, J Evans, D Kounali, G Lewis, J Heron, PG Ramchandani, et al. Maternal depression during pregnancy and the postnatal period: risks and possible mechanisms for offspring depression at age 18 years. *JAMA Psychiatry.* 2013;70(12):1312–19.
30. KS Betts, GM Williams, JM Najman, R Alati. The relationship between maternal depressive, anxious, and stress symptoms during pregnancy and adult offspring behavioral and emotional problems. *Depress Anxiety.* 2015;32(2):82–90.
31. J Hahn, DR Gold, BA Coull, MC McCormick, PW Finn, DL Perkins, et al. Prenatal maternal depression and neonatal immune responses. *Psychosom Med.* 2019;81(4):320–7.
32. H Cookson, R Granell, C Joinson, Y Ben-Shlomo, AJ Henderson. Mothers' anxiety during pregnancy is associated with asthma in their children. *J Allergy Clin Immunol.* 2009;123(4):847–53 e11.
33. A Rodriguez, U Waldenstrom. Fetal origins of child non-right-handedness and mental health. *J Child Psychol Psychiatry.* 2008;49(9):967–76.
34. Hu J, J Ly, W Zhang, Y Huang, V Glover, I Peter, et al. Microbiota of newborn meconium is associated with maternal anxiety experienced during pregnancy. *Dev Psychobiol.* 2019;61(5):640–9.
35. SM O'Mahony, G Clarke, TG Dinan, JF Cryan. Early-life adversity and brain development: is the microbiome a missing piece of the puzzle? *Neuroscience.* 2017;342:37–54.
36. G Buffa, S Dahan, I Sinclair, M St-Pierre, N Roofigari, D Mutran, et al. Prenatal stress and child development: a scoping review of research in low- and middle-income countries. *PLoS ONE.* 2018;13(12):e0207235.
37. PD Wadhwa, S Entringer, C Buss, MC Lu. The contribution of maternal stress to preterm birth: issues and considerations. *Clin Perinatol.* 2011;38(3):351–84.
38. A Duchesne, A Liu, SL Jones, DP Laplante, S King. Childhood body mass index at 5.5 years mediates the effect of prenatal maternal stress on daughters' age at menarche: Project Ice Storm. *J Dev Orig Health Dis.* 2017;8(2):168–77.
39. S Entringer, ES Epel, J Lin, C Buss, B Shahbaba, EH Blackburn, et al. Maternal psychosocial stress during pregnancy is associated with newborn leukocyte telomere length. *Am J Obstet Gynecol.* 2013;208(2):134 e1–7.
40. M Weinstock. Gender differences in the effects of prenatal stress on brain development and behaviour. *Neurochem Res.* 2007;32:1730–40.
41. M Weinstock. Sex-dependent changes induced by prenatal stress in cortical and hippocampal morphology and behaviour in rats: an update. *Stress.* 2011;14(6):604–13.
42. M Darnaudery, S Maccari. Epigenetic programming of the stress response in male and female rats by prenatal restraint stress. *Brain Res Rev.* 2008;57(2):571–85.
43. SG Matthews, DI Phillips. Transgenerational inheritance of stress pathology. *Exp Neurol.* 2012;233(1):95–101.
44. PO McGowan, SG Matthews. Prenatal stress, glucocorticoids, and developmental programming of the stress response. *Endocrinology.* 2018;159(1):69–82.

45. DP Laplante, G Simcock, L Cao-Lei, M Mouallem, G Elgbeili, A Brunet, et al. The 5-HTTLPR polymorphism of the serotonin transporter gene and child's sex moderate the relationship between disaster-related prenatal maternal stress and autism spectrum disorder traits: the QF2011 Queensland flood study. *Dev Psychopathol.* 2018;5:1–15.

46. J Hill, A Pickles, N Wright, E Braithwaite, H Sharp. Predictions of children's emotionality from evolutionary and epigenetic hypotheses. *Sci Rep.* 2019;9(1):2519.

47. LM Hicks, DA Swales, SE Garcia, C Driver, EP Davis. Does prenatal maternal distress contribute to sex differences in child psychopathology? *Curr Psychiatry Rep.* 2019;21(2):7.

48. F Tibu, J Hill, H Sharp, K Marshall, V Glover, A Pickles. Evidence for sex differences in fetal programming of physiological stress reactivity in infancy. *Dev Psychopathol.* 2014;26(4 Pt 1):879–88.

49. C Monk, C Lugo-Candelas, C Trumpff. Prenatal developmental origins of future psychopathology: mechanisms and pathways. *Ann Rev Clin Psychol.* 2019;15:317–44.

50. G Zagron, M Weinstock. Maternal adrenal hormone secretion mediates behavioural alterations induced by prenatal stress in male and female rats. *Behav Brain Res.* 2006;175(2):323–8.

51. N Khalife, V Glover, A Taanila, H Ebeling, MR Jarvelin, A Rodriguez. Prenatal glucocorticoid treatment and later mental health in children and adolescents. *PLoS ONE.* 2013;8(11): e81394.

52. K Raikkonen, S Martikainen, AK Pesonen, J Lahti, K Heinonen, R Pyhala, et al. Maternal licorice consumption during pregnancy and pubertal, cognitive, and psychiatric outcomes in children. *Am J Epidemiol.* 2017;185(5):317–28.

53. EP Davis, CA Sandman, C Buss, DA Wing, K Head. Fetal glucocorticoid exposure is associated with preadolescent brain development. *Biol Psychiatry.* 2013;74(9):647–55.

54. LS Bleker, TJ Roseboom, TG Vrijkotte, RM Reynolds, SR de Rooij. Determinants of cortisol during pregnancy: the ABCD cohort. *Psychoneuroendocrinology.* 2017;83:172–81.

55. P Kratimenos, AA Penn. Placental programming of neuropsychiatric disease. *Pediatr Res.* 2019;86(2):157–64.

56. V Glover, K Bergman, P Sarkar, TG O'Connor. Association between maternal and amniotic fluid cortisol is moderated by maternal anxiety. *Psychoneuroendocrinology.* 2009;34(3):430–5.

57. KJ O'Donnell, A Bugge Jensen, L Freeman, N Khalife, TG O'Connor, V Glover. Maternal prenatal anxiety and downregulation of placental 11beta-HSD2. *Psychoneuroendocrinology.* 2012;37(6):818–26.

58. C Monk, T Feng, S Lee, I Krupska, FA Champagne, B Tycko. Distress during pregnancy: epigenetic regulation of placenta glucocorticoid-related genes and fetal neurobehavior. *Am J Psychiatry.* 2016;173(7):705–13.

59. PM Blakeley, LE Capron, AB Jensen, KJ O'Donnell, V Glover. Maternal prenatal symptoms of depression and down regulation of placental monoamine oxidase A expression. *J Psychosom Res.* 2013;75(4):341–5.

60. L Hantsoo, S Kornfield, MC Anguera, CN Epperson. Inflammation: a proposed intermediary between maternal stress and offspring neuropsychiatric risk. *Biol Psychiatry.* 2019;85(2):97–106.

61. ER Blackmore, JA Moynihan, DR Rubinow, EK Pressman, M Gilchrist, TG O'Connor. Psychiatric symptoms and proinflammatory cytokines in pregnancy. *Psychosom Med.* 2011;73(8):656–63.

62. V Glover, TG O'Connor, K O'Donnell. Prenatal stress and the programming of the HPA axis. *Neurosci Biobehav Rev.* 2010;35(1):17–22.

63. S Osborne, A Biaggi, TE Chua, A Du Preez, K Hazelgrove, N Nikkheslat, et al.

Antenatal depression programs cortisol stress reactivity in offspring through increased maternal inflammation and cortisol in pregnancy: the Psychiatry Research and Motherhood - Depression (PRAM-D) Study. *Psychoneuroendocrinology.* 2018;98:211–21.

64. S Nazzari, P Fearon, F Rice, N Dottori, F Ciceri, M Molteni, et al. Beyond the HPA-axis: exploring maternal prenatal influences on birth outcomes and stress reactivity. *Psychoneuroendocrinology.* 2019;101:253–62.

65. TG O'Connor, K Bergman, P Sarkar, V Glover. Prenatal cortisol exposure predicts infant cortisol response to acute stress. *Dev Psychobiol.* 2013;55(2): 145–55.

66. EC Braithwaite, SE Murphy, PG Ramchandani. Effects of prenatal depressive symptoms on maternal and infant cortisol reactivity. *Arch Womens Ment Health.* 2016;19(4):581–90.

67. KJ O'Donnell, V Glover, J Jenkins, D Browne, Y Ben-Shlomo, J Golding, et al. Prenatal maternal mood is associated with altered diurnal cortisol in adolescence. *Psychoneuroendocrinology.* 2013;38(9):1630–8.

68. A Qiu, M Shen, C Buss, YS Chong, K Kwek, SM Saw, et al. Effects of antenatal maternal depressive symptoms and socio-economic status on neonatal brain development are modulated by genetic risk. *Cerebral Cortex.* 2017;27(5): 3080–92.

69. L Chen, H Pan, TA Tuan, AL Teh, JL MacIsaac, SM Mah, et al. Brain-derived neurotrophic factor (BDNF) Val66Met polymorphism influences the association of the methylome with maternal anxiety and neonatal brain volumes. *Dev Psychopathol.* 2015;27(1):137–50.

70. KJ O'Donnell, V Glover, JD Holbrook, TG O'Connor. Maternal prenatal anxiety and child brain-derived neurotrophic factor (BDNF) genotype: effects on internalizing symptoms from 4 to 15 years of age. *Dev Psychopathol.* 2014;26(4 Pt 2):1255–66.

71. Z Nemoda, M Szyf. Epigenetic alterations and prenatal maternal depression. *Birth Defects Res.* 2017;109(12):888–97.

72. L Cao-Lei, SR de Rooij, S King, SG Matthews, GAS Metz, TJ Roseboom, et al. Prenatal stress and epigenetics. *Neurosci Biobehav Rev.* 2017;198:198–210.

73. VR Mileva-Seitz, MJ Bakermans-Kranenburg, MH van IJzendoorn. Genetic mechanisms of parenting. *Horm Behav.* 2016;77:211–23.

74. I Lacal, R Ventura. Epigenetic inheritance: concepts, mechanisms and perspectives. *Front Mol Neurosci.* 2018;11:292.

75. C Jensen Pena, C Monk, FA Champagne. Epigenetic effects of prenatal stress on 11beta-hydroxysteroid dehydrogenase-2 in the placenta and fetal brain. *PLoS ONE.* 2012;7(6):e39791.

76. TF Oberlander, J Weinberg, M Papsdorf, R Grunau, S Misri, AM Devlin. Prenatal exposure to maternal depression, neonatal methylation of human glucocorticoid receptor gene (NR3C1) and infant cortisol stress responses. *Epigenetics.* 2008;3(2):97–106.

77. CJ Mulligan, NC D'Errico, J Stees, DA Hughes. Methylation changes at NR3C1 in newborns associate with maternal prenatal stress exposure and newborn birth weight. *Epigenetics.* 2012;7(8):853–7.

78. KM Radtke, M Ruf, HM Gunter, K Dohrmann, M Schauer, A Meyer, et al. Transgenerational impact of intimate partner violence on methylation in the promoter of the glucocorticoid receptor. *Transl Psychiatry.* 2011;1(7):e21.

79. F Serpeloni, K Radtke, SG de Assis, F Henning, D Natt, T Elbert. Grandmaternal stress during pregnancy and DNA methylation of the third generation: an epigenome-wide association study. *Transl Psychiatry.* 2017;7(8):e1202.

80. TD Tran, H Nguyen, J Fisher. Attitudes towards intimate partner violence against women among women and men in 39 low- and middle-income countries. *PLoS ONE.* 2016;11(11):e0167438.

81. MN Khan, A Chiumento, M Dherani, K Bristow, S Sikander, A Rahman. Psychological distress and its associations with past events in pregnant women affected by armed conflict in Swat, Pakistan: a cross sectional study. *Confl Health.* 2015;9:37.

82. JA Goldstein, SA Norris, DM Aronoff. DOHaD at the intersection of maternal immune activation and maternal metabolic stress: a scoping review. *J Dev Orig Health Dis.* 2017;8(3):273–83.

83. CM Herba, V Glover, PG Ramchandani, MB Rondon. Maternal depression and mental health in early childhood: an examination of underlying mechanisms in low-income and middle-income countries. *Lancet Psychiatry.* 2016;3(10):983–92.

84. LE Capron, PG Ramchandani, V Glover. Maternal prenatal stress and placental gene expression of NR3C1 and HSD11B2: the effects of maternal ethnicity. *Psychoneuroendocrinology.* 2017;87:166–72.

85. AL Teh, H Pan, L Chen, ML Ong, S Dogra, J Wong, et al. The effect of genotype and in utero environment on interindividual variation in neonate DNA methylomes. *Genome Res.* 2014;24(7):1064–74.

86. J Teixeira, D Martin, O Prendiville, V Glover. The effects of acute relaxation on indices of anxiety during pregnancy. *J Psychosom Obstet Gynaecol.* 2005;26(4):271–6.

87. M de Witte, A Spruit, S van Hooren, X Moonen, GJ Stams. Effects of music interventions on stress-related outcomes: a systematic review and two meta-analyses. *Health Psychol Rev.* 2019:6:1–62.

88. C Nwebube, V Glover, L Stewart. Prenatal listening to songs composed for pregnancy and symptoms of anxiety and depression: a pilot study. *BMC Complement Altern Med.* 2017;17(1):256.

89. A Pickles, H Sharp, J Hellier, J Hill. Prenatal anxiety, maternal stroking in infancy, and symptoms of emotional and behavioral disorders at 3.5 years. *Eur Child Adolesc Psychiatry.* 2017;26(3):325–34.

90. M Strom, EL Mortensen, US Kesmodel, T Halldorsson, J Olsen, SF Olsen. Is breast feeding associated with offspring IQ at age 5? Findings from prospective cohort: Lifestyle During Pregnancy Study. *BMJ Open.* 2019;9(5):e023134.

91. TF Oberlander, W Warburton, S Misri, J Aghajanian, C Hertzman. Neonatal outcomes after prenatal exposure to selective serotonin reuptake inhibitor antidepressants and maternal depression using population-based linked health data. *Arch Gen Psychiatry.* 2006;63(8):898–906.

92. A Rahman, J Bunn, H Lovel, F Creed. Association between antenatal depression and low birthweight in a developing country. *Acta Psychiatr Scand.* 2007;115(6):481–6.

93. J Milgrom, C Holt, CJ Holt, J Ross, J Ericksen, AW Gemmill. Feasibility study and pilot randomised trial of an antenatal depression treatment with infant follow-up. *Arch Womens Ment Health.* 2015;18(5):717–30.

94. MT Kinsella, C Monk. Impact of maternal stress, depression and anxiety on fetal neurobehavioral development. *Clin Obstet Gynecol.* 2009;52(3):425–40.

95. S Pawlby, D Hay, D Sharp, CS Waters, CM Pariante. Antenatal depression and offspring psychopathology: the influence of childhood maltreatment. *Br J Psychiatry.* 2011;199(2):106–12.

96. M Fernandes, A Stein, K Srinivasan, G Menezes, PG Ramchandani. Foetal exposure to maternal depression predicts cortisol responses in infants: findings from rural South India. *Child Care Health Dev.* 2015;41(5):677–86.

97. M Mennes, P Stiers, L Lagae, B Van den Bergh. Long-term cognitive sequelae of antenatal maternal anxiety: involvement of the orbitofrontal cortex. *Neurosci Biobehav Rev.* 2006;30(8):1078–86.

98. LE Capron, V Glover, RM Pearson, J Evans, TG O'Connor, A Stein, et al. Associations of maternal and paternal

antenatal mood with offspring anxiety disorder at age 18 years. *J Affect Disord.* 2015;187:20–6.

99. EP Davis, LM Glynn, F Waffarn, CA Sandman. Prenatal maternal stress programs infant stress regulation. *J Child Psychol Psychiatry.* 2011;52(2):119–29.
100. S Entringer, R Kumsta, DH Hellhammer, PD Wadhwa, S Wust. Prenatal exposure to maternal psychosocial stress and HPA axis regulation in young adults. *Horm Behav.* 2009;55(2):292–8.
101. R Brannigan, M Cannon, A Tanskanen, MO Huttunen, FP Leacy, MC Clarke. The association between subjective maternal stress during pregnancy and offspring clinically diagnosed psychiatric disorders. *Acta Psychiatr Scand.* 2019;139(4):304–10.
102. RF Hentges, SA Graham, A Plamondon, S Tough, S Madigan. A developmental cascade from prenatal stress to child internalizing and externalizing problems. *J Pediatr Psychol.* 2019;44(9):1057–67.
103. C Obel, M Hedegaard, TB Henriksen, NJ Secher, J Olsen. Psychological factors in pregnancy and mixed-handedness in the offspring. *Dev Med Child Neurol.* 2003;45(8):557–61.
104. SL Jones, R Dufoix, DP Laplante, G Elgbeili, R Patel, MM Chakravarty, et al. Larger amygdala volume mediates the association between prenatal maternal stress and higher levels of externalizing behaviors: sex specific effects in Project Ice Storm. *Front Hum Neurosci.* 2019;13:144.
105. P Maki, J Veijola, P Rasanen, M Joukamaa, P Valonen, J Jokelainen, et al. Criminality in the offspring of antenatally depressed mothers: a 33-year follow-up of the Northern Finland 1966 Birth Cohort. *J Affect Disord.* 2003;74(3):273–8.
106. DJ Walder, DP Laplante, A Sousa-Pires, F Veru, A Brunet, S King. Prenatal maternal stress predicts autism traits in 6 (1/2) year-old children: Project Ice Storm. *Psychiatry Res.* 2014;219(2):353–60.
107. J Li, J Olsen, M Vestergaard, C Obel, JK Kristensen, J Virk. Prenatal exposure to bereavement and type-2 diabetes: a Danish longitudinal population based study. *PLoS ONE.* 2012;7(8):e43508.
108. V Glover, TG O'Connor, J Heron, J Golding, ALSPAC Study Team. Antenatal maternal anxiety is linked with atypical handedness in the child. *Early Hum Dev.* 2004;79(2):107–18.
109. M Peterka, R Peterkova, Z Likovsky. Chernobyl: prenatal loss of four hundred male fetuses in the Czech Republic. *Reprod Toxicol.* 2004;18(1):75–9.
110. F Torche, K Kleinhaus. Prenatal stress, gestational age and secondary sex ratio: the sex-specific effects of exposure to a natural disaster in early pregnancy. *Hum Reprod.* 2012;27(2):558–67.
111. S Sarkar, MC Craig, F Dell'Acqua, TG O'Connor, M Catani, Q Deeley, et al. Prenatal stress and limbic-prefrontal white matter microstructure in children aged 6-9 years: a preliminary diffusion tensor imaging study. *World J Biol Psychiatry.* 2014;15(4):346–52.
112. H El Marroun, H Tiemeier, RL Muetzel, S Thijssen, NJ van der Knaap, VW Jaddoe, et al. Prenatal exposure to maternal and paternal depressive symptoms and brain morphology: a population-based prospective neuroimaging study in young children. *Depress Anxiety.* 2016;33(7):658–66.

Chapter 34

Holding the Baby in Mind

How Does Infant Observation Contribute to Perinatal Practice?

Biddy Youell

Introduction

The mental health of babies can be overlooked in perinatal services when there is such an urgent need to care for the welfare of a mentally unwell mother. This chapter focuses on the ways in which training in infant observation can enhance the clinician's capacity to see and make some sense of interactions between mothers (or other carers) and infants, and to notice and reflect on aspects of the baby's early development. Developmental checklists help to assess whether a particular child has reached essential milestones or conforms to expected norms, but in the very early days, weeks and months, the questions are more qualitative ones. What has been the infant's experience of arriving in the world; what kind of relationships are on offer; and how is the baby responding?

The First Year of life

'To become a person with what is often called "a sense of self" requires large amounts of input from other people early in life, and an experience of ourselves as reflected back through the eyes and minds of those around us' [1]. Music lays stress on the broadly accepted idea that babies are born primed to relate to other humans, and much will depend on what they see in the faces of those around them, particularly in the face of their primary caregiver [2]. This suggests that a vital role of the parent is to celebrate the arrival of the baby, to show ongoing, lively curiosity in getting to know their child and, as Winnicott, paediatrician and psychoanalyst, put it, to introduce the child to the world 'in small doses' [3]. Winnicott spoke persuasively to colleagues and students about 'good enough mothering' and was at pains to stress that he and others were never suggesting that mothers should strive for perfection [4]. In fact, he also wrote about what he called 'too good mothering' in which an over-anxious, over-watchful mother fails to give the child enough experience of ordinary separation and frustration [5]. A little later, the psychoanalyst Wilfred Bion developed a theory which he called 'container-contained' to describe the function which a mother, or primary caregiver, fulfils for an uncomfortable, distressed or fearful baby [6]. He suggests that she accepts the baby's wordless communication, does her best to understand what the baby is experiencing and endeavours to relieve the distress one way or another and without panicking or retaliating. The baby has an experience of a mother who can bear negative feelings and who is confident that the world is not about to end! Bion's theory was that through repeated experiences of having his anxiety 'contained' in this way, the baby internalises aspects of his mother and comes to identify with a thoughtful, reliable 'other'.[1] In Melanie Klein's theory of primary splitting, the baby separates good from bad in his mind and later, over time, comes to understand that both can reside in the same person; the mother is both the person who frustrates him and the one who meets his needs [7].

All babies develop ways of coping in the temporary absence of a care-giving adult. Esther Bick drew attention to the way in which distressed, frightened babies can look as if they are literally 'falling apart' as they cry, thrash about and shudder [8]. She coined the phrase 'second skin' to describe the ways in which an infant might 'hold himself together' emotionally, just as the skin holds the body together. They may fix their gaze on a light or a window or develop repetitive movements or sounds when mother is temporarily not present or emotionally unavailable. Observers of babies have been able to see how these kinds of defensive manoeuvres function within ordinary development, and they predate more socially recognised supports such as dummies, finger sucking or clutching favourite toys as reminders of mother or father. There are also examples of babies in whom these kinds of defensive behaviours become habitual and are carried forward into childhood and sometimes beyond.

Observation

Observation is very much part of the day-to-day work of all medical practitioners. This is particularly true in psychiatry where clinicians have to undertake assessments and make nuanced judgements about the mental health of patients without the concrete diagnostic evidence provided by physical tests. Diagnosis and treatment decisions are based on medical knowledge and experience is brought to bear on what is observed about the patient's state of mind. This includes observation of her behaviour and appearance as well as her verbal communication. If these check out against established criteria, the psychiatrist can feel reassured that her judgement and treatment plan is in the best interest of the patient. In the perinatal period, this can mean decisions are made with the woman regarding medication, psychological and social interventions and, in severe cases, whether the mother and baby need the added support of inpatient care.

What About the Baby? Some Commonly Heard Comments

'Babies are resilient. Don't worry about him; he wouldn't even be aware of what was going on.'

'The baby seemed fine. Good as gold. Not a squeak out of him the whole time I was there.'

'Baby? Oh, I didn't think to look. He seemed to be asleep.'

'Luckily, she has a very good baby. Makes no demands. Sleeps through the night and naps lots in the day too.'

In spite of compelling evidence from neuroscience and child development research, one still hears comments such as these from practitioners. There continues to be a tendency in our society to think of babies as needing only physical care and protection.

[1] 'He' and 'him' refers to the baby, and 'she' to mother, father or other caregivers, simply for clarity throughout this chapter.

The idea persists that so long as babies are fed appropriately and are kept clean and safe from harm, they will be fine. Even though it is known that babies can display rudimentary imitation as soon as 20 minutes after birth and that most adults naturally respond to a baby by cooing, smiling, talking and even tickling, there is a tendency to underplay the importance of this kind of interaction [9]. The baby is hardwired to relate and has been interacting with his environment in utero from full physical formation at 12 weeks' gestation [10].

Observation of the baby is therefore a vital part of the assessment for all clinicians in perinatal services. This is both in relation to the baby himself and also about looking at the way he and his caregiver relate. It is a very different challenge from that presented by an adult patient. The pre-verbal, not-yet-mobile infant has a limited repertoire of communication tools at his disposal. He is entirely dependent on those around him for food, shelter and protection. He is also dependent on those same people for the early foundations of his sound mental health.

Infant Observation

The approach which underpins this chapter is usually described as 'infant observation' or 'psychoanalytically informed observation'. It is a method, a skill, a way of looking, seeing and thinking which is at the root of clinical practice in psychoanalytic psychotherapy and in parent–infant work. Esther Bick first introduced the practice into clinical training at the Tavistock Clinic with the support of John Bowlby who later developed attachment theory [8]. It remains a preclinical requirement for most psychotherapy trainings but also attracts participants from many different professions (e.g. teaching, medicine, nursing, social work). The way in which infant observation is taught remains consistent, whether it is a brief experience (perhaps as little as 10 weeks) or the recommended 1- or 2-year period. Participants spend an hour each week observing a baby in the baby's home setting, starting as soon as possible after the birth. Observations may take place when only the mother and baby are at home, but observers often find they are visiting busy families with fathers, siblings, grandparents and friends present at varying times. On occasion, observers see the developing relationship between a baby and a grandparent or a nanny. For this reason, it is a naturalistic observation; there is no attempt to create laboratory conditions. It is worth stressing that families who agree to an observation do so on the understanding that the observer is *learning* and not there as an expert in parenting or in child development. One of the challenges involved in undertaking an observation is to put one's professional identity aside and clear one's mind of prior knowledge or responsibility to assess, judge or intervene, although safeguarding responsibilities remain a priority at all times. Observers are advised to find a family where there are no immediately apparent complicating psychosocial factors.

Observers do not make notes during the hour but are asked to write as much detail as they can recall after the event. These written accounts are taken to a weekly seminar, where a group of observers, with the support of an experienced infant observation seminar leader, take turns to present and work together to try to understand the observation material. Over time, a picture is built up of the emotional and social development of the baby and his emerging personality within the family context. The seminar discussions take place against a framework of psychoanalytic theory, with ideas about containment, defences against anxiety, projection, splitting, transference and countertransference at the core [11].

The Impact on the Student Observer

Observers are supported in opening themselves up to unconscious as well as conscious communication, and notes and subsequent discussions may include reflections on feelings evoked in the observer (countertransference). These are explored in the seminar as to whether they are personal to the observer or whether they shed light on what might be the experience of the baby, parents or other family members. The assumption is, that during the observational hour, an observer will become part of the unconscious, as well as the conscious life of the baby and his family and will be the recipient of all kinds of projected feelings. The opportunity to reflect on these and to tease out what belongs to whom is very much part of the experience (e.g. was I anxious because I was in an unfamiliar situation or was I picking up the anxiety of mother?). The observer is interested in what is going on in the mind of the baby, his mother and other family members as well as in her own mind.

Observers are strongly discouraged from premature judgement or theoretical formulation. They are actively encouraged to be open-minded and to bear with not having ready answers to questions. Reflection and rigorous discussion may lead to a degree of confidence about what has been understood, but it is neither an exact nor a complete science. The students may have to confront their own tendencies to look for certainty and often have to face challenges to their assumptions and prejudices. Aspects of the relationships they are seeing may revive unwelcome memories of their own childhoods or call into question their own capacities as parents. Allowing oneself to be open to feeling states as well as to thoughts is not easy, but the discipline of looking and listening and only later trying to work out what belongs to whom is a fundamental part of any psychotherapeutic training. It is the active emotional involvement of the observer which marks this method out from other forms of observation.

Observers usually have a variety of reactions to being asked to temporarily relinquish their professional identity or work role. Some express relief at the new-found freedom; others feel anxious as to where to place themselves (sometimes literally unsure about where to stand or sit in the room). Some feel under pressure to make comments or ask questions and are naturally drawn to getting to know the adults; it is a challenge to feel comfortable in a role which is neither friend nor professional. Others confess to anticipating boredom. They may be unsure that observing a baby for a whole hour can be sufficiently absorbing. Some worry about feeling intrusive when watching the intimacy of a baby being breastfed. With very few exceptions, participants come around to discovering that they can be completely engrossed in what they see; that their capacity to notice and remember detail increases and that they look forward to the opportunity to present 'their baby' at the seminar. In most cases, what they are experiencing at close quarters is a weekly snapshot of a new baby's experience with all the many ordinary ups and downs. Some see a baby and his parents slowly recover from a difficult start; others see a baby and family having to negotiate unexpected challenges including ordinary life events such as loss of income, illness and bereavement.[2] They come to recognise the significance of times of transition; perhaps most significantly, the baby being weaned or adjusting to alternative care arrangements. They come to witness and understand more

[2] The author has written about the impact of the world financial crisis in 2008 as seen through infant observation reports in Greece and Italy at the time [12].

about the place and role of the father in their particular observation family; the experience of siblings and the wider family network. They also learn a great deal about themselves; often about their own vulnerabilities as well as about their capacity to manage themselves in complex situations.

The following is an extract from a 2-year observation completed as part of a training in child psychoanalytic psychotherapy. The baby girl, Laura, is the third child of Jennifer and Duncan.

4 Weeks Old

Laura was crying loudly … breathless cries, all at the same pitch. Jennifer had been chopping vegetables but put down the knife, and went over to the basket and took Laura out of it, carrying her to a comfortable chair, talking reassuringly. She always talks in a soft voice but when she speaks to Laura, she drops it even more and it is very soothing. Laura stopped crying. Jennifer settled her on her lap so that they looked at each other's faces and commented that it had been a busy afternoon and all Laura really needed was a bit of peace and quiet. They gazed at each other for a few moments in silence but then Laura's brother burst in demanding loudly that his mother look at his homework book, 'now!' Laura's body tensed and she let out a loud screeching cry. Jennifer answered that she would look at the work a bit later and suggested he show it to me (the observer). He did so a little grudgingly but soon warmed up when I showed interest in what he was learning. Jennifer held Laura closer to her tummy but she continued to protest vigorously. She began to thrash about and I found her cries heart-rending. Sighing, Jennifer said she would have to try a feed and she put Laura to the breast. I was struck by the ease and confidence with which she lifted and turned Laura into position, explaining to her baby what she was doing. I could not see the baby's face now, but I could hear hungry sucking. I thought how lucky Laura was to have this mother and what a good-natured baby she seemed to be. Jennifer stroked Laura's face as she fed. She commented that Laura was growing up already. She sounded a little sad as she said that the baby days are over very quickly.

11 Weeks Old

As we went into the hall, there was a definite sound from upstairs and Jennifer said. 'Yes, it's her.' She called out, 'Oh poor Laura. Poor thing. Did you think I'd forgotten you?' We went into her room and saw that the baby was looking reproachfully towards the door. Her hair was tousled and face blotchy from being rubbed on the sheet. She looked offended as she continued to grumble but was immediately quiet in her mother's arms. I felt she gave me a hostile glance but maybe that was my imagination. Jennifer asked, 'Are you hungry? Is that the problem? Are you a hungry girl? Let's go downstairs and have a feed.'

Downstairs, she talked to Laura about the busy day they had had and put her to the right breast. She apologised as she pushed the nipple too energetically towards her. 'Whoops, sorry, didn't mean to choke you.' Laura began to suck hungrily, cheeks moving in and out. Jennifer was quiet for a few minutes, stroking her baby's cheek and hair and tracing the outline of her ear. After a while, she seemed to remember I was there and asked me a question. Laura immediately took her mouth from the breast and looked over at me. Her face crumpled. Jennifer moved her to the other side. I was struck by how actively Laura seemed to be searching for the nipple with her hands as well as with her mouth.

13 Weeks Old

Laura looked a little uncertain as the spoon approached her mouth, but she allowed the food to be slipped in. As she worked the banana around her mouth, a look of surprise and pleasure spread across her face. After this, her mouth became very active every time the spoon came near, working as if at the nipple. She smiled at her mother and smiled again in response to our amused laughter.

34 Weeks Old

As Jennifer busied herself with supper, I watched Laura playing under the baby-gym in the middle of the carpet. I was thinking about the various stages I had seen her go through with this toy. She was now sitting steadily, looking into the mirror which dangled from one of the straps. She reached out to the various hanging toys, bringing one and then another to her mouth and chewing thoughtfully, looking slightly put out each time one slipped from her grasp. She then allowed the toys to swing freely, watching them intently and hitting them to make them swing all the more. She looked towards the kitchen area whenever her mother spoke and then at me when I replied . . . but when we were quiet, she looked back at what she was doing in her play.

These four brief extracts from a student's notes illustrate something of a healthy baby's development in a busy family home. Laura has a mother who has a lot to juggle, but is confident that she can make sufficient space in her day and in her mind for her new baby. The extracts include clear examples of what Bion would call maternal containment [6]. The baby is welcomed by the family but, as Jennifer said during one observation, 'the third baby just has to fit in'. Laura's brothers, particularly the younger of the two, were often resentful at having to make space for a sister, but they did so, most of the time, with the sensitive support of their mother and probably their father. (He was not present during the observations.) Laura was prioritised in those early weeks and months, but there were increasingly significant periods of time when she had to wait; watching and listening to what was going on around her. She had had plenty of experience of being in intimate interaction with her mother and did seem able to get to a point quite quickly in which she had internalised a sense of security. In the final two extracts we see a little girl who is able to welcome new experiences; she is learning new things and is developing new skills.

It should be said that Laura was clearly a rewarding child to care for. She gave her mother and the rest of the family lots of positive feedback. Not all babies are so responsive and, where they are more difficult to look after, a negative feedback cycle can very easily become established. It is also the case that not all families are able to hold together in the way described above.

The observation extracts also illustrate some of the ways in which the student had to adjust to this new and unusual task. As well as the ordinary challenges involved in dividing her attention between the baby, the mother and the brother, she comments on feeling that Laura looked at her with hostility on one occasion and a bit later that she felt the baby's cries to be 'heart rending'. She seemed to feel a degree of admiration for Jennifer which was maybe bordering on envy . . . envy of the baby or envy of the mother? Even in a situation in which everything seemed to be going well, the observer was being brought up against some of her own very powerful feelings.

Psychoanalytically Informed Infant Observation in the Perinatal Period

Naturalistic infant observation provides us with a way of looking into the lives of very young babies in order to be able to understand something of what they are making of their experiences. The aim in observation training is to observe a baby in 'ordinary' circumstances. However, over a period of more than 50 years of infant observation practice, it has been possible to recognise some common patterns of behaviours in babies whose care is, for whatever reason, suboptimal. There have been innovative programmes which have integrated observation of babies into a range of services such as in maternity wards, special care baby units, postnatal outpatient clinics, family assessment centres and social worker home visits to looked-after babies.

Winnicott famously said: 'There is no such thing as a baby. There is a baby *and* someone' [13]. This is very often quoted to emphasise the dependent nature of the newborn and to underline the importance of the caregivers. It is also used to promote parent–infant therapeutic work. However, it is essential to recognise that, although dependent for survival and for relationships on others, the baby is a distinct individual with a separate and different mind. Very early in life whatever the external circumstances, there is also 'somebody' in the mind of the baby, an internalised representation of the external caregiver, which will influence his responses to what is on offer in the external world.

Young babies have a limited repertoire at their disposal with which to communicate when they are in difficulty. Common 'symptoms' include sleeplessness, crying, feeding difficulties, vomiting, etc. All babies can have a bout of one or more of these but when any become severe or chronic in a baby whose physical health is otherwise good, it is very likely to be a sign of something not working well in their primary relationship. Babies sometimes get a label of 'difficult' when they are actually responding to a mother who is anxious, intrusive or who simply mistimes her attempts to soothe them. Babies may be observed to arch away from an intrusive mother, clench their fists and feet as they anticipate an approach, close their eyes and mouth when the mother's face comes too close and so on. A little later in babyhood, infants may seek to bite, scratch, poke at eyes, pull hair and kick out in 'self-defence'.

Less obvious perhaps, is the baby who does not alert adults through behaviours of this kind but who simply withdraws from contact. We have been able, over time, to recognise that the baby who is described as 'a good baby' may or may not be thriving. A baby who makes no demands, who sleeps too much or rarely cries, is as worrying as one who sleeps or cries incessantly. Babies who are neglected or who are maltreated *should* protest but we know that many give up, sometimes very quickly and fall into states of withdrawal or even of despair. This may begin as a way of not making demands on a troubled mother or may be a self-protective manoeuvre in the face of a volatile parent, but it can all too easily become a way of being.

Being aware of the baby's experience is everybody's responsibility. Awareness of this kind requires a willingness to observe; not just to look with our eyes but to be curious about what we see and to be open to what may be the complex emotional experiences of the baby. Is the baby responsive to his mother? Does he avoid eye contact or seek it out? Does he startle at sudden noises? Does he freeze? Are his hands relaxed or does he clench his fists? What is his response to being touched? Is it possible to engage him in a lively exchange? Does he switch off and turn away? Does he seem to be responsive to his father or other family members? How does he respond to strangers? The behavioural responses in a very small baby are not necessarily obvious. Taking the time to notice small signals which occur repeatedly, and which are outside what might normally be expected in a baby of a particular age and stage of development, is very important. These signals include:

- sleeplessness or oversleeping
- crying incessantly and inconsolably
- overeating or poor appetite
- vomiting
- arching away
- wincing when spoken to or when being touched
- pulling feet away from contact or flapping at a hand which is trying to stroke his face
- shuddering, kicking and waving arms agitatedly
- startled response to noises
- clenching fists and tensing whole body
- avoiding eye contact
- going blank . . . dissociating
- staring at a fixed object
- blank response to smiles and cooing
- little or no crying
- yawning

Selma Fraiberg and her colleagues wrote persuasively about 'ghosts in the nursery'; that is, intruders from the mother's past which can have a significant effect on a woman's ability to parent her baby [14]. These 'ghosts' may have a transient and largely unconscious impact on the experience of becoming a parent. Mothers and fathers often express surprise at finding themselves repeating patterns which they recognise as coming from their own experience of being parented. Usually, the 'ghosts' do not impact negatively on the mother–infant relationship, as the baby imposes himself on the relationship and the mother discovers her own parental capacities. However, for some parents, the 'intruders' remain unconscious and they do not realise that they are acting according to unresolved, internalised patterns of behaviour.

For the purposes of thinking about the longer-term effects of negative early experience, I am focusing on broad descriptions of disturbance in the mother–infant relationship, where infant observation practice can help to understand the baby's experience, which in turn, can inform decisions about intervention. Neglect, intrusiveness and unpredictability are broad headings and are not attached to any one psychiatric diagnosis in the mother or caregiver.

Emotional Neglect

We know that babies need what Colwyn Trevarthen (in Alvarez 1992) called 'live company' [15]. Anne Alvarez, child psychotherapist, chose this phrase as the title of her influential book in which she argues cogently for active parenting. She also linked this to ideas about a more active child psychotherapy technique in cases where there is developmental delay or withdrawal in child patients. She writes about the importance of a way of talking to babies and the risks of failing to go in pursuit of the 'withdrawn' or 'undrawn' infant. She describes 'claiming' the baby and about 'reclamation' of a baby who has withdrawn.

The concept of neglect as observed between mothers and their infants, in this context, refers to a level of self-preoccupation in the mother which means that she is simply unable to prioritise her baby, and the baby is left to find ways of holding himself together while he waits for brief moments of contact; both physical and emotional. Like the baby faced with a severely depressed mother, the neglected baby may also give up and withdraw.

An observation of 7-month-old Kylie provides a vivid example of this kind of withdrawal [16]. Kylie was in a placement with a foster carer who delivered her to the family centre as if she were a parcel. Kylie slept through the morning, apparently oblivious of the crowd of noisy children all around her. She accepted a bottle at lunchtime but showed no enthusiasm for it; she simply sucked on the teat until the bottle was empty. The following is an account of the author's attempt to make a connection with her.

I placed Kylie on her tummy on a blanket and got down on the floor so as to be alongside her and within her view. She made one attempt to lift her head and there was a slight twist in her torso such that I thought she might be trying to turn over. I made encouraging sounds but she soon flopped her head onto the floor and remained very still, showing no response to my voice. I turned her onto her back, and she seemed more comfortable. However, she did not meet my gaze as I spoke to her and her head remained in the mid-line regardless of what was going on on either side of her. She showed no reaction to sound or to movement. When I put a toy in her hand, she held it for a moment, but it quickly slipped from her grasp. I concentrated on trying to make contact and talked to her in a lively way, moving my hands and taking hold of hers to clap them together as I sang to her softly. Eventually we made eye contact and I felt hugely rewarded and redoubled my efforts to maintain contact with her. I tickled her tummy and her mouth moved in what I thought was the beginning of a smile or a giggle. I put the toy in her hand, and she held it, making faint gurgling sounds. There was a knock at the door, and I looked up. When I looked back seconds later, she had switched off and was staring blankly.

Kylie did not have organic brain damage, nor was she given a diagnosis of autism when she was older. A very determined long-term foster carer took her on and set about what she described as 'helping her come out of herself'. She was developmentally delayed at 3 years old but was not out of reach.

Kylie certainly needed her new carer to 'reclaim' her. She had retreated into a very remote place. Her early weeks had been spent in a household where her mother had neglected her physical care and had not paid her any attention. It appeared that by the time she was removed from home and placed in foster care, she had all but given up hope of there being anybody who would really be interested in her. There are, of course, babies whose retreat is much less extreme and others who cannot be reached. Some learn not to make demands on their parents when the signals are that the adults will respond with hostility or are emotionally preoccupied and unavailable. Babies are, of course, very different one from another. Each has a unique set of attributes and characteristics, as well as a unique inter-uterine and birth experience.

Lynne Murray, Peter Cooper and associates focused some of their early research on the effect of diagnosed maternal depression on infants [17, 18]. They were able to demonstrate the way in which some babies do their utmost to engage their mothers' attention while others give up and turn away. Even where the depressed mother is trying to keep up her care of the baby, the unconscious communication will be one of lifelessness; absence of curiosity, joy or lively welcome for the baby. The researchers concluded that the children of severely depressed mothers were more likely to fail to meet their milestones and to struggle in nursery [19].

Intrusiveness and Unpredictability

As well as needing lively stimulation, babies need peace and quiet in which to take in and digest their experience and gradually to manage being alone for periods of time. In ordinary infant observations, observers can see the moments when the baby naturally takes a rest from intense interaction; even from those which have been pleasurable. For example, watching a baby playing a rudimentary version of peek-a-boo, there is usually a point at which the baby has 'had enough' and will pause the game. After a moment's respite, they may come back and pick it up again. They rely on the adults to notice these moments and to be willing to wait for the restart of play. Mentally unwell mothers cannot read these nuanced signals, or they may take the baby's withdrawal as a rejection. In other words, they do not hold on to a realistic picture of their actual baby. Instead, they attribute all kinds of characteristics to the baby which have to do with their own state of mind and feeling states. The baby in the worst of circumstances gets very little respite from these projections. The mother may attribute motives to him which are unrealistic or way beyond his developmental stage; for example, a mother may see her baby as being deliberately selfish or full of hate, reflecting her underlying disorder.

The following extract from an observation of a mother, Julie, with her 7-month-old son, Billy, may serve to further illustrate this unconscious dynamic. It is possible to see the way in which Billy struggles to get away from his mother's intrusiveness.

Julie sat down with her baby in her arms. Both mother and baby looked uncomfortable. Billy was wriggling as if he wanted to get off his mother's lap. The more he struggled, the more she held on tightly. She decided he was hungry and put him on the floor while she fetched his bottle. On her return with the bottle of milk, she scooped him up with no words and plonked him back on her lap. He twisted his head this way and that to avoid the bottle. He struggled for a moment longer and then gagged momentarily as she pushed the teat into his mouth. He managed to adjust his hold on the teat and made a half-hearted attempt to suck. Milk was pouring down his front and Julie wiped at it with a cloth. 'Why are you being like this?' she asked. 'You know mummy loves you.' Billy let go of the teat, turned his head from side to side and arched away. Julie rubbed her face into Billy's face making a 'yum, yum' noise before trying to push the teat back into his mouth. When he twisted away, she grabbed his feet and began to open and close his legs rhythmically, humming a tune as she did so. Suddenly, she gave up. 'OK then,' she said, 'have it your way.' She plonked him on the floor again and turned to look at her phone. He did not look at all surprised or distressed.

Babies who do not give in to despair sometimes seem to learn about what Selma Fraiberg called a sadomasochistic way of relating [14]. The following is an interaction between a mother and her 6-month-old son, Tyrone, as observed by a health visitor at a home visit.

Tyrone snatched at his mother's mobile phone and his mother snatched it back immediately, pushing his hands away and snapping at him, 'Don't snatch. It's rude.' She held it out of reach above her head and said triumphantly that it was hers. A moment later, she lowered her arm and he grabbed at it again. 'Do you want to make a call?' She lifted it out of reach again, grinning. She then gave it to him, but after just a moment, complained that he would drop it and break it and she snatched it back again. He kicked and flapped his arms in frustration.

One could see the way in which this kind of interaction could become entrenched with Tyrone's mother being unable to pause for a moment to wonder why her phone was such an attractive (and provocative) item for Tyrone. Even young babies can develop a habit of retaliating or getting in first with an attack. A few months later, Tyrone and his mother were observed in an escalating tickling game in which Tyrone was observed to grin as he dug his fingernails into his mother's face.

Fraiberg offers a detailed example of a baby who became caught up in this kind of dynamic in his relationship with his mother [14]. Sixteen-year-old Annie, baby Greg and father Earl, were given a great deal of professional support from a parent–infant psychotherapist. Annie's own history was such that it sometimes seemed that good enough mothering would never be a possibility for her. Her own childhood had been blighted by cruelty. Over a long period of time, things improved for this young family but there were elements in Greg's development which were of concern. One observation, when Greg was 16 months old, describes the way in which Annie struggled to manage when Greg became fractious or had mishaps. She would become 'strident and scary'. Greg would register this and then grin and giggle in a manic way. Annie had described this kind of manic response as having been her way of coping as a child and Fraiberg suggests that it was perhaps a result of an unresolved identification with the aggressor.

Unpredictable parenting can have a significant effect on a baby's development in the early months and years. Babies who never know which version of their parent they are going to get have to develop all kinds of ways of protecting themselves against shocks. This kind of relationship is characterised by sudden changes of mood in the parent; for example, tenderness giving way to hostility with no warning. In this kind of interaction, the babies, at best, live with a constant ebb and flow of hope and disappointment. At worst, they have to be constantly on the alert for that moment when their mother's mood and behaviour changes.

These kinds of observations are borne out by more recent scientific evidence. Schore suggests that the '[s]till forming neural pathways are flooded with internal chemical reactions to stress, threat and trauma' [20]. Cirulli et al. point out the possible long-term effects: 'The longer and more often an infant is left alone in a dysregulated, dissociated or hyper-aroused state, the more enduring the damaging, biochemical consequences for the developing brain' [21]. In this way, they may succeed in the short term, in protecting themselves, but there is the risk that this manoeuvre becomes entrenched and is carried forward into relationships with other carers, and later with teachers. There is evidence that this kind of hyperarousal in infancy can lead to impairments of thinking, decision-making and planning as well as to difficulties with interpersonal relationships [22].

Infant Observation in Perinatal Mental Health Services

This brings us back to the question as to why it is that so many people cling to an idea that babies are resilient and have minimal needs in the first few months of life. It is perhaps intolerable to think that damage can be done so early in life and can be done by mothers whose conscious wish is to do the very best for their child. Watching mothers and babies in 'ordinary' circumstances is enjoyable and life-affirming. Watching a struggling mother with a struggling baby can be acutely painful. This is particularly challenging for those working in perinatal mental health services when the needs of the mentally unwell mother are so present and compelling. Noticing that a baby is not doing well also means having to consider what can be done to improve matters.

Where an assessment is made that a mother might actively wish to harm her baby, protective measures are put in place. For the most part, babies are moved out of the reach and sole care of mothers who are judged as being intent on hurting them and contact between the two is carefully monitored and supervised. However, such protective measures are never absolutely fail-safe, and disasters do sometimes occur where mothers impulsively hurt their babies; often whilst reassuring themselves and the professionals that this is the one thing they will not do.

It is also important to observe the baby in less extreme circumstances, when mothers are struggling with unexpected postnatal mood changes or have long-term mental illness or personality difficulties, which affect their maternal function. An experience of doing an infant observation as part of a training course, as described in the early part of this chapter, sharpens awareness of the baby and provides a framework for understanding what may be being communicated by infants as well as by their mothers. Some services benefit from having members of staff, trained in infant observation, who can conduct observations themselves, or be available to discuss the observations of colleagues or family members. However, being curious and taking note of the baby should be a part of the normal practice of all perinatal professionals, whether working in community-based services, hospitals or Mother and Baby Units. Whilst it is important to guard against overdeterministic assumptions about negative early experience, reflecting on what one observes and talking to colleagues when one is concerned or puzzled, is an essential part of good practice.

Infant Observation as Intervention

If a mother is emotionally unavailable, there may be a need for somebody else to spend time with the baby, to offer the kind of companionship which babies need alongside food, shelter and protection. There may be a need to talk explicitly with the father, a partner, a grandparent or another relative about the need to make a lively relationship with the baby whilst the mother receives treatment. If this resource is not available within the family, the task of spending time with the baby may fall to a member of staff, a professional or to a volunteer. The task of spending time and interacting with the baby does not require particular training. It is about keeping the baby company, being friendly and curious and working hard to maintain a connection when the baby appears to switch off too readily or drift away from contact. The capacity for play and playfulness begins in the very first few days of life and the importance of laying these foundations cannot be overemphasised. There are circumstances in which the recovery of the mother is too slow for the baby and something else may need to happen in the interim.

One of the objections to professionals or volunteers stepping in to make a relationship with a baby has always been that it can undermine the confidence of the mother. When a woman who is ill or feeling guilty and inadequate is faced with somebody who makes it look easy, she can feel very undermined. However, if an intervention in the early stages is restricted to observation rather than parenting skills training or parent–infant psychotherapy, this can be effective and less persecuting. Being interested in the baby and sharing that interest with his mother can be supportive for both mother *and* baby. It may be possible to set this up in a fairly formal way with regular, predictable time spent with mother and baby, observing rather than intervening.

One of the most common misconceptions is that when a mother's mental health improves, the baby will immediately benefit. The benefits of having a psychologically healthy mother are unquestionable, but if a baby has experienced a very difficult start, without the support of having relationships with alternative attachment figures, it is likely that the mother–baby relationship will need time and additional support to develop and recover.

Summary

Infant observation can make an important contribution in enabling professionals to keep the baby's needs in mind, alongside those of an unwell mother or struggling family. Babies have needs which go beyond physical care and protection. They need to feel welcomed into the world and drawn into relationships with significant adults who can prioritise them. They need repeated and consistent experiences of friendly, lively, playful interaction as well as needing to feel loved and understood when they are experiencing discomfort, fear and frustration. Without this in the early weeks and months, babies may be ill-equipped to deal with later challenges, even the relatively ordinary ones of separation and transition into a wider social world.

References

1. G Music. *Nurturing natures: attachment and children's emotional, sociocultural and brain development.* London: Routledge; 2016.
2. D Poulin-Dubois. Infants' distinction between animate and inanimate objects: the origins of naive psychology. In: P Rochat, editor. *Early social cognition.* Mahwah, NJ: Erlbaum; 1999. p. 257–80.
3. DW Winnicott. The world in small doses. In: DW Winnicott. *The child, the family, and the outside world.* London: Penguin; 1957. p. 69–74.
4. DW Winnicott. *Playing and reality.* London: Penguin; 1971.
5. J Hopkins. The dangers and deprivations of too-good mothering. *J Child Psychother.* 1996;22(3):407–22.
6. WR Bion. The psycho-analytic study of thinking. *Int J Psychoanal.* 1962;43:306–10.
7. M Klein. Notes on some schizoid mechanisms. *Int J Psychoanal.* 1946;27:99–110.
8. E Bick. Notes on infant observation in psycho-analytic training. *Int J Psychoanal.* 1964;45:558–66.
9. AN Meltzoff. Imitation, objects, tools, and the rudiments of language in human ontogeny. *Human Evol.* 1988;3(1–2):45–64.
10. K Karmiloff, A Karmiloff-Smith. *Everything your baby would ask: if only babies could talk.* London: Firefly Books; 2004.
11. L Miller, M Rustin, M Rustin, J Shuttleworth. *Closely observed infants.* London: Karnac; 1989.
12. B Youell. The impact of the global financial crisis on children and families as seen through infant observations in three European countries: the role of education professionals in containing anxiety and holding on to hope and hopefulness. *Infant Obs.* 2015;18(2):154–66.

13. DW Winnicott. The theory of the parent-infant relationship. *Int J Psychoanal.* 1960;41:585–95.

14. S Fraiberg, E Adelson, V Shapiro. Ghosts in the nursery: a psychoanalytic approach to the problems of impaired infant–mother relationships 1. In: J Raphael-Leff, editor. *Parent-infant psychodynamics: wild things, mirrors and ghosts.* London: Routledge; 2018. p. 87–117.

15. A Alvarez. *Live company: psychoanalytic psychotherapy with autistic, borderline, deprived and abused children.* London: Routledge; 1992.

16. B Youell. Observation in social work practice. In: M Bower, editor. *Psychoanalytic theory for social work practice: thinking under fire.* London: Routledge; 2004. p. 49–60.

17. L Murray, A Fiori-Cowley, R Hooper, P Cooper. The impact of postnatal depression and associated adversity on early mother-infant interactions and later infant outcome. *Child Dev.* 1996;67(5):2512–26.

18. L Murray, A Arteche, P Fearon, S Halligan, T Croudace, P Cooper. The effects of maternal postnatal depression and child sex on academic performance at age 16 years: a developmental approach. *J Child Psychol Psychiatry.* 2010;51(10):1150–9.

19, L Murray, PJ Cooper. Effects of postnatal depression on infant development. *Arch Dis Childhood.* 1997;77(2):99–101.

20. AN Schore. *Affect regulation and the origin of the self: the neurobiology of emotional development.* London: Routledge; 2015.

21. F Cirulli, N Francia, A Berry, L Aloe, E Alleva, SJ Suomi. Early life stress as a risk factor for mental health: role of neurotrophins from rodents to non-human primates. *Neurosci Biobehav Rev.* 2009;33(4):573–85.

22. BD Perry, RA Pollard, TL Blakley, WL Baker, D Vigilante. Childhood trauma, the neurobiology of adaptation, and 'use-dependent' development of the brain: how 'states' become 'traits'. *Infant Ment Health J.* 1995;16(4):271–91.

Chapter 35

Mother–Infant Focused Interventions

What Works to Improve the Mother–Infant Relationship?

Jane Barlow

Introduction

The postnatal period is now recognised to be a significant time in terms of the impact of the environment on the developing infant, due in large part to the fact that this is a sensitive developmental period, in particular in terms of the infant's emotion regulation and wider neurological development. Specifically, parents play a key role in helping the infant to begin to regulate themselves – known as the 'dyadic regulation of affect' – and in the development of neuronal pathways. Maternal mental health problems in the postnatal period have been identified as a factor affecting the ability of the mother to interact with her baby, and thereby as having a potential impact on both the short- and long-term development of the child.

This chapter will present the most recent evidence concerning the ways in which a range of maternal postnatal mental health problems can have an impact on the interaction, in addition to some of the tools that have been developed to identify dyads where the interaction has been adversely affected. The chapter will conclude by describing some of the key dyadic interventions currently available, in addition to the evidence supporting their use.

Dyadic Regulation of Infant Affect

One of the key developmental activities of infancy is the baby's growing ability to regulate their affective states, and it is the interaction with key caretakers that enables this to take place. Infants have a range of self-organising neurobehavioral capacities but are on the whole highly dependent on their caregiver to help them to regulate their internal states [1]. It is now recognised that this is done through reciprocal interactions with attachment figures [2], and that this is a key developmental task in the first year of life leading to the infant being either securely or insecurely attached [3]. Securely attached infants have received caregiving that meets their needs in a sensitive and timely way, and who as a consequence have developed trust in their caregiver and a sense of themselves as being lovable and having agency. Infants who receive caregiving that is either intrusive or erratic/dismissive on the other hand are likely to be insecurely attached (i.e. known as insecure avoidant and insecure anxious/ambivalent respectively). These children have less trust in their caregivers to meet their needs and adopt defensive strategies aimed at securing the parenting they need; children who are avoidant downregulate their emotional state and do not show their distress while children who are anxious/ambivalent upregulate their emotional state and appear demanding. Children exposed to frightening or severely erratic parenting behaviours (see the What Characterises Severely Suboptimal Parent–Infant Interaction? section below) are likely to be categorised as 'disorganised'. Longitudinal studies show that children who are securely attached have more optimal outcomes across all developmental domains [4], while children who are insecure or disorganised have less optimal outcomes, including externalising disorders [5], dissociation [6], post-traumatic stress disorder (PTSD) [7] and personality disorder [8].

Based on the use of a range of microanalytic observations of parent–infant interaction [9, 10], infant mental health researchers have highlighted the importance for attachment security of the moment-to-moment interactions, in which parents observe infant cues and respond contingently to them. Parenting that is sensitive and attuned is an important part of such 'contingent' interaction, in terms of enabling infants to become securely attached to their primary caregiver [11]. Research has also highlighted the importance of 'midrange' interaction, which is characterised by parent interaction that is neither too intrusive nor too passive (i.e. optimally in the midrange) [9]. Dyadic interaction that is consistently outside the midrange is associated with insecure and disorganised attachment [9]. There is also evidence to suggest that maternal sensitivity has an impact on specific aspects of neurodevelopment [12], as well as on cognition and language development [13].

Other aspects of early parenting have also been identified as being important. For example, the term 'reflective function' refers to a parent's capacity to treat their infant as an intentional being rather than simply viewing them in terms of physical characteristics or behaviour [14]. Such reflective functioning (RF) has been shown to be associated with positive maternal parenting behaviours such as flexibility and responsiveness, and use of the mother as a secure base on the part of the infant, while low RF has been found to be associated with emotionally unresponsive maternal behaviours such as withdrawal, hostility and intrusiveness [15]. Similarly, the term 'mind-minded' refers to a mother's ability to treat her infant as an individual with a mind. Parental mind-minded comments during interaction with 6-month-old infants have been shown to be significantly correlated with behavioural sensitivity and interactive synchrony, and are a better predictor of attachment security at 1 year than maternal behavioural sensitivity [16, 17].

What Characterises Severely Suboptimal Parent–Infant Interaction?

In addition to what is now known about the type of interaction that is necessary for optimal development, a number of aspects of parent–infant interaction have been identified as playing a significant role in derailing the development of children, particularly in terms of their attachment organisation. 'Fr-behaviour' refers to parent–infant interaction that is both frightened and frightening. Such behaviours can be subtle (e.g. periods of being dazed and unresponsive) or more overt (deliberately frightening children) [18], also known as hostile–helpless states of mind [19]. Fr-behaviours are distinct from neglect and express a distorted image of the child and are often a result of the parents' unresolved trauma and losses [18].

More recent research has suggested that such hostile and helpless states of mind are part of a broader context of disrupted affective communication between parent and infant. This research highlights the importance of 'atypical' or 'anomalous' parenting behaviours that consist of parental withdrawing responses (i.e. maternal behaviours that are rejecting of the infant); negative-intrusive responses (i.e. where the parent is mocking or pulls at part of the infant's body); role-confused responses (i.e. where the mother seeks attention from the infant to meet her own emotional needs); disoriented responses (i.e. the mother adopts a frightened expression or has a sudden complete loss of affect) and affective communication errors (i.e. in which the mother might be positive while the infant is distressed) [20].

There is a strong association between such 'atypical' or 'anomalous' parent–infant interactions at 12–18 months and disorganised attachment, which is highly stable and associated with wide-ranging psychopathology in childhood [21].

Impact of Parental Mental Health Problems on the Interaction

There is now extensive evidence in terms of the potential impact of maternal mental health problems on the interaction between the mother and baby. Overall, this body of research suggests that all mental health problems, irrespective of how common or severe they may be, have the potential to have a negative impact on the interaction, although there is currently little research indicating the proportion of dyads in which the interaction may be affected or the factors that contribute to it being affected (see the Assessing the Interaction section for further detail).

Depression is possibly one of the most common perinatal mental health problems, being experienced by as many as 15% of new mothers. Evidence from a recent meta-analysis that quantified the magnitude of the association between such depression and maternal sensitivity, the latter being defined as contingent and appropriate responding to infant cues, found an effect size of −0.35 for studies that involved a control group [22]. For example, research suggests that postnatal depression (PND) can result in the mother being less sensitively attuned to her infant and less affirming and more negating of infant experience [23]. There is, in addition, evidence about the impact on the development of infants who have experienced interaction that is affected by depression, including deficits in their interpersonal functioning such as less affective sharing, lower rates of interactive behaviour, poorer concentration, increased negative responses with strangers and reduced secure attachment at 12 and 18 months [24, 25, 26]. Longitudinal research shows an impact on cognitive [27] and emotional development [28], with 42% of such children being more likely to experience depression by age 16 [29]. There is evidence to suggest that subclinical depressive symptoms may also influence the mothers' affective facial expression during early face-to-face interactions with their infant [30].

Although research about the impact of anxiety on the interaction is limited, the findings appear to be similarly negative in terms of both the interaction and the attachment status of the infant. Evidence from one study that examined the characteristics of interactions that are 'anxious' (i.e. as opposed to the mothers having been diagnosed with anxiety) identified the presence of interactive contingencies that are both heightened (vigilant) in some modalities and lowered (withdrawn) in others [4]. For example, this study based on micro-analysis of interaction found that interactive contingency patterns in mothers having anxious interactions were characterised by intermodal discrepancies or confusing forms of communication across different systems such that 'mothers vigilantly monitored infants visually, but withdrew from contingently coordinating with infants emotionally, as if mothers were "looking through" them' [4]. The evidence also suggests that the impact of this type of interaction on the infant is an increased likelihood of an insecure or disorganised attachment [9]. Chronic maternal physiological stress, as indicated by raised cortisol levels, was also found in one study to be related to infant cortisol levels, with evidence of more intrusive and lower positive engagement synchrony in the infant, suggesting that maternal stress may contribute to upregulating the infants' developing stress system [31]. The evidence in relation to PTSD is, however, inconsistent in relation to maternal interactional behaviour, possibly reflecting methodological limitations in the studies including the use of self-report measures [32].

Research on mothers with eating disorders is limited to one study, which found that this group of women were likely to be involved in major episodes of mealtime conflict with their infants. Interactional difficulties included poor detection and responsiveness to infants' signals, and difficulty in allowing their infants to express age-appropriate needs for autonomy through self-feeding and experimentation with food [33].

There is also evidence to suggest that more severe mental health problems such as borderline personality disorder (BPD) can affect the interaction. One review found that BPD was associated with an increased prevalence of interactional difficulties with one included study showing evidence of less structuring in mothers' interactions with their infants, and their infants being less attentive, less interested and less eager to interact with their mother [34]. Other included studies found disrupted communication, frightened and disoriented behaviours [35], impaired sensitivity [36] and increased intrusiveness [37]. One qualitative study found that some mothers with BPD reported being less satisfied, less competent and more distressed [38]. A recent study also found that, by 3 months postpartum, infants of mothers with BPD are more likely to be developing dyadic adaptive mechanisms to dysfunctional interactions through self-regulatory mechanisms that may differ according to gender [39], and another study found that more babies of mothers with BPD show signs of a disinhibited attachment behaviour compared with mothers who are depressed or have no diagnosis [40].

The evidence with regard to parents with a history of psychosis also suggests interactional changes, the findings of a recent meta-analysis indicating evidence of disturbed maternal behaviour, and more limited evidence of disturbances in infant behaviour and mutuality of interaction [41]. For example, a number of studies have found that the interaction is less responsive and sensitive, and more remote, intrusive and self-absorbed than their counterparts with affective disorders [42, 43, 44, 45]. A second systematic review found that outcomes, both direct (i.e. interaction) and indirect (i.e. involvement of social services), are affected by the nature of the psychosis (i.e. acute versus chronic) [46], and one further study found that interaction may be partially mediated by the level of cognitive function [47].

Overall, this evidence suggests that mental health problems in the postnatal period can have a significant impact on the interaction and thereby the importance of assessing whether it has been affected.

Assessing the Interaction

Not all women who experience perinatal mental health problems show signs of interactional problems, and very little is currently known about the specific factors that influence whether the interaction is adversely affected. Likely risk factors include poverty, low social support, cognitive function [47] and chronicity of the condition [46], affect regulation [48] and low reflective functioning [49] or capacity for Theory of Mind [50]. This points to the importance of the interaction with the infant being assessed by mental health clinicians in all mothers who are experiencing mental health problems, and a range of tools have been developed for this purpose.

The Royal College of Psychiatrists (2019) Framework for Routine Outcomes Measures in Perinatal Psychiatry [51] identified a number of clinically useful methods of assessing the interaction between the parent and infant. Clinician-rated outcome measures (CROMS) of the interaction include the Parent–Infant Interaction Observation Scale [52], which has been designed as a screening tool for use by frontline practitioners such as health visitors and social workers, and comprises a 13-item scale that can be used to code a 3-minute observation of interaction. The tool involves three levels of classification – no problems; some problems; and significant problems – and can be used as part of the Healthy Child Programme [53] with feedback to the parent being built into a 1-hour video feedback session, preparation for which is provided as part of the training to use the tool. Two other tools that were identified as being potentially useful are the National Institute of Child Health and Human Development study of early childcare mother–infant interaction scales [54] and the CARE-Index [55].

Patient-reported outcome measures (PROMS) of the parent–infant relationship that might be used to assess relational issues include the Postpartum Bonding Questionnaire [56] which is 25 items long and the Brief Mother–Infant Interaction Scale which is a 7-item scale measuring the mother's perceptions about the interaction, and was designed for use on Mother and Baby Units (MBUs). The Mother–Object Relationship Scale – Short Form [57] is only 7 items long and measures the mother's representations about the baby.

One of the concerns about the use of PROMS on their own (i.e. without the additional use of at least one CROM), however, is that some parents do not have insight about the ways in which their relationship with the baby has been affected by their mental health. As such, it is strongly recommended that PROMs are only used alongside a CROM.

Dyadic Models of Working

One of the key features of interventions that are provided to women (with or without mental health problems) who are experiencing interactional problems is that they are dyadic. Unlike interventions in which the mental health profession simply has the baby present in the treatment room, dyadic interventions involve actively intervening with the parent and infant together and some involve what is known as 'in vivo' methods (i.e. live demonstrations).

Dyadic methods are underpinned by a number of theoretical approaches that can be broadly classified as follows: a) psychotherapeutic interventions (e.g. parent–infant psychotherapy); b) mentalisation-based treatments (e.g. Minding the Baby (MTB) and the Mothers and Toddlers Programme (MTP)); c) sensitivity-based interventions, both individual (e.g. Videotape Feedback Intervention to Promote Positive Parenting and Sensitive Discipline (VIPP SD) and Video Interaction Guidance (VIG)) and group-based (e.g. infant massage and Circle of Security); and d) eclectic approaches underpinned by a range of theories such as behavioural and attachment (e.g. Mellow Babies).

The above programmes are on the whole delivered for limited periods of time (up to 20 weeks) in a range of both home and clinical settings, and by a range of practitioners (e.g. psychologists, health visitors, nursery nurses, social workers, family support workers, etc) who have received additional training and who usually receive ongoing supervision.

A majority of dyadic interventions are explicitly aimed at improving the interaction between the mother and baby, although a number of them aim to do this by improving aspects of the mother's functioning such as affect regulation. The different underpinning theories of change can be classified in term of the primary 'ports of entry' through which a programme is used to bring about change.

Ports of Entry

Ports of entry was the term originally used by Stern (1995) [58, 59] to describe the five entry points that could be used within psychotherapy to bring about change, but it is being used here to depict and classify interventions in terms of the primacy of one or more port of entry, and thereby the potential reach or complexity of the intervention.

Figure 35.1 depicts some of the different ports of entry in terms of whether they involve the baby, mother or therapist, and whether they target actions/behaviours or representations. The primacy in terms of the port of entry in the current formulation is driven explicitly by the underpinning theory of change (e.g. where the primary focus is in terms of what the programme targets, such as behaviour or maternal representations). However, some interventions provide the therapist with skills and techniques that enable them to move across different ports depending on the presenting clinical material.

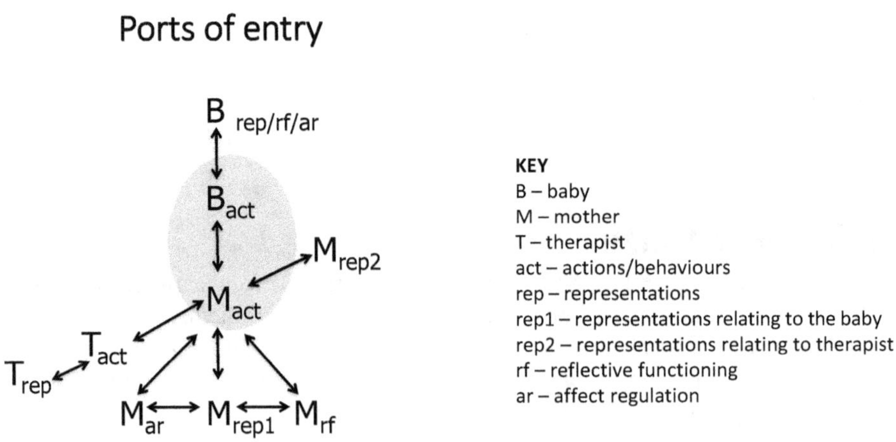

Figure 35.1 Ports of entry.

Single Port of Entry Interventions

A behavioural intervention such as infant massage focuses primarily on one port of entry (i.e. the mother's actions or sensitivity to her infant's cues), with the aim of improving her responsiveness through the teaching of massage strokes that are attuned to the infant's needs in the moment. Infant massage classes do not typically involve the use of other ports of entry but one of the additional outcomes beyond improved sensitivity may be improved maternal mood (e.g. postnatal depression), which appears to be in part a consequence of the opportunity to socialise with other mothers in the group.

The Neonatal Behavioral Assessment Scale (NBAS) or the Newborn Behavioral Observations (NBO) (see section on Sensitivity-Based Approaches for further information) function in a similar way (i.e. through the one port that targets sensitivity by focusing directly on behaviours) but using a slightly different approach to improving such behaviours that focuses on demonstrating to the mother the infant's sensorimotor capabilities.

Dual Port of Entry Interventions

While video feedback has been defined as being behavioural in focus with the port of entry once again being the mother's behaviours towards the infant, it actually involves at least one other port in the sense that the process of watching moments of interaction also involve the guider using probes (e.g. what do you think your baby might be feeling?) that might also improve the mother's reflective functioning. This means that this particular intervention is both more complex and potentially more far-reaching than single port of entry interventions, although there have been no evaluations to date that have explicitly assessed its benefits in terms of maternal reflective functioning.

Multiple Ports of Entry Interventions

Psychotherapeutic approaches are even more complex and comprehensive in the sense that while the focus of the intervention is primarily the mother's internal representations in order to address the 'ghosts in the nursery' (i.e. the way in which the mother's internal world influences her current interactions with her baby), the therapist will utilise a range of different ports of entry as appropriate. For example, the therapist might use the baby's behaviours in the current moment to try to increase the mother's capacity for reflective functioning. This is also one of the few interventions in which the therapist might reflect on their own actions and representations as a port of entry into the mother–baby system in order to bring about change.

Ports of entry can as such be used to conceptualise the focus and complexity of an intervention, and thereby to make clinical decisions about their suitability for particular mother–infant dyads.

What Works for Mothers–Infant Dyads in Which the Interaction Is Affected by Postnatal Mental Health Problems

The final part of this chapter provides a summary from recent updates of the evidence [60, 61] about interventions that have been shown to be effective in terms of the interaction of mother–infant dyads. It should be noted that the chapter explicitly focuses on dyadic interventions (i.e. that target the parent and infant conjointly). Furthermore, while much of the evidence is taken from recent systematic reviews, where possible, reference will be made to studies that have explicitly focused on women with mental health problems. The evidence has been organised in terms of the theoretical underpinning of the intervention.

Sensitivity-Based Approaches

Sensitivity-based approaches typically focus, as their name suggests, on improving the sensitivity of parents, and possibly one of the earliest approaches that has been developed to date is the NBAS [62] or the shorter clinical variation, the NBO. The NBAS, for example, consists of 28 behavioural and reflex items that are demonstrated by a trained practitioner, with the aim of highlighting the infant's unique social-interactive and neurodevelopmental capabilities, including orientation to human voices and other sounds, muscle tone and ability for self-soothing. The aim of this is to increase the parent's awareness of the infant's ability for communication and to promote contingent responsiveness on the part of the parent. There is, however, currently only low-quality evidence to suggest that this improves parental sensitivity in mostly low-risk populations of parents, with the NBO performing better than the NBAS [63].

Possibly one of the most widely used sensitivity-based approaches is infant massage, which is on the whole delivered to groups of parents. As suggested above, this intervention focuses on helping mothers to provide sensitive and timely responses to their infant's cues and signals, through the process of learning how to provide infant massage. The group basis also provides women with the opportunity to obtain support from other women in the group, and most groups provide time to socialise. Despite the existence of numerous systematic reviews, most of which point to the importance of delivering infant massage to targeted groups of women (i.e. experiencing post-natal depression or socio-demographic deprivation), there is only one randomised controlled trial (RCT) to date that explicitly demonstrates that infant massage improves interaction in women with PND [64]. There is also some evidence to suggest that it might improve the mother's mood [65] or depression [66].

Video feedback is the generic term for a more complex method of intervening in terms of ports of entry, comprising a strengths-based approach to supporting parents, that can be delivered using one of the available standardised programmes (e.g. VIPP-SD [67]) or as part of a more flexible model of service provision (e.g. VIG [68]). Both of these approaches involve the use of brief videotaped interactions between the mother and their infants that are then reviewed, with selected moments of positive interaction being discussed with the parent, with the aim of reinforcing sensitive behaviour. These discussions between the guider and parent while watching themselves eliciting a positive response from the baby is also aimed at improving metacognitive functioning in terms of the parent's feelings about themselves as a parent. The conversations can also be used as an opportunity to promote parental reflective functioning as suggested above. The guider aims to model these practices in terms of their relationship with the parent.

As a result of its flexibility, VIG is now being used extensively by a range of practitioners across the UK including health visitors and social workers, and is being delivered as part of the Children and Young Peoples 0–5 Improving Access to Psychological Therapies training programme. It is also being used in specialist perinatal mental health services in the UK.

A systematic review shows that video feedback is effective in improving maternal sensitivity [69] but evidence that it improves children's attachment security has not yet been provided, and there are also few evaluations of effectiveness specifically with mothers experiencing mental health problems. There is, however, some evidence of its potential effectiveness from a number of small one-group evaluations, when delivered to women with severe mental illness receiving inpatient care in MBUs [70, 71].

A group-based version of the use of video feedback is also available. Circle of Security is delivered over the course of 20 sessions of around 90 minutes duration and involves the use of individualised treatment plans based on a brief assessment of the interaction between the parent and child, which is used to identify a set of specific issues that are then addressed in the group, using video feedback guidance. However, there is currently no evidence to date regarding the effectiveness of this programme with parents who have mental health problems, and very limited evidence (i.e. pre- and post-group design) or its effectiveness in improving child outcomes (e.g. attachment) [72].

Mentalisation-Based Approaches

Mentalisation-based approaches are aimed explicitly at improving parental reflective functioning, and two such programmes have now been developed – MTB and MTP [73, 74]. The first is a home-visiting programme for first-time young mothers (aged 14–25 years) who are experiencing a range of problems such as depression, homelessness, poverty or violent relationships. It is designed to increase parental sensitivity and reflective functioning in order to strengthen infant attachment security. The programme comprises weekly home visits from the seventh month of pregnancy until the child is 1 year old, followed by biweekly visits for a year. A qualified nurse and social worker provide developmental guidance, crisis intervention, parenting support and practical support during alternating visits. The nurse provides ongoing help in relation to health and caregiving, while the social worker provides infant and parent mental health services and social services support. Both practitioners receive supervision from highly qualified specialists in either mental health or nursing backgrounds.

Two studies have now been conducted to evaluate the programme's effectiveness – one by Yale University in the US [68] and one by the National Society for the Prevention of Cruelty to Children in the UK [75]. Initial results of the Yale RCT found no significant impact on attachment at 4 months, but at 12 months significantly more babies in the intervention group were securely attached to their mothers compared with the control group, who were significantly more likely to have a disorganised attachment [76]. There was no significant impact on maternal mental health or capacity for reflective functioning. However, the findings of the UK-based version of the programme found limited evidence of effectiveness, and further work needs to be done to address the reasons for this.

The group-based MTP is a 12-week individual psychotherapy intervention that has been used to date with mothers who are substance dependent [68]. As with other psychotherapeutic and attachment-based approaches (see next section on Psychotherapeutic Approaches: Parent–Infant Psychotherapy) the aim is to address the mothers' representations that are based on early life experiences and to increase her capacity for mentalisation (i.e. reflective functioning). The early sessions focus on building a therapeutic alliance and providing help with immediate crises including need for food, housing, health and employment. Subsequent sessions focus on promoting mentalising about both the mothers' behaviour generally and more specifically in relation to the child through the identification of underlying feeling states as well as the way in which such feeling states influence behavior and relationships [68]. Videotaped play sessions are also used in which the therapist preselects specific moments when the mother and child are experiencing emotional synchrony or dysynchrony and the therapist encourages the mother to reflect on the underpinning state of mind.

The results of a small RCT with 47 mothers of infants/toddlers enrolled in substance abuse treatment found evidence of better reflective functioning, and improved representational coherence and sensitivity, and better caregiving behaviour compared with mothers in a parent education group [68], with some maintenance of effect at 6-week follow-up [77].

Psychotherapeutic Approaches: Parent–Infant Psychotherapy

Parent–infant psychotherapy (PIP) is a dyadic (or triadic if both parents are involved) intervention that is explicitly focused on supporting parents experiencing significant problems in the interaction, and working with parents experiencing a range of mental health problems. A parent–infant psychotherapist works by listening and observing the interaction, identifying areas of concerns and helping the parent observe and find different ways to relate to their baby. This work may take place in the home, clinic or hospital setting, and aims to address a wide range of problems that can arise during the antenatal and postnatal periods. The intervention is usually delivered to individual dyads but can also be delivered to small groups of dyads.

Parent–infant psychotherapy focuses on improving the parent–infant relationship and infant attachment security by targeting parental internal working models (i.e. representational world) and by working directly with the parent–infant relationship in the room. The approach is essentially psychodynamic in that it involves identifying unconscious patterns of relating, and the earliest approach, developed by Selma Fraiberg (1980) [78], focused primarily on the mother's 'representational' world ('representation-focused' approach) or the way in which the mother's current view of her infant is affected by interfering representations from her own history. The aim of such therapy is affected to help the mother to recognise the 'ghosts in the nursery' (i.e. the unremembered influences from her own past) and to link them to her current functioning, in order to improve the parent–infant relationship directly, thereby facilitating new paths for growth and development for both mother and infant [79].

Fraiberg's model has been further developed and evaluated by others, and this representational approach has now been combined with more behavioural techniques. For example, Watch, Wait and Wonder is an 'infant-led' PIP that involves the mother spending time observing her infant's self-initiated activity, accepting the infant's spontaneous and undirected behaviour, and being physically accessible to the infant (behavioural component). The mother then discusses her experiences of the infant-led play with the therapist with a view to examining the mother's internal working models of herself in relation to her infant (representational component) [80]. Parent–infant psychotherapy may also work with the father or other primary carer, or with two parents together.

The duration of this intervention depends on the presenting problems but typically ranges from 5 to 20 weeks, usually involving weekly sessions. Parents may be referred to this service by a clinician (e.g. general practitioner or health visitor in the UK) or may self-refer to privately run services. Parent–infant psychotherapy services typically target infants less than 2 years of age at the time of referral and may also offer help to vulnerable mothers during pregnancy. This reflects the importance of the first 2 years of life in terms of children's later development.

A recent systematic review of the effectiveness of PIPs found that they appear to be a promising method of improving attachment security in a range of high-risk groups of parents (including depressed, maltreating and incarcerated women), although the evidence showed that they were not necessarily better than other available methods such as video feedback. This finding is consistent with a more recent study that evaluated the effectiveness of a dyadic psychotherapy for first-time mothers with postnatal depression that showed no additional benefits over usual care plus monitoring by phone [81]. The authors suggest that a stepped care approach is needed to identify which subset of depressed mothers might benefit from this model of working, and it seems likely that this complex intervention should be targeted at women with more severe problems in terms of the interaction and their reflective functioning.

Parenting Programmes

Mellow Babies is a good example of a small number of group-based parenting programmes that are (at least in part) dyadic. This programme was explicitly developed to support women experiencing depression, and is delivered over the course of 14 weeks in sessions that take place over the course of a day (i.e. 5 hours). During the morning sessions babies are cared for in the creche while the mothers take part in a group-based session that is aimed at helping women to develop ways of managing depression underpinned by cognitive behavioural therapy, and development of understanding about the relationship between their current problems and their early life experiences. The afternoon sessions involve a range of targeted interactions between mother and baby using infant massage, video feedback and other play techniques. The final part of the day, in which babies are returned to the creche, involves the use of videotape modelling to demonstrate sensitive parent–infant interactions.

This appears to be a promising model of working, with existing evidence from a small RCT involving 20 mothers suggesting significant improvements in both maternal depression and parent–infant interaction [82].

Parenting programmes such as Baby Triple-P are not dyadic, and a recent RCT showed no evidence of effectiveness when delivered to mothers with postnatal depression [83].

Service Contexts for Delivery

In England, the Five Year Forward View for Mental Health [84] and specifically the Implementation Plan [85] has a number of components that will shape the delivery of dyadic interventions over the next decade, perhaps most significantly being the increase in both community (i.e. specialist perinatal mental health teams) and inpatient settings (i.e. MBU). The equivalent service development programme in Scotland has, in addition, mandated the inclusion of parent–infant therapists in MBU teams and is rolling out dedicated infant mental health services across all health boards [86, 87]. In terms of the effective delivery of dyadic interventions these specialist services will need to ensure that there are clinical staff who can undertake assessment using at least one CROM and that there are both individual and group-based methods of working dyadically for women with both moderate and severe interactional problems. This will require that a parent–infant pathway is established within the service to ensure that there is a recognised process for guaranteeing that all women are assessed in terms of the interaction, and that where necessary a dyadic intervention is delivered in addition to the treatment addressing the mental health problem.

Conclusion

Parent–infant interaction is now recognised to be key to the later emotion regulation abilities of the child and their wider neurological development, and there is extensive evidence suggesting that perinatal mental health problems can derail the interaction in ways that may as such compromise the child's long-term development. There is currently little evidence regarding which parents are at risk of in terms of the interaction, and clinicians working with parents experiencing perinatal mental health problems should ensure that an assessment of the interaction is undertaken in all cases, using a CROM. This assessment will provide some indication as to whether there is any evidence of interactional problems and, if so, whether they are moderate or severe. The evidence suggests that moderate-level problems (i.e. where reflective functioning is not significantly compromised) can be treated using infant massage, video interaction guidance or a parenting programme such as Mellow Babies. More significant problems in terms of the severity of the mental health problem and the related reflective functioning may benefit from a more intensive intervention such as PIP.

References

1. G Spangler, M Schieche, U Ilg, U Maier, C Ackermann. Maternal sensitivity as an external organizer for biobehavioural regulation in infancy. *Dev Psychobiol.* 1994;27:425–37.
2. J Bowlby. *Attachment, vol 1: attachment and loss.* 2nd ed. New York: Basic Books; 1999 [1969].
3. LA Sroufe, EA Carlson, AK Levy, B Egeland. Implications of attachment theory for developmental psychopathology. *Dev Psychopathol.* 1999;11:1–13.
4. LA Sroufe. Attachment and development: a prospective, longitudinal study from birth to adulthood. *Attach Hum Dev.* 2005;7(4):349–67.
5. RP Fearon, MJ Bakermans-Kranenburg, MH van IJzendoorn, GM Lapsley, GI Roisin. The significance of insecure attachment and disorganization in the development of children's externalizing behavior: a meta-analytic study. *Child Dev.* 2010;81(2):435–56.
6. K Lyons-Ruth. Attachment relationships among children with aggressive behavior problems: the role of disorganized early attachment patterns. *J Consult Clin Psychol.* 2005;64(1):64–73.
7. HZ MacDonald, M Beeghly, W Grant-Knight, M Augustyn, RW Woods, et al. Longitudinal association between infant disorganized attachment and childhood posttraumatic stress symptoms. *Dev Psychopathol.* 2008;20(2):493–508.
8. H Steele, L Siever. An attachment perspective on borderline personality disorder: advances in gene–environment considerations. *Curr Psychiatry Rep.* 2010;12(1):61–7.
9. B Beebe, J Jaffe, S Markese, K Buck, H Chen, P Cohen, et al. The origins of 12-month attachment: a microanalysis of 4-month mother–infant interaction. *Attach Hum Dev.* 2010;12(1):3–141.
10. EZ Tronick, H Als, L Adamson, S Wise, TB Brazelton. The infant's response to entrapment between contradictory messages in face-to-face interaction. *J Am Acad Child Adolesc Psychiatry.* 1978; 17:1–13.
11. MS De Wolff, MH Van IJzendoorn. Sensitivity and attachment: a meta-analysis on parental antecedents of infant attachment security. *Child Dev.* 1997;68:604–9.

12. A Bernier, F Degeilh, E Leblanc, V Daneault, HN Bailey, MH Beauchamp. Mother-infant interaction and child brain morphology: a multidimensional approach to maternal sensitivity. *Infancy.* 2019;24(2):120–38.
13. L-E Malmberg, S Lewis, A West, E Murray, K Sylva, A Stein. The influence of mothers' and fathers' sensitivity in the first year of life on children's cognitive outcomes at 18 and 36 months. *Child: Care, Health Dev.* 2016;42(1):1–7.
14. A Slade, J Grienenberger, E Bernbach, D Levy, A Locker. Maternal reflective functioning, attachment, and the transmission gap: a preliminary study. *Attach Hum Dev.* 2005;7(3):283–98.
15. J Grienenberger, K Kelly, A Slade. Maternal reflective functioning, mother-infant affective communication, and infant attachment: exploring the link between mental states and observed caregiving behavior in the intergenerational transmission of attachment. *Attach Hum Dev.* 2005;7:299–311.
16. E Meins, C Fernyhough, R Wainwright, M das Gupta, E Fradley, M Tuckey. Maternal mind-mindedness and attachment security as predictors of theory of mind understanding. *Child Dev.* 2002;73(6):1715–26.
17. E Meins, C Fernyhough, M deRosnay, B Arnott, SR Leekam, M Turner. Mind-mindedness as a multidimensional construct: appropriate and nonattuned mind-related comments independently predict infant–mother attachment in a socially diverse sample. *Infancy.* 2012;17(4):393–415.
18. D Jacobvitz, NL Hazen, S Riggs. Disorganized mental processes in mothers, frightened/frightening behavior in caregivers, and disoriented, disorganized behavior in infancy. In: *Proceedings of the biennial meeting of the Society for Research in Child Development.* Washington, DC; 1997;17:329–47.
19. K Lyons-Ruth, C Yellin, S Melnick, G Atwood. Childhood experiences of trauma and loss have different relations to maternal unresolved and Hostile-Helpless states of mind on the AAI. *Attach Hum Dev.* 2003;5(4):330–52.
20. K Lyons-Ruth, C Yellin, S Melnick, G Atwood. Expanding the concept of unresolved mental states: Hostile-Helpless states of mind on the Adult Attachment Interview are associated with disrupted mother-infant communication and infant disorganization. *Dev Psychopathol.* 2005;17(1):1–23.
21. S Madigan, M Bakermans-Kranenburg, M Van IJzendoorn, G Moran, D Pederson, D Benoit. Unresolved states of mind, anomalous parental behavior and disorganized attachment: a review and meta-analysis. *Attach Hum Dev.* 2006;8(2):89–111.
22. K Bernard, G Nissim, S Vaccaro, JL Harris, O Lindhiem. Association between maternal depression and maternal sensitivity from birth to 12 months: a meta-analysis. *Attach Hum Dev.* 2018;20(6):578–99.
23. L Murray, P Cooper. Effects of postnatal depression on infant development. *Arch Dis Child.* 1997;77(2):99–101.
24. L Murray, A Fiori-Cowley, R Hooper, PJ Cooper. The impact of postnatal depression and associated adversity on early mother infant interactions and later infant outcome. *Child Dev.* 1996;67:2512–26.
25. EZ Tronick, T Field, K Lyons-Ruth, D Zoll, D Connell, HU Grunebaum. The depressed mother and her one-year-old infant: environment, interaction, attachment and infant development. In: EZ Tronick, T Field, editors. *Maternal depression and infant disturbance: new directions for child development.* San Francisco: Jossey-Bass; 1986. p. 61–82.
26. A Stein, H Woolley, L Murray, P Cooper, S Cooper, F Noble, et al. Influence of psychiatric disorder on the controlling behaviour of mothers with 1-year-old infants: a study of women with maternal eating disorder, postnatal depression and a healthy comparison group. *Br J Psychiatry.* 2001;179:157–62.

27. DF Hay. Postpartum depression and cognitive development. In: P Cooper, LJ Murray, editors. *Postpartum depression and child development.* New York: Guilford Press; 1997. p. 85–110.

28. DF Hay, S Pawlby, A Angold, GT Harold, D Sharp. Pathways to violence in the children of mothers who were depressed postpartum. *Dev Psychol.* 2003;39(6):1083–94.

29. L Murray, A Arteche, P Fearon, S Halligan, I Goodyer, P Cooper. Maternal postnatal depression and the development of depression in offspring up to 16 years of age. *J Am Acad Child Adolesc Psychiatry.* 2011;50(5):460–70.

30. HC Braarud, S Skotheim, K Hoie, MW Markhus, M Kjellevold, IE Graff, et al. Affective facial expression in sub-clinically depressed and non-depressed mothers during contingent and non-contingent face-to-face interactions with their infants. *Infant Behav Dev.* 2017;48:98–104.

31. AR Tarullo, AM St John, JS Meyer. Chronic stress in the mother-infant dyad: maternal hair cortisol, infant salivary cortisol and interactional synchrony. *Infant Behav Dev.* 2017;47: 92–102.

32. N Cook, S Ayers, A Horsch. Maternal posttraumatic stress disorder during the perinatal period and child outcomes: a systematic review. *J Affect Disord.* 2018;225:18–31.

33. A Stein, H Woolley, S Cooper, J Winterbottom, CG Fairburn, M Cortina-Borja. Eating habits and attitudes among 10-year-old children of mothers with eating disorders: longitudinal study. *Br J Psychiatry.* 2006;189:324–9.

34. S Laulik, S Chau, K Browne, J Allam. The link between personality disorder and parenting behaviors: a systematic review. *Aggress Violent Behav.* 2013;18(6):644–55.

35. RP Hobson, MP Patrick, JA Hobson, L Crandell, E Bronfman, K Lyons-Ruth. How mothers with borderline personality disorder relate to their year-old infants. *Br J Psychiatry.* 2009;195(4):325–30.

36. LE Crandell, RP Hobson, MPH Patrick. "Still-face" interactions between mothers with borderline personality disorder and their 2-month-old infants. *Br J Psychiatry.* 2003;183:239–47.

37. P Hobson, M Patrick, L Crandell, R Garcia-Perez, A Lee. Personal relatedness and attachment in infants of mothers with borderline personality disorder. *Dev Psychopathol.* 2005;17:329–47.

38. L Newman, C Stevenson, LR Bergman, P Boyce. Disorder parent psychotherapy for mothers with borderline personality. *Iss Infant Clin Child Psychol Psychiatry.* 2008;13(4):505–14.

39. V Garez, G Apter, M Valente, B Golse, E Devouche. Infant gender and maternal borderline personality: what impact on mother-infant interaction at 3 months postpartum? *Neuropsychiatr Enfance Adolesc.* 2014;62(3):147–53.

40. K Lyons-Ruth, C Riley, MPH Patrick, RP Hobson. Disinhibited attachment behavior among infants of mothers with borderline personality disorder, depression, and no diagnosis. *Pers Disord: Theory Res Treat.* 2019;10(2);163–72.

41. KA Davidsen, S Harder, A MacBeth, JM Lundy, A Gumley. Mother-infant interaction in schizophrenia: transmitting risk or resilience? A systematic review of the literature. *Soc Psychiatry Psychiatr Epidemiol.* 2015;50(12):1785–98.

42. D Riordan, L Appleby, B Faragher. Mother–infant interactions in post-partum women with schizophrenia and affective disorders. *Psycholog Med.* 1999;29:991–5.

43. MW Wan, MP Salmon, D Riordan, L Appleby, R Webb, KM Abel. What predicts mother-infant interaction in schizophrenia? *Psycholog Med.* 2007;37:537–8.

44. MW Wan, V Penketh, MP Salmon, KM Abel. Content and style of speech from mothers with schizophrenia towards their infants. *Psychiatry Res.* 2008;159: 109–14.

45. MW Wan, K Warren, MP Salmon, KM Abel. Patterns of maternal responding in

postpartum mothers with schizophrenia. *Infant Behav Dev.* 2008;31:532–8.

46. J Steadman, S Pawlby, A Mayers, RS Bucks, A Gregoir, M Miele-Norton, AM Hogan. An exploratory study of the relationship between mother–infant interaction and maternal cognitive function in mothers with mental illness. *J Reprod Infant Psychol.* 2007;25(4):255–69.
47 B Ramsauer, S Achtergarde. Mothers with acute and chronic postpartum psychoses and impact on the mother-infant interaction. *Schizophr Res.* 2018;197:45–58.
48. SJ Healy, J Lewin, S Butler, K Vaillancourt, F Seth-Smith. Affect recognition and the quality of mother-infant interaction: understanding parenting difficulties in mothers with schizophrenia. *Arch Womens Ment Health.* 2016;19(1):113–24.
49. S Krink, C Muehlhan, P Luyten, G Romer, B Ramsauer. Parental reflective functioning affects sensitivity to distress in mothers with postpartum depression. *J Child Fam Stud.* 2018;27(5):1671–81.
50. J Rigby, S Conroy, M Miele-Norton, S Pawlby, F Happe. Theory of mind as a predictor of maternal sensitivity in women with severe mental illness. *Psycholog Med.* 2016;46(9):1853–63.
51. Royal College of Psychiatrists. FROM-Perinatal. Framework for routine outcome measures in perinatal psychiatry. 2018.
52. PO Svanberg, J Barlow, W Tigbe. The Parent–Infant Interaction Observation Scale: reliability and validity of a screening tool. *J Reprod Infant Psychol.* 2013;31:1–10.
53. Department of Health. *The healthy child programme: pregnancy and the first five years of life.* London: Department of Health; 2009.
54. MT Owen. The NICHD study of early child care mother–infant interaction scales [Unpublished manuscript]. Timberlawn Psychiatric Research Foundation, Dallas, TX; 1992.
55. P Crittenden. CARE-Index: manual. 2004. Family Relations Institute.
56. IF Brockington, C Fraser, D Wilson. The Postpartum Bonding Questionnaire: a validation. *Arch Womens Ment Health.* 2006;9:233–42.
57. JM Oates, J Gervai. Mothers' object relational scales. Poster presented at the XIth European Conference on Developmental Psychology, Milan, Italy. 2003.
58. DN Stern. *The motherhood constellation: a unified view of parent–infant psychotherapy.* New York: Basic Books; 1995.
59. AJ Sameroff. Ports of entry and the dynamics of mother–infant interventions. In: AJ Sameroff, SC McDonough, KL Rosenblum, editors. *Treating parent–infant relationship problems.* New York: Guilford Publications; 2004.
60. K Asmussen, L Brims. *What works to enhance the effectiveness of the Healthy Child Programme: an evidence update.* London: Early Intervention Foundation; 2018.
61. N Axford, J Barlow, J Coad, et al. *A best start at home: What works to improve the quality of parent-child interactions from conception to age 5 years? A rapid review of interventions.* London: Early Intervention Foundation; 2015.
62. TB Brazelton. The Brazelton Neonatal Behavior Assessment Scale: introduction. *Monogr Soc Res Child Dev.* 1978;43(5–6):1–13.
63. J Barlow, NINS Herath, C Bartram-Torrance, C Bennett, Y Wei. The Neonatal Behavioral Assessment Scale (NBAS) and Newborn Behavioral Observations (NBO) system for supporting caregivers and improving outcomes in caregivers and their infants. *Cochrane Database Syst Rev.* 2018;3(3): CD011754.
64. K Onozawa, V Glover, D Adams, N Modi, RC Kumar. Infant massage improves mother-infant interaction for mothers with postnatal depression. *J Affect Disord.* 2001;63(1–3):201–7.

65. M Fujita, Y Endoh, N Saimon, S Yamaguchi. Effect of massaging babies on mothers: pilot study on the changes in mood states and salivary cortisol level. *Complement Ther Clin Pract.* 2006;12(3):181–5.

66. ZR Dehkordi, FS Hosseini-Baharanch, A Kazemian, MR Madiseh, M Reisi, B Motaghi. The effects of infant massage on maternal postpartum depression: a randomised controlled trial. *Nurs Midwif Stud.* 2019;8:28–33.

67. F Juffer, MJ Bakermans-Kranenburg, MH Van IJzendoorn. Video-feedback Intervention to promote Positive Parenting and Sensitive Discipline (VIPP-SD): development and meta-analytical evidence of its effectiveness. In: H Steele, M Steele, editors. *Handbook of attachment-based interventions.* New York: Guilford Press; 2017. p. 1–26.

68. H Kennedy, K Ball, J Barlow. How does video interaction guidance contribute to infant and parental mental health and well-being? *Clin Child Psychol Psychiatry.* 2017;22(3):500–17.

69. L O'Hara, ER Smith, J Barlow, N Livingstone, NINS Herath, Y Wei, TF Spreckelsen, G Macdonald. Video feedback for parental sensitivity and attachment security in children under five years: a systematic review and meta-analysis. *Cochrane Database Syst Rev.* 2019;11(11):CD012348.

70. M Kenny, S Conroy, CM Pariante, G Seneviratne, S Pawlby. Mother-infant interaction in mother and baby unit patients: before and after treatment. *J Psychiatr Res.* 2013;47(9):1192–8.

71. R Schacht, E Meins, C Fernyhough, LCM Centifanti, JF Bureau, S Pawlby. Proof of concept of a mind-mindedness intervention for mothers hospitalized for severe mental illness. *Dev Psychopathol.* 2017;29(2):555–64.

72. K Hoffman, R Marvin, G Cooper, B Powell. Changing toddlers' and preschoolers' attachment classifications: the Circle of Security intervention. *J Consult Clin Psychol.* 2006;74(6):1017–26.

73. LS Sadler, A Slade, N Close, DL Webb, T Simpson, K Fennie, LC Mayes. Minding the baby: enhancing reflectiveness to improve early health and relationship outcomes in an interdisciplinary home-visiting program. *Infant Ment Health J.* 2013;34:391–405.

74. NE Suchman, C DeCoste, D Leigh, J Borelli. Reflective functioning in mothers with drug use disorders: implications for dyadic interactions with infants and toddlers. *Attach Hum Dev.* 2010;12:567–585.

75. P Fearon, et al. *Supporting young mothers (aged 14–25) in the first two years of life: a randomized controlled trial of the NSPCC UK Minding the Baby home visiting programme.* London: NSPCC; forthcoming.

76. MR Ordway, LS Sadler, J Dixon, N Close, L Mayes, A Slade. Lasting effects of an interdisciplinary home visiting program on child behaviour: preliminary follow-up results of a randomized trial. *J Pediatr Nurs.* 2014;29:3–13.

77. N Suchman, C DeCoste, T McMahon, B Rounsaville, L Mayes. The Mothers and Toddlers Program, an attachment-based parenting intervention for substance-using women: results at 6-week follow up in a randomized clinical pilot. *Infant Ment Health J.* 2011;32:427–49.

78. SH Fraiberg. *Clinical studies in infant mental health: the first year of life.* New York: Basic Books; 1980.

79. B Cramer, DN Stern. Evaluation of changes in mother-infant brief psychotherapy: a single case study. *Infant Ment Health J.* 1988;9(1):20–45.

80. NJ Cohen, E Muir, M Lojkasek, R Muir, CJ Parker, M Barwick, M Brown. Watch, wait, and wonder: testing the effectiveness of a new approach to mother–infant psychotherapy. *Infant Ment Health J.* 1999;20(4):429–51.

81. JH Goodman, J Prager, R Goldstein, M Freeman. Perinatal dyadic psychotherapy for postpartum depression: a randomized controlled pilot trial. *Arch Womens Ment Health.* 2015;18(3):493–506.

82. C Puckering, E McIntosh, A Hickey, J Longford. Mellow Babies: a group intervention for infants and mothers experiencing postnatal depression. *Couns Psychol Rev.* 2010;25(1):28–40.
83. ZL Tsivos, R Calam, MR Sanders, A Wittkowski. A pilot randomised controlled trial to evaluate the feasibility and acceptability of the Baby Triple P positive parenting programme in mothers with postnatal depression. *Clin Child Psychol Psychiatry.* 2015;20(4):532–54.
84. NHS England. The five year forward view for mental health. A report from the independent Mental Health Taskforce to the NHS in England. 2016. The Mental Health Taskforce.
85. NHS England. Implementing the five year forward view for mental health. 2016.
86. Perinatal Mental Health Network Scotland. Delivering effective services. 2019. www.pmhn.scot.nhs.uk/professionals/delivering-effective-services
87. Scottish Government. Perinatal and infant mental health services update. 2022. www.gov.scot/publications/perinatal-infant-mental-health-services-update

Chapter 36

Child Safeguarding

Lucinda Green

Introduction

Child safeguarding is an integral part of the work of perinatal mental health services and the health and social care services they work in partnership with. Although mothers with mental health problems rarely intentionally harm their children, serious case reviews repeatedly identify parental mental illness as one of the most significant risk factors for child maltreatment and infants under 1 year old as the most vulnerable group of children [1, 2]. Perinatal mental health services and pathways focus on early identification of women with current or previous mental disorders, proactive care planning, relapse prevention and achieving the best outcomes for women, their infants and families. This provides a context in which child safeguarding concerns can be identified early. Interventions and additional support for families can be provided even before babies are born. There is an opportunity to prevent babies experiencing abuse and neglect and to protect infants and older children from harm.

Child safeguarding is the action taken to promote children's welfare and protect them from harm. *Working Together to Safeguard Children* (2023) [3] defines safeguarding and promoting the welfare of children as:

- providing help and support to meet the needs of children as soon as problems emerge
- protecting children from maltreatment, whether that is within or outside the home, including online
- preventing impairment of children's mental and physical health or development
- ensuring that children grow up in circumstances consistent with the provision of safe and effective care
- promoting the upbringing of children with their birth parents, or otherwise their family network, through a kinship care arrangement, whenever possible and where this is in the best interests of the children
- taking action to enable all children to have the best outcomes in line with the outcomes set out in the Children's Social Care National Framework [4]

Child protection is a part of the safeguarding process. It refers to action taken to identify and protect a child who is suffering, or likely to suffer, 'significant harm' (the Children Act 1989) [5].

Infants at Risk of Abuse and Neglect

Child abuse and neglect affect the health and well-being of children worldwide [6] and is associated with negative short- and long-term consequences for cognitive, behavioural and social functioning, physical and mental health, attachment and relationships [7, 8]. Adverse childhood experiences (ACEs) include abuse, neglect and family dysfunction, parental mental illness and parental drug and alcohol abuse. Around 60% of adults globally report having experienced at least one ACE [9]. Experiencing at least four ACEs is associated with an increased risk of poor outcomes in adulthood including mental illness, alcohol and drug abuse, suicide attempts, serious physical illness such as cancer and heart disease, and being a victim or perpetrator of violence [9, 10, 11].

Comparing international prevalence rates for child abuse and neglect is challenging due to different definitions of abuse and neglect and inconsistencies in data collection [12]. The Crime Survey for England and Wales [13] estimated that one in five adults aged 18–74 years experienced at least one form of child abuse (emotional, physical or sexual abuse or witnessing domestic violence or abuse) before the age of 16 years.

The Department for Education collects data on children who come to the attention of local authority children's services in England. Similar data is collected for Scotland, Wales and Northern Ireland. These figures are likely to underestimate the number of children experiencing abuse or neglect [14]. Department for Education data for the year ending March 2019 identified 76 per 10,000 infants under the age of 1 year old being the subject of a child protection plan (CPP) in England [15]. Infants are the most likely age group to be the subject of a CPP. Neglect is the most common initial category of abuse (Table 36.1) and is a feature in 75% of child serious case reviews in England [1, 2]. However, neglect is often normalised, not noticed and the long-term impact is not adequately considered [2].

Infants under 1 year old have also been repeatedly identified as being the most vulnerable group of children in serious case reviews [1, 2, 16, 17, 18]. An analysis of 235 serious case reviews in England from 2017 to 2019 found that 37% of children were under the age of 1 year at time of death or serious harm. Of these, 47% were under 3 months old [2]. This is consistent with previous analyses of serious case reviews in England from 2005 to 2017 which found 36% to 46% of children were under 1 year old [2]. A 10-year review of child homicides in England and Wales also found that 51% were infants under 1 year and 23% were under 3 months old [19] (see Chapter 38).

Table 36.1 Children who were the subject of a CPP on 31 March 2019 in England (ONS, 2019)

	Total number of children subject to a CPP	Number of unborn babies subject to a CPP	Number of infants under 1 year old subject to a CPP	% of all children subject to a CPP who are unborn or infants under 1 year old
Neglect	25,330	820	4,820	22.2
Emotional abuse	18,460	230	1,350	8.6
Physical abuse	4,170	110	590	16.8
Sexual abuse	2,230	20	140	7.2
Total	52,260	1,210	4,820	11.5

Table 36.2 Parent, child and family characteristics associated with serious and fatal child maltreatment [1, 2, 17]

Factor	Characteristics
Parental factors	Mental health problems Drug misuse Alcohol misuse ACEs Intellectual disability Criminal record Young mothers Ambivalence about the pregnancy Known to children's social care in childhood
Child factors	Disability
Family and contextual factors	Parental separation Multiple partners Domestic abuse Social isolation Transient lifestyle Insecure housing Poverty Large families Bereavement, loss or threat of loss

A wide range of family and environmental risks can combine to affect outcomes for children. Analyses of child serious case reviews highlight parent, child and family characteristics associated with serious and fatal child maltreatment (Table 36.2).

In these analyses of child serious case reviews, more than half of the children who experienced serious or fatal maltreatment had a parent with a mental illness [1, 2, 16]. A meta-analysis of 17 studies showed that perinatal mental health problems increase the risk of child maltreatment (odds ratio 3.04; 95% confidence interval 2.29–4.03) [20]. When mental health problems are combined with other adversities the risk increases. The 'toxic trio' of domestic violence, parental substance misuse and parental mental health problems has repeatedly been identified in child serious case reviews [1, 2, 16, 17, 18, 21]. Complexity and cumulative risks of harm are often apparent, with a variety of the risk factors in Table 36.2 frequently evident in combination and over time [1, 2, 18].

UK Legislation and Guidance

England, Scotland, Wales and Northern Ireland each have their own laws and statutory guidance to safeguard and protect children. These are all based on similar principles.

All four nations have mechanisms to bring together senior professionals in local areas from health organisations, the local authority and police, with other relevant partners, to coordinate effective inter-agency working to safeguard and protect children. In England, safeguarding partnerships (the local authority, the local integrated care board and the chief constable of the police) make arrangements to work together and with other agencies locally to identify and respond to the needs of children. Scotland has a system of chief officers (the chief constable, chief executives of health boards and local authorities) and multi-agency child protection committees. Northern Ireland has a national safeguarding board and local safeguarding panels. Wales has regional safeguarding children boards. These bodies have a responsibility to ensure that national and local policies, procedures and guidance are implemented.

This chapter focuses on the laws and guidance in England as an example, with limited information about the other UK countries where there are many similarities but also some notable differences. It is essential for perinatal mental health professionals to be familiar with, and guided by, child safeguarding legislative frameworks and practice in the areas where they work.

Working Together to Safeguard Children (2023) [3] is the statutory government guidance in England. This focuses on the core legal requirements and makes it clear what individuals, organisations and agencies must do to safeguard and promote the welfare of children, including unborn babies. The guidance emphasises that everyone who works with children has a responsibility to keep them safe. Organisations, including the National Health Service (NHS), need to have safeguarding policies and processes and should provide safeguarding training. Key principles include: having a child-centred approach within a whole family focus; ensuring that the welfare of the child is paramount; working in partnership with whole families; providing early help in preference to reacting later; information sharing; effective multi-agency working; approaching families with empathy, respect and compassion and avoiding shame, suffering and blame.

In addition to being familiar with national guidance, perinatal mental health professionals must be familiar with local safeguarding policies in both acute and mental health trusts. Many areas also have local multi-agency joint working protocols involving adult mental health, children's social care and other agencies. Safeguarding needs to be embedded in local perinatal mental health pathways so that concerns can be identified as early as possible.

Child Safeguarding in Perinatal Mental Health Services

Referrals to Perinatal Mental Health Services

Midwives routinely ask all women about mental health, substance misuse and domestic abuse [22, 23, 24] and consider these and other potential safeguarding concerns at the booking appointment and during subsequent care. Midwives, primary care physicians, health visitors and general adult mental health professionals should highlight current or previous safeguarding concerns in referrals to the perinatal mental health service. For many women with current or previous mental health problems there will be no significant concerns about risk to children. However, all professionals should be encouraged to refer to children's social care if safeguarding concerns are identified. Assuming that this can wait until the woman is seen by the perinatal mental health service can cause unnecessary delay, for example if women do not attend appointments.

It is important for all professionals to be mindful that many women are fearful that being referred to perinatal mental health services will lead to negative judgements about their parenting, automatic referral to children's services or even that their children may be removed from their care [25]. All professionals working with women in the perinatal period have to strike a careful balance between being mindful of the risk factors associated with abuse and neglect, and taking action when concerns are present, whilst also being able to reassure women appropriately when there are no concerns and no indication for referral to children's services.

Assessment by Perinatal Mental Health Clinicians

At the initial assessment, and throughout a woman's care, perinatal mental health clinicians need to carefully balance their role in supporting women and families with the need to protect children. They must always hold in mind that the welfare of the child is paramount (the Children Act 1989). This is the case even if the best interest of the unborn baby, infant and/or other children conflicts with the best interest of the woman. Child safeguarding must be considered as part of every perinatal mental health assessment, even though in many cases there may be no safeguarding concerns. A decision should be made, and documented, about whether a referral to children's social care is needed or not. Women's concerns about being judged negatively as parents, and that their baby might be removed from their care, should be sensitively addressed, whether or not a referral to children's services is needed.

Assessment must include consideration of historical and current concerns, taking into account risk factors for child abuse and neglect already highlighted, as well as identifying the woman and family's strengths. This requires a thorough psychiatric history and review of the woman's previous medical records. The following are some specific areas of the assessment that should be considered in relation to child safeguarding.

Diagnosis, Symptoms, Functioning and Risk

Although some diagnoses, particularly schizophrenia and emotionally unstable personality disorder [26, 27, 28, 29], are associated with greater concerns about parenting capacity, risks need to be considered in each individual case taking into account a range of factors. Substance misuse diagnoses should be identified, being mindful of the increased risk to children when both mental illness and substance misuse are present [1, 2, 18]. Some individual symptoms clearly indicate a high level of immediate risk, for example if a child is incorporated into delusional beliefs [30]. Other symptoms may adversely impact children over a long period of time, for example emotional dysregulation or negative symptoms which may affect children's emotional development [31, 32].

It is important to clarify the extent to which a woman's daily functioning is affected by her illness. For some women there may only be concern during episodes of severe illness, for example women with bipolar disorder, who often have a high level of functioning when well. In contrast, women with a diagnosis of schizophrenia, who live in supported accommodation and cannot manage independent living, may be unable to meet their children's needs. The impact of learning disabilities on functioning and parenting capacity also needs careful consideration, recognising the potential increased risk to children when a parent has a mental illness in addition to a learning disability [1, 2, 18]. In some cases, a specific assessment of activities of daily living by an occupational therapist may be helpful. Assessment of social functioning and the implications for the child's social development is also important.

It is essential to consider previous and current risk to self or others, and vulnerability to risk from others, and to consider how these may potentially affect the child/children. If a woman has suicidal thoughts, or has a history of serious suicide attempts or plans, the risk of extended suicide should be assessed. If she has a history of aggressive behaviour during psychotic episodes, or related to a personality disorder, there may be a risk of the baby being harmed during a similar episode in future. Thoughts or plans to harm the baby or child should be elicited and the risk of actual harm assessed. If these thoughts are linked to psychotic symptoms the risk to the child may be very high. Obsessional (intrusive) thoughts about violently harming a child can be alarming for women and professionals, but the risk that the woman will actually harm her child if the intrusive thoughts are a symptom of obsessive-compulsive disorder (OCD) are very low [33, 34, 35]. However, in OCD, avoidance may include avoiding some aspects of baby care, and compulsions can take up many hours which can unintentionally lead to the baby or child being neglected.

There also needs to be consideration of how parenting may affect mental illness. All parents find parenting stressful at times, but this stress may exacerbate a woman's pre-existing illness. For some women, specific challenges for new parents, such as sleep deprivation, may trigger relapse.

The Woman, Partner and Family's Understanding of Illness

There will be greater concern about the children of a woman who lacks insight into her illness and who has a history of poor adherence to treatment and poor engagement with services, than a woman who proactively seeks help, has a good understanding of relapse indicators, takes professionals' advice and engages with the pre-birth planning process (see Chapter 23). It is also important to assess the partner and/or family's understanding of the woman's illness and any potential risk implications for her child. If a partner or relative understands the woman's risk of relapse, recognises her relapse indicators and would alert professionals if concerns arise, this can be protective. In contrast, if a woman with a history of psychotic illness lives alone with no reliable support and nobody to notice early signs of relapse, or if her partner discourages the woman from engaging with mental health services and taking medication, there may be a greater risk to the child.

Personal History, Relationships and Partner

Assessing the woman's attachment history and understanding her current and previous relationships is essential when considering child risk. Women who have experienced childhood maltreatment and who have had no positive adult attachment figures may find parenting challenging for many reasons [36] and in some cases can present a risk to their children [1, 37].

Serious case reviews highlight a lack of professional curiosity and a failure to consider all the significant figures in the family context and the roles they play in family functioning and dynamics [1, 2, 18]. The NHS England Long Term Plan (2019) [38] introduced assessment and signposting for partners of women seen by perinatal mental health services. Understanding whether partners have a current or previous mental illness and ensuring they have care and treatment is important. The effect of a woman's mental health problems on her partner and the couple relationship should be clarified [39] and the risks to children who witness parental conflict or experience parental separation should be considered [1, 2]. Women who have mental health problems in the perinatal period are particularly vulnerable to domestic abuse, and this in turn can lead to a range of negative outcomes for children as described above and in Chapter 34. The assessment should identify any history of abuse in the current and previous relationship and whether the woman recognises the potential implications for her unborn baby, child and/or children.

It is important to acknowledge the family's strengths and how partners and relatives can act as protective factors. The other parent, partners and extended family are important for children growing up with a parent with a mental illness. If a woman needs frequent or long admissions to hospital, the impact on the child can be minimised if another parent or relative cares for the child and maintains their usual routine during her admission. The child's experience will be very different if foster care is needed. Also, without another parent or relative involved, the child may become a young carer.

Assumptions should not be made about how much practical help and support partners or relatives can provide. Professionals should clarify who has parental responsibility and which adults are actually providing care for the baby and/or other children. If the mother cannot care for her baby due to severe mental illness, or a learning disability, but lives in the family home with her partner or another relative as the child's main carer, there need to be clearly identified plans for how her partner or family will ensure she has the support she needs, especially during episodes of acute illness, whilst at the same prioritising the child's safety and well-being. Where there has been a family history of abuse and neglect, grandparents and other relatives may not have a positive impact on children's lives [1].

Family Environment, Cultural Factors and Social Circumstances

Pressure on the woman and family associated with housing, financial difficulties or immigration issues should be identified. Learning from serious case reviews highlights the impact of other factors including transient life styles and social isolation. The impact of poverty, especially when combined with other risk factors, has been increasingly recognised in serious case reviews [2]. The endemic levels of poverty in some areas can result in a blindness to poor living conditions. The interaction between poverty and neglect and the normalisation of neglect has been identified among professionals who work with families in areas of high socio-economic deprivation [2].

Cultural factors need to be considered from a variety of perspectives when working with families in the perinatal period. Serious case reviews highlight gaps in professionals' cultural competence. Families can sometimes be seen through the lenses of bias and stereotype. Prejudices can affect judgements about parenting [2]. There may also be a fear of being seen as racist or prejudiced which may stop professionals challenging parenting practices or acting to protect children when families are from a different background to their own [39].

Attitude to Baby

The woman's attitude to her baby should be clarified. If she is ambivalent about the pregnancy, the risk to her child should be assessed. Serious case reviews have identified increased risk associated with refused requests for termination [1, 2, 18]. Children with disabilities have also been identified as being at greater risk of neglect and serious harm [1, 2]. Clinicians should sensitively enquire about parents' thoughts about and feelings towards a child who has a disability and consider their ability to care for a child who has additional needs and the support available. It is important to listen to parents who describe difficulty caring for a child who has additional needs and to discuss with the other relevant professionals the need for additional support.

Previous Children's Social Care Involvement with the Family

The reasons for any previous children's social care involvement with the family, particularly if other children have been the subject of a CPP or removed from the woman's care, should be identified. It is also important to recognise what has changed since that time. For example, a woman with a diagnosis of emotionally unstable personality disorder may have had a psychological intervention resulting in significant changes in her ability to regulate emotions, use positive coping strategies and maintain a stable relationship. A woman with a history of psychotic illness who has had multiple admissions, poor engagement with services and poor adherence to treatment in the past but who has since had several years of engaging well, with improved insight may now be better able to safely care for a baby.

Ongoing Care and Partnership Working

Partnership working is key to effective perinatal mental health care and child safeguarding. Serious case reviews [1, 2, 18] and statutory guidance [3] highlight the importance of effective multi-agency working, a clear understanding of roles and responsibilities, good communication and information sharing. An important distinction has been made between information exchange and effective communication. In some cases information is shared but is not understood, or its significance in terms of the risk to a child is not appreciated by another agency. An example of this may be that the significance of a specific mental illness diagnosis for a woman's parenting capacity may not be appreciated by a children's social worker. It is considered good practice for there to be conversations and professional meetings, rather than only sharing documents.

Joint assessments and reviews with professionals from maternity, health visiting, general adult mental health and children's social care are often helpful. Meetings focusing on individual women or children bring all these professionals together with women and families, and provide an opportunity for information sharing, review and joint care planning. This can include perinatal mental health pre-birth planning meetings (see Chapter 25) as well as child in need meetings, child protection conferences and core group meetings. Child safeguarding should be routinely discussed at the perinatal mental health team's clinical meetings.

In some maternity services, regular safeguarding meetings bring together professionals from maternity, health visiting, children's social care and perinatal mental health services. This enables multi-agency discussion about potential safeguarding concerns and referrals to children's social care. Progress and feedback about cases where an unborn baby is the subject of a child in need plan or CPP and when care proceedings are planned can also be discussed. In some cases, especially when children's social care has a pre-birth team, there may be a link social worker who can liaise with the perinatal mental health team, or even attend the team's clinical meeting, to discuss individual cases. All perinatal mental health services need to foster joint working relationships with local children's social care services and maternity safeguarding leads.

There may sometimes be differences of opinion between professionals focusing on the needs of the parents and those focusing on the needs of the child and these should be explored. Sometimes adult mental health professionals may see the baby as a chance for the woman to have a new start. Perinatal mental health professionals may need to inform child social workers and health visitors about the potential short- or longer-term risks to a child linked with a specific mental disorder such as schizophrenia or emotionally unstable personality disorder. Professionals should be able to question and challenge decisions or lack of an appropriate response. Systems of escalation should be clearly established [1, 2, 18].

There are many other lessons from serious case reviews that all professionals should be mindful of when working with families [1, 2, 18]. Continuity of care, effective multi-agency working, good relationships with families and having a good understanding of a family's context make a positive difference. It is important to have a compassionate approach and to recognise that parents can perceive questions about a child as implying blame. Professionals have to balance the need to be supportive and empathic with the need to be curious, to enquire about concerns and to challenge parents in a sensitive and respectful manner when concerns are evident [2, 40]. Strengths and protective factors should be recognised, as well as risks. There must be a constant focus on the needs of the unborn child, the infant and other children's perspectives and their likely experience. Professional optimism can lead to risks being underestimated. Professionals may empathise with parents who are doing their best but must still recognise when this is insufficient to consistently meet the child's needs. Professionals should be able to see the woman interacting with her baby and to engage with all adults in the infant's life and understand who is doing the care. Multi-agency plans should be developed with families and reviewed regularly. Sometimes a focus on small improvements can mean a lack of recognition that the overall care of the child is not improving enough to ensure their developmental needs are met. In other cases, disguised compliance may be evident; families may appear to cooperate with professionals to allay concerns, without meaningfully engaging or changing.

Risk is dynamic and there needs to be frequent review, particularly if the woman's situation changes [1, 2, 18]. For example, a woman with bipolar disorder may have been well for many years, but if she chooses to stop medication in pregnancy and does not accept her high risk of postpartum psychosis and the importance of having a plan to ensure signs of relapse are detected promptly, the risk to her infant needs to be addressed. A woman who has a diagnosis of emotionally unstable personality disorder may have a period of relative stability whilst she is in a relationship, but her symptoms and functioning may deteriorate when the relationship ends, with a return to previous maladaptive coping strategies such as substance misuse. A vulnerable woman with a history of mental illness may become involved in a relationship with a partner who, unknown to her, has previously been a perpetrator of domestic abuse or child maltreatment. A plan may have been made with a woman who has a history of psychotic illness that her partner will alert mental health services if she stops her medication or if there is any evidence that her mental state has deteriorated, but if the relationship ends there may be nobody to recognise relapse indicators.

Interventions

Many different interventions offered by perinatal mental health services can make a difference to children's well-being and safety. These are described in other chapters throughout this book. They include interventions for the mother, including medication, individual psychological therapies, pre-birth planning meetings or Mother and Baby Unit admissions. Other psychological interventions may focus on the parent–infant relationship, the couple or family. Parenting interventions, mother and baby groups that enable the woman to develop social networks, peer support and support for partners can all make a difference to families.

Providing help for children before problems develop, or at an early stage, can prevent unnecessary harm and improve long-term outcomes [41]. Early help services include a wide range of interventions, for example parenting programmes, family nurse partnerships and third-sector organisations such as HomeStart which provide practical help and peer support. Interventions can address a range of difficulties and might include advice and support regarding domestic abuse or housing.

Training and Support for Staff

All clinicians working with women during the perinatal period should have training in child safeguarding relevant to the perinatal period [42, 43, 44, 45] incorporating learning from serious case reviews. Child safeguarding should routinely be discussed in perinatal mental health team clinical meetings, in supervision and team case discussion meetings. Reflective practice can provide a helpful space for teams to consider the emotional impact of this work on clinicians.

Recording, Reporting and Audit

Mental health and acute trusts have child risk assessments and reporting systems to capture data in relation to children referred to children's social care and those who are the subject of a CPP or care proceedings. Electronic record systems in acute and mental health trusts and primary care should have alert systems to highlight child safeguarding concerns.

Children's Social Care: Referral, Child in Need and Child Protection

Referral to Children's Social Care

When there is concern about a child, or an unborn baby's welfare, a referral should be made to children's social care. If there is concern that a child is suffering, or likely to suffer, significant harm the referral should be made immediately.

Referrals should include information about the child's developmental needs, the capacity of the parents to meet those needs and any additional factors which might affect parenting capacity. Some areas have Multi-Agency Safeguarding Hubs (MASH) which include professionals from the local authority, health and the police. The MASH teams facilitate early information sharing, joint decision-making and a timely response to referrals [46]. Children's services should give feedback to referrers to inform them whether or not an assessment will be initiated. Clinicians should also follow up to clarify the outcome of the referral and should escalate concerns if needed. If a midwife or health visitor has made the referral, mental health professionals may need to provide additional information about the woman's mental health history to enable the social worker to decide whether an assessment is needed.

All professionals need to be mindful of how anxiety-provoking children's social care involvement can be for women. Even where there are no safeguarding concerns, women are often very fearful that disclosing mental health history will lead to their baby being removed from their care [47, 48]. If there is a need to refer to children's social care it is important to be honest about the reasons for this.

Police Protection Powers and Emergency Protection Orders

Police Protection Powers (Section 46 Children Act 1989) allow police to remove children to a safe location for up to 72 hours to protect them from 'significant harm'.

An application can be made to the Family Court for an Emergency Protection Order (Section 44 Children Act 1989) for up to 8 days, which can be extended for a further 7 days. The order grants the applicant (usually the local authority) parental responsibility when there is reasonable cause to believe that the child would otherwise be likely to suffer significant harm.

Social Worker's Assessment

The social worker's assessment includes consideration of the child's developmental needs, whether they are suffering or likely to suffer significant harm, parenting capacity and the impact and influence of family and environmental factors. Assessments are child centred, holistic, recognise strengths as well as difficulties and focus on action and outcomes for children. Families and other professionals, including perinatal mental health clinicians, are involved and relevant correspondence can be requested. Health professionals have a duty under section 27 of the Children Act 1989 to assist the local authority with their assessment if requested to do so.

A decision is made about whether no further action is needed or whether the child is either 'in need', or there is 'reasonable cause to suspect that the child is suffering, or likely to suffer, significant harm' requiring assessment under section 47 of the Children Act 1989.

Unless there is an immediate need for protection, *Working Together to Safeguard Children* (2023) [3] requires that assessments should be completed within 45 working days from the date of referral.

Child in Need

A child or unborn baby is regarded as a 'child in need' under section 17 of the Children Act 1989 if they have a disability, or if they are unlikely to achieve or maintain, or to have the opportunity to achieve or maintain, a reasonable standard of health or development, or if their health or development is likely to be significantly impaired or further impaired, without provision of services from the local authority. For these children, a multi-agency child in need plan will be developed, outlining services and support which will be provided for the family from statutory and third-sector services. This is reviewed within 3 months and then every 6 months until it is decided that the plan is longer needed. Perinatal mental health clinicians will be invited to child in need meetings.

Child Protection

Under section 47 of the Children's Act 1989, the local authority has a duty to make enquiries and investigate if there are reasonable grounds to suspect that a child, or unborn baby, is suffering or likely to suffer 'significant harm'. Perinatal mental health professionals may be invited to the strategy discussion, convened and chaired by children's social care. This is to confirm whether there are 'reasonable grounds' for a section 47 investigation, to ascertain the child's welfare and plan any actions to be taken. If a legal framework for the plan is considered necessary, the local authority may convene a legal planning meeting. Legal planning meetings can also happen at a subsequent stage if needed.

If the outcome of the section 47 enquiry is a decision that an initial child protection conference (ICPC) is needed, this should take place within 15 working days of the strategy discussion. For an unborn baby, the ICPC should be held before the child is born. In some areas there are recommendations about the timing of the initial pre-birth child protection conference. For example, the London child protection procedures recommend this should be held 10 weeks before the estimated delivery date and Scottish national guidance states that it should take place by 28 weeks' gestation [49]. However, even when there is a history of previous care proceedings, a large proportion of pre-birth conferences happen late in pregnancy, or after birth [50].

Perinatal mental health professionals will be invited to write a report and attend the ICPC. The ICPC brings together the family and the involved professionals to make decisions about the child or unborn baby's future safety, health and development. If it is agreed that the child, or unborn baby, should become the subject of a CPP, an outline plan with clear timescales is agreed. Perinatal mental health clinicians will usually be included in the 'core group' of practitioners and family members who will develop and implement the CPP, which should have clear actions and timescales. The aim of the CPP is to ensure the child is safe from harm, to promote the child's health and development and to support the family to safeguard and promote the welfare of their child. The core group meets within 10 working days of the child protection conference and at regular time intervals subsequently. A review child protection conference should be held within 3 months of the ICPC and then every 6 months until a CPP is no longer needed.

Wales, Scotland and Northern Ireland have child protection registers, which are a list of all children and unborn babies who are the subject of a CPP. This is no longer the case in England.

Women and Families' Experience

Understandably, parents are often anxious about child protection investigations. They have a better experience of this process if the social worker demonstrates empathy and understanding, communicates well and provides support, but many find having their parenting questioned and being treated as a risk to their child dehumanising and belittling [51]. The child protection conference is often a stressful and emotional experience [51]. Perinatal mental health professionals should explain each step of the process, and offer support, whilst being honest and acknowledging concerns and risks.

Concerns about Parenting Capacity

Care Orders

It is recognised that children are best looked after within their families whenever possible [3, 4]. If there is sufficient concern about parenting capacity the local authority may consider the need for a formal parenting assessment or, as a last resort, separating a mother and baby.

An application can be made to the family court for an interim care order (ICO) or an interim supervision order, which lasts for 26 weeks. This allows the local authority to share parental responsibility with the parents. This application to the court cannot be made until the child is born. The court appoints a children's guardian, whose role is to look after the child's best interests. An application for an ICO does not necessarily mean that the local authority plans to separate the mother and baby. There may be parallel planning to allow for a formal parenting assessment (see below), whilst having a safe alternative in case the parenting assessment has to be rapidly terminated if there are sufficient risk concerns.

In England, Wales and Northern Ireland (but not in Scotland), if an application for an ICO is being considered, and provided there is no urgency, parents will receive a written invitation to a pre-proceedings meeting, with their legal representative. This is to outline the concerns and discuss what would need to change, or possible alternative plans, to avoid going to court. In Scotland a referral is made to the children's reporter, who decides whether there should be a children's hearing for compulsory measures of supervision. A supervision order allows a child to live in foster care or residential care, or to continue living at home under the supervision of the local authority.

An ICO can be made if the court has 'reasonable grounds' to believe that the child has suffered, or is at risk of suffering, significant harm and that this is as a result of care provided by parents falling below a reasonable standard. Removing a baby from parents is a last resort and must be proportionate to the risk of harm to which he or she will be exposed in the parents' care.

A full care order may be made subsequently if the court is satisfied that the child is suffering, or is likely to suffer, significant harm and that the level of harm is due to the care the child is receiving or likely to receive if the care order is not made. If a mother is unable to care for her child, other options within the family will always be considered. Once an adoption order is made parental responsibility is transferred to the adoptive parents. In Scotland a permanence order is made if it is not safe for a child to return home, which gives parental responsibility to the local authority.

In some cases, a woman may voluntarily agree that the local authority can accommodate her child through section 20 of the Children Act 1989. This may allow a child to live with grandparents or other family members, but can also mean that that the baby can be placed with foster carers.

In 2017/18 at least 50% of care proceedings were issued within 4 weeks of birth [52]. In 47% of cases these babies were born to mothers who had previously appeared before the family courts regarding an older sibling. At 31 March 2019, 3,180 children in England looked after by their local authority because of experience or risk of abuse or neglect were infants under 1 year old.

In a study of recurrent care proceedings [50], mothers had experienced multiple adversities and had high levels of maltreatment and abuse in their own childhood. Half had been in the care system themselves as children and 55.9% had experienced four or more ACEs. At the index proceedings 50.6% of mothers had mental health issues, 65% were victims of domestic abuse and 55.9% engaged in substance misuse.

Parenting Assessments

When there are significant concerns about a woman's parenting capacity a formal parenting assessment may be required. This sometimes includes the woman's partner.

Approaches to assessing parenting capacity vary, and concern has been expressed about a lack of valid and reliable assessment tools [27]. Perinatal mental health clinicians may be asked to assess parenting or to give opinions about parenting capacity. Whilst it is important to highlight actual and potential concerns, and to contribute to multi-agency discussions, it is also important for professionals to be mindful of their role and the limits of their expertise (see Chapter 40).

Parenting assessments can take place in a variety of settings:

- a small number of psychiatric Mother and Baby Units (MBUs) have specific parenting assessment beds
- non-psychiatric residential parenting assessment centres
- mother and baby foster placements, where the mother and baby stay together with a foster carer
- the baby can be placed with a foster carer, or another family member, and the mother can have observed contact with her baby at a contact centre several days each week
- there may be an assessment while the mother and baby stay at home

When a parenting assessment is needed, the perinatal mental health team should work closely with children's social workers to ensure that a plan is agreed in advance of the estimated date of delivery. The most appropriate setting for the parenting assessment should be agreed, a parenting assessment bed or a suitable foster carer should be identified and the local authority should approve funding. Parenting assessments should start when the woman is well, or at her best, to maximise her chance of success. In some cases, a period of treatment in an MBU is needed prior to a parenting assessment. Some women may do relatively well in the supported environment of a residential unit but may have more difficulty when they return home, particularly if they have little support or if they are vulnerable to abuse.

When there are concerns about parenting capacity and there is a plan to initiate care proceedings once the baby is born, and/or for a formal parenting assessment, a plan needs to be agreed with the children's social worker and maternity safeguarding lead to ensure the safety of the baby on the maternity unit. This may include 24 hour 1:1 supervision by a health care assistant or maternity support worker. If the mother is sufficiently unwell, 1:1 supervision by a registered mental health nurse may also be needed. Unless there are immediate concerns about the baby's safety, which is rare, the mother and baby will often remain together on the postnatal ward until the court date, or until a parenting assessment bed or mother and baby foster placement is identified. Plans to separate mother and baby during this time should be avoided, although pressure on maternity beds can make this challenging. If the woman has a high risk of postnatal mental illness her mental health should be closely monitored by the perinatal or liaison mental health team. In some cases, where there is a high chance of separation, it may be appropriate to discuss whether breast or bottle feeding is most appropriate and whether the mother wants to meet potential foster carers.

The majority of studies which look at the number of women with mental illness separated from their babies, relate to women admitted to psychiatric MBUs for treatment [27, 53]. The largest of these studies [26, 54] found that 14–15% of mothers and babies were separated at the time of discharge from the MBU. A review of consecutive admissions to a psychiatric MBU over a 6-year period specifically for assessment of parenting, and not in the context of acute psychiatric illness [28], found that less than half of women were discharged together with their babies and less than a third were still caring for the children at follow-up (mean 26 months later). These studies found that mothers with a diagnosis of psychotic illness, particularly schizophrenia or a personality disorder, had the greatest chance of losing care of their baby. Other factors associated with separation included behavioural disturbance, psychiatric illness in the partner, social class, single marital status and lack of high-quality supportive relationships. However, not all women with a diagnosis of schizophrenia or personality disorder will be admitted to an MBU for treatment or parenting assessment. Women who are relatively well, or whose partner can provide good care, do not need admission. At the other end of the spectrum, when it is clear that a woman cannot safely parent her child; for example if she is unable to manage independent living or if there has been no change since previous children were removed from her care, an admission to an MBU for treatment or for a parenting assessment would not be considered. A small study looking at outcomes for 39 women with a current or previous psychotic illness seen as outpatients by a perinatal mental health team found that 7 out of 16 (44%) of women with a diagnosis of schizophrenia or schizoaffective disorder did not have care of their baby at 1 year postpartum [55]. The only other woman who did not have care of her baby at this time had diagnoses of both bipolar disorder and emotionally unstable personality disorder.

Women and Families' Experience and the Need for Ongoing Assessment, Care and Support

A study of women who had babies removed from their care in England [50] found that, not surprisingly, women experience acute grief following removal of their children, which is enduring and difficult to resolve. It is complicated by women's anger towards children's services and feelings of being insufficiently understood or helped. There is often a strong sense of shame and isolation. Women's own experiences in the care system creates great anxiety about their own children's futures in care or with adoptive parents. This study also found that women's mental health can deteriorate and that self-harm and suicidal thoughts are common after being separated from their children. There is a lack of access to psychological therapies recommended by experts in care proceedings. Reports of the confidential enquiries into maternal deaths in UK highlight the increased risk of suicide for women who have a child taken into care and the importance of offering additional monitoring and support for this group [56, 57].

The NHS Long Term Plan recognises the current gap in care for women who are separated from their infants [38]. In England, these women should be offered care within maternal mental health services. Some voluntary programmes, such as Pause, work with women who have experienced, or are at risk of, repeated removal of children from their care [58]. The Pause project aims to improve women's well-being, resilience and stability and to address a broad range of emotional, psychological, practical and behavioural needs to improve the chance of women being able to care for a subsequent child.

Conclusion

Infants under 1 year old have repeatedly been identified as being the group of children at greatest risk of serious harm and neglect [1, 2, 16, 17, 18]. Parental mental illness is one of the most significant risk factors for child maltreatment [1, 2, 16, 17, 18]. The risk to children is increased when parental mental illness is combined with other significant risk factors [1, 2]. For the majority of women under the care of perinatal mental health services, there will be no child safeguarding concerns. However, perinatal mental health clinicians work with women and families with significant complexity and risk. There is a need to constantly hold in mind and balance the need to support women and families and to recognise strengths, with the needs of unborn babies and children and being able to identify and act on safeguarding concerns. Professionals need to be aware of women's anxiety about being judged negatively as parents and that their child may be removed from their care because of their mental illness diagnosis. They need to be compassionate and avoid blame, particularly when children's services do need to be involved.

All professionals working in perinatal mental health services need to work in accordance with national and local safeguarding policies and guidance. Having a child-centred approach, identifying and acting on concerns as early as possible, effective multi-agency working in partnership with families, being curious, being prepared to question and challenge decisions and to escalate concerns when necessary are all essential. Learning from child serious case reviews needs to be implemented in the work of perinatal mental health teams.

Working in perinatal mental services can be emotionally demanding for staff, and this is often the case when working with families where there are complex child safeguarding concerns. Team working, partnership working with other services and agencies, training, supervision and reflective practice will all help clinicians to acquire the knowledge and skills, and to access the advice and emotional support, they need. This will enable them to support women and families to provide the best possible care for children, to act promptly to safeguard and protect unborn babies and children, and to support women when safeguarding concerns are identified.

Further Reading

https://learning.nspcc.org.uk/child-protection-system

www.legislation.gov.uk

https://learning.nspcc.org.uk/key-topics

References

1. M Brandon, P Sidebotham, P Belderson, H Cleaver, J Dickens, J Garstag, et al. *Complexity and challenge: a triennial analysis of serious case reviews 2014–2017.* London: Department for Education; 2020.
2. J Dickens, J Taylor, L Cook, J Cossar, J Garstang, N Hallett, et al. *Learning for the future: final analysis of serious case reviews, 2017 to 2019.* London: Department for Education; 2022.
3. Department for Education. *Working together to safeguard children: a guide to multi-agency working to help, protect and promote the welfare of children.* London: Department for Education; 2023.
4. Department for Education. *Children's Social Care National Framework: statutory guidance on the purpose, principles for practice and expected outcomes of children's social care.* London: Department for Education; 2023.
5. The Children Act 1989. www.legislation.gov.uk/ukpga/1989/41/contents
6. M Stoltenborgh, MJ Bakermans-Kranenburg, LRA Alink, MH van IJzendoorn. The prevalence of child maltreatment across the globe: review of a series of meta-analyses. *Child Abuse Rev.* 2015;24:37–50.
7. RE Norman, M Byambaa, R De, A Butchart, J Scott, T Vos. The long-term health consequences of child physical abuse, emotional abuse, and neglect: a

systematic review and meta-analysis. *PLoS Med.* 2012;9(11):e1001349.

8. A Dodaj, K Sesar. Consequences of child abuse and neglect. *Central Eur J Paed.* 2020;16:168–81.
9. S Madigan, A-A Deneault, N Racine, J Park, R Thiemann, J Zhu, et al. Adverse childhood experiences: a meta-analysis of prevalence and moderators among half a million adults in 206 studies. *World Psychiatry.* 2023;22:463–71.
10. VJ Felitti, RF Anda, D Nordenberg, DF Williamson, AM Spitz, V Edwards, et al. Relationship of childhood abuse and household dysfunction to many of the leading causes of death in adults: the Adverse Childhood Experiences (ACE) Study. *Am J Prev Med.* 1998;14(4):245–58.
11. K Hughes, MA Bellis, KA Hardcastle, D Sethi, A Butchart, C Mikton, et al. The effect of multiple adverse childhood experiences on health: a systematic review and meta-analysis. *Lancet Public Health.* 2017;2(8):e356–e366.
12. D Fry, T Casey. *Bringing the global to the local: review of global trends in the prevalence and services for child maltreatment in order to inform research, policy and practice in England.* London: NSPCC; 2017.
13. Office for National Statistics. Child abuse extent and nature, England and Wales, year ending March 2019. 2020. https://tinyurl.com/469pza5n
14. A Miles. A crying shame: a report by the Office of the Children's Commissioner into vulnerable babies in England. 2018. Children's Commissioner for England.
15. Department for Education. Table 14: children who were the subject of a Child Protection Plan (CPP) on 31st March 2019 in England. 2019. ONS. https://tinyurl.com/4shkuzd9
16. M Brandon, S Bailey, P Belderson, R Gardner, P Sidebotham, J Dodsworth, et al. *Understanding serious case reviews and their impact: a biennial analysis of serious case reviews 2005–07.* London: Department for Children Schools and Families; 2009.
17. S Bailey, P Belderson, M Brandon. *Building on the learning from SCRs: a two-year analysis of child protection database notifications 2007–2009.* London: Department for Education; 2010.
18. P Sidebotham, M Brandon, S Bailey, P Belderson, J Dodsworth, J Garstang, et al. *Pathways to harm, pathways to protection: a triennial analysis of serious case reviews 2011 to 2014: final report.* London: Department for Education; 2016.
19. SM Flynn, JJ Shaw, KM Abel. Filicide: mental illness in those who kill their children. *PLoS ONE.* 2013;8(4):e58981.
20. S Ayers, R Bond, R Webb, P Miller, K Bateson. Perinatal mental health and risk of child maltreatment: a systematic review and meta-analysis. *Child Abuse Negl.* 2019;98:104172.
21. M Brandon, C Belderson, D Warren, D Howe, R Gardner, J Dodsworth, J Black. *Analysing child deaths and serious injury through abuse and neglect: what we can learn? A biennial analysis of serious case reviews 2003–2005.* London: Department for Children Schools and Families; 2008.
22. National Institute for Health and Care Excellence. Pregnancy and complex social factors: a model for service provision for pregnant women with complex social factors. Clinical Guideline (CG11). 2010.
23. National Institute for Health and Care Excellence. Antenatal and postnatal mental health: clinical management and service guidance. Clinical Guideline (CG192). 2014.
24. Royal College of Obstetricians & Gynaecologists. Providing quality care for women: a framework for maternity service standards. 2016.
25. E Moran, M Noonan, MM Mohamad, P O'Reilly. Women's experiences of specialist perinatal mental health services: a qualitative evidence synthesis. *Arch Womens Ment Health.* 2023;26(4): 453–71.
26. LM Howard, G Thornicroft, M Salmon, L Appleby. Predictors of parenting outcome in women with psychotic disorders discharged from mother and baby units.

Acta Psychiatr Scand. 2004;110(5):347–55.

27. J Hammond, M Lipsedge. Assessing parenting capacity in psychiatric mother and baby units: a case report and review of literature. *Psychiatr Danub.* 2015;27 Suppl 1:S71–83.
28. G Seneviratne, S Conroy, M Marks. Parenting assessment in a psychiatric mother and baby unit. *Br J Soc Work.* 2004;33(4):535–55.
29. A Cès, B Falissard, NMC Glangeaud-Freudenthal, AL Sutter-Dallay, F Gressier. Pregnancy in women with psychotic disorders: risk factors associated with mother-baby separation. *Arch Womens Ment Health.* 2018;21(6):699–706.
30. H Cleaver, I Unell, J Aldgate. *Children's needs – parenting capacity: child abuse – parental mental illness, learning disability, substance misuse and domestic violence.* 2nd ed. London: The Stationery Office; 2011.
31. MA Hameed, AJ Lewis. Offspring of parents with schizophrenia: a systematic review of developmental features across childhood. *Harv Rev Psychiatry.* 2016;24(2):104–17.
32. E Aktar, J Qu, PJ Lawrence, MS Tollenaar, BM Elzinga, SM Bögels. Fetal and infant outcomes in the offspring of parents with perinatal mental disorders: earliest influences. *Front Psychiatry.* 2019;10:391.
33. BD Booth, SH Friedman, S Curry, H Ward, SE Stewart. Obsessions of child murder: underrecognized manifestations of obsessive-compulsive disorder. *J Am Acad Psychiatry Law.* 2014;42(1):66–74.
34. FL Challacombe, M Bavetta, S DeGiorgio. Intrusive thoughts in perinatal obsessive-compulsive disorder. *BMJ.* 2019;367: l6574.
35. N Fairbrother, F Collardeau, SR Woody, DA Wolfe, JM Fawcett. Postpartum thoughts of infant-related harm and obsessive-compulsive disorder: relation to maternal physical aggression toward the infant. *J Clin Psychiatry.* 2022;83(2):21m1400.
36. C Chamberlain, G Gee, S Harfield, S Campbell, S Brennan, Y Clark, et al. Parenting after a history of childhood maltreatment: a scoping review and map of evidence in the perinatal period. *PLoS ONE.* 2019;14(3):e0213460.
37. CA Greene, L Haisley, C Wallace, JD Ford. Intergenerational effects of childhood maltreatment: a systematic review of the parenting practices of adult survivors of childhood abuse, neglect, and violence. *Clin Psychol Rev.* 2020;80:101891.
38. NHS England. The NHS long term plan. 2019.
39. B Ruffell, DM Smith, A Wittkowski. The experiences of male partners of women with postnatal mental health problems: a systematic review and thematic synthesis. *J Child Fam Stud.* 2019;28:2772–90.
40. H Laming. The Victoria Climbie inquiry: report of an inquiry by Lord Laming. 2003. https://tinyurl.com/yw39cbzy
41. Early Intervention Foundation. Realising the potential of early intervention. 2018.
42. Health Education England. The competency framework for professionals working with women who have mental health problems in the perinatal period. 2018.
43. NHS Education for Scotland. Perinatal mental health curricular framework: a framework for maternal and infant mental health. 2019.
44. Royal College of Psychiatrists. Standards for community perinatal mental health services. 4th ed. 2018.
45. Royal College of Psychiatrists. Standards for inpatient perinatal mental health services. 6th ed. 2018.
46. Home Office. Multi agency working and information sharing project final report. 2014.
47. L Khan. Falling through the gaps: perinatal mental health and general practice. 2015. The Centre for Mental Health and the Royal College of General Practitioners.

48. Royal College of Obstetricians & Gynaecologists. Maternal mental health – women's voices. 2017.
49. The Scottish Government. National guidance for child protection in Scotland. 2014.
50. K Broadhurst, C Mason, S Bedston, B Alrouh, L Morriss, T McQuarrie, et al. Vulnerable birth mothers and recurrent care proceedings: final main report. 2017. Centre for Child & Family Justice Research, Lancaster University.
51. R Smithson, M Gibson. Less than human: a qualitative study into the experience of parents involved in the child protection system. *Child Fam Soc Work.* 2017;22:565–74.
52. K Broadhurst, B Alrouh, C Mason, H Ward, L Holmes, M Ryan, et al. *Born into care: newborn babies subject to care proceedings in England.* London: Nuffield Family Justice Observatory for England and Wales; 2018.
53. K Connellan, C Bartholomaeus, C Due, DW Riggs. A systematic review of research on psychiatric mother-baby units. *Arch Womens Ment Health.* 2017;20:373–88.
54. NMC Glangeaud-Freudenthal, AL Sutter-Dallay, AC Thieulin, V Dagens, MA Zimmermann, A Debourg, et al. Predictors of infant foster care in cases of maternal psychiatric disorders. *Soc Psych Psych Epid.* 2013;48:553–61.
55. L Green, S Elliott, L Anwar, E Best, M Tero, A Sarkar, et al. An audit of pregnant women with severe mental illness referred during the first 2 years of a new perinatal mental health service. *Arch Womens Ment Health.* 2008;11(2):149–58.
56. M Knight, D Tuffnell, S Kenyon, J Shakespeare, R Gray, J Kurinczuk, editors, on behalf of MBRRACE-UK. *Saving Lives, Improving Mothers' Care – Surveillance of maternal deaths in the UK 2011–13 and Lessons learned to inform maternity care from the UK and Ireland Confidential Enquiries into Maternal Deaths and Morbidity 2009–13.* Oxford: National Perinatal Epidemiology Unit, University of Oxford; 2015.
57. M Knight, K Bunch, D Tuffnell, H Jayakody, J Shakespeare, R Kotnis, et al., editors, on behalf of MBRRACE-UK. *Saving Lives, Improving Mothers' Care – Lessons learned to inform maternity care from the UK and Ireland Confidential Enquiries into Maternal Deaths and Morbidity 2014–16.* Oxford: National Perinatal Epidemiology Unit, University of Oxford; 2018.
58. K McCracken, S Priest, A FitzSimons, K Bracewell, K Torchia, W Parry, et al. Evaluation of pause. Research report. 2017. Department for Education.

Chapter 37

Violence against Women

Claire Wilson, Roxanne Keynejad, Siofra Peeren and Louise M. Howard

Introduction

Violence against women includes domestic violence and abuse (DVA) by intimate partners or family members and non-partner sexual violence, which are the most common forms, but also female genital mutilation and trafficking. One in three women will experience physical or sexual violence in their lifetime [1]. Violence is associated with far-reaching impacts on women's health and well-being, including their sexual, reproductive and mental health, making it a major public health problem. Moreover, users of mental health services are disproportionately affected by DVA and other forms of violence [2]. In this chapter, we discuss the relationship between violence and perinatal mental health and the role of psychiatrists in the assessment and management of women experiencing violence in the perinatal period.

Epidemiology

Domestic Violence and Abuse and Mental Health

The UK Home Office defines DVA as 'controlling, coercive or threatening behaviour, violence or abuse between people aged 16 or over, who are or have been intimate partners or family members, regardless of gender or sexuality' [3]. This includes, but is not limited to, psychological, physical, sexual, financial and emotional abuse. Crime Survey data for England and Wales revealed that 5.7% of women aged 16–59 years had experienced domestic abuse within the last year in the year ending March 2023 [4].

Much of the literature on DVA focuses on physical violence but emotional or psychological abuse can be as detrimental to mental health [2]. Cross-sectional studies support an association between DVA and a range of mental disorders. Most of the evidence pertains to intimate partner violence. A meta-analysis found a four times increased risk of lifetime intimate partner violence in women with anxiety disorders (from five studies), three times in women with depressive disorders (from seven studies) and seven times in women with post-traumatic stress disorder (PTSD) (from four studies) [5]. There is also evidence for an association between DVA and eating disorders, personality disorders, psychosis and substance use [5, 6] and with suicide [7]. Indeed, it is now known that users of mental health services are disproportionately affected by DVA, including the more severe forms of DVA such as non-fatal strangulation [2]. In women with severe mental illness, another meta-analysis found that 15–22% of them were affected by DVA (from six studies) [8]. It is difficult to establish the direction of these relationships (DVA leading to mental disorder or mental disorder leading to DVA) in these cross-sectional study designs but longitudinal studies also find relationships in both directions [9].

Sexual Violence and Mental Health

While much sexual violence is perpetrated by partners or ex-partners [10], it can also be perpetrated by non-partners. This is reflected in this definition from the World Health Organization (WHO): 'any sexual act, attempt to obtain a sexual act, unwanted sexual comments or advances, or acts to traffic, or otherwise directed, against a person's sexuality using coercion, by any person regardless of their relationship to the victim, in any setting, including but not limited to home and work' [11]. The Crime Survey for England and Wales reported that, in 2018, 3.4% of women aged 16–59 years had experienced sexual assault within the past 12 months [12]. Women with mental disorder are also over-represented among victims of sexual violence. In a meta-analysis of 11 studies, median prevalence of sexual violence for women with severe mental illness was 9.9%, although this included studies measuring 3-year prevalence [8].

Crime Survey data also estimate that 11.5% of women have experienced some form of sexual abuse before the age of 16 years [13]. It can be difficult, when investigating the association between violence and mental health, to disentangle the effects of chronic and complex trauma dating back to childhood from that of current violence, which often co-occur. There are also a number of challenges to measuring the extent of violence within a population. Victims may choose not to report their experiences due to self-blame and/or stigma. Moreover, they may not recall the events or identify their experiences as abusive [2].

Other Forms of Violence against Women and Mental Health

Trafficking is the recruitment and movement of people, by force or coercion, for the purpose of exploitation; for example, forced labour or sexual exploitation. Over 70% of those trafficked are women and girls [14]. Those who are trafficked are vulnerable to violence, abuse and exploitation prior to, during and after being trafficked. There is evidence that exposure to violence in those who are trafficked increases the risk of mental disorder in the short and longer term [2]. The duration of trafficking, severity of harm caused, unmet social needs and poor social support following escape are additional risk factors for mental disorder [15]. A systematic review of 31 studies conducted predominantly in low- and middle-income countries reported high levels of PTSD, anxiety and depression among those who had been trafficked [16]. In the UK, a cross-sectional survey of those in contact with post-trafficking services at a median time of 16 months following escape, found that 78% of women reported high levels of anxiety, depression or PTSD, 24% ongoing injuries and 23% sexually transmitted infections [17]. Substance use disorders and psychotic disorders have also been reported in people in contact with secondary mental health services who have previously been trafficked [18].

Female genital mutilation (FGM) is another form of violence against women which may also be associated with an increased risk of anxiety, depression and PTSD [19, 20]. FGM is defined by the WHO as: 'the partial or total removal of external female genitalia or other injury to the female genital organs for non-medical reasons' [21]. It is mostly carried out on young girls up to 15 years of age. More than 200 million girls and women alive today are estimated to have been affected by FGM across 31 countries in Africa, the

Middle East and Asia, where FGM is most commonly practised [22]. In the UK, 1,990 women and girls (including some women born in the UK) were recorded as affected by FGM by the National Health Service between January and March 2019 [23]. It is illegal in the UK and individuals can be prosecuted for a number of offences related to its conduct [24]. In addition to the adverse impacts on mental health, immediate consequences of FGM include life-threatening sepsis and haemorrhage. It can also lead to longer-term genito-urinary problems, such as chronic pain and infection [21].

Perinatal Mental Health and Well-Being

Women exposed to violence prior to or during pregnancy may experience poorer obstetric and neonatal outcomes, such as low birth weight and prematurity [25]. Violence can also be a direct cause of maternal death or indirectly by increasing the risk of suicide [26]. Moreover, the risk of DVA is known to increase in the perinatal period, particularly in women with unplanned pregnancies (which may reflect reproductive coercion) [27]. A meta-analysis found that the pooled prevalence of DVA during pregnancy across 92 studies was 28.4% for emotional abuse, 13.8% for physical abuse and 8% for sexual abuse. The strongest risk factors for DVA during pregnancy appear to be lower education level and pre-pregnancy abuse [28].

There are a number of means by which the presence of violence in a woman's life may exert a negative impact on her childbearing experiences. Physical injuries associated with prior or current violence can increase the risk of physical ill health in women during the perinatal period. For example, FGM can increase the risk of obstetric complications [21]. For women with psychological trauma associated with violent experiences, there are also many events during pregnancy which can recreate the dynamics of past abuse and can be retraumatising; commonly reported triggers include medical examinations or the loss of control sometimes experienced during labour and delivery [29, 30].

There is an increased risk of mental disorder in the perinatal period among women exposed to violence. There are cross-sectional associations between current or previous DVA and depression, anxiety and PTSD in the perinatal period [31]. Meta-analysis of three longitudinal studies provided evidence for an increased risk of postnatal depression in women exposed to intimate partner violence during pregnancy [31]. There is also evidence from large cohort studies of pregnant women experiencing intimate partner violence, that they have higher rates of perinatal substance use, including alcohol and tobacco [32, 33].

Exposure to such obstetric and neonatal adversities may impact offspring's long-term development, exacerbated by any further violence and abuse in infancy and childhood [34]. There is also some evidence for an adverse impact of DVA during pregnancy on the developing mother–infant interaction; poorer attachment has been observed both during pregnancy [35] and in the postpartum [36] in women exposed to antenatal DVA compared to those unexposed. Furthermore, there is some limited evidence from a recent systematic review that women who experienced intimate partner violence during pregnancy may exhibit reduced breastfeeding initiation, shorter duration and earlier termination of exclusive breastfeeding, compared to unexposed women [37].

Assessment and Management

Considering how common a history of previous or current exposure to violence is among women in contact with mental health services and the potential deleterious effects on the woman and her infant, mental health professionals supporting women in the perinatal period should enquire about violence as part of their assessment. There are a number of guidelines, including from the WHO and UK National Institute for Health and Care Excellence (NICE), advising on how best to ask about this and how to create an environment conducive to disclosure [38, 39, 40].

How to ask about violence when assessing women in the perinatal period [38, 39]:

- Ensure your service is a disclosing environment by providing information about violence in waiting rooms, toilets and other spaces occupied by patients. This may include posters or leaflets with information, including contact details of relevant local and national organisations and helplines. Such information should be available in a range of formats and languages.
- Ensure women are routinely seen alone (without the potential abuser present) in a private setting at some point during the assessment and subsequent contacts.
- Do not use family, friends or carers as interpreters.
- Enquire sensitively and non-judgementally.
- For all women, routinely ask open questions followed by behaviourally descriptive questions about events and avoid using generic terms such as 'violence', as women may not identify their experiences as a form of violence or abuse.
- Reassure women that they are believed and not to blame for their experiences.

In addition to presenting with mental ill health, there are a number of other additional signs that may indicate that the woman is experiencing violence.

Additional signs that a woman may be experiencing violence [41]:

- Unexplained chronic gastrointestinal, genito-urinary or gynaecological symptoms, such as pelvic pain, vaginal bleeding or sexually transmitted infections.
- Adverse reproductive events, such as unintended pregnancies, terminations, delayed antenatal care, miscarriages, preterm labour and stillbirth.
- Unexplained or implausible traumatic injuries.
- Repeated health consultations with no clear diagnosis or non-engagement or poor engagement with services.
- Intrusive other person in appointments, such as partner or family member.

There is an emphasis in the NICE and WHO guidelines on being able to provide appropriate support and ensure safety following disclosure, in order to provide a comprehensive response regardless of whether the woman chooses to leave or remain in an abusive relationship [38, 39]. Feeling ill equipped to respond has been identified by mental health professionals as a barrier to enquiry in their patients [42]. There are a number of training packages available for mental health professionals [40, 43]. Box 37.1 provides examples of questions to ask women to prompt discussion about violence and explore it further. Box 37.2 provides further advice for remote consulting. However, recent confidential enquiries into maternal deaths in the UK as a result of DVA underscore the importance of being able to adequately mobilise safeguarding procedures, which may require face-to-face intervention even during crises such as pandemics, natural disasters and armed conflict [44]. It is also important for mental health services to ensure that support is available for staff who may find work with women who are or have been victims of violence challenging. Staff who have been victims themselves may find it particularly difficult, which may act as a further barrier to disclosure.

Box 37.1 Example Questions to Ask about Current and Previous Experiences of Violence

- Has anybody ever done anything to you that they shouldn't have done?
- How are things with your partner/ex-partner/family?
- Has anyone close to you ever hurt or upset you?
- Are you afraid of anybody close to you?
- What happens when your partner/ex-partner/family argue?
- Do you ever change your behaviour because you are worried about how somebody at home might react?
- Does anybody ever stop you doing things that you would like to do such as leaving the house?
- Has anybody been monitoring your emails, texts or location?
- Does anybody consistently put you down, insult or belittle you? (emotional abuse)
- Has anybody ever forced you to have sex when you did not want to? (sexual abuse)
- Has anybody ever forced you to take out a loan or controls your finances? (economic abuse)
- Have you ever had any operations, been cut or had something done to change the appearance of your vagina/genitals/'down below'? (FGM)
- What type of work do you do and can you leave your job if you want to? (trafficking)

Box 37.2 Further Advice for Remote Consulting

- Be mindful that perpetrators may hear conversations with health professionals in the home
- Consider whether or not contact via phone, text, email or messaging apps is a safe and feasible alternative to face-to-face contact
- For all telephone and video consultations, check who else is in the room or at home and if it is safe to talk
- For remote contact via email, text messaging or apps, discuss with the woman whether an abusive partner has access to her phone or computer
- Consider using closed 'yes' or 'no' questions so that the content of the discussion cannot be understood by someone else in the room
- Create a safe word/phrase with the patient to identify risk of harm without the knowledge of a perpetrator ('if the situation changes can we use a phrase for you to let me know that X has returned? e.g. thanks but I'm not interested'). Agree how you will contact her to follow up, if the call is terminated in this way.

Assuming the woman has mental capacity, decisions must involve a consideration of the many factors that may influence actions taken, including whether to continue or end an abusive relationship. The clinical priority is safety planning; this is particularly important given that women are at greatest risk of homicide in the months immediately following separation [45]. While involvement of other agencies is usually indicated, any referrals and/or sharing of information with other parties should be discussed with the woman first, balancing the professional duty of confidentiality alongside the risks to the woman, her child(ren) and wider family. Mandatory legal reporting by healthcare professionals is not recommended [39]. Fear of such actions by professionals following disclosure has been identified as a key barrier to disclosure by victims of violence [42].

Multi-agency risk assessment conferences are meetings in the UK for sharing information between agencies about people experiencing violence or abuse, particularly those at high risk. The person experiencing the violence may be represented by an independent domestic violence adviser or advocate or an independent sexual violence advocate. The aim is to devise a coordinated safety plan.

How to provide a safe and effective response following disclosure of violence [38, 39]:

- Prior to asking about abuse, become familiar with any local referral pathways for those who disclose violence including local agencies who provide support to victims of violence and abuse.
- Prioritise safety.
- Consider referral to local agencies who provide support to victims of violence and abuse after discussion with the woman.
- Liaise with local safeguarding leads.

There is evidence that making health professionals aware of guidelines and training is insufficient to create sustained improvements in the identification and response to violence against women in mental health services [2]. Widespread culture change is also needed. However, there is some evidence from both primary care and mental health services that integrating DVA advocates within clinical teams, including antenatal care, in addition to training, can improve the identification of DVA and outcomes for victims [46, 47]. There is systematic review evidence that advocacy interventions in antenatal settings for women experiencing intimate partner violence are associated with reductions in physical and emotional abuse and depressive symptoms [48].

There have been a number of trials of interventions for pregnant women experiencing intimate partner violence. A systematic review of these interventions included several involving psychotherapy with some evidence for reduced symptoms in the perinatal period of depression and PTSD in women participating in the intervention [49]. There is also evidence that a trauma focus in psychological therapies for mental disorders such as PTSD in survivors of abuse results in improved outcomes. For example, a Cochrane review of the effectiveness of psychological therapies for the treatment of chronic PTSD found evidence (albeit low quality) that trauma-focused cognitive behavioural therapy (CBT) and eye movement desensitisation and reprocessing are superior to non-trauma focused CBT at 1 and 4 months following treatment [50]. More research is required to investigate the outcomes of these approaches in the perinatal period.

In some cases, couples may wish to stay together, particularly in the perinatal period when both will want to be involved in parenting. This may reflect a power imbalance within the couple including reflecting reproductive coercion so each case must be assessed carefully, with awareness of their complexity. When judged safe and appropriate, mental health professionals need to continue to ensure safety by seeing couples individually as well as together and ensuring regular discussion within the multidisciplinary team. There is some evidence, that over time, when DVA has been recognised as an issue, many will decide to leave the relationship [51].

Trauma-Informed Approaches

There is an increasing recognition that practices within mental healthcare can harm those who have experienced violence and abuse, often through re-creating the power imbalances characteristic of interpersonal violence. Trauma-informed approaches are an organisational change process, focused on preventing (re)traumatisation within services. Trauma-informed approaches are distinct from trauma-specific services such as trauma-focused CBT and trauma-specific services are not inherently trauma-informed [52].

The principles of trauma-informed approaches [53, 54, 55]:

1. Seeing through a trauma lens: understanding and acknowledging the links between trauma and mental health.
2. Adopting a broad definition of trauma beyond PTSD that recognises social trauma and the intersectionality of multiple traumas.
3. Safety: ensuring physical and emotional safety; for example, considering how healthcare environments might make a patient feel unsafe and making adjustments such as ensuring single-sex wards and limiting the number of professionals to which a person has to repeat their traumatic history.
4. Trustworthiness: building trust; for example, through prioritising choices, informed consent and confidentiality.
5. Choice: encouraging patients to maintain control and exercise choice; for example, co-production of care plans.
6. Collaboration: clinician and patient working together to set goals and establish priorities.
7. Empowerment: helping patients to recognise their skills and ability to overcome adversity.
8. Adopting strengths-based approaches that reframe symptoms as coping adaptations, for example seeing trauma responses such as dissociation as an adaptive strategy that can help a patient to cope with unbearable experiences.
9. Referring people to evidence-based, trauma-specific support, where indicated.

Conclusion

Violence is a frequent occurrence in the histories of women using mental health services in the perinatal period. As the perinatal period is often the first time in a woman's life that she engages with health services regularly and frequently, this represents an opportunity to support women and their families. Mental health professionals can play a role in sensitive enquiry, assertive safety planning and longer-term support of women affected by violence in all its forms and should be supported to do so through training and advocacy within clinical teams.

References

1. World Health Organization. Global and regional estimates of violence against women: prevalence and health effects of intimate partner violence and non-partner sexual violence. 2013. https://apps.who.int/iris/handle/10665/85239
2. S Oram, H Khalifeh, LM Howard. Violence against women and mental health. *Lancet Psychiatry.* 2017;4(2):159–70.
3. UK Home Office. Information for local areas on the change to the definition of domestic violence. 2013. https://tinyurl.com/bdd8sd6d
4. Office for National Statistics. Domestic abuse in England and Wales overview: November 2023. 2023. https://tinyurl.com/y6jyyet7
5. K Trevillion, S Oram, G Feder, LM Howard. Experiences of domestic violence and mental disorders: a

systematic review and meta-analysis. *PLoS ONE.* 2012;7(12):e51740.

6. S Jonas, H Khalifeh, PE Bebbington, S McManus, T Brugha, H Meltzer, et al. Gender differences in intimate partner violence and psychiatric disorders in England: results from the 2007 adult psychiatric morbidity survey. *Epidemiol Psychiatr Sci.* 2014;23(2):189–99.
7. CL Palladino, V Singh, J Campbell, H Flynn, KJ Gold. Homicide and suicide during the perinatal period: findings from the national violent death reporting system. *Obstet Gynecol.* 2011;118(5):1056–63.
8. H Khalifeh, S Oram, D Osborn, LM Howard, S Johnson. Recent physical and sexual violence against adults with severe mental illness: a systematic review and meta-analysis. *Int Rev Psychiatry.* 2016;28(5):433–51.
9. S Oram, HL Fisher, H Minnis, S Seedat, S Walby, K Hegarty, et al. The Lancet Psychiatry Commission on intimate partner violence and mental health: advancing mental health services, research, and policy. *Lancet Psychiatry.* 2022;9(6):487–524.
10. S Walby, J Allen. Domestic violence, sexual assault and stalking: findings from the British Crime Survey. 2004. Home Office.
11. World Health Organization. Violence against women: intimate partner and sexual violence against women. 2011. https://apps.who.int/iris/bitstream/handle/10665/77434/WHO_RHR_1237_engpdf?sequence=1
12. Office for National Statistics. Sexual offending: victimisation and the path through the criminal justice system. 2018. https://tinyurl.com/56s2r269
13. Office for National Statistics. Child sexual abuse in England and Wales: year ending March 2019. 2020. https://tinyurl.com/mrx8etm2
14. United Nations Office on Drugs and Crime. Global report on trafficking in persons. 2018. www.unodc.org/documents/data-and-analysis/glotip/2018/GLOTiP_2018_BOOK_web_small.pdf
15. M Abas, NV Ostrovschi, M Prince, VI Gorceag, C Trigub, S Oram. Risk factors for mental disorders in women survivors of human trafficking: a historical cohort study. *BMC Psychiatry.* 2013;13(1):204.
16. L Ottisova, S Hemmings, LM Howard, C Zimmerman, S Oram. Prevalence and risk of violence and the mental, physical and sexual health problems associated with human trafficking: an updated systematic review. *Epidemiol Psychiatr Sci.* 2016;25(4):317–41.
17. S Oram, M Abas, D Bick, A Boyle, R French, S Jakobowitz, et al. Human trafficking and health: a survey of male and female survivors in England. *Am J Public Health.* 2016;106(6):1073–8.
18. S Oram, M Khondoker, M Abas, M Broadbent, LM Howard. Characteristics of trafficked adults and children with severe mental illness: a historical cohort study. *Lancet Psychiatry.* 2015;2(12):1084–91.
19. SM Abdalla, S Galea. Is female genital mutilation/cutting associated with adverse mental health consequences? A systematic review of the evidence. *BMJ Global Health.* 2019;4(4):e001553.
20. RC Berg, EM-L Denison, A Fretheim. Psychological, social and sexual consequences of female genital mutilation/cutting (FGM/C): a systematic review of quantitative studies. 2010. https://fhi.brage.unit.no/fhi-xmlui/handle/11250/2378046
21. World Health Organization. Female genital mutilation. 2020. www.who.int/news-room/fact-sheets/detail/female-genital-mutilation
22. UNICEF. Female genital mutilation (FGM). 2020. https://data.unicef.org/topic/child-protection/female-genital-mutilation
23. NHS Digital. Female genital mutilation January–March 2019. 2019. https://tinyurl.com/7jc25kp9
24. UK Home Office. Female genital mutilation. 2020. www.gov.uk/

government/collections/female-genital-mutilation

25. A Hill, C Pallitto, J McCleary-Sills, C Garcia-Moreno. A systematic review and meta-analysis of intimate partner violence during pregnancy and selected birth outcomes. *Int J Gynaecol Obstet.* 2016;133(3):269–76.

26. M Knight, K Bunch, A Felker, R Patel, R Kotnis, S Kenyon, et al., editors. *Saving Lives, Improving Mothers' Care – Lessons learned to inform maternity care from the UK and Ireland Confidential Enquiries into Maternal Deaths and Morbidity 2019–21.* Oxford: National Perinatal Epidemiology Unit, University of Oxford; 2023. www.npeu.ox.ac.uk/mbrrace-uk/reports

27. H Finnbogadóttir, A-K Dykes. Increasing prevalence and incidence of domestic violence during the pregnancy and one and a half year postpartum, as well as risk factors: a longitudinal cohort study in Southern Sweden. *BMC Pregnancy Childbirth.* 2016;16(1):327.

28. L James, D Brody, Z Hamilton. Risk factors for domestic violence during pregnancy: a meta-analytic review. *Violence Vict.* 2013;28(3):359–80.

29. L Halvorsen, H Nerum, P Oian, T Sørlie. Giving birth with rape in one's past: a qualitative study. *Birth.* 2013;40(3):182–91.

30. E Montgomery, C Pope, J Rogers. The re-enactment of childhood sexual abuse in maternity care: a qualitative study. *BMC Pregnancy Childbirth.* 2015;15:194.

31. LM Howard, S Oram, H Galley, K Trevillion, G Feder. Domestic violence and perinatal mental disorders: a systematic review and meta-analysis. *PLoS Med.* 2013;10(5):e1001452-e.

32. HA Flynn, MA Walton, ST Chermack, RM Cunningham, SM Marcus. Brief detection and co-occurrence of violence, depression and alcohol risk in prenatal care settings. *Arch Womens Ment Health.* 2007;10(4):155–61.

33. IE Udo, JB Lewis Lmft, JN Tobin, JR Ickovics. Intimate partner victimization and health risk behaviors among pregnant adolescents. *Am J Public Health.* 2016;106(8):1457–9.

34. AL Murray, D Kaiser, S Valdebenito, C Hughes, A Baban, AD Fernando, et al. The intergenerational effects of intimate partner violence in pregnancy: mediating pathways and implications for prevention. *Trauma Violence Abuse.* 2018;21(5):964–76.

35. C Pires de Almeida, E Sá, F Cunha, EP Pires. Violence during pregnancy and its effects on mother–baby relationship during pregnancy. *J Reprod Infant Psychol.* 2013;31(4):370–80.

36. JA Quinlivan, SF Evans. Impact of domestic violence and drug abuse in pregnancy on maternal attachment and infant temperament in teenage mothers in the setting of best clinical practice. *Arch Womens Ment Health.* 2005;8(3):191–9.

37. AK Normann, A Bakiewicz, F Kjerulff Madsen, KS Khan, V Rasch, DS Linde. Intimate partner violence and breastfeeding: a systematic review. *BMJ Open.* 2020;10(10):e034153.

38. National Institute for Health and Care Excellence. Domestic violence and abuse: multi-agency working. Public Health Guideline (PH50). 2014. www.nice.org.uk/guidance/ph50/chapter/glossary#indicators

39. World Health Organization. Responding to intimate partner violence and sexual violence against women: WHO clinical and policy guidelines. 2013. www.who.int/publications/i/item/WHO-RHR-13.10

40. E Yapp, S Oram, H Lempp, R Agnew-Davies, G Feder, K Trevillion, et al. LARA-VP: a resource to help mental health professionals identify and respond to domestic violence and abuse (DVA). 2018. www.kcl.ac.uk/psychology-systems-sciences/research/lara-vp-download-form

41. MC Black. Intimate partner violence and adverse health consequences: implications for clinicians. *Am J Lifestyle Med.* 2011;5(5):428–39.

42. D Rose, K Trevillion, A Woodall, C Morgan, G Feder, L Howard. Barriers and facilitators of disclosures of domestic violence by mental health service users: qualitative study. *Br J Psychiatry.* 2011;198(3):189–94.

43. L Howard. Domestic violence and abuse: identifying and responding to victims and perpetrators. 2019. https://elearning.rcpsych.ac.uk/learningmodules/domesticviolenceandabuseiaspx

44. M Knight, K Bunch, A Cairns, R Cantwell, P Cox, S Kenyon, et al., editors. *Saving Lives, Improving Mothers' Care Rapid Report: Learning from SARS-CoV-2-related and associated maternal deaths in the UK March–May 2020.* Oxford: National Perinatal Epidemiology Unit, University of Oxford; 2020. www.npeu.ox.ac.uk/mbrrace-uk/reports

45. JC Campbell, D Webster, J Koziol-McLain, C Block, D Campbell, MA Curry, et al. Risk factors for femicide in abusive relationships: results from a multisite case control study. *Am J Public Health.* 2003;93(7):1089–97.

46. G Feder, RA Davies, K Baird, D Dunne, S Eldridge, C Griffiths, et al. Identification and Referral to Improve Safety (IRIS) of women experiencing domestic violence with a primary care training and support programme: a cluster randomised controlled trial. *Lancet.* 2011;378(9805):1788–95.

47. K Trevillion, S Byford, M Cary, D Rose, S Oram, G Feder, et al. Linking abuse and recovery through advocacy: an observational study. *Epidemiol Psychiatr Sci.* 2014;23(1):99–113.

48. C Rivas, J Ramsay, L Sadowski, LL Davidson, D Dunne, S Eldridge, et al. Advocacy interventions to reduce or eliminate violence and promote the physical and psychosocial well-being of women who experience intimate partner abuse. *Cochrane Database Syst Rev.* 2015;(12):Cd005043.

49. KH Howell, LE Miller-Graff, AJ Hasselle, KE Scrafford. The unique needs of pregnant, violence-exposed women: a systematic review of current interventions and directions for translational research. *Aggress Violent Behav.* 2017;34:128–38.

50. JI Bisson, NP Roberts, M Andrew, R Cooper, C Lewis. Psychological therapies for chronic post-traumatic stress disorder (PTSD) in adults. *Cochrane Database Syst Rev.* 2013;(12):CD003388.

51. For Baby's Sake. Final evaluation report. 2021. www.forbabyssake.org.uk/wp-content/uploads/2021/02/FBS-1165-Full-Report-A4-v1-1.pdf

52. A Sweeney, C Perôt, F Callard, V Adenden, N Mantovani, L Goldsmith. Out of the silence: towards grassroots and trauma-informed support for people who have experienced sexual violence and abuse. *Epidemiol Psychiatr Sci.* 2019;28(6):598–602.

53. RD Fallot, M Harris. A trauma-informed approach to screening and assessment. *New Dir Ment Health Serv.* 2001;2001(89):23–31.

54. DE Elliott, P Bjelajac, RD Fallot, LS Markoff, BG Reed. Trauma-informed or trauma-denied: principles and implementation of trauma-informed services for women. *J Comm Psychol.* 2005;33(4):461–77.

55. A Sweeney, B Filson, A Kennedy, L Collinson, S Gillard. A paradigm shift: relationships in trauma-informed mental health services. *BJPsych Adv.* 2018;24(5):319–33.

Chapter 38

When Mothers Kill Their Children

Gwen Adshead

Introduction

The tragedies of Sophocles and Aeschylus contain some of our earliest accounts of mothers who kill; of which *Medea* is probably the best known for its description of a mother who kills her children to punish and distress her husband. *Medea* is a reminder that, for centuries, mothers who kill have been the objects of horrified fascination and condemnation, reflecting the public horror at the idea that a mother could deliberately kill her own child. The very word 'mother' is so closely associated with nurturance and care that it seems unthinkable that any mother could act in such a way; and the women who do so are often seen as unfeminine as well as inhuman.

Every year in every country across the world, national statistics report cases of women who have killed their children: their babies, their toddlers, even their older children. However, in general, fatal violence by women is rare, and it is perhaps that rarity that makes society demand explanations for how mothers could act in this way. It is also perhaps inevitable that the courts and the general public have turned to psychiatry and psychology to provide an explanation and understanding of what makes mothers kill their own children.

In this chapter I will describe some of the available data about women who kill their children and in what circumstances. I will discuss the killing of children under 1 year (infanticide), killing of newborns (neonaticide) and the killing of all other children (filicide). I go on to describe the legal process in England in relation to homicide; how the courts approach the criminal trials of mothers who kill; and how psychiatric evidence might be utilised by defence and prosecution. I discuss how professionals have formulated the motivations of mothers who kill, and the role of mental illness and psychological disorders as risk factors for the killing of children, especially in light of recent studies of the attachment security of high-risk mothers. I conclude with a discussion of the implications for psychiatrists in relation to management, treatment and risk assessment.

Mothers Who Kill: Data from Different Jurisdictions

International data suggests that there are three main forms of homicide: crime related; politically motivated; and relational [1]. In peacetime and in most organised social democracies, relational homicide is the commonest form. The term implies that *the relationship* between the killer and their victim is key to understanding the homicide, and it is that relational context that makes the homicide emotionally meaningful.

It follows that the killing of strangers by strangers is rare, and most people who kill have a relationship with their victims, typically one of closeness and dependency.

The killing of a child by their mother falls firmly within this category. The data on such homicides is likely to be incomplete in many countries, even in wealthy countries with good record-keeping. Researchers in this field suggest that child homicides are almost certainly under-reported [2]. There are still countries and jurisdictions where child deaths are not always criminally investigated; especially if those deaths appear to be the result of concurrent illness or accident.

It may surprise readers that of all age groups of homicide victims, children under the age of one are statistically most at risk of being a homicide victim, and the perpetrator is typically their mother or father or another adult in a parental role [3, 4]. Once over the age of one, the risk of a child being killed by anyone drops steadily, with children aged 10/11 being at lowest risk. However, the teenage years are associated with increasing risk of being killed, although the likely perpetrator is an acquaintance, rather than a parent [4, 5].

Where the child victim is under the age of five, both mothers and fathers are equally likely to be perpetrators but for babies under 1 year, mothers are the most likely perpetrator. The evidence confirms that for children and young people, the risk of being attacked or killed by a complete stranger is low: we warn children and young people not to be trusting of strangers, but the statistics suggests that misplaced trust in carers is a major contributor to risk of death. Small children and babies, of course, have no choice in terms of the adults they 'get' to trust and depend on for safety and protection.

Criminologists differentiate between neonaticide, infanticide and filicide. Only infanticide is a specific legal offence; mothers who kill their newborn babies may be charged with infanticide, but a mother who kills a child older than a year will be charged with murder. Forensic psychiatric studies of mothers who have killed their children usually draw on convenience samples of women facing criminal charges, remanded into custody or detained in secure psychiatric facilities.

Legal Processes after the Death of a Child

Where a child has died in suspicious circumstances, the processes are as for any other homicide investigation. If the mother is a suspect, she will be invited to participate in a police interview, where she should be legally represented. If there is any question of mental vulnerability, an appropriate adult may also be present. The police will make a decision whether or not to charge on the basis of that interview and the evidence; it is common for perpetrator mothers to confess at this stage. Police interviews may also be the first source of evidence that a suspect mother is mentally unwell.

If the mother is charged with the murder of a child, the first step will be a decision about whether she is remanded in custody or is released on bail. Defendants who are charged with murder are rarely released on bail, but in the case of the death of a child, it has been known for mothers to get bail. If a defendant mother is obviously mentally unwell, this is the point at which a psychiatric assessment will be urgently sought for admission to a psychiatric service. Although such mothers could be admitted to open wards, the fact that they are suspects in a criminal case means that it is more usual for them to be admitted to forensic psychiatric services, usually a medium secure facility. Women charged with a crime related to the death of a child will usually be detained under local mental health legislation (e.g. in England and Wales, the Mental Health Act 1983). It is a marker of how attitudes have changed to note that 100 years ago, most women in England who were accused or found to have killed a child were sent to high secure hospitals like Broadmoor; whereas now, it would be rare for a woman detained under English mental health legislation to be seen as requiring high secure provision.

Whether remanded to prison or secure hospital or in the community, the defendant mother will be advised by her criminal solicitors about the basis of a defence to a charge of murder. Solicitors will then instruct expert reports to explore whether there is evidence that the mother was suffering from any kind of mental disorder at the time of the killing. The charges made depend on the age of the child: if the child was under a year old (which includes neonates), the mother may be charged with infanticide, not murder; and if she pleads guilty to this charge, then she is effectively pleading guilty to manslaughter, which means that the judge has a range of sentences at their disposal. The offence of infanticide is a Victorian piece of legislation, but is a convenient way for courts to dispose of mothers who kill their babies when frankly mentally ill with conditions like postpartum psychosis.

If the child is over a year old, the infanticide charge is not available, and mothers will have to explore other defences to a murder charge. Their criminal defence teams will usually explore the psychiatric defences of diminished responsibility or insanity. The insanity defence, if successful, would result in a mother being acquitted, but also results in a hospital order with restrictions and a potentially lengthy stay in secure hospital. Therefore, if there is evidence that the woman was suffering from a mental disorder at the time which 'explains' the killing, then this will be the basis of a diminished responsibility defence. Like infanticide, if successful, the diminished responsibility defence results in a conviction for manslaughter, which allows the judge discretion in sentencing. A mother convicted of manslaughter may be sent to hospital under a hospital order (section 37) with or without restriction of time (section 41). She may also be sent to prison to serve a prison term, which can vary in length.

Readers will note that both women in Box 38.1 committed similar offences but had different outcomes at court. In both cases, the court would have heard expert testimony

Box 38.1 Two Cases

Mr and Mrs S were happily married but had fertility problems. Using IVF, Mrs S eventually conceived and gave birth to twins. Sadly, the relationship between Mr and Mrs S broke down in the first postnatal year, and Mr S announced that he would be seeking a divorce. On the weekend of the twins' second birthday, Mrs S drowned the children and made a serious suicide attempt. After her arrest, she was sent to a medium secure unit and had treatment there for a mood disorder. At the trial she was said to have had a 'catastrophic mental decline'. She pleaded guilty to manslaughter on the grounds of diminished responsibility, and was sentenced to 10 years in prison after she had finished her treatment in hospital. In a letter read to the court, she said, 'I'm in torment. The fact the children are not alive because of me is the hardest part of all.'

Ms G met Mr N online and they had a relationship for two years. Ms G fell unexpectedly pregnant and had a baby girl. The relationship broke up, and Mr N sought to have joint custody of his daughter. There were family legal proceedings which gave Mr N rights to contact his daughter and prohibited Ms G from taking her daughter out of the country as she wished. Ms G drowned her daughter, then aged 20 months; and attempted to leave the country. She was detected and arrested. She was remanded in custody and made a serious suicide attempt while in prison. She was convicted of murder and sentenced to life imprisonment, to serve a minimum of 15 years.

from psychiatrists about the women's mental state at the time of the killing, and for their view about criminal responsibility and treatment needs. In cases like Mrs S's, who did receive treatment of her mental disorder while waiting for her trial, the treating psychiatrist should not act as an expert but only as a professional witness. The expert witnesses may consult the treating psychiatrist and may require access to the clinical notes, subject to the usual consents (see Chapter 40 on writing reports for court).

Different Kinds of Filicide by Age of Child

Women who kill their newborn babies (neonaticide) have been identified as a subgroup distinct from women who kill older babies or small children [6]. These newborn babies are often the outcome of an unplanned and unwanted pregnancy, outside an established relationship. Women in this situation are typically young, still living at home and often without a close supportive relationship within their family. They often deny the pregnancy, either to themselves and/or their families and do not seek antenatal care or help with labour. They may conceal or otherwise dispose of the body of the child; this author is aware of two cases where the young women threw the newborn baby in a rubbish bin. These young women may be socially isolated but rarely have any history of criminal rule breaking or mental illness.

Both Reznick and Spinelli argue that women who kill their newborn babies (often in the context of a 'hidden' or denied pregnancy) should be considered as having different psychopathology from mothers who kill older babies or children, and that neonaticide needs to be distinguished from infanticide or filicide [7, 8, 9]. Specifically, Spinelli argues that these young women dissociate at the time of the birth, and see the baby as a kind of threat, leading to abandonment. However, there is little good quality data on whether this apparent disconnection from a pregnancy and child persists into the future, nor what risk this might pose to future pregnancies.

Filicide studies tend to be either based on criminal justice statistics for a geographical area; or meta-analytic reviews of published papers. Both kinds of publication may include male and female perpetrators of child homicide, while others focus on women. There has been an understandable focus on those women who kill children under a year old while suffering postnatal psychosis. However, the majority of women who kill infants and older children do not meet criteria for postnatal psychosis but may meet criteria for different kinds of personality dysfunction [10].

Motivations for Mothers Killing Children: 50 Years of Research

There have been many attempts to classify the motives of mothers who kill their children, and this work is ongoing. The earliest is that of Resnick, based on a US sample; his work has been replicated in the UK and other countries [11, 12]. Resnick's classification has five categories of possible motivation for filicide: active mental illness at the material time; killing a child who is unwanted; killing as a consequence of physical abuse and neglect; killing as a form of revenge on the child's father; and killing for what Resnick called 'altruistic reasons' (typically, the belief that the child would be spared suffering by their death).

Resnick's typology has not changed much in the last half century. Both hostility towards the child and jealousy of the child have been added as motives [13, 14].

Oberman and Meyer suggest that some mothers may be coerced or assisted into killing their children by other family members, and have social vulnerabilities that make motherhood stressful [15].

Sidebotham argues that research in this field focuses on two distinct perspectives: either the perpetrator mother's consciously expressed motives and her mental health; or a perspective based in work in child protection, which looks at the child's experience and the links between their social circumstances and other kinds of maltreatment [4]. It is true that the many typologies based on maternal motivation tend to be disconnected from the mother's social environment and do not see the child and mother as part of a wider social system. However, neither of these research strands appear to take account of the *relationship* of the child with the mother, or how that relationship is represented in the mother's mind, or what motherhood might mean to this particular mother.

The mother's mind is one aspect of the child's environment and may be influenced by other factors such as a history of childhood adversity, substance misuse and exposure to domestic violence. For example, a recent review by Dekel et al. found that many people who killed their children had experienced adversity and trauma which was relevant to their state of mind at the time of the killing, and for which they had not received support [16]. With regard to domestic violence and substance abuse, two separate studies of fatal child abuse reviews describe a 'toxic triad' of parental mental health problems, parental substance misuse and domestic violence as potent risk factors associated with fatal child abuse in the home [17, 18].

All the filicide typologies include maternal mental illness as a separate category, especially postpartum psychosis and schizophrenia [19, 20]. In such cases, paranoid delusions and hallucinations (both visual and auditory) relating to the baby may act as drivers for fatal violence. For example, beliefs that the baby is possessed by evil and/or perceptions that the baby has 'demonic eyes' and is looking at mother in hostile or frightening way are the kind of phenomena that can be associated with unpredictable violence, even in mothers who seem otherwise calm and loving. Paranoid beliefs about a baby should always be taken seriously, including fears of harming the baby or beliefs that both mother and child are in a dangerous or hopeless situation. Postnatal psychosis is one of the rare diagnoses that does have a strong causal relationship with homicide of a child; one study reports that 8% of women with postpartum psychosis report infanticidal thoughts [21].

However, apart from postnatal psychosis from any cause, the relationship between maternal mental illness and child homicide is complex; just as it is for mental illness and homicide generally. Mental illness is common but homicide is rare; therefore, most people with any kind of mental illness do not kill, perhaps *especially* mothers with mental illness. Mothers who kill resemble other people who kill family members in that they may not always have a clearly diagnosable mental illness; although at the time of the killing they are often experiencing high levels of distress, and other painful affects such as rage, sadness, fear or despair. Only in very few cases (such as in psychosis) do mothers have symptoms that appear to be directly linked to the commission of the offence.

It can be difficult to distinguish motives driven by mental illness from other motives. The typologies for filicide suggest that motives for violence can be easily distinguished from each other and are discrete. However, in reality, human violence is often driven by multiple motives that interact and create a justification that seems to make sense to the perpetrator at the time. For example, mothers with depressive postpartum psychosis may kill because they believe their child is ill or possessed and would be better off dead; a motive which would 'count' as altruistic *and* evidence of mental illness. Similarly, a woman with severe health anxiety before birth may postnatally become convinced that her child is unwell and requires treatment, and may administer medication inappropriately and fatally (e.g. opiates that are risky for young children and babies). In such cases, the woman's prenatal anxiety continues into her relationship with the child and leads to maltreatment which blurs into filicide.

Studies of maternal mental illness associated with filicide find a range of diagnoses, including both antenatal and postnatal diagnoses, such as depression, postpartum psychosis and personality disorder [22, 23]. Studies of motivation in filicide may be subject to sampling bias as they often rely on samples of women who have been referred for psychiatric assessments in relation to a criminal trial; where the stakes are high in terms of outcome, and where the legal defence team is likely to want to emphasise the presence of a mental disorder. There are also sociological issues here about how women's violence is seen as different to men's violence, because it is unusual; and how both mental illness and 'trauma' are seen as explanations for women's violence, but not for men's [24].

For many professionals, the 'classic' case of a mother who kills is a woman with a severe postnatal mental illness who develops paranoid delusions about the baby and herself, but whose deluded mental state is not detected, or is dismissed as ordinary adjustment to the maternal role. When such a mother then kills the baby (typically in the first postnatal year), there are real concerns about the mother's risk of suicide, and associated questions about risk to other or subsequent children. Such women usually have no previous history of either mental illness or criminality; what Putkonen described as a 'pro-social psychotic' [25]. Women who have known prior histories of affective or psychotic disorders at the time of conception should be considered at increased risk of developing postnatal psychosis, and followed up carefully in the first postnatal year. However, where there is no prior history, the first signs of a postnatal psychosis can be subtle, and women who are quite unwell can maintain a 'good front'.

Well-meaning professionals and family may be reluctant to pathologise signs of mental distress, and it is possible for a mother's mental state to deteriorate rapidly and for the risk to escalate abruptly. Each year in the UK, a small number of women do kill their babies and themselves in this context, possibly as a form of 'extended suicide', although recorded data suggests it is thankfully rare. A painful example is that of Daksha Emson who killed herself and her baby while under psychiatric care [26]. It is not known exactly how many women try (but fail) to kill themselves after killing their children; but suicidal risk in the perpetrator is increased after other forms of domestic homicide [27, 28] and, anecdotally, the risk of maternal suicide persists for a long time after a filicide of any sort.

Mothers Who Kill: Maternal Attachment Insecurity and the Breakdown of Maternal Care

It might seem trite or obvious to suggest that if a mother kills her child, it is likely that her relationship to the child is dysfunctional and disordered. Fraiberg first suggested that a mother's own experience of being cared for as a child can have an impact on how she 'sees' her child and their needs, and how their relationships develops [29]. Fraiberg argues that mothers who struggle to care for their children are unconsciously repeating a pattern of poor care that they received as children; what Fraiberg poetically referred to as the presence of 'ghosts in the nursery' that affect the mother's mind in relation to the baby.

A mother's relationship with her baby is the product of many factors, which include factors relating to the child and the woman's social environment. Any maternal mental disorder could in theory affect the relationship with the child, as well as having a major impact on the social environment in which the child is cared for. However, it is arguably the mother's state of mind in relation to the child that is key to her actions, and this representation of motherhood in the mind can be studied using tools based on attachment theory.

Bowlby's account of attachment theory argues that attachment between carers and infants is instinctual in group primates like humans, where young children are dependent and vulnerable for extended periods [30]. Being attached to a parent or carer offers protection, but also helps the child develop an interpersonal sense of self and a capacity to reach out to others when in need. Based on animal studies, Bowlby argued that if the attachment process was disrupted in childhood, then the child's attachment to the parent/carer would be insecure (as opposed to secure) and this might manifest in childhood anxiety and distress. He later theorised that children form internal working models of attachment relationships (similar to cognitive schemas) which persist into adulthood and affect both adult relationships and *crucially* relationships with their own children.

Both prospective and retrospective studies over the last 30 years have confirmed Fraiberg's and Bowlby's work. Children with insecure attachment styles can be identified as early as 18–24 months, and the insecurity can be categorised as 'anxious attachment' or 'avoidant' attachment [31]. Later studies identified another category of disorganised attachment, where children respond to separation from carers with fright and apparent dissociation [32]. Prospective studies of childhood attachment have found that insecurely attached children tend to grow up to be insecurely attached adults [33].

These studies have particular significance for women who become mothers. Prospective studies of attachment insecurity in pregnant women have provided solid evidence that a mother's attachment security has a major impact on how she 'sees' her child's mind and how she embodies her maternal role as carer [34, 35]. In particular, maternal attachment insecurity has an influence on how mothers interpret and respond to their baby's emotional cues [36, 37]. This ability to 'read' a baby's emotional communications is an aspect of 'mentalising' function, which is that capacity to 'read' other people's intentions and keep 'mind in mind' [38]. Insecurity of attachment can be associated with impairments in mentalising [39] which then form a potential mechanism by which attachment insecurity is transmitted from mother to child.

Insecurity of attachment is common (40%) in the general population, which would suggest that a similar proportion of women conceiving children have insecure attachment [40]. Maternal attachment insecurity of mind is more likely if as a child, a mother experienced adverse childhood experiences (ACEs) such as neglect, abuse, chronic fear or traumatic bereavements, especially in the first 5 years of life: a time when children develop mood and arousal regulation capacities and also develop mentalising skills. Some recent studies have found high levels of ACEs in pregnant women, [41] which may suggest that attachment insecurity prevalence might be higher than 40% found in the general population. Exposure to ACEs is known to be associated with unplanned pregnancies and ambivalence towards pregnancy, both of which are often found in teenage pregnancies [42, 43].

Attachment insecurity is not a pathology in itself, but it is a risk factor for a range of mental health problems, because attachment insecurity makes it difficult to regulate painful emotions and thoughts. When a woman who has an insecure attachment system falls pregnant, it activates attachment memories and associated anxieties. This activation is not always conscious and is identifiable at a neurobiological level. For example, studies using fMRI imagery have shown that maternal attachment affects how a mother responds to an infant's facial expressions and how they become attuned to their babies postnatally [37, 44]. Maternal attachment insecurity may influence a woman's transition to motherhood (or matrescence) and explain why some women's mental health deteriorates during pregnancy, why there are high rates of anxiety reported in the antenatal period [45] and the increased risk of breakdown of mental health in the first postnatal weeks.

Attachment Insecurity and the Risk of Killing a Child

Although the majority of mothers with attachment insecurity will never pose a risk of direct harm to their children, it is reasonable to hypothesise that mothers who kill their babies do so in part because they 'see' the babies through a lens of insecure attachment in their own mind. A South African study of 22 parents who killed found that they all reported abuse, neglect and rejection [16]. For such parents, the transition to parenthood may have activated unresolved memories of intense attachment distress and trauma, which are then further activated by the baby's ordinary emotional needs and vulnerability.

The risk of homicide may be associated with a particular type of attachment insecurity, known as disorganised attachment, where a maternal state of mind may oscillate rapidly between feeling settled, feeling frightened and feeling hostile towards the baby. These so called hostile-helpless states of mind affect the ways mothers emotionally relate to their babies and can result in atypical maternal behaviour [46, 47]; whereby the mother feels helpless to manage the baby's ordinary needs or may react to them in a hostile way.

Three recent studies of maternal attachment security have found high rates of hostile-helpless states of mind in both mothers who abuse and neglect their children and in mothers who kill their children [48, 49]. A strength of both studies is the comparison with both a community group of mothers and mothers with mental illness who had not harmed their children. Barone and Carone found that mothers with a mental illness who kill their children (of any age) are more likely to have a hostile-helpless attachment organisation; to have lower mentalising skills; and more severe experiences of child abuse and neglect, compared to mothers with mental illness who did not kill [48]. Filicidal mothers report feelings of helplessness as if the child was a source of threat or fear. A more recent study found that disorganised attachment distinguished those women with poor mental health who killed and those who did not [50, 51]. A possible model is that both disorganised attachment and mental illness impaired women's mentalising skills, and the combination may have led to poor reality testing and the development of beliefs that the child's death would be a kind of solution.

The strength of this model is that it integrates the risk of attachment insecurity and the risk of maternal mental illness in a relational model of risk, that could be used by psychiatrists who are assessing pregnant women with mental health issues and/or when giving conception advice. Such an explanatory model could be applied to other kinds of risk; for example, insecurity of attachment is a risk factor for child maltreatment of a kind which may lead to the involvement of social services and the need to remove a child for the child's protection [52, 53]. If a woman with an insecure attachment system also has postnatal problems with mental illness, or suffers any kind of social stressor (such as domestic violence), the interaction of all these risk factors may bring a woman into the state of mind where the unthinkable becomes 'real', and a thought that was ego-dystonic now becomes ego-syntonic and justifiable.

Treatment and Management: What Can Mental Health Services Offer?

Psychiatrists will meet women who have killed, in a variety of circumstances. Perhaps the most traumatic are those situations where a woman is admitted into a Mother and Baby Unit or is being managed by a perinatal mental health community service because of concerns about her mental disorder; and who then goes on to kill her baby. If she does not also kill herself, such a woman will be transferred into secure psychiatric services for care during the subsequent period of remand, trial and disposal. The impact on professionals can be painful and even traumatic; and staff in perinatal services who have this experience need an opportunity to discuss and reflect on what happened, to learn and to grieve. A paper by Stanton and Simpson provides a useful account of the impact on staff working with filicide and the value of reflective practice groups that meet regularly to validate and discuss staff emotions [54].

Forensic psychiatrists who have to manage such women in their secure units may find that the admission of such women is emotionally disturbing for the staff and the other patients in the unit [55]. It can be hard to keep such offence histories confidential especially when there is local and national press coverage; and highly mentally unwell women may disclose their offences themselves. The chief management concern is the suicide risk, especially as women recover their mental health, and the risk of suicide may be prolonged and not directly associated with obvious distress. Important anniversaries, especially those associated with family celebrations and previous happiness, can be potent triggers for hopelessness suicidal ideation.

Pre-homicide mental illness may be exacerbated by the offence and the trial process, so there may be a recurrence of severe mood disorders, exacerbation of psychotic illness and an increased suicide risk which is persistent and easy to miss. Like other family homicide perpetrators, mothers who kill may suffer post-traumatic stress disorder for which they require treatment, especially for flashbacks, nightmares and insomnia. The timing of this treatment is complex as the regaining of insight is painful and may precipitate intense suicidality; often at a time when legal processes are also active. Clinical teams therefore need to think carefully about how to pace treatment for mothers who have killed, and ensure that all treatments are integrated together.

For most women who kill their own child or children, their offence has changed their identity forever, and they have lost their past as well as having an uncertain future. Two studies discuss the depths of distress experienced by mothers who have killed [56, 57].

Guilt, shame, helplessness, hopelessness and intolerable regret are emotions that cannot be easily managed away with medication or therapy; and therapies for complex grief were not devised with the perpetrator in mind. There may be particular challenges for those who have other living children from whom they may now be separated; and who are now considered to pose a risk to all children, including their own. Mental health teams who are caring for such women will have to engage with both the criminal justice process and the family court process, which work differently and have different priorities. The traditional duty of care towards the patient may be superseded by a duty of child protection, leading to powerful ethical and emotional tensions in teams and inter-professional disputes. These often mirror the tragedy of the homicide where the relationship between the mother and the child was distorted and disorganised. Stanton and Simpson highlight the importance of supervision [54]; and it is my experience that this is especially valuable in those cases where mothers deny the offence or seem to lack concern or distress about it.

Conclusion

Maternal filicide is an unspeakable tragedy; and perhaps even more so when maternal mental illness played a part and professionals later have a sense of a risk that could have been averted. We may not be able to prevent every such tragedy but we could be more alert to the idea that conception, and the move to motherhood, is not always a joyful experience for women. The idealisation of motherhood and babies is arguably a defence against the emotional labour of caring, especially for mothers whose own experience of being cared for as children was chaotic and frightening. We need to be brave enough to ask the questions of vulnerable mothers, and show that we are also brave enough to listen to what they have to say.

References

1. UN Office of Drugs Control. Global study on homicide 2013: trends, context, data. 2013.
2. A Wilczynski. The incidence of child homicide: how accurate are the official statistics? *J Clin Forensic Med.* 1994;1(2):61–6.
3. Office of National Statistics. Homicide in England and Wales: year ending March 2024. https://tinyurl.com/42vvpkpm
4. P Sidebotham, A Retzer. Maternal filicide in a cohort of English serious case reviews. *Arch Women's Ment Health.* 2019;22(1):139–49.
5. H Stöckl, B Dekel, A Morris-Gehring, C Watts, N Abrahams. Child homicide perpetrators worldwide: a systematic review. *BMJ Paediatr Open.* 2017;1(1): e000112.
6. SH Friedman, PJ Resnick. Child murder by mothers: patterns and prevention. *World Psychiatry.* 2007;6(3):137–41.
7. PJ Resnick. Child murder by parents: a psychiatric review of filicide. *Am J Psychiatry.* 1969;126(3):73–82.
8. PJ Resnick. Murder of the newborn: a psychiatric review of neonaticide. *Am J Psychiatry.* 1970;126(10):1414–20.
9. MG Spinelli. A systematic investigation of 16 cases of neonaticide. *Am J Psychiatry.* 2001;158(5):811–13.
10. SM Flynn, JJ Shaw, KM Abel. Filicide: mental illness in those who kill their children. *PLoS ONE.* 2013;8(4):e58981.
11. PJ Resnick. Filicide in the United States. *Indian J Psychiatry.* 2016;58(Suppl 2): S203–9.
12. KD Dodson, LN Cabage. Mothers who kill. In: TL Freiburger, CD Marcum,

editors. *Women in the criminal justice system: tracking the journey of females and crime*. Boca Raton, FL: CRC Press/ Routledge; 2015. p. 189–208.

13. P Scott. Parents who kill their children. *Med Sci Law*. 1973;13(2):120–6.
14. A Wilczynski. Child killing by parents: a motivational model. *Child Abuse Rev*. 1995;4(5):365–70.
15. M Oberman, CL Meyer. *When mothers kill: interviews from prison*. New York: NYU Press; 2008.
16. B Dekel, M Andipatin, N Abrahams. Exploring adversities among parents convicted of killing their children. *PLoS ONE*. 2020;15(7):e0235812.
17. P Sidebotham, S Bailey, P Belderson, M Brandon. Fatal child maltreatment in England, 2005–2009. *Child Abuse Negl*. 2011;35(4):299–306.
18. M Brandon, P Sidebotham, P Belderson, H Cleaver, J Dickens, J Garstag, et al. *Complexity and challenge: a triennial analysis of serious case reviews 2014–2017*. London: Department for Education; 2020.
19. R Lawrence. Understanding fatal assault of children: a typology and explanatory theory. *Child Youth Serv Rev*. 2004;26(9):837–52.
20. D Biron, D Reynald. Developing a revised typology of child homicide. *Child Aust*. 2016;41(1):8.
21. AM Kamperman, MJ Veldman-Hoek, R Wesseloo, E Robertson Blackmore, V Bergink. Phenotypical characteristics of postpartum psychosis: a clinical cohort study. *Bipolar Disord*. 2017;19(6): 450–7.
22. PT D'Orban. Women who kill their children. *Br J Psychiatry*. 1979;134:560–71.
23. D Bourget, J Grace, L Whitehurst. A review of maternal and paternal filicide. *J Am Acad Psychiatry Law*. 2007;35(1):74–82.
24. A Wilczynski. Mad or bad? Child-killers, gender and the courts. *Br J Criminol*. 1997;37(3):419–36.
25. H Putkonen, S Amon, G Weizmann-Henelius, M Pankakoski, M Eronen, MP Almiron, CM Klier. Classifying filicide. *Int J Forensic Ment Health*. 2016;15(2):198–210.
26. North East London Strategic Health Authority. Report of an independent inquiry into the care and treatment of Daksha Emson and her daughter Freya. 2003.
27. M Liem, R de Vet, F Koenraadt. Filicide followed by parasuicide: a comparison of suicidal and non-suicidal child homicide. *Child Abuse Negl*. 2010;34(8):558–62.
28. J Kivivuori, M Lehti. Homicide followed by suicide in Finland: trend and social locus. *JSSCCP*. 2003;4(2):223–36.
29. S Fraiberg, E Adelson, V Shapiro. Ghosts in the nursery: a psychoanalytic approach to the problems of impaired infant-mother relationships. *J Am Acad Child Psychiatry*. 1975;14(3):387–421.
30. J Bowlby, M Ainsworth, I Bretherton. The origins of attachment theory. *Dev Psychol*. 1992;28(5):759–75.
31. MD Ainsworth, MC Blehar, E Waters, SN Wall. *Patterns of attachment: a psychological study of the strange situation*. New York: Psychology Press; 2015.
32. E Hesse, M Main. Disorganized infant, child, and adult attachment: collapse in behavioral and attentional strategies. *J Am Psychoanal Assoc*. 2000;48(4):1097–127.
33. LA Sroufe. Attachment and development: a prospective, longitudinal study from birth to adulthood. *Attach Hum Dev*. 2005;7(4):349–67.
34. P Fonagy, H Steele, M Steele. Maternal representations of attachment during pregnancy predict the organization of infant-mother attachment at one year of age. *Child Dev*. 1991;62(5):891–905.
35. MH Van IJzendoorn. Adult attachment representations, parental responsiveness, and infant attachment: a meta-analysis on the predictive validity of the Adult Attachment Interview. *Psychol Bull*. 1995;117(3):387–403.

36. MA Zeegers, C Colonnesi, GJ Stams, E Meins. Mind matters: a meta-analysis on parental mentalization and sensitivity as predictors of infant–parent attachment. *Psychol Bull.* 2017;143(12):1245–72.

37. L Strathearn, P Fonagy, J Amico, PR Montague. Adult attachment predicts maternal brain and oxytocin response to infant cues. *Neuropsychopharmacology.* 2009;34(13):2655–66.

38. JG Allen. *Mentalizing in the development and treatment of attachment trauma.* London: Routledge; 2018.

39. P Fonagy, AW Bateman. Adversity, attachment, and mentalizing. *Compr Psychiatry.* 2016;64:59–66.

40. MJ Bakermans-Kranenburg, O Dagan, RA Cárcamo, MH van IJzendoorn. Celebrating more than 26,000 adult attachment interviews: mapping the main adult attachment classifications on personal, social, and clinical status. *Attach Hum Dev.* 2025;27(2):191–228.

41. KC Young-Wolff, J Wei, N Varnado, N Rios, M Staunton, C Watson. Adverse childhood experiences and pregnancy intentions among pregnant women seeking prenatal care. *Womens Health Issues.* 2021;31(2):100–6.

42. KS Hall, JL Beauregard, ST Rentmeester, M Livingston, KM Harris. Adverse life experiences and risk of unintended pregnancy in adolescence and early adulthood: implications for toxic stress and reproductive health. *SSM-Popul Health.* 2019;7:100344.

43. MA Bellis, K Hughes, N Leckenby, C Perkins, H Lowey. National household survey of adverse childhood experiences and their relationship with resilience to health-harming behaviors in England. *BMC Med.* 2014;12:72.

44. U Iyengar, P Rajhans, P Fonagy, L Strathearn, S Kim. Unresolved trauma and reorganization in mothers: attachment and neuroscience perspectives. *Front Psychol.* 2019;10:399678.

45. LM Howard, E Molyneaux, CL Dennis, T Rochat, A Stein, J Milgrom. Non-psychotic mental disorders in the perinatal period. *Lancet.* 2014;384(9956): 1775–88.

46. K Lyons-Ruth, E Bronfman, E Parsons, J Vondra, D Barnett. Atypical maternal behaviour and disorganised attachment strategies: frightened, frightening and atypical infant attachment. *Monogr Soc Res Child Dev.* 1999;64(3): 67–96.

47. K Lyons-Ruth, E Spielman. Disorganized infant attachment strategies and helpless-fearful profiles of parenting: integrating attachment research with clinical intervention. *Infant Ment Health J.* 2004;25(4):318–35.

48. L Barone, A Bramante, F Lionetti, M Pastore. Mothers who murdered their child: an attachment-based study on filicide. *Child Abuse Negl.* 2014;38(9):1468–77.

49. L Barone, N Carone. Childhood abuse and neglect experiences, hostile-helpless attachment, and reflective functioning in mentally ill filicidal mothers. *Attach Hum Dev.* 2021;23(6):771–94.

50. N Giacchetti, GM Lattanzi, F Aceti, N Vanacore, R Williams. States of mind with respect to attachment: a comparative study between women who killed their children and mothers diagnosed with post-partum depression. Nordic journal of psychiatry. 2023;77(1):3–13.

51. GM Lattanzi, CR Martin, VR Preedy, VB Patel. Attachment theory, intergenerational trauma, and their role in maternal filicide. In: CR Martin, VR Preedy, VB Patel, editors. *Handbook of anger, aggression, and violence.* Cham: Springer International Publishing; 2023. p. 709–30.

52. CK Lo, KL Chan, P Ip. Insecure adult attachment and child maltreatment: a meta-analysis. *Trauma Violence Abuse.* 2019;20(5):706–19.

53. M Terry, B Finger, K Lyons-Ruth, LS Sadler, A Slade. Hostile/helpless maternal representations in pregnancy and later child removal: a pilot study. *Infant Ment Health J.* 2021;42(1):60–73.

54. J Stanton, A Simpson, T Wouldes. A qualitative study of filicide by mentally ill mothers. *Child Abuse Neglect*. 2000;24(11):1451–60.
55. P Murphy, J Lee, V Bisht, L Dodge. Female filicide perpetrators: challenges facing clinicians and secure services. *BJPsych Advances*. 2021;27(6):405–13.
56. J Stanton, AI Simpson. The aftermath: aspects of recovery described by perpetrators of maternal filicide committed in the context of severe mental illness. *Behav Sci Law*. 2006;24(1):103–12.
57. G Milia, M Noonan. Experiences and perspectives of women who have committed neonaticide, infanticide and filicide: a systematic review and qualitative evidence synthesis. *J Psychiatr Ment Health Nurs*. 2022;29(6):813–28.

Chapter 39

Mental Health and Capacity Legislation in the Perinatal Period

Livia Martucci, Alex Ruck Keene and Lucy Stephenson

Scope of This Chapter

This chapter examines the key principles of applying mental health and capacity legislation in the perinatal period. The four nations of the United Kingdom have different legislative frameworks. England and Wales are governed by the same legislation – the Mental Health Act 1983 (MHA 1983) and the Mental Capacity Act 2005 (MCA 2005), although with some minor variations. Scotland has an entirely different framework – the Mental Health (Care and Treatment) Act 2003 and the Adults with Incapacity Act 2000. Northern Ireland is in a (slow) transition from having mental health legislation (the Mental Health (Northern Ireland) Order 1986) sitting alongside, in effect, no formal framework for thinking about capacity, to 'fused' legislation (the Mental Capacity Act (Northern Ireland) 2016) with no stand-alone mental health legislation. This chapter focuses on the position in England and Wales, primarily because it has the largest body of case law to help understand how to think through the dilemmas covered; for those in other parts of the United Kingdom grappling with those dilemmas, the most useful resource is the British Medical Association's Ethics Guidance which has specific sections for each of the nations [1].

The Perinatal Frame of Mind and Medico-Legal Assessment

The Perinatal Competency Framework (Health Education England & Trust, 2018) lists the 'perinatal frame of mind' as a core competency for perinatal mental health professionals [2]. This involves a focus on holding the needs of all parties in mind; the mother, the infant, the mother–infant relationship and the partner/father. This frame of mind should be maintained when conducting medico-legal assessments under the MCA. In this context further particular features of the perinatal period have relevance. These are:

1. timing of assessments
2. degree of fluctuation in decision-making capacity for treatment (DMC-T)
3. severity of the risks involved.

Timing of Assessments

Two ends of a spectrum exist in the perinatal period; on the one hand for women who have known severe mental illness it is possible to predict with a high degree of accuracy when they are likely to become unwell in the postnatal period. The need for MCA and MHA assessments can be predicted and planned. On the other hand, a woman's mental state may change rapidly, within a few hours, and urgent, unplanned assessment may be required to initiate compulsory treatment.

Degree of Fluctuation in Decision-Making Capacity

Women experiencing psychotic episodes in the postpartum period characteristically have high and rapid degrees of fluctuation in their DMC-T.

Severity of the Risks Involved

The severity of the risks to mother and infant in the perinatal period can mean that risk thresholds in medico-legal assessments need to be lowered and intervention considered at an earlier stage.

The Legal Framework

In principle, a woman is entitled to make any decision that she wishes about her birth arrangements. Whilst she cannot demand a specific intervention be provided to her, she has, on the face of it, an absolute right to decide what, if any, medical interventions proposed by her medical team she will agree to. She can refuse interventions even where they may lead to her death, or the death of her fetus, and any healthcare professional providing treatment in the face of her refusal will be guilty of both a criminal offence and liable in damages.

However, the law provides a framework within which to ask a number of important questions:

1. Does the woman have the mental capacity to make decisions about her birth arrangements?
2. Does the woman have the mental capacity to make decisions about medical treatment?
3. If she lacks such mental capacity, what steps should be taken in her best interests?
4. Are there grounds to intervene even where the woman *has* the capacity to make these decisions?

This chapter looks at the legal frameworks both in principle, and then, by way of case studies, in practice.

The Mental Capacity Act 2005

The most important part of the legal framework is the MCA 2005. This provides a framework for deciding, for most purposes, whether a person has or lacks capacity to make a decision, including to consent to medical treatment. It also provides a framework for making decisions where a person does not have that capacity, based on the concept of best interests.

In principle, care and treatment must be provided to a person over 18 on the basis of their consent. Day to day, however, the MCA 2005 is relied upon by professionals to deliver care and treatment to those whose capacity to consent is impaired; if they take reasonable steps to establish whether the person lacks capacity, and reasonably believe that they are acting in the person's best interests, then s.5 MCA 2005 means that they can lawfully provide that care and treatment even though the person is unable to consent. In cases of doubt or disagreement, the Court of Protection must be involved.

The MCA 2005 is governed by a set of principles, which can best be thought of as a moral compass to help apply the Act. The principles are not a substitute for the application of the relevant part of the Act (e.g. the test for capacity), but they are enormously helpful, and important, in helping reach the right answer in any given case.

The principles are that:

- a person must be assumed to have capacity unless it is established that she lacks capacity
- a person is not to be treated as unable to make a decision unless all practicable steps to help her to do so have been taken without success
- a person is not to be treated as unable to make a decision merely because she makes an unwise decision
- an act done, or decision made, under the MCA 2005 for or on behalf of a person who lacks capacity must be done, or made, in her best interests
- before the act is done, or the decision is made, regard must be had to whether the purpose for which it is needed can be as effectively achieved in a way that is less restrictive of the person's rights and freedom of action.

Capacity

The law gives a very specific definition of what it means to lack capacity for purposes of the MCA 2005. It is a legal test, not a medical test, and is set down in s.2(1) MCA 2005, which provides that 'a person lacks capacity in relation to a matter if at the material time he is unable to make a decision for himself in relation to the matter because of an impairment of, or a disturbance in the functioning of, the mind or the brain'. Crucially, capacity is decision-specific; that a person may have impaired decision-making capacity in relation to a number of areas does not mean that they cannot make a decision in relation to (say) consenting to a blood test.

To apply the test, and as the Supreme Court has confirmed [3] it can best be broken down into three questions:

1. Is the person unable to make the decision in question? If so:
2. Is there an impairment or disturbance in the functioning of the person's mind or brain? If so:
3. Is the person's inability to make the decision because of the identified impairment or disturbance?

Section 3(1) states that a person is unable to make a decision for themselves if they are unable:

- to understand the information relevant to the decision; or
- to retain that information; or
- to use or weigh that information as part of the process of making the decision; or
- to communicate her decision (whether by talking, using sign language or any other means).

Further guidance about each of these points can be found in the Code of Practice to the MCA 2005 (under revision at the time of writing), in the Law Society/British Medical Association work [4] and the Capacity Guide website [5]. Experience has shown that it is particularly important:

1. To identify what the actual decision is in respect of which capacity is being considered.

2. To identify what information is actually relevant to that decision, but narrowing that information to the 'salient' information [6], so as not to set the bar too high by requiring the person to be able to process 'too much' information.
3. To be clear as to whether a person is *unable* to use and weigh relevant information, or *capable* of using that information but simply applying a different value set to the professionals involved [7]. This is particularly the case where the decision that the person is taking or wishes to take appears to be very risky, because it may well be the case that this will rub up uncomfortably against the tolerance for risk of the professionals involved.

Best Interests

As we have seen, it is a legal requirement to provide the person with all practicable support to enable them to make their own decision (s.1(3) MCA 2005). However, if, even with that support, they cannot make the decision, then it will be necessary to proceed on the basis of what is in their best interests. If the woman in question has made a valid and applicable advance decision to refuse a specific treatment (or treatments), then she has made her own decision as to what she considers to be in her best interests. If the woman has granted a lasting power of attorney, then, subject to certain formalities, she has granted the power to decide as to what is in her best interests to her attorney. We address both of these below. In some cases, a deputy may have been appointed by the Court of Protection to take decisions in the best interests of the person.

Otherwise, Parliament's intention was that, wherever possible, a decision as to what is in the best interests of a person unable to take the relevant decision would be reached informally and collaboratively between those involved in their care or interested in their welfare, whether that be paid/professional or unpaid. There is, therefore, strictly, no such thing as a 'decision-maker' under the MCA 2005, but it still makes sense to think of a 'decision-maker' because of the way in which the Act works in practice. In any complex situation, most of those who will be relying upon the defense in s.5 MCA 2005 will be proceeding on the basis of a plan that has been agreed upon by those involved. The 'decision-maker' will therefore be the person with ultimate responsibility for the plan; for instance, the consultant in charge of the patient's care should be thought of as the decision-maker.

Guidance as to best interests decision-making can be found in the MCA Code of Practice, books [4] and online [2]. What will be required in any given case will depend upon the urgency and gravity of the situation. As the Court of Appeal has emphasised, the defence under s.5 MCA 2005 afforded to health and social care professionals delivering routine acts of care and treatment is 'pervaded by the concepts of reasonableness, practicability and appropriateness' (*Commissioner of Police for the Metropolis* v *ZH* [2013] EWCA Civ 69). What will be required to have a reasonable belief as to a person's best interests in the context of an A&E department at 3:00 am will be very different to what may be required in the context of planning for birth arrangements weeks in advance of the due date.

'Best interests' is – deliberately – not defined in the MCA 2005. However, s.4 sets out a series of matters that must be considered whenever a person is determining what is in the person's best interests. It is *extremely* important to recognise that the Act does not specify what is in the person's best interests. Rather, it sets down a process by which that conclusion should be reached, aiming to construct a decision on behalf of the person who cannot make that decision themselves. That decision must take into account all the factors set out in s.4 MCA 2005, but, as the courts have made clear, must be predicated in particular upon the person's wishes and feelings: lack of decision-making capacity is not an 'off-switch' for their rights and freedoms [8].

Ultimately, as the Supreme Court emphasised in *Aintree University NHS Hospitals Trust* v *James* [2014] USKC 67, 'the purpose of the best interests test is to consider matters from the patient's point of view'. The purpose of the process is therefore to arrive at the decision that professionals reasonably believe is the right decision for the person themselves, as an individual human being – not the decision that best fits with the outcome that the professionals desire. Pregnancy is an especially personal matter, and the Court of Appeal emphasised that in best interests decision-making in relation to pregnancy not merely must the woman's wishes and feelings be considered, but also that they can be determinative even if the woman lacks capacity to make the relevant decision [9]. Although the fetus does not have its own independent rights, the courts have frequently identified that a woman's known wish to be delivered of a healthy baby is a matter that can be taken into account as part of the best interests exercise [10].

Involving the Court of Protection

If there is no dispute as to or doubts about the woman's capacity or best interests, then in most cases there will be no need to go to the Court of Protection, even if the consequence of taking the step in question is the death of the woman and/or her fetus (e.g. not proceeding with a blood transfusion in face of the refusal of a woman in labour with capacity to make that decision).

However, the Supreme Court has made clear that, if at the end of the process of decision-making outlined above, it is apparent that the way forward is finely balanced, or there is a difference of medical opinion, or a lack of agreement to a proposed course of action from those with an interest in the patient's welfare, an application should be made to the Court of Protection [11]. In any situation where an intervention is contemplated on a best interests basis that will have the effect of preventing the woman having a further child, the resulting serious infringement of her right to private and family life means that 'in most, if not all, cases, professionals faced with a decision whether to take that step will conclude that it is appropriate to apply to the court to facilitate a comprehensive analysis of best interests, with [the woman] having the benefit of legal representation and independent expert advice' [12]. This will also be the case where the intention is to use deception during the course of either pregnancy or labour in the best interests of the woman.

The courts have repeatedly emphasised that if it becomes clear that a court application is required, then it is necessary to bring it as soon as possible to allow proper consideration and investigation of the position [9].

In Scotland, the Adults with Incapacity Act (2000) contains a similar set of principles on which the Act is based. They include: (i) benefit: (ii) least restrictive intervention; (iii) consideration of the person's wishes; (iv) consultation with relevant others; and (v) encouraging the person to use existing skills and develop new ones. To have capacity under the Act, a person must be able to: (i) understand the treatment and why it is being proposed; (ii) understand the principal benefits, risks and alternatives; (iii) understand the consequences of not receiving the proposed treatment; (iv) retain the information long enough to use and weigh in the balance to arrive at a decision; and (v) communicate their decision. Further details can be found in the Code of Practice to the Act.

The Mental Health Act

Sitting alongside the MCA 2005 is the MHA 1983, whose purpose is to provide the statutory framework for the compulsory care and treatment of people for their mental disorder when they are unable or unwilling to consent to that care and treatment, and when it is necessary for that care and treatment to be given to protect themselves or others from harm. The key point for the exercise of these powers is the inability or unwillingness of the patient who suffers from a mental disorder to consent to the relevant care and treatment. This encompasses people who, notwithstanding their mental disorder, have capacity to do so – and it is entirely possible for someone detained under the MHA 1983 to have capacity in relation to a treatment decision. Inability to consent will also include people who do not have capacity, but the question whether an individual patient has or does not have decision-making capacity is not the key determinant of whether the powers conferred by the MHA 1983 should be used.

Where a woman is detained under the MHA 1983, it is in principle possible for many decisions in the perinatal sphere to be taken within the framework of the MHA 1983, because of the breadth of the definition of 'medical treatment for mental disorder' within the Act. However, it is now generally accepted that decisions about birth arrangements, in particular, should be considered by reference to the MCA 2005 and the framework set out above, not least as this provides a more calibrated way of determining the right course of action to take in relation to the sometimes difficult situations that can arise in the context of mental disorder.

Advance Planning

Almost more than in any other sphere of medicine apart from palliative care, perinatal psychiatry is an area where advance planning is critical. This is particularly so where the woman has a condition such as bipolar where there is a clearly identifiable risk that at some point during her pregnancy or labour she may in consequence be unable to take relevant decisions. The MCA 2005 provides a framework within which the woman is able:

1. To set out factors that she would wish any person considering her capacity to take into account – most importantly (if counter-intuitively) factors that she considers should trigger a determination that she *lacks* capacity to take any material decision even if she might to others who do not know her well appear still to have capacity.
2. To set out specific medical treatment(s) she will not accept, by way of an advance decision to refuse that treatment(s). Although no case law has addressed this, the plain language of the MCA would suggest that this could include a caesarean section; it is likely that in any such case the clinical team would want to be very careful to ensure that it is satisfied that the woman has capacity to make such a decision (if they are involved at the planning stage) or had capacity to make it (if they are involved at the delivery stage), given the seriousness of the consequences.
3. To appoint a person to take decisions for her, by appointing a health and welfare attorney.

4. (In practice perhaps most importantly) to set out her preferences for treatment to be taken into account in any best interests decision-making as a 'relevant written statement made by her when she had capacity' (s.4(6)(a).

If the woman is detained under the MHA 1983, and the medical treatment in question is being delivered under the framework of Part 4 of that Act, then she is in law unable to prevent that treatment taking place by way of an advance decision. However, it is clear both from the Code of Practice to the MHA 1983 [13] and case law [14] that proper consideration must be given to any advance decision even in relation to such treatment. The Mental Health Act 2026 will amend the MHA 1983 to give statutory weight to advance choices in relation to medical treatment for mental disorder.

The Mental Health (Care and Treatment) Act (Scotland) (2003) allows for advance statements to be prepared, with a duty on medical practitioners to have regard to what they contain in drawing up a treatment plan. Advance statement wishes can be overridden but there is a requirement to justify that decision to the Mental Welfare Commission for Scotland.

'Contingent' Declarations and the Inherent Jurisdiction

Whilst advance planning is very important in the context of caring for a woman who may lose capacity to make decisions about her birth arrangements during labour, there are some situations in which it may not be possible to undertake such care planning, or the circumstances under which the treating team consider the baby may have to be delivered if the woman is in mental health crisis during labour will be so restrictive as to require court authority. In such cases, the courts have confirmed that it is possible to make 'contingent' declarations under the MCA 2005 as to what steps should be taken in the event that the woman does lose capacity, even though, at the time that the case is before the court, she *has* capacity.

In *Guys and St Thomas NHS Foundation Trust & Anor* v *R* [2020] EWCOP 4, the vice-president of the Court of Protection held that any deprivation of liberty to which the woman might be subject during labour could only be authorised by the High Court exercising what is known as its inherent jurisdiction. In deciding whether an application to court should be made in such circumstances, we suggest that two key questions will be:

1. Is there a 'real risk' that the woman will lose capacity to make the relevant decisions? [15]
2. Are the steps proposed those that the woman would regard as supporting her in her wishes? If they are not, then this is a red flag for – at a minimum – seeking legal advice.

The Law in Practice

In the balance of this chapter, we illustrate how the frameworks set out above operate in practice.

Case 1: AB

AS is a 35-year-old woman in her third pregnancy. She came to the attention of the perinatal service at 25 weeks' gestation. She has a diagnosis of paranoid schizophrenia and is care coordinated. She is on a regular regime of antipsychotic medication. She also suffers from Huntington's chorea. She lives with her husband, and a friend of the family helps care for her and the children. The family as well as the carer do not have English as a first language and require an interpreter.

Because of her neurological condition, AB's mobility is limited. She can walk if helped, and her arm movements are quite limited so she needs help to dress and eat. Her speech is also altered, to the point that interpreters struggle to understand her, and her facial mobility is reduced. However, she is able to express discomfort and fear.

There is no clear indication of her mental state as communication is difficult. However, since becoming pregnant, she has steadfastly refused all investigations, including blood pressure monitoring, booking bloods, fetal heart beat monitoring and scans. When told that an investigation such as described above is due, she looks frightened and just repeats loudly 'No!' 'No!' 'No!' until she is reassured that it won't be done. On one occasion at 28/40, her husband and carer have been able to persuade her to be examined and a normal fetal heartbeat is detected. It is unclear why she does not wish for any maternity monitoring, as when asked she just does not answer. No other behavioural abnormality is reported by husband or carer, and the care coordinator has not found that there are any changes in behaviour that may warrant a change to medication plan or admission to hospital in her vulnerable condition.

The perinatal mental health service consultant is concerned that there is no clear plan should an obstetric intervention be warranted, such as induction, forceps/ventouse or c-section, in case she refuses it.

Case 1: Comment

Decision-Making Support

In this case there are clear grounds to have concerns about this woman's DMC-T. Given that communication seems to be a key issue it would be especially important to consider acting according to the second principle of the MCA and take all possible steps to support decision-making and communication before determining that she lacks capacity for any specific decision. Furthermore, this case highlights the importance of family members who can provide help and support but could possibly also be coercive. Here the relevant information the woman requires is around the pros and cons of antenatal monitoring and modes of delivery. The specifics of these decisions should be distilled and documented before a capacity assessment takes place. An obstetrician would be best placed to determine and deliver this information. To communicate this information in an appropriate way there may be language considerations, for example using a translator experienced in working with people who have cognitive problems. Other tools such as visual aids or videos could also be tried along with identifying a comfortable location and time of day [16].

AB has a complex medical and psychiatric history and is likely to have been seen by many previous professionals in the past. Prior to carrying out an assessment it would be advisable to attempt to track this history to clarify the nature of her 'impairment', her values history and any risks. This background information may help determine the 'causal nexus', whether this woman's refusal of treatment is likely to be due to mental disorder, for example paranoid delusions, or whether it could be due to long-held beliefs about the importance of non-interference in the natural process of pregnancy and birth.

A further measure is ensuring the presence of someone the woman trusts is available during consultations. AB is reliant on a social network for help with activities of daily living and support with childcare. Their collateral information will be vital in helping to communicate with this woman and understanding her personal history. However, it would be essential to establish the dynamics of these relationships to determine whether there is any potential that this woman could be coerced into making decisions by those caring for her. In practice, this could be achieved with meetings with AB, her family and professionals who have known her for a long time, hopefully prior to her neurological deterioration when communication was easier, such as her community mental health team care coordinator, the older children's health visitor or her primary care physician. If there is suspected coercion, or if it is not possible to determine whether the family is coercive rather than caring (e.g. if there is no third party who can give a historical perspective on the family) then if this is the case an independent advocate should be found.

More detail as to how to assess and record capacity can be found in [5], but critically the record will show that the team has:

- been clear about the capacity decision that is being assessed
- ensured AB has had the concrete details of the choices available
- identified the salient and relevant details she needs to understand/comprehend (ignoring the peripheral and minor details)
- avoided the protection imperative (i.e. erring on the side of finding incapacity on the basis that this would help secure AB's interests)
- demonstrated the efforts taken to promote AB's ability to decide and, if unsuccessful, explained why
- recognised that assessment is not necessarily a one-off matter, and that the team have taken the time to undertake to gather as much evidence as was required to reach the conclusion – including, for instance, returning to have a further conversation with AB or obtaining corroborative evidence
- evidenced each element of the assessment:
    i. Why could AB not understand, or retain, or use/weigh, or communicate in spite of the assistance given?
    ii. What is the impairment/disturbance? Is it temporary or permanent?
    iii. How is the inability to decide caused by the impairment/disturbance (as opposed to something else)?
- answered the question: why is this an incapacitated decision as opposed to an unwise one?

Best Interests Decision-Making in the Perinatal Period

If it is confidently established that this woman lacks the capacity to make decisions around antenatal treatment and the safe delivery of her baby it would be essential to proceed with the process of making plans around antenatal monitoring and birth which are in her best interests. This process should include anticipating that she may refuse potentially life-saving interventions.

In the perinatal context identifying the best interests 'decision-maker' may be complex as joint working between professionals is common. For example, for decisions about psychiatric medications the perinatal psychiatrist is likely to be best placed for this role. For decisions around antenatal monitoring and delivery the obstetrician is likely to have access to the most relevant information. Therefore, in these scenarios a series of multidisciplinary best interests meetings may be required to establish the scope of the decisions that are likely to be made, what is known about the pre-existing and current views of AB (including advance decisions and advance statements) and the views of her family/carers. Careful documentation of the outcome of these meetings should be recorded in her maternity records. This documentation should include: the nature of the decision that is to be taken on AB's behalf; the rationale for the decision that AB does not have DMC-T to make a specific decision; the available treatment options and their risks and benefits; the views of all parties (including the known views of AB herself) on her best interests; and the rationale for the final decision. More information is contained in [17]. Given the limited time that pregnancy offers to make complex decisions, meetings should begin as soon as possible. This is with a view to having sufficient time to contact the Court of Protection if there is disagreement between the parties involved or concern over the level of coercive intervention that may be required to act in AB's best interests. AB should be involved as much as possible in the decision-making. It should be anticipated that several meetings with her are likely to be required to attempt to build trust and develop a greater understanding of her evolving wishes.

Case 2: CP

CP is a woman in her late 30s who was surprised to discover she was pregnant at 24 weeks' gestation, as the result of a casual affair which has now ended. She has had sporadic contact with mental health services before, and at one point she was told she may have some traits of emotional instability. She is also a heavy alcohol drinker and has had alcohol regularly, to the point of harmful use, until she discovered the pregnancy. She has been able to decrease but not stop alcohol consumption after finding out she was pregnant. She also smokes 10 cigarettes per day (decreased from 15–20 per day) and occasionally (once per month or so) smokes cannabis with some of her friends. CP has struggled in childhood, especially in the relationship with her mother who she describes as dismissive of her and always critical of her. She was told that her mother was severely depressed after her birth, and for the first 6 months or so had relinquished her care to other relatives. Their bond was never really recovered in CP's opinion.

CP has been feeling ambivalent about this pregnancy, and is especially concerned that due to her age she might not become pregnant ever again. This was her main reason for not having a termination. Her mood deteriorates as her due date approaches with increasing distress and anticipatory anxiety, especially concerning how she will cope with this baby. Her alcohol consumption increases. A social worker has been in contact with her for an initial assessment following referral done by maternity.

At delivery, labour is not progressing well. CP is on her own and is quite distressed, irritable, snapping at midwives and doctors, tearful. The obstetrician informs CP that the fetus is in distress, and that they will need to consider a c-section. An anaesthetist is called and she is given information about general anaesthesia and epidural. CP was already aware before that anaesthesia can be associated with an increased risk of thromboembolism, and refuses to go through with the c-section. The risks to the fetus are explained to her again, but she remains determined that she will not consent to an operation. The only reason she gives for her refusal is the risk of thromboembolism, and does not agree that this risk is minimal compared to the risks faced by her unborn, which she appears able to understand. The medical team and the midwives remain with her in case she should change her mind, and they all listen as the fetal heartbeat slows down and eventually stops. CP then delivers naturally a stillborn baby.

Case 2: Comment

Urgent Capacity Assessment

In this case there was the need for an urgent decision about this woman's mental capacity with high stakes. Given the history there may have been uncertainty about the presence of mental disorder and how emotional instability, depression and anxiety could be contributing to this woman's decision-making. Assessing how emotional instability might impact a person's ability to 'use and weigh' is complex and poorly established [18]. In this scenario there may have been concerns that CP was in an extreme state of emotional dysregulation which was diminishing her DMC-T. In addition, it could have been important to consider how CP's own early experiences could impact her relationship with her baby and the interactions between her and the professionals attempting to offer help. In standard emergency psychiatric care this kind of capacity assessment could be possible and even therapeutic [19]. However, the time constraints of this obstetric emergency are likely to have made the ideal kind of reflective assessment extremely challenging to the point of being impossible.

When these complexities abound, the advice is often to balance the certainty of the capacity assessment with the severity of the risks. If the risks of treatment refusal involve life or limb, a high level of certainty about the individual's capacity to refuse would be preferable [20]. Of course, here the additional layer of uncertainty comes from balancing the health risks to the mother with those of the unborn infant who has no rights.

Either outcome of a mental capacity assessment in this scenario could be controversial. Practical advice to the team in this scenario would be to ensure there was clear, contemporaneous documentation of the rationale for whatever decision they took rather, in this complex case, than reliance on the presumption of capacity. This might include describing the events and the woman's responses to information that was given to her verbatim. An option that could have been considered is an urgent application to the Court of Protection. There is precedent for out-of-hours judgments following remote hearings, which can authorise compulsory treatment.

If the team had decided CP lacked the capacity to refuse obstetric intervention and it was decided a c-section was in her best interests the practicalities of enforcing this would have to be tackled. Examples of such cases include *NHS Trust* v *JP* [2019] EWCOP 23.

Ideally, this scenario could have been prevented or more carefully managed if this conflict was anticipated and planned for. Enhanced and consistent personal and emotional support from healthcare professionals could have been offered during her pregnancy and delivery. If it became clear that, on discussing delivery options, the woman may refuse life-saving treatment and there were concerns about her capacity, a more thorough assessment could have been made. This could have facilitated an earlier application to the Court of Protection to plan compulsory treatment.

Case 3: AT

In this case (leading to two reported court judgments, [21] and [22]), a young woman with moderate learning disabilities and an increased risk of perinatal psychiatric illness (primarily postpartum psychosis) was staying with her family in Nigeria and, in circumstances which were unclear, became pregnant; a fact that was discovered by her adoptive mother (CD) upon AT's return to this country in April 2019.

Capacity assessments were undertaken early in May 2019 which concluded that AT lacked the capacity to decide whether to continue with the pregnancy. CD was wholly opposed to abortion both from a religious and cultural point of view; she was a devout Roman Catholic and in Nigeria, she said, terminating a pregnancy was 'simply unheard of'. On 16 May 2019, by which time AT was about 16 weeks pregnant, CD arrived at the hospital with AT, together with all of AT's possessions packed into three suitcases and two rucksacks. CD told the hospital that she was 'handing over' the care of AT. Since that time, AT had lived in a residential unit. In her statement, CD said that she did not do this for fear of being ostracised by her community if AT had a termination, but because she felt she could not support AT in having a termination.

The NHS Foundation Trust responsible for the antenatal care of AT concluded that it would be in her best interests for the pregnancy to be terminated on the basis of both obstetric and psychiatric risks if pregnancy were to continue. CD was implacably opposed to the proposal and, accordingly, the Trust made an application to court. By the time that the matter came before the Court of Protection, AT was 22, going on 23, weeks pregnant, which meant that there was considerable urgency to the decision as the latest possible date under the Abortion Act 1967 (in a case such as AT's) for termination is 24 weeks' gestation. CD maintained, contrary to her initial position, that she would then wish to have AT back to live with her even if she had a termination. The first judge who looked at the matter held that it was in AT's best interests for her pregnancy to be terminated. The Court of Appeal held that the judge had gone wrong because she had not taken sufficient account of AT's wishes and feelings and/or her Article 8 right to motherhood. The Court of Appeal emphasised:

> Part of the underlying ethos of the Mental Capacity Act 2005 is that those making decisions for people who may be lacking capacity must respect and maximise that person's individuality and autonomy to the greatest possible extent. In order to achieve this aim, a person's wishes and feelings not only require consideration, but can be determinative, even if they lack capacity. Similarly, it is in order to safeguard autonomy that s1(4) provides that 'a person is not to be treated as unable to make a decision merely because he makes an unwise decision'. [22]

The Court of Appeal held that the medical evidence upon which the judge had placed reliance did not, itself, convincingly demonstrate the need for a termination in light of the fact that all agreed that AT, insofar as she was able to express herself, wished to have her baby. The Court of Appeal had also been very concerned at the fact that the proceedings had not been issued earlier, and suggested:

> [W]here it appears to a Trust that there is a potentially intractable divergence of views with the family, consideration should be given to an application being made at an early stage following the making of the 'best interests' decision. The application should then be listed as a matter of urgency, even if it is subsequently withdrawn. If the pregnancy is allowed to reach a very late stage and a termination is then determined to be in the best interests of the

mother, she will be unnecessarily exposed to what is on any view a highly invasive and, for a woman lacking capacity, bewildering procedure. [22]

Case 3: Comment

We have highlighted this case because it reinforces how seriously the courts have taken the identification of the woman's wishes and feelings in the context of termination, and also – where possible – the need for applications to be made in a timely fashion where there is any suggestion that a termination is to be proposed as being in the woman's best interests.

Case 4: E

E is a 30-year-old woman, 16 days postnatal. She had a long and traumatic labour and finally delivered by emergency c-section due to fetal distress. She became psychotic in the week after delivery, believing that her baby was dying and that she was already dead, hearing voices that told her so. Her mental state was fluctuating with times when she was more coherent and rational, and times when she was perplexed and appeared confused. She was admitted to a psychiatric Mother and Baby Unit (MBU) under section 2 of the MHA, and started treatment with antipsychotic and antidepressant medication. She became a little more settled and could sleep with her medication, but there were no significant changes to her delusional beliefs yet. After 4 days in the MBU she developed a temperature, her scar from the c-section became more painful, and on examination by the ward staff it looked infected. Staff advised her she should go to the general hospital to treat the infection but E refused as she did not want to leave her baby, as she maintained her delusional beliefs that her baby was dying and that she was already dead, therefore she saw no threat in having a serious infection. She resisted and became distressed and agitated when staff insisted she needed to be transferred. When her husband, who had been informed, pleaded with her to get the treatment she needed, she accused him of wanting their baby to die alone. The staff at the MBU had no choice but to organise a formal capacity assessment and invited E's obstetrician to attend and join the psychiatrist on the MBU. Together they assessed E's capacity to decide whether to have her infection treated and both agreed that she lacked capacity to make this decision because of her psychotic beliefs.

The questions they needed to answer were:

1. Does she lack capacity to consent to the treatment?
2. If she does, then is it in her best interests to investigate/treat the infection?
3. If it is, then is it necessary and proportionate to the risk of harm she would suffer otherwise to restrain her to carry out the investigation/treatment or to bring about the transfer to the general hospital to be investigated/treated?
4. If yes to all of these, then they could in principle rely upon s.5 and 6 MCA to restrain her.

They were left with the dilemma of waiting for E's psychotic symptoms to respond to treatment for a day longer risking a deterioration in physical health, or treat her in her best interest, using the MCA, even if this involved the use of restraint.

In the end they decided that E's physical condition was severe enough to warrant treatment under the MCA, and that the use of restraint would be necessary and proportionate to the harm she would suffer otherwise.

Case 4: Comment

Deprivation of Liberty

A particular facet of E's case is that it raises potentially complex issues relating to deprivation of liberty. Guidance about deprivation of liberty in the hospital setting can be found in [23]; the key points as they arise in E's case are set out here.

If she were to be transferred on s.17 MHA 1983 leave to the general hospital, then the general hospital will need to have in place a Deprivation of Liberty Safeguards (DoLS) authorisation before she arrived (if possible) to authorise the deprivation of liberty to which she was subject there [24]. However, if time did not allow for the authorisation to be put in place before she arrived, the authorisation process would have to be started as quickly as possible thereafter, firstly by the general hospital granting itself an urgent authorisation and applying to the relevant supervisory body for a standard authorisation.

The general hospital may have to consider, separately, whether it needs to go to the Court of Protection to endorse its decision to treat (as treatment is not covered by DoLS), but on the facts of this case it appears sufficiently obvious that the treatment is in her best interests and that the general hospital could treat her on the basis of the defence in s.5 MCA 2005. It would only be if they were going to have to use extreme or deceptive methods that they would then have to start thinking about getting a court order.

It may be possible that the restraint required to get her to the general hospital will go beyond restraint into deprivation of liberty, for instance if there is either to be a very extended journey or she is to be sedated covertly. DoLS cannot be used to cover the period prior to arrival, so court authority might be required simply to cover the transfer.

Note that, if she stays at the MBU, and if the restraint is likely to be prolonged or repeated, then it is very likely that her circumstances will give rise to a deprivation of her liberty. In that case, the Trust responsible for the MBU could not use DoLS because she is detained under the MHA and, because of the wording of s.16A MCA, the Court of Protection cannot authorise deprivation of liberty in relation to a person detained under the MHA. The Trust would therefore need an order from the High Court under its inherent jurisdiction, as was confirmed in the case of *NHS Trust* v *Dr A* [2013] EWCOP 2442.

What Should Be Done

Joint capacity assessment: When assessing capacity to make a decision, correct, comprehensive and relevant information must be made available to the individual in order to ensure they have capacity. Therefore joint, multi-disciplinary assessments are necessary to support decisions about physical and mental health.

Documentation: Consideration must be given to a formal documentation of the presence or lack of capacity to make a decision, and to what risks the individual faces if professional advice is not followed. Consideration should also be given to documenting what the individual's views would have been in normal circumstances, that is, E's views about receiving treatment for her infection were she not psychotic. In this case it would be difficult to ascertain as she became known to MBU staff only at admission but possibly her husband and family as well as other professionals that may have been involved in her care could give a view, and this should be documented.

If the acute hospital is not able to complete the process to put in place a standard DoLS authorisation before E arrives, the acute hospital will need to grant itself an urgent authorisation lawfully to deprive E at the hospital for purposes of providing her with treatment.

Case 5: FA

FA is a 33-year-old woman with bipolar disorder who is 20 weeks pregnant. The pregnancy was planned, and she worked with a psychiatrist to optimise her medications for conception and the first trimester. She works in an advertising firm and is married with one child. She became pregnant with her first child aged 25 and had a severe manic episode in the early postpartum period. She became rapidly unwell and ran away from her family home. She was returned after a few hours by police after being seen walking into traffic by members of the public. She was admitted to an MBU under section 2 of the MHA and treated with olanzapine, her symptoms were persistent, and she was also started on lithium which was successful in treating the mania. FA was not able to breastfeed her first baby due to the severity of her symptoms and later the medication she was taking. During her recovery she found this distressing and became depressed.

Between pregnancies her mood has been relatively stable and she has had no further admissions. She has established clear routines and practices that she has found help her maintain her mental health. FA is extremely anxious that she will become unwell after the birth of her second child but would like to remain only on medications that are compatible with breastfeeding.

To achieve this FA would like to make plans for the postnatal period and feel confident that if she becomes unwell again, she will receive rapid help. In addition, she would like to know that even if she loses the capacity to make treatment decisions and needs admission under section, she will not be started on medications that in the longer term will prevent her breastfeeding.

FA has heard of advance directives and writes the following document:

FA Advance Directive

I had a very traumatic time when I was unwell after the birth of my first baby. I want to avoid some of the things that happened to me. So I request that if I become very unwell again after the birth of this baby people involved in my care read and use this document.

I am normally someone who enjoys their life. My husband, son and the baby that is coming mean everything to me and I have a busy, responsible job that I enjoy in a marketing firm. I like cooking, walking our dog and meeting up with friends. I am very worried that if I become unwell again it might have an enormous impact on my family and work life.

I have a diagnosis of bipolar and was very unwell with mania when my son was born. Usually I manage my mental health well – I take my medication and I see my psychiatrist and care coordinator.

When I start to become unwell I talk very fast, start lots of new projects at work and buy lots of things on Amazon. I can also post embarrassing things on Instagram. I can convince health professionals that I am well and sometimes they have not believed my family and friends that how I am acting is not normal for me.

When I have been unwell in the past I have had Home Treatment Team support. I like this team but it hasn't always worked out as I get really unwell very quickly. They are better for support when I am coming out of hospital.

If I need to be admitted after my baby is born I ***only*** *want to go to a local Mother and Baby Unit. I need to be near my family and with my baby.*

Medication:

I had olanzapine when I was last unwell, this worked for me in the short term but I do not want to take it in the long term because it makes me put on weight and become very drowsy.

I am happy to take lorazepam, diazepam and zopiclone – I have had all of these in the past.

I ***do not*** *want lithium under any circumstances or any other medication that will stop me breastfeeding, this is very important to me.*

If I am admitted I may be feeling frightened and angry, having leave from the ward and going on walks with my husband and dog can be really helpful for me. I like to eat healthily and would prefer food brought in from home to hospital food.

My husband has always been involved in my care and I trust his judgement completely. I want him to be given all information about my care and be involved in all decisions. I do not want any decision made without his input. If there are decisions about what medications I need and if I need to be admitted and I am too unwell to make them I want him to decide on my behalf.

I have talked with my mum about who should look after my children if I am unwell and she will come and stay at our house and help my husband look after them.

Case 5: Comment

Advance Decision-Making

The legal status of this document is complex. The term 'advance directive' is commonly used to refer to planning documents. It is not a meaningful legal term in England and Wales but originated in the US to describe advance decision-making documents following the introduction of the Patient Self-Determination Act. However, this document could count as a legally binding advance decision to refuse treatment (ADRT) under the MCA 2005 (the refusal of medical treatment with lithium). Throughout the following the term advance decision-making (ADM) is used as an umbrella term to describe any form of planning activity for mental health crises.

The rest of this document would best be described as an advance statement of wishes and feelings (AS). It is not legally enforceable but should be consulted by professionals and followed as closely as possible during the process of best interest decision-making.

The legal status of the document would change if FA were admitted under the MHA 1983. The ADRT would no longer be legally binding, and she could not guarantee that she would not be started on lithium. However, the MHA Code of Practice [13] states that these sorts of statements should be followed wherever possible, and it would be best practice for clinicians deviating from the instructions in an ADRT or AS to document their rationale for doing so.

FA has described somebody she would trust as a substitute decision-maker. This would not have legal status unless she went through the process of officially appointing that person as having Lasting Power of Attorney for Health and Welfare under the MCA 2005. However, it would be best practice to consult this person as part of a process of best interest decision-making.

Using Legal Provision for Advance Decision-Making in the Perinatal Period

There are several measures FA could take to use the current legal provision to add the maximum possible support to her advance treatment requests and refusals.

Using the Language of the MCA

The document could be explicitly labelled as an advance statement within the meaning of the MCA, rather than an advance directive, and her ADRT highlighted. This may help ensure professionals assessing her in crisis understand the legal significance of the document.

Personalised Capacity Assessment

In FA's document she specifies it should come into effect when she appears to be experiencing a particular mental state or diagnosis. It does not make reference to her decision-making capacity. We have already discussed the complexities of capacity assessment in the perinatal period; in order to guide future professionals a personalised capacity assessment could be documented with all parties using their knowledge of previous episodes to create a clear picture of how this woman presents when she has lost DMC-T.

In addition there is no evidence of a documented capacity assessment at the time FA wrote this document. This is not legally required. However, it could increase the confidence of future professionals that they are reading a document which is highly likely to 'exist', that is, have been made with the requisite decision-making capacity.

Co-producing an Advance Decision-Making Document

FA's document contains one legally binding element, the ADRT. However, as discussed, the *legal* weight of this element fails if she is admitted to a psychiatric hospital under the MHA 1983. FA will then have to rely on the *clinical* weight of the document. This could be ensured by co-producing the document with trusted family members/friends/advocates and senior clinicians who are familiar with the woman's case. Future clinicians could be reasonably assured of the applicability of such a document and, if preferences are agreed amongst all parties, are more likely to be inclined to have confidence in following them. When the Mental Health Act 2025 comes into force, advance decision-making documents will have statutory force, even if they cannot ultimately prevent treatment for mental disorder where sufficient justification exists.

Practical Considerations

During the process of creating the ADM document a plan for storage and access should be thought through. This should include consideration of which parties should be aware of the document and hold paper and/or electronic copies, for example family, primary care physicians, mental health teams, midwifery teams.

To give maximum assurance to professionals using the document in a crisis thought should be given to when the contents of the document should be reviewed. This could be in terms of time periods, such as every 3 years, or according to a change in circumstances, such as when a woman becomes pregnant again. The document would not necessarily expire; however, if a person's circumstances have changed, professionals may have reason to doubt the applicability of the contents.

Supporting Collaborative, Legal ADM with the ADM Templates

These issues have been distilled during studies with professionals, service users and carers which resulted in the co-production of ADM templates (called a PACT (preferences and advance decisions for crisis and treatment) and Crisis PACk (preferences for admission, treatment and care) in successive implementation studies [25, 26]. These documents incorporate crisis planning and explicit use of the MCA provision to provide maximum legal and clinical weight to collaborative advance decisions [25]. The templates and guidance are available in the published articles and can be adapted for use in local settings.

Advance planning offers important opportunities to make use of the predictable nature of perinatal risk periods, that is, post-delivery or if a woman decides to stop medications and to put lived expertise of previous episodes to good use. This has the potential to return some control to the woman and increase her sense of autonomy. As one perinatal care coordinator put it, 'with women within their pregnancy, it's very empowering that decisions in such an important period of their life, are not taken away because of their mental health' [25]. It has also been suggested that the process of drafting such a document can be therapeutic. Below is a quote from a partner of someone who experienced an episode of mania in the perinatal period and who then took part in creating an ADM document:

> It can help families to come together around the illness in a way that we hadn't before we did this kind of process . . . to realise that my view of what I had seen and understood of her illness was so different from her experience of it. And to come to some kind of shared understanding of it, and understanding the other person's memories of it. [25]

A properly considered advance planning framework that places emphasis on the woman's views offers the woman, her loved ones and professionals assurance that well thought through plans, which may take a great deal of time and commitment to produce, have the greatest possible chance of being used to navigate crises as well as possible for the family. Recommended future work in this area should include adapting templates which have been created for use in general mental health and tailoring them to be specific to issues that occur in the perinatal period.

To emphasise once more: advance decision-making is an evolving area of law. In the future such documents would most helpfully incorporate explicit use of provision under the MCA 2005 and the upcoming inclusion of 'Advance Choice Documents' in the reformed Mental Health Act.

Conclusion

For professionals involved in undertaking medico-legal assessments the perinatal period can seem to be a unique time of threat in that some of the most complex and urgent clinical decisions must be made during this time. It is important to recognise that opinions, personal beliefs and emotions can be deeply polarised and complicate the clinical decision-making process. Therefore, it is vital for professionals to be aware of the relevant legal frameworks, have clarity on the legal implications of available care options and to feel confident to seek legal advice early.

However, the perinatal period also offers a unique opportunity to reduce and mitigate the difficulties of urgent, complex medico-legal assessments. This can be achieved through the use of high-quality, collaborative advance decision-making as at least in some cases there is definite predictability of relapse risk. Advance decision-making in the perinatal period offers women and their families the best chance to make autonomous, informed choices about their care. Future work is needed to explore the application of the new provisions for Advance Choice Documents in the Mental Health Act 2025 for women in the perinatal period.

References

1. British Medical Association. Ethics guidance. 2024. www.bma.org.uk/advice-and-support/ethics
2. Health Education England. The competency framework for professionals working with women who have mental health problems in the perinatal period. 2018. https://tinyurl.com/4fbxw9yu
3. *A Local Authority* v *JB* [2021] UKSC 52.
4. A Ruck Keene, editor. *Assessment of mental capacity.* 5th ed. Law Society; 2023.
5. Mental Health and Justice project. The capacity guide. n.d. www.capacityguide.org.uk
6. *LBJ* v *RYJ* [2010] EWHC 2664 (Fam).
7. *Kings College NHS Foundation Trust* v *C and V* [2015] EWCOP 80.
8. *Wye Valley NHS Trust* v *Mr B* [2015] EWCOP 60.
9. *Re AB (Termination)* [2019] EWCA Civ 1215.
10. A Ruck Keene, M Friedman. Best interests, wishes and feelings and the Court of Protection 2015–2020. *J Elder Law Capacity.* 2020;Winter:31–53.
11. *NHS Trust* v *Y* [2018] UKSC 22.
12. *Re P (Sexual Relations and Contraception)* [2018] EWCOP 10.
13. Department of Health. Code of Practice to the MHA 1983. 2015. The Stationery Office.
14. *Nottinghamshire Healthcare NHS Trust* v *RC* [2014] EWCOP 1317.
15. *North Middlesex University Hospital NHS Trust* v *SR* [2021] EWCOP 58.
16. Department for Constitutional Affairs. Mental Capacity Act 2005 Code of Practice. 2007. The Stationary Office.
17. 39 Essex Chambers. Mental capacity guidance note: best interests. 2021. www.39essex.com/information-hub/insight/mental-capacity-guidance-note-best-interests
18. K Ayre, G Owen, P Moran. Mental capacity and borderline personality disorder. *BJPsych Bulletin.* 2007;41(1):33–6.
19. G Szmukler. Personality disorder and capacity to make treatment decisions. *J Med Ethics.* 2009;35(10):647–50.
20. A Buchanan. Mental capacity, legal competence and consent to treatment. *J R Soc Med.* 2004;97(9):415–20.
21. *Re AB (Termination of Pregnancy)* [2019] EWCOP 26.
22. *Re AB (Termination of Pregnancy)* [2019] EWCA Civ 1215.
23. 39 Essex Chambers. Mental capacity guidance note: deprivation of liberty in the hospital setting. 2019. www.39essex.com/mental-capacity-guidance-note-deprivation-liberty-hospital-setting
24. *NHS Trust & Ors* v *FG* [2014] EWCOP 30.

25. LA Stephenson, T Gergel, A Ruck Keene, L Rifkin, G Owen. The PACT advance decision-making template: preparing for Mental Health Act reforms with co-production, focus groups and consultation. *Int J Law Psychiatry.* 2020;71:101563.

26. LA Stephenson, T Gergel, A Ruck Keene, L Rifkin, G Owen. Preparing for Mental Health Act reform: pilot study of co-produced implementation strategies for Advance Choice Documents. *Wellcome Open Res.* 2022; 7(182):182.

Chapter 40

The Preparation of Psychiatric Reports for Court

Gertrude Seneviratne and Susan Conroy

Introduction

Psychiatrists working in perinatal psychiatry may be required to assist within a wide range of medico-legal matters, in a variety of legal contexts. A significant role will be supporting the family court when there are questions about whether a parent is able to care for a baby safely and adequately, both in the short and longer term within the child's minority (i.e. until they reach 18 in the UK). This may be in the context of new onset or chronic perinatal mental health conditions, where an opinion is offered by the psychiatrist about the parent's capacity to remain well, insight into their mental disorder, any impact on the baby of the disorder and other factors such as the existence of substance misuse, learning disability or domestic violence. The psychiatrist will also have to comment on protective factors such as the stability of the mental disorder, presence of good insight, good enough care of baby/child, adequate support for the parent, absence of domestic abuse or substance abuse and impact of all these factors on the developing baby/child. In perinatal psychiatry, this is usually about the index patient who is the pregnant or postnatal mother but may include the partner and wider family. Clinicians will have to keep up with guidance as law and practice are constantly evolving. This chapter has been written using predominantly the frameworks available in the jurisdictions of England and Wales and it goes without saying that one must understand the relevant local processes.

Research carried out by the Family Justice Data Partnership since 2018 has revealed the 'increasing numbers of newborn babies and infants who are subject to care proceedings in England and Wales – a figure that has more than doubled in the last decade' [1]. The corollary to this is that more psychiatric experts are required in family courts and there is a lack of such experts (child and adult psychiatrists). There are concerns about the number of experts available and the quality of reports. Thus, it is essential that perinatal clinicians have adequate skills in writing court reports [2].

To support psychiatrists with this work it is strongly recommended that the updating report by the Royal College of Psychiatrists CR193 'Responsibilities of psychiatrists who provide expert evidence to courts and tribunals' is read [3]. This lays out in greater detail the requirements of an expert in court proceedings, including some of the requirements in other jurisdictions across the UK. Psychiatrists have a duty not to give evidence or opinion on matters outside their areas or fields of expertise. For example, if the clinician is going to comment on the parenting or care of the baby, then it is essential that adequate observations have been made to inform any evidence or opinion. Other useful guidance includes the General Medical Council's Good Medical Practice [4], Acting as a Witness in Legal Proceedings [5], Protecting Children and Young People [6] and the

Academy of Medical Royal Colleges' 'Acting as an Expert or Professional Witness: Guidance for Professionals' [7]. Furthermore, all those who act as experts may be required to comply with certain procedural rules and 'practice directions'. These rules and practice directions for experts vary by court or 'jurisdiction' and are constantly evolving. In England and Wales, the rules and practice directions with which psychiatrists are likely to need to be familiar with are the Civil Procedure Rules Part 35 and its practice directions, the Criminal Procedure Rules Part 19 and its practice directions, the Family Procedures Rules Part 25 and its practice directions [8, 9] and the Expert Witness Code of Practice in Scotland [10].

The clinician may be asked to write a report as either the treating clinician who has knowledge of the patient *or* as an independent expert with no prior knowledge of the individual. The following list of potential instances where a report may be requested to support the work of the courts (to include Family, Criminal, etc.) whilst not exhaustive is applicable to both circumstances above:

- the mental health of parent(s) and babies/children in family cases, including commenting on diagnosis, treatment and prognosis of the mental disorder and the safeguarding of baby/children
- capacity to parent a baby/child in the short and longer term in the context of a perinatal or other mental illness/disorder, including personality disorder, intellectual disability, substance misuse and domestic violence
- the risk of physical or emotional harm, or of neglect posed by parents with mental health problems to their babies/children
- parental custody cases involving a parent or parents with perinatal or other mental disorders
- the effect of the mental illness/disorder on fitness to work
- the mental capacity of parents making various types of decision, such as capacity to understand the family court process
- allegations of negligent perinatal psychiatric care, for example if there has been perinatal suicide or near-miss event for mother or baby
- the state of mind of defendants in criminal cases related to perinatal mental illness – this may include cases of harm/neglect to babies/children or cases of infanticide/neonaticide/filicide.

Perinatal psychiatrists would not be expected or advised to comment on the sentencing of offenders (usually in the context of a perinatal mental disorder) unless trained in forensic psychiatry.

As part of ongoing continuous professional development, it is advised that multi-source feedback is obtained for work as a medico-legal expert. To help with this the Royal College of Psychiatrists has developed a Multi-Source Assessment for Expert Psychiatric Witnesses [11].

Examples of How Mental Illness Affects Capacity to Parent

Although a serious mental illness can adversely affect the ability to care for a child, with adequate resources and support, many parents with a serious mental illness are able to successfully care for their children. As Brockington pointed out, 'it is not so much the diagnosis that confers the risk, but the severity and chronicity of psychopathology' [12].

The level of risk is also affected by the interaction of genetic and child, parent, family and community factors. It has also been noted that children become more vulnerable to abuse and neglect when parental mental illness coexists with other problems such as substance misuse, domestic violence, childhood abuse or poverty [12]. It has been suggested that different psychiatric disorders have their effects through common pathways such as preoccupation, emotional unavailability, anger and disturbed behaviour [13, 14]. Parenting may also be adversely affected by other factors which tend to accompany serious psychiatric disorder, such as poverty, deprivation, stigma, and separations caused by the parent's hospital admissions, or beneficially influenced by protective factors such as good support networks [13, 14].

Schizophrenia, for example is a serious mental illness and parents may struggle in their parenting role [4]. However, this illness does not prevent safe and adequate parenting in all. Studies have shown that, although the rate of custody loss in this group was high, most women with schizophrenia value their roles as mothers, and their adult children remain attached to them [4]. There can be serious harms, however, associated with being the child of a mother with psychotic illness. Poorly controlled illness, including so-called negative symptoms, such as lack of volition, a blunted affect, diminished empathy, lack of emotional availability, cognitive impairment, poor memory and difficulty planning ahead may all impact on parenting.

The presence of acute psychotic symptoms such as delusions may mean that the parent is unable to provide a safe environment for their child [15, 16, 17]. The majority of the serious harm appears to be mediated not by the illness itself but by associated risks, for example poverty, substance misuse, domestic violence, social isolation and/or substandard housing. Whilst schizophrenia in mothers poses problems for offspring, it does not preclude effective parenting in all [18].

There are many requests for medico-legal reports related to mothers/parents who may have a personality disorder. One review of personality disorder posited that parental personality disorder may represent a risk to child development, both in terms of transmission of genetic vulnerability and the environmental stress of living with a parent who has a personality disorder that negatively affects parenting capacity [19]. However, Adshead argued that there are two compelling reasons to offer services for adults with personality disorders that specifically focus on their parenting [19]. Firstly, effective therapies for personality disorder are now available; and secondly, there is a strong argument for improving parental mental health in order to reduce the economic and psychological burden of their offspring's future psychiatric morbidity [19].

Prevalence

While a number of studies show that a significant proportion of women with mental illness are involved in the care of their children, studies in the field of child protection suggest that the prevalence of identified mental illness increases with the level of enquiry and consequent greater knowledge of family circumstances [14]. At the stage of referral to social care, 13% of parents are recorded as having some form of mental illness [20], but this increases to 43% of cases where children are the subject of care proceedings [14].

The 'Born into Care' study by the Nuffield Family Justice Observatory [21] used population-level data (2007/8 to 2016/17) held by the Children and Family Court Advisory and Support Service (Cafcass) to provide the first estimate of the proportion of care proceedings for infants (less than 12 months old) in England, that are issued for newborns (less than 7 days). Cases of newborns in the family justice system comprised a substantial proportion of all care proceedings issued for infants. The study also showed that the likelihood of newborns in the general population becoming subject to care proceedings has also increased over time; the incidence rate has more than doubled, increasing from 15 newborns per 10,000 live births in the general population in 2008 to 35 per 10,000 in 2016 [21].

Babies and very young children are particularly vulnerable to abuse and neglect [22] and, where a woman has a serious mental illness, professionals in mental health and children's services are likely to be concerned about her capacity to care for her child. Parents with pre-existing mental illness or postpartum psychiatric disorders may be at risk of disturbed parent–infant interactions, and their infants may have an increased risk of an unstable early foundation. They may be particularly vulnerable to environmental stress and have a higher risk of developing some psychiatric disorders in adulthood [23] (see Chapter 36, 'Child Safeguarding').

Making recommendations about the potential impact of the parental mental disorder on parenting capacity is complicated as there may be numerous factors which affect the overall capacity to provide safe and adequate care, including the comorbidities of substance and alcohol use, intellectual disability or autistic spectrum disorder to name a few, as well as numerous social and environmental factors.

Writing a Medico-Legal Report during the Perinatal Period

In a Community Perinatal Mental Health Team or Mother and Baby Unit

Clinicians may have to give opinions about parental mental illness, including the consistency and adequacy of parenting skills [24] and may be called upon to act as expert witnesses in child safeguarding cases [25] both in the antenatal and postnatal period, as well as subsequently. Concerns about a mother's mental illness, and ability to care for the baby may arise in pregnancy or following an admission to a Mother and Baby Unit (MBU). In the community, there may be requests following pre-birth planning meetings (Chapter 25, 'Pre-birth Planning'). If there are serious concerns in the antenatal period about a mother's capacity to parent, it may be likely that a pre-birth planning report is requested and a parenting assessment recommended following the birth of the baby. This may be in the context of a first pregnancy or a subsequent pregnancy, or if previous children have already been taken into care.

It is important to distinguish writing a report as the treating psychiatrist versus writing a medico-legal report as an instructed independent expert witness for the court. A treating psychiatrist does have a duty to support the assessment process when it comes to safeguarding the child. The treating psychiatrist may want to limit this to the actual care and treatment offered to the patient and err away from giving an opinion about prognosis, although this may be requested. For the treating clinician, the patient is known to them, whilst an independent expert instructed in a case will not previously know the patient. An instructed independent expert has a duty to speak with the treating psychiatrist or team as part of the assessment process. They will have a range of questions posed in a letter of instruction and they have a duty to offer an opinion.

On a psychiatric MBU, it may become apparent that the mother is having difficulties caring for the baby. This then becomes the duty of the treating team to alert the child safeguarding team about potential parenting concerns. The concerns may be in the context of a perinatal mental illness, lack of recovery from the illness despite best efforts to treat, ongoing psychiatric symptoms such as residual psychotic symptoms, severe mood disorder, severe emotional dysregulation, cognitive impairment, lack of insight into the mental illness, significant attachment problems to the baby, comorbid intellectual disability, inability to care adequately for the baby, poor performance in activities of daily living assessments, inability to care for self, to budget, to cook, etc. There may be significant difficulties with both the practical and emotional care of the baby, with inconsistent care and a struggle to care for the baby whilst trying to carry out other activities. It may become apparent that the baby's own physical, social and emotional development is being affected. It may be easier to notice concerns about baby care on an MBU compared with the community setting. Other factors may come to light such as significant domestic violence, comorbid addiction issues in mother or partner, and other social factors such as poverty, lack of housing or unsuitable home environment.

Perinatal mental health services, both community teams and MBUs, are governed by and work in accordance with the relevant legislation, health and social care policies including child care law. In England this would include the Public Law Outline [26], Children Act 1989 [27] and subsequent Children and Families Act 2014 [28], *Working Together* guidance [29], the London Child Protection Procedures [30], the recommendations of the *Munro Review of Child Protection: A Child-Centred System* [31] and *Decision-Making within a Child's Timeframe* [32], as well as mental health and human rights legislation. There may also be issues related to the safeguarding of adults to be addressed.

When writing a report for a parent on the MBU, the psychiatrist may be the one asked to write the report, but it is important to include information from the multi-disciplinary team as part of the report content.

Areas to include in the report include:

1. medical and psychiatric/psychological assessment of the mother, to include psychiatric and psychological history, diagnosis, psychological formulation, comorbidities, response or lack of response to treatment, insight into mental illness; other psychological difficulties
2. impact of the psychiatric disorder on ability to parent adequately, description of how residual psychiatric symptoms, such as mood disorder, psychosis, cognitive impairment, etc., might affect both practical and emotional care of baby and the ability to provide care around the clock
3. the mother's social functioning.
4. psychological investigations, including psychometric testing to include any cognitive impairment, intellectual disability or neurodiversity
5. mental health nursing and nursery nurses' observations of the mother's mental health and the mother and baby dyad, such as observations and evaluation of mother–infant interactions and their relationship, and information on the ability to provide safe and adequate routine physical and emotional care of the baby, preferably using established protocols on the unit or responses to video guidance [33]

6. developmental assessment of the infant
7. occupational therapy review of daily living skills such as cooking, shopping, budgeting or multitasking with baby
8. social work assessment / social factors to include factors such as existence of domestic abuse, substance misuse difficulties, poverty, environmental stressors such as poor housing or victimisation, etc.
9. relationship with partner, family and wider support networks
10. ability to work with the professional network.

The above list may also be used for women under the care of community perinatal teams. In the antenatal period, the pre-birth planning process allows the team to identify any potential concerns about the mother's mental health, her ability to care for the baby when born and for multi-agency planning (see Chapter 25, 'Pre-birth Planning'). This may include relevant safeguarding frameworks for the unborn child, planning a prophylactic admission to a psychiatric MBU for prevention of relapse, treatment of illness or a planned parenting assessment in a suitable facility. In the postnatal period, concerns may also arise about a parent's mental illness, other comorbidities and their effects on the parent's ability to care for the baby.

As well as updating clinical information, the psychiatrists may also be asked to make recommendations as to whether or not the mother/parent should be the primary carer of the infant, usually in the context of a legal framework, and to comment on what further interventions and support are required. Predictions about future risk are based on the mother's prognosis and the child's developing needs. Writing a report and making recommendations may be difficult and needs to be finely balanced. Ultimately, a decision about whether a baby or child remains with the index parent is decided by the judge in the family court, having weighed up evidence/reports from all parties, for example treating clinician in MBU or community perinatal team, expert independent witnesses, the local authority, the guardian ad litem (independently appointed for the child), parenting assessment reports and reports from other parties such as the partner or grandparents. When writing reports, either as the treating clinician or the independent expert, it is important to consider the positive and negative prognostic factors which may contribute to recommendations on whether the mother or parent has the capacity to provide safe and adequate care not just in the short term, but into the future and throughout the child's minority. The clinician may be asked to make a comment on longer-term prognosis and it is important to be as realistic as possible, whilst making it very clear that there is a difference between the treating clinician and an expert witness.

Assessment Methods Available in the Perinatal Period

Although a number of standardised tools have been developed for assessing and analysing information gathered about whether a child is suffering, or likely to suffer significant harm, a review by Barlow et al. concluded that there is limited evidence about their effectiveness in the field of child protection [34]. There is even less evidence about the effectiveness of tools for evaluating risk to infants in the presence of maternal mental illness. There are several key areas that need to be addressed, including not only the mother's mental illness and its impact on her capacity to nurture her child, but also the social and physical environment within which mother and child are located [29].

The Framework for the Assessment of Children in Need and their Families provides a systematic basis for collecting and analysing information to support professional judgments about how to help children and families in the best interests of the child [29, 35]. The Assessment Framework emphasises the need for a systematic approach, taking into account the interaction of three domains: the developmental needs of the child, the capacity of the parents or caregivers to respond appropriately to those needs, and the impact of the wider family and environmental factors on parenting capacity and the child. Each domain has several critical dimensions which need careful exploration during the assessment to understand how they affect the child in the family. In assessing the child's developmental needs, the critical dimensions of health of the child, education, emotional and behavioural development, identity development, social presentation and self-care skills, and the family and social relationships are explored. When assessing parenting capacity, the ability of the caregivers to provide basic care, to ensure safety of the child, to provide emotional warmth and the ability to provide stimulation, guidance, boundaries and stability are assessed. Family and environmental factors include family history and functioning, role of the wider family, housing and employment status of the caregiver, income, the family's social integration and the availability and accessibility of community resources.

Parenting Assessments

Either in the community or following an admission to an MBU, it may be necessary to recommend a parenting assessment before a mother/parent and baby can be placed in the community independently. Depending partly on considerations about the level of risk, assessment of parenting capability may take place in a variety of settings – the family home, a family centre or day assessment unit, a parent and child foster placement or a residential facility. The mother's mental health must be at what is deemed to be an optimal level before any parenting assessment commences. It would be unethical to conduct these assessments if the parent is still unwell and not fully recovered from an episode of perinatal mental illness.

Three MBUs in England used to facilitate residential parenting assessment in addition to treating women with severe perinatal mental illness. However, for a number of reasons – including funding, training of staff, service models and impact of the Covid-19 pandemic – these parenting assessment facilities on MBUs no longer operate, although there are plans to reopen them. If a parenting assessment is required for a woman under a perinatal mental health service, these are conducted in community or residential independent, local authority facilities or through mother and baby fostering placements.

A key strength of residential parenting assessments identified in a research study was that they can provide relative safety without separating children from parents when the risks are high and/or there are significant gaps in knowledge about parental functioning or relationship dynamics [36]. The intensive nature of a residential parenting assessment may also provide evidence about whether the parents are consistently able to provide 'good enough' parenting.

Concerns have been expressed, however, that parenting assessments lead to unnecessary delays in court proceedings and the Family Justice Review recommended that 'the court should seek material from an expert only when the information is not available, and cannot properly be made available, from parties already involved' [37].

In an earlier study of 61 parenting assessment cases admitted to the MBU during the 1990s, fewer than half of the mothers were discharged together with their babies at the end of the assessment period, and at follow-up, less than a third were still caring for their children [38]. The main factor determining whether a mother continued to care for her child both at discharge and at follow-up was her diagnosis. A lack of antenatal planning was associated with increased rates of separation of mother and infant. The findings illustrated the need for more integrated coordination between professionals in mental health and children's services to ensure early planning for mothers and infants at risk.

In England and Wales, the demand for parenting assessments has recently increased with the introduction of pre-birth assessment teams and planning by local authorities with an emphasis on preventative or 'frontloading' planning prior to babies being born. Since the introduction of the Public Law Outline in 2014, there has been a growing understanding of the need for robust early parenting assessments to be undertaken to establish a plan of permanence for the baby [26]. Any delay in a baby's permanent family is considered unacceptable, and there are now stringent timetables for care proceedings, for example 26 weeks from the granting of the initial interim care order (ICO). This means that local authorities are placed under increasing pressure to identify and fund independent specialist parenting assessments within a short timeframe. However, there remain significant fluctuations in the political and cultural landscape affecting thresholds for safeguarding procedures and decision-making for mothers with mental illness and their babies.

Inter-agency Working

Women referred for medico-legal reports and parenting assessments frequently have complex mental health and social needs, which warrant close collaboration between health and social care professionals. However, lengthy safeguarding and legal proceedings and/or multiple assessments may also be involved, leading to delays in decision-making and subsequent placement of children. This is particularly relevant in the case of babies, where delays, and possibly multiple carers, may have longer-term effects on the child's psychological development. There is potential for mistrust and disagreement between professionals at several stages during the process, for example, differing definitions and thresholds, differing understanding of factors contributing to risk and the validity of assessment processes, and disagreements regarding decisions about future planning.

In their review of 15 UK government-funded studies on safeguarding children from abuse and neglect, Davies and Ward addressed some of the reasons for 'a lack of resolve' on the part of social work practitioners [39]. These include a lack of awareness of the long-term impact of abuse and neglect, of the need to take decisive action in the case of babies, and of the importance of a family's previous history. In addition, there is evidence that practitioners can become desensitised to indications of neglect and that the parents' difficulties may overwhelm their ability to recognise the child's needs. Finally, an issue is the expectation of many professionals, both in social work and other agencies, and in keeping with the Children Act 1989 [27], the Children and Families Act 2014 [28], that children are best looked after within their birth families, and this adds to the complexity and difficulty of making decisions to separate children from their parents.

Timescales

In recognition of the importance of children's developmental timescales, greater emphasis is now being placed on early decision-making, particularly for babies [40]. In England, *Working Together to Safeguard Children* specifies a maximum timeframe of no longer than 45 days for an assessment to conclude [29]. It is expected that it should be possible to reach a decision on next steps, for example to agree on a child in need plan or child protection plan, within 45 working days from the point of referral into children's social care. Care proceedings are now expected to be completed within 26 weeks. There have also been changes to adoption policies and practices [41].

The key components of the Public Law Outline (Practice Direction 12A) [26] are a reorganised court system, which prioritises judicial continuity; a higher test for ordering expert assessments (that should be 'necessary' rather than 'reasonably required'); and a new framework for the submission of required documents, case allocation and timetabling [42]. The new care proceedings process in England and Wales, with its 26-week timescale, provides only a limited time for parents to show change or to recover from mental illness. However, given what is known about the impact of abuse and neglect on early childhood development, and the time it takes for parental change to become established, delayed assessment and decision-making may not only compromise a child's life chances, but may also deny parents the support they need to overcome adverse behaviour patterns within an appropriate timeframe. In the perinatal period, this may also mean that women who develop or relapse with mental illness postnatally are under an additional pressure to recover quickly and stabilise, such that the court timescales may be met. Extending this 26-week period if a mother were to relapse would be considered a reasonable reason to extend; nevertheless, the situation poses significant stress on an already unwell mother and it may paradoxically take longer for her to recover.

The Legal Context of Writing the Report

When there are concerns about the mother's or parent's mental health and capacity to care for the baby in the perinatal period, a psychiatrist (or clinician) may need to write either as the treating clinician or as an independent expert. For the purposes of this section the legal frameworks used in England and Wales have been used to illustrate the process, but of course this will be different in different jurisdictions and countries. In most cases, an independent expert report by a psychiatrist/clinician will be part of the family court process and will not be in the context of a parenting assessment. The treating clinician and independent expert will be contributing to a complex process in court.

As mentioned previously, it is important to make it clear whether the psychiatrist (clinician) is writing either as the *professional witness* (treating clinician) or as an *independent expert* witness. As a treating psychiatrist or clinician there is a duty to share good, accurate and detailed clinical information which may support a pre-birth or post-birth case conference or a local authority assessment. Usually, the consent of the parent is sought before disclosing reports, unless there are safeguarding matters or risks which override this. As a treating psychiatrist or clinician there may be a conflict of interest in also being an expert witness because of the impact on the therapeutic relationship. Consideration needs to be given to general codes of practice, such as the General Medical Council in the UK, whose recommendations regarding the ethics of report writing needs to be followed and understood. This may be difficult and complex in specialist areas such as perinatal psychiatry. However, efforts must be made to distinguish between evidence given as a professional witness and as an expert witness in a case. In the event of being an expert witness, there will also be an independently appointed expert or experts within the family court process. All local authority, medical and other relevant papers should be disclosed to the expert. Each party to the proceedings will be represented by their legal team, so the mother, father or partner, baby (who has a guardian ad litem appointed via court), grandparents and local authority each have separate legal representation.

The psychiatrist may be asked whether the mother/parent has capacity to instruct a solicitor and understand the process within the family court. There is a certificate of capacity to conduct proceedings which need to be completed – this is also referred to as 'litigation capacity'.

There is significant support and guidance in writing expert reports for the family courts. Duties of an expert and the expected content of the report are set out in Practice Direction 25B (PD25B): The Duties of an Expert, the Expert's Report, and Arrangements for an Expert to Attend Court [9]. This came into effect in England and Wales in October 2014. These practice directions vary by jurisdiction. For the purposes of this chapter, we will use this practice direction. The Royal College of Psychiatrists' 'Responsibilities of psychiatrists who provide expert opinion to courts and tribunals' College report CR193 [3] is also recommended as a useful guide in understanding the expert's role and process.

Who Is an Expert?

An 'expert' is defined as a person who provides expert evidence for use in family proceedings and excludes social workers, Cafcass officers and guardians from the scope of expert evidence. An expert may include an expert team. Expert witnesses involved in family proceedings (involving children) in England and Wales must comply with the standards. Significantly, this requirement applies whatever their field of practice or country of origin. There are several minimum standards now required of an expert [3, 9]:

1. The expert's area of competence is appropriate to the issue(s) upon which the court has identified that an opinion is required, and relevant experience is evidenced in their curriculum vitae.
2. The expert has been active in the area of work or practice (as a practitioner or an academic who is subject to peer appraisal), has sufficient experience of the issues relevant to the case, and is familiar with the breadth of current practice or opinion.

   This is especially relevant in perinatal psychiatry as the clinician may be able to comment on the psychiatric illness of the mother/parent but not on parenting capacity or the development of the baby.
3. The expert has working knowledge of the social, developmental, cultural norms and accepted legal principles applicable to the case presented at initial enquiry and has the cultural competency skills to deal with the circumstances of the case.
4. The expert is up to date with continuing professional development appropriate to their discipline and expertise.
5. If the expert's current professional practice is regulated by a UK statutory body, they are in possession of a current licence to practise or equivalent.

6. If the expert's area of professional practice is not subject to statutory registration (e.g. child psychotherapy, systemic family therapy, mediation, and experts in exclusively academic appointments) the expert should demonstrate appropriate qualifications and/or registration with a relevant professional body on a case-by-case basis.
7. The expert is compliant with any necessary safeguarding requirements, information security expectations, and carries professional indemnity insurance.
8. If the expert's current professional practice is outside the UK, they can demonstrate that they are compliant with the Family Justice Courts' 'Guidelines for the instruction of medical experts from overseas in family cases'.
9. The expert has undertaken appropriate training, updating or quality assurance activity relevant to the role of expert in the family courts in England and Wales within the last year.
10. The expert has a working knowledge of, and complies with, the requirements of practice directions relevant to providing reports for and giving evidence to the family courts in England and Wales.

Duties of the Expert

An expert in family proceedings has an overriding duty to the court that takes precedence over any obligation to the person from whom the expert has received instructions or by whom the expert is paid.

The duties are [3, 9]:

(a) to assist the court in accordance with the overriding duty; and to comply with standards for expert witnesses in child proceedings in the family court
(b) to provide advice to the court that conforms to the best practice of the expert's profession
(c) to answer the questions about which the expert is required to give an opinion (in child proceedings, those questions will be set out in the order of the court giving permission for an expert to be instructed, a child to be examined or otherwise assessed or expert evidence to be put before the court)
(d) to provide an opinion that is independent of the party or parties instructing the expert
(e) to confine the opinion to matters material to the issues in the case and in relation only to the questions that are within the expert's expertise (skill and experience)
(f) where a question has been put which falls outside the expert's expertise, to state this at the earliest opportunity and to volunteer an opinion as to whether another expert is required, including the need for a second opinion.

This is especially relevant in perinatal psychiatry as the clinician may be able to comment on the psychiatric illness of the mother/parent but not on parenting capacity or the development of the baby.

(g) when expressing an opinion, to take into consideration all of the material facts including any relevant factors arising from ethnic, cultural, religious or linguistic contexts at the time the opinion is expressed
(h) to inform those instructing the expert without delay of any change in the opinion and of the reason for the change.

What to Include in an Expert's Report

The expert's report must be addressed to the court and prepared and filed within the court's timetable and include the following [3, 9]:

(a) qualifications and experience

The curriculum vitae must illustrate clearly the competencies required to be acting as an independent expert for the purposes of the family court. It is important that the expert does not stray beyond their area of expertise. This may be difficult in the cases during the perinatal period where experts from both an adult and child background may be required for a complete assessment. For example, it may be possible to assess and give an opinion about the mother's mental illness, treatment and prognosis, but not be able to comment about the parenting capacity of the baby. Professionals in perinatal mental health services should be able to offer opinion about both. The legal professions may not fully understand the areas of expertise of various mental health professionals, the differences in training between adult and child psychiatry, for example. It is therefore the expert's duty to be clear about their area of expertise and ensure the court understands this, as well as recommending additional experts if required.

(b) a statement identifying the document(s)

As well as the reason for the report, it is important to list the full range of sources of information from local authority chronology, assessments and papers, previous medical and psychiatric notes, as well as relevant statements. The chronology of medical/psychiatric notes must summarise previous treatments, diagnosis, engagement with service and insight into mental health issues, where possible. Sources of information will include the assessment process as well as any discussions with third parties for collateral information. This should also include the treating psychiatric team or other professionals involved.

(c) a statement of those involved

State who carried out any test, assessment or interview which the expert has used for the report and whether the test, examination or interview has been carried out under the expert's supervision; this will include the clinical assessment and psychometric testing.

In the case of opinions about parenting of the baby, this may only be offered if the clinician has the requisite training and skills to offer this opinion.

(d) providing an opinion. This must:

(i) take into consideration all of the material facts including any relevant factors arising from ethnic, cultural, religious or linguistic contexts at the time the opinion is expressed, identifying the facts, literature and any other material, including research material, that the expert has relied upon in forming an opinion

(ii) describe the expert's own professional risk assessment process and process of differential diagnosis, highlighting factual assumptions, deductions from the factual assumptions, and any unusual, contradictory or inconsistent features of the case

(iii) indicate whether any proposition in the report is a hypothesis (in particular, a controversial hypothesis) or an opinion deduced in accordance with peer-reviewed and tested technique, research and experience accepted as a consensus in the scientific community
(iv) indicate whether the opinion is provisional (or qualified, as the case may be), stating the qualification and the reason for it, and identifying what further information is required to give an opinion without qualification.

(e) where there is a range of opinion:

(i) it is important to summarise the range of opinion
(ii) identify and explain, within the range of opinions, any 'unknown cause', whether arising from the facts of the case or from limited experience or lack of research, peer review or support in the relevant field of expertise
(iii) give reasons for any opinion expressed: the use of a balance sheet approach to the factors that support or undermine an opinion can be of great assistance to the court.

(f) contain a summary of the expert's conclusions and opinions

This should contain a statement that the expert:

(i) has no conflict of interest of any kind, other than any conflict disclosed in his or her report
(ii) does not consider that any interest disclosed affects his or her suitability as an expert witness on any issue on which he or she has given evidence
(iii) will advise the instructing party if, between the date of the expert's report and the final hearing, there is any change in circumstances which affects the expert's answers to (i) or (ii) above
(iv) understands their duty to the court and has complied with that duty
(v) is aware of the requirements of the Family Procedure Rules Part 25 and this practice direction
(vi) in children proceedings, has complied with the Standards for Expert Witnesses in Children Proceedings in the family court which are set out in the annex to this practice direction

(g) be verified by a statement of truth in the following form:

I confirm that I have made clear which facts and matters referred to in this report are within my own knowledge and which are not. Those that are within my own knowledge I confirm to be true. The opinions I have expressed represent my true and complete professional opinions on the matters to which they refer.

Where the report relates to children proceedings in England and Wales the form of statement of truth must include:

> I also confirm that I have complied with the Standards for Expert Witnesses in Children Proceedings in the family court which are set out in the annex to Practice Direction 25B: The Duties of an Expert, the Expert's Report and Arrangements for an Expert to Attend Court.

Example of a Fictional Case X

A young woman, X, with a previous history of depression and anxiety, develops a first episode of psychosis following the birth of her first baby. She has a complicated past psychiatric history with depression and self-harming. The relationship with the father of the baby is under strain as he is unsure about the relationship; mother has little other support. She has been admitted to a psychiatric MBU and takes several months to recover from a mixed affective state, fluctuating between mania and depression. Due to the severity of the illness, not responding to medication and other therapeutic input including psychological and occupational therapy, she requires treatment with electroconvulsive treatment, which does result in improvement in her mental health. When unwell, the mother is not able to focus on the practical, emotional and cognitive needs of the baby. However, as she gets better, which has taken almost 6 months, she is starting to provide sensitive, consistent care for her baby. There are no other comorbidities and she decides she will parent her baby as a single parent, as she is now estranged from the baby's father.

Examples of Possible Questions Posed in a Letter of Instruction for Case X and Baby Y

(a) Describe Ms X's mental health. Does she suffer from a mental health illness/disorder or personality or other difficulty? If yes, how have her experiences impacted on her?
(b) What treatment if any do you recommend for Ms X?
(c) Do any mental health/personality issues you identify affect her parenting capacity?
(d) Does Ms X pose a risk to others, in particular baby Y, and what is the nature of such risk? Does she pose a risk to herself?
(e) What is her insight and her capacity to engage in work and any treatment/therapy? What is the likelihood of success and within what timescale?
(f) Consider her ability to meet baby Y's needs, her insight into those needs, what changes if any she would need to make. Consider her ability to make such changes within the children's timescales.
(g) If baby Y does remain in/return to Ms X's care, what further support do you think she and baby would benefit from?

Opinion and Recommendations in Case X and Baby Y

In the framework for assessment there are several factors to consider:

1. Mental illness – diagnosis, risk assessments, insight, impact on parenting. A history and assessment must consider relevant factors including history of trauma. As well as a psychological and psychiatric formation, diagnosis using the DSM-V [43] or ICD-11 [44] classification systems is required. There must be a detailed discussion and formulation of comorbidities. Response to treatment (biological, psychological and social aspects), progress and capacity to remain well in the context of parenting must be discussed.
2. Psychological assessment including coping mechanisms.
3. Impact of her own experiences of being parented and consideration of how this might be the same or different for her infant.

4. Comment on parenting ability in terms of the ability to provide practical, emotional and cognitive care of the infant, including an understanding of the parent's ability to understand the changing developmental needs of the child. It may require more than one expert to comment on this. Various assessment frameworks may assist this process such as the Crittenden CARE-Index [45].
5. An assessment of the infant's physical, emotional and cognitive development, including any developmental delays which may mean that parenting requires additional support.
6. A mother/parent's independent living skills.
7. The contribution of partners and extended networks.
8. The ability to engage with the necessary services and actual engagement with services.
9. A discussion of relevant safeguarding children's and adult's factors.

The overall recommendations must include a balanced opinion about the various positive and negative prognostic factors and a balanced evaluation of prognosis in the short and longer term. This may include recommendations about whether the dyad should remain together or not, and in which circumstances, either as a sole parent, in a co-parenting role, with the support of an extended network, and with the relevant therapeutic input and multi-agency support to ensure that both the mother/parent's and infant's welfare is looked after. Importantly, if therapeutic input is being recommended, there must be a clear plan as to where and with whom this will take place and the likelihood that this will effect sufficient change in the mother/parent in a timescale suitable for the developing baby. There may be recommendations for further assessments either in a residential or community setting.

Summary

This chapter has focused on writing medico-legal court reports in the context of being either a) the treating clinician or b) an independent expert, with a focus on reports for child safeguarding and family court processes. We have attempted to highlight the range of parenting issues that might arise in the context of perinatal mental illness. We have also outlined the roles and duties of writing a report, as well as areas to include within the report and its structure. We have used the legal frameworks in England and Wales to describe this, whilst mindful that the relevant processes in different jurisdictions must be adhered to. At the time of writing, it is concerning that there are insufficient experts available to write perinatal psychiatric and psychological medicolegal reports in family courts, as highlighted in the data in England and Wales [2]. The need for skills in this area is pressing, as sadly there has been a significant increase in the number of babies born into care proceedings, especially in England and Wales [1, 21]. It is essential, therefore, that the growing number of clinicians practising within perinatal psychiatry and psychology acquire these skills. The primary objective for family courts is to ensure that children remain with birth parents unless there are overriding risks of significant harm and neglect to the child. Psychiatrists and clinicians therefore have a duty to be able to write high-quality professional witness and expert witness reports which assist courts in the case of maternal/parental mental health conditions and their potential effects on developing infants and children. Whether a baby remains in the care of the birth mother (and family) or not has profound effects on both, over lifetimes. However, it is ultimately the task of the judge in the family court to weigh up the available evidence submitted by different experts and parties and make the final recommendations.

It is hoped that policy, professional guidance and assessment frameworks for families will take a much greater proactive, anticipatory stance in the future. Supporting parents to manage their caregiving roles alongside parental serious mental illness successfully has been recognised as a public health priority and much more research is needed into how this can best be achieved with better outcomes for both the parents and their offspring [46].

References

1. The role of the Nuffield Family Justice Observatory is to improve the lives of children and families by putting data and evidence at the heart of the family justice system. www.nuffieldfjo.org.uk/our-work/newborn-babies
2. Family Justice Council. The President of the Family Division Working Group on Medical Experts in the Family Courts final report. 2020. https://tinyurl.com/5p72jyub
3. Royal College of Psychiatrists. Responsibilities of psychiatrists who provide expert evidence to courts and tribunals. College Report (CR193). 2023.
4. General Medical Council. Good medical practice. 2013. www.gmc-uk.org/guidance/good_medical_practice.Asp
5. General Medical Council. Acting as an expert witness. 2008. www.gmc-uk.org/ethical-guidance/ethical-guidance-for-doctors/acting-as-a-witness
6. General Medical Council. Protecting children and young people: the responsibilities of all doctors. 2012. https://tinyurl.com/27wvxkd4
7. Academy of Medical Royal Colleges. Acting as an expert or professional witness: guidance for professionals. 2019. https://tinyurl.com/yck7v9bb
8. Law Commission. Expert evidence in England and Wales. 2009. https://tinyurl.com/mspcvdju
9. Lord Chief Justice. Practice direction 25b: the duties of an expert, the expert's report and arrangements for an expert to attend court. 2014. https://tinyurl.com/bdd8s27h
10. Law Society of Scotland. Expert witness code of practice. n.d. www.lawscot.org.uk/members/business-support/expert-witness/expert-witness-code-of-practice
11. Royal College of Psychiatrists. Multi-source assessment for expert psychiatric witnesses (MAEP). 2023. www.rcpsych.ac.uk/improving-care/ccqi/multi-source-feedback/maep
12. I Brockington, P Chandra, H Dubowitz, D Jones, S Moussa, J Nakku, IQ Ferre. WPA guidance on the protection and promotion of mental health in children of persons with severe mental disorders. *World Psychiatry*. 2011;10:93–102.
13. A Reupert, D Maybery, J Nicholson. Towards the development of a conceptual framework. In: A Reupert, D Maybery, J Nicholson, M Göpfert, M Seeman, editors. *Parental psychiatric disorder: distressed parents and their families.* 3rd ed. Cambridge, UK: Cambridge University Press; 2015. p. 1–15.
14. H Cleaver, I Unell, J Aldgate. *Children's needs – parenting capacity. child abuse: parental mental illness, learning disability, substance misuse and domestic violence.* 2nd ed. London: Department for Education; 2011.
15. H Dipple, S Smith, H Andrews, B Evans. The experience of motherhood in women with severe and enduring mental illness. *Soc Psychiatry Psychiatr Epidemiol.* 2002;37(7):336–40.
16. RE Gearing, D Alonzo, C Marinelli. Maternal schizophrenia: psychosocial treatment for mothers and their children. *Clin Schizophr Relat Psychoses.* 2012;6(1):27–33.

17. MV Seeman. Schizophrenia and motherhood. In: A Reupert, D Maybery, J Nicholson, M Göpfert, MV Seeman, editors. *Parental psychiatric disorder: distressed parents and their families*. 3rd ed. Cambridge, UK: Cambridge University Press; 2015. p. 107–16.
18. MV Seeman. Parenting issues in mothers with schizophrenia. *Curr Womens Health Rev*. 2010;6(1):51–7.
19. G Adshead. Parenting and personality disorder: clinical and child protection implications. *Adv Psychiatr Treat*. 2015;21(1):15–22.
20. J Gibbons, S Conroy, C Bell. *Operating the child protection system: studies in child protection*. London: HMSO; 1995.
21. K Broadhurst, B Alrouh, C Mason, H Ward, L Holmes, M Ryan, S Bowyer. *Born into care: newborn babies subject to care proceedings in England*. London: The Nuffield Family Justice Observatory; 2018.
22. R Brown, H Ward. Cumulative jeopardy: how professional responses to evidence of abuse and neglect further jeopardise children's life chances by being out of kilter with timeframes for early childhood development. *Child Youth Serv Rev*. 2014;47:260–7.
23. NM-C Glangeaud-Freudenthal, A-L Sutter-Dallay, A-C Thieulin, V Dagens, M-A Zimmermann, A Debourg, et al. Predictors of infant foster care in cases of maternal psychiatric disorders. *Soc Psychiatry Psychiatr Epidemiol*. 2013;48:553–61.
24. M Gopfert, J Webster, J Pollard, JS Nelki. The assessment and prediction of parenting capacity: a community oriented approach. In: M Gopfert, J Webster, MV Seeman, editors. *Parental psychiatric disorder: distressed parents and their families*. Cambridge, UK: Cambridge University Press; 1996. p. 271–309.
25. J Hammond, M Lipsedge. Assessing parenting capacity in psychiatric mother and baby units: a case report and review of literature. *Psychiatria Danubina*. 2015;27(suppl. 1):S71–83.
26. Lord Chief Justice. Practice direction 12a: care, supervision and other part 4 proceedings: guide to care management. 2014. www.justice.gov.uk/protecting-the-vulnerable/care-proceedings-reform
27. The Children Act 1989. www.legislation.gov.uk/ukpga/1989/41/contents
28. The Children and Families Act 2014. www.legislation.gov.uk/ukpga/2014/6/contents
29. HM Government. Working together to safeguard children: a guide to inter-agency working to safeguard and promote the welfare of children. Updated 2025. www.gov.uk/government/publications/working-together-to-safeguard-children–2
30. London Safeguarding Children Partnership. London child protection procedures. 2020. www.londoncp.co.uk/local_resources.html
31. Department for Education. Munro review of child protection: a child-centred system. 2011. https://tinyurl.com/4m2ktbw6
32. Department for Education. Decision making within a child's timeframe. 2012. https://tinyurl.com/du4w9y9e
33. R Kumar, AE Hipwell. Development of a clinical rating scale to assess mother-infant interaction in a psychiatric mother and baby unit. *Br J Psychiatry*. 1996;169(1):18–26.
34. JD Barlow, J Fisher, D Jones. *Systematic review of models of analysing significant harm*. London: Department for Education; 2012.
35. Department of Health. *Framework for the assessment of children in need and their families*. London: HMSO; 2000.
36. ER Munro, K Hollingworth, V Meetoo, K Quy, S McDermid, T Trivedi, et al. Residential parenting assessments: uses, costs and contributions to effective and timely decision-making in public law cases. 2014. Childhood Wellbeing Research Centre.
37. Ministry of Justice. Family justice review final report. 2011. www.gov.uk/

government/publications/family-justice-review-final-report

38. G Seneviratne, S Conroy, M Marks. Parenting assessment in a psychiatric mother and baby unit. *Br J Soc Work.* 2003;33(4):535–55.

39. C Davies, H Ward. *Safeguarding children across services.* London: Jessica Kingsley; 2012.

40. J Masson, J Dickens. Protecting unborn and newborn babies. *Child Abuse Rev.* 2015;24:107–19.

41. Department for Education. An action plan for adoption: tackling delay. 2011. https://tinyurl.com/e89zerxe

42. J Dickens, J Masson. The courts and child protection social work in England: tail wags dog? *Br J Soc Work.* 2016;46: 355–71.

43. American Psychiatric Association. *Diagnostic and statistical manual of mental disorders.* 5th ed. Washington, DC: American Psychiatric Association; 2013.

44. World Health Organization. International classification of diseases for mortality and morbidity statistics. 11th revision. 2018.

45. PM Crittenden. CARE-Index. Infants. Coding Manual, unpublished manuscript, Miami, FL. 2010.

46. CI Harries, DM Smith, L Gregg, A Wittkowski. Parenting and serious mental illness (SMI): a systematic review and metasynthesis. *Clin Child Fam Psychol Rev.* 2023;26:303–42.

Index

Abortion Act (1967), 64, 672
abuse, *see* child abuse and neglect; domestic violence and abuse (DVA)
Acacia Family Support, 107, 530
Academy of Medical Royal Colleges, 415
acamprosate, 330
achondroplasia, 59, 67
Action on Postpartum Psychosis, 107, 213, 215, 450, 526, 530, 532
adult learning, 345
Adults with Incapacity (Scotland) Act 2000, 344
Advance Choice Document (ACD), 35, 677, 678
adverse childhood events (ACEs), 8–9, 245, 246, 248, 258–9, 557, 620, 654–5
affection, 77, 87
Affinid XL, 362
Afghanistan, 548
Africa, 282, 546, 550–1, 553, 639
agoraphobia, 187, 197
alcohol, 61, 247, 324, 329–30, 332–3, 423–4, 620, 670
  detoxification, 325, 330
  effects on fetus, 61
alcohol use, 59, 326, 330, 332, 560, 684
  global prevalence of, 324
Alcoholics Anonymous, 329
Alliance of African Maternal Mental Health (AAMMH), 551
Allied Health Professionals (AHP), 565
allopregnanolone, 166
alogia, 224, 232
Alvarez, Anne, 594
amenorrhea, 39, 284
American Psychiatric Association (APA), 171, 174, 192, 338
amphetamines, 360, 362–3, 367, 368
amitriptyline, 318–19
AN, *see* anorexia nervosa
anaemia, 42, 65, 173
Anganwadi workers (AWW), 549
anhedonia, 88, 99, 168, 171, 172, 222, 224, 232
Anna Freud Centre, 251
anorexia nervosa (AN),114, 281–6, 294–5, 297, 299–300, 323, 370, *see also* eating disorders
antidepressants, 165–6, 176–7, 252, 272, 318–19, 470–3, 480–1, 483
  combined seotonergic/noradrenergic, 319
  SSRI, 177, 195–8, 318–19, 369, 470–3, 481
  tricyclic, 177, 197, 318, 471
  withdrawal symptoms, 481
anti-emetics, 46
antipsychotic medication, 177, 215, 228–31, 232, 473–5, 478–81, 483, 491
  discontinuing, 231
  in-utero, 231
  second-generation, 229
antisocial personality disorder (ASPD), 505
anxiety disorders, 117, 129–30, 186–90, 192, 193–4, 198, 357–8, 498–500, 571–5
  aetiology, 188–9
  assessment, 189–90
  comorbidity, 191
    borderline personality disorder, 170
    depression, 173, 187
  course and outcomes, 187–8
  economic cost, 146
  fathers, 86
  fertility treatment and, 117, 119
  generalised anxiety disorder (GAD), 173, 186, 194, 496
  incidence, 98, 99, 117
  loss of child and, 129
  management, 152
  not otherwise specified (ADNOS), 187
  obsessive compulsive disorder (OCD), 172–3, 186–7, 195–6, 377, 490–1, 493, 498, 624
  panic disorder (PD), 82, 186–7, 197–8, 311, 491, 496
  phobias, 82, 186–7, 196
    agoraphobia, 187, 197
    social phobia, 166, 186–7, 189, 196–7, 490–1, 496, 498, 524
    tokophobia, 8, 187, 193–4, 198, 501, 518, 520
  prenatal, 578, 653
  prevalence, 186–7
  as risk factor, 83
  screening, 14
  symptoms, 82
anxiety disorders,treatment, 190–2
Approachable Parenting, 107, 530
Argentina, 552–3
aripiprazole, 231, 473–6
arthrogryphosis, 67
asenapine, 475
Asian/Asian British women, 12, 29, 97, 98, 100–1, 124
asociality, 222, 224, 232
assisted reproductive technologies (ART), 120
Attachment and Bio-behavioural Catch-up (ABC), 271
attachment insecurity, 246, 654–6

attention deficit hyperactivity disorder (ADHD), 283, 355, 357–9, 360, 363–6, 369–70, 371, 473, 573, 578
  adult, 355–6
  breastfeeding and, 369
  comorbidities, 355
  comorbidity
    anxiety, 187
    eating disorders, 283, 289
  defined, 355
  diagnosis, 355, 358–9
  diangosis, female ADHD, 357–8
  during pregnancy, 365–9
  features, 356–7
  medication in pregnancy, 366–7
  pre-conception issues, 364–5
  risk factors, 472, 475
    genetic, 578
    prenatal stress, 573–4
    stress, 62
    tobacco use, 62
  treatment, 359–60
    coaching, 364
    non-stimulant drugs, 363
    psychoeducation, 364
    psychotherapy, 363–4
    stimulant drugs, 360–3
autism, 62, 283, 376–80, 381, 388–90, 473, 475–6
  antenatal period, 382–3
  comorbidity
    anxiety, 187
    eating disorders, 283, 289
  comorbidity, ADHD, 355
  definition, 376–7
  delivery and, 383–4
  diagnosis, 378–81
  identity and terminological issues, 376
  maternal risk factors, 472
    antipsychotic agents, 231
  parenting challenges, 386–8
  as perinatal mental health issue, 377–8
  postnatal period, 384–5
  risk factors, genetic, 62
  sex and conception and, 381
  undiagnosed patients, 388–90
Autism Quotient, 389
avolition, 222, 224, 228, 232
Baby Triple-P, 611
Baby-Friendly Hospital Initiative, 552
Barker, David, 423, 571
Beckwith–Wiedemann syndrome, 59, 67, 68
BED, *see* binge eating disorder.
behavioural activation, 496, 498, 507
behavioural couples therapy (BCT), 123, 271, 496, 506
benevolent childhood experiences (BCE), 262
benzodiazepines, 198, 215, 230, 325, 330, 331–2, 462, 480
bereavement, 128, 130, 171, 266, 494, 500, 590, 654
Best Use of Medicines in Pregnancy (BUMPS), 466
Beyond Blue, 174
BICA (British Infertility Counselling Association), 121
Bick, Esther, 588, 589
binge eating disorder, 265, 281–6, 288, 289, 293–4, 295, 300, 496
Bion, Wilfred, 587, 592
bipolar disorder, 28–30, 31, 129–30, 170–1, 173, 207–13, 221, 477–8
Bipolar UK, 28, 34, 213
Birmingham and Solihull Mental Health Foundation Trust, 107
birth planning, 383–4, 518
birth trauma, 192, 193, 292, 519, 520, 527, 540
Black African, 98, 100, 102
Black British, 98, 124
Black Caribbean, 98, 99–100, 102
Black Lives Matter movement, 103
blood tests, 63, 65, 360, 382, 448, 452, 663
blunted affect, 224, 683
BMI, 115, 284, 289–92, 294–7, 298, 457, 605
  maternal, 469
  pre-pregnancy, 292–3
BMI/weight, 292
BN, *see* bulimia nervosa
bodily distress disorder, 307, 311
Bolivia, 552
borderline personality disorder (BPD), 244–5, 248–9, 262–5, 491, 502–3, 505, 604
bottle feeding, 632
Bowlby, John, 246, 562, 589, 654
brain development, 56, 59, 61–2, 77, 558, 575, 577
brain-derived neurotropic factor (BDNF), 188, 578
breastfeeding, 167, 188, 299, 370, 448, 463–4, 480, 482, 483
  advantages of, 463
  advice provision, 429, 448, 463
  autism and, 386
  benefits of, 332, 448, 464
  child development and, 71, 428
  eating disorders and, 299–300
  epilepsy and, 344
  initiation, 225, 640
  lack of, social anxiety and, 196
  medications and, 318, 330, 399, 411, 416, 431, 458, 463
    ADHD medications, 369–70, 371
    antidepressants, 177, 229, 231, 481
    antipsychotics, 232, 481
    lamotrigine, 482
    lithium, 482
    prescribing principles, 483
    relative infant dose, 481
  nutritional requrements, 299
  partial, 463, 480, 482
  promotion, 552
  recommendations, 480
  substance use and
    alcohol, 332
    benzodiazepines, 332
    tobacco, 332
  see also mixed feeding

brexanolone, 178
British Association in Counselling and Psychotherapy (BACP), 121
British Association of Psychopharmacology (BAP), 330, 359, 362, 426, 476, 483
British Infertility Counselling Association (BICA), 121
British National Formulary (BNF), 360–2, 464
Bucharest Early Intervention Project, 77
bulimia nervosa (BN), 281–6, 288, 294–5, 299–300, 358, 491
bullying, 101, 266, 379
buprenorphine, 330–1, 332
bupropion, 177, 228, 330, 363, 471, 473

CAMHS, *see* Child and Adolescent Mental Health Services (CAMHS)
Camouflaging Autistic Traits questionnaire, 389
Canadian Network for Mood and Anxiety Treatments (CANMAT), 174
cancer, 11, 31, 126, 225, 309, 620
cannabis, 61, 225, 247, 323, 325, 328, 332, 358
carbamazepine, 57, 463, 476–7, 479, 480
cardiac arrest, 46–7
cardiac arrhythmias, 295
cardiac defects, 68
cardiac disease, 45, 51–2, 360, 395
cardiac ischaemia, 51
cardiac output (CO), 39–41
care proceedings, 452, 626, 630, 632–3, 681, 684, 688–9, 695
centrality of motherhood, 23, 25, 26, 27
child abuse and neglect, 8, 619, 620, 688, 689
  diagnosis, 623–4
  eating disorders and, 284
  effects, 619
  emotional neglect, 595
  incidence, 551, 620
  mitigation, 625
  by partners, 627
  post-traumatic stress disorder and, 260
  prevention, 552, 688
  resulting in death, 651–2
  risk assessment, 417, 623
  risk factors, 619, 622, 695
    complex comorbidities, 683
    insecure attachment, 656
    personality disorders, 241, 248
    poverty, 625
  young infants, 631
  see also adverse childhood experiences; filicide; sageguarding
Child and Adolescent Mental Health Services (CAMHS), 14, 17, 249, 365, 564
Child Death Overview Panel, 128
Child Health Action Plan, 525
Child in Need, 629
child maltreatment, *see* child abuse and neglect
child protection, 441, 619, 628, 629, 652, 657, 683, 686
Child Protection Conference, 449, 626, 630
Child Protection Plans (CPP), 452, 540, 620, 626, 628, 630, 689
Child Protection Register, 630
child removal, 227, 342, 346, 400
child safeguarding, *see* safeguarding
childhood trauma, 167, 222, 242, 263, 265, 266–7, 270, 272
  chronic, 244
  parental, 342
  see also adverse childhood experiences; child abuse and neglect
Children Act (1989), 619, 623, 629, 631, 685, 688
children's centres, 453, 514, 525
children's services, 622–3, 633–4, 684, 688
Children's Social Care, 451, 621, 628
Children's Social Care National Framework, 619
Chile, 552–3
Chile Crece Contigo programme, 552
China, 282, 547, 549, 553, 572
chronic diseases, 225, 550
chronic illness, 24, 60, 414, 520
chronic pain, 355, 640
cigarettes, 330, 414, 670
  electronic, 330
Circle of Security, 271, 609
clonidine, 363, 368, 370
clozapine, 231, 232, 448, 463, 474
Cochrane reviews, 122, 643
coeliac disease screen, 292
cognitive analytical therapies (CAT), 297
cognitive behavioural therapy (CBT), 122, 197–8, 329, 363–4, 490–1, 493, 496–8, 507
cognitive reprocessing therapy (CRT), 269
cohabiting women, 30
Colombia, 551–3
complex post-traumatic stress disorder (CPTSD), 8, 257–72
Concerta XL, 362
Confidential Enquiries into Maternal Deaths, 131, 393–9, 401–4, 417, 419, 536, 542, 543
confidentiality, 19, 327, 399, 410, 527, 528, 642, 644
congenital anomalies, 127, 468, 470, 471
congenital malformations, 62, 231, 367–8, 469, 470, 473, 476, 484
contraception, 52, 212, 228, 229, 342, 450, 466, 477
CORE, 189–90, 412
corpus callosum, 59, 65
corticotropin-releasing hormone (CRH), 196, 576
counselling, 34, 52, 88, 121–2, 132, 133–4, 551, 552
  abuse, 232

counselling (cont.)
  exercise, 229
  genetic, 125, 213
  infertility, 121
  nutritional, 491
  pre-conception, 28, 30, 34, 52, 212, 369, 547
  relationship/marital, 364
  reproductive, 477, 484
couple relationship, 10, 80, 84–5, 87, 131, 134–5, 271, 505–6
couples therapy for depression (CTD), 496, 506
Couvade syndrome, 311
Covid-19, 98, 409, 521, 542, 687
CPTSD, *see* complex post-traumatic stress disorder
Crime Survey for England and Wales, 100, 620, 638–9
criminality, 102, 313, 648–50, 651, 653, 657, 662, 682
cultures, 3, 5, 15, 97, 98, 106, 223, 226
Cusk, Rachel, 4
custody loss, 23–4, 26–8, 226–7, 407, 649, 650, 682, 683
cyclothymia, 355, 365

death of a child, 649
dehydroepiandrosterone, 285
delusional disorder, 223
delusions, 206, 214, 222–3, 228, 561, 683
  paranoid, 222, 652–3, 668
denial of pregnancy, 12, 222
depression, 123, 129–30, 133–4, 165, 166–70, 500–1, 572, 574
  antenatal, 193, 286, 550, 576, 577–8
  associated conditions, premature birth, 472
  bipolar disorder and, 33, 212
  case identification, 170–1
  comorbidity, 5, 173, 189, 195, 286, 308
    ADHD, 357, 366, 369
    anxiety, 173, 187, 191, 198
    autism, 289
    eating disorders, 285
    PTSD, 192, 270
  course, 169
  developmental effects, 572–4, 578
  diagnosis, 169, 171–3, 174, 175, 472
    mental state examination, 316
  following loss of child, 129–31, 132
  history of, 83, 130, 188, 311, 694
  hypochondriachal cognitions, 309, 313
  major depressive disorder (MDD), 117, 120, 130, 133, 171–3, 206–7, 210
  management, 178, 505, 611
    antidepressants, 10, 103, 165–6, 175, 176, 177–8, 191, 197, 230, 247, 252, 272, 318–19, 320, 455, 457, 470–3, 480–1, 483, 484, 491, 504, 548, 673
    CBT, 122, 495
    couples therapy, 496, 506
    emerging therapies, 178
    interpersonal psychotherapy for, 491
    interpersonal therapy, 500–1
    NHS talking therapies, 524
    parenting programmes, 611
    pharmacological, 34
    prevention, 175
    psychodynamic therapy, 505
    psychosocial treatments, 132–4, 176, 490
    support group, 528
  maternal sensitivity and, 603
  moderate, 176, 272
  outcomes, 169–70
    filicide, 653, 694
  paternal, 77, 81–3, 86–7
  postpartum, 98–9, 118, 166, 167–70, 286, 341, 603
  presentation, 168
  prevalence, 165
  protective factors, 85
  psychotic, 177, 206, 408
  risk, 167
  risk assessment, 174
  risk factors, 85
    ethnicity, 98
    fertility treatment, 117, 119
    genetic, 167
    obesity, 33
    previous history, 120
    psychiatric history, 165
    social, 167–8
    social support, 100
  risk factors for, 165, 176, 507
  risk factors,neuroendocrine, 166–7
  screening, 14, 153, 547–8, 553
  severe, 174, 177, 178, 342, 441, 491, 520, 548
  subthreshold, 102
  symptoms, 81, 86, 130, 132, 168, 170, 472, 500, 572, 573
  unipolar, 173
deprivation, 99, 106, 514, 674, 683
  sociodemographic, 608
  socio-economic, 99, 124, 625
dexamphetamine, 362, 367, 370
diabetes
  gestational, 46–7, 169, 231, 283, 292, 423, 425, 474
  type 2 293, 295, 341, 355, 428, 571, 575
dialectical behavioural therapy (DBT), 250, 251, 270, 364, 491, 496, 502–3, 506
diarrhoea, 126, 295, 323
diazepam, 330, 331, 676
discrimination, 31, 72, 102, 154, 233, 339
diseases, liver, 8, 11
disorganized thinking, 222
dissociation, 261, 264–5, 268, 500, 594, 644, 654
disulfiram, 330
divorce, 83, 167, 266, 355, 358, 650
domestic violence and abuse (DVA), 85, 100, 346, 619–20, 638, 640, 641–3, 682–3, 684
  assessment, 226, 313, 414, 432, 640–3

child abuse and, 620, 621, 622, 624, 631, 683
filicide, 652, 654
defined, 638
developmental effects on children, 557, 572, 640
during childhood, 83
during pregnancy, 100, 190
enquiry about and response to disclosure, 88
epigenetic effects, 579
independent domestic violence advocates, 518
infant attachment and, 560
post-traumatic stress disorder and, 261
prevalence, 638
response following disclosure, 643–4
retraumatisation, 640
as risk factor, 85, 87, 100, 232, 241, 621
risk factors, 322, 324, 640
sexual abuse, 7, 259, 265, 446, 620, 639, 640,
trafficking, 639
see also child abuse
domestic violence and abuse (DVA) prevalence, 85
doulas, 345, 552–3
Down's syndrome, 66, 68
Drugs and Lactation Database (LactMed), 466
duloxetine, 471
dyadic interaction, 563, 602

Early Help services, 628
Early Pregnancy Units (EPUs), 64
eating disorder services, 289, 292, 293, 297–8, 299, 301, 450
eating disorders
anorexia nervosa, 114, 281, 283, 294, 297, 323, 370, 496
assessment, 288–94
binge eating disorder, 265, 281–6, 288, 289, 293–4, 295, 300, 496
birth outcomes, 285–6
breastfeeding and, 300
bulimia nervosa (BN), 281–6, 288, 294–5, 299–300, 358, 491
care and treatment
exposure-based therapies, 498–500
mentalisation-based treatment, 505
perinatal, 296–8
postnatal, 298–9
psychological therapies, 491
psychotropic medication, 299–301
comorbidities, 262, 286, 299–300
ADHD, 358
autism, 377
personality dysfunction, 246, 249
as coping strategy, 248
diagnostic classification, 281–2
during pregnancy, 284–5
fertility and, 8, 114, 284
morbidity and mortality, 282–4
not otherwise specified (EDNOS), 281, 285, 286
parent–child interactions and, 604
prevalence, 282
remission rates, 286
risk factors, adverse childhood experiences, 259
risks, 294–6
screening, 287–8
Ebstein anomaly, 478
echocardiography, 41
Edinburgh Postnatal Depression Scale (EPDS), 14, 98–9, 170–3, 174, 547–8, 549, 553
electroconvulsive therapy (ECT), 175, 177, 215, 230, 517, 553, 694
embryo transfer (ET), 114
emotional neglect, 594
emotionally unstable personality disorder, *see* borderline personality disorder
Emson, Daksha, 653
endometriosis, 114, 381
epigenetics, 247, 261, 578
epilepsy, 59, 341, 344, 476, 477, 482
Equasym XL, 362
Erb's palsy, 46
Estrin, Lockwood, 7, 542
Ethiopia, 550, 553
ethnic inequalities, 11, 101
ethnic minorities, 12, 15, 97–103, 107, 402
ethnicity, 11, 15, 97–100, 106, 124, 282, 579
EUPD, *see* borderline personality disorder (BPD)
European Mental Health Action Plan, 553
executive dysfunction, 222, 224
external cephalic version (ECV), 64
extinction-based learning, 494
eye movement desensitisation and reprocessing (EMDR), 122, 191, 198, 269–70, 493, 498, 501, 643

factitious disorder imposed on another, 313
factitious disorders, 245, 307, 308, 309, 312, 313, 320
family courts, 629, 631, 681, 686, 690, 691–2, 693, 695–6
family hubs, 525
family members,1, 80–1, 89–90, 410, 447, 449, 565–6, 638, *see also* fathers; partners
Family Nurse Partnership, 628
Family-Centered Maternity Model, 552
fathers, 9–10, 82–3, 86, 87, 88–9, 594, 649, 694
child involvement, 81, 86
depression, 77, 81, 86, 87
engagement and inclusion, 87–8
healthcare professionals and, 83, 89
mental health, 81, 82–3
child outcomes and, 226, 271
risk factors, 83
partner support, 85

fathers (cont.)
  relationship quality and child outcomes, 87, 434
  social role, 81
  as sole parent, 541
  see also partners
fatigue, 4, 12, 171, 172, 222–4, 228, 308, 310
  chronic, 318, 355
fear generalisability, 188
feigning of symptoms, 309, 312–13
female genital mutilation (FGM), 103, 638, 639–40,
FertiQoL, 121
fetal abnormalities, 11, 56, 64, 65, 461
fetal alcohol spectrum disorder (FASD), 61, 560
fetal alcohol syndrome (FAS), 61
Fetal Anomaly Screening Programme (FASP), 63
fetal development, 11, 56, 186, 230, 423–4, 459, 468, 571–2
fetal growth, 60–1, 287, 292–4, 324, 326, 460, 468
fetal medicine unit (FMU), 62, 64
fetal programming, 423, 429, 571, 573, 575
FGM, *see* female genital mutilation
fibromyalgia, 306, 308, 310, 318, 355
filicide, 12, 214, 222, 248, 397, 648–53, 655–6
  maternal, 657
  motivations for, 651–3
  studies, 248, 651
  typologies, 652
First Episode Rapid Early Intervention for Eating Disorders (FREED), 297
Five Year Forward, 103, 611
floppy infant syndrome, 231
fluoxetine, 177, 300, 473, 481
folate, 57, 292
follicle-stimulating hormone (FSH), 284
fragile X syndrome, 59
Fraiberg, Selma, 594, 596–7, 610, 653–4
FRAMES model, 327
Fr-behaviours, 602
functional disorders, 310
Fybogel, 300

GAD2, *see* Generalised Anxiety Disorder scale
gap analysis, 106
Gavin, Hector, 312
gay men, 82
gender, 15, 23, 82, 99–100, 168, 174, 357, 410
General Medical Council (GMC), 415, 681, 689
generalised anxiety disorder (GAD), 173, 186–7, 189, 190, 194–5, 435, 496
Generalised Anxiety Disorder scale (GAD), 14, 189, 547
genetic counsellors, 122
gestational diabetes, 46–7, 169, 231, 283, 292, 423, 425, 474
gestational thrombocytopenia, 42
gestational trophoblastic disease (GTD), 126
gestational trophoblastic neoplasia (GTN), 126
Gidget Foundation, 553
GPs, *see* primary care
grief, complicated, 129, 130, 132, 133
guanfacine, 363
guilt, 23–4, 26–7, 129, 171, 172, 465, 499, 580

hallucinations, 206, 222, 228, 652
healers, 16
Health of Nation Outcome Scales (HONOS), 412
HELLP syndrome, 49–50
holoprosencephaly, 59, 65
Honduras, 552
Hong Kong, 547
honour, 15
Hopkins, Gerard Manley, 156
housing insecurity, 560–1, 621
Howard, Louise, 35
husband, 103, 297, 385, 648, 668, 673, 674, 675–6
hyperemesis gravidarum (HG), 45–6, 126, 287, 289, 297, 311
hypersomnia, 168, 171, 172, 323
hypochondriasis, 307, 309–10, 320
hypoglycaemia, 61, 472
hypokalaemia, 283
hypomania, 172
hyponatraemia, 46, 283
hypophosphatemia, 296
hypoplastic left heart syndrome (HLHS), 471
hypothalamic-pituitary-adrenal (HPA) axis, 166, 212, 314, 577–8

immigrants, 99, 167, 411, 448, 579, 625
impulsivity, 250, 265, 344, 355, 356, 359, 505
India, 547–8, 549
Indonesia, 546, 547, 549, 553
infant affect, 601
infant massage, 73, 606, 608, 611, 612
infant observation, 587, 589, 596, 597–9
infant sleep, 176
infanticide, *see* filicide
infertility, 11, 113–16, 118, 119–23, 134–5, 490
  anovulatory, 114
  counselling, 121
  diagnosis of, 116
  diagnosis and treatment of, 114, 115
  emotional impact of, 120, 135
  secondary, 113, 115
Initial Child Protection Conference (ICPC), 630
inpatient units, 298, 301, 478
insomnia, 168, 171, 308, 310, 323, 362, 370, 656
intellectual disabilities (ID), 338–47, 348, 376
  abuse risk, 346
  autism and, 376
  child outcomes, 342
  comorbidity, 684–5

definition, 338–9
lifestyle factors, 342
mental capacity assessment, 343–4
mental health and, 340–1
mental health assessment, 343
parenting and, 339
perinatal services, 347
physical health and, 341
pregnancy outcomes and, 339–40
psychological therapies, 345
psychotropic medication, 344
safeguarding, 346–7
screening, 685
sexual health and, 341
social support, 344–5
Interim Care Order (ICO), 631, 688
International Classification of Disease (ICD), 130, 171, 207–8, 242–3, 257, 263–4, 281, 307
International Society of Traumatic Stress Studies (ISTSS), 270
International Trauma Questionnaire (ITQ), 262
interpersonal therapy (IPT), 133, 175, 176, 271, 491, 496, 500–1, 503–4
interpreters, 15, 409, 432, 445, 641, 668
intracytoplasmic sperm injection (ICSI), 114
irritability, 88, 206, 264, 323, 332, 356, 369–70, 413
isolation, 23, 24, 26–8, 129, 174, 222, 226–7, 526
IVF, *see* in vitro fertilisation

Japan, 282, 548, 549, 553
Jones, Ian, 28
Jones, Lucy, 3

kangaroo model, 551
killing (of children) *see* filicide
Klein, Melanie, 588

labour, preterm, 231, 641
lactulose, 300
lamotrigine, 476–7, 478, 481, 482, 484
laxatives, 289, 296
leadership, 20, 146–51, 155, 156–7, 159, 162
failures, 162
see also management
Leadsom, Andrea, 525
learning disabilities, 338, 348, 445, 477, 623, 625, 681, *see also* autism, intellectual disabilities
Learning Disability Improvement Standards, 347
left ventricular end-diastolic dimension (LVEDD), 41
Lesotho, 550
LGBTQ+ people, 80, 82, 89, 381, 528
lifestyle factors, 11, 118, 128, 342, 416, 433–5, 470, 491
lisdexamphetamine, 360, 362, 370
lithium, 31, 177, 215, 448, 451, 478–9, 482, 675–6
Lived Experience speakers, 531–2
local authorities, 523, 621, 628–32, 686, 688, 690
Long Term Plan (NHS England), 103, 524, 540, 624, 633
lorazepam, 452, 676
low birth weight, 169, 186, 198, 225, 228, 322–4, 329, 330–1
lung volumes, 44
lurasidone, 475
luteinising hormone, 284

macronutrients, 299
Madre Bonita, 553
major depressive disorder (MDD), 117, 120, 130, 133, 171–3, 206–7, 210
Malawi, 551
Malaysia, 546
malingering, 307, 308, 309, 312–13, 320
management,146–50, 155, 165, 174–6, 226–30, 329, 537, *see also* leadership
managers, 100, 146, 149–53, 155, 516, 527, 529
Marcé, Louis Victor, 205
married women, 30, 340, 385, 650, 675
massage, 73, 75, 606–7, 608, 611, 612
maternal deaths, 169, 205, 322–4, 393, 394–5, 401–4, 536, 543
maternal mental health services (MMHS), 133, 408, 519–20, 537, 540, 550, 553, 633
maternal-perinatal mental health, 553
maternal well-being, mental health and life experiences, 262
Maternity and Neonatal Psychological Interventions (MNPI), 133, 408, 519–20, 524, 538, 540
Maternity and Neonatal Voice Partnership (MNVPS), 519
Matoride XL, 362
matrescence, 2, 655
Maudsley Cultural Psychiatry Group, 106
Maudsley Model of Anorexia Nervosa Treatment for Adults, 297
MBRRACE-UK, 11, 51, 301, 397, 399, 403
MCA, *see* Mental Capacity Act (2005)
mebeverine, 300
media exposure, 76
Medicaid, 227, 473
medical leadership, 149–50
medically unexplained symptoms (MUS), 306–9, 314–20
Medikinet XL, 362
Meflynate XL, 362
Mellow Babies, 568, 606, 611, 612
men, 81, 82–5, 88–9, 100, 116–17, 120–1, 170, 456–7
menopause, 14, 209, 457
menstrual cycle, 284, 365, 456
menstruation, 42, 206, 209, 414
Mental Capacity Act (2005), 343, 661–8, 672, 673–4, 676–7, 678

Mental Capacity (Northern Ireland) Act (2016), 344
mental capacity assessment, 343, 663, 671
Mental Health Act (1983), 298, 649, 661, 666–7, 673, 674–5, 676, 677
Mental Health Act Review, 104
mental health assessments, 81–2, 89, 134, 135, 343, 409, 430
mental state examination, 316, 398, 411–13, 414, 416, 419
mentalisation-based treatment (MBT), 16, 249, 496, 504–5, 568, 605, 609
methadone, 324, 329, 330–2
methylphenidate, 360–2, 367–8, 370
metoclopramide, 46, 300
Metyrol XL, 362
Mexico, 551–3
MHA, *see* Mental Health Act (1983)
micro-aggressions, 101
micronutrient intake, 299
micronutrients, 299, 423
midwives, 63, 152, 451, 499, 514–15, 517–20, 552–3, 564
migrants, 15, 45, 98–9, 103, 167
Military Moms Mental Health Assessment Act, 553
milk
  breast, 73, 177, 231, 332, 369–70, 463, 480, 481
  donor, 483
  formula, 74, 419, 481
mindfulness, 122, 194, 363–4, 502, 507
mindfulness-based cognitive therapy (MBCT), 194, 507
minority groups, 98, 100, 103
miscarriage, 45, 56–7, 124–8, 130–1, 132, 191
mixed feeding, 299, 429, 448, 452, 481
Model of Anorexia Nervosa Treatment for Adults (MANTRA), 297
molar pregnancy, 124, 126, 128
monoamine oxidase inhibitors, 177
monoamine oxidase-A (MAOA), 166, 167
morning sickness, 45
mortality, 6–7, 47, 52, 249, 283, 393, 401–2, 673
Mother and Baby Units (MBU), 298, 546–7, 553, 632–3, 673, 674–6, 684–8
MotherHope Indonesia (MHI), 549
Mother–Infant Interaction Scale, 605
mother–infant relationship, 131, 269, 400, 412–15, 417–18, 564, 567–8, 594
Mother–Object Relationship Scale, 605
Mothers and Toddlers programme (MTP), 568, 605, 609
Mozingo, John, 32
MRI, 64, 316
multiple sclerosis, 435
multivitamins, 296, 299
Munchausen's syndrome, 313
Munro Review, 685
Murray, Lynne, 563, 595
MUS, *see* medically unexplained symptoms

naltrexone, 330
narrative exposure therapy, 269
National Bereavement Care Pathways (NBCP), 133
National Centre for Mental Health (NCMH), 262
National Institute of Mental Health and Neurosciences (NIMHANS) (Sri Lanka), 546–7, 549
natural pedagogy, 76
negative reassurance, 317
neglect, *see* child abuse and neglect
neonatal abstinence syndrome (NAS), 225, 324–6, 330, 331, 560
neonatal adaptation syndrome, 448
Neonatal Behavioural Assessment Scale (NBAS), 74, 607–8
neonaticide, 222, 648–51
Nepal, 548
neural tube defects, 57–8, 59, 62, 66, 231, 424
Newborn Behavioral Observations (NBO), 607–8
NHS England, 18, 330, 358, 376, 515, 519–20, 521, 537
NHS England Long Term Plan, 103, 537, 540, 624
NHS Race and Health Observatory, 104
Nicaragua, 552
NICE Antenatal and Postnatal Mental Health (APMH) guidelines, 13–14, 461, 462, 479, 517
nicotine replacement therapy (NRT), 330
Nigeria, 550, 672
nocebo effect, 318–19
Northern Ireland, 125, 515, 537, 539, 620, 621, 630–1, 661
Norwegian Mother and Child Cohort (MoBa), 285
nutrition, 60, 214, 232, 289–90, 298–300, 364, 484, 560

Oates, Margaret, 536, 542
obesity, 10–11, 213, 355, 423–4, 425, 428, 458, 484
obsessive compulsive disorder (OCD), 172–3, 186–7, 195–6, 377, 490–1, 493, 498, 624
occupational therapy, 229, 297, 694
oedema, 44, 49–50, 68, 296
  cerebral, 295
  interstitial, 50
  peripheral, 39, 49, 52
  pulmonary, 41, 49–50
olanzapine, 231, 232, 300, 426, 473–4, 475, 675–6

opioid substitution therapy (OST), 330–1
opioids, 323, 324, 326, 328, 331, 332
  detoxification, 331
  illicit, 324, 330
Osiander, F.B., 205
Osler, William, 2
other specified feeding or eating disorders (OSFED), 281–2

PACT, 98, 678
pain disorders, 311, 318
pain management, 331, 384, 451
Pakistan, 546, 548, 553, 579
Pan American Health Organization (PAHO), 552
panic disorder (PD), 82, 186–7, 197–8, 311, 491, 496
parental leave, 81
Parent–Infant Interaction Observation Scale, 605
parent–infant psychotherapy (PIP), 249, 271, 568, 605, 610–11, 612
Parent–Infant Research Institute (PIRI), 553
parenting assessments, 451, 631–2, 633, 684, 686, 687–8, 689
parenting capacity, 227, 385, 623, 628–9, 630, 631–2, 687, 691–2
parenting programmes, 28, 611–12, 628
partners, 9, 81, 87, 88, 120, 122, 626, 640, 641
  abuse by, violence, 578
  abuse towards mothers, 100
    violence, 10, 85, 167, 174, 230, 248, 261, 346, 364, 370, 550, 551–2, 577, 638, 640, 643
  attitudes, 434
  attitudes towards pregnancy, 413
  autistic, 379, 381, 383, 385
  childcare from, 33
  communication with, 13, 16, 195, 363, 412, 416, 450, 462, 480, 526
  confidentiality and, 410
  depressed mothers, 87
  effects of mental disorder on, 624
  expectations of, 88
    as barrier to engagement, 409
    gender bias towards, 89
  expectations of mothers, 3, 10
  feeding methods and, 448
  infertility, 115, 119
  interpersonal therapy, 501
  LGBTQ+, 82, 131
  life priorities, 85
  marginalisation and exclusion of, 89, 215
  mental health assessments, 81, 90
  mental health of, 10, 80, 81, 84, 87
    depression, 88, 165, 170
    interventions, 89
    PTSD, 193
  non-parent, 10
  opposition to having children, 30
  partner support groups, 547
  perinatal loss and, 135
  pre-birth planning process and, 449
  pre-conception consultation, 430, 432
  relationship quality, 84
    effects of poor, 261
  response to mother's disorder, 10
  same-sex, 84, 114, 131
  socially anxious women, 197
  stress on, 81
  substance misuse, 326, 332
  suicide attempts and, 447
  support from, 26, 27, 30, 33, 84–5, 120, 188, 550, 553
    lack of, 118, 167, 174, 188, 506
    postpartum, 453
    postpartum psychosis and, 210
  understanding of mother's mental disorder, 10, 13, 80, 598
partners, inclusion in care process, 297, 318, 399
partners therapy, behavioural couples therapy, 506
Patel, Vikram, 1
Patient and Carer Race Equality Framework (PCREF), 104–6
Patient Health Questionnaire (PHQ), 170, 547
Patient Self Determination Act (USA 1990), 676
PD, *see* panic disorder; personality disorders
Peach Tree Perinatal Wellness, 553
peer support, 26, 27, 525, 526, 527–30, 531, 539, 628
  bipolar disorder, 28, 33
  depression, 176
  ethnic minority women, 107
  illness cover and succession planning, 530
  ingredients of effective, 526
  long-term support, 528
  models, 526–7
  perinatal loss, 132
  postpartum psychosis, 215, 450, 526
  protocols, 528–9
  quality assessment, 527
  recruitment, 528
  severe mental illness, 26, 34
  telephone, 176, 525
  telephone based, 525
  third-sector providers, 531
  training, 527, 529
  trauma-informed care, 121
Perinatal Anxiety and Depression Australia Organization (PANDA), 553
Perinatal Depression e-Consortium (PDeC), 553
perinatal depressive symptoms, 118, 166, 170
perinatal frame of mind, 1, 9, 14–15, 16, 17–20, 465, 492, 661
Perinatal Mental Health Care Package, 436
Perinatal Mental Health Care Plan, 440–5, 450, 452, 453
Perinatal Mental Health Project (PMHP), 551

Perinatal Quality Network (PQN), 536–7
Permanence Order, 631
persistent pulmonary hypertension of the newborn (PPHN), 472, 474
personality disorders
  aetiology, 246–7
  child development and, 683
  child welfare implications, 248–9
  comorbidity
    depression, 173, 267
    post-traumatic stress disorder, 262
    schizophrenia, 221, 225
  course and outcomes, 247–8
  diagnosis, 242–4, 263, 266, 365
  domestic violence and, 638
  epidemiology, 244–5
  filicide and, 653
  parent–child interactions and, 604, 623, 626
  presentation, 245–6
  screening, 434
  somatisation disorder and, 311
  treatment, biopsychosocial, 249–52, 491, 502
Person-Centred Therapy (PCT), 269
Peru, 552
phobias, 82, 186–7, 196
  blood/injection, 188
  needle, 187
physical health, 10, 15, 213, 298, 327, 341–2, 414, 674
physical illness, 1, 31, 310, 314–15, 320, 417, 469, 620
Pierre Robin syndrome, 66
placenta, 53, 68, 232, 429, 457, 468, 576–7, 579
polycystic ovarian syndrome (PCOS), 8, 284, 355, 381, 434
postpartum psychosis
  aetiology, 210, 211–12
  depressive, 652
  family history of, 211, 425
  risk factors, 209, 211, 425, 447–8
postpartum psychosis (PP), 24–5, 27–8, 173–4, 205–16, 403, 516, 526, 652–3
post-traumatic stress disorder (PTSD), 129, 132, 192–3, 262, 270, 272, 451, 490, 491
  adverse childhood experiences and, 8, 242
  comorbidity
    depression, 166
    personality disorders, 251, 263, 266–7, 269
  complex, 8, 263
  course and outcomes, 187
  definition, 192
  diagnosis, 173, 192–3, 257, 259–60, 263–5
  domestic violence and abuse and, 85, 643
  fertility and, 118
  filicide and, 656
  incidence, 187, 262, 639
  parent–child interactions and, 604
  partners, 83
  risk factors, child loss, 129–32
  treatment, 191, 193, 250, 269–72, 284, 377, 490, 498–9, 501, 503, 520, 524
potassium, 295–6, 299
Practical Approach to Care Kit (PACK), 550
pre-conception care, 176, 423, 424, 430, 432–3
pre-conception consultation, 424, 425–6, 430
pre-eclampsia, 48, 50, 225
pre-eclamptic toxaemia (PET), 48, 425
pregnancy loss,11, 83, 124, 131, 416, 490, *see also* stillbirth
pregnancy planning, 230, 325–6, 328, 333, 413, 424–5, 466
pregnancy, timing of, 6–8
prescribing, 329, 399, 426, 428, 458, 464, 465, 475, 476
primary care, 293, 298–301, 311, 415–16, 514, 515, 517–18, 520–2
progesterone, 43, 44, 166, 490, 494
prolactin, 8, 117, 370
prolonged exposure (PE), 257, 269–70
prolonged grief disorder (PGD), 130
prolonged grief disorder therapy (PGDT), 496, 498, 503–4
prothrombin time, 42, 53
pseudocyesis, 222–3, 311
psychiatric history, 174, 315, 401, 413–14, 434, 483, 623, 668
psychoeducation, 134, 194, 233, 251, 364, 504, 546, 550
psychological therapies, 345, 416, 491–2, 493, 494–6, 507, 537–8, 643
psychological treatments, 176–7, 194–5, 196, 198, 300, 345, 435, 491–2
psychosis, 520
  anxiety disorders and, 198
  chronic, 25
  comorbidity, 638
  ethnicity and, 98, 99, 101
  filicide and, 652
  management
    peer support, 527, 529
    pharmacological, 177, 215, 228–31, 232, 473–5, 478–81, 483, 491
  non-affective, 206, 425
  perinatal, 146, 558
  postpartum, *see* postpartum psychosis
  psychotic episodes, 205–6, 207, 208, 412, 624, 662
  screening for, 173
  suicidality and, 397
psychotherapy, 176–7, 251–2, 269–70, 271, 491, 504–5, 605–6, 609–10
  psychoanalytic, 589
  psychodynamic, 297, 505
psychotic disorders, 207, 221, 222, 223–4, 227, 232–3, 403, 633
psychotic episodes, 205–6, 207, 208, 412, 624, 662

PTSD, *see* post-traumatic stress disorder
puerperal sepsis, 42
purging disorders, 282, 283, 286, 289, 292, 295–6, 299, 300

quetiapine, 231, 252, 272, 473–4, 475

racism, 9, 101
  institutional, 101
  interpersonal, 101
  structural/systemic, 98, 99
Raphael, Dana, 2
RCPsych, *see* Royal College of Psychiatrists
RCPsych Community Perinatal Quality Network, 537
reassurance, 195, 214, 309, 313, 317, 385, 415, 455
rebound hypophosphatemia, 296
refeeding syndrome, 295–6, 298
referral management, 407
relationship quality, 84, 85–6
relationship satisfaction, 84–5, 194
relative infant dose (RID), 369–70, 428, 464, 481, 483
relatives, 399, 412, 440–1, 447, 452–3, 557, 625, 670
religion, 15, 16, 29, 64, 97, 102–3, 160, 691–2
renal changes, 43
renal function, 67, 479
renal stones, 67
renal systems, 75, 231
renal tumours, 68
renin-angiotensin-aldosterone system (RAAS), 43
repetitive transcranial magnetic stimulation (rTMS), 175, 178, 297
resilience, 3, 9, 18, 60, 146, 262, 563, 633
respite services, 232–3
Rich, Adrienne, 4
Richards, Mike, 154
Richmond, Laura, 258
risk assessment, 12, 174, 189, 294–5, 343, 416–17, 648, 694
risk management, 170, 399, 401, 404, 407, 411, 416–17, 436
risk, explaining, 462
risperidone, 229, 231, 473–4
Ritalin, 362
Ritvo Autism Asperger's Diagnostic Scale, 389
role modelling, 151, 526, 528
Romania, 77
Royal College of Psychiatrists, 18, 151, 415, 536–7, 543, 559, 563, 681
rTMS, *see* repetitive transcranial magnetic stimulation (rTMS)
rubella, 59
Rwanda, 550

safeguarding, 16–17, 449, 619, 621–3, 626, 634, 684–6, 688–9
  perinatal frame of mind and, 17
safety studies, 469
same-sex couples, 84, 114, 131
schizoaffective disorder, 209, 221, 223, 231, 408, 425, 441, 633
schizophrenia, 11, 24–5, 221–8, 232, 573–4, 633, 683
SCOFF questionnaire, 288
Scotland, 133, 515, 517–20, 538–40, 621, 630–1, 661
Scottish Intercollegiate Guidelines Network, 174, 464, 543
screening, 11, 132, 170, 173, 288–9, 548, 551–2, 553
screening tools, 63–4, 99, 171, 178, 359, 434, 553, 605
selective serotonin reuptake inhibitors (SSRIs), 177, 195–8, 318–19, 369, 470–3, 481
self-harm, 99, 174, 263, 265–6, 398–9, 401, 413–14, 417
self-image, 264, 502
self-induced vomiting (SIV), 281, 289, 294–5
sensitivity-based approaches, 608
sensory deprivation, 76–7
sensory development, 60
sensory hypo/hypersensitivities, 380
sertraline, 177, 300, 319, 473
service provision, 24, 26, 407, 430, 536, 543, 608, 629
sexual abuse, 7, 259, 265, 446, 620, 639, 640,
sexual health, 341, 518
sexual healthcare, 228, 229
sexual violence, 5, 192, 365, 370, 552, 638–9
sexually transmitted infections (STI), 224, 229, 360, 365, 370, 381, 639, 641
Shanghai Centre for Women's and Children's Health, 553
Shanghai Mental Health Centre, 549
Shaw, George Bernard, 160
shoulder dystocia, 45, 46, 61
Singapore, 547, 548, 579
Skills Training in Affect and Interpersonal Regulation (STAIR), 270
skin-to-skin contact, 32, 71, 225, 551
sleep, 70–3, 74, 167, 171, 212, 362, 451
sleep deprivation, 5, 33, 224, 232, 429, 431, 446, 448
sleep disorders, 355
sleep disturbances, 88, 168, 211, 357, 472
sleep loss, 211–12
  limited work linking, 212
sleep problems, 573
sleep protection, 73, 175, 176
sleep regression, 74
sleeplessness, 168, 593, 594
smoking, 10–11, 62, 225, 328, 332, 365–6, 423, 425
  abstinence, 228
  cessation, 62, 225, 228, 230, 328, 330, 426, 480
social anxiety, *see* social phobia
social care, 18, 260, 430, 431, 622–3, 626, 628–9, 688–9
social graces, 160
social media, 3, 35, 529, 532
social networks, 9, 24, 27, 162, 326, 327, 628, 669

social phobia, 166, 186–7, 189, 196–7, 490–1, 496, 498, 524
social services, 17, 34, 100, 195, 396, 402, 430, 540
social support, 16, 29–30, 117–18, 167, 214, 500, 526, 639
social workers, 229, 388, 416, 452–3, 608–9, 626–9, 632
somatic symptoms disorder (SSD), 248
somatisation, 247, 262, 309–10, 311, 320
somatoform syndromes, 306, 310–11, 317
Sotos syndrome, 59
South Africa, 550–1, 553
South Asian women, 11, 98, 101, 102
South London and Maudsley Trust, 104
spirometery, 44
stepped care model, 515, 516–17, 549, 550
stereotyped movements, 379, 385
stigma, 16–17, 25, 27–32, 89, 101, 387, 550–1
stillbirth, 11, 61–2, 101, 124–8, 129, 130–1, 225
  intra-partum, 126
stimulant drugs, 360, 363, 366–7, 370–1
Stirling Antenatal Anxiety Scale (SAAS), 189–90
stress, 83–4, 85, 118, 119, 121–2, 171, 247, 264, 571, 572, 573, 575, 576, 577, 578, 579, 580
  depression and, 169, 171
  developmental effects on children, 34, 225, 263, 560, 571–4
    biological mechanisms, 575–7
    brain structure, 577–8
    epigenetics, 578
    gender differences, 575
    physical, 575
  dissociation due to, 260, 268
  effects
    milk supply, 463
    pregnancy outcomes, 574
  fathers, 83–4
  fertility, 122
  financial, 171
  gender-based differences in response to, 457
  offspring as stressor, 267
  personality disorder and, 247
  postpartum psychosis and, 210, 211
  regulation, 246
  relief, 233
    peer support, 526, 529
    skin-to-skin contact, 551
    therapy, 506, 580
  social support and, 340
  somatisation, 310, 311
  sources of, 80, 83, 84, 165, 167, 169, 170, 171, 174, 225, 247, 260, 264, 326–7, 384, 414, 434, 446, 560, 571, 576, 686
    breastfeeding, 448
    childbirth, 519
    children, 247, 248
    environmental, 247, 572, 683–4
    fertility treatment, 117, 119
    financial, 448
    pregnancy, 245, 247
    pregnancy loss, 129
    psychosocial, 572, 576, 579
    relationship, 197, 247
substance use disorders, 12, 173, 187, 228, 340, 365, 505, 639
suicidal ideation, 169, 174, 193, 214, 311, 401, 623, 633
suicide, 130–1, 169, 171, 283, 394–7, 401–2, 413–14
  deaths by, 295, 394–6, 397, 400, 553
  extended, 397, 624, 653
  increased risk of, 331, 633
  non-fatal, 283
  risk of, 174, 268, 283, 396, 541, 640, 653, 656
suicide death, 174
suicide plan/attempt, 172
supermom ideology, 25
supervision order, 631
Sweden, 99–100
systems approach, 562
tDCS, *see* transcranial direct current stimulation (tDCS)
teenage pregnancies, 6–7, 245, 360, 551, 655
television, 76, 263
teratogenic drugs, 56, 61
termination, 124, 125–6, 131, 133, 228, 311, 640–1, 672–3
Thailand, 546, 549
thalidomide, 61, 572
theory of mind (ToM), 378, 605
Thinking Healthy Programme (THP), 548
thromboembolism, 47, 53, 670–1
  venous, 11, 45, 54, 225, 339
thyroid dysfunction, 173, 435
tobacco, 56, 57, 61–2, 65, 325–6, 328, 332–3, 640
tokophobia, 8, 187, 193–4, 198, 501, 518, 520
Tommy's, 35
Tourette's syndrome, 355
trafficking, 638, 639,
training, 17–18, 150, 346–8, 527–30, 550–3, 565–6
transcranial direct current stimulation (tDCS), 178
trauma, 8–9, 118, 173, 192–3, 258, 265–6, 269–70, 644
trazodone, 272
Trevarthen, Colwyn, 594
twin pregnancies, 60, 64, 68, 126, 188, 210, 282, 650

Uganda, 550
UK Adult ADHD Network (UKAAN), 358–9
UK Teratology Information Service (UKTIS), 61, 426, 466
ultrasound scans, 59, 63, 65
unplanned pregnancies, 83, 85, 222, 245, 284, 446, 640, 655

valproate, 33, 57, 61–2, 231, 428, 470, 476–7, 479
varenicline, 228, 330
venlafaxine, 368, 471, 481

video feedback, 607, 608–9, 611
video feedback intervention to promote positive parenting (VIPP), 271
video interaction guidance (VIG), 271, 568, 605, 608, 612
violence, 9–10, 85, 101, 192, 578, 620, 638–44, 652–3
vitamin B12 292
vitamin D, 291
in vitro fertilisation (IVF), 114–16, 117, 121, 650
vomiting, 45, 50, 287, 308, 311, 323, 325, 593

Wales, 97–8, 620, 621–2, 630–1, 638–9, 661, 681–2, 688–91
Watch, Wait and Wonder (WWW), 610
weight, 281, 285–7, 289, 292–4, 298–9, 310, 360, 677
  gain, 10, 33, 47, 228, 292–4, 342, 370, 482
  loss, 45, 172, 284, 295–6, 300, 360, 402
  management, 228, 480
Whooley questions, 99, 170, 174, 190
Williams, Niall, 8
Winnicott, Donald, 3–4, 561, 587, 593
withdrawal symptoms, 322, 325–6, 331–2, 368, 469, 474, 482
World Health Organization (WHO), 322, 330, 331–2, 395, 548, 551, 559, 639

Xaggitin XL, 362
Xenidate XL, 362

Yangihara, Hanya, 5

Zika, 59
Zimbabwe, 550

www.ingramcontent.com/pod-product-compliance
Lightning Source LLC
LaVergne TN
LVHW052204200926
848481LV00001B/30

* 9 7 8 1 9 1 1 6 2 3 5 0 2 *